The 1956 Hungarian Revolution

NATIONAL SECURITY ARCHIVE
COLD WAR READERS

Series Editor
Malcolm Byrne

Previously published:
The Prague Spring '68
Uprising in East Germany, 1953

Forthcoming:
Poland 1980–1981
The Collapse of Communism in Eastern Europe:
Soviet Policy toward Eastern Europe, 1985–1989
Poland, 1986–1989
Czechoslovakia, 1987–1989
Hungary, 1989–1990

Produced in collaboration with:
The Institute for the History of the 1956 Hungarian Revolution

THE 1956 HUNGARIAN REVOLUTION:

A HISTORY IN DOCUMENTS

Compiled, edited, and introduced by
Csaba Békés
Malcolm Byrne
János M. Rainer

Assistant Editors
József Litkei
Gregory F. Domber

C E U PRESS

Central European University Press
Budapest   New York

Published in 2002 by
Central European University Press

An imprint of the
Central European University Share Company
Nádor utca 11, H-1051 Budapest, Hungary
Tel: +36-1-327-3138 or 327-3000
Fax: +36-1-327-3183
E-mail: ceupress@ceu.hu
Website: www.ceupress.com

400 West 59th Street, New York NY 10019, USA
Tel: +1-212-547-6932
Fax: +1-212-548-4607
E-mail: mgreenwald@sorosny.org

ISBN 963 9241 48 2 cloth
ISBN 963 9241 66 0 Paperback
ISSN 1587-2416

Library of Congress Cataloging-in-Publication data

The 1956 Hungarian revolution : a history in documents / compiled,
edited, and introduced by Csaba Békés, Malcolm Byrne, János M. Rainer ;
assistant editors, József Litkei, Gregory F. Domber.
   p. cm. — (National Security Archive Cold War readers)
Includes bibliographical references and index.
   ISBN
   1. Hungary—History—Revolution, 1956—Sources. 2. Soviet
Union—Foreign relations—1953–1975—Sources. I. Békés, Csaba. II.
Byrne, Malcolm. III. Rainer M., János. IV. Series.
   DB956.7 .A15 2002
   943.905'2—dc21
                        2002007516

Printed in Hungary by
Akadémiai Nyomda, Martonvásár

CONTENTS

PART ONE
HUNGARY BEFORE THE REVOLUTION

PART TWO

FROM DEMONSTRATIONS TO REVOLUTION

PART THREE
HUNGARY IN THE AFTERMATH

DOCUMENTARY EPILOGUE

PREFACE

Hungary emerged defeated from the two most brutal wars of modern European history. It took part in triggering World War I, and it held out bitterly to the last man in World War II. After the first war, Hungary saw herself as a ravaged victim, while after the second, her self-perception was that of an innocent victim who had only tried to reclaim what she believed to be rightly hers. The law of war, however, gives the victor the right to draw the portrait of the defeated. This picture is no more authentic than the defeated's self-image: both are biased and self-justifying, one simply conceals the other. Our country's name was removed from the ranks of the Western world without apparent anguish outside our borders. Twice-plundered, occupied, deprived of her autonomy, and cast out of Europe, Hungary began a new era of her history after a brief democratic interlude. Just as world public opinion simplistically identified all Russians with Stalin, although it was they who suffered the most from Stalinist tyranny, the picture of the Hungarian nation became identical to that of Rákosi. With the advance of the cold war, however, the world often referred to Hungary as a "captive nation," to be "liberated" sometime in the distant future. These two words, "captive nation," suggests vulnerability, surrender, inertia, and a lack of will power: that is, the image of lost human dignity. An image of a nation which is totally harmless can be at most a source of nuisance for the "enslaver" or a point of reference for the potential "liberator," but never a determining factor in the balance of great powers.

Enslavers and liberators were separated by an iron curtain that ran along the border of the enslaved nations. They both knew each other very well, each side sizing up the vulnerability of the other, weighing momentary changes in balance in their power games, and taking the propaganda slogans directed against each other not so much at face value, but rather according to their actual significance. While this rhetoric presaged danger not only for both sides, but indeed for the entire world, it was at the same time a systematically planned political opium, concealed in portioned-out rhetorical flourishes.

Naturally, all this leaked through the cracks of the iron curtain, resulting in misconceptions on both sides by those who failed to recognize what lay behind the balance of fear. West of the iron curtain, people created a biased and undifferentiated image of communists and the nations under communist rule: an image in which human features were indiscernible. In the East, on the other hand, we were not aware of the community of interests that reached far beyond the virtual boundary of the iron curtain.

Nonetheless, deep inside society lay hidden the explosive reality, even if in a stifled and invisible way. Something that everybody knew but never talked about until the very last moment: the fear that interlaced everything; the lethal and unfounded violence; the contagious and poisonous lies; the Stalinist caricature of socialism, whose nature was, by that time, recognized by both the followers and opponents of socialism. Let it be said to the formers' credit that, due to their position, they were the first who were able to call it by name, although it is true that back then their aim was nothing more than to make improvements. And when the double fuse of the unrest in Poland and the stupidity of Stalinist policy led to the explosion of the revolution, shattering the fraudulent castle of Stalinism into bits and pieces over a turbulent three days—a split second in historical terms—the world was flabbergasted. The vulnerable, paralyzed, inept, and harmless captive nation of Hungary did not wait listlessly to be liberated, but decided to free itself and assert its human dignity, which had been denied for eight long years. Hungarians did not even ask for or expect a predetermined model for their self-proclaimed freedom. The unanimous "NO" (their rejection of oppression) gave the workers enough strength to socialize the state and exert control over the means of production with a single motion. The same repudiation empowered villages to feed Budapest, the capital city burdened with armed conflict, without any central directives or system of forced agricultural delivery. Those who for decades had viewed the people of the outskirts as a homeless mob, and believed that the youth had completely degenerated, were now surprised to see how working class youths halted Russian tanks, and how female students rescued casualties, blood-soaked Russian soldiers among them, by defying and dodging a lethal shower of bullets. A whole nation became larger than life in a vehement fight for freedom, setting an example for the entire world by showing how human integrity can defy death.

The events of 1956 fundamentally changed the image of Hungary, and this image is still confirmed and maintained in the eyes of the world by the message of 1956.

Official politics and public opinion in Western society were sharply separated after the revolution. Politics followed the ruthless logic of the balance of power, regardless of how much they paid tribute to the Hungarian revolution with beautiful phrases, and gladly acknowledged that most of the progressive forces around the world were grossly disappointed with the fact that Soviet policy had turned out to be dishonest and based upon brute force. But political assistance to the crushed country barely went further than expressions of praise for Hungary and resounding condemnation of the Soviet intervention.

The western public, especially the younger generation, however, backed Hungary's cause with all their heart and soul--perhaps due to the half-hearted political support that came from their governments. Refugees were thoroughly welcomed abroad. Many of today's western politicians, prime ministers and presidents were among those students who at the time demonstrated and protested in front of Soviet embassies and embraced young Hungarian refugees, introducing them to their fellow students or colleagues at work. For them, the Hungarian revolution was a decisive experience of freedom, an uplifting experience that continues to benefit us. For the world, the name of Hungary has become synonymous with freedom and an elementary wish for democracy.

I believe that István Bibó was right when he called 1956 the revolution of human dignity. Our national feelings and desire for freedom are organic elements of our human dignity. What we fought for and achieved, what our youth died for, was no less than the freedom of our nation. The revolution of human dignity consequently includes the notion of a struggle for independence as well. The two are impossible to separate.

Forty-six years have now passed and we have become forty-six years older. Had we not told our children the truth about what happened in 1956, they could not tell their children either. Our grandchildren, however, will unearth the truth for themselves. From archival sources and written memorials. From facts. Mercilessly. Out of the desire for knowledge. Without having lived in that age and breathed the air of those days. It may well be that the story they reconstruct will be more accurate than our own version. Hosts of young researchers abroad and in Hungary are working on that narrative already—as typified by the editors of this extraordinary volume—and I am sure that they will sincerely answer the prevailing questions of "why" and "how". With this outstanding volume, the scholars at the 1956 Institute in Budapest and the National Security Archive in the United States are helping to lead the way in this important historical exercise. We should be aware that in the future our memory will be preserved in both simplistic commonplaces and in objective scholarly works—studies more objective than our own. And this remembrance will also recall the eternal example of a nation—the Hungarian nation—and the memory of a belated but indisputable victory over the violence of a superpower.

Árpád Göncz
Former President of the Republic of Hungary

FOREWORD

The story of the 1956 Hungarian revolution is as complex as it is full of paradoxes.

The revolution's complexity stems primarily from the difference between its leaders and followers. Most of the leaders were members of a disillusioned communist elite, notably intellectuals; the followers were young freedom fighters. True, both leaders and followers sought the removal of Soviet power from Hungarian territory. But the intellectuals and their reformist allies in the Hungarian communist hierarchy, who had prepared the way since 1953 for what eventually happened in 1956, envisaged a peaceful, negotiated transition to a new pluralist political order that would also retain some features of a socialist economy. Showing considerably less patience, the young freedom fighters embraced similar political and economic goals but they had little or no confidence in a negotiated agreement with Moscow and its Stalinist Hungarian diehards.

Paradoxically, a communist, albeit a reformer, was the uncontested, widely admired symbol of this anti-communist revolution. His country's prime minister for two years after Stalin's death in 1953, Imre Nagy occupied the same position again for twelve short days in October-November 1956. Indeed, Nagy's reinstatement was the initial demand of the students whose demonstration on October 23, 1956, sparked the revolution. Yet Nagy was not only a communist; he was a Moscow-trained communist who had spent more than a decade in the Soviet capital before and during World War II. There, like other communist exiles, Nagy almost certainly served as an informer for the Soviet political police. Perhaps for this reason, Moscow did not oppose his reappointment as Hungary's prime minister on October 23–24, expecting Nagy to respect its most basic interests in Hungary. Ironically, then, Nagy was—initially—both the man needed, if not trusted, by the Kremlin and the hero of the freedom fighters as well. Only at the very end of October, after Soviet troops had reentered the country, did Nagy fully understand that the Soviet leadership was not interested in finding a political solution to the crisis. From the communist believer he used to be, this is when Nagy became a Hungarian revolutionary. When he died for it in 1958, he did so without recanting his last, final stance.

What emerges clearly from the documents collected for this immensely rich volume is that both Moscow and Washington were caught off guard by the outbreak of the revolution.

Of the two, Moscow was better informed, of course. Already in mid-1956 it had removed from power Mátyás Rákosi, Hungary's much-hated Stalinist dictator. But the Russians decided to replace Rákosi with another Stalinist rather than with Nagy, because by then they considered Nagy to be too stubborn and too independent. The documents also show that the Soviet Presidium was divided about what to do. At first, military intervention was but one possibility. The man who practically commuted between Moscow and Budapest, Politburo member Anastas I. Mikoyan, clearly preferred to look for a peaceful resolution of the crisis. He seemed to believe that military intimidation and economic and political pressure would be sufficient—over a period of time—to return Hungary to the Soviet fold. To the extent the Kremlin was divided over the course it should follow, it was because it had not perceived such widespread and determined anti-Sovietism to exist in Hungary. Throughout the crisis, members of the Soviet Politburo spoke of the "enemy," especially the United States, instigating the crisis. The records of the most secret meetings of the Presidium show that no one understood that the Hungarian people themselves—among them students raised in a communist educational environment—wanted nothing to do with Communism or the Soviet Union.

The United States was also unprepared for the revolution. Despite the Eisenhower administration's declared policy of rolling back Communism from Eastern Europe—the policy of "liberation"—there were no specific plans to take advantage of the confusion that came to characterize the Soviet bloc after Stalin's death. While Washington had correctly understood the general significance of Titoism as a realistic phase on the path from Communism to democracy, when the opportunity presented itself to support Imre Nagy, a more gentle version of Yugoslavia's Tito, Washington was unable to come up with a proper response. Radio Free Europe (RFE), which at the time was official Washington's very influential mouthpiece, kept hammering on the theme that the Nagy government was still pro-communist and that the freedom fighters should wait for a message from József Cardinal Mindszenty (who was freed from a communist jail during the revolution). Thus, instead of encouraging the Hungarians to support the only realistic alternative of the moment, which was Nagy's Titoist formula, RFE egged on its vast audience to press for maximalist demands. Worse yet, RFE's subsequent self-assessment, which is reproduced in this volume, was but an attempt to cover up its historic error.

When Hungary became free and independent in 1989, it embraced the goals of 1956, together with new goals, of course. In important ways, 1989 was not 1956. In 1956, Hungary stood alone in the world. In 1989, by contrast, favorable international winds helped the Hungarian cause. Mikhail S. Gorbachev's Soviet Union no longer opposed Hungary's steps toward pluralism and the free market. The anti-communist momentum spearheaded by U.S. President Ronald Reagan in the early 1980s certainly helped advance the momentous changes happening in Hungary and elsewhere. Meanwhile, within Hungary itself, the so-called "democratic opposition," which became active as early as 1977, kept pressing for the historical truth about 1956. Its *samizdat* or illegal publications kept talking about '56, and even printed parts of the hidden record of the 1953–55 reform-communist era, the revolution itself, and the trials and murders that took place after Moscow crushed the revolution. On the eve of the collapse of Communism—on June 16, 1989, the 31st anniversary of Imre Nagy's juridical murder—some 200,000 Hungarians attended and millions watched a truly historical event: the ceremonial reburying of Nagy and his fallen comrades. Thus, while 1989 might well have happened without 1956, the fact is that it did not. After 1956, and especially after 1977, reform-communists and anti-communists kept alive the memory of what had happened, and it was that memory, combining pain and hope, that contributed so significantly to the eventual end of communist rule in 1989.

Since 1989, historians have had an opportunity to examine the historical records in Hungary, in Russia, and in other countries too. A free Hungary has produced many outstanding volumes about what happened and why. Concurrently, however, political parties and their leaders have also sought to make "1956" theirs and theirs alone. Especially on various anniversaries, such as June 16th and October 23rd (when, in 1956, the revolution began), right wing and even right-of-center politicians keep offering assessments of the revolution that are essentially ahistorical and politically motivated. Generally speaking, these politicians are so anxious to dissociate themselves from *today's* ex-communists that their version of 1956 lacks appreciation for the critical role once played by *yesterday's* ex-communists.

True, studies of 1956 sponsored by the current government led by Prime Minister Viktor Orbán, for example, do describe Imre Nagy as a brave man who died as a patriot. But his closest advisers have become non-persons so that the revolution could be described simply as a nationalist rising against Soviet imperialism. While 1956, of course, did witness a nationalist rising against Moscow's rule, it was prepared since 1953 largely by former Muscovites, fellow travelers, and the like. At some time or another in their lives, most of Nagy's closest associates in 1956 had been fanatical communists. For example, Ferenc Donáth, Nagy's political adviser, headed the brutal, Stalinist Rákosi's party secretariat in the late 1940s. At that time he led a vicious polemic against Nagy's views on agriculture. Yet the same Donáth in 1956—together with Géza Losonczy and Miklós Vásárhelyi, two totally disillusioned former communist editors—opened Nagy's eyes to the validity of the people's demands. Political acrobatics? Probably not. Donáth as well as Losonczy, Vásárhelyi, and Imre Nagy himself were part of the 20th century in Central and Eastern Europe; their struggle for a free and independent Hungary in 1956 was fueled by their revulsion over having allowed themselves to be fooled.

This volume is important precisely because the documents speak for themselves. Thanks to judicious selection from an impressive array of sources, the volume reflects the very real complexities of 1956. How better to understand those events than by taking a retrospective look through the eyes of participants themselves—at the time, before they have had the chance to rewrite the history to their own advantage? The 120 top-level, formerly secret records included here not only offer a glimpse into the deliberations of the Hungarians, their fellow satellite regimes and beyond them the superpowers themselves, they provide us today with the unusual opportunity to watch the revolution unfold from a variety of perspectives—national, institutional and personal—from each of the dozen countries whose documents are represented here. It is an important achievement and one that is made even more valuable by the inclusion of detailed introductory essays, headnotes for each document, a wealth of footnotes, and other research aids that will help student and expert alike place these complex events in a meaningful context.

Charles Gati
Washington, D.C.
October 2001

INTRODUCTORY ESSAY
Forty Years On[*]

What happened in Hungary in 1956? Here is a fairly typical brief Western summary, from the Columbia Encyclopedia:

> On Oct. 23.1956, a popular anti-Communist revolution, centered in Budapest, broke out in Hungary. A new coalition government under Imre Nagy declared Hungary neutral, withdrew it from the Warsaw Treaty, and appealed to the UN for aid. However, János Kádár, one of Nagy's ministers, formed a counter-government and asked the USSR for military support. In severe and brutal fighting, Soviet forces suppressed the revolution. Nagy and some of his ministers were abducted and were later executed. Some 190,000 refugees fled the country. Kádár became premier and sought to win popular support for Communist rule.

In Hungary itself, the history of the 1956 revolution was obliterated or traduced for more than thirty years, while János Kádár progressed from Soviet quisling to domestic father figure and the West's favorite "liberal" communist. Yet through all those years, Kádár himself seems to have been haunted and driven by the memory of the comrades he had betrayed and, finally, condemned to death. Imre Nagy was his Banquo—and he was always Macbeth.

A part of the true history was written abroad. Another part was gradually rediscovered by independent historians and oppositional writers inside Hungary in the 1980s, interviewing survivors, publishing suppressed writings, and drawing their own conclusions. Then, in June 1989, Imre Nagy and his closest associates were ceremonially reburied. Beside the coffins of the leaders lying in state on Heroes' Square, there lay a symbolic sixth coffin of the Unknown Insurgent. This was the great symbolic turning point in Hungary's transition from communism to democracy. Banquo's ghost was enthroned.

In a free Hungary, the true history of 1956 could surely at last be revealed. A whole institute was established for this single purpose: the Institute for the History of the 1956 Hungarian Revolution. Archives were opened. Survivors could now talk freely. Young historians set to work. The 1956 Institute produced a new short history of the revolution, which became the Hungarian school textbook.[1]

With the end of communism elsewhere, more evidence also emerged from the Soviet Union, from Yugoslavia, even from China. Not all the evidence, of course, but more. Meanwhile, American, British, French, and other Western official documents became available under the "thirty-year rule." Some, perhaps the most interesting, remained classified, but scholars pressed for further access and, in the United States, used the Freedom of Information Act to demand it.

1

Now, forty years on, scholars and survivors assemble in the handsome rooms of the Hungarian Academy of Sciences, its high windows looking across the Danube from naughty Pest to haughty Buda. Inside, it looks like just another academic conference.[2] We might be in London, at a confer-

---

[*] This essay was written immediately after a conference organized in 1996 by the Institute for the History of the 1956 Hungarian Revolution in Budapest and the National Security Archive in Washington, D.C., to mark the fortieth anniversary of the Hungarian revolution. It is reprinted here, with the kind permission of the author, exactly as it appears in *History of the Present: Essays, Sketches, and Dispatches from Europe in the 1990s,* (New York: Random House, 1999).

[1] The excellent English-language edition is György Litván, ed., *The Hungarian Revolution of 1956: Reform, Revolt, and Repression, 1953–1963,* ed. and trans. János M. Bak and Lyman H. Legters (London: Longman, 1996).

[2] Entitled "Hungary and the World 1956: The New Archival Evidence," the conference was organized by the Institute for the History of the 1956 Hungarian Revolution and the Hungarian Academy of Sciences, in Budapest, and the National Security Archive and the Cold War International History Project, both of Washington. D.C.

ence about the Suez crisis that so fatefully coincided with the Hungarian revolution. This forty-year moment is an interesting one even in more normal countries: the first and generally the last occasion when reasonably digested findings from the archives can be confronted with the reasonably coherent memories of surviving participants. Thirty years after the event, most of the archives are still closed; fifty years on, most of the participants are no longer with us. Yet in Budapest, the witnesses have survived not just, say, too many good dinners at the Carlton Club in London but a death sentence commuted at the last minute to fourteen years in prison. So the occasion is not ordinary at all.

Being tested here is the central proposition of modern historical writing since Ranke: that with the passage of time we know more about the past. This is supposed to be the case because we have greater distance from the past: because we are (supposedly) more impartial: because we can see the longer-term consequences and therefore the larger historical "meaning" of the events in question: and, above all, because the documents are now available. The subtitle of this conference is "The New Archival Evidence." Following Ranke, we should now learn "how it really was." But do we, can we?

In important ways, we certainly learn more. For example, here, from the Soviet archives, are the notes made by V. N. Malin, head of the General Department of the Central Committee of the Communist Party of the Soviet Union, on the Soviet leaders' hectic debates in the Party Presidium.[3] We see them dithering and agonizing in the days after the outbreak of the revolution on 23 October: "C[omra]de Khrushchev [says] . . . the matter is becoming more complicated .... The workers are supporting the uprising." And, later, "The English and French are in a real mess in Egypt. We shouldn't get caught in the same company." And their meetings with Chairman Mao's emissaries on 30 October. "Cde. Khrushchev . . . there are two paths. A military path . . . one of occupation. A peaceful path . . . the withdrawal of troops, negotiations."

So might it really have happened differently? What Gorbachev did in 1989, done by Khrushchev in 1956? These documents warn us against what the French philosopher Henri Bergson called "the illusions of retrospective determinism"—against the conviction, so hard to resist, that what actually happened had to happen. For years, most of us have lived with the assumption that the Soviet Union could never have tolerated what was happening in Hungary—otherwise, it would not have been the Soviet Union. But Soviet leaders plainly did not know that at the time. What would have happened if . . .?

The openness did not last long. On 31 October, Malin records Khrushchev saying. "We should re-examine our assessment and should not withdraw our troops from Hungary and Budapest. We should take the initiative in restoring order in Hungary." What factors were decisive? How important, for example, were concerns about the unity of the international communist movement, with the Italian communist leader Palmiro Togliatti and, finally, also Chairman Mao urging the "restoration of order?" What difference was made by the assurance given by John Foster Dulles that "We do not look upon these nations as potential military allies?" What was the impact of Suez? "If we depart from Hungary," Khrushchev goes on, "it will give a great boost to the Americans, English, and French—the imperialists. They will perceive it as weakness on our part and will go on to the offensive . . . To Egypt they will then add Hungary."

"Agreed: Cdes. Zhukov, Bulganin, Molotov, Kaganovich, Voroshilov, Saburov"—and behind this sentence the Russian historian Vyacheslav Sereda hears a sigh of relief. The notes continue, "We should create a Provisional Revol. Govt (headed by Kádár)." But then, incredibly, "If Nagy agrees, bring him in as dep. premier."

Another area of old controversy and new discoveries is the role of Radio Free Europe (RFE), the American-run radio station, which broadcast in all the languages of Eastern Europe. Here we have a hitherto unpublished memorandum from William Griffith, then political adviser to RFE.[4]

---

[3] The Malin notes are translated and expertly annotated by Mark Kramer, a Harvard specialist on Soviet-Eastern European relations, in a compendium of declassified documents prepared for the conference by the 1956 Institute and the National Security Archive. A larger collection of documents is due to be published by Central European University Press.

[4] The memorandum is included in ibid.

Dated 5 December 1956, it reviews the Hungarian output of RFE and concludes that there were important "policy violations" by the Hungarian radio journalists involved. One program on 28 October gave detailed instructions to Hungarian soldiers on the conduct of partisan warfare. "In the Western capitals," a commentary on 4 November declared, "a practical manifestation of Western sympathy is expected at any hour." Griffith's own conclusion in December 1956 is that the Hungarian service did not *incite* the revolution and "(with one exception) made no *direct* promise or commitment of Western or UN military support or intervention. Its broadcasts may well, however, have encouraged Hungarians to have false hopes in this respect; they certainly did little or nothing to contradict them."

Now William Griffith, today a distinguished professor emeritus of political science at MIT, is on the platform, together with other surviving participants. He makes essentially the same argument that he did forty years ago. But a journalist who then worked for RFE's Hungarian service angrily suggests that the Hungarian journalists are being scapegoated. They were only following American policy guidance, which, in particular, urged criticism of the communist Imre Nagy and support for the militantly anticommunist Cardinal József Mindszenty. An American working in RFE at the time jumps up to support him. He remembers the discussions in the newsroom and quotes from the policy guidance given at the time by Griffith, who was, however, himself subject to policy guidance from New York. An old Hungarian, identifying himself as a listener to Radio Free Europe, emotionally declares that it was to blame for the deaths of thousands of Hungarian youngsters.

Pale-faced, her voice trembling, Mária Wittner, one of the street fighters who paid for her part in the revolution with more than fourteen years in prison, reads out extracts from RFE broadcasts in Hungarian. The interpreter gives us some idea of the fiery language: "The tanks come in . . . invited by the bloody-handed Imre Nagy." (Basing their judgments too much on official Hungarian radio broadcasts, RFE initially thought Nagy was co-responsible for the first intervention by Soviet troops.) Or, again, "Where are the traitors . . . who are the murderers? Imre Nagy and his government . . . Only Cardinal Mindszenty has spoken out fearlessly . . . Imre Nagy is a base Muscovite." But afterward there is some confusion. Are these quotations from RFE's own broadcasts or from Hungarian radio stations taken over by the insurgents—the "freedom stations"—some of whose programs RFE rebroadcast? Jan Nowak, then head of RFE's Polish service, draws the important contrast with Poland, where both the freshly released Cardinal Stefan Wyszyński from inside and RFE from outside immediately and firmly backed Władysław Gomułka, the Polish Nagy.

After this dramatic confrontation of documents and memories, of written and oral history, we can see the historical picture more clearly. With the best of intentions on all sides, and quite understandably, in a confused and drastic situation, which changed literally minute by minute, both Hungarians and Americans at RFE got it wrong. Not all of them and not all the time, of course. But in the crucial days of late October, their broadcasts attacked Imre Nagy (while the Polish service was supporting Gomułka), and some encouraged armed resistance, with broad hints of imminent Western aid that, in fact, the United States (let alone the Suez-embroiled British and French) had no intention of giving. We can never know what difference this made to the course of events; it probably made little or none to the final result. That does not diminish the moral responsibility.

Here, then, are two cases which seem to justify the implicit, neo-Rankean assumption: that with the passing of time and careful study of the documents we know more about what really happened. Yet this is, on a moment's reflection, a very odd assumption. It was not shared by historians for more than two thousand years before Ranke. And it is not one we usually make in everyday life. Our rather reasonable everyday assumption is that the closer you are to an event, in both time and place, the more you are likely to know about it. "Well," we say, "of course you'd know better, because you were there."

The fact is that so much of history with a small *h*—most of it, in fact—is simply lost. To be sure, in some respects we do know more after forty years; but in others we know less. This is particularly true of times of crisis and rapid change, and above all of wars and revolutions. Tolstoy reminds us in *War and Peace* of the mystery at the heart of battles. So also with revolutions. Even now—especially now—do we really know how and why it came to the storming of the Bastille?

The Hungarian revolution of 1956 is an event of that kind—perhaps the last in Europe with the popular, violent, and genuinely spontaneous character that we still associate with the word *revolution*. All subsequent European revolutions—Czechoslovakia 1968, Portugal 1974, Poland 1980–1981, the many-in-one of 1989—have to be qualified with an additional adjective: "interrupted," "self-limiting," "peaceful," "velvet," "negotiated." For that reason, and because of the subsequent decades of political repression and historical falsification, there is a part of its history that is virtually impossible to recover. It may also be the most important part. It concerns, for example, the experience of the mainly young men and women who took up arms on 23 or 24 October 1956: the workers, students, street-fighting kids who, after all, actually made this a revolution. Without them, it might have remained a high-level political crisis, an attempt at radical reform, an affair largely of the party and the intelligentsia, with the people playing only a supporting role. Why did they act as they did? What was it like for them? What did they hope to achieve? What kept them fighting? What did they think of in the moment before they died?

I read the contemporary reports, watch the newsreels, look at the black-and-white photographs of those smiling boys and girls amid the broken glass, so like the photos of the Warsaw Rising in 1944. I think of Yeats: "a terrible beauty is born." Then I look at some of the meticulous reconstructions of the street fighting by Hungarian historians, using long interviews with survivors. I talk with Mária Wittner, described to me by another survivor as the revolution's Joan of Arc. It is a deeply moving conversation. But even she cannot really explain to me how, as a nineteen-year-old girl from a convent school, she came to pick up that ammunition belt and start reloading the guns for the boys on the roof, shooting back at the guards of the Budapest radio station on 23 October. She talks of "something in the air," of the "vibrations." But the filters of retrospection are too strong.

She wants to speak for those who can no longer speak: her dead comrades, the unknown insurgents. Much of her life since 1989 has been devoted to that purpose. Yet their experience is lost, irrevocably. We don't know, we will never know, what it was really like at the eye of the storm. Beside history regained, there is history lost. In history, too, there is always a sixth coffin.

2

The other thing that we are supposed to know more about is the consequences, and hence the larger "meaning," of the event. For this we plainly have to consider the alternatives. Purely hypothetical counterfactuals can be fun and illuminating too, but more important are the alternatives that were considered seriously at the time. As we have found from the documents, major alternatives were considered—for example, by Khrushchev. What if the advice from Togliatti, Tito, and Mao had been different? What if American policy had been clearer, one way or the other? What if the British and French had not launched the Suez adventure at exactly the same time? Might the Soviet leadership then at least have tried the second path—withdrawal, negotiations—a little longer and more seriously?

But what would have been the impact of that on Poland? For if the Hungarian revolution started with a demonstration beneath the statue of the Polish General Bem, who himself had been a hero of the Hungarian revolution of 1848–1849, the Polish October was hugely influenced by what happened in Hungary. Khrushchev's "peaceful path" in Hungary would surely have encouraged the Poles to ask for the same or more. If the Soviet Union might just have been prepared to countenance an Austrian status for Hungary—in which, after all, even Stalin had proposed only a fifty-fifty split with the West, in his famous "percentages agreement" with Churchill—it was another thing to countenance that for Poland.[5] This, in turn, would have meant countenancing it for Germany—the larger, Western part of which was already in NATO.

Or take another if: What if Hungary had stopped at radical reform, rather than revolution,

[5] See my review essay, "From World War to Cold War," *The New York Review of Books,* June 11, 1987.

as the reform communists around Imre Nagy would have wished, and as Poland did? What might have happened then? Well, look what happened in Poland, where the hopes invested in Gomułka in 1956 were progressively and comprehensively disappointed. Is there any reason to believe that the same would not have happened in Hungary?

Orwell once remarked that "All revolutions are failures, but they are not all the same failure." The consequences appear different at different times, and some emerge only decades later. To describe 1956 as "the victory of a defeat," as the exiled Hungarian historian Miklós Molnár did in his book of 1968, was not merely romantic hyperbole and wishful thinking.[6] Perhaps the simplest and most direct consequence is one that could be seen immediately but has endured. This is quite simply the sympathy and positive feeling toward Hungary on the part of people around the world who either had hardly noticed its existence before or had had a rather negative image of the country, seeing it as an oppressor of minorities before 1914 and Germany's ally in two world wars. This basic positive association from 1956, supplanting a negative or nonexistent one, has persisted and remains a national treasure—or asset, to use language more appropriate to the 1990s—as the country strives to join the EU and NATO.

Another consequence that emerged immediately but also endured was the impact on the left throughout the world. This was a moment of bitter disillusionment with Soviet communism, of growing doubts in communist hearts, and the parting of ways between democratic and undemocratic socialists. The Chinese historian Jian Chen argues that it also hastened the great split between communist China and the Soviet Union.

Beyond this, however, someone reflecting on the tenth anniversary of the revolution, in 1966, would have been pushed to find many more elements of positive legacy, of clear gain to set against the obvious loss. On the twentieth anniversary, in 1976, one could already add something more. By this time it was clear that the Kádár regime was, if not more "liberal" than other communist regimes in Eastern Europe—that label was always misplaced—then certainly more cautious, circumspect, indirect, subtle, velvet-gloved in the way it treated its own people.[7] This could be and was traced back to the trauma of 1956, when the communist party and state had collapsed in a matter of a few days, and perhaps also, more even than we guessed at the time, to Kádár's personal sense of guilt. On the thirtieth anniversary, in 1986, one might have added the growing importance in Hungarian independent and oppositional thinking of the rediscovery of intellectual and political tendencies of 1956—for example, the work of the distinguished political thinker István Bibó, author of a famous last declaration on behalf of the Nagy government.[8]

The great temptation, of course, is to draw a straight line from 1956 to 1989. There is a very narrow boundary between the historian's privilege of hindsight and Bergson's "illusions of retrospective determinism." Nonetheless, there are connections to be made. For example, I do not think that it is fanciful to make a connection between Soviet policy toward Eastern Europe in 1956 and that in 1989. Top Soviet policymakers, starting with Gorbachev, clearly remembered the political cost to the Soviet Union of the interventions in 1956 as well as 1968. In 1956, the Soviet leaders did not know what to do and therefore used force. In 1989, the Soviet leaders also did not know what to do—but they did know what not to do: use force.

Nor is it fanciful to see Hungary 1956 as an important milepost in what may be described as the cumulative learning process of Central European oppositions and governments, from the sheer outburst of popular fury in East Berlin in 1953, through 1956 in Poland and Hungary, 1968 in Czechoslovakia, 1980–1981 in Poland, to the sophisticated peaceful change of system in

---

[6] *Victoire d'une défaite* is the title of the original French edition (Fayard, 1968). The English edition is entitled *Budapest 1956: A History of the Hungarian Revolution* (London: Allen and Unwin, 1971).

[7] Suitably enough, Miklós Haraszti's book on the position of artists under Kádárism was entitled *The Velvet Prison* (New York: Basic Books, 1987). See also my "The Hungarian Lesson" in *The Uses of Adversity: Essays on the Fate of Central Europe*, new ed. (London: Penguin, 1999).

[8] See István Bibó, *Democracy, Revolution, Self-Determination: Selected Writings*, ed. Károly Nagy (Boulder, Colo.: Social Science Monographs, 1991).

1989–1990, which I christened "refolution."[9] Moreover, it is undeniable that the largest symbolic event in the Hungarian refolution of 1989 was the ceremonial reburial of Imre Nagy on 16 June, the anniversary of his execution in 1958. The six coffins laid out on Heroes' Square, the revolutionary flags once again hanging from the lampposts: an occasion unforgettable to anyone who was there. And the past was a catalyst of the future.

However, the emergence of new evidence already slightly changes our view even of that very recent event. Documents found in the Interior Ministry archives by the longtime oppositionist János Kenedi now show how both the party leadership and the still active secret police used all possible means at their disposal—including, for example, "agents of influence" who had access to the American ambassador—to ensure that the reburial and attendant ceremonies passed off peacefully.[10] Kádár's successors, the new reform communists of 1989, appealed directly and indirectly to Nagy's surviving comrades, the reform communists of 1956.

The kaleidoscope does not stop turning. Now, in 1996, it is a free Hungary. The president of the republic, Árpád Göncz, was himself imprisoned for his attempts to mediate after the 1956 revolution, having been tried together with István Bibó. Wise, warm, avuncular, he is supremely fitted to mark the anniversary. The famous Plot 301 in a remote corner of the municipal cemetery, where Nagy and his comrades were given indecent burial after their execution in 1958, was a site of weeds and rubbish dumps when I first visited it in 1988 and still a place of freshly turned earth and recent clearing at the reburial in 1989. Now it has neat turf, marble tablets, paving stones, a monument—everything that belongs to an official place of public memory.

So far, so good. But the current government of the country is dominated by the Hungarian Socialist Party, the main successor to the ruling communist party. The socialists were elected, with a landslide majority, in 1994 and govern in coalition with the Alliance of Free Democrats, the main heirs to the liberal-democratic opposition of the 1980s, who now find themselves a junior and uncomfortable partner of the post-communists. And the prime minister, Gyula Horn? Well, he was a reform communist in the 1980s, and as foreign minister he was partly responsible for opening the Iron Curtain to Austria in 1989 and letting the East Germans out later that year—thus beginning the end of the Berlin Wall. But in 1956? No, in 1956 young Gyula, aged twenty-four, was a member of the feared and hated volunteer militias, known on account of their distinctive heavy quilted jackets as the *pufajkások* (roughly, "quilted-jacket guys'), who fought, detained, and beat up those who continued to resist.

He has explained his actions. He was young, and he blamed the revolutionaries for the death of a much-loved elder brother. He has, up to a point, apologized. He has, in a way, tried to make amends—for example, by increasing special pensions for the survivors. But his way of dealing with the problem is deeply ambiguous. For it also involves trying to draw a line under the past—and to claim Nagy's inheritance. Soon after becoming prime minister, he joined Imre Nagy's daughter in a ceremony at Plot 301 to mark the anniversary of the revolution. Then, earlier this year, it was Horn who proposed in parliament a special commemorative law to mark the hundredth anniversary of the birth of Imre Nagy. The Free Democrats did not know which way to turn. Of course Nagy should be honored, but at the initiative of a man like Horn? In the end, they abstained. This strange custom of the commemorative law, incidentally, has a history in Hungary reaching back into the nineteenth century. The hero of the 1848–1849 revolution, Lajos Kossuth, for example, was thus commemorated after his death. However, the last person to have been so honored by the Hungarian parliament was Joseph Stalin. And the man who proposed that tribute? The then president of the parliament, Imre Nagy. In Hungary, the ironies and ambiguities just never seem to stop.

How many more turns of the kaleidoscope will we see? As it looks now, Hungary has a very good chance of celebrating the fiftieth anniversary of the revolution as a full member of what we

[9] "Refolution in Hungary and Poland," *The New York Review of Books*, August 17, 1989.

[10] János Kenedi, *Kis Állambiztonsági Olvasókönyv a Kádár-korszakban* (A small reader on the state security services in the Kádár period) (Budapest: Magvető, 1996).

unreflectingly call "Europe" and "the West." Of the EU, that is. And of NATO. It will thus become, to recall John Foster Dulles's words in 1956, a military ally of the United States. But what will those two things mean in 2006? What will the internal condition of Hungary be then, and how will it affect Hungarians' views of 1956? How much more, and how much less, will we then know about the revolution? It is precisely the mark of great events that their meaning constantly changes, is forever disputed, with some questions never finally answered. Questions such as, What happened in France in 1789?

Timothy Garton Ash
Oxford University

EDITORS' INTRODUCTION AND ACKNOWLEDGMENTS

The Hungarian revolution was the most dramatic event in an extraordinarily eventful year. Beginning with Soviet leader Nikita Khrushchev's denunciation of Stalin and Stalinism in a secret speech at the Twentieth Party Congress of the Soviet Communist Party in February 1956, pressures for reform in Eastern Europe accelerated the unraveling of the system of oppression and centralized control that had previously held sway. Nowhere were these broad social forces more prevalent than in Hungary where the process of lifting the lid on social and political freedoms brought widespread expectations for meaningful change—including the possibility of outright independence from Soviet domination.

At first, the Kremlin even encouraged the idea of reform, albeit within the framework of communist rule. Khrushchev understood the need on a number of levels to end the most extreme forms of repression that Stalin's protégés—the leaders of the East European communist parties—had exercised since coming to power after World War II. But he was most keenly interested in finding a solution to the economic crisis that was engulfing the socialist camp and that had been one of the most unwelcome by-products of Stalinism. By granting limited social and political freedoms, he hoped to channel a burst of public energy toward revamping the region's agricultural and industrial base. His goal was always to solidify the socialist community, not to help it disintegrate or to dilute Moscow's control.

But conditions in the camp, especially in Hungary, were too advanced and complex to be responsive to this kind of fine-tuning. When nationalist and democratic impulses finally exploded into a nation-wide revolt beginning on October 23, 1956, the Soviets, after some internal vacillation, finally resolved to crush the uprising before it weakened their position in the empire any further. The impact of this decision affected not only developments in the region but world politics as well, including the superpower rivalry. For more than 30 years, the natural movement toward political independence was put in something of a deep freeze as even public mention of the revolution in Hungary was taboo. This forced suppression of national memory ultimately magnified the significance of 1956 when communist rule finally collapsed in Hungary more than three decades later. Even today, the uprising, which was a far more complex social and political phenomenon than is sometimes understood, is seen by Hungarians as a defining moment in the country's history.

Only after the demise of the communist regimes in the region in 1989 did it become possible to begin to piece together the full story of what happened during the previous 40 years. The substantial opening of most national archives allowed scholars and the public to explore for the first time the internal secrets of their former rulers to try to understand the circumstances, decisions and events that surrounded key crises like the Hungarian revolution.

This volume represents the first major English-language attempt to systematically cull the newly opened archives of all the countries in the region, including the former Soviet Union, as well as presenting key documents from U.S., British and French archives, to produce a multinational account of the Hungarian revolution. There are, naturally, several monographs and many other publications in Hungarian based on similar research, and in recent years there has been one major English-language study of the period in monograph form written by a team of scholars at the 1956 Institute.[11] But this volume goes beyond that earlier effort in several ways. Most importantly, it combines two functions—it is both a compendium of recently declassified, primary source documentation, and a detailed description and analysis of the revolution. Moreover, it is the first to reproduce significant numbers of records from the highest levels of the party and state in both Hungary and the USSR, including some of their most sensitive intel-

---

[11] György Litván, ed., *The Hungarian Revolution of 1956: Reform, Revolt and Repression, 1953–1963* (London: Longman, 1996).

ligence and military files, as well as similar materials from seven other national archival repositories giving readers a truly multinational perspective on the subject.

The volume is divided into three sections. The essay and documents in Part I. describe the immediate history leading up to the revolution from 1953–1956 when Moscow's nod toward reform unleashed pent-up nationalist, social, and political feelings in Hungary, which led to the public outpouring that began on October 23. Part II. covers the uprising itself incorporating the local Hungarian, regional, Soviet, and Western viewpoints. It focuses particularly on the complex political and social picture inside Hungary and the wavering of Kremlin decision-makers. Part III. deals with the revolution's aftermath and its impact on Hungary, the region, and the superpowers. The final section is a brief documentary epilogue which presents the post-1989 Soviet and later Russian governments' apologies for Soviet actions in 1956.

As with the other volumes in this series of documents readers, this book is structured to offer readers information in a variety of forms. First and foremost, the 120 documents in this collection are among the most important primary source records available on the events themselves and on the calculations of the key players. They are the core of the book. Secondly, the introductory essays for each chapter provide an analytical framework and historical context for the documents. These concise yet detailed introductions go well beyond standard prefatory accounts and are based on extensive research over a number of years. The editors' aim was to provide an analytical account that could either accompany the documents or stand alone. Another unique feature of this series is the use of "headnotes" at the beginning of each document that give important supplementary information about the events described in the documents, or about the documents themselves and the context in which they were produced. In addition, the editors have provided hundreds of footnotes to flesh out obscure details for a general, international audience about the people, places, and events being covered. Finally, the volume includes glossaries of key individuals, organizations, and abbreviations, a chronology and a bibliography as additional background and as guides for further research. A note on spellings: the editors have followed the original language spellings of most East European names; however, the renderings of those names in original English-language documents have been retained.

Many of the documents included here were first compiled for use at an unusual conference held in Budapest in September 1996. On the revolution's 40th anniversary, scholars from Hungary, Russia, the United States, Canada, Great Britain, France, Israel, Italy, Poland, and Romania joined veterans of the events themselves to recollect and reassess what had happened. Among the veterans were Gyula Borbándi, William Griffith, Miklós Molnár, Miklós Vásárhelyi, and Mária Wittner. The scholars included some of the best known specialists on Hungary and on the Cold War in Eastern Europe. Topics covered included the legacy of the revolution in Hungary, new evidence on Soviet policy toward Hungary, the uprising's impact on Eastern Europe and its relation to the Polish crisis, the impact on the superpowers, the role of Radio Free Europe, and the connections between the events of 1956 and 1989. More than just an anniversary event, the gathering produced an invaluable mix of documented history with oral history—at a point in time far enough removed from the events for a decent written record to be available, but not too many years afterwards so that first-hand accounts were still possible.[12]

The leading organizer of the 1996 conference was the Institute for the History of the 1956 Hungarian Revolution. The 1956 Institute was established in 1991 with the mission of conducting research on the previously prohibited topic of the revolution. In the years since then, the organization has become a center for the broader study of contemporary Hungarian history, and has developed a wide reputation in the international scholarly community. The scholarship presented in this volume builds on more than 10 years' analysis and archival research conducted by the staff of the Institute, often in conjunction with fellow scholars in Hungary and abroad.

In 1992, the Institute became a partner of the National Security Archive, a research organiza-

---

[12] The 1956 Institute published the conference papers in Hungarian in their Yearbook: *Évkönyv V.* 1996–1997 (Budapest: 1956-os Intézet, 1997).

tion, freedom of information advocate, and publisher of declassified documents, which at the time was initiating a project to promote cooperative research into, and broad public access to, the previously hidden history of the region. The Openness in Russia and Eastern Europe Project involved organizing multinational research groups to explore previously closed archival sources, sponsoring conferences (such as the 1996 event) where new findings could be brought to light for scholars and the general public, and publishing collections such as this volume. Funding for the Openness Project has come primarily from the Open Society Institute, the John D. and Catherine T. MacArthur Foundation, the Smith Richardson Foundation and the German Marshall Fund of the United States. The editors gratefully acknowledge their generosity over the years.

In the course of preparing this volume, the editors have received support of many other kinds as well, which they are pleased to acknowledge.

First mention must go to József Litkei and Gregory F. Domber, whose extraordinary contributions of time and mental energy were felt in all phases of the project.

We would also like to thank the staffs of the 1956 Institute and the National Security Archive for their consistent support for, and patience with us. The following people deserve particular mention. At the Institute, Kata Somlai helped with the collection and organization of materials at an early stage of the project. Attila Szakolczai contributed to the writing of the essay for Parts I. and II., provided editorial assistance on the glossaries and other research aids, as well as co-authoring the chronology. Gusztáv Kecskés helped draft a number of headnotes and footnotes. László Eörsi, Pál Germuska, László Győri and Réka Sárközy also contributed in various ways.

At the Archive, Executive Director Thomas S. Blanton provided intellectual and moral support throughout the project. James G. Hershberg, archive fellow and also professor of history and international relations at George Washington University, was a fount of knowledge and ideas. Christian Ostermann, now director of the Cold War International History Project at the Woodrow Wilson International Center for Scholars, contributed to the original conception and organization of the volume. Catherine Nielsen played a key role, helping to research, collect and organize archival documents as well as copy-edit drafts of the manuscript. Aliza Saivetz, Mary Burroughs, and Sue Bechtel contributed much appreciated administrative support to the project. Special thanks to Suzanne R. Peake for preparing the index.

For their invaluable contributions of documents, advice or other assistance to the project, we thank Jordan Baev, László Borhi, William Burr, Raymond L. Garthoff, Timothy Garton Ash, Charles Gati, Leo Gluchowski, William Griffith, Tibor Hajdu, Paul Henze, Melinda Kalmár, János Kenedi, Béla Király, Mark Kramer, James Marchio, James C. McCargar, Valerii Musatov, Vladimir Pechatnov, Mihai Retegan, Zoltán Ripp, Svetlana Savranskaya, Vyacheslav Sereda, Alexander Stykalin, János Tischler, and Vladislav Zubok.

The book would not have been possible without the translating expertise of Benjamin Aldrich-Moodie, András Bocz, Mónika Borbély, Victoria Isabela Corduneanu, Mark Doctoroff, David Evans, Csaba Farkas, Johanna Granville, Leo Gluchowski, Velichka Hristová, Attila Kolontári, Mark Kramer, József Litkei, Christa Matthews, Maya Nadkarni, József Reiter, Claudia Rossi, Svetlana Savranskaya, Kata Somlai, István Török and Vladislav Zubok. Paul E. Zinner was particularly generous in sharing translations from his book, published just one month after the revolution, *National Communism and Popular Revolt in Eastern Europe (New York: Columbia University Press, 1956).*

Numerous archivists and access professionals have played a key, if generally unrecognized, part in establishing the new historical record on Hungary 1956. Those whose role we know of first-hand include: Mária Bozsics and György Lázár at the Hungarian National Archives; the archival staff of the National Archives and Records Administration at College Park, Maryland, the Dwight D. Eisenhower Library, the archives of the United Nations, the Library of Congress, NATO Archives, Brussels, the former Center for the Preservation of Contemporary Documentation (Moscow), the History and Records Department of the Russian Foreign Ministry; and the Freedom of Information staffs of the State Department, Defense Department and Central Intelligence Agency.

Key collaborating and supporting institutions for the 1996 conference were the Cold War International History Project at the Woodrow Wilson International Center for Scholars in Washington and the Hungarian Academy of Sciences in Budapest (co-sponsors of the 1996 conference), and also in Budapest the Europa Institut, the Institute of History of the Hungarian Academy of Sciences, Central European University, and the Open Society Archives.

Finally, we are very pleased to continue the publication of this series through CEU Press. Our warm thanks to all our colleagues there, especially to former Director and Editor Klára Takácsi-Nagy for all her kind support and cooperation over the past several years; to her successor, István Bart; and to Mária Magyar, Richárd Rados, Ágnes Sümegi and Martin Greenwald.

ACRONYMS AND ABBREVIATIONS

ÁVH	State Security Authority, *Államvédelmi Hatóság* (Hungarian secret police, name adopted in 1948)
ÁVO	Department of State Security, *Államvédelmi Osztály* (Hungarian secret police, name in use from 1946 until 1948)
BCP	Bulgarian Communist Party, *Bulgarska Kommunisticheska Partiya*
CC	Central Committee
Cde.	Comrade
CIA	Central Intelligence Agency
CMEA	Council of Mutual Economic Assistance
COMECON	See, CMEA.
CPC	Communist Party of China, *Zhongguo Gongchan Dang*
CPSU	Communist Party of the Soviet Union, *Kommunisticheskaya Partiya Sovietskogo Soyuza*
CPCz	Communist Party of Czechoslovakia, *Kommunistická Strana Československá*
ČSR	Czechoslovak Socialist Republic
DISZ	Union of Working Youth, *Dolgozó Ifjúság Szövetsége*
FO	Foreign Office (Great Britain)
FPRY	Federal People's Republic of Yugoslavia
FRG	Federal Republic of Germany
GDR	German Democratic Republic
HPR	Hungarian People's Republic
HWP	Hungarian Workers' Party, *Magyar Dolgozók Pártja or MDP*
HSWP	Hungarian Socialist Workers' Party, *Magyar Szocialista Munkáspárt or MSZMP*
ICP	Italian Communist Party
KGB	Committee for State Security (USSR),
KMT	Greater Budapest Central Workers' Council, *Nagybudapesti Központi Munkástanács*
MEFESZ	Hungarian Association of University and College Unions, *Magyar Egyetemista és Főiskolai Egyesületek Szövetsége*
MID	Soviet Ministry of Foreign Affairs, *Ministerstvo Inostrannykh Del*
MP	Member of Parliament
NATO	North Atlantic Treaty Organization
NIE	National Intelligence Estimate
NPP	National Peasant Party, *Nemzeti Parasztpárt*
NSC	National Security Council (U.S.)
OCB	Operations Coordinating Board (U.S. State Department)
PC	Political Committee
PCC	Provisional Central Committee, *Ideiglenes Központi Bizottság*
PEC	Provisional Executive Committee, *Ideiglenes Intéző Bizottság*
PZPR	Polish United Workers' Party, *Polska Zjednoczona Partia Robotnicza*
RFE	Radio Free Europe
RPR	Romanian People's Republic
RWP	Romanian Workers' Party, *Partidul Muncitoresc Român*
SED	German Socialist Unity Party (GDR), *Sozialistische Einheitspartei*

	Deutschlands
SNIE	Special National Intelligence Estimate
SZDP	Social Democratic Party, *Szociáldemokrata Párt*
SZOT	National Council of [Hungarian] Trade Unions, *Szakszervezetek Országos Tanácsa*
U.N.	United Nations
UNGA	United Nations General Assembly
UNSC	United Nations Security Council
USIA	United States Information Agency
USSR	Union of Soviet Socialist Republics
WTO	Warsaw Treaty Organization
YLC	Yugoslav League of Communists, *Savez Kommunista Jugoslavije*

ABBREVIATIONS USED IN DOCUMENT
SOURCE CITATIONS

AAN	Archive of Modern Acts (Warsaw), *Archiwum Akt Nowych*
AMSZ	Archive of the Ministry of Foreign Affairs (Warsaw), *Archiwum Ministerwstwa Spraw Zagranicznich*
AMVR	Bulgarian State Security Archives (Sofia), *Archiv Ministerstvo Na V'treshnite Roboti*
APRF	Archive of the President of the Russian Federation (Moscow), *Arkhiv Prezidenta Rossiiskoi Federatsii*
Arh. CC al PCR	Archive of the Central Committee of the Romanian Communist Party (Bucharest), *Arhivele Comitetul Central al Partidul Comunist Român*
AÚV KSČ	Archive of the CPCZ CC (Prague), *Archiv Ústředního Výboru Kommunistická Strana Československa*
AVPRF	Foreign Policy Archive of the Russian Federation (Moscow), *Arkhiv vneshnei politiki Rossiiskoi Federatsii*
D.	*Delo*
Dok.	*Dokument*
FRUS	*Foreign Relations of the United States*
HL/HM	Hungarian Military History Archive (Budapest)
Ll.	*listy*
MOL	Hungarian National Archives, *Magyar Országos Levéltár*
NA II	U.S National Archives (College Park, Maryland)
Op.	*Opis*
Pap.	*Papka*
Per.	*Perechen'*
Por.	*Portfel'*
PRO.FO	Public Record Office, British Foreign Office (Kew Gardens)
RG	Record Group
TsKhSD	Center for the Storage of Contemporary Documentation (Moscow), *Tsentr khraneniia sovremennoi dokumentatsii*

CHRONOLOGY OF EVENTS

1953

March 5: Soviet dictator Joseph Stalin dies. A major reorganization of the Soviet leadership follows.

March 8: The Hungarian Parliament passes legislation perpetuating the "undying memory" of Stalin and orders a national period of mourning.

May 17: Parliamentary elections in Hungary take place, following the Stalinist pattern.

June 1: Disturbances break out in Czechoslovakia. Workers demonstrating in Plzeň occupy the city hall and display national and U.S. flags. The movement is suppressed by the special police.

June 13–16: Hungary's party and state leaders are summoned to Moscow. Mátyás Rákosi's monopoly on power is ended. He is instructed to hand over the reins as prime minister to Imre Nagy but is allowed to remain as head of the communist party. The main lines of a "New Course" are drawn. The talks, and even the fact that they took place, remains a secret for 30 years.

June 15: The Soviet Union resumes diplomatic relations with Yugoslavia and with Israel.

June 17–18: A workers' uprising takes place in East Berlin and other cities of the German Democratic Republic (GDR). It is the first major protest of its kind in the Soviet bloc. The Soviet military is called in to suppress the insurrection.

June 26: Soviet secret police chief Lavrentii Beria is arrested in Moscow, dismissed from all his positions and excluded from the party. The move is part of the ongoing Kremlin leadership struggle.

July 4: Prime Minister Imre Nagy, in a speech to the new Parliament, outlines the New Course featuring a general relaxation of centralized political, economic and administrative controls mirroring the attitudes of the post-Stalin leadership in the Kremlin.

July 21: A unified Ministry of the Interior is established in Hungary, reintegrating the ÁVH (security police) into the new Ministry's structure.

July 25: As part of Imre Nagy's reform program, a partial amnesty for political prisoners is declared in Hungary.

July 26: The Hungarian Council of Ministers passes a resolution ending the practices of internment and internal exile.

August 8: Soviet Prime Minister Georgii Malenkov announces that the Soviets have successfully tested a hydrogen bomb.

Autumn: Sharp cuts in the size of the Hungarian People's Army begin. By November 15, its strength has been reduced to 150,000 men.

September 6: The Hungarian government announces wide-ranging price reductions.

September 9: Hungary and Yugoslavia resume diplomatic relations.

September 13: Nikita Khrushchev is elected first secretary of the Communist Party of the Soviet Union (CPSU).

December 11: The U.S. National Security Council re-examines its policy towards Eastern Europe. Described in NSC 174, the new policy provides for a scaled-back approach to fomenting dissent in the Soviet bloc after the June uprisings in East Germany.

December 24: A Hungarian court finds former head of the ÁVH, Gábor Péter, and 17 others guilty of abuse of power and crimes against the people.

1954

May 5: Consultations take place between the CPSU Presidium and a HWP delegation in Moscow. While criticizing both Rákosi and Nagy, the Soviets continue to express support for Nagy's reform program.

May 24–30: The Third Congress of the HWP is held in an atmosphere of political uncertainty and leadership deadlock.

July 7: ÁVH Lieutenant-General László Piros is appointed minister of the interior, replacing Ernő Gerő. Gerő remains a deputy prime minister.

October 20: The central party daily, *Szabad Nép* ("Free People"), carries an article by Imre Nagy that is unusual in that it makes clear that the party leadership is engaged in serious in-fighting, and offers the first analysis of the reasons for the conflict.

October 23–24: The founding congress of the Patriotic People's Front elects the writer Pál Szabó as president and the Reformed Church minister Ferenc Jánosi as general secretary. Imre Nagy's speech on national unity later leads to charges of nationalism against him.

November 8: Soviet–Hungarian joint ventures are transferred to 100 per cent Hungarian ownership in a series of economic transactions.

November 21: An article in *Szabad Nép,* instigated by Mihály Farkas, initiates an attack on Nagy's policy line and the reform movement among writers and journalists.

December 1: Rákosi reports to the HWP Political Committee on a message received from the Presidium of the CPSU Central Committee. This begins the process of ousting Imre Nagy from power.

December 15: The HWP Political Committee, in Nagy's absence, passes a resolution pointing out the existence of a "right-wing danger" and condemns Nagy's policies. There is a purge among the staff at *Szabad Nép.*

1955

January 8: During consultations with a HWP delegation that includes both Nagy and Rákosi, the Presidium of the CPSU Central Committee in Moscow strongly criticizes Nagy's policies.

January 25: The Supreme Soviet in Moscow issues a decree declaring the state of war between the Soviet Union and Germany to be over.

March 2–4: At a meeting of the HWP Central Committee, the leadership does not annul the earlier resolution of June 1953, but it identifies the "right-wing, anti-Marxist, anti-party, opportunist" views represented by Imre Nagy as the main danger.

March 25: The Petőfi Circle is founded as an adjunct of the Union of Working Youth (DISZ). Following the Twentieth Congress of the CPSU in February 1956, it becomes a center for vibrant socio-political discussion among intellectuals and the general public.

April 14: A resolution adopted at a meeting of the HWP Central Committee accuses Nagy of anti-party activity and factionalism. Nagy, who still refuses to express regret for his activities, is removed from the Political Committee and the Central Committee and deprived of all party functions. By the end of April he is compelled to resign his seat in Parliament and on the Budapest City Council, as well as all other official positions.

April 18: András Hegedüs is appointed prime minister, as proposed by Rákosi.

May 9: The FRG is admitted into NATO, as the Paris treaties come into force.

May 14: The Warsaw Pact is formed.

May 15: The Austrian State Treaty is signed, making Austria an independent, neutral country.

May 26–June 2: A delegation led by Khrushchev, Bulganin, Mikoyan and Shepilov visits Belgrade. Relations between the Soviet Union and Yugoslavia are normalized.

July 17: Cardinal József Mindszenty, primate of the Hungarian Catholic Church, is moved from prison to house arrest in Felsőpetény, Nógrád County.

July 18: An article in *Szabad Nép* blames former ÁVH chief Gábor Péter and his "gang" for the deterioration in Yugoslav-Hungarian relations.

July 18–23: The Geneva summit between the Soviet Union, the Unites States, Britain and France takes place.

November 20 and 22: Two groups of about 1,200 political prisoners return from the Soviet Union. Among them is Béla Kovács, former general secretary of the Smallholders' Party (FKgP).

December 14: Hungary, Bulgaria and Romania are among 16 new members admitted to the United Nations.

1956

January 1: The ÁVH undergoes a major reduction in size.

January 23: Nikolai Bulganin, the Soviet prime minister, proposes in a letter to President Eisenhower that their two countries conclude a friendship and mutual non-aggression treaty.

February 14–25: The Twentieth Congress of the CPSU marks a turning point in the policy and ideology of the Soviet party and of the international communist movement. The concluding resolution declares that a third world war is no longer inevitable and proclaims "peaceful coexistence" between the two world systems. In a four-hour secret speech, Khrushchev denounces Stalin's crimes in detail.

March 8: The Hungarian government abolishes the restricted border zone between Hungary and Yugoslavia.

March 12–13: Rákosi reports on the Twentieth Congress to the HWP Central Committee. He declares that the HWP has already been working along the lines prescribed by the congress.

March 17: The Petőfi Circle holds its first major event: an informal meeting of former leaders of MEFESZ (the Hungarian Association of University and College Unions).

March 27: Speaking at a meeting of regional party activists, Rákosi admits that the 1949 treason trial of László Rajk was a show trial.

April 7: The COMINFORM is disbanded.

April 10: Poland rehabilitates Władysław Gomułka, former general secretary of the communist party, who was convicted of anti-communist activities in 1951.

April 27: The guidelines for Hungary's Second Five-Year Plan are put forward for public discussion.

May 18: Mátyás Rákosi makes what is to be his final public appearance, at a meeting of HWP activists in Budapest.

June 1: Vyacheslav Molotov, a leading hard-line rival of Khrushchev and one of the main opponents of reconciliation with Yugoslavia, is dismissed as foreign minister. He is allowed to hold on to the posts of deputy prime minister and member of the CPSU Presidium.

June 6: A small circle of Nagy adherents, along with a number of prominent public personalities, meets at Imre Nagy's house to celebrate his 60th birthday.

June 6–14: Soviet Presidium member Mikhail Suslov holds talks in Budapest with members of the HWP leadership, as well as with János Kádár personally.

June 27: A Petőfi Circle debate on aspects of the press and information, held at the Central Officers' Hall, attracts an audience of 5,000–6,000.

June 28: In Poznań, Poland, 100,000 workers take to the streets calling for improvements in living and working conditions and free elections. Security forces break up the crowds, leaving about 100 dead and several hundred wounded. About 600 demonstrators are arrested.

June 30: The HWP Central Committee drafts a resolution that condemns the "anti-party leanings" of the Petőfi Circle.

July 3: Szabad Nép publishes the June 30 CPSU Central Committee resolution on the cult of personality.

July 10: Speakers at a party meeting in the Writers' Union openly criticize the June 30 resolution of the HWP Central Committee.

July 12: The U.S. National Security Council issues NSC 5608 reconsidering American policy toward Eastern Europe.

July 13: Soviet Presidium member Anastas Mikoyan arrives unexpectedly in Budapest to oversee the dismissal of Rákosi.

July 18: At a HWP CC meeting, Rákosi, citing his "state of health," steps down and departs for the Soviet Union. He is replaced by Ernő Gerő. András Hegedüs remains as prime minister.

September: Residents displaced from the Hungarian–Yugoslav border zone are allowed to return to their homes.

September 1: The Presidential Council rehabilitates 50 previously convicted social democrats.

September 17: The General Assembly of the Writers' Union demonstrates in support of Nagy.

September 19: The Petőfi Circle resumes its public debates after a break of two-and-a-half months.

September 19: Authorities complete the final stages of the removal of technical equipment sealing the Hungarian-Austrian border.

September 30: Tito and Gerő meet in the Kremlin, continuing the process of political reconciliation between Hungary and Yugoslavia. Gerő reports on their discussions at the HWP Political Committee meeting on October 8.

October: Troop reductions in the Hungarian People's Army continue. The strength of the army at the outbreak of the revolution is 120,000–130,000 men.

October 4: The Soviet government provides Hungary a loan of 100 million rubles for 1957.

October 4: High-ranking ÁVH officers are arrested.

October 6: László Rajk and his associates, executed for treason in a 1949 show trial, are formally reburied. *Szabad Nép* carries a lengthy front-page article entitled "Never Again" about communists who were executed seven years before. A crowd of 100,000 attends the funeral.

October 8: The newspaper *Hétfői Hírlap* ("Monday News") begins publication. It is the first example of a more relaxed style of newspaper to appear since 1948.

October 12: Mihály Farkas, former member of the inner leadership, is arrested on orders of the Chief Public Prosecutor's Department and eventually sentenced to 16 years in prison.

October 13: After lengthy efforts by Nagy, The HWP Political Committee passes a resolution readmitting him into the party.

October 15: A party and government delegation consisting of Ernő Gerő, Antal Apró, András Hegedüs, János Kádár and István Kovács leaves for a week's visit to Belgrade.

October 15: Reacting to the improvement in Soviet–Yugoslav relations, the United States supends aid deliveries to Belgrade.

October 16: An assembly of about 1,600 undergraduates in the city of Szeged founds the Hungarian Association of University and College Unions, MEFESZ, a student organization independent of the party-sanctioned DISZ and the HWP.

October 19: Soviet leader Khrushchev heads a top-level delegation on an unannounced visit to Warsaw after the Polish party Central Committee votes for Władysław Gomułka to become first secretary. Gomułka persuades the Kremlin not to intervene militarily in Poland, promising to maintain Poland's military and ideological commitments to the Soviet bloc.

October 19: Soviet troops stationed in Hungary are placed on alert in connection with the events in Poland.

October 19: MEFESZ holds a meeting at Szeged University. After accepting demands of a partly political nature, the organization dispatches delegates throughout the country to spread the word about the formation of the organization and the demands that have been formulated.

October 22: A large student assembly from across Hungary convenes at Budapest Technical University and debates the demands put forward by the MEFESZ delegates from Szeged. Several other student meetings take place in the capital during the day. The students adopt the first version of the so-called "16 points," a set of demands that would become the standard reference point for the demonstrations of the following days.

October 23: Szabad Nép publishes a front-page article entitled "New Spring Parade," welcoming the demands being put forward by the country's youth.

October 23: The Hungarian party and government delegation returns from Yugoslavia in the early morning. An expanded meeting of the HWP Political Committee is held to discuss the unfolding socio-political crisis.

October 23, 11 a.m.: A student demonstration begins in the university city of Debrecen.

October 23, 12:53 p.m.: Radio Kossuth broadcasts a statement by the interior ministry banning a public demonstration planned for later in the day. However, at 2:23 p.m., the decision is reversed and permission for the rally is granted.

October 23, 3:00 p.m.: A student-led march leaves the Petőfi statue on the Pest embankment, crosses the Margaret Bridge and heads for the statue to Polish General Bem on the Buda side of the Danube. Meanwhile other groups of students march toward the statue along the Buda embankment.

October 23, about 5:00 p.m.: The first protesters arrive in Kossuth Lajos square (5th District). An hour later, the square is filled with a crowd estimated at 200,000. Also around 5:00, demonstrators gather at the Hungarian Radio building in Bródy Sándor street (8th District) to read out the students' 16 points. The force defending the building is strengthened, but some soldiers support the protesters. The siege of the Radio building starts at about 10 p.m. and lasts until dawn.

October 23, about 6:00 p.m.: In Debrecen, ÁVH forces fire on demonstrators killing three people— the first casualties of the revolution.

October 23, about 8:00 p.m.: The HWP Central Committee begins an emergency session that continues until dawn. Ernő Gerő requests that Moscow authorize Soviet forces to intervene.

October 23, 9:00 p.m.: Nagy delivers a speech from a second-story balcony of the Parliament building. Although intended to respond to demonstrator concerns, it falls well short of expectations, leading the crowds to continue their protests.

October 23, 9:37 p.m.: Demonstrators on Dózsa György road (14th District) topple a giant statue of Stalin. There are also attacks during the evening on telephone exchanges, printing presses and several arms factories in various parts of the city. Late that night, rebels also attack police stations and semi-military and military institutions. The offices of *Szabad Nép* are stormed as well.

October 23, about 11:00 p.m.: An order is given for Soviet special forces stationed at Székesfehérvár to pacify Budapest.

October 23: Demonstrations take place in other university cities around Hungary.

October 24, 3:00–4:00 a.m.: The first Soviet armored units enter the capital.

October 24, early morning: Rebel forces occupy the Radio building. However, government broadcasting has already moved to the Parliament building.

October 24, 8:13 a.m.: Hungarian radio announces that the HWP Central Committee has confirmed Ernő Gerő as first secretary. Nagy is to be prime minister, with the incumbent András Hegedüs as his deputy.

October 24, 8:45 a.m.: Hungarian radio declares a state of emergency. Factories and schools are closed. Trains continue to run, and basic food supplies as well as utilities are available more or less continuously during the coming weeks.

October 24, noon: Rebels temporarily occupy the Athenaeum Press about midday.

October 24: ÁVH men open fire on marchers in Roosevelt square near the building of the Ministry of Interior (5th District). Soviet soldiers open fire on demonstrators outside Székesfehérvár Town Hall. Six lives are lost.

October 24, 12.10 p.m.: Speaking on the radio, Nagy appeals for calm and an end to the fighting.

October 24: Fighting continues in the neighborhood of the Radio building. A fire breaks out in the natural history section of the National Museum during the afternoon, burning part of it down.

October 24: The first workers' council in Budapest is formed.

October 24: Groups of rebels come together in Baross square (7th and 8th districts), in the southern parts of the 8th and 9th districts, at Corvin Passage (8th District), and on Tompa and Berzenczey streets (9th District).

October 24: Insurrectionists seize large quantities of arms from the Bem square barracks (2nd District).

October 24: Extra Soviet troops are transferred to Hungary from the USSR and Romania. TASS issues a statement in Moscow announcing the defeat of the "counter-revolutionary uprising."

October 24, 8.45 p.m.: János Kádár, speaking on the radio, terms the events a counter-revolution.

October 25: Soviet and Hungarian units reoccupy the Radio building in the early morning hours. The first revolutionary newspaper appears under the title *Igazság* ("Truth").

October 25: Rebels occupy the main police station in the 9th District.

October 25, about 11:15 a.m.: Soviet and Hungarian forces guarding the Parliament building open fire on some 8,000–10,000 people gathered in Kossuth square. Between 60 and 80 lives are lost; 100–150 people are injured.

October 25, 12:32 p.m.: A communiqué from the HWP Political Committee is read out on the radio announcing that Ernő Gerő has been dismissed and János Kádár, who was imprisoned during the Rákosi era, has been appointed first secretary. Colonel Pál Maléter, in command at the Kilián Barracks (8th District), reaches a ceasefire agreement with the Corvin Passage rebels.

October 25: A Soviet division of reinforcements arrives from Romania as protests break out in villages and towns across Hungary.

October 25: The University Revolutionary Student Committee is established at the Arts Faculty of Eötvös Loránd University.

October 25: Workers councils are formed at the Csepel Iron and Metal Works in Budapest (21st District).

October 25: Serious fighting takes place at the junction of Grand Boulevard (Nagykörút) and Üllői road, in Corvin Passage (8th District).

October 25: Demonstrators carrying "bloody banners" protest against Ernő Gerő, the Soviet intervention and the bloodshed in front of Parliament.

October 25: Rebels fire a mortar at the radio transmitters at Lakihegy.

October 25: The Borsod County Workers' Council forms in the important industrial city of Miskolc. The major factories and the university of Miskolc send a delegation to Imre Nagy, led by the county's first party-secretary.

October 26: Demonstrations and fighting continue to spread around the country. In the city of Kecskemét, for example, volleys fired by soldiers claim three lives early in the day while by evening a battle breaks out in which MiG 15 fighters strafe the city's Gypsy quarter. Rebel forces make considerable inroads despite the number of casualties.

October 26: Various national and workers' councils spring up in cities such as Győr, Debrecen, Veszprém and Nyíregyháza.

October 26: In the afternoon, rebels occupy the Csepel police headquarters in Budapest (21st District).

October 26, 4:13 p.m.: Hungarian radio broadcasts a statement by the HWP Central Committee promising a new, national government, Hungarian–Soviet negotiations conducted on an equal basis, elections for factory workers' councils, pay raises, and economic and political changes.

October 26, 5:32 p.m.: Hungarian authorities broadcast an amnesty declaration by the Presidential Council. It applies to everyone who lays down their arms by 10:00 p.m.

October 26: A consignment of blood and medicines sent from Warsaw arrives at Budapest's Ferihegy Airport. This is the first aid to reach Hungary from abroad.

October 26: Rebel groups form in the Thököly road-Dózsa György road area (7th District) and at Széna square (2nd District). Rebels also occupy Móricz Zsigmond square (11th District) and the Danuvia Arms Factory.

October 26: Border guards at Mosonmagyaróvár fire on demonstrators, killing 52 and wounding 86. Soldiers shoot at protesters in Esztergom, causing 15 deaths and at least 50 injuries. At Zalaegerszeg, police and party functionaries also open fire on the crowd. There are fatalities and injuries in Nagykanizsa from shots fired from the party headquarters, while ÁVH men shoot at demonstrators in Miskolc. In Miskolc and in Mosonmagyarovár, the insurgents lynch several officers.

October 26: Pope Pius XII in Rome issues an encyclical on the uprising and prays for a rebel victory.

October 27: The United States, Britain and France jointly propose that the U.N. Security Council convene to discuss the Hungarian question.

October 27: The revolution continues to unfold in Hungary. In Budapest and elsewhere, rebels seize or hold onto key facilities such as police stations and local party and government head-quarters while mounting sporadic attacks against Soviet and Hungarian army detachments. On the Romanian border, railroad tracks are pulled up to impede Soviet troop advances into the country. Heavily outgunned, the insurrectionists continue to sustain sizable losses. The first shipments of aid from the International Red Cross arrive.

October 27, 11:18 a.m.: Hungarian radio announces the composition of the new government.

October 27: Free Győr Radio begins broadcasting. Other than the Western radios (RFE, BBC), this station becomes the most important source of information for the public until October 30.

October 27: In a major address in Dallas, Texas, Secretary of State John Foster Dulles declares that the American leadership do not regard the Eastern European states potential military allies of the United States.

October 27–November 3: The U.N. ambassadors of the United States, Britain and France hold a series of secret discussions on the Hungarian uprising.

October 28: Soviet forces attack the Corvin Passage unit at dawn, but are repelled. New groups of insurgents form in the capital's 8th District. Across Hungary, slain revolutionaries are buried as rebel attacks and army counterattacks continue.

October 28, 1:20 p.m.: Hungarian Radio announces a cease-fire.

October 28, 2:00 p.m.: The new government is sworn in. It duly approves the government statement put forward by Nagy that seeks to meet many of the revolutionary demands. Besides remedying past grievances the program promises to legalize revolutionary organizations and to bring about the immediate withdrawal of Soviet forces from Budapest. This indicates a fundamental turn in party policy.

October 28, 5:25 p.m.: Nagy announces the new government program in the radio.

October 28: Hungarian party leaders who are the most seriously compromised since the accession of the new government, including Ernő Gerő, András Hegedüs, István Bata, László Piros, Erzsébet Andics, Andor Berei and István Kovács, flee overnight to Moscow aboard Soviet air-craft. *Pravda* reports on the Hungarian revolution under the headline "Collapse of the Anti-People Adventure".

October 28, 10:00 p.m.: The new government lifts the curfew. There is a radio announcement calling on young people to join the national guard that is being organized.

October 28: The Revolutionary Committee of the Hungarian Intelligentsia, the Buda University Revolutionary Committee and the Revolutionary Party of Hungarian Youth are established.

October 28: The free communist Róka (Fox) Radio is established at the 20th District party headquarters.

October 28: The Hegyeshalom frontier crossing into Austria is closed.

October 28: Khrushchev reports on Hungary to the Presidium of the CPSU Central Committee, which decides to reinforce the troops stationed in the country.

October 28: The U.N. Security Council places the "Hungarian situation" on its agenda.

October 28: Hungary receives offers of aid from the Soviet Union, Yugoslavia, the GDR, Poland, Czechoslovakia, Switzerland, the United States, Austria and other countries, as well as from agencies of the International Red Cross.

October 29: Further clashes between Soviet troops and insurgents occur in the 8th and 9th Districts of Budapest. The 7th District party headquarters is occupied. The leaders of the Corvin Passage rebels begin combining groups in the area, so that the number of organized rebels reaches 1,000–1,200.

October 29: Revolutionary committees and workers' councils grow in numbers all over the country.

October 29: At Záhony, on the Hungarian border with the Soviet Union, the entrance to a rail station is blown up. Several locomotives are incapacitated.

October 29: Talks with representatives of rebel groups are held at the Ministry of Defense in Budapest. At about 8:00 p.m., cease-fire talks begin in Corvin Passage, and later at Budapest Police Headquarters, between the police and military and representatives of the insurrectionists.

October 29: The Hungarian National Revolutionary Committee moves onto the premises of *Szabad Nép*.

October 29: Hungarian radio announces that Soviet forces will begin to withdraw from Budapest the following day. Hungarian troops begin to replace Soviet guards at public buildings.

October 30, 7:20 a.m.: The Defense Ministry announces on the radio that the withdrawal of Soviet forces from Budapest will continue.

October 30: A fire fight breaks out between rebels and guards at the headquarters of the HWP Budapest Committee in Köztársaság square (8th District). After the rebels storm the building, suffering considerable losses in the process, 23 of the defenders either die in the siege or are subsequently lynched by the crowd.

October 30, 2:30 p.m.: Nagy announces on the radio the end of the one-party system and the formation of a coalition government. Minister of State Zoltán Tildy announces that the compulsory-delivery system for farm produce has been abolished and that preparations are being made for free elections.

October 30: The government recognizes the local self-governing bodies created during the revolution.

October 30: In Budapest, the Széna square rebels occupy the ÁVH barracks on Maros street (12th District), a national guard unit is formed in the 8th District, and several political prisoners are freed from the National Prison.

October 30: The Smallholders' (FKgP), Social Democratic (SZDP) and National Peasants' (NPP) parties are re-established.

October 30: The Újpest National Committee sends out armed men to release Cardinal Mindszenty from house arrest in Felsőpetény. His ÁVH guards disperse and he is accompanied to the barracks in nearby Rétság before a detachment from Újpest arrives.

October 30: Revolutionary committees continue to be elected in more towns around the country while organization of national guards continues in several locations. The free Vörösmarty Radio begins broadcasting in the town of Székesfehérvár. The Transdanubian National Council forms in Győr. A communist "officers' brigade" is set up in Salgótarján.

October 30: The International Red Cross begins relief flights of aid to Budapest. The air bridge operates until the onset of the second Soviet occupation.

October 30: Hard-liners in Moscow are temporarily pushed into the background at a meeting of the CPSU Presidium. The leadership approves a remarkable document, published the next day in *Pravda*, declaring Moscow's intent to respect the sovereignty and territorial integrity of its Warsaw Pact allies, including Hungary. The prospects for a peaceful settlement of the Hungarian crisis are at their strongest at this point.

October 30: The U.N. Security Council convenes to debate the unfolding Suez crisis.

October 30: Demonstrations and rallies take place throughout Poland in support of the Hungarian revolution.

October 30: A rally of about 2,500 students at Timişoara, Romania, Technical University is dispersed by the Securitate, Romania's secret police. Protests continue the next day, and almost 3,000 students are arrested in the two-day period.

October 30: Austria seals its borders. Only relief supplies and journalists are allowed to pass into Hungary.

October 31, 6:00 a.m.: A procession consisting of soldiers from Rétság and armed rebels from Újpest escorts Cardinal Mindszenty from Rétság, arriving at Buda Castle at 9:00 a.m.

October 31: The Revolutionary National Defense Commission (FHB) is formed at the Defense Ministry.

October 31: Béla Király is appointed commander-in-chief of the national guard and military commander of Budapest. Pál Maléter is named first deputy to the defense minister, and István Kovács chief of staff. The Revolutionary Committee of the Armed Forces (FKB), overseeing the national guard, is established at the Kilián Barracks (8th District).

October 31, about noon: The withdrawal of Soviet forces from Budapest is completed.

October 31: The HWP Presidium declares the party dissolved. A new party, the Hungarian Socialist Workers' Party (HSWP), is founded.

October 31: The Christian Democratic People's Party and the Hungarian Peasants' Association are re-established. The National Peasant Party (NPP) is also recreated under the name "Petőfi Party," after the heads of the party reject the leadership of Ferenc Erdei who re-organized the NPP at a meeting the day before.

October 31: A delegation of the Transdanubian National Council negotiates with Imre Nagy and Zoltán Tildy.

October 31: Free Csokonai Radio and Free Debrecen Radio begin broadcasting.

October 31: During the night, additional Soviet troops enter Hungary.

October 31: Pravda publishes an extraordinary Kremlin declaration on relations with Eastern Europe on the basis of mutual equality, respect and noninterference. The publication is taken by many, including the U.S. government, as a sign that the Hungarian crisis will be resolved peacefully.

October 31: Notwithstanding the declaration just published in *Pravda*, the CPSU Presidium reverses its position and agrees to a proposal by Khrushchev to intervene militarily in Hungary.

October 31: In Washington, President Eisenhower delivers an address over radio and television expressing his admiration for the Hungarian people. At the same time, he assures the Soviet Union that the United States does not view either the new Polish or the new Hungarian leaderships as potential allies.

October 31: Student demonstrations supporting the Hungarian revolution take place in several Transylvanian cities of Romania.

November 1, 7:30 a.m.: Soviet troops surround Budapest's Ferihegy Airport along with virtually every other Hungarian airfield in the country.

November 1: The Nagy government files a protest with Soviet Ambassador Yurii Andropov at the arrival of new Soviet troops in the country and the encircling of Budapest. The Budapest Armed Forces Command draws up a defense system for the city. Nagy dismisses the idea of leaving the capital for his own safety.

November 1: After Andropov fails to satisfy Hungarian concerns about Moscow's intentions, the government announces Hungary's withdrawal from the Warsaw Pact, declares the country's neutrality, and appeals to the United Nations for help. It calls on the four great powers to help defend the country's neutrality.

November 1: At a meeting of the National Security Council, U.S. officials celebrate the apparent turn of events in Hungary as reflected in the Kremlin's declaration published in *Pravda* the previous day. Unaware that the Kremlin has already decided to intervene, CIA Director Allen Dulles calls the rebels' seeming victory a "miracle."

November 1: The Capital City National Committee, the Democratic People's Party, the Christian Hungarian Party, the Christian Front, the National Association of Former Political Prisoners (POFOSZ) and the Hungarian Scouts Association, all organizations whose existence would not have been tolerated under the previous regime, are established.

November 1, 7:50 p.m.: Nagy announces Hungary's neutrality on the radio. The government forbids Hungarian military units from resisting the Soviet troops.

November 1, about 10:00 p.m.: Hungarian radio broadcasts a speech by János Kádár. However, by the time it is broadcast, Kádár is no longer in the country. He and Ferenc Münnich have left Budapest for secret consultations in Moscow which eventually lead to their return at the head of a Soviet-backed regime.

November 1: At night, Soviet troops surrounding Budapest begin to reconnoiter the city.

November 1: Soldiers change sides during a demonstration in Kaposvár and six officers are arrested.

November 1: Khrushchev tells a Polish delegation led by Gomułka at a meeting in Brest that Soviet intervention in Hungary is imminent.

November 1: Demonstrations continue in Romania as students demand democratic rights and full freedom of study. Emergency measures are introduced throughout the country, especially in areas with large Hungarian communities.

November 1: The Yugoslav army is placed on full alert and begins to advance towards the Hungarian border.

November 2, 9:00 a.m.: The Hungarian cabinet meets. Government delegations are appointed to negotiate with the Soviet Union and to travel to the U.N. General Assembly, which is set to convene on November 12.

November 2: Revolutionary and workers' councils decide on a countrywide basis to return to work on Monday, November 5.

November 2: Soviet forces establish their Hungarian headquarters in Szolnok. Marshal Ivan Konev, commander-in-chief of Warsaw Pact forces, arrives from Moscow to take command.

November 2: János Kádár arrives in Moscow and, along with Ferenc Münnich and István Bata, attends an expanded meeting of the CPSU Presidium.

November 2: Khrushchev and Malenkov meet with Romanian and Czechoslovak leaders in Bucharest, then with the Bulgarian leadership in Sofia to brief them on the impending invasion.

November 2, 7:00 p.m.: Khrushchev and Malenkov begin talks with Tito on the Yugoslav island of Brioni. They succeed in persuading Tito to support the invasion.

November 3: The National Government in Hungary is reshuffled.

November 3: At a press conference, Cardinal József Mindszenty calls for political and economic aid from the Western nations, especially the great powers.

November 3, noon: Hungarian-Soviet negotiations on details of the troop withdrawals begin at the Parliament building. The Soviets promise to halt the occupation. Additional Hungarian units occupy defensive positions around the capital.

November 3: The Petőfi Circle is revived.

November 3, 10:00 p.m.: After Hungarian–Soviet military negotiations move to Tököl, outside Budapest, Soviet secret police forces headed by General Ivan Serov arrest the Hungarian delegation.

November 3: Soviet forces surround Debrecen and Győr, occupy Záhony railway station on the Soviet border and close the frontier with Austria.

November 3: The CPSU Presidium works out the details of forming a counter-government headed by János Kádár and Ferenc Münnich.

November 3: The U.N. Security Council continues its debate on the Hungarian situation. U.S. representative Henry Cabot Lodge introduces a resolution calling on the Soviet Union to withdraw its troops from Hungary. But, in accordance with American delaying tactics, it is not put up for vote. The session is adjourned until November 5.

November 4, dawn: Soviet troops cross the Hungarian border from Romania. From Uzhgorod (Soviet Union), Kádár's pre-recorded proclamation is broadcast on behalf of the Soviet-sponsored "Hungarian Revolutionary Workers' and Peasants' Government."

November 4, 4:15 a.m.: Soviet troops launch a general attack. Five divisions under the command of Soviet Major General K. Grebennik move on Budapest. Nagy does not issue an order to resist, yet national guard units and others put up a considerable fight. Heavy casualties are sustained on both sides as the Red Army advances through the country.

November 4, 5:20 a.m.: Nagy broadcasts a short declaration informing the world about the Soviet intervention. It is repeated several times in English, French, German, Russian, Czech and Polish.

November 4, 6:00–8:00 a.m.: Communist members of the Nagy government take refuge in the Yugoslav Embassy. Cardinal Mindszenty is given asylum in the U.S. Legation. István Bibó is the only member of the Hungarian government remaining in the Parliament building. The Soviets occupy the Defense and Interior ministries and surround the Parliament building.

November 4, 7:00–8:00 a.m.: National guard units in the Jutadomb area force the Soviet convoy carrying the captured Hungarian negotiators to turn back.

November 4, 7:57 a.m.: An appeal for assistance by the Writers' Union is broadcast in Hungarian, English, German and Russian.

November 4: János Kádár and Ferenc Münnich are flown from Moscow to Szolnok by military aircraft.

November 4: A meeting of the U.N. Security Council is called in response to news of the Soviet intervention. Through a "uniting for peace" procedure the Hungarian issue is transferred to the Emergency Special Session of the General Assembly, convening the same day. The UNGA adopts a U.S.-sponsored resolution condemning the intervention.

November 5: Soviet forces occupy the Radio building. Resistance continues in Thököly road (14th District), Zalka Máté square, Liget square, 10th (District), around Lehel road (13th District), and in the 9th, 13th and 21st districts. A Soviet attack on Corvin Passage begins at 1:00 p.m.

November 5: There is fighting in the towns of Pécs, Komló, and Veszprém. The Rákóczi free radio station begins broadcasting from Dunapentele (Sztálinváros, Dunaújváros). The Soviets enter Tatabánya.

November 5: The Moscow-supported Hungarian Revolutionary Workers' and Peasants' Government in Szolnok appeals for help from other socialist countries. The Soviet Union sends a message offering help.

November 5: Several thousand demonstrators in Krakow, Poland, protest the Soviet intervention.

November 6: The Soviets break the resistance in Széna square (2nd District), Gellérthegy (1st and 11th districts) and Óbuda (3rd District). Almost 300 members of the Corvin Passage group set out toward the Austrian border. The strength of the Hungarian resistance decreases sharply, although rebels in Móricz Zsigmond square (11th District) and Thököly road (14th District) continue to defend their positions as do several hundred resisters in the Buda Castle district, armed with heavy weapons. A Soviet plane is shot down over Csepel (21st District). The Soviets, at negotiations held at the Kossuth Academy, demand unconditional surrender, which the national guard refuses to accept.

November 6: Soviet troops in the Mecsek Hills attack the rearguard of the national guard retreating to Vágot-puszta (Mecsek Hills).

November 6: A Soviet armored convoy carrying János Kádár leaves Szolnok for Budapest in the late evening.

November 7: Soviet armored vehicles carrying Kádár and several members of his government arrive at Parliament. The Kádár government takes the oath of office in the afternoon even though the Nagy government has not resigned. The Kádár government restores the state administrative apparatus that existed before the reforms which began on October 23 and bans the new revolutionary committees. At the same time, Kádár takes several steps designed to appease Hungarians, such as declaring November 7, the anniversary of the Bolshevik Revolution, a working day, lifting the requirement to teach Russian in schools and confirming the disbanding of the ÁVH.

November 7: Some 300 national guards in the Buda Castle district retreat into the National Archives building. The Soviets attack them with tanks and heavy artillery. Red Army forces continue to battle other pockets of resistance in the city and countryside.

November 8: Resistance ends at the Schmidt Mansion in Óbuda (3rd District), in Kőbánya (10th District) and in Thököly road (14th District). Soviet tanks enter Csepel (21st District). Elsewhere in Hungary, the Red Army continues to overwhelm rebel forces.

November 8: In New York, the 2nd Special Session of the U.N. General Assembly continues its debate on the Hungarian question.

November 9: Kádár's Presidential Council declares the Hungarian Revolutionary Workers' and Peasants' Government to be the highest organ of state administration.

November 9: The Kádár government begins organization of the National Armed Force. An Officer's Declaration is published requiring unconditional support for the Kádár government.

November 9: Sporadic fighting continues in Széna square (2nd District) and Vajdahunyad street (8th District). The Soviets launch a general offensive to recapture Csepel (21st District), with fighter planes and heavy artillery keeping up a steady bombardment.

November 9: Soviet artillery bombards the rebel headquarters in the Mecsek Hills while armored troops fire on revolutionaries fleeing from Budapest towards Austria. Béla Király and the remnants of the national guard prepare to defend themselves at Nagykovácsi.

November 9: The Soviets inform Kádár that Nagy and his associates, who have taken refuge in the Yugoslav Embassy, may not leave for Yugoslavia as the Nagy group had hoped to do.

November 9: The 2nd Emergency Special Session of the U.N. General Assembly passes a further resolution on the situation in Hungary.

November 10: The Kádár government announces pay raises of 8–15 per cent and abolishes the tax on childless adults. The First Special Forces Officers Regiment begins operations.

November 10: Nagy informs Yugoslav Ambassador Dalibor Soldatić by letter that he is not willing to resign as prime minister.

November 10: Sporadic fighting continues in Budapest while the Soviet attack forces the Mecsek rebels to fall back into the Eastern Mecsek Hills.

November 10: The International Red Cross resumes aid shipments.

November 10: Polish journalists posted in Budapest are expelled.

November 10: Members of the Békés County Revolutionary Council are arrested, provoking a strike in the Békéscsaba factories. The national guard in Sátoraljaújhely lays down its arms. The Soviets attack the national guard units commanded by Béla Király at Nagykovácsi. After brief resistance, the rebels retreat westward.

November 10: The Kádár government accepts a U.N. offer of aid. A Swiss government proposal calls for a conference of the four great powers and India.

November 10: The Yugoslav government confirms the right of Nagy and his associates to claim asylum, a matter that increasingly aggravates Moscow's relations with Belgrade.

November 11: The Provisional Executive Committee of the HSWP hears a report from Kádár on his activity during the revolution. Later, he delivers his first radio address since November 4.

November 11: Delegates of the factories and mines in Baranya County endorse a statement condemning the Kádár government and demanding the withdrawal of the Soviet forces.

November 11: Tito, in an unusually forthright speech to party workers in the town of Pula, describes the events in Hungary as counter-revolutionary and justifies the Soviet intervention by pointing to the danger posed to socialism. On the other hand, he also asserts that Hungarian popular animosity toward the Rákosi regime and "Stalinist methods and practice" was an understandable sentiment. The speech further complicates relations with Khrushchev.

November 12: The Kádár government continues to consolidate its position. The official party organ publishes a decree by the Presidential Council dismissing the Nagy government and recognizing the make-up of the Kádár government. Kádár also criticizes the U.N.'s resolutions on Hungary as interference in the country's internal affairs. Meanwhile, various social groups, among them the Writers' Union and the Újpest Revolutionary Workers Council, continue to press their demands and appeals to the population.

November 12: The 11th session of the U.N. General Assembly places the Hungarian question on its agenda. The debate begins on January 9, 1957.

November 13: The Kádár government issues an order permitting the workers' councils to operate. The underground Hungarian Democratic Independence Movement (MDFM) is established. The planned creation of a centralized workers' council is postponed because Soviet tanks block the entrance to the meeting at the Újpest town hall.

November 13: The Soviets capture several rebels in the Mecsek Hills. Workers' councils form in the Oroszlány and Tatabánya coal mines. Rebels blow up the railway line between Dorog and Leányvár.

November 14: The Greater Budapest Central Workers' Council (KMT) is established at a rally at the United Incandescent Lamp Factory (Egyesült Izzó). The same evening, a KMT delegation negotiates with leaders of the Kádár government in Parliament.

November 14: Eisenhower refers briefly to the Hungarian question at a press conference, saying the U.S. would do nothing to encourage the Hungarians to continue to fight.

November 15: The KMT elects Sándor Rácz as its chairman. Further talks between the KMT and the Kádár government take place in Parliament overnight.

November 15: The Hungarian Democratic Independence Movement issues its "Ten Commandments for Hungarian Rebirth" and launches an illegal paper, *Október Huszonharmadika* ("October 23").

November 15: The Csepel workers' council calls for a return to work, responding to Kádár's appeals for a return to normalcy. A few other councils and workers' groups also decide to resume production.

November 15: A Polish party and government delegation in Moscow wins important concessions in favor of greater freedom from Moscow's tutelage.

November 16: Kádár, at a secret meeting, agrees with Moscow that the Nagy group should be deported to Romania instead of being allowed to travel to Yugoslavia.

November 16: István Angyal, leader of the Tűzoltó street rebels, is arrested. A journalists' strike begins in Budapest.

November 16: The KMT issues an appeal for a return to work while reserving the right to strike. Meanwhile, the KMT delegation has further negotiations with Kádár.

November 16: The Mecsek rebels manage to break through the Soviet encirclement unobserved.

November 16: The U.N. secretary-general appoints a committee to investigate the Hungarian situation.

November 17: Kádár calls on the Yugoslavs to hand over Nagy and his associates to the new government.

November 17: The central party daily *Népszabadság* ("People's Freedom") goes to press despite the journalists' strike.

November 18: The Yugoslav leadership insists on honoring the guarantee of asylum given to Nagy and his group, but registers no objection to their leaving for Romania.

November 18: The Kádár government issues a statement denying that mass arrests and deportations have taken place.

November 19: Nagy and his associates declare that they do not want to leave the country.

November 19: Organizations still loyal to the revolution—the KMT, Peasants' Association, National Union of Hungarian Journalists (MUOSZ), Revolutionary Committee of the Hungarian Intelligentsia, Hungarian Union of Fine and Applied Artists, Hungarian Musicians' Union and Writers' Union—address a letter to Indian Prime Minister Jawaharlal Nehru. They call on him to intervene on Hungary's behalf.

November 19: The KMT issues a call for the establishment of a National Workers' Council. Work resumes at most factories.

November 19: János Szabó, commander of the Széna square rebels, is arrested.

November 19: A number of Hungarians who have been deported to the Soviet Union are handed over to the Hungarian authorities.

November 19: Pravda, commenting on Tito's November 11´speech in Pula, accuses the Yugoslav president of intervening in Hungary's internal affairs.

November 19: The U.N. General Assembly again debates the Hungarian question on November 19 and 20.

November 20: The armed resistance in the Mecsek Hills comes to an end.

November 20: An East German delegation holds talks in Budapest on providing assistance to the country.

November 20: Officers who have not signed the Officer's Declaration are discharged.

November 21: The Kádár government gives a written guarantee to Yugoslavia that Nagy and his associates will not be prosecuted.

November 21: An attempt to form a National Workers' Council fails when Soviet tanks surround the National Sports Hall, where the rally was to be held. The KMT calls a 48–hour protest strike.

November 21: After a three-day debate, the U.N. General Assembly passes several resolutions on the Hungarian question. Three minutes' silence is observed in Switzerland to commemorate the Hungarian independence struggle.

November 22: Nagy and his associates leave the Yugoslav Embassy with assurances of safe conduct from the Yugoslavs. However, as soon as the group boards a bus outside the Embassy, Soviet security officers arrest them and take them to KGB headquarters in Mátyásföld (16th District). From there they are flown secretly to Romania the following day. The abduction apparently catches Yugoslav officials unaware.

November 22: Talks between a KMT delegation and Kádár take place at night.

November 23: Nagy, his associates and their families are taken from Bucharest Airport to Snagov, Romania.

November 23: Yugoslavia files a diplomatic protest at the abduction of the Nagy group.

November 23: The Kádár government recognizes the KMT as a negotiating partner. The KMT calls for a return to work. After an appeal by the Revolutionary Council of the Hungarian Intelligentsia and the KMT to commemorate the revolution, traffic in Budapest comes to a halt between 2:00–3:00 p.m.

November 24: The Nagy issue continues to demand the Kádár government's attention. An official Hungarian communiqué is issued on the departure of Nagy and his group. Two days later, Kádár delivers a major radio address but then makes no further official mention of the matter for the next 18 months.

November 24: Government commissioners are appointed to oversee operations at the country's larger factories.

November 24: Poland sends Hungary aid worth 100 million zlotys.

November 29: Reflecting ongoing domestic political instability, the All-University Revolutionary Committee and the Central Workers' Council of the Csepel Iron and Metal Works are established, and more than 300 miners at Pécsbányatelep go on strike.

November 29: West Germany sends Hungary food and medical aid worth 10 million marks.

November 30: The Soviets call upon Kádár to begin reprisals, naming at least six revolutionaries (József Dudás and János Szabó, for example) whom they believe should be executed immediately.

November 30: The KMT issues a call for readers to boycott the HSWP newspapers until the KMT receives a press permit. The public-supplies commissioner lifts the ban on alcohol sales.

December 1: The Kádár government publishes a decree granting a general pardon to everyone who has emigrated illegally since October 23.

December 1: A security-force regiment of 2,000 is formed under the Ministry of the Interior.

December 1: A strike by miners in Pécsbányatelep ends without result but work stoppages by miners in Tatabánya and Salgótarján continue.

December 2: A crucial three-day meeting of the Provisional Central Committee of the HSWP begins. The events of October are described as counterrevolutionary, setting the stage for reprisals against participants in the uprising.

December 4: Several thousand women march to Hősök tere (Heroes' Square, 14th District), where they place flowers on the Tomb of the Unknown Soldier and display the flag of the revolution. There is also a demonstration in Szabadság square (5th District), in front of the U.S. Legation.

December 5: The U.N. General Assembly passes a resolution on sending observers to Hungary.

December 5: The Central Committee of the Czechoslovak Communist Party announces that proceedings have started in 674 cases linked with the events in Hungary.

December 5, evening: About 200 members of the intelligentsia and of workers' councils are arrested. The first volume of the 'White Book' (The Counter-revolutionary Forces in the October events in Hungary) appears.

December 6: A KMT memorandum states that its negotiations with the government have failed because of government inflexibility. The KMT protests the successive arrests of leaders of the workers' councils. It calls a national meeting to establish a national workers' council.

December 6: The government organizes communist rallies in several locations in Budapest. Workers at the end of their shifts attack communists carrying red flags. Crowds hurling stones at the demonstrators are dispersed by security forces and the Soviets. Gunfire is exchanged near November 7 square (Oktogon), and security men fire into a crowd of workers by the Western Railway Station.

December 6: There are demonstrations in Békéscsaba, Gyula, Tatabánya and Sarkad. A strike breaks out in Békéscsaba the next day to protest the arrests. Coal miners in Nógrád County also go on strike after workers' leaders in the county are arrested.

December 7: The KMT sends a letter to the Soviet premier proposing direct relations between the KMT and the Soviet government.

December 7: Kádár receives Yugoslav Ambassador Dalibor Soldatić and holds out the prospect of settling the Nagy affair peacefully.

December 7: Demonstrations take place around the country.

December 7: The 14th Summer Olympics in Melbourne close. A highlight of the games occurred when Hungary's water polo team defeated the Soviets on its way to winning the gold medal. Many Hungarian athletes refuse to return home after the games.

December 8: In the town of Salgótarján, Soviet and Hungarian security forces open fire on a crowd of demonstrators. The massacre, which lasts for 8–10 minutes, leaves 52 dead and about 150 wounded. The shooting convinces the KMT to call a 48–hour strike.

December 9: The government outlaws the territorial workers' councils, including the KMT. The workers' council delegates assembled at the headquarters of the building trade union in Budapest are arrested. KMT representatives personally deliver the call for a strike to the major provincial centers.

December 9: Demonstrations and protests take place in a number of towns over the next two days. Numerous arrests are made. Security officials murder two national guard leaders in Salgótarján; several demonstrators are killed in confrontations with Soviet forces in the country.

December 11: The 48–hour strike called for by the KMT begins, halting production, rail traffic and public transport throughout the country. The central workers' council at the Csepel Iron and Metal Works comes out against the strike again, but all factories stop work nonetheless. In response, the Kádár government declares a state of emergency—martial law—and orders the disarming of factory guards. KMT leaders Sándor Bali and Sándor Rácz are arrested at the Parliament building.

December 11: The Hungarian U.N. delegation walks out of the General Assembly following attacks against the Kádár government.

December 12: Hungarian internment camps are reopened. Security forces continue to disperse demonstrations by force.

December 12: The U.N. General Assembly passes a further resolution condemning the Soviet intervention.

December 14: The CPSU passes a resolution on sending Soviet advisers to Hungary.

December 15: József Soltész is executed in Miskolc. It is the first execution of a participant in the revolution.

December 24: In an attempt to win over public opinion, the Christmas issue of *Népszabadság* publishes articles on religious subjects. Authorities lift the curfew to allow worshippers to attend midnight mass.

December 28: A members' meeting of the Writers' Union accepts Áron Tamási's piece "Sorrow and Confession" as a statement of principle, upholding the cause of the revolution.

December 30: A decree of the Presidential Council transfers the duties of the reviled ÁVH to a department of the police.

1957

January 1–4: Soviet, Bulgarian, Czechoslovak, Romanian and Hungarian leaders meet in Budapest. They discuss the draft of a forthcoming Hungarian government declaration that includes the prospect of multi-party elections; they also talk about Nagy's role and its "legal consequences."

January 4–7: The deputy secretary-general of the United Nations holds talks in Budapest on aid for Hungary.

January 5: The government sanctions the death penalty for anyone refusing to return to work.

January 5–7: The emigré Hungarian Revolutionary Council holds it founding meeting in Strasbourg.

January 6: The Kádár government publishes its program, "Statement of the Revolutionary Workers' and Peasants' Government on the Main Tasks."

January 7–11: Chinese Prime Minister Zhou Enlai visits Moscow. He calls for strong reprisals against participants in the Hungarian uprising.

January 10: A Special Committee on Hungary is established by the U.N. General Assembly consisting of the representatives of Australia, Ceylon, Denmark, Tunisia and Uruguay.

January 12: An order is issued introducing accelerated criminal proceedings. A state of emergency, hitherto mainly applied to armed actions, is extended to the act of instigating strikes in factories employing more than 100 workers.

January 17: The interior minister suspends the activities of the Writers' Union. Shortly afterwards, all arts associations are placed under the ministry's supervision.

January 19: József Dudás and János Szabó are executed.

February 2: Kádár, speaking in Salgótarján, accuses Nagy of fomenting a counter-revolutionary uprising and calls him a traitor. The secure border zone along the Yugoslav frontier is restored.

February 18: A legal decree is issued establishing the Workers' Militia.

March and April: Nagy's book, *On Communism: In Defense of the New Course,* appears in Western countries.

March 15: Security forces assert control over Budapest and other larger cities on the anniversary of the 1848 Hungarian Revolution. In Romania by this time, more than 20 prisoners are executed and several hundred arrests are made in connection with the Hungarian uprising. The first issue of the exile publication *Irodalmi Újság* ("Literary Gazette") appears in London.

March 21–28: A Hungarian delegation headed by János Kádár visits Moscow. This is the first official visit abroad by representatives of the Revolutionary Workers and Peasants Government.

April 5: Kádár writes to the Yugoslav government requesting that the "right of asylum" accorded in November to Nagy and his associates be formally annulled.

April 6: The People's Tribunal Council of the Supreme Court is established. It serves on the one hand as the general court of appeals for legal proceedings connected to the retaliation, while on the other hand it acts as the court of first instance for especially important cases, without the possibility of further appeal. The people's tribunals together with the Act of People's Jurisdiction become the primary mechanisms for the legal reprisals that followed the revolution.

April 13: The curfew in force in Budapest for the last six months is lifted.

April 14: Members of the Nagy group who have been arrested are brought back to Budapest from Romania.

April 21: The interior minister dissolves the Writers' Union.

May 1: On the traditional May Day holiday, a mass demonstration of 100,000 is organized at Budapest's Heroes' Square in support of the Kádár government.

May 1: Work begins on installation of the first landmine barrier along the Hungary-Austria border.

May 7: A hunger strike breaks out in the Hungarian refugee camp in Austria after emigration to the United States is halted. Some 100–120 Hungarian students demonstrate in front of the U.S. Embassy in Vienna calling for emigration to be permitted again.

May 9: Parliament meets for the first time since August 3, 1956. The Kossuth coat of arms is replaced by a design for the People's Republic, known as the Kádár coat of arms.

May 23: István Bibó and Zoltán Tildy are arrested.

May 27: An agreement normalizing the legal position of Soviet troops stationed in Hungary is signed in Budapest.

May 28: The interior minister orders a political purge of the police force. Some 25–30 per cent of the force is dismissed.

May 30: The Kádár government calls on the International Committee of the Red Cross to cease its activities in Hungary by June 30.

June 20: The U.N. Special Committee submits its report on Hungary. The document becomes a best-seller in the United States. The Kádár government describes it as interference in Hungary's internal affairs. In September, the U.N. General Assembly formally adopts the report.

October 22: The Hungarian Freedom Association, the Hungarian Writers' Union Abroad, the Social Democratic Party, the Free Hungarian Trade Unions and the British Association of Hungarian University Students hold a ceremony on the eve of the first anniversary of the revolution.

October 23: The Hungarian public commemorates the first anniversary of the revolution in various ways, but no large-scale incidents occur. Nevertheless, several hundred people are arrested. Commemorations also are held throughout the West.

November 3: The system of summary justice is abolished in Hungary.

November 17: Hungarian authorities abolish the factory workers' councils.

December 21: Géza Losonczy dies in the prison.

December 30: László Iván Kovács is executed.

1958

February 5–6: After numerous delays to spare Hungary and the Soviets international embarrassment, the secret trial of Nagy and his associates begins—only to be suspended after two days again at Moscow's request.

April: The Soviet Union introduces economic sanctions against Yugoslavia.

April 2–10: Khrushchev leads a Soviet delegation to Hungary.

April 24: József Szilágyi is executed.

May 24: Khrushchev receives Kádár in Moscow. Sizable cuts are made in the level of Soviet forces stationed in the occupied countries. Kádár opposes this. (Soviet forces are withdrawn from Romania permanently.)

June 9–15: After further delays, the secret trial of Nagy and associates continues. Nagy, Miklós Gimes and Pál Maléter are sentenced to death, Sándor Kopácsi to life imprisonment, Ferenc Donáth to 12 years imprisonment, Ferenc Jánosi to eight years, Zoltán Tildy to six years and Miklós Vásárhelyi to five years.

June 16: Nagy, Gimes and Maléter are executed at the Budapest National Prison. They are buried in anonymous graves.

June 17: The verdicts in the Nagy trial are published. News of the executions provokes protests in several Western countries.

September: The remaining members of the Nagy group, who were never formally arrested, return with their families from Romania.

October 23: Commemorations of the Hungarian revolution are held worldwide.

November 16: The first parliamentary elections since the revolution are held.

December 1: István Angyal is executed.

December 11: The U.N. General Assembly again places the Hungarian question on its agenda. The United States resolves to keep the matter alive until 1962 when Washington finally agrees to drop it following secret negotiations with the Kádár regime.

1959

April 4: A partial amnesty is declared for those serving sentences of less than two years

1960

April 1: A further partial amnesty is declared.

1961

August 26: The Baross square rebels are the last people to be executed for acts committed during the 1956 revolution.

1962

October 20: It is agreed at secret Hungarian-U.S. talks to drop the Hungarian question from the UN agenda in return for a general amnesty for most of those being punished for revolutionary activities in 1956.

December 18: The United States proposes at the U.N. General Assembly that the Hungarian question be dropped from the agenda. The proposal is accepted on December 20.

1963

March 21: Kádár, addressing the opening session of the new Parliament, announces a general amnesty for most of those remaining in prison for their actions during the revolution.

PART ONE

HUNGARY BEFORE THE REVOLUTION

INTRODUCTION

By summer 1952, Hungarian communism had reached a state of crisis. Since the introduction of Stalinist rule just three years earlier, societal pressures had been building steadily under the combined weight of imposed economic rigidity and political excesses in the form of purges, show trials, and other extreme methods of control. The first cases of mass resistance against the system came in the critical agricultural sphere where peasants refused to go along with compulsory agricultural quotas and grain threshers went on strike leading to outbreaks of violence between farmers and local authorities.

Hungarian communist party leader Mátyás Rákosi's instinct for dealing with the crisis was, as always, to imitate his benefactor, Soviet dictator Joseph Stalin. Just as Stalin was then in the midst of his final campaign of political vengeance at home, Rákosi decided to turn the system's repressive apparatus against his own colleagues in the leadership. At the beginning of January 1953, he ordered the arrest of Gábor Péter, head of the State Security Authority (ÁVH), and several other ÁVH officers, as well as a number of leading party functionaries. He sacked two other members of the top-level Hungarian Workers' Party (HWP) Political Committee, István Kovács and Zoltán Vas, and exiled them to the provinces. Their Jewish background suggested the influence of Stalin's own "anti-Zionist" purges. Far from being resolved, then, the crisis that had been bubbling up from below for months was now beginning to take its toll on the leadership. This was the state of affairs when news of Stalin's death arrived on March 5, 1953.

Soviet Policy after Stalin

After the dictator's passing, the new Soviet leadership tried to make significant changes in both the domestic life and foreign policy of the empire. In the late 1940s, the Soviet Union, whose economy had still not recovered from the trauma of World War II, had begun spending heavily in order to keep pace in the budding arms race with the United States. Following the pattern set in the 1930s, Moscow had planned to generate the capital for weapons production by diverting extensive resources from the agricultural and consumer goods sectors of the economy. But the new Kremlin leaders, especially during the premiership of Georgii Malenkov (1953-1955), were sensitive to potential domestic unrest and chose instead to create a more balanced economic structure featuring less emphasis on heavy industry, particularly arms production. However, any cuts in weapons expenditures could only come in the context of a general improvement in East-West relations, which until then had been based mainly on mutual fears of direct confrontation.

As a result, beginning in 1953 Soviet foreign policy adopted a much more flexible stance, exhibiting a willingness to negotiate and compromise with the Western powers for the first time since the closing stages of World War II. This change in Soviet behavior ultimately opened the way to the end of the Korean War and led to such significant reduction in East-West tensions that the mid–1950s are justifiably referred to as the first period of détente.

A distinctive feature of the new Soviet foreign policy between 1953 and 1956 was its emphasis on creating a rapprochement with the West, particularly Britain, France and the United States. During Stalin's rule, the West lived in constant fear of the possibility of a Soviet attack. After 1953, however, the Kremlin's new tack, based on growing parity in the balance of power and mutual respect for the post-World War II status quo, gave rise to a greater sense of security in Western Europe. Yet, even under Stalin, Moscow had never had any serious intention of altering the European status quo. The Soviets respected the Allies' spheres of influence even during the chilliest years of the Cold War, but their increased penchant for negotiations stemmed mostly from a sense of vulnerability in the military balance, despite having the hydrogen bomb.[1] The Soviet shift to a more conciliatory international policy also had another, more concrete motivation: preventing West German rearmament by creating divisions within the Western alliance.

During this period the Soviets clearly set the limits of the compromises they were willing to make in negotiating with the West, and it was soon obvious that they were most ready to discuss the very issues over which the Western powers were split. Resolving the question of German reunification, for example, was unworkable because the Soviet and Western positions were irreconcilable. When West Germany joined NATO in 1955, the matter was finally taken off the agenda for an extended period. But the signing of the Austrian State Treaty that same year showed that the Soviet leadership was willing to bargain with the West. In exchange for a pledge to withdraw its troops from the country, the Kremlin got the Western powers to agree to Austria's permanent neutrality and to allow the East European countries that were not already members of the United Nations to join the world organization. However, one issue Moscow never considered to be negotiable was the status of the satellite countries; after resolution of the Austrian question removed the legal basis for stationing troops in Hungary and Romania, the USSR moved to tighten its grip on the region by creating a communist bloc military alliance, the Warsaw Treaty Organization (WTO), just one day before the Austrian treaty's signing.[2]

Western Attitudes toward Eastern Europe

Meanwhile, the policy of the first Eisenhower administration (1953–1957) toward East-Central Europe featured a peculiar duality.[3] President Dwight Eisenhower and especially his soon-to-be secretary of state, John Foster Dulles, had made the peaceful "liberation" of the region a major part of their election platform, firmly believing that the Truman administration's containment policy had been ineffective and that only a more aggressive posture would force the USSR to surrender Eastern Europe. This led the new administration to spend considerable sums to support clandestine radio stations and other semi-official entities, as well as various underground Eastern European émigré organizations. References to the liberation of captive nations were, until October 1956, a staple of most high-level administration pronouncements, which Radio Free Europe, Voice of America, and other propaganda organizations faithfully transmitted to Eastern Europe. Other activities included such spectacular ploys as launching balloons to distribute printed materials to the populations behind the Iron Curtain (Document No. 6). But despite the rhetoric and the unceasing barrage of propaganda aimed at Eastern Europe, there was never much likelihood that the West could unilaterally effect serious change.

In fact, by the time of the 1953 East German uprising, the Eisenhower administration had already recognized that the United States could not dramatically "roll back" Soviet influence except

---

[1] The USSR would not acquire a reliable intercontinental ballistic missile capability that could threaten North America until the end of the 1950s.

[2] The Warsaw Pact was established on May 14, 1955, while the Austrian State Treaty was signed on May 15. For recent multi-archival research on the establishment and the early period of the Warsaw Pact, see Vojtech Mastny, "'We are in a Bind': Polish and Czechoslovak Attempts at Reforming the Warsaw Pact," *Cold War International History Project Bulletin,* no. 11 (Winter 1998): 230–250.

[3] For important accounts of Eisenhower administration policy vis-a-vis Eastern Europe, see Bennett Kovrig, *The Myth of Liberation: East-Central Europe in U.S. Diplomacy and Politics since 1941* (Baltimore: Johns Hopkins University Press, 1973); Bennett Kovrig, *Of Walls and Bridges: The United States and Eastern Europe* (New York: New York University Press, 1991); Richard H. Immerman, ed., *John Foster Dulles and the Diplomacy of the Cold War* (Princeton, N.J.: Princeton University Press, 1990); James David Marchio, *Rhetoric and Reality: The Eisenhower Administration and Unrest in Eastern Europe, 1953–1959,* (Ph.D. dissertation, The American University, 1990), (Ann Arbor, MI: UMI Dissertation Services, 1993); and László Borhi, "Az Egyesült Államok Kelet-Európa politikájának néhány kérdése, 1948–1956," *Történelmi Szemle* 37, no. 3 (1995): 277–300.

through direct military action, an option the president himself ruled out early on because of the unacceptable risk of global war. By late 1953 then, the U.S. had quietly begun to aim only at gaining the "eventual" freedom of the satellites—adopting a more gradual, evolutionary program centering modestly around "sustaining their spirit of resistance to Soviet imperialism" (Document No. 3). Unfortunately, the effort to boost morale relied so heavily on a rhetorical campaign stressing the shrinking of Soviet power that it had the unintentional consequence of creating the illusion, not only in Eastern Europe and the United States but throughout the world, that the liberation of these nations remained a cornerstone of Eisenhower's foreign policy and of East-West relations in general.

In reality, American foreign policy during this era was based on a clear recognition of the post-World War II European status quo and the prevailing balance of power with the Soviet Union. With Moscow's acquisition of thermonuclear weapons, the U.S. was even more determined to avoid superpower conflict at all costs. By the mid-1950s, the Eisenhower administration's attempt to find an acceptable *modus vivendi* with the USSR—on issues ranging from the Korean War to disarmament—would become part of the concept known as peaceful coexistence. One of its main features was the implicit acceptance of the Soviet Union, the world's other superpower, as Washington's principal negotiating partner on the world stage. For its part, Moscow had made it clear that it would not consider discussing the status of previously conquered territory such as Eastern Europe.

Thereafter, the West saw Eastern Europe as secondary to the larger imperatives of global security—entirely understandable from an international political perspective. Although they had not given up hope for the peoples of Eastern Europe, by the beginning of 1956 Western officials generally no longer expected any significant change in the status of the satellite states. Despite perceptible fractionalization within the Soviet bloc, reports on probable developments in these countries assumed Moscow's continued ability to maintain control (Document No. 7). Moreover, the prospects for open resistance were minimal (Document No. 8). Therefore, West European experts, like their American counterparts, stressed the importance of evolutionary changes and concluded that, for the time being, the Yugoslav political model of "national communism" offered the best opportunity for these countries to gain any degree of internal or external autonomy (Document No. 17). This in no way implied abandoning the goal of gradually undermining communist rule, but the east bloc's more moderate course did encourage some NATO circles to contemplate a somewhat more flexible approach toward Eastern Europe (Document No. 16).[4]

Soviet Goals Regarding the Satellites

One of the new Soviet leadership's primary objectives after 1953 was to refurbish relations with Yugoslavia. The momentous Yugoslav-Soviet split of 1948 had created serious fissures in the socialist bloc, which Stalin's successors tried steadily to repair. Finally, in May 1955, Nikita Khrushchev and Nikolai Bulganin traveled to Belgrade to try to make amends with President Josip Broz Tito, blaming Stalin's policies for the deterioration in relations between the two countries and their ruling communist parties. Throughout 1955 and 1956, the Soviets made several conciliatory gestures toward Yugoslavia, such as giving public sanction to the notion that there could be more than one valid way to build socialism. In fact, Moscow was fundamentally unprepared to accept the Yugoslav model for its East European satellites (Document No. 14). The Kremlin's real goal was to bring Yugoslavia amicably back into the socialist camp (i.e. under Soviet control) and, more specifically, to make it a member of the Warsaw Pact. Because of its significance for broader satellite policies, the Yugoslavia issue loomed as a constant challenge for the Soviet leadership throughout the period leading up to (and during) the Hungarian revolution.

---

[4] For another example, see a report by the British NATO delegation to the Foreign Office on the October 24 meeting of the NATO Council, October 24, 1956, PRO FO, 371 122081 N 1059/9.

Within East-Central Europe, another overarching aim of Soviet foreign policy was simply to maintain stability. In spring 1953, the Kremlin faced the first serious post-Stalin challenge to its domination of the region in the form of mounting social unrest in East Germany. Alarmed at the GDR's decision to press ahead with the Stalinist pattern of "forced construction of socialism," the Soviets summoned top East German party officials to Moscow and instructed them to adopt more liberal political and economic policies. The short-lived "New Course," introduced in June, was marked not only by a reduction in heavy industrial production and a corresponding growth in the manufacture of consumer goods, but by a suspension of the collectivization of agriculture, an end to curbs on religious practices, reduced restrictions on travel abroad, and, for a short time, removal of the word "socialism" from the regime's propaganda vocabulary. Ironically, the New Course backfired. The sudden abandonment of much of the hard-line dogma that had been used to legitimize the regime, coupled with the GDR leaders' refusal to ease production quotas for workers, quickly led to an outbreak of strikes and riots in Berlin on June 17, which immediately spread to the rest of the country.[5] The turmoil shocked the Kremlin and had a profound effect on Khrushchev's plans for intra-bloc reform.

Hungary was just as susceptible to the economic and social problems that flared up in East Germany. Through a network of Soviet "advisers" stationed at every level of Hungary's state administration, the Kremlin had been receiving bleak assessments of the situation since at least summer 1952. Shortly after their reprimand of the GDR's party leadership, the CPSU CC Presidium summoned top HWP representatives to the Kremlin from June 13–16 (on the eve of the East German unrest), to deliver the same stern message. At one point, secret police chief Lavrentii Beria[6] told the Hungarians pointedly: "If the great Stalin made mistakes, comrade Rákosi can admit that he made mistakes too" (Document No. 1). The Soviet Communist Party (CPSU) Presidium's recommendations, dictated to the Hungarians at this meeting, were designed both to support a partial change in Moscow's own political line and to avert an imminent economic collapse in Hungary. Their intention was not so much to reform Hungary's socialist system as to prevent an incipient crisis from getting out of control, and to forestall any other developments that might interfere with larger foreign policy ambitions.

Imre Nagy and the New Course

By the spring of 1953, the Soviets could certainly cite some economic justifications for their concern. In its few years of rule since 1948, the HWP had brought Hungary to the brink of economic ruin. Reports reaching Moscow from various sources spoke of heightening tensions and a menacing level of discontent. Real income of wage-earners in 1953 had already fallen by 20 percent since 1949.

After his return to Hungary in mid-June, Rákosi reported to the HWP Secretariat on his instructions from Moscow. At a full meeting of the Central Committee on June 27–28, the leadership dutifully passed a detailed condemnation of past policies, including forced industrialization and the neglect, exploitation, and forcible collectivization of agriculture. These misguided policies, the CC obediently declared, had led to a steep decline in living standards. The leader-

---

[5] For recent scholarship on the Berlin uprising, see the primary document compilation edited by Christian F. Ostermann, *Uprising in East Germany, 1953: The Cold War, the German Question, and the First Major Upheaval Behind the Iron Curtain* (Budapest: Central European University Press, 2001), and id., *The United States, the East German Uprising of 1953, and the Limits of Rollback,* Cold War International History Project Working Paper, no. 11 (Washington D.C.: Woodrow Wilson International Center for Scholars, 1994); also James Richter, *Reexamining Soviet Policy during the Beria Interregnum,* Cold War International History Project Working Paper, no. 3 (Washington D.C.: Woodrow Wilson International Center for Scholars, 1992).

[6] Lavrentii Beria was people's commissar for internal affairs, then minister of state security from 1938 to 1953, from which post he played the leading role in carrying out the Stalinist terror. Beginning in 1939, he was a candidate member, and later a full member of the CPSU Politburo and Presidium. He was arrested in 1953 and executed.

ship's mistakes—but especially the errors of the four figures at the head of the regime, Rákosi, Ernő Gerő, Mihály Farkas and József Révai—had been compounded by a campaign against society itself through the use of arbitrary administrative methods and mass terror. The whole country, including the ruling party, according to the CC resolution, had in effect been left at the mercy of a handful of men (Document No. 2).

Rákosi, until then the country's undisputed leader, responded in Hungary as he had in Moscow, by going through the Bolshevik ritual of self-criticism and confessing his mistakes—or at least some of them. Far from conceding defeat, however, he did his utmost to restore his authority and resuscitate his discredited policies. He was powerless to alter the Central Committee resolution—which would have amounted to open opposition to Moscow—but he managed at least to prevent its publication in the party-controlled press. Instead, the text informing the party of his errors was turned over to the Political Committee, and the critical resolution did not become public.

Rákosi could not, however, prevent his own demotion, nor a number of other important personnel changes. For his central role in creating Hungary's predicament, he lost his post as prime minister and was replaced by Imre Nagy, whose name soon became emblematic of reform in Hungary. From then on, the posts of prime minister and party leader were split. The size of the government was to be reduced, and younger, intellectual "cadres" who had "grown up" since 1945 were to be involved more directly in the leadership.

On July 4, 1953, a new Hungarian Parliament, elected the previous May, convened. This was the venue Nagy chose to announce the party's more "people-friendly" New Course. Thus the general public learned about the new policy line not from the party, as usually happened, but from the new prime minister over the radio. Aside from its content, his speech was a marked departure in tone and style from the impersonal and flavorless addresses normally heard from functionaries of the party-state. This had a noticeable impact on the population.

Nevertheless, Nagy's task was enormous. He was taking control of the leadership of a country in fundamental crisis and was not adequately prepared for the role. Even his insights into the situation must have been limited. As a member of the HWP Secretariat and a deputy prime minister, he had depended on the foursome at the top of the leadership for the information he needed to carry out his work. All he could trust now, apart from his own convictions, was the judgment and good will of the Kremlin (over which he had little influence), and the sincerity of its professed opening to the outside world. Predictably, this was far too little to allow him to gauge Hungary's true state of affairs and devise a comprehensive policy program for the new government.[7]

The New Course concentrated on five areas of policy. First and foremost was the economy. The absolute priority previously given to industry, especially heavy industry, ended. Industrial investment was curbed and the rate of industrial expansion slowed. This released funds which could be redirected to consumer goods production, housing construction, and agricultural development.

These radical changes caused a number of problems. For one thing, the shift in priorities undermined the officials who had put the old policies into place, leaving Nagy at a disadvantage when he needed to call on them for support. The person most directly compromised was Gerő, who ran the economy and would be someone Nagy would have to rely on to implement his economic program and to form a political alliance against Rákosi. Gerő had shown some willingness to cooperate with Nagy early in 1954—no doubt hoping to exploit the rivalry between his counterparts—but he had quickly pulled back, making it clear to Nagy at that point that he could not count on him. The new economic measures also alienated lower-level functionaries who had been part of the forced development of heavy industry or were closely identified with it: factory managers, party branch secretaries, production managers, local-government officials, as well as powerful members of the central apparatus.

The second area of policy covered by the New Course concerned measures to stimulate agriculture. In industry, the new policy still operated in the old way—through centralized decision-making. In agriculture, Nagy began to shift to a more rational economic approach. He put an end

---

[7] On Nagy and the New Course, see János M. Rainer, *Nagy Imre. Politikai életrajz,* 2 vols. (Budapest: 1956-os Intézet, 1996–99), 1:509–543 and 2:9–37.

to the forced collectivization of land and gave peasants the option of withdrawing from agricultural cooperatives. Individual farmers were allowed to rent uncultivated land on favorable terms, while the targets for compulsory deliveries of produce were eased. With the involvement of his university colleagues[8] and other experts, Nagy devised a long-term development program for agriculture. These steps helped to dissolve the immediate crisis, increase supplies to the general public, and provide a foundation for the long-range improvement of the agricultural sector.

Yet these new measures, too, encountered some strong resistance. One objection was that agricultural policy could not be divorced from the economy as a whole. If private farming gained predominance, central control of the whole economy would be shaken. Furthermore, reducing the pressure on the villages would stem the flow of money available for investment in heavy industry. This, according to government operatives affected by the changes, would hurt workers whose jobs could be cut. Even more dire predictions surfaced, including the possibility of urban famine and village "rebellions." Since the immediate beneficiaries of the New Course policies were the peasantry, especially property-owning peasants—some of whom had previously been discriminated against as "kulaks," or rich peasants—there were warnings about the imminent collapse of the worker-peasant alliance, which formed the basic foundation of socialism.

The third important set of measures aimed at raising the nation's living standard. During the earlier period the level of state appropriations had characteristically exceeded what the general public could bear. These funds had fueled the program of forced economic growth, and sustained the regime's main base of support: the military, police and security forces. By bringing down prices, raising wages, and setting lower performance norms, Nagy hoped to reduce the bloated state bureaucracy and ease the intolerable burden on society. He recognized that no one could expect a strong performance from a famished country or base a socialist society on a harassed, impoverished population. He also realized that if the working class knew its basic needs would be met, then its will to produce, and consequently its performance, would rise. In the longer term, he believed, this would yield the greater accumulations needed to generate a moderately higher level of personal consumption.

In practice, the effect of the price cuts was reduced by a steady drop in the quality of goods produced. Also, the new steps led to generally sluggish deliveries, even though the number of items in short supply dropped. In 1954, there was a marked rise in personal consumption, to a level about 20 per cent higher than in 1950, but this still fell far short of what the growth in national income during the intervening period might have allowed. A similar situation obtained in the government's housing-construction campaign, eased only a few of the most pressing problems in that area.

The most important, and certainly most spectacular, New Course measures targeted excessive official coercion.[9] In order to redress years of oppression against society and establish credibility, the authorities would have to curb dramatically the reliance on terror that had played such a key role in running the political and economic system.[10]

A major step in this direction was the declaration of a broad amnesty. The authorities released large numbers from confinement, excused fines, or dismissed legal claims. The government also closed internment camps and abolished sentences such as internal exile and the designation of a

---

[8] From 1948 to 1955, Nagy taught at the University of Economics and the University of Agricultural Science. A great number of his later adherents and members of the "Imre Nagy circle" were his academic colleagues and students.

[9] The issue of the repression was already a topic of discussion in the HWP CC Secretariat as early as August 1952. According to a joint report by the justice and interior ministries and the party's Administrative Department on the period between 1949 and 1951, the courts sentenced 72,300 prisoners in 1949, 98,000 in 1950, and 125,000 in 1951. By the final year covered by the report, the courts found 87,000 of the 212,000 accused not guilty, while the prosecution authorities proffered no charges in 150,000 cases out of 300,000. In the same year, 500,000 penalties had been imposed by police and local administration for petty offenses alone. See, Minutes of the August 27, 1952, meeting of the HWP Secretariat, MOL, 276. f. 54/208 ő.e.

[10] János M. Rainer, The New Course in Hungary in 1953, Cold War International History Project Working Paper, no. 38 (Washington D.C.: Woodrow Wilson International Center for Scholars, 2002).

6

compulsory place of residence. As the releases from captivity continued, the issue of legal and moral rehabilitation came up, which in turn led to the question of responsibility for miscarriages of justice. Since so many people——mainly communist politicians—were now being declared innocent of any crime, whoever had originally condemned them must logically be at fault. At first, some officials tried to shift the blame onto Gábor Péter, the former head of the ÁVH who had already been arrested. But it was undeniable that Péter, whatever his personal responsibility, had run the ÁVH at the pleasure of the party leadership; he also never exercised authority over the courts or the rest of the power apparatus that had been involved in the repression. Many Hungarians remembered, for example, that Rákosi had claimed sole credit for exposing the "Rajk gang" (see below). Clearly, the real culprits were the top leaders of the HWP and, beyond them, their patrons in the Soviet Union itself.

Hungarian society's thirst for justice intersected with Nagy's political instincts. He felt a personal need to point out the main guilty party—Rákosi—by name, while recognizing as a politician that the party chief was also the greatest obstacle to the June 1953 program. Rákosi would have to be removed from power completely before the New Course could develop. If Nagy succeeded, that in itself would be one of the great achievements of the new policy. So efforts to stamp out illegalities, start the rehabilitation process, and carry it through consistently rose to the top of Nagy's agenda in 1954. Deposing his main rival and trying to build broad popular support for his policies made it seem worth the risk of alienating other officials.

Rákosi, of course, also understood what was at stake and made every effort to prevent Nagy's "rummaging in the past" and "exorbitant pursuit of rehabilitation." He charged the prime minister with undermining the credibility of the party's leaders and the party itself, which he said raised the danger that the socialist system itself might collapse. Rákosi had help from the ÁVH, which had essentially remained intact and was able to play a role in obstructing the rehabilitation process. Also, the official investigating bodies continued to answer to the old leadership and were fully prepared to generate evidence they thought the authorities wanted to see——evidence that, naturally, did not taint Rákosi himself or disclose the Soviet role in the terror campaign. The main obstacle to the process, however, was that the Kremlin had absolutely no interest in a public investigation of responsibility; their idea of reform would be more than satisfied with just the release of communists who had been wrongly condemned. So although Nagy's crusade managed to rehabilitate many communist detainees, including future leader János Kádár, the most important case of political abuse by the Party—the László Rajk trial—was not reopened until 1956.[11] Nonetheless, Nagy's achievement in reducing society's fears of regime-imposed terror was probably the most significant development of the New Course. Although it would still be possible to revert to some of the pre-1953 economic policies after Nagy's dismissal in 1955, there was no way to restore the atmosphere of fear that had existed under Stalin and Rákosi.

The fifth area of Nagy's activity consisted of measures, especially from 1954 on, to create an institutional, political framework for the New Course. An essential requirement was to break up the HWP's monolithic power by freeing government bodies from party control. Nagy had the same motive in creating a "popular front" organization: to establish institutional structures to allow for political activity by the majority of the population—who were not members of the HWP—and give them a say in running the country's affairs. In other words, the front was meant to allow room for a plurality of interests under a relatively democratic structure, albeit within the

---

[11] László Rajk, a high-ranking party official who belonged to the non-Muscovite segment of the communist leadership, was arrested in the summer of 1949. Along with several other officials, he was accused of a variety of implausible crimes, including Trotskyism, Titoism, and espionage, and was executed after a celebrated show trial. While Rajk's case was an important part of the anti-Yugoslav campaign resulting from the split between Stalin and Tito, Rajk probably also fell victim to Rákosi's personal suspicions. The trial of the "Rajk gang" was one of several strikingly similar cases that were brought almost simultaneously throughout Eastern Europe at the time. These show trials had their origins in the Stalinist logic of power, according to which continuous purges served as an important means of controlling society and disciplining the party membership. See, George H. Hodos, *Show Trials: Stalinist Purges in Eastern Europe*, 1949–1956 (New York: Praeger, 1987).

framework of a government-sanctioned forum operating within a one-party system. The danger of even this degree of decentralization was apparent to Rákosi and his followers, who ultimately managed to dilute the new organization so thoroughly that it was indistinguishable from any of its communist-controlled predecessors. Nagy was also unable to boost the number of reformers in the Central Committee or the Political Committee during the 3rd Congress of the HWP in May 1954. He managed to get Zoltán Szántó elected to the CC, but his other candidates lost. Moreover, the Secretariat, headed by Rákosi, actually strengthened its power over the party.

These setbacks can be partly explained by the Soviet leadership's increasing ambivalence towards Nagy's policies. Although the New Course had brought some important results by autumn 1954, it had not led to any breakthroughs, often because of resistance by the Rákosi group. In the end, a number of Kremlin officials thought Nagy's approach had only brought more turmoil—not the order Moscow had sought. Soviet Presidium member Lazar Kaganovich summed up the ambiguity of the post-Stalin period when, in May 1954, he criticized the Hungarian delegation for following precisely the economic policy Moscow had stipulated: "You are living in greater style than your means permit. You are building socialism on credit" (Document No. 4).

Retrenchment

By late 1954, Soviet dissatisfaction with Nagy's policies had grown to the point where they were ready to withdraw their support. The worsening international climate, particularly Western moves to rearm West Germany and include it as a member of NATO, had only magnified their concerns. Rákosi, coming back from a lengthy stay in the Soviet Union, immediately made the most of this shift in Soviet thinking. On December 1, he reported to the HWP Political Committee that Moscow's views on reform had changed. Although the Political Committee did not retract its resolution of June 1953, it introduced a new one which warned that a "rightist" deviation from communist doctrine represented the main danger confronting the regime. They condemned Nagy's policy accordingly. This was not enough for Rákosi, however, whose ambition was to squeeze his rival out of public life altogether. He proposed that a party delegation travel to Moscow to discuss the Hungarian situation directly with the Soviets, an idea Nagy opposed unsuccessfully.[12]

The CPSU Presidium met with Hungarian party leaders on January 8, 1955 (Document No. 5). The Soviet side was interested in only three things. One was the state of the Hungarian economy, which was still not improving the way the Kremlin had hoped. This topic received the least emphasis at the talks. A second subject, which the Soviets viewed far more seriously, was an article Nagy had written in *Szabad Nép* ("Free People"), the official party daily and the country's largest circulation paper, on October 20, 1954.[13] In the article, he advocated democratizing the party, castigated the errors brought about by one-man rule, and called on party members to take on independent political activity. Moscow saw Nagy's appeal as an invitation to factionalism, which violated the cardinal principle of party unity and constituted a serious crime. The third item discussed in Moscow was the Soviets' anger at Nagy's stubbornness in insisting that he could not work with Rákosi in implementing the New Course. Although this was the truth, he was directly implying that Rákosi should be dismissed, but this kind of major personnel decision was traditionally a jealously guarded purview of the CPSU Presidium.

In spite of all these problems, Khrushchev did not recommend a complete break with the 1953 program. He insisted only that order be imposed in Hungary once and for all. The economic crisis certainly concerned him, but he wanted to deal with it in a way that would preserve the larger interests of socialism, which meant maintaining agricultural cooperatives and heavy industry in general, especially the arms industry. No rhetorical changes or even shifts in economic policy

[12] Minutes of the HWP PC, December 1, 1954, MOL, 276. f. 53/206. ő.e.

[13] Imre Nagy, "A Központi Vezetőség ülése után," *Szabad Nép*, October 20, 1954.

could alter the fundamental principle of Kremlin ideology that industry was the foundation of all socialist economic activity, while agricultural cooperatives were the main guarantor of the worker-peasant alliance, and thus held the system together. Khrushchev further directed that Rákosi's leading role be restored but, at the same time: "the authority of Comrade Nagy has to be safeguarded as well"—mainly to retain the image of complete unity at the top of the HWP. Khrushchev was thus offering Nagy an opportunity to remain active in politics, if not in the top ranks, but only if he subscribed to the restored policy and condemned his own mistakes.

Interestingly, neither Nagy nor Rákosi obeyed their instructions after their return from Moscow. Nagy, instead of accepting Moscow's criticisms unquestioningly, tried to salvage certain elements of the New Course while holding on to some degree of personal control over national policy. Rákosi remained determined to claim victory over Nagy and, with the HWP Political Committee behind him, set about drafting a resolution condemning his rival and his policies, a task Nagy made easier by flouting the unwritten rules of Bolshevik discipline.

By 1955, however, Rákosi and the hardliners could no longer pick up the reins of government where they had dropped them in 1953. Neither domestic nor international circumstances were right for doing so. In foreign policy, despite Soviet worries about suffering a number of reverses, East-West détente continued. Furthermore, the Austrian State Treaty, followed by the Geneva conference in July 1955, the first four-power summit since Potsdam, and the establishment of diplomatic relations with the Federal Republic of Germany that autumn (Document No. 9) reassured Moscow of its international standing, and particularly its hold on Eastern Europe. Khrushchev's handling of bloc affairs betrayed a certain ambivalence about revising the reform program, but he was genuinely intent on doing away with some of the excesses of the Stalinist system, like those Rákosi had implemented in Hungary, and his renewed international confidence helped to keep him moving in that direction.

Domestically, the hardliners discovered that Hungary was a different country after Nagy's reforms. Despite Nagy's refusal to be involved in self-criticism, his opponents found it hard to marginalize him, let alone resort to the more radical measures available before 1953. Hardly a year after the amnesties and the start of the rehabilitation process it was already impossible to try the prime minister and imprison him (although Rákosi did raise the possibility). In fact, Rákosi could not even have him dismissed right away. A HWP CC resolution in early March 1955 denounced Nagy's policy, but various domestic and foreign policy considerations intervened, forcing Rákosi to be content with isolating Nagy under virtual house arrest until mid-April—using Nagy's (actual) illness as an excuse. At that point, Rákosi pushed through another CC resolution charging Nagy with anti-party activity and removing him from all party posts and the premiership. (He was succeeded by András Hegedüs.) His expulsion from the party did not come until December 1955, while the hard-liners never managed to put to rest the "Nagy question"—that is, the complete repudiation of his political agenda—by the time the revolution broke out on October 23, 1956.

Convinced he was in the right, the deposed prime minister refused to stay quietly on the sidelines. Instead, he wrote a stream of protest memoranda and polemics to the Hungarian and Soviet party leaderships, which also circulated among a narrow circle of his political adherents.[14] Under the old regime, he would never have been allowed to keep so active politically. Thus, one essential factor behind Nagy's staying power, apart from his perseverance and sense of principle, was the change in the country's political atmosphere thanks to the New Course.

Another important reason for Nagy's survival was the increasingly conspicuous group of supporters that had gathered around him by the end of 1954. This group consisted partly of colleagues and students who had helped him devise a radical reform program for agriculture, and partly of politicians, writers and journalists. They came to be known collectively as the "Party Opposition." Despite the sanctions Rákosi tried to impose against them, the group stayed faithful to the New Course, even after the prime minister had lost his official posts.

[14] These writings were later smuggled out to the West and were published in several languages. For the English version, see Imre Nagy, *On Communism: In Defense of the New Course* (New York: Praeger, 1957).

Nagy's policies also gained ever-wider support in the Hungarian press during 1954. At the end of October, a number of senior employees at a *Szabad Nép* staff meeting came out in support of the New Course and against the forces holding it back—including senior party officials Ernő Gerő and Mihály Farkas as well as the paper's own editors. In November, support for socialist reform came from Miklós Gimes, and later Géza Losonczy who worked for another daily paper, *Magyar Nemzet* ("Hungarian Nation"), which had just become the organ of the Patriotic People's Front.

Meanwhile, prisoners continued to be released from confinement, although not at the pace Nagy had wanted. Among other notables, Anna Kéthly gained her release at the end of 1954, followed in 1955 by Simon Papp, who had been sentenced in the MAORT (Hungarian-American Oil Company) trial, and Cardinal József Mindszenty, followed by József Grősz, archbishop of Kalocsa.[15] In November 1955, Béla Kovács, formerly general secretary of the Smallholders' Party, got permission to return from the USSR with several of his associates. The rehabilitation of Noel Field, who had played a key part in the East European show trials, added impetus to calls to re-examine the Rajk case. After the release of condemned communists, non-communist politicians and defendants in economic trials also won their freedom or had their sentences reduced.[16]

The Twentieth Party Congress and the Reemergence of the Reform Movement

The Twentieth Congress of the CPSU marked a turning-point in the politics and ideology of the Soviet party and the international communist movement. Overturning the doctrine that a third world war was inevitable and proclaiming the concept of peaceful coexistence, Soviet leader Khrushchev laid out new tasks for the leaders of the bloc. Although Khrushchev's secret speech revealing the crimes of Joseph Stalin was not to be published in full for 30 years, news of it spread immediately. It confirmed the worst beliefs of Stalinism's opponents, and overcame the resistance of many members of the old guard.[17]

The Twentieth Congress placed the Hungarian party leadership in a virtually impossible position. Rákosi, the man most identified with Stalinism in the country, was given the job of spearheading the de-Stalinization process, unveiling the mistakes and crimes of the past, and condemning the guilty. Meanwhile, Moscow unrealistically required that the top party leader (himself) not lose prestige in the process. It is hard to imagine how the Kremlin's rulers thought this could be accomplished.

The Soviets stuck with Rákosi for several reasons. For one thing they worried that a high turnover of personnel would destabilize the leadership and the country even further. The changes since 1953 had already caused enough trouble for the party. For another thing, the Kremlin saw in Rákosi a personal guarantee that Hungary would not follow an independent policy of reform that might clash with their interests. Finally, in their minds there was no suitable alternative to Rákosi on the horizon.

Not surprisingly, pro-reform forces in Hungary gathered strength after the Twentieth Congress. This was the case inside the HWP as well, where calls for real change and a radical renewal of the party steadily widened. The Petőfi Circle, begun as a regime-sanctioned intellectual discussion group, started to take on a more vocal, anti-Stalinist cast. Their public debates

[15] József Grősz, arcbishop of Kalocsa, was arrested in 1951 and sentenced after a show trial to 15 years in prison. Although he was released in 1955, he remained under house arrest until receiving an amnesty in May 1956.

[16] Valéria Révai, ed., *Törvénytelen szocializmus: A Tényfeltáró Bizottság jelentése* (Budapest: Zrínyi Kiadó–Új Magyarország, 1993), 215–331.

[17] See, V. P. Naumov, "Bor'ba N. S. Khrushcheva za edinolichnuyu vlast'," *Novaya i Noveishaya Istoriya* 24, no. 2 (1996): 10–31; and Rudolf G. Pikhoya, "O vnutripoliticheskoi bor'be v sovetskom rukovodstve 1945–1958 gg," *Novaya i Noveishchaya Istoriya* 23, no. 6 (1995): 3–14.

went well beyond cautious reformist formulations to include everything but the two topics that remained utterly off-limits: the stationing of Soviet troops in Hungary and the one-party system. The Circle gradually drew broader segments of society into debates about national conditions as audience members took what they heard back to their work places and to the provinces, and started similar discussions.[18] Soon, the authorities began to see the danger involved. Soviet Ambassador Yurii Andropov, after listening to one of the debates, reported to Moscow that it had "essentially degenerated into a demonstration against the party leadership."[19] On June 30, the HWP CC took action, condemning the debates and suspending the group's activities.

Undeterred, the reform camp continued to broaden and strengthen its base, and to clarify its program in spite of Nagy's dismissal. At the same time, Rákosi and his supporters were proving unable to handle the spreading crisis; a succession of half-measures had only further weakened their authority. Many party members who disagreed with the existing system were not so much in favor of reforming it as eliminating some of its excesses—especially the mechanisms of repression. (The main advocate of this was János Kádár.) But the leadership rejected these criticisms as right-wing deviations, examples of Nagy's corrupting influence, or symptoms of ignorance and backwardness. Significantly, the party's higher-ups were spared this kind of censure. For example, Kádár, despite his expressed point of view, joined the top-level Political Committee in July 1956.

By summer 1956, Moscow had decided it was time for another political intervention in Hungary (Document Nos. 11 and 14). Unraveling conditions there were raising concerns throughout the socialist camp that "unexpected and unpleasant" events could "happen in Hungary" (Document No. 15). The likelihood seemed to increase after the uprising in Poznań, Poland, on June 28, where security units forcibly broke up a demonstration of workers who were demanding improvements in living and working conditions. The clash cost almost a hundred lives, with several hundred wounded.

To prevent a similar outbreak in Hungary, Anastas Mikoyan, one of the more moderate members of the CPSU Politburo, arrived in Budapest on July 13 with a broad mandate to put an end to the crisis. Mikoyan initiated two measures: a change of leadership and a crackdown on the opposition. Reversing the earlier Soviet position, he declared that Rákosi had to step down as HWP first secretary. In his place, a new, unified group would be appointed to bring fresh blood to the leadership. Officially, the Soviets attributed Rákosi's removal to poor health and allowed him to keep his membership in Parliament and on the Central Committee (Document No. 15).

But Rákosi's replacement by the ineffectual Ernő Gerő, whose main appeal for Moscow was his unquestioned loyalty, only made matters worse. The move disconcerted Rákosi's supporters who had lost their benefactor, and left his opponents dissatisfied over the prospect of another period of no meaningful change (even though they may have had less to fear from Gerő personally). In fact, no other high-level changes took place, which meant that Rákosi's followers largely retained their influence and the splits within the Political Committee remained. If anything, it became even harder to agree on the most basic questions much less to respond to the country's growing problems.

Mikoyan's second measure accomplished nothing either. The authorities never attempted the assault on the opposition. Even Rákosi understood that this sort of tactic would not help, since anyone they arrested would quickly be replaced by other activists. In any event, the shaken leadership no longer had the will to take serious action (Document No. 19). Far from becoming more hard-line, the party actually began showing signs of moderation, readmitting Nagy as a member in October, for example, despite his refusal to practice public self-criticism.

[18] On the Petőfi Circle, see András B. Hegedűs, "The Petőfi Circle: The Forum of Reform in 1956," in *Hungary 1956— Forty Years On,* ed. Terry Cox, (London: Frank Cass, 1997), 108–134.

[19] "Zapis besedi Yu. V. Andropova s A. Hegedushem," after June 27, 1956, in *Sovietskii Soyuz i vengerskii krizis, 1956 goda: Dokumenty,* ed. and comp. by E. D. Orekhova, Vyacheslav T. Sereda and Aleksandr. S. Stykalin (Moscow: ROSSPEN, 1998), 122.

Another reason for not carrying out domestic reprisals was the regime's decision to focus on long-neglected foreign policy problems. During his three months in power, Gerő spent barely a month in Hungary. High on his agenda was the need to resolve the Yugoslav question—no simple matter since Tito had made clear his unhappiness with the uninspired choice of Gerő. Thus, Gerő spent much of his time away from Hungary in Moscow preparing for the delicate talks with Belgrade (Document No. 18). Meanwhile, Kádár, the second most powerful figure in the party, was also largely absent, representing Hungary at prolonged talks in China. This left the party and the country without the capacity for making vital decisions at a very difficult stage.

Hungary on the Eve of Rebellion

Even without a renewed crackdown, Hungarian society by mid-1956 was feeling the effects of ever more burdensome political and economic demands. Nagy's dismissal in 1955 had led to increased popular resentment that was only compounded by a series of tougher economic policies. In agriculture, a new wave of collectivization accompanied a redistribution of peasant holdings and higher compulsory delivery quotas. Industrial production norms and employees' pension contributions also rose. The combined results were painful. Housing shortages became critical with many people having to live in shanties, or worse. Workers on high-priority, large-scale production projects were forcibly separated from their families and worked under extreme conditions. New industrial towns suffered from severe shortages of basic goods and became breeding grounds for crime. Overall, living standards in 1956 sank below 1938 levels, which was already far from prosperous compared with other European countries.[20] By the time the guidelines for the Second Five-Year Plan were released for public discussion in April 1956, Hungarians realized that the regime was going to do no better than continue the same outmoded and failed economic policies of the previous era.

Gradually, Hungarians came to the conclusion that this was no way to live, and opposition forces began to gain strength again. Even before Rákosi's dismissal, Mikoyan was reporting that "day after day the comrades are further losing their grip on power. A parallel center is forming from enemy elements operating actively, decisively, and self-confidently. The press and radio are not under CC control any more" (Document No. 15). Mikoyan's observations were accurate. By autumn, not only writers, journalists and other intelligentsia, but the vast majority of Hungarians had become active opponents of the regime. The authorities, who had shown themselves to be weak and hesitant, had lost the confidence of the people, a fact that local Soviet officials reported regularly to Moscow (Document No. 19). Soon, the final barriers of fear began to crumble as well. It was becoming clear not only that Hungarians no longer wanted to live under the current system, but that the regime no longer had the power to defend it.

On October 6, 1956, a turning point came with the ceremonial reburial in Budapest of László Rajk and others who had been executed with him in 1949. Rajk's rehabilitation had been a long-standing demand of pro-reform elements. Now that Rákosi, who had played a major part in the show trial, was out of favor, the regime had found it easier to seem responsive to the population. At the reburial, following the obligatory party speeches, a former co-defendant of Rajk's named Béla Szász spoke. Capturing the feeling of the crowd of some 200,000, he declared: "As hundreds of thousands pass by the coffins, they are not simply paying their last respects to the victims; they have an ardent desire and an unswerving resolve to bury an era."[21]

The Rajk funeral not only deepened the overall moral crisis of the HWP and strengthened the positions of the inner party opposition (Document No. 21), it also sparked an unprecedented student

---

[20] On the economic situation in Hungary before the 1956 Revolution, see Iván Pető and Sándor Szakács, *A hazai gazdaság négy évtizedének története*, vol. 1 (Budapest, Közgazdasági és Jogi Kiadó, 1985); László Varga, *Az elhagyott tömeg. Tanulmányok 1950–1956-ról* (Budapest: Cserépfalvi–Budapest Főváros Levéltára, 1994), 7–85.

[21] *Szabad Nép*, October 7, 1956.

demonstration in the streets of Budapest that included displays of anti-Stalinist slogans.[22] The march was the first open protest of its kind and set the stage for more demonstrations leading up to the revolution itself. While the party's leadership stayed mired in the old ways, the students had struck out in a radically new direction. On October 16, for example, a student assembly at the University of Szeged decided to withdraw from the communist-controlled Union of Working Youth (DISZ) and reconstitute an earlier students' association known as MEFESZ. This development was not just a stage on the road to revolution, it was revolutionary in itself: for the first time under communist rule, a self-governing organization had been founded independently and had elected its leaders without HWP screening. At the time, no public entities were allowed to function outside of party control. The notion that alternative institutions would be needed to represent differing interests ran directly counter to official ideology, which denied that such differences could exist in a socialist society. By the time the uprising broke out on October 23, MEFESZ had established a nationwide membership.

On October 19, another major development occurred that had a direct impact on the Hungarian crisis. On the eve of its 8th Plenum, the leadership of the Polish United Workers Party (PZPR) had decided to elect the once-discredited Władysław Gomułka[23] first secretary and to exclude pro-Soviet officials from the top levels of the party. The Kremlin reacted with alarm at the implications for Soviet control. Khrushchev and a top-level Kremlin delegation made a surprise visit to Warsaw to confront the Polish authorities. At the same time, Red Army units in the country moved into strategic positions in and around the capital in case military force was needed. In a dramatic face-off, Gomułka convinced Khrushchev to compromise: the Soviets accepted the new Polish leadership, while Gomułka gave assurances that the political reforms in Poland would not threaten either local communist rule or the unity of the Soviet bloc. Hungarian society reacted in different ways to the crisis. The internal party opposition took heart from Gomułka's rise from political outcast to party leader, and especially from his bold defense of a "Polish road to socialism." They hoped that they would also be able to effect meaningful change from within Hungary's existing socialist system. On October 22, the party daily *Szabad Nép* reprinted a speech by Gomułka from the day before describing the successful outcome of the talks with the Soviets.

Hungary's youth learned a different lesson from the Poles. On the same day that Gomułka's speech appeared in the newspaper, a student gathering at Budapest Technical University decided not only to join the new independent organization, MEFESZ, but to formulate a list of political demands inspired by Gomułka's showdown with Khrushchev (Document Nos. 23 and 27). They announced a demonstration of solidarity with anti-regime protestors for the next day. The "Sixteen Points" the students presented broke crucial new ground. They ignored the taboos that the Petőfi Circle had respected in the spring, explicitly demanding the withdrawal of Soviet forces from Hungary and the restoration of a multi-party system (Document No. 24). Neither the press nor the radio would agree to reproduce their demands in full, but the students ruled out any changes. Instead, they made stenciled copies and circulated them around Budapest.

Just one day later, the groundswell of popular frustration erupted into full-scale revolution, sweeping aside the naive hopes of the party opposition for producing reform "from within."

---

[22] The demonstration began at the memorial to the country's first parliamentary prime minister, Count Lajos Batthyány, who was killed by the Austrians after the crushing of Hungary's war of independence in 1849. Because both his execution and that of thirteen Hungarian army generals in Arad took place on October 6, that day became a national day of mourning for Hungarians. Given its dense historical meaning, October 6 might seem like a strikingly unsuitable choice for Rajk's reburial, since it inevitably connected the injustices committed under Stalinism to the theme of lost national independence. Surprisingly, evidence suggests that the communist leaders simply forgot about the significance of the date when they consented to Rajk's public reburial.

[23] Gomułka, a long-time Polish communist, had been accused of "rightist-nationalist deviationism" in 1948, expelled from the party in 1949 and imprisoned from 1951–1954. His political resurrection in 1956 was a serious concern to the Kremlin, which did not trust his loyalty to Moscow. For documentation and discussion of this crucial confrontation, see L. W. Gluchowski, "Poland, 1956: Khrushchev, Gomulka and the 'Polish October,'" *Cold War International History Project Bulletin* no. 5 (Spring 1995): 1, 38–49. Ironically, Gomułka would turn out to be more of a traditional Soviet-line communist than Nagy.

DOCUMENT NO. 1: Notes of a Meeting between the CPSU CC Presidium and a HWP Political Committee Delegation in Moscow, June 13 and 16, 1953

By Spring 1953, the political, economic and social situation in Hungary had deteriorated to such an extent that the Kremlin had begun to urge Hungarian leader Mátyás Rákosi to implement fundamental reforms. These measures included moving away from the Stalinist economic model of emphasizing heavy industry at the expense of consumer goods, and, in the political sphere, such steps as separating the posts of prime minister and party leader. When the Hungarians failed to comply, Rákosi and several colleagues were summoned to Moscow for "consultations" with the CPSU Presidium in mid-June 1953. Earlier in the month, a similar meeting had taken place with senior members of East Germany's Socialist Unity Party, whom the Kremlin coerced into formulating a "New Course," the first program of reform in the eastern bloc designed to correct the "mistakes" of the past.

During their talks with the Hungarian "comrades," the Soviets proposed discussing three major issues: economic development, "the selection of cadres" and the problem of "authoritarianism." Although Rákosi would claim that Hungary's mistakes had already been corrected according to earlier guidelines, the Soviet leaders harshly criticized the Hungarian party's policies, including the excesses in connection with collectivization, compulsory deliveries of agricultural goods, and the use of extreme administrative measures against the peasants, as well as an exaggerated emphasis on industrialization and an excessive reliance on repression. Beria, for one, strongly condemned Rákosi for his personal handling of the state security apparatus, for intervening in individual investigations, and even for ordering the use of physical violence. He declared that Rákosi would have to resign as prime minister in favor of Imre Nagy. Khrushchev was even more explicit in singling out Rákosi for blame.

The Soviet leadership ordered the Hungarians to prepare a written plan for correcting their many errors, and to compile a list of party personnel changes they intended to make. The Hungarians completed the two documents on the spot. They were then discussed with the Presidium during the second round of negotiations on June 16 (also presented in part below). At this meeting, the Soviets insisted that Rákosi's, Ernő Gerő's, Mihály Farkas', and József Révai's personal responsibility be explicitly spelled out. The result was the promulgation of the June 1953 resolution of the HWP CC (see Document No. 2), and Nagy's replacement of Rákosi as premier.

KREMLIN, 13 JUNE 1953.

Cde. Malenkov: There was a discussion recently with Comrade Rákosi about the Hungarian situation. After that conversation, it seemed necessary to discuss certain questions in a wider scope. He recommends as the procedure for discussion that the Hungarian comrades lay out their views primarily regarding three questions that relate to fields where not everything is in order in Hungary:

1. certain questions of economic development
2. the selection of cadres
3. certain questions of state administration (abuses of power).

After discussing these questions, the manner of correcting the mistakes must be discussed. [...]

Cde. Malenkov: We view Hungary's situation with a critical attitude. We would like the comrades to be critical as well, and to tell us their opinions about the problems. Our impression is that the Hungarian comrades underestimate the problems. Without a thorough debate of the issues, it is impossible to find proper solutions. The facts that we are familiar with indicate that the situation in the field of agriculture is not good. The quality of animal husbandry is not improving; on the contrary, it is declining. Regarding the [agricultural] cooperatives, the situation is not too good there either. As far as we know, 8,000–10,000 families left the cooperatives last year. They say the harvest was bad. That cannot explain everything. There were excessive orders during the compulsory delivery of the [agricultural levy]. It was not proper to collect the entire sunflower and rice harvest. Many peasants are sentenced by the courts because they do not fulfill their obligations to the state. There are problems in the area of trade as well. They provide few commodities for the population.

Prosecutions were initiated against 250,000 people in the second half of 1952. It is true that 75 percent of the prosecutions were stopped; yet, the number is still rather high. In 1952, they brought sentences in about 540,000 cases of transgressions within 9 months. All these provoked dissatisfaction among the population.

To return to the [question of] cooperatives, there is evidence according to which the income of the cooperatives' employees is less than that of farmers working individually. It is also a mistake that [only] a small sum is appropriated for investments in agriculture. Regarding the cadres. It is appropriate that many [of them] study. But if the leaders are always studying, they are not working. The leaders are virtually turned into students. [...]

Cde. Beria: He agrees with what comrade Molotov said. When comrade Rákosi was here last time, it was brought up that certain questions should be discussed with more comrades. Not that they do not trust comrade Rákosi or that comrade Rákosi does not represent Hungary, but just so that they would get to know more comrades.

Comrade Rákosi himself suggested this on several occasions.

It cannot be said that there is no improvement in Hungary. The positions of the people's democracy are continuously becoming stronger. The point is that the situation should become even better. The international and internal conditions will not always be this favorable. This is exactly why the internal situation must be strengthened now. We must be stronger than we are now.

Let us look at agriculture from this point of view. The collective sector in Hungary could work much more effectively if the Central Committee and the government paid more attention to agriculture. In that case, there would not be 750,000 hectares of fallow land. The situation wouldn't be such that the peasants leave agriculture and move into industry. The situation wouldn't be such that the peasants are significant debtors to the state. This debt constitutes 400 million forints, according to our information. The situation wouldn't be such that the peasants would not know how much levy they had to surrender to the state the following year. Comrade Imre Nagy was excluded from the PC because he recommended that the collective movement be developed more slowly. This was not correct. The comrades who lead the CC and the Council of Ministers do not know the countryside well, and they do not want to get to know the countryside.

The large number of major investments contributes to the bad situation in the villages. Hungarian industry is not small. If Hungarian industry were rectified and broadened a bit, it would be possible to develop metallurgy and certain other industrial branches more slowly. This would allow them to pay more attention to light industry, to the industry that serves the population.

Regarding legality and law enforcement, comrade Malenkov is right. Comrade Rákosi once again misunderstands us on this question. The issue is not that comrade Rákosi mentioned 30-40,000 arrested, and [that] their number is somewhat higher.

Could it be acceptable that in Hungary—a country with 9,500,000 inhabitants—prosecutions were initiated against 1,500,000 people? Administrative regulations were applied against 1,150,000 people within two-and-a-half years. These numbers show that the interior and judiciary organs and the ÁVH work very badly, and the Ministry of the Interior and the ÁVH must merge precisely because of this. A respectful comrade must be placed in the leadership of the Ministry of the Interior; someone who will be able to change the situation that developed there. Several leaders replaced each other at the ÁVH and the M. of Interior; it is not even possible to know exactly what the situation is now. And Hungary will be the object of attention of many capitalist countries, of the USA, and of England for a long time. There is a large and well-qualified group of Hungarian émigrés in the West that keeps in touch with leading foreign imperialist circles. It is to be expected that certain capitalist countries will try to flatter; others will send diversionists to Hungary. They have one goal: to overthrow the existing authorities and restore the capitalists' power. There are many elements in Hungary who could be exploited by the enemy. And there are many who are unsatisfied with the policies of the party. Why does he treat this question so extensively? Because it has great significance in the relations of the peoples' democracies, but also in the Soviet Union.

There is another way to improve the situation. The personal intervention of the chairman of the Council of Ministers[24] or of the party's first secretary in matters concerning the Ministry of the Interior. Comrade Rákosi does that. This intervention is not always appropriate. Even comrade Stalin made a mistake in this question. He directly gave instructions for questioning those arrested, etc. Comrade Rákosi would be even more likely to make mistakes.

It is not right that comrade Rákosi gives directions regarding who must be arrested; he says who should be beaten. A person that's beaten will give the kind of confession that the interrogating agents want, will admit that he is an English or American spy or whatever we want. But it will never be possible to know the truth this way. This way, innocent people might be sentenced. There is the law, and everyone has to respect it. How investigations should be conducted, who should be arrested, and how they should be interrogated must be left to the investigating organs.

Thus, there are two ways to improve the situation. One of the methods: a responsible person is placed at the top of the Ministry of the Interior who becomes the supervisor of the area and corrects the mistakes. The other method: comrade Rákosi directly manages the work of the Interior and ÁVH organs. This latter method is not correct. Comrade Rákosi tells who is to be arrested, etc. This is how we reach the point that comrade Rákosi is never wrong; all the other comrades are wrong. This situation leads to a point where comrade Rákosi will not be respected, but feared. [He] is the party's [first] secretary, the chairman of the Council of Ministers, and the director of the ÁVH in one person.

Cde. Malenkov: Here we are correcting the mistakes that we made in this area.

Cde. Beria: The issue of Péter's[25] arrest. Bielkin, a person arrested by Soviet State security, confessed that he spied together with Gábor Péter. Later he withdrew his confession.

Comrade Rákosi said that Péter could not be released because he had other sins.

Two people were beaten at the ÁVH until they died. This [was] a serious mistake. Comrade Rákosi appears as a most important person. It is not right that he does everything. It was not even right for comrade Stalin to be everyone in one person. One person is only one person. When comrade Rákosi says the people would not understand if he were released from his position as first secretary, he overestimates himself. Those comrades who are here and the other comrades at home are not accidental [sic] people either. It would be better if the chairman of the Council of Ministers were Hungarian.[26] Comrade Stalin told comrade Rákosi several times that Hungarians should be promoted more. It is said that many of them served Horthy.[27] If they are honest people and now they serve us, they must be supported. Today the Red Army is still in Hungary, but it will not be there forever. Therefore, we must prepare and become stronger so that nobody can do any harm to us.

If comrade Nagy becomes chairman of the Council of Ministers, comrade Rákosi should remain at the head of the party as a comrade rich in experience who is faithful to the party's cause. Comrade Nagy would be satisfactory as the chairman of the Council of Ministers (faithful to the party, Hungarian, knows the agricultural sector).

Comrade Rákosi in his telegram misinterpreted the suggestion that comrade Gerő should be the Minister of the Interior.

Comrade Molotov: The comrades had a chance to be convinced that even though we are talking about Hungary, the issue is not only Hungary, but all of the peoples' democracies.

---

[24] That is, the prime minister.

[25] Gábor Péter, head of the Hungarian political police from 1945–1953, was arrested in 1953 for "trespasses against socialist legality" and sentenced to life in prison. His arrest was part of the Stalinist purges of the period, and presumably served to lay the groundwork for an "anti-zionist" trial.

[26] As opposed to Jewish—a reflection of the prevalence of anti-Semitism at the time.

[27] As regent of Hungary from 1920 to 1944, Admiral Miklós Horthy was the head of the country's authoritarian regime during the entire interwar era.

The criticism is severe, but the comrades have to get used to severe criticism. He [Molotov] agrees with cde. Malenkov's and cde. Beria's speeches. He also agrees with what has been said about comrade Rákosi. The tendency for bossiness [*vezérkedés*] that plagued comrade Rákosi originated in the Soviet Union. This mistake must be corrected as soon as possible.

Is the HWP's political line correct? In my opinion, it is not entirely correct. There have been many mistakes made in the economic field that must urgently be corrected. The speed of industrialization is exaggerated; it is beyond our capabilities. There is a disease in almost all of the peoples' democracies that leads them to want to establish autarky. This is a child's disease. They do not take into account the Soviet Union's existence. What happened in Hungary? The number of people working in industry grew by 500,000 people within 3 years. This is dangerous and detrimental for Hungary.

They want to invest 19 billion [forints] this year.

There is a virtual wave of oppression against the population. They initiated prosecutions against 1,500,000 people in three and a half years in a population with 4.5 million adults. There were 1,500,000 violations during this time. They punish for everything, and punish insignificant acts arbitrarily. The constitution was established in 1949 according to which a Bureau of State Attorney was to be set up. It still has not been set up. This state of affairs is intolerable.

They resort to all kinds of manipulations to ensure forced industrial development. For instance, there was [only] 57 percent wool in a particular fabric. They left the name and price of the material in place, but they took the wool out of it. They significantly decreased the quality of milk. This resembles fraud. They have lost contact with the population; they do not express the interest of the population on many questions. Is this why we chased the bourgeoisie away, so that afterwards the situation would be like this? Comrade Rákosi's bossiness played a role in this. He knows everything, sees everything, and is capable of doing anything.

We are speaking with you, comrades, in a totally frank and honest way. The necessary conclusions must be drawn.

Cde. Bulganin: We have not discussed anything in advance; we have no such habits. There are many facts that I only heard for the first time from comrade Beria's presentation. All that the comrades have said permits me to observe that a catastrophe will occur if we do not improve the situation. The whole situation might be entirely different if the Red Army were not there. It is a fact that elements of power abuse exist; the population's standard of living has declined. This is not the road to socialism, but the road to a catastrophe.

The question of the army. It is intolerable and impermissible that the army is constantly being purged. Of course, there should be no dubious elements in the army. But it is not possible to keep purging the army for 8 years. Continuously purging the army and keeping it in a feverish state means morally disarming the army and counterbalancing it [with the party]. In 1952 and in the first quarter of 1953, 460 officers and generals were discharged for political reasons. The army was not established in 1952. Why was it necessary to discharge this many people for political reasons? If comrade Rákosi and the CC looked at these 460 people, it would become clear that some of them are our friends, our people. Thus they turn honest people into traitors. There were 370 desertions in 1952. There were 177,000 disciplinary punishments in the army in one year and 3 months. There was almost one punishment for each person.

There are many signals coming in that comrade [Mihály] Farkas likes glamour too much and strives to present himself as a great commander. Rather thorough steps must be taken urgently to improve the situation.

Cde. Mikoyan: Comrade Malenkov and comrade Beria brought up these questions as openly as they would have [just] between themselves. This is a sign of great trust and friendship.

I have known comrade Rákosi for a long time. The comrades analyzed comrade Rákosi's mistakes correctly. Comrade Rákosi has become very full of himself. There is a certain kind of adventurism in the question of economic planning, for instance, the forced development of their own metallurgy. Hungary does not have its own iron ore, nor its own coke. All this must be imported from abroad. Nobody has calculated yet how much 1 ton of raw iron and steel costs Hungary. They are building ironworks in Hungary for which nobody had promised the iron ore. In 1952, they had a lack of 700,000 tons of coke. [Russians] helped based on the instruction from comrade Stalin so that the ironworks would not stop. The coke is not secured for next year either. There are great excesses in the field of major investments. The construction of the metro could have waited 5–6 years. The amount of money invested in heavy industry has quadrupled since 1950. They are implementing [agricultural] collectivization without the appropriate economic basis, and, as a consequence, the cooperatives had a lower productivity rate than the individual producers.

This is a serious mistake.

The party newspaper reported [cases of] sentences in which [a] peasant was imprisoned for one year and fined 3,000 forints because he fed 1.5 q. sugar cane [to his animals]. The peasantry cannot respect a system like this.

They ask for equipment for the army in the value of a quarter million rubles when Hungary has problems with food supplies. Hungary has a debt of 360 million rubles to the people's democracies.

They draw up strenuous plans that they cannot fulfill. The goods available to the populace in Hungary are of bad quality and expensive. There are no goods of high quality because they export those in order to try to achieve trade balance somehow. The situation is not improving but getting worse. Everything is growing in Hungary, but the amount of goods provided for the population is decreasing. (Examples of decreasing quantity: textiles, soap, etc.)

Hungary has all the potential to bloom. It was generally developing well until 1951, until success blinded the leaders and they started to make audacious plans.

The mistakes must be corrected instantly.

Cde. Khrushchev: He agrees with the criticism that the comrades developed. Comrade Beria's passionate criticism was aimed at helping to correct the mistakes. Certain comrades think that the Russian comrades did not form an entirely correct opinion when they directed their criticism against comrade Rákosi. Comrade Rákosi is primarily responsible for the mistakes. Comrade Rákosi observed that coal production grew by 25 percent, and in spite of this there were no protests in certain schools or hospitals. Even though Comrade Rákosi commented on this in the form of self-criticism, he is still responsible for it. It is possible that comrade Rákosi practiced self-criticism because he saw that things were going badly and this way he could avoid criticism.

Hungary used to be famous for her well-developed agriculture and for being a rich country. Now, even the middle peasantry is in uncertainty because of the extremely rapid pace of collectivization. The peasantry needs oxen, power for the ploughs, etc. If the peasantry sees that sooner or later they will have to join the cooperatives, they will not develop their farms. This is how individual farming declines. We should not even be surprised if all of a sudden they started to do away with the vineyards.

My impression is that there is no real collective leadership, [that] a true collective leadership has not developed. Comrade Nagy criticized the leadership; therefore, they excluded him from the Politburo. What kind of respect for [critical] opinions is this? Far-reaching consequences must be drawn from the criticism toward Comrade Rákosi. Is it not possible to produce a collective leadership made up of Hungarians? It is impossible that a people with 9.5 million cannot produce people who are suitable leaders. This situation which has not been fully studied yet, the other one which has just started, must be changed; thus, there are no leaders with sufficient values.

Comrade Rákosi cannot work collectively. There are capable people; they must be promoted and the relationship [of the party] with the Hungarian people must be improved.

They are building the metro in Budapest. In the Soviet Union they only started to build it in 1932. Moscow is the capital of a country with 200 million people. The Hungarian comrades are mistaken to start with the assumption that since it exists in Moscow it must therefore be quickly built in Budapest as well.

Cde. Malenkov: Certain questions must have surprised the comrades. They would need to stay for another 2–3 days to develop and discuss the main regulations. We should meet once again. We could meet on Tuesday afternoon.

The [Hungarian] comrades who spoke said themselves that things were not going very well in Hungary. It is not an issue of minor details; rather correcting the political line has become necessary, because there are problems on fundamental issues, and it also has to do with the question of leadership. Last time, when comrade Rákosi was here, we talked with him in more immediate circles. Comrade Rákosi could not name anyone among the Hungarians as his primary deputy. This was an unpleasant surprise for us. Whenever someone's name came up, comrade Rákosi always immediately had some kind of objection, thus finally he could not name any Hungarian as his primary deputy. In connection with this came the idea that the comrades should be invited, and we should discuss certain questions together. No matter what kind of candidate's name came up, there were always immediate objections. This was what worried us, and made it necessary to speak with more comrades, this way. Comrade Rákosi's telegram also had this kind of effect. And then we saw that we needed to help the comrades and we would have to talk about this question openly. It is not a coincidence that the question of bossiness came up. It is one thing to paint things very beautifully in the movies, but reality is another thing.

Why do we bring these questions up so harshly? We, as Communists, are all responsible for the state of things in Hungary. The Soviet Union is also responsible for what kind of rule exists in Hungary. If they say that the Communist Party of the Soviet Union advised certain incorrect things, we admit to that, and we correct the mistakes too. We admit to the extreme military demands, but the comrades executed these demands even beyond what was expected. Why should an so large an army be maintained that it bankrupts the state[?] The point is, we have to develop regulations together that are suitable for correcting the mistakes, and these regulations must be put in writing. It must be determined how power can be allocated to the right places and distributed properly. We have to come to the conclusion that the chairman of the Council of Ministers should be Hungarian. Comrade Rákosi will find his own important position as the [first] secretary of the party. A respectful person must be recommended as the minister of the interior; comrade Gerő should take over the leadership of the Ministry of the Interior. The Politburo must take its own place; the Secretariat and the Council of Ministers should also take their own place. It is an impossible state of affairs that persons in the Council of Ministers keep silent regarding the question of the [agricultural] levy [only] because it had been previously decided on by the Secretariat.

Recommendations must be made as to who should be placed where. They must not favor anyone with regard to who should be placed in what field. It is our sacred responsibility to place everyone in the proper position. Whoever is placed in a responsible position must be respected, and full rights must be insured for him. There is no reason for people in responsible positions to work as employees next to the master. Nothing good could come of it, besides all the harm. That is a petit-bourgeois habit.

These questions must be considered thoroughly, and recommendations must be prepared. We will meet on Tuesday, and then we will discuss the recommendations.

Cde. Rákosi: Regarding hubris, that's an illness that one cannot detect, just like one cannot smell one's own odor. If the comrades say this is the case, I accept it. (Beria: Comrade, what do you think?)

It must be said that I never wanted to be the chairman of the Council of Ministers. (Comrade Molotov: But you wanted a chairman for the Council of Ministers that would have had no say in decisions.)

Comrade Beria: We like you and respect you, that's why we criticize you. You had told comrade Stalin even before being elected chairman of the Council of Ministers that power was already in your hands. Comrade Stalin reported this.

Cde. Rákosi: The comrades said that it was we who wanted a big army and military industry.

Cde. Malenkov: We wanted you to develop the army. We [will] correct this mistake. There are 600,000 people in the army. (Comrade Rákosi: Including the reserves.) So you carried the Soviet Union's wishes to the extreme.

Cde. Beria: The development of the army was discussed with comrade Stalin. Comrade Stalin gave incorrect instructions.

Cde. Rákosi: We tried to execute the instructions. My heart was aching about the fact that we had to maintain such a large army.

Cde. Malenkov: When you asked us to decrease our demands to build barracks, we withdrew our requests immediately.

Cde. Rákosi: 26 percent of the farmland is in the hands of cooperatives. We achieved this in 5 years. The peasantry knows that collectivization will happen sooner or later.

Cde. Beria: The policy toward the middle peasantry must be changed.

Cde. Malenkov: One or two things can be explained, but not everything. The issue of comrade Rákosi's telegram. Comrade Rákosi started to expand in the telegram on something other than what they had talked about and agreed upon. The issue is that there should not be three Jews in the leadership.[28] However, in the telegram comrade Rákosi made it sound like we had given such advice, and answered that he did not really understand it, but he accepted it.

Cde. Beria: If the great Stalin made mistakes, comrade Rákosi can admit that he made mistakes too. It must not be prescribed who should be beaten by the ÁVH. Everyone will be afraid. Comrade Hidas[29] is afraid too; that's what his speech reflects. Provocation can reach everything [sic], if the methods are like these. People must not be beaten.

The Council of Ministers must make decisions about important questions regarding production. The organs of the party's Central Committee must be preoccupied with education and the question of cadres.

Why is it necessary to invest 1 billion forints in crude oil production? Romania has got enough oil. In Hungary, the aluminum industry should be developed more.

Cde. Gerő: The criticism is justified and correct not just in general, but also regarding the question of bossiness. The leadership is not collective, and we did not raise Hungarian cadres. He often wanted to raise the question but never got to it. The situation really got to the point that whenever comrade Rákosi gave a speech, the newspapers really exalted it, and the KV's staff made sure that it would appear before the people as some extraordinary achievement. Such bossiness undoubtedly exists, and I am primarily responsible for it, second to comrade Rákosi. I did not have the courage to bring up the question. By expressing our mistakes this openly, the comrades have helped us tremendously. It is a shame that we could not do this ourselves. It must be admitted that such bossiness happened in my case too, but I stopped during the last few years. The enemy tries to take advantage of these things. Bossiness is also practiced by comrade Farkas. In fact, there is bossiness even at the lower levels, at the smaller organs. The county and village secretary, the cooperative president, everyone is a boss in their realm. This kind of bossiness exists, and it must be uprooted thoroughly. In our case, bossiness is intertwined with petit-bourgeois phenomena; he [Gerő] also agrees with the comrades on that. We just had parliamentary elections. After the elections, a picture was published in *Szabad Nép* depicting Comrade Rákosi voting together with his wife. Comrade Rákosi did not arrange for this himself, but he did not protest it either.

Regarding mistakes in the economy. We noticed on a number of issues that there were mistakes, but we did not bring up these questions so openly. For instance, the issue of the metro. It is actually fortunate that they did not listen to the military advisers who recommended that the metro be built so that tanks and military trains could commute on the metro line. There was great excess in the case of the metro.

[...]

Cde. Malenkov: It seems like we all agree on recommending comrade Imre Nagy. He [Malenkov] explicitly asked for comrade Rákosi's and comrade [István] Dobi's opinions. Comrade Rákosi and comrade Dobi agreed with the proposal, too.

[...]

* * *

---

[28] All four top Hungarian Communist leaders—Mátyás Rákosi, Ernő Gerő, Mihály Farkas and József Révai—were of Jewish background.

[29] István Hidas was a member of the HWP PC and Secretariat from May 1951 on, and vice-chairman of the Council of Ministers from November 1952–July 1953 and from October 1954–October 1956.

Present are: Comrades Malenkov, Beria, Molotov, Khrushchev, Bulganin, Mikoyan, Kiselev,[30] and Boiko [Sic: Baikov][31], and Comrades Rákosi, I. Nagy, Dobi, Gerő, Hegedüs, Hidas, [Rudolf] Földvári, and [Béla] Szalai[32]

[The] Soviet comrades had received the attached document[33] prepared by the delegation in advance. [...]

Cde. Beria: The document means a step forward. But the document must be made more concrete and it must be supplemented. The question of industrialization must be dealt with in a separate section. Numbers must be included also in the section that deals with industrialization and the over-intensified investments, because it cannot be understood without them. It must express what the projections are according to the current plans, and to what extent we will change those. Agriculture must also have its separate section in the resolution. Numbers must be included here as well. It must clarify what "fallow lands" are, what led to these fallow lands, and what the reason is for such an abundance of "fallow land."

The productivity of the cooperatives must also be discussed. It must be expressed honestly that in our country the yield of the land is less in the cooperatives than on the land of middle peasants working individually. It must be stated that the pace of collectivization will be decreased. The peasants' flight into the cities—an important question. It must be determined what causes this and how the mistake will have to be corrected. The question of the cooperatives' debt must be examined. There is a suggestion to terminate the kulak list. This is not correct. The problem is not the kulak list. The important issue is that it must be determined correctly who is a kulak.

The question of lawfulness is mentioned in too vague a form. This is insufficient. What happened in the past needs to be stated, that court procedures were initiated against 1,200,000 people in 3-and-1/4 years, and during the same period 1,150,000 people were prosecuted for violations. The people will understand it better if the numbers are in the document. It also must be shown how unlawfulness needs to be corrected.

[...] It must also be discussed in the resolution that it was incorrect for comrade Rákosi to interfere with the running of the ÁVH and the Ministry of the Interior, and that the way he interfered was incorrect; he gave directions for investigations, for the arrest of certain people, and for their physical mistreatment. If we do not admit this in the resolution, comrade Rákosi could repeat the mistake, or anyone else could do something similar. Such methods can have rather serious consequences, and we would never learn the truth.

It also must be stated that the practice of unifying the functions of the party secretary and the chairman of the Council of Ministers in one person was incorrect.

As a consequence, comrade Rákosi thought he could do anything. In reality, he could not do a thorough job in either position. What comrade Molotov said regarding the mistakes in the ideological field also points to this. [...]

---

[30] Evgenii D. Kiselev was Soviet ambassador in Hungary from 1949–1954.

[31] Originally, all four copies of the Hungarian minutes indicated the name Boiko; however, this was later corrected on one copy to Boikov. Although there was a Soviet official named Boiko involved in Soviet policy toward Hungary— Lieutenant-General Vasilii R. Boiko, head of the team of Soviet military advisers in the country—it is clear from Rákosi's memoirs that the person present at the meeting was in fact Vladimir S. Baikov, an official of the CPSU CC department dealing with relations with foreign communist parties from the early 1950s, and a specialist in Hungarian affairs. After the revolution Baikov was sent to Budapest to work with Kádár, and served as a liaison between the Kádár government and the Soviet leadership from November 4, 1956, to March 1957. See, Mátyás Rákosi, *Visszaemlékezések, 1944–1956* (Budapest: Napvilág Kiadó, 1997), 2:912.

[32] Béla Szalai was a member of the HWP CC from 1953 to October 28, 1956, a member of the PC beginning in 1954 and HWP CC secretary from 1955 until October 24, 1956.

[33] Not reprinted here.

Cde. Molotov: Agrees with comrade Beria. He has a couple of supplementary comments.

Regarding the ideological work: criticism must be further developed. Criticism—self-criticism—must also be discussed in the document. What the document contains regarding economic policy is correct; a few things, however, are worded coarsely. For instance, where moderating industrial development is mentioned, it should also be mentioned that this is being done so that quality of life for the population will rise.

The situation in the village and the population. This is the weakest part of the document. It must be stated that the agricultural sector has been neglected, and in the future great attention must be paid to the improvement of agriculture. Dispersing cooperatives should not be feared where they were established by administrative methods. Collectivization need not be rushed; it is important to have good relations with the working peasants.

The working class is not mentioned in the document. Where we discuss in the document that over-intensified industrialization had a negative effect on the population's standard of living, it also must be stated that [it had a negative effect] primarily on that of the working class. We must not be afraid to show that the working class' standard of living declined in the last few years in Hungary. When we observe that major investments must be reduced [and] certain construction projects must be stopped, it also must be added that new opportunities for work must be created for the workers. With regard to housing construction, it must be stated that we are primarily building houses for workers.

The falsification of the quality of products and the price increase that accompanied it must be condemned in the resolution as impermissible.

[...] *Cde. Molotov:* The cooperatives do not have to be dissolved, but if they want to disperse at their own initiative, that must not be stopped.

Cde. Mikoyan: The section regarding the standard of living of the population is not convincing enough. It must be included in the resolution that the flow of products in small business decreased last year.

Cde. Khrushchev: Agrees with Comrade Beria's and Comrade Molotov's comments. There is no need for a Secretariat with 7 members. A Secretariat with 7 members besides a Politburo with 12 members, for instance, would mean that the Secretariat is a majority in the Politburo. Though not all the members of the Secretariat must be PC members. It would be better to organize a Secretariat with 3 members.

Cdes. Beria, Malenkov: The Secretariat could have 3–4 members. There should not be a Presidium but a Politburo, which should have 9 members and 2 candidate members. The members of the Secretariat could be the members of the PC at the same time, but it's not necessarily essential for all the members of the Secretariat to be members of the PB.

Cde. Malenkov: The observations made by the comrades who spoke before me were correct. If there is no objection on the side of the Hungarian comrades, the above observations should be included in the document.

[...]

Cde. Beria: It does not depend on one person only, but on the entire leadership. And if comrade Rákosi does not help to correct the mistakes, he will demolish himself.

Cde. Imre Nagy: The connection with the CC CPSU has not been as direct for the last few years as it was 3–4 years ago.

Cde. Beria: The connection existed before and it exists now, but it was not the proper kind of relationship, and this led to negative consequences. Celebratory meetings and applause constituted the relationship. In the future, we will create a new kind of relationship, a more responsible and serious relationship. We will inform the comrades about this.

Cde. Malenkov: The comrades will see; this relationship will be entirely different from that of the past.

Cde. Rákosi: I am very sorry that I did not receive this kind of lesson before, and I was not given this kind of a mirror to face myself. Regarding the future, I can assure the comrades that I will do everything to correct the mistakes. However, correcting the mistakes does not depend on one person, but on the entire party leadership.

[...]

Cde. Beria: A stubbornness is evident from the Hungarian comrades' attitude—primarily from that of comrade Rákosi—regarding the reexamination of the Péter case. Four comrades were sent to Hungary to investigate the case. Comrade Rákosi had convened a meeting of these comrades before his departure for Moscow. (Comrade Rákosi: They came; I did not invite them.) The discussions lasted for two hours. Of that, the Soviet comrades talked for 12 minutes, comrade Rákosi talked for 1 [hour] 50 minutes, and he lectured them about how they should conduct the investigation. If we made mistakes, those must be revealed, because stubbornness leads to even worse mistakes.

Cde. Malenkov: There is no need to certify the resolution. The Hungarian comrades will be able to work out the draft resolution and will be strong enough to correct the mistakes.

[....]

[Source: Magyar Országos Levéltár (MOL), 276. f. 102/65. ő.e. - Typed revision. Published in György T. Varga, "Jegyzőkönyv a szovjet és a magyar párt- és állami vezetők tárgyalásairól (1953. június 13–16)," Múltunk 37, no. 2–3 (1992): 234–269. Translated by Mónika Borbély and Csaba Békés.]

DOCUMENT NO. 2: "Resolution of the Central Committee of the Hungarian Worker's Party Concerning the Mistakes Committed in the Policy and Practice of the Party, and the Tasks Necessary to Correct These Mistakes," June 28, 1953

After the Hungarian delegation's return from Moscow, the party leadership was under orders from the Kremlin to discuss the political, economic, and personnel changes urged by the Soviet leaders, and to formulate a public resolution outlining the changes that were to be made.

A HWP CC meeting was convened on June 27 and lasted for two days, at which point the resolution printed below was adopted. At the time, it was an unprecedented admission of mistakes and a blueprint for a fundamental reevaluation of the regime's approach to society and its problems.

The resolution (of which only a fraction is published here) consisted of four main parts. The first deals with mistakes committed in the past, including the domination of the economy by sectarian policies and the imposition of heavy taxes and other economic and administrative burdens that resulted in a considerable decline in the standard of living. Society generally was said to have suffered massive oppression at the hands of the authorities. The second section lays out the causes of the regime's errors, which center around the activities of party leader Mátyás Rákosi and three of his colleagues who are accused of placing their personal concerns above the requirements of the collective leadership. The third part outlines a series of necessary economic and political remedies, while the last section discusses organizational changes to be carried out within the political leadership.

The party heads also recommended that Imre Nagy take over from Rákosi as prime minister, among other personnel shifts, but otherwise the leadership's composition did not fundamentally change. Rákosi kept his post as party first secretary and Ernő Gerő, one of those singled out for criticism, retained considerable power as deputy prime minister and minister of internal affairs.

Ultimately, on Moscow's advice, the resolution was not published in 1953.[34] In part, this decision reflected the power struggle underway in the Kremlin after the death of Joseph Stalin. The main instigator of the reforms, secret police chief Lavrentii Beria, was arrested in Moscow on June 26, just two days before this resolution was drafted.

The full meeting of the Central Committee of the Hungarian Worker's Party states that in the past few years the party leadership headed by Comrade Mátyás Rákosi has committed several grave mistakes in its policy and practice. These mistakes have had an unfavorable impact on the living standard of the population, particularly that of the working class, have weakened the party's relations with the working class, and in general have undermined the relationship between the party, the state, and the working people, and thus have brought about serious difficulties in the national economy.

I.

The most important mistakes are as follows:

1. The leadership of the party set an overly ambitious target for rapid industrialization, especially concerning the development of heavy industry, disregarding the actual conditions in the country and the needs of the working class and the working people.

Drunk from the impressive success it achieved in economic development, the party leadership proposed a policy of excessively rapid industrialization at the 2nd Party Congress. As a result, the 2nd Congress adopted an incorrect line of economic development. Based on the

---

[34] The text of the document was first published by the Hungarian samizdat publication *Hírmondó* in 1985. The next year it appeared in a non-public party journal, soon followed by publication in a selection of documents from the Stalinist period. See, *Hírmondó*, no. 2 (1985); *Propagandista*, no. 4 (1986): 136–167.

Congress resolution, the production of crude iron had to be raised from 398,000 tons in 1949 to 1,280,000 tons in 1954. This rate was all the more immoderate since the country has hardly any iron ore or burnt coal production, without which the rapid development of the iron industry has no sound foundation. Similarly, the directive that the amount of coal to be mined had to be increased from 11,5 million tons of 1949 to 27,5 million tons in 1954 was also unrealistic. The five-year plan for the manufacturing industry was also overextended inasmuch as production in 1954 had to reach 310 percent of the 1949 base level, and within this the production of heavy industry had to surpass the 1949 level by 380 percent.

The overly ambitious targets for production demanded an excessive investment program. Thus the five-year investment program originally set at 50,9 billion forints was raised to 85 billion. In addition, the distribution of the money appropriated for various investments was also improper, allocating only 11 billion for agriculture and 3,5 billion for light and food industry, while 37,5 billion was directed to heavy industry.

This mistaken economic policy did not reckon with the actual resources of the country and failed to take into consideration how economical and functional the planned investments appeared to be. In a number of cases, investments were accomplished, or at least started, which could have been postponed to a later time (the Budapest Underground), or which were not desirable with regard to the economic capabilities of the country.

This sectarian policy regarded socialist industrialization as an end in itself, neglecting the real needs and interests of the working class and the working people. This improper economic policy also showed some signs of megalomania, and at the same time it involved elements of adventurism by basing the excessive development of heavy industry partly on resources and raw materials that were not available within the country. This policy also reflected an endeavor to achieve a kind of "self-supply" autarchy, ignoring the fact that Hungary was building the foundations of socialism not on a remote, uninhabited island but within the socialist camp, and failed to reckon sufficiently with the possibility and necessity of the division of labor and economic cooperation among the Soviet Union and the people's democracies.

2. The leadership of the country neglected agricultural production and imposed an overly accelerated pace on the socialization of agriculture.

Excessive industrialization necessarily led to the neglect of agricultural production, for the country's resources did not make it possible to invest enough money into agriculture when excessive targets had to be reached in industry. As a result, the agriculture's share of the overall investment in the national economy decreased in the past couple of years, though the amount of money invested into agriculture increased in absolute terms year-by-year over the course of the five-year plan. Thus in 1952, agricultural investment amounted to 15.3 percent of the overall investment, while in 1953 only to 13.7 percent. Production by private farmers was especially neglected. For instance, farmers cultivating their land on their own were given 50 percent less chemical fertilizers in 1951 than in 1949. The amount of work done by machines also decreased significantly in private farms.

The insufficient development of agricultural production was significantly influenced by an excessively rapid socialization of agriculture that was not in accord with the political and economic conditions in the country. The immoderately rapid development of agricultural cooperative farms, the occasionally violent methods and administrative pressure, coupled with the ever-changing and complicated system of compulsory delivery, resulted in insecurity among the peasants and deteriorated the relationship between the party and the middle peasantry, simultaneously hindering the economic consolidation of cooperative farms, the improvement of their management, as well as the ability to increase the income of their members.

This policy of imposing rapid changes upon the socialization of agriculture was all the more serious, since Comrade Imre Nagy had already spoken against it within the party, but the leadership of the party—rather than adopting his position—had qualified it as "opportunistic" and adopted punitive measures against Comrade Nagy. [...]

Grave mistakes were made concerning the regulations imposed on the kulaks. The original restrictions soon turned into a policy that aimed at eliminating the kulaks for good. This was shown by the fact that in the past five years the area of land owned by the kulaks has shrunk to some 30 percent of the original amount. And the majority of the remaining kulaks abuse their land in many ways: they cultivate it inefficiently, they reduce their livestock. [...]

3. The leadership of the party neglected and de-emphasized the basic needs of the people, and a bad economic policy led to a significant decrease in the standard of living.

Excessive industrialization particularly the immoderate development of heavy industry and the national defense industry, the lack of attention to the development of agricultural production, and the unnecessarily rapid establishment of cooperative farms and state-owned agricultural farms all contributed in the failure to meet the basic needs of the people. Other factors also played a role [in the failure of this policy], such as the excessive and rapid development of the armed forces and the explosive growth of the state apparatus.

As a result, the people's standard of living, including the working class, has not increased sufficiently in the past few years; moreover, the real value of workers' and employees' wages has decreased. Although the extraordinarily bad harvest of 1952 contributed significantly to this decrease of living standards and real wages, the essential reason was to be found in the mistakes committed in the party's economic and general policy line. [...]

Another reason for the deterioration of supplies and services was that private retail trade and private small-scale industry were displaced too rapidly. As a result, the service industry (plumbers, electricians, locksmiths, glass-workers, painters, etc.) in particular cannot meet the people's needs. A number of villages lack a shoemaker, a tailor, a hairdresser; moreover, water-supply is poor and insufficient in several places. Only 45 percent of the plan for building streets and sidewalks in cities and villages was accomplished in 1952.

Excessive industrialization also exerted an unfavorable effect on the people's living standards, in that the housing program was pushed into the background for the sake of large-scale investments in heavy industry and industrial production. As a result, the number of newly-built houses decreased year after year from 1950, and a significant increase can only be observed in 1953. The number of privately built houses decreased significantly with respect to the three-year plan, which was largely due to the fact that the available building materials were almost exclusively used up by heavy industry and state-run building programs, so that virtually nothing was left for private house-building. The housing issue is further worsened by the fact that house maintenance and renovation has also decreased significantly due to the shortage of materials, equipment, and labor. Therefore, though the Council of Ministers approved 30 percent, only 22 percent of the money coming from rents was used for such purposes in the second half of 1952.

Excessive industrialization, primarily the immoderately rapid development of heavy industry, challenged economic organs with a task so hard that they intended to fulfill it by having their employees work overtime and over weekends. Especially intolerable is the situation in mining and metallurgy where the Labor Code is violated regularly, production work on Sunday is common, so-called big production shifts are held regularly, and workers' rest time is not ensured as required by the law. Overwork often led to safety regulations being ignored, to the proliferation of accidents, and provided ample reason for justifiable dissatisfaction among the workers. At the same time, it disturbed the required rate of production and increased prime costs.

4. The proliferation of administrative measures, the excessive number of judicial processes and police procedures in minor offenses, authoritarianism with the people.

The mistakes committed by the party in the general line of policy and in economic policy considerably contributed to the fact that administrative measures were, and still are, applied in large scale against the working people. The police and the courts penalize masses of people, the authorities treat the people in a rigorous manner, and domineering treatment [önkényeskedés] is quite common.

Between 1951 and May 1, 1953—that is, over a period of 2 years and 4 months—the police, acting as a court of minor offenses, inflicted punishment in 850,000 cases altogether. Though in 831,000 of these 850,000 cases the punishment was a fine; in 760,000 out of the 831,000 cases the fine was under 100 Hungarian forints; and only 19,000 involved imprisonment (most of which were suspended). Nonetheless, the number of minor offense cases is intolerably high. This high number clearly shows that administrative measures are applied against the people in Hungary to an unacceptable extent in a people's democracy, in a country of the working people.

The same problem is reflected by the way in which the courts operate. Between 1950 and the first quarter of 1953—that is, over a period of 3 and a quarter years—the courts dealt with 650,000 cases and pronounced a negative judgment against 387,000 people.

Similarly, the system and praxis of punishing failure to meet compulsory delivery quotas with mass fines is also incorrect and unallowable. So far, nearly 400 million forints in fines have been levied on working peasants, cooperative farms, and kulaks who failed to meet the required quotas, most of which compensation are unjust and unlawful even by the existing laws.

The interment system is still utilized in our country, which provides ample opportunity for abuse and authoritarianism, and which, 8 years after the end of the war, is unjustifiable. Cases of abuse similar to the one that took place in Kiskőrös and made public in the press are by no means isolated, especially in rural areas. In a number of cases citizens are arrested with no grounds at all, and the legal and constitutional regulations which are meant to defend the rights of citizens, their personal safety, and their security are often breached.

The proliferation of administrative procedures, the significant increase in the number of judicial and minor offense procedures, and abuses against the people were strongly influenced by the lack of a Chief Prosecutor's Office, though its establishment was ordained by the Constitution of the People's Republic passed in 1949.

II.

The most important reasons for the serious mistakes committed in the general policy line and party practices can be found in the internal conditions within the party and party leadership, in the incorrect methods used by the leadership, in their mistaken cadre-policy, in the inadequate relationship between the party leadership and the leaders of the state, and in the backwardness of ideological work.

1. The main source of all the mistakes and flaws was the lack of collective leadership, that is, the replacement of collective leadership by one-man leadership, although it is evident that in a Communist party the only correct method is collective leadership. One-man leadership was coupled with a cult of personality and bossiness [*vezérkedés*], which did much harm to the party and the development of people's democracy. This incorrect leadership method prevented the active participation of all leaders in elaborating party policy, and made it extremely difficult to detect mistakes quickly and correct them in due time.

It is chiefly Comrade Rákosi who must be held responsible for replacing collective leadership with one-man leadership, coupled with a cult of personality.

Bossiness and the cult of personality characterized the army too, where it was coupled with the excessive development of the armed forces, with blatant disregard for what the country's economy could afford. For this Comrade Farkas must be held primarily responsible.

Personal leadership also hindered and made impossible the formation of a collective body to lead the party and the state. Only a very small number of people of Hungarian origin[35] were promoted to higher positions, and even these were mostly formal rather than functional positions. In fact the leadership was rather like a clique, with all the power concentrated in the hands of four comrades: Comrades Rákosi, Gerő, Farkas and Révai. These comrades did not criticize each other even on fundamental issues, or at best they did it in private rather than at the plenum of leading party organizations. As a necessary consequence criticism and self-criticism, as a fundamental method in communist leadership, were not utilized in the party leadership, difficulties and mistakes were often covered up, in general the leaders did not trace mistakes back to their roots, and they did not radically wipe out what was wrong. [...]

[35] See footnote 26 above.

2. The party's improper economic policy led to a separation from the masses. This was largely due to the reduction of collective leadership and its replacement with one-man leadership.

This can be seen clearly in that complaints—fair and justifiable criticism by working people, peasants, intellectuals, and the common man—often did not get through to the highest leaders. On the other hand the clique-like leadership did not pay any attention to signals sent by the workers, the party, state and social organizations, or occasionally by certain members of the party leadership themselves. These signals were often stigmatized as "opportunistic." Even when they did attend to some of these warnings, they failed to view them in the right context and merely applied superficial treatment. They did not bring themselves to trace troubles to their roots. The same equally applies to economic policy, supplying workers with material goods, and serious difficulties in the relationship between the masses and the state and party. [...]

It is Comrade Gerő who is chiefly responsible for the mistakes committed in economic policy because it was mostly he who was in charge of economic matters both in the party and in the state leadership. The exaggerated concentration of control in the hands of one person was wrong and harmful.

3. Separation from the masses also manifested itself in the failure of the party leadership to respond appropriately to the signals sent by the people with respect to: the proliferation of the breaches of law; the incorrect and rigorous treatment of the people by the police and the security authorities; the wrong, often unfair and unlawful measures introduced by the local councils against the people; and the large number of court sentences.

[The party leadership] failed to realize that the organs of the state and other authorities often did not represent the interests of the people; moreover, the local party organizations often not only failed to represent the just needs of the people but they themselves often played a part in violating their rights and in their harassment. The immediate leadership virtually closed their eyes to the series of atrocities committed against the kulaks. The lack of collective leadership played a significant role in that the party leadership did not try to uncover the fundamental reasons for the proliferation of administrative measures, how these reasons related to economic policy and the party leadership's incorrect methods, and therefore they were unable to eliminate the harmful and intolerable relationship among the party, the state, and the working masses. As a result of all this, the party's relationship with a significant part of the population had deteriorated considerably.

The proliferation of administrative methods (e.g. fines) aroused discontent in certain layers of the working class too. In particular, it did significant damage to the party and state's relationship with the middle peasantry. The extensive use of administrative methods, the violation of existing laws, and the lack of legal security brought about disheartenment among the old intelligentsia as well.

4. Mistakes were committed largely as a result of the lack of progress in the fields of ideology and theory.

The party's central committee did not discuss fundamental ideological or theoretical issues in any of the cases that emerged. Nor was there any serious discussion of ideological issues in the Political Committee or Secretariat. No ideological issues concretely relating to Hungarian matters were discussed either in the party's central newspaper, in *Szabad Nép*, or in the theoretical-political journal *Társadalmi Szemle* ("Social Review"). The party leadership and its press did not uncover the serious lag in ideological work and the shallow level of ideological activity. Ideological issues were brought up only in general, not in a combative way. Actual mistakes were not condemned with any regard to who was responsible.

Ideological issues—which are of utmost importance for the development of the party, for its entire policy, for the progress of the party cadres and for educating communists and people alike—were rented out, as it were, to Comrade Révai, who had been taking a monopolist position in ideological matters for years. This incorrect method, that is, the method of personal control in ideological matters instead of collective leadership, blocked the possibility of training good, ideologically well-educated party officials and hindered the party's ideological development. As a result, the confrontation of viewpoints could not become a major driving force of development in literature, science, and the arts.

It is, therefore, mostly Comrade Révai who must be held responsible for the serious mistakes in the ideological work of the party.

5. The reduction of the party leadership, that is, the replacement of collective leadership by one-man leadership, led to a decrease in state leadership as well, with the party leadership largely appropriating the functions of the state leadership, including those of the Council of Ministers. The Council of Ministers did not have an independent role to play, but rather became a shadow of the party leadership.

This was largely due to the fact that two positions, secretary general of the party and chairman of the Council of Ministers, were concentrated in one person—the person of Comrade Rákosi—which was not right.

The State Security Authority [ÁVH] was led by the party and personally by Comrade Rákosi in an incorrect fashion. It was improper that Comrade Rákosi gave direct orders to the State Security Authority, telling them what and how to investigate and who to arrest, and, moreover, ordering the physical mistreatment of those arrested, which is forbidden by law. In addition, Comrade Rákosi's orders were wrong in a number of cases, making it extremely difficult to discover the truth. [...]

III.

Because of the urgent and pressing need to fix the mistakes committed in the area of industrialization, in the supplies provided for the population, and in the relations of the state and the people, the central committee has made the following decisions:

1. The party's economic policy must be changed radically, the rate of developing industry, above all heavy industry, must be decreased, and the national economic development projects and related investments must be revised.

The major goal of this radically modified new economic policy is to achieve a fundamental and continuous increase in the people's living standards, especially the working class, and to improve the social and cultural services for working people, while simultaneously continuing, at a slower pace, the policy of socialist industrialization which remains the party's main economic policy line.

In keeping with these goals, the rate of industrial development must be decreased by as early as 1953. The amount of investment planned for 1953 must also be reduced. The target for the growth in industrial production for 1954 must be set at 8 percent.

The ratio of development between heavy industry and light and food industry must be changed radically in favor of light and food industry, maintaining and implementing the basic principle that the creation of the means of production must develop relatively faster than that of consumer goods. To this end, investment into light industry, and especially into food industry, must be increased significantly because Hungary has very good prospects in this branch of industry, and we are now particularly behind in this area. Investment must also be increased in agriculture.

All the investment projects, particularly those in heavy industry, must be revised keeping in mind which should be continued and which should be terminated temporarily or permanently. When revising the projects, ample care must be taken to evaluate how economical and necessary a given investment is. In addition, possibilities of economic cooperation and division of labor with the Soviet Union and the other socialist countries must also be taken into consideration, and autarchy must be avoided by all means. [...]

2. Investment in agriculture must be increased, agricultural production and yield must be improved, including those of private farms; development in the number of cooperative farms must be slowed down; state-owned farms should not be permitted to increase their area of land.

Considerable support must be given to private farmers so that they can develop their farms, meet the quotas of compulsory delivery, pay their taxes, and, in addition to meeting their own needs, deliver a sufficient amount of goods to the free market. Private farmers should be given access to the machines of machine stations. It must be ensured that private farmers can freely buy chemical fertilizer in large amounts at the official rate as early as this coming fall. The possibilities of developing fertilizer production must be reviewed, and by next year the amount of chemical fertilizer available for agriculture must be increased significantly.

The coercive nature of production contracts must be eliminated. These contracts must be made more appealing by allocating large amounts of industrial goods. Veterinary services must be made free of charge for all agricultural producers.

Cooperative farms remain the socialist way of developing villages, but in forming cooperatives it is not the number of new cooperative farms that should be set as the next task, but rather strengthening already existing farms, increasing their yields, improving their productivity in animal husbandry, and enhancing their profitability.

In order to enforce the voluntary principle in the cooperative farm movement, modification of the clause in the cooperative farm charter which stipulates that members of these farms not be allowed to resign their membership for three years must be revised, so that anybody who wishes to do so may be given the chance to terminate their membership at the end of the economic year. The dissolution of cooperative farms must be permitted in the event that the majority of the members so choose. In the future, the Minister of Agriculture should authorize establishing new cooperative farms only at the proposal of the district council's executive committee.

The cooperative farms' approximately 450 million forints of overdue debt to be paid back to the state must be revised, and those debts which can not be supported with proper documents by the state authorities, or the ones whose recovery is unrealistic, must be canceled. In this way, more than 200 million forints of debt must be remitted.

The 400 million forints levied as compensation money to be paid by the cooperative farms and by private farmers for not meeting the compulsory delivery quotas must be fully remitted. The arrears of those who accurately meet the delivery quotas this year must be canceled. [...]

As of 1954 a new compulsory delivery system must be introduced so that the whole system and the quotas to be met by the various farmers be kept unchanged for several years. While the policy of isolation and restriction toward the kulaks must be continued, their harassment must be stopped. To this effect the kulak-lists must be terminated. In the new compulsory delivery system, required quotas for the kulak farms must be reduced and so must their tax burdens. However, it must be required by all means that they fully meet the obligations which are in accord with what they can actually afford. [...]

3. The level of material goods supplies for the population, and especially of the working class and the peasants, must be improved radically. The incorrect measures of excessive industrialization, which have lead to the deterioration of the living standards of the working class and the population in general, must be eliminated. New measures must be introduced which can improve the standard of living of the working class, the peasantry, and the population of the country. In addition care must be taken to ensure that the working class' and the population's consumption should increase, especially in basic consumable goods and manufactured goods.

We must be firm in ending the common practice whereby the state or cooperative farms sell poor quality goods at the same price, or sell the same articles under a different name or in a different packaging at a higher price. Such practices must be punished by the law in all its rigor.

After the harvest, the price of flour must be set again at 4,60 forints. The supply of meat products must be improved urgently, and the unhindered supply of bread and fat must be ensured. As of fall 1953, large amounts of goods favored by the population, which are now not available or are hard to find in the shops (high quality ox hide and calfskin shoes, boots, rubber boots, snow boots, good quality textile goods, etc.), must be put into circulation. The quality of goods made of plastic, artificial leather, and pigskin must be improved. It must be insured that various manufactured goods which are not now commercially available (various kinds of buttons, knitting needles and crochet hooks, high quality razors and razor blades, pails, coffee mills, etc.), or which can only be found in small amounts and in bad quality, must be manufactured and made commercially available. The high retail prices of several articles of clothing and other consumer goods must be reduced significantly. [...]

It must be ensured that the workers are provided with protective foods and protective clothing as stipulated by law. Unjustified and unnecessary overtime should be reduced in production work, in civil transport, and in the whole economy in general, including Sunday shifts. Labor Code regulations must be enforced fully so that the workers can have their one day-off every week.

The fine, as a means of enforcing discipline among workers and employees, must be terminated. [...]

The communal services in cities and villages (water supply, baths, streets, sidewalks, public sanitation) must be improved radically, and it must be ensured that basic manufacturing and service cooperatives, local industrial companies, and local artisans meet the people's needs in every city and village.

It must be ensured that manufacturing cooperatives and local industrial companies primarily meet the demands of the population rather than those of large plants and public institutions. As need arises, private artisans should be given trade licenses.

The housing projects must be accelerated, especially for the working people and most importantly in Budapest, in the county seats, and in the major industrial areas. At the same time, the small-scale building of houses in the villages and the campaign to build houses for miners must also be facilitated with state subsidies.

By reducing or slowing down investment in heavy industry, it must be ensured that 40,000 new apartments be built from state resources and partly with state subsidies in 1954, in contrast to the 24,000 built in 1953.

The renovation of houses and apartments must also be sped up. [...]

In sum: as a result of correcting the mistakes in economic policy we will have to achieve a considerable increase in the population's living standard as early as this coming fall, and this increase should continue in the future.

4. A correct relationship between the people's democratic state and the population must be established.

Unlawfulness and violations of law by the police, the security police, the judicial bodies, and the councils must be eliminated. By October 1, 1953, the Chief Prosecutor's Office must be established as the primary guarantor of lawfulness.

An amnesty bill must be submitted to the upcoming session of Parliament, and based on this act of amnesty, all those whose offenses were not so serious that their release would pose a threat to the security of the state, the public, or property must be released from prison. The system of internment must be canceled, and the detention camps must be dissolved.

The judicial function exercised by the police must be eliminated by law.

It must be made possible for all those deported to choose their place of residence freely, in accordance with the laws and regulations binding any citizen of the country.

Lawfulness must be fully restored by all possible means.

IV.

An essential precondition for correcting and radically eliminating the mistakes in the party's general policy line, its economic policy, and practice is to change the internal conditions within the party, to modify the methods of leadership, cadre policy and ideological work, as well as to establish the proper relationship between the party and the state leadership.

To this effect the following objectives must be accomplished:

1. A collective leadership must be established which has full collective responsibility for the party's policy and its entire activity. Personal, one-man leadership must be eliminated, and the cult of personality must be abolished in both the party and the country so that no one person should be regarded as superior to the party, to the Central Committee.

The party's policy must be elaborated and determined in a collective manner by the party's principal organ, the Party Congress, while in the interim period between two congresses [this task must be carried out by] the Central Committee. It must be ensured that the Central Committee becomes a truly collective leading body of the party.

With a view to making the party leadership more uniform and collective in its nature, the Secretariat and the Organizing Committee now performing the function of leading political bodies must also be dissolved. The composition and the character of the Political Committee must also be changed. A Political Committee must be established which is capable of leading and controlling the party with full responsibility and in a collective manner during the period between the full sessions of the Central Committee. The Political Committee should consist of 9 full members and 2 candidate members.

Subordinated to the Political Committee, a Secretariat of the Central Committee must be established whose task should be to ensure that resolutions of the party's leading bodies be executed properly, to supervise the execution of resolutions, and to decide upon the distribution of those cadres working in the party, in mass organizations, and the state apparatus, who belong to its sphere of authority. Care must be taken to prevent the Secretariat from turning into the party's leading, directive body, thus replacing the Politburo and the Central Committee, as has been the case in the past. Therefore the Secretariat must have a small number of members (3 or 4 at most) who are not all necessarily members of the Political Committee.

The office of the Secretary-General, which contributed to one-man leadership in the party, must be eliminated. Secretariat members are the secretaries of the Central Committee. One of them should be the first secretary of the Central Committee. [...]

2. Criticism and self-criticism must be boldly introduced in the party in a top-down manner, making it an integral part of everyday life and work, an essential working method of the party leadership. This—in addition to correcting the mistakes committed in economic policy and eliminating the violent administrative methods of the authorities—should play a decisive role in making the members, the organizations, and the leaders of the party more attentive to the signals and warnings sent by the workers so that they can detect mistakes and fix them in due time before they become too serious and cause even greater trouble. Developing criticism and self-criticism—irrespective of the people involved—will also aid the party in improving its relations with the working people and with those who are not party members, so that our party should become—in spite of the grave mistakes it has committed in the past—not only a recognized but a passionately beloved leader of our people. [...]

3. Backwardness in the realms of ideology and theory must also be eliminated. Collective leadership must be ensured in this respect too. Care must be taken to ensure that not only *Szabad Nép* and *Társadalmi Szemle*, but also other daily papers and journals, regularly raise issues of ideology and publish criticisms openly, not in a general but in a concrete fashion, relating to Hungarian issues, disregarding the people involved in them. A healthy ideological debate serving progress should be launched or facilitated in the most diverse fields of literature, science, and the arts. [...]

4. In addition to finding the correct line of policy, most of the party leadership's attention should be paid to the education, selection and promotion of party officials. [...]

5. The right relationship must be found between the party leadership and the state leadership, the Council of Ministers. It must be ensured that the Council of Ministers fully play its role in leading the state and the country.

To this effect, the two offices of the first secretary of the party and the chairman of the Council of Ministers must be separated and filled by different individuals.

It must be proposed to the Presidential Council of the People's Republic and the Parliament that the number of ministries be reduced by merging several ministries, so that the Council of Ministers should consist of no more than 20 members, becoming a true consultative and decision making body that—following the main policy line determined by the party—can handle the matters of the country with full responsibility. Simultaneously with the merger of the ministries, the ministers' sphere of authority must be broadened and their personal responsibility strengthened. [...]

* * *

The Central Committee is aware that the enemies of the party and the Hungarian people will try to take advantage of our party's open and bold self-criticism—something that only a strong party and a strong system is capable of—and to break up our unity and undermine our people's democracy. Therefore the Central Committee calls every party member and party organization to be alert. Let us all be always on the alert against any kind of possible provocation! Let us all listen to and discuss the criticisms and proposals of honest working people, but let us also disclose and repel every adversary attack from whichever direction it might come.

The honest, unsparing, but fair self-criticism exercised by our party will make the Hungarian Worker's Party even more unified than it was before! It will raise the prestige of our party's leadership and government in the eyes of our people. It will establish an even closer relationship between the party, the working class, the working peasantry, the old and new intelligentsia, and the people outside the party. It will make the unity of our party, our government, our people's democratic state, and our people stronger! It will greatly facilitate the strong, secure, and sound grounds on which the building of socialism and the ever-growing welfare of our people should rest!

[Source: Sándor Balogh, ed., Nehéz esztendők krónikája 1949–1953. Dokumentumok *(Budapest: Gondolat, 1986), 496–510. Translated by András Bocz.]*

DOCUMENT NO. 3: NSC 174, "United States Policy Toward the Soviet Satellites in Eastern Europe," December 11, 1953

NSC 174 was a major restatement of U.S. policy towards Eastern Europe, developed in the wake of the June 1953 East German uprisings.[36] Intended to replace NSC 58/2 and NSC 158, the new policy reflected somewhat diluted aims after the East German events gave the Eisenhower administration its first concrete indication of the limits of the doctrine of "rollback" and "liberation" of the "captive peoples," which it had espoused during and after the 1952 presidential campaign. The new directive concluded that "the detachment of any major European satellite from the Soviet bloc does not now appear feasible except by Soviet acquiescence or by war." Still, the administration maintained the goals of disrupting Soviet relations with the Eastern Europe countries, undermining the satellite regimes, and strengthening the "spirit of resistance" inside the bloc. To that end, the new directive authorized a host of political, diplomatic, economic, and covert actions designed to further the more moderate end of "fostering conditions which would make possible the liberation of the satellites at a favorable moment in the future."

DRAFT

STATEMENT OF POLICY

Proposed by the
NATIONAL SECURITY COUNCIL

on
UNITED STATES POLICY TOWARD THE SOVIET SATELLITES IN EASTERN EUROPE
(Except as otherwise indicated, parenthetical
references are to paragraphs in the Staff Study)

GENERAL CONSIDERATIONS

1. Soviet Control over the Soviet satellites in Eastern Europe (Poland, Czechoslovakia, Hungary, Romania, Bulgaria, Albania and East Germany[37]) has contributed importantly to the power disequilibrium in Europe and to the threat to the security of the United States. Despite economic dislocation and administrative difficulties, the Kremlin has made considerable progress in exploiting the industrial capacity of the satellites and expanding their military capabilities for use as a coordinated whole with those of the Soviet Union. (2–4, 37)

2. Barriers to the consolidation of the Soviet Union are:
   a. The anti-communist attitude of the great majority of the population in each satellite. This anti-communism is intensified particularly by loss of personal freedom and a reduced standard of living, as well as by outraged religious and national feelings, but its undiminished survival over the long run is jeopardized by communist control over every aspect of the lives of the people, particularly the young.

[36] For the most complete and up-to-date research on the 1953 crisis and its impact on the Cold War, see Ostermann, *Uprising in East Germany.*

[37] This paper is not concerned with Berlin, which is treated in NSC 132/1 on maintaining the U.S. position in West Berlin. It is recognized that Albania and East Germany possess specific features differentiating each of them in important ways from the other satellites. The inclusion of these two has, however, made possible the treatment of the satellite area as a whole. The situation of each satellite is sketched in Annex B of the staff study. East Germany is also considered in NSC 160/1. [Footnote in original.]

b. The continued refusal of the West to accept the permanence of the imposed satellite regimes as compatible with the freedom and self-determination of nations. (5–6)

3. Despite the widespread popular opposition to communism in each of the satellites, known underground groups capable of armed resistance have survived only as scattered remnants in a few areas, and are now generally inactive. The recent uprisings in East Germany and the unrest in other European satellites evidence: (a) the failure of the Soviets fully to subjugate these peoples or to destroy their desire for freedom; (b) the dependence of these satellite governments on nearby Soviet armed forces; and (c) the relative unreliability of satellite armed forces (especially if popular resistance in the satellites should increase). These events necessarily have placed internal and psychological strains upon the Soviet leadership. Nevertheless, the ability of the USSR to exercise effective control over, and to exploit the resources of, the European satellites has not been appreciably reduced, and is not likely to be, so long as the USSR maintains adequate military forces in the area. (3)

4. The death of Stalin created for Soviet dominion over the satellites new problems which may lend themselves to exploitation. Although there is as yet no evidence that Soviet capability to dominate the satellites has been impaired since the death of Stalin, the possibility nevertheless exists that a greater concentration of effort may be required to maintain control and that the new Soviet leaders may have to moderate the pace and scope of their programs in the satellites. Such moderation is indicated by the new economic measures, recently announced by the satellite regimes. (7)

5. Although nationalist opposition to Soviet domination is a disruptive force within the Soviet orbit, and even within the communist movement itself, it does not appear likely that a non-Soviet regime on the Tito model will emerge in any of the satellites under existing circumstances. The combination of basic factors which made possible the successful Yugoslav defection from Moscow is lacking in any of the satellites. In addition the Kremlin has taken drastic measures since the Yugoslav defection to guard against further defections. (6, 8–17)

6. Tito's establishment of an independent communist regime, nevertheless, has brought valuable assets to the free world in the struggle against aggressive Soviet power. It provides a standing example of successful defiance of the Kremlin and is proof that there is a practical alternative for nationalist communist leaders to submission to Soviet control. There are further advantages flowing from Yugoslavia's political and military cooperation with the West, its association with Greece and Turkey in a Balkan entente,[38] and its role as a vigorous propaganda weapon against Soviet Communism. (18–21)

7. East Germany poses special and more difficult problems of control for the USSR than do the other satellites. The fact that the main body of the German nation in the Federal Republic has made continued advances in freedom and economic well-being, and the fact that West Berlin provides a means of contact with the free world, serve to keep alive the hope for an eventual escape from Soviet domination. By utilizing these special advantages the West can probably continue to exploit strong popular anti-communism, maintain East Germany as a focal point and example of disaffection for the rest of the Soviet satellites, make difficult full utilization of East Germany's economic resources, and keep alive Soviet doubts as to the reliability of the East German population in time of war. At the same time, U.S. policy toward East Germany must take into account the latter's relationship to the problem of German unification, the integration of the Federal Republic with Western Europe, and the importance of, and dangers inherent in, preserving our access to and position in Berlin. (24, 41, Annex B.)

8. The detachment of any major European satellite from the Soviet bloc does not now appear feasible except by Soviet acquiescence or by war. Such a detachment would not decisively affect the Soviet military capability either in delivery of weapons of mass destruction or in conventional forces, but would be a considerable blow to Soviet prestige and would impair in some degree Soviet conventional military capabilities in Europe. (NSC 162/1, para. 5–b)

---

[38] After the signing of an agreement on mutual friendship and cooperation in 1953, relations between the three countries were further tightened through formation of the Balkan Pact, a mutual assistance treaty, in 1954.

POLICY CONCLUSIONS

9. It is in the national security interests of the United States to pursue a policy of determined resistance to dominant Soviet influence over the satellites in Eastern Europe and to seek the eventual elimination of that influence. Accordingly, feasible political, economic, propaganda and covert measures are required to create and exploit troublesome problems for the USSR, complicate control in the satellites, and retard the growth of the military and economic potential of the Soviet bloc. Decisions on such measures to impose pressures on the Soviet bloc should take into account the desirability of creating conditions which will induce the Soviet leadership to be more receptive to acceptable negotiated settlements. Accordingly, this policy should be carried out by flexible courses of action in the light of current estimates of the Soviet Government's reactions and of the situation in the satellite states concerned, after calculation of the advantages and disadvantages to the general position of the United States in relation to the USSR and to the free world. (37–42)

BASIC OBJECTIVES

10. *Long-range:* The eventual fulfillment of the rights of the peoples in the Soviet satellites to enjoy governments of their own choosing, free of Soviet domination and participating as peaceful members in the free world community. (2, 37)

11. *Current:*
   a. To disrupt the Soviet-satellite relationship, minimize satellite contributions to Soviet power, and deter aggressive world policies on the part of the USSR by diverting Soviet attention and energies to problems and difficulties within the Soviet bloc. (35, 39)
   b. To undermine the Satellite regimes and promote conditions favorable to the eventual liberation of the satellite peoples. (35, 36, 38, 39)
   c. To conserve and strengthen the assets within the satellites, and among their nationals outside, which may contribute to U.S. interests in peace or war, and to the ultimate freedom of the satellites. (29–32, 39)
   d. To lay the groundwork, as feasible with reasonable risk, for resistance to the Soviets in the event of war. (29–30, 35)

COURSES OF ACTION

12. Use appropriate means short of military force to oppose, and to contribute to the eventual elimination of Soviet domination over the satellites; including, when appropriate, concert with NATO or other friendly powers, resort to UN procedures, and, if possible, negotiation with the USSR. (23–32, 36)

13. Encourage and assist the satellite peoples in resistance to their Soviet-dominated regimes, maintaining their hopes of eventual freedom from Soviet domination, while avoiding:
   a. Incitement to premature revolt.
   b. Commitments on the nature and timing of any U.S. action to bring about liberation.
   c. Incitement to action when the probable reprisals or other results would yield a net loss in terms of U.S. objectives.[39] (26, 29, 30, 40)

---

[39] For example, account should be taken of the undesirability of provoking the liquidation of important resistance movements or of creating false hopes of U.S. intervention. [Footnote in original.]

14. Develop and encourage, as appropriate, increased use of passive resistance by the peoples of the satellites. (5, 40)

15. Be prepared to exploit any future disturbances similar to the East German riots of 1953 by planning courses of action which would best serve U.S. interests in such events. (29, 30)

16. Foster satellite nationalism as a force against Soviet imperialism, while avoiding commitments to national ambitions which would interfere with U. S. post-liberation objectives. (6, 16)

17. Cooperate with other forces—such as religious, cultural, social—which are natural allies in the struggle against Soviet imperialism. (5)

18. Stimulate and exploit conflicts within the communist ruling groups in each satellite, among such groups, and between them and the Kremlin. (16)

19. Foster disaffection in satellite armed forces and police, to diminish their reliability in suppressing domestic disturbances and their will to fight in the event of war. (3)

20. Encourage democratic, anti-communist elements in the satellites; but at the same time be prepared to exploit any Titoist tendencies, and to assist "national communist" movements under favorable conditions, making clear, as appropriate, that opportunities for survival exist outside the Soviet bloc. (8–16, 41)

21. Exploit the developing organizations of Western unity (NATO, OEEC, CSC,[40] etc.) as a force of attraction for the satellites. (22)

22. Encourage defection of key satellite personnel and possible VFC[41] recruits, but not mass defection; and assist in the resettlement and rehabilitation of refugees who do escape. (32)

23. Support or make use of refugees or exile organizations which can contribute to the attainment of U.S. objectives, but do not recognize governments-in-exile. (32)

24. Strengthen covert activities in support of the objectives in paras. 10 and 11 above. (29–32)

25. Maintain flexibility in U.S. economic policies toward the Soviet bloc, and toward individual satellites, in order to gain maximum advantage with the limited economic weapons at hand (both restrictions and incentives). (27, 28)

26. Continue U.S. diplomatic missions in Poland, Czechoslovakia, Hungary, and Rumania as long as may be in the U.S. interest, and keep under review the possibility of resuming diplomatic relations with Bulgaria. (25)

27. Exploit the existence, and encourage the development, of the Yugoslav-Greek-Turkish entente as a means of weakening Soviet power in the Balkan satellites and as an example of free association of independent Balkan nations serving as a potential alternative to Soviet rule. (22)

28. Keep the situation with respect to Albania under continuing surveillance with a view to the possibility of detachment of that country from the Soviet bloc at such time as its detachment might be judged to serve the over-all U.S. interest. (15, 31, Annex B.)

29. Exploit, to the fullest extent compatible with the policies regarding Germany as a whole and Berlin, the special opportunities offered by West Berlin and the facilities of the Federal Republic to undermine Soviet power in East Germany. Place the Soviets in East Germany on the defensive by such measures as may be taken to keep alive the hope of German reunification. (24, 41)

30. Emphasize (a) the right of the peoples of Eastern Europe to independent governments of their own choosing and (b) the violation of international agreements by the Soviet and satellite Governments, whereby they have been deprived of that right, particularly the Yalta Declaration on Liberated Europe and the Treaties of Peace with Bulgaria, Hungary and Rumania. (2, 37)

---

[40] These entities are, respectively, the North Atlantic Treaty Organization, the Organization for European Economic Cooperation, and the Coal and Steel Community.

[41] The Volunteer Freedom Corps was to be made up of émigrés from Eastern Europe who could be deployed in the region to carry out military and paramilitary operations. First proposed in 1948, the idea was debated intermittently by the Truman and Eisenhower administrations but never fully implemented.

NSC STAFF STUDY

on

UNITED STATES POLICY TOWARD THE SOVIET SATELLITES IN EASTERN EUROPE

PROBLEM

1. To determine what policies with respect to the Soviet satellites of Eastern Europe (Poland, Czechoslovakia, Hungary, Rumania, Bulgaria, Albania, and East Germany[42]) will best serve the national interests of the United States, and in particular will contribute to the resistance to and eventual elimination of dominant Soviet influence over those satellites. It is necessary to reexamine and revise, where necessary and desirable in the light of intervening developments, the conclusions of NSC 58/2.

BACKGROUND

Importance of the Satellites

2. The satellites are of importance in the current balance of power in Europe because they augment the political, military and economic power of the Soviet Union and extend Soviet power into the heart of Europe. The permanent consolidation of Soviet control in this area would represent a serious threat to the security of the United States and Western Europe. It is likewise our traditional policy to recognize and support the right of such peoples to independence and to governments of their own choosing. The elimination of dominant Soviet influence over the satellites is therefore, in the fundamental interest of the United States.

Soviet Domination of the Satellites

3. Soviet domination of the satellites remains a basic fact; there is no evidence as yet to indicate that Soviet capability to dominate the satellites has been significantly affected by anything that has happened since the death of Stalin. However, Soviet suppression of the riots in East Germany suggests that the satellite regimes themselves may be unable, without Soviet armed forces available, to maintain the population in subjection to the will of the Kremlin.

4. The Kremlin has pushed forward with considerable success its plans to expand the industrial and military capabilities of the satellites and to coordinate their Sovietized political system, military establishments and economies with those of the USSR in a working totality. Although the Kremlin permits and encourages programs of cultural, economic and technical collaboration among the satellites, it appears determined to bind the satellites individually to the USSR rather than to unify them. Whether and when the Soviet leaders will take the formal step of incorporating any or all of the satellites into the USSR itself is unpredictable.

Opposition to Soviet Domination

5. The great majority of the population in each satellite continues to be opposed to the communist regime and resents the lack of personal freedom and hard living conditions for which the

---

[42] This paper is not concerned with Berlin which is treated in NSC 132/1 on maintaining the U.S. position in West Berlin. It is recognized that Albania and East Germany possess specific features by which they are differentiated in important ways from the other satellites. The inclusion of these two has, however, made possible the treatment of the satellite area as a whole and even the other satellites have in a lesser degree certain special aspects. The situation of each satellite is sketched in Annex B. [Footnote in original.]

regime is responsible. The aggrieved religious feelings resulting from the communist attack on religion have also served to intensify this widespread anti-Communism. The anti-communist majorities are not in a position to carry on active resistance which would represent a serious challenge to Soviet power in any of these satellites with the possible exception of Albania, as is noted hereafter. Nevertheless, by passive resistance they can impede the process of Sovietization and afford a main element on which must be based eventual elimination of dominant Soviet influence. It is recognized at the same time that, if the process of exclusive communist indoctrination and education proceeds without interruption for an indeterminate period, it is uncertain how strong this anti-communist sentiment may remain.

6. In addition to anti-communism per se, nationalism is a significant factor of opposition to Soviet control in all the satellites. These peoples will not reconcile themselves in a few years to the loss of national independence, a disregard of national traditions and the enforced glorification of the USSR. The nationalist sentiment focuses on the memory of better times in the past, hopes for the future, and the resentment felt at the injuries and insults experienced under the present regime. In many respects it is the strongest leverage available for strengthening the morale of the satellite populations, sustaining their spirit of resistance to Soviet imperialism, and encouraging their defiance of servile communist regimes. Nationalism is, however, a double-edged weapon, raising a number of operational problems, as we have discovered in our propaganda work and dealings with the refugees. Besides arousing anti-Soviet feeling, nationalist sentiment also creates divisions among these peoples themselves, Magyars against Slavs and Rumanians, Slovaks against Czechs, Poles against Germans and Germans against the Slavs. A problem which will become increasingly serious as nationalist sentiment ferments is that of the Polish-occupied areas of Germany east of the Oder-Neisse line.

7. The death of Stalin created for Soviet dominion over the Satellites new problems which may lend themselves to exploitation. Although there is as yet no evidence that Soviet capability to dominate the Satellites has been impaired since the death of Stalin, the possibility nevertheless exists that a greater concentration of effort may be required to maintain control and that the new Soviet leaders may have to moderate the pace and scope of their programs in the Satellites. Such moderation is indicated by the new economic measures recently announced by the Satellite regimes, which give priority to increasing the output of consumer goods in order to improve popular morale and to stimulate labor productivity. In promulgating the new policy, the Satellite regimes have admitted that an economic dislocation has developed, mainly because of an over-emphasis on the development of heavy industry and a neglect of agricultural development. The Satellite regimes now seek a modification of industrial and agricultural programs to bring about a more normal balance between industry and agriculture and to raise the level of popular morale. The Communists have rationalized that this corrective will provide a healthier foundation for future economic growth and for further sovietization of the Satellite countries.

Possibilities of "Titoism"

8. NSC 58/2 laid down a policy of fostering communist heresy among the satellites and encouraging the emergence of non-Stalinist regimes as temporary administrations even though communist in nature. However, as was noted in the third Progress Report on implementation of NSC 58/2, dated May 22, 1951, the Kremlin and its local agents have been successful in warding off any trend in the satellites comparable to that which led to the break between Moscow and Yugoslavia. In fact, in none of the satellites have there developed the capabilities such as rendered Tito's defection successful.

9. Of all the European satellite leaders, only Tito achieved controlling power. He created an impressive military force, as well as a political organization, responsive to his own leadership which maintained itself inside Yugoslavia during the war and which, following withdrawal of the Nazi forces, possessed requisite power to impose its will upon the Yugoslav people without

substantial assistance from the Red Army. All the other Communist regimes, with the exception of Hoxha's[43] government in Albania, were placed in power by the Red Army itself or by threat of force which the Red Army represented. These regimes, therefore, were from the outset dependent on Soviet military power for their very existence and have remained so. In East Germany, Poland, Hungary and Rumania, the physical presence of sizeable Soviet forces bears daily witness to Soviet domination of these satellites. In Poland the Minister of Defense is a Soviet marshal, and Soviet officers occupy the higher posts throughout the Polish armed forces. In all the satellites there are large Soviet military missions which are supervising the reorganization of the satellite armed forces, and Soviet commanders, advisers, and technicians are located in key command and staff positions in the military forces and in the defense ministries.

10. Thus, the ultimate basis of Soviet control in the satellites is Soviet military domination of these countries. The Soviet forces stationed within the satellites and in the Soviet Zone of Austria in April 1953 consisted of 538,000 personnel from the Soviet Army (including military missions), 24,000 security troops, and 2,400 Soviet-manned aircraft.

11. Of all the satellite leaders of Eastern Europe, only Tito could claim to exercise effective control over the state security apparatus. His security forces were built up on the basis of personal loyalty demonstrated in the heat of battle, and Tito knew that he could trust the overwhelming majority of the higher echelons of his command. None of the current satellite leaders can count on this kind of allegiance from the key personnel of their security establishments. Soviet liaison personnel maintain close supervision over the leading satellite officials, and it is doubtful whether far-reaching orders issued by those leaders to any of their respective security organs would be executed without confirmation from Soviet controlled sources. In contrast, it was Tito's steadfast denial to Soviet liaison officials of uncontrolled access to his security organization which contributed extensively to the friction climaxed by the break between Tito and the Kremlin.

12. Poland, Czechoslovakia, Hungary, and Rumania have a common land frontier with the USSR. Bulgaria has a common sea frontier. These states are accordingly more exposed to Soviet military intervention and hence more readily susceptible to Soviet pressure and control than was Yugoslavia which shares no common frontier with the USSR. Furthermore, with Yugoslavia's long sea coast facing the West, greater possibilities to obtain material support from the Western powers in the event of a break with Moscow were available to Tito than there would be to the other satellites, with the exception of Albania.

13. Since Tito's defection in 1948, the Soviets have taken stringent and thorough measures to guard against a similar development in other satellites. Leaders in whom any taint of Titoism was suspected have been either shorn of all power, imprisoned, or actually liquidated. If any leader through long tenure in office or for any other reason seemed to be gaining too much power, he has been ruthlessly eliminated. The customary security safeguards have been tightened and expanded. A series of friendship and mutual assistance pacts have been concluded among the various satellites (except Albania and East Germany) and with the USSR which in effect obligate the parties signatory to go to each others' aid in the event of action from without. The relationship of the USSR to the satellite regimes raises every probability that the Soviets would in effect intervene in the face of internal action threatening the overthrow of the Soviet-controlled regimes, except possibly in the case of Albania.

14. In the light of the foregoing considerations, the chances are negligible at the present time that any existing satellite communist regime would or could break away from Moscow under its own power, or, with the possible exception of Albania, that any anti-Soviet faction could seize or hold power in a satellite and bring about its detachment from the Soviet bloc.

15. Albania is to some extent an exception in that, unlike the other satellites, it does enjoy geographical isolation from the rest of the Soviet bloc and access to the West by sea. Although the other factors which rendered Tito's defection successful are generally not present, Soviet

[43] Enver Hoxha was first secretary of the Albanian Communist Party (renamed the Albanian Party of Labor) beginning in 1943, and prime minister between 1945–1954.

control in Albania is challenged by the inherent potential of the internal anti-Communist majority whose resistance could be supported by the large Albanian population in the neighboring Kossovar region of Yugoslavia. The necessity of Western cooperation with Yugoslavia would of course be a complicating factor. Albanian refugees in the West might also be used although their disunity would seriously hamper any such action.

16. Nationalism may, nevertheless, continue to be a disruptive force within the Communist movement open to exploitation by the United States. Not all communists in the satellites are able or willing to serve Moscow's interest without any regard for that of their own nation; the very problems of governing their respective territories and of meeting the goals which have been set seem to require at least a minimum of cooperation from the people and may lead certain local communists to oppose as best they can those Kremlin demands and policies which put too great a strain upon their own position. In any of the satellite communist parties there are likely to be personal antagonisms and other differences which might be exploited from the outside.

17. Since the relation of Communist China to the USSR is believed to involve considerably less subordination than that of the European satellites, the diplomatic, trade and cultural connections between the satellites and Communist China represent a potentially troublesome factor in Soviet-satellite relations. While this factor is not easily susceptible to exploitation by the U.S., it should be closely watched for whatever opportunities it may offer.

Significance of Yugoslavia in Policy toward the Satellites

18. Even though no other Satellite has followed or seems capable (with the possible exception of Albania) of following the path of Tito's Yugoslavia under existing conditions, the example of Yugoslavia continues to be a significant factor in the satellite picture. Tito's success in maintaining Yugoslavia's independence constitutes a standing insult to Soviet prestige and a challenge to Soviet infallibility. His political and ideological counteroffensive has been a disturbing factor within the satellite communist parties.

19. In terms of Yugoslavia's foreign relations, Tito is steadily moving toward closer integration with the defensive system being built up by the free world. An important step in this direction is the recent inauguration of contingent military planning talks first with the United States, United Kingdom and France and shortly thereafter with Greece and Turkey. In the political field, a Friendship Pact between Greece, Turkey, and Yugoslavia has recently been concluded.

20. These developments point toward ultimate integration of Yugoslav military capabilities with those of the NATO powers and the consequent marked enhancement of Yugoslav defensive strength against any aggression. Their significance in relation to the satellites lies in the extent to which it is demonstrated that a practical alternative to continued acquiescence in Soviet domination is being created.

21. The relationship which the United States has developed with Yugoslavia is of vital importance in this process of augmenting Yugoslavia's effectiveness in the struggle against Soviet domination. In addition, means of cooperation may be worked out with the Yugoslav Government on such matters as action in the United Nations, propaganda, the reception and treatment of refugees from the satellites and the exchange of intelligence. Moreover, the mere fact of substantial United States economic and military assistance to Yugoslavia must have its effect on both communists and non-communists in the satellite countries. The exposition before the world by Yugoslavia of its experience with Soviet domination as a member of the Soviet bloc also provides excellent refutation of Soviet propaganda.

Significance of Western European International Organizations

22. While there has been considerable discussion among the exiles of federation in Eastern Europe following liberation, no concrete plans toward this end have been advanced. Neither have the Western powers attempted to offer any specific proposals for unity of the satellite peo-

ples or their association with Western Europe after they are freed. The growing international organization of the West reflected in NATO, the Coal and Steel Community and similar bodies nevertheless acts as a disruptive influence upon the satellite orbit by helping to keep alive the hopes of the captive peoples. Such organizations hold out to them (a) evidence of developing unity and strength of the West essential to their ultimate emancipation, and (b) as an inviting alternative to the compulsory dominion of the false internationalism to which they now belong, a glimpse of an integrated Europe of free constructive possibilities in which they may take part once they are liberated.

MEANS OF ATTACKING SOVIET DOMINATION OF THE SATELLITES

23. The means available to the United States to assist resistance to, and the eventual break-down of, the dominant Soviet influence in the satellites fall into the following general categories: (a) political and diplomatic; (b) propaganda; (c) economic; (d) covert; and (e) military. It must be recognized that, owing to the actual presence of Soviet power and the apparatus of Soviet control, all these means, with the exception of the military, are of limited effectiveness, except possibly in the case of Albania, whose peculiarly exposed position renders it susceptible to some measure of economic pressure and to a greater degree of covert activities.

Political and Diplomatic

24. The major political and diplomatic capability is to exert the pressure of the unalterable United States position as to the fundamental right of the satellite peoples to freedom, upon the existing Soviet controlled regimes. The United States can also utilize its position of free world leadership to rally the support of the free world to this position and thus to strengthen and broaden the pressure on the USSR and on those regimes. The United States can also exploit the German desire for unity and a peace treaty in order to undermine the Soviet position in East Germany.

25. The United States still maintains diplomatic missions in Poland, Czechoslovakia, Hungary and Rumania. This is advantageous in that it (a) provides useful opportunities for reporting and intelligence acquisition, (b) shows American concern for the rights, welfare and eventual independence of the satellite peoples, (c) makes possible direct contact with the government concerned and facilitates dealing with such problems as the protection of American citizens and property, (d) provides a vantage point which could be useful in the event of future developments that cannot be predicted, such as a major defection, and (e) provides a means for evaluating and guiding our propaganda effort. The principal disadvantages are (a) the impression created in some quarters that diplomatic relations indicate the acceptance of the legitimacy of the communist regimes, (b) the pressures and harassments to which American representatives in the satellite states are subjected, to the detriment of United States prestige, (c) the brake which the existence of diplomatic relations may exercise on covert operations directed against satellite governments, and (d) the continued presence of satellite missions in the United States. The possibility of opening diplomatic relations with Bulgaria should be kept under review.

Propaganda

26. The progressive denial to the satellite peoples of access to truth and means of contact with the outside world has limited the possibilities in the propaganda field almost entirely to broadcasting, although balloons, air drops, etc., may be used occasionally with some effect to supplement this medium. The operation of adequate technical facilities for broadcasting to the satellites and the preparation of effective programs assume increasing importance in the effort to conserve and promote anti-communist sentiment against the possible inroads of the communist monopoly over the various media of information. Utilization of our propaganda facilities is

conditioned by the necessity of, on the one hand avoiding any commitments regarding when and how these peoples may be liberated and any incitement to premature revolt, and on the other hand seeking to maintain their faith in the eventual restoration of freedom.

Economic

27. Western controls of exports to the Soviet bloc and the Soviet drive for self-sufficiency have reduced trade with Eastern Europe to a relatively low level. The economic measures available are consequently of limited efficacy as implements to accomplish the general purposes of this paper. They might, however, have some harassment value or could serve as auxiliaries to a coordinated program based primarily on other measures. Existing trade controls have already made the economic problems of the satellites more difficult and to this extent contribute to realizing the specific purposes of United States policy toward the satellites.

28. Other economic measures, however, in so far as latitude is allowed by relevant legislation and over-all United States policies, should be considered on a case-by-case basis, bearing in mind the balance of advantage in each instance between the USSR and the free world. It is desirable to maintain flexibility in U.S. economic policies toward the Soviet bloc and toward individual satellites, in order that maximum advantage may be gained with the limited economic weapons at hand (both restrictions and incentives). It is also desirable to have in reserve sufficient economic weapons to bring pressure to bear against particular satellite regimes at particular times if doing so serves U.S. interests. The application of such controls on a general basis, aside from the question of whether they are worth while in terms of general aspects of United States relations with the USSR and our free world allies, would tend to facilitate the integration of the satellites with the USSR, and would make it impossible to maintain the desired flexibility. Only in the case of Albania is this perhaps not true, for general economic measures by the West could serve to emphasize Albania's political and economic isolation, while effective integration by the Soviets as a countermeasure would be under present conditions most difficult.

Covert

29. Covert operations can be directed to the satellites (a) to gain intelligence, (b) to build up organizational arrangements which will strengthen capabilities for resistance and constitute an asset in the event of war or other situation where action against the regimes may be feasible and desirable, and (c) to reinforce official United States propaganda, especially with the purpose of keeping up the morale of the anti-communists and sowing confusion among the communists. To be most effective, operations of this kind should be conducted so as to avoid encouraging divisive forces among the anti-communists at home or the exiles abroad.

30. It is recognized that the difficulties of conducting covert operations have steadily increased because of the mounting concern of the Kremlin for security throughout the Soviet bloc and the growing effectiveness of the bloc-wide security apparatus. In consequence of these considerations, as well as of physical difficulties, the mounting of any specific operations necessarily requires considerable time for adequate preparation. Furthermore, in view of recent experience it is of the utmost importance to proceed with extreme care in this field with a view to solid accomplishment for the long run rather than to seek quick results in building up resistance capabilities (for military utilization on the hypothesis of the early outbreak of war) at the greater risk of infiltration, detection and embarrassment of United States political action and propaganda. The latter course may well result in defeating the immediate aim of covert activity by disrupting any embryonic resistance organization already created; it may also deliver a most serious blow to the broad efforts of the United States in behalf of freedom for the people concerned.

31. Albania probably offers the best opportunity for the implementation of United States policy through effective use of covert activities. Any undertakings designed either to promote internal resistance or to introduce resistance forces from outside must take into consideration the

43

impact of any such development on the USSR and on other satellite nations. A careful and thorough estimate of Soviet capabilities and intentions in regard to retaliatory action is essential. Also, full attention must be given to the conflicting interests of Albania's immediate neighbors and of our western allies. The conflicting aims and aspirations of Yugoslavia, Greece and Italy in regard to Albania and Albania's territory could give rise to serious international complications if not fully balanced on the basis of full understanding with them and other interested western powers prior to any undertaking. Further, should any such covert operation require the collaboration of any of the directly interested nations (Yugoslavia, Greece and/or Italy), the western powers should take steps to ensure that their basic interest in reference to the ultimate independence of Albania be not jeopardized.

32. Among the means at hand to assist in the attainment of United States objectives are defectors and refugees from the satellites. It is questionable whether the mass flight of refugees from those areas (or an increase in the mass flight in the case of East Germany) would be desirable from the standpoint of United States interests, in view of the magnitude of the welfare and settlement problem it would create and the loss of strength to any actual or potential resistance movements within the satellite area. However, the defection of key personnel and potential recruits for a Volunteer Freedom Corps offers considerable benefits to the United States and should continue to be encouraged in accordance with existing policy. Defectors, exiled leaders and other refugees can contribute to United States objectives by virtue of (a) their knowledge of conditions, trends and personalities in their homelands, (b) such symbolic value as they may have to the peoples of their homelands, and (c) their military potential. Although recognition of exile organizations, under existing circumstances, as governments-in-exile would be inconsistent with the maintenance of diplomatic relations with the satellite regimes and would be undesirable for other reasons, notably because recognition would constitute a measure of commitment to groups whose value might be altered by eventual developments, such organizations which are united and broadly representative of the non-totalitarian elements in the satellite populations can be given general moral support and other appropriate encouragement in their activities on behalf of the freedom of their peoples. When they operate in the United States or with American funds the United States should seek by appropriate means to have them abide by its general over-all guidance.

ALTERNATIVE COURSES OF ACTION

The Three Alternatives

33. One alternative is to take direct action for the liberation of the satellite peoples from the USSR by military force, either through direct military measures or through armed support of revolutionary movements. Such exercise of military force would in all probability start a global war, except possibly in Albania. In the case of the latter the probability of Soviet military counter action is somewhat less than in the other satellites and the risk commensurately diminished but nevertheless real and worthy of most careful consideration. This alternative could not be adopted by the United States unless it were willing to undertake a global war for this purpose, and to wage it in all probability without the wholehearted support of allied nations and of the United Nations.

34. The contrary alternative is to accept the fact of Soviet control of the satellites for an indeterminate period, possibly as a basis for reaching some kind of negotiated accommodation with the USSR, while United States' efforts are devoted to areas beyond the present limits of Soviet control in order to block Soviet expansion. To follow such a course, besides being inconsistent with the fundamental principle of the right of the satellite peoples to freedom, would be to deny ourselves means of reducing the over-all Soviet power position vis-a-vis the United States and its allies. It may be reasonably assumed, moreover, that our

acceptance of the legitimacy of the present satellite regimes, even if it should require Soviet assent to some limited agreement with the West, would be the course which the Kremlin would desire the United States to follow.

35. There is a large area between the extremes mentioned in the two preceding paragraphs in which policy and action can be developed with the purpose of limiting and impeding the Soviet grip on the satellites. Policy within that field would be determined with a view to contributing toward the eventual elimination of dominant Soviet power over these peoples, but its usefulness need not depend on its effectiveness in achieving this purpose within any given period of time. The more immediate criteria for judging the desirability of any particular measures would be their effectiveness in slowing down Soviet exploitation of the human and material resources of the satellites, in maintaining popular resistance to and non-cooperation with Soviet policies, and in strengthening those forces and factors which would minimize Soviet assets and maximize Soviet liabilities in this area in case of war. Progress in this regard might bring the question of liberation of one or more satellites to a status of greater actuality and immediacy; any acceleration of or change in the United States policy could then be considered in the light of the situation existing at the time.

36. Adherence to this middle course, though it may preclude reaching any general accommodation with the Soviet Union in the foreseeable future, might contribute to the creation of conditions which will induce the Soviet leadership to be more receptive to negotiated settlements in line with U.S. objectives toward the satellites. Action of this type, when it has reference to areas of direct concern to certain western nations, can have far reaching consequences to our relation with our own allies. It is desirable that every effort be made to obtain British and French support for this general course of action. Any action regarding Albania, for example, which did not adequately take into account the legitimate interests of Italy, Greece, and Yugoslavia might well result in a net loss rather than gain to Western solidarity and hence to our fundamental interests. In addition to considerations of Soviet capability of reacting in Albania itself, the possibilities of Soviet retaliatory action elsewhere in the world must be taken into account.

U. S. Policy

37. Soviet domination of the satellite peoples violates the principle of freedom and self-determination of nations. It has also, by bringing Soviet power into the heart of Europe, created a fundamental disequilibrium on the continent and a continuing pressure on Western Europe. So long as it remains, the task of achieving security, stability and orderly progress in Europe must encounter grave difficulties. The United States should make clear by its words and deeds that it does not accept this situation as right or as permanent and that no accommodation with the Soviet Union to the contrary effect can be countenanced.

38. A deliberate policy of attempting to liberate the satellite peoples by military force, which would probably mean war with the USSR and most probably would be unacceptable to the American people and condemned by world opinion, cannot be given serious consideration. The United States should, however, direct its efforts toward fostering conditions which would make possible the liberation of the satellites at a favorable moment in the future and toward obstructing meanwhile the processes of Soviet imperialism in those areas. The possibility of early action in this regard in Albania should be kept under continuing review in cooperation with our major allies.

39. In general, full advantage should be taken of the means of diplomacy, propaganda, economic policy and covert operations to maintain the morale of anti-Soviet elements, to sow confusion and discredit the authority of the regimes, to disrupt Soviet-satellite relationships, and generally to maximize Soviet difficulties. Policies and action to be undertaken by the United States should be judged on the basis of their contribution to these purposes, limited of course by such other factors in the global policy situation as may be pertinent. For exam-

ple, such questions as the maintenance of diplomatic relations with satellite states, or the nature of economic pressures to be applied to these states, should be decided strictly in terms of general advantages and disadvantages to the United States, not of legalistic considerations or of the degree of indignation felt as a result of the acts of satellite governments.

40. In its efforts to encourage anti-Soviet elements in the satellites and keep up their hopes, the United States should not encourage premature action on their part which will bring upon them reprisals involving further terror and suppression. Continuing and careful attention must be given to the fine line, which is not stationary, between exhortations to keep up morale and to maintain passive resistance, and invitations to suicide. Planning for covert operations should be determined on the basis of feasibility, minimum risk, and maximum contribution to the fundamental interest of the United States.

41. The United States should vigilantly follow the developing situation in each satellite and be prepared to take advantage of any opportunity to further the emergence of regimes not subservient to the USSR, provided such regimes would have reasonable prospects of survival. Considerations of the relative vulnerability of the several satellites must enter into our calculations. In the case of East Germany, such action will be within the framework of unification under acceptable conditions. In the case of Albania it may prove possible to move more directly towards the removal and replacement of the present pro-Soviet regime. United States action in any individual case would have to be determined in the light of probable Soviet reactions in the immediate area involved, or elsewhere, risks of global war, the probable reaction of our allies, and other aspects of the situation prevailing at the time.

42. United States interests with respect to the satellites can be pursued most effectively by flexible and adaptable courses of action within the general policy of determined opposition to, and the purpose of the eventual elimination of, dominant Soviet influence over those peoples. Such action should be within the limits of our capabilities as conditioned by our general policies. Thus the existing power situation, the current policies of the Soviet Government, the effect of any action on the satellite peoples, and the attitudes of the American people and of other free peoples must be borne in mind.

[In the original, a map of "The European Soviet Satellites" (including Poland, Czechoslovakia, Hungary, Bulgaria, Yugoslavia, Albania, and Rumania), with selected railroads outlined, follows.]

ANNEX A

ESTIMATED SATELLITE GROUND FORCES
APRIL 1953

COUNTRY	ARMY	SECURITY TROOPS	TRAINED AND PARTIALLY TRAINED RESERVES
E. GERMANY	100,000	25,000	11,000
POLAND	330,000	65,000	1,535,000
CSEHOSLOVAKIA	185,000	35,000	1,195,000
ALBANIA	40,000	10,000	80,000
HUNGARY	185,000	35,000	450,000
RUMANIA	267,000	56,000	1,275,000
BULGARIA	210,000	40,000	500,000
TOTAL	1,317,000	266,000	5,046,000

BRIEF SURVEY OF THE SITUATION IN THE EUROPEAN SATELLITES

POLAND

Poland has a population of 25 million and is the largest of the satellites both in number of inhabitants and in amount of territory. Strategically and economically it is of high importance to the USSR. It occupies the main approach to Germany and Western Europe and has been occupied since the end of the war by Soviet military forces nominally serving as line-communication troops, to the number of several divisions. This fact, together with the country's easy accessibility to Soviet troop movements, and the direct control of its own armed forces by Soviet officers, ensures Soviet military and political domination.

Economically, Poland is important to the Soviet bloc primarily as the chief coal-producing country of Eastern Europe, but also because of its merchant fleet and some of its other products such as railway cars. Polish industry, emphasized over agriculture in the current Six-Year Plan (1950–1955), is less developed than those of Czechoslovakia and Eastern Germany, but is more important than the industry of the Balkan satellites. Polish agriculture since the war has not kept pace with the requirements of increased industrialization. This has been one factor in a tight supply and distribution problem, particularly in foodstuffs, which has led the Communist regime into extensive experimentation with market management, including a system of rationing and dual prices that had to be abolished as unworkable early in 1953. Farm collectivization, though currently being pushed more rapidly than ever before, is still in its early stage; only some 20 percent of the arable land is as yet embraced in "producer cooperatives" and state farms together.

The Soviet-imposed Communist regime lacks the foundation of a historically strong Communist Party, as the prewar Party prior to its dissolution in 1938 was numerically small, illegal and without major influence. The present organization (called the United Polish Workers' Party), though numbering 1.2 million members, is almost entirely a postwar creation based on Soviet support and on the opportunism of thousands of job-holders. It also includes several thousand former Socialists whose party was annexed under pressure in 1948, most of whom probably remain inwardly critical of Soviet policy and Communist leadership. The Party is thought to harbor a strong latent tendency toward what Moscow calls "nationalist deviation," though its principal symbol, Gomulka, was purged in 1948. In particular the distrust and antipathy toward Germany which is traditional in the nation at large is widely shared in the Party, despite the current Soviet line calling for German unification and for close relations between the Polish and Eastern German Communist regimes.

Poland's overwhelmingly Roman Catholic character (95 percent of the people are Roman Catholic), its strong sense of cultural and political community with the West, and its historic antagonism toward Russia combine to render political assimilation to the Soviet system difficult. The Soviet wartime annexation of the eastern two-fifths of Poland, the Katyn Forest massacres, and the Soviet refusal to aid the Warsaw uprising of 1944 against the Germans have deepened the anti-Soviet disposition of the nation. Moreover, the successful large-scale wartime underground movement against the Germans established a precedent for resistance to alien rule. Nevertheless, the physical presence of strong Soviet military forces, combined with the efficiency of Communist police controls, at present holds organized underground resistance to a minimum. The skeleton organizations of a few formerly strong anti-Soviet underground movements are thought to exist still, and to maintain tenuous contact with Polish exile groups in the West, but they do not currently engage in any significant operations against the Communist regime.

A special feature of the Polish situation is the role of the territories annexed from Germany after the war, which amount to approximately one-fourth of the total area of present-day Poland. Most of the nation, regardless of political attitudes, supports the Polish claim to these territories. The Communist regime exploits this popular feeling by stressing the fact that only the Soviet bloc is willing to guarantee these territories to Poland. A major Communist propaganda theme, which has not been entirely without effect among many Polish elements, is the charge that any retreat of Soviet and Communist power from Poland under Western pressure would be bound to involve a new hegemony of Germany over Poland and the forced retrocession of the Oder-Neisse territories to Germany.

CZECHOSLOVAKIA

Czechoslovakia, with a population of over 13 million, is the fourth largest European satellite (following Poland, Eastern Germany and Rumania). Its special importance to the USSR lies in its highly developed industry, particularly the size and diversity of its engineering industry and the many-sided skill of its industrial population.

Owing to Czechoslovak industrial capabilities, Moscow has laid particularly heavy economic tasks on Czechoslovakia. From a country of medium and light industry widely engaged in international trade it has been forced to change over into a producer of heavy and medium industrial equipment primarily for the USSR and the Soviet bloc. This change, involving Soviet demands for drastically increased output in heavy industry, has brought manpower and raw material shortages, consumer-goods scarcities and consequent inflationary pressure. The result is a more severely strained economy than any other in the orbit.

Czechoslovakia presents Moscow with a complex problem of assimilation. Despite a pan-Slav and pro-Russian cultural tradition, the nation is socially less akin to the USSR than most of the other satellites. Like Eastern Germany it is more markedly middle-classed, urban and commercial in character than the other satellites, and psychologically more closely tied to Western and Central Europe. Its relatively long and successful practice of parliamentary democracy between the wars, coupled with a highly conscious cultivation of a late-won right of national self-determination renders its accommodation to dictatorship and alien institutions psychologically difficult. Among the workers, the Communists have not been able to destroy entirely the strong democratic trade union traditions established in the inter-war period. The difficulties of adjustment by the workers to the changed role of trade unions under Communist dictatorship, together with the strains caused by Soviet economic demands, result in dissatisfactions which the Communists are impelled to recognize.

Unlike the situation in most of the other Soviet bloc countries, the Czechoslovak Communist Party was legally recognized and relatively large in the pre-war period and had experiences in techniques of winning popular support. It has continued to be a mass party with present membership of 1.7 million, the largest Communist party in the world in proportion to the population, and therefore remains heterogeneous in character harboring nationalist, trade-unionist and pro-Western attitudes to a degree. Furthermore, the sudden accession to full control by a coup in February 1948 and tensions caused by Soviet demands led to difficulties in adjustments of the leadership to the new situation, and drastic wide-spread purges developed culminating apparently in the elimination of dissident factions and consolidation of the top leadership.

Ethnic problems which contributed in 1938–39 to the downfall of the democratic Republic, involving particularly the Sudeten German and Slovak questions, still play a disturbing role. Agitation in Germany for the return of the expelled Sudeten population and the possible reemergence of Germany as a united and dominant power are feared by the Czechs, including the non-communist majority. The Slovaks, who inhabit the eastern two-fifths of the country and comprise a fourth of the population, are of different historical and cultural background from the Czechs, though they are closely related ethnically. The Slovaks are much less highly industrialized, more strongly Catholic, and less anti-German than the Czechs. Slovak nationalist tendencies find expression in the desire for a clearly defined and established autonomy of the Slovak people in a free Czechoslovakia or, with a number of the Slovaks, for the formation of an entirely separate Slovak state. The Czechoslovak Communist Party has had to combat these nationalist tendencies in the party itself. On the other hand, the Slovak question tends to divide anti-Communist forces.

Few if any genuine underground resistance organizations exist in Czechoslovakia, and although there are no Soviet troops stationed there, Moscow's close control over the party police and armed forces assures an effective security system which makes acts of overt resistance rare.

HUNGARY

Hungary, with a population of 9.1 million, is one of the smaller satellites. However, its economic contribution to the USSR and its strategic situation on the Soviet lines of communication with Austria and on the approaches to Italy and the Balkans make it a key satellite from Moscow's viewpoint. Though it has only a narrow and mountainous common frontier[44] with the USSR and hence is less accessible geographically to the latter than Poland or Rumania, it is securely under Soviet military domination owing to the presence of strong Soviet occupation forces within the country and in neighboring Austria and Rumania.

Economically Hungary is important to the USSR as a large producer of foodstuffs, a supplier of certain important raw materials (such as bauxite), and a well developed manufacturing country specializing in fine machinery and electrical equipment. A very rapid development of engineering, backed by an unprecedented increase in output of such basic materials as coal and steel, was scheduled in the Five-Year Plan of 1950–54, which was revised drastically upward after the outbreak of the Korean war. The speed and concentration of this buildup in the sphere of producer-goods, to the neglect of consumer-goods and agriculture, has created the same supply problems as in other industrial satellites. Once a big exporter of foodstuffs, Hungary (following two bad drought years in 1950 and 1952) is now experiencing food scarcities. A factor here has been the steady socialization of agriculture, which now ranks with that of Czechoslovakia in proportion of arable land (about 40 percent) in collectives and state farms.

Sovietization and Soviet control face peculiar difficulties in Hungary, owing to historical Russophobia and to the traditional cultural pattern, which is directly antithetical to the Slav-Byzantine cultural forms. This antipathy is reinforced by memories of an earlier Soviet-type regime in 1919, the only such case of repetition in the orbit. In religion the strong Roman Catholic and Calvinist traditions work as primary institutional forces tying the nation to the West and delaying psychological socialization, though the church leadership has largely bowed to state control.

The Hungarian Communist regime does not have a historically strong Communist party behind it to provide even minority support of any significance. The Hungarian Workers' (Communist) Party is largely a postwar creation out of heterogeneous elements and contains internal tensions of its own, including latent enmity between Moscow-trained and domestically produced leaders. A distinctive feature is the fact that the now dominant, Moscow-trained leadership is headed almost solidly by Jews—a fact of widely ramifying implications for party cohesiveness in a country with traditional anti-semitic tendencies.

RUMANIA

Rumania, with a population of 16 million, is the third largest of the Soviet European satellites and is of strategic and economic importance to the USSR. Geographically it is the key to Soviet control of the Danube basin and Balkan peninsula. Its long common land and sea frontier with the USSR and topographic continuity with the Soviet Ukraine and Moldavia facilitate Soviet military access and domination, which is further ensured by the presence of strong Soviet occupation forces nominally serving as line-of-communication troops for Soviet forces in Austria.

---

[44] In reality the Soviet-Hungarian border was on a plain.

Modern Rumanian cultural and political life has been oriented very pronouncedly toward Western Europe. The national tradition inclines to Russophobia, intensified by hostility to the Soviet system. The Communist Party was never large nor strong. No Communist-dominated partisan forces developed during the war, and the Party played no significant role in the events of August 1944 by which on King Michael's initiative the country was realigned on the side of the Allies. The subsequent establishment of a Communist dictatorship was due exclusively to Soviet military occupation and the importation of Rumanian and Bessarabian exile Communists from the USSR. The latter were placed in controlling posts through direct Soviet dictation to King Michael by Soviet Foreign Minister Vishinsky[45] in March 1945. Unlike the other satellite regimes, the Rumanian Communist Party underwent no major purges or shifts during the first seven postwar years. The first significant purges, involving Foreign Minister and Politburo member Ana Pauker[46] and two other top Communists, occurred only in 1952 and resulted in the concentration of party and state powers in the hands of the new Premier and Party secretary-general Gheorghe Gheorghiu-Dej. Though Gheorghiu-Dej has some personal following in the Party and among the workers, a large part of the 700,000 Party members are loosely attached, opportunistic postwar recruits to the movement.

Economically Rumania's chief contribution to the Soviet Bloc is its oil industry. Soviet control of this industry and of other enterprises is in part exercised through Soviet-Rumanian joint companies. Under the current Five-Year Plan (1951–55) a number of new manufacturing industries are also being developed, while the electric power base is being greatly expanded. While these developments apparently are proceeding with fewer complications than in Czechoslovakia and Hungary, the inevitable inflationary pressures of the Communist-type development program are much in evidence, resulting, for example, in the imposition of a discriminatory currency reform (January 1952) which does not appear to have provided a basic alleviation or permanent solution for the problem. Rationing and the dual price system are still in effect. In agriculture, which is traditionally the larger sphere of the Rumanian economy, approximately 23 percent of the arable land has been socialized in either collective farms ("producer cooperatives") or state farms, and collectivization is gradually being pushed further.

Though both economic and political conditions cause general dissatisfaction, particularly among the peasantry, there is virtually no attempt to conduct organized resistance or evasion, except on the part of occasional scattered bands in mountain districts. Popular disaffection is expressed mainly through individual acts of evasion or economic sabotage, listening to Western radio broadcasts, and occasional individual flights abroad.

BULGARIA

Bulgaria, with a predominantly agricultural population of 7.3 million, is one of the smallest and economically least developed of the satellites. Owing however to its numerically strong and highly sovietized armed forces and to its forward geographical position at the southern end of the orbit, it has an important role for Moscow as a military and strategic outpost of the USSR. Soviet military access to Bulgaria is limited to the northern land frontier with Rumania and to the sea frontier on the east; on the other sides the country is exposed to anti-Soviet states allied with the West: Turkey and Greece on the south and Yugoslavia on the west. Nevertheless Soviet military domination, based on the proximity of strong Soviet forces in Rumania and the USSR and on direct control of the Bulgarian armed forces themselves by Soviet officers, appears secure.

[45] Andrei Ya. Vishinskii was in fact deputy foreign minister when this mission took place; he became foreign minister in 1949.

[46] Anna Pauker was a member of the Politburo and foreign minister from 1949–1952. Charged with offenses against the collective leadership and right-wing deviation, she was relieved of her posts and expelled from the party in 1952.

This direct control through Soviet personnel, which extends also to the key branches of the government, is a more pronounced feature of the Bulgarian Communist regime than of most other satellites. It originated in the Soviet military occupation at the end of the war, and in the fact that the Soviet-installed regime consisted in large part of Soviet-trained Communists, many of them Soviet-Bulgarian dual citizens who had spent the war years in the USSR. The relatively greater direct control by the USSR in Bulgaria is also undoubtedly motivated by the relatively backward character of the country and by its strategic importance.

The Bulgarian Communist regime is based on a party with a well-marked tradition, whose leadership in the 1920's and 1930's was the strongest of any of the Balkan Communist parties. Since the war, however, the leadership has undergone more top-level alteration through death and purging than most other satellite regimes and has been reduced to mediocrity. At present it is composed of remnants both of the "Muscovite" (i.e. dominant Moscow-trained) element and of the "nativist"-element, which are subservient to Moscow without being either efficient or (in the Kremlin's view) completely dependable.

Economically Bulgaria remains essentially a backward agricultural country in the rudimentary stages of partial industrialization. The first phase of industrialization initially involved expansion of textile and food-processing industries and at present is concerned with construction of electric power facilities, certain basic processing industries (principally chemicals and building materials), and a few machinery assembly installations. It should also be noted that there are several uranium mines in the Balkan mountains northeast of Sofia. In agriculture, collectivization has been pushed farther, and at an earlier date, than in any other satellite. Today over 50 percent of the arable land is comprised in the so-called socialist sector—mainly in the producer cooperatives, as there are few state farms.

Bulgaria is linked closely to Russia culturally and historically, and has a Russophile tradition. Russia played a prime role in helping establish an independent Bulgarian state in the 19th century, free of Turkish rule. Nevertheless the effects of present Soviet control over Bulgaria have negated rather than enhanced this tradition owing to widespread resentment of the Soviet-imposed dictatorship and Soviet economic exploitation.

ALBANIA

Albania is the smallest and most primitive of the satellites, and has a population of only 1.2 million—mainly peasants—of whom a large proportion are mountaineers. It is also the only one of the Soviet European satellites which is geographically isolated from the rest of the Soviet bloc. As such, it presents a peculiar problem to the Soviets whose only uninterrupted access to Albania is by sea. Because of this, Soviet control is based not so much upon military domination as it is upon a strategic infiltration, by reliable Soviet personnel, of the entire Albanian political, economic, and military structure, coupled with skillful exploitation of traditional Albanian fears of the territorial aspirations of neighboring states.

Soviet control is, of course, exercised through the Communist puppet regime under the dual leadership of the Premier and party Chairman Enver Hoxha and Interior Minister Mehmet Shehu.[47] There was never any significant Communist movement in Albania before the war, and the present regime stems from the successful efforts of a small group of determined Communists who won control of the Albanian underground movement during the war and seized power with aid from the Yugoslav communists as the Germans withdrew.

In its beginnings the Albanian communist regime was closely dependent upon Yugoslavia. After Tito's split with the Cominform in 1948 the regime went through a series of drastic purges of alleged pro-Titoist elements. At present it appears firmly wedded to the Cominform and fully capable of controlling any potential internal opposition.

---

[47] Mehmet Shehu was a member of the Albanian Party of Labor's Political Committee, minister of the interior and deputy prime minister beginning in 1948, and became head of the government in 1954.

The regime maintains its control through reliance on an elaborate security system, a number of concentration and forced labor camps and the other communist methods of police terror and intimidation. Its weakness lies in its failure to convert the majority of Albanians. Hostility to the regime is reported to be widespread, extending even into the ranks of the army and into elements of the security and police forces. The party itself, on the local level, is loosely organized and composed in many cases of those who have joined for opportunistic rather than ideological reasons. While not of a degree actually to endanger the regime's control, there is probably more passive and active opposition to the Communist regime in Albania than in most of the other European satellites.

Economic conditions in Albania have deteriorated markedly under the Communists. The situation is aggravated by the country's present isolation from its natural trade sources in the west and Soviet insistence on development of mining and industry at the expense of agriculture. At present the food supply is very insufficient and determined efforts to collectivize agriculture, which have resulted to date in socialization of approximately 6 percent of the arable land, have not served to increase production. Malnutrition and lack of clothing, fuel and medical assistance have had serious repercussions on the morale of the people. In recognition of this situation the USSR and other satellites have been forced to extend substantial economic assistance to Albania. Without this assistance the Hoxha regime could not remain in power for any length of time.

Albania's geographic isolation makes it the most vulnerable of any of the satellites. Albanians, however, fear that Albania's liberation from the Soviet orbit might result not in an independent Albania, but in a partition of the country between some or all of the neighboring states of Yugoslavia, Greece, and Italy. All of these countries have traditional aspirations to Albania or Albanian territory which none has convincingly renounced. Further, these neighboring countries mistrust each other's intentions toward Albania. As a result of this situation the present regime has been able to represent itself to the Albanians, with considerable success, as the only true guarantor of Albanian territorial integrity.

EASTERN GERMANY

The Soviet Zone of Occupation in Germany, which was nominally transformed into a satellite by Soviet creation of the puppet Communist regime of the "German Democratic Republic" in October 1949, is the latest of the orbit states formed on this model and is the second in size, with a population of 18.5 million. In addition to its high strategic importance to Moscow in the struggle for control of all of Germany, Eastern Germany makes an important economic contribution to Soviet power by virtue of its highly developed and specialized industries.

East German progress toward effective satellite status has been slowed by its peculiar character as part of a larger Germany under divided occupation, and by Soviet overall German policy, including Moscow's professed desire for restoration of a unified and independent Germany. The proximity of free German territory, a West German government, and strong Western military forces in conjunction with the unsettled and dynamic character of the struggle of the Western Powers and the USSR in Germany, has tended to encourage hopes of a change and resistance to Soviet controls among the East German population, despite the presence of a powerful Soviet army of occupation. In mid-1952 Soviet strategy shifted toward a more rapid and undisguised creation of a completely bolshevized state in Eastern Germany. There is no evidence that this goal has been abandoned though progress toward it has again been slowed since early June 1953.

The East German state apparatus is for all practical purposes managed through and by the Socialist Unity Party (SED), a Communist-dominated organization formed in 1946 through the Soviet-prompted fusion of Social Democrats with the Communists of the Soviet Zone. The Communists have attempted to convert the SED into a Soviet-type Communist party, but it still remains a rather heterogeneous and unwieldy organization, with 1.4 million members. It has been unable to obtain strong working-class support. A portion of the youth, owing to intensive indoctrination and a youth-slanted Communist program, apparently has come to furnish the largest single element of support for the regime outside of the SED itself.

Within the framework of SED control of political life, a number of non-Communist political parties are permitted to continue on a very limited basis, as part of the Soviet policy of maintaining a facade of political freedom in Eastern Germany. These include the Christian Democratic Union (155,000 members), the Liberal Democratic Party (100,000), the National Democratic Party (50,000), and the Democratic Peasant Party (30,000). All are subservient to and dependent on the SED. Aside from political parties the Protestant Church, embracing approximately three-fourths of the East German population, represents the only other major institution retaining some independence. As a competing center of spiritual allegiance, however, it too is currently under strong state pressure to conform to the program of the regime.

In the absence of mass support, the regime exerts control by the normal authoritarian methods. In mid-1952 its efforts to isolate the population physically from contact with the West increased sharply, particularly with regard to movement between East and West Germany. These efforts have been only partially successful. Movement continues on a significant scale across the frontier between East and West Berlin. This gap in the East German security belt is also a gap in psychological control since relatively easy access to West Berlin has facilitated refutation of Communist propaganda regarding Western conditions. Moreover, the presence of Western forces in Berlin is a major obstacle to the full consolidation of Communist control over East Germany. The principal East German vulnerabilities to Western political warfare are the continuing East German sense of remaining a part of the community of the West; the desire for a united Germany, the example and attractive power of West Germany; and the fact that the East German regime patently represents Soviet rather than German interests and is recasting East Germany in the Soviet and satellite mold.

In early June, 1953 the East German Government announced a series of measures largely economic and social in nature modifying and in some cases apparently halting aspects of the Sovietization program. This change may have been motivated in part by the realization that the pace of industrialization and rearmament was too ambitious for East German resources and was, along with increasing political repression, creating dangerous popular resentment though the new program also conformed with current Soviet moves in the international sphere. Popular resentment was at any rate demonstrated by a wave of strikes and riots on June 16 and 17 which forced the employment of Soviet troops and the declaration of martial law. Despite some continuing reprisals against participants in the disturbances and other possible steps to counteract future riots, the regime seems for the present to be continuing certain measures of relaxation.

[Source: NARA, FOIA (Mandatory Review Release to the National Security Archive). Fully declassified version available from the National Security Archive, "Soviet Flashpoints" Collection.]

DOCUMENT NO. 4: Notes of Discussion between the CPSU CC Presidium and a HWP Leadership Delegation in Moscow, May 5, 1954

Early in 1954, a stalemate between the orthodox Stalinist Mátyás Rákosi and the reformist Imre Nagy paralyzed the Hungarian communist leadership. However, in early May, the CPSU Central Committee Presidium summoned leaders of the HWP to Moscow for talks. The Soviet leadership reprimanded Rákosi and his associate, Ernő Gerő, who was responsible for running the Hungarian economy. Nagy came in for criticism as well, but the Presidium supported his basic program of reforms which gave him a temporary advantage in the power game with Rákosi. These minutes of the negotiations also shed light on the highly unequal relationship that existed between the Soviet party leadership and the rulers of the satellite states. Khrushchev and his colleagues' authority to rebuke and give orders to the HWP leaders is unquestioned by the Hungarians here.

Present: comrades Malenkov, Khrushchev, Voroshilov, Kaganovich, Bulganin, Mikoyan, Suslov, Zorin[48] and Kiselev; and comrades Rákosi, Nagy, Gerő, Farkas, Hidas and Hegedüs.

(These notes were compiled on the basis of memos by comrades Farkas, Hidas and Hegedüs.)

1. Comrade Rákosi presents the report of the delegation.
2. Questions:

Comrade Bulganin: Do the delegates find the proposed changes in the Central Committee too farfetched, and the role of the ex-social democrats too meager?

Comrade Malenkov: How do you describe the new course?

Comrade Voroshilov: What is there about the unity of the Political Committee? Is it not unclear in the report? Did the delegates reveal the situation honestly?

Comrade Kaganovich: What is the situation of the class struggle in the villages and separately in the urban areas? What is the attitude towards the *kulaks*?

Comrade Khrushchev: What is their idea about developing agricultural cooperatives? How do they secure the conditions necessary for planned development?

The response of Comrade Rákosi.

Debate:

Comrade Mikoyan: Hungary has undoubtedly achieved remarkable results, but not without mistakes. I mainly want to focus on economic policy.

Economic difficulties are debilitating. It was a good year in agriculture, yet the gathering of crops and taxes is slower than expected. This is the reason behind inflation in Hungary, as there are not enough goods produced to counterbalance the extra money that was issued. A sure sign of inflation is the 600 million Forint deficit in the foreign trade balance.

This is the most dangerous enemy of reinforcing the worker-peasant alliance in a country like Hungary, where small-scale farming has such significance. Curbing investments is not the only solution to the problem.

The situation is all the more serious, because in 1953 there were fewer textiles, shoes, and soap produced for the peasantry than in 1952. The first quarter of 1954 brought no improvement either.

It is obvious that these are by no means healthy phenomena for the Hungarian people's economy.

Many investments are stalled, the total sum of deferred investments has mounted from 5 to 13 billion. Administrative expenses are extremely high. Solutions to economic problems are being sought timidly and only under the pressure of circumstances.

---

[48] Valerian A. Zorin was a candidate member of the CPSU CC Presidium from 1956 and deputy foreign minister between 1947–1955 and 1956–1965.

The National Planning Office is anticipating the intense development of heavy industry for the second five-year plan. If 87 billion is targeted, as opposed to 45 billion in the first five-year term—naturally more will be achieved—then this is exactly the old policy.

One telling example is that although you have no foundry coke and iron ore, you intend to raise crude iron production by 86 percent in the second five-year plan. On the other hand, you have idle capacities as well. You suffer a shortage of energy, yet 35 percent of your power generation is unused. Wine growing is a traditionally important branch of agriculture in your country, and yet overall grape production was halved last year.

Expenditures and income must be balanced. A favorable situation has to be created so that peasants are willing to sell their products for money.

Comrade Khrushchev: There seem to be problems concerning mutual agreement and consensus within the Political Committee. The comrades are not quarreling but apparently they are not in complete harmony either.

These questions are not to be dismissed or shrugged off. But you get together and dismiss them. There is no mutual agreement between comrades Rákosi and Nagy.

Comrade Rákosi embellishes the situation prior to June [1953]. He deeply embraces the mistakes, so it is hard for him to accept that those were mistakes.

We consider his case similar to that of our office worker, whom we asked if he believed in God; he replied, "When in the office, I don't, when at home, I do."

Comrade Rákosi acknowledges the mistakes when at Political Committee and the Central Committee meetings, but then denies or belittles them when at home. Party members, however, are aware of this duality, and it does not help party unity.

Comrade Rákosi blames Beria's provocation to explain bringing up the mistakes so sharply, and he thinks that, once we have shot Beria, the criticism has to be shot down as well. This is not correct, though. Actually there were mistakes, and we too, criticized those mistakes, not just Beria.

Mistakes must be considered, criticized and corrected. Mostly because your mistakes are the mistakes of the party as well.

Comrade Rákosi is a venerable and experienced communist, and he has to find courage to admit the mistakes and take the wheel in correcting them.

Comrade Nagy, on the other hand, is the other extreme. His criticism is correct, but it is not the right thing to point out only mistakes to the party membership. One has to be just and appreciate the positive results as well.

Comrade Nagy only emphasizes the mistakes; although he knows that there are achievements too, he never mentions those.

Comrade Nagy is talking about mistakes, comrade Rákosi is presenting the results. That is why the party is said to have a dual line of policy, which is most unfavorable.

Comrade Nagy has to tell about achievements, and comrade Rákosi has to face the mistakes. If so, people will understand that there are not two lines.

Comrade Rákosi mentioned that prisoners in Hungary now all want to prove their innocence. This is not a crime in itself. However, their innocence or culpability is not a question of making an agreement with them, but a matter of justice, a decision based on facts.

Comrade Rákosi has not a small responsibility for many people being unjustly convicted, since these verdicts were agreed upon with him. Nonetheless, comrade Rákosi is slow to correct the mistakes. These questions have to be handled with manly courage, and the process of releasing those innocently convicted must be speeded up. Hosts of people were arrested and convicted innocently in your country; true enough, some of these cases were prompted from here.

These questions are not being resolved in your country because comrade Rákosi has no firm opinion in the matter. I remind you that there was a time when the air was palpably electrified around comrade Nagy as well, when people did not trust him. This is another question to clear up and answer.

Maybe mistakes have to be corrected in a different way in Hungary than in our country, considering that the CPSU is stronger than your party. Mistakes have to be corrected so that comrade Rákosi can preserve his dignity, because his [dignity] involves the party's dignity at the same time. We criticize comrade Rákosi but do not widely publicize our criticism.

It is not the right opinion, though, that the arrested should stay in prison until they can prove their innocence. Comrade Rákosi refrains from handling this issue with due courage because he himself had a lot to do with these convictions. Comrade Nagy, on the other hand, is more courageous in the matter, as he gave no orders for arrests.

Mistakes are to be corrected discreetly so that the reputation of both comrade Rákosi and the central commitee is preserved.

These are the fundamental questions, and if you resolve them properly, you resolve all the other problems properly at the same time. Failing, however, could sever the whole leadership.

As to the issue of agriculture. I witnessed a discussion between comrade Rákosi and comrade Stalin about the collectivization of agriculture. Comrade Stalin was warning against hasty collectivization at that time, and suggested a circumspect pace instead.

Collectivization, however, needs constant attention; its process cannot be left unguarded. At the time of collectivization I was working in Ukraine, where we had to face a serious class struggle. All the same, we finished collectivization three years earlier than in Belorussia. As a result, cooperatives are much more stable in Ukraine than in Belorussia.

Naturally we have to create the right environment for the development of cooperatives, but one has to accept the fact that it coincides with an intense class struggle with the *kulaks*, and it is impossible to achieve any results without exerting pressure on the middle peasantry.

We have to create the conditions of collectivization, something that comrade Rákosi forgot to talk about. We need technical background. Lenin was talking about 100,000 tractors; you have proportionately more than that. Party workers who can become leaders of cooperatives also have to be trained.

Much attention has to be paid to the existing cooperatives, that 18 percent.[49] If productivity is higher in cooperatives, individual farmers will join, otherwise they will stay away.

We used to transfer 25,000 workers who had no agricultural skills to the villages. You can do it on a higher professional level.

The problem is that you have no detailed plan for collectivization. A definite plan has to be made.

The error in your agricultural strategy is that the area sown with corn is to be reduced.

I am afraid that Soviet consultants gave you incorrect advice.

We have [made] serious achievements in the cereals production, but root crops are more problematic. We had no machinery to cultivate root crops. We have solved this problem by now; we have square drills, cultivators, corn harvesters, etc. This is a decisive factor when it comes to meat production.

Through the system of machine parks, you have to equip cooperatives with these machines. It is a mistake that you do not ask us for square drills for checkrow sowing, while other people's democracies have already bought some.

If you find a solution for the motorized farming of root crops, you will be more productive, which creates a different situation, and you will be able to achieve the target set for the year 1960 earlier.

It is far from me to hasten the process of collectivization, but I do not agree with its retardation either.

Comrade Voroshilov: On the question of unity, I share the views of comrade Khrushchev.

Last time, when we were discussing the relationship of the party and the state with you, comrades, the question came up: who is subordinated to whom? In fact, there is no subordination at any level—everyone is subordinate to the will of the party.

Comrade Nagy says that everything was wrong. Comrade Rákosi says that everything was right. Neither of them is right, though.

---

[49] Khrushchev is confusing different pieces of information here. The material sent by the HWP did not state that 18 percent of cooperatives remained after 1953, but that 18 percent of cultivated land belonged to the cooperatives.

An enormous task is awaiting you, and if you cannot find the common denominator you will see no results. However valuable you are individually for the party and the state, this cannot lead to party interests being relegated into the background. I disagree with the fact that you both have a separate circle of friends.

It is needless to talk about who ranks first and who comes second.

I have seen your cooperatives; they are extremely weak. You have to aim at creating sample cooperatives. Hungarian peasants are intelligent—if they see that it is better to be in a cooperative, they will not shy away. In your cooperatives, there is too much freedom for withdrawal on the one hand, and nobody should be kept from joining on the other hand. Spontaneity has to stop.

The problem of those who have been arrested but are innocent is indeed a serious issue. Revisions have to be carried out more quickly yet thoroughly.

The issue should not be overemphasized either, as there are real criminals and spies who should not be confused with the innocent.

Revisions in Hungary are disappointing for the time being.

These mistakes ought to be presented as if they were committed by Gábor Péter.

Once again, I have to stress that unity in the leadership is a decisive issue.

Comrade Kaganovich: The Bolshevik openness of comrade Khrushchev is most appropriate and much needed. It is not the first time that we bring up these issues, yet there have been no fundamental changes so far. Economic policy mistakes have not been corrected. The [state] apparatus is changing your policy when it comes to practical execution.

While the production of heavy industry increased by 18 percent in 1953, light industry decreased.

The ratio of industrial and agricultural production shows defects as well.

The numbers that comrade Rákosi was talking about are reconstructed.

You are living in greater style than your means permit. You are building socialism on credit. You want to build everything at once, that we have been building for 30–35 years now. You are building too many sanitariums, schools, technical schools, etc.

You are determined to make changes but you are slow to carry out those changes.

I do agree with the remarks of the preceding speakers; there are three fundamental issues:

1. Rendering unity in the leadership, restoring the correct relationship between comrades Rákosi and Nagy.

2. Collectivization of agriculture, and generally the situation of the villages.

We were guarding our remaining cooperatives as the most precious treasure. You, on the other hand, made serious mistakes and veered from the path of cooperative agriculture. There are ideas, according to which socialism can be achieved in two different ways: through cooperatives and by means of individual peasant farming. You have given up your positions in the villages.

You were basically on the right path in collectivization but made mistakes.

If you keep spending lavishly and do not support agricultural cooperatives, the mistakes will prevail.

3. The party leadership's method.

It is most undesirable that you copied the CPSU's post-war leadership techniques. Leadership has to emphasize democracy. It is most disagreeable that the June Central Committee decree has not been announced yet, and the guidelines that were presented instead do not comply with the Central Committee decisions.

The prevailing shortcomings need to be criticized without reserve, because this is the only way to enhance the party's reputation.

Comrade Bulganin: I do agree with the notes of my comrades, the previous speakers.

Comrade Rákosi said that he had discipline problems in the army, that there is opposition between the general staff and the political chief division, besides other problems.

The CPSU Central Committee discussed the issue of their relationship to the military forces of people's democracies. The general opinion is that the Soviet Union's Ministry of National

Defense has to deal with the people's democracies' armies with a more direct approach. One of our Soviet army generals has been commissioned to manage the task.

We would like to see for ourselves the situation in your army. Organizational statutes must not be issued. Such questions need delicate handling when it comes to the military.

Last autumn I met comrade [István] Bata, and I was much impressed by him. He needs support and assistance; his reputation has to be increased. It is necessary that comrade Farkas help him as much as he can.

Comrade Malenkov: I would like to address comrade Rákosi. I do agree with the previous speakers. We are seriously worried about the situation in the HWP leadership.

What is the problem with comrade Rákosi?

We acknowledge comrade Rákosi's merits as leader of the HWP. His reputation has to be retained by all means.

We repeatedly discussed the mistakes but their correction is an all-too-slow process, especially because comrade Rákosi could not take the lead in correcting the mistakes.

The main problems are those of the villages and of planning.

Your second five-year plan is still aiming at an excessive rate of industrialization. True enough that you rejected this guideline, but you also failed to come up with an alternative for the future work. That is why the National Planning Office is making the plans alone, which are therefore wrong. The administration is managing you. You forget that a plan that has not been rejected still lingers on in people's consciousness.

You have to correct the mistakes of wrongful arrests, but not in a crude and demonstrative manner. Comrade Rákosi has to deal with this issue himself.

Comrade Rákosi says he is tired, but that is not the issue here; rather, he has lost faith in correcting those mistakes.

[It is] comrade Nagy's misapprehension, on the other hand, that he cannot see what is right. In correcting the mistakes, though, it is comrade Rákosi who has the lion's share.

As to the people's economy, things are changing to the worse. We suggested comrade Gerő concentrate solely on economic issues. This question has to be solved.

The question of why the National Planning Office is making plans that oppose party policy has to be examined.

Mistakes must be discussed with due openness.

What good was it to negotiate without the presence of comrade Nagy in this situation, as comrade Rákosi previously suggested? It is necessary that comrade Rákosi acknowledge his mistake.

From words we must turn to action. It is not good that it was we who had to initiate the exploration of mistakes; this is first of all comrade Rákosi's responsibility.

You are looking forward to a party congress, so this is the time to reveal the mistakes.

4. Speeches of the delegates.

(Comrades Nagy, Gerő, Farkas, Hegedüs and Hidas)

The following important notes were made:

Comrade Khrushchev noted concerning the speech of comrade Nagy:

It is not enough that the leadership has shown improvement since last June, the leadership has to be good.

Comrade Nagy is mitigating the mistakes; he is being too diplomatic.

5. *The concluding speech of Comrade Khrushchev:*

The speeches of the Hungarian comrades, especially that of comrade Hidas prompt me to ask to speak again. I would not like anyone to misunderstand what I have said about comrade Rákosi's reputation. What I said, I do maintain, without regret, but it does not mean that the mistakes of comrade Rákosi deserve temperance. All the more so, as he seems to be sticking to his mistakes obstinately. I would like you to understand that by preserving his reputation I do not mean to gloss over his mistakes. The reputation of the leader need not be preserved at all costs, at the expense of the party's reputation. The party's reputation is of highest importance.

If comrade Rákosi is not willing to take the initiative in correcting the mistakes, then this has to be carried out by the community, otherwise the reputation of comrade Rákosi, the Political Committee, and the whole party will be destroyed. If he is reluctant to lead in correcting mistakes, then it will happen above his head, which is a true catastrophe for a leader.

In the meantime, comrade Malenkov made the following notes:

It is unreasonable that comrade Rákosi keeps mentioning the differences in quality between the older and younger members of the Political Committee. Instead of emphasizing the disparity, young members need to be raised to a higher level.

Comrade Khrushchev also brought up the following:

It is disagreeable to emphasize the increase in the ratio of intellectuals within the party's leading organizations. First and foremost, we are the party of the working classes, which has to be taken into account. It is the working class who engage in the struggle against capitalism.

András Hegedüs
Mihály Farkas
István Hidas

[Source: MOL, 276. f. 102/66. ő.e. Published in János M. Rainer and Károly Urbán, eds., "'Konzultációk:' Dokumentumok a magyar és szovjet pártvezetok két moszkvai találkozójáról 1954–1955-ben," Múltunk 37, no. 4 (1992): 143–141. Translated by Csaba Farkas.]

DOCUMENT NO. 5: Notes of Discussion between the CPSU CC Presidium and a HWP Leadership Delegation in Moscow on January 8, 1955

These notes on the negotiations between the CPSU CC Presidium and the Hungarian Politburo, held in the Kremlin on January 8, 1955, convey information about a new chapter in the political struggle between Mátyás Rákosi and Imre Nagy that had been unfolding since June 1953. By the time he returned from a long health-related vacation in November 1954, Rákosi had already learned of the latest shift in Moscow's political line away from supporting reform. Western moves to include the Federal Republic of Germany in NATO, along with political fermentation in Hungary caused by Nagy's policies, were arousing uneasiness in Moscow. Soviet criticism was therefore directed mainly at the "rightist mistakes" of the Hungarian premier. In a peculiar but characteristic way, the Soviet leaders also blamed Nagy for introducing policies which they themselves had originally proposed. Nonetheless, at this point Khrushchev had not yet planned Nagy's removal from the Hungarian leadership. As he put it: "We sharply criticized comrade Nagy but always from a party-minded position. We want to be on your side." Nagy's unwillingness to practice self-criticism, however, foreshadowed his imminent fall from power.

JANUARY 12

Present: comrades Bulganin, Voroshilov, Kaganovich, Malenkov, Molotov, Mikoyan, Pervukhin,[50] Saburov,[51] Khrushchev and Suslov—members and candidate members of the Presidium of the Soviet Union [sic], comrade Andropov, the Soviet Union's ambassador in Hungary, and comrade Stepanov, head of the International Department of the Communist Party of the Soviet Union.

Delegates of the Hungarian Workers' Party's Political Committee were comrades Mátyás Rákosi, Imre Nagy, Mihály Farkas, Lajos Ács[52] and Béla Szalai.

Date of the meeting: January 8, 1955, 3 to 7 p.m.

Once comrades Rákosi, Nagy, Farkas, Ács and Szalai had presented their opinion about the main issues of Hungary's political and economic situation, with special emphasis on the palpable conflicts within the party leadership and their possible causes, members of the Communist Party of the Soviet Union's Presidium made remarks on the proposed questions.

Comrade Voroshilov: It is most peculiar that very soon after the successful 3rd Congress of the Hungarian Workers' Party, and despite the serious discussion that followed the congress, the situation within the party has become aggravated. Most of all, comrade Imre Nagy is to blame. However, it is not only his fault; the mistakes and responsibility of other members of the Political Committee have to be looked at. Criticism must be aligned with party principles.

The article by comrade Nagy[53] is not in keeping with party principles, as it leads to the discrediting of certain comrades. (Interruption by comrade Khrushchev: It only happens when someone holds a different line within the party. Comrade Nagy holds a different line.)

The country's political and economic issues should not be considered exclusively with the peasantry in mind. The ratio of small-scale farming is still very high in Hungary. (Comrade Rákosi: 1,600,000 peasant families.) Smallholders' farms revitalize capitalism by the day. Land is not nationalized in Hungary. Those who do not take this into consideration are undoubtedly

---

[50] Mikhail G. Pervukhin was a member of the CPSU CC from 1939–1961 and of the CC Presidium from 1952–1957, and served as first deputy prime minister from 1955–1957.

[51] Maxim Z. Saburov was a member of the CPSU CC Presidium from 1952–1957 and first deputy prime minister from 1955–1957.

[52] Lajos Ács was a member of the HWP CC and PC, and served as CC secretary from 1953 to October 24, 1956.

[53] Imre Nagy, "A Központi Vezetőség ülése után" (After the meeting of the Central Committee), *Szabad Nép*, October 20, 1954.

wrong, representing false opinions. Comrade Nagy is intelligent and smart, but he is not firm enough in his principles. He wanted to defer the implementation of land reform.

Comrade Nagy is conceited and undisciplined. It is a shame that the Political Committee lacks discipline. How can we expect discipline within the party if the nine members of the leading body are without control? Who has authorized comrade Nagy to do whatever he pleases, and disregard what the majority wants, even if his opinion is contrary to that of the majority? He is obliged to keep to the decisions of the majority, instead of turning to the public against certain members of the Political Committee. Discipline in the party is most important, above all.

Neglecting industry is not only incorrect but outright dangerous. If there is no heavy industry and it does not develop gradually, then we cannot advance.

These questions have to be considered thoroughly and on an even keel. You are all intelligent and communists—mistakes can be corrected. Comrade Nagy has to admit his mistakes unconditionally. These are grievous mistakes—appealing to the public against certain members of the Political Committee—bordering on treason.

Comrade Molotov: Is there an economic and political crisis in Hungary? Perhaps crisis is too strong a word, but the situation is certainly very serious. Had it not been for the neighboring Soviet Union, which granted economic support to Hungary, and for the friendly neighboring states, you would not be able to conduct such debates. The people's democracy would not be sustained for long in Hungary. Productivity has not increased over the year, which is a sure sign of economic decline [*razlozhenie*]. You created a public climate that is most unfavorable for productivity, without which a single year cannot be survived. What would have happened if the Soviet Union and the friendly countries had not helped?

In July 1953, comrade Nagy was lobbying in his speech for the peasants to leave the agricultural cooperatives. (Interruption by comrade Nagy: it was not my idea. We were given advice here. Comrade Dobi objected to the idea at the time.) Indeed, Beria gave you such advice at the time, but after Beria's arrest we warned you to think twice and be careful. Comrade Nagy supported the withdrawal from the cooperatives with much pathos, which aggravates his mistake.

Comrade Nagy's article on October 20, 1954, is not our article. He does not discuss the questions from a communist point of view. The main question is the worker-peasant alliance. Is the heart of the alliance really the exchange of goods between the town and the village? An entirely false opinion. When we communists refer to the worker-peasant alliance, we always point out that the leading role of the working class has to be strengthened. The worker-peasant alliance must always serve the building of socialism. Comrade Nagy believes that collectivization in the Soviet Union was not conducted in the right way. Nonetheless, what would have happened to the Soviet Union if we had not accomplished collectivization? We constantly raise the productivity level in industry and agriculture and strengthen cooperatives in the Soviet Union. This is a path that one can walk. Comrade Nagy's opinion reflects the view of the petit bourgeoisie. You have to correct this mistake.

The party and people's democracy came to life in June 1953? Your decision of June 1953 is a manifesto? You only started to correct the mistakes you made the previous year. We made many mistakes as well. All the same, our work, just as yours, was fundamentally correct until June 1953. You could achieve serious results before June 1953. Just think about the achievement of [creating a] people's democracy and the Constitution, etc. Disregarding all this is a serious mistake.

Most people in Hungary are not communists. If comrade Nagy relies predominantly on them instead of the party, you will ruin what you have built so far. Counting on the petit bourgeoisie is a dangerous game.

You said that you are unable to work together with comrade Rákosi. There is no better leadership in Hungary than that of comrade Rákosi. Comrade Rákosi used to be one of the leaders of the Comintern. He is experienced and well-known all over the world. Comrade Nagy has two choices: [to stand] with the party or against the party. Mistakes must be corrected—in writing.

Comrade Kaganovich: The article of October 20, 1954, is very much like the manifesto of the Provisional Government. Most dangerous. The Soviet Union liberated Hungary. Why did comrade Nagy fail to mention that in the article? You do not write about what happened in the last ten years either. You think that everything is wrong. This is not our opinion. Comrade Nagy is under considerable pressure from the enemy. His aggressive attitude is very dangerous. His ideas reflect the opinion of the petit bourgeoisie and partly that of the enemy. In the past, the Communist Party of the Soviet Union had to retreat sometimes. Yet we never withdrew with pathos. It is inappropriate that you talk about mistakes with pathos. The definition "new era" is wrong. This is not a Marxist definition. Comrade Nagy does not understand Marxism and the class struggle. The *kulaks* are getting stronger. When you talk about the standard of living, you support the village bourgeoisie. The motto of prosperity was the catchword of Bukharin. There is nothing new in your slogan. You simply rehash some ideas that have been already smashed in the Soviet Union.

Why is comrade Nagy so aggressive? Because he relies on others around him. It was a mistake that comrade Farkas suggested writing the article. Comrade Nagy relies on him. The situation was the following: comrade Rákosi is away, so comrade Nagy poses as the leader of the Hungarian people and proclaims a manifesto. As comrades, we have to say what we think, and we would like you to admit your mistakes. Comrade Rákosi is well-known all over the world; he is a venerable Comintern member. How can you say that either you go or Rákosi goes? Why does the party have to be without you? It would be much better if you could correct your mistakes and carry on working as before.

Comrade Malenkov: He read the article with considerable anxiety. Had it not been signed by comrade Nagy, we would have thought that it was written by someone alien to the notion of Marxism. Rotten movements hide behind comrade Nagy. For instance, there is the proposition to dismiss the DISZ.

Such a fact in itself should suffice for comrade Nagy to become anxious. What good is it if he is outright against a majority of the party leadership? Should the others come out too? It is enormously damaging to the party.

Comrade Nagy has false opinions about the peasantry, about party direction of the people's front, questions of economy and discipline. These false opinions are deplorable. He caused serious damage to the party. Allegedly some 50 people heard about the intention to lower the standard of living in Hungary. You thought you might write your opinion for the whole country now. It has to be admitted that the rightist danger is very great for you [in Hungary]. The source of danger has to be eradicated. Mistakes have to be admitted honestly. It is not right to quote the mistakes of the past all the time. The term "new course" is not right either.

Comrade Nagy is working in the wrong environment. The idea that he refuses to work with Rákosi is disreputable for a party member. Comrade Farkas was not doing the right thing. We are not aware of all the facts but he encouraged Nagy with his behavior. When the article was published, comrade Farkas was outraged that it was not presented to him in time. Then the article by Vas[54] was published. Why did you fail to make sure that more articles of this kind would not be printed again? (Comrade Khrushchev's interruption: Vas is hiding behind comrade Nagy, while comrade Nagy stalls him.) (Comrade Voroshilov's interruption: Vas is not an honest man, he has to be dismissed.)

The leadership's reputation is decreasing in Hungary, mostly because some are demonstrating against the CC. (Comrades Nagy and Vas.) We have to concentrate on comrade Nagy's mistakes. He has to condemn his mistakes—this is the only way to go. Comrade Farkas also has to draw the right conclusion. Comrade Nagy has to write down for himself what kind of mistakes he has made, then he has to submit it to the Political Committee. Perhaps the Central Committee needs to take part in the decision-making, as the affair has had considerable publicity.

Comrade Bulganin: He completely identifies with the previous speakers.

Comrade Nagy, I consider your line alien to party principles. How can a member of the Political Committee behave like this? The Political Committee decided that you would make a report about topical economic questions in the Central Committee, which is a great honor and is

---

[54] Zoltán Vas, "Az új szakasz gazdaságpolitikájáról" (On the Economic Policy of the New Course), *Szabad Nép*, October 27, 1954. Vas' main "sin" was that his article exposed differences within the party leadership concerning the upcoming economic policy.

a reflection of confidence in you. It was a grave violation of party principles not to give that speech. What would we do in this case in our party? Such a situation is inconceivable in our party.

About your article of October 20, comrade Molotov has expressed our common opinion.

The opinion that comrade Nagy was expressing today goes against party principles. He said he cannot work with Rákosi. Comrade Rákosi is a well-known leader in the international communist movement. He is known in every country and has an international reputation. Raising the question in this way and speaking about resignation is against party principles.

What goal did you have in mind when writing the article? What forces did you want to set in motion, and against whom? You wanted to mobilize ordinary party members and non-party members against the Central Committee. This is anti-party policy. We are all too aware of the technique and consequences of such a struggle. Comrade Nagy has two paths before him. He either admits the mistakes and corrects them, or he turns against the party.

There is no order in the Central Committee. Comrade Rákosi! The Central Committee needs order. You are also responsible for the unruly situation.

Comrade Farkas has not yet expressed his theoretical position concerning the comrade Nagy's mistakes.

Comrade Mikoyan: The comrade Nagy's opinion is incomprehensible. He is alone in the Political Committee with his ideas. He crudely disregarded the Political Committee's decision. He showed the worst traits of individual leadership. When comrade Rákosi made mistakes, we criticized him and he corrected his mistakes. However, he is a man of principles. Such a situation within the party is intolerable. It will lead to fractionalizing. Comrade Nagy already has his own people. The political platform appeared in the paper. Such a situation is intolerable.

Comrade Nagy said: "I am unable to work with Rákosi." This is the language of ultimatums. This is not our language; it is alien to us.

Comrade Nagy made serious mistakes. If he cares for the party's interests and for Marxism, he [should] condemn his mistakes.

Comrade Khrushchev: He shares the previous speakers' opinion.

What comrade Nagy said about comrade Rákosi has some reason after all. There are mistakes that comrade Rákosi is held responsible for, but he has not yet overcome them. However, this is not the main issue right now; comrade Nagy's mistakes are more in the forefront. That is why we give full support to Rákosi against Nagy. Comrade Nagy represents anti-party ideas, and we support the party and comrade Rákosi against anti-party views. Is comrade Nagy unable to work with comrade Rákosi? What should this mean? You are not given the opportunity to realize your program, so you say you are not accountable and resign. Your resignation and reticence are nothing but attacks on the party. Your silence would suggest that you are weak—you meant well but the others hindered you. Dear comrade Nagy, maybe you have different thoughts in your soul. What you bear in your heart, you know and no one else. We only know what you put down on paper. You are not without merits. But then again, Zinovyev and Rykov were not without merits either; perhaps they were more meritorious than you are, and yet we did not hesitate to take firm steps against them when they became a threat to the party.[55] You need to be rebuked as well. It will be far more difficult if others do it. If we do not intercede in time, later the whole party might be against you. There is no other way out.

You came to us for advice. The outspoken judgment of a friend is more helpful than a friendly handshake and a smile. You should read [sic] the "Voice of America"—[do you know] what they say? The bourgeoisie likes you. They hope that you become a traitor. They hope that there will be Soviet, Yugoslav, and Hungarian [versions of] socialism. What you wrote was the best gift for the bourgeoisie. Churchill is rubbing his hands now. He thinks that it has already begun.

---

[55] Grirorii E. Zinovyev and Aleksei I. Rykov were both top Soviet party officials who fell victim to the purges in the 1930s. Zinovyev was head of the Comintern between 1919–1926, but in 1927 he was expelled from the party and executed in 1936. Rykov served as chairman of the Council of People's Commissars (head of the government) from 1924–1930 and was executed in 1938.

(Intervention by *comrade Voroshilov:* they hope that Hungary will be the same as Yugoslavia.) Comrade Nagy is at a fork in the road: he either stays with the party or turns against the party. There is no other way.

Why did you stop the construction of the foundry in Sztálinváros? We criticized your far-fetched industrial development but it does not mean that industrialization must stop—it has to go on within rational constraints. Without the support of industry, especially a strong machine industry, we are unable to keep up with the enemy. Whether or not there will be a war, we have to carry on with industrial development. Even if we have enough bacon to eat, it is to no avail without aircraft.

You are a bad leader for the Council of Ministers. How can the chairman of the Council of Ministers publish such an article? You consider yourself a Marxist economist, yet you forget to mention production costs and productivity. You have come under the influence of the masses. People have to be told the truth. The standard of living can only rise if the people themselves are producing more. Even the bourgeoisie knows that much; even Churchill is aware of it. Production must exceed consumption to expedite investments. No victory is possible without investments.

The principle of voluntary membership in cooperatives is not to be mistaken with the principle of withdrawal. We have to maintain the principle of voluntary membership, but not the principle of withdrawal. The [possibility of] withdrawal from cooperatives must be abolished.

You say that the fight was against those in the Central Committee who wanted to reduce the standard of living—comrade Gerő and his colleagues. According to you they represent the old line. However, it is far from being the old party line. We would not have supported it because it is against the interest of the workers. (*Comrade Molotov:* The old days were much better [because at the time] there were greater successes.)

Why do you need Zoltán Vas? He is a dangerous man. The editor-in-chief of your newspaper is not an honest man either.[56] If he had been an upstanding man he would have refused to print the articles by comrade Nagy. Nor [would he have printed] the article by Zoltán Vas. He has the right to refuse, but he failed to do so.

Mistakes are to be corrected. When we correct mistakes it means that the party's reputation is strengthened. We suggest you do the same. Comrade Rákosi's reputation must be defended, because it is an asset to the party. It must be taken care of, for the benefit of the party. Comrade Rákosi has to express criticism himself.

Comrade Farkas was not as ingenious as he should have been, even though he is the second secretary. He pushed comrade Nagy, instead of holding him back. He is an energetic, honest man, but he has played an unfortunate role in this matter.

We sharply criticized comrade Nagy but always from a party-minded position. We want to be on your side. Think about the criticism. "The authority of Comrade Nagy has to be safeguarded as well." His reputation is also an asset for the party. We support him, provided that he corrects his mistakes.

(Intervention by *comrade Voroshilov:* What is going on with the People's Front in your country? Individual membership is no good. The People's Front has to be firmly under the auspices of the party leadership.)

Educating the youth on the principles of proletarian internationalism is in a rather poor state in Hungary. Allow me to quote two examples: 1. At football matches and sports events, outbursts of nationalist feelings are quite frequent. This is unparalleled in friendly states, it only occurs in Hungary. 2. We have recently received a report about a Hungarian student who came to study in the Soviet Union: he was openly denouncing Soviet conditions. This is not a unique case. Educating the youth needs more careful attention.

These notes are not a verbatim record of the speeches but only a condensed version, absolutely exact in places, and roughly corresponding to the original in other places.

Béla Szalai

---

[56] Márton Horváth was editor-in-chief of the party daily *Szabad Nép* from 1954-1956.

[Source: MOL, 276. f. 102/66. ő.e. Published in János M. Rainer and Károly Urbán, eds.,
"'Konzultációk:' Dokumentumok a magyar és szovjet pártvezetok két moszkvai találkozójáról
1954–1955-ben," Múltunk 37, no. 4 (1992): 143–141. Translated by Csaba Farkas.]

DOCUMENT NO. 6: Dispatch 1086, "Balloons to Hungary," March 24, 1955

One of the most effective weapons in the U.S. arsenal against the Soviet bloc during the Cold War was "propaganda" designed to accentuate the harshness of Soviet methods and the difficulties of life behind the Iron Curtain. Radio was the preferred medium, through outlets like Voice of America and Radio Free Europe. But covert operations planners often resorted to leaflet drops by using unmanned balloons to target specific areas and make sure that their message literally got into the hands of the intended audience. This report from the American Embassy in Vienna, where many Hungary-related operations originated, highlights the advantages of this type of activity. Until very recently, U.S. documentation about these sorts of covert operations within the Soviet bloc were kept almost entirely secret.

FOREIGN SERVICE DISPATCH

FROM: AMEMBASSY, VIENNA   DISP. NO. 1086

TO: THE DEPARTMENT OF STATE, WASHINGTON   MARCH 24, 1955

SUBJECT: PERIPHERAL: COMMENTS OF HUNGARIAN ESCAPEES CONCERNING BALLOONS AND LEAFLETS SENT TO HUNGARY.

Five Hungarian escapees who left Hungary separately between November 11, 1954 and January 30, 1955, agreed that the release of balloons with anti-Communist propaganda material for Hungary was a clever maneuver because:

(1) It reminded the people of Hungary that they had not been forgotten nor abandoned to their oppressors;
(2) It delivered into Hungarian hands valuable material which was read and retained;
(3) It embarrassed the Communist authorities by forcing them to maintain constant watch for arrival of balloons and for anti-Communist propaganda material, which the authorities were unable to stop;
(4) It added to the Communists' chores by requiring them to collect such material and to prevent the population from obtaining possession of it;
(5) It forced the Communists into a defensive position in their efforts to combat "this insiduous means of propaganda directed against the welfare of the people of the Hungarian People's Republic";
(6) It created a "balloon psychosis".

The leaflets and the manner of their delivery constituted an inexhaustible and interesting topic of conversation. Information concerning leaflets dropped in remote parts of the country spread rapidly by word of mouth.

Steps Taken by AVH [ÁVH] and by Regular Police against Collection, Retention and Distribution of Leaflets by the Population.

This action varied by districts and localities. The "leaflet war" placed the Hungarian authorities in an awkward situation. The AVH did its best to stop the distribution of leaflets by announcing that distributors would be arrested as reactionaries and enemies of the people. The authorities, however, had not announced the penalties awaiting violators. In actual practice, apprehended violators received jail sentences of varying length depending upon their age and social standing. One source had heard that a two-year jail sentence had been imposed on a kulak boy and that a

16 year old schoolboy had been banned from attending any school in Hungary. Sources had not heard of the police searching private homes for leaflets. Persons in the vicinity of balloon landings had, in some cases, been searched but not arrested, even though suspected of having hidden such leaflets.

Preventive Measures Ordered by Police.

These steps were not of uniform character. Local police were evidently left some discretion in the action to be taken. Instructions issued by police in various localities were: (1) to destroy leaflets by burning; (2) not to pick up leaflets but to notify police of their landing; (3) to collect the leaflets and to deliver them to the police.

Distribution of Leaflets.

Juveniles were the most active distributors of leaflets. The AVH had occasionally asked for assistance of school-children in collecting leaflets strewn over a large area. While doing so, some children secreted a number of these in their pockets. Erik NEHIBA, 15 years of age, found a number of leaflets on November 10, 1954, in the Brenner woods (12 kilometers southeast of Sopron). He and a number of his schoolmates distributed them to spectators at a local football match. Even his school principal received a handful. The police, however, learned of his activities and he had to flee Hungary. He escaped to Austria on November 11, 1954.

Type of Leaflets.

The material which reached western Hungary was: (1) The "Twelve Points" (about 4 x 8 inches in size) and (2) the folding booklets (about 4 x 18 inches). The latter containing a RAKOSI caricature, pictures of American scenes, helicopters, Churchill, etc., were specially appreciated. Many persons were anxious to obtain them.

Efforts Made by Police to Destroy Balloons in Flight.

These attempts have not been a success. Lajos KANTOR, 19 years of age, and Joseph KARDOS, both of Sopronkővesd (25 kilometers southeast of Sopron), who escaped from Hungary on January 30, 1955, on or about January 15 saw a number of balloons floating over Sopronkővesd in an easterly direction at an altitude of about 150 meters. The AVH, which was alerted at once, marched out to a field "in battle formation" and fired at the balloons with rifles and machine guns. Much to the joy of the population of Sopronkővesd, which watched the maneuver, the AVH fire did not bring down a single balloon. Most of them floated freely on. The police obtained possession only of those balloons which settled there or in the vicinity. Lajos Kantor overheard a Security Police sergeant, who had directed operations, say that the Frontier Guard garrison at Sopronkővesd had exhausted its entire ammunition supply during the balloon hunt. Civilian spectators of the "battle" were asked to help the Security Police in collecting leaflets. It was observed that almost every participant in the collection, including the guards, kept a few leaflets for himself.

Balloons Sighted in Eastern Hungary.

Janos SZAKSZON, 23 years of age, of AJAK, Szabolcs District (35 kilometers northeast of Nyiregyhaza and 20 kilometers from the Soviet frontier) was shown a "Twelve Points" leaflet found near Ajak. He was told that a number of "American balloons" had been sighted early in November flying at a great altitude in an easterly direction. Szakszon escaped from Hungary on November 24, 1954.

Leaflets on Austrian Soil.

Some of the escapees, who had entered Austria between Szentgotthard (near Furstenfeld in Austria) and Sopron, reported that many Hungarian language leaflets had landed on Austrian soil, near the Hungarian frontier.

FOR THE AMBASSADOR:

RICHARD H. DAVIS
COUNSELOR OF EMBASSY

cc:
Budapest
Munich (MRC)
Frankfurt (PR)

[Source: NARA, RG 59, Internal Affairs of Hungary, 1955–1959, Decimal File, 764.00/3-2455.]

DOCUMENT NO. 7: National Intelligence Estimate (NIE) 12–56, "Probable Developments in the European Satellites," January 10, 1956

National Intelligence Estimates, such as this one, were prepared regularly by the U.S. intelligence community and covered a full range of foreign policy issues. The "12" series dealt specifically with Eastern Europe. Representing the consensus view of all U.S. intelligence agencies, NIEs tended to offer broad-brush examinations and contain little in the way of controversial analysis, but for historians they serve as useful indicators of the general state of U.S. understanding of a given issue. NIE 12–56 reflects the widely held view at the time that the Soviet Union was in full control of the region and was likely to remain dominant through 1960. Few, if anyone, in the West would have predicted Khrushchev's denunciation of Stalinism at the CPSU's Twentieth Party Congress the following month, or the liberalizing forces that would be unleashed throughout Eastern Europe as a result, seriously threatening Moscow's domination over the region. Yet, the analysis did predict—to a point—that the Soviet Union was inclined to introduce a more flexible policy toward Eastern Europe out of a belief that the satellite countries were sufficiently secure to handle such a change. The NIE's statement that Moscow would have to resolve latent differences among the regimes "from time to time" was also an accurate, if dramatically understated, foretelling of events in October-November 1956.

PROBABLE DEVELOPMENTS IN THE EUROPEAN SATELLITES THROUGH 1960

THE PROBLEM

To estimate the current situation and probable developments in the European Satellites[57] through 1960.

CONCLUSION

1. The military, political, and economic significance of the Satellites to the USSR is so great that Moscow almost certainly regards the maintenance of control over the area as an essential element of its power position. The Satellites provide the Soviet Union with a defense in depth and an advanced position for launching attacks on western and southern Europe. The Satellite regimes themselves are valuable to the USSR as instruments in the conduct of Soviet foreign policy, propaganda, and economic and subversive operations. The Satellites represent an important element of over-all Bloc economic strength. The total gross national product (GNP) of the Satellites is roughly two-fifths that of the USSR and includes significant production of certain key materials and heavy manufactures. (Paras. 12–16, 48–51)

2. The USSR now has, for all practical purposes, complete control over the Satellite regimes and will almost certainly be able to maintain it during the period of this estimate. Within the limitations suggested below with respect to East Germany and Albania, we believe that it will remain firm Soviet policy to retain such control. This control rests fundamentally on the USSR's military capability of maintaining its domination over the area. Control is exercised primarily through the Satellite Communist parties, assisted and guided by a complex of Soviet diplomatic and military establishments, economic advisors, and police agencies. Moscow has made clear that the status of the Satellites is not a matter for international negotiation. In the case of Germany, the USSR has held open the possibility of reunification on the basis of negotiations between the East and West German regimes. We believe, however, that the USSR will not voluntarily relinquish East Germany except in exchange for a solution of the German problem

---

[57] As used in this paper the term "European Satellites" includes East Germany, Poland, Czechoslovakia, Hungary, Rumania, Bulgaria, and Albania. [Footnote in original.]

favorable to Soviet interests. It is also possible that the USSR might be willing to reconsider its position with regard to Albania. For example, there is a slight chance that the physical isolation of Albania from the Soviet Bloc and its minor strategic value to the Bloc would induce Moscow to use Albania as a pawn in Balkan intrigue. (Paras. 14,17, 22)

3. The maintenance of effective Soviet control over the Satellites does not preclude policy modifications calculated to take greater account of local conditions, to promote smoother economic development, and to diminish the impact of Soviet rule on Satellite national sensibilities. In addition, Moscow might expect that such measures would document the claim of Satellite independence, and would thereby impress opinion in neutral and underdeveloped countries and improve the propaganda position of Free World Communist parties.

4. Despite Moscow's firm control of the Satellites, there are a number of local factors which hamper the execution of Soviet policy. In some of the Satellites factionalism has become evident in the party leadership and has caused confusion in the program. Some elements privately resent dictation by Moscow and favor a reduction of political terror and an increase in consumer goods. There are many party members with a nationalist tinge who constitute a potential for "deviation." All the governments are still confronted with problems arising from their unpopularity with the masses and from the difficulties inherent in developing an efficient administration in a totalitarian state under an alien ideology. We believe, however, that none of these difficulties will jeopardize either the control by Moscow-oriented Communists or the implementation of Soviet policy.[58](Paras. 27–28)

5. Dissidence[59] is widely prevalent in the Satellites. It is unlikely that an additional five years of Communist rule will appreciably reduce this dissidence, or greatly diminish the traditional national aspirations of the East European peoples. On the other hand, dissidence is offset by a tendency of the Satellite population to become resigned to Communist rule and by the gradual increase in the number of Communist-indoctrinated youth. We believe that, except possibly in East Germany, no development short of a drastic impairment of Communist controls or the approach of friendly forces in time of war would be sufficient to stimulate important outbreaks of open-resistance. (Paras: 31–35)

6. The Satellite regimes have as fundamental goals the expansion of industry, the collectivization of agriculture, and the Sovietization of the countries generally. In 1953, however, faced with mounting difficulties, they reduced the pressure for rapid achievement of these goals. Industrialization and collectivization of agriculture were slowed and police controls became somewhat less obtrusive. In early 1955, however, pressures for increasing output were revived, the priority of heavy industrial development was reaffirmed, and collectivization efforts were renewed. These modifications do not appear to represent a full return to the pre-1953 program. (Paras. 36–40)

7. We estimate that the Satellite economies, taken together, will increase their GNP through 1960 at the rate of slightly less than four percent per annum, a substantial decline from the extraordinary average annual rate of over seven percent achieved in 1949–1954. Satellite agricultural output in 1960 will probably be about 11 percent greater than in 1954, while nonagricultural production will increase by about 28 percent. Meanwhile, total population is expected to increase about seven percent by 1960. Manufactured consumer goods will account for the major part of the small prospective rise in living standards. (Paras. 43–47)

8. During the period of the estimate Satellite trade with the Free World may continue to rise somewhat faster, in percentage terms, than total Satellite trade. For economic as well as political reasons, the Satellites apparently desire to increase their trade with the Free World. In the

---

[58] The Assistant Chief Of Staff, Intelligence, Department of the Army and the Deputy Director for Intelligence, The Joint Staff while conceding the existence of certain ideological and administrative problems in the Satellites, nevertheless, believe these problems are currently of no great magnitude and are likely to diminish during the period of this estimate. They would therefore omit this conclusion. [Footnote in original.]

[59] On this subject, see NIE 10–55, "Anti-Communist Resistance Potential in the Sino-Soviet Bloc," dated 12 April 1955. "Dissidence" is defined as a state of mind involving discontent or disaffection with the regime. "Resistance" is defined as dissidence translated into action. [Footnote in original.]

70

absence of substantial medium- or long-term credits from Free World countries, however, an early expansion of Satellite exports will be necessary to balance any increase in imports from the Free World. This confronts the Satellites with the problem of adjusting the character and prices of their exports and their way of doing business, in order to improve their position in Free World markets. It will probably be easier for the Satellites to increase trade with the underdeveloped areas than with the industrial countries of the West. (Paras. 52–54)

9. We believe that the scope of Bloc-wide[60] regional planning will substantially increase as compared with the period 1949–1953. During the period of this estimate, this policy will probably not contribute greatly to the growth of the economy or to the resolution of basic economic problems, although some benefits can be expected. Over a longer period, integration may make significant contributions to the economic strength of this area. (Paras. 55–58)

10. The Satellite armed forces constitute a substantial element in the balance of military power in Europe. Ground forces now number 77 divisions, which, given extensive Soviet logistical support, could be expanded to 188 divisions by M+180 days. There are currently about 3,000 Satellite operational military aircraft of all types. We believe that the capabilities of these forces will be substantially augmented by continued conversions to newer weapons and equipment and by an increase in numbers of aircraft. (Paras. 70–71, 77, 80)

11. The combat effectiveness of the Satellites armies varies considerably from country to country. However, we estimate that up to 50 percent of present Satellite divisions could be employed initially in combat alongside Soviet forces. Several of the armies, with Soviet logistical support, would be capable of sustained independent operations against traditional enemies. The reliability of these armies is such that they would be unlikely to defect on a substantial scale until victorious Western forces approached the Satellite area. Indoctrination and improved personnel selection have increased the political reliability of the Satellite air forces. We believe that the combat effectiveness of these air forces is such that they could be employed in a defensive role in the event of general war and would have some offensive capability, particularly against traditional enemies. The Satellite navies are small in size and poorly equipped and constitute only a minor contribution to Bloc naval strength. (Paras. 73–74, 77, 82)

DISCUSSION

I. SOVIET POLICY IN THE SATELLITES

Basic Soviet Interests in the Area

12. The military, political, and economic significance of the Satellites to the USSR is so great that Moscow probably regards the maintenance of control over the area as an essential element of its power position.

13. The Satellites provide the Soviet Union with defense in depth, a consideration which may become of increasing importance to the USSR in view of the prospective rearmament of West Germany. The fact that the Satellites are being given current Soviet aircraft and that their air defenses are being integrated with those of the USSR, indicates the importance which Moscow assigns to the area as an advanced line of air defense. Similarly, Satellite ground forces constitute increasingly effective obstacles along the land approaches to the Western USSR. For offensive purposes, control of Poland, Czechoslovakia, and East Germany provides the USSR with an advanced position for an assault on Western Europe; Hungary, Bulgaria, and Rumania provide a base from which to operate against the States on the northern shore of the Mediterranean and against the Dardanelles.

---

[60] The terms "Soviet Bloc," "Bloc-wide," or "Intra-Bloc" refer to the USSR and the European Satellites. Where Communist China is also referred to, the term "Sino-Soviet Bloc" will be used. [Footnote in original.]

14. The Soviet leaders probably regard continued control over the Satellites as essential to prevent the recreation of a German state of prewar size and power, which in their view might once again exert dominant influence in Eastern Europe and threaten the security of the USSR. Directly, or through the Satellites, the USSR controls not only East Germany, but also the formerly German areas of Silesia, Pomerania, and East Prussia, from which most of the German population was expelled in 1945. In 1938 the eastern provinces of Germany now held by Poland and the USSR had a population of nine million, and the territory of present-day East Germany 17 million. In other words, Moscow now controls territories which constituted one-fourth the area of 1938 Germany, and sustained more than a third of its population. We believe that the USSR will not voluntarily relinquish any of these territories except in exchange for a solution of the German problem favorable to Soviet interests.

15. The Satellites represent for the USSR an important economic component of power in the over-all East-West struggle. Satellite gross national product and Satellite population are approximately two-fifths as large as those of the USSR, and the area provides the USSR with important strategic raw materials and manufactured goods. Economically, the three most important Satellites are Poland, Czechoslovakia, and East Germany, which together contain 61 percent of the Satellite population and account for 85 percent of Satellite GNP.

16. Finally, control of the Satellites has great political value for the Soviet Union and the international Communist movement. The Satellite regimes are used by the USSR in the conduct of foreign policy, propaganda, and subversive operations. In addition, the mere existence of the "People's Democracies," with their population of almost 100 million, proclaims to the outside world that Communism is on the march. Communist domestic and foreign propaganda has made capital of the fact that these varied and populous states are members of the "progressive camp."

17. The USSR has made clear that it regards incorporation of these areas into the Soviet Bloc as an accomplished fact, and that the status of the Satellites is not a matter for international negotiation. In the case of Germany, the USSR has held open the possibility of reunification on the basis of negotiations between the East and West German regimes. We believe, however, that the USSR will not voluntarily relinquish East Germany except in exchange for a solution of the German problem favorable to Soviet interests. It is also possible that the USSR might be willing to reconsider its position with regard to Albania. For example, there is a slight chance that the physical isolation of Albania from the Soviet Bloc and its minor strategic value to the Bloc would induce Moscow to use Albania as a pawn in Balkan intrigue.

Tactical Shifts in Soviet Policy in the Satellites

18. Soviet policy in the Satellites has followed a changing but generally consistent course since Soviet troops occupied the area in the wake of the German retreat. From 1944 to 1947 the Soviet tactic was to direct and assist the local Communist parties in gaining control of the East European governments under a facade of legality. The Communists championed causes which could give them some initial popular support, such as land reform, the expulsion of some 12 million Germans from East European territories, and the transfer of the property of these Germans to Poles, Czechs, and Slovaks. Coalition cabinets were the order of the day, and prime ministers sometimes came from non-Communist parties, but key ministries were held by the Communists. The Communists most in view were frequently those who had acquired local stature as underground resistance leaders, rather than those who had spent the war years in the USSR. On the economic front, the USSR exploited the Satellites, particularly those identified as ex-enemies, for its own benefit, and simultaneously introduced Soviet-type institutions into the nonagricultural sectors of their economies. The USSR as yet showed little interest in the long-range economic development of the area.

19. In 1947 the next phase of Soviet policy began to develop. The Communists, well established in key positions, proceeded to consolidate their power and to sovietize the Satellites. In some countries coalition governments were eliminated by means of intimidation and rigged

elections. In September 1947 the Cominform was founded, in part to provide Moscow with closer control over the Satellite parties. Early in 1948 the vestiges of freedom in Czechoslovakia were wiped out by a coup d'etat. In June 1948 the Yugoslav party was expelled from the Cominform for "nationalist deviation." In September, Wladislaw Gomulka was dismissed as secretary general of the Polish party on the same charge. There followed a series of purges, the object of which was to decapitate nationalist Communist factions throughout the Satellites. Communist leaders especially loyal to Moscow, men who had spent long years in the Soviet Union and who in many cases were Soviet citizens, openly took over the direction of the local parties. A beginning was made at screening undependable elements from the large Communist parties which had been built up in the period 1945–1948. After 1948 direct exploitation of East Germany, Hungary, and Rumania was gradually eased, and every effort was devoted to the rapid development of heavy industry throughout the Satellites. This development was patterned after Soviet practice, which involved a high rate of forced savings through depressed consumption levels, and concurrent neglect of agricultural development. A policy aimed at full agricultural collectivization was inaugurated. Security measures were tightened. Western correspondents were expelled, or arrested as spies, and Western embassies were cut off from contact with the local populations. Pressure on the churches was intensified, and religious leaders were imprisoned on charges of treason. This pattern continued until the death of Stalin, in March 1953.

20. Beginning in mid-1953, a shift in Soviet tactics in the Satellites became evident. This shift emerged primarily in the economic field with announcements of a "new course" which held out the promise of a higher standard of living for the Satellite populations. Planned rates of economic growth were cut back to more realistic levels, and the emphasis on the development of heavy industry was toned down. In general, collectivization of agriculture was greatly slowed, and in some countries it actually lost considerable ground. Investment in agriculture was increased substantially. Most of the joint Soviet Satellite companies, which had become symbols of Soviet exploitation, were dissolved, and other overt signs of Soviet economic control were reduced. In early 1955, however, there was some modification of the "new course" economic approaches, concurrent with the consolidation of the present regime in the USSR. Pressures for increasing output were revived; heavy industrial development was re-emphasized; and collectivization efforts were renewed. At the same time, Soviet and Satellite planners began to place more emphasis on Bloc-wide coordination of economic planning and on regional specialization in economic activity.

21. In the political field, security and police pressures became somewhat less obtrusive. Mass deportation of urban middle class elements in Hungary came to a halt. In a few countries, some representatives of former opposition parties were released. A special effort was made to persuade political refugees to return home. The isolation of the Western diplomatic corps was somewhat reduced, and a few Western correspondents were permitted entry.

II. THE FUTURE OF SOVIET POLICY IN THE SATELLITES

22. The USSR now has, for all practical purposes, complete control over the Satellite regimes and will almost certainly be able to maintain it during the period of this estimate. Within the limitations suggested in paragraph 6 with respect to East Germany and Albania, we believe that it will remain firm Soviet policy to retain such control. Control rests fundamentally on the USSR's military capability of maintaining its domination over the area for an indefinite period. Soviet control is exercised primarily through the Satellite Communist parties, assisted and guided by a complex of Soviet diplomatic and military establishments, economic advisors, and police agencies. Under the aegis of the Soviet security apparatus, the various Satellite security services have become in effect a part of the Soviet police mechanism. These controls are so designed as to bind the Satellites to the USSR individually, rather than as a group.

23. The Soviet leaders will continue the policy of controlling the Satellite area in such a way as to produce the greatest possible internal and foreign policy advantages for the USSR. This

aim does not preclude Soviet policy modifications calculated to take greater account of local conditions and to procure smoother economic development. Such flexibility may also diminish the impact of Soviet rule on Satellite national sensibilities and support Soviet claims that these states are independent. Bloc statements on the importance of "local conditions for the development of socialism" may portend increasing flexibility in planning and in socialization, aimed at a more realistic program of economic development for the area as a whole. Moreover, Communist control being well established, the regimes can now afford to grant minor relaxations of political pressure and police control. In addition, Moscow might expect that such measures would document the claim of Satellite independence, and would thereby impress opinion in neutral and underdeveloped countries and improve the propaganda position of Free World Communist parties.

24. The USSR may somewhat reduce or refine its more visible means of control. Soviet troops might be withdrawn from Rumania and Hungary, where the USSR probably estimates their presence is not essential. Abolition of the Cominform would be an even more inexpensive gesture, since this agency has become largely a Soviet Bloc information and propaganda link with the West European Communist parties, rather than an instrument of control. In matters essential to Soviet control, such as the building up of a reliable and subservient Satellite Communist leadership and the staffing of key positions with Soviet or Moscow-oriented personnel, the Soviet rulers will almost certainly continue to maintain the policies of the Stalin era.

25. Soviet leaders are almost certainly aware, however, that some of the actions they have already taken involve certain risks for their position in the Satellites. The visit to Belgrade, for example, had the effect of building up the prestige and influence of Tito, and the public acknowledgment of Yugoslavia's right to pursue its own "way to socialism" aroused hopes in the Satellites for a substantial lessening of Soviet control. The case of the Imre Nagy regime in Hungary indicates the existence of latent conflicts within the Satellite party leadership which may have to be resolved by Moscow from time to time.

26. We believe that Soviet authorities will avoid any actions which, in their judgment, would jeopardize their control of the Satellite regimes or the regimes' control over the local populations. There are, therefore, narrow limits to the freedom of action which Moscow can afford to permit the Satellite regimes to develop.

III. INTERNAL DEVELOPMENTS IN THE SATELLITES: POLITICAL

27. The Communist regimes, backed by the ultimate sanction of Soviet power, almost certainly have firm control of the Satellite populations. Nevertheless, there are indications of factionalism within some of the party leaderships, and all governments are still confronted with problems arising from their unpopularity with the masses and from the difficulties inherent in developing an efficient administration in a totalitarian state. We believe, however, that during the period of this estimate, Soviet dominated regimes will be able to maintain their control over the populations and gradually to increase their administrative effectiveness.

28. Since the Communist parties are the basic instrument of the regimes' control over the populations, any weakness or inefficiency within these parties acts as a conditioning factor on the execution of policy. Approximately seven percent of the total Satellite population, or 6.5 million persons, are Communist party members. This means that one of every 10 adults in the Satellites is a party member. Obviously, the development of such large parties from very small beginnings (there were probably less than a thousand Communists in Rumania in 1944) could not have been accomplished without taking in large numbers of people who were not dedicated to Communism. In staffing positions at the lower echelons of the bureaucracy, the party has often had to sacrifice technical qualification in favor of political loyalty. At higher levels an element of the party membership with technical qualifications is opportunistic. Some elements privately resent dictation by Moscow and favor a reduction of political terror and an increase in

consumer goods. There are many party members with a nationalist tinge who constitute a potential for "deviation." We believe, however, that these "unreliable" elements will not attain sufficient influence within the parties to jeopardize either the control by the Moscow-oriented Communists or the implementation of Soviet policy.[61]

29. In the field of education, Communist attempts to indoctrinate the adult generation have apparently had little success. Within the youth, however, intensive indoctrination, coupled with the bait of advanced schooling, career opportunities, and other material benefits, has begun to produce a greater degree of cooperation with the regime. Educational opportunities, especially for favored classes, have in fact been greatly increased, particularly in technical fields.

UNIVERSITY STUDENTS PER THOUSAND POPULATION[62]		
COUNTRY	1937–1939	1953–1954
BULGARIA	1.7	4.1
CZECHOSLOVAKIA	1.9	3.7
HUNGAY	1.3	5.7
POLAND	1.4	5.3
RUMANIA	1.4	3.8

As a result, the regimes will probably become increasingly able to find adequate personnel for positions in the state apparatus and the nationalized economic enterprises. Some of these younger people are likely to constitute an element with a vested interest in the Communist regimes, even though the majority of youth will probably not become convinced Communists during the period of the estimate.

30. In relations between church and state, the Satellite regimes have avoided a head-on collision with popular devotion to traditional religious observances, which appears to have been increasing. Instead, they have directed their policy primarily toward strangulation of the independent organizational and institutional features of the churches, in the hope of making these churches subservient to the regime. This aim has to a large extent been realized in the case of the Orthodox, Protestant, and Moslem churches of the area. Even the Catholic Church has been forced to adopt a policy of avoiding open controversy with the regime, in order to conserve the position of its clergy and as much as possible of its traditional functions.

31. All available evidence indicates that throughout the Satellite area the regimes have made no appreciable progress in inducing the people to give active support to the Communist system and its program. For a number of reasons, of which economic hardship and regimentation, hatred of Soviet domination, and fear of the police state appear uppermost, a substantial majority of the people continue to be antipathetic toward the regimes. Dissidence is widely prevalent among the peasantry, which stubbornly resists collectivization, and is a significant factor even within groups which are ostensibly favored by the regimes, such as youth and industrial workers.

[61] The Assistant Chief of Staff, Intelligence, Department of the Army, while concurring in the estimative conclusion contained in the last sentence of this paragraph, considers that the paragraph as a whole conveys an impression of weakness in the Satellite Communist parties that is not supported by intelligence and recommends the substitution of the following for paragraph 28: "Satellite Communist parties are large in comparison to immediate postwar size, and membership now consists of seven percent of the total Satellite population or 6.5 million persons. Although the parties probably contain some unreliable elements, we believe that these elements either will remain submerged or will be eliminated and will not exercise significant influence on control by the hard-core Communists or implementation of Soviet policy." [Footnote in original.]

[62] The comparable figure (1954) for the U.S. is 15.2, for the USSR 5.4, for West Germany 2.7, and for the UK 1.4. [Footnote in original.]

32. The effectiveness of the Satellite governments in combating dissidence and promoting Communist indoctrination will be limited by a number of factors. A shortage of capable and ideologically grounded teachers and writers will probably continue. The traditional affinity of the Satellite intelligentsia for Western culture will probably remain strong in the older generations. Western broadcasts will probably continue to reach the Satellite populations, and there may be greater exchange of cultural, technical, and sport delegations with Western countries.

33. The failure of the Satellite governments to win mass support will be partly offset by a tendency of the population to become resigned to Communist rule. Next to general positive support, the Communist regimes probably regard a growth of popular acquiescence and resignation as the second best development for their purposes. If the Soviet policy of "relaxation of international tensions" continues, attitudes of resignation among many elements of the population will be reinforced. The Satellite populations have placed their main hope for eventual liberation on Western Europe and the U.S., and they have tended to believe that this could be accomplished only through war. This hope of liberation apparently remained fairly strong up to 1953, but since then has been diminishing. The Summit meeting at Geneva intensified the belief that the Western Powers were determined to avoid war and, if necessary, to accept a modus vivendi with the USSR involving the maintenance of the status quo in Eastern Europe.

34. So far as is known, no active resistance organizations survive in the Satellite area at present. There are today, and probably will be for many years to come, a few elements of potential resistance scattered throughout Satellite society which may be able to survive by remaining inactive and deeply concealed. Only in the event of war, however, would they be likely to attempt conspiratorial activity. Except possibly in the case of East Germany, we believe that no development short of a drastic impairment of Communist controls or the approach of friendly forces in time of war would be sufficient to stimulate important outbreaks of open resistance.

35. While the number of Communist supporters will probably increase over the period of the estimate, it is unlikely that anything like a majority within the Satellite populations will accept Communism, or that the national aspirations of the East European peoples will be extinguished. These peoples have a long history of suffering under oppressive masters. While submitting to the exploitation of the Turk, or the Tsarist Russian, or the German over many centuries, they yet managed to maintain their national identity. They will probably continue to do so. Nevertheless, there will probably be some increase in support of the government by more favored elements in the population and, among the people generally, an increasing resignation to life under Communist rule.

IV. ECONOMIC

Trends in Economic Policy

36. While Satellite economic policy in the period 1914–1953 resulted in a considerable growth of heavy industry, this was accomplished at the expense of consumer goods and agricultural production. Moreover, a considerable imbalance developed in heavy industry, resulting from over rapid build-up of manufacturing facilities without corresponding expansion of the raw material, fuel, and power base. By the end of 1952 rates of industrial growth began to fall at a pace which made it apparent that many of the augmented plan goals set in 1951 would not be met. The growth rates of previous years had been realized primarily as a result of substantial additions to the industrial labor forces and of fuller utilization of capacities. By 1953, additions to the total labor forces and transfers of workers from agriculture to industry had greatly diminished, so that further economic growth depended increasingly on improved labor productivity. Disaffection of both workers and peasants, however, seriously hampered efforts to achieve such an improvement.

37. Beginning in mid-1953 all the Satellites adopted, under Moscow's guidance, an economic "new course." This new policy involved an acceptance by the Satellite regimes of much

lower planned rates of industrial growth than they had foreseen in 1951 for the period 1953–1955. It entailed some shift in emphasis within industry from heavy machinery to basic raw materials, power, and consumer goods. In agriculture, the "new course" called for increased investment and for the enhancement of incentives through such concessions as the lowering of delivery quotas and, in some countries, permission to withdraw from the collectivized sector. By means of such a program, the regimes also hoped to improve the economic response of workers and peasants and thereby to alleviate the major economic difficulties of the previous period.

38. During 1954 some progress was made in altering the structure of industry. However, the "new course" ran into serious economic difficulties and even created a certain political threat. Slowness in implementing unrealistic promises of improved living standards led to widespread disillusionment and skepticism. Non-cooperation was encountered from almost all elements of the population. The doctrinaire elements in the Communist parties objected to what they considered a "deviationist" economic course. The workers and peasants were inclined to hold out for greater and more effective concessions. Changes in production and allocation patterns adversely affected industrial schedules and unfavorable weather reduced crop yields. As a result, performance in both industry and agriculture was extremely disappointing during 1954. Even the reduced industrial goals were not fulfilled, and rising wage levels without corresponding increases in productivity began to cause fiscal problems for the regimes.

39. Early in 1955 modifications of the "new course" were undertaken, coinciding with the ouster of Malenkov and Soviet reaffirmation of the primacy of heavy industry. These modifications called for restoration of some degree of emphasis to heavy industry, reaffirmed the eventual goal of full collectivization, and reintroduced some of the earlier discipline into economic activities. During 1955, the stress was placed on the restoration of discipline in such matters as workers' norms, wage payments, and peasant delivery obligations. In some countries, collectivization activity was resumed. The implementation of the renewed emphasis on heavy industry, however, was put off, at least in part, until 1956.

40. The early 1955 modification does not appear to represent a full return to pre-"new course" programs. Emphasis on heavy industry is coupled with a determination to keep development plans more in line with capabilities and with a recognition of the danger of neglecting agricultural development. In some respects discipline has been restored, but many of the "new course" incentives remain intact.

41. The present industrial program emphasizes for the immediate future the full utilization of existing industrial capacities. Such an effort will continue the "new course" stress on the production of raw materials, fuel, and power. Only limited major new investments in the field of heavy manufactures are scheduled. Industrial investments are to be concentrated to a greater degree on replacement and modernization of outmoded equipment and on technological improvements, rather than on wholesale expansion of industrial capacity. The program also seeks to reduce the disparity which had existed prior to 1953 between the rate of expansion in the output of producer goods and that of consumer goods. It envisages, moreover, greater use of heavy industrial plant for the production of agricultural equipment and durable consumer goods.

42. The Satellite regimes are faced with thorny policy problems in the field of agriculture. As a matter of doctrine, they continue to insist that full collectivization of agriculture is a prerequisite for the "building of socialism," yet they have an acute awareness that rapid and forced collectivization depresses agricultural production. Consequently, they can increase agricultural output significantly over the next five years only if collectivization is carried out at a slow pace, and private agriculture is given at least limited encouragement. They will be faced with a delicate problem of maintaining a judicious balance between the incentives given the collectives and those provided the free sector. In any case, as long as a substantial private sector remains, the regimes will have difficulty in getting maximum results from the collectivized sector. On balance, in view of the serious concern of the Satellite leaders to increase agricultural output, we believe there will be only moderate increases in collectivization during the period of this estimate.

43. The application of the "new course" was accompanied by a reduction in the rate of growth of Satellite GNP. In 1954 estimated GNP was only five percent greater than in 1953, a modest rate as compared with preceding years. Only Poland was able, to fulfill its initial industrial production goal for that year. In all seven Satellites, the announced percentage gains in industrial output over the previous year were smaller than in 1953. The average gain in the productivity of labor was also significantly less than in previous years; in the case of Hungary, output per industrial worker actually declined. Total Satellite production of agricultural commodities showed no increase in 1954 over the preceding year.

44. We estimate that even with the modifications of the "new course" undertaken in 1955, the rate of increase in the total GNP of the Satellites for the years 1955–1960 will average somewhat less than four percent per annum. This is lower than the projected Soviet rate of about five to six percent, and represents a substantial decline from the extraordinary Satellite average of over seven percent for the years 1949–1954.

ESTIMATED GROSS NATIONAL PRODUCTS OF
THE EUROPEAN SATELLITES
(excluding Albania)

	BILLION 1951 U.S. DOLLARS				PERCENT INCREASE 1960 OVER
	1938	1948	1954	1960	1954
EUROPEAN SATELLITES	44.5	32.4	49.4	61.4	24
POLAND	14.5	11.0	17.1	21.1	23
EAST GERMANY	16.1	9.0	15.8	19.3	22
CZECHOSLOVAKIA	7.3	6.8	9.2	11.6	26
RUMANIA	3.1	2.6	3.0	4.1	36
HUNGARY	2.5	2.0	3.0	3.7	24
BULGARIA	1.0	1.0	1.3	1.6	29

45. Assuming only moderate increases in the collectivized sector, we estimate that Satellite agricultural output in 1960 will be about 11 percent greater than in 1954. Relatively large increases are projected for Hungary and Rumania, where agricultural output is still far below the prewar level, but the anticipated increase for the Satellites as a whole is much smaller than during the period 1949–1954. Realization of the projected 11 percent increase would still leave Satellite agricultural production about 10 percent below the prewar level. The agricultural labor force is expected to increase slightly rather than decline as in the past, even though mechanization is to be accelerated. The increased use of labor in agriculture, where productivity is low, rather than in industry where productivity is higher, will tend to have an adverse effect on the rate of economic growth.

46. We estimate that nonagricultural production will increase by approximately 28 percent in the period 1954–1960. This will be made possible by an estimated increase of 11 percent in the nonagricultural labor force and by an expected growth in output per worker on the order of two to three percent per year. The productivity of labor in the Satellite area in 1960 will still be considerably less than that of the industrialized countries of the West.

47. We estimate that there will be a small increase in Satellite living standards by 1960. The total population of the European Satellites is expected to increase about seven percent from 1954 to 1960, approximately from 93 to 100 million persons. Since the projected increase in total agricultural production amounts to 11 percent, only a very small per capita increase in agricultural output is probable. Even with some increases in imports of agricultural products, comparatively

little improvement in the per capita consumption of foodstuffs will result. The diet will remain low in proteins and high in starchy substitutes, and the caloric intake will not be substantially increased. Manufactured consumer goods will account for the major part of the small prospective rise in living standards. Producer goods output will increase at a more rapid rate than consumer goods, and investment will rise more rapidly than consumption.

Satellite Contributions to Bloc Strength

48. The European Satellites represent an important element of over-all Bloc economic strength. Satellite GNP in 1954 is estimated at roughly two-fifths that of the USSR. The ratio probably will be somewhat smaller in 1960, since the estimated rite of growth of GNP is significantly lower for the Satellites than for the USSR.

49. Satellite production of basic materials such as uranium, coal, petroleum, bauxite, calcium carbide, and caustic soda represents a particularly significant contribution to Bloc strength. The largest Satellite reserves of bituminous coal are in Poland, which ships important quantities to the USSR and East Germany, and lesser amounts to Czechoslovakia and Hungary. Hungary has the largest bauxite reserves in Europe and accounts for approximately 60 percent of Soviet Bloc production. Although Satellite oil reserves are estimated to constitute only seven percent of the reserves of the Soviet Bloc, the Satellites currently provide 16 percent of Bloc production.

50. It is estimated that, in 1954, the Satellites provided approximately two-thirds of Bloc uranium ore production. East Germany alone provided almost 50 percent of the Soviet Bloc total. The uranium production of East Germany can be expected to remain about the same during the period of this estimate, and the other Satellites may show a slight increase. The USSR, however, is not dependent upon Satellite sources. If necessary the Soviet atomic energy program could probably be supported at its present level of operation from internal Soviet sources alone. Nevertheless, the USSR will almost certainly wish to continue its rapid and large-scale exploitation of Satellite ores in order to accumulate maximum reserves.

51. The Satellites also produce some types of machinery and equipment which the USSR continues to import in large quantities. Most of the production of rolling stock has been exported to the Soviet Union, leaving Satellite railway systems in a deplorable condition by Western standards. Satellite shipbuilding capacity has been expanded, and the bulk of the output, consisting chiefly of merchant ships, has been exported to the USSR, thus freeing Soviet shipyards for construction of naval vessels.

Foreign Trade and Bloc Economic Integration

52. After having steadily increased since 1948, the trade of the Satellite countries within the Sino-Soviet Bloc remained constant in 1954, while their trade with the Free World increased. During the period of this estimate, trade with the Free World may continue to rise somewhat faster, in percentage terms, than total trade. However, the intra-Bloc trade will probably again begin to show annual increases and, in any case, will remain the predominant part of the trade of each Satellite.

53. For political as well as economic reasons, the Satellites apparently desire to increase their trade with the Free World. Politically, the development of trade ties with the Free World coincides with the current Soviet drive to extend Communist influence, particularly in underdeveloped areas. Economically, the achievement of the planned rates of growth and the improvement of living standards will be significantly facilitated if the Satellites can import from the Free World certain key commodities, such as agricultural products, iron ore, nonferrous metals, and machinery. Some items in these categories are at present embargoed by the COCOM countries.

54. In the absence of medium- or long-term credits from Free World countries, which are unlikely to be offered on any substantial scale during the period of this estimate, an early expansion of Satellite exports will be necessary to balance an increase in imports from the Free World.

Thus, the Satellites are now facing the problem of adjusting the character and prices of their exports and their way of doing business in order to improve their position in Free World markets. Except in East Germany and to some extent in Czechoslovakia, products of the newly-created Satellite manufacturing industries have been high in cost and indifferent in quality. The large agricultural surpluses formerly used by some Satellites in their foreign trade have dwindled rapidly. Moreover, Satellite regimes have gained a bad reputation in the Free World for abruptly terminating the exchange of particular commodities and for unsatisfactory performance on commitments and deliveries. Under these circumstances, it will probably be easier for the Satellites to increase trade with the underdeveloped areas, particularly in South Asia, the Middle East, and Latin America, than with the industrial countries of the West.

55. Despite this interest in East-West trade, Soviet planners are also placing greater stress on the economic integration of the Soviet Bloc. The particular aspects of integration to which they are giving attention are regional coordination of production planning and a more rational adjustment of the industrial structure of the Satellite area. Beginning in 1956, the Five-Year Plans of all the Satellites except Bulgaria will cover the same time period as the Soviet plan, and it has been officially announced that these plans will be coordinated with one another and with the Soviet plan to a greater extent than heretofore. As in the past, the plans will reflect broad economic policies and goals laid down by the USSR. The Council for Mutual Economic Assistance (CMEA) will probably play the major coordinating role. The planners apparently hope that, as a result of closer coordination of production plans for particular commodities, together with a continued high volume of intra-Bloc trade and increasing exchange of technical information, critical deficiencies in materials, plant or labor can be avoided during the next five years. They further hope that the concept of better balanced economic development applied to the area as a whole, with individual countries concentrating on their most efficient economic activities, will increase the benefits of intra-Bloc trade and help avoid imbalances, strains, and bottlenecks. Such an adjustment would presumably require the maintenance or elevation of the already high priorities established for expanding the output of coal in Poland, petroleum in Rumania and Hungary, machines and equipment in Czechoslovakia and East Germany, and chemicals in East Germany and Poland. In agriculture the highest priorities would logically be assigned to Hungary and the Balkans.

56. We believe that during the period of this estimate the scope and effectiveness of Bloc-wide regional planning will substantially increase as compared to the period 1949–1953. Economic interdependence of the Soviet-Satellite area has already grown significantly through the forced shift of the Satellites during the past seven years to intra-Bloc trade at the expense of trade with the Free World. The benefits from such trade could be increased by further developing the complementary character of the Satellite economies.

57. The success of these efforts will, however, be limited by a number of factors. The task of coordination is intrinsically difficult, and its extension will almost certainly encounter practical and doctrinal obstacles. Centralized planning and organization of supply channels on an international scale are much more complex than on a national scale. Greater interdependence will multiply the area-wide repercussions of plan failures in individual countries. While it would be rational for each country to intensify concentration on its most efficient production lines, it will apparently be necessary, at least during the period of this estimate, for individual Satellites to maintain or even increase their efforts along certain uneconomical lines, pending anticipated production increases by their Bloc trading partners. Finally the nationalistic and doctrinaire position that each Communist country should concentrate on the development of heavy industry will probably militate against the full acceptance of the concept of interdependent economies.

58. On balance, we view the current stress on economic integration as indicative of a long-term policy which will increasingly influence Satellite development plans. During the period 1956–1960 this policy will probably not contribute greatly to the growth of the economy or to the resolution of basic economic problems, although some benefits can be expected. Over a longer period, integration may make significant contribution s to the economic strength of this area.

V. SCIENTIFIC DEVELOPMENTS

59. During the period 1956-1960 Satellite capabilities in many fields of science will continue to grow. At the same time, however, the USSR will probably cease to be dependent upon the Satellites for its basic research and development needs in such fields as scientific instruments, precision tools, optical goods, photographic equipment, and electronics. This trend will probably result in a general redirection of effort toward the development of items for the domestic economy and foreign trade.

60. Since World War II, East Germany and, to a lesser extent, Czechoslovakia have made significant contributions to the scientific and technological development of the USSR by supplying instruments for scientific research and development and for industrial process measurement and control. During 1955, the USSR cancelled large contracts for instruments, probably reflecting an increased supply from domestic sources. The loss of these contracts may at least temporarily reduce funds allocated for East German instrumentation research and development. Unless Soviet support is revived, East German research and production in this field will depend upon the development of other trade outlets, including the West. Progress, in any case, will probably be slower than prior to 1953.

61. Competent scientific manpower is still in short supply, but there are many young and well-trained research workers in East Germany, Czechoslovakia, Poland, and Hungary whose capabilities are increasing with experience. The current trend toward the decentralization of scientific research, which has been noted particularly in East Germany, may release a number of scientists from administrative duties and make them available for more productive work. While the scientific-technical manpower shortage will not be overcome during the period of this estimate, it will probably be considerably alleviated.

62. Satellite restrictions on the dissemination of scientific-technical information have been eased, and the controlled interchange of such information has been encouraged. Greatly increased attendance at international scientific meetings, together with any easing of security policy, have permitted contacts with scientific colleagues on a world-wide basis. Such exchanges of ideas and experience, if they continue, will be of considerable benefit to the Satellites.

63. There has been a sharp increase in nuclear physics research. In East Germany, Poland and Czechoslovakia new institutes of nuclear physics have been established, and capabilities in this field are expected to increase. The Soviet Union has announced a broad program of assistance to the Satellites, including the supply of nuclear reactors and fissionable materials. Such a program, if carried out, would considerably broaden the base and enhance the capabilities of the Soviet Bloc in the nonmilitary aspects of nuclear research. In any case, the full impact of this program would not be felt before 1960.

64. The direct contribution of the Satellites to the Soviet Bloc air, ground, and naval weapons research and development program is of little significance. There is a small amount of work being done in Czechoslovakia and in East Germany which gives support to Soviet weapons programs. Soviet policy, however, has been to limit Satellite research and development work on weapons. The Satellites have been encouraged to apply their scientific and technical effort to the development of test and research equipment, of ancillary military items, and of industrial techniques related to military production. We believe that, during the next five years, there will be no significant change in this policy.

VI. MILITARY DEVELOPMENTS

65. Soviet control of the Satellites has moved the Soviet military frontier into Central Europe. In view of the strategic importance of this region, the USSR has given great emphasis to its development for military operations. It has maintained and modernized large forces of its own in the area, and has intensively developed airfields and communications. It has sought to build reliable Satellite forces and has increasingly supplied them with modern weapons and equipment.

Soviet Forces Stationed in the Satellites

66. Of an estimated 494,000 Soviet Army ground forces (plus 24,000 security troops) stationed in the Satellites, approximately 400,000 (22 line divisions) are located in East Germany, while the remaining 94,000 (6 line divisions) are located in Hungary, Poland, and Rumania. It is possible that the Soviet troops in Hungary and Rumania will be withdrawn during the period of the estimate, since their presence is probably not considered necessary to the maintenance of Soviet control. The Soviet leaders might make such a move in support of their diplomatic and propaganda campaign against NATO. At present, however, the indications are that these troops will remain. Provided there is no basic change in the German situation, the number of divisions in East Germany and Poland will probably not change substantially during the period of the estimate, although their combat effectiveness will be increased through the re-equipment and reorganization program which has been in progress since late 1954.

67. The most significant change in Soviet air strength in the Satellites over the past year has been a sizeable increase in jet light bomber strength. This substantially enhances Soviet capabilities for direct and indirect support of ground force operations. Of the 14 light bomber regiments currently in the area, 9 are based in East Germany, 2 in Poland, and 3 in Hungary.

68. About 25 percent of the Soviet FAGOTS (MIG 15) based in the Satellites on 1 July 1954 have been replaced by FRESCOS (MIG 17). This represents a significant increase in combat effectiveness. All indications point to the probability that this re-equipment program will continue until all FAGOTS are replaced by improved fighter types by mid-1957. At present there are a limited number of jet all-weather fighters which are probably being used for training purposes. While these planes do not materially increase the over-all combat effectiveness of the Soviet air force in the Satellites, their presence portends a buildup in all-weather fighter strength and defensive capabilities. It is also expected that all BEAST (IL–10) attack aircraft will be phased out by mid-1959 and replaced in the attack role by jet fighters and light bombers. In short, present Soviet authorized air strength of some 2,500 military aircraft of all types stationed in the Satellites will probably not change substantially over the period of the estimate. Actual strength is presently estimated at about 85 percent of TO&E.[63] The capabilities of this force will be increased by the continued phasing in of new types; actual strength could be brought up to the TO&E figure in a relatively short time.

69. The USSR bases a small number of patrol vessels and minesweepers in several Satellite ports on the Baltic and Black Seas. The primary purpose of these forces is to direct the training of the Satellite navies in the use of Soviet equipment and operating procedures. In the size, composition, disposition, or capabilities of the Soviet naval forces based in the Satellites there have been no significant changes and none are anticipated over the period of the estimate.

Satellite Forces[64]

70. *Ground.* The Satellite ground forces have become a substantial element in the balance of military power in Europe. We estimate that currently the ground forces of the Satellites comprise 1,085,000 men organized in 77 divisions, of which six are tank and 15 mechanized. Recently cuts have been announced for the major Satellite forces ranging from nine to 18 percent.[65] Even if these cuts are actually carried out, the over-all effectiveness of the ground forces will not be significantly impaired. These ground forces are supplemented by Satellite security troops which total 321,000 men. By M+180 days the Satellites could mobilize 4,700,000 men in 188 divisions, provided there was extensive Soviet logistical support.

---

[63] Tables of Organization and Equipment.

[64] See the tables in the Appendix for detailed figures on the strengths of Satellite military forces. [Footnote in original. The tables are not reprinted here.]

[65] In the case of Albania the figure is 29 percent. In East Germany no cut has been announced in the strength of the military forces. [Footnote in original.]

71. We do not believe that there will be significant increases in the Satellite standing armies over the period of the estimate, with the possible exception of the East German army. If conscription is adopted the latter could be doubled in size (from 100,000 to 215,000 men), but quality and political reliability would sharply decline. Such a development will probably depend in large part upon the extent of West German rearmament.

72. There appears to have been little joint planning or training among Satellite armies. The recent formation of a unified Soviet-Satellite armed forces command has changed only the forms under which the established Soviet control over military affairs is effected. There is as yet no conclusive evidence of inter-Satellite or Soviet-Satellite training under direction of the unified command. There is no evidence of plans for tactical integration of Bloc forces in wartime. It is probable, however, that integrated planning is under way and that combined maneuvers will be held within a few years. In the meantime, in the event of general war, the Satellite forces would probably be used separately under the direction of the Soviet high command and might be placed directly under Soviet officers.

73. The morale and reliability of Satellite ground forces has increased over the past year and will probably continue to improve during the period of the estimate. This trend will be largely the result of continued indoctrination and training. We believe that the reliability of these armies is such that they would be unlikely to defect on a substantial scale until victorious Western forces approached the Satellite area.

74. The combat effectiveness of the Satellite armies varies considerably so that no over-all generalization is possible respecting their probable performance in the event of general war. The amount of transport and mechanized equipment allocated to major Satellite forces has increased significantly in the last year, and mobility approaches that of Soviet forces. We believe that up to 50 percent of existing Satellite divisions could be employed initially in combat alongside Soviet forces. With Soviet logistical support, several of the armies would be capable of sustained independent action against traditional enemies. In general, the Bulgarian army is probably the most reliable, best trained, and effective of all the Satellite forces; division-level maneuvers have been held each year for the past five or six years. Bulgarian reserve training is extensive and thorough. Against such traditional enemies as the Turks or the Greeks, the Bulgars would fight with their maximum effectiveness. If the enemy forces included sizeable German contingents, the Czechoslovak and Polish armies would probably give a good account of themselves, for the Poles would fear the loss of the "recovered" lands and the Czechs the reoccupation by Germans of the Sudeten areas. The Hungarians and Rumanians, on the other hand, would probably regard a revival of German influence in Eastern Europe as favoring their chances of liberation from the USSR, and consequently their troops would suffer from poor morale if pitted against German units. The Satellite army with the lowest combat potential except for the small Albanian force, is that of East Germany. The Garrisoned People's Police (KVP), as this army is still called, could probably not be used for operations against NATO forces in West Germany, especially if the latter included components of German Federal Republic troops. KVP units would, in this case, have to be used for guarding lines of communication and in other secondary roles.

75. The Satellite militarized security forces have not changed significantly in strength over the past several years, although they have probably become more efficient. It is believed that they will retain approximately their present status through the period of this estimate, and that they will remain capable of protecting the local regimes against any threat of internal subversion. The one exception to this general capability is provided by East Germany where, until recent years, most security functions were performed by Soviet security forces. During the past year, however, there has been a strengthening and reorganization of East German security forces, probably in anticipation of their assuming greater responsibility for security operations.

76. The total Satellite output of arms and ammunition will remain a small share of total Soviet Bloc production. Although these countries will manufacture small arms, artillery, tanks, ammunition, personal and optical equipment, no significant increase in production of army equipment is expected.

77. *Air.* The Satellite air forces now have an estimated TO&E strength of 4,400, and an estimated actual strength of 3,000 operational aircraft of all types. We estimate that by 1960 TO&E strength will probably be 5,000, and that actual strength by that date will be nearly 4,000. Personnel strength is at present estimated to be 102,600. The capabilities of the Satellite air forces will probably be augmented as a result of an over-all increase in available aircraft and in the proportion of jet aircraft. We believe that, even if the recently announced manpower cuts are actually carried out, the over-all air capabilities will not be affected. No heavy bombers are expected to be introduced but piston medium bombers could be made available to the Satellite air forces as they are phased out of the Soviet air force. The greatest stress will continue to be placed on air defense, with secondary emphasis on air support of ground operations. Throughout the period of this estimate, the Satellite air forces will continue to constitute a significant increment to Soviet air strength in Europe.

78. The USSR provides intensive training for carefully selected Satellite pilots in the doctrines, techniques, and tactics of the Soviet air force. Soviet policy appears to be directed toward the attainment of a high degree of coordination between the air force of each Satellite and the Soviet air force, and the integration of the Satellite air forces into the Soviet air defense system. There has been little coordination among the individual Satellite air forces. While the Eastern European Defense Pact (EEDP)[66] suggests that such coordination is contemplated, probably no significant progress in this direction will be made. We estimate that the policy of close Soviet control of the Satellite air forces will continue through 1960.

79. After the Polish defections of 1953, the USSR strengthened its control over flying activities in all Satellite air forces. Concomitantly, there were increased efforts to improve personnel selection and political indoctrination. Emphasis was also placed upon the role of each Satellite air force in the defense of its own territory, thus stressing the national interest. These measures have increased the political reliability of the Satellite air forces. We believe that the combat effectiveness of these air forces is such that they could be employed in a defensive role in the event of general war and would have some offensive capability, particularly against traditional enemies.

80. Combat aircraft production in the Satellites now accounts for 11 percent by number and five percent by airframe weight of Bloc production. This share will probably increase to 14 percent by number and seven percent by weight by 1960. We believe that aircraft models now being produced in the Soviet Union will gradually replace obsolescent models on Satellite production lines, after the Soviets have converted to newer models. For example, we estimate that the FAGOT (MIG 15), the only jet fighter now being produced in the Satellites, will be phased out and will probably be replaced by the FRESCO (MIG 17) jet fighter in Czechoslovakia and in Poland by mid-1956. The FRESCO will probably be phased out after about three years and be replaced by either the FARMER jet fighter or the FLASHLIGHT all-weather fighter, or by both. The BEAST (IL–10), a ground attack aircraft, was phased out in Czechoslovakia in December 1954, and it is expected that the production of a light jet bomber, probably the BEAGLE (IL-28), will begin in 1956. The BEAGLE will probably be phased out by about 1960 and be replaced by a new light jet bomber. A new plant under construction in Rumania will probably begin production of FRESCO jet fighters in 1956. No production of guided missiles in the Satellites is expected during the period of the estimate.

81. An extensive program of airfield improvement and construction is being continued in all the Satellites. Principal emphasis has shifted from East Germany to Poland, but other Satellites continue to pursue a vigorous airfield construction effort. Runways now being built are at least 7,000 feet long and many are 8,000 or more. There are more than 400 airfields available to Soviet forces in the Satellites. Currently the number of major airfields (permanent runways of 6,000 feet or more) in the Satellites is 117, of which more than one-half are located in Poland and East Germany. If recent trends in construction continue, this figure would be almost dou-

[66] The Warsaw Pact.

bled by 1960. Airfields in the Satellites are numerous enough to support elements of the Soviet air force, as well as the Satellite air forces, in a general war occurring during the period of this estimate. Many Satellite fields are being equipped with night lighting, radio navigation aids, radar, increased POL facilities,[67] and improved structures. This growing network of modern well-equipped air facilities, as it progresses toward completion, will add materially to Soviet Bloc air capabilities.

Satellite Naval Forces[68]

82. The Satellite navies are small in size and poorly equipped and constitute only a minor contribution to Bloc naval strength. At present their primary function is the development of trained and politically reliable cadres for coastal patrol operations. They are gradually attaining some degree of defensive capability. Offensively they could give limited seaward support to ground forces. The Polish and East German navies have the capability of providing appreciable assistance to the Soviet Navy in such fields as minesweeping, mine laying, escort and coastal defense. In addition Poland has a limited potential for defensive submarine operations within approaches to Polish waters. The Rumanian and Bulgarian navies, however, will be capable of rendering only token assistance. Satellite ports and bases provide the USSR with a considerable extension of naval logistic and operational facilities. While in the past, Satellite navies have not been considered entirely reliable, the recent acquisition of several submarines by Poland and a steadily increasing number of mine warfare and patrol vessels in the East German Sea Police attest to increasing Soviet confidence in their reliability. However, it is not expected that any long-range program to build up the strength of the navies will be undertaken until the USSR is certain of their reliability.

83. The Polish Naval Air Arm, the only naval air arm in the Satellites, has progressed slowly to its present strength of one regiment of jet fighters and a possible regiment of piston attack type aircraft. It is considered to have limited capabilities for fighter defense and air strikes on surface vessels in the South Baltic area. The effectiveness of this air arm will probably remain limited. A small East German naval air arm may also be formed during the period of this estimate.

[Source: NARA, (Mandatory Review release to the National Security Archive), published in Jeff Richelson, The Soviet Estimate, *(Alexandria, V.A.: Chadwyck-Healey, Inc. and the National Security Archive, 1995), Document no. 00185.]*

[67] Most likely a reference to petroleum, oil, and lubrication facilities.

[68] For detailed figures on Satellite naval strength, see Table 6. [Footnote in original. Table not reprinted here.]

DOCUMENT NO. 8: Study Prepared for U.S. Army Intelligence, "Hungary: Resistance Activities and Potentials," January 1956

This detailed study, prepared for the U.S. Army several months before the Hungarian uprising, examines Hungary "as a potential theater for Special Forces operations." It not only analyzes the level and nature of dissidence in the country, but considers geographical and other factors in determining whether Hungary represents a suitable target for direct U.S. action. The report, too lengthy to reproduce in its entirety, is remarkable for the painstaking survey it includes of forced labor camps, prisons and other relevant data.

The report was one of a series of studies of conditions in Warsaw Pact countries conducted during the 1950s (and beyond), and provides evidence of the U.S. military's active search for ways to exploit the vulnerabilities of regimes in Eastern Europe. In this case, however, the authors found that "Hungary is singularly unpromising" as a potential special operations area. Geographic obstacles—the country is described as mostly "a flat plain" offering "few evasion possibilities"—and the "notably" low level of active resistance compared with other East European countries are the main reasons given. Superpower politics aside, there were clearly very practical considerations preventing an American military or paramilitary operation in Hungary in 1956.

On the other hand, the report also notes the relatively "widespread, intense, and current" nature of passive resistance in the country, and points to the prospect that "what is now dissidence may be converted into active resistance with the proper leadership." As it happened, this view mirrored the thinking of President Eisenhower and his close advisers, although they drew very different conclusions about the desirability of tapping reservoirs of popular discontent. Far from contemplating intervention in Hungary during the uprising, Eisenhower worried instead about inflaming the situation, possibly to the point of general war with the Soviet Union.

HUNGARY: RESISTANCE ACTIVITIES AND POTENTIALS (C)[69]

PROJECT NO. 9570

INFORMATION CUT-OFF
5 JANUARY 1956

[69] This study was prepared by an external research agency: (The) Georgetown University, Washington, D.C., research project, under contract to G2, Department of the Army, and does not necessarily represent the official views of ACSI, D/A. [Footnote in original.]

[70] Since the document is too lengthy to include in its entirety in this volume, the Table of Contents has been provided for the information of the reader. Page numbers listed correspond to pages in the original document.

Appendices[71]

Maps[72]   Following

***

CONCLUSIONS

I. Purpose of Report

To examine Hungary as a potential theater for Special Forces operations and to analyze those resistance, sociological and geographical factors which pertain to Special Forces planning.

1. Sources of dissidence and resistance potential in Hungary.
2. Major dissident elements.
3. Extent and currency of passive resistance.
4. Extent and currency of partisan resistance activity.
5. Extent and currency of underground resistance activity.
6. Suitability of Hungary for guerilla-type activities.
7. Localities of greatest dissidence and resistance.

II. Scope

This report goes beyond, and in some respects is less than, a supplementary to the general survey of the primary sociological characteristics and institutions of the people of Hungary which was presented in the Georgetown study, *Resistance Potentials: Hungary*, November 23, 1953. It is broader in scope because it will be principally guided by the requirements of Special

[72] Not reprinted here.

[71] Not reprinted here.

87

Forces; it is less than a supplementary because it omits several sections which were integral parts of the old Resistance Potentials outline. The objective of this report is to analyze, chiefly in light of recent available information, those factors relating to Special Forces interests which have not been fully treated elsewhere. The geographical suitability of Hungary for Special Forces operations is analyzed to the extent that these operations require a theater which provides places of refuge and/or bases of operations, places of concealment from observation and where pursuit is difficult. Because of their accessibility and economic and strategic importance, the railroads in Hungary stand out as the most notable Special Forces targets. However, because of various limitations, no attempt has been made to formulate a list of such targets.

The report undertakes to synthesize existing finished intelligence. The chapters in the original Georgetown report dealing with sociological and resistance factors relevant to Special Forces operations have been brought up to date. G–2 Project 6550 and appropriate NIS sections are the major source of information for the brief analysis of areas geographically suitable for Special Forces operations. G–2 files of resistance incidents in Hungary (maintained in Eurasian Branch), a summary translation of items appearing in *Magyarorszagi Hirek* (1954–55) which indicate dissidence and resistance (provided by Air Information Division), and recent G–2, CIA, and Department of State intelligence reports, have been employed for measuring the degree of dissidence and resistance potential which exists in Hungary. Throughout consideration was given to the requirement that no unnecessary duplication occur of other intelligence studies on Hungary, such as G–2 Project 6550 and NIS sections.

III. Factors Bearing Directly Upon the Conclusions

Viewed as a potential theater of Special Forces operations, Hungary is singularly unpromising. The geography of the country is forbidding: in view of the fact that most of Hungary is a flat plain, there are few evasion possibilities and the selection of Special Forces operational areas is consequently quite limited. Active resistance, of both the partisan and underground variety, has been notably less than in the other European satellites. Special Forces planners who would require the operational conditions of suitable terrain in proximity to appropriate targets, favorable resistance and sociological factors, and the absence of security forces, will find a very small area of selection in Hungary.

Nevertheless, Hungary must not be discounted in Special Forces planning. It may be argued that in no other European satellite is passive resistance so widespread, intense, and current. The conclusions which follow suggest that what is now dissidence may be converted into active resistance with the proper leadership. If the objective of Special Forces is to rally dissident elements in active opposition to the regime, the possibilities of success are favorable, at least in some localities and particularly among some elements of the population. Furthermore, hot war conditions may radically change the resistance picture and other actors related to the feasibility of Special Forces operations.

IV. Conclusions

1. Theoretically and practically Communism is the very antithesis of Hungarian nationalism which, on its positive side, is Christian and pro-Western. In international and national politics, in its agricultural policy of collectivization, in its program of industrialization, in its policy of Sovietization, in its persecution of religion, its regimentation of workers and widespread use of forced labor, the Communist regime has completely thwarted Hungarian nationalism and provided all elements of the population with numerous reasons for being dissident.

2. Dissidence and resistance potential appear to be strongest among *peasants*, whose continuing opposition has substantially contributed to the failure of the regime's agricultural program; *youth*, whose cynicism and apathy has caused growing concern in Communist circles; *industrial* workers, whose disillusionment is widespread; and the Roman Catholic *clergy*, the majority

of whom have not joined the regime-inspired "peace priest" movement and are respected by a large segment of the population.

3. Passive resistance is perhaps more common in Hungary that in any other European satellite. There are indications that this kind of resistance has grown in intensity since the Communist coup in 1948. The abandonment of the "new course" in early 1955 was partially responsible for this growth, and the predictable failure of the regime to achieve economic stability under a stricter program will probably continue to stimulate it.

4. Partisan activity during World War II was minor and probably consisted of little more that a few feats of individual heroism. Incomplete and poorly authenticated reports of partisan bands have placed them in those few areas of Hungary where the topography provided some possibilities of cover and concealment. There is no evidence that any armed partisans in Hungary endured for any length of time, and some of those reported may have consisted entirely of criminals and army deserters. There is no evidence of any current partisan activity in Hungary.

5. An analysis of the available information leads to the conclusion that underground activity of the early postwar period was poorly organized and haphazard. Further, there is evidence that the Communist regime itself either sponsored some of the organizations reported in order to entrap disloyal persons or invented them for the purpose of building up a case against individuals whose removal from positions of public influence was desirable. It is possible that remnants of underground groups currently exist, and are responsible for occasional acts of resistance. More probable, however, is the conclusion that current reports of underground activity are an expression of hope rather than of fact.

6. There are few areas in Hungary in which the terrain affords possibilities of cover and concealment. The forests in these areas are deciduous and provide only limited concealment during the winter months. Of the seven geographically feasible areas listed in this report at least three— the Bakony Forest, and the Pilis and Borzsony ranges—must be ruled out because they either coincide with, or are very proximate to, closely guarded summer training and maneuver areas of the Hungarian Army. The Bukh [Bükk], Matra and Hegyalja ranges and the Meksec [Sic: Mecsek] Hills appear to provide limited possibilities for successful guerilla-type operations.

7. The resistance picture in Hungary is such as to permit only questionable generalizations about the comparative intensity of peasant and worker resistance. Apart from reports of resistance incidents which may serve as a reliable index of current local dissidence, there is no feasible method of estimating resistance potential in various parts of the country.

HUNGARY: RESISTANCE POTENTIALS AND ACTIVITIES

A. Dissidence in Hungary

Dissidence,[73] a state of mind involving discontent or disaffection with the regime, is widespread in Hungary. By its very nature unorganized, it is not unified by any institutions such as church or political party. Though it is widespread—in 1954, an estimate placed the regime's ideologically convinced popular support at about 10 percent[74]—and hampers the efficiency of the Communist regime, it does not constitute an immediate threat to its security. The factors productive of dissidence and resistance potential spring mainly from the sociological characteristics of the people, and the measure taken by the Communist regime in opposition to them. Every vulnerability in the Communist system tends to generate dissidence; every passing day, without the hope of outside help, tends to diminish it.

[73] Definitions of dissidence and resistance are taken from Resistance Intelligence Report, RIR-1, July 20, 1954, *Anti-Communist Resistance Activities and Potentials in Poland,* prepared by the Resistance Intelligence Committee— approved by the Intelligence Advisory Committee (SECRET). [Footnote in original.]

[74] Dept. of State, *Psychological Intelligence Digest,* II/14, July 15, 1954 (S). [Footnote in original.]

1. Sources of Dissidence

Hungarian nationalism is anti-Slav, anti-Rumanian, anti-Czechoslovakian, anti-Semitic, and anti-Communist. On the positive side it is Christian, pro-German (as the lesser of two evils), and pro-Western, consisting of a deeply ingrained sense of the historic role of Hungary as a Christian nation and an outpost of Western civilization and culture. Although many fundamental and largely irreconcilable differences remain between Hungarian mentality and German character, the cultural affinity of the two peoples are based on a common Western heritage. Magyars bear a deep-rooted resentment toward the concept of Slavic supremacy. Their animosity toward Rumania and Czechoslovakia is an expression of revisionist ambition—to regain some of the territories lost to these countries by the World War II settlement, ratified by the Treaty of Trianon.[75] In contrast with some of the other satellites, Hungary has no territorial issues to settle with Germany. Because Communism is diametrically opposed to each element of Hungarian nationalism its acceptance involves a complete rejection of the latter. That Hungarians realize this can be presumed in view of their memory of the short-lived Bela Kun government of 1919[76] and their current experience under a Communist regime. The Sovietization of Hungarian society and culture, the rejection of Hungarian revisionist ambitions, the disproportionate number of Jews in high official positions, the savage attempts to collectivize the peasants, and the persecution of religion are forceful illustrations that Communism is the very antithesis of Hungarian nationalism.

On the reasonable assumption that the majority of Hungarians retain their nationalistic outlook and sociological characteristics, the following measures and policies implemented by the Communist regime are productive of dissidence and resistance potential:

a. After World War II Hungarian revisionist ambitions were completely thwarted. Whereas Hungary suffered losses of both territory and people, receiving no compensation whatsoever, Poland was granted administration of the so-called "Recovered Territories"; Northern Transylvania, which had been ceded to Hungary August 30, 1940, was returned to Rumania; Czechoslovakia received the Teschen area.

b. Although the experience of Hungarians with multi-party democracy in the inter-war years was very limited, the elections of 1945 and 1947 gave strong endorsement to parties representing democratic politics. The suppression of the multi-party system and the tyrannical Communist domination of every aspect of political life have intensified the antipathy of politically-conscious Hungarians.

c. The following measures taken by the Communist regime in the implementation of its agricultural policies have caused widespread discontent among Hungarian peasants, who in 1949 comprised nearly 50 percent of the total population:[77]

(1) collectivization, with its pressures against the peasants;
(2) the gradual but constant abrogation of the Land Reform Act of 1945;

---

[75] The Treaty of Trianon, in which Hungary lost two-thirds of its former territory, was part of the settlement of World War I.

[76] The Hungarian Soviet Republic (Tanácsköztársaság) was established by a coup on March 21, 1919, after the merger of the Hungarian Party of Communists and the Hungarian Social Democratic Party. Although, formally, the head of the government was the Social Democrat Sándor Garbai, real power was in the hands of the communist, Béla Kun, who was commissar for foreign affairs. The "Red terror" and collectivization of land soon made the Soviet Republic unpopular, and by August 2 it was overthrown through a combination of internal counterrevolution and foreign intervention.

[77] According to Hungarian official statistics, 40 percent of the total population of 9,750,000 in June were urban residents and 60 percent, rural residents. (Free Europe Committee, *News From Behind the Iron Curtain* (hereafter referred to as *NBIC*), May 1955). [Footnote in original.]

(3) the transfer of agricultural laborers into industry, contrary to the peasants' traditional dislike of industrial work, and which has deprived many independent peasants of the normal supply of farm labor;

(4) the quota delivery system, under which large portions of crops are sold to the state at low fixed prices;

(5) heavy taxation and the withholding from independent peasants of necessary supplies of seed, fertilizer, machinery, and other essentials;

(6) restrictions on freedom of action of peasants and their frequent intimidation by Communist officials.

Since the abandonment of the "new course" the regime has renewed its program of collectivization. In an article published in the Cominform journal (the official organ of the East European Communist parties) in September 1955, Janos Matolcsi,[78] now Minister of Agriculture, stated the Hungarian government aims at the socialization of 50 percent of the crop area by 1960.[79] According to Matolcsi, 43,000 new members were brought into the collectives since June 1955, and the total number of such farms now stands at 4,600. Although the collectivization goal is still fairly modest, the outlook for the private farmer is bleak. He is still being courted by the regime with promises of material aid, but it is made abundantly clear that the reason for this is simply that he and his fellows still farm 70 percent of the arable land and Hungary must have food. If the drive for more collectives is successful, the private farmer knows that he will become an ever less important member of the community, and that his treatment by the regime will deteriorate to the same degree.[80] Meanwhile, in view of his rather open resistance to the regime, the private farmer must be kept under constant surveillance.[81]

d. The Communist program of industrialization has been carried out with little regard for the welfare or desires of the Hungarian people. The industrial labor force has been expanded from a pre-war figure of about 300,000 to a total of approximately 1,000,000. Additional workers have been drawn from the peasantry, the former middle class, and the female and child population. With the exception of a few favored groups, industrial workers have suffered a marked reduction in their standard of living. The spectre of unemployment raised by large-scale layoffs in August and September 1954 so intensified the negative attitude of the population that the regime was forced to announce, in the wake of dismissals, apparently unplanned pension increases and emergency measures to aid the employed.[82]

e. Most independent craftsmen and merchants have been forced out of business. Nationalized domestic commerce has not fulfilled the needs of the people, and the introduction of inferior equipment and machinery of Soviet manufacture into Hungarian industries has caused many breakdowns.

f. The Communists have assumed control of all education in Hungary. Academic freedom has been abolished, textbooks have been rewritten from the Soviet point of view, and a rigid system of state control has been introduced at every level. Teachers of elementary and advanced schools are under close supervision of the government, and Party teachers who failed to follow Communist ideology have been dismissed. Students applying for a university education must satisfy Communist standards of loyalty.

g. The Sovietization of Hungarian culture has been relentlessly promoted on all fronts. Hungary is represented as a junior partner in the Pan-Slavic movement. The Russian

---

[78] János Matolcsi was a member of the HWP CC from 1951–1956, CC Secretary beginning 1953 and Minister of Agriculture from November 1955 to October 25, 1956.

[79] *New York Times,* September 20, 1955; Dept. of State, OIR, *Soviet Affairs,* April 1955 and July 1955 (S). [Footnote in original.]

[80] Dept. of State, OIR, IB No. 1794, June 16, 1955 (OUO); *The Economist,* June 18, 1955. [Footnote in original.]

[81] CIA, *Current Intelligence Digest,* OCI 0011/55, January 14, 1955, ID 0117305 (C). [Footnote in original.]

[82] Dept. of State, IR No. 6771, December 14, 1954 (S); IR No. 6853, February 1, 1955 (S). [Footnote in original.]

language is compulsorily taught in the schools and the history textbooks are being re-written to show that Hungary is a natural and traditional ally of the Soviet Union.

    h. Apart from the Land Reform Laws of 1945 which provided for the nationalization of all landed properties of the churches exceeding 100 hold (approximately 141 acres) and may have enjoyed popular support, the Communist regime has carried on a steady campaign against religious institutions in Hungary. Among the measures enacted against the various churches are the following:

(1) The privilege of clergymen to serve in the ranks in the military service was abolished.

(2) The Jewish denominational organizations were deprived of their autonomy when their officers, previously elective, were made subject to appointment by he government. At the same time two of the Jewish denominational organizations were merged by decree.

(3) Several laws and decrees were issued which deprived the churches of their schools and progressively restricted religious instruction in schools until it was all but abolished.

(4) A large number of national and local charitable, cultural, and economic associations under religious auspices were dissolved by the Ministry of Interior.

(5) Many ecclesiastical holidays were declared regular workdays.

(6) In violation of a previous agreement between the churches and the regime, the clergy were forced to take an oath of loyalty to the government.

(7) Most Roman Catholic religious orders were disbanded and their monasteries confiscated. Only the Franciscan, Benedictine, and Piarist orders were spared and are currently permitted to conduct two high schools each.[83]

(8) The appointment of bishops and prelates was made subject to government approval with retroactive effect.

(9) A "Movement of Peace Priests" has been developed by the Communists in order to split the unity of the Roman Catholic Church.

In addition to these measures, which in reality provide only the legal framework for the destruction of the churches, atheist propaganda, intense police terrorism, and brutal treatment of the clergy provide the most impressive evidence of the intentions of the regime. People who have continued to practice their religion have been discriminated against, and it was apparently common knowledge in some areas that regular church attendance could cause loss of employment.[84]

The Roman Catholic Church, of which approximately 70 percent of the population are members, has been a primary target of the regime. The arrest and trial of Cardinal Mindszenty, Primate of Hungary, was perhaps productive of more dissidence and resistance potential than any other single action of the regime. The "peace priest" movement has apparently failed to achieve its objective and is regarded with suspicion by the majority of the people. During the "new course" the campaign against the Catholic Church was suspended. Radio Vatican stated that in the 18 months of Imre Nagy's government religion in Hungary enjoyed an almost privileged position, and that celebrations of the Marian Year, the normal exercise of pastoral functions, and other imposing privileges granted to the Church had quieted the minds of the people.[85] The dismissal of Nagy and the abandonment of the "new course" have been followed by an intensification of the campaign against the Catholic Church. According to Radio Vatican, as soon as the new Premier, Hegedus, took office, the secret police resumed close watch on the churches, bishops' palaces, priests and Catholic lay leaders.[86] The announced release of Cardinal Mindszenty, and the reportedly imminent release of Archbishop Groesz [Grősz] and other clergymen, may signify another pause in the campaign against the Church. Recent

[83] *New York Times*, November 2, 1955. [Footnote in original.]

[84] JIC, USFA, March 12, 1955 (DOI: 1953), Eval: F-None (C). [Footnote in original.]

[85] FBIS, Paris AFP, March 12, 1955. [Footnote in original.]

[86] FBIS, May 11, 1955. [Footnote in original.]

reports of a new program of so-called cooperation between Church and State—the people being urged to believe in God and go to church—indicate a more lenient attitude.[87] At best, however, these are only tactical maneuvers and most probably are recognized as such by the Hungarian people.

i. General labor restrictions apply to every worker in Hungary. Prohibitions against leaving one's job, rules concerning work performance, and a carefully detailed system of disciplinary regulations, hem in the worker and subordinate him to Communist economic plans. Some of the specific forms of the coercion of free labor are:[88]

(1) Youth Brigades, organized and administered by the Communist Working Youth Association (DISZ), for work during summer vacations. The Fact that scholarships and even the individual's school record depend upon his cooperation in this regard belie the so-called "voluntary" nature of this work. Youth brigades have been reported at Kolocsa-Baja, Kazincbarcika, and other places.

(2) The assignment of graduating students and technical personnel to work designated by the state.

(3) Forced labor "on the job." This is a marginal case between free and forced labor and it applies to individuals sentenced to "corrective-educative" labor. The worker is generally left on his job but is fined from 10 to 25 percent of his wages. "On-the-job" forced labor has been reported from Hodmezovasarhely and other places.

j. Special restrictions have been imposed on many persons whose loyalty to the regime has been questioned. These restrictions amount to forced labor, of which there are the following types:[89]

(1) *Area arrest,* or assignment to a new place of residence with the obligation to work. Individuals included in this category are not physically detained in a camp or prison, but on the basis of a court sentence or administrative police order are made to perform work under police surveillance at an arbitrarily assigned location.

(2) *Army labor service battalions.* These labor units are recruited under military draft for seasonal or more permanent work. The draft for these units is similar to the pre-war anti-Jewish measures and is based on political discrimination. Young kulaks and unreliable elements serve three-year terms under armed guards, working conditions being very similar to those of forced laborers in camps and prisons.[90]

(3) *Forced Labor under total restraint.* This category includes workers in all types of camps or prisons engaged in economic activity. More that 200 forced labor camps and prisons have been reported as existing in Hungary. (See Tab A)[91]

k. Deportations (see Tab B),[92] as a means of carrying out various objectives of the regime, have been conducted by the Hungarian Communist regime since the coup in 1948. (Prior to 1947, they were initiated by the Soviets to supply labor for the Soviet Union.) Deportees, whose number it is impossible to estimate with any degree of accuracy, eventually became forced laborers. Large-scale deportations have resulted in the virtu-

---

[87] *Time Magazine,* October 17, 1955; *New York Times,* November 2, 1955. [Footnote in original.]

[88] *Forced Labor in the "People's Democracies,"* Mid-European Studies Center, Free Europe Committee, Inc. (New York: 1955), ID 948099 (U). [Footnote in original.]

[89] *Forced Labor in the "People's Democracies,"* op.cit. [Footnote in original.]

[90] Army Labor Brigades (*Muszaki Dandar—MJSZ*) were reportedly abolished in 1953. See American Embassy, Vienna, Desp. No. 1045, March 14, 1955 (C). [Footnote in original.]

[91] Not reprinted here.

[92] Not reprinted here.

al elimination of the upper and middle classes. As a result of the amnesty provisions of the "new course," none who were released from detention camps were allowed to return to their original places of residence.

During 1955 a renewed campaign of deporting undesirables has been reported. According to one report, 1700 persons were deported from Budapest, Gyor and Miskolc during May and June 1955, and for the first time the relatives of persons who have fled the country are being deported for that reason.[93] The deportees were reportedly being taken to emergency accommodations in Bekes (4646–2108) near the Rumanian border and their homes were being confiscated.

2. Major Dissent Elements

Whether the discriminatory measures of the Communist regime have destroyed more resistance potential than they have created is difficult to determine. The measures have been largely directed against those elements of Hungarian society which, if uncontrolled, might eventually generate resistance leaders. The campaign to eliminate potential resistance leaders has been thorough and probably effective. At the same time it has served to crystallize the opposition of various groups who have been clearly marked out for destruction by the regime. Whereas there are apparently few potential resistance leaders remaining in Hungary, there are dissident elements in almost every walk of life. Dissidence and resistance potential appear to be strongest among the following groups:

a. *Peasants.* The term "kulak," loosely used to refer to all farmers who have remained outside the collectives, has become almost synonymous with "enemy of the people." Even those persons with a kulak background are regarded as suspect. The fact that approximately 278,000 farmers (one out of every four) withdrew from the collectives during the 1953–54 period is a clear indication of the unpopularity of the collectivization program. Despite every pressure to join the collectivization program, only approximately 30 percent of the arable land in Hungary has been collectivized.[94] Disaffection toward Communist rule and popular apathy toward Communist measures became so pronounced in the rural areas as to compel the regime to admit its weakness in an unprecedented manner during the local elections held in November 1954.[95] These elections were distinguished from previous ones held in the satellites in that never before had any Communist regime allowed the admitted small minority of negative votes to affect the actual outcome of the election. In announcing the results, the Hungarian regime claimed 97.9 percent of the vote cast, but admitted the rejection by the voters of 586 candidates out of 106,000. Virtually all of the rejections occurred in the villages where the candidates were close to the electorate. Furthermore, there is evidence that farmers' clubs, whose organization was recently authorized by the regime in order to bring "Communist culture" to the rural population, have come under the influence of "kulaks." The rural population readily responded to the invitation to form these clubs, many respected anti-Communist peasants joining. In an editorial, January 13, 1955, *Szabad Nep* wrote: "In the farmers' clubs, certain elements under the influence of the enemy try to incite the working peasants against the Party . . . Everywhere kulaks penetrate these clubs."[96]

[93] Washington Post and Times Herald, August 8, 1955 (letter from Bela Fabian, member of the Executive Committee of the Hungarian National Council); New York Times, August 5, 1955 (from Austrian Socialist Press Service). [Footnote in original.] This information seems to be incorrect since there is no indication of such deportations as late as 1955. In fact, this period was characterized by the elimination of the entire deportation system and by the release of those who had been previously deported.

[94] Soviet Affairs, July 1955 (S). [Footnote in original.]

[95] Dept. of State, IR 6853, February 1, 1955 (S). [Footnote in original.]

[96] Magyarorszagi Hirek, No. 4, January 22, 1955, item 5. [Footnote in original.]

94

b. *Youth.* Contrary to early predictions of Communist success in the indoctrination of youth, the whole youth program has been far from successful, and the resistance of youth is one of the most serious problems facing the Communists. There have been several "official criticisms" of the DISZ (the Communist youth organization), and Hungarian youth, particularly students, have reacted to Communist propaganda with apathy and cynicism. Over the past few years, the Party has issued many complaints about the young people's bourgeois attitudes and emulation of Western customs.[97] Resentment of Communism has been manifested by "hooliganism," which often amounts to nothing more than wearing American-style ties, chewing gum, listening to American jazz, reading and distributing "westerns," as well as by indifference to Marxist-Leninist courses and Communist youth activities. For example, *Szabad Ifjusag* (Budapest, April 25, 1954) stated:

This year there were 1,200 disciplinary cases at the Polytechnical University. In some cases, such as in the fourth year thermodynamics class, whole circles of students refused to perform the obligatory tasks. Often, on days when only one or two classes are given, 25 percent of the students are absent.[98]

c. *Industrial Workers.* Only a small percentage of industrial workers originally supported the Communists. As a result of the regimentation of labor, stakhanovite methods of speeding up production, and deteriorating living standards, many have been alienated. One report states that the regime believes that resistance is most likely to arise from the disappointed working class and in particular from old Social Democrats, and that, as a result, industrial workers are more closely watched than kulaks or members of the middle class who are materially and morally depressed and incapable of organizing any resistance.[99]

d. *Clergy.* Despite intensive pressure, the "peace priest" movement has apparently failed. In July 1955 the official organ of the movement, *Kereszt*, was placed on the Index of Forbidden Books by the Vatican. Church attendance is reportedly greater than ever before and the majority of the clergy are at least recognized as non-conformists and have great influence on the people. It has been reported that Communist influence is stronger in the Protestant areas of Hungary.[100] Since the abandonment of the "new course" there have been new arrests of priests and the Communists have reportedly issued a warning that priests will be held responsible for peasants who fail to meet their quotas and for any general effort to resist the authorities.[101] In the vicinity of Szeged priests have been warned that in case of sabotage they will be required to pay for all the damage.[102]

B. Passive Resistance

Conducted within the framework of the resisters' normal life and duties, passive resistance[103] involves the deliberate non-performance or the malperformance of acts which would directly or indirectly benefit the regime, or deliberate nonconformity with standards of conduct established by the regime. Under a Communist regime the simplest and safest method by which the ordinary citizen may offer resistance is by carrying out his work in a slipshod manner and only exter-

---

[97] See American Legation, Budapest, Desp. No. 386, June 3, 1955 (LOU). [Footnote in original.]

[98] NSIC, August 1954; *Magyarorszagi Hírek*, No. 18, May 29, 1954, item 7. [Footnote in original.]

[99] CIA, CS-X-48559, November 30, 1954, B–3 (S). [Footnote in original.]

[100] G–2, USFA, R–1317–54, 22 July 1954 (DOI: Dec. 1953), F–3 (O). [Footnote in original.]

[101] FBIS, May 11, 1955, Source: Radio Vatican. [Footnote in original.]

[102] *Ibid.* [Footnote in original.]

[103] Definitions of dissidence and resistance with its various types are taken from Resistance Intelligence Report, RIR–1, July 20, 1954, Anti-Communist Resistance Activities and Potentials in Poland, prepared by the Resistance Intelligence Committee—approved by the Intelligence Advisory Committee (S). [Footnote in original.]

nally complying with the regulations of the government. This is especially true in Hungary where an effective Soviet control system and other factors such as physically and psychologically exhaustive work norms, material want, and compulsory political activities have restricted Hungarian resistance to passive, unorganized manifestations.

If the public complaints of the regime are accepted at their face value, resistance of this type has been widespread in Hungary.[104] Prior to the "new course," passive resistance took the forms of absenteeism, job-hopping, shoddy work, waste, frauds in computing norms, and often culminated in deliberate sabotage. Peasants formed the largest section of the population which offered resistance to the regime.[105] In the factories, excessively high labor norms, long hours with little pay, poor working conditions, inefficient bureaucratic management, defective materials, ever-increasing demands for speedier output, and expanded "socialist competitions," had alienated the Hungarian workers. Shortages of food and consumer goods, poor housing conditions, currency reforms which reduced purchasing power and wiped out savings, added to the grievances of the Hungarian people. The evidence is that the Hungarian people at first regarded the "new course" as a manifestation of the weakness of the regime. In response to Premier Nagy's announcement of July 4, 1953 that the dissolution of the kolkhozes [collective farms] would be permitted, many peasants started a movement for leaving and breaking up the collectives. The announcement, coming during the harvest period, was ill-timed: desertions from the kolkhozes disrupted the harvesting of crops, and individual peasants rushed onto the kolkhoz land to pillage crops, reclaim their individual holdings, and incite collective farm members to revolt. During the "new course" period approximately one-fourth of the collective farms were disbanded. Further, many peasants, believing that the regime would abandon its agrarian policy entirely, grew bolder in their refusal to meet delivery quotas, which they believed would be reduced even more. On October 30, 1953, Radio Budapest pointed out that the "new course" was in no way a sign of regime weakness:

> The enemy described cancellation of delivery arrears and concessions granted under the new produce collection as a sign of weakness; the enemy spreads lies that the present concessions will be followed by others and that peasants therefore much not surrender their produce. A number of out local councils do not stand up to such hostile views with sufficient determination.

Other farmers decided that the "new course" concessions were only wasted maneuvers and that the regime was "fattening peasants for a future kill." This attitude was so widespread that on September 29, 1953, Nagy saw fit to denounce "enemy propaganda" which claimed that government aid to farmers was a "transitory phenomenon."[106] The "new course," in some ways an admission that the regime no longer found it expedient either politically or economically to disregard the welfare of the people, failed to achieve its objective of pleasing the people and was abandoned in early 1955. According to the admissions of the regime, Hungary faces falling agricultural production, the need to import "considerable quantities" of grain, the non-fulfillment of even the reduced compulsory deliveries, and "rampant indiscipline" in the local councils and on some of the farms.[107] The dismissal of Imre Nagy as Premier (announced officially April 18, 1955) signaled the formal abandonment of the "new course" and a return to the rule of force and fear. Circumstances surrounding Nagy's dismissal from all Party and government posts emphasized the central position of agriculture in regime planning.[108] (Among the crimes imputed to Nagy was failing to carry on class warfare in the vil-

---

[104] NIE 10–55, April 12, 1955, p. 19 states: "Passive resistance in Hungary appears to have been more widespread and effective than elsewhere in the satellites." [Footnote in original.]

[105] G–2, GSI/TRUST/BETFOR, R–189–53, 2 July 1953 (DOI: up to Oct. 1951), ID 1181961, F–6 (S). [Footnote in original.]

[106] *NBIC*, August 1954. [Footnote in original.]

[107] *The Economist,* June 18, 1955. [Footnote in original.]

[108] See American Legation, Bucharest, Desp. No. 338, May 11, 1955 (S); Dept. of State, OIR, IB No. 1769, April 20, 1955. [Footnote in original.]

lages—eradication of kulaks—and to encourage the development of collective farming.) For the peasant the abandonment of the "new course" means a more rigorous enforcement of the collectivization program. For the churches it means new persecution and a tightening of controls. For the worker it means more stringent restrictions.

The anticipated withdrawal of Soviet troops from Hungary, as a consequence of the peace treaty with Austria, may have been one of the motives for the recent tightening of controls. In an effort to brace itself for a possible reaction to a withdrawal of Soviet troops, promised by Soviet leaders in July 1955,[109] the Hungarian regime has renewed its campaign to eliminate potential resistance leaders. However, Hungarian officials have pointed out that Soviet troops would remain in their country while NATO existed, and that, on the basis of the Soviet-bloc military pact signed in Warsaw in May 1955, troops of the signatory powers could be assigned to any one of the member nations.[110] During 1955, deportations have been reported and there have been an increasing number of regime attacks on kulaks, speculators, and peasants who have not fulfilled delivery quotas.

As a result of passive resistance by the people and poor planning by the regime Hungary's economic situation borders on the critical.[111] In addition to larger admissions of failure in the fields of agriculture and industry, the Communist press has publicly acknowledged many instances of production failures. These, together with reports of unrest among the peasants and other sectors of the population, provide an index of the extent of passive resistance in Hungary (see Tab C).[112]

It is reasonable to assume that the majority of Hungarians regard themselves as a captive people and resent this status. Motivated by expediency and the necessity of achieving a *modus vivendi*, many have come to accept the status quo and, with the motive of "making the best of a bad situation," to cooperate with the regime. Certainly, after several years of Communist domination, some people are becoming desperate and giving up hope of outside help. Others are perhaps bitter at the West for what they consider as broken promises. Nevertheless, the Communist tyranny has not become more palatable with the years and national pride and ambitions have not been destroyed in a decade. The causes of dissidence remain in Hungary and will probably continue to produce passive resistance for several years to come.

C. Resistance Activities

Resistance, which is dissidence translated into action, may be organized or unorganized, and, in either case, may be *active* or *passive*. Organized *active* resistance is either *overt* (partisan activity in open revolt against the regime) or *covert* (underground resistance which is carried out in secrecy and is designed to collect and disseminate intelligence, and to prepare for the overthrow of the government).

There is no tradition or history of active resistance in Hungary, and all the evidence indicates that this tradition has not been broken.[113] During World War II there were several military and civilian underground groups active in German-occupied Hungary, but their exploits are probably best described as feats of individual heroism. Hungary is a relatively small country with few inaccessible areas and a large and efficient police force which is probably loyal to the regime. It has been suggested that there is resistance in Hungary and that it is purposely scattered and indefinable so that it will be more difficult to detect.[114] However, this purposiveness would seem to require a direction and organization which does not appear in any of the reports which describe resistance activity. Closer to the true situation is the conclusion that most of the resistance in Hungary is of a passive character, and that there are few potential underground leaders.

[109] *Washington Post and Times Herald*, July 31, 1955. [Footnote in original.]

[110] *New York Times*, September 14, 1955. [Footnote in original.]

[111] See M/A Hungary, R–455–53, December 15, 1953 (DOI: August 1, 1953), ID 1192960 (C); Dept. of State, IR No. 6771, December 14, 1954 (S). [Footnote in original.]

[112] Not reprinted here.

[113] See M/A Hungary, R–455–53, *op. cit.* [Footnote in original.]

[114] CIA, OO–W–26725, June 29, 1953 (DOI: April 10, 1953) (R). [Footnote in original.]

Since the Communist coup in 1947 active resistance has been largely unorganized. There are only a few instances of alleged partisan activity, and much of the underground activity reported appears to have been invented or "inspired" by the regime. Since the coup, the Communists have publicized a number of alleged conspiracies, such as in the Cardinal Mindszenty trial (1949), the Rajk case (1949), the imprisonment of Archbishop Groesz (1951), and General Gabor Peter (1953–54). The Communist press, especially during the 1951 to 1953 period, carried frequent accounts of the arrests and trials of saboteurs. Although there is a report which states that there are 1,000 Hungarians in the penal prisoner area around Tayshet (Eastern Siberia) who were sentenced because of activities on June 17, 1953,[115] there is no other evidence that there were large-scale disturbances on the occasion of the East German uprising.[116] Neither did the purge of [Beria] in the USSR cause any covert or popular reaction in Hungary. There is evidence that some of the underground movements alleged to exist in Hungary were "inspired" by the regime for the purpose of apprehending dissident elements of the population. On the whole, admissions by the regime of specific acts of popular resistance diminished considerably after the inauguration of the "new course" in July 1953. However, since late 1954 reports of arrests have been more numerous, and there have been recent avowals of a renewed vigilance campaign against the "traditional enemies of socialism."

1. Partisan Activity

It is highly unlikely that there is any organized partisan activity in Hungary today. Considering the strength of the regime, the pervasiveness of its control, and the fact that most of Hungary is geographically unsuitable for partisan warfare, it would indeed be quite surprising if partisan groups still existed. Reports of partisan bands in the past have placed them in those areas where the topography provided some possibility of cover and concealment. There is no evidence that any armed bands in Hungary endured for any length of time, and some of those reported may have consisted entirely of criminals and army deserters. An unsuccessful attempt by five men to penetrate a large ammunition dump located in a wooded area near Erdotelek (4741–2019) in December 1953 is apparently the most recent resistance incident which might be construed as partisan activity.[117]

Following is a summary account of several incomplete and inadequately authenticated reports of partisan activity in Hungary. Since these activities took place prior to 1954—mostly in 1950—they are of interest only because they highlight the areas within Hungary which are suitable for this type of active resistance.

  a. In July 1950 a partisan camp was reportedly located near Bukkszentlaszlo (4804–2040) and Bukkszentkereszt (4804–2038). There were also 10 small encampments between Lillafured (4805–2037) and Ujmassa (cannot locate), each quartering from 30 to 50 partisans. Partisans allegedly had a transmitting and receiving radio station at Ujmassa and large supply depots in the woods between Ujmassa (cannot locate) and Omassa (4807–2032).[118]
  b. In late November 1950 there were reportedly partisan groups in the mountainous regions of Nagyszal (4752–1707), Karancs (4809–1947), Czerbat [Cserhát] (4755–1919), Bukh (4804–2035) and Matra (4750–2000). These probably crossed the Danube from Eastern Slovakia and were allegedly composed of Hungarians, Slovaks,

---

[115] USAREURIC, 513th MISG, RVPET-950–54 (EI–2558), October 19, 1954 (DOI: Feb.–Mar. 1954), ID 1264080, F–6 (C), p. 42. [Footnote in original.]

[116] In fact, there were no disturbances at all in Hungary at the time of the East German uprising.

[117] M/A Hungary, R–471–53, December 22, 1953, B–3, ID 1194807 (C) (Source: member of a friendly legation). The official comment on this information was that the attempted penetration was the work of some resistance groups in need of ammunition or merely an act of sabotage. [Footnote in original.]

[118] CIA, SO–59549, April 4, 1951 (DOI: July 1950), ID 777145 (S). (Washington comment: The identity of these "partisans" is unknown.) [Footnote in original.]

Balkan Volksdeutsche, Ukranians and Ruthenians. The partisans were reportedly poorly armed, only an estimated 30 percent having weapons.[119]

c. In September and October of 1950 the authorities at Vac (4746–1908) reportedly organized extensive expeditions in the regions of Kosd (4748–1910), Osagard (4751–1912), Alsopeteny (4752–1915), and farther north to seek out these groups. These expeditions failed, and despite the use of agents provocateur to single out those who may have been helping the partisans, did not discover any disloyal elements in the local populace. According to the source of this information, it was mostly Slovak peasants (presumably in Slovakia) who were aiding these partisans.[120]

d. In late 1950 independent partisan bands were reportedly operating in the marshy regions of the Hortobagy river on the plain north of Szeged.[121] Consisting of five to ten men, these groups were composed of Russian and Hungarian deserters, fugitive peasants from the collective farms near the Yugoslavian frontier, and ordinary criminals. Equipped with Russian arms and supplies, these groups limited themselves to banditry.

e. In late 1950 some partisan groups allegedly maintained contact with the Yugoslav authorities and there was an organized contact group of a permanent character along the Yugoslavian frontier supported by Yugoslavian officials.[122] Yugoslav patrols allegedly made contact with partisan groups, usually along the lower course of the Danube where it is difficult for Hungarian police to guard the border effectively.[123]

f. Because of numerous troops in the area, the mountainous region of Mecsek (4606–1813) was abandoned by partisans, but small groups were reportedly coming back in late 1950.[124] It was reported that, on August 2, 1950, a Hungarian resistance group of 15 attacked a Soviet military store in the vicinity of Villany (4552–1827), killed five Soviet guards and took 150 automatic pistols and rifles and large quantities of ammunition and food rations.[125] In 1952 a meeting of an anti-Communist youth group in the woods of Mecsek was reportedly raided by the AVH and 80 of the participants were arrested.[126] In May 1954 there was hearsay information that this group still existed and held meetings in the same wooded area.[127]

g. In 1951 the White Guard (see following section), according to the source,[128] had its headquarters at Kismaros (4750–1901) in the Bukh mountains and partisan centers in the Bakony mountains (4715–1750) (the leader living in Papa), in the area of Lake Balaton (with headquarters in Siofok), and a fourth group between the Danube and the Tisza. The Guard reportedly had a 200-man unit at Kismaros, 50 men at Siofok near Lake Balaton, and 280 men at a spot somewhere east of the Danube—each unit having a secret arms cache and instructions not to take action until a propitious time.[129]

h. Sometime after 1947 one source reported hearsay information of partisan activities in the Pilis mountains (4741–1852).[130]

---

[119] CIA, SO–73847, October 23, 1951 (DOI: late Nov. 1950), C–6, ID 845578 (S). [Footnote in original.]

[120] *Ibid.* [Footnote in original.]

[121] *Ibid.* [Footnote in original.]

[122] *Ibid.* [Footnote in original.]

[123] It may be significant that in August 1955 Yugoslavia received a friendship pledge from Hungary, a fact which may mark the end of the open enmity of several years standing between the two countries. [Footnote in original.]

[124] *Ibid.* [Footnote in original.]

[125] CIA, OO–W–15025, November 8, 1950 (DOI: 1950), ID 731177 (C) (from *Hungaria*, an émigré newspaper published in Munich). [Footnote in original.]

[126] JIC, USFA, R–6676–54, December 21, 1954, ID 1268756 (C). [Footnote in original.]

[127] *Ibid.* [Footnote in original.]

[128] American Embassy, Vienna, Desp. No. 1124, April 23, 1951, ID 805567 (S). [Footnote in original.]

[129] G–2, D/A, Weekly Intelligence Report, August 10, 1951 (S); USFA, Bi-Weekly Report No. 145, June 8, 1951 (DOI: Jan. 11, 1951), F–3 (S). [Footnote in original.]

[130] JIC, USFA, R–0060–55, October 30, 1954 (DOI: 1947–June 1954), C–None, ID 1274369 (C). [Footnote in original.]

2. Underground Activity

If one were to believe the claims of émigré organizations and the reports of the Communist press, there has been considerable organized active resistance of the covert variety in Hungary. However, an analysis of the available information leads to the conclusion that there is really no organized underground movement at the present time and that underground activity of the early postwar period was poorly organized and haphazard. Further, there is evidence that the Communist regime itself was either the sponsor of some of the organizations reported or invented them for the purpose of building up a case against individuals whose removal from positions of public influence was desirable. Tab D[131] lists 15 underground organizations which have been reported in the postwar period.

There is no feasible method of determining to what extent the Communist regime promotes "resistance" groups under the names of White Guard, Black Eagle, etc., for the purpose of apprehending disloyal citizens. Certainly some of the anti-regime elements in Hungary have learned to be very careful in joining resistance groups. An incident reported in the Domsod (4705–1900) area depicts the astuteness of the regime in weeding out dissident elements and forestalling the growth of resistance movements:

> According to an F–2 source (an American businessman), the potato crops in the Domsod area in 1952 were so poor that none of the uncollectivized farmers were able to meet their quotas and their temper was "pre-revolutionary." The AVH secretly distributed pamphlets in English and Hungarian calling for recruits in a resistance group. Applications were accepted only with payments of 300 forints. Nine men were hanged after applying. The news of this was apparently suppressed because recruiting continued in this area as well as in another village 20 km south of Budapest.[132]

In the last two years no new underground movements have been reported. There have, however, been several defector reports which rather vaguely affirm that there is still a distinct underground movement in Hungary.[133] A non-commissioned officer of the Hungarian Army, who defected in January 1954, state that there still is a NEM (see Tab D–15)[134] underground movement in the Hungarian Army, operating on a cell system.[135] According to this defector, only a few officers belonged to this movement but there was a conscript cell in almost every army unit. Considering the available evidence, the most probable conclusion which can be drawn is that it is highly doubtful that there ever was a large organized underground in Hungary, and the organized resistance which continues to be reported is more an expression of hope than fact.

3. Resistance Incidents

In contrast to Poland, Rumania, and Czechoslovakia, there has been very little, if any, organized resistance in Hungary, and the volume of incidents of active resistance appears to be proportionately smaller. Arrests and trials of persons for anti-regime activity are listed in Tab F[136] and provide information valuable for determining the extent of both passive and active resistance. Many of the incidents of active resistance which have occurred appear to be spontaneous outbursts of pent-up opposition to the regime; others, such as the distribution of anti-regime literature, indicate some planning. Considering the oppressive measures of the regime and the absence of a reasonable expectation on the part of the Hungarian people that these will be of short duration, it is to be expected that such incidents will con-

---

[131] Not reprinted here.

[132] CIA, SO–94806, October 16, 1952 (DOI: August 12, 1952) F–2 (S). [Footnote in original.]

[133] USFA, R–9236–54, May 13, 1954, ID 1254092 (C). [Footnote in original.]

[134] The National Resistance Movement or Nemzeti Ellenállási Mozgalom. Tab D is not reprinted here.

[135] American Embassy, Vienna, Desp. No. 1045, March 14, 1955 (C). [Footnote in original.]

[136] Not reprinted here.

tinue. Such resistance obviously does not constitute any threat to the security of the regime, and indeed may even have been provoked by the regime in some cases for the purpose of uncovering subversive elements of the population. From an anti-Communist point of view, however, resistance incidents, of whatever type, serve to index the strength of passive resistance, and may cumulatively provide information concerning attitudes of a definitive sector of the population. Examples of resistance incidents which have occurred in different parts of Hungary are listed n Tab E.[137]

4. *Arrests and Trials of Anti-Russian Elements*

Charges made in courts and convictions obtained should not be construed as acceptable evidence of the extent of active resistance. Many arrests and trials are undoubtedly largely motivated by the necessity of finding scapegoats for failures to meet production quotas or to keep promises of better economic conditions; others, probably those of real resistance leaders, are not publicized. According to Communist policy near relatives of the accused are also arrested on the grounds that they have violated security laws in not reporting subversive activity. For the purpose of swaying the public conscience, all of those accused of anti-regime activity are also charged with petty crimes such as fraud and theft.[138] It appears reasonable to assume that the persons arrested can be regarded at least as potential resistance leaders, and, in some cases, may indeed have been involved in some effort, however disorganized, to defeat the objectives of the government. Consequently, Tab F presents a partial list of arrests, trials, and sentences passed in the last three years which may reveal elements in the population and/or localities which the regime regards as potential trouble-spots, and may thus serve as a criterion for appraising resistance potential.

There are continuing reports of arrests in Hungary: In early July 1955, reports reaching Vienna stated that in mid-June hundreds of police arrived in Budapest and raided homes, cafes, and coffee houses. At about the same time the Hungarian Communist news agency (M.T.I.) confirmed that widespread tension existed by reporting numerous arrests of Hungarians charged with acting as "American spies and saboteurs."[139] According to *Neue Zuercher Zeitung*, August 1, 1955, ". . . police terror in Hungary is on the increase and security has been tightened: Budapest was literally occupied by police; cars were stopped and passengers searched; anti-West posters appeared on the walls of buildings; all groupings of people were immediately dispersed and food warehouses were placed under heavy guard; large military units were dispatched towards the Austrian and Yugoslavian borders."

D. *Suitability of Hungary for Special Forces Operations*

One of the principal reasons why Hungarian resistance is more or less restricted to passive unorganized manifestations is geographical. Poor terrain impedes the formation of nuclei for future guerilla operations and certainly would inhibit Special Forces operations. There are relatively few areas in Hungary which offer possibilities of refuge and concealment for guerilla-type activity. With the exception of a semi-circle of forested hills to the west and northwest and the Meksec [Mecsek] Upland (northwest of the city of Pecs), Hungary is a flat plain, the Alfold. Areas of the country which are suitable for Special Forces operations requiring terrain offering such possibilities are the *Northern Hills* region and the *Meksec Hills*.

Map A[140] shows geographically suitable refuge areas and/or bases of operations for Special Forces. These areas are identical with those selected by G–2 Project #6550 on the basis of cartographical inspection of terrain and cultural features. Refuge areas on Map A are referred to by the same numbers and letters under which they are described in the text. Training and maneuver

---

[137] Not reprinted here.

[138] G–2, USFA, R–1317–54, July 22, 1954 (DOI: Dec. 1953), ID 1257339 (S). [Footnote in original.]

[139] *New York Times,* July 6, 1955. [Footnote in original.]

[140] Not reprinted here.

areas of the Hungarian Army—most of them used only in the summer when the deciduous mountain forests provide the best concealment—are also plotted because of their proximity to the refuge areas.

1. Geographical Suitability

a. *The Northern Hills region*, a narrow northeast-southwest-trending series of forested hills, lies between Satoraljaujhely on the Hungarian-Czechoslovakian border and Keszthely at the Western end of Lake Balaton.[141] This region varies in width from 13 to 28 miles and can be subdivided as follows:

(1) *Bakony Forest:* The Bakony range overlooks lengthy and shallow Lake Balaton from an escarpment. It is covered by discontinuous forests of oak and hornbeam and has many steep and stony slopes. The range is interrupted by valleys and, on the gentler slope, by small villages and towns. Relatively speaking, the mountains are sparsely populated, but lumbering and mining are common. None of the following cover areas listed by G–2 Project 6550 is truly isolated, all of them being fairly easy of access, having many roads and trails crossing them:

   (a) An area (Area H–1, Refuge Area E) located just north of the western tip of Lake Balaton near Keszthely, approximately 10 km east-west and 8 km north-south.
   (b) An elongated strip of forested land (Area H–1, Refuge Area C), approximately 30 km long with an average width of 4 km, lying along the crest of the mountains north of Veszprem.
   (c) A forested area adjacent to (b) (Area H–1, Refuge Area D), about 20 km east of the city of Papa and about 10 km east-west and 7 km north-south. This area is bisected by a secondary north-south road (82); height 704 m. commands the low ground to the north.
   (d) A circular, well-forested area (Area H–1, Refuge Area B) of approximately 100 sq. km between the cities of Mor and Csakvar. The mountains are quite low in this area which is easily accessible from either of the towns mentioned.

(2) *Pilis Mountains:* The Pilis Mountains are located approximately 10 km northwest of the outskirts of Budapest. There is a refuge area (Area H–1, Refuge Area A) of approximately 300 sq. km of hilly to mountainous forest which, from its center, is only about 25 km to the heart of Budapest. The Danube bends guard the approaches from the north and east, and there is good observation of the surrounding lowlands from heights 757 m. and 950 m.

(3) *Borzsony Mountains:* The Borzsony Mountains are located north of the Danube River bend above Budapest. A refuge area (Area H–3, Refuge Area D) is approximately 18 km long and 12 km wide and consist of mountainous forest terrain. The mountains are low but have steep slopes; streams are deeply incised. There are dense forests of beech and oak with scattered stands of pine at the higher elevations. Heights from 585 m. to 939 m. provide a good view of the Danube River valley to the south. The area is sparsely populated, but there is mining and lumbering in the mountains.

(4) *Matra Mountains:* The Matra Mountains are located north of Gyongyos. A refuge area (Area H–3, Refuge Area B) is roughly 30 km east-west and 15 km north-south and consists of mountainous forested terrain. The mountains have steep slopes and are extensively dissected by deeply incised narrow-stream valleys. There is a pronounced escarpment along the southern border of the mountains and the height increases (from west to east) from 803 to 1010 m. At the lower elevations there are dense forests of beech mixed

---

[141] NIS 19–21, Fig. 21–1: Map of Military Geographic Regions and areas suitable for guerilla bases. [Footnote in original.]

102

with oak; scattered stands of pine appear at the higher elevations. On the southern slopes there are numerous vineyards and orchards. Good roads (routes 24 and 217) cross the area from east to west and lead south to Gyongos; numerous trails traverse the mountains. Off-road movement, however, is impossible for vehicles. The area is sparsely populated but there is considerable lumbering and mining activity in the mountains.

(5) *Bukh [Bükk] Mountians:* The Bukh (Beech) Mountains are located 8 km west of Miskolc and only three km west of the steel mills at Diosgyor. A refuge area (Area H–3, Refuge Area A) consists of forested mountains extending 30 km from east to west and 20 km from north to south. The mountains are extensively dissected below 670 m. and have steep slopes and deep narrow-stream valleys. The upland area above this is comparatively less rugged but is rimmed by an escarpment with slopes up to 50 percent. Several roads, notably route 22, and numerous trails penetrate the area. However, traversability on foot is limited.[142]

(6) *Hegyalja Mountains:* The Hegyalja Mountains, northwest of the Bodrog River, are located near Tornyosnemeti and Satoraljaujhely. A refuge area (Area H–3, Refuge Area C) covers more than 200 sq. km, extending 15 km from north to south and 20 km from east to west. The terrain consists of low mountains which are extensively dissected by numerous streams and characterized by sudden changes in the slope. There is a dense beech forest with some oak at the lower elevations. Extensive clearings occur along the southern border of the mountains, and there are scattered clearings on some peaks and in the valleys. Numerous roads and trails cross the area but the drainage pattern makes cross-country movement difficult.

b. *The Meksec [Mecsek] Hills* are a part of the Somogy-Meksec Upland, an area of hills and dissected plateaus southeast of Lake Balaton. This Upland rises 70 to 150 m. above the surface of the surrounding plain, and peaks within the fringing hill belt are 600 to 680 m. in elevation. The plateaus and hills are covered by discontinuous dense forests of broad-leaved trees which, except during the winter months, provide good concealment. In comparison to the sheltering plain, the Upland is sparsely populated. The best refuge or cover area in this region is located in the Meksec Hills northwest of Pecs (Area H–2, Refuge Area A). Here the elevation varies between 200 and 600 m. and the terrain is dissected by shallow, steep-sided valleys. Broad-leaved forests cover the entire area—oak and hornbeam on the lower and red beech on the higher slopes. The forests at the lower elevations are more open; orchards, vineyards, and cornfields planted along the lower slopes and in the valleys provide limited concealment.

2. Training and Maneuver Areas of the Hungarian Army

The scope of this study does not call for a detailed discussion of the Hungarian Army and internal security forces. In general, the reliability estimate of these organizations which appears in the Georgetown Study, *Resistance Potentials: Hungary,* November 23, 1953, is still valid, and there is additional evidence of the poor morale of the conscript element.[143] The curtailment of the formerly free-wheeling State Security Authority (AVH) and imprisonment of its chief, Gabor Peter, after the introduction of the "new course" has not had any observable bad effects on the efficiency of police controls.[144]

Because changes in order of battle occur relatively often in peacetime, and may be radical and sudden in time of war, and because current Order of Battle is available from G–2, no attempt is made to describe the present location of Hungarian Army and security components. Training

---

[142] The telecom exchange of the Soviet High Command is housed in bombproof headquarters in Lillafured. (NIS 19, Sec. 38, September 1952). [Footnote in original.]

[143] American Embassy, Vienna, Desp. No. 1045, March 14, 1955 (C). [Footnote in original.]

[144] Dept. of State, IR No. 6771, December 14, 1954 (S). [Footnote in original.]

and maneuver areas of the Hungarian army are plotted on Map A—showing geographically suitable refuge areas and/or bases of operation—because they are relatively stable and may directly affect the utilization of these areas.

Map A is not intended to present definitive information on training and maneuver areas. These areas are approximately located on the basis of information contained in files maintained by G–2, Eurasian Branch, Special Projects Section, and their size on Map A is only a rough approximation of their actual size. Most training and maneuver areas are located in the plains regions, but some also appear in the Northern Hills. Following is a list of the areas referenced on Map A:

Bekes (4646–2108) - Doboz (4644–2115) - Sarkad (4644–2123)

Berkesd (4604–1824)

Bőhőnye (4624–1723) - Nagybajom (4623–1730)

Bugacmonostor (4641–1941)

Csakbereny (4721–1819)

Debrecen (4731–2139) - Hajduhadhaz (4740–2140)

Deg (4652–1826) - Enying (4656–1814)

Diosjeno (4756–1902) - Dregelypalank (4803–1903) - Vamosmikola (4758–1847)

Dombovar area (4623–1808)

Eger (4754–2022 - Verpelet (4751–2014) - Tarnamera (4739–2010) - Vamosgyork (4741–1956) - Gyongyos (4747–1956)

Esztergom (4747–1845) - Dobogoko (4741–1854)

Janoshalma (4618–1919) - Melykut (4613–1922)

Jaszbereny (4730–1955)

Kalocsa (4632–1859) - Kiskoros (4637–1917)

Kecel (4631–1915) - Soltvadkert (4634–1923) - Bocsa (4636–1929)

Kenyeri (4723–1705)

Kisbodak (4754–1725)

Kiskunhalas (4625–1929) - Sandorfalva (4622–2006)

Marcali (4635–1725)

Nyiregyhaza (4758–2143)

Ozd (4813–2018)

Paks (4638–1851)

Papa (4720–1728) - Keszthely (4649–1715) - Sumeg (4658–1717)

Paszto 94755–1942)

Petervasara (4801–2006)

Pomaz (4739–1901) - Szentendre (4740–1905)

Pusztavam (4726–1813)

Solt (4648–1900)

Szeged (4615–2009) - Mindszent (4632–2012) - Szentes (4635–2037) - Bekescsaba (4639–2105)

Tab (4643–1802)

Tamasi (4638–1817) - Kocsola (4632–1812)

Tata (4739–1819)

Tiszadob (4801–2110)

Tiszafured (4737–2045) - Kiskore (4730–2030)

Zalaegerszeg (4650–1651) - Bak (4643–1651)

Zirc (4716–1752) - Lokut (4712–1752) - Penzeskut (4714–1747)

In choosing some training areas the Hungarian Army apparently places emphasis on the concealment factor. Some camps are located in mountainous and wooded areas which do not appear to offer good training facilities. Map A shows that of the geographically suitable refuge areas all but two or three should be eliminated either because they coincide with, or are in close proximity to, training and maneuver areas. The entire Bakony Forest appears to be a vast training area. Near the Pilis refuge area there is a training and maneuver area probably used by motorized rifle troops. In the Borzsony mountain area there are extensive firing ranges and summer training areas. It is reasonable to assume that, when in use, all these areas are closely guarded and it would be quite hazardous to use them as Special Forces refuge areas and/or bases of operations.

3. Locale of Dissidence and Resistance

The resistance picture in Hungary is such as to permit only questionable generalizations about the comparatively intensity of peasant and worker resistance, and there is no feasible method of estimating resistance potential in various parts of the country. There are no sizeable communities of ethnic minorities, and no institutions of local or national importance which have organizationally survived the approximately seven years of Communist domination. A study of dissidence and resistance in Hungary reveals no definite patterns: passive resistance has been widely spread and scattered; similarly, incidents of active resistance largely appear to represent sporadic outbursts of pent-up opposition which cannot be accurately related to any particular locale as indicating the mood and temper of the people.

Incidents of passive and active resistance which have occurred during the last three years are listed in Tabs C and E. These have occurred in both the cities and the outlying areas, but in no particular locality with such frequency as to suggest a greater degree of opposition to the regime. Current reports of resistance incidents which can be verified may, however, serve as an index of local dissidence which can be exploited. The dozen or more underground groups, reported as existing at one time or another since 1948, operated largely in the major cities (see Tab [illeg.]). Possible remnants of some of these organizations still exist in a dormant state, and it is probable that more underground groups will appear at least as symbols of opposition to the regime.

As noted in Section C of this study which deals with resistance movements, there has been very little, if any, genuine partisan activity in Hungary. Incomplete and inadequately authenticated reports of partisan bands generally place them in those areas where topography provides some possibility of cover and concealment. Partisan activity has been reported in the Bakony, Pilis, Borzsony, Bukh, Matra and Mekesc [Mecsek] mountainous regions. Most of this activity allegedly occurred in 1950, a fact which may be explained by spotty reporting and/or the unavailability of earlier or later information for this study. No resistance whatsoever has been reported in the Hegyalja mountain area. Of the areas listed, the Meksec Hills[145] have been cited most often and most recently as the scene of partisan activity; the Bakony Forest and the Pilis and Borzsony mountain areas are referred to most vaguely and infrequently in connection with such activity. A seemingly plausible report names the Matra-Bukh range[146] as a refuge area for partisan groups from Eastern Slovakia.

All-in all, the few reports of partisan resistance do little but confirm the general principle that partisan groups do not develop save in those geographic regions where there is terrain offering possibilities of cover and concealment. The incomplete reports of partisan activity available barely suggest that, of the limited mountainous areas in Hungary offering such terrain, the most advantageous are the Meksec Hills and the Matra-Bukh mountain areas.

[Source: U.S. Army Military History Institute, Carlisle Barracks, Pennsylvania, (non-integrated collection of military studies). On file at the National Security Archive, "Soviet Flashpoints" Collection.]

[145] In connection with the interest of the Special Forces, it is noteworthy that the Meksec Hills and the Matra-Bukh range coincide with areas of great economic and strategic importance to Hungary. In view of Hungary's major economic weaknesses—her lack of minerals and sources of hydro-electric power—the coal mines near Pecs (the only natural source of coking coal in Hungary) and the lignite reserves of Salgotarjan and the Matra foothills are outstanding economic targets. Furthermore, one of the main industrial regions in Hungary is located in the Matra-Bukh area (at Salgotarjan, Ozd, Diosgyor and Miskolc), a fact that highlights the strategic importance of the rail network in this area. [Footnote in original.]

[146] *Ibid.* [Footnote in original.]

DOCUMENT NO. 9: Soviet Foreign Ministry Notes on Current Issues in Soviet Global Policy, January 4, 1956

This memorandum provides a useful perspective on the Soviet Foreign Ministry's view of the situation facing the socialist bloc at the beginning of 1956, and sketches out a broad, proposed course of action for the USSR and its allies. With the East European crises of 1956 still in the future, the Ministry displays considerable confidence, viewing global developments since Stalin's death as evidence that the socialist camp is gaining strength. The document also reveals a duality characteristic of Moscow's new international approach after March 1953. On the one hand, it repeatedly invokes concepts such as "peaceful coexistence" to reaffirm publicly a determination to avoid confrontation with the West while privately hoping to reduce Soviet military spending, which was inordinately high relative to the country's economic potential. On the other hand, the memorandum also betrays plans to carry out a dynamic and expansive foreign policy in the name of "intensifying the ideological war against the aggressors"—a propaganda slogan meant to sway public opinion both in the West and in the emerging countries of the third world. Containing elements of both ideology and political realism, the authors envision a unified, global foreign policy that centers around a determination to play an active role in world politics.

In addition to increasing propaganda and resorting to new methods of economic penetration, the memorandum places great emphasis on the need for a concerted initiative by the socialist countries. In fact, the document was produced to prepare for negotiations on a new framework for political consultation within the Warsaw Pact. It was presented to participants at a summit meeting of communist leaders held in Moscow starting on January 6, 1956.

TOP SECRET

NOTES FROM MID[147] USSR
CONCERNING QUESTIONS OF FOREIGN POLICY
(MATERIAL FOR THE JANUARY 6 MEETING)[148]

I.

1. In the last year, the Soviet Union, the People's Republic of China, Poland, Czechoslovakia, the German Democratic Republic, Hungary, Romania, Bulgaria, Albania, and other countries of the socialist camp have achieved significant success in the fight for peace and in strengthening their foreign policy positions. In 1955, they took a series of foreign policy steps that had international significance and contributed to an increase in the prestige of the socialist countries, and to the easing of international tensions as well.

To these results belong primarily: [a] radical shift towards friendship and collaboration in relations between Yugoslavia [on the one hand] and the Soviet Union and the people's democracies [on the other]; the settlement of the Austrian question with the declaration of Austria's political neutrality;[149] the improvement in relations between the Soviet Union and Finland due to the Soviet Union's relinquishing of its Porkkala-Udd military base on Finnish territory, and extending the term of the Soviet-Finnish mutual assistance treaty;[150] the establishment of diplomatic relations between the Soviet Union and the German Federal Republic;[151] the important

---

[147] *Ministerstvo Inostrannykh Del*, or Ministry of Foreign Affairs.

[148] This line is crossed out by hand in the original Russian document.

[149] The Austrian State Treaty was signed on May 15, 1955.

[150] The Soviet and Finnish prime ministers signed the agreement on September 19, 1955.

[151] This took place on Sept. 13, 1955.

political results of the Bandung conference of Asian and African countries, achieved due to the active participation of the People's Republic of China;[152] the socialist countries' joint measures in the area of disarmament on the basis of the Soviet government's proposals of May 10, 1955;[153] the expansion of international ties of the Soviet Union and the countries of people's democracy; the admission of 16 new countries—including Albania, Bulgaria, Hungary, and Romania—to the United Nations, which strengthens the international positions of these countries, and which will not fail to have a positive influence on the situation in the U.N.[154]

The conference of the four great powers in 1955 in Geneva was a rather significant international event, showing that the imperialist powers have to take into account the growing popular demand to bring an end to the Cold War, and to find ways to settle unresolved international issues through negotiations.

The foreign ministers conference of the four states in Geneva[155] did not lead to consensus decisions on the issues under consideration, but it did contribute to the strengthening of the positions of the Soviet Union and of the entire socialist camp, primarily on such issues as European security and the German question. It also reaffirmed that the Western countries' infamous "power politics" has no enduring basis. Regarding that conference, the Western powers' attempt to solve the German question and other problems discussed at the conference [sic] on the basis of their demands, which do not meet the requirements of European security and of a further relaxation in the international tensions, were rebuffed.

2. The trips by Comrades N. A. Bulganin and N. S. Khrushchev to India, Burma, and Afghanistan[156] had great international political significance from the perspective of strengthening the cause of peace in the Asian countries, and for developing cooperation and friendship between the Soviet Union and the entire socialist camp and the states of the East. This trip showed, more clearly than ever before, the weakness of the leading capitalist states' influence on such Asian countries as India, Burma, and Afghanistan; it also showed how strong the Asian countries aspire for independence and for a closer relationship with the Soviet Union and the countries of the entire socialist camp at the present time. The speeches delivered by Comrades Khrushchev and Bulganin, which propagated the Leninist principles of national politics aimed at the struggle against the colonial system, helped strengthen the socialist camp's positions in the struggle for peace, and increased the Soviet Union's prestige in the eyes of the peoples of the East. The peoples of the countries, which had the status of colonies and lived in colonial dependence until recently, are now rising up against colonial slavery with an increasing intensity, becoming our active allies in the struggle for peace against the aggressive policies of the imperialist states.

3. The international success of the socialist camp is based on the achievements of the peoples' concerted fight for peace and for the strengthening of their economic and military power, and on [the fact] that our peoples unite around the Communist and workers' parties. The socialist camp's foreign policy, which is based on Leninist principles, ensures us of the support of millions of working people in all the countries of the world; it undermines the plans of the aggressive circles, [and] makes their preparations for a new war more difficult.

At the same time, however, one cannot consider the danger of a new war to have become a thing of the past. We are reminded of it by the continuing arms race, especially in the area of nuclear weapons production, by the construction of numerous American military bases in for-

[152] Twenty-nine countries met between April 18–24, 1955 in Bandung, Indonesia.

[153] In August and September 1955, several members of the Soviet bloc announced their intention to decrease the size of their armies. The USSR, for example, pledged to cut its forces by 640,000 troops. Hungary reduced its armed forces by 20,000 troops.

[154] The U.N. admitted these new member states on December 14, 1955.

[155] The conference was held from October 27–November 4, 1955.

[156] Khrushchev and Bulganin left for India, Burma and Afghanistan on November 18, 1955, and returned to Moscow on December 21.

eign territories, by the building of military blocs under the auspices of the Unites States and England, by the signing of the Paris treaties,[157] which ordain West Germany's remilitarization and its entry into NATO, and by the Western powers' refusal to agree with the Soviet Union on the issue of creating a system of collective security in Europe.

It is precisely this [kind of] action by the Western powers that necessitated putting the question of the creation of the Warsaw Pact on the agenda[158] with the purpose of coordinating the efforts of the countries of the socialist camp in both foreign policy and military spheres.

4. The international situation and the interests of the struggle to strengthen the positions of socialism require an even more active mobilization of our forces in the foreign policy sphere. Besides this, it must be mentioned that there are still significant opportunities, which we have not taken advantage of, to develop the foreign policy activities of each individual country and of the socialist camp as a whole, for the sake of strengthening our mutual positions in the struggle for peace and socialism.

We have not yet fully taken advantage of opportunities to improve our relationship with a number of Western capitalist countries, with the countries of Asia, the Middle and Near East, and the countries of Latin America, or of the opportunities to undermine and weaken the imperialist military blocs. The talks held by the Soviet government with Norwegian Prime Minister Gerhardsen;[159] the increasing conflicts in French leading circles regarding Germany's rearmament and the aggravation of French-German contradictions in the Saar,[160] which was reflected in the latest parliamentary elections;[161] the growing disagreements among NATO members, for example between Greece and England, [and] Greece and Turkey regarding the Cyprus question; the intensifying disagreements between West Germany on the one side and the United States, England, and France on the other due to the escalating fight for markets, and because of the establishment of diplomatic relations between the Soviet Union and the Federal Republic of Germany—these and other [examples] testify to the existence of such opportunities.

It would be desirable to exchange opinions on these questions for the sake of coordinating our countries' international activities in the future.

II.

1). The future foreign policy course of the Soviet Union and other countries of the socialist camp will also be determined by the interests of the struggle to strengthen peace and ease international tensions, because this is appropriate for the cause of building socialism and communism in our countries and a vital interest for the peoples of the world. The realization of this line is possible only by means of an active fight for peace against the imperialist policies of preparing for the new world war, by comprehensively strengthening the positions of the socialist camp and other anti-imperialist forces, by thoroughly weakening the positions of the reactionary forces, which conduct the policies of the arms race, the creation of aggressive military blocs, [and] the subjugation and suppression of the colonial and dependent countries and peoples. The countries of the socialist camp are guided by the Leninist principle of peaceful coexistence in their relations with the capitalist coun-

---

[157] Under the Paris treaties, signed on October 23, 1954, the United States, Britain, and France eliminated West Germany's occupation zones and established full sovereignty for the country. Among other effects, the FRG gained the right to join NATO. The Paris treaties took effect on May 5, 1955.

[158] The Soviet Union and its East European allies established the Warsaw Treaty Organization, with China represented as an observer, on May 14, 1955.

[159] Einar Henry Gerhardsen was prime minister from 1955–1963 and chairman of the Norwegian Labor Party between 1945–1965.

[160] Placed under French control after World War II, the Saar region later became part of the FRG through an agreement between the two countries signed on October 27, 1956.

[161] This is a reference to the French parliamentary elections of January 2, 1956, in which the Communists gained 57 seats over their showing in 1951.

tries. The consistent and flexible application of Leninist principle made it possible for our countries to achieve serious results in easing international tensions. It is obvious that our measures for normalizing and improving relations with the capitalist countries have not been and should not be implemented at the expense of our countries' interests, whereas the appropriateness of compromise decisions made in some cases (Korea, Indochina)[162] was justified by [the fact] that they strengthened the positions of the countries of the socialist camp. Meanwhile, the imperialist states under the leadership of the United States, however, are striving to gain precisely unilateral concessions from the Soviet Union and the countries of people's democracy, trying to make it appear as if the Soviet Union's "stubbornness" was the obstacle to the easing of international tensions.

In our efforts to ease international tensions, we have to start from the assumption that we do not want just any relaxation of tensions. We cannot agree to have the relaxation of tensions proceed at the expense of concessions on our part on matters of principle, which could seriously undermine our positions and weaken the influence of the socialist camp in international matters. We cannot and should not give up criticizing imperialism, exposing "power politics;" and moreover, we should not assume a position of ideological disarmament. [Our] task is to try to make our common foreign policy—the Leninist policy of people and friendship among peoples—exert influence on more and more people in the capitalist countries by conducting our policy consistently and unswervingly, thus strengthening our position while ensuring support among the peoples of all countries of the world.

All this proves the necessity of intensifying the ideological war against the aggressors and encourages us to take advantage of the opportunities for mobilizing the masses of working people—the working class, the peasantry, and the democratically-minded intelligentsia—in the capitalist countries as well as the dependent and colonized countries of the East, in order to intensify the political struggle against reactionary imperialist circles and to support the foreign policy steps of the Soviet Union and the countries of the socialist camp. It must be noted that our propaganda on international issues is not sufficiently active, and that it is often not of an offensive but rather of a defensive nature.

2). It is entirely natural that the countries of the socialist camp act as a united front in the diplomatic field in the interests of socialism and in expressing the interests of the working classes. However, there are still a number of problems here. The necessity of mutually informing each other on foreign policy questions is irrefutable, and the Soviet side in particular must improve [its procedure of] informing the ambassadors accredited to Moscow from the countries of people's democracy. It should not be excluded that some of the countries of the socialist camp might find it necessary to be able to discuss certain foreign policy questions or [questions] regarding relations among socialist countries. For the sake of exchanging ideas and working out a common line on the most important foreign policy questions, we should probably hold closed conferences of representatives of our countries [in corresponding areas]. The existing close and friendly relationship between the Soviet Union and the countries of people's democracy makes it possible to strengthen the coordination of our steps considerably in the sphere of foreign policy, as well as in the economic, cultural and military spheres.

While maintaining our unity on foreign policy issues, each of the countries of the socialist camp should substantially increase their own initiative on those issues. Opportunities for this exist, especially following the admittance of Albania, Hungary, and Romania into the U.N. Coordinated and yet enterprising actions of our countries aimed at the development of foreign trade can also seriously contribute to strengthening the international positions of the socialist camp.

3). Under conditions where the Western powers are striving by all their means to strengthen NATO and other organizations established within the NATO system, the West European Union, and other military blocs, the need emerges to step up the activities of the Warsaw Pact, especially its political activity. In particular, it would be desirable to discuss the expediency of convening a meeting of Warsaw Treaty member countries in the near future, during which we could exchange views regarding the international situation and the tasks of the Warsaw Pact member-states. It would

[162] Cease-fire agreements were signed in Korea, on July 27, 1953, and Vietnam, on July 20, 1954.

be expedient to publish a mutual declaration at the completion of these discussions about our countries' position on such important international questions as: European security, the German question, disarmament, our attitude toward the national liberation movements in the countries of Asia and Africa, our support for the policy of neutrality and non-participation in military blocs, and our attitude toward the five principles of peaceful coexistence as formulated in the communiqué of negotiations between the governments of the People's Republic of China and India.[163]

We could also discuss some organizational issues at this conference: establish the political committee prescribed by the agreement, approve the composition of military organs, and also listen to the report on measures taken to coordinate our countries' efforts in the defense sphere.

4). It would be expedient to exchange views regarding the further development of relations with Yugoslavia. The Belgrade Declaration,[164] as well as the exchange of letters between the Central Committee of the YLC and the Central Committee of the Communist Party of the Soviet Union, have created advantageous conditions for the further development of cooperation with Yugoslavia in all spheres—political, economic, cultural—and also for the development of contacts along party lines. At the same time, it must be kept in mind that some countries of people's democracy still have some open questions regarding Yugoslavia, the resolution of which must be accelerated, taking [our] mutual interests into consideration of course. The restoration of normal treaty relations with Yugoslavia, which is very important for creating a solid foundation for [our] relations with Yugoslavia at the state level, will require a certain amount of time and attention.

Our mutual interests require the development of economic cooperation with Yugoslavia: assistance in strengthening Yugoslavia's economic situation and decreasing its financial dependence on the capitalist countries. The possibility of engaging Yugoslavia in cooperation within the CMEA framework must be examined, especially since the Yugoslavs exhibit a certain interest in the CMEA's activities.

Furthermore, it is necessary to develop cooperation with appropriate Yugoslav social organizations (labor unions, women's and youth organizations, etc.) while keeping in mind the desirability of involving Yugoslavia in the work of international democratic organizations as well.

Special attention should be devoted to strengthening the relationship with the Yugoslav League of Communists, with the purpose of further strengthening our rapprochement with Yugoslavia and our communist influence in Yugoslavia, and so that we can provide assistance to the Yugoslav comrades in solving the problems the country faces in the area of building socialism, while at the same time upholding the ideas of Marxism-Leninism in a tough and relentless manner.

5.) For the sake of further relaxing international tensions, it is necessary to devote our attention to the task of improving relations of the countries of the socialist camp with certain capitalist powers, including countries that are members of this or that Western organization.

In [our] relations with the capitalist great powers—with the United States, England, France, and also with West Germany, Italy, and Japan—we should take account not only of what is common among, or what unites, the imperialist ruling circles of these countries, but also of the significant contradictions among them, and we have to take better advantage of opportunities to strengthen our influence on the progressive forces inside those countries. In the diplomatic field, efforts must be made to hinder the hostile activities of the great powers' leading circles against the Soviet Union, the People's Republic of China, and the countries of people's democracy.

Thus, while exposing the desires of American imperialism to establish its global hegemony, efforts must be made to normalize relations with the United States, to strengthen U.S. [public] opinion in favor of improving relations between the countries of the democratic camp and the USA, and to provide support for those segments of the American population who stand up for such normalization [of relations]. It would be necessary to think about what kinds of steps should be taken in the future to normalize diplomatic (Albania and Bulgaria) and economic relations with the United States, and to encourage cultural ties and contacts in other spheres.

---

[163] India and China signed the declaration on June 28, 1954.

[164] Khrushchev and Nikolai Bulganin visited Belgrade between May 26–June 2, 1955, where they apologized for slandering Yugoslavia during Stalin's rule, and proceeded to reestablish bilateral relations.

110

The contradictions existing between American and British imperialism, as well as between other capitalist countries, could be taken advantage of in the interests of peace and socialism.

In implementing our foreign policy regarding England, we have to take into consideration existing contradictions between American and British imperialism as well as the known differences between the British and American positions on the issues of China and international trade. At the same time, it must be taken into consideration that England is a leading colonial power and the initiator and ring-leader of such aggressive a bloc as the Baghdad Pact.

In relations with France, the serious contradictions that exist between the United States and France, as well as West Germany and France must be taken into account. France's influential bourgeois circles are working to loosen France's dependency on the United States and to strengthen France's positions vis-à-vis West Germany. Considering these tendencies in French foreign policy, a certain degree of movement toward the countries of the socialist camp can be expected by France on certain issues, especially issue of collective security and the German question. France's traditional, cultural and economic relationship with the Soviet Union, Poland, and Romania can be taken advantage of from the perspective of our mutual interests.

6.) The development of relations between the people's democracies and their neighboring capitalist countries deserves serious attention. The struggle for further normalization of relations with such countries, development of economic ties, cultural exchanges, and all kinds of contacts could contribute to the improvement of the international situation as a whole. It would be a mistake to forget that under certain conditions the leading circles of the surrounding capitalist countries are forced to improve and develop their relations with the countries of people's democracy, which in the end boosts our influence on increasingly broader social circles in these countries.

Regarding the concrete questions of relations between the countries of our camp and the capitalist countries, we should put special emphasis on our relations with the Scandinavian countries, Austria, Italy, Greece, Turkey, Iran and Japan.

The signing of the Austrian State Treaty has created more favorable conditions for the development of good neighborly relations between our countries and Austria, which could have a certain influence on the positions of other capitalist countries in Europe.

The opportunities for developing relations with Italy, which exhibits a certain interest in economic ties with such countries as Czechoslovakia, Hungary and Albania, have improved to some extent.

It is well known that the contradictions between Greece on the one hand, and England and Turkey on the other, on the issue of Cyprus have intensified so much that there is a growing dissatisfaction with NATO among certain Greek circles; furthermore, statements were made in some influential Greek bourgeois parties in favor of improving relations with the Soviet Union and the countries of people's democracy, which should be taken into consideration as far as Greece is concerned.

It is in our common interest to look for opportunities to normalize our relations with Turkey, while keeping in mind that the current situation in Turkey can only be changed with persistent work in this direction. As a consequence of this [work], the patriotic forces that are more connected with the people could get the opportunity to wage a more active struggle for Turkey's national interests, and weaken U.S. influence in Turkey.

As far as Iran, which has joined the Baghdad pact, is concerned, it seems necessary to apply economic pressure by sharply cutting trade with Iran, criticize its current foreign policy, and condemn its reactionary regime and the bloody terror in the country. At the same time, we should think about actions that would prevent further strengthening of the U.S. and British positions in Iran while weakening Iran's ties with the Baghdad Pact.

The next question is the normalization of relations with Japan, and the task of helping the Japanese people terminate their dependence on the United States, so as to contribute to Japan's turn toward rapprochement with the peace-loving countries as well as Japan's shift to at least a position of neutrality.

The importance of developing relations with the capitalist countries in the fields of culture, science, sports, tourism, etc., must be emphasized. At the same time, of course, it has to be taken into account that the capitalist countries' ruling circles will try to take advantage of such contacts for hostile purposes, which requires that we exhibit the necessary vigilance.

7.) As is known, the Soviet government notified the three Western powers that any further discussions of the German question would be meaningless until the GDR and the FRG agree with each other on ways to resolve it, and that the German question cannot be resolved without the GDR or at the expense of the GDR's interests. Such a definition of the German question helps to strengthen the GDR's international position and prestige, and also serves the interests of the entire socialist camp.

All of us should give even more active support to the GDR government's proposal for creating an all-German Council,[165] because this would help mobilize national forces for the struggle for a democratic solution of the German problem.

At the same time, it must be taken into consideration that the competition between the socialist and capitalist systems is proceeding in a particularly intense manner in Germany, and that millions of Germans could be and are drawing the wrong conclusions from the current economic boom in West Germany, which can be explained by the known causes of market fluctuations. This is exactly why we have to use all our strength to help our German comrades to realize their main goal—to overcome the existing economic difficulties in the GDR's economic situation, and in creating conditions superior to West Germany in terms of the working class' living standards.

With the purpose of further strengthening the GDR's foreign policy positions, we should also give more active support to steps that the GDR government is undertaking to improve relations with such countries as India, Finland, Egypt, Burma, Austria, Syria, Afghanistan, Sweden and Switzerland, and provide assistance regarding the GDR's admittance to appropriate international organizations, in particular to specialized organizations of the United Nations. At the same time, taking into account the intense struggle surrounding the German issue, one cannot disregard the fact that the struggle to strengthen the GDR's international positions at the present time represents one of the most important foreign policy tasks for all our countries.

At the same time, it is necessary to note that the West German bourgeoisie is trying to conduct a more independent policy, both in the sphere of their economic ties with foreign states and in the sphere of foreign policy, sometimes creating clear contradictions with the three Western powers' policies (for example, establishing diplomatic relations with the Soviet Union in spite of the Western powers' positions on this issue). In the course of our struggle against the remilitarization of West Germany, we should simultaneously pursue a course to normalize relations with the FRG.

8.) At the present time quite favorable conditions have emerged to further expand the democratic camp's influence in the countries of Asia, the Near and Middle East and also Latin America, and to undermine the influence of the imperialist forces in those countries through moral and political support for the peoples' of those countries national liberation struggle against colonialism, by providing assistance to the countries which have chosen a course of strengthening their national independence. The substantial improvement of the People's Republic of China's political and economic position plays a particularly important role in all of this. The trip by comrades N. A. Bulganin and N. S. Khrushchev to India, Burma, and Afghanistan is clear proof of the existence of yet unused opportunities for improving our relations with the countries of the East, and for increasing our influence on these countries' policies.

The development of [our] relations with Egypt—and especially the agreement on Czechoslovak arms deliveries to Egypt—shows what serious results intensifying the socialist commonwealth states' foreign policy can produce in that region. The resistance organized by the Trans-Jordanian people against the efforts to pull that country into the aggressive Baghdad Pact deserves attntion. Without our support for the actions of countries like Egypt, Syria, and others aimed at strengthening their national independence, such resistance would have been impossible, just as it would have been impossible if the People's Republic of China had not achieved significant improvement in their internal and international positions.

---

[165] The idea was to form a consultative body consisting of representatives from the governments of the GDR and FRG. The Soviets proposed this in Geneva on November 2, 1955, but it was rejected by the West on the grounds that it would have formalized the division of Germany and amounted to de facto recognition of the GDR.

We should devote more and more attention to the development of all forms of political, economic and cultural cooperation, as well as personal contacts between statesmen of the Soviet Union and the countries of people's democracy on the one hand, and those of the countries of Asia, and the Near and Middle East, on the other. It would be desirable to exchange our views regarding existing opportunities in this respect.

In addition, taking into account substantial interest regarding economic and technological assistance expressed by a number of countries in Asia and the Near and Middle East, and also countries of Latin America, it appears expedient to study opportunities to further increase the volume of our foreign trade with those countries, and also to follow a course of more active assistance to them in the construction of industrial enterprises, deliveries of spare parts, and so on. We have to keep in mind that as the experiences of India, Egypt, Syria and the Sudan show, the leading circles of those countries are usually interested in having relations not with just one country of the socialist camp, but with several countries of this camp. Regarding this connection, the fact that Poland, Czechoslovakia, and other countries of the socialist camp received proposals for the construction of enterprises in economically backward countries deserves our attention. For instance, we know that Poland received a total of 270 proposals for construction of various enterprises, primarily in the countries of the East and Latin America. It is characteristic that among those proposals, there are 52 requests from Turkey, 35 from Egypt, and 18 from India. In this connection, the question arises as to whether it would be expedient to accept some of those proposals in order to use our assistance toward some of those countries to strengthen our influence on the respective countries' policies. Of course, we are talking about undertaking such projects, particularly in those countries that are of most interest [to us]. We should also share our views regarding the possibility of coordinating our countries' actions in considering and implementing some of those requests. In connection with the task of strengthening our influence in those countries of Latin America with which the USSR and some other countries of the socialist camp do not have normal diplomatic relations, there is a need to establish and expand such relations with those countries, or at least with some of them. At the same time, as regards those countries with which, for example, the Soviet Union does not have normal diplomatic relations, we should, in our own general interests, make use of the possibilities afforded by the presence of diplomatic representatives from other states, for example, Czechoslovakia and Poland.

9.) A number of states' growing aspiration to conduct a policy of non-participation in military blocs and coalitions and [to pursue] a policy of neutrality, represents one of the most important signs of the weakening front of the aggressive powers.

In Europe, due to the Soviet Union's initiative, Austria assumed a neutral position; in Asia it was Afghanistan. The neutrality movement is growing in West Germany, Denmark, Norway, and Iceland. The movement against participation in military blocs unfolded with a special intensity in the Asian and Near and Middle Eastern countries where [the movement] is closely connected with the peoples' movements for national independence and liberation from the colonial yoke. Such states as India, Burma, Indonesia, Egypt, Syria, and Saudi Arabia decisively refuse to take part in the military blocs constructed by the Western powers.

These are some of the foreign policy issues on which it would be expedient to exchange views at the coming conference, along with other issues.

JANUARY 4, 1956[166]

[Source: MOL, M-KS-267. f. 62/75. ő.e. Published in Hungarian in József Kiss, Zoltán Ripp and István Vida, eds., Magyar-jugoszláv kapcsolatok, 1956: Dokumentumok, *(Budapest: MTA Jelenkor-kutató Bizottság, 1995), 33–40. Translated by Mónika Borbély and Svetlana Savranskaya.]*

---

[166] This line is crossed out by hand in the original Russian document.

DOCUMENT NO. 10: British Foreign Office Minutes concerning Developments in Eastern Europe, June 5, 1956

The following report from the British Foreign Office forwards important information to the effect that the Soviet leadership was preparing to reevaluate its relations with the East European satellites as early as Spring 1956. This new policy was eventually published in the Soviet government's declaration of October 30, 1956, during the midst of the Hungarian crisis (see Document No. 50).

FOREIGN OFFICE MINUTES TAKEN BY MISS BROWN, 5 JUNE 1956

CONFIDENTIAL

There have been one or two indications recently that Moscow was preparing to make some special announcement about the Satellites.

2. Moscow Telegram No. 621 of May 14 reported a remark to this effect apparently made by Khrushchev to the French socialist party delegation.[167] He then said that at the next meeting of the Supreme Soviet an announcement would be made about the Satellites, but as he also said they would make an announcement about disarmament[168] which was in fact issued quite independently, the report may not be accurate.

3. H.M. Ambassador at Warsaw had heard rumors a little earlier of the possibility of a withdrawal of Soviet troops from Satellite territories. However, one would have expected the announcement to be made at the same time as that on disarmament published on May 15, since it made a reference to the reduction of 30,000 troops in Eastern Germany.

4. On May 29 a Hungarian radio broadcaster, commenting on Tito's visit to Moscow[169] said that Hungarian-Yugoslav relations had not yet progressed to the extent desired "but we trust that the Moscow talks, in the course of which—according to the press—the East European countries will also be discussed, will promote the solution of questions still unsolved". It still seems possible, therefore, that an announcement on Satellite policy can be expected shortly.

5. Mr. Matthews, News Department, has drawn my attention to telegram No. 621 reminding us that although we had warning that troop reductions would take place we were not ready with any comment when it happened. He would therefore have like us to be prepared with a comment about the Satellites.

6. I think it is too early to say what announcement, if any, will be made about the Satellites. It is quite possible that a withdrawal of forces from these areas could take place, since Soviet control can be maintained by economic and administrative means without the actual presence of the Red Army. Any comment we made would have to depend partly on the strings attached to such a withdrawal; we could however probably say in general terms, that any steps which brought alleviation to the peoples of the Satellite would be welcome but it would be unrealistic to suppose that Soviet control depended solely on the presence of the Red Army.

7. If discussions take place in the Yugoslav context, it is, I suppose, just possible that they might relate to closer Yugoslav association with C.M.E.A. I hope it would be over pes-

---

[167] A French Socialist Party delegation headed by Prime Minister Guy Mollet visited Moscow between May 15–20, 1956.

[168] On May 14, 1956, the Soviet government announced that it would reduce its armed forces by 1.2 million men by May 1, 1957.

[169] Tito's visit began on June 2 and lasted for three weeks. On the results of the negotiations, see Document No. 14.

simistic to suggest that there would be any possibility of Yugoslavia being linked with the Warsaw Treaty.

[SIGNED]
(G.G. BROWN)
JUNE 5, 1956.

[Source: Public Records Office, London, Kew (PRO). Foreign Office General Correspondence (FO.371).122068.194235.]

DOCUMENT NO. 11: Memorandum from Kliment Voroshilov to the CPSU CC Presidium regarding His Meeting with Mátyás Rákosi, June 26, 1956

This record of a meeting between CPSU CC Presidium member Kliment Voroshilov and Hungarian First Secretary Rákosi was written a few weeks before the latter's demotion in July 1956. As the head of the Allied Control Commission in Hungary between 1945 and 1946, Voroshilov had direct experience with Hungarian conditions. The document clearly shows how untenable Rákosi's position had become after the CPSU's Twentieth Congress in February 1956. Soviet-Yugoslav rapprochement on the one hand, and exposure of the personality cult and the unlawfulness of the show trials on the other, undermined Rákosi's domestic and international policies. At this point, however, the Soviet leadership still believed he should retain his position.

TO THE PRESIDIUM OF THE CC CPSU

Yesterday, Comrade Rákosi came to visit me before his departure for Hungary.[170]

I asked him about the situation in Hungary, and especially in the party.

Comrade Rákosi generally characterized the situation in the HWP as extremely difficult, as a result of a whole series of events that took place in Hungary over the last three years.

In most general terms, Comrade Rákosi told me that in 1953 they started on the course of industrialization, then, in 1954, the party was re-oriented toward the development of light industry and improving the living standards of working people. Then, in 1955, they had to reconsider their plans once again—this time preference was given to heavy industry. All this could not help but create a number of problems in the life of the party.

To my question of how Imre Nagy was behaving in this situation, Comrade Rákosi responded that Imre Nagy and his supporters still believe that they were right when they emphasized the development of light industry and individual peasant farms. Those rotten opinions still find sufficient fertile soil in the country among a segment of backward party members, and among, unfortunately, quite a large layer of the former big and petty bourgeoisie, the kulaks, old officers, and bureaucrats.

Touching upon the Farkas case, Comrade Rákosi expressed considerable concern and anxiety regarding the future discussion of this issue at the HWP CC Plenum. According to Comrade Rákosi, Farkas would undoubtedly try to involve as many leading party officials as possible in the Rajk case, in hopes of diminishing his guilt in that way. In this connection, Comrade Rákosi noted the great assistance and support which Comrade Suslov has given to the HWP CC Politburo. In particular, with great satisfaction, the Hungarian comrades welcomed Comrade Suslov's statement that the CPSU CC Presidium considered the work and the political line of the HWP CC to be correct.[171]

Then Comrade Rákosi touched upon his personal situation. According to him, among the backward segment of party members—and there are many such people because approximately 9 percent of the Hungarian population are part members—and also among the intelligentsia, there are rumors that Rákosi is not capable of carrying out the decisions of the Twentieth Congress, and that for that purpose they would need leaders who are not connected with the past. Now one hears in Hungary that Rákosi was close to Stalin, that they used to call him Stalin's loyal student, and that after Dimitrov, Gottwald, and Bierut[172] had passed away, Rákosi

---

[170] Rákosi was in Moscow to participate in the non-official summit of Eastern European communist leaders on June 22–23, during which the Soviet leadership informed the satellite leaders of Tito's recent visit to the Soviet Union.

[171] Suslov visited Hungary between June 8–14 and consulted with several Hungarian leaders, eventually reinforcing Rákosi's position.

[172] Georgii Dimitrov secretary general of the BCP beginning in 1948. Klement Gottwald was prime minister of Czechoslovakia from 1948. Bolesław Bierut was secretary general, chairman (later first secretary) of the PZPR from 1948–1956. Dimitrov died in 1949, Gottwald in 1953, and Bierut in 1956.

remained "the last of the Mohicans" of the Stalin school; and, therefore he did not fit the spirit of the times. In particular, they point out that Rákosi, being an internationalist, would not be able to accept the decisions of the Twentieth Congress, according to which socialism must be built keeping the nationally and historically special features of particular countries in mind.

Western propaganda against Hungary has recently been heating up those feelings.

Comrade Rákosi believes that Comrade Tito's visit to the Soviet Union[173] was a great event in the normalization of relations of the USSR and countries of people's democracy with Yugoslavia.

I briefly summarized the results of Comrade Tito's visit to the USSR, and pointed out to comrade Rákosi how important it was to further improve the relations between Hungary and Yugoslavia. I emphasized that Comrade Tito assured us of the YLC's desire of to do everything necessary for friendly relations with the countries of people's democracy.

Rákosi said that Hungary was ready for the closest friendship with Yugoslavia. Mutual financial claims with Yugoslavia have been fully settled.[174] Comrade Rákosi emphasized that during negotiations regarding those claims, the Yugoslavs did not act in a modest manner—they demonstrated rudeness and arrogance—and that he had to correct and restrain the Hungarian comrades in order to keep the negotiations going.

During the discussion of practical steps toward further normalizing relations with Yugoslavia, comrade Rákosi was notably reserved and expressed a number of critical remarks regarding the Yugoslav leadership. In particular, he noted that after their successful visit to the USSR, the leaders of the YLC might begin showing arrogance and intolerance. Comrade Rákosi said that now they could write and say only positive things about Yugoslavia, because the Yugoslav comrades perceive the slightest critical remarks as insults. Moreover, they have many problems; suffice to say that they fulfilled only 80 percent of the sowing plan, and, if not for assistance from the Americans and the Soviet Union, they would have experienced hunger in the country. In this connection he told me about his recent conversation with Vukmanović-Tempo.[175]

At the beginning of the Korean War, said Comrade Rákosi, the turncoats brought us the order for mobilization in Yugoslavia. At our meeting, I asked comrade Vukmanović-Tempo what the origin of that order was. Comrade Vukmanović-Tempo responded that Yugoslavia had to take that step because they expected an attack from the East. And he honesty admitted that they organized guerrilla bases against a possible attack by the Soviet Army in Yugoslavia in that period.

Comrade Rákosi said that as a result of the Soviet-Yugoslav Belgrade Declaration[176] and Tito's visit to the USSR, some people in Hungary started saying that now Yugoslavia would use its situation to get material benefits from both East and West, and that it would be good for Hungary to follow this road as well.

I told comrade Rákosi that Yugoslavia was undoubtedly on the right course right now, and that Hungary should follow our example to decisively break with the mistakes of the past and courageously follow the course of improving friendly relations with Yugoslavia.

Comrade Rákosi said that they understood this very well, and that they were going to address Tito with an appropriate letter in the nearest future.[177]

In conclusion, comrade Rákosi touched upon the rumors that emerged in the HWP as a result of the publication by the Americans of Comrade Khrushchev's report to the Twentieth Congress

---

[173] Concerning Tito's visit, see Document No. 14.

[174] On May 29, 1956, as a result of long negotiations, the two counties signed an economic and financial agreement, in which Hungary agreed to pay $85 million over the following five years as compensation for Yugoslav claims. For the agreement, see József Kiss, Zoltán Ripp and István Vida, eds., *Magyar-jugoszláv kapcsolatok, 1956: Dokumentumok* (Budapest: MTA Jelenkor-kutató Bizottság, 1995), 56–63.

[175] Svetozar Vukmanović-Tempo was a member of the Executive Committee of the YLC CC beginning in 1952 and vice chairman of Yugoslavia's Federal Executive Council (government) from 1953–1958.

[176] "See footnote 164 above".

[177] For the letter, see Document No. 18.

of the CPSU CC on the personality cult. Upon receiving the text of comrade Khrushchev's report from Moscow, we selected excerpts and made copies for reading in the party organizations, but at that time, the Voice of America began broadcasting the full text of the report.

In this connection, comrade Rákosi mentioned comrade Togliatti's statement,[178] which he characterized as hasty and incorrect.

I had a general impression from our conversation that comrade Rákosi was seriously concerned about the forthcoming discussion of the Farkas case at the HWP CC; apparently, he is worried that some facts about him, which are not known to the party, might be revealed.

Comrade Rákosi spoke at length about those conversations that involved his name in connection with criticism of the personality cult. This worries him and leads to a lack of confidence.

As far as normalization of relations with Yugoslavia is concerned, it seems to me that Rákosi has not yet fully removed the burden of the past. He exhibited a lot of anxiety and tension regarding this issue.

JUNE 26, 1956.

[Source: Arkhiv Prezidenta Rossiiskoi Federatsii (APRF), Fond (F.) 3, Opis (Op.) 64, Delo (D.) 483, Listy (Ll.) 11–14. Published in Sovietskii Soyuz i vengerskii krizis, 1956 goda: Dokumenty, edited and compiled by E. D. Orekhova, Vyacheslav T. Sereda and Aleksandr. S. Stykhalin (Moscow: ROSSPEN, 1998), 97–100. Translated by Svetlana Savranskaya.]

[178] This refers to Togliatti's interview in *Nuovi Argumenti* on Stalin and the Twentieth Congress which was also published by *l'Unitá* (the organ of the ICP) on June 17, 1956. In this interview, Togliatti found the criticism voiced at the Twentieth Congress—which discussed Stalin's mistakes only in the framework of the "cult of personality"— insufficient, and emphasized the need for a more fundamental explanation of the distortions. He also criticized the Eastern European countries for their uncritical imitation of Soviet methods.

DOCUMENT NO. 12: NSC 5608, "U.S. Policy Toward the Soviet Satellites in Eastern Europe," (excerpts) July 6, 1956

As early as fall 1955, not long after the Geneva summit, momentum began to build within the Eisenhower administration for a reevaluation of basic U.S. policy toward Eastern Europe. The most recent review had taken place in 1953, after Stalin's death, and resulted in the formulation of NSC 174 (see Document No. 3). The NSC considered a new draft policy statement, NSC 5608, at its 290th meeting on July 12, along with the accompanying NSC staff study. When the study was published in the State Department's Foreign Relations of the United States series, the portions dealing with possible covert activity and "alternative courses of action," the often hidden aspects of U.S. policy, were still considered secret. Those sections have only recently been declassified and are reproduced below.

JULY 6, 1956 TOP SECRET

NSC STAFF STUDY

ON

U.S. POLICY TOWARD THE SOVIET SATELLITES IN EASTERN EUROPE

BACKGROUND

Importance of the Satellites

1. The satellites are of importance in the current balance of power in Europe because they augment the political, military and economic power of the Soviet Union and extend Soviet power into the heart of Europe. The permanent consolidation of Soviet control in this area would represent a serious threat to the security of Western Europe and the United States. It is our traditional policy to recognize and support the right of all peoples to independence and to governments of their own choosing. The elimination of Soviet domination of the satellites is, therefore, in the fundamental interest of the United States.

Soviet Domination of the Satellites

2. Soviet domination of the satellites remains a basic fact; there is no evidence that Moscow's ability to control them has been fundamentally affected by anything that has happened since the death of Stalin. While it rests in the last analysis on Soviet military domination of Eastern Europe, the immediate basis of Moscow's control is the reliable Communist leadership in each satellite, flanked by Soviet advisers in the state apparatus and armed forces and by a Soviet-supervised security police system. A contributing factor is the high degree of Soviet-satellite economic interdependence systematically developed since the war. In East Germany a large Soviet military occupation force furnishes an added element of control, without which the Communist government might be unable to maintain the populace in subjection; this was demonstrated when Soviet military force was required to suppress the 1953 riots. The smaller Soviet forces, totaling around 100,000, which are stationed in Poland, Hungary and Rumania are probably not essential to the maintenance of Soviet control over those countries; in them (as in Albania, Czechoslovakia and Bulgaria, where no Soviet forces are stationed) what counts is rather Moscow's over-all military ability to dominate the region.

3. The Kremlin has pushed forward with considerable success its plans to expand the industrial and military capabilities of the satellites and to coordinate their Sovietized political system, military establishments and economies with those of the USSR in a working totality. While tending on the whole to bind the individual satellites separately to the USSR, Moscow has permitted programs of cultural, economic and technical collaboration among them. Through such devices as the Council of Mutual Economic Assistance (CMEA) and the Warsaw Security Pact it has geared them collectively with one another and with the USSR for specific economic and military purposes. To all intents and purposes the satellites are as much at Moscow's disposal, economically, politically and militarily, as if they were formally member-republics of the USSR. On the other hand, the convenience to Moscow of their nominally independent status for purposes of UN activity (Albania, Bulgaria, Hungary, and Rumania were admitted to the UN in 1955), foreign trade promotion, propaganda, and other roles abroad, makes the actual incorporation of any of the satellites in the USSR appear unlikely in the foreseeable future.

Opposition to Soviet Domination

4. The great majority of the population in each satellite continues to be deeply dissatisfied with the Communist regime, resenting the hard living conditions and lack of personal freedom for which the regime is held responsible. Aggrieved religious feelings resulting from Communist attacks on the churches have also served to intensify this widespread anti-Communism. The dissident majorities are, however, not in a position to develop active resistance of a kind which would seriously challenge Soviet control. Nevertheless, by passive resistance they have long impeded and undoubtedly will continue to impede the process of Sovietization, and they form the main element on which must be based eventual elimination of Soviet domination. At the same time, however, if the process of exclusive Communist indoctrination and education of the young proceeds without interruption and if Moscow continues its new policy of allowing the satellites greater latitude in the conduct of their own affairs, the prevailing anti-regime sentiment may be jeopardized over the long run.

5. In addition to anti-Communism *per se,* nationalism is a significant factor of opposition to Soviet control in all the satellites. These peoples will not reconcile themselves in a few years to the loss of national independence, a disregard of national traditions and the enforced glorification of the USSR. The nationalist sentiment focuses on the memory of better times in the past, hopes for the future, and the resentment felt at the injuries and insults experienced under the present regime. In many respects it is the strongest leverage available for strengthening the morale of the satellite populations, sustaining their spirit of resistance to Soviet imperialism, and encouraging their opposition to servile Communist regimes. Nationalism is, however, a double-edged weapon, raising a number of operational problems, as we have discovered in our propaganda work and dealings with the refugees. Besides arousing anti-Soviet feeling, nationalist sentiment also creates divisions among these peoples themselves, Magyars against Slavs and Rumanians, Slovaks against Czechs, Poles against Germans, and Germans against the Slavs. A problem which will become increasingly serious as nationalist sentiment ferments is that of the Polish-occupied areas of Germany east of Oder-Neisse line.

6. Since the death of Stalin the new Soviet leadership has tried certain new approaches in its rule of the satellites. There has been a trend away from the enforced uniformity of the Stalin era, and more emphasis on individual satellite problems and local ways of carrying out socialization within the general framework of Communist dogma. The purge of Beria has been reflected in the satellites in a greater degree of subordination of their police apparatuses to Party control, and in a toning down of some of the more arbitrary and terroristic police-state practices of the Stalin era. Along with an increasing propaganda emphasis on "socialist legality" in the treatment of the ordinary citizen by the state, there has been a tendency to amnesty imprisoned opposition elements. In foreign relations the Soviet bloc has begun to encourage tourism, to expand cultural relations, and to urge the study of non-Soviet as well as Soviet achievements. In these and other

ways it has sought to create the feeling that its increasing strength and stability justify a more confident and conciliatory approach to its own peoples and to other countries than in the past. In the economic sphere the USSR has gradually cut down its direct participation in the satellite economies by liquidating all but a few of its holdings of satellite industrial properties both in and outside of the Soviet-satellite joint companies. The satellites have been allowed to relax their previous over-emphasis on heavy industrial development and devote more resources to agriculture. They have been encouraged both to develop more economic interdependence through coordination of planning and development of regional specialization among themselves, and to expand trade with the free world. All evidence so far points to Soviet confidence in the maintenance of its economic power over the satellites under this new regime. The USSR still has ample diplomatic and party mechanisms for overseeing satellite economic programs, and still dominates the trade of each satellite, thus maintaining their prime economic dependence on the USSR. The USSR, furthermore, oversees their inter-satellite economic relations, and probably also their economic approaches to the free world, through the mechanism of the Soviet-dominated Council of Mutual Economic Assistance (CMEA).

7. Accompanying these developments over the past months has been a sense of relaxation which in varying degrees, depending on the circumstances in each country, has in general given the population a greater feeling of ease and personal security. Moreover, the denigration of Stalin and Moscow's acceptance of Titoism have created difficulties in Soviet relations with the satellites; they have raised questions as to the infallibility of Soviet leadership among important elements of the satellite Communist parties; they have aroused to varying degrees latent popular aspiration for relaxation of oppression, restoration of national independence, and the establishment of governments responsive to popular will. As a result, criticism of the regime and its policies, first encouraged as Communist "self-criticism", has appeared in a number of the satellites and has undoubtedly gone beyond the bounds originally envisaged by those in authority. The intelligentsia, in particular, have seized this opportunity to express in vehement terms diverse criticisms of the regimes and their policies. The recent Writers' Congresses in Poland, Czechoslovakia and Hungary offer strikingly similar examples of this phenomenon; the May demonstrations of Czech students and the resolutions adopted at Czech student meetings are other examples.[179] This has led the regimes to seek to impose definite limits on criticism, which they saw was leading to questioning of basic policies and even Communist doctrine itself, and they have already threatened a crackdown where those limits were exceeded. However, it may be expected that the Eastern European intelligentsia will seek to utilize to the fullest opportunities for free expression and that they will exert pressure on the regimes for more freedom.

Possibilities of "Titoism"

8. Nationalism in the satellites, even within the Communist movement itself, remains a disruptive force in Soviet-satellite relations. There is a real and growing split in most satellite parties between those amenable to close Soviet control and the "national Communists." However, since the combination of basic factors which made possible the successful Yugoslav break with Moscow is lacking in the satellites, it is unlikely that the Yugoslav experience will be repeated in any of them. Moreover, by its reconciliation with Tito, Moscow has sought with some success to neutralize the competing attraction originally exercised on the satellite governments by Belgrade's independent position and policies.

9. Tito is unique among the European satellite leaders in the degree of power that he achieved independently. He created an impressive military force, as well as a political organization, responsive to his own leadership which maintained itself inside Yugoslavia during the war and

---

[179] On the student demonstrations in Czechoslovakia see John P. Matthews, *Majales: The abortive Student Revolt in Czechoslovakia in 1956*, Cold War International History Project Working Paper, no. 24 (Washington D.C.: Woodrow Wilson International Center for Scholars, 1998).

which, following withdrawal of the German forces, possessed the requisite power to impose its will upon the Yugoslav people without substantial assistance from the Soviet Army. Only the Hoxha regime in Albania achieved a similar success, on a much smaller scale. All the other Communist regimes were placed in power by the Soviet Army itself or by the threat of force which the Soviet Army represented. These regimes, therefore, were from the outset dependent on Soviet military power for their existence and have remained so. In East Germany, Poland, Hungary and Rumania the physical presence of sizable Soviet forces bears daily witness to Soviet domination of these satellites. In Poland the Minister of National Defense is a Soviet marshal,[180] and Soviet officers occupy many of the higher posts throughout the Polish armed forces. In all the satellites there are Soviet military missions, some of them large, which supervise the build-up and Sovietization of the satellite armed forces, and Soviet advisers and technicians hold key positions in these forces as well as in the defense ministries.

10. In contrast to the leadership in the other satellites, Tito preserved exclusive control over his state security apparatus. His security forces were built up on the basis of personal loyalty demonstrated throughout the crucial wartime resistance struggle, and Tito knew that he could trust the overwhelming majority of the higher echelons of his command. In other satellites the security organs were created with a large measure of Soviet assistance and participation which continues to this day. In contrast, Tito steadfastly denied the Soviet liaison officials uncontrolled access to his security organization, a fact which contributed much to the friction that later reached its climax in the break between Tito and the Kremlin.

11. Poland, Czechoslovakia, Hungary, and Rumania have a common land frontier with the USSR. Bulgaria has a common sea frontier. These states are accordingly more exposed to Soviet military intervention and hence more readily susceptible to Soviet pressure and control than was Yugoslavia, which shares no common frontier with the USSR. Furthermore, with Yugoslavia's long sea coast facing the West, greater possibilities to obtain material support from the Western powers in the event of a break with Moscow were available to Tito than there would be to the other satellites, with the exception of Albania.

12. Following Tito's defection in 1948 Stalin took stringent and thorough measures to guard against any similar development in other satellites. Leaders in whom any taint of independence was suspected were either shorn of all power, imprisoned, or liquidated. Sovietization was accelerated. The customary security safeguards were tightened and expanded, and contacts with the West restricted. A series of bilateral mutual assistance pacts was created among most of the satellites and between them and the USSR, signifying that they would go to each other's aid in case of action from without—a commitment which in 1955 was transformed into a multilateral security pact embracing all of the satellites and the USSR and providing for a joint military command.[181] The resultant relationship between the USSR and the satellites made it appear highly probable that the Soviet leaders could count on the satellite regimes to stay under their control, and that any unforeseen local challenge to that control would precipitate swift Soviet intervention.

13. The safeguards built up by Stalin against satellite Titoism have in general retained their effectiveness up to now. Viewed together with the geographic difficulties, they make the chances appear negligible that any existing satellite Communist regime would or could break away from Moscow under its own power or that any anti-Soviet faction could seize or hold power in a satellite and bring about its detachment from the Soviet bloc.

14. Albania represents a partial exception, albeit an extremely hypothetical one, in that, unlike the other satellites, it is geographically isolated from the rest of the Soviet bloc and has close access to the West by sea. However, this circumstance and the potentiality of the anti-Communist majority of the Albanian population for action against Soviet rule are offset by the current strength the regime. The present Albanian leaders are loyal to the Kremlin and rule the

---

[180] Marshal Konstanty Rokossowski, see footnote 246 in this chapter.

[181] This refers to the establishment of the Warsaw Treaty Organization on May 14, 1955.

country with an effective security apparatus. It is clear that they prefer allegiance to distant Moscow, without whose economic aid they could not exist for any length of time, to domination by some nearer neighbor. An important factor militating against any Albanian move away from the soviet orbit is the bitter rivalry with respect to Albania of its three neighbors—Italy, Yugoslavia and Greece.

15. Nationalism may, nevertheless, continue to be a disruptive force within the Communist movement, open to exploitation by the United States. The fact that Moscow and the satellite Communist parties are giving increasing lip-service to the principle of national autonomy and diversity shows that they are conscious of its importance in the popular mind and would like to twist it to their own advantage. Writers, teachers, scientists, technicians, artists, and similar elements on whom the regime depends to help implement its program, are apt to be deeply imbued with the national tradition, or keenly aware of the local problems, and impatient of limitations or controls dictated by the requirements of distant Moscow or of Soviet-imposed policies. Even within the regime itself, not all satellite Communists are able or willing to serve Moscow's interest without any regard for that of their own nation; the very problems of governing their respective territories and of meeting the goals which have been set seem to require at least a minimum of cooperation from the people and may lead certain local Communists to oppose as best they can those Kremlin demands and policies which put too great a strain upon their own position. Moreover if the Soviet leaders, out of awareness of these satellite stresses and strains, permit somewhat more local flexibility so as to ease the task of their satellite proteges, it is conceivable that such flexibility might at some point tend to get out of hand, inspire wider unrest, and even impair the general effectiveness of Soviet control. The latter possibility, however, so far appears to be remote.

Significance of Yugoslavia in Policy Toward the Satellites

16. Even though no other satellite has followed or seems capable of following the path of Tito's Yugoslavia under existing conditions, the Yugoslav example continues to be a significant factor in the satellite picture. Tito's success in maintaining Yugoslavia's independence constitutes a reflection on the past political competence and infallibility of the Soviet leadership. His political and ideological counter-offensive has been a disturbing factor within the satellite Communist parties. He has provided an example of a Communist alternative to Soviet domination. Though he has latterly tended to swing partly away from the Western allies, including Greece and Turkey, his close relationship with the Western allies has undoubtedly made a strong impression on the satellite peoples. The mere fact of substantial U. S. economic and military assistance to Yugoslavia has had an effect on both Communists and non-Communists in the satellites.

17. In connection with its new, conciliatory tactics toward Tito over the past year, Moscow has caused the satellites to cease their criticism of him and to adopt a conciliatory posture. Some of them have gone so far as to repudiate formally the charge of "Titoism" that was included in the indictment of certain of their major purge victims executed in 1949–52. Nevertheless, the Yugoslav leaders so far have moved slowly and cautiously with respect to the reestablishment of contacts with the Communist parties of the Soviet Union or the satellites. The Soviet Government, for its part, has been in no hurry to reshuffle satellite leaders who are distasteful to Tito; most of the satellites are still headed by Communists who spoke out strongest against him in 1948–53, such as Rakosi in Hungary, Hoxha and Shehu in Albania, and Gheorghiu-Dej in Rumania. One such leader, Chervenkov[182] in Bulgaria, was recently removed, although internal party reasons also appeared to play a role in his ouster; and it was significant that reliable Bulgarian proteges of Moscow were just as prominent in the reshuffled leadership as before.

---

[182] Vulko Chervenkov, secretary general of the Bulgarian Communist Party between 1950–1954 and prime minister from 1950–1956, lost the latter post in March 1956 after being criticized by the Central Committee.

18. Since 1945 none of the organized political émigré groups from the Eastern European countries have been recognized by any of the free world countries as governments-in-exile. The passage of time, the proliferation of exile organizations, and the diverse voices raised in claim to represent the views of the peoples behind the Iron Curtain, have tended to discourage Eastern European political leaders and to diminish the effectiveness of their émigré organizations. In recognition of this trend, the exile leaders joined forces in 1954 to create the Assembly of Captive European Nations (ACEN) in order to provide a unified and cohesive forum for their national voices. Through periodic deliberations and actions in this forum, the exiles have been able to attract more serious attention of the U. S. and foreign press and of the free world states-men, and thus the ACEN has become to date the most effective device of the Eastern European political exiles to exercise influence on and expound their views before public opinion outside and within the Iron Curtain.

19. For the past year or more the Soviet Union and satellite governments have conducted an intensified "redefection" campaign aimed at rendering ineffective and, if possible, eliminating the organized activities abroad of the political exiles. Although few exiles have been persuaded to return to their native countries (1158 known cases in the period January 1955-March 1956), this campaign has had a disturbing psychological effect in exile circles. The United States has countered this Soviet action with a program emphasizing (a) increased material assistance to escapees, (b) a propaganda counter-offensive, and (c) protection and security of the émigrés. The United States should continue to combat by all feasible means Soviet redefection efforts and should encourage and assist the exiles in opposing the redefection campaign.

Means of Attacking Soviet Domination of the Satellites

20. The means available to the United States to assist opposition to, and the eventual break-down of, Soviet domination of the satellites fall into the following general categories: (a) polit-ical and diplomatic; (b) economic; (c) propaganda; (d) covert; and (e) military. It must be rec-ognized that, owing to the actual presence of Soviet power and the apparatus of Soviet control, all these means, with the exception of the military, are of limited effectiveness.

Political and Diplomatic

21. The major political and diplomatic capability is to exert upon the existing Soviet-con-trolled regimes the pressure of the long-standing U. S. position defending the fundamental right of the satellite peoples to freedom. The United States can reaffirm its position on this subject on all appropriate occasions in discussions both with its free world partners and with Soviet and satellite representatives, with a view to strengthening and broadening pressure on the USSR and the satellite regimes.

22. The United States maintains diplomatic missions in Poland, Czechoslovakia, Hungary and Rumania. This is advantageous in that it (a) provides useful opportunities for reporting and intelligence acquisition, (b) shows American concern for the rights, welfare and eventual inde-pendence of the satellite peoples, (c) makes possible direct contact with the government con-cerned and treatment of such problems as the protection of American citizens and property, (d) provides a vantage point which could be useful in the event of future developments which might be exploited in the U. S. interest, and (e) provides a means for evaluating and guiding our prop-aganda effort. The principal disadvantages are (a) the impression created in some quarters that diplomatic relations indicate the acceptance of the legitimacy of the Communist regimes, (b) the pressures and harassments to which American representatives in the satellite states are subject-ed, to the detriment of U. S. prestige, and (c) the security problems created by the presence of satellite missions in the United States. Diplomatic relations with Bulgaria and Albania should be

resumed whenever those governments give satisfactory guarantees for the treatment of our missions and their personnel and exhibit a willingness to negotiate satisfactory settlements of outstanding bilateral issues between our governments.

Economic

23.[183] Western controls of exports to the Soviet bloc, as well as the Soviet bloc drive for self-sufficiency, reduced the trade of Eastern Europe with the free world to a low level by 1953. Subsequently, the Eastern European countries have begun to show more interest in increasing imports from the free world, including the United States, and have taken steps to expand their exports to those areas, with a result that their trade with the West has increased substantially, though it continues to be small as compared to trade within the Bloc. The relatively low level of East-West trade and the size and strength of the Soviet bloc economy, together with Soviet autarchic policies, serve to limit the efficacy of economic pressures as implements to accomplish the general purposes of this paper. They might, however, have some harassment value or could serve as auxiliaries to a coordinated program based primarily on other measures. Existing trade controls have already made the economic problems of the satellites more difficult and to this extent contribute to realizing the specific purposes of U. S. policy toward the satellites. On the other hand, the application of controls on a general basis going beyond commodities of a primary strategic character, requires a large measure of agreement and cooperation among the free world countries, and the question accordingly arises whether they are worthwhile in terms of the general aspects of U. S. relations with the USSR and with our free world allies. Such general controls may also be self-defeating in so far as they tend to facilitate the integration of the satellites with the USSR. The unilateral application of economic pressures by the United States should therefore be considered on a case-by-case basis, bearing in mind the balance of advantage in each instance between the USSR and the free world.

24.[184] The existing low level of trade makes relatively more important economic incentives as a measure to promote U. S. policy toward the satellites. The ability of the United States to offer such incentives, however, is presently inhibited by legislative obstacles to trade with the Soviet bloc. Legislative restrictions on trade in U. S. Government-owned foodstuffs and the provisions of the Trade Agreement Act, which deny to Soviet bloc countries the benefits of most-favored-nations treatment, are presently applied to the bloc as a whole. They do not permit individual treatment as circumstances may warrant. It is desirable to attain greater flexibility in U. S. economic policies, in order that maximum advantage may be gained with the limited economic weapons at hand (both restrictions and incentives). Favorable Congressional action should be sought on amendatory legislation where necessary to provide the flexibility required to utilize increased trade as an incentive to promote the objectives of U. S. policy toward the satellites.

Propaganda

25. The denial to the satellite peoples of access to truth and means of contact with the outside world has limited the possibilities in the propaganda field principally to broadcasting, although balloons, air drops, etc., are being used to supplement this medium. The operation of

---

[183] The Treasury Department objects to paragraph 23 on the ground that it appears to be weighted against the retention of multilateral controls over lists II and III items and in favor of a relaxation of the unilateral U. S. export controls over these items on shipments to the satellites. The Treasury Department feels that this is an issue which should be carefully reviewed by EDAC and ACEP before broad sweeping conclusions are reached with respect to the efficacy of multilateral controls or the revision of U. S. export controls. [Footnote in original.]

[184] The Treasury Department objects to paragraph 24. It sees no justification, at the present time, for requesting broader authority from Congress which would permit either local currency sales of agricultural surpluses to the satellites or the granting of most-favored-nation treatment to the satellites under the Tariff laws. [Footnote in original.]

adequate technical facilities for broadcasting to the satellites and effective programming assume increasing importance in view of the need to conserve and promote anti-Communist sentiment in the face of the Communist monopoly over the various media of information. Utilization of our propaganda facilities is conditioned by the necessity of avoiding, on the one hand, any commitments regarding the time and means of achieving freedom from Soviet domination and any incitement to premature revolt, and, on the other hand, seeking to maintain faith in the eventual restoration of freedom.

26. One important means of sustaining the hope and faith of the satellite peoples in eventual freedom and independence, would be a program of reciprocal exchanges, especially on the non-official level. The travel of Americans in the satellites and reciprocal visits to the United States can become an effective means of serving to remind the captive peoples of U. S. interest in their ultimate freedom, and correcting the distorted image of the West as mirrored in Communist propaganda media.

Covert

27. Covert operations can be directed to the satellites (a) to gain intelligence, (b) to build up organizational arrangements which will constitute an asset in the event of war or other situation where action against the regimes may be feasible and desirable, and (c) to reinforce official U. S. propaganda, especially with the purpose of keeping up the morale of the anti-Communists and sowing confusion among the Communists. To be most effective, operations of this kind should be conducted so as to avoid encouraging divisive forces among the anti-Communists at home or the exiles abroad.

28. It is recognized that the difficulties of conducting covert operations are considerable because of the concern of the Kremlin for security throughout the Soviet bloc and the effectiveness of the bloc-wide security apparatus. In consequence of these considerations, as well as of physical difficulties, the mounting of any specific operations necessarily requires considerable time for adequate preparation. Furthermore, in the light of recent experience it is of the utmost importance to proceed with extreme care in this field with a view to solid accomplishment for the long run.

29. Among the means at hand to assist in the attainment of U. S. objectives are defectors and refugees from the satellites. The defection of key personnel offers considerable benefits to the United States and should continue to be encouraged in accordance with existing policy.

30. However, the effectiveness of émigré leaders and their organizations in promoting U. S. objectives toward the Eastern European satellites remains problematical. Particularly, in a fluid situation such as has developed since the death of Stalin, effectiveness of political exiles will depend to considerable degree upon their own flexibility and resourcefulness. Many variable factors are involved. In addition to the exiles' cohesiveness and substantive activities, there are such factors as adequate financial support, the amount of publicity given to them by free world media directed at their captive countries, and the policies and actions of the United States and its allies. Manipulation of these factors can act to modify up or down the degree of favor, indifference, or disfavor with which the exile leaders and their organization are regarded by the Communist regimes and the captive peoples. U. S. moral and covert financial support of political émigrés has not and should not be directed at restoring any particular group of émigrés to power or at establishing any particular economic or social system in any of the satellites should independence and freedom be achieved by one or more of the captive nations. Under present conditions exile organizations can accomplish only limited objectives. Nevertheless, they form an asset, which, when the aforementioned variable factors are skillfully handled, may encourage developments in the satellites in the direction sought by U. S. policies.

ALTERNATIVE COURSES OF ACTION

The Three Alternatives

31. One alternative is to take direct action for the liberation of the satellites peoples from the USSR by military force, either through direct military intervention or through armed support of revolutionary movements. Such use of military force would in all probability start a global war. This alternative is not in accordance with current U. S. policy and must therefore be rejected.

32. The contrary alternative is to accept the fact of Soviet control of the satellites for an indeterminate period, possible as a basis for reaching some kind of negotiated accommodation with the USSR, while U. S. efforts are devoted to blocking Soviet expansion in areas beyond the present limits of Soviet control. Such a course, besides being inconsistent with the U. S. position in defense of the right of the satellite peoples to freedom, would deny us the possibility of seeking to reduce the over-all Soviet power position vis-à-vis the United States and its allies. It may be reasonably assumed, moreover, that our acceptance of the legitimacy of the present satellite regimes, even if it should require limited Soviet concessions to the West, would be the course which the Kremlin would desire the United States to follow.

33. There is a large area between the extremes mentioned in the two preceding paragraphs in which policy and action can be developed with the purpose of limiting or weakening the Soviet grip on the satellites. U. S. policy should be directed toward the weakening and the eventual elimination of dominant Soviet power over these peoples, although the accomplishment of this goal in the near future cannot be expected. The more immediate criteria for judging the desirability of any particular measures would be their effectiveness in promoting and encouraging evolutionary change toward the weakening of Soviet controls and the attainment of national independence by the countries concerned. Increased freedom of communication, increased cultural and technical exchanges, American tourism, increased trade, all offer us opportunities to exert greater influence on developments in satellites and should give us a leverage in our dealings with them which has previously been lacking. However, there is a constant danger that efforts on our part to influence the situation, to build up or exploit pressures, might easily be counter-productive if they have the effect of associating the opposition forces with the United States and hence stimulating and justifying the regimes in a crackdown.

U.S. Policy

34. Soviet domination of the satellite peoples violates the principle of freedom and self-determination of nations. It has also, by bringing Soviet power into the heart of Europe, created a fundamental disequilibrium on the Continent and a continuing pressure on Western Europe. So long as it remains, the task of achieving security, stability and orderly progress in Europe must encounter grave difficulties. The United States should make clear by its words and deeds that it does not accept this situation as right or as permanent and that no accommodation with the Soviet Union to the contrary effect can be countenanced.

35. A deliberate policy of attempting to liberate the satellite peoples by military force must be rejected. The United States should, however, direct its efforts toward fostering conditions which would make possible the attainment of national independence by the satellites in the future and toward obstructing meanwhile the processes of Soviet imperialism in those areas.

36. In general, full advantage should be taken of the means of diplomacy, economic policy, propaganda, and covert operations, to maintain the morale of anti-Soviet elements, to foster desired changes in Soviet-satellite relationships, and to maximize Soviet difficulties. Policies and action to be undertaken by the United States should be judged on the basis of their contribution to these purposes within the context of over-all U. S. policy.

37. In its efforts to encourage anti-Soviet elements in the satellites and keep up their hopes, the United States should not encourage premature action on their part which will bring upon

them reprisals involving further terror and suppression. Continuing and careful attention must be given to the fine line, which is not stationary, between efforts to keep up morale and to maintain passive resistance, and invitations to suicide. Planning for covert operations should be determined on the basis of feasibility, minimum risk, and maximum contribution to the fundamental interest of the United States.

38. The United States should vigilantly follow the developing situation in each satellite and be prepared to take advantage of any opportunity to further the emergence of regimes not subservient to the USSR. U. S. action in any individual case would have to be determined in the light of probable Soviet reactions, risks of global war, the probable reaction of our allies, and other aspects of the situation prevailing at the time.

39. U. S. interests with respect to the satellites can be pursued most effectively by flexible and adaptable courses of action within the general policy of determined opposition to, and the purpose of the eventual elimination of, Soviet domination over those peoples. Such action must be within the limits of our capabilities as conditioned by our general policies.

[Source: Dwight D. Eisenhower Library, White House, Office of the Special Assistant for National Security Affairs: Records 1953–1961, NSC Series, Policy Papers Subseries, Box 17.]

DOCUMENT NO. 13: Minutes of the 290th NSC Meeting, July 12, 1956

This National Security Council session focuses on a new draft policy statement toward Eastern Europe, NSC 5608 (see previous document). Much of the discussion is about ensuring that the United States has sufficient flexibility in pursuing policies, particularly economic actions, toward individual countries in the Soviet bloc. The relevant FRUS volume reproduces only a small portion of this discussion, omitting most of the lively debate over what U.S. trade and economic goals in the region should be. In the previously unpublished sections that appear below, Secretary of State John Foster Dulles clarifies a hidden purpose behind the proposed U.S. policy to tender food aid to the Eastern Europe regimes. Acknowledging that in making "our offer recently to the people of Poznan, we never seriously thought that we would be able to provide food to these people," he discloses that "our main idea was to embarrass the Government of Communist Poland." Even after the 1953 East German uprising, Dulles still aims to promote "spontaneous manifestations of discontent and opposition to the Communist regime, despite risks to individuals." This phrasing would survive in the final policy statement, NSC 5608/1 (Document No. 17). In another memorable moment that does not appear in FRUS, Vice President Richard Nixon, who is presiding at the session, reflects his stark realpolitik approach, commenting that "it wouldn't be an unmixed evil, from the point of view of U.S. interest, if the Soviet iron fist were to come down again on the Soviet bloc."

JULY 13, 1956

MEMORANDUM

SUBJECT: Discussion at the 290th Meting
of the National Security Council,

THURSDAY, JULY 12; 1956

[....][185]

There follows a summary of the discussion at the meeting and the main points taken.

1. U.S. POLICY TOWARD THE SOVIET SATELLITES IN EASTERN EUROPE
(NSC 5608 and Annex to NSC 5608; NSC Action No. 1530–b; NSC 5505/1; NSC 174; Memos for All Holders of NSC 5608, dated July 5 and 6, 1956; Memo for NSC from Executive Secretary, same subject, dated July 11, 1956)

Mr. [Dillon] Anderson[186] briefed the Council on the main features of the proposed new policy, particularly as it differed from the existing policy on the subject, NSC 174. When he reached paragraph 25, Mr. Anderson pointed out the split views. As proposed by the majority of the Planning Board, the paragraph would read:

"Seek authority for and use, as appropriate, greater flexibility in U. S. economic policies (both incentives and restrictions) toward the satellites."

The Treasury member of the Planning Board wished to delete the first four words. Mr. Anderson suggested that this might be a suitable time for the Council to determine which ver-

---

[185] This paragraph contains a lengthy list of participants.

[186] Dillon Anderson was special assistant to the president for national security affairs from April 1955 until September 1956.

sion it preferred, and invited [Treasury] Secretary [George] Humphrey to speak to the Treasury position.

Secretary Humphrey said that the position of the Treasury Department was quite a simple one. It seemed to them that, with all the difficulties which the Administration was now encountering with the Congress, it was wholly unrealistic to go to the Congress and ask them to agree to legislation which would permit us to give surplus agricultural commodities to the Soviet satellites. It was simply impossible, according to Secretary Humphrey, to get any such concession from Congress. They were opposed to any liberalization of Public Law 480 vis-a-vis the Soviet satellites. To make the attempt to induce a liberalization would only succeed in arousing a storm of protest in Congress and further complicate our already involved situation.

Dr. [Arthur] Flemming[187] inquired whether the Secretary of State and the Secretary of Agriculture had not already requested authority from Congress for greater flexibility in carrying out economic policies toward the satellites. Secretary Dulles replied that all that they had sought was authority to barter goods with countries behind the Iron Curtain. Moreover, he added, he had not in mind asking anything more of the Congress by way of authority in this area.

[Defense] Secretary [Charles] Wilson said that he went along with the position taken by Secretary Humphrey toward this course of action, but that he did so for different reasons than Secretary Humphrey. He was not opposed to seeking additional authority from Congress simply because to do so was inexpedient at this time, but rather because he did not wish to see the standard of living in the satellites raised through the agency of U.S. surplus food. If the satellite standard of living was raised, it would indirectly promote both the political stability and the military power of the satellite states. In sum, trading on a preferred basis with the Communists in items of food value was a very doubtful course of action. It would be doubtful even if the people of the United States and the Congress could be induced to support it.

Secretary Dulles said that he believed there was a misunderstanding of the intention of this paragraph. It was not the objective of this paragraph or this paper to encourage any level of trade with the Soviet satellites. The objective was simply to put the U.S. Government in a position to be able to make offers of surplus materials to the satellite governments which these governments could not reject without simultaneously putting pressure on the USSR to match the U.S. offer of surplus food. Moreover, no satellite government would be able to accept any U.S. offer of surplus food without affording the United States increased political influence in that satellite. Essentially, therefore, this was not a matter of trade, but rather of economic and political warfare. The United States simply must be in a position to be able to make these gestures and feints in its dueling with the Communists. Thus, for example, when we made our offer recently to the people of Poznan, we never seriously thought that we would be able to provide food to these people. Our main idea was to embarrass the Government of Communist Poland. In concluding, Secretary Dulles once again repeated that he was not now seeking any new authority, along the lines suggested by paragraph 25, from the Congress at this time.

Mr. Anderson pointed out that it was generally understood that an effort would be made to secure Congressional agreement for the sale of surplus commodities in return for local currencies. This, he believed, underlay paragraph 25.

Secretary Humphrey said that in general when this Government sold surplus agricultural commodities to foreign countries, it gave back the local currencies thus generated to the country which received the surplus food. This being the general pattern of our performance, Secretary Humphrey predicted that we would get into terrible trouble if we followed this pattern of operations in dealing with the satellites.

The Vice President agreed that from the practical standpoint the language of paragraph 25, calling for additional authority and greater flexibility in U.S. economic policies toward the satellites from the Congress, posed a political impossibility at this time. Later on we may educate Congress into understanding more clearly our reasons for seeking such additional flexibility.

---

[187] Dr. Arthur S. Flemming was director of the Office of Defense Mobilization.

130

Accordingly, the Vice President said he agreed with the Treasury proposal to delete the first fourwords of the paragraph.

Secretary Dulles again stated emphatically that he hadn't the slightest idea of going before Congress for anything at the present time; and if any such proposal as this was inherent in paragraph 25, it was nothing less than ridiculous, particular [sic] with the Congress about to adjourn. Was anybody, he asked, actually suggesting that the Administration should now go to Congress for more authority for carrying out flexible economic policies vis-a-vis the satellites? Accordingly, he said, he was quite prepared to agree to drop the bracketed four words. Subsequently, if the situation warranted, we could seek authority for more flexible action from the Congress.

Secretary Wilson agreed, and pointed out that Secretary Dulles was essentially engaging in a poker game. It was a poker game which Secretary Wilson said he understood but did not like. In any event, if the Secretary of State needed more authority later on, he could probably get it.

The Vice President commented that he rather inclined to support of Secretary Dulles' poker playing, though he was not very hopeful that the results would be successful. Secretary Dulles again pointed out that he had little idea that the satellite governments would ever accept our offers of surplus food, but the very fact that we made these offers would serve to embarrass the Communist governments of the satellite states. The Vice President noted that the Soviets themselves were now engaged in playing much the same game as Secretary Dulles was proposing to play against them. The Soviets were making offers of assistance to our allies. They know that our allies are not likely to accept these offers, but they hope that the mere offers will prove embarrassing to us.

Mr. Anderson proposed deletion of the first four words of paragraph 25, the Council agreed, and Mr. Anderson went on to conclude his briefing of the remainder of the paper. (A copy of Mr. Anderson's brief is filed in the minutes of the meeting.)

When Mr. Anderson had finished, Secretary Dulles stated that he had a proposed new paragraph which he would like to suggest should be inserted after the present paragraph 20, which paragraph 20 read as follows:

> "Encourage the satellite peoples in passive resistance to their Soviet-dominated regimes when this will contribute to minimizing satellite contributions to Soviet power or to increasing pressures for desirable change. [2 1/2 lines excised.]

Paragraph 20, continued Secretary Dulles, seemed to him and to some of his associates in the State Department, as rather too negative in character. He thought a somewhat different note and a more positive one would be struck by his proposed new paragraph, which he read to the Council as follows:

> "In general, however, do not discourage, by public utterances or otherwise, spontaneous manifestations of discontent and opposition to the Communist regime, despite risks to individuals, when their net results will exert pressures for release from Soviet domination. [3 1/2 lines excised.]

Secretary Dulles added that he and some of his associates felt that the statement on passive resistance in paragraph 20, particularly as it was explained and delineated in the corresponding paragraphs of the Staff Study (Annex to NSC 5608) did not adequately recognize the fact that [4 1/2 lines excised.] Of course, continued Secretary Dulles, we want to see a lot of low-level officials running around and stirring up riots and uprisings in the satellite countries. [2 1/2 lines excised.] This, in sum, was the purport of his proposed new paragraph.

Secretary Wilson wondered why the Council could not agree to take out some of the "soft words" from the present paragraph 20, instead of adding some harsher words in a new paragraph 21. He then referred to the Dirksen Amendment.[188] He said he did not think that this was a wise amendment, because it would put the United States on record before the world as appropriating

---

[188] Amendment to the Mutual Security Act. [Footnote in original.]

money to stir up trouble behind the Iron Curtain. This he thought was unwise. Secretary Dulles agreed with Secretary Wilson, and pointed out that the Soviets were already publicizing the purport of the Dirksen Amendment to the disadvantage of the United States.

The Vice President said that he would be most reluctant to approve any policy which seemed to follow the George Kennan line that there was essentially nothing we could do about the unhappy *status quo* now existing in the Soviet satellites. If our policy paper were to be couched in terms that would be discouraging to the democratic elements in the satellite populations, this would be a very great error. Moreover, continued the Vice President, it was naive to imagine that the existence of a lot of neat little independent Communist states throughout the world would help to solve the security problem of the United States, though the Vice President admitted that the existence of such states might be more advantageous than the present situation, in which the satellite states were under the thumb of the Soviet Union. Summing up, the Vice President said he did not relish the tenor of the present paper in suggesting that the United States should relax because it can do nothing to remedy the unhappy conditions in the satellites.

Dr. Flemming said that his thoughts ran along the same line as the Vice President's. For this reason he strongly supported the new paragraph proposed by the Secretary of State.

Turning to Mr. William Jackson[189] and Mr. Allen Dulles, the Vice President called on them for their views. He inquired what the effect on the activities headed up by these individuals the adoption of the proposed new policy on the satellites would have.

Mr. Jackson replied that adoption of NSC 5608 would have the effect of encouraging this Government to be more active in the satellites short of violence. The current scene in the satellites was more favorable today for U.S. action than it had been for a long time, and the United States should exert itself vigorously vis-a-vis the satellites. [1 1/2 lines excised.] Moreover, Mr. Jackson doubted the wisdom of actually inserting the Secretary of State's proposed new paragraph in the policy paper.

In his reply to the Vice President's question, Mr. Allen Dulles said that if the new paper were adopted the CIA could easily continue all the activities which it is now carrying on vis-a-vis the satellites—such things as support of Radio Free Europe balloons, support of exile groups, defection, and the like. [5 lines excised.]

Secretary Dulles said that Mr. Allen Dulles' s suggestions were perfectly agreeable to him, and he had no objection [4 lines excised.] He therefore suggested that the sentence in question could be put in a specific covert appendix to NSC 5608, or else in a memorandum having very limited circulation. After further discussion, Mr. Anderson said he gathered it was the consensus that we should add the first sentence of the Secretary of State's proposed new paragraph to the end of the present paragraph 20, and omit the second sentence of the Secretary of State's proposed new paragraph. This was agreed.

The Vice President then said he wanted to get back to his earlier question. Turning to Mr. Allen Dulles and to Mr. [Theodore] Streibert,[190] he said he wanted to test out his understanding of what this paper would mean to officials like these who would have to carry out the policy. As he understood it, adoption of this new policy statement would involve the attempt to achieve two objectives vis-a-vis the Soviet satellites. The first of these was the same objective as in the old satellite paper—namely, the restoration of a democratic and popular government to the satellite nations. Second, a new and possibly a more realistic objective was to support the development of national Communist states, free of Soviet domination, like Yugoslavia. This was, in short, another string to our bow, but, as the Vice President understood it, we still proposed to play on both strings. Mr. Streibert replied that this was his understanding of NSC 5608, and he strongly favored the addition of the Secretary of State's first sentence, which he believed would be helpful to the operations of the USIA.

Secretary Dulles pointed out that the adoption of the language he proposed would help to mitigate the implications of the language set forth in paragraph 37 of the Staff Study (Annex to

[189] William Jackson was special assistant to the president.

[190] Theodore C. Streibert was director of the U.S. Information Agency.

NSC 5608). This language in the Staff Study had worried him a good deal, because of its negative quality, especially taken in conjunction with paragraph 20 of the policy statement. If we had nothing but this language in paragraph 20, we would be prevented from taking any actions to encourage manifestations like the East German revolt of July 1954 [sic: June 1953] and the recent uprising in Poznan. Sometimes unrest of this sort and uprisings like these were an important part of the way we have to play the game in the present situation we are confronting with the Soviet Union.

Mr. Anderson suggested that the same reasons which dictated the elimination of the last sentence of the paragraph proposed by the Secretary of State, also applied to the phrase "despite risks to individuals" which occurred in the first sentence of the Secretary of State's proposal. On the other hand, the Vice President thought that this phraseology should continue to be included because it represented a realistic understanding. After all, we are not saying that we are going to initiate uprisings and violence in the satellites. We are merely saying that we will not always discourage such uprisings and violence if the uprisings should occur spontaneously. The policy paper, concluded the Vice President, should not be too "soft" in character.

At this point Mr. Allen Dulles expressed concern about the content of paragraph 23, reading. as follows:

> "As a means of encouraging the eventual establishment of freely elected governments in the satellites and not as an end in itself, be prepared on a case-by-case basis to assist 'National Communist' movements where U.S. and free world cohesion would not be jeopardized thereby. While avoiding the appearance of encouraging the export of Tito's Communism, use Yugoslavia's unique position in Eastern Europe to promote the weakening of the Soviet grip on the satellite countries."

Mr. Allen Dulles pointed out that if this Government undertook to encourage national Communism, the effect would be very damaging to democratic, idealistic, and religious people in the satellites who looked to the United States for guidance and ultimate relief. Mr. Dulles said that he was not actually opposing a carefully selected assistance to national Communist movements by the U. S. in certain circumstances, but he insisted that such assistance [1 line excised.]

Secretary Wilson said he strongly disapproved of the whole idea of support for any national Communist movement as set forth in paragraph 23. Secretary Dulles explained that the object of supporting in certain instances a national Communist movement was simply to loosen the ties, between a satellite and the Soviet Union. Once these ties were loosened by the development of a national Communist government, it might ultimately be possible to go much further and to change the character of the Communist government in the satellites. He agreed, however, that we should certainly not openly commit ourselves to a policy of support for national Communist movements in the satellites.

The Vice President expressed his emphatic agreement with this last statement of Secretary Dulles. What it got down to, he said, was that we encourage such national Communist movements where we believe the effect will be to disrupt the tie between the satellite state and the USSR. We certainly do not support such national Communist movements because we approve of national Communism as such. Accordingly, this paragraph would have to be implemented with the utmost caution. Mr. Allen Dulles then suggested language for inclusion in paragraph 23 which he believed would meet the point he had raised and which had found general support among the members of the Council. Secretary Wilson commented that in a kind of a way this was like telling a man how to play poker and even how to cheat if he doesn't like one of the players.

The Vice President said he had one other point to add. He could think, he said, of nothing which would, from the point of view of domestic politics or of our international relations, be worse than the occurrence of a leak tending to indicate that we at the highest levels were agreeing on a policy for national Communism under any circumstances. Accordingly, he hoped that everybody, from those present all the way down the line, would keep their mouths shut on this subject. Secretary Humphrey expressed warm agreement, and wondered whether it was essential that all these papers had to be passed all the way down the line. Imagine what would happen if portions of this paper were ever published in the newspapers. The effect on the Administration would be murderous.

The Vice President wondered whether it would be possible to classify certain portions of the paper as ultra-Top Secret. Mr. Anderson suggested that the covering Note by the Executive Secretary could call attention to the extreme sensitivity of the contents of NSC 5608. Under Secretary [Herbert] Hoover, on the other hand, pointed out that it was inevitable, from the point of view of OCB, that these policy papers receive a wide circulation. Indeed copies of them have to be sent all over the world. Accordingly, it was almost impossible to preserve absolute secrecy as to any particular portion of the policy statement. Secretary Humphrey said that in any case we should do our best to minimize the risk of a leak, for if one occurred on this paper it would be the worst we had ever had.

On the same subject, Secretary Dulles pointed out that NSC 5608 was rather a rarity among our policy papers, in that in this paper we were dealing with [1 1/2 lines excised] He agreed that it would be very dangerous indeed if the contents of the paper should leak. Agreeing with Secretary Dulles, Secretary Wilson commented adversely on the moral tone which the paper would seem to give rise to. In turn, Mr. Streibert wondered whether it might not be possible to work out a more limited distribution for this paper than the distribution normally given to a policy paper.

Mr. Anderson said that questions of the security of policy papers had often arisen before, and asked if the Council would not like to hear from the Executive Secretary as to how these matters had been handled in the past. Mr. [James] Lay pointed out that for this paper, as for past papers, it was perfectly possible to resort to a very limited and restricted distribution, so that the precise text would be known only by the heads of agencies, who could pass on the required information in some carefully guarded form. Mr. Lay's remarks prompted the suggestion from Secretary Hoover that certain sensitive paragraphs in the paper should be extracted and made the subject of a special annex to NSC 5608.

Secretary Wilson pointed out that it was, after all, the responsibility of officials in the several departments to carry out these policies. This did not mean that they had to pass the policy papers all over the place. The Defense Department leaked like a sieve, and Secretary Wilson said he couldn't seem to stop these leaks.

Secretary Dulles indicated that it would be possible to remove certain sentences and paragraphs and give them a higher, classification, though in general, of course, these papers had to circulate as guidance for those who were to carry out the policy. He personally favored the suggestion of Under Secretary Hoover for a special annex.

The National Security Council:

> a. Noted and discussed the draft statement of policy contained in NSC 5608, prepared by the NSC Planning Board pursuant to NSC Action No. 1530–b, in the light of the views of the Joint Chiefs of Staff transmitted by the reference memorandum of July 11.
> b. Adopted the statement of policy contained in NSC 5608, subject to the following amendments:

> (1) *Paragraph 20:* Add the following sentence: "In general, however, do not discourage, by public utterances or otherwise, spontaneous manifestations of discontent and opposition to the Communist regime, despite risk to individuals, when their net results will exert pressures for release from Soviet domination."
> (2) *Paragraph 23, line 2:* After the word "satellites", insert the words "as a disruptive device".
> (3) [3 lines excised.]
> (4) *Paragraph 25:* Delete the bracketed phrase and footnote relating thereto.

c. Agreed that the NSC Planning Board would delete from the statement of policy in NSC 5608 especially sensitive statements as indicated in the discussion, and that such statements, with the addition of the sentence discussed at the meeting which would require the authorization of the Secretary of State for certain operations, should be circulated as a separate Appendix with special limited distribution.

NOTE: The statement of policy in NSC 5608, as amended and edited in accordance with the actions in b and c above, subsequently approved by the President subject to the following additional amendments:

Paragraph 23, lines 3 and 4: Substitute for "'National Communist' movements" the words "nationalism in any form where conducive to independence from Soviet domination and".

[Three lines excised]
The statement of policy in NSC 5608 as amended, edited and approved by the President, subsequently circulated as NSC 5608/1 and the Appendix thereto; and referred to the Operations Coordinating Board as the coordinating agency designated by the President.
[...]

6. SIGNIFICANT WORLD DEVELOPMENTS AFFECTING U.S. SECURITY

[...]
Continuing his intelligence briefing, Mr. Allen Dulles pointed out that the Soviet leaders are now trying to cut off debate on the Khrushchev speech to the Twentieth Party Congress. The United States, of course, wants to keep the debate going, and indeed it is still going on, as witness Togliatti's continuing statements and those of the French Communists and other foreign Communist parties. One vehicle we are going to use, said Mr. Dulles, to keep the pot boiling, is to collect and publish all relevant data bearing on the Khrushchev speech and its implications. [1 line excised.]
The Vice President commented that it wouldn't be an unmixed evil, from the point of view of U.S. interest, if the Soviet iron fist were to come down again on the Soviet bloc, though on balance it would be more desirable, of course, if the present liberalizing trend in relations between the Soviet Union and its satellites continued.
Mr. Dulles then pointed out indications of considerable unrest in Czechoslovakia and Hungary. Our attention had been diverted from these significant developments by the more spectacular events in Poznan.
[...]

The National Security Council:

Noted and discussed an oral briefing by the Director of Central Intelligence on the subject, with specific reference to the results of the recent Japanese elections; the continuing debate on the Khrushchev de-Stalinization speech; unrest in Czechoslovakia and Hungary; and the situations in Iceland, the Middle East, and Cambodia.

[signed]
S. Everett Gleason[191]

[Source: Mandatory Review Release to the National Security Archive from the Dwight D. Eisenhower Library.]

---

[191] S. Everett Gleason was deputy executive secretary of the NSC.

DOCUMENT NO. 14: Nikita Khrushchev's Letter to Mátyás Rákosi and Other Socialist Leaders, July 13, 1956

In June 1956, high level Soviet-Yugoslav negotiations took place in Moscow. Nikita Khrushchev's circular letter to the leaders of East European socialist countries contains a summary of these meetings. The course of Soviet-Yugoslav relations particularly affected Rákosi's position in Hungary because of his role in carrying out a concerted propaganda campaign against Tito since 1948, which prominently featured the László Rajk show trial. It must have been disquieting for Rákosi to read that both the Soviets and Yugoslavs were now ready to try to resolve their differences. Moscow hoped to persuade Belgrade to loosen its ties with the United States, while Tito wanted to ease his country's economic problems through Soviet support. Although, according to the letter, settling bilateral party ties still seemed difficult, Khrushchev's message to the socialist countries is clear: "We believe that the 'Declaration on Relations between the Yugoslav League of Communists and the Communist Party of the Soviet Union' paves the way for the successful development of cooperation between the [YLC] and other fraternal parties."

Strictly confidential!

During the visit of the Yugoslav government delegation to the Soviet Union, headed by comrade Tito, negotiations were conducted concerning state-level relations between the Soviet Union and Yugoslavia, and representatives of the Communist Party of the Soviet Union and the Yugoslav League of Communists discussed the relationship, and cooperation between, the peoples of both countries.

In the course of the negotiations the Soviet delegates relied on the premise that the Soviet-Yugoslav Declaration, which was announced on 2 June 1955, and recent initiations by the Communist Party of the Soviet Union effectively brought about fundamental changes in the relations between the Soviet Union and Yugoslavia. The relationship between the Soviet Union and Yugoslavia improved, as well as Yugoslavia's liaison with other people's democracies. A connection was established between the Communist Party of the Soviet Union and the Yugoslav League of Communists.

Developing and strengthening Soviet-Yugoslav relations, as well as the mutual flow of information at party level, positively influenced the domestic and foreign policy of the Yugoslav League of Communists and the Yugoslav government.

In this way the necessary conditions were established to shift cooperation by the Soviet Union and Yugoslavia into a new era, both in state and party affairs, based on Marxist-Leninist principles.

Nonetheless, the Soviet delegation had to bear in mind that Yugoslavia still receives economic and military aid from the United States of America. The Americans are supporting Yugoslavia, making considerable effort to encumber the development of Soviet-Yugoslav relations, and impeding the rapprochement between Yugoslavia and other socialist countries.

Delegates also considered that certain questions between Yugoslavia and the people's democracies are still unanswered.

In the course of negotiations the Soviet delegation aimed at the following achievements:

    a) broadening and strengthening the governmental relationship between the Soviet Union and Yugoslavia in every respect;

    b) further rapprochement between the Communist Party of the Soviet Union and the Yugoslav League of Communists, on the basis of Marxist-Leninism, considering that it is one of the most important factors in developing Soviet-Yugoslav relations for the sake of peace, democracy, and socialism. At the same time, it would expedite the rapprochement of Yugoslavia with the people's democracies, and weakened their relationship with capitalist countries, who are unfavorably influencing the Yugoslav government's domestic and foreign policy.

While in Moscow, comrade Tito had four official meetings with the Soviet delegation, whose members were: N. A. Bulganin, K. Y. Voroshilov, A. I. Mikoyan, V. M. Molotov, N. S. Khrushchev, and D. T. Shepilov. Members of the Yugoslav delegation were: J. B. Tito, E. Kardelj, K. Popović,[192] M. Todorović,[193] and J. Blažević.

They discussed Soviet-Yugoslav relations, the international state of affairs, and the problems concerning the relationship between the Yugoslav League of Communists and the Communist Party of the Soviet Union.

Soviet-Yugoslav state relations

Discussing the improvement of Soviet-Yugoslav relations, the negotiating partners agreed that fraternal cooperation in political, economic, and cultural issues needs to be broadened and strengthened, and the wide scope of experiences in building socialism need to be exchanged. As a result of negotiations, we specified a wide series of measures, giving special emphasis to: exchanging political and other information mutually important for both countries; further improving economic relations; increasing the exchange of goods; widening cooperation in the fields of science, culture and arts with the elaboration of appropriate plans for this purpose; and exchanging experiences connected to building socialism. Negotiations proved that for the time being there is no significant obstacle which could hinder the improvement of multilateral cooperation between the two countries. The Yugoslav comrades expressed that even though Yugoslavia has no formal obligations towards the West, they had to maintain the embargo on trading with the Soviet Union and people's democracies. Yugoslavia needs a few more months to get rid of their obligations to the United States of America.

The Yugoslav delegation was convinced that Yugoslavia would cancel American military aid in the course of this year, and refrain from another military agreement. J. B. Tito said that the Americans ship obsolete military material to Yugoslavia without spare parts, which in reality means, in the words of comrade Tito, not so much the armament as the disarmament [of Yugoslavia]. He added that they do not want to break relations with the United States of America first—it is better if the Americans do it themselves.

The Soviet delegates expressed understanding for Yugoslavia's situation, and declared that these conditions should not hamper the further development of Soviet-Yugoslav cooperation. The Yugoslavs fully agreed. In order to realize their ambitions regarding the American aid process, the development of economic and trade relations between the Soviet Union and Yugoslavia is of utmost importance. The Yugoslav comrades said that their economy's greatest problem currently is the state deficit, which is directly related to the import of foodstuffs. Due to the increasing ratio of urban inhabitants, and the slow development of agriculture, Yugoslavia has to import 1–1.3 million tons of wheat every year. So far Yugoslavia solved the problem with American aid and the purchase of Canadian and Turkish grains. Nonetheless, Yugoslavia does not want to become economically and politically dependent on the United States, and they would like to receive grains from the Soviet Union instead.

The Soviet delegation expressed that the Soviet Union is ready to help Yugoslavia. Considering [this year's] good crop, the Soviet Union can provide Yugoslavia with the necessary quantity of grains. At the same time, we suggested that they buy some wheat from on the markets of third countries. Regarding economic questions, the Soviet delegation said that together with Czechoslovakia and the German Democratic Republic, the Soviet Union is will-

[192] Koča Popović was a member of the LCY CC and Yugoslav minister of foreign affairs from 1953–1965.
[193] Mijalko Todorović was a member of the YLC CC from 1952 on, and of the Yugoslav government beginning in 1953.

137

ing to invest in building an aluminum works in Yugoslavia. The parties agreed that they would carry on with specific questions of building the metal works in the usual form of bilateral negotiations.

Parallel with the government delegates' negotiations, both countries' foreign trade organs engaged in a discussion about how to increase the exchange of goods. They agreed that both countries increase the volume of trade into the other country to the sum of 20 million dollars each. This means that the Soviet Union will rank first in the Yugoslav export index.

Cooperation in international political issues

In the course of negotiations between Soviet and Yugoslav delegates, opinions about the international situation were exchanged, so that a unified point of view and concurrent political behavior is articulated on the most important international issues. They discussed the possibility of specific measures for strengthening peace and socialism. The exchange of ideas proved that since last year's negotiations in Belgrade both countries' opinions regarding the most crucial international issues have come closer, and that presently the two governments' opinions about international affairs and controversial international crises are largely the same.

The joint declaration about the Soviet-Yugoslav negotiations basically covers all the issues on which the delegations came to an agreement. The Declaration of the Soviet and Yugoslav governments refers to the fact that both countries will try to have the mandate and rights of the People's Republic of China accepted in the United Nations. The government declaration stresses the possibility for resolving such international issues as the questions of disarmament and collective security—issues that the Soviet Union has steadily represented lately in negotiations with Western powers.

It is of utmost importance for the socialist bloc, and especially for the German Democratic Republic, that the Declaration of the two governments finds the German Democratic Republic and German Federal Republic's negotiations about the unification of Germany most expedient. It would create more favorable conditions for the democratic forces in Germany, who are fighting for a peaceful and democratic unification of Germany.

Apart from issues dealt with in the Declaration, other questions were raised in the course of negotiations. Discussing international problems and relations with third countries, specific attention was given to Yugoslavia's relationship with the countries of people's democracy. The Yugoslav comrades explained that since the Belgrade negotiations with Soviet government delegates in May and June 1955, Yugoslavia's relationship with Poland, Czechoslovakia, Romania, and Bulgaria has considerably improved. As to their relations with Albania, the Yugoslav comrades desire a total restoration of governmental relations, which is—as they put it—not quite normal at the moment. They said that Albania is allegedly not aiming at normalizing their relationship with Yugoslavia. The Soviet delegates stressed their conviction that the Albanian comrades are sincerely determined to restore the fraternal relationship with Yugoslavia, and that the relationship between the two countries will be settled as it should be in the case of two socialist states. Apart from that, our delegation called the Yugoslav partners' attention to the fact that certain Yugoslav public personalities' and diplomats' behavior makes the Albanians cautious, because this seems to prove that there are apparently still people in Yugoslavia who do not unconditionally support the development of Yugoslavia's relations with other socialist countries.

The Yugoslav delegation raised the issue of relations between Yugoslavia and the German Democratic Republic. The Yugoslav comrades announced that they decided to establish trade relations with the German Democratic Republic, which will be followed by further steps. They emphasized that, for the time being, Yugoslavia cannot recognize the German Democratic Republic, as it would mean the immediate termination of their relations with the Federal Republic of Germany, which would cause economic losses in Yugoslavia. Comrade Tito asked that the German comrades be informed [of this], so that they do not believe that Yugoslavia has an incorrect foreign policy regarding the German Democratic Republic. The Soviet delegates accepted the Yugoslav comrades' standpoint. At the same time, we emphasized how important it is that socialist countries support the German Democratic Republic, making a contribution to strengthening peace and socialism in the long run.

The Yugoslav comrades agreed with us that no allowances are to be made on the German issue and that the existence of the German Democratic Republic is most important for ensuring peace and security in Europe.

Comrade Tito explained that West German representatives informed them of their intention to form a good relationship between the German Federal Republic and Poland, and that they are prepared to concede German-Polish border revisions. In actual fact, in comrade Tito's interpretation, the Federal Republic of Germany's real aim is to induce unrest in Poland, so that the background of the German Democratic Republic becomes weakened.

The Yugoslav delegation raised the issue of the Balkan Pact.[194] The Yugoslav comrades expressed their view that in the present state of affairs this pact has only economic importance for Yugoslavia. They added that Turkey finds it unnecessary from a military point of view as well.

When discussing the state of international affairs, the Yugoslav delegates emphasized that Yugoslavia had returned to the socialist camp. At the same time, they expressed their doubt about the correctness of such expressions as "socialist camp" and "capitalist camp."

The Soviet delegates explained that the word "camp" is not necessary to use. One can refer to the close cooperation or alliance between socialist countries. The main thing, though, is that mutual agreement between socialist countries is stressed. If we say that we are countries that are heading in the same direction and we coordinate our activities, then this demonstrates our unity in the eyes of the West, and weakens western efforts to separate us from one another. The Soviet delegation put special emphasis on the fact that socialist states need to align in a unified front. Should the communist parties fail to coordinate their activities, it would seem to be a step backward, leading to segregation instead of unification.

The Yugoslav delegation said that Yugoslavia stands outside [all] camps, but not outside the socialist camp. Referring to Yugoslavia's relationship to other people's democracies, the Yugoslav comrades stressed that it is out of the question for the West to use Yugoslavia to split these countries off from the Soviet Union. Yugoslavia will cooperate with the Council of Mutual Economic Assistance, on the basis of multilateral agreements. The Yugoslav delegation emphasized that irrespective of Yugoslavia's special situation, Yugoslavia and the Soviet Union share general objectives and have the same duties.

About the relationship and cooperation between the Communist Party of the Soviet Union and the Yugoslav League of Communists

The Yugoslav comrades were informed that according the opinion of the Central Committee of the Communist Party of the Soviet Union, the successes achieved in the field of normalizing relations and strengthening confidence between the Soviet Union and the Yugoslav Federal Republic, as well as between the Communist Party of the Soviet Union and the Yugoslav League of Communists, created the conditions for restoring relations between our parties according to the principles of Marxism-Leninism.

The Yugoslav comrades agreed with our opinion, then proposed a document for discussion, entitled "Draft Declaration on relations between the Yugoslav League of Communists and the Communist Party of the Soviet Union."

In the Central Committee of the Communist Party of the Soviet Union's opinion, the document proposed by the Yugoslav comrades lacks momentum in many respect, and contains a series of theoretically erroneous items. The Central Committee of the Communist Party of the Soviet Union could not and cannot agree with the Yugoslav comrades' proposal. We informed them that the drafted declaration meant a set-back, as compared to what we have actually

---

[194] See footnote 38 in this chapter.

achieved in the course of negotiations regarding our parties' relationship. Had we accepted the draft in the form that the Yugoslav comrades presented it to us, it would disorient communist parties, and it would mean a concession to socialists and social democrats. Although not without scruples, they [the socialists] could accept such a declaration, yet it would not satisfy the communists. The Yugoslav draft does not differentiate between parties that operate on the basis of Marxist-Leninist principles and other communist parties that maintain relations with socialist and social democratic parties. Furthermore, the draft fails to clearly outline the ideological basis for cooperation between the Yugoslav League of Communists and the Communist Party of the Soviet Union and other communist parties. The draft declaration emphasized that one of the basic principles of cooperation is mutual respect for differing opinions, regardless of the nature of these opinions, which would entail respect for non-Marxist views as well. It is obvious that we cannot accept the correctness of the statement that the Yugoslav comrades formulated: that "both parties accept that the development of scientific socialist theory in the international labor movement has failed to keep pace with material growth in the past ten years." The Communist Party of the Soviet Union's delegates told the Yugoslav comrades that, in their opinion, the declaration must contain a detailed description of objectives and tasks for cooperation between the Communist Party of the Soviet Union and the Yugoslav League of Communists. They suggested adding [a section] to the declaration, [stating] that cooperation is necessary for "the further strengthening and prosperity of our socialist countries, for the sake of our mutual fight for world peace, and against [both] the unauthorized intervention of imperialist reactionary forces and attacks on the national independence and freedom of the people. Furthermore, cooperation is required to expedite the united action of the international labor movement, in order to mobilize the forces that stand up for peace and the mutual co-existence of different social systems."

The Communist Party of the Soviet Union's delegates explained to the Yugoslav comrades that naturally stronger contacts must be maintained with political parties which accept Marxist-Leninist principles as the basis of their activities. We put special emphasis on the continuing importance of cooperation and exchanging ideas between communist and workers' parties, which together build socialism. This makes it possible for socialist experiences, which real life has justified, to be put to the best use. The exchange of ideas would promote the processing of the most apt and appropriate ways to build socialism, taking into consideration both international relations and the national characteristics of each and every country.

The delegates of the Communist Party of the Soviet Union suggested that the declaration express more firmly that both parties embrace the principles of Marxism-Leninism in all their activities, and that they set building full socialism in their countries as their general objective.

We proposed to the Yugoslav comrades our draft declaration, which contained the above-mentioned paragraphs. Influenced by our draft and rationale, they agreed to make a series of changes to their proposition. At the same time—although they basically expressed their accord with our ideas about closer cooperation between communist parties, about the necessity of fighting imperialist reaction because of its unauthorized intervention against people's national independence and freedom, and about the exchange of ideas and cooperation between communist and workers' parties which build the communist system—the Yugoslav League of Communists' delegation said that in their opinion these issues should not be added to the declaration now. Comrade Tito said that in principle they agree with these propositions; however, as the Yugoslav delegation is a government delegation, setting these principles in a declaration would complicate Yugoslavia's relationship with western countries.

Although the declaration's amended text did not satisfy us, we thought it inadvisable to insist on the acceptance of our version and therefore agreed to the Yugoslav proposal, bearing in mind that the present text could be an appropriate vehicle for improving relations between the Yugoslav League of Communists, the Communist Party of the Soviet Union, and other fraternal party organizations. We are convinced that the declaration will play an important role in developing relations between Yugoslavia, the Soviet Union, and the people's democracies, both on the level of party and state organizations, exerting a favorable socialist influence on the Yugoslav League of Communists' policy.

During negotiations the question of improving relations between the Yugoslav League of Communists and other communist and workers' parties, and the possibility of forming an international organization, were also raised.

We told the Yugoslav comrades that the Communist Party of the Soviet Union and other fraternal parties are very disturbed by the fact that while, the Yugoslav League of Communists is busy settling its relations with French, English, Belgian, Norwegian, and other socialists and social democrats, they haven't established a working relationship with the communist parties of these countries so far. Biting and unjust criticism of certain communist parties still appears in the Yugoslav press every so often.

We expressed the view that we are glad to witness the developing fraternal relations which state, social, and other institutions of the Soviet Union and Yugoslavia have established. However, we noted that certain responsible Yugoslav personalities obviously have not cast off the heritage of the past, and have indulged in an unfriendly response towards the Communist Party of the Soviet Union and the Soviet Union. We are informed about the inappropriate behavior of certain Yugoslav diplomatic corps representatives in the people's democracies, which could harm the socialist countries' mutual understanding and firm fraternity. For example, the Yugoslav ambassador to Bulgaria, [Mita] Miljković, celebrating the national day of Yugoslavia on November 29, 1955, organized a reception and invited Bulgarian leaders as well as persons who had been removed from different state offices and no longer represented anybody. Former Yugoslav Ambassador to Albania [Pedrag] Ajtić, celebrating his return to Yugoslavia, organized a reception in Tirana in April 1956 and invited dismissed Albanian leaders, many of whom had been ousted from the Albanian Labor Party. Reportedly, the Yugoslav Embassy in Tirana keeps direct contact with people who treated the Albanian Labor Party's leadership in a hostile manner. Possibly this served as a basis for unjust pronouncements against the Albanian Labor Party's central leadership during the Third City Party Conference in Tirana. We also mentioned that it was inconsiderate of the Yugoslav government to deny granting an entry visa to certain members of the Bulgarian parliamentary delegation, because defining the members of such a delegation is the sovereign right of a state. We also mentioned that the conflict regarding the composition of the delegation could have been settled in a different way. We listed further instances where responsible Yugoslav personalities have acted inappropriately.

The Yugoslav comrades said that they are taking into account all these remarks, although they doubted the credibility of some of the facts that were presented. They noted that lately they had achieved considerable improvement in mutual relations between the Yugoslav League of Communists and the communist and workers' parties of Romania, Czechoslovakia and Poland, and that they had laid the foundation for cooperation with the Italian Communist Party. Comrade Tito said that he thinks that their relations with the Hungarian Workers' Party will also develop well. At the same time, the Yugoslav comrades admitted that normalizing their relations with certain communist parties was still hindered by obstacles. Comrade Tito mentioned the Albanian Labor Party as a prime example.

Comrades Tito and Kardelj said that relations between the Yugoslav League of Communists and the Communist Party of the Soviet Union provides an impetus for improving relations between the Yugoslav League of Communists and other communist and workers' parties.

"We shall meet the representatives of other communist parties and make an agreement with them, so that our case may be advanced more efficiently," said comrade Kardelj.

As far as the form of cooperation between communist parties is concerned, the Yugoslav comrades were informed that relationships can be maintained via regular meetings with representatives of communist and workers' parties, keeping in mind that every communist party may openly raise the issue of meeting and negotiating fundamental problems together. Obviously it is not topical to form an organization for international relations for communist parties at the present time. Nonetheless, our delegation emphasized that this is a tactic and not a principle, since forming such an organization at the right time could be expedient.

141

On the whole, we assess the negotiations with delegates of the Yugoslav League of Communists positively. The ongoing negotiations have proved that there is a favorable climate for improving relations and cooperation between our parties, based on the principles of Marxism-Leninism. The negotiations showed us that although the Yugoslav comrades came closer to our views on the principal questions of Marxism-Leninism, the Yugoslav comrades still interpret certain fundamental questions in a different way than our Marxist-Leninist party, as the above examples prove. With regard to this, the Central Committee of the Communist Party of the Soviet Union considers the opinion of comrade Bulganin, which he expressed at an official breakfast in Moscow on June 5, labeling comrade Tito a Leninist slightly premature. Such labeling makes it difficult for us to merge our ideologies and disorients fraternal communist parties and members of the Communist Party of the Soviet Union.

We believe that the "Declaration on relations between the Yugoslav League of Communists and the Communist Party of the Soviet Union" paves the way for successfully developing cooperation between the Yugoslav League of Communists and other fraternal parties.

If the most important achievement of the Belgrade talks was normalizing state-level relations between the Soviet Union and Yugoslavia, then the most significant result of the negotiations in Moscow was the further steps we made toward normalizing relations between the Yugoslav League of Communists and the Communist Party of the Soviet Union, according to the principles of Marxism-Leninism.

[Source: MOL, 276. f. 65/117. ő.e. Published in Hungarian in József Kiss, Zoltán Ripp and István Vida, eds., Magyar-jugoszláv kapcsolatok, 1956: Dokumentumok, *(Budapest: MTA Jelenkor-kutató Bizottság, 1995), 77–84. Translated by Csaba Farkas.]*

DOCUMENT NO. 15: Report from Anastas Mikoyan on the Situation in the Hungarian Workers' Party, July 14, 1956

Between July 13 and 21, CPSU CC Presidium member Anastas Mikoyan visited Budapest incognito to hold meetings with leaders of the Hungarian Workers' Party. In this report, he judges the situation to be far more serious than Mikhail Suslov depicted it a month before, when Suslov was on a similar mission: "One can see how day after day the comrades are further losing their grip on power," Mikoyan observes. "A parallel center is forming from enemy elements operating actively, decisively, and self-confidently." Mikoyan sees the impotence of the HWP leadership and weakening party influence on the press as real dangers. The subordination of the HWP to Moscow is again illustrated by the fact that the Political Committee fully accepts Mikoyan's scenario for handling the crisis, including consenting to their own leader, Rákosi's, resignation. The Soviet leader's comments to his negotiating partners in Budapest are essential to understanding the Soviet Union's behavior during the revolution: "it was impermissible that anything unexpected and unpleasant should happen in Hungary. . . if they needed any help—advice or anything else—our CC was ready to come through for the Hungarian comrades in order to correct the situation."

JULY 14, 1956

TOP SECRET
MAKING COPIES IS FORBIDDEN. COPY NO. 12
TOP PRIORITY. SPECIAL.

CPSU CC

On July 13, at 11:00 a.m., immediately upon my arrival in Budapest, I had a two-hour conversation with cdes. Hegedüs, Rákosi, Gerő, and CC Secretary Vég,[195] who also came to meet us. Cde. Andropov was present. After the conversation, we all dined together, and agreed to convene a conference of Politburo members, candidate members and secretaries of the CC immediately afterwards; it lasted over four hours. All Hungarian comrades spoke sincerely without any time limitations. I am sending the record of speeches separately. Below I present our impressions, and also the outlined decisions.

I asked the Hungarian comrades to inform us about what was going on in the country and in the party, and what the CC was undertaking to implement [the measures] that were discussed with cde. Suslov. I emphasized that our CC and the entire socialist camp were concerned about the state of affairs in Hungary, because it was impermissible that anything unexpected and unpleasant should happen in Hungary. I stated that if they needed any help—advice or anything else—our CC was ready to come through for the Hungarian comrades in order to correct the situation.

In an open conversation, all the comrades acknowledged the unpleasant picture.

Apart from the published CC resolution of June 30 directed against the enemy elements,[196] nothing is being done; the comrades prepare reports for CC Plenums, while enemy elements act among the masses and in the country unpunished; they expand their influence further and further, and engage new circles, including the workers, in the struggle to remove the party leadership.

One can see how day after day the comrades are further losing their grip on power. A parallel center is forming from enemy elements operating actively, decisively, and self-confidently.

The press and radio are not under CC control any more.

---

[195] Béla Vég was secretary of the HWP CC from 1953 to October 24, 1956.

[196] This was a HWP CC resolution targeting the Petőfi Circle and suspending its activities.

Although the CC resolution of June 30 was made unanimously, there is no unity in the CC either on issues of principle or on practical questions of party management. Some CC members, who voted for that resolution, now not only do not support the resolution, but also do not obey the CC's instructions, and even speak against the CC decision. The editor of the party's central organ,[197] the most widely distributed paper, does not agree with the CC line, and the CC still has not done anything about it because, you see, he is a CC member.

Discipline among CC members has fallen apart, and many Communists, especially among the intelligentsia, have dispersed into the petty bourgeois milieu, which opposes the government. The Petőfi discussion club has turned into an active ideological and opposition center. A practically parallel CC, opposed to the CC of the party, has been created, which acts freely and without any impediments. Leading Hungarian comrades have not taken any measures against those enemy elements, and they do not even have any plan in that respect.

Every day, the influence of the hostile, opposition mood—supported by hostile Western radio propaganda and agents residing in the country, as well as Yugoslav radio, press, and agents supporting and encouraging those opposition elements—is expanding. Right-wing elements within the party, in particular those oriented toward Imre Nagy, in addition to several hundred party activists who were previously subject to reprisals and have now been released from prison and are residing mostly in Budapest, cannot tolerate having Rákosi and his supporters, who caused their misfortunes, remain in power.

To my question, "Why did they not undertake reprisals and arrests of the leaders of the hostile elements?," Rákosi stated that the situation had worsened and tensions had increased so much that arrests would not help: if we arrest some, others would appear, and if we arrest those the third wave would arise, and there would be no end to that.

I explained to the Hungarian comrades that it is an intolerable violation of internal party discipline when officials of the CC apparatus do not carry out the decisions of the elected party organs, i.e. the collective leadership, and conduct their own policy directed against the CC. The CC apparatus should not have its own policy; it should be an executor of the CC's decisions. Therefore it is necessary to expel all such elements from the CC apparatus immediately. A situation where newspapers and the radio cease to serve as channels of the CC line also represents a violation of internal party democracy. Therefore, it is necessary to get rid of all press and radio staff who are unwilling to implement the CC's line.

In this dangerous situation, the party leadership practically exists in a state of prostration [prostratsiya].

After the discussion, the Hungarian comrades had to admit that, although in practice, power had not yet slipped from their hands, it was slipping away and the process was leading to a loss of power.

Comrades like Gerő, Hegedüs, [István] Kovács, and others understand all the danger of such a situation, but they have not proposed anything; although from their statements one could glean that everything comes down to the question of Rákosi, but none of them wanted to pose this question.[198] It was apparent that all of them were waiting for us to raise the issue of Rákosi, because they feel bound by our line on this matter which was transmitted to them on behalf of our CC by cde. Suslov, who stated that Rákosi's removal now would be a gift for the Americans. Cde. Kovács stated this directly in his conversation with cde. Andropov.

When I raised this issue, they emphasized that the main problem, the biggest obstacle, was the issue of responsibility for violations of the law, i.e. the issue of responsibility for reprisals against communists which took place before 1953. The Central Committee is under attack on

[197] Márton Horváth, as indicated earlier in this chapter, was editor-in-chief of Szabad Nép from 1954–1956.

[198] The last phrase "...but none of them wanted to pose this question," does not appear in Sovietskii Soyuz i vengerskii krizis, but does in the original document and also in the version published in the Hungarian-language edition of Vyacheslav T. Sereda and Aleksandr S. Stykhalin, eds., Hiányzó lapok 1956 történetéből: dokumentumok a volt SZKP KB levéltárából (Budapest: Móra Ferenc Könyvkiadó, 1993), 40–46.

this issue from all sides, and the CC cannot defend itself. Everybody thinks that it is not so much Farkas as Rákosi who is to blame.

When, during a preliminary discussion in a narrow circle, I raised the question of whether it would have been better, in the interests of the party and taking the existing circumstances into account, for Rákosi to resign on his own in order to make it easier for the party to preserve its leading position and defeat the opposition and the hostile elements, it was clear that cdes. Gerő, Hegedüs and Vég were pleased with the suggestion, and even breathed easier. Cde. Kovács also received that suggestion with a certain pleasure, as he told me in a personal meeting.

Later, during a Politburo session, everybody spoke in favor of expediting cde. Rákosi's resignation. Gerő even said: "We dragged the decision on this issue on to the last hour."

The Hungarian comrades agreed with my statement that cde. Rákosi's departure from the leadership would help to achieve a genuine unity in the Central Committee and would make it easier to fight against the opposition and hostile elements. Success here could ensure simultaneous implementation of the following order of measures: first, the resignation of Rákosi, who was the target of all the opposition strikes and whom everyone considers responsible for the violations of law to a greater extent than Farkas; second, the inclusion within the leadership of a new group of officials, especially of Hungarian nationality, who have shown themselves to be steadfast in the struggle for the party line during the latest period of complications; third, a simultaneous blow against the leaders of the hostile elements and defeat of their centers. Further, it is necessary to engage in an active struggle on the ideological front against the anti-Marxist, anti-Leninist positions and statements from among party members. Finally, they need to reinstate party discipline among all party members, regardless of personalities, as Lenin did at our Tenth Congress after the Central Committee had been practically split on the eve on the Congress.

When I asked what the issues were on which there were disagreements of principle among the CC members, one CC member noted that those CC members who disagree mostly drop hints and do not say everything they are thinking. Many of them hide their views. Then Gerő responded to this question in the following manner, with which everybody apparently agreed: the CC members who disagree with the CC line do not have either a defined platform or any system of views. One can speak only about separate issues. The first group of issues is related to the collectivization of agriculture. CC member Zoltán Vas formulated it more directly than anyone when he said that collectivization should be postponed for another ten years, and that tractors, for instance the "Universals," should be sold to individual peasants. There were also other statements, for example: to allow the law of costs [*zakon stoimosti*] to work in the economy without any limitations, by permitting competition; and to build the system of economic management not after the Soviet, by after the Yugoslav model, which they regard as the more democratic one, in their opinion. And finally the question of democratization: many of them, especially under the pressure of Western propaganda, are sliding down the slope toward formal bourgeois democracy.

As far as Imre Nagy is concerned, I said that our CC did not discuss him, but that I had my own opinion and I know the opinions of some of our CC members. We believed previously, and we believe now, that it was a mistake to expel him from the party, even though he deserved that with his behavior. Had Imre Nagy remained in the party, he would have had to obey party discipline and carry out the party's will. By expelling him, the Central Committee has complicated its own struggle against him. It is necessary to explain to Nagy very directly that he cannot return to the party by fighting against it. The path of fighting against the party is one that will inevitably lead him to prison. Alternatively, if he changes his behavior, he can count on being reinstated to the party. A number of comrades stated that although this was correct, if they reinstate Imre Nagy to the party in the existing situation it would be perceived as his victory, and the right wing of the party would grow stronger. Some time later, after he takes a number of steps on behalf of the party and in the direction of correcting his own mistakes, then they could return him to the party. During my conversation with cde. Kovács on this issue, he told me that such a conversation [initiated by the Hungarian CC] with Imre Nagy would not make any impression on him. However, if you—Kovács said addressing me—could speak to Imre Nagy on behalf of your CC, that would be a totally different matter.

Cde. Rákosi conducted himself correctly during both the preliminary session and the session of the Politburo. He stated that the idea of resignation had come to him long ago, but that he kept postponing raising this issue because he wanted to correct his mistakes in leading the party through his own efforts, and then to resign. He was not able to do this, and now taking into account the party's interests, which are ultimately important for him, he considers it necessary to resign.

Szalai essentially said that he was in favor of removing Rákosi from the leadership, but he expressed his concern that the hostile elements wanted to remove not only Rákosi, but also his supporters—as he has put it, "all his milieu"—from the leadership. He expressed his own opinion, as well as the opinion of the younger Politburo members and CC secretaries promoted by Rákosi—such as Hidas, Vég, Bata, Egri, and Mekis[199]—who expressed concern about their fate.

Many comrades expressed the opinion that the Plenum of the CC could possibly overthrow the entire Politburo.

Szalai personally introduced a proposal, taking these concerns into account and also—lest the enemy perceive Rákosi's resignation as their victory—to relieve Rákosi of his duties as first secretary, while at the same time establishing the honorary position of Party Chairman for him. Nobody supported his proposal, and many people openly spoke against it. Szalai himself did not insist on it.

At the Politburo [session] they agreed to undertake the following measures:

1. To satisfy cde. Rákosi's request to resign his post as first secretary and CC Politburo member, and to give him permission to make an appropriate statement at the CC Plenum. In this connection, it was decided that it should be not Rákosi but another comrade who should make a presentation on the internal political situation at the CC Plenum.

2. To prepare proposals to enlarge the composition of the CC by including young cadres of Hungarian nationality who have proven themselves during the struggle with the opposition, and who are connected with the masses; and to introduce this proposal at the CC Plenum.

3. To prepare and carry out a practical plan for striking a blow against the hostile, anti-party groups, and to defeat the established centers of their activity in the next several days.

4. Without waiting for the CC Plenum, to begin an attack against the opposition immediately, toward which end:

   a) to immediately start publications in the press and on the radio of resolutions of party organizations, especially the party organizations of industrial enterprises, which support the party and which are directed against the opposition; up until now the press has refused to publish such resolutions;
   b) to publish articles against incorrect statements in the party press;
   c) to remove from their posts those newspaper editors and radio officials who refuse to implement the CC line; to bring them to account before the party;
   d) to carry out measures to remove all officials from the CC apparatus who disagree with the CC line or are engaged in a struggle against the CC line;
   e) to prepare a Politburo discussion on the behavior of those CC members who speak against the CC decision on fighting the opposition and the hostile elements, having in mind in this way to achieve a restoration of party discipline for CC members.

During the break between sessions, I spoke with cde. Kovács. He makes a good impression as a party person, does not come across as someone likely to be involved in intrigues. He reflects the opinion of his Budapest party organization, and fully trusts the Soviet Union. Everybody

---

[199] József Mekis was a member of the HWP CC from 1948–1956 and deputy prime minister from 1954–1956.

says that his party apparatus within the City Committee holds up much better than the CC apparatus.

The Politburo decided to consider questions about the composition of the Politburo, about the post of first secretary, and about the CC tomorrow, and to consult with us.

MIKOYAN

[Source: APRF, F. 3. Op. 64. D. 483. Ll. 165–175. Published in Sovietskii Soyuz i venger-skii krizis, 1956 goda: Dokumenty, *edited and compiled by E. D. Orekhova, Vyacheslav T. Sereda and Aleksandr. S. Stykhalin (Moscow: ROSSPEN, 1998), 152–157. Translated by Svetlana Savranskaya.]*

DOCUMENT NO. 16: Memorandum from J.G. Ward to the British Foreign Office, "British Policy towards the Satellites," July 17, 1956

After the Geneva summit in July 1955, and especially following the visit of Khrushchev and Bulganin to Great Britain in April 1956, a lengthy process began in the Foreign Office to reevaluate the British Government's attitude towards the East European Communist countries. Until then, the basic policy had been that these regimes were not legitimate; therefore, contacts with them should be reduced to the lowest level possible while still maintaining formal diplomatic relations. This memorandum, prepared in mid-July, shows the generally prevailing view in the British government that the model for the satellites to achieve greater internal and external independence would be Yugoslav-style national communism, not a genuine parliamentary democracy. It is interesting that the U.S. government made a similar assessment at virtually the same time (see Document No. 17).

BRITISH POLICY TOWARDS THE SATELLITES. SECRET.

17 JULY 1956

I submit the attached paper in an attempt to draw certain conclusions from recent discussion among officials in The Foreign Office and correspondence with H.M. Missions concerned.

J.G. WARD[200]   JULY 17, 1956

Private Secretary

Copies to: Lord Reading   Sir H. Caccia
            Mr Dodds-Parker   Sir J. Ward
            Mr Dean/Mr. McDermott   Mr. Wright
            Mr Grey/Mr. Rennie   Mr. Hohler

POLICY TOWARDS THE SATELLITES

Problem

What changes are required in general British policy towards the Soviet Satellite States?

2. The Soviet Government's "new course" has been accompanied by a loosening of Soviet control of the Satellites and the development of a considerable internal ferment in at least Poland, Hungary and Czechoslovakia. Tito's success in imposing on the Russians his concept of "various roads to Socialism" has had repercussions in the other Communist states of Eastern Europe. Tito's policy can be described as the promotion of "national Communism" and any progress towards greater independence and internal freedom in the Satellites is more likely to be along the road of "national Communism" than towards forms of government which we would recognize as democracy.

3. We may hope that more "liberal" and independent-minded personalities will come into power in the Satellites. There is no evidence that the émigrés have any influence in Eastern Europe and it is unlikely that they have any future prospects. It is in our interest to encourage

---

[200] Sir John Ward was undersecretary of state in the British Foreign Office in 1956.

national independence and internal relaxations in these Satellites and thus to reduce their at present important contribution to the Soviet Union's military potential and to its policy of economic and political penetration of the free world particularly in the Near East.

4. But we must recognize that our power to influence the course of events in Eastern Europe is limited. Moreover, we must be careful about expressing approbation of "national Communism", as although preferable to "Soviet Communism", that is not a way of life that we wish to see adopted in the unstable or emergent countries of Asia and Africa.

5. If it is now accepted that there is no prospect of restoring the pre-war regimes in the Satellites, our best way of exercising a favorable influence might be to establish closer relations with their present governments. Since the visit of the Soviet leaders to this country,[201] the Satellite Governments have in fact been angling for closer relations, including exchanges of Ministerial and Parliamentary visits, and other manifestations calculated to increase their international standing. We have hitherto held back as we regard the Satellite Governments as fraudulent in that they were imposed on these countries by Soviet power and do not represent the will of their peoples. (In his despatch on the Poznan riots[202] H.M. Ambassador at Warsaw estimates that only 5% of the population of Poland support the Government and the percentage in the other Satellites cannot be much higher). We have been at pains to make a clear distinction between our stand-off attitude towards the Satellite regimes and our friendship and good-will towards the peoples of Eastern Europe as expressed in the overseas services of the B.B.C.

6. However, this distinction has become increasingly blurred. The Satellites have now achieved membership of the United Nations.[203] Under our free system we cannot prevent, even if we wanted to, the ever more numerous contacts in the fields of trade, the arts, sport and travel. As every activity in a Communist-run country has some official character we have inevitably been drawn a long way into association with the Satellites. Our distinction between Governments and peoples has become rather artificial and it is for consideration how far it can or should be further maintained.

"Pros" and "Cons"

7. *The arguments in favor* of a more forthcoming attitude towards the Satellite Governments may be summarized:

   i) If we wish to restore freedom and independence to the countries concerned, we have no option but to accept and work upon the present regimes, exploiting to the full the new post-Stalin atmosphere and the opening given to us by overtures from the Satellite side.
   ii) The improvement of relations in the political and cultural fields might lead in time to an increase in trade.
   iii) Blank refusal to accept ostensibly friendly advances is an awkward posture, as well as largely frustrated by our inability in practice to refuse United Kingdom entry visas, or to prevent British subjects from responding, to Satellite overtures.

8. *The contrary arguments may* be summarized:

   i) Closer links with the Satellite Governments, which are not essential, would result in further blurring the continuing menace of Communism.

---

[201] The visit of Khruschchev and Bulganin to Great Britain—the first by a delegation of top-level Soviet leaders to a western country since the Potsdam conference in 1945—took place between April 18–27, 1956.

[202] On June 28, almost 100,000 workers took to the streets in Poznań demanding free elections and improved living and work conditions. Polish armed forces crushed the demonstration, leaving several hundred dead and wounded.

[203] In December 1955, 16 new member states were admitted to the United Nations, including Albania, Bulgaria, Hungary and Romania. Czechoslovakia and Poland were founding members of the organization.

ii) A deliberate policy of developing relations with the Governments would be regarded by the émigrés, and by wide circles both here and in the U.S.A., as a betrayal and would attract considerable criticism.

iii) There is still no evidence that the Soviet Union will allow real independence of any Satellite.

iv) The Poznan riots and reports of other effervescences cast doubt upon the stability of the cliques at present in power in the Satellites.

v) Trade will rise or fall according to what the Satellite Governments and their Soviet masters consider to be their self-interest and without regard to other developments, and will in any case continue to be restricted by the general policies of the Communist bloc.

vi) Any policy for promoting relations by Government action would involve considerable expenditure. We can better use our limited resources in the uncommitted countries.

Conclusions

9. There is no clear balance of argument in favor of a deliberate policy of cultivating the Satellite Governments. On the other hand, it will be increasingly difficult to maintain a rigidly negative policy towards them. The situation points towards continuing much as hitherto, but with a rather greater degree of empiricism.

Recommendations

10 a) It is neither necessary nor desirable for H.M.G.[204] to adopt in present circumstances a new high policy line towards the Satellites. We should wait on developments and not exclude progress via "national Communism".

b) We should continue to assert in official statements and in our propaganda, friendship for the Satellite peoples and our desire to see national independence and internal freedom restored to them by peaceful processes.

c) Our day-to-day business dealings with the Satellite Communist Governments (e.g. over trade) should be governed by a realistic assessment of where the British interest lies.

d) Our political relations with the Satellite Governments and our response to their "goodwill" overtures should continue to be restrained. We can permit ourselves a more flexible and empirical course of conduct. But we should still be chary—in default of very special circumstances—of lending ourselves to acts such as the exchange of Ministerial visits which could be interpreted as acceptance of the permanent character of the Communist regime.

e) Below the Ministerial level we can support, where conditions are appropriate, a greater degree of contacts, such as exchanges of visits by officials, expert delegations, sportsmen etc., and of "goodwill gestures," such as Naval visits.

f) We should emphasize to the Satellite Governments that if they want closer relations it is up to them first to (i) stop jamming the B.B.C.; (ii) fix a realistic exchange rate; (iii) concede full freedom of travel, particularly to journalists

g) *Information*

i) The B.B.C. overseas service should continue to broadcast to the Satellites straight news and material showing that freedom is preferable to Communism.

ii) If money permits, and local relaxations make it worth while we might aim at restoring some information services at H.M. Missions.

h) *Culture*

We can approve in suitable cases, and administratively facilitate, cultural exchanges, except where organized by British fellow-traveling societies. But there is no for diverting exiguous official resources to the Satellites in their present condition of subservience to the USSR. If how-

---

[204] Her Majesty's Government.

ever, the Satellites produced realistic exchange rates we might undertake a modest expansion of the British Council foothold in Poland and consider re-opening in Hungary and Czechoslovakia.

i) As far as divergent attitudes make possible we should seek to concert out attitude towards the Satellites with the U.S.A., France and out other NATO allies. We might make more use of the NATO Council for this purpose.

j) We should devote priority interest to Poland, and in second place to Hungary and Czechoslovakia.

J.G. WARD   JULY 17, 1956

[*Source: PRO.FO.371.122081. Previously published in Eva Haraszti-Taylor, comp.,* The Hungarian Revolution of 1956, *(Nottingham, U.K.: Astra Press, 1995), 65–68.*]

DOCUMENT NO. 17: National Security Council Report NSC 5608/1, "U.S. Policy toward the Soviet Satellites in Eastern Europe," July 18, 1956

The following updated statement of U.S. policy toward Eastern Europe, the first since NSC 174 (see Document No. 3), was approved by President Eisenhower on July 18 after review by the National Security Council (see Document Nos. 12 and 13). The generally optimistic conclusion of NSC 5608/1 was that the "fluid situation" following the denunciation of Stalin at the Twentieth CPSU Party Congress and Soviet acquiescence to Titoism had "increased the previously limited U.S. capabilities to influence a basic change in Soviet domination of the satellites." The document proceeds to lay out a variety of possible approaches toward that goal. NSC 5608/1 remained in force until the adoption of NSC 5811 in May 1958 (see Document No. 118). The document below was heavily excised when first published in the State Department's FRUS series (only the first nine numbered paragraphs were released), but it appears here in full, having only recently been declassified.

STATEMENT OF POLICY

ON
U. S. POLICY TOWARD THE SOVIET SATELLITES IN EASTERN EUROPE

GENERAL CONSIDERATIONS

1. Soviet control over the Soviet satellites in Eastern Europe (Poland, Czechoslovakia, Hungary, Rumania, Bulgaria, Albania, and East Germany[205]) has contributed importantly to the power of disequilibrium in Europe and to the threat to the security of the United States. Despite economic dislocation and administrative difficulties, the Kremlin has made considerable progress in exploiting the industrial capacity of the satellites and expanding their military capabilities for use as a coordinated whole with those of the Soviet Union. Formation of the Warsaw Pact in May 1955 as a counter to NATO, which had just admitted West Germany, institutionalized and extended existing Soviet coordination and control over the military potential of the Eastern European bloc. The Soviet military position in Europe was affected little, if at all, by the withdrawal of Soviet troops from Austria in October 1955.[206]

2. Impediments to the consolidation over the Eastern European satellites are:

   a. The anti-Communist attitude of the great majority of the population in each satellite. This anti-Communism is intensified particularly by loss of personal freedom and a reduced standard of living, as well as by outraged religious and national feelings; but its undiminished survival over the long run is jeopardized by Communist control over every aspect of the lives of the people, particularly the young, as well as by the new Moscow policy of allowing the satellites greater latitude in the conduct of their own affairs.
   b. The continued presence of nation[al]ist sentiment among the people and even within the satellite Communist parties themselves.

---

[205] While many of the considerations set forth in this paper with respect to the Eastern European satellites area as a whole also apply to East Germany, the specific problems of East Germany and Berlin are treated respectively in a supplement to NSC 160/1, being prepared pursuant to Council action on June 15, 1956, and in NSC 5404/1. [Footnote in original.]

[206] Soviet troops were withdrawn from the Eastern part of Austria following the signing of a state treaty between Austria and the four Great Powers on May 15, 1955. The treaty restored the country's independence and the American, British, French and Soviet occupying troops were withdrawn from its territory.

c. The continued refusal of the West to accept the permanence of the imposed satellite regimes as compatible with the freedom and self-determination of nations.

3. Despite these impediments, Soviet domination of the Eastern European satellites remains firm and there appears little immediate prospect of basic change in this regard. While the satellite regimes have not been able to overcome widespread popular dissatisfaction with their Communistic program and with their inclusion within the Soviet world, nevertheless there are no known underground groups capable of coordinated, sustained resistance activities to the governments in power in any of the countries concerned. As long as a Moscow-dominated Communist leadership remains in power in these countries and is backed by Soviet military force or threat of force, it is unlikely that Soviet ability to exercise effective control over and to exploit the resources of the European satellites can be appreciably reduced.

4. On the other hand, the many changes in the USSR since the death of Stalin—particularly the introduction of collective leadership, Moscow's acceptance of Titoism and acknowledgment that there are "different roads to Socialism", and the denigration of Stalin—are being reflected in current satellite developments. These developments have varied in pace and scope in each of the satellites and are continuing, but common to them all are a reduction in the role of the secret police embodied in the emphasis on the need for "socialist legality" and the admission of past errors attributed to the "cult of personality." Some personnel changes have occurred at the top in certain satellite governments and others may follow. Although the basic political and economic policies and objectives have not been successfully challenged nor the fundamental subjection of the satellites to the Soviet Union effectively threatened, there are indications that Moscow now recognizes the advantage of using greater flexibility as well as more camouflage in its control of the satellites, and of giving them certain latitude or responsibility of decision on matters of local detail within the general framework of Soviet bloc policy.

5. Nationalism in the satellites, even within the Communist movement itself, remains a disruptive force in Soviet-satellite relations. There is a real and growing split in most satellite parties between those amenable to close Soviet control and the "national Communists." However, since the combination of basic factors which made possible the successful Yugoslav break with Moscow is lacking in the satellites, it is unlikely that the Yugoslav experience will be repeated in any of them. Moreover, by its reconciliation with Tito, Moscow has sought with some success to neutralize the competing attraction originally exercised on the satellite governments by Belgrade's independent position and policies.

6. Tito's establishment of an independent Communist regime provides a standing example of successful defiance of the Kremlin and a demonstration that the West is prepared to assist nationalistic Communist leaders to assert their independence of Moscow. Despite Moscow's apparent reconciliation with Belgrade, it may be still possible to exploit Yugoslavia's unique position in promoting future changes in the Soviet satellite relationship. Any diminution of Yugoslavia's independence of the Kremlin will limit its usefulness in this regard. On the other hand, a Yugoslavia which maintains a position of independence between East and West, would be an important asset in promoting possible future changes in the Soviet-satellite relationship.

7. U.S. strategy and policy with respect to the German problem and the satellite issue are so closely interrelated that each must be considered in the light of its effect on the other. The intransigence of the Soviets on German reunification, at Geneva and subsequently, arises in part from their German policy and in part from their regard for Eastern Germany as an advanced position for control of the satellite area. These considerations provide strong Soviet incentives for postponing an agreement on German reunification. The inability of the West to make the satellite issue an agenda item at the negotiating table or to offer substantial promise of the early elimination of Soviet control depresses the hopes of the satellite peoples for

freedom and reduces their will to resist, thereby increasing the tendency to accept accommodation with Moscow.

8. Nevertheless, Eastern Germany poses a special and more difficult problem of control for the USSR than do the other satellites. While the Eastern German regime has made some progress with the program of basic industrial development and socialization, and while there are various factors operating to weaken resistance of the Eastern German population to the Communist regime, there is little likelihood that the East Germans can be brought to accept the Communist system imposed on them. The fact that the main body of the German nation in the Federal Republic has made considerable advances in freedom and well-being, and the fact that West Berlin provides a means of contact with the Free World, serve to keep alive in Eastern Germany the hope for an escape from Soviet domination. The situation in East Germany provides opportunities for the West to exploit strong popular anti-Communism, to maintain East Germany as the focal point and example of disaffection for the rest of the Soviet satellites, and to make difficult full utilization by the Soviet Union of East Germany's economic resources.

9. The denigration of Stalin and Moscow's acceptance of Titoism have created difficulties in Soviet relations with the satellites; they have raised questions as to the infallibility of Soviet leadership among important elements of the satellite communist parties; they have aroused to varying degrees latent popular aspirations for relaxation of oppression, restoration of national independence, and establishment of governments responsive to popular will. This fluid situation in the satellites has increased the previously limited U.S. capabilities to influence a basic change in Soviet domination of the satellites. Although the Eastern European peoples continue to feel that liberation is remote, they remain responsive to our interest in their independence, provided it is expressed persistently and in terms which make it clear that this is our basic objective. There is a possibility that an internal relaxation might result in the long run in the development of forces and pressures leading to fundamental changes of the satellite system in the direction of national independence and individual freedom and security.

POLICY CONCLUSIONS

10. It is in the national security interests of the United States to oppose Soviet control of the satellites in Eastern Europe and to seek the eventual elimination of that control. At the same time it must be recognized that the attainment by any of the present satellites of national independence free of Soviet domination is remote, and that whatever degree of independence may be granted from Moscow or may evolve in differing circumstances in individual satellites, Soviet Russia by reason of its power status and its geographical position is bound to possess and exercise strong influence in the Eastern European area.

11. The United States is not prepared to resort to war to eliminate Soviet domination of the satellites, nor does attainment of this goal through internal revolutionary means appear likely or practicable. Therefore, the principal emphasis of our efforts should be directed to the encouragement of evolutionary change resulting in the weakening of Soviet controls and the attainment of national independence by the countries concerned, even though there may be no immediate change in their internal political structure. While some policies and actions may be applicable for the Soviet bloc as a whole, others may be suitable only for one or more of the satellites. Treatment of the satellites as a bloc without regard for significant differences among them may support and encourage Moscow's dominating position.

12. Flexible courses of action involving inducements as well as pressures are required to create and exploit troublesome problems for the USSR, complicate Soviet control in the satellites, and retard the growth of the military and economic potential of the Soviet bloc while encouraging the growth of forces in the satellites tending to assert national independence aims. This policy should be carried out in the light of current estimates of the Soviet Government's reactions and of the situation in the satellite states concerned.

BASIC OBJECTIVES

13. *Long-range*: The eventual fulfillment of the rights of the peoples in the Soviet satellites to enjoy representative governments resting upon the consent of the governed, free of Soviet domination and participating as peaceful members in the free world community.

14. *Interim:*

a. To foster changes in the character and policies of the satellite regimes by influencing them and their peoples toward the choice of those alternative lines of action which, while in their national interests, do not conflict with the security interests of the United States.
b. To minimize satellite contributions to Soviet power and to encourage changes in the present Soviet-satellite relationship toward national independence for the individual countries concerned.
c. To conserve and strengthen the assets within the satellites, and among their nationals outside, which may contribute to U. S. interests in peace or war, and to the ultimate freedom of the satellites.
d. To lay the groundwork, as feasible with reasonable risk, for resistance to the Soviets in the event of war.

GENERAL COURSES OF ACTION

15. Use appropriate means short of military force to oppose, and to contribute to the eventual elimination of, Soviet domination over the satellites; including, when appropriate, concert with NATO or other friendly powers, resort to UN procedures, and diplomatic negotiations.

16. Seek to create and increase popular and bureaucratic pressures through the exploitation of discontents and other problems to promote evolutionary changes in Soviet-satellite policies and relationships which will advance U. S. objectives.

17. When appropriate, depict the causes of the discontents and other problems which are to be exploited not as conditions reparable only by revolution but as susceptible to correction by the satellite regimes if they should choose to take the necessary action.

18. Continue basic opposition to the Soviet-Communist system and continue to state its evils; but stress evolutionary rather than revolutionary change.

19. Seek to cause each satellite regime to occupy itself increasingly with internal problems and to pose difficult decisions tending to create uncertainty or divisions within the regime.

20. Encourage the satellite peoples in passive resistance to their Soviet-dominated regimes when this will contribute to minimizing satellite contributions to Soviet power or to increasing pressures for desirable change.

21. Foster satellite nationalist sentiment as a force to weaken and disrupt Soviet domination while avoiding commitments to national territorial ambitions in the Eastern European area.

22. Encourage democratic, anti-Communist elements in the satellites. Cooperate with other forces—such as religious, cultural, social—which are natural allies in the struggle against Soviet imperialism, and seek to revive and revitalize the centuries-old bonds between these peoples and the West.

23. While avoiding the appearance of encouraging the export of Tito's Communism, use Yugoslavia's unique position in Eastern Europe to promote the weakening of the Soviet grip on the satellite countries.

24. When appropriate to achieve the basic objectives set forth in this paper, stimulate and exploit conflicts within the Communist ruling groups in each satellite, among such groups, and between them and the Kremlin.

25. Use, as appropriate, greater flexibility in U. S. economic policies (both incentives and restrictions) toward the satellites.

26. Exploit the developing organizations of Western unity (NATO, OEEC, CSC, etc.) as a force of attraction for the satellites, and emphasize on appropriate occasions the concept of a free European community to include ultimately the Eastern European countries.

27. Support or make use of those refugees or exile organizations which can usefully contribute to the attainment of U.S. objectives, but do not recognize governments-in-exile. Encourage exile unity and combat the Communist campaign to fragment and repatriate the emigration.

28. Continue propaganda and special operations by official and unofficial means, with appropriate adjustments as Communist controls and obstructions of communications are relaxed.

29. Be prepared to negotiate issues between the United States and the individual satellite regimes, taking into account varying conditions in the different countries with a view to:

a. Protecting and advancing the interests of the United States and its citizens.
b. Removing obstacles to communications between the peoples of these countries and the outside world.
c. Encouraging changes in the satellite regimes in line with the objectives set forth in this paper.

30. Emphasize (a) the right of the peoples of Eastern Europe to independent governments of their own choosing, and (b) the violation of international agreements by the Soviet and satellite Governments, whereby they have been deprived of that right, particularly the Yalta Declaration on liberated Europe and the Treaties of Peace with Bulgaria, Hungary and Rumania.

[Appendix to NSC 5608/1, July 18, 1956]

SUPPLEMENTARY STATEMENT OF POLICY BY THE NATIONAL SECURITY COUNCIL

ON
U. S. POLICY TOWARD THE SOVIET SATELLITES IN EASTERN EUROPE

1. Avoid incitements to violence or to action when the probable reprisals or other results would yield a net loss in terms of U.S. objectives. In general, however, do not discourage, by public utterances or otherwise, spontaneous manifestations of discontent and opposition to the Communist regime, despite risks to individuals, when their net results will exert pressures for release from Soviet domination. Operations which might involve or lead to local violence will be authorized only by the Secretary of State with the approval of the President on the basis of feasibility, minimum risk, and maximum contribution to the basic U.S. objectives in NSC 5608/1.

2. As a means of encouraging the eventual establishment of freely elected governments in the satellites as a disruptive device and not as an end in itself, be prepared on a case-by-case basis generally, covertly and under appropriate policy guidance to assist nationalists in any form where conducive to independence from Soviet domination and where U.S. and free world cohesion would not be jeopardized thereby.

[Source: NARA, Record Group 59, Lot 63D351, Box 88.]

DOCUMENT NO. 18: Letter from Ernő Gerő to Josip Broz Tito, July 19, 1956

Ernő Gerő, the newly elected first secretary of the HWP, sent this letter to Tito at the prompting of the Soviet leadership. Following the June 1956 Soviet-Yugoslav negotiations in Moscow, Khrushchev had called on then-leader Mátyás Rákosi to normalize the Hungarian party's relations with Yugoslavia. Rákosi originally signed the letter with this goal in mind, but he was forced to resign before it was sent. In the letter, Gerő apologizes for the problems caused by the László Rajk trial and the fierce propaganda campaign against Yugoslavia, in which Rákosi had played a leading part. Apparently preoccupied with the unfolding Suez crisis, Tito's official response came only on September 11, but significantly, he raised no objections to starting negotiations. The talks eventually took place between October 15 and 22 in Belgrade, but their significance was immediately overtaken by the revolution, which broke out on October 23.

Strictly Confidential!

Dear Comrade Tito,

The Central Committee of the Hungarian Workers' Party has investigated the development of relations between our two countries—the Yugoslav Federal People's Republic and the Hungarian People's Republic—and has taken pleasure in concluding that as a result of our common efforts to improve inter-state relations, significant improvements have taken place in the last few years; trade, cultural, sport and academic relations between the two countries are developing healthily. At the same time, for its part the Central Committee believes it necessary for comradely, friendly relations to emerge between the Yugoslav League of Communists and the Hungarian Workers' Party, as between parties whose countries are working hard to build socialism.

In the years following the war, a close relationship developed between the Yugoslav Communist Party and the Hungarian Communist Party, which played a vital role in forming neighborly relations between the two states, and in establishing friendship between the Yugoslav and Hungarian people. These connections, which had been useful for both parties and both countries, deteriorated as a result of unfortunate circumstances from 1948 onwards when we rashly took sides on questions raised against the Yugoslav League of Communists. The Rajk trial, which, as the Central Committee's investigation concluded, was based on provocation and false charges and which was one of origins of a completely unfounded slander which was insulting to the Yugoslav League of Communists and the Yugoslav Federal People's Republic, played an important part in the development of bad relations between the two parties and the two countries. We greatly regret that this seriously damaging event occurred. We are aware of the fact that it caused considerable harm to the people of our countries and to the cause of the entire communist movement.

For its part, the Hungarian Workers' Party Central Committee, while correcting past mistakes in the interests of peace and the socialist cause, is working hard to completely rebuild confidence between the two parties in order to promote the emergence of a truly neighborly relationship—a close bond of friendship, between our countries and peoples. In our opinion, achieving this goal would be greatly furthered by a renewal of ties between the two parties, which would provide a foundation for us to finally defeat and eliminate all those things that in the past few years have undermined the relations between our two countries and parties.

To discuss renewing ties between the Yugoslav League of Communists and the Hungarian Workers' Party, we would regard it as proper for representatives of the two parties to meet. To the extent that you agree with this suggestion, we suggest that a delegate from each party meet in the near future, in either Budapest or Belgrade, to make preparations for the meeting recommended above.

Trusting that our suggestion will meet with your approval, we await your reply.

Communist regards
Leadership of the Hungarian Workers' Party

Ernő Gerő

[Source: MOL, 276. f. 53/295. ő.e. Published in József Kiss, Zoltán Ripp and István Vida, eds., Magyar-jugoszláv kapcsolatok, 1956: Dokumentumok, *(Budapest: MTA Jelenkor-kutató Bizottság, 1995), 99–100. Translated by David Evans.]*

DOCUMENT NO. 19: Report from Ambassador Yurii Andropov on Deteriorating Conditions in Hungary, August 29, 1956

More than a month after the July 1956 meeting between the HWP leadership and Anastas Mikoyan, Soviet Ambassador Andropov wrote the following report to Moscow on the state of affairs in Hungary. He states that "notwithstanding certain improvements which followed the decisions of the July HWP CC Plenum, the political situation in Hungary continues to be quite complicated and requires constant attention." In an ideologically fueled analysis, Andropov blames the crisis and increasing social unrest on the "subversive activity" of "hostile elements." The most worrisome factors in his opinion are the weakness of, and lack of public respect for, the party leadership. He suggests that Moscow actively intervene to raise the prestige of Hungarian leaders, launch a pro-Soviet press campaign, and promote firmer ideological cooperation among the socialist countries.

SECRET, Copy No. 3
August 29, 1956

TO THE PRESIDIUM OF THE CPSU CC

On the eve of the July Plenum of the Central Committee, the internal political situation in the country has sharply deteriorated. Hostile elements, who see Hungary as one of the weakest links among the countries of the socialist camp, have stepped up their activities, and have spoken openly against the Hungarian Workers' Party leadership. They conduct their subversive activity from their base among the affluent segment of Hungarian peasants, the dissatisfied elements from among the former right-wing social democrats, and the intelligentsia. They were able to use the considerable influence that Western propaganda enjoys among the population of the country, in particular the Catholic Church, and various nationalist elements. The mistakes made by our friends in the sphere of economic policy, the violations of socialist legality which took place in the past, and the weakening of intra-party democracy—all of which were consequences of the lengthy period of Comrade Rákosi's personality cult in Hungary—aggravated the situation in the country even more, and led to the revival of activity by hostile elements in the country.

The mistakes made by the HWP leadership led to serious dissatisfaction among some party members and, above all, among party activists who were concerned that comrade Rákosi's personality cult could be revived under convenient circumstances, and that the persecution of honest communists could be revived as well. The decisions of the Twentieth Congress of the CPSU, which were received by members of the Hungarian Workers' Party with great enthusiasm, were implemented very slowly by the HWP leadership. All that led to a situation where the leadership and comrade Rákosi, above all in the eyes of some party members, looked like people who were resisting implementing the decisions of the Twentieth Congress. Hostile and opposition-inclined elements used that factor, and began their advance against the party leadership under the slogan of the decisions of the Twentieth Congress of the CPSU. The situation in the country was also becoming more complex because the party did not have a clear and precise program of action. The Politburo, and comrade Rákosi personally, being burdened with past mistakes, acted indecisively in the struggle with hostile elements, and exhibited signs of confusion and passivity.

Under these circumstances, the HWP CC Plenum was convened on July 18, which discussed pressing issues of life in the party and the country and outlined a program of party actions. The CPSU CC's assistance to the Hungarian comrades and comrade Mikoyan's personal participation in the work of the Plenum ensured the Plenum's success. Only one month after the Plenum, it is difficult to give a comprehensive analysis of the changes that occurred in the country; however, already now, one can say that after the Central Committee Plenum the political situation in the country has become less tense. Party activist meetings, with party and Hungarian government leaders participating, have shown that the overwhelming majority of Hungarian workers [people] approved of the decisions of the HWP CC Plenum, as well as the party and the government measures which followed those decisions. The party activist meetings have shown that the decisions of the CC Plenum provided a good basis for uniting party members, for raising their trust of party leadership, and for strengthening the people's democratic regime in Hungary.

At the same time we believe that notwithstanding certain improvements which followed the decisions of the July HWP CC Plenum, the political situation in Hungary continues to be quite complicated and requires constant attention.

Of most concern to us is the fact that the Hungarian comrades have so far achieved only insignificant results in the struggle to strengthen their power in the country. After the HWP CC Plenum, our friends implemented a number of steps directed at further democratizing the government administration. Those steps included: strengthening the Parliament's role, expanding the independence of the local councils, transferring local industrial enterprises, communal services, and cultural institutions under their authority. The Hungarian public positively received our friends' measures, such as the introduction of interpellations in the Parliament, the announcement regarding the rehabilitation of persons who were subjected to wrongful arrests in the past, the organization of press conferences with the Chairman of the Council of Ministers and other leading figures of the Hungarian government, and so on. However, our friends do not combine those measures with the implementation of firm policies, which would ensure the strengthening of power in the country; they use power very indecisively even in those cases where it is absolutely necessary.

The HWP CC and the Council of Ministers of the Hungarian People's Republic were not able to firmly set before the party and the government such tasks as increasing labor productivity, strengthening work discipline, lowering production costs, and fighting for the most economical production methods. Without resolving those tasks they will not be able to achieve any success in the economy. At the same time, many Hungarian officials made a number of promises regarding increasing living standards, providing new benefits for peasants, giving them additional credits, and so on. The hostile elements, who were confused and could not find any firm base for their subversive activity immediately after the July Central Committee Plenum, are now beginning to use the our comrades' indecisiveness for their own purposes. Playing on the widespread feelings of dependency on the government among certain Hungarian workers, the enemies and the opposition increasingly inspire new demands addressed to the government regarding increasing living standards, as well as on a number of political issues. Thus, during workers' meetings, which took place recently, some participants raised demands to repeal taxes, to increase wages, to open the Austria-Hungary border, to stop the collectivization of the agriculture, and so on. The hostile elements use such tactics to place our friends in a difficult position, while understanding that it would be impossible to satisfy those demands at the present time. In fact, some of them cannot be satisfied at all without harming the policy of the party and of the people's democratic state itself. It is clear from our conversations with our Hungarian comrades that they have noticed those facts themselves; however, so far they have not undertaken any decisive measures that would ensure implementation of a firm line.

The hostile elements are trying to portray such steps as comrade Rákosi's retirement, the decision not to issue state bonds this year, and several others, as their victory, and as our comrades' retreat. In these circumstances, as we believe, it would be especially important to demonstrate the firmness of the party line and the strength of the regime. Meanwhile, the Hungarian comrades continue to follow the course of [making] concessions, trying to avoid all possible complications. In doing so, in our opinion, they are only heating up hostile and opposition elements' activity. This is especially apparent in the sphere of ideology. We know that during a June 27 discussion in the Petőfi club, a number of writers—[Tibor] Déry[207] and [Tibor] Tardos above all—put forward the reactionary demands of a "new

---

[207] Tibor Déry was a well known writer and a leading figure of the opposition around Imre Nagy. After being expelled from the party in the summer of 1956, he was elected into the Writers' Union Presidium in September. During and after the revolution he became a spokesman for the writers and a member of the Revolutionary Council of Hungarian Intellectuals. Arrested in 1957, he was sentenced, together with Tibor Tardos, in the so-called "great writers' trial" to nine years in prison but was amnestied in 1960.

revolution" in Hungary, slandered the party leadership in various ways, and so on. Some time ago, the Politburo was correct to condemn their counter-revolutionary statements, and the party control commission expelled Déry and Tardos from the party. However, now, according to the statements by comrades Gerő and Szalai, our comrades intend to agree with Déry's election to the leadership of the Hungarian Writers' Union. Moreover, they are planning to entrust him with editing a new literary-esthetic magazine, and they have also made statements to the effect that it could be possible to reinstate him in the party. Here is a characteristic example: a month ago, a writers' party meeting discussed the HWP CC resolution from June 30 of this year, which condemned the counter-revolutionary statements in the Petőfi circle.[208] All the writers who attended that meeting spoke against that decision, and only one person—the editor of *"Csillag"* magazine, comrade [István] Király—voted to approve the decisions of the HWP CC, accompanied by laughter and ironic exclamations from the other writers. Recently, we learned that Király was summoned to the city party committee, and it was suggested that he resign as the magazine's editor on the basis of a possible writers' boycott, because "Király's leadership at that time differed sharply from the line of other writers." Such steps, in our opinion, do not describe the firmness of the leadership's positions.

Many Hungarian comrades, especially county party committee secretaries with whom we have had conversations, expressed their opinions to the effect that the HWP leadership had made certain concessions to the reactionary elements, thus attempting to pacify them. Such a course could actually help our friends to avoid conflicts with the opposition elements for some period of time, but essentially it is an incorrect and dangerous line because it could lead our Hungarian comrades to abandon the positions of Marxism-Leninism.

Our friends are facing a serious task in terms of socialist reconstruction of agriculture. According to the Ministry of Agriculture of the Hungarian People's Republic, as of June 30 this year, Hungary had 4,863 cooperatives and cooperative groups, which included 343,400 members. The cooperatives unite 2,479,000 holds[209] of land, or approximately 20 percent of all cultivated land in the country. In the first half of 1956, the collectivization of agriculture progressed faster than during the same period last year. Whereas in the first half of last year, 101 cooperatives with 25,000 members were added, in the first half of this year 327 new cooperatives were organized, and 55,000 members joined those cooperatives. At the July Plenum, the Central Committee subjected the mistakes committed by several county committees (Zala, Somogy, Borsod, and others) in the collectivization of agriculture, to sharp criticism. The hostile elements are trying to use our criticism of those mistakes for their own purposes. They organized quite an extensive propaganda campaign among the peasants, enticing them to leave the cooperatives. One has to note that all this propaganda is not without some results. According to the information that we have, in the counties of Zala, Somogy, and Vas the peasants from approximately 100 villages submitted requests to disband cooperatives and withdraw from them. In the last 2 or 3 months, the pace of organizing peasant farm cooperatives has slowed considerably. If from May 1 to June 15, 5,591 people joined the cooperatives, in comparison only 1,000 people did so in the period between June 15 to August 1.

The solution to the issue of strengthening the regime's authority in the country is linked to the need to consolidate the HWP, and to raise the authority and influence of the Politburo in the party.

Currently, the Hungarian Workers' Party is quite loose, and embraces approximately 10 percent of the entire Hungarian population (870,000 members and candidates). There are between 300–350,000 former social democrats among the ranks of party members, and in addition to those a significant number of petty bourgeois and other random elements joined the party and brought hostile, anticommunist influences into the party domain. One has to keep in mind the fact that there are many dissatisfied people among the Hungarian party activists who were offended by the leadership at some time in the past. Some of these comrades exert a negative influence on the rank-and-file party members. All this complicates Hungarian leadership's posi-

---

[208] This refers to the July 10 meeting of the Writers' Union's party organization.
[209] A "hold" is a Hungarian unit of measure equaling 0.57 hectares.

tion and creates considerable difficulties for the party to direct the country. It used to be that the party leadership's authority was perceived by rank-and-file communists to be linked with the comrade Rákosi's personality cult. At the present time, the Hungarian Workers' Party has done considerable work to overcome that anti-Marxist phenomenon; however, having debunked the personality cult, the Hungarian comrades were still unable to increase the authority of the HWP's collective leadership. The absence of the necessary authority of the Politburo and the individual leaders is one of the main reasons for the Hungarian comrades' lack of confidence and inconsistency.

Therefore, the embassy believes that our Hungarian friends face the task of strengthening the authority of the party leadership, as they have never had before. We believe that we could provide them with considerable assistance on our part.

1. We believe it would be expedient to invite a Hungarian government delegation—a mission of friendship—to the Soviet Union at the end of this year, to be led by comrade István Dobi and include leading figures of the HWP and the Hungarian government (comrades Gerő, Kádár, Rónai, Hegedüs, and others). A visit of such a delegation and meetings with our party leadership would undoubtedly help to increase the authority of the Hungarian leaders in the party and in the country. In our opinion, it would be expedient to cover this delegation's visit to the Soviet Union in the press, and at its conclusion to publish a joint communiqué to the effect that the Soviet and Hungarian sides enjoyed full understanding, both on the issues of foreign policy and on the issues of building socialism in our countries.

2. It would be helpful to publish a number of articles in the Soviet press on the issues of building socialism, above all on such matters as, for example, the leading role of the party, the need to strengthen the dictatorship of the working class, democratic centralism, and other subjects. It would be very important to utilize specific materials and facts from the experience of building socialism in the countries of people's democracy in the process of preparing such articles.

3. It would be expedient to send a party delegation from the CPSU CC to Hungary before the end of this year, which should include a number of prominent party officials. The official goal of the visit of such a delegation should be to study the experience of party work in Hungary (as Hungarian comrades do it here). Essentially, such a delegation could provide considerable assistance to the Hungarian comrades by sharing the CPSU's experience with them.

4. It would also be expedient for us to organize conversations between CPSU leaders and some of the Hungarian comrades who would come to the Soviet Union for a vacation. Such conversations would be especially useful with comrades Gerő, Kádár, Rónai and Márton Horváth. Such a measure would help our Hungarian comrades to grow politically, and to increase their confidence and level of leadership.

5. We believe it is necessary to ask the Ministry of Agriculture and the Ministry of State Farms of the USSR to develop a plan for an exchange of agricultural delegations with the Hungarian People's Republic. Before the end of this year, it would be very desirable to send to Hungary a delegation of our best agricultural workers, who would be able to tell the Hungarian peasants and party activists about Soviet achievements in the agricultural sphere.

* * *

Relations between Hungary and Yugoslavia represent a serious issue for our comrades. In the last six months, the intensity of this relationship has subsided somewhat. This became especially noticeable after the agreement on the payment of reparations to Yugoslavia had been reached; as a result, new opportunities to establish contacts between the HWP and YLC have emerged. The course of improving relations between the two parties has so far been slowed by the fact that comrade Rákosi, of whom the Yugoslav government was very critical, was a member of the Hungarian Workers' Party's leadership. The Yugoslav comrades are not trying to hide the fact that they are not satisfied with Gerő's candidacy for the position of first secretary of the HWP CC. Until recently, the Yugoslav press quite decisively supported the opposition elements in Hungary. After comrade A. I. Mikoyan's conversation with Yugoslav leaders in Belgrade,[210] the Yugoslav press's rhetoric in its coverage of Hungarian events became somewhat more reserved. However, until recently, there have been statements in the Yugoslav press and on the radio, which in our Hungarian friends' opinion, represented interference in the internal affairs of the Hungarian state. Thus, for example, the newspaper *Politika* wrote on July 20 of this year: " . . . after the removal of Rákosi, an optimistic revival prevails in the country. One serious obstacle was removed, but that is not all." The newspaper *Republica* published an article about Gerő on August 7 of this year, in which his work was linked to comrade Rákosi's activities in various ways. By the way, the article says: " . . . party observers do not think that this compromise will last. Supporters of Imre Nagy are trying to place control of the party in their own hands." On April 21 of this year, the Yugoslav weekly political magazine *Nin* published an article by Iván Iványi,[211] "Hungary without Rákosi." That article pointed out that the intelligentsia believed that Rákosi was not capable of finding a Hungarian way to build socialism independently, that he was blindly following the USSR, and that only Moscow was maintaining him in his position. Then Iványi wrote that many people with whom he had spoken were disappointed by Rákosi's replacement as Central Committee first secretary, because comrade Gerő's authority was very insignificant and his policy would be essentially a continuation of comrade Rákosi's. On August 23 of this year, the newspaper *Borba* published fictitious information about the rehabilitation of Imre Nagy, stating that it was necessary to rehabilitate not only Nagy as an individual, but his policy as well. The Hungarian comrades characterize this article as a sign of the Yugoslav's desire to put certain pressure on the Hungarian leadership.

The Yugoslav mission is engaged in very active work in Budapest, organizing all kinds of receptions, inviting Hungarian opposition figures, and spreading propaganda about the benefits of the so-called, "Yugoslav way" of building socialism. Unable to stay even within those limits, some mission officials, particularly trade adviser Mijatović, make visits to enterprises, where they try to praise the "Yugoslav way" of building socialism and in a number of cases make anti-Soviet statements in their conversations with the Hungarian comrades.

This kind of behavior by the Yugoslav comrades negatively affects the situation in Hungary and in the Hungarian Workers' Party. One has to take into account that there are some people in the HWP, especially from among the intelligentsia, who are positively inclined toward the position taken by the Yugoslav press. Some party members openly say that allegedly, due to special national conditions, the "Soviet way of building socialism" is less appropriate for Hungary than the Yugoslav way. These people are engaged in spreading the so-called theory of "national communism," mentioned above. At one of the district party activist meetings in Budapest, the district party committee secretary stated that the Hungarian way of building socialism should lie "in the middle, between what is now being done in Hungary and what is being done in Yugoslavia." There are conversations among some Hungarian party activists to the effect that Tito now enjoys great respect in the Soviet Union, because some time ago he was not afraid to follow a line independent of the Soviet Union.

The Hungarian comrades do not have a sufficiently firm and clear line in their relations with Yugoslavia. If several months ago they exhibited an undeserved mistrust in their attitude toward the Yugoslav leaders, now, to the contrary, in some of the statements by several leading comrades, one can hear traces of ingratiation before the Yugoslav leadership. The fact that the Hungarian comrades still have not given explanations for misunderstandings and mistaken opinions which have emerged from time to time among party members in connection with certain statements of the Yugoslav leadership, has a negative impact on the situation. It turns out that the Yugoslav comrades are openly presenting their point of view, whereas the Hungarian leadership remains silent; although, in the conversation with us, comrades Gerő, Hegedüs, [István]

[210] Mikoyan traveled to Belgrade after paying a crisis-management visit to Hungary between July 13–21. See Document No. 15.

[211] Iván Iványi was a Yugoslav journalist working on the newspaper *Mladost*.

Kovács and other Politburo members admitted that the position they took on this matter was wrong. Unfortunately, the Yugoslav comrades, despite the promises given by comrade Tito in his conversation with comrade Mikoyan, still have not responded to the HWP CC regarding their proposal on establishing contacts between the parties. We believe that it would be very important to look for possibilities for providing some assistance in mending Hungarian-Yugoslav relations. It would be very useful if the YLC leadership found it possible to respond to the HWP CC letter of July 21,[212] and to support the proposal made by the Hungarian comrades regarding a meeting between Yugoslav and Hungarian delegations in the nearest future.

* * *

Strengthening Hungary's international ties with the Soviet Union and other people's democracies would have great significance for improving the situation in Hungary and in the HWP. One has to say that the hostile and opposition elements' activities after the decisions of the Twentieth Party Congress were directed precisely toward weakening those ties and, if not to split away, then to separate Hungary from the socialist camp, primarily the USSR, as much as possible. Recently, in various discussions at meetings and in Hungarian newspapers and magazines, it is possible to detect more frequent statements containing criticism of the Soviet Union, or of certain aspects of Soviet life. Along with correctly condemning the practice of excessive praise for Soviet reality, which was prevalent before, some statements have recently been made in Hungary in which the authors cast doubts on the achievements of the Soviet Union in building socialism; at a minimum, there were publications that were silent about the Soviet people's achievements, and at the same time inappropriately emphasized our problems. One can cite the essays of Hungarian journalist Pándi Pál,[213] who recently visited the Soviet Union, as one such example. He attempted to treat the phenomena of Soviet reality with an objectivist approach, trying to diminish the USSR's successes in improving living standards for the Soviet people, but in essence he painted certain aspects of our life black. At a philosophical discussion that took place recently, Hungarian philosopher [György] Lukács made a biased statement in which he tried to portray the state of Marxist-Leninist science in the USSR by placing almost exclusive emphasis on the fact that Soviet philosophers were dogmatic and trying only to score points. The Hungarian literary newspaper *Irodalmi Újság* has recently published numerous critical articles also. Radio propaganda from the Western countries, and especially from a station such as "Free Europe," plays a large role in instigating nationalist feelings. Day after day, broadcasts of this station follow the line of discrediting Soviet foreign policy, compromising international contacts among the socialist camp countries, and sowing mistrust toward the Soviet Union among the Hungarian people. In the past several days, the radio station "Free Europe" paid great attention to the presence of Soviet Army units in Hungary. According to confidential information available to us, this campaign was prepared and materially supported by the American mission in Budapest. Radio station "Free Europe" recently reported that, as a result of the presence of a large number of Soviet Army officers and their families, who, allegedly, get huge paychecks in Hungary, prices in the markets in cities where Soviet military units are stationed grew considerably higher. Comrade Gerő spoke with me about this same issue several days ago. He said that the HWP CC received letters from the population with complaints that families of Soviet officers were causing inflated market prices, and had "in general, conducted themselves incorrectly."

In light of the information presented above, it is becoming especially important to implement measures to strengthen Hungary's international contacts with the countries of people's democracy, especially Hungarian-Soviet friendship. In our view, the following measures would help to fulfill this goal.

---

[212] See Document 18. Although the letter was written on July 19, 1956, it was handed over on July 21 when Tito received Hungarian Ambassador Sándor Kurimszky.

[213] Pál Pándi was editor of the cultural column at *Szabad Nép* from 1955–1956.

1. The Hungarian comrades admit the great significance of Soviet assistance to Hungary. However, the Hungarian press mentions this assistance in only general phrases, without specifically stating what is included in that assistance. Therefore, it is not incidental that there are rumors among the population that trade with the Soviet Union is unfavorable to Hungary, and that the Soviet Union extracts profits from Hungary only for itself, "rubs Hungary," and so on. Some time ago, comrades Rákosi and Gerő told us that even among leading officials there were conversations regarding the fact that Hungary should be selling uranium ore not to the Soviet Union, but on the world market in order to receive hard currency. We believe that it is extremely important that the Hungarian press describe the concrete assistance which is being provided to Hungary by the Soviet Union. It would be good if the Soviet press, radio, and cinema also described that assistance, because there is hardly any sense in keeping secrets about such forms of aid as credits, supplies of equipment, deficit goods, and so on, which the Soviet Union gives to Hungary.

2. Sending Hungarian delegations to our country would have invaluable significance for the developing Hungarian-Soviet relations. However, the practice that has developed in this sphere does not allow us to achieve the desired results from those visits. As a rule, the delegations include leading party and state officials who rarely speak before the working people after their visits to the Soviet Union.

It would be expedient to take into account the composition of the Hungarian delegations when inviting them to the Soviet Union, in order to include as many representatives of workers, peasants, rank-and-file intelligentsia, low level party officials, and so on as possible. There is a need to further strengthen cultural cooperation between the USSR and Hungary. When we form our cultural delegations which are sent to the Hungarian People's Republic, we often include persons who, in terms of their artistic skills, are much weaker than Soviet performers who visited Hungary in past years, whereas we send the best performers of our country to the capitalist countries. It has to be noted that we have never yet sent one of our best theater collectives to Hungary, although there is no doubt that such a tour would create great interest in the Hungarian audience. The plan of cultural cooperation with Hungary has not been approved yet, although agreement on issues of cultural cooperation were already signed in June 1956, and the Hungarian side presented their draft plan simultaneously with the drafting of that agreement. Beginning in 1953, the Ministry of Culture repeatedly promised the Hungarian leaders that they would stage the Hungarian national opera *Bánk Bán* at the Bolshoi Theater; however, that performance is not even in the plans, which offends the Hungarian intelligentsia considerably.

I believe it would be expedient to draw the USSR Ministry of Culture's attention to the need to step up work on cultural exchanges with Hungary, having in mind sending our best performers and high-level theater groups to the Hungarian People's Republic. The same principle should be followed in selecting materials for various artists' exhibitions that are being sent to Hungary, etc.

3. The Embassy believes that there is a pressing need for closer cooperation and coordination between the countries of the socialist camp on ideological issues, including such aspects as press, radio, cinema, theater, publishing, and others. In recent years, Soviet propaganda in Hungary clearly has not matched the level of existing relations, cooperation, and mutual assistance between our two countries in the economic sphere. Soviet radio and press propaganda is often conducted in a general manner, bureaucratically, without introducing concrete and accessible materials that would characterize Hungarian-Soviet relations. In the last three years, the Hungarian comrades have systematically complained about the unsatisfactory work of the Soviet Information Bureau, which sends materials of very poor quality to Hungary.

It would be expedient to establish closer contacts between the leaders of fraternal Communist and Workers' Parties involved in ideological issues, as well as between particular leaders of various areas of ideological work, for example radio, publishing, and so on.

4. Timely information about the situation in the fraternal parties is very important for strengthening international ties in the socialist camp. At the present time, the only systematic information about the work of Central Committee Plenums, and about other important develop-

ments, has been coming from the CPSU. The Hungarian comrades do not have a system for exchanging such information with other countries. Our Hungarian comrades repeatedly told us that they learned about many important events in the socialist camp from the Western press. Thus, for example, the Hungarian comrades learned about the developments in Poznań from Reuters. One has to say that the Hungarian leaders themselves do not show any particular concern about informing fraternal Communist and workers' parties about the most important events that have taken place in the HWP. We are aware that such practices by the Hungarian leadership have led to serious dissatisfaction on the part of our German, Polish, and Bulgarian comrades. In our opinion, it would be good if we showed initiative by raising the issue of exchanging information on the most important issues and also on the most pressing issues in the work of our parties, before all the fraternal Communist and workers' parties of the socialist camp.

5. It would be expedient if the Soviet Army's political department gave appropriate instructions to the command of Soviet forces stationed in Hungary about strengthening their work with officers' families.

6. The Embassy believes that resolving the following issues would greatly improve the situation in the HWP and in the country.

a) Control figures on the collectivization of agriculture. After the Third Congress of the HWP, the Hungarian press published information that the party was planning to collectivize 60 to 65 percent of peasant farms by the end of 1960. In comrade Hegedüs' report about the directives for drafting the 5-year plan given at the July Central Committee Plenum, it was again stated that by the end of 1960, the socialist sector should include 55 to 60 percent of all cultivated land in the country. The above-mentioned control figures were repeatedly mentioned in various meetings. We think that such open publication of control figures on the collectivization of agriculture, in which individual peasants essentially see the decisions [being made] about their destiny, irritates them and encourages hostile activity against our friends. On the other hand, publishing those figures has led, and will lead, to a campaign approach and excesses in the process of collectivization, as well as to violations of the principles of voluntary participation. Since this issue is a very important one, it seems that it would be expedient to suggest to the Hungarian leadership that the control goals regarding collectivization be available only to the Central Committee and the local party organs for their orientation, without making them public.

b) On Imre Nagy. After the July Plenum of the HWP CC, the Hungarian leadership made several attempts to speak with Nagy, to force him to make a critical statement concerning his mistakes, so that subsequently they would have an opportunity to bring him back into the party. According to our Hungarian comrades, Nagy refused to admit his mistakes, and sent a letter to the Central Committee in which he insisted on holding a discussion within the framework of the entire party, or at least in the Central Committee. In our opinion, such behavior is incorrect because, if he were accepted in the party with such ideas, it would lead not to the strengthening but to the weakening of HWP unity. On the other hand, it would be remiss not to mention that comrade Gerő exhibited a tendency to put an end to the Nagy issue, to remove it from the agenda. Until now, only secondary party officials—Egri, Nógrádi,[214] and Köböl—have spoken with Nagy. It would be difficult for them to influence Nagy (especially because, up until recently, Nógrádi and Köböl were themselves in opposition to the leadership). Meanwhile, the issue of Nagy cannot simply be removed from discussion in the present situation, because it is being actively raised in a number of party organizations. This question is also being heated up by publications in the Yugoslav press. It would be good if comrade Gerő himself spoke with Nagy, together with other members of the Politburo, and tried to persuade Nagy to make a self-critical statement. If Nagy makes such a statement, at least on the most important issues (mistakes in the sphere of industrialization, collectivization of agriculture, and the leading role of the party), he should be reinstated in the party and given some insignificant work. However, if Nagy persists

---

[214] Sándor Nógrádi was a member of the HWP CC and head of the Army's Political Division between 1949 and 1956. In 1956 he was head of the HWP CC Department for Agitation and Propaganda.

in his opposition, then it would be necessary to expose him in the eyes of Communists as a member of the opposition and as a dissenter.

Some Hungarian comrades expressed an opinion that the CPSU CC Presidium would want to see Nagy among the party leadership. It seems to us that it would be useful to explain our position on this issue to the Hungarian comrades, using comrade Gerő's visit to the USSR this September for that purpose.

c) About comrade Rákosi. From our conversations with the Hungarian comrades, we had the impression that comrade Rákosi was planning to return to Hungary and to take an active part in the leadership of the party and the country in the nearest future. Comrade Rákosi himself expressed such feelings on the eve of his last trip to the USSR.

In this connection, one cannot disregard the fact that there are conversations among a certain segment of party members to the effect that comrade Rákosi's retirement was only temporary, and that after his health improves he would return to the HWP leadership.

If upon his return to Hungary, comrade Rákosi really tries to interfere with the Politburo's work, then it could again lead to an aggravation of the situation in the HWP, because there are elements in Hungary who would find it profitable to contrast Rákosi with the new leadership. On the other hand, the hostile elements will cry about Rákosi "holding the entire Central Committee in his hands" again, and that would not be helpful in terms of strengthening the authority of the HWP leadership.

USSR AMBASSADOR TO HUNGARY   YU. ANDROPOV

[Source: Arkhiv vneshnei politiki Rossiiskoi Federatsii (AVP RF), F. 077, Op. 37, Papka (P.) 190, D. 33, Ll. 65–79. Published in Sovietskii Soyuz i vengerskii krizis, 1956 goda: Dokumenty, edited and compiled by E. D. Orekhova, Vyacheslav T. Sereda and Aleksandr. S. Stykhalin (Moscow: ROSSPEN, 1998), 240–252. Translated by Svetlana Savranskaya.]

DOCUMENT NO. 20: North Atlantic Council Document C-M(56)110, "The Thaw in Eastern Europe," September 24, 1956

The recent partial opening of the NATO Archives has significantly increased the possibilities for reconstructing Western policy concerning Hungary.[215] This document gives a comprehensive analysis, from a NATO perspective—and therefore that of Western foreign ministries—of the process of de-Stalinization in Eastern Europe, which began with the death of Stalin and was accelerated by the CPSU Twentieth Congress in February 1956. Moreover, the analysis offers an outline for a possible Western approach toward the region. This document has special significance because the highest consultative and decision-making forum of the North Atlantic Treaty Organization, the NATO Council, began to discuss this material on October 24, exactly one day after the outbreak of the Hungarian revolution. Created by the Political Division of the NATO International Secretariat and checked by a working group dealing with developments inside the Soviet bloc,[216] the document was meant to prepare participants for a ministerial meeting of the North Atlantic Council scheduled for the middle of December 1956.

The first part of the report (the excerpts dealing with Hungary are published below), describes the thaw in each East European country, giving special emphasis to local characteristics—noting, for example, the fundamental differences in the origins of the turmoil in Poland and Hungary. Written just a few weeks before the revolution, the report forecasts the possible sudden acceleration of developments. The second part of the study describes the general features of the "thaw: its essence, origins and possible consequences—and does so quite successfully given the limits on the ability of NATO missions in the Soviet bloc to gather information. Besides examining the interaction between the four "main actors" (the Soviet Union, the satellite leaders, the intellectuals, and the people), the study also draws attention to the fact that the "thaw" in Eastern Europe fit the global strategy of post-Stalin Soviet foreign policy, which continuously emphasized an interest in the process of détente. Concerning Western conduct, the report emphasizes that although certain signs of greater freedom should be welcomed, caution was still necessary when gauging the real aims of the Soviet Union. Given the realities of the bipolar world order and the risk of a possible thermo-nuclear war, the authors of the report were aware of the restricted means available to promote the thaw. Therefore, although the authors found it important to show sympathy for the changes that were unfolding at the time, they suggest refraining from encouraging the "captive peoples" to initiate "futile rebellions." In light of this report, it is easier to understand the contemporary statements of Western statesmen which made clear their intention not to intervene in Poland and Hungary.[217]

CONSEIL DE L'ATLANTIQUE NORD
NORTH ATLANTIC COUNCIL

ORIGINAL: ENGLISH

24TH SEPTEMBER, 1956

DOCUMENT

C-M(56)110.

---

[215] As of early 2001, only those document series generated by the North Atlantic Council and its committees, and the Military Committee and its main subordinate organs between 1949 and 1965 are open for research at the NATO Archives Reading Room in Brussels.

[216] The Working Group on Trends of Soviet policy worked since 1952.

[217] See, for example, the remarks by French Foreign Minister Christian Pineau in Paris before journalists on October 26, the speech by Secretary of State John Foster Dulles in Dallas during the presidential campaign on October 27 and the response by the British government representative on behalf of Foreign Minister Eden to a question in Parliament on November 1; all are referenced in Csaba Békés, *The 1956 Hungarian Revolution and World Politics*, Cold War International History Project Working Paper, no. 16 (Washington, D.C.: Woodrow Wilson International Center for Scholars, 1996), 15, 17–18.

THE THAW IN EASTERN EUROPE

Note by the Chairman of the Working Group on Trends of Soviet Policy
This paper was prepared by the Political Division and subsequently examined by the Working Group on Trends of Soviet Policy.

2. In compliance with the request of the Working Group, the Secretary General[218] has agreed to list the paper on the Agenda for the meeting of the Council to be held on Wednesday, 24th October.

(Signed) A. CASARDI[219]

Palais de Chaillot, Paris, XVIe.

[...]

HUNGARY

Hungarian ferment–1953–55

23. The background to the current ferment in Hungary is substantially different from that in Poland.[220] During Stalin's lifetime, the regime in Hungary seemed to be one of the most "Stalinist" in Eastern Europe. Social and economic policies were as extreme as the rulers could possibly impose. The police terror and repression of the population were very severe. The government's attitude toward the West and toward Tito was most hostile. A "cult of the personality" on the Stalin model was developed around Rakosi, particularly after he had eliminated Rajk in a purge trial closely modeled on the Moscow trials of the thirties.

24. Then in the period just after Stalin's death, the pendulum swung back perhaps more sharply than in any other satellite. Rakosi became much less prominent, though he clearly retained considerable power. The "New Course" under a new leader, Imre Nagy, seemed to promise a substantial slackening of the pressure on the Hungarian people, especially in the economic field.

25. The "New Course" ended in confusion and disarray. The promised relief had not materialised and the people were at least as restive as before the rise of Nagy. Rakosi was returned to full authority and the screws were tightened again both in the economic area and in the general control of the population. However, the situation by no means reverted to what it had been before 1953. During the 16 months of Rakosi's second tour of duty (March 1955–July 1956), a number of conflicting tendencies were apparent, as though the regime were not really clear about the course to be followed.

26. On the one hand the leaders plainly would have to get the country back on the pre-1953 programme of building heavy industry, pushing the rapid collectivisation of agriculture, and organizing a monolithic state and party on the Russian model. On the other hand they were not willing to use the sort of repression which would have been required to force Hungary back on to this line of development. It is not clear how far this restraint was the result of orders from Moscow, dissension within the leadership or increased resistance from below. Very likely all three factors were involved and interacted. In any case, from the beginning Rakosi seemed to be trying to steer a middle course between his old "hard" line and Nagy's excessive "softness".

[218] Lord Ismay was NATO secretary general from 1952–1957.

[219] Alberico Casardi was deputy secretary general for political affairs from 1956–1958.

[220] The section of this document dealing with Poland concluded that there were no significant changes in Polish politics or economy during the period immediately after Stalin's death. In 1954, a centrally organized campaign began against schematic art. This brought a wave of criticism which the regime was no longer able to keep under control.

27. Since late 1955 the signs have been multiplying that Rakosi's compromise was not working out. Criticism from below of various aspects of Hungarian life grew sharper and Rakosi reacted with a series of stern but ineffective calls for discipline.

28. As in Poland, it was the intellectuals within the Party whose complaints came to the attention of the outside world. In the Nagy period, there have been a measure of relaxation and Rakosi's efforts throughout 1955 were directed toward "containment" and "roll-back" of these dangerous tendencies. Toward the end of the year the intellectuals seemed to realise that the régime would not or could not turn loose on them its full powers of repression. They resumed the initiative at a meeting on 10th November of the Writers' Federation.[221] The Party Central Committee in December roundly condemned this and earlier signs of "rightist deviation"—a striking contrast to the not unfriendly, though cautious, attitude of the Polish authorities. However, reprisals do not seem to have been taken against the individuals concerned.[222]

29. The intellectuals in Hungary, as elsewhere behind the curtain, were emboldened by the Moscow Party Congress in February. Although the régime handled the dethronement of Stalin in a very restrained way, word of Khrushchev's speech was slowly disseminated and had its usual unsettling effect on Communists and sympathisers. A meeting of the Writers' Union in March is reported to have been suspended and another meeting in April was no less hostile.[223] Meanwhile a broader forum was developing in the meetings of the Petőfi Club. Apparently organized by the régime in March as a grouping of discussion circles, the Club[224] had by June become the focus of complaints against the régime. A tumultuous all-night meeting on 27th June turned into a public demonstration against Rakosi and his policies.

Other political developments

30. A feeling of relative security against reprisals is necessary before intellectuals behind the Iron Curtain will speak out in even indirect criticism of the party or régime. To a certain extent, the shake-up in the Hungarian secret police in 1953 served this function. The head policeman, Gabor Peter, was denounced for various crimes and linked to Beria. Rakosi's revived influence in 1955 brought some increase in police activity but evidently not a real wave of terror. Then following the Moscow Party Congress, there was renewed stress in the newspapers on "socialist legality". There has not, however, been any campaign on the Polish model against past abuses and those responsible for them.

31. There was an amnesty in Hungary which curiously enough coincided with the fall of Nagy (April 1955). It seems not to have had very significant results, at least for some time after its promulgation. However, in March 1956 Rakosi admitted that the notorious purge trial of Rajk and seven associates was an error. Subsequent reports indicated an increased tempo of releases from imprisonment, including some leading Social Democrats.

32. The Hungarian press in recent months has carried hints that some revival of the role of Parliament might be under consideration. As yet, however, this revival remains even more hypo-

---

[221] At a meeting of the party organization of the Writers' Union on November 2–4, the majority of members accepted a memorandum worded by Communist writers, journalists and artists on October 18, which demanded the elimination of administrative measures in cultural life. This memorandum was forwarded to the HWP CC.

[222] In reality, there were retaliations against the writers of the memorandum, after most of those who signed it were forced to withdraw their signature. (For example, Sándor Haraszti and Miklós Vásárhelyi were expelled from the party).

[223] Most likely this refers to the party assembly of the Writers' Union on March 30, 1956, which was interrupted by party officials because of the sharpness of the criticisms that were being expressed. The meeting was continued on April 13, 16 and 18, in no less tense an atmosphere. See Éva Standeisky, *Írók lázadása: 1956-os írószövetségi jegyzőkönyvek* (Budapest: MTA Irodalomtudományi Intézete, 1990), 32–36.

[224] The Petőfi Circle was in fact formed a year earlier on March 25, 1955, although its political activity began only after the Twentieth Congress of the CPSU, in March 1956.

thetical than in Poland. There has also been greater emphasis on decentralisation of authority and on the role of the trade unions.

The fall of Rakosi

33. During the first half of 1956, the No. 1 political issue in Hungary was Rakosi—would he maintain his position or not? He was clearly unpopular, not to say reviled, among the masses as a whole. For them he personified the worst features of a bad régime. Among the intellectuals sympathetic to Communism he was looked on as an anachronism, a Stalinist survival who was blocking progress toward an improved "Hungarian" socialism. Even within the Central Committee of the Party there seem to have been critics of his methods. And of course he was anathema to Tito and, as such, was a real handicap to the Moscow drive for better relations with Yugoslavia.

34. On the other hand, it seems clear that he had considerable, though not unqualified support from the Soviet leaders. During the past spring the Russians made a series of gestures indicating their high opinion of Comrade Rakosi. For them he must have represented a very desirable force for stability and guarantee of pro-Soviet orientation, especially welcome after the disorder of Nagy's last months. Rakosi should also have been able to count on the support of the top figures in the Party and government: they were his own creatures and had been for years closely associated with his policies and actions. They must have been aware of the difficulties inherent in Hungary's situation, difficulties calling for ruthless, able leadership.

35. As late as 1st July, the Central Committee resolution on the Petőfi club[225] indicated that Rakosi was still in firm control and intended to crack down strongly on his critics. Then, for reasons which are not clear, though certainly related to the general considerations above, the balance suddenly shifted against him. On 18th July he announced that his health plus his past mistakes made his resignation as Party Secretary desirable.[226]

The "new" régime

36. There seems to be little doubt that Rakosi's eclipse is definitive this time. Barring a bloc-wide revival of Stalinism, it does not seem possible for him to make yet another comeback.

37. The immediate effect of his departure has not been very great. His successor, Geroe [Gerő], is a very old associate of Rakosi whose main field of activity has been economic. He is thus closely linked with the régime's policy of industrialising at all costs and stands for the maintenance of this policy in the Five Year Plan which has just begun. Although his first speech as Party Secretary contained some concessions to consumer needs, close examination indicates that they are largely verbal concessions. Moreover, one of Rakosi's last acts was to exclude his old rival, Nagy from the Communist Party and one of Geroe's first acts has been to reaffirm that "right deviations" centering around Nagy are just as dangerous as "left-wing sectarianism", (i.e. Stalinism). Geroe's line thus seems to bear a very close resemblance to the sort of half-and-half policy which Rakosi tried to pursue, "liberalisation" and "democratisation", but as little as possible, all essential elements of Communist control and policy remaining untouched.

38. There is a general tendency to doubt whether this compromise can be a lasting solution. Geroe and the Prime Minister, Hegedus, are looked on as second-rate figures whose only advantage over Rakosi is that, living in his shadow, their names have not become symbols, like his, of the evils of the past. This is a transient advantage. Moreover, as their difficulties grow, their relative lack of stature will make it difficult for them to impose their authority in the Rakosi manner.

39. Probably the most important consequence of Rakosi's fall will be its effect on the intellectuals and the middle ranks of the Party. It seems to have been their pressure which in the end

---

[225] The actual date of the HWP CC resolution denouncing the Petőfi Circle's activities was June 30.
[226] Concerning Rákosi's resignation, see Document No. 15.

"got" Rakosi and their self-confidence cannot fail to be bolstered by their success. It can be expected that their increasing influence will be felt over the longer run in the sense of growing liberalisation along the lines being followed by Poland. The admission to the Politburo of a Social-Democrat[227] only recently released from prison is an indication that now that the log-jam has been broken, events may move with surprising speed.

Economic and military questions

40. It has been noted that all the turmoil in intellectual and political circles has not strikingly affected the economic policies of the régime. Even Rakosi's fall has brought no sharp change in direction. However, the current Five Year Plan does represent some moderation or caution when compared with its Stalinist predecessor. Or, to put it another way, their remain [sic] some elements from the "New Course" of the Nagy period. Investments are to take a lower share of the national income, goals in general are more modest, there is more emphasis on raw materials and energy than on further expansion of the engineering industries. Along with increased attention to agriculture, the use of force to achieve collectivisation is deplored, even though a fully collectivised agriculture remains the goal.

41. The Hungarian régime also has been reducing its military expenditures. Budget allocations this year were over 25% below the 1953 level and a further reduction of 15,000 men was announced in August. Certain spokesmen have even gone so far as to blame the low standard of living on excessive spending for defence in the past.

[...]

PART II

THE THAW IN PERSPECTIVE

73. Development in the satellites during the past year or so have a sufficient number of features in common to justify generalisations about the bloc as a whole. Plainly the people and the régimes in these states are in roughly similar situations, subject to roughly similar social and political forces, (e.g. governments of unpopular cliques ultimately dependent on Moscow and struggling with economically and politically backward areas).

74. The outstanding symptoms of the thaw are two: (a) a considerable limitation of the role played by the security apparatus and police terror; (b) greater freedom of expression for intellectuals and sharper and more basic criticism of many practices of the various régimes. To these two principal symptoms have been added in certain cases a variety of secondary phenomena: revival of parliamentary activity, lessened hostility to the West, rejuvenation of trade unions, reduction in military expenditures, shifts of top personnel, lessened sycophancy toward the Soviet Union.

75. It would be wrong to look on the thaw either as something forced on unwilling régimes by discontent from below or as concessions freely dispensed by Moscow and imposed on the local Communists from the "Centre". Rather it should be viewed as a response to the political and economic situation which Stalinism had created: —a situation which may be characterised as an impasse in both domestic and foreign affairs. Internally, the Stalinist techniques of ruthless exploitation had extracted from the masses everything that they had to give. Further economic progress was becoming increasingly difficult, the working classes were becoming, if not disaffected, at least apathetic, the agricultural situation (not just in the satellites but in the Soviet Union as well) was in danger of passing from an incipient to real crisis. Externally, the advances

---

[227] This probably refers to György Marosán who was elected a member of the Political Committee during the June 18–21 meeting of the HWP CC.

of the immediate post-war period had been consolidated but the very process of consolidation had created effective barriers to further advances. A new approach seemed in order.

76. The response which Moscow has been making to this situation was not the only possible one. However, a number of factors seem to have ruled out the most important alternatives (widespread purges and foreign adventure, for example, or at the other extreme, a genuine shift away from heavy industry), and in this sense one might say that the passive resistance of the masses and the more active resistance of the West imposed the thaw on the Communist leaders.

77. The decisive moment was Moscow's downgrading of the security apparatus. (One can hardly doubt some connection between this event and the fall of Beria, though the nature of the connection may be debated for years.) The downgrading was generalised to the satellites and in a very real sense the whole of the subsequent thaw may be said to have developed from this event. (The climate within the Bloc began to change, of course, from the moment of Stalin's death. The fall of Beria and subsequent police shake-ups were able to have the importance and the far-reaching effects we have seen only because of this alteration in the general atmosphere).

78. The most important consequence has been the ferment of discussion and criticism in the circles called "ideological activists", writers, journalists, lecturers, scholars, artists, etc. This group, whose function in a Communist state is to enlist the support of the masses for the projects of the régime, was very aware that under Stalinism its relationship to its audience had withered away. The pupils had learned all the standard responses but they were not really paying any attention to the teacher. It was to remedy this situation that the régimes very gingerly opened the door to criticism from below.

79. The leaders were from the beginning fearful that this criticism might get out of hand. They viewed it as a necessary evil—necessary if the "transmission belt" from the leadership down to the masses was to be repaired and put back in operation, but evil if through its pressures were exerted on the leadership to alter its fundamental policies. As Morawski[228] (a leading Polish ideologist) explained it: "We want to encourage discussion of various topics from the fields of politics, culture, economic policy in order to clear the path of our ideology more effectively and spread understanding of our political line".

80. However, the "activists" became very active indeed when they understood that a measure of genuine criticism would be tolerated. Their complaints and Moscow's instructions converged on the local Party leaders. The reaction of these unhappy creatures has differed widely from one satellite to another. Judging by results one would suppose that the Polish Politburo almost welcomed the thaw, yet we have the testimony of a writer in a Polish journal last March that the thaw "has happened despite the fact that the leadership has not only not done all in its power to speed up this process but has often tried to restrain it." The régimes in the southern satellites have not merely tried to restrain it, they have nipped it in the bud.

81. Once the régimes began to give ground to the intellectuals the process fed on itself. Each concession made it more difficult to refuse the next demand. In order to halt the process a really serious effort became necessary. For example, in Poland throughout 1954 and 1955 the régime repeatedly set limits to criticism only to see them overstepped. In Hungary in 1955, the régime made a vigorous attempt to reverse the trend: it ended after 16 months in the fall of Rakosi. In Czechoslovakia, after making only the most minimal concessions to the new trends, the leadership in June roused itself to a general counter-attack whose outcome is not yet apparent.

82. It is interesting to examine the reasons why the course of the thaw has varied so widely from one satellite to another. One can, for example, distinguish the "northern tier" (Poland, Czechoslovakia, Hungary) from the southern group, with East Germany a rather special case.

83. It has been suggested above that, the four "actors" in the drama are Moscow, the satellite leaders, the satellite intellectuals and the people. The role actually played by the first is the most difficult to analyse accurately. There is little doubt that some sort of general instructions

---

[228] Most likely this refers to Jerzy Morawski, who was a member of the PZPR CC as of 1954 and of the Politburo from 1956.

have gone out from Moscow to "liberalise, democratise", with the concrete measures to implement this order being left to the local bosses. The Soviets then appear to have sat in judgement on the satellite performance, interposing their veto when a situation seemed to be developing dangerously (as in Hungary in early 1955), encouraging a shift when the old leadership seemed unduly conservative or hopelessly discredited (Chervenkov and Rakosi). The Russians thus have engaged in a "two-front" action. Having given the thaw a push originally, their influence now seems generally to be a restraining one. Soviet pressure, when a new leader had to be named, has clearly been in favour of the "hardest" candidate acceptable to the local machine (Ochab,[229] Geroe, Yugov[230]). One should be in no doubt about Soviet determination to retain ultimate control over the satellites, nor about Soviet ability to exercise control so long as the thaw does not proceed a great deal further than it has in the passing three years. There seems to be no basis for attributing the differences along the various satellite thaws to differential handling by Moscow; simply the Soviets have allowed national differences to be reflected in the actions of the various régimes, perhaps pushing Bulgaria a bit and certainly holding back on Poland (vide Bulganin's speeches in Warsaw during August), but realistically refraining from forcing everyone into the same mould as Stalin used to do.

84. The satellite leaders probably have approached the thaw from slightly differing points of view. Even under Stalin the Poles managed to show a certain variation from the norm, for instance in never holding an anti-Tito show trial, so that Gomulka alone of the important "Titoists" could be rehabilitated alive. It has not, therefore, been surprising to find them in the lead in their de-Stalinisation process. Rakosi may be considered the other extreme. He made a good try over a period of more than a year at reimposing Stalinism (minus Stalin) on what is surely one of the most unruly nations in Europe. In general, it would seem to have been easier for the governments in the northern tier to make the shift (still very incomplete) away from compulsion toward persuasion in their relationship to the governed. The northern satellites all had Communist parties with a certain footing in the life of their countries. Marxism was once respectable among their intellectuals and trade unionists. In Czechoslovakia the Party had over a million members in 1946 and polled more than a third of the votes in the election of that year. Naturally the leaders who disposed of this sort of base (even though now comprised by the excesses of communist rule) could afford to take chances, to permit a degree of liberalisation unthinkable to the tiny Albanian clique around Hoxha.

85. The role played by the third actor, the intellectual class, has also differed from one country to another. It is difficult to deal in any sound way with the complex question of national character. However, it does not seem unfair to say that in Poland and Hungary the national character has produced a very widespread ferment, often addressed at the most fundamental faults of the Communist system. In Czechoslovakia, the "activists" have been appreciably more cautious in their complaints, while in the southern satellites only isolated individuals have spoken up. Discontent in East Germany has been expressed chiefly through the continuing exodus.

86. The attitude of the people toward their régime is, of course, also affected by "national character" and history. It has been suggested that apathy, not active resistance, has been the principal force compelling the régimes to seek an improved relationship with their working classes. Yet this apathy is less effective when, as in Rumania and Bulgaria, it is the attitude the people have always had toward each of the succession of unpopular rulers which history has foisted on them. The development of this passive resistance will have been a greater cause for concern in Poland where even the Communist government was able, in the early post-war years, to harness considerable popular enthusiasm to its reconstruction and development projects, particularly among the youth. The Poznan riots must have been particularly frightening to the régime, not

---

[229] Edward Ochab was a member of the PZPR Politburo beginning in 1954. After Bierut's death he became first secretary of the PZPR in March 1956 but was replaced by Gomulka in October of the same year.

[230] Anton Tanev Yugov replaced Chervenkov as Bulgaria's prime minister from 1956–1962.

because their hegemony was threatened but because the riots made clear just how bad the relationship between the Party and the masses has become.[231]

87. One factor cuts across the attitude of all three national groups, the leaders, the intellectuals and the people: the factor of nationalism. Its action is, however, not a uniform one. In Poland and East Germany the historic hostility toward the Russians must be one of the most serious problems faced by the régimes. The thaw in Poland has even brought a surprising amount of it out into the open. In Czechoslovakia and Bulgaria, nationalism plays a rather different role, being historically directed against other neighbours. In fact the Soviets have even benefited to some degree from the old pan-slavist sentiments. In Hungary the contemporary facts of a régime imposed from without and supported by Soviet troops, whose arrival in 1944 was not a pleasant experience, are probably of greater weight than historical attitudes. The Rumanians may be presumed to resent the loss of Bessarabia and the imposition of a government which can scarcely count any genuine Rumanians in its upper levels. This presumed resentment seems, however, to be expressed in a relatively passive attitude. The Albanians are perhaps the most interesting for their nationalism has tended to support the close relationship to Moscow. Territorially the Albanians have nothing to fear from the Russians, everything to lose to the Yugoslavs. This consideration was probably the determining factor in enabling Hoxha to purge his rival Xoxe[232] and come down on Stalin's side in the Stalin-Tito feud. Fear of being swallowed up by Tito remains today an important factor inhibiting the development of a new look in Albania.

88. It is not easy to weigh the influence of Tito separately from the other factors working toward a change in the satellites. It seems reasonable to suggest that the effects of his reconciliation are greater in the four states which border Yugoslavia than in Poland and Czechoslovakia. Still, it appears likely that the rehabilitation of Gomulka is at least indirectly linked with Tito's new relationship with Moscow. Very probably Tito's influence is felt more on leadership questions than on policy matters. He may thus be accorded a share or the responsibility for Rakosi's fall and Chevenkov's demotion; he surely deserves little credit for the increasing intellectual freedom in Poland. Tito, after all, is not a liberal democrat. Before the break he was one of the most violent "leftists" among the satellite leaders, and the "Titoists" in, other countries, Gomulka, Rajk, Slansky,[233] etc. were also extremely "hard" in their general outlook. It would thus seem an illusory hope on our part to suppose that Tito, now more or less back in the Communist Camp, is destined to lead the other satellites out of their ideological bondage and away from the "dictatorship of the proletariat" toward a truly democratic way of life. One may also doubt whether Yugoslavia will play any important part in bringing about in the Satellites greater political independence from Moscow. It may, nevertheless, be significant that Poland is the only satellite with which Tito has so far been willing to establish party-to-party relations. And the NATO countries should in any case consider carefully if in any way Yugoslav influence within the Bloc might be made to further Western interests.[234]

SUMMARY

89. The thaw in the satellites has been seen as a process with its origin in the passive resistance of the people to further sacrifices on behalf of the projects of their unpopular régimes. The Soviet response, generalised in all the satellites in greater or lesser degree, has been to loosen

---

[231] See footnote 202 above.

[232] Koci Xoxe was minister of interior between 1946 and 1949, and leader of the Albanian Communist Party's Cadre Department. In 1949, he was arrested for treason and executed.

[233] Rudolf Slánsky was first secretary of the Czechoslovak Communist Party between 1945–1951. He was arrested and executed following a show trial in 1952.

[234] Several participants at the October 24 session of the NATO Council thought that the report did not adequately emphasize the effects of Titoism as an ideology in Eastern Europe. (NATO Archives, Brussels, CR(56)56).

the screws a few notches, especially those binding the intellectuals into Stalinist forms. This Soviet policy has, of course, fitted into the world-wide strategy of the détente. The satellite leaders, under attack from below as each concession generated fresh demands, have uniformly resisted the thaw. In some countries they have had considerable success, in others they have had to retreat to new lines of defence.

90. The picture today, as compared with that of three years ago, presents a relatively considerable movement in social, intellectual and even political factors in at least some of the satellites. Some powerful currents are at work, but it would be an over-optimistic and ultimately a "Marxist" interpretation, to suggest that the movement has become irresistible and that a radical transformation of the satellite societies has become inevitable in the near future. The régimes could still reverse it if they are willing to pay the price: rigorous repression on the old Stalinist lines.

91. The danger to the West is the tendency to substitute hope for reason and to assume that the "thaw" has gone considerably further than it has in fact. The interest of the West presumably lies in the future development of the "thaw": in any event the thaw cannot be other than welcomed by the West, which its traditions of freedom.

92. For the West, then, the question must be: what can we do to accelerate the thaw? Certainly we should not exaggerate our resources in this field. Fundamentally, the immediate future of Poland must be decided in Warsaw and Moscow and the West can play only a marginal role. Yet it can have some influence.

93. With the leaders of the Soviet bloc in Moscow and in the satellites the West has certain contacts: diplomatically, sometimes through visits of top personalities, and, of course, via the policy statements of Western leaders on developments within the bloc. The Communist leaders now feel a strong desire (coldly calculated but still real) for a more friendly attitude on the part of the West. Clearly, this fact can be a weapon if it is discriminatingly used. Either rigid hostility or fatuous amiability would deprive the West and the satellite peoples of whatever concessions can be extracted by this method.

94. The West also has certain contacts with the intellectuals and the common people of the satellites: exchanges of visits, radio broadcasts the increasing circulation of Western publications within the bloc. These channels can be used to encourage the activists in their struggle with their own leaders. (They can, for example, spread word of developments in the leading satellites to the intellectuals in those countries where the thaw is slow in developing.) The West must also use these channels to assure the captive peoples of its moral support in their efforts to free themselves. As we are not prepared to use force to liberate them, we should not encourage futile rebellions on their part. Rather, as the best guide for the future, we should point to the concessions already extracted from the régimes by the people through their patient, unspectacular withholding of support.

QUESTIONS

95. The foregoing description of the thaw in the satellites suggest certain questions to which the Council might address itself.

(1) Does your government agree or does it differ substantially with the analysis of events put forward in this paper?

(2) What has been the broad line of development of the recent and current policy of your government vis-à-vis the Satellites, particularly in respect of:

    (a) cultural contacts and information effort;
    (b) exchange of visits by government officials and political leaders;
    (c) relations in the economic and trade field;
    (d) renewal of normalisation of diplomatic relations.

(3) Are there, in the view of your government, any aspects of Western policy in relation to the Satellites which could fruitfully be examined further in the NATO forum with a view to co-ordinating Western policy and activities in the Satellites?

[Source: NATO Archives, Brussels, Document C-M(56)110. Obtained by Gusztáv Kecskés.]

DOCUMENT NO. 21: Record of Conversation between Yurii Andropov and Ernő Gerő, October 12, 1956

Following talks with HWP leader Gerő, Soviet Ambassador Andropov reported to Moscow on the worsening situation in Hungary: unrest was spreading quickly from intellectuals to workers and peasants, anti-Soviet feelings were intensifying, and opposition elements were gaining influence with the army and state security forces. Gerő did not see things as starkly as Andropov, reflecting a characteristic divergence of views between Hungarian leaders and their Soviet patrons at this stage. In the document, Andropov acknowledges Gerő's loyalty to Moscow, as indicated by his intention to report on talks with other foreign leaders (the Chinese and Yugoslavs), but depicts him as "rather nervous and uncertain." He warns that if this general pattern by "our friends" continues, Imre Nagy will "most likely" take over leadership of the party and country.

STRICTLY CONFIDENTIAL
HIGH PRIORITY
SPECIAL IMPORTANCE

I had a meeting with Comrade Gerő, who informed me about his negotiations with leaders of the CPSU, and with comrades Tito and Ranković in the Crimea.[235] Commenting on his consultation with the Yugoslav comrades, comrade Gerő expressed his belief that he "succeeded in coming to an agreement with the Yugoslavs." At the same time, he noted that in the course of negotiations comrade Tito strongly stressed the mutual economic interests of Hungary and Yugoslavia, adding that the two countries are "able to make considerable achievements together." Comrade Gerő believes that these remarks refer to an old plan of comrade Tito for unifying the Balkan countries. Regarding his negotiations with comrades Mikoyan and Suslov, comrade Gerő remarked that it was most useful, although upon returning to Hungary he realized that the situation was much more complicated and critical than he had thought while in the Soviet Union. Consequently, the measures that the Hungarian delegation agreed on with CPSU leaders in Moscow are "not sufficient any longer." Comrade Gerő said that the political situation has worsened considerably during the one-and-a-half months while he was in the Soviet Union, and now it is not only the party but the whole country which is in a "serious situation." The principal source of danger is that three or four months ago only the intellectuals gave voice to their discontent, whereas now the mood of dissatisfaction is spreading among the workers as well, not to mention peasants, who are apparently on the verge of a rebellion, demanding the abolition of agricultural cooperatives. Economic hardships are making things even worse. Crops have significantly fallen behind last year's results. Coal, oil and raw material shortages have caused companies to suffer serious work disruptions. Some six hundred scheduled runs of the national rail service were canceled, mostly passenger trains. All this seriously mars the workers' interests, and has a negative effect on their attitude.

Reactionary forces have come forward again, taking advantage of the economic and—above all—political hardships, virtually joining forces with the opposition within the party. Since the burial of Rajk's mortal remains,[236] the opposition has become especially arrogant. They openly demand the Imre Nagy's return to the Political Committee, the indictment of Rákosi and Farkas, as well as the ousting of several comrades from the party. Some are called upon to resign because they used to be members of the old Political Committee and they are morally account-

---

[235] From the end of August until October 7, Gerő was on vacation in the Soviet Union. He met Tito and Ranković in the presence of Khrushchev on September 30.

[236] The reburial of Rajk and his associates took place on October 6, 1956, at an official ceremony attended by 200,000 people. (See the essay to this section.)

able for unfounded repression (Gerő, [István] Kovács and Apró); while others from among the young party leaders [are called upon to resign] because of their lack of experience and respect (Szalai, Mekis, Bata, Egri and others). Palpable pro-Yugoslav emotions are running high in the party, with a clear determination to embrace "the Yugoslav experiences of building socialism," as they say. Such convictions were present even before in the party, but now they have strengthened to the extent that it poses a potential danger.

Comrade Gerő believes that the burial of Rajk's mortal remains caused serious harm to the party leadership, whose esteem had been rather tarnished anyway.

A situation has evolved in which the Political Committee has no real say in the actual solution of certain problems. The opposition, and especially Imre Nagy, are taking advantage of this. The Political Committee had a discussion with Imre Nagy on October 9. According to comrade Gerő, Imre Nagy behaved in an unconcerned manner. He was not willing to add a paragraph to his letter in which he would reject his association with the opposition, although he promised that he would "think about how to improve" the letter. The Political Committee has not decided yet about Nagy's reinstatement into the Hungarian Workers' Party. Nevertheless, they told Nagy that the Political Committee was considering this possibility.[237] As to admitting mistakes, comrade Gerő said that Nagy flatly refused to do so, adding that, so far, life showed that he was right on every single issue. Similarly, Nagy mentioned that he had once been reprimanded in Moscow because he demanded the total rehabilitation of Rajk and other comrades in a letter of October 20, 1954. What has been done now in Hungary is exactly what he demanded in 1954. Comrade Gerő said that the problem of Imre Nagy remains a tough issue for the Hungarian Workers' Party, as Nagy obviously wants to return to the party with his own political program. It must be expected that Nagy will probably have to be reinstated in the party leadership soon, in the Central Committee, possibly in the Political Committee as well, since there is considerable pressure in this direction. Once in the Political Committee again, Nagy will possibly "take the upper hand." His policy of "cutting back for a short period" on industrial development, his pseudo democracy, and attitude against cooperatives are rather popular in the party, because they mark the line of least resistance and require little effort. Comrade Gerő expressed his firm conviction that the forces who want to detach Hungary from the Soviet Union and the whole socialist camp will use Nagy for their own purposes, even though Nagy is not our enemy but holds "very dangerous views." Should Nagy be granted the possibility to realize his policy—which is a potential danger right now—then Hungary will certainly undergo changes in the near future, which will distance the social and economic system of the country from the socialist ideal even further than Yugoslavia's. Hostile forces and opportunists are trying to push Hungary in a direction where it becomes a kind of intermediary state (in between socialism and capitalism), and so the political program of Nagy is completely suitable for their purposes.

Comrade Gerő touched upon the issue of Hungarian-Soviet relations. He mentioned that the question came up in the course of the negotiations between Hungarian delegates and comrades Mikoyan and Suslov, and that they finally agreed they would intensify the exchange of various delegations. However, comrade Gerő added that these measures will hardly improve the state of affairs. Comrade Gerő thinks that the estrangement of Hungary and the Soviet Union has gone too far, and anti-Soviet attitudes have become palpably stronger [in the country]. Recently, comrade Kovács delivered a speech at a rally of workers and employees of the Ganz factory. He noticed that workers cheerfully expressed their sympathy when he talked about the successes that China had achieved, yet they became quite reticent when it came to talking about the Soviet Union. Their mood did not change a bit, even when Kovács brought up the issue of Soviet aid to Hungary.

Comrade Gerő said that reportedly the same public mood is palpable in Poland as well.

Comrade Gáspár,[238] president of the National Council of Trade Unions, has recently returned from Sofia, Bulgaria. He said he was truly startled by the cold reception that comrade Grishin,

---

[237] Eventually, Nagy was readmitted to the HWP on October 13, 1956.

[238] Sándor Gáspár was secretary general of SZOT from 1956–1959, a member of the HWP PC between October 23–28, 1956, and of the HSWP PCC beginning in November 1956.

president of the All-Union Council of Trade Unions received at the 8th session of the World Association of Trade Unions. This is most disquieting news, which needs further analysis, said comrade Gerő. Taking a closer look at the issues that currently induce anti-Soviet propaganda in Hungary, the following problems seem to be on the agenda:

a. Protests against the presence of Soviet troops in Hungary;
b. Protests against the selling of [former] German properties as a form of Hungarian payment to the Soviet Union;
c. Protests against the alleged short selling of Hungarian uranium to the Soviet Union (even though the country received a Soviet loan before shipping [the raw materials], added comrade Gerő);
d. Complaints that Hungary is involved in unfavorable trade relations with the Soviet Union.

Although these opinions are quite sharp on their own, said comrade Gerő, it does not sufficiently explain why a segment of Hungarian workers became alienated from the Soviet Union, even within the party membership. Comrade Gerő said that he had been thinking about it lately and he came to the conclusion that the explanation must be found in the following: hostile forces in Hungary exploit the fact that Stalin's personality cult, so to speak, hindered democratic development of both the party and the state in the Soviet Union for many years. At the same time, other countries—where allegedly there was no personality cult (like China and Yugoslavia)—went much further in the desired direction, so that we now have to align with them rather than with the Soviet Union. Now that the personality cult has been disclosed in the Soviet Union, it is a common opinion in Hungary that no fundamental "democratic" changes were made in the Soviet Union after the Twentieth Congress of the CPSU, that criticism of leading institutions is still censored in the Soviet press, and CPSU CC plenary sessions are not summoned regularly, and so on. Comrade Gerő believes that roughly these opinions are the main reason why the general attitude towards the Soviet Union has changed lately in Hungary. He noted that these are only attempts at giving a sufficient answer and unfortunately they in Hungary "have not yet learned" to fight back such views.

In order to illustrate what he mentioned above, comrade Gerő said that a Hungarian delegation in Beijing[239] conducted a three hour-long negotiation with Zhou Enlai. In the course of negotiations, Zhou Enlai made a remark that "roughly suggested" that the Chinese leadership disagrees with the way Stalin's personality cult was raised at the Twentieth Congress of the CPSU.

Zhou Enlai stated that Chinese communists had disagreed with Stalin on certain issues even in his lifetime. For example, they think that the leftist deviation of Wang Ming can be placed upon Stalin's influence.[240] The Chinese leadership disagreed with Stalin concerning the Chinese people's armed action for political power. Zhou Enlai said that after the Great patriotic War Stalin advised China not to use armed forces, referring to the fact that China, "according to agreements, is in the American sphere of interest."

The Chinese communists did not listen to Stalin on this question and they turned out to be right.

Despite all this, added Zhou Enlai, the Chinese communists did not want to openly criticize Stalin because they wanted to preserve respect for the Soviet Union. He added that the Twentieth Congress should have inquired into Stalin's mistakes with a clear statement that leaves no doubt: his merits "outweighed his mistakes."

According to comrade Gerő, comrade Zhou Enlai also said that the Twentieth Congress made a mistake when it failed to clarify the responsibility of other Soviet leaders. Until this

---

[239] The Hungarian party delegation headed by János Kádár participated in the 8th Congress of the CCP from September 15–27, 1956.

[240] Wang Ming was a CCP leader in the 1930s. As Mao Zedong's rival, Wang Ming advocated a more Moscow-oriented policy line.

question is clarified, there will be difficulties to account with, he added. Comrade Gerő said that he could not guarantee the exactitude of his account, as he only interpreted the words of Kádár second-hand.

I asked comrade Gerő whether he informed comrades Mikoyan and Suslov about these facts. He said that he could not inform them, as it was agreed that comrade Kádár would do it in the course of negotiations. Nonetheless, Kádár did not do it, saying that "there was no opportunity for that." Eventually they agreed that they would inform the CPSU leadership through the Soviet ambassador to Budapest.

Comrade Gerő said that he assumes that the Chinese comrades have in all probability informed the CPSU CC of their opinion. However, he wanted to make sure that the CPSU CC is familiar with the fact that the Chinese comrades had raised these issues in the course of their negotiations with the Hungarian delegation.

At the end of our discussion, comrade Gerő returned to the political situation in Hungary. He was seemingly worried and downhearted by the problem. He said that he wanted to avoid being accused of panic-mongering, but once again he feels obliged to express his view that the situation in Hungary is "exceptionally serious and is worsening further." Consequently, comrade Gerő asked for the following questions to be reconsidered:

1. He said that comrade Khrushchev provisionally agreed in a personal meeting that he would visit Hungary around November 20. Taking into account the complexity of the situation, comrade Gerő asked about possibly hastening the visit of comrade Khrushchev to Budapest.

2. Comrades Mikoyan and Suslov promised him in the course of their meeting that someone from the CPSU leadership would talk to Rákosi and convince him to stay in the Soviet Union as long as possible. Comrade Gerő asked about expediting this discussion because comrade Rákosi keeps making phone calls to comrades Hegedüs and Ács, saying that he wants to return to Hungary and resume work, and that his wife has already returned to Hungary. Comrade Gerő thinks it advisable that a short news item be published in the Hungarian press, saying that comrade Rákosi is staying in the Soviet Union for prolonged medical treatment. Comrade Gerő is asking the CPSU leadership to give their consent.

3. Comrade Gerő expressed his wish that the Economic Relations Department of the Council of Mutual Economic Assistance should examine the development of the Hungarian economy, with special emphasis on the most essential economic aid.

Listening to comrade Gerő, I had the impression that he is rather nervous and uncertain. I asked him how he and other Political Committee members wish to tackle the said difficulties; comrade Gerő said that neither he nor other comrades have any idea about the way out of the present situation. It must be noted that most Political Committee members are of the opinion that the political situation is becoming aggravated once again. We think that the reason behind the aggravation, which has just become conspicuous, is that the Hungarian comrades—even before comrade Gerő went on vacation—failed to exploit the resolutions that the HWP CC plenary session made in July or the favorable situation that ensued after the plenum for strengthening their position.

Uncertainty in the Political Committee and a series of concessions against principle, which were made without achieving any political advantage, seriously shook the Hungarian leadership's position. The burial of Rajk's mortal remains has contributed to this. We think that comrade Gerő's opinion regarding the dangerously spreading discontent and anti-Soviet attitude among the working class is not quite correct. It would be more precise to say that agitation by the reactionary part of the intelligentsia has disoriented workers to a considerable extent, resulting in political passivity, while leaders of the HWP are too inert to explain and defend their own policy, let alone fight to strengthen the party's influence among workers.

Regarding comrade Gerő's statement about Hungary's economic hardships, I find it necessary to note that these difficulties can blamed to a great extent on the fact that our [Hungarian] friends have lately given up keeping an eye on the national economy. Several questions concerning industrial control are pending, most of them are not being taken care of at all. Sowing

181

the winter corn is especially problematic. By September 30 only 6 percent of grain crops had been sown, compared to 21 percent in the previous year. Private farms have sown ten times less wheat than last year. It is worth noting that while lately the Hungarian comrades are constantly receiving advice from the CPSU leadership on various issues, and even though they agree with these suggestions, afterwards they are too feeble when it comes to enforcing their execution. This is especially relevant regarding measures that need to be taken to strengthen political power in the country.

Hostile and opposition elements use every possible means to revile party leaders, and our friends either keep silent or try to convince their adversaries; however, their arguments always end with a retreat. Comrade Ishchenko, our chief advisor at the Ministry of Interior, informed me that an unhealthy attitude is also increasingly manifest among staff members of state security institutions. We have received several indications about leading military functionaries speaking against the party leadership. If our friends continue a policy of avoiding confrontation with the opposition, clearly it is most likely that Imre Nagy will soon become the leader of the party and the country.

ANDROPOV
OCTOBER 12, 1956

[Source: APRF, F. 3. Op. 64. D. 484. Ll. 64–75. Published in Sovietskii Soyuz i vengerskii krizis, 1956 goda: Dokumenty, *edited and compiled by E. D. Orekhova, Vyacheslav T. Sereda and Aleksandr. S. Stykhalin (Moscow: ROSSPEN, 1998), 300–305. Translated by Csaba Farkas.]*

DOCUMENT NO. 22: Memorandum from the British Foreign Office to the British NATO Delegation, October 16, 1956

The Foreign Office memorandum below conveys the official British reaction to the NATO International Secretariat's proposal, completed on September 24 (Document No. 20), concerning Western policy toward the satellite states. Prepared as guidance for the British representative at the upcoming NATO Council meeting on October 24, the memo declares that it is "in our interest to foster the thaw by whatever means are available to us." However, as for the concrete steps to be taken, only a very cautious line emerges from the document—that of developing cultural, trade, and sport relations with Eastern Europe at a non-governmental level.

The memorandum contains another interesting reference to the effect that "the CPSU will seek a new theoretical basis for the relations between itself and the Satellite parties, which would not require all power to inhere in Moscow".

The fact that the British appeared totally unprepared for the events that would occur in Budapest a week later is illustrated by the statement of the (otherwise well-informed) Foreign Office official that "the popular pressure which is so remarkable a feature of the Polish scene seems almost non-existent" in Hungary.

N. 1012/13 OUTFILE
CONFIDENTIAL

FOREIGN OFFICE, S.W.1.
OCTOBER 16, 1956[241]

We have read the Working Group's paper on the Satellites with great interest; if I may say so, it is an admirable production. The answers to the questions, for which you asked in your letter 22807/105 to Given, are as follows.

2. We agree generally with the analysis of events put forward in the paper; some points on which we think the emphasis might have been different are set out in the annex to this letter.[242] Briefly, we are inclined to the view that the thaw arose from two sets of causes: the failure of the Stalinist repression to get results from Satellite workers, and internal causes in the Soviet Union, at the nature of which it is unnecessary for this purpose to guess. The first led to attempts, in Poland at least, to enlist the cooperation of the workers by encouraging them to criticize management (not policy); this could only be done by causing journalists to write articles for the purpose. As a result, there was a good deal of vaguely critical talk in intellectual circles in Poland long before criticism became orthodox, for the writers refused to be restricted to the criticism they were told to produce. The second caused the destalinization campaign; we suspect that the Soviet leaders did not give much thought to its possible consequences in the Satellites.

3. The present position in Poland appears to be that a considerable number of intellectuals, both inside and outside the Party, are trying to get away from Party dictatorship and the totally planned economy; they are encouraged by popular discontent with material conditions and by national and religious feelings among the people. We doubt if these intellectuals have any very clear idea of where they want to go, although the economic ideas expressed by Professor Lange[243] are quite specific and shock the more *dirigiste* members of a group of British economists who met him recently. It would be a mistake to think that even if the thaw in Poland became complete there would necessarily be a return to parliamentary democracy and free enter-

---

[241] In the bottom margin of the original, the letter is addressed to: D. H. Greenhill, Esq., U.K. Delegation to NATO, Paris.

[242] Not reprinted here.

[243] Oskar Lange, internationally respected economist and member of the PZPR CC since 1948, belonged to the more "liberal" wing of the Polish party leadership.

prise; still less would there be much possibility of a Poland independent of Russia in international affairs.

4. Nevertheless, the Russians cannot take any risks as long as they have troops in Germany. They can estimate, probably better than we can, the temper of the Poles, and realize that if they let things go too far they may not be able to maintain their position (i.e. control of the Polish economy and secure communications with their troops in Germany) without the kind of naked repression which they have themselves denounced. They are therefore trying to put the brakes on before it is too late—hence Bulganin's speech in Warsaw during the Polish National Day celebrations, and more recent directives to the Satellite parties to return to the paths of orthodoxy. The Americans have suggested that the CPSU will seek a new theoretical basis for the relations between itself and the Satellite parties, which would not require all power to inhere in Moscow; it is of course a common Marxist trick to try to change the premises when they lead to a dilemma, but we feel sure that any new theory will be a means of hiding the continued residence of power in Moscow. We are convinced that, at least for the next few years, the Russians will hang on to their empire and not abandon the influence which it gives them in Europe, unless their circumstances change in some radical fashion, a remote possibility which is outside the scope of this discussion.

5. The foregoing applies only to Poland; of the other Satellites, only Hungary has made any real progress, but there the popular pressure which is so remarkable a feature of the Polish scene seems almost non-existent. The Czechoslovaks are accustomed to come to terms with their oppressors, while the southern Satellites are little better than colonies.

6. Faced with those developments, we have been gradually moving towards the conclusion that we ought to adapt a more flexible and empirical attitude towards the satellites, in order not to lose any possible advantages. While it would be futile to hope in the next few years for any revival of national independence in Eastern Europe, our position will be improved relatively to that of the USSR by any decrease of the latter's control of the Satellites; it is therefore in our interest to foster the thaw by whatever means are available to us. Moreover, we are the object of a large-scale cultural and economic offensive, which we cannot simply ignore without conceding many advantages to the other side. The answers to the second question in the Working Party's paper are as follows.

7. As regards cultural contacts, we are not prepared to spend money on manifestations of Satellite culture, but if reputable private persons wish to arrange visits in either direction by bodies such as orchestras, theatrical or ballet companies, or to arrange exhibitions, we shall treat them as if the other country concerned were not communist; in other words, it must be a commercial venture. We were prepared to spend money on Anglo-Soviet cultural exchanges because we hoped to gain on balance, and because there was real public demand. Neither of these considerations applies to the Satellites, and we hope that most of the rather dreary manifestations of Satellite culture which have been inflicted on us lately will become unprofitable once the novelty has worn off. When "friendship societies" are concerned in these ventures, we do not help them and we avoid anything which would indicate official countenance, but we feel we must not appear to set up our own iron curtain; we therefore do not actively oppose the efforts of these societies, which are now pretty well discredited in this country.

8. Our information effort is concentrated on the countries of Asia and Africa, where we believe the communist menace to be most immediate. We have no resources to spare for information work in the Satellites, although we keep on with a few activities which were established before the reorientation of our effort, such as the information office in Budapest. The British Council office in Warsaw also falls into this category. We also supply technical periodicals to a small number of specialists in various iron curtain countries.

9. We are not really in favor of "exchanges" in any field, but prefer visits to take place as the need arises. For example, veterinary experts have gone to Hungary and Romania at H.M.G.'s expense to report on animal diseases, so that the competent authorities here can decide on the restrictions to be placed on imports of e.g. poultry. Satellite officials visit the U.K. in consider-

able numbers, and receive facilities from commercial firms which hope to get contracts; but no official facilities are extended unless we are satisfied that we shall serve British interests by so doing. We approach the subject of ministerial visits with the greatest reserve; British Ministers would go to the Satellites only if it were clear on a realistic assessment that the West would gain.

10. The trade position is not such that we can afford to neglect any opportunities to export, subject to the requirements of the strategic controls. The Export Credits Guarantee Department deals with the Satellites on a strictly commercial basis, and we make no special payment arrangements. We do, however, refuse to issue import licenses for "less essentials" exported by Satellites which have refused to come to terms with us about the repayment of their debts and on compensation for nationalization and war damage; the last applies only to the ex-enemy Satellites, which have obligations under the Peace Treaties.

11. Diplomatic relations are correct with all the Satellites except Albania and East Germany. Relations with the former were broken off as a result of the Corfu Channel incident, when Albania refused to pay compensation awarded by the International Court in respect of the mining of a British destroyer. We have at present no intention of resuming relations with either.

12. We think that it will be useful for NATO members to keep in touch with each other through the Organization, so that they keep generally instep as regards their relations with the Satellites. In particular, it my be useful, when resources are so limited, to divide the effort among NATO members to ensure that there is the minimum of undesirable duplication, and that members' own interests are best served. It will be clear from the whole tenor of this letter that we should prefer to concentrate on Poland, where we already have a British Council office, and with which we already have closer trade links than with the others.

13. This letter has been drafted with regard only to the non-German Satellites. Special considerations affecting Eastern Germany are set out in the second annex.[244]

14. I hope this will give you something to argue from in future discussions. We are to meet an American group led by Frank Wisner later this month; we shall go into that debate on the lines of this letter, and if we are persuaded to change our minds about any of it, I will write again. After the American meetings we may also have consultations with the French before the subject comes up in NATO.

(T. BRIMELOW)[245]

[Source: PRO.FO.311.122063.]

---

[244] Not reprinted here.

[245] Thomas Brimelow was head of the Northern Department of the Foreign Office which dealt with Hungarian affairs, among other things.

DOCUMENT NO. 23: Working Notes from the Session of the CPSU CC Presidium, October 20, 1956

The Hungarian revolt was not the only crisis facing the Soviet leadership in October 1956. Just days before the uprising began in Budapest, the Polish United Workers' Party (PZPR) seemed on the verge of making fundamental political changes in the country. On October 19, Khrushchev personally led a delegation on a surprise visit to Warsaw to try to prevent both the election of former internal opposition figure Władysław Gomułka as first secretary of the party and the ouster of Soviet Marshal Konstanty Rokossowski[246] from the Politburo. Negotiations with Polish party leaders—which began at the airport as Soviet tank columns marched towards the capital—finally ended with the Soviet delegation's return to Moscow after accepting Gomułka's assurances that Poland would not turn its back on the Warsaw Pact or demand the withdrawal of Soviet troops.[247]

When reconstructing Moscow's decision-making process in the Polish and Hungarian crises, the handwritten notes of Vladimir Malin, head of the CPSU CC General Department, are an essential source of information. Several of these documents, which were first publicly disclosed in 1995, are reproduced in this volume. They do not give a verbatim account of the Presidium's discussions, they are notes in outline form. But in virtually every case, they are the only contemporaneous record available of the Kremlin's highest-level debates.

Notes of this Presidium session on October 20 deal mostly with Poland and only briefly with Hungary. They add several important details to our knowledge of the Polish crisis. We learn that on returning to Moscow, the Kremlin delegation immediately reported on their mission to the rest of the CPSU leadership, which then came to a stark conclusion: "There is only one way out—put an end to what is [taking place] in Poland." Plans were made to carry out another military action, or at least to exert political pressure under cover of a military exercise. However, the decision to go ahead depended on the fate of Marshal Rokossowski: "If Rokossowski is kept, we won't have to press things for a while." Finally the campaign was called off, even though the PZPR Central Committee ultimately acted in ways that were detrimental to Moscow.

Participants: Bulganin, Kaganovich, Malenkov, Mikoyan, Molotov, Pervukhin, Saburov, Suslov, Khrushchev, Brezhnev, Zhukov, Shepilov, Furtseva,[248] Pospelov,[249] Serov.

I. Briefing from the CPSU Delegation about the Trip to Warsaw.
(Khrushchev, Mikoyan, Molotov, Kaganovich, Konev, Zhukov)

1. There is only one way out—put an end to what is in Poland.
If Rokossowski is kept, we won't have to press things for a while.
Maneuvers.
Prepare a document.
Form a committee.
2. The ambassador, Cde. Ponomarenko,[250] was grossly mistaken in his assessment of Ochab

---

[246] Konstanty Rokossowski was a Soviet marshal of Polish origin who became, despite his Soviet citizenship, Polish defense minister and member of the PZPR Politburo from 1949–1956. Relieved from his post on October 20, 1956, he returned in November to the Soviet Union where he served as deputy defense minister until 1962.

[247] For a discussion of recent evidence on the Soviet-Polish meetings in Warsaw, see L.W. Gluchowski, "Khrushchev, Gomulka, and the 'Polish October,'" *Cold War International History Project Bulletin*, no. 5 (Spring 1995): 1, 38–49.

[248] Ekaterina A. Furtseva was a CPSU CC secretary from 1956–1960 and a candidate member of the CPSU CC Presidium from 1956–1957.

[249] Piotr N. Pospelov was a CPSU CC secretary from 1953–1960.

[250] Panteleimon K. Ponomarenko was ambassador to Poland from 1955–1957 and a candidate member of the CPSU CC Presidium from 1953–1956.

and Gomułka.

3. We should invite to Moscow representatives from the Communist parties of Czechoslovakia, Hungary, Romania, the GDR, and Bulgaria. Perhaps we should send CC officials to China for informational purposes.

4. Send information. Take notice of information. Think through the questions that have been raised.

II. On Hungary.

We need to think it over, perhaps send Cde. Mikoyan.
Cdes. Mikoyan and Zhukov must consider recalling soldiers to their units.

Cde. Mikoyan is to draft information for the fraternal parties.

Pull out the KGB advisers

[Source: Tsentr khraneniia sovremennoi dokumentatsii (TsKhSD), F. 3, Op. 12, D. 1005, Ll. 49–50, compiled by V. N. Malin. Originally published in the Cold War International History Project Bulletin *no. 8–9 (Winter 1996/1997): 388. Translated by Mark Kramer.]*

DOCUMENT NO. 24: The "Sixteen Points" Prepared by Hungarian Students, October 22–23, 1956

On October 16, the student organization MEFESZ was formed in the city of Szeged with a ground-breaking program that included a series of openly political demands. By forming an organization independent of the party system, disseminating its program widely, and promising strikes and demonstrations, the student movement went significantly further than even the party's intellectual opposition, which had initiated the country's revolutionary ferment. Spreading throughout the country in a matter of days, the student movement managed to produce a fundamental change in Hungarian political life.

The student meeting held on October 22 at the Budapest Technical University can be seen as one of the immediate precursors to the revolution. An analysis of parts of the famous "Sixteen Points," which were formulated before several thousand students, shows how their demands became increasingly radical. The more pragmatic aims that characterized the reform communist opposition (such as the appointment of Imre Nagy as Prime Minister, the convocation of a party congress, and the revision of the compulsory delivery and norm system) were supplemented by broader democratic and nationalist demands (including a multi-party system, free elections, civil rights, economic independence, and a return to traditional national holidays and symbols). Although the withdrawal of Soviet troops later headed the list as the precondition for all of these demands, this change was made only on October 23. In the version of the students' list formulated on October 22, this demand appeared only fourth on the list. It was typical of the spontaneous nature of events that the "Points" appeared in several different versions (containing 10, 14, or 16 points), according to when it was disseminated or how it was remembered. The version below, for example, was presented to a Budapest construction company; it was chosen for this collection because it reflects the most complete list of demands that were considered as of October 23, and follows the order of priorities that was eventually accepted across the country.

Adding to the document's historical significance is the fact that the official Hungarian Radio's refusal to broadcast the points—because of their radicalism—led to the idea of organizing the critical demonstration on October 23.

Copy and Distribute among Hungarian Workers!

The main political, economic and ideological points of the declaration made at the student assembly of the MEFESZ at the Building Industry Technical University:

1) We demand the immediate withdrawal of all Soviet troops from Hungary, in accordance with the declarations of the peace treaty.

2) We demand the election of new low-, mid-level, and central leaders of the Hungarian Workers' Party, by a secret ballot that moves from bottom to top. In the shortest time possible, the elected representatives should convoke a Party Congress and elect a new central commitee.

3) The government needs to be reshuffled under the leadership of comrade Imre Nagy. All the guilty leaders of the Stalinist Rákosi-era must be dismissed immediately.

4) We demand that the criminal case against Mihály Farkas and his accomplices be tried in open court. Mátyás Rákosi, who is primarily responsible for all the crimes of the recent past and for Hungary's deterioration must be returned home from abroad and tried by the people's tribunal.

5) We demand general, impartial, and secret elections in Hungary with the participation of several parties, with the purpose of electing a new National Assembly. We demand that workers be granted the right to strike.

6) We demand the reconsideration and revision of Hungarian-Soviet and Hungarian-Yugoslav political, economic, and cultural relations on the basis of total political

and economic equality and the principle of noninterference in one another's internal affairs.

7) We demand that the whole Hungarian economy be reorganized with the participation of our experts. The entire planned economy system should be re-examined, with an eye on local conditions and the essential interests of the Hungarian people.

8) Hungary's foreign trade contracts should be published, and the actual figures of reparations, which we will never be able to pay, should be revealed. We demand open and straightforward information concerning Hungary's uranium ore resources, their exploitation, and the Russian concessions. We demand that Hungary be able to trade uranium ore freely in exchange for hard currency at world market prices.

9) We demand the total revision of industrial norms and the immediate and fundamental settlement of the wage demands of workers and intellectuals. We demand that subsistence wages be set for workers.

10) We demand that the system of compulsory delivery be fundamentally revised, and that the collected produce be used rationally. We demand that individual farmers be treated and supported equally [with cooperatives].

11) We demand that all political and economic legal cases be retried in an independent court, and that the innocent be released and rehabilitated. We demand that prisoners of war and civilians deported to the Soviet Union—including those sentenced outside Hungary—be immediately transferred back to Hungary.

12) We demand freedom of opinion, freedom of speech, a free press and radio, and a new daily paper with significant circulation for MEFESZ. We demand that personal files [káderanyag] be opened to the public and eventually destroyed.

13) We demand that the statue of Stalin—the symbol of Stalinist despotism and political oppression—be immediately removed and replaced with a monument commemorating the heroes and martyrs of the 1848–49 war of independence.

14) We wish to restore the old Hungarian Kossuth coat-of-arms, thus replacing the existing one, which is alien to the Hungarian people. We demand new uniforms for the Hungarian army that are worthy of our national traditions. We demand that March 15 and October 6 be declared national and public holidays.

15) The students of Budapest Technical University unanimously declare their solidarity with the workers and students in Warsaw and the whole of Poland, in connection with their movement for national independence.

16) The students of the Building Industry Technical University are determined to immediately set up local organizations of MEFESZ, and they have decided to convoke a Youth Parliament in Budapest on October 28 (Saturday), where the whole of Hungarian youth will be represented by delegations. Tomorrow, the 23rd of this month, at 2:30 p.m., students of the Technical University and other institutes of higher education will gather in front of the Technical University, then march to Pálffy square (now Bem square), to express their solidarity with the Polish freedom movement by laying wreathes at the statue to Bem. Factory workers are free to join the march.

This evening, both Hungarian Radio and the Hungarian press refused to publish the above declaration *verbatim*, primarily because of the first point. We printed the declaration in the periodical *Engineer of the Future*, copied it by means of a typewriter and a stencil duplicator, and are now distributing it among the people of Budapest via a chain-letter campaign.

We are still determined to publish the entire document in the Hungarian press. On October 24, MEFESZ will initiate a countrywide debate concerning crucial issues faced by the Hungarian nation. We demand that Hungarian Radio provide live coverage of the assembly.

The present declaration was made at the dawn of a new Hungarian history, on October 22 in the foyer of the Building Industry Technical University, as the result of a spontaneous action by thousands of young Hungarian patriots.

The declaration was presented to the workers' assembly of the Mélyépterv construction company on October 23. The assembly welcomed the declaration with an ovation and decided to give the youth movement their full support.

[Source: Magyar Nemzeti Múzeum, Legújabb-kori Főosztály, Röpiratgyűjtemény (Hungarian National Museum, Department for Contemporary History, Leaflet Collection) Published in Izsák Lajos, József Szabó and Róbert Szabó, eds., 1956 Plakátjai és röplapjai: Október 22-november 5 *(Budapest: Zrínyi Kiadó, 1991), 18–19. Translated by Csaba Farkas.]*

PART TWO

FROM DEMONSTRATIONS TO REVOLUTION

INTRODUCTION

On the morning of October 23, 1956, *Szabad Nép* ran a lead article entitled "New Spring Parade." The title was taken from a revolutionary poem written in 1911 which referred to traditions of modernization and intellectual revolution that had been current at that time. Appearing the day after the demonstration at Budapest Technical University, the article warmly welcomed Hungary's "politicizing youth" as partners in the struggle to democratize socialism. The students, who had initiative on their side but who still lacked political influence, had suddenly gained support and protection from an important source. Alongside these encouraging remarks, the paper published a communiqué from the Writers' Union enthusiastically greeting the recent changes in Poland, although the organization still dissociated itself from the students' ground-breaking, and politically hazardous, demonstration.

The situation remained unsettled, however. Hungarian radio reported that there would be a march to show support for the developments in Poland, but there was no way to tell whether the authorities would back it or even tolerate it. The views of the intellectuals and politicians around Imre Nagy were not clear either. Nagy himself came out strongly against the students' demonstration because several of their demands went well beyond what he had in mind. He was justifiably worried that their radicalism might jeopardize the gains which had already been made, and which looked even more promising after the Polish events.[1]

That same morning, the party and government delegation led by Ernő Gerő, and including Prime Minister András Hegedüs and János Kádár, returned from Belgrade after concluding a historic reconciliation with Yugoslav President Tito. Gerő and his colleagues were astonished at the turn of events and immediately called a meeting of the HWP Political Committee.[2] After hearing Gerő's account of the Yugoslav negotiations, the group turned to Lajos Ács, the senior Political Committee member who had remained in Hungary, for a report on the domestic situation and the student demonstration set to take place later in the day. Two strongly opposing views surfaced. One was advanced by József Révai and György Marosán who warned about the threat of "counterrevolution" and urged the strongest possible reaction: canceling the demonstration and authorizing the security forces to fire on anyone who defied the ban. The interior and defense ministers were confident their forces could handle the situation. At the other extreme was Ács who disagreed that a revolt was imminent and supported the political remedy of bringing Nagy back into the government.[3]

In the end, buffeted by their own internal conflicts, the leadership voted to ban the rally but withheld authorization to use deadly force against the populace. Political Committee members

[1] On the role of Imre Nagy during the 1956 Hungarian Revolution see: Rainer, *Nagy Imre*, 2:237–336.

[2] For the most thorough study of the activities of the HWP's leadership during the revolution, see Julianna Horváth and Zoltán Ripp, eds., *Ötvenhat októbere és a hatalom: A Magyar Dolgozók Pártja vezető testületeinek dokumentumai, 1956. október 24–28* (Budapest: Napvilág Kiadó, 1997). Besides publishing all preserved minutes of the meetings of the leading party organizations held during this period (that is, the Central Committee meetings on October 25, 26 and 28; the Political Committee meetings on October 24 and 28; and the Military Committee resolutions of October 26 and 27), this volume contains a separate study written by Hungarian scholar Zoltán Ripp, which provides a detailed description of the events, including a reconstruction of the meetings for which minutes did not survive.

[3] The general history of the revolution outlined in this part is based on the following publications: György Litván, János M. Bak and Lyman H. Legters, eds., *The Hungarian Revolution of 1956: Reform, Revolt and Repression, 1953–1963* (New York: Longman, 1996); András B. Hegedűs, ed., *1956 Kézikönyve*, 3 vols. (Budapest: 1956-os Intézet, 1996); Békés, *The 1956 Hungarian Revolution*; Jenő Györkei and Miklós Horváth, eds., *Soviet Military Intervention in Hungary, 1956*, trans. Emma Roper-Evans (Budapest: Central European University Press, 1999); and Rainer, *Nagy Imre*, 2:237–336.

fanned out to key locations to implement the resolution and help maintain order, but they soon realized they could not enforce their own directives. The all-powerful party discipline of old had broken down. During the morning, the majority faction in the leadership became the target of denunciations not only by ordinary citizens but by an increasing number of party functionaries. Several party organizations protested the ban, and DISZ, eager to hold on to its lingering influence over the country's youth, decided to ignore it altogether, resolving instead to join the demonstration and try to take control of it. One critical factor in their thinking was that growing numbers of workers had begun to add their voice to the students' demands.

Meanwhile, party loyalty within the officers' academies, the institutional base of the security forces in Budapest, was also wavering as cadets, approached by their university counterparts, promised to lend their support. Furthermore, Sándor Kopácsi, the Budapest chief of police, announced that his forces would not take up arms against peaceful demonstrators. Even the reliability of the army was in doubt. This meant that the security police—the detested ÁVH—were the only armed force the authorities could completely rely on. These developments finally convinced party leaders that they did not have the power to crush the demonstration. Reluctantly they lifted the ban, then called on party organizations in Budapest to join the march in order to try to water down its impact and to control the spread of opposition demands. Defense Minister István Bata even allowed soldiers to participate as long as they were unarmed and did not appear as part of an official unit.

Elsewhere, the authorities took other steps to try to maintain order. They deployed armed reinforcements across the city, including to the Radio station, where, since the previous evening, students had been calling for their demands to be read on the air.

At 3:00 in the afternoon, the demonstration got underway. Beginning simultaneously from the Pest and Buda sections of the city (on the east and west banks of the Danube, respectively), the march grew rapidly in size as the protestors' demands and slogans became more and more radical. Workers coming off the morning shift joined in, along with other segments of the population. Onlookers from windows and sidewalks urged the marchers on. The two streams of protestors met at Bem Square, on the Danube bank opposite Parliament. This location was symbolically significant because the square was named after a Polish general who had fought with the Hungarians against the Hapsburg and Russian monarchies during the revolution and fight for independence of 1848–1849.[4] Now, Hungarians were marching in support of Poles. In Bem Square the symbol of the revolution was also born—the Hungarian tri-colored flag with the coat of arms of Rákosi's Soviet-style regime cut out of the center.

From the square, most of the crowd, now numbering several tens of thousands, marched across Margit Bridge shouting slogans that had turned blatantly political, such as, "Rákosi into the Danube—Imre Nagy into the government!" Once on the Pest side, the marchers made their way the short distance to Kossuth Square, in front of Parliament, and called out for Nagy. Meanwhile, other demonstrators gathered at the Radio station and at the huge statue of Stalin in City Park, about a mile from Parliament.

Although the situation was already tense, it still may have been possible to keep it from developing into an armed uprising. Unfortunately, the authorities acted with a destructive combination of weakness and inflexibility. Heavy reinforcements were dispatched to the Radio station, but it was a long while before the regime felt bold enough to authorize the use of force. At the same time, they were unwilling to yield an inch to the marchers' demands. Instead, they resorted to a series of petty tactics that were ultimately self-defeating. Outside the Radio station, they gave the protestors a microphone that appeared to be hooked up to transmission equipment in order to make them think their demands were going to be broadcast. At Kossuth Square, they turned off the street lights in hopes that the crowd waiting for Nagy would disperse. But the demonstrators simply lit improvised torches—mostly made from rolled-up copies of *Szabad Nép.*

---

[4] The profound influence of the events of 1848 on 1956 can be seen in the borrowing of names of revolutionary organizations and coats of arms, as well as in the rhetoric of newspapers.

These developments placed one of the keys to resolving the crisis directly in Nagy's hands. Nagy had fallen into official disgrace the year before and was still an outcast of the party, but at that moment the HWP leadership realized they needed help to mollify the growing popular dissatisfaction with the regime and were preparing to reinstate him to office. Nagy's reaction was not encouraging, however. Despite the public outcry and the urgings of friends and followers, he refused to leave his home, fostering the impression either that he did not grasp the seriousness of the situation or that he was unprepared to take the initiative. Only when the party leadership specifically called on him did he act—addressing the crowd from a second-story balcony of the Parliament at about 9:00 in the evening. However, the speech was a major disappointment. It was not only that he started with the formal, party-style greeting—"Comrades!"—or that much of what he said could not be heard. The problem was also what could be heard. Nagy promised no more (or less) than to implement his 1953 program consistently—in effect to carry out moderate socialist reform through the mechanism of the ruling party. Just a few days before, this kind of remedy might have helped stem the tide, but this particular crowd, fed up after years of frustration and filled with a new sense of empowerment, had expectations that far outstripped Nagy's outdated and inadequate prescriptions. By now, the opportunity for any communist leader to win the public's respect and trust—and avert an armed conflict—had disappeared. Nagy's call on the protestors to go home did have some effect, but many simply moved on to other parts of the city and continued to demonstrate.

At the Radio station, where protestors had been facing off all day against units of the ÁVH, police and, later, soldiers (who were not carrying ammunition), violence finally broke out. At 8:00 p.m., First Secretary Gerő delivered a previously scheduled nationwide address. Relayed to the crowds from radios perched in windows, the speech was filled with denunciations of the protests. Its harsh and uncompromising tone sparked outrage in the streets. Until then, only a few small clashes had broken out, and no shots had been fired. But by now, the demonstrators had gotten hold of weapons, either from workers at munitions factories, from sympathetic soldiers, or from diverted deliveries to troops guarding the Radio station. The first shot came from the Radio building at about 9:00 p.m., under circumstances that have never been made clear. It was followed by a siege of the station—the event that now marks the beginning of the armed conflict. The battle lasted until dawn when the protestors finally managed, temporarily, to take control of the building.

The same evening, in a highly symbolic move, demonstrators at City Park managed to topple a massive statue of Stalin. A truck dragged the colossus to Blaha Lujza Square, in front of the National Theater, where crowds smashed it to pieces.

October 23 also witnessed important developments in the provinces. Demonstrators took to the streets in several university towns, most significantly in the city of Debrecen in the eastern part of the country. In the late afternoon, before the confrontation at the Radio building in Budapest, ÁVH forces fired on some 20,000–30,000 people as they paraded in front of the county's police headquarters. Three people died and six were injured—the first casualties of the revolution.[5]

The Soviet and Hungarian Leaderships React

Meanwhile, despite streams of alarming reports emanating from Hungary in previous weeks, the Soviets hesitated momentarily before opting for a show of military force against the revolt. One factor in their delay was undoubtedly the fact that a peaceful resolution had been found to the crisis in Poland, a country with even greater strategic and political significance for the USSR. This seemed to hold out hope for a similar outcome in Hungary. Furthermore, Moscow clearly preferred not to use force, partly because it might disrupt the process of international détente, which Khrushchev was nurturing at the time.

---

[5] For a history of the revolution in Debrecen see Tibor Filep, *A debreceni forradalom 1956 október: Tizenkét nap krónikája* (Debrecen: Piremon, 1990).

Nonetheless, barely an hour after the battle had broken out at the Radio station, the CPSU first secretary was on the telephone to Budapest. After repeated prompting from Gerő and based on Soviet Ambassador Yurii Andropov's evaluation of the situation, the CPSU Presidium agreed to allow Soviet troops stationed in Hungary to take part in restoring order (Document No. 25)—on the condition that the Hungarian Council of Ministers (the government) deliver a formal written request to Moscow to that effect (Document No. 27).[6] András Hegedüs signed the appeal—but only several days after the fact, when he had already been dismissed from the post of prime minister—and Andropov forwarded it to the Kremlin (Document No. 42). At the same time, Moscow sent the head of the KGB, Ivan Serov, and the deputy chief of staff of the armed forces, Army General Mikhail Malinin, to Hungary to oversee the operation. At 9:00 p.m., local Red Army units received their orders to advance on Budapest. This marked the end of any hope of a relatively bloodless solution to the crisis. In addition to dramatically raising the stakes, the joint Kremlin and Hungarian decision to introduce troops inadvertently gave the resistance the character of a national liberation struggle.[7]

Apart from providing military help, Moscow also dispatched two CPSU Presidium members on the 24th to oversee the political side of the campaign. They were Anastas Mikoyan, first deputy chairman of the Council of Ministers and the only Presidium member to oppose military intervention, and Mikhail Suslov, secretary of the CPSU Central Committee and a hard-liner. These two senior officials, representing sharply differing points of view on Hungary, would be Moscow's principal eyes and ears on the crisis until the very end of October when the Soviets decided to invade with overwhelming force.

The HWP Political Committee and the Central Committee sat in continuous session from the evening of 23 October until dawn the following day. Nagy, who arrived straight from addressing the crowds at the Parliament Building, had to wait to take part until the leadership formally voted him back into office. He had just regained his party membership, and was about to be nominated both prime minister and a member of the Politburo, which would give him a major voice in the decisions reached that night.

The HWP leadership started from the assumption that the Soviet troops arriving in Budapest would break up the disturbances without serious resistance. The party's main task, then, would be to support the Red Army and lay the groundwork for political changes. They opted for a strategy of deterrence. Moments after his election was announced at 8:30 a.m. on October 24, Nagy declared a state of emergency. The armed forces went on alert, and a curfew and ban on public gatherings took effect. A Military Committee was formed with István Kovács at its head to provide coordination between Soviet and Hungarian forces. The Central Committee then issued a blanket statement condemning the armed uprising, calling the rebels a "dark horde of reaction," whose aim was to "rob our people of their freedom and restore the rule of capitalists and landlords."[8]

---

[6] For the notes taken at the CPSU Presidium meetings during the Hungarian Revolution see Mark Kramer, "The 'Malin Notes' on the Crises in Hungary and Poland, 1956," *Cold War International History Project Bulletin*, no. 8–9 (Winter 1996/1997): 385–410. Minutes of nine Presidium meetings are printed in this volume, see Document Nos. 23, 25, 40, 49, 53, 70, 78, 84, and 89.

[7] On the role of the Soviet Union, see: János M. Rainer: "The Yeltsin Dossier: Soviet Documents on Hungary, 1956," *Cold War International History Project Bulletin*, no. 5 (Spring 1995): 22, 24–27; the introductory essay by János M. Rainer in Vyacheslav Sereda and János M. Rainer, eds., *Döntés a Kremlben, 1956: A Szovjet pártelnökség vitái Magyarországról* (Budapest: 1956-os Intézet, 1996); Györkei and Horváth, *Soviet Military Intervention*; Mark Kramer, "New Evidence on Soviet Decision-Making and the 1956 Polish and Hungarian Crises," *Cold War International History Project Bulletin*, no. 8–9 (Winter 1996/1997): 358–384; Csaba Békés, "Hidegháború, enyhülés és az 1956-os magyar forradalom," in *Évkönyv V, 1996–1997*, ed. András B. Hegedűs et al. (Budapest: 1956-os Intézet, 1997), 201–213; *Sovietskii Soyuz i vengerskii krizis*; Valerii L. Musatov, *Predvestniki buri: Politicheskie krizisy v Vostochnoi Evrope* (Moskva: Nauchnaya Kniga, 1996).

[8] See, "Az MDP Központi Vezetőségének felhívása," in Lajos Izsák, József Szabó and Róbert Szabó, eds., *1956 plakátjai és röplapjai: Október 22–november 5* (Budapest: Zrínyi Kiadó, 1991): 40.

At the same time, the leadership understood they needed to take steps to soothe popular frustrations. One of these had been the reappointment of Nagy.[9] After further debate, other personnel changes were ordered in the party's top ranks, with Nagy managing to have two of his reform-minded supporters, Ferenc Donáth and Géza Losonczy, elected to the Central Committee while several Stalinists were dropped. However, Nagy was unable to force out Gerő as first secretary, even though that had been a condition of his accepting the premiership. Despite his low public standing, Gerő still had the backing of Nagy's own candidate for the party job, János Kádár, as well as of most of the Central Committee; Nagy saw no choice but to relent.

During the night of the 23rd, before the Soviet troops arrived, rebel groups attacked munitions factories, printing presses, telephone exchanges, and even police stations and military institutions. They also briefly took over the offices of *Szabad Nép*. The fighting intensified after the Red Army reached Budapest at dawn on the 24th. Armed groups immediately formed, mainly along the main transport routes, to try to keep the Soviets from entering the capital.

Despite being poorly armed, the rebels, mostly young people brought up on Soviet war films and novels, put up a remarkable fight against the invading tanks. One element in their favor was the fact that the Soviets had deployed no infantry support since they had not expected to encounter meaningful resistance, a miscalculation that led to serious losses early on. The fiercest clashes occurred around the Radio station, the offices of *Szabad Nép*, and on the routes leading to them: in Boráros Square at the Pest end of Petőfi Bridge; at the junction of Üllői Road, a main artery leading east from downtown, and Grand Boulevard; and in Baross Square, outside the Eastern Railway Station. Because of the intense fighting, the Soviets could not even get near the Radio station on the morning of the 24th, which by then had been occupied by the insurrectionists.[10]

The authorities' decision to resort to stiff measures overnight temporarily prevented the uprising in Budapest from escalating or spreading to the provinces. There were demonstrations in a few towns on October 24, but local party and military leaders stayed in control. This was partly because most Hungarians only had access to spotty information about events in the country. Uncertain of what was happening, they could only wait and watch. The curfew also kept less committed people off the streets and made it harder to communicate news; it could not, however, stop the spread of information by word of mouth, for instance in the work place, where increasingly bold public discussions of the latest developments occurred. In some cases, reports of isolated assaults against advancing Soviet forces managed to filter through from outside the capital, just as more tangible help occasionally reached the rebels in Budapest as well.

Despite expectations, the emergency measures, in tandem with the presence of Soviet armor, failed to bring an immediate end to the uprising. The rebels' stunning success in keeping the rebellion alive over the next several days, in the face of vastly superior forces, began to create real hopes among the population for a political victory—and growing alarm on the part of the Hungarian and Soviet authorities.

When the CPSU Presidium delegates, Mikoyan and Suslov, arrived in Budapest early on the 24th, however, a very different attitude prevailed. After getting a briefing on the military situation, they held talks in the afternoon with a small group of HWP leaders. The Soviets agreed at first that the uprising could be suppressed in a matter of hours. As they reported to Moscow, "All the hotbeds of the insurgents have been crushed; liquidation of the main hotbed, at the Radio station, where about 4,000 people are concentrated, is still going on" (Document No. 26). In fact, they scolded the Hungarians for exaggerating the dangers in their earlier messages to Moscow.

The Red Army's arrival and the optimism of the CPSU's emissaries also gave the Hungarian authorities a dose of confidence. In talks with Mikoyan and Suslov, they focused mostly on how to consolidate the situation after the revolt. Publicly, they announced that the curfew would be

---

[9] The new government was not inaugurated right away; the cabinet of András Hegedüs actually remained in office until October 27.

[10] In a practical sense, the occupation was inconsequential since the authorities had already transferred broadcast operations to an emergency studio in the Parliament.

lifted temporarily the next day to allow people to buy food, but also to signify that order had been restored. They even authorized a bulletin to be read over the radio at 4:30 a.m. on the 25th, declaring: "The counterrevolutionary gangs have largely been eliminated." Two hours later, the Council of Ministers issued an even bolder statement: "The attempted counterrevolutionary coup has been eliminated! The counterrevolutionary forces have been routed!" According to the radio, life was already returning to normal: public transportation was running again; employees had been called back to work; pensions were posted on time. One senior officer at National Police Headquarters felt so certain of the situation that he gave orders to pursue any rebels fleeing to the provinces.

After the appearance of Mikoyan and Suslov, Nagy found himself in a curious position. He did not have strong support from Khrushchev, nor even from some of his own Hungarian political allies, at least initially. Donáth and Losonczy, for example, rejected several of the measures the leadership had adopted to restore order, and even refused their own election to the Political Committee. Their temporarily independent course had some unintended risks, however. Isolated from advisers who shared his ideas, Nagy could have become more susceptible to hardline influences or failed to follow through on the goals that had prompted him to take on his new leadership role. It was also possible that Nagy would pick up where he had been forced to leave off on the night of October 23 and reclaim his place at the head of the reform movement. The ambiguities of his character made it hard to predict which route he would take. Over the next few days, he ultimately chose the latter.

The Regime Falters

Of course, all talk of political solutions would have been irrelevant if the Soviet army had managed to sweep the rebels aside. But the events of October 25 marked the transformation of the insurgents into full-fledged freedom fighters and forced the Kremlin and its Hungarian allies to choose between large-scale military intervention, with its potentially major loss of life and international repercussions, and a political solution which carried its own unpredictable consequences.

The problem of control resurfaced almost immediately when crowds poured into the streets after repeal of the curfew on October 25. Those who ventured out discovered just the opposite of what they had been told over the radio, until then their main source of information. The armed struggle was not over. Nor had the city been overrun with looters; goods were still intact behind broken shop windows. Clearly, the rebels were not the hooligans or fascists they had been painted as, but ordinary workers, students, neighbors and friends. Instinctively, people began to try to convince the Soviet soldiers posted throughout the city that the rebellion was not a fascist movement. Hungarians could be seen gathered around Soviet tanks everywhere, gesticulating and using the sparse Russian they had been forced to learn at school to explain the national, democratic—and in important respects, socialist—character of the uprising. In more than a few cases, they actually succeeded. Groups of young people, riding on or accompanied by Soviet tanks flying the Hungarian tri-color flag, set off spontaneously for Parliament. Even without reliable news services, word of this extraordinary development spread across the city, sometimes taking on a larger-than-life quality. So it was an ever more jubilant and self-confident crowd, certain of victory, that began to mill around in Kossuth Square outside Parliament during the morning hours of October 25.

Many of the Soviet and Hungarian armed forces deployed around Parliament reacted with alarm at what they saw. Far from the situation "normalizing," as the authorities had expected, the scene unfolding before them consisted of throngs of boisterous insurrectionists consorting with armed units of uncertain loyalty to create an atmosphere of growing confusion and tensions.

Suddenly, shooting broke out. The demonstrators panicked, as did the Soviet soldiers who moments before had been socializing with them. These troops also opened fire, both in the direction of the initial shots and at the protestors, apparently thinking they had been led into a trap. The situation became so chaotic that a Hungarian unit detailed to guard the party headquarters began shooting at their Soviet counterparts. It was one of the bloodiest episodes of the revolution.

The question of blame for the atrocity has not yet been entirely answered, but two hypotheses have emerged. According to one theory, KGB General Serov was responsible. While at a HWP Central Committee meeting at nearby party headquarters, Serov heard about the crowds around Parliament and went to make a personal inspection. He was reportedly so incensed at the sight of Red Army troops fraternizing with the "enemy" and at Hungarian forces openly changing sides, that he unilaterally gave the order to open fire on the crowd.[11] The other theory blames Hungarian Border Guard forces positioned on the roof of the Ministry of Agriculture building opposite the Parliament. Believing that the crowd was about to attack Parliament, they allegedly began shooting.[12] It is also possible that both versions are true, and that the two units began to fire almost simultaneously. All told, the massacre claimed 100 lives and left 300 wounded.[13]

Crowds escaped from the square and merged with another demonstration, now with blood spattered on their banners, shouting "The ÁVO are killers, down with the ÁVO!"[14] News of the massacre flashed to the provinces where more demonstrations and strikes were reported. The short-lived period of relative national calm had ended.

The developments of October 25 bankrupted the regime's approach to handling the crisis. The Hungarian military command, despite Soviet aid, proved helpless at stopping the uprising from spreading and at reestablishing the order needed for a political settlement. Even so, some members of the leadership continued to press for a military solution, urging tougher actions against the rebels, reimposition of a total curfew, and relentless use of emergency measures. But this hardline perspective lost ground during the afternoon. The first blow came when Gerő, on Soviet instructions, stepped down as first secretary and was replaced by János Kádár. Though Kádár was not an active reformer, he was not seen as an opponent of reform either (Document No. 33).

The decline of the hardliners, however, did not produce a firm plan of action. The Political Committee continued to lean toward using force, granting the Military Committee absolute powers. But they also looked ahead to the consolidation period and were not convinced that order could be restored by Soviet military might alone. The question of relying on a foreign army— especially the Red Army—was a sensitive one given the deeply nationalistic character of the rebellion. Yet it had already become clear that the Hungarian army was unreliable. As for the Budapest police, commanded by Sándor Kopácsi, they had played no part so far in restoring order and in fact appeared to be devastated by the bloodshed at Kossuth Square, which had prompted Kopácsi to initiate talks with a delegation of demonstrators and subsequently to release a number of political prisoners who had been in police custody. Thereafter, the police became more active participants—but not on the side of the regime.

Proponents of real reform within the Political Committee gained ground at this stage. For example, the views of Donáth and Losonczy won the support of József Köböl, who proposed

[11] Györkei and Horváth, *Soviet Military Intervention,* 38.

[12] From the very beginning, a wide-spread belief among the public attributed the massacre to the ÁVH, on the assumption that the aim of this deliberate provocation was to prevent the people from fraternizing with the Soviet soldiers. For a study emphasizing the planned nature of the shooting, see, László Varga, "A harmadik napon," in *Az elhagyott tömeg: Tanulmányok 1950–1956-ról,* László Varga, ed. (Budapest: Cserépfalvi–Budapest Főváros Levéltára, 1994), 99–126. Recent research by military historian Miklós Horváth seems to partly support this view, indicating that there were indeed Hungarian units involved in the shooting. These were not the ill-famed state security forces, however, but regular border guard units, which—being organizationally subordinated to the ÁVH—wore very similar uniforms.

[13] For the most thorough study of the event, see András Kő and Lambert J. Nagy, *Kossuth Lajos tér, 1956* (Budapest: Teleki László Alapítvány, 2001).

[14] Although its official name was changed in 1948, people continued to call the ÁVH by its former abbreviation, ÁVO (State Security Department).

that negotiations on a complete withdrawal of Soviet troops begin after order had been restored. This was strongly opposed by the Soviet emissaries, who sat in on the meeting on the morning of October 25; but a reference to troop withdrawals nevertheless found its way into a speech approved by the Political Committee, which Nagy delivered in the early afternoon.

The afternoon session of the Central Committee also failed to yield a solution to the crisis. By then the main obstacle was no longer the leadership's hesitancy or inaccurate reading of events (although these factors persisted), but the deepening division of the CC into two strongly opposed camps. For the moment, neither side had the power to impose its will on the other—and consequently on the increasingly paralyzed party apparatus—but each had enough weight to block the other's initiatives. Vacillation continued. The news that the uprising was spreading haunted the leadership and left it unable to make clear, logical decisions. Kádár, the new party leader, also wavered, promising simultaneously to institute radical government reform and tough measures against the resistance.

Meanwhile, new institutions designed to lend organization to the revolution and support to the insurgents began to form. A University Revolutionary Students' Committee was established at the History Faculty of Budapest's Eötvös Loránd University. The first revolutionary newspaper, *Igazság* ("Truth"), appeared, marking the *de facto* end to the communist monopoly of the press—a major objective of the rebels.

October 26: The Revolution Spreads

During the course of October 26, the rebels and the growing number of soldiers who joined them kept control of their main bases of operation and organized fresh acts of resistance, despite the escalating superiority of forces arrayed against them. They were strongest in the 8th and 9th Districts of Pest, where they took control of several major thoroughfares, including Grand Boulevard between Petőfi Bridge and the Oktogon, as well as Rákóczi Road and Üllői Road, which radiated eastward from the city center. The most important rebel units were the Corvin Passage group, commanded initially by László Iván Kovács[15] and later by Gergely Pongrátz, and the Tompa Street group under János Bárány.[16] These forces had captured a cache of heavy weapons to augment the small arms they had obtained in the early days of the fighting. Some of the Buda units were also gaining a reputation—at Széna Square (commanded by János Szabó), at Móricz Zsigmond Square, and in the Castle District.

The tactic of these spontaneously formed groups was simple: to keep watch on major thoroughfares and assault Soviet military units as they passed. After each strike they would withdraw into the narrower side streets where the tanks either could not or did not dare to follow, only to reemerge and attack again. They owed their many successes, in part, to the lack of Soviet infantry support, but also to their familiarity with the city, the unconditional support of the local population, and their seemingly inexhaustible inventiveness. Occasionally they managed to fend off tank attacks with home-made small arms or Molotov cocktails. At other times they made do with no weapons at all, placing frying pans in the roads to make them look like anti-tank mines, or pouring oil in the path of oncoming vehicles. Destroyed equipment made good barricades for the next skirmish, so every Soviet loss helped the increasingly confident rebels twice over.[17]

---

[15] László Iván Kovács was commander of the Corvin passage resistance group from October 25 to November 1. Arrested in March 1957, he was executed on December 30 of that year.

[16] János Bárány, who commanded the Tompa street group from October 25 on, was arrested in April 1957 and executed on February 18, 1959.

[17] On street fighting and rebel group activities, see: László Eörsi, *Ferencváros 1956: A kerület fegyveres csoportjai* (Budapest: 1956-os Intézet, 1997), and id., *Corvinisták, 1956: A VIII. kerület fegyveres csoportjai* (Budapest: 1956-os Intézet, 2001); Györkei and Horváth, *Soviet Military Intervention*; Györgyi Bindorffer, Pál Gyenes and Gyula Kozák, eds., *Pesti utca-1956: Válogatás fegyveres felkelők visszaemlékezéseiből* (Budapest: Századvég Kiadó-1956-os Intézet, 1994); Gergely Pongrátz, *Corvin köz-1956* (Budapest: Magyar Szinkör Kisszövetkezet, 1989).

By October 26, the battles were no longer confined to the capital. The number of provincial demonstrations and armed clashes multiplied daily and strikes spread throughout the country. Demonstrations erupted in virtually every town. Crowds on the streets made more or less the same demands from place to place, including an end to the fighting and an amnesty for the rebels. But in several instances they went further than the 16 Points drawn up at Budapest Technical University on October 22, and now called for Hungary's withdrawal from the Warsaw Pact and a declaration of neutrality (see Part One). As in Budapest, protesters systematically began taking down the much despised symbols of the old regime, ripping up red flags, pulling down red stars from building tops, toppling Soviet memorials, and destroying portraits and statues of communist idols.

During this phase of the uprising, events unfolded in four basic ways, depending mainly on how the local authorities reacted. In some instances, the local party or military leadership used force to prevent a take-over of power. This was the case in Esztergom, just north of Budapest on the Danube, and in Kecskemét, about 50 miles southeast of the capital, where army commanders used particularly harsh measures to crush any acts of resistance.[18]

The second type of reaction occurred where the regime's aggressiveness failed to bring about the desired outcome. Usually, these operations only fanned the flames and led to a complete collapse of authority, which then helped the revolutionaries to seize power. This happened in the northeastern city of Miskolc, where a demonstration gathered outside police headquarters. At first, the authorities tried to negotiate, then abruptly fired into the crowd. Local miners and factory workers moved in on the police and a siege developed. The crowd took over the building and massacred every person thought to be responsible for the shootings. The bloodiest episode of the day, however, took place in Mosonmagyaróvár, near the western border with Austria. A demonstration organized by students and joined by factory workers and others, started out like any other: protesters removed official symbols from public buildings, set out demands, and made speeches. Then they marched to the local military barracks to call on the soldiers to join them. No attempt was made to stop them as they approached the barracks gate. But as soon as they reached the entrance they were unexpectedly met with gunfire. As in Miskolc, the crowds eventually took control and several officers were beaten to death.

In the third variant of revolutionary events, the old leadership simply relinquished authority to the rebels. This was the pattern followed in many cities and towns, including several county seats. Revolutionary councils, choosing names harkening back to the 1848 revolution, took power in Debrecen, Veszprém, Győr and many other places with little or no resistance.

Areas where merely embryonic revolutionary forces posed no major challenge to the local authorities constituted the final variant of local reactions to events.[19]

Back in Budapest, in the early morning of the 26th two closely related issues topped the agenda of the Political Committee and subsequently the Central Committee. One was a change of government. Here Nagy attempted to push through several radical changes. His candidates included relatively well-known and increasingly respected public figures committed to his notions of reform: József Szilágyi, Géza Losonczy, Ferenc Donáth, László Kardos,[20] Gábor Tánczos,[21] Sándor Kopácsi, Áron Tamási,[22]

---

[18] On the brutality of the crackdown in different parts of the country, see Frigyes Kahler, ed., *Sortűzek 1956*, 2 vols. (Lakitelek: Antológia Kiadó, 1993–1994).

[19] On the events in the countryside during the revolution, see Zoltán Simon, ed., A vidék forradalma: Az 1991. október 22.-én, Debrecenben rendezett konferencia előadásai (Debrecen: Az 1956-os forradalom történetének Hajdú-Bihar Megyei Kutatócsoportja, 1992); Lajos Izsák, József Szabó and Róbert Szabó, eds., *1956 vidéki sajtója* (Budapest: Korona, 1996).

[20] László Kardos, director of the Ethnographic Museum, was one of the leaders of the Revolutionary Committee of Hungarian Intellectuals and was imprisoned between 1957–1963.

[21] Gábor Tánczos was secretary of the Petőfi Circle from the beginning of 1955. As a member of the Nagy group he also took refuge in the Yugoslav embassy on November 4. Sentenced in 1958 to 15 years in prison, he was amnestied in 1962.

[22] Áron Tamási was one of the leading exemplars of the so-called populist writers school. On September 17, 1956, he was elected co-chairman of the Writers' Union, and on October 31 he became a member of the Petőfi Party's leadership. His "Sorrow and Confession" became, on December 28, 1956, the writers' statement of loyalty to the cause of the repressed revolution.

and the staunchest reformer among the existing party leadership, József Köböl. The Smallholders' Party leader, Béla Kovács, was also mentioned as a gesture toward coalition government (Document No. 32). But this slate was ultimately unacceptable to the party leadership, and Béla Kovács was the only one to gain a seat in the cabinet announced the next day.[23]

In the second, more dramatic part of the morning meeting, Ferenc Donáth put forward another set of proposals. Donáth drew a sharp distinction between a political and a military solution, bifurcating the two approaches the leadership had previously treated together and leaving no doubt that he favored the former. He declared that the party had to radically revise its assessment of events. The party had to acknowledge that blame for the October 23 demonstration and the subsequent outbreak of fighting lay in its own mistaken policies. Consequently, the uprising had to be recognized as a national democratic movement and not a "counterrevolution." The demonstrators' democratic, socialist and national demands had to be met, he insisted, and the party, after restoring order, should be required to begin negotiating a complete withdrawal of Soviet troops from the country. Donáth warned that a failure to do so would not only cost the party its remaining influence with the public but further radicalize popular sentiment in an increasingly polarized environment.

Donáth's presentation was convincing, and Kádár raised it at the Central Committee meeting, which began immediately afterwards at 9:00 p.m. Kádár's somewhat softened presentation won agreement from a majority of the CC. Losonczy and Donáth then went a step further by advancing another set of proposals, including direct negotiations with the rebels. But while Donáth was speaking, members of the Military Committee, who had not been told about the meeting ahead of time, rushed in to try to block the reformers. They argued that a reappraisal of the situation was impossible because to imply that the uprising was national and democratic in nature meant that anyone opposing it must be anti-national and anti-democratic. They claimed there was no going back for the communist party, which proclaimed itself to be the vanguard of all revolutionary efforts and human progress. The hardliners also declared that a military solution was feasible. The main impediment, they insisted, was not weakness in the armed forces but treachery in the party leadership. The harshness of their attack had its effect: the Central Committee made an astonishing about-face and adopted a policy statement without a single new reform initiative (Document No. 33).[24]

In so doing, the party leadership picked the worst possible course of action and showed that, for the moment, they still could not settle on an effective and consistent response to events. Instead, they insisted on a military solution while trying to split the opposition with minor policy adjustments that were already long overdue. The promises they made on October 26 targeted some of the mainly financial demands of the working class, while the October 27 list of ministers was an attempt to woo the peasantry by including two Smallholders' Party members in the government: Zoltán Tildy and Béla Kovács. These "cosmetic" changes, however, were no longer enough to satisfy a revolutionary society. Eventually, even the party hierarchy would be forced to come to this realization.

October 27: Nagy Takes the Initiative

It became clear by the morning of the 27th that the regime's appraisal of the situation and the Military Committee's solutions bore no relation to reality. This short-sightedness was mirrored in the Political Committee's final decision that morning on the composition of the new government, and in the evident self-confidence of their public statements (Document No. 38). The hardliners had claimed that there was no broad base of worker support for the rebels, and that those who had drifted toward the opposition could be won back by limited reforms. In fact,

[23] From the morning of October 26 until it was finally approved on the 27th, the composition of the government was debated by three top-level bodies in four consecutive meetings, producing a number of different lists of potential ministers.

[24] For a detailed reconstruction of the meeting, see Horváth and Ripp, *Ötvenhat októbere és a hatalom*, 50–88.

the programs of the so-called Workers' Councils, established in large numbers at factories and local municipalities after the Central Committee's appeal the previous day, featured the same far-reaching demands that Nagy and the central authorities were hearing from other revolutionary organizations all over the country. They called for the withdrawal of Soviet troops, the dissolution of the ÁVH, the removal of all remnants of the Rákosi regime from public life, an amnesty for anyone who had taken part in the fighting, and the introduction of a multi-party system. Likewise, the economic platform of the Workers' Councils reflected the ideas of the party opposition: providing for some degree of private ownership and enterprise, but preserving the overall socialist character of the economy.

The realization eventually dawned on some of the leadership that the party could not recover its popular base of support with just limited reforms. Workers on the whole had not even reacted to the government's promises to them. Furthermore, the new government itself was a non-starter: its claims to be a true coalition representing all Hungarians' interests were patently false; all of the prominent candidates of the Nagy group had been left out; and of the two Smallholder politicians included, Tildy did not have the political prestige the communists assumed he had. Far from regaining public confidence, installing a new government only brought a fresh wave of civil disobedience and demands for the dismissal of individual ministers.

While the top levels of the party tried to enforce the previous day's political line, Nagy increasingly realized that this line was unsustainable. By the end of the day on the 27th, he finally came to the conclusion that change could no longer be postponed. He may have been told that the hardliners were contemplating a military dictatorship, although that is not clear. He certainly knew they were planning a final, brutal showdown with the Corvin Passage unit, which would have led to another civilian bloodbath and wiped out all hopes for reconciliation. But, the decisive factor for Nagy probably was a meeting he had with a group of laborers who called themselves the Angyalföld Workers' Delegation. This discussion, which gave him the chance to hear a workingman's evaluation of events firsthand, coupled with urgings from his allies, convinced him to take the initiative and claim leadership of the reform movement.

As evidence of this change of heart, Nagy took the floor at a critical meeting of the Emergency Committee (often referred to as the Directory) on the night of the 27th to insist that a cease-fire be declared, that security forces be ordered off the streets, and that the government begin to negotiate the withdrawal of Soviet troops. He threatened to resign as prime minister and bring down the new government unless the leadership approved his proposal. At this stage, he had the support of János Kádár, the man who would soon help drive him from office.

In an informal discussion following the meeting, Nagy and Kádár persuaded the Soviet envoys—who still backed Nagy—of the necessity of a shift in policy. Whether Mikoyan and Suslov acted independently or whether Khrushchev immediately approved their decision is not entirely clear, but based on the emissaries' report the CPSU Presidium ultimately gave its blessing to the change (Document No. 40). There was no real alternative. The uprising had spread across the country and, at this juncture at least, could not be suppressed by available Soviet forces alone. Furthermore, the regime had made no preparations for the political consolidation that would necessarily follow the crushing of the rebellion.

Nagy's approach of finding a political solution that would obviate new street fighting benefited Moscow by avoiding the embarrassment of an eventual forced withdrawal by the Red Army. What was more, nothing in his proposals implied a threat to the leading role of the communist party, or to Hungary's membership in the Warsaw Pact; in other words, the foundations of the so-called "people's democracy" seemed safe. At this point, there was still no mention in Hungary of changing the power structure or altering the system itself. The cease-fire and troop withdrawals were specifically designed to prevent this from happening and to allow the country's rulers—the prime minister and the party first secretary—to resolve the crisis politically. Still, at the October 28 Political Committee session, Mikoyan and Suslov warned the Hungarians to take every precaution to prevent a further drift to the right, a sign that Nagy's current proposals marked the limits of Soviet tolerance (Document No. 39).

Meanwhile, throughout the first days of the rebellion, several other bloc states were experiencing spill-over effects from the Hungarian and Polish crises. For example, word reached Moscow from the GDR about the "danger of open anti-government protests," with dissent rising mainly from the ranks of intellectuals and students, but also among segments of the working class and well-off peasants.[25] In Romania, secret cables reported a "revival of hostile activities by internal reactionary forces"[26]—mostly Hungarian minorities—including non-sanctioned meetings, the distribution of leaflets and minor sabotage. In Bulgaria, "reactionary elements" among the intelligentsia and student population, but also the party, showed signs of dissatisfaction with the government and increasing "anti-Soviet sentiments" (Document No. 52).[27]

In fact, popular support for the Hungarian cause was widespread in the region. Even in the Soviet Union opposition surfaced, especially in the Baltic republics and the Caucasus, where animosity toward the system always ran high. Alarmed, the authorities reacted quickly. Aside from easing economic obligations, boosting wages, and intensifying ideological propaganda and control over information, the responses included reinforcement of security forces and the adoption of administrative measures against malcontents (Document Nos. 29, 36, 51, and 60). In the process, party members were expelled while dissidents were arrested, beaten, and even executed.[28]

The Western Reaction

The Hungarian leadership's decision, so long in the making and now enjoying Soviet approval, had become even more urgent because of international considerations.

Although the U.S. government had produced a succession of intelligence reports since 1953 on possible developments inside the "captive nations," the Hungarian revolution had taken the Eisenhower administration by surprise.[29] With few significant policy options available, Eisenhower and his aides were reduced to improvising while trying to balance conflicting expectations.[30] On the one hand, the uncertain advantages to be gained from exploiting the uprising at this stage were outweighed by the drawbacks of upsetting the geopolitical status quo in Europe that had been operating relatively smoothly since 1945, and of jettisoning the ongoing process

---

[25] I. Tugarinov, deputy head of the Committee of Information of the Soviet Foreign Ministry, to N.S. Khrushchev, July 29, 1957. TsKhSD, F. 5, Op. 30, D. 230, L. 215.

[26] A. Zhigulev and K. Kravchenko, correspondents for TASS, to N. G. Palgunov, [otvetstvennyi rukovoditel'], "On Certain Questions Concerning the Internal Political Situation in Romania during the Hungarian Events," March 12, 1957. According to a cover sheet, Palgunov forwarded the memo to Shepilov, with copies to the rest of the top Soviet leadership, on the same day. TsKhSD, F. 5, Op. 30, D. 230, Ll. 49, 51.

[27] See also I. Tugarinov, deputy head of the Committee of Information of the Soviet Foreign Ministry, to N.S. Khrushchev, February 14, 1957. TsKhSD, F. 5, Op. 30, D. 230, L. 17.

[28] See Békés, *The 1956 Hungarian Revolution*, 28.

[29] Characteristically, a U.S. military report on resistance potential in the country, dated early 1956, concluded that the chances for active opposition were minimal and that Hungary made a poor target even for indirect military action (see Document No. 8).

[30] On the U.S. role during the Hungarian crisis, see the following papers presented at the international conference, "Hungary and the World, 1956," Budapest, September 26–29, 1996, organized by the Institute for the History of the 1956 Hungarian Revolution, the National Security Archive, and the Cold War International History Project: Raymond L. Garthoff, "Hungary 1956: The Washington Reaction" and Ronald W. Pruessen, "John Foster Dulles and 1956." All of the conference papers were published in Hungarian in *Évkönyv V, 1996–1997*, ed. András B. Hegedűs et al. (Budapest: 1956-os Intézet, 1997), the yearbook of the 1956 Institute. They will also appear in a forthcoming English-language volume to be published by the Woodrow Wilson International Center for Scholars. For other works, see John C. Campbell, "The Soviet Union, the United States and the Twin Crisis of Hungary and Suez," *in Suez 1956. The Crisis and its Consequences,* ed. W. M. Louis and R. Owen (Oxford: Clarendon Press, 1989), pp 233–252; and Békés, *The 1956 Hungarian Revolution*.

of international détente.[31] On the other hand, many senior officials felt that the United States had an obligation to live up to the administration's rhetoric about "rolling back" communist control over Eastern Europe and to meet the expectations of a public which gave wholehearted support to the Hungarians' battle for freedom. The popular outcry in the United States induced the administration, on October 24, to raise the possibility of taking the Hungarian question to the U.N. Security Council (Document No. 28). Washington's main allies, Britain and France, gave way to American pressure, even though they were secretly preparing for war over Suez and did not want to set a precedent at the U.N. against intervention (Document No. 37).[32] The three powers jointly called for a meeting of the Security Council on October 27 to debate the situation in Hungary. Since the USSR had a veto there, this move did not pose a real danger to Soviet goals, although a debate would certainly have been uncomfortable for them; the Soviets therefore filed a protest to the secretary general, claiming that the intervention had come at the Hungarians' request and was, in any case, an internal affair not adjudicable by an international organization (Document No. 41).[33]

Outside the United Nations, the United States had one other principal weapon, short of force, to use against the Soviets: Radio Free Europe (RFE). Throughout the crisis, RFE broadcast news bulletins and commentary into Hungary, becoming an essential source of information for the rebels as well as an inspiration for many. But, the value of Radio Free Europe would be partially offset by what many Hungarians (and other Europeans) charged were gross misrepresentations and exaggerations in its Hungarian broadcasts. Despite guidelines received from the CIA, the work of the RFE's Hungarian desk was characterized more by the passions and improvisations of the largely émigré staff. Even the more cautious broadcast supervisors were sometimes caught up in the fervor. In this atmosphere, some broadcasts lost the objective tone of news reporting and became subjective commentaries, giving the impression that RFE was trying to influence events rather than just inform about them. This gap between official policy and practice was an interesting reflection of some of the contradictions in the overall U.S. approach toward Eastern Europe.[34]

October 28: The Turn toward Reform

Nagy announced his new measures on Hungarian radio and on the front page of *Szabad Nép* on October 28 (Document No. 44). He also called the events a national democratic movement—not a "counterrevolution"—and promised to meet most of the rebels' other demands. He planned to reshuffle the party's top echelons to give himself and his faction a majority in a new Presidium, replace the old Political Committee, dissolve the ÁVH, and create a National Guard out of selected police and army units to take over responsibility for public order from the defunct security services.

[31] Even before the revolution, the administration understood that mounting a military response from the West was politically and strategically out of the question.

[32] The British, French, and Israelis agreed to the joint attack on Egypt during secret talks held in Sévres, a suburb of Paris, from October 22–24.

[33] This should have given Moscow another reason to accept the Hungarian proposal to find a peaceful solution to the crisis.

[34] It is worth mentioning that although RFE was one of the most important propaganda outlets of the U.S. government, it never received any comprehensive guidance on the substance of "liberation/roll back" doctrine. Aside from instructions on specific points, RFE from the very beginning depended on some level of improvisation, resulting in an overall policy that its formulators hoped corresponded to Washington's approach. For more on the Hungarian desk of RFE, see Gyula Borbándi, *Magyarok az Angol Kertben: A Szabad Európa Rádió története* (Budapest: Európa Könyvkiadó, 1996), and George R. Urban, *Radio Free Europe and the Pursuit of Democracy: My War within the Cold War* (New Haven: Yale University Press, 1997). See also papers presented at the conference "Hungary and the World, 1956: New Archival Evidence," (see footnote 30 above).

With Soviet approval, the HWP Political and Central committees approved Nagy's October 28 program (Document No. 39). One reason was an increasing number of reports of Hungarian soldiers defecting to the revolutionary councils. Another was the fact that the mass demonstrations were beginning to reach the villages, where local groups were ousting compromised local party and government officials. The Győr National Council then raised the stakes by calling on Nagy to bring an immediate end to the fighting. Otherwise, "the inhabitants of Transdanubia would rush to the aid of the Budapest freedom fighters."[35] There was also a mounting danger that postponing a full political settlement could radicalize or marginalize the revolutionaries who wanted to reach an agreement with the reformers within the communist party. Against this threatening background, Nagy was finally able to present the country with a program that could reasonably be expected to meet popular demands and effect a peaceful settlement. In the process, he had brought about a radical shift in the locus of power from the party to the government.

Meanwhile, the process of consolidation by the rebels had gotten underway in the provinces and villages, although the party resolution had little to do with it. The rapid transfer of power and the almost immediate settlement of the conflict there came about for several reasons. First and foremost, village authorities had no effective apparatus to use against the population. By the time the village demonstrations began on October 27 and 28, the old order had no more reserves to deploy. If the local authorities even bothered to wait for the protesters to arrive, they generally handed over the keys of government with no resistance. At that point, typically, local revolutionary councils and committees would form.

The rebels' political demands in the countryside (which were frequently implemented), corresponded to similar calls around the country. Many localities, for example, decided to dissolve their agricultural cooperatives, although they often put off the task. As a rule, protesters from the villages adopted the same points that were formulated in large nearby towns, then added specific local needs and grievances. The peasants' ultimatums, like the workers', harkened back to 1945–1947, the transitory period between the collapse of the authoritarian Horthy regime and the final Communist takeover. Just as the working class did not want to see the return of capitalist-era factory owners, the villagers had no desire to reverse the 1945 land reform. As soon as local power was transferred to the reformers, life in the villages generally returned to normal. Rural dwellers were then satisfied to leave the job of reaching a political settlement to the people they trusted: the Nagy-led government and the local, county-level revolutionary councils.

Far from bringing the crisis to an end, the HWP Central Committee decision on October 28 started an avalanche. One reason for this was that the two sides had different interpretations of the crisis and the change in the HWP's program. Nagy wanted to strike a compromise with the rebels against the extremists. He was prepared to accede to the maximum demands that would be acceptable to the Soviets in return for rebel cooperation against the seemingly real threat of counterrevolution. For their part, the rebels saw the party leaders' turnaround as a partial victory, which only encouraged them to fight for acceptance of their entire program.

For Nagy, the restoration of order continued to be his most urgent task. He understood that this was the only way he and his policies could secure the backing, or at least the acquiescence, of the Kremlin. This meant that the ceasefire had to be enforced and the workers convinced to return to work so that Moscow could see that the party's concessions were being offset. So, the prime minister, having shifted the leading role in shaping national policy from the party to the government on October 28 and having made the symbolic gesture of moving into the government offices in the Parliament Building the following day, now tried to persuade his rebellious countrymen to set aside their weapons and agree not to go out on strike.

---

[35] For more concerning the developments in the city of Győr, see Győr Megyei Jogú Város Levéltára, *Győr 1956*, 2 vols. (Győr: Győr Megyei Jogú Város Polgármesteri Hivatala, 1996).

Many of the insurrectionists were still wary of the prime minister, though, and even more guarded about the government as a whole. When Soviet troops engaged the rebels in heavy battles in Budapest on October 29, the revolutionaries quickly concluded that either the ceasefire did not apply to the Red Army or that Nagy could not guarantee its observance. In either case, the truce was meaningless. Furthermore, as pointed out above, revolutionaries across the country wondered why they should make concessions right at their moment of triumph, or why specifically they should give up armed resistance and strikes when these seemed to be their best hope of reaching their goals.

While the October 28 statement conceded several of the revolution's demands, it refused to grant two of the main points that had been formulated at Budapest Technical University: free, multi-party elections and the withdrawal of Soviet troops from Hungarian territory. The statement included the promise to start negotiations on the second issue, but the rebels could not consider their victory complete until both ultimatums had been accepted. Their continued insistence on these points after the 28th was more than just cosmetic. Without a multi-party system and full Soviet withdrawal, there was no assurance that a Moscow-backed communist regime would not be reimposed.

As the government kept up its efforts at persuasion on the 29th, problems continued to surface. For one thing, mutual suspicions hampered the negotiations. For another, resistance leaders could not always guarantee that their members would accept the terms agreed to with the regime. One consequence of the spontaneity of the revolt was that relations among revolutionary groups were not always well defined, and cooperation was often on a case-by-case basis. Also, the rebels had no commander-in-chief who could serve as their principal negotiator.

In the course of successive meetings at the Parliament Building, the Defense Ministry, and Budapest police headquarters, the rebels put forward a series of demands. They insisted, for example, that they would only hand over their weapons to Hungarian units—after the Soviet army had left the country—provided the government guaranteed that rebel forces who wanted to join the new security force could do so. Their negotiating position was strengthened by support from the Kilián Barracks and their commander, Colonel Pál Maléter, who drew up a list of ceasefire conditions in conjunction with the rebels. The most insistent rebel demand was for the Red Army to pull out immediately. But for the Nagy government, this was unrealistic because they were sure it would take lengthy negotiations to come to terms with Moscow on the status of the military.

Another serious challenge to the government appeared on October 29 when the Revolutionary Committee of the Hungarian Intelligentsia, founded the day before as an umbrella group for several rebel organizations, announced its own program.[36] While it welcomed Nagy's new measures of the 28th, the committee agreed with other opposition elements that the government's policy did not go far enough. National reconciliation (that is, order and consolidation), they asserted, could only be reached by completely agreeing to the rebels' main demands. The question was not whether the communist party, having lost absolute control, should be deposed, but whether it should be forced to share power with the newly forming democratic parties.

Nagy and Kádár were aware by October 29 that the HWP had largely disintegrated. Some of the central and local leaderships as well as the rank and file had even gone into hiding. Others, notably Ernő Gerő, had fled to the Soviet Union or placed themselves under Soviet military protection in Hungary. Seeing how untenable the situation had become, Nagy decided to make an extraordinary announcement, declaring over the radio in the afternoon of October 30 that the one-party system had been abolished—or at least that it had simply ceased to exist. A coalition "government cabinet," he said, would take over running the country. Kádár, who realized that the government—not the party he headed—was now the only entity capable of exercising centralized control, decided to join the new ruling body.

---

[36] On the role and activity of the intelligentsia during the revolution see: Éva Standeisky, *Írók és a hatalom, 1956–1963* (Budapest: 1956-os Intézet, 1996).

Attempts at Consolidation

October 30 marked the real beginning of the consolidation period. The HWP CC resolution of October 28 had only laid the foundations for the process. Revolutionary councils formed in the few remaining counties that lacked them and proceeded to take control of local governance. In this, they had the firm support of the local press and radio, which now operated under the control of armed civil-military units that had been organized as *de facto* local national guards. Talks at the Budapest police headquarters in Deák Square led representatives of the army, the police, and the armed rebels to form the Preparatory Committee of the Revolutionary Armed Forces Committee. The publicly stated purpose of the new committee was to implement the government order of the 28th to establish a National Guard as a branch of the country's armed security forces. But the underlying aim was to centralize the locally formed units, to integrate the insurgents within the larger apparatus, and thereby gain control over them.

Following an order issued the previous day by Minister of Defense General Károly Janza, revolutionary military councils were also formed to keep order and safeguard the rebel's gains, showing that the army supported the people in the uprising. Officers of the Rétság armored corps freed the Hungarian Catholic primate, Cardinal József Mindszenty, from house arrest at Felsőpetény.[37] And the re-christened Radio Free Kossuth went on the air promising to provide accurate, impartial information.

In addition, Nagy's announcement of the demise of the single-party system led immediately to the revival of previously banned political parties. This was an extremely important development, despite the fact that each of these groups had serious obstacles to overcome. First, there was the question of past conduct. Antagonisms surfaced between political activists who had spent the communist period in obscurity and others who had been (or seemed to be) fellow travelers of the HWP. Considerable numbers of armed rebels also took exception to the reappearance of these parties, resenting the intrusion of potential rivals on their hard-won victory. Other Hungarians worried about the rise of factional politics because of the danger it posed to the fragile national unity produced by the revolution.

Some of the most prominent revived parties deserve mention. The Independent Smallholders' Party, with Béla Kovács as its nominal leader, elected a provisional governing body. The Smallholders wanted to honor the results of the 1945 general elections, the last free parliamentary ballot before communism, because that would restore their own party to preeminent status. The Smallholders were prominent in organizing the Capital City National Committee, a revolutionary body designed to oversee events in Budapest, which became an important factor in the consolidation process.

The Social Democratic Party also chose a governing body, with Anna Kéthly as chair. The SDP won immediate international recognition and a representative was invited to the meeting of the Socialist International on November 1 in Vienna. The SDP's reappearance placed a question mark over the legitimacy of the HWP, which had been created in 1948 through the forced merger of the Social Democrats with the Hungarian Communist Party.[38] Ultimately, the reappearance of the SDP helped speed the collapse of the HWP and brought the prospect of national reconciliation closer. On October 30, a member of the HWP Political Committee, Zoltán Szántó, (among others) proposed dissolving the HWP because it had been tainted by the old regime and was now being undermined by the formation of a new party that was genuinely capable of representing popular interests. However, the Political Committee could not yet bring itself to abolish the party at this stage.

Representatives of another dormant entity, the National Peasants' Party, met on October 31 at Vajdahunyad Castle, in Budapest's City Park, where they reconstituted their organization. The

---

[37] On Cardinal Mindszenty's role during the revolution, see Árpád Tyekvicska, *A bíboros és a katona: Mindszenty József és Pálinkás-Pallavicini Antal a forradalomban* (Budapest: Századvég-1956-os Intézet, 1994).

[38] Those Social Democrats who opposed the fusion (constituting the majority of the leaders and a large number of party members) were expelled from the SDP as early as the first half of 1948.

NPP underlined its break with the recent past by adopting a new name, the Petőfi Party, after the poet, Sándor Petőfi, an instigator of the 1848 revolution. This symbolic step implied both support for the revolution and a continuing link with writers, traditionally an influential element in Hungarian society.[39]

The clear successes of the consolidation process on October 30 were coupled with some serious challenges to the central authorities as they tried to reassert control. The first edition of the newspaper *Függetlenség* ("Independence"), published by the Hungarian National Revolutionary Committee, bluntly declared, "We do not recognize the present government!" Formed the previous day and led by József Dudás, the Committee, unlike the other revolutionary councils and organizations, saw itself as a national body, with aspirations of forming a counter-government. Many Hungarians were critical of the October 27 cabinet because it included party members who had served the discredited Mátyás Rákosi, but the Hungarian National Revolutionary Committee was the only organized group to demand a new government altogether. Dudás had no appreciable forces behind him, but he managed to join with members of the Revolutionary Committee of the Hungarian Intelligentsia in arranging a meeting with Nagy that same day for the purpose of clearing up misunderstandings as quickly as possible. Thereafter, his newspaper (now called *Magyar Függetlenség,* or "Hungarian Independence") continued to attack the government, but drew a distinction between Nagy and the fellow travelers of the Smallholders' and National Peasants' parties, whom it called on to resign.

News of similar threats to the regime's hold on power arrived from Győr, about 100 kilometers west of the capital. The Győr National Council, headed by Attila Szigethy, had been founded on October 26 to cover Győr-Sopron County. The Council repeatedly expressed support for Nagy and his policies, but radical elements in the city urged the organization to turn against the Nagy cabinet and form an alternative government. Anxious to co-opt the radicals, Szigethy met on October 30 with representatives of local area revolutionary councils and established the Transdanubian National Council (TNC), which vowed to ensure "complete implementation of the revolution's demands." There were understandable fears in Budapest that an alternative government might form in Győr. But the TNC did not aspire to this or even to act on the government's behalf. Its aim was only to convince the executive to take all possible steps to bring about complete social reconciliation.

The events in Győr may have contributed to Nagy's decision to form an inner cabinet, which he announced on October 30. Although in formal terms this step entailed hardly any personnel changes within the government, it was tantamount to a reshuffle. The new cabinet, which became the actual locus of decision-making, was made up primarily of representatives of the 1945–1948 coalition parties and specifically excluded the Rákosi loyalists whose presence in the government had been harshly criticized (Document No. 46).

However, the change still did not guarantee adequate representation for the democratic revolutionary organizations. Partly because Nagy relied so much on personal ties, the former coalition politicians he had chosen for the new cabinet had not been the leading figures in their parties during the coalition period. In many cases, either their activities at that time or the fact that they had collaborated with the communists later on meant they could no longer represent their old parties to the extent Nagy had imagined. For example, the reconstituted NPP was not prepared to cooperate with Ferenc Erdei, who had been included in the cabinet ostensibly as its representative. The Smallholders were suspicious of Zoltán Tildy, their erstwhile representative, who had taken on the important post of deputy prime minister with the rank of state minister. Tildy had not even been elected to the party's nine-member provisional steering committee. Meanwhile, the Social Democrats had yet to nominate anyone to represent their party. This left Béla Kovács of the Smallholders as the only accepted representative of his party in the new cab-

---

[39] On the activity of the reemerging political parties see István Vida, ed. *1956 és a politikai pártok: Politikai pártok az 1956-os forradalomban, 1956. október 23 – november 4. Válogatott dokumentumok* (Budapest: MTA Jelenkorkutató Bizottság, 1998).

inet—and he had already been chosen for the October 27 government. Ultimately, for most Hungarians it was not enough simply to have "non-communists" *per se* appointed to the new cabinet; they wanted to see the true representatives of the coalition parties elevated to power.

While the authorities did manage to block attempts to unseat their new government, on October 30 they faced a third danger: mob violence. On that day, as Soviet and Hungarian military units began to withdraw from the capital, and the ÁVH was being disbanded, armed rebels arrived in Köztársaság Square to take control of the HWP Budapest Committee building. Party headquarters in Budapest had been one of the main centers of opposition to the revolution. After gun battle erupted with party loyalists inside, rebel reinforcements arrived and laid siege to the building, which led the authorities in turn to order tanks to the scene. In a bizarre twist, the tank commanders, seeing a Hungarian tank on the side of the revolutionaries, also fired a barrage on the building. This decided the battle, although worse was to come. As some of the defenders surrendered and walked out into the square, three negotiators—two army colonels and Imre Mező,[40] a secretary of the party committee who sympathized with Nagy—were seized and summarily shot. The crowd then stormed the building, forced everyone remaining inside—mostly ÁVH troops—out into the square and proceeded to lynch several of them. A number of rebels managed to intercede and prevent more executions, but the violence had taken its toll: 23 lives had been lost in the siege and its aftermath. John Sadovy of "Life" magazine captured the scene on film; his pictures were published worldwide and ironically became part of the Kádár regime's later propaganda campaign to discredit the revolution.

During the next few days, every revolutionary organization in Hungary condemned the lynchings and called on Hungarians to safeguard the integrity of the revolution. On October 31, another crowd in Budapest killed an ÁVH captain, but after that incidents of mob justice died down, especially with the acceptance of the last remaining rebel demands.

Decisions in Moscow and Washington

In Moscow, the CPSU leadership anxiously followed the ambiguous events of October 30. The Kremlin had vigorously debated the HWP CC proposals of October 28 but eventually accepted them, albeit with certain strict conditions attached (Document No. 40). Nagy was given the authority to form a stable, reliable government that would allow him to restore order in the country. However, he did not get permission to accede to any further rebel demands. Khrushchev made it plain that he saw the call to withdraw the Red Army from Hungary as a hostile move. Even if the Soviets had allowed a pull-out, the Hungarians had to take heed of Mikoyan's warning to the HWP Political Committee on the 28th: "The comrades have to ... behave with firmness in this. If there are further concessions tomorrow, then it cannot be stopped" (Document No. 39).

Contrary to Moscow's wishes, however, the HWP was forced to make several important concessions to the rebels after October 28 because by then the party had lost any remaining influence over the armed forces and the press. *Szabad Nép* ceased publication on October 29 and the local newspapers and radio stations became mouthpieces for the revolution. As Hungary seemed on the verge of restoring a *de facto* multi-party system, the Soviets no doubt recalled the last multi-party elections in 1945, in which the communist party fared poorly under far more favorable conditions than pertained in 1956.

Throughout this period, the CPSU leadership kept regularly informed about the situation in Hungary, but the reports they received were often one-sided. The Soviets' informants tended to accentuate the anti-communist sentiments of the population, and grossly exaggerated the atrocities that were being committed. They kept a thorough account of all the Soviet war memorials

---

[40] Imre Mező was a member of the HWP CC beginning in July 1956 and of the Military Committee as of October 26, 1956.

that had been overturned and war graves desecrated, corroborating this bleak picture with reports of the lynchings at Köztársaság Square. On October 30, Mikoyan and his team reported that it was impossible to halt the armed uprising by peaceful means. The rebels had occupied key facilities, including party buildings, printing presses, and telephone exchanges. They warned that the Hungarian government could be expected to make a change in the country's international policies, a move that called for drastic action: "We think it is essential that Comrade Konev come to Hungary immediately," they advised (Document No. 47).

Across the Atlantic, the United States, along with the other western powers, was struggling to formulate a response to the unexpected developments. The Eisenhower administration had a difficult time backing away from its earlier liberation rhetoric. On October 26, the top-level National Security Council (NSC) met for the first time during the period of the revolution to evaluate the events taking place in Eastern Europe and to plan what kind of official message to communicate regarding U.S. policy toward the region (Document No. 34).

Amid the general confusion of the session, Harold Stassen, the president's adviser on disarmament, made one proposal that seemed particularly astute in retrospect. Stassen suggested that it would be expedient to offer assurances to the Soviets that the United States would not try to exploit the possible independence of the satellite countries in any way that could threaten the security of the Soviet Union. Although the NSC promptly rejected the idea, the next day its backers got the president to endorse an expanded version of it. According to this plan, the United States, either through Yugoslav President Tito or some other diplomatic channel, would try to convince the Soviets that a zone of strictly neutral, non-NATO countries, politically akin to Austria, would offer Moscow just as much security as the existing buffer of satellite countries (Document Nos. 35).

Ultimately, Eisenhower instructed Secretary of State Dulles to build this message into the presidential campaign speech the secretary was set to deliver in Dallas, Texas, on October 27. However, Dulles, who had opposed the proposal from the beginning because he thought it offered exaggerated ideological concessions, watered it down—ultimately gaining approval for this from the president—by dropping any reference to either neutrality or a prohibition on NATO membership. In the end, Dulles' message to Moscow boiled down to the following celebrated sentence: "We do not look upon these nations as potential military allies."[41]

This fundamentally modified version of Stassen's original proposal did not accomplish its original purpose of pacifying the Soviets. Or, more precisely, it achieved it in a different way. The revised variant had a distinctly defensive tone, which the Soviets could logically be expected to take as assurance that the United States would not take any action on behalf of East European independence. The American leadership nonetheless went to great lengths to make sure that the message reached its intended audience: on October 28, Henry Cabot Lodge, the U.S. representative to the United Nations, quoted the relevant passages from Dulles' speech during a session of the Security Council; on October 29, the American ambassador in Moscow was instructed to reiterate these points personally to the Soviet leadership, including Marshal Georgii Zhukov; and on October 31 Eisenhower himself repeated the key passage during a televised address.[42]

Dulles' statement was historically significant, despite its weakened form. The Eisenhower administration's earlier official pronouncements on the satellites were based on the assumption

---

[41] The full context of Dulles' statement was as follows:

> And let me make this clear, beyond a possibility of doubt: The United States has no ulterior purpose in desiring the independence of the satellite states. Our unadulterated wish is that these peoples, from whom so much of our own national life derives, should have sovereignty restored to them and that they should have governments of their own free choosing. We do not look upon these nations as potential military allies. We see them as friends and as parts of a new and friendly and no longer divided Europe. We are confident that their independence, if promptly accorded, will contribute immensely to stabilize peace throughout all of Europe, West and East.

(See, *FRUS, 1955–1957*, vol. 25 (Washington, D.C.: Government Printing Office, 1990), 318.

[42] For the history and an evaluation of the "security garantee" section of Dulles' speech, see Békés, *The 1956 Hungarian Revolution*, 15–16.

that if they gained independence they would in reality join the western world, which also meant joining NATO. Therefore, declaring that the United States did not consider these states potential military allies was a renunciation of the earlier position. It was a turning point in U.S. policy toward the region, eventually wiping out the remaining vestiges of liberation propaganda.

In Moscow on October 31, the CPSU daily *Pravda* published a remarkable proclamation from the Soviet government, which seemed to augur dramatic changes in the prospects for the Hungarian revolution. Dated October 30, and announced that day over Radio Moscow, the declaration was a striking statement in favor of building relations within "the great commonwealth of socialist nations" based on "the principles of complete equality, of respect for territorial integrity, state independence and sovereignty, and of noninterference in one another's internal affairs" (Document No. 50). The declaration focused on the entire socialist camp, but it specifically mentioned Hungary, acknowledging that "the working people of Hungary" were "rightfully" addressing the need to boost economic conditions and fight "bureaucratic distortions" in the country. Although it warned of "forces of black reaction and counterrevolution," the document nevertheless announced that the Soviet military command had been ordered "to withdraw the Soviet military units from the city of Budapest as soon as this is considered necessary by the Hungarian Government."

The new statement prompted immediate, jubilant reactions abroad. Virtually every member of the socialist camp publicly welcomed it. For top officials in Washington too, it was a major event. CIA Director Allen Dulles told the president and the NSC on November 1 that it was "one of the most important statements to come out of the USSR in the last decade" (Document No. 62). The completely unforeseen turn of events in Hungary, he said, was "a miracle." Hungary's revolutionary forces seemed to have won a tremendous victory, with Moscow endorsing the changes of October 28 as well as the momentous introduction of a multi-party system and coalition government within a hitherto socialist state.

But the elation turned out to be fleeting. Within a day of releasing the declaration, on October 31, the Kremlin abruptly changed its position and not only reversed the order to pull out from Budapest but decided to mount an even more massive military intervention. The curious point here is not that the CPSU Presidium, after lengthy debate, reached a consensus on October 31 to intervene, but that it did not do so the day before. The most plausible explanation is that the full import of the previous day's alarming news of general disintegration and violence against communist officials did not become apparent right away. By the 31st, the Soviets realized that communist power in Hungary was about to collapse, if it had not done so already, and that only immediate military action would make any difference.

For Moscow, the prospect of Hungary breaking away from the Soviet bloc was unacceptable on several levels. Firstly, in Soviet eyes, cracking the East European buffer zone would create an intolerable security threat. Secondly, Khrushchev felt he could not allow Moscow's actions in Hungary to be seen as vacillation in the West. As he told the Presidium on the 31st, "If we depart from Hungary, it will give a great boost to the Americans, English, and French—the imperialists. They will perceive it as weakness on our part and will go onto the offensive" (Document No. 53). The Kremlin also worried about the USSR's standing among its socialist allies, especially China (the Chinese delegation that had been visiting Moscow was informed of the Presidium's decision before returning to Beijing). Finally, Khrushchev was sensitive to challenges from within the CPSU. In rejecting the abandonment of Hungary, he reminded the Presidium: "Our party will not accept it if we do this." Clearly, the Soviets believed they had no other option but to intervene militarily.

Interestingly, U.S. intelligence had reached the same conclusion the day before. U.S. analysts noted that Soviet policymakers faced two options—either to accept Hungary's changed circumstances and allow the country to become independent, or to restore communist power by force of arms. They judged accurately that Moscow would most likely choose the latter course.[43] The Soviet decision was quickly followed by the introduction of a fresh wave of troops into Hungary, this time larger, with far more advanced equipment and a more seasoned command than on October 23.

---

[43] *FRUS, 1955–1957*, vol. 25, 330–335; Békés, *The 1956 Hungarian Revolution*, 16.

Internal Developments and the Question of Neutrality

While the superpowers were busy reacting to events, Hungary continued to experience dramatic political transformations. On October 31, the HWP was dissolved and a new party, the Hungarian Socialist Workers' Party (HSWP), took its place. It was a radical change, as the composition of the new, reform-oriented Provisional Executive Committee showed. The Committee's membership included Kádár, Nagy, Géza Losonczy, Ferenc Donáth, Zoltán Szántó, György Lukács, and Sándor Kopácsi. Remarkably, the Soviet emissaries, Mikoyan and Suslov, who returned to Moscow on the 31st, supported the new leadership. In their view, which differed from their Kremlin colleagues', it offered the only remaining hope of having communist doctrine represented by a party and leadership that still enjoyed some credibility and a chance to retain a share of power, even after free elections.

Other important developments occurred that day in the course of government talks with the armed revolutionaries. For one, adults were to be allowed to keep their weapons. Also, the rebels would now be included in the new public-security force—the National Guard formed at the Kilián Barracks. Army General Béla Király took over as commander-in-chief of the Guard, but representatives of younger revolutionaries also became part of its leadership. This move made it possible to begin reining in acts of mob justice and clear the streets of barricades and physical wreckage.

Parallel with the establishment of the Revolutionary Armed Forces Committee on October 30 (as noted above), and the National Guard the next day, a Revolutionary National Defense Commission was set up at the Ministry of Defense. The regime dismissed several Rákosi-era general officers from command positions in the army, opening the way for the military to present itself as a popular force dedicated to defending the revolution. The dilemma that had been facing officers until then—whether to side with the people or obey the government's orders— seemed to have been resolved.

The government and rebels also found a resolution for one of the most serious grievances from the past—the issue of political prisoners—through the release of a number of dissidents being held in the Budapest National Prison. Just the day before, as indicated earlier, Cardinal József Mindszenty had been freed from house arrest and returned to Budapest under the protection of an armored unit and a group of revolutionaries from Újpest.

Meanwhile, Moscow did not inform Nagy of the decision to re-invade. In fact, when the new government indicated that it wanted to negotiate the removal of the Red Army, the Kremlin only pretended to be interested even though the Presidium had already decided to intervene (Document No. 58). But by early in the morning of November 1, the Hungarian leader had learned from his own sources that the direction of Soviet troop movements had changed. Reports from Záhony, Nyíregyháza and Miskolc in the east of the country were essentially confirmed by Soviet Ambassador Andropov when he told Nagy disingenuously that the new troops entering the country were only being deployed to help cover the Red Army's withdrawal. He gave the same explanation for reports Nagy was receiving of other troop movements inside the country, including sealing off airfields.

Realizing that Moscow had again chosen a military solution, Nagy was forced into a predicament. He could either toe the line with the Kremlin, which would give him a chance, albeit a slim one, to stay in power; or he could take independent action. Documents now available on this tense period show that Nagy and his colleagues did not take long to choose their direction. On the morning of November 1, the newly formed inner cabinet decided to summon the Soviet ambassador to protest the Red Army's continued advance into Hungary and to negotiate terms for its withdrawal. They resolved to send further official protests to the United Nations if Andropov's responses were unsatisfactory (Document No. 61).

The same afternoon, the cabinet met with Andropov. When the ambassador again failed to calm Hungarian concerns, the government took the bold step of declaring Hungary's neutrality, renouncing the Warsaw Pact and calling on the four permanent members of the U.N. Security

Council for support (Document Nos. 64 and 65). Formal communications to this effect were sent to the U.N. and to the chiefs of foreign diplomatic missions in Budapest (Document Nos. 66 and 67), and Nagy went on the radio to announce the cabinet's decision (Document No. 68). The logic behind leaving the Warsaw Pact and declaring neutrality was to remove any Soviet claim to the right to intervene by asserting that Hungary was either an ally in distress or, conversely, a security threat. This was the only approach the Hungarians were able to devise under the circumstances.[44]

Hungary's declaration of neutrality did not have the desired diplomatic effect abroad. Great Britain and France supported the idea, but for a specific reason. After the sudden deterioration in relations among the Western powers due to the Suez crisis, discussions about Hungary between their representatives at the United Nations took place in an increasingly icy atmosphere. Instead of genuinely condemning the Soviet intervention, the British and French mainly wanted to exploit the Hungarian crisis for their own interests, which in this case diverged fundamentally from the United States'.

At this point, the British and French tried to move the Hungarian question from the Security Council to the emergency session of the General Assembly, which had been convened to discuss Suez. They hoped that the General Assembly's treatment of both crises simultaneously would mitigate international censure of their own activities. In fact, because there was no veto power in the General Assembly, transferring the Hungarian question there might have helped the reform and revolutionary elements in Hungary, since the Soviets would not be able to block a resolution against the invasion. However, the sole U.S. objective at that point, given the limits on their influence in Eastern Europe, was to resolve the Middle East crisis. They therefore did everything possible to frustrate the British and French strategy, and, until November 4, they succeeded—blocking a draft Hungary proposal in the Security Council and preventing referral of the question to the General Assembly via the "uniting for peace" procedure.[45]

Apart from the maneuvering with their European allies, Eisenhower administration officials disagreed sharply among themselves over whether Hungary's neutrality would serve U.S. interests. The concept gained a good deal of support in the State Department where it had already been under discussion days before Nagy launched his appeals to the United Nations. President Eisenhower himself sympathized with the idea of establishing a zone of neutral states in Central and Eastern Europe but he wanted to achieve it through negotiations with the Soviets within a framework of the general rebuilding of East-West relations. Yet to openly recognize Hungary's neutrality meant that the United States might have to take on a difficult international obligation in the event the Hungarian uprising was suppressed, a possibility which seemed imminent. Even more important for Eisenhower was the likelihood that such a move would jeopardize Soviet-American relations, and indirectly the entire process of détente. Secretary of State Dulles, who had sharp misgivings about the increasingly powerful nonaligned movement, and was generally poorly disposed toward the notion of neutrality, not surprisingly came out against the idea with regard to Hungary. Dulles firmly believed that if, by some chance, Hungary were to succeed in freeing itself from Soviet domination, the United States should not be content with its neutral status when a real possibility existed of incorporating it into the Western sphere of influence.[46]

[44] On the history of the declaration of neutrality, see: Csaba Békés, "A magyar semlegesség 1956-ban," in *Semlegesség: Illúziók és Realitás*, ed. Biztonságpolitikai és Honvédelmi Kutatások Központja (Budapest: Biztonságpolitikai és Honvédelmi Kutatások Központja, [1997]): 111–130.

[45] For an analysis of the interrelationship between the Hungarian and the Middle East crises, see Brian McCauley, "Hungary and Suez, 1956: The Limits of Soviet and American Power," in *Hungary and Suez, 1956: An Exploration of Who Makes History*, ed. Daniel F. Calhoun (Lanham, Md.: University Press of America, 1991); see also Csaba Békés, "A magyar kérdés az ENSZ-ben és a nyugati nagyhatalmak titkos tárgyalásai 1956. október 28.-november 4: Brit külügyi dokumentumok," in *Évkönyv II*, 1993, ed. János M. Bak et al. (Budapest: 1956-os Intézet, 1993): 39–71.

[46] On the U.S. position toward Hungary's neutrality, see Csaba Békés, "Az Egyesült Államok és a magyar semlegesség 1956-ban," in *Évkönyv III*, ed. János M. Bak et al. (Budapest: 1956-os Intézet, 1994): 165–178.

Moscow Prepares for Intervention

Of course, the Soviets were convinced that Dulles' opinions epitomized the prevailing attitude in the Western camp. Since the Kremlin leadership was even more loathe to see Hungary adopt neutrality, they drew up a set of political blueprints—complementing the military operation—to replace the Nagy government with a regime that could be relied on to stay firmly within the Soviet sphere. At the October 31 CPSU Presidium meeting, two Hungarians—Ferenc Münnich and János Kádár—surfaced as consensus choices to head a new, Soviet-installed "provisional revolutionary government." Several Presidium members preferred Münnich but also felt comfortable with Kádár even though he was a member of Nagy's inner cabinet.[47] The day before, based on Mikoyan's assessments from Budapest, Khrushchev had declared that "Kádár is behaving well" (Document No. 49). On November 1, after the Hungarian cabinet voted unanimously on neutrality, Andropov told Moscow that unlike virtually every other Hungarian leader, Kádár's participation in the vote had been reluctant (Document No. 65).

That same day, Kádár, along with Münnich, had secretly gone to the Soviet Embassy to meet with Andropov. The two Hungarians then departed by armored vehicle to Soviet military headquarters at Tököl, from where they were flown to Moscow, arriving early the next day. Kádár had told no one where he was going, leaving his Hungarian colleagues to wonder whether he had been taken prisoner by the Soviets, or even the rebels.

Meanwhile, after the momentous decision to invade, Khrushchev and a small delegation immediately set out to inform other Warsaw Pact members and, where necessary, seek support. On November 1, Khrushchev, Malenkov and Molotov met with Polish leader Władysław Gomułka at Brest. Gomułka had narrowly averted a similar fate for Poland just 10 days earlier and was understandably cool toward the decision (Document Nos. 63 and 69). From there, Khrushchev and Malenkov stopped briefly in Bucharest to inform the Romanian and Czechoslovak party leaders, then quickly visited Sofia, Bulgaria, before flying to Yugoslavia (Document No. 75). The consultations with President Tito took place from November 2–3 on the island of Brioni, where the Yugoslav leader was recuperating from an illness (Document No. 76). Khrushchev was still courting the Yugoslavs in an effort to undo the 1948 split with Stalin, so Tito's consent was particularly important.[48] Tito raised no objections to the intervention despite his positive relationship with Nagy. The Yugoslav leader had already become apprehensive about the turn of events in Hungary by the end of October. He had instructed Belgrade's ambassador to Budapest to inform his contacts in the government and HWP that "no further concessions [to the rebels] can be made" (Document Nos. 55 and 56). Tito now promised to use his influence at the appropriate time to neutralize the Nagy group politically by offering them refuge in the Yugoslav Embassy in Budapest, and to persuade Nagy to resign as prime minister. Tito also backed Kádár to head the new "counter-government" rather than Münnich.[49]

---

[47] The fact that on November 1 Kádár taped a radio broadcast calling the revolution a "glorious uprising of our people" and pointing to the external threat facing the country (i.e. from the East) did not seem to deter the Kremlin. Interestingly, at the Presidium meeting on the 31st, Khrushchev even mentioned Nagy as a candidate for deputy prime minister, possibly in the interests of attracting greater popular support.

[48] Tito also was an influential figure for reformists in East and Central Europe, as well as in the nonaligned movement. Gomułka and Mao were other important players from Khrushchev's perspective.

[49] On Yugoslav policy towards the Hungarian Revolution and its aftermath, see: Veljko Micunovic, *Moscow Diary, 1956–1958*, trans. David Floyd (Garden City, N.Y.: Doubleday, 1980); László Varga, "Moszkva-Belgrád-Budapest: A jugoszláv kapcsolat 1956. október-november," in *Jalta és Szuez között*, ed. by Luca Gábor (Budapest: Tudósítások Kiadó, 1989): 142–175; Pierre Maurer, *La réconciliation sovéto-yougoslave 1954–1958: Illusions et désillusions de Tito* (Cousset (Fribourg): Delval, 1991); Zoltán Ripp, *Belgrád és Moszkva között: A jugoszláv kapcsolat és a Nagy Imre-kérdés, 1956. november–1959. február* (Budapest: Politikatörténeti Alapítvány, 1994); Kiss, Ripp and Vida, *Magyar-jugoszláv kapcsolatok, 1956*, and id., *Magyar-jugoszláv kapcsolatok, 1956. december–1959 február: A magyar-jugoszláv kapcsolatok és a Nagy Imre csoport sorsa, Dokumentumok* (Budapest: MTA Jelenkor-kutató Bizottság, 1995 [1997]).

While Khrushchev was in Brioni, Kádár and his group were in Moscow discussing plans for installing the new regime. Immediately after arriving early on November 2, the Hungarian visitors took part in a CPSU Presidium meeting. Kádár argued for a peaceful solution to the crisis and for retaining the present government and institutions (Document No. 70). There are several possible explanations for his position, which seems anomalous in retrospect. For one thing, without Khrushchev there, Kádár may not have realized how united the Presidium was in its decision. For another thing, even before the October 28 turn of events, Kádár had repeatedly emphasized the dangers of relying on force to defeat the revolution without accompanying political reforms. He clearly understood that a Soviet-led military victory would rule out a genuine political settlement capable of removing the underlying causes of the crisis. Furthermore, any successor government would essentially be a Soviet puppet, an unappealing prospect for Kádár.

Until Khrushchev returned, Kádár also did not know where the other satellite leaders stood, or whether other Warsaw Pact forces would take part in the occupation. For example, Romania's participation, which Bucharest offered, would have complicated the new Hungarian government's position even further because of the two countries' mutual antagonisms. He also had no way of telling what stance the Yugoslavs and the Poles were taking. Finally, he was unclear as to how far the Soviets were willing to go to restore the old regime. There were no apparent guarantees that Rákosi and his supporters might not return to power, which would mean Kádár would have to do battle on two fronts—against both the party reformers and the hardliners. Since he would be facing opposition from virtually the entire country, Kádár's failure would be virtually assured.

On his return to Moscow on November 3, Khrushchev, more secure in his decision to invade despite the Poles' ambivalent reaction, hastened to reassure Kádár. He promised that Rákosi would not be allowed to return to Hungary, let alone re-enter the political picture. He also guaranteed, after his talks with Gomułka and Tito, that Kádár would have the support of the other reform-oriented countries of the region. Finally, Khrushchev made it clear that the Soviet decision to intervene was irrevocable (Document No. 77). Kádár faced only two courses: to cooperate and stay in power, or to stay loyal to the Nagy government and the Hungarian people, and deal with the political consequences. He chose the first alternative, possibly influenced by the recent creation of a new coalition government in Budapest that seemed like it might be more viable.

But Kádár also seemed to agree with some of the Kremlin's basic thinking. He deplored the violence against the HWP—"They're killing communists," he exclaimed—and proclaimed to the Presidium that "surrendering a socialist country to counterrev[olution] is impossible." Notes of his remarks included in this volume show that he reverted more than once to calling the uprising a counterrevolution. At the same time, he insisted that the revolt had a broad base of support—"the whole nation is taking part in the movement"—and stressed the need for an eventual Soviet troop withdrawal. Münnich, for his part, agreed. Finally, Kádár also tried faintly to eke out a claim to independence for the soon-to-be-established replacement regime. "This government must not be puppet-like," he insisted (Document No. 78). In fact, there was no chance of it being anything else. The Soviets drew up the list of ministers. The policy program was composed in Russian; Kádár, who did not speak the language, could not even help to translate it. And to ensure maximum control during the change-over, the Soviets decided to send three Presidium members to accompany Kádár to Hungary: Georgii Malenkov, Anastas Mikoyan and Leonid Brezhnev.[50]

The Revolution's Final Days

While Kádár and his Soviet staff in Moscow prepared for the invasion, the atmosphere in Hungary was a mixture of hope and apprehension. Despite the news of an apparent Soviet retreat

---

[50] Leonid I. Brezhnev was a member of the CPSU CC beginning in 1952, a candidate member of the CPSU CC Presidium between February 1956–June 1957 and CC Secretary between 1956–1960. He later rose to the post of general secretary of the party, and died in November 1982. Eventually the Soviet mission consisted of Malenkov, Suslov and Aristov.

and a truly remarkable national victory, there was a palpable sense of foreboding at what Moscow might do next. The Nagy government kept busy trying to consolidate domestic conditions and seal off the country from the looming threat. On November 2, the Hungarians sent a formal protest note to Moscow about the Soviet troops (Document No. 72). The cabinet also appointed delegations to handle a variety of international issues: Géza Losonczy would lead the group in charge of Hungary's departure from the Warsaw Pact; Nagy would head the delegation to the U.N. General Assembly; and Ferenc Erdei and Pál Maléter were assigned the delicate troop withdrawal talks, which the Hungarians proposed begin immediately (Document No. 71).

On November 3, Nagy moved to broaden the government's base of support. Following demands by the recently revived political parties, he agreed to reshuffle the cabinet and create a more representative coalition. This brought into the government István Szabó of the Smallholders, István Bibó and Ferenc Farkas[51] of the National Peasants' (Petőfi) Party, and Anna Kéthly, József Fischer and Gyula Kelemen[52] of the Social Democrats. The new defense minister was Pál Maléter, who was promoted to the rank of major general. Except for Ferenc Erdei, the other members of the cabinet (Kádár, Béla Kovács, Losonczy and Tildy) remained in office.

On a popular level, society was already attempting a partial return to normalcy. Workers at several locations returned to their jobs on Saturday, November 3, and a succession of Workers' Councils voted to go back to work in full force the next Monday. At the same time, the revolutionary councils, in cooperation with the National Guard units and the army, began to organize and install defenses against a Soviet assault. Partial mobilization was ordered in several places. Soviet troops were kept under observation, as were main access roads. Medical stations were set up. Still, there was general hope that the Soviets would not move in the face of such determined national unity. Even in the worst case, the feeling was that the country could count on the good offices of the United Nations, which Hungary had joined less than a year before.

On the international front, the government had two objectives at this juncture. Through the international press, they wanted to reassure the world, and especially the USSR, that no counterrevolution was occurring in Hungary, that the duly constituted government had unanimously backed the fundamental social changes since 1945, such as land reform and nationalization—in other words a new order that should have been acceptable to Moscow. The other goal was to appeal to Polish and Romanian diplomats to mediate between Budapest and Moscow, and particularly to prevent the Soviet Union from resorting to armed force. Unbeknownst to the Hungarians, the Soviets had already made certain of those governments' support.

In at least one respect, the hopes of many Hungarians were undermined during this period. At 8:00 in the evening on November 3, Cardinal Mindszenty delivered a speech on Radio Free Kossuth that amounted to a political declaration. The influential head of the Hungarian Catholic Church did not come out directly against the Nagy government, but he described its members as "successors of the fallen regime." In sum, the address was calmer than many people had expected. But its tenor led some observers outside the country to conclude that a new center of power, opposed to the Nagy government, might soon emerge. This had ramifications reaching all the way to Washington where officials, not surprisingly, tended to gravitate towards a symbol of religious dissent of Mindszenty's stature rather than to a perceived communist apparatchik such as Nagy. At the November 1 NSC meeting, shortly after Mindszenty's release from house arrest, CIA Director Allen Dulles made the point that Nagy seemed unable to unite the rebel forces, but "in such a heavily Catholic nation as Hungary, Cardinal Mindszenty might prove to be such a leader and unifying force" (Document No. 62). This view was transmitted in several RFE programs as well. The problem, as acknowledged recently, was that Mindszenty probably never had a realistic chance of building an alternative government. On the other hand, Nagy did have a

[51]Ferenc Farkas was secretary general of the Petőfi Party beginning October 31 and minister of state in the Nagy cabinet on November 3–4, 1956.

[52] Gyula Kelemen, who was a member of the Social Democrat leadership after 1945, became secretary general of the SDP in October 1956 and minister of state in the Nagy government between November 3–4, 1956.

viable and growing national base of support, even though American observers consistently, and inaccurately, compared him unfavorably even to the likes of Gomułka (Document No. 30). Some American operatives, such as CIA Deputy Director for Plans Frank Wisner, who had extensive experience in Hungary, recognized the paradox but could not convince the White House to throw its weight behind a Nagy-led coalition.

The Second Invasion

The ambiguity of Soviet actions continued on November 3. Soviet troops, already surrounding the airfields, blocked off the larger cities and closed main roads and the Western frontier. At the same time, negotiations had begun in Parliament on troop withdrawals. Pál Maléter put forward the Hungarian government's position based on instructions from Nagy. Soviet units that had arrived after October 23 were to leave the country by December 31. Negotiations would resume later on the troops stationed in Hungary earlier under the terms of the Warsaw Pact. The two sides agreed to continue talks later that day at the Soviet base at Tököl. However, by then the invasion, code-named "Operation Whirlwind," had already gotten underway. As one of the first steps toward neutralizing the Hungarian leadership, Soviet security forces under KGB head General Ivan Serov arrested Maléter, Ferenc Erdei, and the rest of the Hungarian delegation at 10:00 that evening as they sat at the negotiating table.

The next morning, November 4, the country awoke to the sounds of artillery and armored vehicle traffic. The Soviet attack on Budapest and several other cities began at 4.15 a.m. At 5:05, in a radio transmission from Uzhgorod, a town in Ukraine on the Hungarian border, Kádár announced the formation of the Hungarian Revolutionary Workers' and Peasants' Government. He declared that the mass movement of October 23 had transformed into a fascist uprising, which required the intervention of Soviet troops. He promised immunity to everyone who had "joined the movement for honest, patriotic reasons" and added that several of the revolution's demands would be met, including beginning negotiations on a Soviet withdrawal once order was restored.

At 5:20 a.m., Nagy read a proclamation on Radio Free Kossuth. It was too soon for the Hungarian leadership to have an accurate picture of the situation. Nagy did not yet know, for example, what had happened to the Hungarian negotiators at Tököl the night before. All he could tell the nation at this stage was that the government had not invited Soviet forces in. He did not give orders to resist (and realistically could not have), but he did not forbid resistance either (Document No. 82). Military commanders at the Ministry of Defense, however, did bar the Hungarian army from taking up arms, based on a written order from Major General István Kovács,[53] who had been arrested at Tököl. Nagy called on the Maléter team to return from Tököl immediately, but when this had no effect, he decided that he had no alternative but to accept the offer of asylum at the Yugoslav Embassy. During the day, 42 others, including family members, joined him. Cardinal Mindszenty took refuge in the American Legation. Minister of State István Bibó, the only representative of the lawful Hungarian government to remain in the Parliament Building, addressed a final proclamation to the nation and the world, defending the revolution and the Hungarian people who had conducted it.

---

[53] Major-General István Kovács was appointed chief of the general staff as of October 31, 1956. Along with Pál Maléter, he was arrested by Soviet authorities during the negotiations over Soviet troop withdrawals on November 3. In 1958, he was sentenced to prison but was amnestied in 1961.

DOCUMENT NO. 25: Working Notes from the Session of the CPSU CC Presidium, October 23, 1956

The CPSU CC Presidium gathered at 11:00 p.m. on October 23 to discuss the revolutionary events that stirred Budapest that day. According to Vladimir Malin's notes, the Presidium's primary source of information was probably a report from Marshal Georgii Zhukov, although Ambassador Andropov and Ernő Gerő also telephoned from Budapest with accounts of their own. Following Zhukov's report, Khrushchev proposed an immediate solution: to send troops to Budapest. Anastas Mikoyan suggested an alternative, "Polish type" political way out as a first step, involving retaining Imre Nagy in the Hungarian leadership and leaving the responsibility for forcibly restoring order to the Hungarians—that is, to Nagy himself. Every other Presidium member, however, supported Khrushchev. To monitor political measures which the Hungarian government was expected to take, including invoking a curfew and conducting courts martial, two members of the Presidium were dispatched to Budapest: the "liberal" Mikoyan, and Mikhail Suslov, an ally of the hard-line faction. Shortly after, or possibly even during, the brief meeting, the Kremlin ordered special troops garrisoned in Székesfehérvár to move immediately on Budapest.

Participants: Bulganin, Kaganovich, Mikoyan, Molotov, Pervukhin, Saburov, Khrushchev, Suslov, Brezhnev, Zhukov, Furtseva, Shepilov

On the Situation in Budapest and Overall in Hungary
(Cdes. Zhukov, Bulganin, Khrushchev)

Information of *Cde. Zhukov.*
A demonstration by 100 thous. in Budapest.
The radio station is on fire.

In Debrecen the obkom[54] and MVD[55] buildings were occupied.
Cde. Khrushchev speaks in favor of sending troops to Budapest.
Cde. Bulganin believes Cde. Khrushchev's proposal to send troops is justified.
Cde. Mikoyan: Without Nagy they can't get control of the movement, and it's also cheaper for us. Expresses doubt about the sending of troops. What are we losing? The Hungarians themselves will restore order on their own. We should try political measures, and only then send troops.
Cde. Molotov—With Nagy left on his own, Hungary is coming apart. Favors the sending of troops.
Cde. Kaganovich—The government is being overthrown. There's no comparison with Poland. Favors the sending of troops.
Cde. Pervukhin—Troops must be sent.
Cde. Zhukov—There is indeed a difference with Poland. Troops must be sent. One of the members of the CC Presidium should travel there. Martial law should be declared in the country, and a curfew introduced.
Cde. Suslov—The situation in Poland is different. Troops must be sent.
Cde. Saburov—Troops must be sent to uphold order.
Cde. Shepilov—Favors the sending of troops
Cde. Kirichenko[56]—Favors the sending of troops. Cdes. Malinin and Serov should be dispatched to Budapest.

---

[54] Provincial party committee.

[55] Although this Russian abbreviation is usually used to indicate the Soviet Interior Ministry, in this context it clearly refers to the Hungarian ÁVH.

[56] Aleksei I. Kirichenko was a member of the CPSU CC Presidium from 1955–1965 and first secretary of the Ukrainian Communist Party from 1953–1965.

Cde. Khrushchev—We should recruit Nagy for political action. But until then we shouldn't make [him] a chairman of the government.
Cdes. Mikoyan and Suslov are to fly to Budapest.

[Source: TsKhSD, F. 3, Op. 12, D. 1006, Ll. 4–4ob, compiled by V. N. Malin. Originally published in the Cold War International History Project Bulletin *no. 8/9 (Winter 1996/1997): 388–9. Translated by Mark Kramer.]*

DOCUMENT NO. 26: Situation Report from Anastas Mikoyan and Mikhail Suslov in Budapest to the CPSU CC Presidium, October 24, 1956

Following the CPSU CC Presidium's October 23 decision, Anastas Mikoyan and Mikhail Suslov, along with KGB Director Ivan Serov and Army Deputy Chief of Staff Mikhail Malinin, set off for Budapest, arriving the next day. While Mikoyan and Suslov held official talks with members of the Hungarian leadership, Serov and Malinin arrived incognito to focus secretly on military preparations. Their presence in the country during the revolution was not discovered until the release of documents from the Russian archives in 1992. Mikoyan and Suslov stayed until October 31 and during that time sent seven reports to the CPSU CC Presidium. In this message, they offer a more positive picture of the situation than accounts received in Moscow the previous day, concluding that the situation appeared much less dangerous from the ground. Their depiction of the destruction of the rebels' firing positions, the arrests of hundreds of "instigators," and the involvement of Hungarian authorities in restoring order, in addition to their comment that Imre Nagy had shown loyalty and a co-operative attitude toward Moscow, according to Malin's notes, gave the Kremlin such a feeling of optimism and self-assurance that the Presidium did not raise the Hungarian issue again until October 26.

TOP SECRET
MAKING COPIES PROHIBITED

CIPHERED TELEGRAM
FROM BUDAPEST

OUT OF SEQUENCE

We arrived at the scene after some delay; due to weather conditions, we were unable to land at the airport near Budapest. We landed 90 kilometers to the north. We stopped by the corps headquarters for orientation, and from there, in an armored personnel carrier with comrades [KGB chief Ivan] Serov and [Gen. Mikhail S.] Malinin, we set off for the city. We were accompanied by tanks, because there was shooting in Budapest at this time and casualties on both sides, including Soviet soldiers and officers.

In Buda small groups of people watched the movement of our column calmly; some looked anxious, others greeted it with a smile. The roads approaching the city and in the city were full of Soviet tanks and other materiel.

On the streets with the Soviet troops were Hungarian patrols. In contrast to Buda, where it was calm, in Pest there was continuous shooting between isolated groups of provocateurs and individuals and our machine-gunners, beginning at the bridge and extending to the ministry of defense building, as well as toward the central committee building. Our men did more of the shooting; to solitary shots we replied with salvos.

In the Ministry of Defense we met the ministers of defense and state security, as well as a group of Central Committee members—[István] Kovács, Zoltán Vas, and others, who were authorized to lead the operation for liquidating the riots in the city. There is a field headquarters there, which works in contact with the Hungarians. It should be noted that during a telephone conversation with Gerő from the corps headquarters, he replied to our question about the situation by answering that there is both an improvement and deterioration in the situation, and that the arrival of Soviet troops in the city has a negative effect on the disposition of the inhabitants, including the workers.

After a conversation with army personnel—during which it turned out that, after closer familiarization, the preliminary reports from the Soviet military command and the Hungarian armed forces command were exaggerated in a rather negative way—we stopped by the Hungarian Workers' Party Central Committee, where we conversed with Gerő, Imre Nagy,

Zoltán Szántó, and Hegedüs, who informed us about the situation in the city and the measures they had taken to liquidate the riots.

We had the impression that Gerő especially, but the other comrades as well, are exaggerating the opponent's strength and underestimating their own strength. At five o'clock Moscow time the situation in the city was as follows:

All the hotbeds of insurgency have been crushed; liquidation of the main hotbed, at the radio station, where about 4,000 people are concentrated, is still going on. They raised a white flag, but when representatives of the Hungarian authorities appeared, [the insurgents] presented the removal of Gerő from his post as a condition of surrender, which of course was rejected. Our command is setting for itself the task of liquidating this hotbed tonight. It is significant that the Hungarian colleagues here, above all the state security personnel, put up violent resistance to the insurgents and tolerated defeat here only because ammunition was exhausted and a fresh battalion of Hungarian troops who mutinied, attacked them.

The comrades express the opinion that the Hungarian army conducted itself poorly, although the Debrecen division performed well. Hungarian sailors, who patrolled the banks of the [Danube] River, also performed well, especially, as already noted, state security troops and employees.

Arrests of the instigators and organizers of the disturbances, more than 450 people, are being carried out. Exposing and arresting instigators continues.

The task has been set to completely liquidate the remaining individual groups hiding in buildings. Because a turning point in the events has occurred, it has been decided to use Hungarian units more boldly for patrolling, for detaining suspicious elements and people violating the introduction of a state of emergency, and for guarding important installations (railroad stations, roads, etc.).

The Hungarian comrades, especially Imre Nagy, approved the use of more Hungarian military units, militia, and state security units to lighten the burden on the Soviet troops' and to emphasize the role of the Hungarians themselves in liquidating the riots. The majority of the workers did not participate in the riots, and it is even said that the workers in Csepel, who had no weapons, drove off provocateurs who wanted to incite them to riot. However, some workers, especially young ones, did take part in the disturbances.

One of the Hungarian comrades' most serious mistakes was the fact that, before 12 midnight last night, they did not permit anyone to shoot at the participants in the riots.

The Hungarians themselves are taking measures, and we gave them additional advice with respect to the organization of workers' fighting squads at factories and in the regional party committees, and about arming such squads.

They had already made such a decision, but they didn't carry it out, because they couldn't deliver weapons to the factories, fearing that the opponent would intercept them. Measures were taken to provide for a weapons delivery today, with the help of our armored personnel carriers. Radio addresses by prominent party and government leaders, as well as other public leaders, were organized. Gerő, Imre Nagy, and Zoltán Tildy have already spoken. István Dobi, Hegedüs, Szakasits,[57] Kádár, Zoltán Szántó, Marosán, and Rónai will be speaking. Appeals by the Women's, Youth, and Trades Unions will be published.

Today, not a single newspaper was published, only a bulletin. It has been arranged to have at least one newspaper published tomorrow. It has also been arranged to publicly announce that all citizens who fail to surrender weapons within the next 24 hours will be accused of a criminal offense.

We are not transmitting the information about the changes in the leadership of the party and government, since the embassy has already reported it. While conversing with the Hungarian comrades, we did not touch on that issue. One gets the feeling that these events are facilitating the

---

[57] Árpád Szakasits was secretary general of the Social Democrat Party between 1945–1948, president of Hungary from 1948–1949, and chairman of the Presidential Council from 1949–1950. Imprisoned after a show trial in 1950, he was amnestied in March 1956 but, because of his former cooperation with the HWP, was not invited to join the re-established SDP during the revolution.

unity of the Central Committee and Politburo. When we asked Imre Nagy when and how he joined in the struggle with the party's opponents, he replied that he started to take action in the struggle yesterday at six o'clock in the evening, not by the summons of the Central Committee, but because the youth in the meeting demanded that he go there and speak to them, which he did.

He thinks the majority of the crowd of almost a hundred thousand people approved of his appeals, but many fascist element groups hollered, whistled, and screamed, when he said that it was necessary to work together with the party. Fights took place in the square between the fascist and democratic elements. The whole crowd dispersed peaceably, but then began to regroup in various places in the city and the events, well-known to you, began.

During Imre Nagy's reply, Gerő retorted that they were looking for Imre Nagy before the meeting and couldn't find him. Nagy said that if they had appeared before the crowd earlier and announced the leadership changes before or during the meeting, then events would not have grown complicated. The other comrades met Imre Nagy's assertion with silence.

To our question, "Is there unity in the Central Committee and Politburo in the face of the events that have taken place?," Everyone answered in the affirmative; however Gerő made a remark that more voices are being heard against his election as first secretary of the Central Committee, thinking that he is responsible for this whole thing. To this remark, Imre Nagy said that it is necessary to make a correction; this concerns neither the Politburo, neither the Central Committee members. Such voices, rather, are being heard from below. He cited the letter received from a secretary of one of the factory party committees, protesting the choice of Gerő as first secretary. To our question, "May we report to our Central Committee that the Hungarian comrades are mastering the situation and are confident that they will deal with it?" they answered in the affirmative.

Gerő announced that he hadn't slept for two nights; the other comrades: one night. We prearranged to meet with these same comrades at eight o'clock in the evening. We have the impression that all the Central Committee members with whom we met related well, in a friendly manner, to our appearance at such a time. We said the purpose of our arrival was to lend assistance to the Hungarian leadership in such a way as not cause friction, and for the public benefit, referring especially to the participation of Soviet troops in liquidating the riots. The Hungarian comrades, especially Imre Nagy, related to this with approval.

A.MIKOYAN
M.SUSLOV

[Source: AVP RF, F. 059a, Op. 4, Pap. 6, D. 5, Ll. 1–7. Originally published in the Cold War International History Project Bulletin no. 5 (Spring 1995): 22–3, 29. Translated by Johanna Granville.]

DOCUMENT NO. 27: Jan Svoboda's Notes on the CPSU CC Presidium Meeting with Satellite Leaders, October 24, 1956

The CPSU CC Presidium called a meeting of bloc allies for October 24, inviting representatives of the East German, Bulgarian, Hungarian, and Romanian communist parties. The Soviets originally intended to discuss the Polish situation and inform the "fraternal parties" about the negotiations with the PZPR. But because of the "disquieting events" that had taken place in the meantime, Hungary was also a major agenda item. The following document is a report by Jan Svoboda, secretary to Czechoslovak party leader Antonín Novotný, about this extraordinary session.

This account has special significance because, among all the materials that have been made public so far, it gives the most detailed account of the circumstances underlying the first Soviet intervention of October 23. However, it also differs markedly from the account in Malin's notes (see Document No. 25). For example, it is interesting that Khrushchev emphasizes Gerő's role in Moscow's decision to intervene, reflecting the Soviet leader's attempt to balance the need for strong measures to avoid unraveling the alliance, with a desire to stress principles of mutual assistance and support demands for "legal" requests for assistance from within the socialist alliance. In some ways, Malin's notes, recording an internal CPSU leadership gathering, are a more realistic assessment of the decision on military intervention.

ACCOUNT OF A MEETING AT THE CPSU CC, 24 OCTOBER 1956, ON THE SITUATION IN POLAND AND HUNGARY

On 24 Oct. 1956, I [Novotný] attended a meeting of the CPSU CC Presidium. Comrades from the HWP Central Committee, the SED Central Committee, the BCP Central Committee, and the RWP Central Committee also were invited to take part. But the only ones who were actually present were the comrades from Germany, namely Ulbricht, Grotewohl, and Stoph,[58] and the comrades from Bulgaria—Zhivkov,[59] Yugov, and Damyanov.[60]

Comrade Khrushchev began by informing everyone about the situation in Poland and Hungary. He said that originally the CPSU CC Presidium wanted to inform the fraternal parties about the situation in Poland and about the outcome of the negotiations between the CPSU CC and the PZPR CC. But in the meantime, important events had happened in Hungary. That is why he deemed it necessary to inform us about the situation there as well.

In essence, this is what he said:

When serious reports came in from Poland that far-reaching changes were expected in the top party posts of the PZPR, the CC CPSU decided to send a delegation to Poland.

The delegation negotiated mainly with Comrades Gomułka, Cyrankiewicz,[61] Jędrychowski,[62] Ochab, and the foreign minister.

---

[58] Willi Stoph was a member of the SED Political Committee from 1953–1989, vice chairman of the Council of Ministers from 1955–1962, and minister of defense from 1956–1960.

[59] Todor Zhivkov was first secretary, later secretary-general of the BCP from 1954–1989.

[60] Georgi Damyanov was a member of the BCP CC Politburo beginning 1945 and chairman of the Bulgarian National Assembly from 1950.

[61] Józef Cyrankiewicz was a member of the PZPR CC Politburo and chairman of the Council of Ministers beginning 1948.

[62] Stefan Jędrychowski was a member of the PZPR CC Politburo from 1956–1971 and head of the PZPR CC Planning Committee from 1956–1971.

All of these comrades, especially Gomułka, sought to defend everything that was happening in Poland. They assured the Soviet delegation that the measures being taken would not have an adverse effect on Poland's relations with the Soviet Union and the CPSU. On the question of why so many changes occurred in the [PZPR] Politburo, Comrade Gomułka said that the comrades who had not been reelected to the Politburo had lost the confidence of the party masses. The Soviet comrades are very worried because the [Polish] comrades who were removed from the Politburo were known to the Soviet party as old, trustworthy revolutionaries who were faithful to the cause of socialism. Among them is also Comrade Rokossovskii, who is of Polish origin but never gave up his Soviet citizenship.

While the CPSU CC delegation was in Poland, certain Soviet Army maneuvers took place on Polish territory, which displeased Comrade Gomułka. The discussions between the delegations ranged from being very warm to rude. Gomułka emphasized several times that they would not permit their independence to be taken away and would not allow anyone to interfere in Poland's internal affairs. He said that if he were leader of the country, he could restore order very promptly. The PZPR representatives explained the arguments and factors that had led to the current situation in Poland. These were very unpersuasive and seemed to be outright fabrications. For example, Comrade Gomułka tried to convince the Soviet delegation that most blame should be placed on the presence of 50 Soviet security advisers in Poland and [on the presence] of many generals and other senior officers in the Polish army who still hold Soviet citizenship.

In addition, [Gomułka] said that Poland's obligation to supply coal to the USSR at excessively low prices had caused the difficult economic situation. Comrade Khrushchev emphasized to the Polish comrades, referring to several concrete examples, that on various occasions in the past, this had not been true.

After the CPSU CC delegation returned to Moscow, an official letter was dispatched to the PZPR CC from the CPSU CC saying that it was up to the Polish side to decide whether to send the Soviet advisers and the generals with Soviet citizenship immediately back to the USSR.

A delegation from the PZPR was invited to meetings in the USSR along party lines [*po stranicke linii*]. On Oct. 23, 1956 Comrade Gomułka told the CPSU CC that he would accept the invitation and that he would arrive after Nov. 11, 1956. Comrade Gomułka also asked Comrade Khrushchev to have the Soviet forces return to their camps, as he had been promised. From the telephone conversation between Comrade Gomułka and Comrade Khrushchev, Comrade Khrushchev got the impression that Comrade Gomułka was attempting to earn the confidence of the CPSU CC.

On this occasion the two sides arranged that a long-planned exchange of delegations between *Trybuna Ludu* and *Pravda* would take place in the near future.

Typically, at PZPR CC plenary sessions the majority of speakers would express their wish for friendship with the USSR and other states of people's democracies.

The opinion of the CPSU CC is that in the case of Poland it is necessary to avoid nervousness and haste. It is necessary to help the Polish comrades straighten out the party line and do everything to reinforce the union among Poland, the USSR, and the other people's democracies.

Poland is in a catastrophic economic situation. There is a shortfall of 900,000 tons of grain. Coal mining is in very bad shape also. After the Twentieth CPSU Congress, Poland adopted the same social measures as in the USSR, but did not have sufficient means to carry them out. That is why Comrade Ochab turned to the CPSU CC delegation with a request for a loan. When Comrade Khrushchev remarked that perhaps the USA would give them a loan, [Ochab] answered that Poland would ask for a loan from the USA but he doubts that the USA would give them one. Comrade Khrushchev surmised that Comrade Ochab was answering hastily, on the spur of the moment.

Comrade Khrushchev said that the GDR and ČSR had asked the CPSU CC to resolve the problem with Polish coal at the highest level. But [Khrushchev] believes it would be inappropriate to do that at this time because it would unnecessarily exacerbate the affair and lead to disputes and polemics between fraternal parties about this matter, which the Poles, even with the best of intentions, cannot do much about.

Comrade Gomułka's speech will not be published in the USSR because it would have to be accompanied by commentaries that would lead, in turn, to further disputes and polemics, which would be highly undesirable. It is necessary to help Poland. The USSR is willing to provide the necessary grain. All possible measures will be taken to ensure that by 1958, or at the very latest by 1959, the USSR will no longer be dependent on Polish coal. Most likely the USSR will also agree to the loan request.

Later on, before the meeting ended and after the main discussions, Comrade Ponomarenko delivered a report about a political rally today by workers in Warsaw. Comrade Gomułka gave a speech there. There were more than 150,000 people.

Among other things, Comrade Gomułka said that the PZPR CC had received a letter from the CPSU CC which stated that it was up to the Polish side to determine how to resolve the matter of the Soviet security advisers. He expressed his view that the presence of Soviet advisers in Poland at this time was in Poland's interests. This was greeted with wide and loud applause.

He further emphasized that the presence of Soviet troops on Polish territory was necessary because of the existence of NATO and the presence of American troops in West Germany. And this view, too, was greeted with loud and long applause.

He condemned all those who want, by means of demagogic talk, to undermine trust in the Polish army, which is under the exclusive command of the Polish government and the PZPR CC. He appealed to the crowd to finish the rally and commit themselves to work for the good of the Polish people.

It was the view of Comrade Khrushchev that this speech by Comrade Gomułka gives hope that Poland has now adopted a course that will eliminate the unpleasant state of affairs. He said that finding a reason for an armed conflict now would be very easy, but finding a way to put an end to such a conflict would be very hard.

On the Situation in Hungary

Comrade Khrushchev said he does not understand what Comrades Gerő, Hegedüs, and others are doing. There were signs that the situation in Hungary is extremely serious. That did not prevent Comrades Gerő and Hegedüs from continuing to spend time by the sea. And as soon as they returned home they left on a "trip" to Yugoslavia.

When Comrade Khrushchev talked by phone on Oct. 23, 1956 with Comrade Gerő, whom he summoned for a consultation, Comrade Gerő told him that the situation in Budapest is bad and for that reason he cannot come to Moscow.

As soon as the conversation was over, Comrade Zhukov informed [Khrushchev] that Gerő had asked the military attaché at the Soviet embassy in Budapest to dispatch Soviet troops to suppress a demonstration that was reaching an ever greater and unprecedented scale. The CPSU CC Presidium did not give its approval for such an intervention because it was not requested by the highest Hungarian officials, even when Comrade Gerő had been speaking with Comrade Khrushchev earlier.

Shortly thereafter, a call came through from the Soviet embassy in Budapest saying that the situation is extremely dangerous and that the intervention of Soviet troops is necessary. The Presidium authorized Comrade Khrushchev to discuss this matter by phone with Comrade Gerő.

As it turned out, Comrade Khrushchev informed Comrade Gerő that his request will be met when the government of the [Hungarian People's Republic] makes the request in writing. Gerő responded that he is not able to convene a meeting of the government. Comrade Khrushchev then recommended that Hegedüs call such a meeting in his capacity as chairman of the Council of Ministers. Although that had not happened as of today, the situation developed in such a way that Comrade Zhukov was given orders to occupy Budapest with Soviet military units located on Hungarian territory and in Uzhgorod. The redeployment of the units was slow and difficult because of dense fog. In an effort to protect at least Comrade Gerő, an armored car was sent to Budapest. The vehicle passed right through Budapest without the slightest resistance. The other

Soviet army troop formations did not arrive until Oct. 24, 1956 at 4:00 a.m., when the sessions of the HWP CC plenum were already over in Budapest.

Comrade Khrushchev recommended to Comrade Gerő that he tell everyone that the HWP CC plenum had not taken place before the demonstration was suppressed. It turned out that this did not happen. As was expected, a new politburo was elected at the plenum. It included some members from the previous politburo: Apró, Hegedüs, Gerő, and Kádár. It also had new members: Imre Nagy, Köböl (the head of the 1st department of the HWP CC, who recently spoke out strongly and sharply against the politburo), Gáspár, Szántó (the head of the Institute for Foreign Cultural Relations), Marosán (a persecuted but good comrade), Kiss (the chairman of the C[entral] C[ontrol] C[ommittee]), and Kállai (the head of the department of culture of the HWP CC). Selected as candidates were: Losonczy (a journalist who was very active in campaigning against the leadership of the party) and Rónai (chairman of the parliament).

In the new politburo there are three people who were persecuted in the past and have now been rehabilitated. Among the old members not elected [to the new body] are: Hidas, Szalai, Mekis, [István] Kovács, Révai, Ács, Bata (a candidate), and Piros (also a candidate).

Those elected to the secretariat were: Gerő (first secretary), Kádár, Donáth (director of the Institute of Economics), Köböl, and Kállai. Among them are three persecuted comrades. Of the old secretariat members, those who were dismissed were: Szalai, Egri, Vég, and Kovács.

Within the government, Nagy has been selected as chairman of the Council of Ministers and Hegedüs as first deputy chairman of the Council of Ministers.

There were no longer any demonstrations in Budapest on the evening of Oct. 24, 1956. Near the Danube there were several groups of bandits. These consisted of groups of 15–20 people armed with pistols and weapons seized from soldiers. Resistance is still occurring on certain street corners, roofs, and balconies. On several streets there were barricades. The bandits temporarily occupied two railway stations and one of the two radio stations. The bandits wanted to tear down the statue of Stalin. When they were unsuccessful in this task, they seized a welder's torch and cut the statue to pieces, and then disposed of the whole thing.

The Hungarian internal security forces performed very well, but suffered most of the casualties from among the 25 dead and 50 wounded. Also, one Soviet officer was killed and 12 soldiers were wounded. The unrest has been confined to Budapest so far. Everywhere else, in cities and villages, there is calm. The workers from the Csepel factory defended themselves with bare hands against armed bandits.

In Hungary, after a decision by the government, an "action group" of five [akcni petka] was set up to suppress the uprising. It consists of Bata, Piros, Kovács, Emerich,[63] and Zoltán Vas, who in the past spoke out very strongly against the HWP leadership and now is centrally involved in organizing the fight against the bandits. The group consists entirely of people who were not elected to the Politburo.

On the morning of Oct. 24, 1956, Nagy spoke on the radio. He called for order, and he signed a decree establishing a military tribunal which is authorized to pass immediate sentence on anyone who puts up resistance. Generally, the bandits are spreading the word that Nagy has betrayed the uprising.

He spoke again later in a similar vein. He also mentioned that the Hungarian government had asked Soviet troops to enter Budapest.

In his third speech on the radio today, he said that the positive thing the students had begun was being abused by the bandits to foment turmoil and shoot people. He appealed for order and urged people to give up their arms by 1:00 p.m.

A delegation from the CPSU CC Presidium was sent to Hungary this morning; it included Mikoyan, Suslov, and Serov.[64]

---

[63] "Emerich" is not the name of any known senior Hungarian official. Svoboda probably spelled it phonetically; it might refer to Imre Mező, who was a member of the military committee, or perhaps to Ferenc Münnich.

[64] The mission had a fourth member as well, General Mikhail Malinin, who was in charge of Soviet forces during the first phase of the invasion.

During the [Soviet] Presidium meeting, those comrades informed the Presidium by telephone about the situation [in Hungary]. They said that Comrades Mikoyan and Suslov had attended the [Hungarian] Central Committee meeting. The situation, in their view, is not as dire as the Hungarian comrades and the Soviet ambassador have portrayed it. Budapest itself is more or less calm. Resistance is limited to certain rooftops and house balconies, from which the enemy is shooting. The internal security forces respond quite freely to each of their shots, which creates the impression of a battle. One can expect that by morning there will be total calm. The Soviet embassy let itself be encircled and protected by 30 tanks.

Among the Hungarian leadership, both in the party and in the state, there is an absolute unity of views.

There is no doubt that Nagy is acting courageously, emphasizing at every opportunity the identity of his and Gerő's views. Gerő himself had told the Soviet comrades that protests against his election as 1st secretary were occurring. But Nagy had emphasized and reemphasized that those protesting against him did not include even a single Central Committee member. Only certain individuals were behaving that way.

In Budapest roughly 450 people have been arrested. In response to a question from Comrade Ulbricht about whether it is known who is leading the uprising, Comrade Khrushchev said that according to reports, the insurgents had set up their headquarters in the Hotel Astoria. This had been captured by Soviet troops. It appears that the groundwork for preparing a coup was organized by writers and was supported by students. The population as a whole has reacted passively to everything, but has not been hostile toward the USSR.

Comrade Khrushchev recommends that we not cover the situation in Hungary in our press until the causes of everything have been well clarified.

The representatives of the fraternal parties who were present joined the discussion. All of them expressed support for the CPSU CC Presidium's stance.

Comrade Ulbricht emphasized in his speech that in his view the situation had arisen because we did not act in time to expose all the incorrect opinions that had emerged in Poland and Hungary. He assumed that it would behoove each party to give a response in the press to certain incorrect opinions.

Comrade Khrushchev recommended that they think about the problems in greater depth. We must realize that we are not living as we were during the CI [Communist International], when only one party was in power. If we wanted to operate by command today, we would inevitably create chaos. It is necessary to conduct propaganda work in each party, but we cannot permit this to turn into polemics between fraternal parties because this would lead to polemics between nations. The CPSU CC plenum in December will discuss ideological questions and, a bit later, the question of how to raise living standards, particularly quicker construction of apartments as one of the basic prerequisites for boosting living standards. The extent to which patience is required can be seen from the recent case in Zaporozhe. Here 200 people refused to work because those responsible for guiding the work of the factories, including party functionaries, union leaders, and the top manager, did not do anything to induce the employees to work to the limit. Did they refuse to work because some ideological matters were unclear to them or because they were opposed to the Soviet regime? No, they refused because basic economic and social issues had not been resolved. Ideological work itself will be of no avail if we do not ensure that living standards rise. It is no accident that the unrest occurred in Hungary and Poland and not in Czechoslovakia. This is because the standard of living in Czechoslovakia is incomparably higher. In the USSR more than 10,000 members of the CPSU were rehabilitated and more than a million were released from prison. These people are not angry at us because they see we have done a lot to raise the standard of living in our country. In our country they also listen to the BBC and Radio Free Europe. But when they have full stomachs, the listening is not so bad.

It is necessary to improve ideological and propaganda work and to bolster the quality of the work of the party and state apparatus geared toward managing the economy.

[Source: SUA, Fond 07/16, Svazek 3. Originally published in English in the Cold War International History Project Bulletin *no. 5 (Spring 1995): 53–55. First published in Hungarian by Tibor Hajdu, "Az 1956 október 24-i moszkvai értekezlet," in* Évkönyv 1992, I., *ed. János M. Bak et al. (Budapest: 1956-os Intézet, 1992), 149–156. Translated by Mark Kramer.]*

DOCUMENT NO. 28: Memorandum of Conversation between John Foster Dulles and U.S. Ambassador to the United Nations Henry Cabot Lodge, October 24, 1956

This conversation presents early evidence of the acute discomfort the American leadership felt after hearing news about the revolution. After years of rhetoric about the imminent liberation of the "captive nations" of Eastern Europe, the uprising instantly clarified the conviction quietly held by President Eisenhower and most of his advisers that, in fact, the United States could do nothing meaningful to avert or reverse a Soviet crackdown. Although the United Nations became the principal forum for publicly airing the Hungarian issue, the question of going specifically to the Security Council was more problematic, not only because of the threat of a Soviet veto, but because of the imminent Suez crisis. Unbeknownst to American officials, Israel was about to invade the Sinai Peninsula (the attack occurred on October 29) as part of a secret, joint operation with Britain and France against Egypt.

WEDNESDAY
OCTOBER 24, 1956
6:07 P.M.

TELEPHONE CALL TO AMB. LODGE

Re Hungary—apparently the fighting is developing in quite a big way and there is clear evidence of considerable Soviet military activity in the area to try to repress it. We are thinking of the possibility of bringing it to the [UN]SC. From a political standpoint the Sec. is worried that it will be said that here are the great moments and when they came and these fellows were ready to stand up and die, we were caught napping and doing nothing. L. mentioned Poland. The Sec. said that was different and there is more excuse to take this to the [UN]SC. He wishes L. would think about it and possibly for tomorrow. L. said calling for a cease-fire. The Sec. mentioned asking the British and French to join, and they agreed they would be reluctant to though the Sec. thinks they would vote with us. L. will go to work on it and wait for word. The Sec. said to keep it close. L. will go into the Article to move on.

pdb

[Source: Foreign Relations of the United States, 1955–1957, *vol. 25 (Washington, D.C.: Government Printing Office, 1990), 273.]*

DOCUMENT NO. 29: Minutes of Czechoslovak (CPCz) Politburo Meeting, October 24, 1956

These minutes of the CPCz Politburo's October 24 session illustrate how the satellite party leaders reacted to the challenges presented by the Hungarian revolution and the Polish crisis. These laconic resolutions show that the Czechoslovak leadership judged the Hungarian events primarily from the point of view of their own country's internal situation. Therefore, the orders presented below mainly include taking propaganda measures, although they also encompass some police action. The latter step was necessitated partly by the existence of a Hungarian minority population of several hundred thousand in the southern part of Slovakia, whose possible expressions of sympathy with the revolution were a cause of serious concern for the CPCz leadership.

Minutes of the 147th[65] meeting of the Political Committee of the CPCz CC at 2 p.m., October 24, 1956, at the CPCz CC building.

Comrades Present: Barák, Dolanský, Fierlinger, Kopecký, Široký, Zápotocký, Jankovcová, and Šimůnek.
Comrades on justified absence: Bacílek, Novotný
Comrades invited: Černík, Hendrych, Köhler, Krutina, Pašek.
Presiding over the meeting: cde. Zápotocký.[66]

Agenda:
I. Events in the Hungarian People's Republic.
II. Departure of the government delegation to the People's Republic of China.

Issue discussed:
I. Events in the Hungarian People's Republic (cdes. Barák and Hendrych, orally)

Participated in the debate:
Cdes. Zápotocký, Široký, Kopecký, Fierlinger, Dolanský, Hendrych, Köhler.

Decisions:
1) Minister of the Interior, cde. Barák informed the Political Committee of the CPCz CC about the events of October 23 and 24, 1956 in the Hungarian People's Republic. The Committee gave their consent to the minister of the interior's measures in Slovakia.

2) The CPCz CC Political Committee accepted the measures taken by the Secretariat in order to inform the party and ensure the [proper] press coverage of events in Hungary. At the same time, the CPCz CC Secretariat (cde. Hendrych) is charged with the following tasks:

    a) To inform the party about the facts and point out the reasons behind the events. To emphasize the correct policy of our Central Committee, which we carry out undaunted; our correct steps following the Twentieth Congress of the Soviet Communist Party; the unity of our party, [the unity] of the working class, and the strong alliance between the

---

[65] Although the document indicates this was the 147th meeting, it is very likely it was in fact the 146th session.
[66] Antonín Novotný, first secretary of the CPCz did not attend the PC meeting because he was in Moscow at the meeting of Eastern European party leaders. See Document No. 27.

party and the people. We have to hold up our achievements concerning the people's standard of living, in securing and developing the power of people's democracy. We have to observe the greatest possible wariness and circumspection in all fields. We have to stress the further strengthening of proletarian internationalism within the party and the working classes, as well as among the widest range of the working masses. We must also stress our adamant friendship with the Soviet Union and with the people of the other people's democracies. We have to demonstrate our correct policy in mobilizing the masses in order to develop a planned economy and continuously raise productivity. Moreover, we have to counteract uncontrolled petty bourgeois tendencies in the economy. For now, no public statement about the policies of Gomułka and Nagy should be issued. The transmission of resolutions from party assemblies and meetings should be organized.[67]

b) To modify, as a consequence of the Hungarian and Polish events, the program of the Month of Czechoslovak-Soviet Alliance, making it more combative and demonstrative.

IN CHARGE: CDE. HENDRYCH

II. Departure of the government delegation to the People's Republic of China.

Participated in the debate:
Cdes. Zápotocký, Široký and Barák

1. Government delegations to the People's Republic of China and to other countries need to be delayed temporarily.
IN CHARGE: CDE. ŠIROKÝ

The meeting was closed at 17:30 p.m.
Minutes made by: V. Kadlec.

[Source: MOL–XXXII–16, 11 k. Translated by József Reiter and Csaba Farkas.]

---

[67] The CPCz PC is requesting party 'aktiv' meetings and other assemblies to issue resolutions condemning the Hungarian events.

DOCUMENT NO. 30: Notes on the 38th Meeting of the Special Committee on Soviet and Related Problems, Washington, October 25, 1956

The Special Committee on Soviet and Related Problems was an interagency group chaired by the State Department's Jacob Beam. This was the first time the committee met to discuss the events in both Poland and Hungary, focusing on two important speeches—by Gomułka on October 20 and Nagy on October 25. The Polish leader's speech sparked more intensive American interest because of the breadth of its critique of the previous communist leadership in Poland, mirroring Khrushchev's denunciation of Stalin at the Twentieth CPSU Congress in February 1956. This reaction was reflected in CIA Director Allen Dulles' remark at the time that Gomułka's address was "one of the most dramatic things since Khrushchev's speech."[68] Nagy's public promise to negotiate the withdrawal of Soviet troops met mainly with skepticism, however, as spelled out below. Most U.S. officials tended to see Nagy as toeing Moscow's line and lacking the kind of independent streak they detected in Gomułka. Many Hungarians shared this point of view, based partly on Nagy's extremely cautious public pronouncements up until then. However, unbeknownst to outside observers at the time, Nagy delivered these remarks against explicit Soviet insistence that he omit the subject of a Soviet pull-out from the speech. As such, this represents the first public sign of the prime minister's dissent from the Soviet line, a fact not revealed until Russian President Boris Yeltsin released previously secret archival documents to the Hungarian government in late 1992.

MEMBERS PRESENT

State—Mr. Jacob D. Beam, Chairman
Defense—Colonel Oscar R. Schaaf
Defense—Mr. Roger Ernst
CIA—Mr. Laughlin Campbell
Office of Spec. Asst. to the President—Mr. Oren M. Stephens
USIA—Mr. Alfred V. Boerner
OCB—Mr. Paul B. Comstock, Staff Representative

OTHERS PRESENT

State-Mr. Edward L. Freer
State-Mr. Howard Trivers
State-Mr. Robert O. Blake
State-Mr. Frank G. Siscoe
CIA-Mr. Arthur M. Cox
USIA-Mr. E. Lewis Revey

Mr. Boerner read the President's statement on Hungary.[69]
[The following notes are not exact quotations.][70]
Freers: The statement appears to be laying groundwork for UN action. We're considering UN action in State. Any resolution or statement now would have to be in the Security Council, probably under Article 30—potential threat to peace.[71] Later we may go to the Human Rights

---

[68] Dulles' remark is quoted in *FRUS 1955–1957*, vol. 25, 258.

[69] For text of the President's statement, issued on October 25, see *Department of State Bulletin*, November 5, 1956, 700. [Footnote from source text.]

[70] All brackets are in the source text. [Footnote from source text.]

[71] Reference presumably should be to Article 34, which allows for Security Council investigation of any dispute to determine if the dispute is likely to endanger international peace. [Footnote from source text.]

231

Committee or the General Assembly. There would have to be first policy consultation with other Security Council members.

Boerner: Problems like Cyprus and Algeria could confuse the issue.

Freers: There are some hurdles but all factors are under consideration.

Campbell: Should we not announce that we are going before the UN in order to let the Hungarian people know?

Freers: That is also under consideration. Legation Budapest is very interested in the statements by the President and the Secretary of State, and in UN action. The key point is whether the story about Nagy negotiating troop removal with the Russians can be confirmed.[72]

Siscoe: Radio reports from Budapest indicate this.

Freers: These reports might be coming from Vienna rather than Budapest. We should try to hold Nagy to this commitment. Line should be: Nagy stands or falls on his ability to get Soviet troops out of Hungary.

Boerner: USIA has been reporting events for the people in Hungary but we do not have any definite line.

Freers: Can't have a definite line on Hungary because we don't know what is going to happen. New subject: Mr. Hoover and OCB have recommended wide exploitation of Gomulka speech.[73]

[. . .][74]

Boerner: USIA has sent it to about 20 posts.

Campbell: We will see if we still have the stencils. It is being fully translated.

Boerner: USIA sent it out straight without comment.

Blake: It is important to have IPS comment, e.g., columns comparing this with past promises. It is a strong break from Russian Communist technique. The Chalmers Roberts article is a good start—though not accurate in all points.[75]

Boerner: The Gomulka speech is useful, particularly concerning failure of cooperatives.

Trivers: Failure of collectives is its strongest point.

Blake: It is strong break with the past.

Boerner: It lends authenticity to much of our line. It admits in one statement that Communist statistics are fake, production is off, industrial work is required on Sunday, etc.

Freers: Useful to report it back to Russia.

Revey: It also stresses the cult of the individual.

Freers: It will be possible to exploit the speech for a long time.

Trivers: Gomulka's statements regarding ties with Russia are strong and devoutly meant.

Cox: We should wait to see how much popular support Gomulka has before we establish our line on him.

Blake: Could we get someone with the stature of George Kennan to write a series to appear when hot news tapers off?

Schaaf: Jacobs indicated Gomulka got most applause when he promised to get Russian troops out.

Freers: Gomulka is popular right now and for some unforeseen period because of his apparent anti-Soviet stand. When time passes he will be subject to question for failure to deliver goods.

[Mr. Beam joined the meeting at this point.]

[72] Nagy had indicated such an intent in a broadcast to the Hungarian people on the afternoon of October 25. Earlier in the day, it was announced that Janos Kadar had replaced Gero as party first secretary. [Footnote from source text.]

[73] For a translation of this speech, see "Address by Władysław Gomulka before the Central Committee of the Polish United Workers' Party, October 20, 1956," in Zinner, *National Communism*, 197–239.

[74] State Department officials deleted an unspecified amount of text here for security classification reasons.

[75] Reference is to an article that appeared in the *Washington Post* on October 24. [Footnote from source text.]

Beam: We have been working on circular letter to the Security Council. It will not take any stand on the action of the Hungarian Government itself. It will go after the idea that the Soviets have used their troops. It might even strengthen the hand of the Hungarians against Russia. It should make it possible for anyone to open debate. We are going to ask the support of the French, British, Belgians, and Australians. Planning to circulate it tomorrow. I understand the free Hungarian representatives in New York, the National Council, want to take some action. They want to go to UN.

Trivers: They can present a petition to the Secretary General, but he won't circulate it unless a government sponsors.

[. . .][76]

Siscoe: Sunday[77] is post World War I Liberation Day for Czechoslovakia.

[. . .][78]

Campbell: Should there be a day of prayer for Poles and Hungarians? Perhaps the President could mention it.

Beam: The Catholic Church, rather than the Government, would be the appropriate organ to take such action.

Cox: The Crusade for Freedom[79] was approached by the Upjohn Company with an offer of medical supplies.

Beam: Perhaps something can be worked out through the Red Cross. How are we playing the situation to neutral areas?

[. . .][80]

Blake: We could quote what is being said by socialists and similar groups.

Campbell: Also labor groups.

Boerner: We are cross reporting. We ought to get out a follow-up guidance next week.

Campbell: The Socialist governments in the free world have not made any public statements yet.

Blake: We could put out commentary on use of Soviet troops in Hungary and the fact that they were poised in Poland.

Trivers: Such commentary could be used together with the Gomulka story.

Beam: We should try to get some good pictures for use by our media of the fighting in Hungary and of delivery of U.S. humanitarian assistance.

PBC[81]
OCB Staff Representative

[Source: Foreign Relations of the United States 1955–1957, vol. 25 (Washington, D.C.: U.S. Government Printing Office, 1990), 277–280.]

[76] See footnote 74 above.

[77] October 28. [Footnote from source text.]

[78] See footnote 74 above.

[79] The financial arm of the Committee for a Free Europe, it was later known as the Radio Free Europe Fund. [Footnote from source text.]

[80] See footnote 74 above.

[81] Paul B. Comstock.

DOCUMENT NO. 31: Memorandum from Thomas Brimelow to the British Foreign Office News Department, October 25, 1956

This memorandum by the head of the British Foreign Office department in charge of Eastern Europe reflects the general dilemma facing Western policy-makers: something ought to be done, or at least said, to support those Hungarians fighting for their freedom but, recognizing the West's limited ability to act beyond the Iron Curtain, without creating expectations of Western help in their struggle. Aside from the internal "declaration" of a policy of non-intervention at this early stage in the Hungarian crisis, the document is interesting because of the author's realistic assessment of Imre Nagy's role. While the general evaluation of his activity both within the revolutionary society in Hungary and in the West was highly critical, Brimelow clearly saw that, "At the moment he seems to offer the best prospects for a more liberal Communist régime in Hungary." The declaration mentioned in the text—ultimately never issued—was supposed to express regret for the loss of life in Hungary and to convey the British Government's hope that reforms would continue without similar sacrifices being required.

BUDAPEST RIOTS. GUIDANCE
25 OCTOBER 1956

This is full of pitfalls. We must be careful not to say anything which might encourage hotheads in Budapest to further useless rioting. We might express our disapproval of the intervention of Soviet forces, but the Russians are forearmed with the answer that they went in by invitation. We could criticize Mr. Nagy for calling the Russians in and for suppressing the riots with such brutality. But it may be to our interest to have Mr. Nagy in power. At the moment he seems to offer the best prospects for a more liberal Communist regime in Hungary. It is a bitter irony that he should have had to begin with bloodshed. Hungarian public opinion will almost certainly expect some statement from us condemning their rulers and [ap]proving the rioters. The Legation had many telephone calls asking for armed British intervention. It would be more difficult to avoid comment than it was in the case of Poland.

2. I recommend that we should say as little as possible, but on the assumption that we cannot avoid comment altogether, I submit a draft of a statement which might be made by the Head of News Department.

T. BRIMELOW OCTOBER 25, 1956

[Source: PRO.FO.371.122378.NH.10110/175. Originally published in Eva Haraszti-Taylor, The Hungarian Revolution of 1956 (Nottingham, U.K.: Astra Press, 1995), 102.]

DOCUMENT NO. 32: Situation Report from Anastas Mikoyan to the CPSU CC Presidium, October 26, 1956

This telegram from Mikoyan, his first on October 26,[82] is significant because it mentions for the first time Imre Nagy's suggestion of a "political" solution to the crisis instead of military intervention by the Soviet army. Mikoyan's palpable preference for the former course of action is partly based on his belief that Hungarian military resistance had already essentially been eliminated. He actually quotes Nagy when evaluating the military alternative: "If we follow that path, we will lose." However, having witnessed the local government authorities' incompetence, Mikoyan makes his own worries explicit: "because of their fear of taking these or other steps we would be faced with accomplished facts." Still, according to the Malin notes of CPSU CC Presidium meetings at this time, his concerns fail to exert any significant influence on the Soviet leadership for the time being.

OCTOBER 26, 1956

In the Central Committee of the CPSU

Today, we drove around the central districts of the city and had conversations with the soldiers and officers of the Soviet Army. The troops are conducting themselves in an exemplary manner. The mood is good; so is the level of organization.

The enemy's armed resistance has been destroyed. Our troops have no more targets for their operations; there are only sporadic, minor skirmishes and occasional shots fired from roof-tops in different parts of the city. We have entered a period of minor guerrilla raids as well as resistance from small groups of bandits in various houses. The work of capturing the bandits hiding in houses and of disarming the population is now shifting to the police and civilian organs. This is a task for local organs not the military, which can only offer help on this matter.

The local organs are in a very poor state: they are not able to cope with their own tasks. We are taking steps so that the Hungarian comrades can strengthen this aspect of their work.

At the moment, a session of the party CC is underway. We are not participating in it.

We have just received information that a new government is being chosen.

Taking the current situation into account, the conclusions are the following: the government of the resistance [sic] has been suppressed, however a peaceful popular movement persists. So far, they [the Hungarian authorities] have not been able to gain control over it, and it is growing, especially in the countryside and particularly in Miskolc.

Delegations made up of different segments of the population are arriving—workers, students, the intelligentsia—who are demanding a change in the government.

There are two possible paths before us: [first,] to reject all of these demands and not to make any changes in the composition of the government, relying on the Soviet Army to continue the struggle. But in this case, they would lose all contact with, and the trust of, the peaceful population—the workers and students—and there would be new victims, which would widen the chasm between the government and the population. If we follow that path, we will lose.

Therefore, the Hungarian comrades think the second path would be more acceptable: that is to include in the government several prominent democrats, proponents of the people's democracy, both from the former petty bourgeois parties and from the intelligentsia, the students and the workers—five or six persons out of 20–22 members of the government.

In response to the specific question of which parties would be brought in to participate in the government, Nagy answered that no parties as such would be involved. We are talking about the individual candidacies of various democrats representing the people's democracy.

---

[82] Mikoyan and Suslov sent another telegram to Moscow later the same day. See Document No. 33.

In response to our question of who among the old members would be removed from the government and who would stay, he answered that of all the current deputy [prime] ministers, only cde. Erdei will remain. Cde. Hegedüs is being relieved of his post as a deputy [prime] minister because all the delegations demand it—they do not trust him.

The Communist, Bognár,[83] is being nominated as a deputy minister.

They did not name other candidates for deputy minister positions. They say that all of that is in the process of being discussed and nothing has yet been finalized.

They mentioned the following candidates as more likely possibilities:

defense minister: Münnich, the former ambassador to Moscow;

[Imre] Horváth will remain as foreign minister;

minister of interior: Szilágyi, an old Communist and former police colonel;

minister of education: László Kardos, a Communist;

As minister of agriculture: Béla Kovács, a former member of the Smallholders' Party leadership, has been appointed. According to Nagy, President of the Republic Dobi recommends him well. Nagy himself speaks well of him, as of an honest person, loyal to the people's democracy and capable of bringing calm to the peasantry. He was arrested and held in the Soviet Union; he has only recently returned. In spite of that, they consider him an acceptable candidate.

Nagy says that either we [Hungarians] make a decision along those lines today and immediately publish it throughout the country, which might possibly bring calm to Budapest and the countryside, or, if we do not do it today, we fear that tomorrow could be too late.

In response to our warning that the path of appealing to bourgeois democrats is a slippery one, and that one has to be careful otherwise one could slip and lose the respect of the masses, Nagy responded that they are doing this out of the utmost necessity in order not to lose the government's rudder, and as the minimum required measure.

We asked that before publishing a decision they discuss it with us. We are now going to the CC for that discussion.

Let me add: in response to our question about whether any changes to the composition of the CC or Politburo are anticipated, Nagy said that there are no such intentions right now.

Before yesterday the conviction was forming that because of their fear of taking these or other steps we would be faced with accomplished facts. We have already informed you about a similar circumstance with regard to the withdrawal of Soviet troops. Today, we did not find out about the changes in government from the leadership; apparently, they wanted to make a final decision and then inform us once the decision had already been published.

We asked Nagy, and he promised to refrain from publishing any decisions on this question until our arrival at the CC.

We are now on our way to the CC.

A. MIKOYAN

[Source: APRF, F. 3, Op. 64, D. 484, Ll. 118–121. Published in Sovietskii Soyuz i vengerskii krizis, 1956 goda: Dokumenty, *edited and compiled by E. D. Orekhova, Vyacheslav T. Sereda and Aleksandr. S. Stykhalin (Moscow: ROSSPEN, 1998), 387-389. Translated by Malcolm Byrne.]*

---

[83] József Bognár was a leading Smallholder politician as of 1945, minister of domestic, later foreign, trade from 1949 to October 27, 1956, then deputy prime minister in the Nagy government until November 3.

DOCUMENT NO. 33: Report from Anastas Mikoyan and Mikhail Suslov to the CPSU CC Presidium on Talks with HWP Leaders, October 26, 1956

This telegram from the CPSU CC Presidium's special envoys to Budapest is an especially interesting one because it gives some insight into the Hungarian leadership's internal debates and reflects, at a relatively early stage in the crisis, the limits of political change tolerable to the Soviets. It also reveals that Imre Nagy, who was appointed prime minister on October 24 and who was eager to gain political support from the Soviets to help consolidate the situation, also tried to exert special pressure on Moscow to gain concessions as early as October 25–26.

TOP SECRET
FOR IMMEDIATE DELIVERY

CPSU CC

We had lengthy conversations with the leading figures: a few minutes with Gerő, who then left to attend the ongoing session of the Politburo with the [Hungarian Workers' Party] CC members, then we talked with Cde. Kádár. Imre Nagy was busy negotiating with representatives of the opposition—writers and students who are taking part in organizing demonstrations, but are not participating in the armed revolt. Then he also joined us, and then Hegedüs and a few other Politburo members also arrived by the end of the conversations.

They informed us that at the session, the Politburo, including CC members, formed a Directory—a transitional body of the CC and the government—consisting of Kádár, Imre Nagy, Hegedüs, Apró, Münnich, Szántó.

Cde. Kádár calmly and in detail informed us about the issues that are being discussed in the CC now and which decisions have already been passed.

On the issue of the government's outline, Kádár informed us that the list that he reported to Imre Nagy was approved unanimously by the CC.

Cde. Kádár said that they have approved this government slate [*sostav pravitelstva*]. When we asked if there were counterrevolutionary elements among those who have returned to the government, he firmly said: no, these are decent people, and they accept in principle both socialism and democracy. He also said that the crucial posts will be retained by the party's representatives, but that the cooperation of some public figures, non-Communists, in the government would help the party to win the sympathies of masses of people to its side.

Unfortunately, Kádár said, the masses are now beyond our control. The party's prestige has sunk dramatically, particularly because of past mistakes.

Kádár drew our attention to the fact that strong anti-Semitic and anti-Soviet feelings are predominant among the masses of workers and the rest of the population.

One should distinguish in the anti-government movement, said Kádár, between counterrevolutionary coup-makers who want to destroy the people's democracy's order and with whom a military struggle to the end will be necessary (this is a common opinion within the predominant majority of CC members, he said), and the movement of broad masses of people—students, intellectuals, large segments of workers, and even a considerable share of party members—who are displeased with our activities. The reactionary forces are exploiting this widespread discontent. The task boils down to separating the people's masses from the counterrevolution and bringing them over to our side.

It merits particular attention that the new CC Secretary Donáth took a capitulationist stand and essentially spoke in favor of the counterrevolutionary rebellion, suggesting that a forthcoming address by the government and CC to the nation should recognize this entire movement, including the military uprising, as a popular and revolutionary movement, and thereby, morally justified and legal.

Members of the CC Military Committee Münnich, [István] Kovács, and Hazai[84] harshly objected to Donáth. We spoke firmly to the Hungarian comrades that they should give a strong warning to Donáth; that if he adheres to his capitulationist positions and does not strictly follow the CC's decisions, then one should take necessary measures against him.

The vast majority of CC members were outraged by Donáth's speech, and passed a resolution supporting an uncompromising struggle with the mutineers, in addition to parallel political measures directed at conquering their influence among the working class and popular masses. In particular, they decided to satisfy workers' demands to set up workers' soviets in plants and factories, and to consider proposals to improve the workers' material conditions in the future.

The Central Committee approved yesterday's speeches by Kádár and Imre Nagy.

Imre Nagy repeated, in essence, what he told us earlier and what we reported to you [in Moscow] on the two possible ways they [Hungarians] can act. We decided, said Imre Nagy, along with suppressing the revolt by force, to carry out a policy of reconciliation and rapprochement with the intelligentsia and the masses of people and to embrace the popular movement and national feelings, in order to surmount this popular movement and thereby defeat the counterrevolutionaries and preserve order in the people's democracy. The other way, said Nagy, the masses of people would remain hostile to them and they would have to lean only on Soviet troops and a certain segment of the party isolated from the people; this way would have been tragic and would have paved the way for the Americans to enter.

Imre Nagy informed us about the talks with writers and students: they turned out to be his acquaintances, and the students are communists he had taught some time ago. These people are ready to mobilize students to help the militia in the struggle against the mutineers, but before [doing so] they demand, for instance, replacing the minister of internal affairs, whose fate, according to Imre Nagy, has already been sealed. They also demand not to have special MVD[85] troops in Hungary in the future, because they never existed before in the history of Hungary and they do not exist in other people's democracies; there is a national army, as well as secret and common police. In their opinion, Hungary should have the same. Meanwhile they expressed their indignation at the cruelties the MVD troops perpetrated against the population.

We ended the conversation with the impression that Imre Nagy, deep in his soul, did not mind supporting this demand with regard to the MVD troops. Kádár shook his head as a sign of disagreement.

Imre Nagy informed us that these delegations are also demanding the withdrawal of Soviet troops from Hungary. In this regard we asked Nagy: why in his speech yesterday had he promised to begin negotiations with the USSR about withdrawing Soviet troops from Hungary, while a majority of the [HWP] Politburo, when we declared that the Soviet side cannot agree with the withdrawal of Soviet troops from Hungary, declined the proposal about the troops' withdrawal? Moreover, he made this statement without a preliminary report to us. Imre Nagy and the Politburo members who were present [at this conversation], including Gerő, confirmed that they had later gathered to discuss a draft speech by Imre Nagy. Considering the workers' predominant [*massovikh*] demands—particularly from the largest workers' centers and even from a number of party organizations, in particular the Debrecen and Miskolc regional party committees—about withdrawing troops, and in order to regain control of the situation and preserve their influence over the workers, they had to accept this formula, which is, after all, soft and non-assertive.

Gerő added that initially he had spoken against it, vacillated, then eventually saw no other way out of the situation, and accepted it.

---

[84] Jenő Hazai was chief of the Army's Political Division and a member of the HWP CC from July 1956. Hazai took part in the work of the Military Committee because of his other positions, but he was not a member.

[85] Although the acronym usually stands for the Ministry of Internal Affairs, here it refers to the ÁVH. See also footnote 55 above.

We said that we consider this a grave error, since withdrawing Soviet troops would inevitably bring the entry of American troops. Now as before, we consider it possible for Soviet troops to return to their bases soon after order is restored. We declared that we object to including any kind of promise about withdrawing Soviet troops from Hungary in the upcoming party CC and the Council of Ministers appeal, and that we consider this to be the crucial issue in relations between our countries. Both Imre Nagy and Kádár promised not to include the formula about withdrawal of Soviet troops from Hungary in the CC and government appeal.

From the morning discussion with Imre Nagy we had the impression that his position regarding support for a curfew and a ban on demonstrations is uncertain. With support from the majority of the Politburo and in order to avoid demonstrations, we insisted on preserving a very strict curfew today and, depending on the situation, tomorrow, not only at night but also during the daytime, [in addition to] the ban on street traffic.

Some of our conclusions:

1. A majority of the CC members and Directory members stand firmly for suppressing the counterrevolution to the end. They take into account the vacillations of Imre Nagy who, because of his opportunistic personality, does not know where to stop in his concessions.

We warned them that no further concessions are possible; otherwise, it will lead to the regime's downfall.

2. Under the circumstances, we deem it acceptable and advisable to co-opt into the government a certain number of petty-bourgeois democratic and influential public figures, in order to expand the government's public base.

The replacement of Defense Minister Bata by Cde. Münnich is a decision most favorable to our cause. Cde. Bata, though he is an honest man, lacks the required characteristics and abilities.

3. We take as correct, under present circumstances, their intentions to create workers' councils at plants and factories, because this finds support among the masses of workers.

4. To assess the dangers of capitulation, we believe that the majority of the CC are not capitulationists. Rather, there is a danger there might emerge capitulationist governments in Debrecen and Miskolc. We will take the most resolute measures against them, not only political but also military.

5. We believe that today the most important thing is not military measures, but domination over the masses of workers.

As for the situation at 6 p.m. Moscow time: the situation in the city is calm, except for shelling by our troops from tank cannons and machine-guns against a few attics where some snipers from among the mutineers have become ensconced. Mass disorder and demonstrations did not take place today, and the order imposed by the city commandant has been largely maintained.

A. MIKOYAN
M. SUSLOV

OCTOBER 26, 1956

[Source: APRF, F. 3. Op. 64. D. 483. Ll. 123–129. Published in Sovietskii Soyuz i vengerskii krizis, 1956 goda: Dokumenty, edited and compiled by E. D. Orekhova, Vyacheslav T. Sereda, and Aleksandr. S. Stykhalin (Moscow: ROSSPEN, 1998), 403–407. Translated by Vladislav M. Zubok.]

DOCUMENT NO. 34: Memorandum of Discussion at the 301st Meeting of the National Security Council, October 26, 1956, 9–10:42 a.m.

This memorandum records the first gathering of the NSC after the outbreak of violence in Hungary. CIA Director Allen Dulles asserts that the revolt "constitute[s] the most serious threat yet to be posed to continued Soviet control of the satellites." He accurately notes the "much clearer anti-Soviet and anti-Communist bias" of the Hungarian crisis over the Polish events. Virtually no suggestions are made for how to respond to the uprising. The only major idea comes from Harold Stassen, Eisenhower's adviser on disarmament, who proposes that the United States assure the Soviets that Washington has no aggressive intentions in connection with developments in Eastern Europe. Although Eisenhower rejects the idea on the spot, it resurfaces in Secretary of State Dulles' speech in Dallas, Texas, the next day.[86]

[...]

1. Significant World Developments Affecting U.S. Security

[Here follows discussion of unrelated matters.]

With respect to Poland, Mr. [Allen] Dulles stated that the reporting in the press had been fairly accurate to date. A dramatic cable had been received yesterday in the clear from our Embassy[87] in Budapest.[88] The writer of the report had been obliged to lie down on the floor as he was writing, in order to avoid being shot at. The following were the main points in the cable.

In the first place, Soviet troops had arrived in Budapest at four o'clock in the morning on Wednesday last.[89] These troops were from the First Mechanized Division. In addition, certain reinforcements had arrived from Soviet forces in Rumania. The cable stated that the native Hungarian troops had thus far been held in the background, with the Soviet forces doing the actual fighting. Some Hungarian troops had already gone over to the rebels. It was also being alleged that certain Soviet tanks had gone over to the Hungarian rebels. Mr. Dulles expressed some skepticism at this report of Soviet military defectors, but indicated that it might possibly be true. In any event, at as late as eleven o'clock on Wednesday morning the Embassy had stated that tanks were fighting tanks in the streets of Budapest. The cable went on to provide other details of the fighting in Budapest, including the large demonstration in front of the U.S. Embassy, in the course of which the demonstrators called for U.S. assistance. As late as yesterday evening many sectors of the city were still in the hands of rebel bands.

In addition to the above intelligence, press reports early this morning stated that the situation had quieted somewhat in Budapest itself, and there was a partial lifting of the curfew. On the other hand, there were reports of disorders in at least two other Hungarian cities.

Mr. Dulles stated that it was of course too early to reach any firm conclusions on the intelligence summarized above. Nevertheless, he would give to the Council certain thoughts which he was entertaining on what was happening in Poland and in Hungary.

In the first place, there was bound to be much soul-searching in Moscow as to whether a Gomulka-type regime could be permitted to function in Poland in view of what has happened in Hungary. Secondly, Soviet intervention in Hungary may have been due to Soviet unwilling-

---

[86] See the introductory essay in this part.

[87] At this time, the United States maintained a legation in Budapest, not an embassy.

[88] See "Transcript of a Teletype Conversation Between the Legation in Hungary and the Department of State, October 25, 1956," in *FRUS 1955–57*, vol. 25, 280–286.

[89] October 24.

ness to submit to a second humiliation after Poland. On the other hand, the Hungarian revolt had from the outset exhibited much clearer anti-Soviet and anti-Communist bias than had the Polish disorders.

Thirdly, the Hungarian revolt may demonstrate the inability of a moderate national Communist regime to survive in any of the satellites. What has happened would seem to indicate only two alternatives: One, either to return to a hard Stalinist regime, or two, to permit developments in the direction of genuine democracy. It had become evident that the revolt in Budapest had early taken a far more serious turn than that in Warsaw. Indeed, Mr. Dulles believed that the revolt in Hungary constituted the most serious threat yet to be posed to continued Soviet control of the satellites. It confronted Moscow with a very harsh dilemma: Either to revert to a harsh Stalinist policy, or to permit democratization to develop in the satellites to a point which risked the complete loss of Soviet control of the satellites.

Mr. Dulles then commented on the effect of these events on neutral nations such as India, and on Yugoslavia. He emphasized that while Marshal Tito had approved of what had happened in Poland, he had remained silent on Hungary. The Marshal may well view what has occurred in Hungary with genuine alarm. Certainly any free election would make abundantly clear that there was no popular support for any kind of Communist regime in Hungary or in Poland.

Various members of the Council then commented on the possibility of an ultimate replacement of Soviet influence in the satellites by a Western orientation for these countries. In connection with this discussion Secretary Dulles mentioned a telegram which had come in to the State Department early this morning from our Ambassador in Warsaw. The portions of this message read by Secretary Dulles concerned themselves with the Polish economy and Poland's resources. The Ambassador concluded that the Polish economy could be made viable if the Poles were permitted to trade anywhere they wanted to in normal fashion.

Mr. Allen Dulles, reverting again to the impact of these events on third countries, pointed out that while Communist China had welcomed the developments in Poland, it had been silent on what had occurred in Hungary. Nevertheless, the Chinese Communists may not be unhappy about Hungarian developments. If so, this could be the beginning of the first rift between Communist China and the Soviet Union.

The President inquired whether Mr. Allen Dulles had had any information about the Czech reaction to these events. Mr. Dulles replied that he had very little on this point. In any event, practically all the potential Gomulkas in Czechoslovakia had been pretty well slaughtered.

Turning to the immediate future, Mr. Allen Dulles stated his belief that the Soviet leaders in Moscow would try to convey an outward impression of continued unity of belief and action. Bohlen, for example, has reported that Bulganin and Khrushchev had been seen together at a recent reception in Moscow. However, Bohlen said he had never seen them looking so grim. In any event, the current Soviet leadership was certainly on the defensive, and Khrushchev is probably being held responsible for what has happened. Khrushchev's days may well be numbered. It was quite possible that upon Zhukov would devolve the choice of Khrushchev's successor. Indeed, it was even possible that Zhukov himself would be Khrushchev's successor.

The President then asked if there were further questions. Admiral Radford[90] inquired if there was any information as to the reaction of the United States Communist Party. Mr. Allen Dulles replied that he had read several editorials in *The New York Daily Worker*. These editorials had welcomed what had happened in Poland, but had little to say about Hungary. The President referred to the Attorney General's recent report[91] which had indicated the gradual disintegration of the Communist Party, USA. The President also added that he thought it had been wise of him

[90] Admiral Arthur M. Radford was chairman of the Joint Chiefs of Staff.

[91] Attorney General Herbert Brownell, Jr., sent a memorandum to the President on this subject on October 7. The text was printed in *The New York Times* on October 8. [Footnote from source text.]

to issue his statement with respect to Hungary.[92] He had noted many signs of approval in the course of his visit yesterday to New York City.

Secretary Dulles then informed the Council that the State Department had just sent out messages to all the friendly co-signatories of the Hungarian Peace Treaty, to ascertain if any of these countries was disposed to take any action in the United Nations with respect to Hungary.[93] In the case of Yugoslavia, which was one of the signatories, it had been left to Ambassador Riddleberger's discretion whether to put this problem to Marshal Tito.

The President, referring to the message on Poland's economy and resources, stated that the question of trade interested him immensely, in view of his long-held conviction that the United States should trade as widely as possible with the Soviet satellites. On the same point, Secretary Dulles stated that one sentence in the telegram from Warsaw had emphasized the fact that nearly all the Polish textile mills were geared to use U.S. short-staple cotton rather than Egyptian long-staple cotton. This, thought Secretary Dulles, would be of interest to the Secretary of Agriculture. The President agreed that this was worth thinking about.

Governor Stassen recalled a talk he had had with Gomulka several years ago, before the latter had been put in prison. On this occasion Gomulka had protested his friendliness toward the United States and had also outlined his desire to follow an independent road to Socialism in Poland. With reference to Governor Stassen's observation, Mr. Allen Dulles stated that Gomulka's long speech a few days ago represented the most violent denunciation of the entire Soviet economic system which had ever [been] issued anywhere from any source. He had accordingly sent copies of this speech all over this Government and to many places overseas.

At this point, Governor Stassen inquired whether, in view of the great significance of what was taking place in Hungary and Poland, it would not be advisable for the President to call a special meeting of the National Security Council to discuss the whole problem of Hungary and Poland. The President replied that he was not sure that discussion in the National Security Council was the best initial step. He did believe, however, that the responsible departments and agencies should proceed at once to formulate the clearest possible analysis of what had happened in these two countries. Such an analysis could then be presented to the National Security Council. Such a procedure he believed better than to plunge right into a discussion in the Council on these difficult subjects.

Governor Stassen pointed out that basic decisions would have to be taken presently by the Soviet Union. They would either have to revert to the old harsh policy of Stalin toward the satellites, or else they would have to let things go on as they were going. The President replied that if the Soviets did revert to the Stalin policies, they would stand bankrupt before the whole world. Pointing out that he had a memorandum on his desk,[94] the President said that he was concerned about another question which was possibly being posed for the Soviet Union. In view of the serious deterioration of their position in the satellites, might they not be tempted to resort to very extreme measures and even to precipitate global war? This was a situation which must be watched with the utmost care. After all, observed the President, Hitler had known well, from the first of February 1945, that he was licked. Yet he had carried on to the very last and pulled down Europe with him in his defeat. The Soviets might even develop some desperate mood such as this.

Governor Stassen wondered if it would not be prudent to try to get some message to Marshal Zhukov indicating that the achievement of freedom in the Soviet satellites should not be con-

[92] On October 25, President Eisenhower made a statement expressing his admiration for and sympathy toward those Hungarians who were fighting for their freedom, while carefully avoiding the assumption of any political obligations on the part of the United States.

[93] See "Telegram from the Department of State to the Embassy in the United Kingdom," in *FRUS 1955–1957*, vol. 25, 292–3.

[94] Not further identified. The President noted in his diary for October 26 that he "warned both the Chairman of the Chief of Staff and the Director of the Central Intelligence Agency to be unusually watchful and alert during the crisis occasioned by the Hungarian revolt." (Eisenhower Library, Whitman File, Eisenhower Diaries) [Footnote from source text.]

sidered by the Soviet Union as posing any real threat to the national security of the USSR. We should make clear that this development would not impel the Western powers to make any warlike move against the Soviet Union. The President stated that he did not believe such a move would be worthwhile. He doubted if the Soviet leaders genuinely feared an invasion by the Western powers. He thought that a better procedure would be to ask the NSC Planning Board to provide an analysis of what had happened in Hungary and Poland and to make any suggestions which it could as to what the United States might do in the light of these developments. All of the members of the National Security Council had representatives on the Planning Board and could make their views available.

[Here follows discussion of unrelated matters.]

The National Security Council:

    a. Noted and discussed an oral briefing on the subject by the Director of Central Intelligence, with specific reference to Poland, Hungary, and the Middle East.
    b. Noted the President's directive that the NSC Planning Board prepare a comprehensive analysis of the developments in Hungary and Poland, and possible courses of action in the light thereof which the United States should consider.

[Here follow the remaining agenda items.]

S. EVERETT GLEASON

[Source: Foreign Relations of the United States, 1955–57, *vol. 25 (Washington, D.C.: U.S. Government Printing Office, 1990), 295–99.]*

DOCUMENT NO. 35: Memoranda of Conversation between President Eisenhower and John Foster Dulles, October 26, 1956

These memoranda of conversation show how Harold Stassen's idea to allay Soviet concerns about the possibility of an aggressive American response to the revolution (see Document No. 34) continued to be circulated even after Eisenhower had rejected it earlier that day. Following the NSC meeting that morning, Stassen developed the notion of the United States accepting a neutral Hungary and pressed it on a reluctant secretary of state and president. Dulles put Stassen off, saying he had doubts about "an Austria-type neutralization."[95] But when Eisenhower calls to suggest that he include something along this line in the speech he is to give the next day, Dulles is compelled to treat the point more seriously.

[TELEPHONE CONVERSATION OF 5:50 P.M.]

TELEPHONE CALL FROM THE PRESIDENT

The President said he had been turning over in his mind what Stassen had said in the meeting this morning.[96] As far as the border states were concerned, they [the Soviets] need have no fear that we might make an effort to incorporate them into NATO or make them part of our alliances. We want to see them have a free choice. We have no access to any of these states except through Austria. All we hope is that they have the same likes as Austria. The President said he brought this up because the Secretary was giving a speech and he thought he could put something like this in the speech.[97]

The Secretary said it was extremely difficult to know how to handle this thing. He had seen Stassen a while ago and he was presently engaged in a meeting on the subject in his office.[98] We have given quite a lot of thought to the problem. The Secretary said he did not think we should get into talks with the Russians about it unless through the Security Council. We could have some backstage talks going on during the time the Council was in session, which would be more or less legitimate.[99] The Secretary said it appeared that the British favored taking the matter to the GA two or three weeks hence. The President mentioned calling in the Ambassador and the Secretary said he planned on sending a message to Selwyn Lloyd.[100]

---

[95] See "Memorandum of a Conversation Between the Secretary of State and the Director of Foreign Operations (Stassen), Washington, October 26, 1956, 4:10 p.m.," in *FRUS, 1955–1957*, vol. 25, 305.

[96] See Document No. 34. Stassen also addressed a letter to the President on this date in which he wrote: "The Soviet Union may calculate that if they lose control of Hungary that country would be taken into NATO by the United States, and this would be a great threat in Soviet eyes to their own security. May it not be wise for the United States in some manner to make it clear that we are willing to have Hungary be established on the Austrian basis—and not affiliated with NATO?" (Eisenhower Library, Whitman File, Administration Series, Stassen, Harold E. 1956 (1)) [Footnote from source text.]

[97] See "Address by Secretary of State Before the Dallas Council on World Affairs, October 27, 1956," in *FRUS 1955–1957*, vol. 25, 317–8.

[98] According to FRUS, "The Secretary's appointment book shows that such [meeting] did take place, but no record of the substance of the discussion have been found in Department of State files." See footnote 5, Document 117 in *FRUS 1955–1957*, vol. 25, 300."

[99] The White House transcription of this call has Dulles stating that he did "not want to get into anything that looked as though 'backstage talks' were going on." (Eisenhower Library, Whitman File, Eisenhower Diaries) [Footnote from source text.]

[100] See "Telegram from the Department of State to the Embassy in The United Kingdom," in *FRUS 1955–1957*, vol. 25, 307. [Footnote from source text.]

TELEPHONE CALL TO THE PRESIDENT

The Sec. said he was thinking over the Pres's thought and wondered if he approved the Sec's saying something to the effect—all we want is their genuine independence and that if they once had it that would alter the whole aspect of the European scene and the whole problem of European security would be altered. The Pres. said yes—the whole European and world security would seem to be on the road to achievement. The Sec. mentioned his trying to imply you might not need to build up NATO so much or something to that effect. The Pres. said if they could have some kind of existence, choose their own government and what they want, then we are satisfied and this would really solve one of the greatest problems in the world that is standing in the way of world peace. Then something that [like] this would be of far greater effect than any alliance.

The Pres. said the evening paper looks as if it is spreading. The Sec. said we are sending a cable to Lloyd that it should get before the [U.N.] SC in order to focus attention on it so the Russians will not commit vast reprisals and give us a chance to talk privately with them there. The Pres. said to say to Lloyd it is so terrible we would be remiss if we did not do something.

[Source: Foreign Relations of the United States, 1955–1957, *vol. 25 (Washington, D.C.: U.S. Government Printing Office, 1990), 305–307.]*

DOCUMENT NO. 36: Minutes of the 55th Meeting of the Romanian Workers' Party Political Committee, October 26, 1956

From October 24 on, the Political Committee of the Romanian Workers' Party (RWP PC) focused increasing attention on Hungary. In the first days of the crisis, however, a lack of information from daily embassy reports and radio broadcasts made it impossible for the PC to assess the real extent of the danger. They therefore decided to play it safe by taking measures from across virtually the entire range of policy-making: from tightening controls over Romanian airspace to restoring party membership to selected politicians from national minority groups. It was also at this point that the PC took its first steps to seal the country's borders, aimed at blocking the influx of both people and ideas. These spontaneous decisions, several taken at this PC meeting, formed the basis of a policy developed over the next several months designed to keep a Hungarian-style crisis from spreading to Romania—a theme of concern repeated in several other satellite states. The document below is also interesting because of the insight it gives into the regimented nature of local party meetings. For example, the PC instructs members that "At these meetings, workers and clerks, both young and old, will express their disapproval towards the counterrevolutionary actions of the reactionary and fascist forces in the HPR."

Attended by the following comrades: Apostol Gheorghe,[101] Bodnăraş Emil,[102] Ceauşescu Nicolae,[103] Chişinevschi Iosif, Drăghici Alexandru,[104] Moghioroş Alexandru,[105] Pârvulescu Constantin.

Chaired by: cde. Apostol Gheorghe

The meeting began at 10:00.

Agenda

Information provided on the situation in the Hungarian People's Republic and the political and organizational measures to be taken in the country [Romania].

Cde. Gh. Apostol informs the RWP CC Politburo about the events that occurred in the Hungarian People's Republic in the last two days.

Cde. N. Ceauşescu presents a report on the information received through the party and cde. Al. Drăghici on the information from state organs about the state of affairs and climate of opinion in the country.

After discussion, the following decisions were made:

1. After completing political explanatory work in the lower Party and UTM organizations concerning the events in the Hungarian People's Republic, meetings will be organized in factories and institutions, with the participation of every employee in sections, workshops, trade-union groups or services, etc., in order to inform the working class and [administrative] employees about the situation in Hungary. The information provided will be based on the news published in *Scânteia*. The[se] presentations will be given by the presidents of the trade-union committees in the factories and institutions, in sections or workshops, with the assistance of the secretaries of Party organizations. The meetings will primarily be organized in large factories, plants of particular importance, and in the most important institutions. Care should be taken not to organize too many meetings at the same time, so that control [over these meetings] and the

---

[101] Gheorghe Apostol was RWP first secretary from 1954–1955 and a member of the Politburo between 1948–1969.

[102] Emil Bodnăraş was minister of the Armed Forces between 1947–1955 and deputy prime minister from 1954–1965.

[103] Nicolae Ceauşescu was secretary of the RWP CC from 1954–1965 and then general secretary from 1965–1989.

[104] Alexandru Drăghici was a member of the RWP CC Politburo and minister of interior from 1952–1965.

[105] Alexandru Moghioroş was a member of the RWP CC Politburo beginning in 1948, and vice chairman of the Council of Ministers from 1954–1965.

participation of members from regional, county, and city party committees can be ensured. At these meetings, workers and clerks, both young and old, will express their disapproval towards the counterrevolutionary actions of the reactionary and fascist forces in the HPR. They will express their solidarity with the heroic fight of the Hungarian working class for the ending of the counter-revolution as soon as possible.

The same explanatory work will be carried out with the students of every higher educational institution, either in study-groups or [groups organized] by year. The presentations will be delivered by well-prepared party and UTM activists and by professors (party members).

We will send comrades who were either active in or had contacts with the party during the period of illegality to speak to workers and students.

After finishing the explanatory work within the basic Party and UTM organizations [cells], Party and UTM members will explain the meaning of the events that occurred in the Hungarian People's Republic to the working peasants in the countryside, either individually or in small group discussions.

2. In order to carry out all the measures decided by the RWP CC, the Council of Ministers, and local party and state organs, collectives of 3–4 members will be formed at every regional party committee from the members of the regional committee Bureaus; for a certain period, these collectives will ensure the execution of party and government resolutions.

These collectives will meet twice a day in order to evaluate the situation and the reports received from the region through the party [*pe linie de patid*] and the organs of MAI,[106] with the aim of adopting adequate measures. Information and measures of higher importance will be forwarded to the Secretariat of RWP CC twice a day. (Cde. Nicolae Ceauşescu will deal with the measures decided in point 2).

3. For the operative solution of all problems concerning providing the population—especially urban worker centers—with foodstuffs, a collective will be formed in every region consisting of the vice-president of the regional People's Council (previously responsible for this task), the head of the trade section of the regional People's Council, the person in charge of collecting foodstuffs in the region, and the president of URCC. These collectives will include a member of the Bureau or the secretary of the regional party committee in charge of economic matters.

These collectives will daily inform the Council of Ministers of the RPR (cde. Al. Moghioroş) about the current situation and the measures taken.

4. Party organs will ensure timely payment of salaries and of other rights of workers and other employees; they will also ensure the immediate reimbursement of agricultural products delivered by peasants. The Council of Ministers will also instruct the RPR Bank to disburse the necessary funds.

5. In order to offer an operative and central solution to all the problems of provisioning the population with foodstuffs, a collective will be formed at the Council of Ministers, which will include competent comrades from the Ministry of Food Industry, Internal Trade, Collection [of Agricultural Products], Centrocoop, CCS and from the Sections of Consumer Goods, Transport and Communication of the RWP CC, under the supervision of cde. Al. Moghioroş.

6. At its meeting on October 27, 1956, the Politburo will analyze the problem of the population's provision with consumer goods. Comrades from the CSP, the Ministry of Agriculture, Collection [of Agricultural Products], Food Industry, Internal Trade, Centrocoop and the Sections of Consumer Goods and Financial Planning of RWP CC will be invited to this meeting.

7. The party and state organs will take the proper measures to ensure that foodstuffs sent to certain centers do not fall into the hands of profiteering elements. The Council of Ministers will analyze the possibility of providing corn to the population living in mountainous counties.

8. The CSP, together with the existing commission, should urgently prepare proposals concerning salaries, which will be discussed immediately after the return of the comrades who left with the RWP and Government delegation to the FPRY.

---

[106] (Ministerul Afacerilor Interne) Ministry of Internal Affairs

9. Attention should be devoted to the activities of former leaders of fascist organizations and parties (the Arrow Crossists [*nyilaşişti*], Szálasi-ites [*szalaşişti*][107] and legionnaires[108]) and of former bourgeois parties, as well as to the activities of other active elements, and to former members of these fascist and bourgeois parties and organizations who still hold high rank in the central and regional state apparatus.

The Minister of the Interior will propose a plan for organizing a report on and the strict surveillance of every suspicious element, including suspicious elements from among those lately repatriated from capitalist states to RPR.

10. Additional measures should be taken to strengthen the border guard in the regions of Oradea, Baia Mare, and Timişoara (Arad, Salonta etc.).

11. Preparation of a report for the Politburo concerning the state of mind of MFA[109] and MAI troops.

12. The intensification of political work among workers, peasants, intellectuals and especially among young people and students.

The collection [of agricultural produce] must be made tactfully, with special emphasis given to the method of political explanatory work.

13. Comrades E. Bodnăraş, Al. Drăghici and L. Sălăjan[110] will analyze the measures necessary to strengthen the units of the MFA and MAI, and of the guards at the border to the HPR.

14. Intensification of political explanatory work in the military units of the MFA and MAI. The grave events that recently occurred in the Hungarian People's Republic must be discussed in meetings with all military personnel (divided into small groups).

15. MAI will take measures to ensure military protection of the radio stations at Băneasa, Tăncăbeşti, and Bod, as well as at 13 important sites. For this purpose, the effective troops of the MAI will be reinforced with several hundred soldiers, on the basis of a Council of Ministers decision.

16. MAI will take measures to release some of the students from Bucharest who have been taken into custody, by transferring them to the UTM town committee in order to persuade them of the unhealthiness of their opinions and attitudes.

17. MAI will perform arrests only with previous approval from the party leadership. Cde. Gh. Apostol will coordinate this problem through the party. MAI may perform arrests without approval only in the case of flagrant violations; these cases, however, are to be reported to the leadership within 24 hours.

18. The Politburo approves the suspension of repatriations to the RPR and the deferral of tourist travel to and from the RPR for a certain period. The necessary guidelines will be transmitted to the embassies of RPR abroad. Com[rades] E. Bodnăraş, Al. Drăghici and the Foreign Minister will deal with this issue.

19. A collective consisting of cdes. P. Niculescu-Mizil, Melita Apostol, Vasile Dumitrescu, under the supervision of cde. I. Chişinevschi, will verify all mass-media materials published or broadcast regarding the events from Hungary.

20. By Monday, October 29 of this year, Cde. Popescu-Puţuri[111] must urgently prepare a complete report for the party leadership on the situation in Hungary.

21. Regarding cde. Dr. Petru Groza's[112] wish to come to Bucharest, it has been decided that cde. E. Bodnăraş will leave for Deva in order to inform Groza about the events in Hungary and

---

[107] Actually, both of these first two names refer to the same group: the Nyilaskeresztes Párt (the Hungarian Arrow-Cross Party), the organization of the Hungarian Nazi movement before 1945, which was headed by Ferenc Szálasi.

[108] The legionnaires were members of the Romanian fascist movement, Legion of the Archangel Michael, later known as the Iron Guard (Garda di Fier).

[109] (Ministerul Forţelor Armate) Ministry of Armed Forces (Ministry of Defense before 1950).

[110] Leontin Sălăjan was minister of the armed forces beginning 1955 and candidate member of the Politburo from 1956.

[111] Ion Popescu-Puţuri was Romania's ambassador to Hungary from 1955–1958.

[112] Petru Groza was prime minister from 1945–1952 and chairman of the Presidium of the Great National Assembly (head of state) from 1952–1958.

some of the internal measures taken, as well as to convince him to defer his departure for several days, as his sudden return would not be appropriate without public announcement.

22. For a certain period, the Politburo of the RWP CC will meet daily at 13.00 and 21.00 o'clock to analyze the internal situation and to decide upon proper measures to be taken.

The meeting ended at 13.00 o'clock.

GH. APOSTOL
GH. GHEORGHIU DEJ

[Source: Arh. CC al PCR, fond Biroul Politic, dosar nr. 355, ff. 1–5. Published in Romanian in Corneliu Mihai Lungu and Mihai Retegan, eds., 1956 Explozia: Percepţii române, iugoslave şi sovietice asupra evenimentelor din Polonia şi Ungaria *(Bucharest: Editura Univers Enciclopedic, 1996), 91–95. Translated by Victoria Isabela Corduneanu.]*

DOCUMENT NO. 37: French Foreign Ministry Instructions to United Nations Representative Bernard Cornut-Gentille, October 27, 1956

On the eve of the U.N. Security Council meeting convened to investigate the Hungarian crisis, the French Foreign Ministry sent this telegram to its U.N. mission. The document reflects the complex political situation facing Paris, referring to the war in Algeria, which France fought to protect its influence in North Africa, and which was denounced repeatedly before the U.N. It also points out the only possible courses of action available to the French government concerning the Hungarian revolution under the cold war circumstances of the time: to play to international and Hungarian public opinion. Although not mentioned explicitly, Paris' worries about a possible investigating committee at this point are not due mainly to the situation in Algeria but to what is about to happen in the next two days—the secret, joint Israeli-British-French military attack on Suez.

CHRISTIAN PINEAU, MINISTER OF FOREIGN AFFAIRS
TO THE PERMANENT DELEGATION OF FRANCE AT THE UNITED NATIONS ORGANIZATION

PARIS, OCTOBER 27. 11P.M.

T.N. 3282. ABSOLUTE PRIORITY
SECRET. RESERVED.

To transmit to Mr. Cornut-Gentille[113]

It is essential that the draft resolution which will be put to the Security Council on the Hungarian question should not contain any disposition which may disturb our action in Algeria and our relationship with Morocco and Tunisia.[114] We are particularly against the formation of a committee of inquiry.

On the other hand, the resolution will have a greater impact on international and Hungarian public opinion, the more concise and free of hackneyed formulas it is.[115]

[Source: Ministère des Affaires Étrangères, Documents Diplomatiques Français, 1956, vol. 3, 24. Octobre–31. Décembre (Paris: Imprimerie National, 1990), 49. Translated by Kata Somlai.]

---

[113] Bernard Cornut-Gentille was French representative to the United Nations and chairman of the U.N. Security Council in October 1956.

[114] Beginning in 1954, France was engaged in a brutal war against the independence movement in Algeria, which made Paris the object of repeated criticism in the U.N. French diplomacy was therefore sensitive toward any potential Security Council resolution that might further exacerbate its position. Morocco and Tunisia gained their independence from France in March 1956.

[115] On October 27, at U.S. initiative, the United States, Great Britain and France made a joint request to convene a session of the Security Council to discuss the Hungarian situation.

DOCUMENT NO. 38: Report from Anastas Mikoyan and Mikhail Suslov in Budapest to the CPSU CC, October 27, 1956

In this report, Mikoyan and Suslov, relying on information from the HWP Political Committee, assess the coalition-like government formed by Imre Nagy. They describe the members of the new government as being "as a whole ... reliable and in the social sense more authoritative" than their predecessors. They go on to discuss the military situation in Hungary and plans to restore order, and refer to the discussions within the HWP Central Committee which led Géza Losonczy and Ferenc Donáth, two close associates of Nagy, to leave the CC. There is even a reference to Suslov giving Nagy medicine to treat his "acute overexertion."

TOP SECRET
DELIVER IMMEDIATELY

CPSU CC

I.

Today we participated for more than three hours in a Politburo meeting, where we discussed government appointments and the present situation.

Members of the Politburo made changes to the primary government slate with the intention of improving the political stability of the government. Thus, for example, [Antal] Apró—who is a member of the Directory and a member of the Military Commission,[116] having behaved very well these past few days—has been chosen deputy chairman of the Council of Ministers and, in actuality, he will be the first deputy because the remaining deputies are non-party members and less strong.

The candidacy of [József] Szilágyi for the post of minister of internal affairs was turned down, because politically he was not very reliable, and Münnich was chosen instead. In this connection, the former deputy minister of the military supply service, Károly Janza, was chosen for the post of minister of defense. He is a communist, reliable, and from a workers' background.

The candidacy of László Kardos for the post of minister of culture was also turned down for the same reason. Chosen instead was [György] Lukács, who is a famous philosopher, and although he caused a lot of confusion in the field of philosophy, is more trustworthy politically and authoritative among the intelligentsia.

In order to strengthen the government with non-party elements, Zoltán Tildy, a famous public leader, was chosen to be minister without portfolio. Comrade Imre Nagy suggested that Zoltán Tildy not be selected because he is on poor terms with Béla Kovács. However, that was not accepted.

Characteristically, at night there appeared proclamations in the city, in which Nagy was called a traitor and Béla Kovács was recommended as Premier. [These proclamations] also call for demonstrations, and in his honor.

As instructed by the CC, Nagy called Béla Kovács who lives outside the city, and asked him whether he would join the government. Kovács responded affirmatively, and added that he had been invited to a mass meeting, but that even if he attended, he would speak out against the demonstrators, [and] for the government.

The non-party specialist [Miklós] Ribiánszky has been confirmed as the minister of state farms.

Characteristically, all of these candidates were accepted unanimously and Nagy did not object to the replacement of individual candidates.

In conversations with us, the Hungarian comrades declared that they consider the new government suitable both politically and in terms of efficiency. Imre Nagy especially emphasized this.

[116] The correct form is Military Committee.

The formation of this government was announced on local radio at 12 noon Hungarian time.

We had the impression that as a whole the new government is reliable and in the social sense more authoritative.

II.

Comrade Apró gave a report about the military situation in assured tones. Among other things he reported that about 3,000 injured Hungarians are in the hospital, and of those 250 have died. The number of others killed or wounded is unknown.

In connection with the unsettled situation in the countryside, comrade Kádár asked the question: can we increase the number of Soviet troops?

We declared that we had reserves, and that as many troops as were needed would be provided. The Politburo members were very glad to hear this.

Apró suggested taking a number of actions to help organize further struggle in the city and to restore order to the city.

Apró informed us that people had been surrendering a significant number of weapons and that 700 rifles had been collected.

Apró also informed us that the situation in the countryside was already beginning to stabilize, but Kádár and Hegedüs reacted skeptically to this.

The Hungarian comrades have started to arm the party *aktiv*, which has thus begun to feel more confident. It was decided to bring the armed party members into the city police force. It was also decided to assign military censors to the radio and newspapers.

It was suggested to the ministers that they ensure that the ministries and enterprises functioned smoothly.

III.

Comrade Kádár informed us that new Politburo candidate member [Géza] Losonczy and new CC Secretary [Ferenc] Donáth, who spoke yesterday in a capitulationist manner at the Politburo meeting, and whom several members of the CC called traitors of the working class, declared their disagreement with the CC's policies and submitted their resignations.

Imre Nagy was not present when cde. Kádár gave this information, because he was busy with negotiations with the assigned ministers, and also because he suffered a heart attack due to acute overexertion. (By the way, after a break in the session we found Nagy in a faint state in his office, and the Hungarian doctor did not know what to do, so Suslov gave him Validol [a medicine] which brought Nagy back to normal, and for which later he was very grateful.)

Considering that Losonczy and Donáth are closely associated with Nagy, and, as we mentioned before, that Nagy was not present at the session at that time, the Politburo decided to postpone a final resolution in their case, and put them to work outside of the CC for the time being.

* * *

We agreed to have a heart-to-heart talk with Kádár and Nagy this evening in an unofficial capacity.

A. MIKOYAN
M. SUSLOV

OCT. 27, 1956

[Source: APRF, F. 3. Op. 64. D. 484. Ll. 131–134. Also in TsKhSD, F. 89, Per. 45, Dok. 9. Originally published in the Cold War International History Project Bulletin *no. 5 (Spring 1995): 29–30. Translated by Johanna Granville and József Litkei.]*

DOCUMENT NO. 39: HWP CC Political Committee Meeting, October 28, 1956

These minutes constitute one of the most important documents on the history of the Hungarian revolution, not only because of all the top-level political meetings during this period, this session is supported by the most reliable documentation (stenographic notes along with a contemporary transcription), but also because the minutes themselves illustrate a fundamental change in the Hungarian party leadership's position. By accepting János Kádár's proposal for a peaceful settlement without branding "the people who took part in the fighting ... as counterrevolutionaries," the Party's most influential body radically reevaluated the events that had begun on October 23. The uprising was no longer part of a counterrevolution, as it had been defined from the very beginning, but a national democratic movement against past mistakes, which implied that its aims could be reconciled with socialist goals and be seen as essentially parallel with the party's. This meant that the crisis could be solved by political, not military means.

The choice between those two alternative approaches had been the central dilemma for the Hungarian leadership since the outbreak of the revolution. But by October 27 the party had come to a crossroads. By then it was clear that military actions, including the deployment of the Soviet army, had failed to suppress the movement. In fact, spreading demonstrations in the countryside, strike threats, and the formation of workers' councils made the leadership realize that they were increasingly losing control. Nagy's speech at the evening session of the Emergency Committee finally turned the tide in favor of change, and the committee acknowledged the national democratic character of the uprising.

Still, in order to enforce this decision, Moscow's approval was required. Kádár and Nagy therefore spent the night of October 27 seeking Mikoyan and Suslov's support. The two envoys could see that Soviet military measures had failed and that the situation in the country, as well as within the HWP, was continuing to collapse. In providing their agreement, most likely with Khrushchev's consent, they no doubt were influenced by the fact that Kádár, who represented the views of the rest of the Hungarian party leadership, joined Nagy in urging a policy shift. (It was also easier to agree to remove Soviet troops from Budapest because the current deployment was already due to be rotated out of action.) Also, the latest news of an imminent agreement among the trade unions, university students, and Writers' Union underlined the need for concessions. The Soviets did insist on maintaining the leading role of the HWP, and therefore called for a party resolution on the new approach. To strengthen the party's position, Mikoyan and Suslov further proposed establishing a solid political center, which they called the "directory".

Given this background, the purpose of the October 28 HWP PC session, aside from enforcing a political decision that followed guidelines set the night before, was simply to spell out the main points of the decision and how they were to be interpreted. The lack of serious debate indicates that some of the most influential personalities, above all Ernő Gerő, had agreed to the changes in advance. Similarly, Kádár stressed the presence of the Soviet emissaries and Mikoyan's active part in formulating the resolution.

The HWP Central Committee, which convened that night, also sanctioned the turn, and expressed support in its resolution for Nagy's government declaration, already in preparation.

Present: János Kádár, Sándor Rónai, György Marosán, Zoltán Szántó, András Hegedüs, József Köböl, Ernő Gerő, Imre Nagy, Károly Kiss, Antal Apró, Géza Losonczy.
Comrades Mikoyan and Suslov also participated in the session.

Comrade Kádár: We have to find a way to get the people who took part in the fighting to lay down their arms without regarding them [all] as counterrevolutionaries. Those who live in the provinces cannot be regarded as counterrevolutionaries. They represent a mixed picture. In the future, it has to be made clear that [we must fight] against those who, after this declaration and [given] a certain opportunity for changing sides, continue to use armed force against our People's Republic—until they give themselves up or are destroyed. We must act most firmly against those atrocities which public opinion in the country has also condemned, in line with our view: murders, shootings of prisoners, hangings. I have said nothing about the cease-fire because the declaration [already] provides a standpoint [on this], as well as some means for those still participating in the armed battle to change sides.

At midnight we were informed that the SZOT is negotiating with a student organization, which is an approach that is fundamentally at odds with what we consider a solution.

This would be an agreement [that], independent of the party, would describe the entire movement as it stands as a national democratic revolution. The fact that the SZOT and the students are issuing a separate declaration without [the involvement of] the party and the government shows how our political line has completely split in two. Comrade [Sándor] Gáspár was well-intentioned, but it is patently clear that this is how it would come out. A separate declaration would mean separating the working class from the party. I cannot imagine that the working class would not see the importance of this, if we explained it to them. This is theoretically indefensible, and in practice means that every authority of the CC and the government will collapse; if we say that those who are still fighting at the last minute are revolutionaries, then the workers and the students will not look to the party's Central Committee as their leading body, but to the SZOT or something else.

We see the situation as pressing, and we must establish our position quickly, after the oath is taken. We cannot dictate to the trade unions. As communists, however, we can give this advice to comrades working there.

In answer to individual questions:

1. The movement cannot simply be called a national revolution, because that means that everyone who is against us is a revolutionary, and that we are counterrevolutionaries. The right terminology must be found. *(Comrade Gerő: Szabad Nép's lead article is quite good.)*
2. There are good things in this settlement, too—we haven't permitted it to be released yet, though. The party is completely missing from it. It must include mention of the party. It doesn't necessarily have to appear in the government's declaration, but the opinion must be firm, that the [new] government, which was created by the CC, is the one that works.
3. ÁVH. Some of the comrades were against its abolition. We all raised our hands at the Central Committee session when we voted to put the ÁVH troops into action. The state security troops are workers in military uniform. On our vote they went into battle and cleared their names; we cannot give these people up to the counterrevolution. It would be possible to include in the declaration that we are going to rearrange the structure of the Ministry of the Interior. *(Comrade Gerő : We have to organize a unified state police.)*
4. Soviet troops: we told the people of this country that we invited the troops in; we even gave reasons for it. In the same way that we asked them to engage in the fighting, we can ask them to take their troops out of the fight. And we can ask them to withdraw their troops from the territory of the country. Whether they withdraw them or not is at the sole discretion of the Soviet Union. If such a formula is correct, let us stick to what Comrade Nagy suggested concerning the negotiations because that is good; we can accept it.
5. Two members of the CPSU Presidium are here. The comrades give us no instructions. As a communist, I, however, see it as a fundamental duty that we pay heed to their advice, which combines the interests of our people and of the communists with proletarian internationalism.
6. Last night I told our Soviet comrades my opinion. As I understood it, our comrades approved what I have outlined here. They had a very important piece of advice regarding the party's survival: one of our greatest handicaps in our battle is that we are not unified, not even in terms of politics.[117] We will go to ruin like this because an internal battle is going on and the enemy is

---

[117] In a 1996 transcription of the original stenographic notes, prepared by the Institute of Political History in Budapest, this sentence ends as follows: "...not even in the Political Committee." Because of the imperfect quality of the original notes, significant differences of interpretation sometimes appeared in various transcriptions made over the years. In those instances, the editors of the most recently published version, used here, indicated alternatives by comparing their version to the 1996 transcription. Those alternatives are indicated in the footnotes below.

attacking. Our comrades advised that we create a party directory—this must receive the Central Committee's consent. The party organizations should be left as they are, but the leadership must be strengthened, and such a directory could work until the congress. The number of directory members cannot be too large, for that would decrease its operational effectiveness. According to my experiences so far, this directory is capable of working in its current form. This is a considerable mandate, but it would be nonsensical if there were lengthy debates first in the directory and then in the Political Committee, for even the most simple questions. The Central Committee must be convened immediately for 10:30 [a.m.] through an announcement on the radio.

Comrade Mikoyan: The Political Committee and the Central Committee would not be dissolved, but would give authorization to the party directory that would from time to time report on its work. The right to make decisions is in the directory's hands. Every member of the CC should return to their positions and put every effort into their work there. Long debates only weaken us.

Comrade Marosán: When the CC, following my proposal, elected this directory, this was exactly what my proposal aimed at. This was the way the CC delegated full power concerning military and political decisions. I still regard this to be correct.

Comrade Mikoyan: It has to be said more clearly that there were mistakes in the old leadership.

Ernő Gerő: But we must discuss the old leadership's misdeeds.

Comrade Mikoyan: The government is determined to fight firmly against bureaucracy and tyranny, and for socialist legality. If we want to be at the leading edge of the workers' movement, we must demand that they end the fighting. We should not negotiate during the shooting and use street loudspeakers, but hold meetings, factory meetings. The comrades have to display, and behave with, firmness in this. If there are further concessions tomorrow, then it cannot be stopped. The new government has not yet declared anything—so far only Comrade Imre Nagy has spoken, and on his own behalf. Now he should express the government's position, let us take the initiative. Then the trade union can make a declaration. Preventing the SZOT from wavering is precisely why it should be invited to the meetings, be kept informed, and be involved in the task. Letting the trade union leadership out of our hands will lead to a parallel center, which could become a pawn in the enemy's hands.

We respect Comrade Nagy, he is an honest man, but sometimes he can very easily fall under the influence of others. But, to be strong, a definite stand is needed, which we adhere to and maintain.[118]

Comrade Hegedüs: I agree with what Comrades Kádár and Mikoyan have said. The priority is to breathe new life into our own people. The Southern Railway [station] was reoccupied by members of the party College. Újpest was regained, and members of the Petőfi College captured 40 people. We must not allow any uncertainty to surround the fact that the battle is fundamentally a just battle. If we allow any kind of uncertainty here, I think we are committing a very grave error. On the other hand, we mustn't look at the events in a sectarian way. In the whole movement—I am not looking only at the armed uprising—there are many democratic elements. If we confront these democratic demands, as we have started to do, then we will confront our own workers and peasants. This is what experience confirms. I spoke to the leader of the Worker's Council in Győr County, who is a man of integrity. Should we work against him, or with him?

He supports the government. But what did he ask of me? Three times he asked me for weapons, because their forces have become weak: they have 20 machine guns and some hand grenades. He said that the Arrow Crossists were a trifle compared to what the insurgents are doing now.[119] The Revolutionary Council is in a desperate position. Representative Attila Szigeti addressed a crowd of 5,000; they listened to him; 4,000 left, but a group remained that had demanded weapons from soldiers.

---

[118] The 1996 transcription of the original stenographic notes also includes the following two sentences: "And we have to reach agreement with the delegation; we have to persuade them of the correctness of our line."

[119] According to the 1996 transcription, these two sentences read: "Three times he asked me for weapons, because the police have become weak, and 20 machine guns and hand grenades have fallen into the hands of enemy individuals. He said that those making declarations were a trifle compared to this."

[We must act] on a broad, national basis, including those who stand for the people's democracy, and [then join] them in arms, otherwise our popular democratic system will not survive.

Concerning the cease-fire: I support a cease-fire, but on no account for the bandits and looters. It is not a cease-fire when in Budakeszi they completed a list of the communists and wanted to massacre them. I think it was proper that we sent out the Petőfi Officers' Training College and that they captured those (120 or 160 people).

I mean cease-fire in the following way: a cease-fire in Budapest for 1,000 people who are surrounded; but where they are stealing, murdering, or killing our comrades, I cannot vote for a cease-fire and I think nobody else could do so. We have to order a cease-fire and make as many concessions as we can without risking the power of the people's democracy. Partly, it is not even a question of concessions, rather of correcting our own mistakes.

We mustn't make commitments that we cannot later satisfy and which go beyond the requirements of the people's democracy. I negotiated with Comrade Apró, [who informed me that] they proposed a coalition government, secession from the Warsaw Pact, etc.[120]

If we go further [than the present concessions], there are two possible courses of action: the first is a bourgeois restoration, whether in multiparty or in fascist form. The second is a very forceful Soviet occupation, which is very hard for both the Soviet government and for us. So between these two roads we have to find a new one.

Very smart army officers are leading the military resistance. For example, staff officer Dezső Király by Corvin [Passage]—he was Gömbös' right-hand man. His demands we cannot satisfy.[121] There is a conception among us that those who took up arms have gone a bit too far, but that they are fighting for national freedom. We must see that the majority of the leaders are good army officers, as far as the armed actions are concerned.[122]

Comrade Mikoyan: Let's not talk in generalizations, but say who is saying what and state who is playing a part.

Comrade Hegedüs: 1. Declaration: First publish a party declaration and then a government declaration. If only a government declaration is made about these questions, I am worried that some opposition will emerge between the party and government leaderships. I would [also] agree with a joint declaration. 2. I opt for the reorganization of the ÁVH.

Comrade Mikoyan: The government declaration is more fortunate [sic] since this is a state affair; the party should invite the support of party members.

Comrade Hegedüs: It must be declared, and the proper formulation found, that there is no conflict on these questions between the Central Committee and the government.

[As for] the ÁVH: It would not be ethical if, having sent them into battle, we were to leave them in the lurch. These comrades are in a very difficult situation. They are being denounced, their families are persecuted. I strongly agree with restructuring the ÁVH; it should be a separate division of the police. However I am afraid that if we only talk about restructuring in the declaration, and fail to recognize that they have held out together with the soldiers, then we will stigmatize them.

Comrade Mikoyan: The government and the armed rebels should not enter into negotiations. The SZOT, however, should negotiate by all means—with the young people too. We have to

---

[120] This refers to the unsuccessful negotiations with the leaders of the Corvin Passage rebels after the failed attack in the morning. The insurgents rejected the Soviet ultimatum to immediately lay down all arms, responding instead with a list of demands of their own. These included a new coalition government led by Péter Veres (former chairman of the National Peasant Party and chairman of the Writers' Union since 1954), free elections before the end of the year, and the withdrawal of Soviet troops from Hungary.

[121] This reference is to Béla Király, who was not at the Corvin Passage and whose only connection to Gyula Gömbös was that he married his foster daughter in 1947. Gömbös was a German-oriented right wing politician in the interwar period and Hungarian prime minister from 1932 until his death in 1936.

[122] According to the 1996 transcription of the original stenographic notes, these two sentences read: "We must see that the leaders are bad elements. The majority of them are former army officers."

demand that they support the government and that the youth cannot set conditions for the government. The questions need to be solved after the armed fighting, not during it.

Comrade Gerő: I agree with what Comrade Kádár said. It is extraordinarily important that:

1. The backbone of the armed groups, who, in part, are still to be organized and are partly in the process of being organized, should be the self-conscious [sic] working class. This is fundamental, since there is a conception that the core should be students—not among us here, but this [conception] exists.
2. We must ensure that from the outset we organize this armed force with the party leadership and don't allow it to slip through our fingers.
3. I don't see that a separate State Security Authority is necessary. [We need] a unified Hungarian democratic state police, which would of course include state security bodies. The important thing is not for there to be a separate name and separate uniform. We have to make concessions in this area, but we cannot make concessions concerning the crux of the matter.
4. Those organs who fought against the government in the armed action are demanding amnesty. Amnesty can be granted, but [then] the next step [will be that they] demand that those who put up resistance be brought to justice in a court of law—this cannot be allowed.[123]
5. The directory is a good idea, but the fact that it will lead the party until the congress must by all means be made public.
6. On the basis of this political platform we have to concentrate on pulling together the party, the party committees, and the party organizations, so that work can begin again in Pest. In Budapest, where everyday life presents considerable difficulties, the party, together with the trade unions and residents' committees, etc., should take the lead.

Comrade Apró: There is no solution other than the one Comrade Kádár has presented. The masses will understand. If we did anything else, the party would collapse, the masses would rise against us, and we would become isolated.

The cease-fire must be ordered, without specifying a concluding time. We have to make sure that when we have the Soviet forces withdrawn, the Hungarian authorities in charge of public order are ready, otherwise there will be a vacuum.

Comrade Szántó: Time is pressing; the situation is very serious. At the moment the situation in the provinces is getting worse and worse. In five days the situation has developed very quickly in what, for us, is a bad direction. A peaceful demonstration began and now crowds of workers are rising up against the people's power. They are removing the councils, and the workers, who are not enemies of the people's democracy, are passively watching the slaughter of party functionaries. We cannot go any further down the road toward opening fire on the workers.

Politically and morally, we are tending more and more to isolate the party from the masses who sympathized with us and followed us.

The fact that our Soviet comrades undertook this support created a particularly delicate and awkward situation for us as well.[124] Not only does it offer the imperialist governments hopes for intervention, it also leads to a shattering of faith, faith in socialism on the part of the communists in Western countries. The Soviet Union's foreign policy enabled it to establish contacts with many countries. In the present situation, the intervention makes the Soviet Union's further relations more difficult. We have the duty, not only as Hungarian communists but also as proletarian internationalists, to consolidate the situation. I completely agree with Comrade Kádár.

---

[123] In the 1996 transcription, points 4 and 5 are inverted. This part of the text continues as follows: "The Central Committee decided on this unanimously, the state security organs gave orders, just as the military [organs]. We mustn't give way on this question."

[124] In the 1996 transcription, the final phrase of this sentence reads: "this has had a strongly negative effect."

The cease-fire should not be ordered in a way that makes it effective in some towns and not in others, but as a complete cease-fire; and we must still rise up against the looters, murderers and bandits. [We need] a general cease-fire, and those who attack with weapons should be met with weapons.

I agree with restructuring the ÁVH.

I consider the party directory sensible and necessary. We must make it easier for it to function politically, for it to bring around those crowds and those strata which broke away from us because of the former party leadership's mistakes. That is why we should not burden the party directory with a dead weight that makes [its] work more difficult. Neither should we burden it with Comrade Hegedüs, because he is still a captive of the old methods.

Comrade Rónai: We must prepare a government declaration and [therefore we should] ask Comrade Nagy to expound his position.

Comrade Nagy: In a situation as tragic as today's, the fact that questions arise accidentally exposes the failure of the party leadership. Yesterday evening the Committee concerned itself with the arming of the workers.[125] Yesterday I already proposed that this leadership could not be tolerated any longer. I protest against the directory's working practices when it deals with questions of third-, fourth- or fifth-order importance, and not with what [it is handling] finally today. Comrade Mikoyan turned to me and said that we have to stand more firmly. I'm not going to stand firmly when the party's interests demand going further. Neither did I stand firmly for what the CC and the PC stood for. My position then was correct, I stood for the same position then as I do now. There are two options: If we evaluate the broad-based movement as a counterrevolution, as we initially evaluated it, then there is no option but to suppress it with the help of weapons, tanks, and artillery. This is a tragedy. Now we are able to see that this course of action is not our course of action. We have created an extraordinarily serious situation for the Soviet Union and for our country—that we are being overrun by counterrevolution. This means that if we are not careful we will be exposed to intervention.[126] We have to lean on and take command of the great, powerful people's forces which are on the move. However, this is only possible if we evaluate the events as outlined by Comrade Kádár.

A cease-fire has to be ordered as soon as possible. This morning there was still the greatest amount of uncertainty; at 6:00 this morning they wanted to begin military operations.[127] Comrade Hegedüs was very instrumental in causing the serious instability that exists within the leadership. Yesterday morning he shared our opinion; by today he is again thinking of ordering military operations.

Comrade Mikoyan: Concerning the evaluation of the situation we have to argue with him.[128]

Comrade Nagy: Soviet troops must be withdrawn from armed battle, and Hungarian troops must simultaneously be deployed: the army, the democratic police, [we must] rely on the workers, and I don't rule out students either.

Gerő: Neither do I, but the leadership should be in the hands of the workers.

Nagy: Right. We must definitely discuss the ÁVH. We must now withdraw them from the fighting without evaluating them.

Mikoyan: The Soviet army is fighting against the Hungarian People's Army here. If they change to the rebels' side, then they will be fighting against Soviet units.

---

[125] This refers to the meeting of the Emergency Committee on the night of October 27.

[126] The 1996 transcription uses the expression "imperialist intervention."

[127] Although the night before the HWP Directory had forbidden any further military action, in the early morning of October 28, the Soviet and Hungarian military leaderships, with the knowledge of the Party's Military Committee, ordered a long-planned attack against the Corvin Passage aimed at finally liquidating one of the main centers of armed resistance. When Nagy heard about this, he immediately ordered Defense Minister Károly Janza to abort the operation. Although Nagy believed that his order had been carried out, the attack went ahead. Nevertheless, it soon collapsed after rebel defenders were able to destroy the very first tanks that were sent out for reconnaissance.

[128] In the 1996 transcription of the original stenographic notes, this sentence reads: "We are allowed to develop our arguments."

Comrade Nagy: An amnesty is definitely appropriate.

Comrade Gerő: But we must not call to account those who opposed them [the insurgents] through the courts.[129]

Comrade Nagy: Two types of amnesty are needed: 1. for the participants in the fighting, 2. for all former political prisoners.

Comrade [Károly] Kiss: I agree with Comrade Kádár's report. We must build up a very broad-based unity [on the basis of] people's democracy and in close friendship with the Soviet Union. I agree with "ceasing fire," but we must be very careful that they do not murder our best comrades in the meantime.

I agree that the ÁVH should not remain, but we transferred the working class's best children there and we must protect them, because at this moment people want to kill them. I agree with an amnesty.

Comrade Rónai: I agree with Comrade Kádár. I ask Comrade Apró: can we ensure that order will be maintained without the Soviet army? Can we ensure it with the Hungarian army or other armed units? Only if we can achieve this can we begin withdrawing the Soviet troops.[130]

Comrade Apró: Comrade Rónai asked for a guarantee. This we cannot provide. Maintaining public order has to be organized as soon as possible. The only guarantee is if we are united with the party members, the workers, and [politically] conscious people against the looters and murderers.[131]

Suggestions for a resolution:[132]

1. The platform outlined by cde. Kádár was accepted as the basis for the party's efforts in the current situation. This has to be seen as obligatory, whatever position we hold.
2. We agree that the government declaration should appear, and in our party announcement we [should] state that the government is operating in conjunction with the party.
3. The PC agrees with what cde. Kádár and other comrades have done to prevent the appearance of the SZOT's resolution.
4. A decision is required on what we should call the central party institution: the party Presidium. The Political Committee and the Central Committee give the party Presidium full authority to conduct its work; in this work it relies on the members of the Political Committee and the Central Committee.[133]

Comrade Kádár: Concerning Comrade Hegedüs. I have only really been working with him since June. In my opinion he is useful from the point of view of the committee's work, he is a young man capable of operative work, absolutely honorable in his intentions, dynamic, and hard-working. That his working methods comprise a lot of the old [ways] is true, but because of the committee's composition I do not see a danger.

Comrade Köböl: What Comrade Kádár says is right, knowing the opinion of the party membership and the functionaries. Because of political considerations, however, I am against him staying. The party membership sees no guarantee they could continue to work with him.

Comrade Gerő: I consider him an honest, principled, competent communist. We must listen to the Central Committee on this.

---

[129] The 1996 transcription represents the relevant phrase as those "who are against us."

[130] In the 1996 transcription, the relevant phrase reads: "can I see the withdrawal of the Soviet troops being safe."

[131] In the 1996 transcription the text continues: "I'm afraid that otherwise a vacuum will be generated." This is followed by an interruption by Sándor Rónai that was omitted from the minutes: "If we are united on this platform, then the Party is united."

[132] The suggestions were made by Kádár. The portions concerning Kádár in the stenographic notes were written in the first person singular.

[133] At this point in the 1996 transcription, Károly Kiss interrupts: "We should enlarge the party Presidium by one member, if Hegedüs is excluded."

Comrade Mikoyan: It is best if you don't change the composition. If you change it, there will be no end to it. I assume that Comrade Hegedüs had different views since in such a situation that is inevitable. He has influence in the party; he did not take part in making arbitrary arrangements. His record is also good. He should stay, as he will be useful. Concerning the composition of the directory the CC has already decided and only the CC can change it. Otherwise conflicts will emerge and that is not good.

Comrade Köböl: There must be undivided support for the Presidium, this is why I don't recommend Comrade Hegedüs. *(Result of vote: 4 against, 6 in favor)*

Comrade Köböl: Even this vote shows that there isn't unity of opinion.

Comrade Mikoyan: There is a consensus on the theoretical questions and that is the important thing.

Comrade Szántó: Theoretical consensus is the priority, but what I see is precisely that a theoretical consensus is missing. I don't question his competence or honesty. But Comrade Hegedüs's political conception and working practices developed in such an atmosphere that he cannot escape from them. This has revealed itself over the last few days, too. If a piece of news arrived, [which was incomplete], it immediately changed his political conception, because his old methods pulled him back.

Comrade Kádár: I believe unity is extremely important. We ought to report the result of the vote to the CC, but I am afraid that political debates will begin again. I take back my proposal, let him be left out. An executive apparatus should be set up and Comrade Hegedüs should work in it, as a leader, since he can make arrangements quickly and [thus] would not take part in making political decisions.

Hegedüs: I don't think I would be an obstacle to further work. I fought many times and quite consistently in the Political Committee against sectarian mistakes. Indeed, in the last few days I did not see the military and political situation correctly and clearly. There is only one circumstance in which I could take on the leadership of the Executive Committee, and that is if [the situation] does not deteriorate further.

Comrade Gerő: Comrade Hegedüs cannot carry out this work, because every problem manifests itself in the executive. Everything culminates there, this is why I don't propose that he undertake it.

Comrade Hegedüs: I am afraid that we [sic] will slip further down. My position would be very difficult if I were beaten in more disputes: obviously I will execute the decision even if I am beaten in more disputes, but only if I can participate in the discussion.

Comrade Rónai: Let him be the leader of the Executive Committee with right of consultation.

Comrade Losonczy: There is a contradiction in Comrade Kádár's proposal. If Comrade Hegedüs is not going to agree politically with the majority position of the committee, how can he be nominated to head the Executive Committee? *(Vote: 3–8 votes resulting in the omission [of Hegedüs]; he should participate in the work of the executive apparatus)*

Comrade Hegedüs: As a member of the Executive Committee I will execute every order. *(Comrade János Kádár was unanimously elected leader of the Presidium)*[134]

Comrade Gerő: We should decide that nothing of great importance should happen in the government without it being previously discussed by the Presidium, which leads the party.

Comrade Kádár: Considering the unusual situation and circumstances, we would ask the Soviet comrades to be present at the CC session and help to present the position which has taken shape here.

Comrade Mikoyan: There is no need for that, because they will interpret it as us trying to exercise pressure. The Political Committee members should speak in unison.

Comrade Gerő: I ask permission to present [the proposal] at the CC session for Hegedüs's participation in the committee.

---

[134] The 1996 transcription includes the following: "János Kádár: Does the Presidium need an overall leader? Answer: Yes, János Kádár."

Comrade Mikoyan: I don't agree with this, because then the dispute will begin again. If the Political Committee members speak in unison, then it would not be useful for us to separately reintroduce a contested question.[135] Comrade Hegedüs remains a member of the Political Committee, but let us look at it honestly. He remains a member of the PC, but the PC has in practice no right to make a decision.

Comrade Kádár: In theory I don't think it is right for you to take part in the CC session, but on this occasion I am asking you to take part. If you say no, then we will respect this. I suggest that we make an announcement that we have consulted with the comrades.[136] (The proposal was accepted)

Comrade Losonczy: The Presidium is also obliged to hold regular CC sessions.[137]

[Source: Politikatörténeti Intézet Levéltára (Institute of Political History*), 290 f. 1/15 ő.e. pp. 57–68. Published in Julianna Horváth and Zoltán Ripp, eds., Ötvenhat októbere és a hatalom: A Magyar Dolgozók Pártja vezető testületeinek dokumentumai, 1956. október 24–28 (Budapest: Napvilág Kiadó, 1997), 98–112. Translated By David Evans.]*

[135] The 1996 transcription of the original stenographic notes includes the following sentence as well: "We have faith in Comrade Gerő. What is your opinion?" The debate following Gerő's interruption was left out of the minutes. According the 1996 transcription, the omitted part was the following: *Ernő Gerő:* "If he is the leader of the apparatus, then he must be a member." *Mikoyan:* "If the members of the Political Committee speak in unison, then it would not be useful for us to separately reintroduce a contested question. But he remains a member of the Political Committee." *Gerő:* "He remains so on paper, but not in practice, because he has no right to make decisions."

[136] The 1996 transcription of the original stenographic notes also contains Mikoyan's answer: "That is possible. But the Political Committee must be convened from time to time. We should connect the election and the work of the Presidium to a congress."

[137] The 1996 transcription of the original stenographic notes ends with the following sentence: "At the moment there is no such obligation, because the situation is extraordinary." Logically, it appears that Losonczy must have made this remark, although that is not indicated in the text.

DOCUMENT NO. 40: Working Notes from the CPSU CC Presidium Session, October 28, 1956

Vladimir Malin's cryptic notes of the CPSU CC Presidium session five days after the first Soviet invasion reflect Moscow's confused and changing state of mind concerning Hungary. At this session, the Soviet leaders reassured themselves about the appropriateness of deploying troops into Budapest but recognized that conditions were continuing to deteriorate. Their frustration not only resulted in a decision to condemn the Hungarian leadership, especially Nagy, for "indecisiveness," but even led Presidium hardliners to criticize Mikoyan's activities. In this atmosphere, Nikita Khrushchev outlined the alternative courses of action open to the Kremlin: either to continue to support Nagy's government in hopes that it would be able to consolidate the situation, or set up a new government capable of restoring order. Khrushchev, who had serious concerns about a military solution, seemed to prefer the first alternative.

At this point, Mikhail Suslov, who had been ordered back to Moscow, joined the meeting. His report on the "complicated" circumstances in Budapest not only reflected the dilemmas the Soviet emissaries had to face in Hungary but also depicted the Hungarian leadership's efforts to gain control over the crisis. Emphasizing how unfavorable the conditions were for a military solution (mass support of the movement, increasing anti-Soviet sentiments, and so on), Suslov clearly endorsed Nagy's policies.

Convinced by Suslov's arguments and realizing that at this point the Hungarian leaders were "evidently ... not able to do more," the Presidium supported the Nagy government's October 28 declaration calling for a cease-fire, the dissolution of the secret police, and negotiations on Soviet troop withdrawals. "We must support this gov[ernmen]t" was the almost universal conclusion, "otherwise we'll have to undertake an occupation."

Participants: Voroshilov, Bulganin, Kaganovich, Malenkov, Molotov, Saburov, Khrushchev, Brezhnev, Zhukov, Shvernik,[138] Shepilov, Furtseva, Pospelov, Zorin.

On the Situation in Hungary
(Khrushchev)

Cde. Khrushchev—the matter is becoming more complicated.
They're planning a demonstration.
Kádár is leaning toward holding negotiations with the centers of resistance.[139]

We must set Sobolev right at the UN.[140]
The workers are supporting the uprising (therefore they want to reclassify it as something other than a "counterrevolutionary uprising").

Cde. Zhukov provides information.
They would refrain from stamping out one of the centers of resistance.[141]
An order was given not to permit a demonstration.

---

[138] Nikolai M. Shvernik was a candidate member of the CPSU CC Presidium from 1953–1957 and chairman of the CC Party Control Committee between 1956–1966.

[139] This presumably refers to negotiations between Kádár and trade union leaders during the night of October 27–28, but could also relate to Kádár's views, which he expressed at the October 28 session of the HWP PC (see Document No. 39).

[140] On October 28, Foreign Minister Shepilov instructed U.N. Representative Sobolev to represent the Hungarian events as a fascist movement at the upcoming Security Council session. Khrushchev's remark indicates a revision of this instruction corresponding to the imminent change in the official Hungarian evaluation.

[141] On October 27, the HWP Emergency Committee (Directory) decided that no military action against the Corvin passage group would be launched unless the insurgents attacked first. The October 28 morning session of the PC confirmed this decision after Nagy criticized Gerő and Hegedüs for insisting on a military solution. See also footnote 127 above.

They're dismantling the railroad tracks in a number of localities.
In Debrecen power has passed to our troops.[142]

Cde. Khrushchev provides information.
The situation is complicated.
Cde. Suslov is to fly back to Moscow.[143]
A Directory has not been declared.
They propose that Hegedüs be removed from the Directory (4 in favor, and 6 against).[144]
The plenum is going on now.

Cde. Voroshilov—they are poorly informed.
Cdes. Mikoyan and Suslov are behaving calmly, but are poorly informed.
We're in a bad situation. We must devise our own line and get a group of Hungarians to embrace it.
Cde. Mikoyan is not able to carry out this work.
What we intended to do (to send a group of comrades) must now be done.[145]
We should not withdraw troops—we must act decisively.[146]
Nagy is a liquidator.

Cde. Molotov—things are going badly.
The situation has deteriorated, and it is gradually moving toward capitulation.
Nagy is actually speaking against us.
Our cdes. are behaving diffidently.
It is agreed up to what limit we will permit concessions.
This pertains now to the composition of the government[147] and to the Directory.
They are excluding Hegedüs, and this means they're no longer showing regard for us.
The bare minimum is the question of friendship with the USSR and the assistance of our troops.
Cde. Mikoyan is reassuring them.
If they don't agree, we must consider what will happen with the troops.

Cde. Kaganovich—a counterrevolution is under way.
Indecisiveness of the Hungarian Communists.
Kádár should make certain concessions to the workers and peasants and thereby neutralize the movement.
Decisive action is needed against the centers of resistance; we cannot retreat.

---

[142] This statement was far from accurate; it more correctly refers to the fact that the county's party and state leaders took refuge with nearby Soviet forces from the city of Debrecen, which was already under the control of the local revolutionary committee.

[143] Suslov actually arrived in Moscow while the meeting was underway and reported on the Hungarian situation at this meeting. Until then, the discussions had been based on reports received over the past few days.

[144] See Document No. 39.

[145] This presumably refers to a decision made during the October 26 meeting of the CPSU Presidium, which concerned Hungarian party officials studying in Moscow. The idea, first proposed by Hungarian Ambassador János Boldoczki, was to send these officials back to Hungary, with proper instructions, in order to strengthen the HWP. For the minutes of the meeting see Kramer, "The 'Malin Notes'," 389.

[146] Voroshilov's remark again refers to the October 28 session of the HWP PC (See Document No. 39) where the Hungarians requested the withdrawal of Soviet troops from Budapest without launching a military action against the Corvin passage.

[147] Although the new government formally came into being on October 28, the decision concerning its composition had already been made at the HWP PC session the day before. Mikoyan and Suslov immediately informed the Soviet leadership. See Document No. 38.

Cde. Bulganin—the HWP is acting ambivalently.

Kádár kept lurching. The main thing is to demand greater decisiveness from Kádár.

We must act as follows—summon Mikoyan to the phone and say: The HWP Politburo must act decisively; otherwise, we will take action without you. Perhaps will have to appoint the gov't directly.

Cde. Malenkov—we shouldn't lay blame for the situation on our comrades. They're firmly carrying out a line aimed at suppressing the uprising. Nagy from the government so he can put forth a program [sic].

Cde. Zhukov—regarding Cde. Mikoyan's role, it's unfair to condemn him right now. The situation has unfolded quite differently compared to when we decided to send in troops.

We must display political flexibility.

We must organize the CC for more flexible actions.

We must organize armed workers' brigades.

Our troops must be kept in full readiness.

The main center of resistance must be suppressed.

Cde. Saburov—agrees with Cde. Zhukov. They must take up their positions at large enterprises. A program is needed.

Cde. Khrushchev—we will have a lot to answer for.

We must reckon with the facts.

Will we have a gov't that is with us, or will there be a gov't that is not with us and will request the withdrawal of troops?

What then?

Nagy said that if you act he will relinquish his powers.[148]

Then the coalition will collapse.[149]

There is no firm leadership there, neither in the party nor in the government.

The uprising has spread into the provinces.

The [Hungarian] troops might go over to the side of the insurgents.

We can't persist on account of Hegedüs.

Two options.

The gov't takes action, and we help.

This might soon be completed, or Nagy will turn against us.

He will demand a cease-fire and the withdrawal of troops, followed by capitulation.

What might the alternatives be?

1) The formation of a Committee, which takes power into its hands[150] (this is the worst alternative), when we . . .

---

[148] Nagy threatened to resign over the planned attack against the Corvin passage group; see footnote 127.

[149] "Coalition" here merely means the presence of non-communist politicians in the government, not a coalition of different parties.

[150] The first reference to a "Military-Revolutionary Committee," the formation of a counter-government, was made at the October 26 CPSU CC session. The word "committee" originates from the vocabulary of the 1917 Bolshevik revolution when such "revolutionary military committees" were formed. For the minutes of the October 26 session, see Kramer, "The 'Malin Notes'," 389.

2) This gov't is retained, and officials from the gov't are sent into the provinces.
A platform is needed.
Perhaps our Appeal to the population and to workers, peasants, and the intelligentsia should be prepared, or else we're just shooting.
3) Would it not be appropriate if the Chinese, Bulgarians, Poles, Czechs, and Yugoslavs appealed to the Hungarians?
4) Decisively suppress the armed forces of the insurgents.

Cdes. Brezhnev, Pospelov, Shepilov, and Furtseva are to prepare documents.[151]

It is agreed: the fraternal parties should appeal to the Hungarians.

On the Situation in Hungary[152]
(Cde. Suslov)

Cde. Suslov: The situation is complicated.
On 23 Oct. our troops entered.
On 25 Oct. only one pocket of resistance was left; we found out about it on 26 Oct. It was at the "Corvin" cinema, a group headed by a colonel from the Horthyite army.[153]
Single gunshots are heard (often).
They're beating officers.
3,000 wounded, 350 dead (Hungarians).
Our losses are 600 dead.
The popular view of our troops now is bad (and has gotten worse). The reason is the dispersal of the demonstration on 24 Oct. 56.[154] Shooting began. 70 ordinary citizens were killed. Many flags were hung up on the sidewalk.

Workers are leaving their enterprises.

Councils are being formed (spontaneously) at enterprises (around various cities).
There is an anti-Soviet trend to the demonstrations.

How can we regain control of the situation?
The establishment of a relatively strong gov't.

---

[151] This refers to the appeals, referred to above, that were to be issued. For the actual list of these documents, see Document No. 53.

[152] There is some disagreement among scholars about the proper placement of the following section of Malin's notes, which covers Suslov's report to the Presidium. According to Mark Kramer, who published extensive translations of Malin's notes (including this one) relating to Hungary in the *Cold War International History Project Bulletin,* Suslov's comments must have come late on October 28 or early the following morning (see Kramer, "The 'Malin Notes'," 391–392 and 403, fn 68). The editors of a more recently published compilation of Russian documents on the revolution placed the section as it appears in this volume, which also has the effect of attributing to Suslov (instead of to Khrushchev) the last two lines before Bulganin's next statement, below. (See *Sovietskii Soyuz i vengerskii krizis,* 435–436 for the location of this segment of Suslov's remarks.)

[153] This alleged Horthyite colonel first appears in the October 27 report by Serov with the name "Berlaki." However, since no such person is known to have been at the Corvin passage, it is possible that the report refers to Pál Maléter who was in the neighboring Kilián barracks. For Serov's report (forwarded by Suslov and Mikoyan), see *Sovietskii Soyuz i vengerskii krizis,* 414–415.

[154] This should be October 25. Suslov is referring to the bloodshed at Kossuth Square.

Our line is not to protest the inclusion of several democrats in the gov't.
Yesterday a government was formed.[155]

On the morning of 28 Oct., at 5:00, Kádár arrived and pointed out that the trade unions had demanded a reassessment of the insurgents, reclassifying the events as a national-democratic uprising.[156]
They want to classify it according to the example of the Poznań events.[157]
Kádár reported that he had succeeded in agreeing with the trade unions to eliminate the formula of a national democratic movement and about the organs of state security.

In his address, Nagy inserted a point about the withdrawal of Soviet troops.
They're also insisting on a cease-fire.

Our line now: this time the gov't is recommending a cease-fire, and the military command is devising an order for the withdrawal of troops from Budapest.

Nagy and Szántó raised the question of removing Hegedüs from the Directory.

There's no need to hold elections.[158]

Do we support the present government once the declaration is issued?[159]
Yes, support it. There is no alternative.

Cde. Bulganin: . . .

Cde. Voroshilov: We acted correctly when we sent in troops. We should be in no hurry to pull them out.
American secret services are more active there than Cdes. Suslov and Mikoyan are.[160] A group of comrades should go there. Arrange to form a gov't and then withdraw the troops. We sent you there for nothing.[161]
(Cdes. Khrushchev and Kaganovich object.)

Cde. Bulganin: We acted properly when we sent in troops, but I can't agree with the assessment offered by Cde. Voroshilov. We should endorse the actions taken by Cdes. Mikoyan and Suslov. We must draw the right conclusion: In Budapest there are forces that want to get rid of

[155] See footnote 147, above.

[156] Concerning Kádár's meeting with the leaders of the SZOT, see footnote 139, above.

157 This refers to Gomulka's famous speech on October 20, 1956, at the Eighth Plenum of the PZPR CC, in which he denied that the Poznań uprising was counterrevolutionary in character, and explained it as the result of despair on the part of the workers caused by the grave mistakes committed while building socialism.

[158] Presumably, this refers to the resolution of the October 28 HWP CC session, according to which the Fourth Party Congress was to be convened within the shortest possible time. The word "elections" refers to the election of congress delegates by the party organizations.

[159] For the declaration, see Document No. 44.

[160] Voroshilov may be referring to the report sent by Serov on October 28, according to which U.S. diplomats said during a private conversation that "if the uprising is not liquidated in the shortest possible time, U.N. troops will move in at the proposal of the USA and a second Korea will take place." In fact, this information lacked any foundation. For the report, see *Cold War International History Project Bulletin*, no. 5 (Spring 1995): 30–31.

[161] "You" means Suslov and Mikoyan.

Nagy's and Kádár's government. We should adopt a position of support for the current government.

Otherwise we'll have to undertake an occupation.

This will drag us into a dubious venture.

Cde. Kaganovich: Regarding the sending of troops, we acted properly in sending them.

There is no reason to attack Mikoyan and Suslov.

They acted properly. It's unfair to lay the blame on them.

If we don't offer support, there'll be an occupation of the country.

That will take us far afield.

We should do what is needed to support the gov't.

Changes shouldn't be made in the declaration regarding the withdrawal of troops.

So that they speak about friendship.

The question is how to strengthen the party.

We don't need to send additional people there.

Malenkov: The actions that were taken were correct.

There is no point at all in condemning Cdes. Mikoyan and Suslov.

We should support the new gov't.

We should keep troops there with the approval of the gov't.

Cde. Malenkov: So many people were involved there that there'll have to be a guarantee of an amnesty.

Cde. Molotov: We acted properly when we sent in troops. The initial messages from Cdes. Mikoyan and Suslov were reassuring about their view of the government.

The influence of the party on the masses is weak.

With regard to the new government, we should support it.

But regarding friendship with the USSR, they're talking about the withdrawal of troops. We must act cautiously.

Cde. Zhukov: We must support the new gov't.

The question of a troop withdrawal from Hungary—this question must be considered by the entire socialist camp.[162]

The authority of the HWP CC must be raised.

We should appeal to the fraternal parties so that they, in turn, will issue appeals to the Hungarians.

In Budapest, we should pull troops off the streets in certain regions.

Perhaps we should release a statement from the military command.

With regard to the assessment of Cdes. Mikoyan and Suslov, it's inappropriate to say the things that Cde. Voroshilov did.

Cde. Saburov: We must support this gov't.

The authority of the gov't must be increased in the eyes of the people.

We shouldn't protest their assessments of events, and we shouldn't protest about the withdrawal of troops, albeit not an immediate withdrawal.

Cde. Khrushchev: Agrees with the cdes.

We must support this gov't.

---

[162] This is the first reference to withdrawing Soviet forces from the entire country, not just Budapest. The term "withdrawal" may have been used in this sense during the entire meeting but this cannot be ascertained from the notes.

We must devise our tactics.

We must speak with Kádár and Nagy: We support you; the declaration—you evidently are not able to do more.

We will declare a cease-fire.

We are ready to withdraw troops from Budapest.

We must make this conditional on a cease-fire by the centers of resistance.

Cde. Molotov: Second, we must look after the Hungarian Communists.[163]

Cde. Bulganin—the regime of people's democracy in the country has collapsed.

The HWP leadership no longer exists.

Power has been gained by . . .

Cde. Kaganovich—we're not talking here about concessions, but about a war for the people.

The declaration must be adopted.

A troop withdrawal from Budapest.

Cde. Voroshilov: If only a group could be formed there, we could leave our troops in place.

There's no one to rely on.

Otherwise there's war.

Cde. Khrushchev—I support the declaration.

Politically this is beneficial for us.

The English and French are in a real mess in Egypt.[164] We shouldn't get caught in the same company.

But we must not foster illusions.

We are saving face.

Fundamentally, the declaration must be adopted.[165]

But adopt it with corrections.

Life in the city must be put right.

An appeal from the fraternal parties.

A ciphered cable to Yugoslavia.[166]

Cde. Pospelov is to be included in preparations of the report for 6. XI. 56[167]

If there is to be a leaflet from the military command, let . . .

Hegedüs
Gerő
Piros
them to Bulgaria.[168]

---

[163] This presumably refers to the Soviet aim to evacuate certain Hungarian leaders from the country. See footnote 168 below.

[164] This remark indicates that on October 28 Khrushchev already knew about the imminent attack against Egypt.

[165] Again, this refers to the Nagy government's October 28 declaration, see Document No. 44.

[166] The purpose of this telegram was presumably to arrange for a consultation with Tito, or propose a personal meeting. Nevertheless, the telegram was not sent on the 28th, but on the 31st, see Document 53.

[167] This refers to the speech that Suslov was to deliver on the occasion of the 38th anniversary of the Bolshevik revolution on November 6, 1956.

[168] This is what appears in the original. Eventually, the three officials, together with their families, were flown to Moscow not Bulgaria during the night of October 28. According to Hegedüs' recollection, former Defense Minister István Bata was also evacuated with the group. Piros and Hegedüs remained in the Soviet Union until 1958, while Gerő could only return on 1960.

[Source: TsKhSD, F. 3, Op. 12, D. 1005, Ll. 54–63, compiled by V. N. Malin. Originally published in English in the Cold War International History Project Bulletin *no. 8/9 (Winter 1996/1997): 389–92. Translated by Mark Kramer.]*

DOCUMENT NO. 41: Soviet Foreign Ministry and CPSU CC Presidium Instructions to Yurii Andropov and Arkadii Sobolev, October 28, 1956

On October 27, the U.S., British, and French representatives to the United Nations requested a Security Council meeting to discuss Hungary. The document below is the proposed Soviet response, comprising a draft set of instructions for the Soviet ambassadors to Budapest and the U.N. Following standard Soviet foreign policy decision-making procedures, the drafters formally request Central Committee approval for the most significant steps to be taken. The instructions then give an exact timetable for the Hungarian government to follow in supporting Soviet measures. To the document's authors it is especially important to issue a communiqué describing the crisis as an internal Hungarian affair, emphasizing that Soviet troops intervened at Hungarian government request, and objecting to the issue being placed on the U.N. agenda. At Soviet urging and on instructions from the Hungarian government, Péter Kós,[169] Hungary's minister to Washington and permanent representative to the U.N., handed that communiqué to the secretary general on October 28. Nevertheless, and in spite of further objections by Soviet U.N. Representative Arkadii Sobolev, the issue was raised in the Security Council the same day. Sobolev reacted with the standard argument that this amounted to interference in Hungary's domestic affairs.

CPSU CC

In connection with the fact that the Western powers have raised the issue of the situation in Hungary in the Security Council, the USSR minister of foreign affairs considers it expedient to:

1. Advise the Hungarian comrades to immediately make an appropriate statement by the Hungarian government.
2. Give instructions to the USSR's representative in the Security Council about the stance he should assume.
A draft resolution is attached.
Please consider.

October 1956.

Resolution of the CPSU CC
To approve draft instructions for the USSR Ambassador in Budapest (attached).
To approve draft instructions for the USSR representative in the Security Council on the Hungarian question (attached).

***

Budapest
Soviet Ambassador

As you know, the Western powers introduced a question entitled "The Situation in Hungary" in the Security Council, having in mind to accuse the Soviet Union of interfering in Hungary's internal affairs, and of violating the Peace Treaty with Hungary.

In this connection, you should speak with the Hungarian leadership about the expediency of publishing an appropriate Hungarian government statement. The statement should note that the develop-

---

[169] Péter Kós was Hungarian minister to the United States and representative at the U.N. beginning in 1956. On October 31, 1956, he was recalled but on November 4 received instructions from the Kádár government to return to Washington.

ments occurring in Hungary are the internal affair of Hungary, and that the counterrevolutionary riot, which began on October 23, was a result of subversive activity by the imperialist states, who made use of certain difficulties and problems in the country and systematically incited the reactionary elements with propaganda and interference in Hungary's internal affairs in the struggle against the people's democratic regime. Soviet military forces participation in suppressing the counterrevolutionary riot is a result of the Hungarian government's request to the government of the USSR to provide assistance in reconstructing the legal order and defending the people's democratic regime and the Hungarian state's sovereignty, which, therefore, has nothing to do with the Peace Treaty with Hungary.

The introduction of this issue by the Western powers in the Security Council represents more evidence of interference by those states in Hungary's internal affairs. The statement should end with a protest by the Hungarian government against the introduction of this question in the Security Council and with the demand not to include this question on the agenda.

Tell the Hungarian comrades that in our opinion this statement should be published and broadcast on the radio today, without waiting for the discussion of this issue at the Security Council session, which is scheduled for October 28 at 15:00, New York time. Recommend to the Hungarian comrades to telegraph that statement to the chairman of the U.N. Security Council and to its representative in New York. Simultaneously, the text of the statement should be sent immediately to Moscow.

In your conversation with the Hungarian comrades, express our opinion about the expediency of immediately preparing appropriate materials, drawing their attention to the selection of concrete facts and, where possible, documents characterizing the Western powers' interference in Hungary's internal affairs, which could be used by the Soviet representative in discussing this issue.

Tell the Hungarian comrades that since the inclusion of the Hungarian issue on the Security Council's agenda is probable, it would be expedient for the Hungarian government to send their representative to take part in the discussion, if it is impossible to remove that issue from the Council's agenda. In this connection, the Hungarian U.N. representative should demand that the discussion of this question be postponed until the arrival of the Hungarian government representative, i.e. for 5 to 7 days.

Telegraph implementation.

***

New York
Soviet Ambassador

First. We agree with your proposals.

In case there is a substantive discussion of the issue, you should develop the points you have already mentioned—discount as groundless the Westerners efforts to draw in the Peace Treaty, which has nothing to do with the current developments in Hungary. However, if the Westerners are trying to use Article 2, Section 1 of the Peace Treaty (regarding the protection of human rights), you should point to the groundlessness of accusations of violations of that Article, and cite Article 4 of the same Section obligating the Hungarian government not to allow the existence and activity of fascist organizations that aspire to rob the people of their democratic rights. In your statements, you should maintain a confident and calm tone.

Second. For your information, we are notifying you that the Hungarian government gave its representative at the United Nations direct instructions to reach an agreement with the Yugoslav representatives to speak against including this question on the Council's agenda.

Get in touch with the Yugoslav representative, find out his intentions, inform him about our position, and try to reach an agreement on a common mode of behavior.

[Source: (Original Russian archival citation not on document; document is available as part of the "Flashpoints" collection at the National Security Archive). Translated by Svetlana Savranskaya.]

DOCUMENT NO. 42: Report from Yurii Andropov Transmitting a Back-Dated Request for Soviet Intervention from András Hegedüs to the CPSU CC Presidium, October 28, 1956

This urgent communication from the Soviet ambassador includes a Hungarian government request for Soviet troops to intervene "in order to put an end to the riots that have broken out in Budapest." According to information from the Moscow meeting of satellite party leaders on October 24 (see Document No. 27), Khrushchev had insisted on an official request the day before, to be signed by the Hungarian prime minister. The Soviets needed legal justification for military action to keep from being branded an aggressor; the upcoming U.N. Security Council meeting on October 28 could have yielded just such a pronouncement.

Although under the Soviet-led socialist system the first secretary of the party, in this case Ernő Gerő, was considered to be the de facto leader of the country, under international law only the actions of heads of governments or their designees are recognized. On October 27, Gerő and Andropov therefore tried to persuade Nagy to sign a pre-dated letter of request for Moscow, but Nagy refused, arguing that he had not held the proper post when the decision was made to intervene. It was thus ex-Premier András Hegedüs who provided the signature, probably on October 27 even though the document is dated October 24. While the original letter has not yet been recovered, Soviet Foreign Minister Shepilov read aloud the cable published below at the November 19 U.N. General Assembly session—without mentioning the name of the signatory.

BUDAPEST, OCTOBER 28, 1956
IN CODE

TOP SECRET
NOT TO BE COPIED

SENT FROM BUDAPEST

URGENT

I hereby forward a letter from the Hungarian Government to:

"The Council of Ministers of the Soviet Socialist Republics

Moscow

On behalf of the Council of Ministers of the Hungarian People's Republic I appeal to the government of the Soviet Union to send Soviet troops in order to put an end to the riots that have broken out in Budapest, to restore order as soon as possible, and to guarantee the conditions for peaceful and creative work.
24 October 1956
Budapest
Prime Minister of the Hungarian People's Republic András Hegedüs"

28.X.56 [28 October 1956] Andropov

[Source: AVP RF, f. 059a, op. 4, p. 6, d. 5,1.12. Originally published in János M. Rainer, "1956—The other side of the story: Five documents from the Yeltsin file," The Hungarian Quarterly 34, no. 129 (Spring 1993): 104.]

DOCUMENT NO. 43: Minutes of the First Meeting of the Hungarian National Government, October 28, 1956

These minutes give a detailed account of the discussion that took place at the first session of the new Hungarian government, which was formed between October 25 and 27. As its first priority, the participants approved the text of Nagy's radio speech to be delivered later that day. Based on a resolution adopted at the morning meeting of the HWP Political Committee and approved by the Central Committee, the speech referred to the uprising as "a national democratic movement" instead of a "counterrevolution." With a view to how critical the situation had become, the meeting mostly emphasized the measures that could facilitate consolidation: increased supplies of goods for the public, a possible cut-back on curfews, and actions related to martial law and the compulsory delievy of agricultural products. "We should get ahead of the regional mood on this question, we should take command of events...," was the consensus. The document below sheds considerable light on the government's position and the special nature of its decision-making mechanisms. Decisions on issues with far-reaching consequences had to be made within a short time-frame and based on a severe lack of information. Still, even under conditions of revolution, the new leadership tried to handle emerging problems in a "normal" way.

Session of the Council of Ministers, 28 October 1956

Imre Nagy, the chairman of the Council of Ministers, convened the Council of Ministers at 2 p.m. on the 28th of October, 1956.

István Dobi, the president of the Presidential Council of the People's Republic, administered the oath to the members of the new government.

Agenda of the Session of the Council of Ministers:

1. Report of the chairman of the Council of Ministers on the national situation.
   Speaker: Imre Nagy, chairman of the Council of Ministers.
2. The establishment and agenda of the Government Committee for Public Supplies.
   Speaker: Zoltán Vas.

Budapest, 28 October 1956.

***

Minutes of the first session of the National Government, 28 October 1956

István Dobi: I suggest that, contrary to established practice, the members of the government should take the oath verbally, not only in writing.

(Taking of the oath!)

Imre Nagy: I wish you all a warm welcome, to those not present also. I would like to spend a few words on the great responsibility that has perhaps never before faced a responsible Hungarian ministry on the road to rebuilding the country. On this occasion, in this difficult situation, I would not like to say grave things about the tasks which lie ahead of us. From here I have to go to the radio, so that we can achieve some amelioration of the bloody brawl which is taking place in our country. In my speech to the Hungarian people I think I have succeeded in outlining all the tasks which will hopefully be appropriate to take us and our people down the road by which we will surely overcome our exceptionally serious problems and difficulties. We should be filled with this calm conviction and the belief that we are serving our country and that we will not spare our strength or our lives in its service.

Before I speak to the people of this country, please allow me, esteemed Council of Ministers, to ask you to listen to and approve the words and ideas that might lead us toward improvement.

"People of Hungary!...."(reads the speech)[170]

Esteemed Council of Ministers, we intend to present ourselves to the people with this appeal. I think the appeal represents a turning-point in the life of our People's Republic, and we hope that it opens a new era in which we really will secure all the guarantees which will make it impossible for the sad, grave, and tragic events which have happened in our country to be repeated.

Zoltán Tildy: I suggest we replace "the government ... in the first place on the support of the fighting working class" with "the government wishes to rest in the first place on the support of the fighting working class, but also, of course, on the support of the entire Hungarian working population ..."

Imre Nagy: I hereby raise the question of whether I have the support of the Council of Ministers in turning to the people of this country with this appeal. (Every minister showed his support by raising his hand!)

Items on the agenda: Report on the situation! Report of the Government Commissioner for Public Supplies.

Comrade Erik Molnár:[171] I suggest that we add the question of summary jurisdiction to the agenda.

Comrade Apró:[172] Zoltán Vas would like to speak.

Zoltán Vas: Esteemed Council of Ministers! Yesterday the Government Committee was established, under the authority of the Council of Ministers. Its first activity, its first task, was to inform public opinion that such a committee was established. To the best of my knowledge, the news was very well received, and they see in it an assurance that, after so much anxiety, the government is making effective arrangements to guarantee public supplies.

Having examined the situation as a whole, I have to say I found it satisfactory. The committee has only been formally established in the sense that we are in contact with each other by telephone. We have not yet held an actual session, but we work in complete agreement with Comrades Tausz,[173] Nyers,[174] and Pongrácz[175] and the relevant ministries. In my opinion supplies are sufficient for about three weeks, though not of everything. The exception is milk, which is understandable.

Although the food situation is generally satisfactory, there are difficulties with milk, and if we cannot guarantee delivery there will be certain difficulties with bread and flour; although, there are supplies of grain. It is basically a question of deliveries. At the moment there are certain problems with this, because particular railway regions are not satisfied with the selection of Comrade Bebrits.[176] It is my duty to report this, and in many regions strikes have been started in response to it. I spoke to Comrade Bebrits, who most loyally declared that he will step down on these questions, if there is a personal problem with him, but that he will still do everything he can to guarantee deliveries.

---

[170] For the text of the speech, see Document No. 44.

[171] Erik Molnár was a member of the HWP CC from 1948–1956, minister of justice from 1954 to November 3, 1956, and head of the Institute of History of the Hungarian Academy of Sciences from 1949–1966.

[172] Antal Apró chaired the government meeting on October 28 while Imre Nagy went to the broadcasting studio in the Parliament building.

[173] János Tausz was minister of domestic trade from April to October 31, 1956.

[174] Rezső Nyers was a member of the HWP CC beginning 1954 and minister of food industry from August to November 3, 1956.

[175] Kálmán Pongrácz was a member of the HWP CC from 1949–1956 and chairman of the Municipial Council Executive Committee (mayor) of Budapest between 1949–1958.

[176] Lajos Bebrits was minister of transportation and postal service from 1949 to October 29, 1956 and a candidate member of the HWP CC from 1954 to October 1956.

My opinion is that we will overcome this as well. So at the moment, the main problem is the organization of deliveries, and it is also characteristic that this is not in the region of Budapest but rather in the regions further out. It was my duty to say this, as being the only possible difficulty.

The Záhony region gave up its position regarding the delivery of food and salt: they declared that they were willing to deliver food.

In Budapest the shops are now turning over very significant sales. We have succeeded in increasing deliveries. The only difficulties were on certain Buda hills, and even then it tended to be because we could not get across the bridges in time.

There were interesting initiatives: they did not take the bread into the shops; instead cars stopped in front of the shops and they did their shopping there.

In general the overall impression is that in some form life has begun again on the food front. There are no particular difficulties. The peasantry is preparing for the shipments. Certain larger stocks of goods are at our disposal. A very significant train shipment is on its way to Budapest.

In my opinion the Council of Ministers must deal with [the question of] what kind of work schedule there will be tomorrow. Will the curfew continue, or will work begin again? It has to be said that workers are, in general, very bored of being at home. They would like to go to their workplaces. Their opinion is that if there are fewer loiterers on the streets, these questions will also be cleared up much more effectively.

The overall impression is that the food situation can only get better in the next few days, and in the following weeks—if we work well enough—there will not be any problems.

To conclude: I do not think it would be right to commit ourselves to maintaining the committee on a permanent basis. There is a very great political need for this committee, so that the people can see that the government is making decisive arrangements, but we must not make preparations for any kind of apparatus here.

I am convinced that the ministries and the apparatuses have already shown that they are capable of working well and that they can solve the problems.

Antal Apró: I have a question: Are they dealing with provisions for children—powdered milk, baby food? The situation in children's homes is hard. Attention should principally be turned to this; this is where help must be provided.

Zoltán Vas: I am in constant contact with the secretary-general of the Red Cross. A lot of help is on its way. The first deliveries have already arrived at Hegyeshalom. These have been taken away by those from Győr. No error was in fact made, as those supplies have entered national circulation.

We are receiving serious help from abroad. We agreed with Comrade Nagy and the Foreign Ministry that we will give a positive reply to the offer from the Swiss Red Cross. My opinion is that if they attach the condition that they want to distribute it, we must accept it.

Comrade Bognár: Could we not do it such that we tell them what we need?

Ferenc Nezvál:[177] They offered us the chance to choose.

Zoltán Vas: The secretary-general of the Red Cross made a list of what is practical. Our request was that they add more grain and flour to it.

József Bognár: That does no harm.

Zoltán Vas: Especially as we require serious imports in any case. My feeling is that it will be easy to get supplies from America.

Zoltán Tildy: Who is acting as the government liaison with the Red Cross?

Zoltán Vas: The Foreign Ministry and myself.

Zoltán Tildy: We should request that the foreign minister reply to every such offer immediately and accept the assistance with gratitude. I would also like the matter to be publicized in the Hungarian press and on the radio.

Imre Horváth: We should immediately bring the Hungarian Red Cross in on this task.

---

[177] Ferenc Nezvál was minister for city and village management in the Nagy government from October 27, 1956. In May 1957, he became minister of justice in the Kádár government, and from June a member of the HSWP CC.

Zoltán Tildy: It is certain that agitation will begin. I am especially thinking of the points of view from which the people's mood can be influenced. So far what has happened is that the masses have led, and the government has followed behind them. These things must be taken in hand and my kind friend the foreign minister should put great weight on this.

István Kossa:[178] The food commissioner should handle things for the government from now on.

József Bognár: So he should be responsible for what we receive, for what we ask for, what lists we hand over. The foreign minister should be responsible for other questions, for the political side.

Imre Horváth: The Red Cross should supply the shipments, and Comrade Vas should keep a record of them.

József Bognár: The domestic food situation and political situation should justify what items we ask for. This should be done by Comrade Vas and his comrades, the distribution by the Red Cross, and the political part by the Foreign Ministry.

Mrs. József Nagy:[179] With regard to the work schedule, Comrade Vas recommended that we agree that work should begin again. We must definitely wait to see what the HM [Ministry of Defense] says. It would be better if people stayed at home. Where it is very essential and important, they go in to work anyway.

The other question: I would like to inform the Council of Ministers about how salaries have been paid in the factories. They could not go into every bank. They took the spare keys to three banks. They also took all the money from the food shops. With the workers' councils' signature people received their money; they distributed advances of between 200 and 400 forints. People were satisfied with this.

Rezső Nyers: Concerning what Comrade Vas was saying, I suggest we make shopping hours much longer. There is a lot of overcrowding and queuing in the allotted time. We have to guarantee that every food shop opens. Comrade Tausz can report on this tomorrow. The period for which people can go out should not be restricted to five hours, given that people are on the streets anyway. I suggest people should be able to go out from eight o'clock in the morning until five or six o'clock in the afternoon. This will calm people down. There is something else we should do. Regarding food storage, there are four important centers. These should be supervised or guarded by the army. There have already been instances where people wanted to plunder them.[180]

Antal Apró: Do we have also livestock?

Rezső Nyers: We are feeding them!

Ferenc Nezvál: I would like to be given instructions, as our first task will be to supply the residential buildings with glass. We must investigate how much glass we have at our disposal. If we do not have adequate supplies, they must be imported. We need a huge amount. Instructions must be given to the Ministry of Housing for the glass factories and warehouses to begin deliveries.

József Bognár: We can ask the Czechs, Poles, or Germans for them!

Ferenc Nezvál: They thought that the shipment of existing glass would run into big problems. Apart from putting glass into residential buildings, we must also secure public buildings, so that official work can start again; I ask for help with this. I ask that not just state companies get involved in the completion of these operations, but anyone who understands them.[181]

Lajos Bebrits: With regard to what was said by Comrade Vas, I report the following: two motorized Soviet divisions should have been allowed to enter at Záhony station yesterday. Záhony denied admission to the trains. I received a report on this, took the station manager to

---

[178] István Kossa was minister of finance in the Nagy government from October 27–November 3, 1956.

[179] Mrs. József Nagy was minister of light industry from 1955 to October 31, 1956, and a member of the HWP CC beginning in 1954.

[180] The verb in the original Hungarian, 'szétütni,' implies "to break up" or "strike," however the translation used above seems closer to the intended meaning.

[181] That is, a self-employed craftsman.

account, who replied that the workers' council had forbidden him from accepting goods, soldiers, or troops from the Soviet Union. I spoke to the leader of the workers' council, who said that they had stopped consignments arriving from the Soviet Union in the name of the united workers' council of Hajdú-Bihar [county] and Nyírség [region], nor would they accept any in the future. They can go out but not come in. I gave them an order, to which they replied that ministerial tyranny was over. The Soviet troops still entered. The workers' council of Záhony then sent a circular telegram around the whole country, that this dictatorial minister is unacceptable and must be dismissed. Another such incident happened in the afternoon. A consignment of 28 coaches was arriving from Romania in the direction of Kecskemét. Békéscsaba did not let it through. The Záhony thing was repeated. The workers' council came, citing its instructions from the workers' council of Békés county. They explained that everything is happening most peacefully—they are sending food, but the troops should not come in. Between Békéscsaba and Lökösháza they took up a hundred-meter stretch of track, so the consignment could not enter. I do not recommend that we disturb the peace in Békéscsaba. I can report that three food trains are on their way. About 300-400 coaches, which have to be collected and put to use, are standing in the shunting depot in Budapest. I can report that provisional consignments traveling across Hungary, including animals and perishable foodstuffs, have been stopped. At present we cannot feed the animals, and we cannot pass them abroad. We ordered that they be used for Hungarian ends, given that we have to pay compensation. We will unload them in Budapest and use them.

Work is going on in Budapest. There is a shortage of staff. Three-quarters of Budapest's railway workers live far away. There is no passenger traffic, so there are hardly any staff in today. They are constantly exposed to snipers. Today we raised the staff level, in fact it will rise by tomorrow.

Antal Apró: Are there any other questions?

János Tausz: Esteemed Council of Ministers! The food supply for the population is not really decisively influenced by reserves at the moment—rather it is a question of deliveries and how residents can move around.

During today's opening hours, although service workers made superhuman efforts, they were not able to conduct trade undisturbed. From 10 a.m. to 3 p.m. is not quite enough.

I think Comrade Nyers' suggestion is worthy of consideration, for two reasons. Shop opening hours—despite their extreme importance for supplying the population—must be subordinated to the military situation. The soldiers should say whether it bothers them or not if there are crowds of people on the streets early in the morning or in the evening.

The second thing is the question of transport. Workers must go to work too. Often they walk for one, two, or three hours. I do not think we have to take that many steps, just one step from where we stand at the moment: we should extend morning opening hours to 8 o'clock and leave those in the afternoon as they are. By the time people set off for home in the evening it is dark.

I suggest that, the military situation allowing, the Council of Ministers should decide on opening hours of 8 to 3 or 8 to 4.

I would like to underline the importance of glass. Glass is not just important for the glazing of apartments, but for the glazing of broken shop windows. In addition to the assistance from abroad, I recommend [executing] the decision made earlier by the previous Council of Ministers, that we use the glass stocks of the ÁRHI.[182] However, due to Szijártó's[183] leadership methods, it was impossible to know whether there was any glass there or not.

Antal Apró: I think it is right that you raise these points, but we need shorter speeches, precisely so that we can get to the more important questions. The minister should carry these things out within his own jurisdiction.

János Tausz: I recommend that the president of the OT[184] look to see whether they have any glass at the ÁRHI, and, if so, to remove all of the glass stocks.

---

[182] *Áruraktározási Hivatal,* or Warehousing Office.

[183] Lajos Szijártó was minister of housing and construction from 1951 to October 27, 1956.

[184] *Országos Tervhivatal,* or National Planning Office

Antal Apró: Agreed. We must make a decision on this.

(Imre Horváth reads out the American Government's telegram.)[185]

Antal Apró: We should acknowledge it.

Károly Janza: I do not suggest we change the curfew. There are still serious firearms out there, ammunition and weapons, and until a significant portion of these is surrendered, until these heavily-armed groups have handed them in, I do not suggest that we change the times. With hard work, political and otherwise, we must make every effort to get them to give up their weapons.

I would like to underline the problem of transporting Soviet troop supplies, which is in an exceptionally strained state. There is an army commander[186] here who received a task; if we cannot guarantee to complete the task ourselves, he will make the guarantee himself. We must account for this and make arrangements for it.

Antal Apró: Comrade Bebrits has already spoken about this.

Ferenc Nezvál: Comrade Janza says that the Council of Ministers should not change this schedule and that the Committee[187] should look at it.

Antal Apró: In accordance with established practice, we will have a look at it at Comrade Janza's place. Though I am also afraid that the ammunition and weaponry out there could cause problems, we do not need to maintain the state of war: it can be widened.[188] However we should not make a decision about this here.

Ferenc Erdei: We should recognize that this is the [military] command's[189] decision.

Zoltán Vas: I would ask the Council of Ministers to accept the report on the basis of the debate which has played out. I suggest we make the minutes public. This is politically very important for the Council of Ministers. It would be very reassuring if the Council of Ministers published a communiqué: it listened to the government committee's report and acknowledged that the supply of food to Budapest can be guaranteed.

Zoltán Tildy: This goes without saying.

Zoltán Vas: Politically I think it important for us here to make a note of the fact that the chairman of the Government Committee for Public Supplies gave an account to the Council of Ministers, that the Council of Ministers [will accept] with thanks the assistance offered by Western states and People's Democracies...

Antal Apró: But Comrade Vas! Perhaps there should be some kind of order. The lists must be shown to the chairman of the Council of Ministers. We are thankful, we are thankful, but we don't yet know what for. We will meet tomorrow.

Zoltán Vas: Politically I want to express how important this thing is for the population, and that it should not just be the foreign minister doing it on the quiet.

Antal Apró: We express our thanks for all such help which has come into our country, in the press, and in speeches.

Zoltán Vas: I do not agree with this, but the Council of Ministers has the right to decide. As far as the glass question is concerned, the Government Committee is dealing with this, as it is within its jurisdiction.

---

[185] This telegram from the U.S. Government has not been found in the Hungarian archives. Based on contemporary newspapers and a communiqué broadcast on Kossuth Radio on October 28 at 9:00 p.m. dealing with the government session that day, it seems most likely that the above reference concerned an offer by the Eisenhower administration for humanitarian aid.

[186] It is not entirely clear whether the "army commander" mentioned here is Lieutenant General Piotr I. Lashchenko, commander of the Special Corps stationed in Hungary, or Army General M. S. Malinin, commander of the first soviet intervention. The formulation of the sentence, however, makes it more likely that it refers to Malinin, who was indeed in touch with the Hungarian leaders.

[187] This most probably refers to the Emergency Committee.

[188] Despite the literal meaning of the sentence, the expression "it can be widened" most likely refers to the population's free movement or the opening hours and not the state of war.

[189] The reference to the military command means, in this context, the Emergency Committee which was established on October 26 as a plenipotentiary operative arm and thus had the competence to deal with military issues.

György Lukács: I would like to support one part of Comrade Vas' proposal. It is extremely common knowledge amongst the masses that the Western states want to intervene against our government. If an official communiqué arrives, saying that the Western governments are offering assistance to this government, this cannot be related in a two-line communiqué.

Antal Apró: There is certainly need for a communiqué, but not a two-line one.

Sándor Czottner:[190] I think it is absolutely necessary for the Council of Ministers to deal with the coal situation. It is a well-known fact that the coal supply was already in a very critical state. Now there is an almost 400-thousand-ton shortfall from the October target. If we take this into account, the existing shortage is even worse. We have very quickly to work out the distribution procedure—will we supply the factories, or the population, or both, and if so, how? The two cannot be combined such that both are completely satisfied. That is why I suggest that the Trade Ministry and the National Planning Office, together with the Ministry of Mining, look at the question, and after their examination report to the Council of Ministers as to what, in their opinion, is the right thing to do.

Antal Apró: They should produce a distribution plan!

Zoltán Tildy: Esteemed Council of Ministers! First I would like to settle the theoretical question. I would like to know whether this government can decide on the great decisions facing this country without other forums being asked.[191] This does not mean that I am not aware of the current political set-up. This is a practical question—if the government cannot freely decide on all political, theoretical, and practical questions, then in these times we cannot stand our ground. I would have suggested, if there had not been heartening words, that the party forum[192] should take part in the conference. Here what is needed is for us to be able to make a decision immediately and throughout the country. The decisions must appear to the masses to be allowances. They want to exploit us easily, saying I got this today, so I want that tomorrow, as I know I will get it anyway.

Personally I find it moving that some department leaders are able to talk about their problems, and do talk about them, in such a peaceful mood. They are quite clear about their jurisdiction. A ministry cannot make decisions without other institutions. I think we have to decide that for a while the ministry leaders can, if necessary and in the knowledge of their responsibilities, make immediate decisions.

Every practical question is extremely important, especially the question of salaries. In every practical question there is exactly as much benefit as the political benefit it brings. What I want to mention, what I have seen in this country, particularly worries those living in the provinces. Halting a revolution is only of benefit to the people if we carry it out with peaceful instruments and not with bloodshed.

I suggest that we invite the minister of agriculture in today and that he order the immediate discontinuation of operations of the commassation of land.[193] This order should appear in the newspaper today and has to be announced on the radio. Its benefit is tenfold. I would like the education minister to publish an order that every page must be torn out of textbooks that reminds us of these former sorrowful times.

I suggest that the government tell the individual craftsmen and the craftsmen's cooperatives that their tax systems will be revised urgently.

Zoltán Vas: Their whole situation, principally taxes.

Zoltán Tildy: Concrete examples need to be given, because on its own this is worth nothing.

---

[190] Sándor Czottner was minister of energy and mining from July 30 to November 3, 1956.

[191] By "other forums" Tildy means the HWP's leading bodies.

[192] Tildy is most probably referring to the HWP Political Committee.

[193] Officially, the commassation of land [*tagosítás*], as a facet of agricultural collectivization, aimed at rationalizing land property relations by merging scattered small farm plots into large continuous fields that were more suitable for motorized, large-scale agricultural production. Those non-member farmers whose land lay on the cooperatives' planned fields were "compensated" with plots elsewhere. In practice, however, due to the usually lower quality of land offered in exchange, the effect was to sanction anyone not willing to join the cooperatives.

This is an exceptionally fair requirement. The only thing I ask is that if we decide on what we are recommending, these should be available to public opinion this evening, and we should make the relevant ministers responsible for working out the proposals. We must try to lead things rather than follow them.

Lajos [Sic: Albert] *Kónya:[194]* I have already dealt with Zoltán Tildy's proposals. History textbooks must be withdrawn in their entirety. There is no other way to sort this out. In the case of literature textbooks, I think it is possible just to tear out a few pages. Arrangements can take place within two or three days. Similarly we must announce to the universities that we are postponing examinations in ideological subjects. We must announce that the ideological examinations will be left out of state examinations.

István Kossa: It is in the government's declaration that we will make the 15th of March a national holiday again.[195] Let us publish an order about this.

Imre Nagy: Wait. Let us not pile everything up onto one day.

István Kossa: In two weeks' time it will be the 7th of November.[196] They won't celebrate it, there will be a demonstration again.

Imre Nagy: Before then there will be another Council of Ministers meeting.

Zoltán Vas: They will celebrate the Soviet revolution.

István Kossa: There will be scandal and a demonstration.

Antal Gyenes:[197] Esteemed Council of Ministers! In the list of those problems which Minister Tildy and my other ministerial colleagues have described as the most urgent, the question of collecting surpluses is by no means the least significant. This problem should definitely have been discussed in a period of calm. I myself had some ideas about reforming the collection of surpluses. I previously thought it necessary to follow the course of action in which the government narrows the sphere of compulsory delivery to the state, immediately discontinues the compulsory delivery of a few items, and we put the country's food supply on a different foundation.

In today's circumstances there are no means by which to investigate these questions in an atmosphere of calm. At the same time we know well that collecting surpluses and compulsory deliveries is one of the most burning questions for the peasantry apart from taxes.

I do not know what the current situation is in the country on the question of compulsory delivery. I have information that in a few places they burned compulsory delivery registers in a revolutionary way. It is possible that this has not spread over the whole country. We must take up a position on this question in the Parliament. We should get ahead of the regional mood on this question, we should take command of events, and we should provide something which is outrightly favorable to the peasantry, and which clearly moves us toward political consolidation.

I know very well that this represents an extremely difficult problem. The government is taking on a task which will be difficult to solve. In such a situation I see no option but to repeal compulsory delivery. We cannot stick to this thing; perhaps there are means by which we can increase the government's ethical and political reputation in this way.

Imre Nagy: What do you propose?

Antal Gyenes: The Government should proclaim the discontinuation of the compulsory delivery system, and an alteration of the method of collection, that is that compulsory delivery will be replaced by purchasing.

[194] Albert Kónya was minister of education from July 30 to October 31, 1956. The transcriber mistakenly wrote the name Lajos Kónya, who was a famous poet at the time.

[195] March 15 is the traditional commemoration day of the Hungarian revolution of 1848.

[196] November 7, commemorating the Bolshevik seizure of power referred to officially as "the Great October Socialist Revolution," was in Hungary—as in every communist country—a national holiday.

[197] Antal Gyenes was minister of collection of agricultural surpluses [*begyűjtés*] in the Nagy government from October 27 to November 3, 1956, and a member of the HSWP PCC from November 10, 1956 to June 1957, when he was relieved because he opposed the deportation of the Nagy group.

Imre Nagy: It would be premature for the first Council of Ministers meeting to make a decision on this. We do not know how we stand economically at all. It must be investigated very thoroughly.

Ferenc Erdei: Anyway there is nothing else we can do.

Imre Nagy: That is not entirely the case. We can discontinue certain elements of it. After all, life will return to normal; our premise should not be that these anarchic conditions will continue for a long period.

I suggest that the minister for the collection of surplus produce, having made a study of what lies within his jurisdiction, prepare a proposal together with the food minister and the agriculture minister.

Ferenc Erdei: We should publish this in a communiqué.

Imre Nagy: I do not think that would be right. We do not have to expose all our internal arrangements to the public gaze. It would also be very bad for the Council of Ministers if at the outset a good number of ministers made proposals in their own fields and the Council of Ministers accepted them without examining the situation.

Neither should I be brought into a situation where I have to reject them because I am not acquainted with their content. I am not informed about everything, either. Here there is a whole list of very suitable proposals, but there are also questions here which cannot be decided without more thorough investigation. They should prepare proposals for the next meeting of the Council of Ministers.

Zoltán Tildy: In principle I agree with my friend, Chairman Imre Nagy. Difficult economic questions, that is of course in normal times, require very thorough deliberation. Thorough and fast. I suggest we do the same now. In this regard I am in complete agreement.

But I have talked a lot to workers, to peasants; I have mixed with people. I do not agree with Imre Nagy that the people do not have to be informed about matters. I think this is a priority. Either we will inform them, or others will. If the Council of Ministers publishes a short communiqué, they will say: "These people aren't doing anything either." In certain senses we have to use different instruments from those a competent government would use in a normal situation.

In certain senses we must get down and influence the public mood. The public mood is the decisive political factor in Hungary right now. Imre Nagy should allow us to draw up a communiqué from which it emerges that the government sent out the minister for the collection of surplus produce, the food minister, and the agriculture minister to examine the problems with compulsory delivery, who, after their examination of the situation, will report to the Council of Ministers within a week, and then the Council of Ministers will come to a decision on this question which affects the whole working peasantry. This will have a positive effect.

(?) (Sitting next to Comrade Bognár): In the declaration we must specify the direction these efforts are going in, and this task must be completed within a short space of time. We cannot settle things with the peasantry if these efforts are not going in the direction of lessening and eliminating the collection of surpluses. Every working peasant in Hungary knows that in Yugoslavia there is no collection of surpluses. Everyone in Hungary knows that in Poland a revision of the system of collection of surpluses has begun that will eliminate compulsory delivery. This is all public knowledge in Hungary. I do not think that if the government were to make a declaration that was general in nature, that that would represent [a gain in] political capital. That would suggest that the government is leaving this question open, that it wants to stretch it out, that it does not want to express an opinion. This thing carries great responsibility. I would never have imagined that we could transform it from one day to the next in a revolutionary way. I think Comrade Nagy is right to have qualms that it is hasty. It is certainly necessary to make a declaration which specifies the direction in which the system of collecting surpluses is being reformed. This direction is toward purchasing and contracted cultivation.

József Bognár: Regarding the law on the collection of surpluses, I agree that it should be included in the communiqué that three ministers have been given the task of reviewing this. They have to present a report to the Council of Ministers within a week. It is conceivable that we could give instructions to the three ministers without these instructions being published. In principle this is a tax system. If we eliminate it, it could cost three to four billion [forints]. In order to make a decision on this question, we have to know the whole picture.

There are, however, things which are worthy of consideration. Does compulsory free purchase still go on? Do they still maintain corn "E" contracts?

Imre Nagy: We can only contribute if we are acquainted with the problems. I am not acquainted with the ministerial fields, and neither are my ministerial colleagues acquainted with the situation. Tomorrow is the first time I am coming in to be informed by them. Let us not act in too great a hurry, because that can lead to improper arrangements being made. Today we are making a whole lot of arrangements.

Zoltán Tildy: The government must be at peace for it to be able to work. We should publish a statement that the ministers will make their proposals on the most urgent questions within a week.

György Lukács: I suggest we publish a general statement that these and these ministries are investigating the questions, and within a short period of time they will submit a proposal for measures to be taken. We cannot change everything in one day. We should draw up a communiqué, but not with specific content.

Zoltán Vas: About the problem of collecting surpluses. I will be very brief. Financially, the grain question will arise in 1958. The grain for 1957 is already stored. We are talking about next year's harvest.

They raised the question of "E" corn. There is no more "E" corn, so the whole question is irrelevant. Today's Council of Ministers meeting should be ceremonial. I do not agree that it should be published today—let us publish it in three days' time.

Imre Nagy: Let us not get into disputes, into questions relating to particular departments. Considering the extraordinary circumstances, we should focus on the most urgent things to be done.

Rezső Nyers: I agree that we should investigate it, but we should also refer to its direction, that we will lessen the peasantry's burden of collected surpluses. We can eliminate the collection of eggs, poultry, and wine immediately.

Erik Molnár: On the morning after the uprising, the Council of Ministers declared its summary jurisdiction over the territory of the whole country. According to existing law, the declaration of summary jurisdiction must be communicated to the population via posters put up by county courts. Yesterday evening arrangements were being made to put up posters around Budapest. Should we arrange for county courts to deal with such arrangements, or should we take it off the agenda?

Imre Nagy: We should see what other possibilities there are that are just as rigorous.

Erik Molnár: In any circumstances the chief justice can make a decision within eleven days. The law provides for this.

György Nonn:[198] Linked to this question is what we should do with those we have taken prisoner. There are a couple of hundred prisoners. There are those who only demonstrated. We set them free. There are those on whom we found weapons. We did not set them free. Either we release them, in which case they might join the others, or we wait until arms are laid down, and then release them—this is what I recommend—or we should take them before the courts.

With regard to the summary jurisdiction, we have reports that the forces of order have already captured escaped criminals, looters, and thieves, and I suggest that we have them taken before the courts and that the representatives of these institutions should take part as people's judges.[199]

Imre Nagy: This means that there is no need for summary jurisdiction. We do not use it, but let us not talk about it.

---

[198] György Nonn was a member of the HWP CC beginning in 1948 and chief public prosecutor from February to November 16, 1956.

[199] The term "people's judges" refers to lay judges who assisted the professional judge in passing sentences. In the legal system of the Hungarian People's Republic the institution of "people's judges" was supposed to provide "social control" over the judicial procedure.

György Nonn: After weapons have been laid down, as they have released captives from so many prisons, we should be prepared for the fact that the number of violent crimes will intensify. In my opinion summary jurisdiction should be declared once weapons have been laid down and should involve representatives from the people's institutions.

Zoltán Tildy: Quite right.

Zoltán Vas: It will transpire that summary jurisdiction came about in illegal circumstances.

Imre Nagy: The council meeting is over. I hereby close today's session, our first.

[Source: MOL, XX–5–h, Nagy Imre és társai pere, Minisztertanácsi jegyzőkönyvek, 25. köt. (The Trial of Imre Nagy and his Associates, Minutes of the Council of Ministers, vol. 25.) Also MOL, XIX–A–83–o. 160. d., pp. 75–99. Published by Ferenc Glatz, ed., "A kormány és a párt vezető szerveinek dokumentumaiból, 1956. október 23–november 4," História 11, nos. 4–5 (1989): 47–48. Translated by David Evans.]

DOCUMENT NO. 44: Radio Message from Imre Nagy Announcing the Formation of a New Government, October 28, 1956, 5:25 p.m.

Prime Minister Nagy's October 28 radio address was significant because it informed the public for the first time of the fundamental turn in HWP policy, and of the new interpretation of the revolution as a "national democratic movement," officially replacing the previous label of "counterrevolution" (see Document No. 39).

The program emerging from the government declaration sought to meet the demands of different social groups during the revolution. Besides ordering an immediate cease-fire and promising to legalize various organizations formed during the revolution, such as workers' councils and revolutionary committees, the declaration also promised measures to raise living standards and remedy the many administrative-economic grievances plaguing the country. Most importantly, it announced the immediate withdrawal of Soviet troops from Budapest, along with the promise to start negotiations for their complete removal from all of Hungary.

At the same time, various formulations in the speech (as well as a comparison with earlier drafts) reveal Nagy's efforts to soften the rhetoric and to preserve what remained of the HWP's influence; hence his inclusion of comments to the effect that "reactionary and counterrevolutionary elements had penetrated into the movement," that the "Government wishes to rest in the first place on the support of the fighting Hungarian working class," and that the communist period had also registered some positive achievements.

A similar rationale motivated the 5:40 p.m. broadcast of an HWP CC communiqué issued earlier in the day. Because this broadcast followed immediately after Nagy's radio message, it was meant to give the impression, in accordance with Mikoyan and Suslov's proposal, that the party had initiated the change in policy.

Suslov, who arrived in Moscow around the time of Nagy's speech, reported its main points to the CPSU Presidium, which approved them—even the one pertaining to the withdrawal of Soviet troops from Budapest (See Document No. 40). Despite these concessions, however, the address ultimately fell short of its main goal of bringing the mass movement under control.

During the course of the past week bloody events took place with tragic rapidity. The fatal consequences of the terrible mistakes and crimes of these past 10 years unfold before us in these painful events which we are witnessing and in which we are participating. During the course of 1,000 years of history, destiny was not sparing in scourging our people and nation. But such a thing has never before afflicted our country.

The Government condemns the viewpoints according to which the present formidable movement is a counterrevolution. Without doubt, as always happens at times of great popular movements, this movement too was used by criminal elements to compromise it and commit common criminal acts. It is also a fact that reactionary and counterrevolutionary elements had penetrated into the movement with the aim of overthrowing the popular democratic regime.

But it is also indisputable that in these stirrings a great national democratic movement, embracing and unifying all our people, developed with elemental force. This movement aims at guaranteeing our national freedom, independence, and sovereignty, of advancing our society, our economic and political system on the way of democracy for this is the only foundation for socialism in our country. This great movement exploded because of the grave crimes committed during the past historic period.

The situation was further aggravated by the fact that up to the very last, the [Party] leadership had not decided to break finally with the old and criminal policy. It is this above all which led to the tragic fratricidal fight in which so many patriots died on both sides. In the course of these battles was born the Government of democratic national unity, independence, and socialism which will become the true expression of the will of the people. This is the firm resolution of the Government.

The new Government, relying on the people's power and control in the hope of gaining its full confidence, will at once begin with the practical implementation of the just demands of the people. The Government begins its work in the midst of conditions of unheard-of difficulty. The grave economic situation bequeathed to us by the past has become further aggravated as a consequence of the fighting of the past few days. The next few months facing us will also be very difficult. The Government clearly sees the gravity of the material situation in which our working class, our peasants, and our intellectuals find themselves.

The Government wishes to rest in the first place on the support of the fighting Hungarian working class, but also, of course, on the support of the entire Hungarian working population.

We have decided to work out a broad program, in the framework of which we wish to settle old and justified demands and rectify damages to the satisfaction of the working class, among other things on the question of wages and work norms, the raising of minimum pay in the lowest wage brackets and of the smallest pensions, taking into account the number of years worked, and the raising of family allowances.

To help resolve the exceptionally grave housing crisis, the Government will give its utmost support to all state, cooperative, and private construction of homes and apartments. The Government welcomes the initiative taken by workers for the extension of democracy in their enterprises, and approves the formation of workers' councils. With a firm hand the Government will put an end to the serious illegalities which were committed in the movement of agricultural producer cooperatives and during the course of commassation of land. The Government will work out a great scheme to help the development of neglected and retarded agricultural production to revitalize production in cooperative and individual farms and stimulate productive zeal.

The Government will courageously build on young workers, peasants, students, and the university youth, giving them the means of using their initiative in the framework of a cleaner public life. It will take pains to offer them the best material conditions at the outset of their careers. The Government supports those new organs of democratic self-government which have sprung up at the people's initiative and will strive to find a place for them in the administrative machinery. In order to put an end to bloodshed and in the interest of assuring peaceful development, the Government has ordered a general cease-fire and has commanded the Armed Forces not to shoot unless attacked. At the same time it appeals to all those who took arms to abstain from all military operations and to deliver their arms without fail. In order to assure the safeguarding of order and security new armed forces will be formed without delay from units of the Army, of the police, and of the armed groups of workers and youth.

The Hungarian Government has come to an agreement with the Soviet Government that the Soviet forces shall withdraw immediately from Budapest and that simultaneously with the formation of our new Army they shall evacuate the city's territory. The Hungarian Government will initiate negotiations in order to settle relations between the Hungarian People's Republic and the Soviet Union, among other things with regard to the withdrawal of Soviet forces stationed in Hungary in the spirit of Soviet-Hungarian friendship and the principle of the mutual equality and the national independence of socialist countries.

After the reestablishment of order we shall organize a new and unified state police force and we shall dissolve the organs of state security. No one who took part in the armed fighting need fear further reprisals. The Government will put proposals before the National Assembly for the restoration of the emblem of Kossuth as the national emblem and the observance of March 15 once again as a national holiday.

People of Hungary!

In these hours of bitterness and strife one is prone to see only the dark side of the past twelve years. We must not let our views become clouded. These twelve years contain lasting ineradicable, historic achievements which you, Hungarian workers, peasants, and intellectuals, under the leadership of the Hungarian Workers' Party brought into being by virtue of hard labor and sacrifice. Our renascent popular democracy relies on the strength and self-sacrifice which you have displayed in our founding labors and which constitute the best guarantee of our country's happier future.

[Source: Paul E. Zinner, ed., National Communism and Popular Revolt in Eastern Europe: A Selection of Documents on Events in Poland and Hungary, February–November, 1956 *(New York: Columbia University Press, 1956), 428–431.]*

DOCUMENT NO. 45: Transcripts of Radio Free Europe Programs, Advising on Military Tactics to Use Against a Superior Enemy, October 28, 1956

Among the programs RFE broadcast during the revolution was a series featuring "Colonel Bell," a pseudonym used by more than one member of the Hungarian desk from the very earliest RFE transmissions.[200] In sharp contrast to the U.S. administration's attitude toward support for violent resistance, these programs clearly encouraged Hungarians to take up arms against Soviet forces and even gave direct combat advice to the insurgents. A prime example of this can be seen in the following two programs aired on October 28, which a later internal RFE report not only condemned for excessive optimism and policy violations, but saw as epitomizing the unfortunate attitude which characterized a significant part of the Hungarian RFE staff: "Here at its worst is the émigré on the outside, without responsibility or authority, giving detailed advice to the people fighting at home."[201] Nevertheless, it should be noted that the idea to broadcast military information, even in a "theoretical" vein, was initially approved by American advisers, even though they later admitted that it was a mistake to allow programs to be broadcast on such risky topics.

PROGRAM TITLE: ARMED FORCES SPECIAL NO. B–1
AIR DATE: 28 OCTOBER 1956
AUTHOR: JULIAN BORSANYI
TRANSLATOR: E. BEDE[202]

NARR: Colonel Bell will tell the Hungarian soldiers how ingenious and smart leadership can counter-balance numerical and armed superiority.

BELL: World opinion is full of admiration. The English press, the main characteristics of which is the so-called "understatement" and which always writes calmly and with simple words about the facts, cannot find enough praising and admiring words to describe the Hungarians. This enthusiasm which crossed oceans was brought about by the courage of the young freedom fighters, by the patriotic and brave attitude of our soldiers who remained faithful to their national ideals in spite of communist ideological education. Three days ago we said that every day, every hour gained by resistance is worthy the sacrifice, lessens the risk. This statement of ours is emphasized by the meeting of the U.N.'s Security Council, called together for tonight. It is of tremendous importance that in these next few hours, maybe in a few days, tangible facts should prove the true mood and will of the nation. There could be no more convincing fact, in the interest of this, than the undiminished attitude of those who fight for the idea of freedom, the manifestation of the united sympathy for them and chiefly the uphold of armed forces on the side of the freedom fighters. This latter achieved already enormous results. The calling together of the Security Council would have shrinked to a purely formal demonstration if Imre Nagy and his companions would have liquidated the revolutionary movement within two days. Many, naturally are afraid that what did not happen yet can happen in the course of the next days or hours. There are rumors that Moscow ordered further three or four divisions to Hungary from the Sub-Carpathian area and Rumania. According to pessimists these forces will snap up the freedom fighters in no time. We on the other hand say: let us not be scared of these numbers indicated as overpowering forces.

Two Soviet divisions and a part of a third one were stationed in Hungary, altogether approximately 25,000 men. It is true that in the majority of these were armored divisions but we cannot speak of overpowering forces. In the garrisons of the People's Army there were approximately 100,000

---

[200] See Borbándi, *Magyarok az Angol Kertben*, 31, 256–7.

[201] See Document No 105.

[202] This rough translation is the version RFE officials used in evaluating the Radio's performance after the revolution. It has been retained here despite its somewhat unfinished character.

honvéds [Hungarian patriotic soldiers] on duty two weeks ago. If only one third of them takes an active part in the fights, numerical equality would be reestablished. Much depends on whose side the armored divisions from Esztergom and Gyöngyös will fight. It depends mainly on them if the threateningly announced Soviet military re-enforcement will be able to liquidate the resistance of the freedom fighters in a matter of two or three weeks. Namely, there is no need for further endurance, if only because of political reasons. Naturally four more Soviet divisions are a serious force but their task is even more serious. They have to occupy a very large territory, to pacify and secure it. If the Hungarian national forces are clever and their leadership quick-witted, then the Soviet reinforcement eventually moving from the east and north-east will not even reach the Danube line within two or three weeks. Those who shake their heads incredulously at this, should listen to the following story:

In November 1943 the army command of the Nazi forces in South-Eastern Europe wanted to strike a blow on the Serbian partisan forces which broke out time again from the Podujevo-Pristina area and disconnected the Belgrade-Sofia railway line. After heavy fights they succeeded in crowding together the main force of the partisans south- and south-westwards to Pristina, only the north-east entrance of the pocket remained open. It had to be closed by the German 137th division and the partisans liquidated. The 137th German division was enforced by an armored regiment to accomplish this task. More than 100 tanks and 15,000 Germans were unloaded in Nis and started from Prokupelje toward Pristina 80 kilometers away, planning to reach it in three days. They never reached the place, to be more accurate, when they finally reached it after 10 days, there was no trace of the main body of the partisan forces. The Germans lost more than 2,000 men and 30 tanks. The partisans who had altogether 500 men achieved this daring feat in the following way.

From their 500 men, they formed 12 fighting groups. The strength of these fighting groups alternated between 10 and 100 members. These groups consisted partly of experienced fighters and partly of young men who received improvised training on the spot. Their equipment consisted of automatic weapons, mine throwers, a few 75 millimeter guns, bazookas and different explosives which were all thrown by English-American planes. The fighting groups went into action by attaching themselves closely to the marching German division, popping up on the sides, in front and the rear and by keeping close contact with each other. They did not rest day or night. During the 80 kilometer march not one German soldier was able to shut his eyes for even one minute. The few numbered groups made a tremendous noise, backed by strong artillery giving thus the impression that their numbers are far greater than they were in reality and forcing great German forces to counter-act. The deception was increased by involving the population into the operation, namely they organized false spy-reports to confuse the Germans. The larger groups attacked simultaneously and from different directions in surprise raids. They approached the column without being noticed, usually during the night when the Germans rested and strived to cause them the highest losses possible. When the Germans started a counter-attack, the partisans simply vanished among the population of the nearest village or settlement. Thus the Germans grabbed into nothing. The moment the German covering troops retreated to the marching column, the partisan fighting groups assembled in a matter of minutes and the next attack started immediately. Two smaller partisan groups had the task to make as much noise as possible and to fool the Germans without carrying out real attacks. As it was recorded later by the general staff of the German 137th division: "they made us believe that they were in places where in reality they were not, that they were strong where they had no strength at all and attacked with great strength where they were not expected." This was the secret of their success. It is by these means and not by a supremacy of arms and numbers that they succeeded to stop in a decisive place an enemy army which marched towards a decisive task, causing grave losses without suffering substantial losses themselves.

We have yet to emphasize that ground and road conditions between Nis and Pristina are not much different than those in the Trans-Danubian area and settlement conditions are similar too. It happened in the month of November too, the same month we will start in a few days.

The example of the Serbian partisans could only be followed successfully in our country if the following conditions are realized:

The creation of a united leadership and faultless contacts. An essential condition is the complete co-operation with the population, without their help there can be no question of success.

The co-operation with the population has a further basic condition: and this is the total liquidation of the so-called inner armed forces, the local organs of the ÁVH. The presence of the ÁVH cannot only obstruct the unnoticed absorbation of the partisan troops into the life of villages and farms but endangers also the population engaged in their activities helping the partisans.

NARR: Colonel Bell told the Hungarian soldiers how to obstruct large forces by small ones and by simple arms. This is RFE, the Voice of Free Hungary.

PROGRAM TITLE: SPECIAL ARMED FORCES B-2
AIR DATE: OCTOBER 28, 1956
AUTHOR: LITTERATI
TRANSLATORS: L. MERAN, E. GERECZY[203]

SOUND: SIGNAL

ANNC. (BELL): Dear Listeners, we have recently told our Hungarian soldier comrades how one can outbalance numerical and armamental odds with ingenuity, a resourcefulness of the leadership and clever partisan tactics. As a justification we have mentioned the example of a German division which was halted by 500 Tito partisans for more than ten days and lost 30 medium tanks as well. Since this partisan unit did not have any anti-tank weapons, the example may sound incredible to many. Therefore we have asked our fellow worker Gyula Patkó[204] to report about his own experiences, in order to illustrate the possibilities of partisan warfare against tanks. Our fellow worker Gyula Patkó whose name my listeners know very well from the sports feature and our radio plays, has fought in the last months of WW II as the commander of an armour-piercing gun company and he also fought in the ranks of the defenders of Buda. His company destroyed almost three dozens of Soviet T–34 type tanks, ten out of these only with partisan methods. Let us now listen to the report of our fellow worker:

NARR.: When we hear now that the soldiers and youth of the glorious freedom fight raging now are facing Soviet tanks, the partisans of the last world war are involuntarily recalled to our minds. I am thinking of both, the ten thousands of Soviet partisans in the forest of Briansk and the Tito partisan units fighting in the labyrinths of the Dinarian Alps. These partisans caused serious losses, to the Germans especially, although in most cases they did not even have medium or heavy anti tank weapons. To myself, who fought as an anti tank officer during the entire war, the primitive but very effective anti tank methods used by the partisans caused much worry. We already knew by experience that the regulations compiled on desks describing the procedures were not worth much. Prescriptions like that in case of a tank attack all the light weapons should open fire on the peep-sights while the anti tank (heavy) guns should shoot in the first place at the crawler belt, i.e. the base of the turret, proved useless in practice. On one hand, who could see the peep-sights (measuring a few cms) of a tank approaching at a speed of 50 to 60 kms, on the other hand the gun-layers were happy when they could hit the moving tanks at all, not to speak from the a/m spots. This explains why—if only for reasons of the economy of accumulation—the partisans never fired with hand weapons against the enemy tanks. Hand weapons were not invented for armour plates a few cms thick, but for man-to-man fight.

Naturally it had decisive influence on the choice of methods suitable for the fighting of tanks whether one had to fight single tanks or a mass attack of tanks. It is true that, knowing that they can be destroyed very easily when they are alone, the tanks only turn up alone very seldom. This may take place in street fights in villages or towns when single tanks have to blockade roads. This, by the way, is their favorite occupation. In the course of the fights in Budapest in 1945, we not only did not shoot a single Soviet tank with our heavy anti tank guns, in spite of the fact that in former fights we had already shot many Soviet tanks, but we did not even see any. We could,

---

[203] See the previous footnote.

[204] Gyula Patkó was the pseudonym of Gyula Litteráti-Loótz. RFE staff broadcast almost without exception under pseudonyms in order to protect themselves and any family members still in Hungary from persecution by the Hungarian authorities.

however, destroy five with simple devices which we had made ourselves. We owe it to the methods we learned from the partisans that we succeeded in this.

One of these methods is in the first place the bottle filled with gas which was, at the time, jokingly called "Molotov cocktail." All one needed for this was a wine bottle of one liter filled with gasoline to which we added a few crumbs of yellow phosphor and then sealed it tightly. Armed with this primitive weapon we stood in doorways waiting for the Soviet tank to pass, when it did so we jumped forth and threw the bottle on the grated ventilation slit over the engine from 2 or 3 meters distance.

The moment the bottle broke, the phosphor set the gasoline immediately on fire and the enormous sucking effect of the powerful motor did then the rest. The motor caught fire and the tank became immovable. The crew was forced to leave the tank and our firearms done the rest. I must also mention that we did not always have phosphor. On such occasions we put a rag-stopper on the bottle-mouth so that the rug-end was hanging out from the bottle. Directly before throwing the bottle this piece of rage had to be set on fire and the effect was the same as if we would have put white phosphor into the gasoline.

The so-called mine-pulling method was also very effective whenever we wanted to destroy tanks. Outside a loaded earth-mine (flat earth-mine) we needed only a few meters of strong cord in case we wanted to apply this method. The cord which had to be twice as long as the width of the street had to be put in the middle in two parts and then the ends were tied to the two sides of the mine. The other ends were each held by one-one man who stood out of the sidewalk in order not to be noticed by the observers in the tank. When the tank approached the mine, still in the middle of the street, one man pulled the mine just before the tank, respectively one of its caterpillars. There it blew up the moment the caterpillar run over it. After several experiments this method also proved to be very good.

The immovable tank was not always left by its crew, often they kept on firing in the tightly closed tank. It is an old rule that a tank should only be approached from behind and so mostly two soldiers jumped from behind on the tank in order to finish off or to silence the crew. One of them watched the lid of the tank and when that was opened from the inside he threw a hand-grenade into the inside. We must mention that it is impossible to try open such a lid from the outside. The inside exploding hand-grenade liquidated the crew but we must mention here that it happened seldom that we succeeded to annihilate our enemy by this method. So mostly the other fighter on top of the tank had to step into action. In case he had a chance to do so, he stuffed in very great hurry a handful of mud on the peepsights and gunnersights, taking away thereby the anyway very few observation contrivances. The muted gun, respectively machine gun was the also stuffed in its end with mud and when the next shot was fired the barrels got barrel-protuberances or were blown up. If there was no mud with the attacker then the barrel of the machine gun could be wrecked by a few heavy blows with a hard object. Naturally, gun barrels were much harder to wreck. But for them we had always in readiness so-called concentrated loads. Each of them consisted of 5 pounds of exploding cubes. They were tied together with about 15 to 20 centimeters of cord and fitted with a normal fuse and a very short detonating cord. The two cubes fastened to the cord were then hung over the gun barrel so that the exploding material was at both sides of the barrel. After making everything ready for the explosion, the place behind the turret had to serve for the protection of the two attackers on the tank. After the explosion took place from the gun barrel only a stub was left.

We applied these methods also in case of a mass-attack of tanks. We shall speak about them on the next occasion.

As was already proven on many occasions in the past, the nature of Hungarians is not suited too well for the application of sly and merciless methods as are ordinarily applied by partisans. But we must never forget that the enemy must be defeated by its own arms and methods. However, the slogan of freedom fighters today is: Freedom or Death!

SOUND: SIGNAL

ANNC: With Colonel Bell's program we have read to you a lecture by Gyula Patkó, entitled: "Partisan methods of wrecking tanks."

[Source: Archives of the Hungarian Radio. Obtained by Judit Katona and György Vámos.]

DOCUMENT NO. 46: Proclamation by Imre Nagy on the Creation of a Multi-Party System, October 30, 1956

At 2:28 p.m. on October 30, Imre Nagy delivered a radio address in which he went much further toward accepting the revolutionaries' demands than he had in his speech two days earlier (see Document No. 44). The October 30 address marked a fundamental change in the Hungarian political system by placing "the country's Government on the basis of democratic cooperation between the coalition parties, reborn in 1945"—thus abolishing the one-party system.[205] For the sake of more effective governance and a closer approximation of the multi-party system, Nagy announced the formation of an inner cabinet consisting of seven members. He also raised, with greater resolve than ever before, the issue of withdrawing Soviet troops from Budapest and the entire territory of Hungary. Moreover, not only did he fully recognize "the democratic organs of local autonomy," he also asked them to support the government.

All of these declarations fundamentally shifted the foundations of the government's legitimacy: whereas on October 28, Nagy still spoke as the representative of the disintegrating regime embodied by the HWP, on October 30 he had already moved toward claiming legitimacy based on the popular movement of October 23. This is no better demonstrated than by Nagy's use of the word "revolution" for the first time when asking Hungarians to maintain order and preserve the revolution's achievements. In the same vein, his last sentence celebrated a "free, democratic, and independent Hungary," and specifically omitted the "socialist" attribute. From this point on, the prime minister sought to continue the consolidation process by relying on the goodwill of Hungary's revolutionary society.

Yet this change had its limits, and at this moment in the process it did not yet indicate a complete turnaround from the previous methods of decision-making. After all, it was the HWP Presidium that made the decision announced in the radio address, and it did so probably after negotiating with Suslov and Mikoyan. Moreover, the new multi-party cabinet did not officially replace the full government, which formally remained in place. This cabinet was also formed by "invitation," and not through consultations with the emerging parties.

Despite the significance of this announcement for Hungary, news of the October 30 changes in Budapest, which Mikoyan reported to Khrushchev by telephone, did not appreciably influence discussions in the CPSU Presidium.

Working people of Hungary! Workers, peasants, intellectuals! As a result of the revolution, which is unfolding with tremendous strength, and the mighty movement of democratic forces, our Fatherland has reached a crossroads. The national Government, acting in complete agreement with the Presidium of the Hungarian Workers Party, has arrived at a decision, vital for the nation's life, of which I want to inform Hungary's working people.

In the interest of the further democratization of the country's life, the Cabinet abolishes the one-party system and places the country's Government on the basis of democratic cooperation between the coalition parties, reborn in 1945. In accordance with this it sets up an inner Cabinet within the national Government. The members of this Cabinet are Imre Nagy, Zoltán Tildy, Béla Kovács, Ferenc Erdei, János Kádár, Géza Losonczy, and a person to be

---

[205] In a narrower sense, the allusion to the coalition of 1945 was a reference to the four parties which constituted that earlier partnership (the Communist, Social Democratic, Smallholders, and National Peasant parties). In another sense, however, it could also be interpreted as a reference to the "spirit" of 1945, a fundamentally left-oriented political line, a "people's democratic" platform that excluded the possibility of any return to the pre-war political and economic system and rejected a potential development along the lines of Western-type liberal democracies. The idea to reshuffle the government on the basis of a coalition originated with Zoltán Tildy, but Imre Nagy agreed to it from the very beginning.

nominated by the Social Democrat Party.[206] The Government will submit a proposal to the Presidential Council of the People's Republic to elect János Kádár and Géza Losonczy as Ministers of State.

The national Government appeals to the headquarters of Soviet forces immediately to begin the withdrawal of Soviet troops from the territory of Budapest. At the same time, the national Government informs the people of the country that it will begin negotiations without delay with the Government of the USSR about the withdrawal of Soviet troops from Hungary.

I announce, on behalf of the national Government, that it recognizes the democratic organs of local autonomy which have been brought into existence by the revolution, that it relies on them and asks for their support.

Hungarian brethren, patriots! Loyal citizens of the Fatherland! Safeguard the achievements of the revolution, safeguard order by every means and restore calm. No blood should be shed in our country by fratricide. Prevent any kind of disturbance and safeguard life and property by every means at your disposal.

My Hungarian brethren, workers, peasants! Stand beside the national Government in the hour of this fateful decision. Long live free, democratic, and independent Hungary!

[Source: Paul E. Zinner, ed., National Communism and Popular Revolt in Eastern Europe: A Selection of Documents on Events in Poland and Hungary, February–November, 1956 *(New York: Columbia University Press, 1956), 453–454.]*

---

[206] The Social Democrats actually did not officially name their minister until the government reshuffling on November 3. However, the party then delegated three members to take part in the enlarged government: Anna Kéthly, József Fischer and Gyula Kelemen. But since Kéthly had already left to attend the meeting of the Socialist International in Vienna on November 1, she did not participate on the government meeting on the 3rd.

DOCUMENT NO. 47: Situation Report from Anastas Mikoyan and Mikhail Suslov in Budapest, October 30, 1956

Compared to earlier, more optimistic accounts by Mikoyan and Suslov, their last report from Budapest on October 30 describes a significant "worsening" of the situation. In addition to the dissolution of party organizations, they attach considerable significance to the position taken by the Hungarian army: "[T]he Hungarian units sent against the insurgents could join these other Hungarians, and then it will be necessary for the Soviet forces to once more undertake military operations." Based on Nagy's objections to new Soviet troop deployments they rightly sense the policy shift the Hungarian government is about to make at the U.N.—namely, protesting the Soviet military intervention. These new developments, however, did not immediately change the view of the CPSU Presidium, which had been discussing Hungary almost without a break since October 28 with respect to the Soviet government communiqué of October 30 (see Document No. 50). That document, which appeared in Pravda the following day, held out the prospect of pulling Soviet troops from Budapest and negotiating a complete withdrawal from the entire country.

1. The political situation in the country and in Budapest is not getting better; it is getting worse. This is expressed in the following: in the leading organs of the party there is a feeling of helplessness. The party organizations are in the process of collapse. Hooligan elements have become more insolent, seizing district party committees, killing communists. The organization of party volunteer squads is going slowly. The factories are stalled. The people are sitting at home. The railroads are not working. Hooligan students and other resistance elements have changed their tactics and are displaying greater activity. Now they are almost not shooting at all, but instead are seizing institutions. For example, last night the central party newspaper's printing office was seized.

The new minister of internal affairs sent 100 fighters who met up with more than 200 people, but did not open fire, because the CC advised not to spill blood. That was late at night. Imre Nagy was sleeping in his apartment, and they, apparently did not want complications with Nagy, fearing that opening fire without his knowledge would be an occasion for weakening the leadership.

They [the "hooligan elements"-ed.] occupied the regional telephone station. The radio station is working, but it does not reflect the opinion of the CC, since in fact it is in foreign hands.

The anti-revolutionary newspaper did not come out, because there were counterrevolutionary articles in it and the printing office refused to print it.

2. An opposition group in the region around the Corvin theater negotiated with Nagy to peacefully surrender their weapons. However, as of the present moment the weapons have not been surrendered, except for a few hundred rifles. The insurgents declare that they will not give them up until Soviet troops leave Budapest, and some even say until the Soviet troops leave Hungary. Thus peacefully liquidating this hotbed is impossible. We will achieve the liquidation of these armed Hungarian forces. But there is just one fear: the Hungarian army has occupied a wait-and-see position. Our military advisors say that relations between Hungarian officers and generals and Soviet officers have deteriorated in the past few days. There is no trust as there was earlier. It could happen, that the Hungarian units sent against the insurgents could join these other Hungarians, and then it will be necessary for the Soviet forces to once more undertake military operations.

3. Last night according to Imre Nagy's instructions, Andropov was summoned. Nagy asked him: is it true that new Soviet military units are continuing to enter Hungary from the USSR? If yes, then what is their goal? We did not negotiate this.

Our opinion on this issue: we suspect that this could be a turning point in the change in Hungarian policy in the [U.N.] Security Council.

We intend to state to Imre Nagy today that the troop-movements were in accordance with our agreement, that from now on we do not intend to bring in any more troops on account of the fact that the Nagy government is dealing with the situation in Hungary.

We propose giving instructions to the minister of defense to cease sending troops into Hungary, continuing to concentrate them on Soviet territory.

As long as the Hungarian troops occupy a non-hostile position, these troops will be sufficient. If the situation further deteriorates, then, of course, it will be necessary to reexamine the whole issue in its entirety.

We do not yet have a final opinion of the situation—how sharply it has deteriorated. After the session today in the CC at 11 o'clock Moscow time, the situation will become clear and we will inform you.

We think it is essential that Comrade Konev come to Hungary immediately.

[Source: APRF, F. 3. Op. 64. D. 485. Ll. 22–24. Originally published in the Cold War International History Project Bulletin *no. 5 (Spring 1995): 32. Translated by Johanna Granville.]*

DOCUMENT NO. 48: Cable from Italian Communist Party Leader Palmiro Togliatti to the CPSU CC Presidium, October 30, 1956

One of the Hungarian revolution's effects was to create fissures both within the various national communist parties in Europe, and between Western communist parties and the CPSU. In subsequent years, these splits were partly responsible for the rise of the so-called Euro-Communist movement. Here, Italian party leader Togliatti complains to Moscow about the debilitating effects of the revolt on party unity and on his own attempts to retain power within the Italian party. (See Moscow's draft response in Document No. 54.)

Hungarian events have created a heavy situation inside the Italian labor movement, and in our party, too.

The gap between Nenni[207] and ourselves that seemed to be closing after our initiatives is now rudely and suddenly acute. Nenni's position on Polish events coincides with the Social Democrats. In our party, one can see two polarized and inappropriate positions. On one extreme there are those who declare that responsibility for what happened in Hungary is due to Stalinist methodology being abandoned. At the other extreme are those groups who are accusing the party leadership of not taking a position in favor of the insurrection in Budapest, and who claim that the insurrection was justly motivated and should have been fully supported. These groups firmly insist that the entire leadership of our party be replaced, and they believe Di Vittorio[208] should become the new party leader. They are based on a declaration by Di Vittorio that did not correspond to the party line and was not approved by us. We are going to fight against these two opposing positions and the party will not give up the battle.

Although I assure you that Hungarian events have developed in a way that render our clarifying action in the party very difficult, it also makes it difficult to obtain consensus in favor of the leadership. When we defined the revolt as counterrevolutionary, we had to face the fact that our position was different from the Hungarian party and government's, and now it is the same Hungarian government that is celebrating the insurrection. I think this is wrong. My opinion is that the Hungarian government—whether Imre Nagy remains its leader or not—is irreversibly going in a reactionary direction. I would like to know if you are of the same opinion or if you are more optimistic. I would like to add that there are worries among our party's leaders that Polish and Hungarian events could damage the unity of the leadership of your Party Presidium, as was defined by the Twentieth [CPSU] Congress.

We are all thinking if this occurs, the consequences could be very serious for the entire movement.

[Source: APRF, Moscow. Originally published in La Stampa, *September 11, 1996. Published in English in the* Cold War International History Project Bulletin *no. 8/9 (Winter 1996/1997): 357. Translated by Doc and Claudia Rossi.]*

---

[207] Piero Nenni was secretary general of the Italian Socialist Party from 1943–1963.

[208] Giuseppe Di Vittorio, communist politician, was secretary general of the Italian General Worker's Union (CGIL) from 1947–1957 and chairman of the World Association of Trade Unions from 1949–1957.

DOCUMENT NO. 49: Working Notes from the Session of the CPSU CC Presidium on October 30, 1956 (Re: Point 1 of Protocol No. 49)

On the morning of October 30, Nikita Khrushchev began another round of negotiations on relations within the socialist camp with a visiting top-level Chinese delegation. The Chinese favored greater equality among the socialist countries, particularly between the USSR and China. While these talks went on, the other members of the CPSU CC Presidium met to review Mikoyan and Suslov's latest report from Budapest, which essentially called for preparations for a military intervention. Impressed by the Mikoyan-Suslov report, the Presidium members in attendance immediately decided to send Marshal Ivan Konev to Budapest. At this point, Khrushchev joined the meeting. Ever worried about the consequences of a brutal military solution and reinforced in his views by a Chinese declaration favoring a pull-out and intra-bloc equality, he engineered a reversal of the hard-line course the Kremlin had adopted two days earlier. The Presidium thus approved a remarkable document entitled "Declaration by the Government of the USSR on the Principles of Development and Further Strengthening of Friendship and Cooperation Between the Soviet Union and Other Socialist States," which opens up the possibility of a Soviet troop withdrawal from Hungary as well as other East European satellites (see Document No. 50). The Presidium also considered issuing an appeal to the Hungarian people supporting the Nagy/Kádár government, which the Soviet leadership hoped would be able and willing to consolidate the situation in Hungary on the basis of socialism. Eventually, however, no such declaration was issued. Instead a paragraph dealing with the events in Hungary and containing an appeal to the Hungarians was incorporated into the Soviet government's declaration. Faced with a choice between, in Khrushchev's words, "a military path—one of occupation" and "a peaceful path—the withdrawal of troops [and] negotiations," the "liberal wing" within the Presidium temporarily held sway.

Participants: Bulganin, Voroshilov, Molotov, Kaganovich, Saburov, Brezhnev, Zhukov, Shepilov, Shvernik, Furtseva, Pospelov

On the Situation in Hungary
Information from Cdes. Mikoyan and Serov is read aloud.[209]

Cde. Zhukov provides information about the concentration of mil.-transport aircraft in the Vienna region.[210]
Nagy is playing a double game (in Malinin's opinion).[211]
Cde. Konev is to be sent to Budapest.

On Discussions with the Chinese comrades.[212]
(Khrushchev)

[209] The whereabouts and content of Serov's report is unknown. For Mikoyan and Suslov's report, see Document 47.

[210] The transport aircraft in question were most likely those carrying humanitarian aid to Vienna, from where it was transported to Hungary.

[211] Malinin sent regular reports to Marshall Sokolovskii, the Soviet chief of staff, on the Hungarian situation. These reports have not yet been opened for research.

[212] From October 23–31, a high-level PRC delegation headed by Chinese Communist Party Deputy Chairman Liu Shaoqi was in Moscow for talks with Soviet leaders. While there, they were consulted by the Kremlin on both the Polish and Hungarian crises, and communicated regularly with Mao Zedong in Beijing.

We should adopt a declaration today on the withdrawal of troops from the countries of people's democracy[213] (and consider these matters at a session of the Warsaw Pact), taking account of the views of the countries in which our troops are based.[214]

The entire CPC CC Politburo supports this position.
One document for the Hungarians, and another for the participants of the Warsaw Pact.
On Rokossowski—I said to Gomułka that this matter is for you (the Poles) to decide.

Cde. Bulganin—The Chinese cdes. have an incorrect impression of our relations with the countries of people's democracy. On our appeal to the Hungarians—we should prepare it.
A declaration should be prepared.

Cde. Molotov—Today an appeal must be written to the Hungarian people so that they promptly enter into negotiations about the withdrawal of troops.
There is the Warsaw Pact.
This must be considered with other countries.
On the view of the Chinese comrades—they suggest that relations with the countries of the socialist camp be built on the principles of Pancha Shila.[215]

Relations along interstate lines are on one basis and interparty relations on another.

Cde. Voroshilov: We must look ahead. Declarations must be composed so that we aren't placed into an onerous position. We must criticize ourselves—but justly.

Cde. Kaganovich—Pancha Shila, but I don't think they should propose that we build our relations on the principles of Pancha Shila.
Two documents—an appeal to the Hungarians and a Declaration.
In this document we don't need to provide self-criticism.
There's a difference between party and state relations.

Cde. Shepilov—The course of events reveals the crisis in our relations with the countries of people's democracy.
Anti-Soviet sentiments are widespread.
The underlying reasons must be revealed.
The foundations remain unshakable.
Eliminate the elements of diktat, not giving play in this situation to a number of measures to be considered in our relations.
The declaration is the first step.
There is no need for an appeal to the Hungarians.
On the armed forces: We support the principles of non-interference.
With the agreement of the government of Hungary, we are ready to withdraw troops.
We'll have to keep up a struggle with national-Communism for a long time.

---

[213] See Document 50.

[214] By 1956, under the terms of the Warsaw Treaty, Soviet troops were stationed in Poland, Romania, and Hungary. Although the German Democratic Republic was also a Warsaw Pact member, the Soviet military presence there was based on the Potsdam agreement on four-power occupation of Germany after World War II.

[215] *Pancha Shila*, the five principles of peaceful coexistence, were first formulated in a Sino-Indian agreement signed by Zhou Enlai and Jawaharlal Nehru in 1954 in the context of defining trade and other relations between India and Tibet. The principles of Pancha Shila became a fundamental part of the joint statement of Bandung in 1955. See also footnotes 152 and 163 in Part One.

Cde. Zhukov—Agrees with what Cde. Shepilov has said.

The main thing is to decide in Hungary.

Anti-Soviet sentiments are widespread.

We should withdraw troops from Budapest, and if necessary withdraw from Hungary as a whole.

This is a lesson for us in the military-political sphere.

Cde. Zhukov—With regard to troops in the GDR and in Poland, the question is more serious.

It must be considered at the Consultative Council.

The Consultative Council is to be convened.

To persist further—it is unclear what will come of this.

A quick decision, the main thing is to declare it today.

Cde. Furtseva—We should adopt a general declaration, not an appeal to the Hungarians. Not a cumbersome declaration.

The second thing is important for the internal situation.

We must search for other modes of relations with the countries of people's democracy.

About meetings with leaders of the people's democracies (concerning relations).

We should convene a CC plenum (for informational purposes).

Cde. Saburov: Agrees about the need for a Declaration and withdrawal of troops.

At the XX Congress we did the correct thing, but then did not keep control of the unleashed initiative of the masses.

It's impossible to lead against the will of the people.

We failed to stand for genuine Leninist principles of leadership.

We might end up lagging behind events.

Agrees with Cde. Furtseva. The ministers are asking; so are members of the CC.

With regard to Romania—they owe us 5 billion rubles for property created by the people.[216]

We must reexamine our relations.

Relations must be built on an equal basis.

Cde. Khrushchev: We are unanimous.

As a first step we will issue a Declaration.

Cde. Khrushchev—informs the others about his conversation with Cde. Mikoyan.[217]

Kádár is behaving well.

5 of the 6 are firmly hanging in there.[218]

A struggle is going on inside the [HWP] Presidium about the withdrawal of troops.

[216] Presumably this refers to the compensation Romania had to pay for the property confiscated from Soviet territory during World War II.

[217] No written record is available.

[218] The five HWP Presidium members are Kádár, Apró, Károly Kiss, Münnich and Szántó. Nagy is clearly the sixth.

The minister of defense will issue a directive about the suppression of insurgents in the cinema, using the armed forces.[219] (Malinin, apparently, became nervous and left the session.)[220]

Officers from the state security (Hungarian) are with our troops.

Consideration of the Draft Declaration[221]
(Shepilov, Molotov, Bulganin)

Cde. Bulganin—we should say in what connection the question of a Declaration arose.
Page 2, Par. 2, don't soften the self-criticism.
Mistakes were committed.
Much use should be made of "Leninist principles."

Cde. Khrushchev—expresses agreement. We should say we are guided by Leninist principles.
Page 2, Par. 5—we should say we are making a statement, not an explanation.
Page 3—we should speak about economic equity, make it the main thing.
We should say that no troops are stationed in the majority of countries.
We should say that on the territory of the Polish, Hungarian, and Romanian states the stationing of troops is done with the consent of their governments and in the interests of these gov'ts and peoples.

We should express our view of the government of Hungary.
Measures to support them.
About support for the party and HWP CC and for the gov't. We should refer specifically to Nagy and Kádár.[222]

Cde. Kaganovich, Cde. Molotov, Cde. Zhukov: We should mention the Potsdam agreement and the treaties with every country.

Cde. Zhukov—We should express sympathy with the people. We should call for an end to the bloodshed.

Page 2, Par. 2: We should say the XX Congress condemned the disregard for principles of equality.

Cde. Zhukov—we should speak about economics.
Restructuring was thwarted after the XX Congress.[223]
(Cde. Khrushchev)
We are turning to the member-states of the Warsaw Pact to consider the question of our advisers. We are ready to withdraw them.

---

[219] This sentence is presumably based on earlier information, since according to what is now known, there was no plan by the Hungarian forces to launch an attack on the Corvin passage after the cease-fire agreement on October 28. It is also possible that this represents a partial misunderstanding and the reference is to relief operations that were planned to end the siege of the party center at Köztársaság Square.

[220] This most likely refers to the HWP CC session mentioned in Mikoyan and Suslov's October 30 report. See Document No. 47.

[221] This document has not yet been found. For the final declaration, see Document No. 50.

[222] This expression of support was eventually omitted from the final document, as was the explicit reference to Kádár and Nagy.

[223] This reference was also omitted from the final text.

Further editing.
Transmitted via high frequency to Cdes. Mikoyan and Suslov.

Information from Cde. Yudin[224] on Negotiations with the Chinese Comrades.

What's the situation: Will Hungary leave our camp? Who is Nagy? Can he be trusted? About the advisers.

Those taking part: Bulganin, Voroshilov, Kaganovich, Molotov, Saburov, Khrushchev, Zhukov, Brezhnev, Shepilov, Shvernik, Furtseva, Pospelov, Yudin. Chinese comrades.

On the Situation in Hungary
(Cde. Khrushchev, Cde. Liu Shaoqi)

Cde. Liu Shaoqi indicates on behalf of the CPC CC that troops must remain in Hungary and in Budapest.

Cde. Khrushchev—there are two paths.
A military path—one of occupation.
A peaceful path—the withdrawal of troops, negotiations.

Cde. Molotov—the political situation has taken clearer shape. An anti-revol. gov't has been formed, a transitional gov't. We should issue the Declaration and explain our position. We should clarify our relationship with the new gov't. We are entering into negotiations about the withdrawal of troops.

Nagy—the prime minister.
Kádár—a state minister.
Tildy Zoltán—
Kovács Béla—
Losonczy—a Communist and a supporter of Nagy[225]

[Source: TsKhSD, F. 3, Op. 12, D. 1006, Ll. 6–14, compiled by V. N. Malin. Originally published in English in the Cold War International History Project Bulletin *no. 8/9 (Winter 1996/1997): 392–393. Translated by Mark Kramer.]*

---

[224] Pavel F. Yudin was Soviet ambassador to China from 1953–1959.

[225] This note appears on the back side of the previous page. Apparently, this was the moment when news of the formation of Nagy's inner cabinet reached the meeting. However, the name of Ferenc Erdei, representing the National Peasant Party is missing from the list. It is also not mentioned that one seat was reserved for the Social Democratic Party.

DOCUMENT NO. 50: "Declaration by the Government of the USSR on the Principles of Development and Further Strengthening of Friendship and Cooperation Between the Soviet Union and Other Socialist States," October 30, 1956

On October 28, the CPSU CC Presidium revived its debate over Hungary. The increasingly worrisome news reaching the Kremlin pushed Khrushchev to propose commissioning Politburo members Brezhnev, Pospelov, and Shepilov to draft a government communiqué on the principles governing the relationships between socialist countries. In fact a document of this sort had been in preparation for some time, but the Polish events and particularly the Hungarian crisis suddenly accelerated the work and determined its final character.[226] The declaration appeared in Pravda on October 31.

The most surprising sentence in the document for many contemporaries both inside and outside the bloc was the following: "[T]he Soviet Government is prepared to enter into the appropriate negotiations with the Government of the Hungarian People's Republic and other members of the Warsaw Treaty on the question of the presence of Soviet troops on the territory of Hungary." Reading this after the brutal crackdown that was to begin on November 4, the wording seems utterly cynical. But the Malin notes of the relevant CPSU CC Presidium discussions offer a different impression. The communiqué represented a genuine initiative by the more "liberal" wing of the Soviet leadership to create a more even balance in relations between the USSR and its satellites, and they managed, at least very briefly, to get their hard-line colleagues to agree. At the same time, the document clearly marked the boundaries of change that would be tolerable for the Soviet Union. The Moscow-approved reforms in fact aimed entirely at maintaining a socialist (that is, Soviet-style) system internally, and strengthening the current intra-bloc alliance system (i.e., the Soviet empire). In that context, the subsequent crackdown did not go against the spirit of the October 30 communiqué; it was simply a change in tactics.

"DECLARATION BY THE GOVERNMENT OF THE USSR ON THE PRINCIPLES OF DEVELOPMENT AND FURTHER STRENGTHENING OF FRIENDSHIP AND COOPERATION BETWEEN THE SOVIET UNION AND OTHER SOCIALIST STATES."

A policy of peaceful coexistence, friendship, and cooperation among all states has been and continues to be the firm foundation of the foreign relations of the Union of Soviet Socialist Republics.

This policy finds its deepest and most consistent expression in the mutual relations among the socialist countries. United by the common ideals of building a socialist society and by the principles of proletarian internationalism, the countries of the great commonwealth of socialist nations can build their mutual relations only on the principles of complete equality, of respect for territorial integrity, state independence and sovereignty, and of noninterference in one another's internal affairs. Not only does this not exclude close fraternal cooperation and mutual aid among the countries of the socialist commonwealth in the economic, political, and cultural spheres; on the contrary, it presupposes these things.

The system of people's democracies took shape, grew strong, and showed its great vital power in many countries of Europe and Asia on this foundation after the Second World War and the rout of fascism.

In the process of the rise of the new system and the deep revolutionary changes in social relations, there have been many difficulties, unresolved problems, and downright mistakes, including mistakes in the mutual relations among the socialist countries—violations and errors which demeaned the principle of equality in relations among the socialist states.

The 20th Congress of the Communist Party of the Soviet Union quite resolutely condemned these violations and mistakes, and set the task of consistent application by the Soviet Union of

[226] For Western information on the prospective communiqué, see Document No. 10.

Leninist principles of equality of peoples in its relations with the other socialist countries. It proclaimed the need for taking full account of the historical past and peculiarities of each country that has taken the path of building a new life.

The Soviet government is consistently carrying out these historic decisions of the 20th Congress, which create conditions for further strengthening friendship and cooperation among the socialist countries on the firm foundation of observance of the full sovereignty of each socialist state.

As recent events have demonstrated, it has become necessary to make this declaration of the Soviet Union's stand on the mutual relations of the USSR with other socialist countries, particularly in the economic and military spheres.

The Soviet government is prepared to discuss together with the governments of other socialist states measures ensuring further development and strengthening of economic ties among the socialist countries in order to remove any possibility of violation of the principles of national sovereignty, mutual benefit, and equality in economic relations.

This principle must also be extended to advisers. It is known that, in the first period of the formation of the new social system, the Soviet Union, at the request of the governments of the people's democracies, sent these countries a certain number of its specialists—engineers, agronomists, scientists, military advisers. In the recent period the Soviet Government has repeatedly raised before the socialist countries the question of recalling its advisers.

In view of the fact that by this time the people's democracies have formed their own qualified national cadres in all spheres of economic and military affairs, the Soviet Government considers it urgent to review, together with the other socialist states, the question of the expediency of the further presence of USSR advisers in these countries.

In the military domain an important basis of the mutual relations between the Soviet Union and the people's democracies is the Warsaw Treaty, under which its members adopted respective political and military obligations, including the obligation to take "concerted measures necessary for strengthening their defense capacity in order to protect the peaceful labor of their peoples, to guarantee the inviolability of their borders and territory, and to ensure defense against possible aggression."

It is known that Soviet units are in the Hungarian and Rumanian republics in accord with the Warsaw Treaty and governmental agreements. Soviet units are in the Polish republic on the basis of the Potsdam four-power agreement and the Warsaw Treaty. Soviet military units are not in the other people's democracies.

For the purpose of assuring mutual security of the socialist countries, the Soviet Government is prepared to review with the other socialist countries which are members of the Warsaw Treaty the question of Soviet troops stationed on the territory of the above-mentioned countries. In so doing the Soviet government proceeds from the general principle that stationing the troops of one or another state which is a member of the Warsaw Treaty on the territory of another state which is a member of the treaty is done by agreement among all its members and only with the consent of the state on the territory of which and at the request of which these troops are stationed or it is planned to station them.

The Soviet government considers it necessary to make a statement in connection with the events in Hungary. The course of events has shown that the working people of Hungary, who have attained great progress on the basis of the people's democratic system, are rightfully raising the question of the need to eliminate serious defects in the sphere of economic construction, the question of further improving the living standards of the population, the question of combating bureaucratic distortions in the state machinery. However, this legitimate and progressive movement of the working people was soon joined by the forces of black reaction and counterrevolution, which are trying to take advantage of the dissatisfaction of a part of the working people in order to undermine the foundations of the people's democratic system in Hungary and to restore the old landowner-capitalist ways in that country.

The Soviet government, like the whole Soviet people, deeply regrets that the development of events in Hungary has led to bloodshed.

At the request of the Hungarian people's government, the Soviet Government has granted consent to the entry into Budapest of Soviet military units to help the Hungarian people's army and the Hungarian agencies of government to bring order to the city.

Having in mind that the further presence of Soviet military units in Hungary could serve as an excuse for further aggravation of the situation, the Soviet Government has given its military command instructions to withdraw the Soviet military units from the city of Budapest as soon as this is considered necessary by the Hungarian Government.

At the same time, the Soviet Government is prepared to enter into the appropriate negotiations with the government of the Hungarian People's Republic and other members of the Warsaw Treaty on the question of the presence of Soviet troops on the territory of Hungary.

To guard the socialist achievements of people's democratic Hungary is the chief and sacred duty of the workers, peasants, intelligentsia, of all the Hungarian working people at the present moment.

The Soviet Government expresses confidence that the peoples of the socialist countries will not permit foreign and domestic reactionary forces to shake the foundations of the people's democratic system, a system established and strengthened by the self-sacrificing struggle and labor of the workers, peasants, and intelligentsia of each country. They will continue all efforts to remove all obstacles in the path of further strengthening the democratic foundations, independence, and sovereignty of their countries; to develop further the socialist foundations of each country, its economy and its culture, for the sake of an uninterrupted rise in the living standards and cultural level of all the working people; they will strengthen the fraternal unity and mutual aid of the socialist countries to buttress the great cause of peace and socialism.

OCTOBER 30, 1956

[Source: Paul E. Zinner, ed., National Communism and Popular Revolt in Eastern Europe: A Selection of Documents on Events in Poland and Hungary, February–November, 1956, *(New York: Columbia University Press, 1956), 485–89. The original translation appeared in* The Current Digest of the Soviet Press *8, no. 40 (November 14, 1956): 10–11.]*

DOCUMENT NO. 51: Minutes of the 58th Meeting of the Romanian Politburo, October 30, 1956

The Hungarian events produced an increasingly strong response in Eastern Europe, including Romania. On October 27, students at the technical university in Timişoara organized a meeting and demonstration where they formulated political demands which directly challenged the country's political system. As a result, the RWP PC decided to intensify its earlier measures, and to set up a top-level emergency committee, the General Command, consisting of four PC members with full authorization to take extraordinary steps, such as opening fire on demonstrators and declaring a state of emergency. The Ministry of Defense and Ministry of the Interior, among others, were subordinated to this new entity. Similar reactions to the Polish and Hungarian crises occurred elsewhere in the socialist bloc (see, for example, Document No. 52). In subsequent years, the RWP and Romanian state administration underwent systematic purges, in part as an outgrowth of the types of measures proposed below.

Attended by the following comrades: Gh. Apostol, E. Bodnăraş , P. Borilă,[227] N. Ceauşescu, Chivu Stoica,[228] Al. Drăghici, Gh. Gheorghiu-Dej, Al. Moghioroş, C. Pârvulescu.
Chaired by: cde. Gh. Gheorghiu-Dej

Agenda:

Examination of certain measures to be taken in order to secure order in the country.
Following the discussion, the Politburo of the RWP CC made the following decisions:
Taking into account the agitation of certain reactionary elements and the hostile manifestations of some student groups in Timişoara after the deterioration of the situation in the Hungarian People's Republic, it is necessary to take the following measures:

1. Intensification of political work among the working class in order to strengthen its militancy against the conspiracies of the class enemy.
   The working class that built the people's democratic regime must faithfully defend its accomplishments against the attempts of hostile elements to attack the people's democratic regime. Special attention should be directed to political work among young people, intellectuals, and especially students, who constitute a stratum easily influenced by hostile elements.
2. Measures to improve guarding the party headquarters, as well as regional and municipal People's Councils [*Sfaturi Populare*].
   Also, measures should be taken to strengthen the guard groups [*grupelor de pază*] in factories and to improve the organization of these groups.
   Where it proves necessary, auxiliary groups from the Militia will be organized. The guard groups should be recruited from among the best party members, UTM[229] members, and Trade Unions' members, that is, among comrades totally devoted to the cause of the Party and to the people's democratic regime. The guard groups at the regional, county, and municipal Party committees will be immediately provided with arms. Similarly, gradually arming guard groups in factories will be continued, as approved by the RWP CC Politburo.
3. Immediate measures will be taken in order to organize the protection of central institutions, as well as institutions in the country's main cities. These will be guarded by the organs of State Security [*Securitate*], and supplemented by army troops if needed.

---

[227] Petre Borilă was a member of the RWP CC Politburo beginning in 1952 and deputy prime minister from 1953–1968.

[228] Chivu Stoica was a member of the RCP (later RWP) CC Politburo beginning in 1948 and chairman of the Council of Ministers from 1955–1961. His real name was actually Stoica Chivu, but he came to be addressed by his family name first in leadership circles, chiefly by Gheorghiu-Dej.

[229] *Uninea Tineretului Muncitoresc*, Union of Working Youth.

4. Immediate measures will be taken to strengthen guarding the Hungarian border.
5. Regarding the events that occurred at the Polytechnic University in Timişoara, measures will be taken to arrest those who gathered at the Polytechnic University. They will be transported to a special destination and will be filtered out by state security in order to uncover the hostile elements among them.
6. In order to coordinate the above-mentioned measures and to take some operative measures on the basis of Politburo decisions, a General Command will be constituted, beginning on October 30, 1956, 22.00 hours. Members will be comrades Emil Bodnăraş, Nicolae Ceauşescu, Alexandru Drăghici and Leontin Sălăjan.
7. The General Command will be led by cde. Emil Bodnăraş and subordinated to the RWP CC Politburo and to the Council of Ministers of the RPR. The Command will be in permanent contact with cde. Gh. Gheorghiu-Dej, RWP CC first-secretary, and with cde. Chivu Stoica, chairman of the Council of Ministers.
8. The General Command will have the right to take any measures to secure order where necessary, including the right to order fire.
   In case of a difficult situation in a given region, the General Command may declare a state of emergency in the affected area, which shall be established according to the situation. Subsequently, this measure is to be submitted to the RWP CC Politburo for approval.
9. If the situation demands, the General Command may order the suspension of courses in some institutes of higher education.
10. Every item of information concerning the situation in the country must be forwarded to the General Command.
11. All measures to secure order in the regions and counties must be taken under the supervision of the respective party organs.
12. In order to reduce the number [of subscribers], the propaganda and culture directorate of the RWP CC will submit to the RWP CC Politburo a list of those receiving the special Agerpres[230] bulletins.
13. Proposals will be drafted for measures to be taken related to the former legionnaires, Arrow Crossists [nyilaşişti] and Szálasi-ite [szalaşişti] leaders,[231] as well as former leaders of bourgeois parties in our country.
14. Special attention should be devoted to the CFR[232] and to the PTTR.[233] The Presidium of the Council of Ministers will study the issue of raising the salaries of CFR and PTTR employees.
15. In the coming days, the RWP CC Politburo will meet daily in order to receive the General Command's reports concerning the situation in the country, and to decide upon the measures to be taken.
16. Meetings will be organized in factories in order to explain the resolution of the RWP CC, the Council of Ministers, and the Central Council of Trade Unions regarding improving the current system of salaries and pensions. Telegrams will be sent from these meetings to the RWP CC and the Council of Ministers.

GHEORGHIU-DEJ

[Source: Arh. CC al PCR, fond Biroul Politic, dosar nr. 358/1956, ff.3–5. Published in Romanian in Corneliu Mihai Lungu and Mihai Retegan, eds., 1956 Explozia: Percepţii române, iugoslave şi sovietice asupra eventimentelor din Polonia şi Ungaria (Bucharest: Editura Univers Enciclopedic, 1996), 143–145. Translated by Victoria Isabela Corduneanu.]

[230] The Romanian national news agency.
[231] See footnotes 107 and 108 above.
[232] *Caile Ferate Romane*, Romanian State Railroad.
[233] *Posta Telefon Telegraf Roman*, Postal, Telegraph and Telephone Services.

DOCUMENT NO. 52: Information Report from Bulgarian State Security on the Activities of "Hostile Elements," October 30, 1956

This report by the Bulgarian secret police offers a characteristic view of the reaction prompted by the Polish crisis and the Hungarian revolution in other Eastern Bloc countries. As this document shows, the state security apparatus was mainly concerned about those segments of society which seemed to harbor potential enemies and "troublemakers": the non-communist intelligentsia, which was seen as most immune to ideological indoctrination; journalists, who had access to external news sources; and artists, "actors, painters, writers and others," because of their non-conformist views and influence among other intellectuals.

The fact that Stalinist policies resulted in almost identical grievances all over Eastern Europe shows through in this report where the main complaints are strikingly similar to those in Hungary: a deterioration of living standards especially in the countryside, Sovietization, and dissatisfaction toward the new elite which the party had promoted into top posts. Probably the most unpleasant and alarming phenomenon for the party leaderships in Eastern Europe was the reaction of party intellectuals, which often did not differ significantly from the responses of non-communists.

Top Secret!

Report

On the comments and activities of hostile elements among the bourgeois intelligentsia in regard to the events in Poland and Hungary

In connection with the events in Hungary and Poland, no data has been received regarding vehement hostile activities among the reactionary part of the bourgeois intelligentsia. For the most part, these circles are engaged in lively discussions, which approve of the events and maintain that they should have occurred earlier. Such commentaries try to prove that the primary reason behind the events does not lie in the activities of the enemies of the state, which actually caused some temporary difficulties, but in the roots of the socialist system per se, which was even rejected by nature, and that this will thus come to be the logical end of all socialist states.

Data was received concerning energetically hostile statements among journalists, especially among the employees of the BTA.[234] These journalists have access to enemy radio station broadcasts, along with printed materials from the foreign press, which enables them to spread hostile rumors and slander.

The remarks and hostile statements in these circles are directed against party and government leaders, who are held responsible for the people's poor living conditions, particularly the peasants; for the uncritical application of the USSR experience; and for the promotion of inexperienced and "incapable" individuals to responsible and well-paid positions in the state and administrative apparatus. [According to these opinions,] it seems that our people have a slave characteristic of patience [sic], and what is happening now in Hungary could hardly occur [here]. Some hostile elements from these circles point out that our party stands on a higher level, and this guarantees the security of the present power.

Actors, painters, writers, and others also commented on the events with extreme pleasure. Among the actors, most remarks were initiated by hostile elements, who for some reason consider themselves subject to a professional maltreatment, and who have never received any awards or professional recognition. Most of them spoke indignantly, even with overt criticism, about the Soviet army's intervention in the Hungarian events, which [they considered] an aggression.

---

[234] The Bulgarian National News Agency.

Todor Mladenov, an actor from the "Labor Front" theater, stated in front of a group of actors: "Believe me, I will personally stab a scythe into them if I am given a signal..."

Instigated by the enemy, artists and writers admire the "bravery of the Hungarian and the Polish people" who have risen against tyranny and misery. Included in almost all statements made by hostile elements is that they are waiting with great happiness for such events to occur in our country, which would lead to happier days when they will be able to create art and not follow the "orders" of "idiots" who have already ruined their artistic abilities.

Fervent comments and discussions are also taking place among jurist circles. Quite a few people openly declare that despite the different situation, similar events should take place here as well. Another part of them silently approves of and admires the events without making any special remarks, claiming that [state] power has taken all measures and that one should neither talk a lot nor to anyone.

Along with hostile elements from the bourgeois intelligentsia, communists from the same strata have also commented on the events, while others silently approve [these statements] without undertaking any critical position towards the hostile accusations.

Such was the claim of Docho Dobrev, a member of the BCP who works in "Poligraphizdat," who has stated that "if the same events that occurred in Hungary would also occur in Bulgaria, then I would fight on the side of those fighting against the misery and hunger of the village and the city and against the incapable people who rule...."

The department's present task is directed towards observing the bourgeois intelligentsia, which mainly involves the supervision of hostile elements by agents and checking some signals.

OCTOBER 30, 1956 SOFIA
HEAD OF DEPARTMENT II
CAPTAIN: SIGNATURE

[Source: AMVR, Fond 13, Opis 1, File 1404, p. 36–37. Obtained by Jordan Baev. Translated by Velichka Hristova.]

DOCUMENT NO. 53: Working Notes and Attached Extract from the Minutes of the CPSU CC Presidium Meeting, October 31, 1956

At the October 31 Presidium meeting, Nikita Khrushchev announced, seemingly unexpectedly, that the conclusions reached at the previous day's momentous session should be re-examined. Soviet troops, he said, should not be withdrawn from Hungary and Budapest. On the contrary, the USSR "should take the initiative in restoring order in Hungary," in other words in suppressing the revolution, which had been only one of the possible solutions under discussion just three days before, on October 28.

In stating his position, Khrushchev made no mention of the news coming from Budapest, nor did he refer to the Chinese views he had heard the previous day, nor to the American position. He did raise the weakness of the Hungarian communist government as a factor, but his argument was based mainly on the need to defend the Soviet empire's prestige and on the implications of an eventual withdrawal for Soviet domestic politics. His warning made special reference to those "circles" which might have influence at the top levels of the party, the army, state security, and the party apparatus. He called attention to the risks of a possible power struggle and a rupture within the party. Interestingly, there is no indication in the meeting notes that Khrushchev's measures were meant to be discussed; he seems to have intended simply that they be carried out.

The only detail on which Khrushchev was uncertain was whom to appoint as head of the provisional revolutionary government: Kádár or Münnich. Aside from the amount of time needed to make military preparations, this circumstance explains why the final decision was postponed for four days. Strangely enough, even though the plan was to overthrow the Nagy government, Khrushchev did not exclude the possibility of involving Nagy in the "normalization" process. Within the Politburo, Deputy Prime Minister Saburov was the only one who tried to uphold the "liberal" position, but at this point nobody supported him.

Information about Discussions with Gomulka Regarding the Situation in Poland and Hungary[235]
(Khrushchev)

A meeting with Cde. Gomulka (in the Brest region) was proposed.

On Hungary

Cde. Khrushchev sets forth the various considerations.
We should reexamine our assessment and should not withdraw our troops from Hungary and Budapest. We should take the initiative in restoring order in Hungary. If we depart from Hungary, it will give a great boost to the Americans, English, and French—the imperialists.
They will perceive it as weakness on our part and will go onto the offensive.
We would then be exposing the weakness of our positions.
Our party will not accept it if we do this.
To Egypt they will then add Hungary.
We have no other choice.
If this point of view is supported and endorsed, let's consider what we should do.

Agreed: Cdes. Zhukov, Bulganin, Molotov, Kaganovich, Voroshilov, Saburov

---

[235] This refers to a telephone conversation between Khrushchev and Gomułka during which they agreed that Khrushchev, Malenkov, and Molotov would meet with Gomułka and Cyrankiewicz the next day, November 1, in Brest.

We should say we tried to meet them halfway, but there is not now any government.
What line are we now adopting?

We should create a Provisional Revol. Gov't (headed by Kádár).
Best of all—a deputy.
Münnich—as premier and min. of defense and internal affairs.

This government—we should invite them to negotiations about the withdrawal of troops and resolve the matter.[236]
If Nagy agrees, bring him in as dep. premier.

Münnich is appealing to us with a request for assistance. We are lending assistance and restoring order.
We should negotiate with Tito.
We should inform the Chinese comrades, the Czechs, the Romanians, and the Bulgarians.
There will be no large-scale war.

Cde. Saburov—after yesterday's session this discussion is all pointless.
It will vindicate NATO.

Cde. Molotov—yesterday was only a compromise decision.

Cdes. Zhukov, Voroshilov, Bulganin: We should reject the view that we are reexamining our position.

Cde. Furtseva—What further should be done?
We showed patience, but now things have gone too far. We must act to ensure that victory goes to our side.

Cde. Pospelov—we should use the argument that we will not let socialism in Hungary be strangled.

Cde. Shvernik—Cde. Khrushchev's proposal is correct.

Cde. Molotov—we should not defer the creation of organs in localities. We should act simultaneously in the center and in the localities.

Cde. Zhukov is instructed to work out a plan and report on it.[237]

Shepilov, Brezhnev, Furtseva, and Pospelov are to handle the propaganda side.[238]

An appeal to the people from the military command or the government.
An appeal to the people from the Prov. Revol. Gov't.

---

[236] This sentence can be interpreted in two ways. It might refer to future negotiations with the new government concerning the withdrawal of Soviet troops after the intervention. The more likely interpretation involves a plan to lure the Nagy government into a trap with the promise of negotiations.

[237] See also attached resolution in this document.

[238] The "propaganda side" involved preparing the documents that were to be issued at the start of military operations. See also attached resolution in this document. Probably dissatisfied with their work, the CPSU Presidium on November 3 handed the task over to Mikoyan, Suslov and Shepilov. See Document No. 78.

An order from Cde. Konev.[239]

We should send a group to the region of Cde. Konev's headquarters.

Cde. Rákosi—favors Münnich (as premier)
Cde. Hegedüs— "
Cde. Gerő— "[240]

Apró
Kádár
Kiss Károly
Boldoczki
Horváth[241]

On Negotiations with Tito
(Cdes. Khrushchev, Molotov, Bulganin)

Draft a telegram to Tito about the meeting.
To Brest: Khrushchev, Molotov, Malenkov.
To Yugoslavia: Khrushchev, Malenkov.

To discuss with you the situation that has emerged in Hungary. What is your view of it? If you agree, our delegation will visit incognito from

1. XI in the evening to
2. XI in the morning your time.

Confirm the telegram to the Soviet ambassador in Belgrade.

[RESOLUTION]

Workers of the World, Unite!   Strictly secret
Communist Party of the Soviet Union
CENTRAL COMMITTEE

Extract from Minutes No. 49/VI taken on the October 31, 1956 meeting of the Presidium of the CC

---

[239] All these documents were eventually issued on November 4. The first two communiqués, entitled "Appeal by the Command of Soviet Troops in Hungary to the Hungarian People and the Officers and Men of the Hungarian Army" and "Appeal to the Hungarian People" by the Hungarian Revolutionary Workers' and Peasants' Government addressed the Hungarian population and were broadcast over the radio after the military intervention was underway. For their text, see Zinner, *National Communism*, 480–481 and 474–478. The third document, "The United Armed Forces Commander in Chief's Order No. 1," issued by Marshal Konev, was distributed among the Soviet units prior to the operation. Its English translation can be found in Györkei and Horváth, *Soviet Military Intervention*, 257–258.

[240] This indicates the opinions of the three former Hungarian leading party officials, who at that time were in Moscow. Whether they expressed their views beforehand through consultations with Khrushchev or were present at the Presidium meeting is not clear, but the second possibility cannot be ruled out.

[241] This is the list of politicians to be included in the new government.

[242] Not printed here.

About the situation in Hungary

1. In accord with the exchange of opinions at the session of the Presidium of the CC CPSU, Cdes. Khrushchev, Molotov, and Malenkov are empowered to conduct negotiations with the representatives of the CC PZPR.
2. Confirmed is the text of the telegram to the Soviet Ambassador in Belgrade for Cde. Tito (Enclosed).[242] In the event of an affirmative reply, Cdes. Khrushchev and Malenkov are authorized to conduct negotiations with Cde. Tito.
3. Provide Cde. Zhukov with an account of the exchange of opinions at the CC CPSU Presidium session, [instruct him] to prepare a plan of measures [*plan meropriatii*] in connection with the events in Hungary, and to inform the CC CPSU.
4. Inform Cdes. Shepilov, Brezhnev, Furtseva, and Pospelov on the basis of the exchange of opinions at the CC Presidium to prepare essential documents and submit them to the CC CPSU for review.

SECRETARY OF THE CC

[Source: TsKhSD, F. 3, Op. 12, D. 1006, Ll. 15–18ob, compiled by V. N. Malin. Originally published in English in the Cold War International History Project Bulletin *no. 8–9 (Winter 1996/1997): 393–394. Translated by Mark Kramer. The resolution is located at TsKhSD, F. 89, Per. 45, Dok. 15. Originally published in the* Cold War International History Project Bulletin *no. 5 (Spring 1995): 32. Translated by Johanna Granville.]*

DOCUMENT NO. 54: Draft telegram to Italian Communist Leader Palmiro Togliatti on the Situation in Hungary, (CPSU CC Protocol 49), October 31, 1956

In this response to Italian communist leader Togliatti's cable from the day before, the Soviet leadership hastens to agree with his view that the Hungarian government is moving in a "reactionary" direction, and to dispel the notion that the Kremlin may be divided over its approach to the crisis (see Document No. 48).

WORKERS OF THE WORLD, UNITE!
TOP SECRET

Communist Party of the Soviet Union
CENTRAL COMMITTEE
No P 49/69

To Comrade Shepilov (M[inistry] of F[oreign] A[ffairs]) and to Comrade Vinogradov[243]
Extract from Minutes No. 49, taken at the October 31, 1956 meeting of the Presidium of the CC

Draft of a telegram to be sent to Comrade Togliatti
The CC approves the attached text of a telegram to be sent to Comrade Togliatti in connection with the Hungarian situation.

SECRETARY OF THE CC
TO PARAGRAPH 69 OF MINUTES No. 49

TOP SECRET

ROME

For Comrade TOGLIATTI

In your evaluation of the situation in Hungary and of the Hungarian government's tendencies to develop in a reactionary direction, we are in agreement with you. According to our information, Nagy is occupying a two-faced position and is increasingly falling under the influence of the reactionary forces. For the time being we are not speaking out openly against Nagy, but we will not reconcile ourselves with the turn of events toward a reactionary debaucher.

Your friendly warnings regarding the possibility of the weakening of the unity of the party's collective leadership have no basis. We can firmly assure you that in the complex international situation our collective leadership unanimously [*yedinodushno*] evaluates the situation and unanimously takes appropriate decisions.
CC CPSU

[Source: TsKhSD, F. 89, Per. 45, Dok. 14. Originally published in Cold War International History Project Bulletin *no. 5 (Spring 1995): 32–33. Translated by Johanna Granville and Mark Doctoroff.]*

---

[243] I. T. Vinogradov was first deputy head of the CPSU CC Department for Ties with Foreign Communist Parties from 1953–1957.

DOCUMENT NO. 55: Instructions from Koća Popović, Yugoslav Secretary of State for Foreign Affairs,[244] to Ambassador Dalibor Soldatić, October 31, 1956 (Excerpt)

This excerpt from the Yugoslav Foreign Ministry's instructions to the ambassador in Budapest gives a good sense of Belgrade's position on the Hungarian events. The Yugoslavs, who had long before supported Nagy and his associates against the HWP's Stalinist line, stood by the new government during the first few days of the revolution. They probably knew that by this time Nagy saw Yugoslavia as an example of a socialist yet independent and neutral state with an active foreign policy. After October 23, it would have served Belgrade's interests to have Hungary also become independent of the Soviet Union and the socialist camp, and choose the Yugoslav alternative. At Nagy's request, Tito even sent a letter to the HWP CC expressing his full backing for the Hungarian program communiqué of October 28, which promised democratic and social reforms and supported the rebels' demands.

However, the Yugoslavs watched the Hungarian crisis with growing anxiety, and their position began to shift within a few days. By the end of October, Tito's personal opinion had already changed radically. He now concluded that a "counterrevolution" was underway in Hungary and that the accomplishments of socialism were in danger. This shift helps to explain his eventual support, lukewarm as it was, for the Soviet-led second invasion.

Activate your relationships with the members of the government and the party's central committee. State that we are ready to help them according to our abilities. Inform [them] that you had received instructions for this and also to forward all their requests urgently.

Given that we have received little information about the development of the situation, we have already helped much wherever we could. They have to state in what direction and precisely how we can help them. Therefore, more frequent meetings would be needed.

State that we started to worry seeing the possibilities of a bend toward the right, which threatens the social order, regardless of [the fact] that the working masses do not want this. Therefore, according to our opinion—if we are informed properly—no further concessions can be made. Even though we understand the difficulties, the question emerges whether they had not gone too far in the area of concessions. It is certainly no longer possible to satisfy the frequently unrealistic demands of certain political groups, and certain demands are demagogic and reactionary too. We believe that the most important thing right now is to assume the standpoint of one program, to insist on that rigidly, and to focus on organizational work, which is aimed at gathering those elements that are ready to support the program actively.

[Source: MOL, XIX–J–1–j. 11. d., p. 24. Published in József Kiss, Zoltán Ripp and István Vida, eds., Magyar-jugoszláv kapcsolatok, 1956: Dokumentumok (Budapest: MTA Jelenkorkutató Bizottság, 1995), 144. Translated by Mónika Borbély.]

---

[244] In the Yugoslav state administration this title corresponds to Foreign Minister.

DOCUMENT NO. 56: Record of Conversation between Yugoslav Ambassador Dalibor Soldatić and János Kádár, October 31, 1956[245] (Excerpt)

The following is an excerpt from Ambassador Soldatić's account of his negotiations with Kádár. According to instructions received the same day, the Yugoslav diplomat had contacted the Hungarian leadership expressing Belgrade's concerns about the course of events in Hungary and assuring the HWP of Yugoslavia's support in the fight for "the party and the general interests of socialism." The circumstances surrounding the meeting were rather critical, given that the previous day the HWP Presidium had already begun discussing dissolving the party. On October 31, the Hungarian Socialist Worker's Party was founded.

I talked with János Kádár primarily about reshuffling the government. I underlined that I wanted to talk to him particularly about party questions and I wanted to be informed about how they wish to solve this problem, because the development of events is making our leaders rather uneasy. I told him my opinion of the new party leadership, that in these days of revolution and due to the rapid unfolding of events, the party and the general interests of socialism should be taken into consideration; they should work fast and they should not let events supercede them. Kádár said the party Presidium, which consists of six members, had discussed this question; opinions differ and the decision-making is not easy. I answered that considering the situation's development, the decision should not be delayed for long as it will [soon] be late and, taking no account of the victims, the leadership should be given to those who are not compromised[246] and who are able to advance the party, and they have to be given help in this. I said that I talked to him as a communist, and drew his attention again to the uneasiness of our leading comrades. I let him know that their opinion is the same as the political line I described, but the necessary details are unknown to them and therefore they cannot have full insight into the current situation. I said that we wish to help them, and that their victory or defeat is effecting us, too. Kádár said he want either the one or the other versions to happen, and personally he today will aim at establishing a new party[247] hoping that the Yugoslav comrades will give full support to this, they count on this and trust that it will happen.

[Source: MOL, XIX–J–1–j. 11. d., pp. 25–26. Originally published in József Kiss, Zoltán Ripp and István Vida, eds., Magyar-jugoszláv kapcsolatok, 1956: Dokumentumok *(Budapest: MTA Jelenkor-kutató Bizottság, 1995), 146–147. Translated by Mónika Borbély.]*

[245] Although the Hungarian-language document found in the archives indicates November 1 as the date for this conversation, it is clear from the context that the meeting must have taken place on October 31. Presumably, Soldatić reported the event on November 1 and this may have caused the confusion.

[246] That is, those who played no significant role in the Rákosi-Gerő era.

[247] The HWP Presidium—János Kádár, Imre Nagy, Antal Apró, Károly Kiss, Ferenc Münnich and Zoltán Szántó—discussed the question of disbanding the HWP the previous day, October 30. At that point, however, the Presidium voted down Szántó's proposal that because the HWP had been discredited and had already virtually collapsed, a new party, the Hungarian Socialist Workers' Party, should be formed. The next day, primarily because of pressure from Nagy's followers, that decision was reversed. After the founding assembly that afternoon, Kádár announced the formation of the new party the following day, November 1. The speech was recorded in advance and broadcast at 10:00 p.m. while Kádár, with the assistance of the Soviet Embassy, was already on his way to Moscow. The address was also published in the November 2 issue of *Népszabadság* under the headline "Our party defends our national honor, the cause of democracy and socialism," and the subhead "The Hungarian Socialist Workers' Party is formed." For an English translation, see Zinner, *National Communism*, 464–467.

DOCUMENT NO. 57: Minutes of the Nagy Government's Second Cabinet Meeting, October 31, 1956

On October 30, as a result of the extraordinary situation in Hungary, Imre Nagy established an internal Cabinet within the National Government that had been formed on October 28. Its members were: Nagy, János Kádár, and Géza Losonczy from the HWP; Zoltán Tildy, former president of the Republic (1946–1948); Béla Kovács from the Smallholders Party; and Ferenc Erdei from the National Peasant Party. One seat, reserved for the Social Democratic Party, was to be filled later. The resolutions presented below contain the decisions made at the internal Cabinet's second meeting on October 31. The leadership's main objective was still to consolidate its position in Hungarian society, which partly explains their continued insistence on pressing for Soviet troop withdrawals, a demand being made by all the revolutionary organizations. The new government also made a number of personnel decisions, and called on the population to go back to work and to return public transportation to full service. According to the Malin notes, the new Cabinet's actions had little effect on the CPSU CC Presidium's deliberations over the decision to intervene militarily.

Present:
IMRE NAGY, JÁNOS KÁDÁR, GÉZA LOSONCZY, FERENC ERDEI, ZOLTÁN TILDY.

I.

a) We must prepare a government declaration to the outside world. Géza Losonczy and the Foreign Ministry are responsible. With Comrade Nagy's approval, this should be issued this very day.[248]

b) The Warsaw Pact question. The Government's position is to turn to the Soviet Union today about the Warsaw Pact question in the interests of the withdrawal of Soviet troops, taking note of the Soviet Government's declaration. Géza Losonczy will prepare it, Imre Nagy will sign it. A prominent press statement must be prepared about the letter; the letter should ask for the nomination of a delegation, and the time and place of negotiations.[249]

c) A radio statement must be made as soon as the Soviet troops have left the territory of Budapest and returned to their positions. Géza Losonczy will prepare it.

d) The Soviet declaration concerning the withdrawal of Soviet troops must be translated into Hungarian and published in the press this very day. The Foreign Ministry is in charge of it.[250]

e) An answer has to be given to the questions from the Czechoslovak, Polish and Yugoslav governments. The Foreign Ministry will prepare it.

f) Imre Nagy will summon the Austrian minister, raise with him the possibility of émigré Hungarian divisions crossing into Austria, and put to him questions about this as regards Austria's neutrality.[251]

---

[248] The planned government declaration was never completed. The public learned of the cabinet's resolution through Nagy's speech at Kossuth Square early that afternoon.

[249] For the telegram requesting negotiations, see Document No. 58.

[250] The Soviet declaration was reported in all Hungarian newspapers; its full text was published by *Magyar Függetlenség* on October 31 and by *Népszava* on November 1.

[251] Nagy received Austrian Minister Walter Peinsipp on November 3 when the latter delivered his government's official memorandum concerning measures taken by the Austrian government in accordance with its neutral status. These included the establishment of a closed zone around the Hungarian border and strict control of Austria's western borders as a preventive measure against the entry of émigrés into the country. Peinsipp also informed Nagy about former Hungarian Prime Minister Ferenc Nagy (see footnote 290 below). The Austrian memorandum was broadcast over the radio at 4:11 p.m. the same day. See, László Varga, comp., *A forradalom hangja: Magyarországi rádióadások 1956. október 23–november 9* (Budapest: Századvég-Nyilvánosság Klub, 1989), 92–93.

II.

a) The current deputy defense minister must be relieved of his duties and Pál Maléter should be appointed first deputy. Chief of Staff [Lajos] Tóth should similarly be relieved of his duties and István Kovács appointed in his place. In addition, Béla Király must be appointed commanding officer of Budapest. A press statement must be prepared about these appointments. Ferenc Erdei is in charge, József Szilágyi will carry it out.

b) The government will ask SZOT to arrange a call to the workers that at some point tomorrow they should start work in all factories and institutions.

c) The government instructs the transport minister to immediately make arrangements for the restoration of transportation in Budapest. In Budapest he should, together with the City Council, raise a call for the youth to join the restoration work. György Csanádi[252] must be summoned to discuss these questions. Antal Apró is in charge.

d) The Government entrusts Géza Losonczy with the leadership of the Press Office, and also to arrange the publication of a government paper.

e) Identity cards with Imre Nagy's signature must be issued to ministers. Ferenc Erdei is in charge; György Czilczer will carry it out.

DATE AS ABOVE.

[Source: MOL, XX–5–h, Nagy Imre és társai pere, Minisztertanácsi jegyzőkönyvek, 25. köt., pp. 101–102. ; MOL, XIX–A–83–a. 160. d., pp.101–102. Published in Ferenc Glatz, ed., "A kormány és a párt vezető szerveinek dokumentumaiból, 1956. október 23–november 4," História 11, nos. 4–5 (1989): 47–48. Translated by David Evans.]

---

[252] György Csanádi was minister of transportation and postal service from October 29 to November 3, 1956.

DOCUMENT NO. 58: Telegram from Imre Nagy to Kliment Voroshilov Proposing Negotiations on the Withdrawal of Soviet Troops, October 31, 1956

In this message to the president of the Presidium of the USSR Supreme Soviet, Imre Nagy, referring to the Soviet government declaration of the day before (see Document No. 50), communicated the Hungarian government's desire to start immediate negotiations on withdrawing Soviet troops from the country. Of course, the CPSU CC Presidium had already decided on military intervention on the same day that Nagy sent his telegram. The Soviets did agree to official talks, which started at 12:00 a.m. on November 3 in Budapest, but later that night, when the Hungarian delegation, at Soviet invitation, arrived at the Red Army's headquarters at Tököl to continue discussions, they were arrested.

To His Excellency, Chairman of the Presidium of the Supreme Soviet of the Soviet Union

Your Excellency,

The government of the Hungarian People's Republic desires to undertake immediate negotiations in connection with the withdrawal of Soviet troops from the entire territory of Hungary.

With reference to the latest declaration of the government of the Soviet Union, according to which it is ready to negotiate with the Hungarian government and with the other member states of the Warsaw Treaty concerning the withdrawal of Soviet troops from Hungary, the Hungarian Government invites the Soviet Government to designate a delegation so that conversations can be initiated as soon as possible.[253] At the same time it requests the Soviet government to designate the place and date for these negotiations.

IMRE NAGY
Chairman of the Council of Ministers of the Hungarian People's Republic

[Source: Paul E. Zinner, ed., National Communism and Popular Revolt in Eastern Europe: A Selection of Documents on Events in Poland and Hungary, February–November, 1956, *(New York: Columbia University Press, 1956), p. 462.]*[254]

---

[253] See Zinner, *National Communism,* 485.

[254] Information on the opening address and signature was taken from a Hungarian version of this document.

DOCUMENT NO. 59: Draft Minute by British Foreign Secretary Selwyn Lloyd to Prime Minister Anthony Eden, October 31, 1956

This memorandum documents one of the few instances in which the British foreign secretary dealt personally with the Hungarian situation as it unfolded between 23 October and 4 November. In this minute, Lloyd advises Eden against the British ambassador in Moscow's proposal to send a personal message to Soviet Premier Nikolai Bulganin regarding Hungary. Characteristic of this hectic period, the minute was not even presented to the prime minister, who was preoccupied with the Suez crisis. Only after the Hungarian uprising was crushed did Lloyd support a message to Bulganin, but this time Eden himself rejected the idea.

DRAFT MINUTE
TO THE
PRIME MINISTER

FROM THE
SECRETARY OF
STATE

You will have seen Moscow telegram No. 1481 in which Sir W. Hayter raises the question of sending a personal message to Bulganin about Hungary.

I do not myself think that this is a moment for such a message. We have taken the Russians to the Security Council, we have had to hit them quite hard there and no doubt we shall have to hit them again, since it looks *unfortunately*[255] as if they have not intention of making a quick departure from Hungary. I think you will agree that there is no point in wasting the asset of this personal link with Bulganin upon mere polemics, however satisfying it would be to play back at Bulganin his hypocritical lectures about Suez.

So I suggest that we keep the Bulganin channel in reserve until there seems a better prospect of it helping towards a settlement. But we can encourage Sir W. Hayter to let us know whenever he thinks a message might be useful.

I attach a draft reply to the Ambassador for your consideration.[256]

[Initaled "SL"]

[Source: PRO, Foreign Office General Correspondence, FO 371.12380.]

---

[255] This word was crossed out in the original document.
[256] Not printed here.

DOCUMENT NO. 60: Minutes of the 59th Romanian Politburo Meeting, October 31, 1956

The Romanian leadership used the Hungarian revolution not only as an excuse to beef up internal security but to lay the foundations for a more independent foreign policy, which they hoped would also strengthen their own position inside the country. The Soviet government declaration on October 30 (see Document No. 50) brought to the forefront the recurring question of withdrawing Soviet forces from Romania (a total of at least two armored divisions), a step the RWP PC had been urging since the Austrian state treaty was signed in 1955. The next day, after declaring its loyalty to the Warsaw Pact, the RWP PC proposed reopening negotiations, hoping that the party's actions during the revolution would prove its ability to hold on to power in Romania even without the presence of Soviet troops. According to some sources, the Romanians presented their request when Khrushchev and Malenkov arrived unexpectedly in Bucharest to prepare for the second invasion. Although the Soviets rejected the proposal outright at the time, two years later the Kremlin finally gave in and pulled its forces from Romania.

Attended by following comrades: GH. Gheorghiu-Dej, Gh. Apostol, E. Bodnăraş, P. Borilă, N. Ceauşescu, Chivu Stoica, Al. Drăghici, C. Pârvulescu, D. Coliu, L. Răutu, L. Sălăjan, Şt. Voitec.

The meeting begins at 18.00.

Agenda:

Regarding the position of the RWP and the government of the RPR on the Soviet Government's declaration concerning the basic principles of development and further strengthening of friendship and cooperation between the USSR and other socialist countries.

Cde. Gh. Gheorghiu-Dej presents proposals concerning the position to be adopted by the RWP CC and by the government of the RPR regarding the declaration of the Soviet Government on the principles of development and further strengthening of friendship and cooperation between the Soviet Union and other socialist states.

After discussion, the RWP CC Politburo decided the following with regard to this issue:

1. To affirm on this occasion the RPR's attachment to the socialist camp, emphasizing that we will contribute with all our means to strengthen unity among socialist countries.
2. To underline on this occasion, as always, that the unwavering friendship between the Romanian people and the peoples of the Soviet Union is one of the basic principles of our party and government's policy.
3. To restate the RPR's government's full accordance with the Warsaw Treaty, emphasizing the necessity of maintaining the Warsaw Treaty.
4. The RPR government delegation participating in the next meeting of the Warsaw Pact signatory-states will be charged with the task of discussing with the USSR government the problem of stationing Soviet troops on the RPR's territory.

It should be mentioned in this discussion that the opinion of the RPR's government is that from the viewpoint of the RPR's internal situation, the RPR government does not consider the stationing of Soviet troops on RPR territory necessary; and that the withdrawal of Soviet troops from the RPR's territory would take away a means of anti-Soviet agitation from the hands of internal and external hostile elements.

Similarly, the RPR Government delegation will be instructed to discuss with the USSR Government the problem of recalling from the RPR Soviet advisers, who work in various institutions of the RPR; several specialists will remain in certain state institutions in order to share their expertise.

5. The RWP CC Politburo approves the draft of the resolution by the RWP CC and the Council of Ministers concerning establishing a general command and its sphere of responsibilities (to be annexed).

The meeting finished at 21:00.

DECISION no. 317 (Annex)

Taking into account the deterioration of the situation in the Hungarian People's Republic and the necessity of ensuring calm and order on the territory of the RPR, the Politburo of the Romanian Workers' Party's Central Committee and the Council of Ministers of Romanian Peoples' Republic
Decide:

1. On the establishment of the General Command, beginning October 30, 22:00 hours, charged with taking every measure necessary to secure public order within the entire territory of the RPR.

The General Command consists of the following comrades: Emil Bodnăraş, Nicolae Ceauşescu, Alexandru Drăghici, and Leontin Sălăjan.
The General Command functions under the supervision of cde. Emil Bodnăraş.
For its entire activity, the General Command is responsible to the Council of Ministers and to the Politburo of Central Committee of the RWP.

2. The General Command, as an executive organ, has the following tasks:

  a. The coordination and extension of state information services activities in order to be permanently informed of subversive activities; [and] of the frame of mind among the Army Forces, MAI troops, State Security apparatus, road, naval and air transport apparatus and in communications.
  b. To ensure security measures at:
    - party and state organs
    - the installations of communications and railroad, naval and air transport,
    - plants and factories
    - silos and depositories for food, materials, equipment, medicine, arms and munitions.
  c. to take the necessary measures to ensure greater security along the entire border with [Hungary].
  d. to prepare army units and Securitate apparatus for intervention in case of troubles.
  e. to organize armed detachments of workers in plants and factories.
  f. To repress any action that threatens state order.

3. Subordinated to the General Command are:
    - The Ministry of Armed Forces,
    - The Ministry of the Interior,
    - The guard and security detachments of party sections, enterprises and factories.
    - The military courts
    - The military prosecutor's department
4. Lieutenant-General Ion Tutoveanu is appointed head of the General Military Staff.
5. Lieutenant-General Nicolae Muică is appointed head of the General Command secretariat.
6. The seat of the General Command is at the Council of Ministers.

First-secretary of the Central-Committee of RWP,
GHEORGHIU-DEJ

Chairman of the Council of Ministers,
S. CHIVU[257]

[Source: Arh. CC of PCR, fond Biroul Politic, dosar nr. 359/1956, ff.1–2. Published in Romanian in Corneliu Mihai Lungu and Mihai Retegan, eds., 1956 Explozia: Percepţii române, iugoslave şi sovietice asupra eventimentelor din Polonia şi Ungaria (Bucharest: Editura Univers Enciclopedic, 1996), 147–150. Translated by Victoria Isabela Corduneanu.]

---

[257] As indicated in footnote 228, Stoica Chivu came to be known by his family name (Chivu) followed by his given name among the Romanian leadership.

DOCUMENT NO. 61: Minutes of the Nagy Government's Third Cabinet Meeting, November 1, 1956

This record of the third meeting of Nagy's multi-party inner Cabinet reflects the government's determination to consolidate the internal political situation as soon as possible in hopes of avoiding another outside military intervention. As recently revealed by the full version of the meeting's minutes,[258] which are presented here, the Cabinet discussed in principle the issue of declaring the country's neutrality pending a Soviet explanation for the ongoing influx of Red Army troops into Hungary, which Soviet Ambassador Yurii Andropov had been invited to give.

NOVEMBER 1, 1956

Present:
Imre Nagy
János Kádár
Zoltán Tildy
Ferenc Erdei
Géza Losonczy
Also attending: István Dobi and József Bognár.

1. The division of labor within the Cabinet is as follows: as was customary before, delegations have to be received in the A[gricultural] M[inistry] building where a reception committee is to be set up. The head of the reception committee is appointed by the Secretariat of the Council of Ministers, and the parties of the coalition should send four representatives each to deal with the delegations in two shifts—changing shifts at noon. Their task is to select the minimum number of delegations possible to eventually meet the Chairman of the Council of Ministers.

2. Zoltán Tildy should have a discussion with [Cardinal József] Mindszenty, and at the same time permission should be granted to the organization of the People's Party.[259] The aim of the discussion with Mindszenty is to convince him to make a declaration that he supports the restoration of law and order, and the government. Regarding this issue, István Dobi should negotiate with him.

3. Everything has to be done to restart work [in the country]. Therefore, parties have to be requested to do political work for this sake. Kádár, Tildy, and possibly a social democratic leader—appointed by Imre Nagy—should give speeches to the workers' council delegations at 11:00 this morning.

4. Lacking a firm agreement regarding the government's economic policy, members of the government should refrain from official statements and only speak for themselves on economic issues.

5. The Cabinet fully agrees with Béla Kovács' statement and measures have to be taken to get him to come to Budapest as soon as possible.

6. On the basis of yesterday's decision about the press, Géza Losonczy should reclaim the daily paper *Magyar Nemzet* from the Smallholders' Party and reissue it as a government paper. Zoltán Tildy should personally support this issue.

---

[258] The first version of the minutes that was publicly released omitted paragraph 12 dealing with the declaration of neutrality. See Ferenc Glatz, "A kormány és a párt vezető szerveinek dokumentumaiból 1956 október 23 – November 4," História 11, No. 4–5 (1989). The full version of the document was discovered and first published in Békés, "A magyar semlegesség 1956-ban."

[259] This is the Democratic People's Party, the main opposition party after the 1947 elections but soon eliminated from political life by the communists.

7. Radio broadcasts must continue from the Parliament building with increased control. In order to ensure this, the Cabinet appoints Jenő Széll[260] as government commissioner and Lajos Tamási[261] as his deputy. Every significant political announcement requires their consent before being broadcast. At the same time, the military defense of radio broadcast has to be organized.

8. As regards the repeated entrance of Soviet troops, the government will immediately summon Ambassador Andropov and officially protest these measures. At the same time, the Defense Ministry should send a liaison officer to Soviet headquarters. The defense of Budapest should be maximized, both internally, by restoring law and order, and externally, against a possible attack. An official protest against intervention, depending on the outcome of the negotiations with Ambassador Andropov, should be sent to [foreign] envoys and to the United Nations, and should be announced in a public statement. Said statement is to be written by Géza Losonczy, while the negotiations with Ambassador Andropov will be the task of Imre Nagy.

9. In regard to the proposals concerning the composition of the government, the position is that we should not make changes right now, rather the Cabinet should meet at 4:00 p.m. to discuss the issue. At the same time the Cabinet takes the position that the temporary requisition [of facilities] by the parties must be stopped. Consequently, the two central garages of the HWP, following a proposition from the HWP, are declared the garage of the Council of Ministers and cars can only be issued with the permission of József Halász,[262] head of the Secretariat.

10. In the absence of the Foreign Minister, his duties should be taken over by Imre Nagy.[263]

11. The Cabinet has listened to the reports of Pál Maléter, István Kovács, and Béla Király about the military situation. Reportedly, Soviet troops have left Budapest, save for a few rear guards protecting some of their own institutions. On the other hand, troops are continuously crossing the eastern border, military moves have been registered around Budapest, and Czechoslovak forces are deployed at the Czechoslovak border. Law and order have been restored in Budapest, although there were still a number of atrocities. It can be stated that the army is functioning properly. The National Guard has started its activity but they need more financial and moral support.

12. For the sake of both putting an end to the armed fighting and ensuring the full and final independence of the country, the Cabinet discussed the question of neutrality. The Cabinet unanimously agreed with the position that the government should declare the country's neutrality. For the time being [the Cabinet] refrains from deciding which form of neutrality should be chosen (Switzerland, Austria or Yugoslavia).

This very day, Géza Losonczy will prepare a draft communiqué for public announcement, together with a simultaneous information note for the diplomatic corps, a draft telegram to the Secretary General of the U.N., and finally, an announcement for the press and radio.

The Cabinet acknowledged the report, approving its suggestions and urging the commanders to carry them out without delay. To support the above suggestions, it has taken the following measures:

    a) Military announcements of any kind concerning Budapest can only be issued with the signature of Béla Király, commander of the armed forces in Budapest.

    b) To strengthen the morale of the National Guard, medals and promotions initiated by Béla Király have to be acknowledged and given immediately by István Kristóf,[264] sec-

---

[260] Jenő Széll was a member of the party opposition and worked as Imre Nagy's personal secretary from October 29. Arrested in 1959, he was sentenced to 10 years in prison but was amnestied in the early 1960s.

[261] Lajos Tamási was party secretary of the Writers' Union.

[262] József Halász was head of the Secretariat of the Council of Ministers from 1955 to March 1957.

[263] On the absence of Foreign Minister Imre Horváth, see the headnote for Document No. 79.

[264] István Kristóf was secretary of the Presidential Council from February 1956–1961.

retary of the E[xecutive] C[ommittee]. The Cabinet agrees that the National Guard should be established along the pattern of [18]48, using ranks and badges.[265]

c) The Cabinet appoints Colonel András Márton[266] commander of the outer defense of Budapest, at the same time relieving him from command of the Miklós Zrínyi Military Academy. Major General Béla Székely is relieved of his position as deputy chief of the General Staff, and appointed commander of the Military Academy.

d) The Cabinet finds it necessary to eliminate the Dudás group. Imre Nagy will initiate negotiations with Dudás. Should they fail to reach an agreement, Nagy will authorize Pál Maléter, first deputy minister of defense, to arrest Dudás, and further negotiations should be initiated with one of Dudás' lieutenants.

[Source: MOL, XX–5–h, Nagy Imre és társai pere, Minisztertanácsi jegyzőkönyvek, 25. köt., pp. 105–108.; MOL, XIX–A–83–a. 160. d., pp. 103–106. Published in part by Ferenc Glatz, ed., "A kormány és a párt vezető szerveinek dokumentumaiból, 1956. október 23–november 4," História 11, nos. 4–5 (1989): 48–49. Translated by Csaba Farkas.]

---

[265] On November 2, an article was published in Népszabadság over the signature of Béla Király and entitled "The Revolutionary Armed Forces Committe was established for the defense of the achievements of our victorious revolution." The article announced that on October 31 the irregular armed groups decided to unite as a single national guard which would enjoy equal status with the army and police. Members of the national guard, according to the article, would receive badges and licenses to carry arms. The article also urged the members of the guard to distance themselves from troublemakers.

[266] András Márton was commander of the Miklós Zrínyi Military Academy beginning October 1, 1956. In 1958, he was sentenced to 10 years in prison but was amnestied in 1962.

DOCUMENT NO. 62: Memorandum of Discussion at the 302nd Meeting of the National Security Council, Washington, November 1, 1956, 9–10:55 a.m.

This NSC meeting was supposed to deal mainly with U.S. policy toward Eastern Europe (see Document No. 99). But 20 minutes before it was due to start, Secretary of State John Foster Dulles called the president to tell him that the situation in Hungary had changed dramatically for the better, making it unnecessary to focus on that subject.[267] In his intelligence report to the NSC, Dulles called the apparent victory of the rebels "in a sense ... a miracle," and described the Soviets' October 30 declaration (see Document No. 50) as "one of the most important statements to come out of the USSR in the last decade." He, of course, was completely unaware that the Soviets had reversed themselves on October 31 and decided to send in troops to crush the revolution. Dulles' continuing skepticism about Nagy's ability to lead Hungary was shared by virtually all sides, including the rebels and the Soviet leadership who were debating who would be his replacement (even as the U.S. was of the opinion that Cardinal Mindszenty might be more of a "unifying force"). Few observers at the time seemed to give Nagy credit for the dramatic steps he had just taken, including abolishing one-party rule, forming a coalition government, and declaring Hungary's neutrality.

[Here follows a paragraph listing the participants at the meeting.]

Upon entering the Cabinet Room from his office, the President informed the members of the Council that, except in so far as it was the subject of the DCI's[268] intelligence briefing, he did not wish the Council to take up the situation in the Soviet satellites. Instead, he wished to concentrate on the Middle East.

1. Significant World Developments Affecting U.S. Security

The Director of Central Intelligence said that he had a few remarks to make on the situation in Hungary. In a sense, what had occurred there was a miracle. Events had belied all our past views that a popular revolt in the face of modern weapons was an utter impossibility. Nevertheless, the impossible had happened, and because of the power of public opinion, armed force could not effectively be used. Approximately 80% of the Hungarian Army had defected to the rebels and provided the rebels with arms.[269] Soviet troops themselves had had no stomach for shooting down Hungarians, except in Budapest.

Mr. Dulles then commented that the Soviet statement of October 30, on Soviet relations with the satellite states, was one of the most important statements to come out of the USSR in the last decade.[270] After summarizing the contents of this statement, Mr. Dulles declared that the main problem facing us today in Hungary was the lack of a strong guiding authority to bring the rebels together. Nagy was failing to unite the rebels, and they were demanding that he quit. Somehow a rallying point must be found in order to prevent chaos inside of Hungary even if the Soviets took their leave. In such a heavily Catholic nation as Hungary, Cardinal Mindszenty[271] might prove to be such a leader and unifying force.

In Poland as well as in Hungary, Mr. Dulles described the economic problem as acute.

[....]

---

[267] See *FRUS, 1955–1957*, vol. 25, 358, fn 2.

[268] Director of Central Intelligence—i.e. Allen Dulles.

[269] This statement, in this form, is untrue. The Hungarian army in general behaved rather passively during the revolution.

[270] See Document No. 50.

[271] On the evening of October 30, Cardinal Mindszenty was released from house arrest. [Footnote from source text.]

3. U.S. Policy Toward Developments In Poland And Hungary (NSC Action No. 1623; SNIE 12–2–56; NSC 5616)

The National Security Council:

Deferred action on NSC 5616 until a subsequent meeting.

S. EVERETT GLEASON

[Source: Foreign Relations of the United States, 1955–1957, *vol. 25 (Washington, D.C.: United States Government Printing Office, 1990), 358–359.]*

DOCUMENT NO. 63: Cryptogram from the Polish Ambassador in Budapest, Adam Willman, to Warsaw, November 1, 1956

In this encrypted cable, Polish Ambassador Adam Willman[272] in Budapest reports to the Polish leadership about his conversation with Imre Nagy and János Kádár on October 31. The document is an interesting example of communications between officials of two satellite states. The Hungarians clearly hope that the Poles will be sympathetic to their aim of getting the Red Army to withdraw from their territory. According to Willman, the Hungarians believe this is the "central problem" and that they are not sure the Kremlin intends to pull out. Nagy and Kádár confide in the ambassador that after the Soviet withdrawal, Hungary will immediately leave the Warsaw Pact. They add that they are investigating "Hungarian neutrality of the Austrian, Swiss type or coexistence of the Yugoslav type." The Hungarians were also consulting with the Yugoslavs at this point. As of October 31, they still hoped to negotiate neutral status for Hungary with the Soviets, but the next day's news of impending intervention led them to the desperate step of declaring neutrality unilaterally.

TOP SECRET!

CRYPTOGRAM NO. 17858

FROM BUDAPEST, CABLED 1.11.56, 18:00 HRS., RECEIVED 2.11, 01:44 HRS. RECEIVED AT THE CRYPTOGRAM SECTION 2.11, 03:10 HRS.

FLASH V[ERY] URGENT

[Maria] Wierna

I am communicating the substance of discussions held yesterday evening as requested by comrade Gomułka and comrade Cyrankiewicz with Nagy and Kádár. As requested, the substance of the discussions was transmitted yesterday by telephone directly to comrade Cyrankiewicz.

The discussants each believe that the withdrawal of the Soviet military from Hungary is the central problem. This demand is put forward by the workers, the youth, and the intelligentsia. The workers announced a strike until the time of the withdrawal of the [Soviet] military. This results in a daily loss of about 300 million Ft. The Hungarian government turned to the Supreme Soviet of the USSR to propose immediate negotiations and in the quickest manner possible.

One hundred and thirty [Soviet] tanks arrived at Nyíregyháza, not far from the Soviet-Hungarian frontier, and at Cegléd, the headquarters of the [Soviet] Third Army.[273]

Hungarians are trying to discover [officially from the Soviets] if [they are] securing [strategic areas in Hungary to make a quick] military withdrawal [from the country]. After the Soviet military pulls out of Hungary, the Hungarians will leave the Warsaw Pact. [They are] investigating Hungarian neutrality of the Austrian, Swiss type or coexistence of the Yugoslav type. They are consulting with Yugoslavia on the latter. [They are] also investigating the possibility of friendly bilateral agreements with neighbors. They ask for our advice and opinion. Situation tense, military activities in principle have ceased. [Hungarian] military and security forces are

---

[272] Adam Willman was ambassador to Hungary from 1955–1959. The addressee, Maria Wierna, was director-general of the Ministry of Foreign Affairs.

[273] Nyíregyháza is located about 280 km from Budapest and about 60 km from the former Hungary-USSR border; Cegléd is 70 km east of the Hungarian capital.

far from up to strength and not stabilized. The government's program causes discontent in Győr, Pécs, Miskolc. Submitting themselves to the government in principle are the overwhelming majority of new local authorities in Budapest and in the provinces. Active, small bands of fascist elements or those released from prison search for communists at night and kill them; there are lynchings. For a short period Marosán—the former deputy premier—was taken away. Factories, mines, transport immobilized. Reserve provisions could be drained shortly. The government and Trade Unions appealed to the workers to resume their jobs. The Committee of Young Revolutionaries refused to sign the appeal. Nagy asked the Social Democrats to help in the mobilization with the aim of launching production. New parties: Smallholders, Social Democrats, and National Peasants are actively organizing themselves. In the Smallholders' Party the main role is played by Béla Kovács. He believes that there are too many communists in the Government. He also believes that it is not possible to return to the old world of capitalists and bankers. The Social Democrats are led by the right wing with [Anna] Kéthly at the head. The Government stands firmly in favor of upholding the basic gains made to date in building socialism. It foresees small private enterprise, a completely voluntary cooperative economy, freedom to leave the cooperatives, return the land to the peasants. The HWP has collapsed. From what remains, a Hungarian Socialist Workers' Party is to emerge. Strong battles are being fought over the new party. The parties, except the HWP, will be ready for quick, secret, and free elections based on a multi-party system. There still exists the possibility of Catholic parties. [Cardinal József] Mindszenty as of yesterday has not taken a position. International trade agreements will be checked at a later time. They [Hungarians] will take steps to attempt to change debts from short-to-long term. They expect to bring in a new loan, if at all possible from our [socialist] camp. Yugoslav envoy Soldatić has expressed sympathy for the government; political and often material support. Romania and Bulgaria, besides a declaration of medical assistance, remain silent. The Czechs have taken, according to Nagy, a positive political position. The main effort of Kádár and Nagy is to halt a further move to the right. They had to make concessions for the moment in response to force, and in my opinion the HWP does not possess any forces. Nagy, characterizing the uprising, underlined that the majority of insurgents are workers; very many party members. The current social mood [Nagy] characterized as anger against the continued presence of the Soviet military and lawlessness on the part of the Security Organs; anger against party functionaries. Many communists say: better to die than to live. Nagy and Kádár ask that we uphold their positions regarding [Hungarian] relations with the USSR, the withdrawal of the [Soviet] military and from the Warsaw Pact, especially in the U.N., for medical aid, glass, cement and wood, for coal and foundry coke before the Winter.

They ask that we communicate our positions firstly regarding political matters. I informed them that comrade Cyrankiewicz will forward a reply to us at one in the evening or two in the morning.

(—)WILLMAN

DECIPHERED 2.11.56, 08:10 HRS

[Source: Archiwum Ministerwstwa Spraw Zagranicznich (AMSZ), zespól depesz, wiazka 48, teczka 612. Szyfrogramy ambasady PRL w Budapeszcie do polskiego MSZ, paz dziernik-grudzien 1956 r., k. 90–92. Published in János Tischler, Rewolucja węgierska 1956 w polskich dokumentach *(Warsaw: Instytut Studiów Politycznych PAN, 1995). Translated by L.W. Gluchowski.]*

DOCUMENT NO. 64: Minutes of the Nagy Government's Fourth Cabinet Meeting, November 1, 1956

The Hungarian Cabinet met in the afternoon of November 1 for its second session of the day. Yurii Andropov was invited to the meeting to explain the re-entry of Soviet troops into the country, but his attempt to play up Moscow's good intentions was unconvincing. The Cabinet decided unanimously (János Kádár included) to renounce Hungary's membership in the Warsaw Pact and declare the country's neutrality. Simultaneously, the government turned to the United Nations with the request that the four great powers jointly "help in defending" Hungary's neutral status. The decision amounted to a heroic, last-ditch effort to save the revolution. For the first time under the Soviet empire, an Eastern European government headed by a communist had turned to the Western powers for political assistance. However, Imre Nagy had no illusion about the West's willingness or capability to come to Hungary's rescue. While addressing a second telegram to U.N. Secretary General Dag Hammarskjöld on November 2 (see Document No. 74), Nagy, fully aware of the nature of Soviet imperial thinking, was also doing everything he could behind the scenes to convince the Kremlin that his government was in control of the situation and that Hungary represented no threat to Moscow.

NOVEMBER 1, 1956

Present:
Imre Nagy, Zoltán Tildy, János Kádár, Ferenc Erdei, Géza Losonczy

Also attanding: István Dobi.

1. The Cabinet commissions Deputy Prime Minister József Bognár to temporarily supervise financial affairs and make sure that all financial institutions are working and properly directed. In the case of general economic measures he should involve Zoltán Vas in the decision-making.

2. The Soviet ambassador in Budapest, Andropov, could not satisfactorily answer the questions of the National Government regarding further Soviet troops entering at the eastern border. Consequently Imre [sic: István] Kovács, chief of the General Staff, had to reveal to the ambassador in the presence of the members of the Cabinet details of Hungarian military observations about military movements, which undoubtedly prove that major Soviet military forces had crossed the border and are making their way towards Budapest.

Considering this situation, the Cabinet makes the following decisions:

a) It immediately issues a declaration of neutrality.

b) The Hungarian government immediately renounces the Warsaw Treaty and declares Hungary's neutrality, at the same time seeking recourse to the United Nations, asking the four great powers for help in defending the country's neutrality. The Hungarian government asked the U.N. secretary general in a telegram to put the issue on the agenda with special dispatch.

c) The heads of diplomatic missions resident in Budapest will be informed of the above decisions.

d) Finally, the decisions will be publicly announced partly through a radio speech by Imre Nagy and partly through a government statement on the radio and in the press.

e) At the same time, the Hungarian National Government will take the opportunity for negotiations offered by the Soviet Union, and immediately appoint a committee, asking the Soviet government to set the time and place of negotiations as soon as possible.

f) Finally, the Cabinet told Ambassador Andropov if Soviet troops are withdrawn from Hungary in the shortest amount of time allowed by such a military operation, then they will annul their telegram to the United Nations.

[Source: MOL, XX–5–h, Nagy Imre és társai pere, Minisztertanácsi jegyzőkönyvek, 25. köt., pp. 103–104.; MOL, XIX–A–83–a. 160. d., pp. 107–108. Originally published in Ferenc Glatz, ed., "A kormány és a párt vezető szerveinek dokumentumaiból, 1956. október 23–november 4," História 11, nos. 4–5 (1989): 49. Translated by Csaba Farkas.]

DOCUMENT NO. 65: Report from Yurii Andropov in Budapest to the CPSU CC Presidium, November 1, 1956

The Soviet ambassador gave Moscow an account of the Hungarian Cabinet session held that afternoon. Led by Imre Nagy, he reports, the cabinet protested the influx of Soviet troops into Hungary and informed Andropov for the first time that Hungary would renounce the Warsaw Pact effective immediately and declare neutrality. Interestingly, Andropov makes an effort to record the emotional reactions of everyone present. Although he notes that "Kádár supported Nagy" when the prime minister demanded an explanation from Andropov for the military movements, Andropov believes that Kádár was "reluctant" when Nagy raised the issue of neutrality. That same evening, at Andropov's invitation and through the mediation of Ferenc Münnich, Kádár secretly made his way to the Soviet embassy where he agreed to travel to Moscow for confidential discussions. He left for the Soviet Union the next day.

CODED TELEGRAM

TOP SECRET
NOT TO BE COPIED

FROM BUDAPEST
PRIORITY

Today, on November 1, at 7 p.m.[274] I received an invitation to the inner cabinet meeting of the Council of Ministers of the HPR.[275] Imre Nagy, who chaired the meeting, informed the participants in a rather nervous tone that in the morning he had addressed the Soviet ambassador in connection with the Soviet troops crossing the Hungarian border and advancing towards the heart of the country. Nagy "demanded" an explanation in that matter. The way Nagy said all this suggested that he expected me to affirm that he had really expressed his protests to me. Also, he kept looking at Zoltán Tildy all along, as if expecting support.

Tildy behaved with dignity. He spoke immediately after Imre Nagy, in a tone that was much friendlier and calmer. He said that if the Soviet troops continued their advance on Budapest, there would be a scandal and the government would be forced to resign. Tildy would like to prevent the workers' anger turning against the Soviet Union.

Tildy said that he insisted that the Soviet troops—at least those which are not stationed in Hungary under the terms of the Warsaw Pact[276]—be withdrawn without delay.

Kádár supported Nagy; Haraszti[277] and Ferenc Erdei spoke very nervously and in a manner unfriendly to us. Dobi remained silent.

After they spoke I offered my views—in keeping with the instructions I had received. Nagy immediately replied that although he accepted that my statement was good, it did not answer the Hungarian Government's question.

---

[274] 5:00 p.m. Hungarian time.

[275] For the minutes of this meeting, see Document No. 64.

[276] In addition to the Soviet forces stationed in Hungary under the terms of the Warsaw Treaty, further units entered the country after the first intervention, especially after October 31. This took place without the approval of the Hungarian government, even though it would have been required under the relevant provisions of the Warsaw Treaty.

[277] Sándor Haraszti, journalist, was one of the leading figures of the party opposition around Imre Nagy. He served as editor-in-chief of *Népszabadság* from October 31–November 4. After the Soviet invasion he took refuge in the Yugoslav Embassy and was later deported to Romania. Sentenced to six years in prison in 1958, he was amnestied in 1960. According to the official minutes of the session (see Document No. 64), Haraszti was not present at the government meeting Andropov discusses.

Nagy proposed that, since the Soviet government had not stopped the advance of the Soviet troops, nor had it given a satisfactory explanation of its actions, they confirm the motion passed that morning regarding Hungary's giving notice of cessation of Warsaw Pact membership, a declaration of neutrality, and an appeal to the United Nations for the guarantee of Hungary's neutrality by the Four Great Powers. In the event that the Soviet Government stopped the advance of the Soviet troops and withdrew them beyond its own borders with immediate effect, (the government of the Hungarian People's Republic will form a judgment on compliance on the basis of the reports of its own armed forces) the Hungarian Government would withdraw its request to the United Nations, but Hungary would still remain neutral. Erdei and Losonczy strongly supported this reply by Nagy. Tildy's response was affirmative but more reserved, while Kádár's reaction was reluctant. Dobi remained silent.

One hour later the Embassy received the note from the Ministry of Foreign Affairs, declaring that since a strong Soviet Army force had crossed the border that day and had entered Hungarian territory against the firm protest of the Hungarian government, the government was leaving the Warsaw Pact effective immediately. The Ministry of Foreign Affairs asked the embassy to notify the Soviet government of this decision immediately. They sent notes with a similar content to every embassy and diplomatic mission in Budapest.[278]

Note: we have information that, at the instigation of the Social Democrats, the workers of all the enterprises in Hungary have declared a two-week strike, demanding the withdrawal of Soviet troops from Hungary.[279]

1.11.56

Andropov

[Source:AVP RF. 059a, op. 4, p. 6, d. 5, ll.17–19. Originally published in János M. Rainer, "1956—The other side of the story: Five documents from the Yeltsin file," The Hungarian Quarterly 34, no. 129 (Spring 1993): 108–110.]

[278] See Document No. 66.

[279] The general strike began spontaneously on October 24. The idea of continuing the strikes until Soviet troops had left Hungary was presented by the workers' councils. Nevertheless, on November 1, the day Andropov sent his report, the negotiations between the government and the workers' councils resulted in an agreement to return to work.

DOCUMENT NO. 66: Telegram from Imre Nagy to Diplomatic Missions in Budapest Declaring Hungary's Neutrality, November 1, 1956

Nagy, then serving both as prime minister and acting foreign minister, sent the following telegram to every foreign diplomatic mission in Budapest in a desperate attempt to prevent another Soviet intervention. The Hungarian demand for a withdrawal of Soviet troops, the denunciation of the Warsaw Pact, and a declaration of neutrality meant an open break with the Moscow-led socialist camp. Unfortunately, the appeal to the four great powers and the United Nations to protect Hungary's neutrality was an impossible demand under the circumstances, since firm action by the Western powers would have risked direct confrontation with the Soviet Union and, many in the West feared, even nuclear war.

The prime minister of the Hungarian People's Republic, in his role as acting foreign minister, informs your excellency of the following:

The Government of the Hungarian People's Republic has received trustworthy reports of the entrance of new Soviet military units into Hungary. The President of the Council of Ministers, as acting Foreign Minister, summoned Mr. Andropov, the Soviet Union's special and plenipotentiary ambassador to Hungary, and most firmly objected to the entrance of new military units into Hungary. He demanded the immediate and fast withdrawal of the Soviet units. He announced to the Soviet ambassador that the Hungarian government was withdrawing from the Warsaw Pact, simultaneously declaring Hungary's neutrality, and that it was turning to the United Nations and asking the four Great Powers to help protect its neutrality.[280]

The Soviet Ambassador acknowledged the objection and announcement of the president of the Council of Ministers and acting foreign minister, and promised to ask his government for a reply without delay.

Your Excellency, please accept with this my most sincere respects.

[Source: Hungarian People's Republic, The Counter-Revolutionary Conspiracy of Imre Nagy and his Accomplices *(Budapest: Information Bureau of the Council of Ministers, [1958]). Also published in József Kiss, Zoltán Ripp and István Vida, ed., "Források a Nagy Imre-kormány külpolitikájának történetéhez,"* Társadalmi Szemle *48, no. 5 (1993): 86. Translated by David Evans.]*

---

[280] See Document No. 67.

DOCUMENT NO. 67: Telegram from Imre Nagy to U.N. Secretary General Dag Hammarskjöld, November 1, 1956

In his first telegram to U.N. Secretary General Dag Hammarskjöld, Imre Nagy describes the current crisis, requests that the Hungarian issue be put on the agenda for the next regular meeting of the General Assembly, and asks that Hammarskjöld help persuade the four great powers to come to Hungary's assistance.

However, Nagy was fully aware that the fate of the Hungarian revolution depended mainly on Moscow, and he wanted to hang onto the possibility of negotiations, even under these desperate circumstances. He therefore tells Hammarskjöld that the Hungarian government wants the crisis to be raised specifically at the UNGA meeting set for November 12. The Security Council had begun discussing Hungary as early as October 28, and the emergency special session of the General Assembly was convened on this very day, November 1, to debate the emergency in the Middle East. Most likely, Nagy intended to give the Soviets time to consider the offer made to Andropov the previous day—that if the Soviets pulled back all troops to the borders, the Hungarian government would immediately withdraw its appeal to the U.N., although the country would retain its neutral status. This offer held out much higher hopes for a satisfactory outcome than any potential U.N. resolution, but for it to succeed the U.N. had to be kept from taking any immediate action detrimental to the Soviet Union. This interpretation is supported by the fact that wording in the original draft of the telegram claiming that Hungary "has been attacked by armed force" from the Soviet Union and requesting "immediate action" was omitted in the final version.

The President of the Council of Ministers of the Hungarian People's Republic as designated Minister of Foreign Affairs has the honor to communicate the following to Your Excellency.

Reliable reports have reached the Government of the Hungarian People's Republic that further Soviet units are entering into Hungary. The President of the Council of Ministers in his capacity of Minister for Foreign Affairs summoned M. Andropov, Ambassador Extraordinary and Plenipotentiary of the Soviet Union to Hungary, and expressed his strongest protest against the entry of further Soviet troops into Hungary. He demanded the instant and immediate withdrawal of these Soviet forces. He informed the Soviet Ambassador that the Hungarian Government immediately repudiates the Warsaw Treaty and at the same time declares Hungary's neutrality, turns to the United Nations, and requests the help of the four great powers in defending the country's neutrality. The Government of the Hungarian People's Republic made the Declaration of Neutrality on November 1, 1956; therefore I request Your Excellency promptly to put on the agenda of the forthcoming General Assembly of the United Nations the question of Hungary's neutrality and the defence of this neutrality by the four great powers.

I take this opportunity to convey to Your Excellency the expression of my highest consideration.

[Source: U. N. Document A/3251, November 1, 1956. Originaly published in Paul E. Zinner, ed., National Communism and Popular Revolt in Eastern Europe: A Selection of Documents on Events in Poland and Hungary, February–November, 1956 *(New York: Columbia University Press, 1956), 462–3.]*

DOCUMENT NO. 68: Imre Nagy's Declaration of Hungarian Neutrality (Radio Broadcast), November 1, 1956

On the same day that he forwarded a summary of the declaration on neutrality to diplomatic missions in Budapest (See Document No. 66), Nagy delivered a radio address to the nation announcing the declaration. By the end of October, an announcement of this sort had already become the main demand of every revolutionary group, and enjoyed virtually unanimous public support. By answering this demand, the government thus took a major step toward resolving the national crisis. The Workers' Councils of Budapest responded by calling for a return to work on November 5, and other parts of the economy such as public transportation began to get underway again. Local Workers' Council delegations that had previously been deeply distrustful of the Nagy government assured him of their support. But by this time the die had been cast. Either despite or, in part, because of these important signs of internal consolidation, Soviet preparations for military intervention continued.

People of Hungary! The Hungarian national Government, imbued with profound responsibility toward the Hungarian people and history, and giving expression to the undivided will of the Hungarian millions, declares the neutrality of the Hungarian People's Republic.

The Hungarian people, on the basis of independence and equality and in accordance with the spirit of the U. N. Charter, wishes to live in true friendship with its neighbors, the Soviet Union, and all the peoples of the world.

The Hungarian people desire the consolidation and further development of the achievements of its national revolution without joining any power blocs. The century-old dream of the Hungarian people is thus fulfilled. The revolutionary struggle fought by the Hungarian heroes of the past and present has at last carried the cause of freedom and independence to victory. The heroic struggle has made it possible to implement, in the international relations of our people, its fundamental national interest—neutrality.

We appeal to our neighbors, countries near and far, to respect the unalterable decision of our people. It is true indeed that today our people are as united in this decision as perhaps never before in their history.

Working millions of Hungary! With revolutionary determination, self-sacrificing work, and the consolidation of order; protect and strengthen our country—free, independent, democratic, and neutral Hungary.

[Source: Paul E. Zinner, ed., National Communism and Popular Revolt in Eastern Europe: A Selection of Documents on Events in Poland and Hungary, February–November, 1956 *(New York: Columbia University Press, 1956), 463–4.]*

DOCUMENT NO. 69: Minutes of the PZPR Politburo Meeting Reacting to the Soviet Decision to Use Military Force in Hungary, November 1, 1956

This top-level PZPR session took place after three members of the Polish leadership (Gomułka, Cyrankiewicz and Ochab) learned about the imminent second Soviet intervention at a meeting with Khrushchev and a Soviet delegation at the Soviet-Polish border city of Brest. Gomułka "dissented" at that meeting, saying he could not unreservedly agree with the idea of military intervention by a foreign power since Poland had just faced a similar danger twelve days earlier. Following suit, the PZPR Politburo also reacted negatively to the news. The next day the leadership published a condemnation of foreign intervention in the Polish press, but at the same time they accompanied it with a description of the dangers of reactionary and counterrevolutionary developments. The Politburo also declared that withdrawing Soviet troops from Poland would run counter to the fundamental interests of the Polish state—part of Gomułka's strategy to use the German threat to consolidate the PZPR's position.

Minutes No. 135, meeting of the Political Committee on November 1, 1956

Comrades present: Cyrankiewicz, Gomułka, Jędrychowski, Loga-Sowiński,[281] Morawski, Ochab, Rapacki,[282] Zambrowski, Zawadzki.

Agenda:
1. The Hungarian situation.
2. Personnel issues.

Regarding the first item on the agenda—The Political Committee surveyed the political situation in Hungary and the issue of Soviet troops entering Hungary.

The Political Committee expressed a negative reaction concerning the Soviet Union's armed intervention in Hungary.

The following decision was made: The Political Committee has to communicate to the nation the party's policy, namely, that it is the Hungarian nation that is to defend and sustain the achievements of the people's power and socialism in Hungary, rather than an external intervention.

A further decision was made: On party assemblies of November 2 the report of the Political Committee about the Hungarian situation and the party's opinion on Polish-Hungarian relations must be read out.[283]

[...]

[Source: Archiwum Akt Nowych (AAN), KC PZPR, paczka 15, tom 58. Protokoły Biura Politycznego KC PZPR za rok 1956, numer 73, oryginały podpisane, kart 237. Published in János Tischler, Rewolucja węgierska 1956 w polskich dokumentach (Warsaw: Instytut Studiów Politycznych PAN, 1995), 153–154. Translated by Csaba Farkas.]

[281] Ignacy Loga-Sowiński was a member of the PZPR CC Politburo from 1956–1971 and chairman of the Central Council of Polish Trade Unions.

[282] Adam Rapacki was a member of the PZPR CC Politburo from 1949–1968 and foreign minister from 1956–1968.

[283] In its information release for party organizations, the PZPR PC emphasized that "...the Polish government believes that the armed intervention of foreign troops is a bad thing—even if they do so in the name of defending freedom and socialism—if the Hungarian nation and the Hungarian working class do not demand that." See János Tischler, *Rewolucja węgierska 1956 w polskich dokumentach* (Warsaw: Instytut Studiów Politycznych PAN, 1995), 136.

DOCUMENT NO. 70: Working Notes from the CPSU CC Presidium Session with the Participation of János Kádár and Ferenc Münnich, November 2, 1956

Vladimir Malin's notes document a speech to the CPSU CC Presidium by János Kádár on the situation in Hungary. Nikita Khrushchev and Georgi Malenkov were absent at the time, traveling to Yugoslavia to discuss the impending invasion with Tito. Although Kádár points out the danger posed by counterrevolutionary forces, he emphasizes that "everyone" in Hungary "[has] demanded the withdrawal of Soviet troops." He defends the position of the Nagy-led coalition government—" the coalition parties don't want counterrev[olution]"—and apparently believes that the situation can be consolidated on the basis of socialism if Soviet troops pull out. He relates the Hungarian Cabinet decision to declare Hungary's neutrality and appeal to the U.N. but assures the Presidium that if the ongoing Soviet troop movements turn out to be "just maneuvers, they'll withdraw the question from the U.N." Significantly, Kádár warns that in the event of a military solution to the crisis "the morale of the Communists will be reduced to zero" and the "socialist countries will suffer losses. . . . If order is restored by force, the authority of the socialist countries will be eroded."

Participants: Bulganin, Voroshilov, Kaganovich, Mikoyan, Molotov, Saburov, Suslov, Brezhnev, Cdes. Münnich, Kádár, and Bata

Exchange of Opinions about the Situation in Hungary

[Kádár:][284]
An assessment.
The intelligentsia is taking the lead;
the oppositionists are supporters of Nagy;
the armed groups are headed by
party figures, including
Dudás, an engineer.
When the uprising ended, they spoke with the rebels;
these were workers, the leaders of the group;[285]
they arrived at the coalition government;
they didn't want this;
they're seeking the ouster of the Rákosi clique.

The fought for the withdrawal of troops and for the order of people!s democracy.

Mass demonstrations are taking place on the periphery;
these didn't include any goal—to destroy the order of people's democracy; many demands about democratization, and social demands.

"Initially we did not see this, we classified it as a counterrevolution and with this turned [the people] against us—they did not feel themselves to be counterrevolutionaries."
I personally took part in one meeting (of the conference) and no one wanted counterrevolution.[286]

---

[284] Although it is not indicated in the notes it is clear that the speaker was Kádár. The notes often indicate the third person even when Kádár is actually speaking in the first person.

[285] Kádár's description of the rebel leaders is based on his meeting with the commanders of the Tűzoltó Street group on October 30—the only armed group he had the chance to meet. Reports of this meeting were also announced over the radio, see Varga, *A forradalom hangja*, 244–245.

But when we spoke with the leaders of the armed groups, inside these groups—armed groups of counterrevolutionary nature have emerged.

I have to say that everyone demanded the withdrawal of Soviet troops. We didn't clarify how the counterrevolutionaries managed to disseminate this counterrevolutionary propaganda.

The strike is a demand for the withdrawal of troops: we may starve, but the troops must be withdrawn.

Yesterdey there was a conference.

They were speaking about the Declaration of the Soviet government and the Declaration of neutrality.

Stated that we will go back to work.
But Soviet troops were being redeployed, and the news quickly spread.

The government will not be considered to have any authority because of the coalition nature of the government.
All forces are seeking the restoration of their parties. Each group wants to take power into its own hands. This undermines the authority of the government even further.
The Soc.-Democrats are especially distinctive in this regard.

In the inner cabinet the Soc.-Dems. were given one spot. But they haven't named a candidate; they don't want to act in solidarity with Nagy.[287]
Nagy's policy has counterrev. aspects to it.
The soldiers freed Cardinal Mindszenty.

The Austrians support a fascist organization
(in West Germany—a Hungarian organization) 35 thous. people (Horthyites).[288]

The weak link is the HWP; it has ceased to exist:
some have been killed (workers),[289] some were saved.

The leaders of 1/3 of the obkoms [province committees] are taking part in revolutionary committees (for the region and county [oblast]).
Local bodies have been destroyed.

On Nov. 1 at noon—the point of view in the government is that it's necessary to hold discussions with the Soviet gov't and to have the troops withdrawn by a certain time.
But this isn't accurate.
The coalition parties don't want counterrev.
Tildy and other cdes. are afraid of Ferenc Nagy.[290]

[286] Presumably, this refers to the above-mentioned meeting with the Tűzoltó Street leaders on October 30. See the previous footnote.

[287] See footnote 206 above.

[288] Kádár is presumably referring to the émigré organization the Fraternal Community of Hungarian Fighters which was one of the main targets of the Hungarian intelligence service before 1956. The number is certainly exaggerated, nor does the alleged support of the Austrian government correspond to the facts.

[289] In reality, only a very small number of HWP functionaries were killed during the revolution. See footnote 296 in Part Three.

Those in the émigré community: they're afraid of them.

Tildy is afraid of [Béla] Kovács, but he's better than Tildy and is a smart man.

Kovács gave a speech in Pécs: we are creating a Smallholders party, but we can't struggle on the basis of the old program.

He is against the return of the landowners and capitalists.

But they aren't putting forth demands that are popular in the nation.

Hour by hour the situation is moving rightward.

2 questions:
1) the government's decision about neutrality,
2) the party.

How did the decision about the neutrality emerge?

The strong impression is that there's an organized departure of troops.

The Declaration—a good impression and a reassuring gesture.

But the masses are very stirred-up and are reacting harshly.

There were movements of Sov. troops, which alarmed the government and masses.

The gov't is doing one thing, and the troops another.

They reported that Soviet troops had crossed the border in transport vehicles. Hungarian formations are entrenched.

What should be done—to shoot or not to shoot?

They summoned Andropov. Andropov said that these are railroad workers.

Hungarians at the border sent back telegrams saying that these definitely are not railroad workers.

Then they reported that Soviet tanks are moving into Szolnok.

This was at noon. The government has been thrown into a nervous state.

They summoned Andropov. He responded: the withdrawal of wounded soldiers.

Nagy was convinced that a strike against Budapest is being prepared. Tildy requested that Hungarian tanks approach the parliament.

In the army—a Rev. Council,

Maléter, [István] Kovács, and Király are not subordinate to the gov't.[291]

They don't want bad ministers.

The whole gov't was inclined to the view that if the troops move toward Budapest, the city must be defended.

In this atmosphere the idea of neutrality arose.

The initiator of it was Zoltán Tildy.

Everyone supported it.

I was a supporter of the view that no sorts of steps should be taken without having spoken with Andropov.

The whole cabinet, other than Kádár, declared that the Sov. gov't is deceiving the Hungarian gov't.

[290] Ferenc Nagy was chairman of the Smallholders' Party from 1945 and prime minister from February 1946. In July 1947, he was forced to resign and emigrated to the United States. After the outbreak of the revolution, he immediately traveled to Vienna. The sudden appearance of one of the most prominent emigré leaders caused serious diplomatic complications for the Austrians, who feared that it would throw their neutrality into question. At the request of the Austrian government, Nagy was forced to leave the country after only one day. He returned to the United States via Paris.

[291] When Kádár left Hungary, Major-General Pál Maléter was first deputy defense minister, Major-General István Kovács chief of the general staff and Major-General Béla Király head of the Revolutionary Armed Forces Committee and commander of the National Guard. They were all members of the Revolutionary National Defense Commission established at the Ministry of Defense on October 31. However, contrary to what Kádár stated, they faithfully executed the orders of the government.

They deferred it for two hours.[292]

The Sov. gov't explanation didn't satisfy them. They told Andropov that they'll be taking this step. When Andropov left, they took their step about neutrality and decided to issue an appeal to the UN. If these are just maneuvers, they'll withdraw the question from the UN.

When Andropov left, Kádár voted for neutrality, too.

The renaming of the party: the Hungarian Socialist Workers' Party (a name used back in 1925).[293]

The HWP has been compromised in the view of the overwhelming masses.

The peak of the HWP's authority was in 1948 (the alliance with the Soc.-Dems.).

The Rajk affair shattered its authority.

About the future.

Yesterday I voted for these two decision of the government.

If they will withdraw Soviet troops in the near future (within two-three months)—the decision on the withdrawal of troops is the important thing—our party and other parties would be able to fight against the counterrev.

But I'm not sure this will be successful.

There's no unity within the coalition.

My point of view is: if the Soc.-Dems. and the Smallholders party are going to operate on the basis of their old programs, they will be deceitful.

The people believe in nationalization and regard it as their affair.

If the Communists declare that they support nationalization, the authority of the other parties will stop increasing.

The looming danger—the counterrevolution wouldn't embolden these coalition parties.

My view is that there's another path.

Use the armed forces to support Hungary.

But then there will be squabbles.

The use of military force will be destructive and lead to bloodshed.

What will happen then? The morale of the Communists will be reduced to zero.

The socialist countries will suffer losses.

Is there a guarantee that such circumstances will not arise in other countries?

The counterrev. forces are not meager. But this is a matter of struggle. If order is restored by force, the authority of the socialist countries will be eroded.

Münnich:

A gloomy situation.

Why did this situation arise?

The isolation of the leaders from the masses.

Certainty that the regime exists and is preserved only through the support of the USSR.

This is the source of anti-Soviet sentiments

(facts: soccer,[294] radio broadcasts[295]).

---

[292] This refers to the declaration of neutrality.

[293] In 1925, the left-wing opposition, excluded from the Social Democratic Party, formed a party with an almost identical name. The party also served as a cover organization for the then-illegal communist party.

[294] According to widespread belief, the legendary Hungarian soccer team of the early 1950s, the so called "Golden Team," was not allowed to beat the Soviet team for political reasons (their matches usually ended in a draw). The first Hungarian win actually came only a few weeks before the revolution. For Soviet complaints concerning the "nationalist" atmosphere of the soccer matches, see Document No. 5.

[295] This obviously refers to RFE and other western radio stations.

In Hungary: total chaos.
What would be the result if the troops are withdrawn—this would respond to the sentiment of the masses.

Counterrev. elements are receiving reinforcement, and their actions are not being stopped. We have no more forces left.

On the military nature of the events.
Anti-Soviet sentiments are being spread by counterrev. elements.

Cde. Kádár—a concrete request:
preserve the party cadres.[296]

Cde. Bata:
The question is pointedly raised about the withdraw of Soviet troops. Everything all of them are doing will lead to a confrontation of Soviet and Hungarian troops.
I was a witness when a Hungarian unit opened fire on Soviet troops.
The Soviets didn't respond. Further such restraint couldn't be expected from even the most disciplined army.
Whether deliberately or not, the government is laying the groundwork for a confrontation of Soviet and Hungarian troops.
Order must be restored through a military dictatorship.
Change the policy of the government.

Appendix

WORKING NOTES FROM THE SESSION ON 2 NOVEMBER 1956 (RE: POINT IV OF PROTOCOL NO. 50)

On the Plan for Measures Concerning Hungary
(Zhukov, Serov, Konev, Molotov, Mikoyan, Kaganovich, Bulganin, Voroshilov)

    1) to speak about the threat of fascism posed by the Horthyites;
        the threat to our homeland,
        they want to use it as a base against our country;
        the workers and peasants support us.
        Adopt it with amendments.[297]

2) send Cdes. Mikoyan and Brezhnev
        (decide on 3 Nov. 1956).

        Approve the plan.

[Source: TsKhSD, F. 3, op. 12, D. 1006, Ll. 23–30, compiled by V. N. Malin. Originally published in English in the Cold War International History Project Bulletin *no. 8/9 (Winter 1996/1997), 395–97. Translated by Mark Kramer.]*

---

[296] Kádár's request presumably aimed—in case of a military intervention—at preventing purges among those communist leaders who sided with the revolution.

[297] Given the participants and the order of their contribution, it is likely that this part of the discussion dealt with the military plan for intervention. The amendments were changes proposed to the orders of Marshal Konev. See footnote 239 above.

DOCUMENT NO. 71: Minutes of the Nagy Government's Fifth Cabinet Meeting, November 2, 1956

Based on the Soviet government declaration of October 30 (see Document No. 50), the Hungarian government initiated talks with Moscow the following day on withdrawing Soviet troops from the country. Although the Soviets' real intentions became increasingly obvious in light of the arrival of new forces into Hungary that same day, the Hungarians were pleased with the Kremlin's decision, on November 2, to start negotiations in Budapest immediately. Nagy and his associates assumed—mistakenly—that no military intervention would take place as long as these talks were underway. Reflecting the same hope that the Hungarians could gain time to work toward domestic consolidation, the Cabinet took several other steps, such as nominating the Hungarian delegation to the forthcoming session of the U.N. General Assembly.

Present:
Imre Nagy
Zoltán Tildy
Ferenc Erdei
Géza Losonczy

1. The Cabinet decided to send a letter with regard to further negotiations on the withdrawal of Soviet troops.[298] The content of the letter is as follows. The Cabinet suggested Warsaw as an ideal location for negotiations, which should be held immediately. The delegation should be a government delegation, keeping the coalition nature of the government in mind as far as its composition. Accordingly, the Cabinet set up the five-person delegation in the following way: the head of the delegation is Géza Losonczy; the members are József Antall,[299] András Márton, Ferenc Farkas and possibly a member of a workers' council, appointed by Prime Minister Imre Nagy according to the proposition of Zoltán Tildy. (Press coverage.)

2. The Cabinet sets the size of the delegation to be sent to the forthcoming session of the U.N. General Assembly at five members. Concerning its composition, it should be a government delegation, bearing the coalition nature of the government in mind. The Cabinet appointed Imre Nagy head of the delegation; his deputy is Zoltán Tildy, and Anna Kéthly and Béla Kovács are members. Further suggestions should be made and the composition of the delegation should be finalized tomorrow. Furthermore, the Cabinet decided that the Foreign Ministry should start preparing the material for the negotiations immediately.

3. Since the question of reshuffling the government is increasingly urgent, the Cabinet decided that instead of appointing new ministers, the Cabinet should be expanded with new members, on the one hand involving insurgents, on the other hand appointing professionally competent under-secretaries of state to direct the ministries—instead of ministers proper. These functionaries should essentially have the rank of political under-secretary, with the exception that in cases when the solution of personnel questions is not possible, an administrative under-secretary of state should also be appointed. As to the identity of these would-be under-secretaries of state who will direct the ministries, Ferenc Erdei should make suggestions at the next meeting, bearing in mind that the people in question must be approved by the revolutionary committees of the ministries in question.

4. The Cabinet declares the Hungarian Workers' Party's funds in the National Bank's account to be government property, which should be distributed among the coalition parties immediately, today. Concerning this, Deputy Prime Minister József Bognár is to make suggestions.

---

[298] The letter was published in Kiss, Ripp and Vida, "Források a Nagy Imre-kormány," 88–89.

[299] József Antall was one of the leaders of the Smallholder' Party from 1946–1948. During the revolution he took part in the reestablishment of the party and became its director.

5. The Cabinet finds it necessary to examine the country's economic situation immediately, with special emphasis on food and fuel resources, and how wage-payments could be normalized again. On the basis of the results of this survey, further suggestions should be made about the necessary measures. The survey should consider foreign resources as well, both in the form of foreign trade and aid. Deputy Prime Minister József Bognár will submit his suggestions on this issue to the Cabinet for discussion at tomorrow's meeting; therefore a short summary of his proposition will be sent to members of the Cabinet tonight at the latest. (Press coverage.)

6. The Cabinet finds it necessary to issue an official statement.[300] The draft should be prepared within a week; Prime Minister Imre Nagy should organize the preparations within his own sphere of responsibilities, therefore he is to be excused from his official duties as much as possible.

7. The Cabinet decided that, until further notice, they will hold a meeting regularly at 9:00 every morning.

[Source: MOL, XX–5–h, Nagy Imre és társai pere, Minisztertanácsi jegyzőkönyvek, 25. köt., pp. 109–111.; MOL, XIX–A–83–a. 160. d., pp. 109–111. Published in Ferenc Glatz, ed., "A kormány és a párt vezető szerveinek dokumentumaiból, 1956. október 23–november 4," História 11, nos. 4–5 (1989): 49–50. Translated by Csaba Farkas.]

[300] The statement was ultimately never issued.

DOCUMENT NO. 72: Hungarian Government Protest, November 2, 1956

This is the formal protest which Imre Nagy, who was both prime minister and foreign minister at the time, handed to Soviet Ambassador Andropov after it had become clear that Soviet troop movements were now directly threatening Budapest. To avoid a military confrontation, the document proposed holding bilateral talks in Warsaw on Hungary's departure from the Warsaw Pact, "with special regard to the immediate withdrawal of Soviet troops stationed in Hungary." The choice of Warsaw as the location was not without significance; on one level it was meant to indicate the equal status of the parties, Warsaw being the capital of a third country; on another level, Nagy and his associates probably hoped that Poland would be a favorable setting because of the Poles' recent experience in confronting the threat of Soviet force. But it was already too late. Following the CPSU CC Presidium's decision of October 31, preparations for an attack were well under way, and János Kádár and Ferenc Münnich were already in Moscow planning to suppress the revolution.

The Chairman of the Council of Ministers, in his role as Acting Foreign Minister of the Hungarian People's Republic, informs the Budapest Embassy of the Union of Soviet Socialist Republics of the following, and requests [the Embassy] to forward the [information] included in this note immediately to its government:

On October 26, 1956, the Hungarian government requested the government of the Soviet Union to undertake immediate negotiations in connection with the withdrawal of Soviet troops stationed in Hungary on the basis of the Warsaw Treaty, and stated its desire to settle this question through negotiations. With reference to the October 30, 1956 declaration of the government of the Soviet Union approving the Hungarian government's initiative, as well as to the response to this declaration given and published by the government of the Hungarian People's Republic, and [with reference] to the statement of his excellency the Soviet ambassador in Budapest given on his visit to the chairman of the Council of Ministers of the Hungarian People's Republic on November 1, 1956, the Hungarian government announces the following:

Unfortunately, despite the above-mentioned consultations between the two governments, further Soviet units crossed the Hungarian border between October 31 and November 1, 1956. The Hungarian government exerted all efforts in its power to achieve the withdrawal of the troops, but these attempts proved to be in vain. Moreover, the Soviet troops continued their advance and some units surrounded Budapest. As a consequence of all this, the Hungarian government denounced the Warsaw Treaty on November 1, 1956.

Nevertheless, the government of the Hungarian People's Republic has repeatedly declared its desire to maintain to the utmost [its] friendly relationship with the Soviet Union in the future, as well. This relationship should be based on the principles of complete equality, sovereignty, and non-interference in one another's affairs, as well as on respect for the neutrality that was declared by the government of the Hungarian People's Republic on November 1, 1956.

For the sake of this, the government of the Hungarian People's Republic proposes to start immediate negotiations, on the basis of the above-mentioned principles, between the government delegations from the Hungarian People's Republic and the Union of Soviet Socialist Republics concerning the execution of the secession from the Warsaw Pact, with special regard to the immediate withdrawing Soviet troops stationed in Hungary. The Hungarian government proposes Warsaw as the location of these negotiations. Members of the Hungarian government delegation are:

Géza Losonczy, minister of state, head of delegation
József Kővágó,[301]

---

[301] József Kővágó was member of the Smallholders' Party and mayor of Budapest between 1945 and 1947. On October 30, 1956, he was elected a member of the Executive Committee of the Independent Smallholders' party. From November 1 to 4, he served again as mayor of Budapest.

András Márton,
Ferenc Farkas and
Vilmos Zentai.[302]
The Chairman of the Council of Ministers, in his role as Acting Foreign Minister, takes the opportunity to assure the Union of Soviet Socialist Republics of his high esteem.

[Source: MOL, XIX–j–1–j. 11. d. (1956) p. 36. Originally published in József Kiss, Zoltán Ripp and István Vida, ed., "Források a Nagy Imre-kormány külpolitikájának történetéhez," Társadalmi Szemle 48, no. 5 (1993): 88–89. Translated by József Litkei and Maya Nadkarni.]

---

[302] Vilmos Zentai joined the leadership of the reestablished Social Democratic Party beginning October 31, 1956.

DOCUMENT NO. 73: Imre Nagy's *Note Verbale* to the Chiefs of Diplomatic Missions in Budapest Informing of Soviet Military Movements and Hungarian Intentions to Negotiate, November 2, 1956

On the same day of his protest to Soviet Ambassador Andropov (see the previous document), Nagy dispatched the following note to foreign diplomatic missions in Budapest as part of the effort to alert the international community to the crisis and to try to make it more difficult for Moscow to take military acove findings to the attention of the leaders of all the accredited foreign representations in Budapest, and also announces that at the same time it has informed the U.N. Security Council of the latest developments.

The Prime Minister of the Hungarian People's Republic, in his role as acting Foreign Minister, informs your Excellency of the following:

The Government of the Hungarian People's Republic would at all costs like to settle the question of the withdrawal of Soviet troops from Hungary by the route of peaceful negotiation and agreement. It has repeatedly expressed this intention and has nominated preparatory committees which demonstrate its readiness to negotiate, and whose task it is to complete the arrangements or decide what changes need to be made to them. The Hungarian government has communicated its suggestions concerning the composition of these committees and concerning the time and place of negotiations to the Union of Soviet Socialist Republics' ambassador to Budapest.

But despite all this, reliable intelligence sources and reports from our army reconnaissance show that new and substantial Soviet units have crossed the border into Hungary, and are proceeding towards Budapest; they are occupying railway lines, railway stations, and other railway infrastructure. We also have reports of Soviet troop movements in the Western region of Hungary in an East-West direction.

The government of the Hungarian People's Republic believed it necessary to ask for Mr. Andropov, the Soviet Union's ambassador to Budapest, to clarify this issue, and at the same time repeated its protestations about the movement of Soviet troops within Hungary.

The Hungarian Government brings the above findings to the attention of the leaders of all the accredited foreign representations in Budapest, and also announces that at the same time it has informed the [U.N.] Security Council of the latest developments.

Your Excellency, please accept my most sincere respects.

[....]

[Source: MOL, XIX–j–1–j. 11. d. 008083/1956., 9. o. Originally published in József Kiss, Zoltán Ripp and István Vida, ed., "Források a Nagy Imre-kormány külpolitikájának történetéhez," Társadalmi Szemle 48, no. 5 (1993): 89–90. Translated by David Evans.]

DOCUMENT NO. 74: Telegram from Imre Nagy to U.N. Secretary General Dag Hammarskjöld, November 2, 1956

This is Nagy's second telegram to U.N. General Secretary Dag Hammarskjöld. Printed in full in the Hungarian press the next day, it makes clear that he wanted to maintain communications with the Soviets until the very last minute. Instead of asking for an "immediate intervention" by the Security Council, Nagy appeals to the secretary general only to ask the great powers to recognize Hungary's neutrality and to order the Soviet and Hungarian governments to begin negotiating the withdrawal of Soviet troops. He was not interested in trying to get the United Nations to condemn the ongoing Soviet invasion. His main objective was to use Security Council pressure merely to bring the Soviets to the table.

As the President [sic: Chairman] of the Council of Ministers and Designated Foreign Minister of the Hungarian People's Republic I have the honor to bring to the attention of Your Excellency the following additional information:

I have already mentioned in my letter of November 1st that new Soviet military units entered Hungary and that the Hungarian Government informed the Soviet Ambassador in Budapest of this fact, at the same time terminated the Warsaw Pact, declared the neutrality of Hungary, and requested the United Nations to guarantee the neutrality of the country.

On the 2nd of November further and exact information, mainly military reports, reached the Government of the Hungarian People's Republic, according to which large Soviet military units crossed the border of the country, marching toward Budapest. They occupy railway lines, railway stations, and railway safety equipment. Reports also have come about that Soviet military movements of east-west direction are being observed on the territory of Western Hungary.

On the basis of the above-mentioned facts the Hungarian Government deemed it necessary to inform the Embassy of the USSR and all the other Diplomatic Missions in Budapest about these steps directed against our People's Republic.

At the same time, the Government of the Hungarian People's Republic forwarded concrete proposals on the withdrawal of Soviet troops stationed in Hungary as well as the place of negotiations concerning the execution of the termination of the Warsaw Pact and presented a list containing the names of the members of the Government's delegation. Furthermore, the Hungarian Government made a proposal to the Soviet Embassy in Budapest to form a mixed committee to prepare the withdrawal of the Soviet troops.

I request Your Excellency to call upon the Great Powers to recognize the neutrality of Hungary and ask the Security Council to instruct the Soviet and Hungarian Governments to start the negotiations immediately.

I also request Your Excellency to make known the above to the Members of the Security Council.

Please accept, Your Excellency, the expression of my highest consideration.

BUDAPEST, NOVEMBER 2, 1956

[Source: U. N. Document S/3726, November 2, 1956. Published in Paul E. Zinner, ed., National Communism and Popular Revolt in Eastern Europe: A Selection of Documents on Events in Poland and Hungary, February–November, 1956, *(New York: Columbia University Press, 1956), 468–469.]*

DOCUMENT NO. 75: Resolution of the CPCz CC Politburo Supporting Planned Soviet Measures, November 2, 1956

On November 2 in Bucharest, Khrushchev and Malenkov informed the Czechoslovak and Romanian leaders about the imminent Soviet intervention. That same evening, Czechoslovak First Secretary Antonín Novotný reported the news to the CPCz Political Committee. The minutes below sum up the resolutions passed at this meeting. The Czechoslovak leadership, along with their hard-line East German, Romanian, and Bulgarian counterparts, had watched the Hungarian developments with growing concern, and were actually relieved that the Soviets had finally decided to intervene because it meant their own domestic political positions would be strengthened. According to this document, they were even willing "if need be" to lend a hand in liquidating the "counterrevolution" in Hungary.

Decisions of the 151st[303] meeting of the CPCZ CC Politburo on November 2, 1956.

Agenda: Hungarian events
(cde. Novotný)

Decision:
The Politburo of the CPCz CC has discussed the development of the Hungarian situation and the reports of cdes. Novotný and Široký, and has made the following decisions:

1. The Politburo wishes to state that the position expressed by the CPCz CC delegation in evaluating the Hungarian situation emerges from the unanimous opinion of the CPCz CC; furthermore, it agrees that the people's democracy should be maintained in Hungary with every necessary measure, and, if need be, we not only agree with taking such measures but are willing to make an active contribution and help vindicate them.

2. Considering the spreading of the Hungarian counterrevolution, the Politburo orders minister of national defense, cde. Lomský, and minister of the interior, cde. Barák, to safeguard the vigilance and total security of our armed forces, and make sure that they are on the alert for defending the borders of Czechoslovakia.

3. Cde. Zápotocký, president of the republic, is commissioned to deliver a speech over the radio at 1:00 p.m. on 3 November 1956, addressing the Czechoslovak people and informing them about the latest events in Hungary and in Egypt. The speech will be discussed at the CPCz CC Politburo meeting on Saturday at 11:00 p.m., November 3, 1956.

4. Considering the new situation in Hungary, cde. Novotný, first secretary of the central committee, is asked to make sure that the CPCz CC Secretariat will make the necessary political and organizational measures.

5. Convening an assembly of the CPCz CC has to be considered.

[Source: MOL, XXXII–16., 11 k., 10. o. Translated by József Reiter and Csaba Farkas.]

---

[303] Although the document indicates this was the 151st meeting, it was very likely the 149th session.

DOCUMENT NO. 76: Notes of Yugoslav Ambassador to Moscow Veljko Mićunović on Negotiations between Yugoslav and Soviet Leaders at Brioni, November 3, 1956

In his diary entry for November 3, 1956, Yugoslav Ambassador Mićunović gives a detailed account of what transpired during the crucial talks between Nikita Khrushchev and Josip Tito on November 2–3. As with the rest of his extraordinary diary, this account is a valuable contemporary source. Following the resolution passed by the CPSU CC Presidium on October 31, Khrushchev and Malenkov secretly arrived on the island of Brioni to consult with the Yugoslav leadership about the imminent invasion of Hungary. Although at the beginning of the talks Khrushchev declared that the military action had already been decided upon regardless of the Yugoslav view, the fact that he took the trouble to visit Tito was a clear sign of Yugoslavia's significance to Moscow as the Kremlin tried to woo the Yugoslavs closer to the Soviet camp. The Soviet delegation must have been relieved to find Tito in agreement with their decision. Belgrade had already been deeply concerned about the "swing ... toward counterrevolution" that Hungarian events had taken. The Yugoslavs also insisted on the need to complement military action with political steps. They proposed setting up "something like a revolutionary government composed of Hungarians." Instead of the Soviets' nominee for the top post, Ferenc Münnich, however, they recommended János Kádár, since Kádár was politically further removed from Tito's nemesis, Rákosi, and in fact had been imprisoned by the former Hungarian leader. Khrushchev agreed. Tito also offered to use Belgrade's political influence to apply pressure on Nagy and his circle to resign their positions and clear the way for the new Kádár government to take over formally. However, no agreement was reached on the details of their resignation, which later became a source of serious tension between Moscow and Belgrade.

Although they lacked a certain enthusiasm, the Yugoslav leadership held to the Brioni agreement and publicly supported the intervention, as well as the Kádár government and its program.

The talks with Khrushchev and Malenkov lasted from seven o'clock in the evening of November 2 to five o'clock in the morning of November 3.

Khrushchev said at the outset they had come to consult with us about the situation in Hungary, or rather to inform us about what they were preparing to do. They said that on the previous day, November 1, they had spoken with the Poles in Brest. On the Soviet side there had been Khrushchev, Molotov, and Malenkov and on the Polish side Gomułka, Cyrankiewicz, and Ochab. After that Molotov had returned to Moscow, while Khrushchev and Malenkov had gone to Bucharest, where they had spoken with [Gheorghiu-] Dej and the Romanians. The leaders of Czechoslovakia, led by Novotný, had joined them. Then Khrushchev and Malenkov had gone to Sofia for talks with the Bulgarians. All these visits had been secret. They had also consulted the Chinese. There had been a delegation of the Chinese Communist party led by Liu Shaoqi in Moscow, and they, like all the others had been in complete agreement with the Russians on everything. The Poles had had their own views but even they agreed that the situation in Hungary was turning into a counterrevolution. The Poles knew what the Russians had decided to do and there was no other way out. Khrushchev and Malenkov wanted to inform us about the Soviet Union's decision and to hear our views.

Khrushchev talked about the way events in Hungary were moving toward counterrevolution. He started off emotionally, without giving any serious analysis of the course of events, saying that Communists in Hungary were being murdered, butchered, and hanged. He mentioned Imre Nagy's appeal to the United Nations and the four powers and the withdrawal from the Warsaw Pact. It was a question of whether capitalism would be restored in Hungary. Whether Nagy was just a tool or had himself long been an agent of imperialism was not clear at the moment; what was important was that things had taken this course and that the outcome would be the restoration of capitalism. "What is there left for us to do?" Khrushchev asked, meaning the Soviet Union. "If we let things take their course the West would say we are either stupid or weak, and that's one and the same thing. We cannot possibly permit it, either as Communists and internationalists or as the Soviet state. We would have capitalists on the frontiers of the Soviet Union." He said they had assembled sufficient troops and that they had decided to put a stop to what was going on in Hungary. They still needed a couple of days. He said he had spoken with Bulganin by telephone today, November 2, and the Bulganin had given him the happy news that Ferenc Münnich and János Kádár had succeeded in fleeing from Budapest and were now in a plane on their way to Moscow.[304] Khrushchev said this was tremendously important. He asked whether we knew what had happened to Antal Apró, and said it would be very important if he could get out and be saved. The Russians are doing what they can about this but up to now don't know what has happened to him.[305]

Khrushchev turned again to the question of intervention by the Soviet Army. He said that there were also internal reasons in the Soviet Union why they could not permit the restoration of capitalism in Hungary. There were people in the Soviet Union who would say that as long as Stalin was in command everybody obeyed and there were no big shocks, but that now, ever since they had come to power (and here Khrushchev used a coarse word to describe the present Soviet leaders), Russia had suffered the defeat and loss of Hungary. And this was happening at a time when the present Soviet leaders were condemning Stalin. Khrushchev said this might be said primarily by the Soviet Army which was one of the reasons why they were intervening in Hungary.

Khrushchev explained that the military preparations were going successfully. He mentioned Marshal Zhukov and said that the commander of the military operations in Hungary would be Army General Malinin. He said that some Romanian forces might have taken part but the Russians considered it was not necessary. Khrushchev went on to say that in a matter of two days they would halt and crush all resistance in Hungary. He didn't say when it would begin, but it was clear that it would be very soon-and we were the last to be informed. In fact the Russians are not here because they need our agreement. They will do what they have decided to do in Hungary whether we agree with it or not, in spite of the fact the Khrushchev says it is very important that we should "understand them properly."

Khrushchev said that British and French aggressive pressure on Egypt provided a favorable moment for a further intervention by Soviet troops. It would help the Russians. There would be confusion and uproar in the West and the United Nations, but it would be less at a time when Britain, France, and Israel were waging a war against Egypt.[306] "They are bogged down there, and we are stuck in Hungary," Khrushchev said.

Malenkov let it be known that everything in the Soviet Union was ready for the second military intervention against the Nagy government to start right away. It is clear that the Russians are going to intervene frontally and with great force, because they are completely isolated from the Hungarian people; in fact, the population is opposed to the Russians.

Khrushchev mentioned the workers in the Miskolc region, where Hungarian miners had remained loyal though reactionaries were in power. The Czechs had given the miners some arms and it might be possible to try some political action against Nagy with the help of those Hungarian miners or jointly with them. He repeated that everything was ready to be carried out immediately as he had explained, that there was no other way out, and that the situation would be resolved with the greatest speed and firmness. He mentioned incidentally that Hungary had twice fought in coalition with the West against Russia, and he stressed the bad feeling existing in the Soviet Army against Hungary, which wanted to join the West again against the Russians.[307]

---

[304] The departure of János Kádár and Ferenc Münnich was organized from Budapest by Soviet Ambassador Andropov late in the afternoon of November 1. After arriving in Tököl that evening, they spent the night there and were flown on a special airplane to Moscow on November 2.

[305] On November 1, Yurii Andropov also got in touch with Antal Apró. He escaped from the capital in an armored car late the following evening, together with György Marosán, Károly Kiss, Sándor Nógrádi and others. On November 4, he went from the Soviet airfield in Tököl to Szolnok, where the Kádár government was officially formed.

[306] Khrushchev's calculation concerning the effect of the Suez crisis on the U.N. proved to be accurate: the military operations against Egypt seriously distracted the attention of the world organization from the Hungarian events.

[307] In World War I, Hungary fought against Russia as part of the Austro-Hungarian empire in alliance with Germany, while in World War II Hungary fought against the Soviet Union as an ally of Nazi Germany.

On our side we stated at the outset that we had followed the course of events in Hungary with the greatest attention. The revolt and rioting by the people had been an explosion of pent-up dissatisfaction with Rákosi's policy and the faults and crimes of the past. If the right steps had been taken in good time, what was taking place now would have been avoided. Our attitude toward Nagy's first government, after Kádár replaced Gerő, had been explained by us in the message which Tito sent to the Hungarians.[308] (Khrushchev and Malenkov said they agreed with the contents of Tito's letter and referred to the Soviet Government's declaration of October 30, which followed the same lines and was intended basically as support for Imre Nagy.)

We explained that we were also concerned at the swing of events to the right, toward counterrevolution, when we saw the Nagy government allowing Communists to be murdered and hanged. There would have to be intervention if there was a counterrevolution in Hungary, but it should not be based exclusively on the Soviet Army's weapons. There would be bloodshed, with Hungarians fighting against Soviet troops, because the Communist party of Hungary, as a result of what had happened in the past, had disintegrated and no longer existed. We suggested that in the present situation there should be some political preparation, an effort to save what could be saved, and to set up something like a revolutionary government composed of Hungarians who could give the people some kind of political lead.

Khrushchev said they had a proposal that a new Hungarian government should be formed by Ferenc Münnich, the former Hungarian ambassador in Moscow (who before the revolt had been appointed ambassador in Belgrade). But there was also Kádár. Khrushchev asked what we thought. Tito inquired who Münnich was and Ranković spoke about recent meetings with him. We said it would be better if Kádár and not Münnich formed the new revolutionary government, although we didn't know enough about either of them. The Russians are obviously in favor of Münnich but are not against accepting our proposal.

We pointed out that much depended on what the policy of the new government would be. Some of us suggested that the new government should condemn sharply and categorically the policy of Rákosi and Gerő as well as everything in the past which led to this situation. Khrushchev and Malenkov reluctantly agreed. One had the impression that they would rather talk about the present counterrevolution and the West than about the mistakes of the past, but they agreed. Khrushchev used coarse language about Rákosi and then even worse language about Gerő, who, he said, after being elected secretary went first for a holiday in the Crimea and then to Yugoslavia. Rákosi telephoned to Moscow offering to go and "help" in Budapest, but Khrushchev told him he could "go down there and the people will hang you there." Rákosi asked for a telephone call to Budapest, but the Soviet operator refused to put his call through. Malenkov said the telephone operator proved himself to be politically more mature than Rákosi, adding: "That idiot doesn't understand the most elementary things."

Khrushchev and Malenkov inquired what points ought to be included in the new government's declaration. The main suggestions from the Yugoslav side were: The new government's program should decisively condemn the past and tell the truth frankly about Rákosi and Gerő.

[308] In a letter to the Presidium of the HWP CC dated October 29, Josip Broz Tito assured the Nagy government of his support: "The League of Yugoslav Communists and the working peoples of our countries owe admiration to those progressive people in neighboring Hungary who are making enormous efforts these days to transform this tragic fight into an era of rebirth and to protect the socialist future of their people.Therefore, Yugoslav public opinion unanimously welcomes the new state and party leadership as well as the declaration delivered by the government of the Hungarian People's Republic on October 28. Important elements of the new state and party leadership's political platform such as the democratization of public life, the introduction of self-governance of the workers and democratic self-governance in general, the normalization of relations between socialist countries on the basis of respect for equal rights and sovereignty, the initiation of negotiations about the withdrawal of Soviet troops from Hungary, etc., as well as a realistic evaluation of the nature of the Hungarian events which is included in the above-mentioned declaration by the government serve as proof that the policy of the current state and party leadership and the truly socialist democratic endeavor of the Hungarian working people will weld together." See *Magyar Nemzet*, October 30, 1956. Also published in Kiss, Ripp and Vida, *Magyar-jugoszláv kapcsolatok, 1956*, p 142. Translated by Mónika Borbély.

Then it should suggest how the basic achievements of the socialist system can be defended. The program of the new government should aim at establishing democratic relations on equal terms with countries of the socialist camp and arranging for the eventual withdrawal of Soviet troops. Within Hungary it should appeal to the revolutionary committees, the workers' councils, and the working class. Khrushchev agreed with the condemnation of Rákosi and Gerő, and with the prospect of withdrawing Soviet troops, although he was obviously not inclined to stress it.

These talks lasted for about three hours. After ten o'clock we all moved into the next room for supper. At table Khrushchev resumed the discussion about who should form the government. He was clearly not anxious to accept Kádár, who was not his choice. The Russians again praised Münnich. They said they had only just learned that Münnich had always been against Rákosi and that he was an old Communist whom Khrushchev had known twenty years ago: in the thirties they had been officers together in the Soviet Army on maneuvers in Russia, when they had shared the same tent. It appears that the Russians have already formed the government and that Münnich is to be prime minister. I said that I knew Münnich and that I had often met him in Moscow and that I could say only the very best things about him. But I explained that there was a major political factor to consider in deciding whether it should be Kádár or Münnich: in Rákosi's time Münnich had been ambassador in Moscow, whereas Kádár had been in prison in Budapest. For every Hungarian this would be decisive in Kádár's favor. Khrushchev withdrew and agreed.

We spoke of the need to find new leaders and stressed that the revolutionary government would have influence insofar as it contained no Rákosi people, condemned Rákosi and Gerő decisively, and really pursued a whole new policy. The Russians seemed to understand and to be reconciled to this, although they had arrived with different ideas about who should lead Hungary. For example, Khrushchev proposed that István Bata take over the Ministry of National Defense in the new government, although he had held the same post in Rákosi's government. When the Yugoslav side said that such a decision would be politically weak, the Russians withdrew it.

There was talk about other Hungarian communists. Khrushchev insisted again that everything should be done to get Antal Apró out. We mentioned Losonczy as a person who gave the impression of being honest and capable, but Khrushchev and Malenkov reacted coolly. It emerged from the discussion that the Russians know that Losonczy is in contact with us and regard him as one of Nagy's doubtful characters.[309] There was also a reference to Colonel Maléter, who was appointed head of the Hungarian delegation for discussing the withdrawal of Soviet troops with the Russians. We were not sure who Maléter is; nobody knows him or has any sure information about him. Khrushchev and Malenkov say nothing, although they know Maléter.

After supper, around midnight, the question of political preparations was raised again. Malenkov agreed with our view that this played a very important role. There was further discussion of the principles we had expounded, which Khrushchev and Malenkov once again said they agreed with and would adopt. From what Khrushchev said, one had the impression that the new Hungarian Government's declaration had in fact already been written in Moscow but that it might be changed as a result of these talks and our proposals.[310] When our uncertainty about

---

[309] According to Miklós Vásárhelyi, Géza Losonczy did not have any contact with the Yugoslav diplomats prior to October 23, nor did he even visit the legation (or embassy, after its status was officially elevated on October 12). During the spring of 1956, following the Twentieth Congress of the CPSU, Vásárhelyi and Miklós Gimes, with Péter Erdős acting as intermediary, kept in touch on behalf of the Nagy group with members of the Yugoslav legation, primarily through Secretary Milan Georgijević. They frequently visited the legation in order to exchange information and to hand over copies of Nagy's studies and his letters and petitions written to the Hungarian leaders. (See Kiss, Ripp and Vida, *Magyar-jugoszláv kapcsolatok,* 1956, 156.)

[310] The task of elaborating the declaration of the new Hungarian government was given to Dimitri Shepilov, Leonid Brezhnev, Ekaterina Furtseva and Piotr Pospelov at the October 31 meeting of the CPSU Presidium, where the decision on military intervention was made. At the November 3 CPSU Presidium meeting, Khrushchev indeed expressed the need to make corrections and handed the task over to Suslov, Mikoyan and Shepilov. See Document Nos. 53 and 78.

the Hungarian Communists came up, our comrades said that János Kádár should know them best and that his opinion should be accepted. The Russians agreed.

They again asked what possibilities we had of trying to do something about Nagy. Apart from Losonczy we mentioned Zoltán Szántó, who has already asked for asylum in our embassy because of the danger of reprisals.[311] It seems to us that such people are not to be distrusted, because they are decent folk with good intentions. It was agreed that we would see what we could do in this direction, because the Russians said they had no such possibilities. Khrushchev and Malenkov repeated several times that anything we could do with the Nagy government on the above lines would be of the greatest importance. We pointed out that we didn't know what could be achieved. The Russians still said nothing about when their troops would intervene. We can't ask them, and they don't want to say. For that reason the time factor remains unclear: We don't know what opportunity we may have to influence Nagy and try to reduce the number of casualties and the amount of unnecessary bloodshed. But we agreed that we would try and influence Nagy.

Khrushchev explained that they had had consultations with everybody, and above all with the Chinese. Only the Albanians were not mentioned. He said they had invited a delegation from China. They knew that Mao Zedong would not be able to come, so they had asked for others: Liu Shaoqi, secretary of the Chinese Communist party, and Zhou Enlai (who Khrushchev said was a "great diplomat"). The Chinese had agreed and appointed a delegation of six or seven people led by Liu Shaoqi. The Russians wanted to hear the views of the Chinese because they were further away from the events in Poland and Hungary, were not directly involved, and could see things better than the Russians who were affected by inertia and the habits of the past. The Chinese had apparently agreed to everything and had been in contact with Mao Zedong by telephone. He had agreed completely with the decision to intervene in Hungary.

Khrushchev said that Marshal Zhukov was dealing with the military side of the matter, praised his ability as a military leader, and said that he had fallen into disfavor during the war in a quarrel with Stalin over plans for military operations. When Stalin said that he, Stalin, bore responsibility for the fate of the Soviet Union, Zhukov replied that he, too, was responsible for its fate.

There was mention of Kádár's statement about the tragic course of events in Hungary.[312] Kádár is afraid that socialism and working-class power will collapse there. Khrushchev said that Kádár is a "a good guy" [molodec]. Then there was talk about the terror in Hungary and the arrest of Kádár in Rákosi's day. Farkas' son had distinguished himself particularly in the maltreatment of Kádár.[313] Khrushchev and Malenkov described him repeatedly as "scum."

We said that Kádár, who was in the Hungarian party delegation when it visited Yugoslavia, had made a very good impression. The Russians said Gerő had said that the Hungarian party had had about 900,000 members, but that there was nothing left of it now: It had completely disintegrated.

Several times the Russians mentioned Mikoyan, who had been in Hungary in the summer and again now, but we did not follow up this line of conversation. It must have been clear to

---

[311] On November 1, during a conversation in the prime minister's office, Zoltán Szántó and Géza Losonczy asked Ambassador Dalibor Soldatić unofficially whether it would be possible, considering the uncertain situation in Budapest, for the Yugoslav Embassy to offer asylum to the wives and children of certain leading Hungarian politicians.

[312] Presumably, this refers to Kádár's radio address on November 1, in which he announced the formation of the HSWP. See footnote 247 above.

[313] In his memoirs, former ÁVH officer Vladimir Farkas, son of Mihály Farkas, firmly denied any participation in the torture of János Kádár in 1951. In his last interview, Kádár said that Vladimir Farkas forced him to sign statements that were untrue, although he did not mention Farkas using physical violence against him. See, *Kádár János—végakarat*, interviews by András Kanyó, documents complied and edited by Mária Veres (Budapest: Hírlapkiadó Vállalat, 1989), 78.

Khrushchev and Malenkov that the Yugoslavs have a poor opinion of the part played by Mikoyan and Suslov in Hungary.[314]

We then asked what were the views of individual members of the Soviet Presidium about the situation. This took the Russians by surprise. After a short pause Khrushchev replied that there was complete and absolute agreement. Malenkov added that the same degree of agreement had prevailed at all phases of the events and that it still prevailed.

Khrushchev spoke about Poland with some restraint but still critically. He said nothing bad about Gomułka, but declared that the views of some Poles were unacceptable. For example, some of them (he did not know which ones) were talking about the return of Lvov to Poland. Khrushchev said that the Ukrainians and Byelorussians would raise the question of the Curzon Line,[315] and then there was the fact that East Prussia had been divided between Poland and the Soviet Union, so that these territories might also come into question (obviously only the Polish half), but the Poles would not be able to find anyone in Germany to defend their frontiers on the Oder and the Neisse. According to Khrushchev, the Russians had made this clear to the Poles, and Gomułka had said there was no need at all to discuss such questions.

Khrushchev criticized the Poles for the way they thought they could trade: selling coal for cash to the West and asking for grain on credit from the Russians. This was not trading on equal terms, Khrushchev said, but exploitation of the Soviet Union. He explained which of the socialist countries they were giving grain to and how much. They would let the Romanians have it as a loan, and the Romanians would return it next year. Khrushchev was interested to know how much grain Yugoslavia needed to import. We told him of the agreement on this we intended to sign with the United States Government. Khrushchev and Malenkov approved. Khrushchev spoke ironically about the Poles, who had managed to work out that the Soviet Union was in debt to Poland, although the Soviet Union had given them enormous assistance.

At the beginning of the conversation Malenkov demonstrated that from a purely legal and constitutional point of view Imre Nagy's government was not legitimate or properly established by the constitutional bodies,[316] and that its present program was unconstitutional—as though this line of argument made Soviet military intervention any easier—and as if that itself were constitutional!

As usual when he is talking to Yugoslavs and wants to put them in a good mood, as though he were making some concessions to them, Khrushchev told some unflattering stories about Stalin. This time they referred to Stalin's relations with Rákosi, whom Stalin allegedly could not stand and did not trust. Rákosi used to take his vacation in the Soviet Union in the same place as Stalin, and Stalin was suspicious of this and said he would cure Rákosi of it. At the first opportunity Stalin pressed Rákosi to drink an excessive quantity of alcohol at one gulp. But then they were afraid that Rákosi might die from it and carried him away, although in fact nothing happened to him. Rákosi modeled himself on Stalin to such an extent that he had a steel door made for his office in Budapest as well as some bulletproof clothes to protect him from attempts on his life. Khrushchev and Malenkov concluded by saying Rákosi never had and still did not

---

[314] During his stay in Budapest between June 7 and 14, Suslov consulted several times with members of the Hungarian party leadership, which had the effect of strengthening Rákosi's position. However, when Mikoyan visited Hungary between July 13–21, the first secretary of the HWP was forced to resign. Nevertheless, Yugoslav criticism more likely targeted the two envoys' activities during the revolution since they were unable to obviate the need for a second military intervention, which the Yugoslavs considered a highly negative development.

[315] The Curzon Line was proposed by Lord Curzon, British foreign secretary, as an armistice line between Soviet and Polish forces after World War I. Although the actual border was set further east after the Polish military successes in 1920, Soviet demands in 1945 referred once more to the Curzon line when drawing the final frontier between the two countries. For its territories lost in this way, Poland was compensated with areas in the eastern part of Germany.

[316] The Nagy government was formed according to legal procedures, and its official oath was administered by István Dobi, president of the Presidential Council, on October 28, although the Council itself had not discussed the issue. The convocation of Parliament, where the Nagy government's introduction should have occurred, could not take place because of the Soviet intervention on November 4.

have the most elementary understanding of what needed to be done, that he and Stalin had cooked up a porridge in Hungary that the present Soviet leaders now had to eat.

Whenever the question of Imre Nagy came up, Khrushchev would generally repeat, "They are slaughtering Communists in Hungary," as though it was all being done on decisions taken by Nagy's government and carried out by its services. Later, when there was discussion of how much Nagy could do to ease the whole situation, Khrushchev took a different line, did not keep repeating, "They are cutting Communists' throats there," but accepted a quite different assessment of Imre Nagy, agreeing that he could do much to help and to reserve his reputation as a Communist.

[Source: Veljko Micunovic, Moscow Diary *(Garden City, N.Y.: Doubleday, 1980), 132-140. Reprinted with permission.]*

DOCUMENT NO. 77: Nikita Khrushchev's Recollections of Discussions between the CPSU CC Presidium and Hungarian Leaders János Kádár and Ferenc Münnich in Moscow, November 3, 1956 (Excerpt)

The following excerpt from Khrushchev's memoirs recounts the essence of the crucial strategy session of Soviet leaders with János Kádár and Ferenc Münnich at the Kremlin the day before the second invasion. Khrushchev and Malenkov had just returned from talks with Josip Tito, at which the Yugoslav president had acquiesced to the Soviet intervention, leaving no further obstacles in the Kremlin's path. The purpose of the meeting with the Hungarians was to decide on the make-up of the new government that would replace that of Imre Nagy. Leaving aside the inevitably self-serving nature of memoir accounts, Khrushchev's recollections have largely held up in the light of new documentation, and this account is useful in offering a flavor of the dynamics between the two sides.

[....]

"We reached the Soviet capital only in the second half of the day, closer to the evening. Members of the CPSU CC Presidium gathered immediately, and we went to the Kremlin straight from the airport. We reported on the results of the fraternal negotiations together with Malenkov. Molotov had already spoken about the conversation at the border [with the PZPR delegation]. We confirmed that the majority was in favor of taking urgent and decisive measures. We immediately took up the issue of the composition of the new Hungarian government in consultation with Kádár and Münnich. Molotov spoke sharply against Kádár .... He used an insulting expression referring to Kádár (however, at the moment, Kádár was not present in person). Molotov justified his position by pointing out that Kádár continued to see himself as a member of the leadership together with Nagy, however now, having spent two days in Moscow while Malenkov and I were away, he began to express anxiety and tried to return to Budapest. Yes, I understood Molotov's position: how can one propose a person who sees himself as a member of the leadership against which we are preparing to strike? He would have to lead the struggle against the acting leadership. Molotov insisted: "I am voting for Münnich." ... I said: "Let us invite both of them." They were escorted in. We immediately told them frankly that the counterrevolution had begun in Hungary, and that we had to use troops against it. That it was the only opportunity to return to normalcy and to suppress the rebellion, which was raging in Budapest. I was watching Kádár intently. He was listening silently. Then came his turn to speak: "Yes," he agreed, "you are right, in order to stabilize the situation, we need your assistance now."... Münnich also expressed his support for actions involving the assistance of Soviet troops. Both Kádár and Münnich expressed their confidence that the Hungarian people in general would support the suppression of the counterrevolution. We started forming the government. It was done mostly by Kádár and Münnich—they knew the people."

[Source: Quotation from Khrushchev's memoirs as cited in Sovietskii Soyuz i vengerskii krizis, 1956 goda: Dokumenty, *edited and compiled by E. D. Orekhova, Vyacheslav T. Sereda and Aleksandr. S. Stykhalin (Moscow: ROSSPEN, 1998), 544–545. Translated by Svetlana Savranskaya.]*

DOCUMENT NO. 78: Working Notes from the Session of the CPSU CC Presidium, with the Participation of János Kádár, Ferenc Münnich, and Imre Horváth, November 3, 1956

This document, and the one that follows, record from different perspectives the crucial Kremlin session at which János Kádár and the Soviet leadership agreed on the formation of a regime to replace the Nagy government currently in power in Hungary. The day before (see Document No. 70), Kádár retained some lingering uncertainty, which Khrushchev learned about (according to the most complete version of his memoirs) after his return to Moscow from Brioni. At this session, the Soviet first secretary makes a genuine effort to persuade Kádár to agree to lead the new government. Khrushchev's speech, which was left out of these notes by Vladimir Malin, but is referred to in the summary prepared by Hungarian Foreign Minister Imre Horváth (see the next document), leads to a common platform condemning both Rákosi and Gerő. In his reply, which Malin does record in detail, Kádár first joins Khrushchev in denouncing Rákosi, then declares that Nagy, through his conduct, has been providing "a cover" for the "counterrevolutionaries." At this point, Kádár gives his blessing to the Soviet strategy: "I agree with you. The correct course of action is to form a rev[olutionary] government."

In the next part of Malin's notes, Kádár discusses matters that he would not repeat for more than three decades. One is the disturbing fact that popular support for the uprising was overwhelming; another is the potential for dependency on the Soviet Union, which prompts him to declare somewhat wishfully that "this government must not be puppet-like." In the process, he effectively passes sentence on both his predecessors and on the circumstances of his own selection.

In the end, Kádár reaffirms his agreement with the Soviet leadership. When the CPSU CC Presidium passed its resolution later that evening, Hungary's new government was de facto formed.

Those Taking Part: Voroshilov, Bulganin, Kaganovich, Malenkov, Mikoyan, Molotov, Kirichenko, Saburov, Suslov, Brezhnev, Pospelov

On the Preparation of Documents for Use in Hungary[317]
(Khrushchev, Mikoyan)
The documents are poorly prepared.
Cdes. Suslov, Mikoyan, and Shepilov are to prepare the documents.

On the Composition of the Hungarian Gov't
(Mikoyan)
Cde Mikoyan: At the head of gov't is Kádár.

Kádár— it is worth speaking about mistakes, but for a long while there was no time. About one matter—why in the summer they chose Gerő as secretary.
The Soviet comrades always helped, but there was one mistake: only 3–4 Hungarian cdes. enjoyed the full trust of the Soviet cdes.: Rákosi, Gerő, Farkas.
But among others there are many orderly people.
3–4 individuals monopolized relations between Hungary and the USSR.
This is the source of many mistakes.

Rákosi would say "this is the view of the Soviet cdes.," and that would put an end to the debate.
On the exclusion of Nagy from the party: Rákosi said that the Soviet cdes. share his view.

---

[317] This refers to the documents decided upon at the October 31 CPSU CC Presidium meeting. See Document No. 53.

Cde. Kádár—the decisions of the XX Congress were heartily welcomed.

To critizice Rákosi means speaking out against the Soviet cdes.

The congratulatory telegram in Rákosi's name (caused confusion).[318]

For 12 years: the Soviet comrades were calm with Rákosi at the head and then Gerő (they didn't raise objections to them).[319]

What now?
On Nagy's behavior.
They're killing Communists.
The counterrev. are killing them, and premier Nagy provides a cover.

The government lacks the forces to put an end to it.

What must be done?
Surrendering a socialist country to counterrev. is impossible.
I agree with you.
The correct course of action is to form a rev. government.
I'd like to dwell on one point:
the whole nation is taking part in the movement.
The nation does not want to liquidate the peop.-dem. order.

The withdrawal of Soviet troops from Hungary has great significance.
We are being strengthened in our military relationship, and are becoming weaker in the political.
National sentiments are offended (uniform, title).[320]

Cde. Kádár:
This government must not be puppet-like, there must be a base for its activities and support among workers.
There must be an answer to the question of what sort of relationship we must have with the USSR.

Cde. Münnich:
Believes that Cde. Kádár's assessment and conclusions are correct.

Cde. Kádár—the center of counterrev. is in the city of Győr.
If we declare Nagy's gov't counterrev., all parties will fall under this rubric.
The government does not want to struggle against the counterrev.

The position:
on the basis of defending the peop.-dem. order, socialist gains, and friendship with the USSR and with other socialist countries and cooperation with all peaceloving countries.

At the head of the gov't is Kádár.

---

[318] The CPSU CC sent a telegram of greetings to Rákosi and Hegedüs on April 4, 1956, (on the occasion of the anniversary of Hungary's "liberation" in World War II). The telegram was published in *Szabad Nép* two days later.

[319] Kádár glosses over the fact that it was Soviet pressure that forced Rákosi to resign as prime minister in June 1953.

[320] Kádár refers here to Soviet-style uniforms worn by the Hungarian army and to the naming of streets, cities and institutions after Soviet personalities.

To send: Malenkov, Mikoyan, Brezhnev.[321]
To fly off: (at 2:00–3:00) at 7:00 to 8:00 in the morning.

[Source: TsKhSD, F. 3. Op. 12. D. 1006. L. 31–33ob. compiled by V. N. Malin. Originally published in English in the Cold War International History Project Bulletin *no. 8–9 (Winter 1996/1997): 397–398. Translated by Mark Kramer.]*

[321] This mission presumably did not take place. Malenkov remained in Moscow, while Mikoyan and Brezhnev were absent at the meetings on November 4 and 5. Later in early November a Soviet mission was nevertheless sent to Budapest consisting of Malenkov, Suslov and Aristov.

DOCUMENT NO. 79: Working Notes of Imre Horváth from the Session of the CPSU CC Presidium, November 3, 1956

On October 31, 1956, Hungarian Foreign Minister Imre Horváth was en route to the U.N. General Assembly when an order to return to Budapest reached him in Vienna. Under uncertain circumstances (one report, sent to Nagy, said that he was forced to go), he traveled via Bratislava and Prague to Moscow, where in the first few days of November he took part in discussions aimed at forming the Kádár government. From the CPSU Presidium meeting of the evening of November 3, where the new government's composition, program and immediate tasks were set out, Horváth prepared two pages of rough handwritten notes in a mixture of Hungarian and Russian. (It is possible that he acted as interpreter at all or part of the session.)

What makes these notes particularly interesting is that they include Khrushchev's opening remarks, which are missing from Vladimir Malin's notes (see the previous document). This makes it possible to reconstruct how Khrushchev tried to convince Kádár to accept the leadership of the counter-government. The Soviet first secretary admitted that Moscow had committed serious mistakes on "cadre" policy in the Hungarian party, and took responsibility for having appointed Gerő to head the HWP in July 1956. He also singled out Nagy for criticism. Khrushchev assured Kádár of his personal support, referred to the dangers resulting from the international situation and reported the worries voiced by the satellite countries and Tito.

In his response, Kádár attempted to criticize Soviet policies dealing with Hungary: Moscow had relied exclusively on Rákosi, or at most one or two other people, and its proxies in Hungary had offended Hungarian national sensitivities. Kádár also insisted that his regime not be a puppet government. In the end, overcoming his hesitations from the day before, he agreed to take on the role of Moscow-appointed premier.

NOVEMBER 3, 1956 8:45 PM.

[Present are:]

Khr[ushchev], Bu[lganin], Vor[oshilov], Mal[enkov], Mol[otov], Kaga[novich], Mikoyan, Brezhnev

Khr[ushchev]

Organized	
Counterrev.	*Ev[ents]...sleeplessly*[322]
From the North	The mistakes of R[ákosi] + G[erő] + others.
Miskolc!	We do a lot, but not enough!

It cannot be defended that there is no Hungarian leader!
It is our mistake that we did not intervene in time.
Rákosi became paralyzed, and [they][323] *did not take steps actively.* We have asked [for] his replacement with great delay.

Szalai	R[ákosi]	Gerő was not
Hegedüs	*They are in the same shoes.*	

Gerő must not be nominated/proposed, he is unable to turn against R[ákosi.]
Mikoyan and I made a mistake when we proposed Gerő *instead of* Kádár. *We were taken in by Gerő.*
R[ákosi] *and* G[erő] *are honest, loyal communists. They*

---

[322] Text in italics indicates notes written in Russian.

[323] This probably refers to the Hungarian leadership.

made lots of nonsense.
R[ákosi] *is rough,* G[erő] *is ham-fisted.*
They criticized I[mre] N[agy]. *They thought he was an opportunist, though he is also a traitor.*
The expulsion of I[mre] N[agy] *was a mistake, even compared to Rákosi's stupidity.*
We would have arrested I[mre] N[agy].
We were for him being brought back into the party.
A part of the insurgents are not enemies! They were embittered because of the mistakes of the leadership.
We welcomed your [Kádár] being elected.
They are giving up the achievements of the revolution.
We cannot regard I[mre] N[agy] *as a communist.*
Dulles needs such people as I[mre] N[agy].
We hold to the declaration.[324]
This is impossible with I[mre] N[agy].
Eng[land] + F[rance]. Egypt.
We consulted other parties. *Malen[kov], Khrushch[ev], Poland.*
We cannot be outsider observers.
Yu[goslavia]. Rank[ović], Kard[elj], Mićunović, ambassador to M[oscow] + Malenk[ov], Khrushch[ev]. Worries!
Rev[olutionary] government.
The traitors want to use Kádár as shelter.
If I[mre] N[agy] *does not resign then he is in the service of the enemy.*

- Münnich deputy, interior, def[ense]

- Kádár chairman	- Apró	Hidas
- Kossa finance	- Rónai	Berei[325]
	[Károly] Kiss	Andics[326]
	- Maros[án]	
		[István] Kovács
		Egri
		Vég

They want to isolate Kádár.
- [Imre] Dögei[327] a[griculture] / e[conomy]
Miskolc, Szolnok   Budapest

Kádár: We will have to talk about the mistakes.
One thing about the earlier [issues]. Why we were united in the summer behind G[erő].
One mistake lasted 12 years.

[324] This refers to the Soviet government declaration of October 30. See Document No. 50.

[325] Andor Berei was a member of the HWP CC from 1949 and chairman of the National Planning Office beginning in 1954. On October 28, 1956, he left for Moscow together with his wife, Erzsébet Andics. On November 5, they returned to Hungary and became editors of the republished *Szabad Nép*. On November 16, they were ordered by the HSWP PEC to leave the country again and were unable to return until 1958.

[326] Erzsébet Andics was a member of the HWP CC and the Presidential Council from 1948–1956, and chairperson of the Hungarian Historical Society, 1949–1958.

[327] Imre Dögei was a member of the HWP CC between 1948–1956 and of the HSWP CC from 1956–1960. He served as minister of agriculture from November 12, 1956–1960.

Only 3 were trusted R[ákosi] + G[erő] + [Farkas]
This is the root of the mistakes. There were very decent people in the West as well.
Mihály Keresztes.[328]
R[ákosi] monopolized relations with the SU.
R[ákosi] said that the Soviet comrades agree with the expulsion of I[mre] N[agy].
It seems that the I[mre] N[agy] government covers the slaughtering of communists, but this is only the appearance. The government is powerless.
We often offended national feelings: coat of arms, [uni]form, Transylvania, Upper Hungary.[329]
We should refrain from [being] a Soviet puppet government.[330]
1. Against the counterrevolution.
2. Defense of achievements.
3. Relations with the SU.

Worker-Peasant Government
Declaration.
[Gyula] Uszta.[331]
+ 5 places reserved in the government.
Friendship with the Soviet Union. + people's democr[acy].
with peace-loving countries
Marshall Zhukov
HWP.

[Source: MOL, XIX–J–1–k. 55. d. First published by László Varga, "Hruscsov és Kádár titkos tárgyalásai, 1956. November 3," Magyar Hírlap, *October 22, 1992. Translated by József Litkei.]*

[328] Mihály Keresztes, a former member of the HWP CC, was head of the Agricultural Credit Institute of the Hungarian National Bank in 1956.

[329] Kádár here uses the word "Felvidék", which is a historical Hungarian name for what was then Slovakia. As parts of Hungary prior the Treaty of Trianon of 1920, both Transylvania in Romania and the Southern part of Slovakia had (and have to this day) a significant Hungarian ethnic minority.

[330] In this regard, see also the previous document.

[331] Gyula Uszta, former commander of the Hungarian armored units, was an organizer of the armed security forces in Budapest after November 4 and chairman of the Army's Military Council. He became a member of the HSWP PCC in November and served as first deputy minister of defense from December 1956.

DOCUMENT NO. 80: Hungarian Government Instructions to Acting U.N. Representative János Szabó, November 3, 1956

*On November 3, Imre Nagy sent the following two telegrams to János Szabó, Hungary's acting repre-
sentative at the United Nations (after Péter Kós' recall on October 31). The prime minister's goal continued to be to avert a second Soviet invasion. He instructed Szabó to ask the Security Council at their evening
session "to call on the great powers to recognize Hungary's neutrality and to order the Soviet and the
Hungarian governments to start negotiations with immediate effect." Szabó was also instructed to inform
the Security Council that the high commands of the two armies had already begun to negotiate about the
technical preconditions for withdrawal and that the Soviet delegation had promised not to send more
troops across the border. The probable purpose of telling the Security Council this was to create serious
embarrassment for the USSR in case they decided to break that promise. If so, Nagy's scheme failed to have
the desired effect: Szabó, who by then had probably been in consultation with Soviet U.N. representative
Sobolev, conveyed only the part of his instructions referring to the beginning of negotiations, without even
mentioning the issue of neutrality. This eventually made it easier for the American and Yugoslav envoys to
carry out their respective delaying tactics—the U.S. in order to focus U.N. attention on Suez, the Yugoslavs
probably as a result of collusion with the Soviets. After a short debate that evening, therefore, the Council
session was adjourned until November 5.*

I instruct you to report officially and directly to the Secretary General of the U.N. without
delay that the various telegrams, letters, messages, including the ones sent directly to the
Secretary General, and the information in these that have been sent and will be sent in the future
express the official standpoint of the entire Hungarian government.

FURTHER INSTRUCTIONS TO JÁNOS SZABÓ
ON NOVEMBER 3, 1956

At today's meeting of the Security Council, refer briefly to Prime Minister Imre Nagy's
telegrams that have been sent to the Secretary General of the U.N. so far, since you cannot report
on the Hungarian situation based on personal experience.

Beseech the Security Council emphatically in the name of the Hungarian government to call
on the great powers to recognize Hungary's neutrality and to order the Soviet and the Hungarian
governments to start negotiations with immediate effect.

The joint committee of the commanders of the Hungarian and Soviet armies met today at
noon, and both sides unfolded their standpoints regarding the technical questions of the Soviet
troops' withdrawal.

The joint committee agreed that they would examine the mutually disclosed opinions and
they would meet again at 10 p.m.. Until then, the Soviet delegation promised that no more Soviet
trains carrying troops would cross the Hungarian border.

*[Source: MOL, XIX–J–1–j. 81 d. Originally Published in József Kiss, Zoltán Ripp and István
Vida, ed., "Források a Nagy Imre-kormány külpolitikájának történetéhez," Társadalmi Szemle
48, no. 5 (1993): 93–94. Translated by Mónika Borbély.]*

DOCUMENT NO. 81: Telegram from Jean Laloy, Head of the European Department of the French Foreign Ministry, to the French Delegation in New York, November 3, 1956

This telegram reporting on the views of the counselor of the Soviet Embassy in Paris foreshadowed the forthcoming Soviet intervention. While claiming, on the one hand, that Hungary's assertion of neutrality "cannot be taken seriously," the counselor nevertheless predicts that Moscow's declaration of October 30 (see introduction and footnotes to Document No. 50) would not apply to Hungary if it "were to leave the path of people's democracy."

FOREIGN AFFAIRS

POLITICAL DIRECTOR

EUROPE

TELEGRAM ISSUED:

PARIS, NOVEMBER 3, 1956

CONFIDENTIAL—VERY URGENT

MOSCOW 4446/48 BONN 3207/09
NEW YORK 3540/42 BUDAPEST 908/910
LONDON 11733/35 WARSAW 1419/21
WASHINGTON 11895/97

The Counselor of the Soviet Embassy whom the director of Europe[an Affairs at the French Foreign Ministry] called in this afternoon to speak about French journalists held at the Hungarian border by Soviet troops, made, after having promised to settle the dispute, disturbing comments about the evolution of affairs in Hungary.

According to Mr. Erofeev,[332] the Nagy Government no longer represents anything. It has been deprived of its authority; it denies, against all appearances, having asked for Soviet intervention, and it thus tends to play the role of "provocateur." The neutrality that it has declared therefore cannot be taken seriously.

On the other hand, this government tolerates fascist acts and dictates measures which are against the spirit of socialism. In such conditions, the USSR could invoke Article 4 of the [Hungarian] peace treaty to order that an end be put to the activity of these elements.

Interrogated finally on the scope of the declaration of October 30 regarding Hungary, Mr. Erofeev responded that this declaration only concerned socialist countries; if Hungary were to leave the path of people's democracy, it could not invoke this declaration. If Hungary stays there, many allowances could be granted it.

Warned against resorting to force to save the "People's Democracy," Mr. Erofeev avoided any response by hiding behind vague promises that all would rapidly return to order, and the essential thing was to maintain peace in Europe.

Diplomatic Headquarters
LALOY

[Source: Ministère des Affaires Étrangères, Documents Diplomatiques Français, 1956, vol. 3, 24. Octobre–31. Décembre (Paris: Imprimerie Nationale, 1990), 163–164. Translated by Christa Matthews.]

---

[332] Vladimir Erofeev was counselor at the Soviet Embassy in Paris.

HUNGARY IN THE AFTERMATH

INTRODUCTION

On November 7, Kádár's government formally took power. The tasks he faced were daunting: to re-establish Communist authority over a bitterly divided society and to rebuild a broken economy. Complicating matters, he had almost no personal base of support among the population. Most Hungarians saw him as Moscow's comrade-in-arms, particularly after he announced over Radio Kossuth on November 4 that the incoming Hungarian Revolutionary Workers' and Peasants' Government had asked the Soviet Army "to help our nation." Even Mátyás Rákosi loyalists resented his reappearance, blaming him for preventing their re-ascension to power.

Kádár's first priority was to crush the armed uprising. Over the next several days, pro-Kádár forces cooperated with the Red Army and KGB to isolate and eliminate the last pockets of resistance in Budapest and throughout the country. Ultimately, Soviet forces disarmed the National Guard and the Hungarian Army; the insurgents, realizing that further armed struggle was useless, either went into hiding or fled to the West. By November 9, Soviet Marshal Georgii Zhukov could already report to Moscow that "life is gradually returning to normal in the country."[2] While the costs of putting down the resistance had been high, even for the Soviets,[3] the larger consequence for Hungarians was that the revolution lost both its armed forces and its political core.

After the Nagy government collapsed, the leaders of the non-Communist opposition parties were more-or-less reduced to the status of passive observers. One notable exception was István Bibó, minister of state of the Petőfi Party, who tried to uphold the integrity of the revolutionary government in Parliament, standing his ground until November 6. On the day of the second invasion, he formulated a memorable appeal to his countrymen not to capitulate: "I call upon the Hungarian people to regard neither the occupation force nor the puppet government it may install as a legal authority but rather to employ every means of passive resistance against it..."[4]

Despite the devastation of the Soviet attack, most of Hungarian society seemed to respond to Bibó's plea and continued to defy the new regime, keeping Soviet and Hungarian security forces tied up for months dealing with strikes, demonstrations, sabotage, work slowdowns, and other acts of resistance (Document No. 102). The invasion galvanized the opposition, unifying its many disparate elements through a renewed commitment to the uprising's principal goals of national independence and democratic freedoms. The exhilaration of having achieved so much against overwhelming odds, along with a continued readiness to make sacrifices for their rav-

---

[1] Portions of this part were originally based on János M. Rainer, "The City: Center of Post-Revolutionary Crisis, 1957–63," in *Budapest: A History from Its Beginnings to 1998*, ed. András Gerő and János Poór (Highland Lakes, N.J.: Atlantic Research and Publications, 1997), 233–250. János Rainer and the editors are grateful to Atlantic Research and Publications, Inc. for their courtesy.

[2] For Zhukov's report, see *Sovietskii Soyuz i vengerskii krizis*, 629–630.

[3] Although Zhukov reported on November 9 that from October 24 through November 6, 377 Soviet troops had been killed and 881 wounded, recent data puts the number of casualties significantly higher. According to Russian scholar Alexandr M. Kirov, 640 Soviet troops (including 85 officers) were lost during military actions. Together with the 1251 wounded and 67 missing in action, this makes a total loss of 1958 men due to the military conflict. See Györkei and Horváth, *Soviet Military Intervention*, 187, 204–205.

[4] For the text of Bibó's proclamation of November 4, see István Bibó, *Democracy, Revolution, Self-Determination: Selected Writings*, ed. Károly Nagy (Highland Lakes, N.J.: Atlantic Research and Publications, 1991), 325–327. For details on his proposals after November 4, see *Bibó István összegyűjtött munkái*, vol. 3, ed. István Kemény and Mátyás Sárközi (Bern: Európai Protestáns Magyar Szabadegyetem, 1993), 881–885.

aged country, kept the spirit of resistance alive. Even unrequited hopes for help from the West, which dwindled after November 4, did not die out altogether.

The nature of Kádár's motivations and intentions at this crucial stage remains a fundamental question. The available records, albeit fragmentary, offer some insights into his frame of mind when, after heated debates within the CPSU Presidium on November 2 and 3, he accepted the leadership of the new Hungarian government. For one thing, he had no plans to restore Stalinism to Hungary (Document Nos. 70 and 78). Believing that Kremlin leaders, especially Khrushchev, were anxious about the fragility of the current government, he was ready to go back to Budapest immediately and to hold talks with the reform communists, even if it meant granting concessions. He undoubtedly hoped that Hungarian society would understand that their opposition to the Soviet empire had gone too far and that they would accept the Moscow-dictated compromise: a drastic curtailment of national independence and democratic freedoms in exchange for assurances that neither Rákosi nor his methods would ever be restored. But he was disappointed in virtually all of his expectations. He counted on Nagy's support as the country's second-ranking politician, but Nagy rejected the ultimatum even before it had been completely formulated, choosing instead to follow his own road to tragedy (and in the process embodying the fate of the revolution).[5]

Moreover, Kádár was not able to act with complete independence. Moscow's three emissaries— Georgii Malenkov, Mikhail Suslov, and Averki Aristov—had been sent to Budapest to oversee the transfer of power. Together with KGB head Ivan Serov and Ambassador Yurii Andropov, they directed the first stage of the post-Stalin "normalization" process from early November until mid-December. Moscow's control mechanisms went as far as assigning three security agents to follow Kádár everywhere. In fact, the Soviets left their mark on virtually every aspect of the immediate post-revolutionary period, from Kádár's increasingly tough negotiations with the Workers' Councils, to the introduction of repressive measures in December 1956, and even to the kidnapping of Nagy.

The Nagy Problem

For both Kádár and Moscow, the problem of how to deal with Nagy was perhaps the most immediate one. Nagy's refusal to resign as premier, and the Yugoslav decision to grant him asylum at the Embassy on November 4 directly undermined Kádár's claim to legitimacy. The Yugoslav move sparked a furious round of démarches from both Moscow and the Kádár regime to Belgrade. Khrushchev wrote to Tito personally, warning that the situation could "result in irreparable damage" to Soviet-Yugoslav relations (Document No. 90).

Tito found himself in a difficult spot. At Brioni, he had agreed to help the Soviets by convincing Nagy to turn over power to Kádár in the course of the second invasion. But the embassy had taken Nagy in before realizing that he had defiantly denounced the invasion in a nationwide radio broadcast and refused to resign. Having already acted, the Yugoslavs were understandably reluctant to damage their international prestige by reneging on an offer of sanctuary (Document No. 91). As a compromise, Tito proposed transferring Nagy to Yugoslavia, arguing that this would eliminate him as a political factor in Hungary. But Khrushchev understood that Nagy would always be a rallying point for opponents of the new regime. Tito only aggravated the situation when he delivered a speech to a Yugoslav Party meeting on November 11 which openly criticized Moscow's early handling of the Hungarian demonstrations, and called the invasion a "lesser evil" (Document No. 96).

Over the next two weeks, the Kádár government, the USSR, Yugoslavia, and even Romania held almost continuous talks on the issue. Nagy was a problem nobody wanted, yet no solution could be found that was acceptable to everyone. Belgrade wanted to extricate itself from its uncomfortable position, but refused to agree to Nagy's departure from the embassy without a guarantee of safe passage. Deputy Foreign Minister Dobrivoje Vidić, sent to Budapest by Tito to find a face-saving solution, held several unsuccessful rounds of negotiations with both Kádár and

---

[5] For Nagy's behavior after November 4, 1956 see Rainer, *Nagy Imre,* 2:339–437.

the members of the Nagy group (Document Nos. 100 and 101). Kádár was willing to let Nagy go to Yugoslavia but insisted that he and his associates first admit that they had made mistakes and pledge their support for the regime—something Nagy was unwilling to do. Finally, the Soviet delegation in Hungary (Malenkov, Suslov and Aristov) came up with a dramatic idea: to entice Nagy to leave the embassy grounds, then promptly arrest him, extract an appropriate statement of abdication, and send him to Romania, where Romanian leader Gheorghiu Dej had offered to hold him in custody. Kádár agreed, and the impasse was soon, brutally, resolved. (Document No. 98)

On November 22 at 6:30 in the evening, after Kádár had signed an agreement with the Yugoslavs guaranteeing the safety of the Nagy group,[6] the ex-prime minister, his entourage and their families left the embassy and boarded a bus that they were told would take them to their homes. Once on board, however, and over the protests of the Yugoslav ambassador who witnessed the scene, Soviet NKVD forces arrested the group and drove them to an undisclosed location in the city. Now under confinement, Nagy was pressured to declare his support for the Kádár government, but he refused, whereupon he and his colleagues were forcibly transported to Romania and held *incommunicado* for the next several months. This "solution" temporarily removed Nagy from the scene, but his ultimate fate had yet to be sealed. In the meantime, the episode contributed directly to a further worsening of Soviet-Yugoslav (and Hungarian-Yugoslav) relations at a very sensitive time (Document No. 103).[7]

Crushing Popular Opposition

With Nagy out of the way for the time being, Kádár felt more freedom to act against other sources of opposition to his rule, including intellectuals and workers. The Hungarian Writers' Union, for example, was one of the most active resistance forces in the country at the time. After bringing together other professional and artistic associations, including the Academy of Sciences, the Union of Musicians, and the Hungarian Press Agency, the Writers' Union published on November 12 the first statement of its kind protesting the Soviet intervention. Other organizations soon followed suit, threatening the regime with an intolerable groundswell of popular sentiment.

At the heart of the popular movement was the network of Workers' Councils that had formed in the factories and municipalities during the uprising. Originally created to promote worker self-management and expand popular control over local and community affairs, the idea of Workers' Councils had initially won even Kádár's encouragement.[8] But in early November, as

---

[6] Nagy and eight of his colleagues signed a note agreeing to leave the Embassy based on the assurances provided by the Yugoslavs. It reads: "With reference to Comrade Vidić's statement to us today, according to which a written agreement has been concluded between the Kádár government and the Yugoslav government, which states that we may return home freely and unharmed, together with our families, and without retaliation for our past activities, we declare—expressing our thanks and gratitude—that we are leaving the building of the Yugoslav Embassy of our own free will on November 22, 1956." *Népszabadság* published the note on November 21, 1992.

[7] Leonid Gibianskii, "Soviet Yugoslav Relations and the Hungarian Revolution of 1956," *Cold War International History Project Bulletin*, no. 10 (March 1998): 139–148.

[8] For a history and analysis of the Workers' Councils and the resistance led by the Central Workers' Council, see László Varga, "Munkástanácsok 1956," in *Az Elhagyott Tömeg*, 199–237. For documents of the Central Workers' Council, see Id., "A Nagybudapesti Központi Munkástanács irataiból," parts 1 and 2, *Társadalmi Szemle* 46, nos. 8–9 (1991): 142–155; no. 11 (1991): 79–93. For recollections of leaders of workers' councils, see Gyula Kozák and Adrienn Molnár, eds., "*Szuronyok hegyén nem lehet dolgozni!*" *válogatás 1956-os munkástanácsvezetők visszaemlékezéseiből* (Budapest: Századvég Kiadó—1956-os Intézet, 1993). The recollections of Miklós Sebestyén and Ferenc Tőke can be found in Gyula Kozák, ed., *Szemle: Válogatás a brüsszeli Nagy Imre Intézet Folyóiratából* (Budapest: Századvég—1956-os Intézet, 1992), 50–69. See also Bill Lomax, ed., Hungarian Workers' Councils in 1956 (Highland Lakes N.J.: Atlantic Research and Publications, 1990); István Kemény and Bill Lomax, eds., *Magyar Munkástanácsok 1956-ban* (Paris: Magyar Füzetek, 1986).

the new government asserted control and armed resistance died down, the councils began to organize strikes and other disruptive actions, taking a serious toll on the national economy. On November 14, the stakes grew higher with the creation of the Central Workers' Council of Greater Budapest (KMT), an amalgam of smaller organizations based in the capital. Two days later, its members elected a new leadership—including Sándor Rácz, Sándor Bali, György Kalocsay, and Ferenc Tőke—that was even more radical than the previous group. The powerful new entity proceeded to table several broader political demands—the reinstatement of Nagy, the removal of Soviet troops, and respect for Hungary's neutrality, among other things—and thus seriously increased the political stakes for the new regime.

Despite having no intention of brooking such wide-ranging demands, Kádár had no choice but to negotiate with the KMT. The Workers' Councils occupied the major factories, and the regime needed the cooperation of the labor force in order to restart the economy. Moreover, it was hard to argue that the councils were "alien to the regime:" they had played no role in the excesses of late October and had no connection whatsoever to the armed resistance. On the contrary, they saw themselves as true socialists. These factors ruled out the use of armed force as an option. Instead, the government, surprisingly, offered a number of concessions, including an across-the-board wage increase of 8–15 percent and greater worker self-management. The tactic seemed to work. In return for this gesture, on November 16 the KMT agreed to go back to work.[9]

At the same time, the KMT moved forward with plans to create a national Workers' Council. The organizers set November 21 as the date for the inaugural congress, but Kádár balked. His later policies would show that he was relatively flexible and open-minded when it came to economic reform, but a nationwide workers' organization represented a clear threat to the regime's still tenuous hold on power. Although he continued to offer wage and management concessions on the one hand (in part to split worker unity), on the other hand he shut the door to any broader political demands. He ordered tanks to block access to the National Sports Hall where the first session of the national council was to meet, and began large-scale arrests of labor organizers (Document No. 102). In retaliation, the KMT decided to call a general strike, which took place on December 11–12. It was a defiant gesture, but in the face of tougher retaliation by the authorities it was the last major action the Workers' Council movement would undertake.

The turning point in the regime's handling of the opposition came at a meeting of the HSWP CC on December 2–5. Branding the uprising a "counterrevolution," party leaders blamed its outbreak on the mistakes of both Rákosi and Nagy, and began laying a legal foundation for a far-reaching program of repression lasting over the next several months and years (Document No. 104). Within a week, the regime had outlawed the Workers' Councils and declared martial law as part of a nation-wide emergency decree. A wave of arrests and military reprisals followed. The most tragic of these was the clash at Salgótarján, an industrial town in Northern Hungary, where dozens of people died.[10] On December 16, the first execution under martial law occurred; on average, one or two followed each week thereafter.[11] In early January, the authorities expanded the definition of martial law to include sanctions against fomenting a strike. As a consequence, the Central Workers' Council of Csepel, which had largely taken over the coordinating role of the KMT, dissolved itself. More harsh measures ensued. On January 5, 1957, the government authorized the death penalty for anyone refusing to return to work.[12] On January 17, the Writers' Union was declared illegal, and in mid-February a large-scale show trial began at the

[9] Andrew Felkay, *Hungary and the USSR, 1956–1988: Kadar's Political Leadership* (New York: Greenwood Press, 1989), 92; Litván, Bak and Legters, *The Hungarian Revolution of 1956*, 110.

[10] János Dávid, Sándor Geskó, and Pál Schiffer, *Forradalom, sortűz, megtorlás* (Budapest: Progresszió, 1990).

[11] For background on the imposition of martial law and retaliation in general, see János M. Rainer [Elek Fényes, pseud.], "Adatok az 1956-os forradalmat követő megtorláshoz," *Beszélő*, no. 19 (1987): 43–63. See also János M. Rainer, "The Reprisals," in *Encounters: A Hungarian Quarterly Reader*, ed. Zsófia Zachár (Budapest: Balassi Kiadó, c1999), 249–259.

[12] For a concise account of the KMT and the broader workers' council issue, see Litván, Bak and Legters, The *Hungarian Revolution* of 1956, 108–114.

Budapest Municipal Court. Eventually, the range of essentially political acts treated as crimes widened to encompass virtually any form of dissent.

Another question worth exploring is how to explain the regime's shift from seeking compromise in early November to using repressive methods one month later. Pressure from the Kremlin's envoys does not fully account for the change. Had Kádár wanted to oppose the Soviets, he could have done so even with their presence in the country. For example, he did manage to stop a plan to deport captured freedom fighters and civilians to the USSR.[13] The most likely explanation for Kádár's shifting tactics is that he was surprised by the level of resistance he encountered in Hungarian society. Notes from his meetings in Moscow show that he expected to be able to negotiate with authoritative party officials and leaders of the former opposition, with whom he would have shared experiences from the post-1945 period. Instead, he found himself confronting mainly younger-generation workers who claimed to speak for the broader resistance movement. The party opposition, led by Nagy, who was now at the Yugoslav Embassy, was intransigent, while the intellectuals and others, represented by the Writers' Union, the Journalists' Association, and the Revolutionary Council of Hungarian Intellectuals, supported the KMT. This left the HWP leadership as the only group with whom Kádár felt comfortable. Even there, sympathizers with the party's "moderate opposition" held sway until early December, including György Aczél,[14] Lajos Fehér, Antal Gyenes, József Köböl and László Orbán[15] (Document No. 95). Kádár's "partners" thus had either withdrawn from public activity or had no viable political base. Some had even gone over to the opposition.

Aside from the USSR and other so-called allies such as Romanian party boss Gheorghiu-Dej who advocated suppressing the opposition, Kádár felt compelled to accept help from the former Stalinists who had joined the new HSWP and were already beginning to creep back into middle and upper leadership posts. On the one hand, they were the only faction he could rely on to act decisively. On the other hand, if he resisted them, he feared that he might lose authority or even be replaced, if not by Rákosi himself then by a self-appointed successor. (Toward the end of the year he decided to cooperate with them.) On the other hand, he appeared to undergo another internal shift, setting aside his conviction that the revolution had sprung from a genuine internal Hungarian social and political crisis. He now seemed willing to see the October events as the product of anti-communist plots. And in his mind, plots had to be dealt with firmly.

Kádár's Consolidation of Power

By spring 1957, Kádár had achieved some significant political successes. He had forged a united party leadership and won the support of the Soviet Presidium during his visit to Moscow in late March. In the course of those talks, he reached agreement with the Soviets about the upcoming trial of Nagy, which had become an increasingly important issue for him personally. The court proceeding could be used to show that there had been a plot at the highest levels of the previous government, a "fact" that could explain why the regime collapsed in October and the resistance rose against him in November. Equally important, the Kremlin agreed that Rákosi and his group would not be allowed to return to Hungary (Document No. 112). While Kádár was negotiating in Moscow, signs of his increasing hold on the Hungarian political scene emerged. On March 29,

---

[13] On this issue, see the Report by I. Serov and Yu. Andropov from Budapest on November 14 in *Sovietskii Soyuz i vengerskii krizis*, 651–652 . For another, detailed Soviet report on the deportation see Document No. 97.

[14] György Aczél was a member of the HSWP PCC (later CC) beginning in early November and represented a more lenient position toward the Nagy case. He served as deputy minister of culture from April 1957-February 1958 and played a dominant role in shaping cultural policy during the entire Kádár era.

[15] László Orbán was deputy head of the HWP CC Scientific Department from February 1956 on, and deputy head of the HSWP CC Department for Agitation and Propaganda from November 1956. He was a member of the HSWP CC beginning in June 1957.

György Marosán organized the first communist mass meetings in the capital. On May Day, just before the session of Parliament and the national conference of the party, the two leaders were able to produce a crowd of about 100,000 at Heroes' Square to listen to their speeches.

In addition, large-scale resistance had already ended by January 1957. The kidnapping of Nagy the previous November and the arrest of the leaders of the Central Workers' Council in early December deprived the resistance of its symbolic leaders. The regime now stepped up reprisals, including arrests and other punitive acts targeting average citizens, as well as the issuance of harsh decrees such as the December decision of the provisional Central Committee of the party (Document No. 104) and the government's January 6 declaration on the "main tasks" facing the country.[16] All of these steps made it increasingly clear that no compromise could be expected. What one side perceived as rigidity was seen by the other side as the ultimate concession. While the regime's actions grew more severe, the opposition was simultaneously growing weaker. Not only had the leadership been lost, but the range of groups and individuals representing divergent political ideas had also shrunk significantly. Many of these people had left the country in a surge of emigration that reached its peak in late November and early December.[17] Those who stayed were persecuted in various ways. Ultimately, the Central Workers' Council sat down at the negotiating table and *de facto* endorsed the communist leaders. Although abandoning the revolutionary program entirely was not feasible, compromising on attitudes and behavior was still possible.

In effect, by early 1957 a wave of acceptance had swept over Hungary. The mass public turnout for official celebrations of May Day in Budapest was one indication of this. Force alone could not account for the change. It was as if the population recognized that the cause of the revolution had been lost and the realities of the new situation had settled firmly in place. Every resource had been exhausted—strikes, speeches, mass meetings, and negotiations—and all had failed. For many people, it simply seemed impossible to go on. General frustration contributed to the feeling of political apathy captured in the cliché: "nearly everything was an illusion." The desire for a return to "normal" life grew, even if that meant reinstating the *status quo ante*. At the same time, the public genuinely welcomed the benefits that could be traced back to October (for example, an end to the forced collection of agricultural surpluses, improvements in living standards, and especially a halt to mass purges). Typical sentiments ran along the lines of: "At least we accomplished something ... We couldn't have done anything more." Once life returned to its earlier patterns, many Hungarians simply thought it was wiser to resurrect old customs.

It should also be pointed out that the May Day crowd at Heroes' Square in 1957 included a significant number of Hungarians who had reaped various personal or social advantages from the pre-1956 communist regime—mid- and lower-level members of the vast party and government bureaucracy, for example, as well as other ordinary citizens who either supported the regime or felt no special antipathy toward it. These people had undoubtedly felt terrorized during the revolution because of their status or sympathies, and possibly humiliated or remorseful in its aftermath. On that holiday they celebrated a combination of liberation and victory, some almost certainly harboring hopes of revenge against their countrymen who had turned their way of life upside down. Contrary to general opinion in Hungary today, this group represented a not inconsiderable proportion of the overall population.

[16] For a discussion of the draft of the government declaration, see the minutes of the December 28, 1956, meeting of the HSWP Provisional Central Committee in *A Magyar Szocialista Munkáspárt ideiglenes vezető testületeinek jegyzőkönyvei*, vol. 1, *1956. november 11.–1957. január 14*, ed. Karola Némethné Vágyi and Levente Sipos (Budapest: Intera, 1993), 281–300; for the text of the government declaration, see *Népszabadság*, January 7, 1957.

[17] Between November 1956 and February 1957, approximately 200,000 people escaped from Hungary, mostly to Austria (174,000) and to a lesser extent to Yugoslavia (20,000), prompting a worldwide campaign to facilitate their settlement in various western countries. Some 10,000 refugees soon returned, but most settled either in Western Europe or North America. See the top secret report of the Central Statistical Office from 1957, republished in "A KSH nyilvánosságra nem került felmérése az 1956-os disszidálásról," *Regio* 2, no. 4 (1991): 174–211.

It is clear that in the first flush of victory, Kádár tried to return to the years 1948-1949, which he thought of as the "golden age" of the communist era. This was the period between the forced union of the two workers' parties and the trial of László Rajk. It was a time when party control was nearly total but did not yet feature the excesses of Rákosi. Just as the ÁVH prosecuted large numbers of citizens in the late 1940s on the grounds that they were supposedly "enemies of the people's democracy" and "reactionary elements," Kádár blamed the 1956 revolt on similarly hostile elements—"Horthy-ite army officers, gendarmes and the like"—and declared that they did not "actually have to be tried in-depth," only "brought to justice, sentenced to death and hanged in a procession."[18] On the other hand, in 1948-1949, the regime was still willing to tolerate a degree of autonomy, for example in agriculture, as long as it suited the demands of power. Kádár's conception was thus to restore the party's unquestioned authority, but to retain the ability to act flexibly, without the need to resort to Rákosi's abuses of power.

It would have been more logical for Kádár to look back to the 1953-1954 period, the years of Nagy's reforms. After all, 1948 was the year Moscow imposed the single party system, which in turn led to the purges, beginning with the Rajk trial in 1949, and to the imprisonment of Kádár himself in 1951 on various trumped-up charges. Choosing 1953 as a starting point would have allowed Kádár to draw a line between Rákosi and himself, which he did not manage to do during the first stage of his rule. Beyond that, there were remarkable similarities between Nagy's and Kádár's policies, despite the ambiguity of Kádár's assessment of the 1953 "New Course." For example, Kádár's ideas about expanding the government and promoting a new "policy of alliances," which he outlined in December 1956, resembled Nagy's attempts at political reform through the creation of the Patriotic People's Front in 1954. It was not easy, though, to find the way back to 1953–1954. The rifts created by 1956 and Nagy's own personality raised serious obstacles. Still, a discernible path did exist that connected Nagy's reform policies with the prime minister's goals of 1956. As late as October of that year, even Kádár himself had followed its route until he realized it was too dangerous.

The Politics of the Nagy Trial and Execution

In Kádár's mind, the Nagy problem was not only a challenge to the new regime but in some ways its antithesis because Nagy so directly personified the 1956 revolution.

The matter of the "responsibility and accountability of Imre Nagy and others in the Hungarian events, and their legal consequences" was first raised at a summit of five communist parties (from the Soviet Union, Hungary, Romania, Czechoslovakia and Bulgaria) in Budapest from January 1–4, 1957 (Document No. 108). Interestingly, the protocols of the top HSWP organizations hardly mention these talks. In fact, according to previously secret Russian documents, the meeting originally convened to deal with two crucial but unrelated issues: the possible return to Hungary of Zoltán Szántó, one of the detainees from the Nagy group in Romania, and the question of whether to allow the existence of non-Communist parties in Hungary. The Szántó issue was important for Kádár because, as an experienced party leader who had opposed Rákosi, Szántó was a potential rival for the HSWP leadership. For reasons that remain unclear, the Romanians notified the Hungarians in late December that they were considering allowing Szántó to come back to Hungary (Document No. 107). The question of granting other political parties legal status in Hungary was of greater concern to the Soviets, who, after learning at the end of December that Kádár planned to publish a declaration on January 5 or 6 incorporating a provision to this effect, demanded an immediate summit—regardless of the traditional New

---

[18] Kádár's concluding remarks at the meeting of the Provisional Executive Committee of the Hungarian Socialist Workers' Party on April 2, 1957, appear in *A Magyar Szocialista Munkáspárt ideiglenes vezető testületeinek jegyzőkönyvei*, vol. 2, *1957. január 25.–1957. április 2*, ed. Karola Némethné Vágyi and Károly Urbán (Budapest: Intera, 1993), 357. For other parts of this meeting see Document No. 112.

Year's holiday (Document No. 107). However, although convened for different reasons, the summit also dealt with the Nagy issue. Who raised the subject is uncertain, but the discussion resulted in a fundamental reassessment of Nagy's role and opened the way for instituting legal action against his group.

Later in January, Kádár tried to advance the process by sending Gyula Kállai to Bucharest to create divisions among Nagy's supporters and extract self-critical statements from them. The now-deposed prime minister was no longer a major factor in his own right, but his acknowledgement of political responsibility would have yielded political advantages for Kádár. Yet, Nagy remained true to his decisions of October and November and refused to go along. Reporting on his failed mission on January 29, Kállai, in the first known reference to the idea of a trial, said that perhaps "launching a court procedure could be considered."[19]

Kállai probably did not come up with the idea of a trial himself. It seems to have originated either with Kádár or possibly a narrow circle of Hungarian party leaders. In January, the Provisional Executive Committee decided to "collect information on the activities of Nagy's group in October and November"[20] in order to use it at trial. In February, they confirmed this approach,[21] and the first of a series of "White Books" was produced on Nagy's alleged crimes going back to 1948, although it did not initially circulate to the public.[22]

In early March 1957, again in Bucharest, Kállai informed Boris Ponomarev,[23] head of the CPSU CC department in charge of relations with foreign communist parties, that "the majority of the members of the Executive Committee (Comrades Kádár, Marosán, Münnich, and Kállai) had agreed upon organizing the judicial procedure for Nagy and his group." In his report, Ponomarev mentions an "earlier plan" to call the Nagy group to account, clearly referring to Kállai's mission in January.[24] This required approval at the highest levels, however. The Soviet-Hungarian summit in Moscow in late March offered the opportunity. At that session, as Kádár recalled a few days later at an Executive Committee meeting, "[t]he question of Imre Nagy and the others also arose. We raised it. The comrades think it proper that we call him to account with suitable severity" (Document No. 112). The Executive Committee and the Central Committee endorsed the idea on April 5. On April 9, Kádár pressed the Executive Committee to adopt a decision "on the arrest of certain elements on the recommendation of the Ministry of Interior, and on launching a legal procedure against them."[25] (Interestingly, Kádár generally did not mention Nagy by name in formal situations.)

At this same session, the leadership devised a concept for the investigation and the trial, and a report appeared later under Kállai's name entitled "The Counter-Revolution in Hungary in the

[19] "Az IB 1957 január 29-én tartott ülése első napirendi pontjának jegyzőkönyvi kivonata" (Minute of Resolution of the first point of the agenda of the [HSWP] PEC meeting on January 29, 1957), in A Magyar Szocialista Munkáspárt ideiglenes vezető testületeinek jegyzőkönyvei, vol. 2, 79

[20] Ibid., 75.

[21] See, "Az MSZMP IKB 1957. Február 26-ai ülésének jegyzőkönyve" (Minutes of the HSWP PCC meeting on February 26, 1967). Ibid., 157–237. For the resolution published after this meeting, see Document No. 111.

[22] This first study of Nagy's role was published without indicating the author. See A jobboldali nézetektől az osztályárulásig: Adalékok Nagy Imrének és csoportjának elméleti és gyakorlati tevékenységéhez 1947–1956 (Budapest: Kossuth, 1957). While the document was intended strictly for an internal party audience (with all copies numbered in order to control circulation), a year later another book was published, which, as the fifth volume of the propagandistic "White book" series, already targeted a much larger public. See The Counter-Revolutionary Conspiracy of Imre Nagy and his Accomplices (Budapest: Information Bureau of the Council of Ministers of the Hungarian People's Republic, 1958).

[23] Boris N. Ponomarev was a member of the CPSU CC from 1956, head of the CPSU CC Department for Ties with Foreign Communist Parties from 1955–1957 and of the International Department from March 1957–1986.

[24] For Ponomarev's report on March 12, 1957 see Sereda and Stykalin, Hiányzó lapok, 260–263.

[25] "Melléklet az Intéző Bizottság április 9-i ülése jegyzőkönyvéhez" (Supplement to the Minutes of the Executive Committee meeting on April 9), in A Magyar Szocialista Munkáspárt ideiglenes vezető testületeinek jegyzőkönyvei, vol. 3, 1957. április 5.–1957. május 17, ed. Magdolna Baráth and István Feitl (Budapest: Intera, 1993), 69.

Light of Marxism-Leninism."[26] The phrases it used, particularly in claiming that the Nagy group had deliberately laid the ground for the revolt "in cooperation with the imperialists," were often repeated word for word in investigators' reports, the indictment, and the verdict alike. With the structure and plan for the trial in place even before the arrest of the main character in the drama, all that was left was for the play to move on to its predetermined climax.

In late March 1957, a Hungarian police official traveled with a special unit to Romania to arrest Nagy and his colleagues. Their last stop was in the town of Snagov, on April 14, where they took Nagy into custody and returned him to Budapest. The Interior Ministry then immediately initiated its proceedings, following Kádár's instructions to "draw the poison fang" urgently. In fact, interrogations had already begun in Romania, but it took more than a year before the verdicts were finally reached.

Initially, the problem underlying the delay was that political considerations clashed with the schedule set by the Interior Ministry's Political Investigation Department for bringing the "principal criminals of the counterrevolution" to trial. It took months just to decide whom to indict. The final list included Pál Maléter and Sándor Kopácsi, who had been arrested on November 4 and originally considered for separate trial, and Miklós Gimes, a leading resistance figure after the revolution. General Béla Király, the commander in chief of the National Guard who left the country ahead of arrest, was separated from the main trial. The Interior Ministry also wanted to arrest Zoltán Tildy in early April, but for political reasons waited until late May. The investigation continued to creep ahead because most of the defendants pleaded not guilty, and the authorities chose to avoid the usual resort to torture in order to preserve legal proprieties.

The government eventually charged Nagy and his companions with organizing a plot, beginning in 1955, "to overthrow the people's democratic regime" and "seize power," and with ultimately carrying out the scheme in October 1956. The indictment also accused Nagy and Pál Maléter of high treason. With few exceptions, the allegations centered around the defendants' actual activities at the time, including opposition and government work, public statements and diplomatic initiatives. But now the indictment presented them as criminal.

The defendants, who were kept in solitary confinement, reacted to the charges and the various attendant psychological pressures differently. Most eventually admitted responsibility, but without accepting the official interpretation of the facts. József Szilágyi, Nagy's secretary during the revolution, refused to cooperate altogether. Nagy tried to do the same at first, declining to answer a single question until late May 1957, when he changed his strategy and decided at least to try to establish the facts and explain his decisions. However, along with Maléter, he consistently denied the charges. Géza Losonczy broke down psychologically, then, after undergoing a hunger strike, collapsed physically as well. In his delirium, he confessed to a variety of offenses not even raised by the prosecution. On a number of points, the defendants' accounts did not agree. Nagy, for example, tried to mitigate the opposition's role within the party in order to avoid being accused of conspiracy. The investigators played on these differences, with at least partial success. But in trying to build a credible case they failed completely, and the refusal of the main defendants, especially Nagy, to buckle under made it impossible to hold the proceedings in public. The show trial had to take place *in camera* from beginning to end.[27]

Events continued to move slowly. At a June 22 CC meeting held to prepare for the next party conference, Kádár commented that the "investigation was going on with difficulty and was mak-

[26] Gyula Kállai, *The Counter-Revolution in Hungary in the Light of Marxism-Leninism* (Budapest: Zrínyi, 1957). First published in Hungarian as id., "A magyarországi ellenforradalom a marxizmus-leninizmus fényében," *Társadalmi Szemle* 13, no. 1 (1957): 12–39.

[27] Documents from the trial were carefully guarded in the archives of the Interior Ministry until 1989. Today they can be found at the Hungarian National Archives, see MOL, XX–5–h. *Legfelsőbb Bíróság Népbírósági Tanácsa iratai V–150.000 sz. Nagy Imre és társai pere* (Documents of the Supreme Court's Council of People's Courts. The trial of Imre Nagy and his associates).

ing little progress."[28] He listed several causes but left out the most important one—the international implications of the trial. Days before the CC meeting, Kádár and Interior Minister Béla Biszku traveled secretly to Moscow to inform the Kremlin about preparations for the party conference, but also about the investigation. Because of its significance abroad, the Soviets followed the trial process carefully, although no documents have been found to prove they participated in it directly. Kádár brought three documents with him to Moscow: an update on the investigation including the behavior of the defendants; a list of prosecution exhibits; and a note on the relationship of Nagy and his co-defendants with Yugoslavia.[29]

By early August, the Interior Ministry had prepared the indictment, which Biszku also took to Moscow. He told the Soviets that while the HSWP leadership had not yet decided on the penalties, the inclination appeared to be "to sentence Nagy, Losonczy, Donáth, Gimes, Maléter, Szilágyi and Király to capital punishment." Andropov, who by this time had become head of the CPSU CC department for ties with other socialist parties within the bloc, reviewed the indictment and declared that it was "basically acceptable" but needed to be improved further, "especially ... the part that deals with the treacherous Nagy's group's connection with the imperialists" (Document Nos. 116 and 117).

The Hungarians scheduled the trial to follow a special U.N. session in September, but at Soviet request Kádár postponed it until after the November 1957 communist party summit in Moscow.[30] On December 21, the HSWP CC finally decided that "[l]egal procedures must be allowed to take their course" (Document No. 115). The indictment followed quickly, and the trial began on February 5, 1958. Once again, however, the Soviets asked for a deferral, this time because of an upcoming East-West summit. Kádár had already reflected growing impatience with the delays. "Retaliation would have been more justifiable between November 4–5, but it was then that we were the weakest," he said at the December 21 CC meeting (Document No. 115). "The problem is that the greater the delay, the more complicated the whole case becomes," he noted on February 14, 1958, when the HSWP CC discussed the second Soviet request. "At the time when we could have settled the case, we had not the strength to do so." He proudly declared, however, that "discretion was also maintained, which is very good."[31] Kádár's statements soon filtered out to the West and the London émigré publication *Irodalmi Újság* quoted them in the following distorted form: "When this trial was topical, we had no strength to institute it. Now that we are strong, it is no longer topical."[32]

The problem in moving ahead seems to have been a function not only of settling on a date for the trial, but foreseeing what course it might take. It has never been established whether the Soviets also suggested imposing a sentence other than death, although the Soviet "peace offensive" in early 1958 and Khrushchev's imminent visit to Budapest might even have warranted a political amnesty from Moscow's viewpoint. After the December decision, Khrushchev indicated his interest in a solution along these lines through Moscow's new ambassador, Yevgenii I. Gromov. Kádár informed his colleagues about this in December in the following way: "Comrade Khrushchev said he approved of our efforts to get to the bottom of this matter. He asked how we were going to do it. He was probably interested in what we were going to do: to send them to

[28] "Jegyzőkönyv a Központi Bizottság 1957. Június 22-ei üléséről" (Minutes of the June 22, 1957 Central Committee meeting), in *A Magyar Szocialista Munkáspárt ideiglenes vezető testületeinek jegyzőkönyvei*, vol. 4, *1957. május 21.–1957. június 24*, ed. Magdolna Baráth and Zoltán Ripp (Budapest: Intera, 1994), 192–193.

[29] Regarding Kádár's and Biszku's preparations for their visit to Moscow, see Éva Gál, András B. Hegedűs, György Litván and János M. Rainer, eds., *A "Jelcin Dosszié:" Szovjet dokumentumok 1956-ról* (Budapest: Századvég Kiadó-1956-os Intézet, 1993), 193–199. The CPSU CC Presidium dealt with these documents at its meeting on June 19, 1957. These documents are to be found at TsKhSD, F. 89. Op. 2. D. 5, Ll. 35–137.

[30] See Andropov's recommendation to this effect in Document No. 117.

[31] Minutes of the HSWP CC meeting on February 14, 1957. Published in Karola Némethné Vágyi, László Soós, György T. Varga and Gábor Ujváry, eds., *A Magyar Szocialista Munkáspárt Központi Bizottságának 1957–1958. évi jegyzőkönyvei* (Budapest: Magyar Országos Levéltár, 1997), 237–245.

[32] "Budapesti jelentés" (Report from Budapest), *Irodalmi Újság* (London), May 1, 1958.

prison, reprimand them or what? He approves of finishing the matter."[33] But Kádár disagreed with the idea of a reprieve. "Should we grant amnesty now, it would include the principal criminals, which would weaken the people's democratic order," he explained, to the approval of nearly all other members of the party leadership. Thus, in February 1958, when the HSWP CC finally agreed to postpone the trial, they were also hoping to avoid imposing a lighter sentence.

However, the February debate over postponement created a rift in the party leadership. One Central Committee candidate member, Márton Valkó, argued that pronouncement of the death sentence, a term scrupulously avoided until then, should be followed by an immediate pardon. "This is not feasible," Kádár replied indignantly.[34] In March, when John Gollan, general secretary of the British Communist Party, asked Kádár if the Hungarian leaders were sensitive to the interests of other communist parties, he answered roughly as follows: "Had we not taken the interests of the international Communist movement into consideration, we would have done away with the gang of Imre Nagy long ago."[35]

By the spring of 1958, Kádár had dug in hard enough to get what he wanted. "If you compare the climate of public opinion now with that of a year-and-a-half ago," he said after Khrushchev's visit in April, "frankly speaking, no one could have imagined the political success that is within [our] reach [now]."[36] At the same time, Kádár was extremely cautious. The Political Committee ordered that a CC plenary meeting be convened later that month to deal with the Nagy trial, among other topics. But Kádár postponed the meeting until early June. In the meantime he went to Moscow once more to gather information on the all-important international context—particularly the deteriorating Soviet-Yugoslav relationship and the West's negative reaction to Soviet initiatives for a summit. On May 27, the Political Committee held a secret meeting and resolved that "the court procedure against the special counterrevolutionary group guilty of intending to overthrow the legal order of the people's democracy should take its course."[37] A secret CC session on June 6 confirmed the decision.

The trial resumed between June 9 and 15 behind closed doors. As before, Nagy consistently denied the charges and refused to acknowledge the competence of the court. At sentencing, he declined to plead for mercy, declaring instead that the final verdict would be up to the Hungarian people and the international working class. Nagy, Maléter, and Gimes were executed on June 16.[38] The authorities made public the facts of the trial and the sentences on June 17, after the executions had already been carried out.

The Era of Reprisals

The fate of Nagy's group epitomized the atmosphere of reprisal in the late 1950s in Hungary. During his March 1957 visit to Moscow, Kádár agreed with the Soviets on the need to accelerate retaliation against the rebels and to try their cases in closed session. This was probably deemed necessary because of world-wide protests against the regime's harsh tactics. By then, the last vestiges of serious resistance had disappeared; even the legally constituted Workers' Councils had been replaced by party organizations.

The period of massive reprisals lasted from April 1957 until spring 1959. The people's courts instituted in April 1957 tried not only those people who continued to resist authorities after November 4, but large numbers of others who had only taken part in the revolution before that

[33] Meeting of the HSWP Political Committee on December 28, 1957, see MOL, 288 f. 5/59. ő.e.

[34] Némethné Vágyi et al., *A Magyar Szocialista Munkáspárt Központi Bizottságának 1957–1958. évi jegyzőkönyvei,* 242, 244.

[35] Vyacheslav T. Sereda and Elena D. Orekhova, "V. Sz. Bajkov naplójából: Feljegyzés Nemes Dezső et.-tel az MSZMP KB póttagjával folytatott beszélgetésről 1958 áprilisában," *Tekintet* 8, nos. 5–6 (1995): 201.

[36] Meeting of the HSWP Political Committee on April 15, 1958, see MOL, 288. f. 5/75. ő.e., p. 34.

[37] Meeting of the HSWP Central Committee on June 6, 1958, see MOL, 288. f. 4/17. ő.e., p. 1.

[38] József Szilágyi, whose case had been tried separately, was executed in April.

date or in its preparations. After April, the police began to make mass arrests, and the prosecutor's office and the people's courts soon became overloaded. By early Spring 1959, a variety of factors led to a slight relaxation of the terror, including a partial amnesty. Domestically, there was no further evidence of civil unrest that might have justified continuing the process; superpower relations had improved; and by then even the country's leaders had become nervous about the overzealousness of the police. Even more than security, the authorities were preoccupied with economic concerns, especially the collectivization of agriculture, and understood the need to ease those burdens on society. However, the use of coercion by no means ended altogether. Intellectuals who kept up resistance after the uprising, along with certain other political offenders, continued to be tried and condemned.

Besides being a "mass" phenomenon, the reprisals were also extremely cruel. Between December 1956 and the summer of 1961, when the last death sentence was carried out for offenses committed in 1956, 341 people were hanged, as many as in the darkest years of the Rákosi regime. Of that total, 229 received death sentences because of their role in the revolution.[39] Most were workers or soldiers in their 20s who had taken part in street fighting. During the first three years of the reprisals, 35,000 people faced legal action for insurrectionist activities; 26,000 went to trial; and 22,000 cases proceeded to sentencing. Prison terms were severe: almost half of those brought to trial were sentenced to terms of more than five years. In addition, between 1957 and 1960, approximately 13,000 people went to internment camps at Tököl and Kistarcsa. Tens of thousands were banned from their homes, dismissed from jobs (including over 1,000 teachers, mostly outside Budapest), or placed under police supervision. In all, the oppression affected more than 100,000 individuals and their families.

As repressive as it was, Kádár's brand of reprisal differed from the reign of terror of the Rákosi era in one important respect. Rákosi was at war with all of Hungarian society—from "class enemies" to the highest-ranking party leaders. After 1956, the Kádár regime targeted reprisals against fairly distinct groups. These groups had certain common features such as age and occupation; most were in their 20s and 30s, for example. The determining factor, however, was whether they had participated in the uprising and what their presumed attitude was toward the Kádár regime.

Aside from deterrence and revenge, Kádár's reprisals served various long-range goals. For one, the regime had to find an explanation for the revolution and the collapse of the old regime in October 1956. Kádár and the new elite had personally experienced the spontaneous and "mass" character of the rebellion. Many of them had even shared some of its democratic, anti-Stalinist goals and aspirations for independence. Yet they chose to interpret the uprising as a conspiracy by anti-communist, reactionary forces. This was why they labeled many ordinary citizens' actions as crimes. Critical opposition attitudes were described as "a plot to overthrow the people's democratic regime," and workers and peasants who took part in the revolt were called "jail-birds, ragamuffins, and kulaks." Armed resistance to occupying forces became "murder and wrecking state property." This kind of terminology became part of the official ideology of the regime toward the outside world.[40]

---

[39] The rest were sentenced for committing common crimes, mostly murders, or war crimes committed during World War II, and in one case for activities during the "White terror" that followed the fall of the first Hungarian Communist regime in 1919. See Attila Szakolczai, "A forradalmat követő megtorlás során kivégzettekről," in *Évkönyv III, 1994*, ed. János M. Bak et al. (Budapest: 1956-os Intézet, 1994), 237–257. It is worth mentioning that this new wave of trials dealing with World War II crimes served the propaganda goal of associating the revolution with fascism and linking 1956 to the history of "anti-communist terror" reaching back as far as 1920. See, István Rév "Counterrevolution" in *Between Past and Future*, ed. Sorin Antohi and Vladimir Tismaneanu (Budapest: CEU Press, 2000), 247–271. Concerning literature on reprisals in general, see footnote 11 above.

[40] For a typical survey of propaganda intended for distribution abroad, see the so called "White Books" entitled, *The Counter-Revolutionary Forces in the October Events in Hungary*, 4 vols., (Budapest: Information Bureau of the Council of Ministers of the Hungarian People's Republic, 1956–1957). The documents were published in German, French, and Russian, as well as the languages of most of the socialist countries. The White Books published in the individual counties of Hungary in 1957–58 summarized local "counterrevolutionary" events.

Another long-term goal for Kádár was to isolate activist opposition elements from the rest of the population once and for all. Those who played any part in the revolution could count on retaliation of some kind, but anyone who stayed passive was left alone. The main lesson of the reprisals was that it paid to keep silent. As early as the June 1957 HSWP conference, Kádár declared that in general people were not interested in grand political affairs, only in their own material well-being. In fact, as indicated above, many Hungarians who had been shaken by the suppression of their revolution were truly glad to see even minor signs of freedom and opportunity. The regime understood this and offered a wide array of benefits as part of a calculated effort to coopt the population, including a growing range of goods in the shops; tourist visas and the chance to buy $70 worth of foreign currency; and removal of the category "social background" from university applications. In addition, state intervention into the private lives of citizens became less obtrusive, and in some cases disappeared altogether. There were no compulsory political seminars in the work place. The party daily was no longer read out loud and discussed with workers every morning. Synchronized applause no longer accompanied official speeches. Individuals did not even have to demonstrate active support for the regime. All that was required was to keep quiet and go along.

Of course, this new social contract did not come without a cost. A "nationwide suppression" of feelings and memories followed, as described by the psychologist, Ferenc Mérei[41]. Discussion of the uprising and its repression was taboo and no one dared to mention the revolutionaries who were, or had been, in jail. This brand of "peace" opened up new vistas of personal comfort but at the same time destroyed social unity—the very solidarity that had been such a hallmark of the revolution. It was a tragic consequence of the period, and particularly of the reprisals, that democratic activity became impossible for almost two decades until the appearance of an entirely new generation.

Soviet-East European Relations after the Revolution

In the immediate aftermath of the uprising, the Soviet leadership found itself sharply divided over the direction Hungary should take. Their disputes covered a range of issues, and were closely linked to the ongoing power struggle in the Kremlin. At the height of the crisis, the debates over whether Hungary might "go the route of Yugoslavia" and become overly independent of Moscow, or whether changing the name of the HSWP in order to put distance between Kádár's group and "the Rákosi-Gerő clique" would undermine the entire party, became highly personal. At one point, Khrushchev and his colleagues scoffed at Molotov and his hardline allies for spreading "pernicious ideas" (Document No. 84) and viewing things too "simplistically and dogmatically" (Document No. 89).

Khrushchev won this round of the debate over the management of Eastern Europe. But the revolution had clearly come as a shock to him, exposing his failure to anticipate how quickly the unrest could spiral out of control, and leaving him vulnerable to later political attack. Even though he had understood the need to alleviate the satellites' economic plight and shape a more equitable balance in relations between the satellite states and the USSR, he was determined not to allow another outbreak to occur. The period following the revolution thus saw an ongoing back-and-forth between two priorities: reform and control.

In this confusing atmosphere, the heads of state of the bloc countries responded with a mixture of uncertainty and opportunism. As loyal members of the socialist camp, they looked to the Kremlin for direction. But as political leaders facing potential explosions at home, they had other pressures which required immediate action. In order to stabilize their power base against the chal-

---

[41] Ferenc Mérei was a well known scholar and a leading figure of the People's College movement before 1950. Arrested in 1958 for his participation in the revolution and in the following intellectual resistance, he was sentenced to ten years in prison but was amnestied in 1963.

lenge of the Hungarian events, bloc leaders in general were more inclined to use repression than to recast their previous policies. Khrushchev and his reform-oriented colleagues, no less disturbed at the unrest, saw no choice but to support the crackdowns while the East European leaders used the turmoil to promote themselves to Moscow as guarantors of stability and to oppose further reforms.

Nevertheless, Khrushchev strongly felt the need to tackle the region's underlying economic problems, which meant having to pursue a more flexible approach toward the bloc. With opponents of reform on two fronts—hardliners in the Kremlin and among the satellites—Khrushchev faced a lengthy battle. In early January 1957, two months after the uprising, he called the first meeting of allied leaders since the Hungarian events to discuss future relations and policies (Document Nos. 108). The gathering did little to clarify major questions, though. Moscow discovered it was difficult to grant greater independence of action to the satellites—as spelled out in the October 30 Declaration—yet still retain the desired degree of control. By spring 1957, Foreign Minister Andrei Gromyko felt constrained to appeal to Khrushchev to deal with instances of "excessive restraint" on the part of several Soviet embassies in Eastern Europe. In a rare example of soviet-style political correctness, the staffs of those embassies had begun to worry that "a manifestation of interest on their part in one issue or another involving the host country could be regarded as interference in [that country's] internal affairs."[42]

A turning point came at the June 1957 Plenum of the CPSU Central Committee. At this now-famous session, Khrushchev finally managed to overcome the opposition of the so-called "anti-party group" spearheaded by Molotov, Malenkov, and Lazar Kaganovich (Document No. 114). The victory left Khrushchev and his allies free to pursue a more reform-oriented policy toward Eastern Europe that encompassed a greater sense of balance in the relationship between Moscow and its partners. Encouraging the concept of "*sodruzhestvo*," or socialist commonwealth, the Kremlin worked on ways to convince, rather than compel, their allies to tighten the unity of the bloc. While some of the impetus came from Khrushchev, he also was forced to some degree to respond to the spurt of demands that had come from the East European regimes in the wake of the Polish and Hungarian events.

In the economic sphere, over time, Khrushchev ended the most exploitative forms of resource extraction by the USSR, withdrawing some of the legions of advisers that honeycombed each country's party and government bureaucracies, and significantly boosting economic and financial support to the satellite economies.[43] Institutionally, the Kremlin breathed life into the Council of Mutual Economic Assistance (CMEA), originally created in 1949 as a showpiece of socialist cooperation, so that by the early 1960s it had begun functioning as a mechanism for greater economic partnership.

Another major focus for the Kremlin was the military relationship of the bloc countries. The East European party leaders accepted the Soviet Union's dominance partly because they understood that their political positions depended on Moscow. Still, resentment festered over the unevenness of the relationship, institutionalized in a series of bilateral "mutual defense" treaties with Moscow, and then in the May 1955 establishment of the WTO. Designed to advance Khrushchev's plan to place Moscow at the center of a new European security framework, the Warsaw Pact also incorporated secret provisions reinforcing the Soviets' right to deploy troops in Eastern Europe and control the disposition of satellite armed forces.[44] After the revolution, and particularly after publication of the October 30 Declaration, Khrushchev opened the door to renegotiation of some of these issues. Among the first to take advantage were the Poles, who as early as November 3 began drawing up a scheme for "a thorough analysis and revision" of both the WTO and the previous bilateral military agreements on the grounds that they "do not correspond to the policy of independence and sovereignty of our country."[45] Moscow consented to some of these demands, signing a more equitable "status of forces" treaty on December 17, 1956, which

[42] A. Gromyko to N. S. Khrushchev, May 25, 1957, in TsKhSD, F. 5, Op. 30, D. 230, L. 21.

[43] See Document No. 114.

[44] For important new research and analysis on the Warsaw Pact, see Mastny, "We are in a Bind," 230–250.

[45] "Memorandum on the Warsaw Treaty and the Development of the Armed Forces of the People's Republic of Poland," January 10, 1957, in Mastny, "We are in a Bind," 237.

regulated (on paper, at least) such principles as the stationing of Red Army forces on Polish territory. Over the next several months, similar agreements followed between the USSR and East Germany, Hungary, and Romania. Khrushchev also reduced overall troop levels in these countries and removed some of the cadres of "advisers" who had helped stifle allied military independence. But he stopped well short of any moves, such as rotating the Warsaw Pact's top command positions, which might shift meaningful decision-making authority away from Moscow.

Khrushchev's goal was never to fully relinquish control over his allies. He merely wanted to loosen restraints enough to allow the emergence of more creative and effective policies toward the problems facing the region. He certainly had no intention of undoing the bonds that strapped the system together. After 1956, Moscow would no longer tolerate the Yugoslav model of following different roads to socialism. The trick, however, was to accomplish one result without risking the other. His initial efforts at reestablishing control within a more flexible framework culminated at a world conference of communist parties in Moscow in November 1957, on the fortieth anniversary of the Bolshevik revolution. The conference produced a final declaration, signed by 12 leading parties, which attempted to spell out a new ideological foundation and statement of principles for the socialist world. Among its key passages was the following:

> The socialist countries base their relations on principles of complete equality, respect for territorial integrity, state independence and sovereignty and non-interference in one another's affairs. These are vital principles. However, they do not exhaust the essence of relations between them. Fraternal mutual aid is part and parcel of these relations. This aid is a striking expression of socialist internationalism...[46]

The statement gave the satellite states approval of the notion of sovereignty and non-interference, but its impact was strongly diluted by the reference to "fraternal mutual aid" which could only be seen in the context of the intervention in Hungary just one year before.

The Soviet leadership was satisfied with the overall results of the conference because it formally enshrined the USSR at the head of the socialist camp. But the process had been difficult. Mao Zedong and the Chinese Communist Party had asserted an influential role, while the Yugoslav delegation and the Poles had objected to the propositions the Soviets wanted to insert in the final documents.

For the rest of his tenure as CPSU first secretary, Khrushchev wrestled with the contradictory impulses of reform and control. Where possible, he encouraged and cajoled the satellite leaders to be flexible and unleash creative forces inside their countries—albeit with the aim of strengthening the bloc as a whole, and always under the direction of Moscow. But whenever the situation showed signs of spinning out of control, he made it clear that he would choose repression over independence.

United States' Reactions to the Crisis

The immediate U.S. reaction to the crushing of the revolution was shock and revulsion. President Eisenhower called it "a bitter pill for us to swallow," and "shocking to the point of being unbelievable" (Document No. 92). Just days before, victory had seemingly been in the hands of the Hungarian people. Magnifying the blow was a feeling of general helplessness, a grim awareness that the United States and the West could have done virtually nothing, short of declaring war, to stop what had happened (Document No. 86). Worse, there was the added sensation of responsibility for having put the Hungarians in harm's way.

At the heart of the criticisms of the administration was the accusation that a significant gap existed between Eisenhower's shrill rhetoric promising the "liberation" of "the captive peoples" and the reality of how limited America's capabilities actually were. More acutely, critics charged that the president and his secretary of state had deliberately encouraged the Hungarians

---

[46] Quoted in Jonathan Steele, ed., *Eastern Europe since Stalin* (New York: Crane, Russak & Company, Inc., 1974), 90–91.

to revolt by implying that Western help would be forthcoming.[47] Eisenhower himself, shortly after the invasion, privately acknowledged worrying about the possibility, raised by U.N. Ambassador Henry Cabot Lodge, that "we have excited Hungarians for all these years, and now [are] turning our backs to them when they are in a jam" (Document No. 94).

The principal medium for this message of encouragement had been Radio Free Europe (see Part Two). Therefore, one of the administration's first acts after the revolution was to investigate allegations in Europe and the United States that RFE broadcasts had urged on the violent rebellion. On November 20, CIA Director Allen Dulles sent a report to the president which minimized the Radio's culpability, concluding that "[f]rom all information available to date, RFE did not incite the Hungarian people to revolution," nor did it "directly or by implication offer hope that American military help would be forthcoming to the patriots."[48] But this opinion was far from universal. RFE's own internal inquiry concluded that in some cases programs included serious policy violations and could have led to potential misunderstandings (Document No. 105). In a peculiar way, RFE became an emblem for the remorse felt in the Western world: just as its operations during the revolution underscored the emptiness of the "roll-back" doctrine, the accusations the Radio faced called the behavior of the West as a whole into question.

Meanwhile, the public outcry in the United States against the invasion was tremendous and brought a flood of demands for immediate action. Fed by vivid images and dramatic accounts in the press, members of Congress, union groups, and newspaper editorialists pressed for bolder initiatives, from refusing the Kádár government a seat at the United Nations to airdropping weapons to the rebels, to mounting military counter-strikes. Ironically, some of the most extreme ideas came from the president's own aides. C.D. Jackson, Eisenhower's former adviser on psychological warfare, had persistently called for a tough response during the uprising, even proposing major U.S. military action. Eisenhower rebuffed him, saying, "to annihilate Hungary, should it become the scene of a bitter conflict, is in no way to help her."[49] The same answer would have held for an idea put forward by Robert Amory, Jr., deputy director of the CIA, who wanted to launch a nuclear attack on Soviet communications routes into Hungary.[50] Amory had worked directly on Hungary and was deeply affected by the brutality of the Soviet move. His plea went nowhere but it reflected the strength of feeling of many Americans, even inside the administration.[51]

In the end, the administration limited its response to far more modest steps aimed at ending the repression: for example, pressuring Moscow to comply with a U.S.-sponsored U.N. resolution on November 4;[52] publicly condemning the Soviet action; focusing world attention on events in both Hungary and Poland through a broad propaganda campaign; urging key foreign leaders such as Indian Prime Minister Nehru to join the outcry; and supplying aid to refugees fleeing the country[53] (Document No. 99). Eisenhower considered two stiffer alternatives—a trade embargo against the

---

[47] For the most detailed and thoughtful analysis of this question, see Marchio, *Rhetoric and Reality.*

[48] Memorandum from the Director of Central Intelligence (Dulles) to the President, "Radio Free Europe," November 20, 1956, in *FRUS, 1955–1957*, vol. 25, 473–475.

[49] Eisenhower message to C.D. Jackson, November 19, 1956. Also cited in *FRUS, 1955–1957*, vol. 25, 463.

[50] Martin Ben Schwartz, *A New Look at the 1956 Hungarian Revolution: Soviet Opportunism, American Acquiescence* (Ph.D. diss, Fletcher School of Law and Diplomacy [Tufts University]) (Ann Harbor, Mich.: University Microfilm International, 1988), 321.

[51] The U.S. reacted similarly to the only known West European proposal for armed intervention, which came from Spain and its right-wing, anti-Communist leader, Gen. Francisco Franco, who offered to send military forces to help the Hungarian insurgents. It is difficult to gauge the seriousness of the Spanish offer, given that Washingto's almost immediate negative response and the denial of U.S. logistical support made the plan impossible to carry out. See László Borhi, ed., "Franco és az 1956-os magyar forradalom: Dokumentumok a spanyol segítségnyújtás tervéről," *História* 20, no. 9–10 (1998): 60–62.

[52] This and several other resolutions passed during November and December, demanded that the Soviets remove their forces from Hungary and that the Kádár regime allow U.N. Secretary General Hammarskjöld to make an inspection visit to the country.

[53] See footnote 17 above.

USSR and breaking off diplomatic relations if the Soviets failed to abide by the U.N. resolution—but never followed through on them since Moscow repeatedly snubbed the U.N. demands.

At the same time, Washington took steps to anticipate, and try to prevent, a follow-on Soviet intervention in Poland. Eisenhower ordered studies as to whether the U.S. should initiate or support the use of force in the event of a Soviet attack and a Polish government appeal for help to the U.N. The chairman of the Joint Chiefs of Staff, for one, strongly endorsed being ready to strike Soviet military targets, even though he acknowledged: "There is a risk of general war if the United States adopts this course of action."[54]

Despite their emotions, the near universal conclusion inside the administration was that there was nothing more that could be done. Eisenhower himself lamented: "[W]hat can we do that is really constructive? Should we break off diplomatic relations with the USSR? What would be gained by this action? The Soviets don't care." In the end, the U.S. turned mainly to the United Nations, keeping the "Hungarian question" on the U.N.'s agenda beginning in late 1956, despite the fact that arrests had stopped and various amnesties had been granted in 1959 and 1960. After secret negotiations, the U.N. removed Hungary from the agenda in December 1962. In March 1963, the Kádár regime declared a general amnesty covering the release of most of the remaining victims of the reprisals of 1956.

Not surprisingly, the revolution prompted a fundamental review of U.S.-Eastern Europe policy. The process had actually begun in mid-1956 (Document No. 17), resulting in a report on "U.S. Policy Toward Developments in Poland and Hungary" dated October 31, just before the uprising had reached full force. Immediately after the second invasion, the NSC ordered yet another reevaluation. At this stage, the reassessments produced surprisingly little change, but gradually a shift began to occur, first in the administration's public pronouncements and later in basic policy documents.

The most notable change involved moving away from the concept of "liberation" and "roll-back," which implied the goal of outright victory by the "captive peoples" over their Soviet oppressors, to the notion of "evolution" and the more peaceful, gradual process that term suggested. Although the origins of this new "pacific" approach were evident by summer 1956, probably its earliest formal articulation came in a set of guidances on Poland produced by the Operations Coordinating Board (OCB) in March 1957. In keeping with earlier administration goals, the document called for sustaining "the morale and the hopes of the Polish people," but it now stressed that any change would be "evolutionary" and only take place over a prolonged period of "patience and enduring quiet effort."[55]

The administration's revised long-term policy logically called for a different set of tools. Rather than emphasize rhetoric and radio propaganda to sharpen antagonisms between the opposition and the authorities (and possibly encourage overt acts of resistance that risked violent suppression), the new approach sought to broaden direct contacts with "the dominated peoples" in order to develop "means of exerting more effective U.S. influence upon future developments."[56] Ironically, to be successful, this approach meant reaching out to engage the regimes themselves through a program of economic aid, cultural exchanges and tourism. The Budapest Legation first raised the need for a less rigid approach in October 1957 and it quickly picked up support inside the State Department where frustration at "our present extremely rigid tactics" had been on the rise.[57] Within a few months, the proposal gained formal acceptance. "It is now apparent," various policy papers explained:

---

[54] The order to study a military response to an invasion of Poland appears in paragraph 15 of NSC 5616/2 (Document No. 99).

[55] Operations Coordinating Board, "Operational Guidance with Respect to Poland," April 2, 1957, cited by James Marchio in id., *Rhetoric and Reality*, 439. This passage is based on Marchio's analysis on 438–439.

[56] See Operations Coordinating Board, "Report on Soviet-Dominated Nations in Eastern Europe (NSC 5811/1) in *Foreign Relations of the United States, 1958–1960*, vol 10, pt. 1 (Washington, D.C.: Government Printing Office, 1993), 95–98.

[57] See Despatch from the Legation in Hungary to the Department of State, "Certain Aspects of U.S. Policy Toward Hungary," October 11, 1957, in *FRUS, 1955–1957*, vol. 25, 669–671. See also a follow-up telegram sent during the revolution, Despatch from the Legation in Hungary to the Department of State, "Review of United States Policy Toward Hungary," Ibid., 679–684. Finally, see the memorandum advancing the idea within the Department, Memorandum from the Deputy Director of the Office of Eastern European Affairs (Leverich) to the Assistant Secretary of State for European Affairs (Elbrick), "Future U.S. Policy Toward Hungary," November 8, 1957, Ibid., 685–690; the quote appears on 686.

that, as a practical matter, substantial expansion of direct U.S. contacts with the peoples of these nations, and the development through such contacts of popular pressures upon the regimes for increased internal freedom and independence from Soviet control, cannot be achieved without more active U.S. relationships with and through these governments (Document No. 118).[58]

In other words, while the long-range goals of U.S. policy—helping East Europeans acquire representative governments enjoying full national sovereignty—remained in place, the means to be used had changed dramatically. The next logical step was to formalize the concept of "differentiation" among the various countries of the region. Already effectively in place for Yugoslavia and Poland, this idea posited that the United States (and increasingly other Western countries) could nudge individual regimes toward further internal liberalization or greater independence from Moscow by offering preferential treatment as a reward.[59]

One other major revision in Eisenhower's East European policy occurred in the realm of covert action. Along with diminished interest in other, more aggressive tactics that had held sway during Eisenhower's first term, came a decision to downplay clandestine activities. To the disillusionment of veteran operations hands, such as Frank Wisner and C.D. Jackson, there appears to have been a wholesale dismantling of the web of programs and networks that had been created in the years following World War II. The Volunteer Freedom Corps and Operation Red Sox/Red Cap,[60] for example, were among the quiet casualties of the administration's reassessment of ways and means.

It took approximately 18 months for the United States' new policies towards Hungary and the region to take shape. They remained intact through the end of Eisenhower's second term, although their results were by no means always satisfactory. With modest changes, the new model formed the basis for the policies of Eisenhower's successors for the next three decades.

Superpower Relations after the Crisis

Despite the Eisenhower administration's genuine repugnance at the Soviet invasion, Washington was reluctant to intensify problems in the superpower relationship. Two years earlier, the ground-breaking Geneva summit had crowned expectations for a new post-Stalin era of détente and for diminished international tensions. In suggesting responses to the Hungary events to the OCB on November 7, the State Department's Jacob Beam concluded: "It is not recommended that we revive the cold war on the scale of intensity of the late Stalin period. [...] we would not wish to jeopardize some of the gains, small as they may be, resulting from the Geneva conference."[61]

---

[58] Aside from appearing in NSC 5811, this justification is repeated a year later in Operations Coordinating Board, "Operations Plan for the Soviet-Dominated Nations in Eastern Europe," July 2, 1959, see *FRUS, 1958–1960*, vol. 10, pt. 1, 79–94.

[59] As James Marchio points out, the term "differentiation" came into vogue during the Johnson presidency, but the roots of the policy clearly extend to the period immediately following the Hungarian revolution. See Marchio, *Rhetoric and Reality*, 444, footnote 78.

[60] The Volunteer Freedom Corps (VFC) and Operation Red Sox/Red Cap were programs to recruit escapees from Eastern and Central Europe into armed units and infiltrate them back into their own countries to help agitate nationalist forces against the region's Soviet-backed regimes. The VFC came into existence in May 1953, and Red Sox/Red Cap reportedly appeared at around the same time. There have been reports that émigré forces under these programs took part in the Hungarian uprising. Although there is disagreement on this point, it seems clear that the revolution's tragic ending contributed to the U.S. decision to terminate these and other émigré operations shortly thereafter. See Marchio, *Rhetoric and Reality*, 139–144, 376–377, 446–447; also Stephen E. Ambrose, *Ike's Spies: Eisenhower and the Espionage Establishment* (Garden City, N.Y.: Doubleday & Co., 1981), 238, and William R. Corson, *The Armies of Ignorance* (New York: The Dial Press, 1977), 360, 366–372.

[61] Notes for an Oral Report to the Operations Coordinating Board by the Chairman of the Special Committee on Soviet and Related Problems (Beam), "Steps with Specific Reference to Hungary," November 7, 1956, *FRUS, 1955–1957*, vol. 25, 416–418.

Nonetheless, the revolution did temporarily kill hopes for continuing "the spirit of Geneva." The United States made sure the Soviet action remained squarely in the focus of world attention, and clearly wanted to do more. But the reality of the power imbalance in Eastern Europe, secured at the Yalta conference, imposed sharp constraints on Washington's options. Moscow's successful development of an ICBM capability in August 1957, followed by the launch of Sputnik soon afterwards, only heightened Eisenhower's fears about sparking a global war.

Ultimately, the United States concluded—just as the Budapest Legation had with respect to the Kádár regime—that there was an overriding need to engage the Soviets in order to contain global tensions. The Kremlin's offer on arms reduction in mid-November 1956 found no takers in Washington, coming so soon after the bloodshed, but by the following spring the United States had begun to reconsider its position and to move toward a renewed dialogue with Moscow. By year's end, both sides were actively preparing for a new summit. All signs pointed in the direction of a fresh period of détente until the next crises, over Berlin and Cuba, combined to derail the process again.

Photo 1: A demonstrator in Budapest on October 23

Photo 2: **Demonstrators at Deák Square on October 23**

Photo 3: **Crowds gather at Bem Square on October 23**

Photo 4: **Demonstrators mass behind the Parliament building on the evening of October 23**

Photo 5: Children wave their caps from the boots of the toppled Stalin statue at Budapest's City Park

Photo 6: Communist propaganda materials being burned in front of the Horizon bookshop

Photo 7: **Zoltán Tildy, Imre Nagy and Pál Maléter in the Prime Minister's office on November 2**

Photo 8: **A Hungarian soldier paints the "Kossuth" coat of arms on a tank**

Photo 9: Soviet tanks block access routes outside Keleti railway station

Photo 10: A Soviet tank burns on Rákóczi Road

Photo 11: **An insurgent patrols the streets**

Photo 12: Freedom fighters at Killián Barracks on the corner of Ferenc Boulevard and Üllői Road

Photo 13: Grand Boulevard, one of Budapest's main thoroughfares, after the fighting

Photo 14: Coffins litter the corner of Ferenc Boulevard and Üllői Road

Photo 15: A destroyed Soviet tank at Boráros Square

Photo 16: Demonstrators fraternize with Red Army soldiers in front of Parliament on October 25 …

Photo 17: … then later run for their lives as Soviet and Hungarian units open fire on the crowd

Photo 18: Leaflets and posters pasted on a Budapest shopwindow

Photo 19: Dead ÁVH soldiers lie outside Budapest Party headquarters at Köztársaság Square

Photo 20: János Kádár with Nikita Khrushchev

Photo 21: Soviet tanks at Móricz Zsigmond Square

DOCUMENT NO. 82: Radio Statement by Imre Nagy Announcing an Attack by Soviet Forces on the Hungarian Government, November 4, 1956

Imre Nagy's laconic radio announcement about the second Soviet military intervention was broadcast at 5:20 a.m. on November 4. By that time, the Hungarian army had already been ordered not to engage the Soviet forces, whose hostile movements had concerned the Hungarian leaders for days. Therefore, the announcement that "our troops are fighting" was not strictly true, since only the irregular forces put up any resistance in the coming days. After his radio speech, Nagy took refuge inside the Yugoslav Embassy to forestall his possible arrest. His statement indicates that, despite Soviet expectations, he was unwilling to resign or to side openly with the counter-coup even after the revolution had been crushed. The speech was repeated in several languages as the Nagy government's last cry for help to the outside world.

This is Imre Nagy, chairman of the Council of Ministers of the Hungarian People's Republic, speaking. In the early hours of this morning, the Soviet troops launched an attack against our capital city with the obvious intention of overthrowing the lawful, democratic, Hungarian Government. Our troops are fighting. The Government is in its place. I inform the people of the country and world public opinion of this.

[Source: Paul E. Zinner, ed., National Communism and Popular Revolt in Eastern Europe: A Selection of Documents on Events in Poland and Hungary, February–November, 1956 (New York: Columbia University Press, 1956), 472.]

DOCUMENT NO. 83: Report from Georgii Zhukov to the CPSU CC, November 4, 1956, 12 a.m.

In the days following the November 4 intervention, Marshal Georgii Zhukov, the Soviet minister of defense, reported regularly on the situation to the CPSU CC Presidium. The document presented below summarizes the events of the first day, consisting of planned military operations against Budapest and major cities in the provinces. According to the Malin notes, however, these triumphant reports had little effect on the Presidium, whose November 4 session centered instead on political issues such as the future name of the Hungarian party.

At 6:15 on Nov 4, Soviet troops began to conduct the operation for restoring order and rehabilitating the government of the people's democratic rule of Hungary. Acting according to an earlier thought-out plan, our units mastered the most stubborn points of the reaction in the provinces, as they existed in Győr, Miskolc, Gyöngyös, Debrecen, and even in other regional centers in Hungary.

In the course of the operation Soviet troops occupied the most important communication centers, including the powerful, radio broadcasting station in Szolnok, the depots of military supplies and weapons, and other important military objectives.

The Soviet troops operating in Budapest, having broken the resistance of the insurgents, occupied the Parliament building, the Central Committee of the Hungarian Workers Party, and even the radio station in the region near the Parliament building. Also seized were three bridges across the Dunai [Danube] River, joining the eastern and western parts of the city, and the arsenal of weapons and military supplies.

The whole staff of the counterrevolutionary government of Imre Nagy was in hiding. Searches are being conducted.

One large hotbed of resistance of the insurgents remains in Budapest around the Corvin Theater in the southern-eastern part of the city. The insurgents defending this stubborn point were presented with an ultimatum to capitulate. In connection with the refusal of the resisters to surrender, the troops began an assault on them.

The main garrisons of the Hungarian troops were blockaded. Many of them gave up their weapons without a serious fight. Instructions were given to our troops to return to their command the Hungarian officers who were captured by the insurgents, and to arrest the officers who were assigned to replace the captured ones.

With the objective of not allowing the penetration of Hungary by the hostile agency and the escape of the resistance leaders from Hungary, our troops have occupied the Hungarian airports and solidly closed off all the roads on the Austro-Hungarian border. The troops, continuing to fulfill the assignment, are purging the territory of Hungary of insurgents.

G. ZHUKOV
NOVEMBER 4, 1956

Sent to Khrushchev, Bulganin, Malenkov, Suslov, etc.

[Source: TsKhSD, F. 89, Per. 45, Dok. 23. Originally published in the Cold War International History Project Bulletin *no. 5 (Spring 1995), pp. 33–34. Translated by Johanna Granville.]*

DOCUMENT NO. 84: Working Notes from the Session of the CPSU CC Presidium, Protocol No. 51, November 4, 1956

Published below are Vladimir Malin's notes of the CPSU CC Presidium session which coincided with the second Soviet intervention. The most important development during this meeting was Molotov's opposition to Kádár in favor of restoring the Rákosi-Gerő regime. Based on the Presidium's earlier rejection of a more lenient attitude towards the Hungarian events, and on Khrushchev's vacillation and eventual siding with the hard-liners during the negotiations, Molotov saw this as his opportunity to make the restoration final, as symbolized by the reinstatement of the name Hungarian Workers' Party.

However, according to Malin's notes, Khrushchev with noticeable exasperation rebuffed this latest attempt by the hard-liners. Molotov reacted in kind, demanding that the first secretary be reprimanded, but with the exception of Foreign Minister Shepilov every other Presidium member took Khrushchev's side. The subsequent debates of November 5–6 strengthened the latter's position even further.

Participants: Bulganin, Voroshilov, Kaganovich, Malenkov, Molotov, Pervukhin, Saburov, Suslov, Khrushchev, Zhukov, Shepilov, Furtseva, Pospelov.

On the Operations and Situation in Hungary

Cde. Kaganovich's ciphered cable from Cde. Malinin
at Cde. Khrushchev
(4 XI).[62]
1) Bring back Cdes. Mikoyan and Brezhnev.[63]
2) Provide assistance to Hungary.[64]
3) More actively take part in the assistance to Egypt.
Think through a number of measures (perhaps a demonstration at the English embassy).
More widely in the newspapers.

Cde. Molotov—think about Hungary.
Exert influence on Kádár so that Hungary does not go the route of Yugoslavia. They made changes in the Declaration—they now condemn the Rákosi-Gerő clique—and this might be dangerous.[65]
We must convince them that they should refrain from this reference to the Rákosi-Gerő clique.

Kádár is calling (1 XI) for a condemnation of Stalinism.[66]

---

[62] This sentence is as it appears in the original. The number in parentheses refers to the date November 4.

[63] Compare with footnote 321 in Document No. 78. Mikoyan and Brezhnev were probably already preparing for the journey.

[64] This refers to a financial aid package that was discussed in detail at the next Presidium meeting on November 5. The aid consisted of foodstuffs and building materiel valued at 44 million rubles and of advancing Soviet transports that were set in the previous exchange trade plans between the two countries.

[65] The reference here is to Kádár's November 4 radio address entitled "Appeal to the Hungarian People!," which was elaborated following a decision by the CPSU Presidium on October 31 (see Document No. 53). The draft of this declaration, almost certainly a translation from a Russian original, was indeed amended by either Kádár or Münnich, replacing the original phrase concerning "numerous big mistakes committed under the leadership of Rákosi and Gerő" with the more severe "grave mistakes of the Rákosi-Gerő clique." As can be seen from the discussion at the Presidium's next meeting (see Document No. 89), the main issue that worried some Soviet leaders was not the criticism of Rákosi, but use of the term "clique," which indicated a more thorough disapproval of the entire Rákosi era. See Gál et al., *A "Jelcin Dosszié,"* 88 and 92. For the text of the final version, see Zinner, *National Communism*, 474–478.

[66] This reference is to János Kádár's November 1 radio address announcing the formation of the HSWP. See footnote 247 in Part Two.

The title of Hungarian Workers' Party should be retained.

We should come to agreement with them and prevent them from shifting to Yugoslav positions.

Cde. Molotov—reinforce the military victory through political means.

Cde. Khrushchev—I don't understand Cde. Molotov. He comes up with the most pernicious ideas.

Cde. Molotov—you should keep quiet and stop being so overbearing.

Cde. Bulganin—we should condemn the incorrect line of Rákosi-Gerő.

Cde. Khrushchev: The declaration is good—we must act honorably.

Cde. Shepilov—during the editing they added the phrase "the clique of Rákosi and Gerő." We are giving them legal opportunities to denigrate the entire 12-year period of the HWP's work.

Cde. Shepilov—is it really necessary to disparage cadres? Tomorrow it will be the "clique of Ulbricht."

Cde. Saburov—if they themselves don't comprehend their mistakes, we will deal at length with the matter.

Reward the military personnel.

Take care of the families of those who perished.

V. On Purging the Higher Educational Institutions of Unsavory Elements[67]
(Cdes. Zhukov, Khrushchev, Furtseva, Pervukhin, Voroshilov)

Furtseva, Pospelov, Shepilov, and Elyutin[68] are to come up with recommendations for purging the higher educational institutions of unsavory elements.

IV. On the Response to Cde. Kardelj and the Telegram About Imre Nagy[69]
Affirm the text of the response.[70]

On Instructions to the Soviet Ambassador in Hungary

On the Raising of the Question at the Gen. Assembly's Session on Hungary

Cde. Kádár is to say that he will withdraw the question from the UN.[71]

[Source: TsKhSD, F. 3, Op. 12, D. 1006, Ll. 34–36 ob. Compiled by V. N. Malin. Originally published in English in the Cold War International History Project Bulletin, *no. 10 (March 1998), 398–99. Translated by Mark Kramer.]*

[67] This refers to Soviet students sympathizing with the Hungarian revolution.

[68] V. P. Elyutin was minister of higher education from 1954–1959.

[69] This was a telegram sent by Nikolai Firyubin, the Soviet ambassador in Belgrade. See footnote 72 below.

[70] See Document No. 85.

[71] The Kádár government sent a telegram dated November 4 to U.N. Secretary General Dag Hammarskjöld claiming that Nagy's November 1 appeal (See Document No. 67) had been illegal and indicating that the Hungarian Revolutionary Workers' and Peasants' Government "categorically protests" the discussion of the issue at either the UNGA or Security Council because it was exclusively a matter for the Hungarian People's Republic. The telegram was published in *Szabad Né*p on November 6.

DOCUMENT NO. 85: Instructions to Soviet Ambassador Nikolai Firyubin to Inform the Yugoslavs of the Soviet Position Concerning Imre Nagy, November 4, 1956

As early as November 4, Edvard Kardelj, the Yugoslav vice president, disclosed to Soviet Ambassador Firyubin that following the agreement in Brioni the Yugoslavs had made contact with Imre Nagy; he also reported that Nagy and his colleagues were at the Yugoslav Embassy in Budapest, although he did not mention how they got there. He also announced that Belgrade wanted to persuade Nagy to make a declaration supporting the Kádár government. On behalf of Tito, he asked for Moscow's opinion on whether to continue negotiating with the leaders of the uprising. Furthermore, Tito appealed to the Soviets to ask Kádár and his associates not to retaliate against any Communists who had joined the insurrection.[72]

The telegram published here contains the Soviet leadership's reply to Kardelj. According to the document, the Soviets were surprised to learn that Nagy and his circle had been given political asylum inside the Yugoslav Embassy, an eventuality not discussed in Brioni. Their reaction was blunt. They rejected the idea of negotiating with Nagy, claiming that any statement from him would come too late, and they demanded that the Hungarian leaders be handed over immediately to Soviet military authorities. In response, Tito personally wrote to Khrushchev the next day disclosing that the Hungarians wanted to go to Yugoslavia, and asking Moscow's permission to take this step. He also made clear that the Yugoslavs would not turn Nagy and his followers over to the Kádár government.

It is easy to see from these stiff exchanges how the Nagy issue contributed to the deterioration of Soviet-Yugoslav relations that followed.

To Part IV of Minutes No. 51.

Top Secret!
Top Priority
Special
To the Soviet Ambassador
Belgrade

Regarding special [telegram] No. 1059–1060. Inform Comrade Kardelj that the CPSU CC discussed this question. The CC's opinion is as follows:

When, at our comrades' meeting with you, we found that a public statement by Imre Nagy would be expedient, he was still the prime minister and his statement could have facilitated the defeat of the counterrevolution.

Our opinion is such that no statement from Nagy is necessary now.

As for the Yugoslav Embassy, we gave instructions to our troops to watch over the Embassy.

Regarding Nagy and his group's further stay at the Embassy, it is not only the [forces of] reaction but also revolutionary elements who could carry out violent acts against them. In this connection, and also having in mind that the Hungarian Revolutionary Workers' and Peasants' Government does not possess security organs at the moment, it would be expedient to entrust Nagy and his group to our troops for transfer to the Revolutionary Workers' and Peasants' Government in Szolnok.

[Source: TsKhSD, F. 3, Op. 14, D. 72, Ll. 2, 7. From protocol No. 51. APRF, F. 3, Op. 64, D. 485, Ll. 103–104. Published in Sovietskii Soyuz i vengerskii krizis, 1956 goda: Dokumenty, *edited and compiled by E. D. Orekhova, Vyacheslav T. Sereda and Aleksandr. S. Stykhalin (Moscow: ROSSPEN, 1998), pp. 587–588. Translated by Svetlana Savranskaya.]*

---

[72] For the text of Kardelj's telegram, see *Sovietskii Soyuz i vengerskii krizis*, 582–593. First published in Hungarian in Gál et al., *A "Jelcin Dosszié*," 108.

DOCUMENT NO. 86: Action Taken as a Result of White House Decision, November 4, 1956

The main significance of this brief document is that it records the United States' decision not to consider sending a U.N. force to Hungary. Although this might have seemed a logical step in the context of the Cold War—in both establishing a multinational monitoring effort and creating at least some degree of additional difficulties for the Soviets and their allies—the Eisenhower administration chose instead to pursue a different interest: maintaining the possibility for a broader dialogue with Moscow on issues that transcended the Hungarian crisis.

DEPARTMENT OF STATE
EXECUTIVE SECRETARIAT

NOVEMBER 4, 1956

Action taken as a result of White House decision in consultation with Mr. Hoover on November 4.

Hungary

a. A statement by the President was approved for release by Mr. Hagerty.

b. A letter from the President to Premier Bulganin was approved.

c. The text of a resolution to be introduced at the 4:00 p.m. session of the Special Session of the General Assembly was approved and telephoned to New York.

d. A Departmental text of a speech for Ambassador Lodge was also telephoned to New York

e. It was decided there should be no UN force for Hungary

JOSEPH N. GREENE

cc: G—Mr. Murphy
EUR—Mr. Elbrick
IO—Mr. Wilcox

[Source: NA II, RG 59, Decimal Files FIN 761.00/11–4 56.]

DOCUMENT NO. 87: RFE Press Review on U.N. Action against the Soviet Union, November 4, 1956

One of the most severe criticisms of RFE after the Hungarian revolution was that it encouraged mili-tary opposition even after the second Soviet intervention, and called for continuing the fight with the prom-ise of immediate U.S. military aid. This widespread view was based primarily on a press review broadcast on November 4, published below, which aimed at reporting the world's reaction to the Soviet intervention, and was considered even by RFE's own internal investigation to constitute "the most serious [policy] vio-lation of all" (see Document No. 105). The most ambiguous part of this report was the review of an arti-cle published in the prestigious British newspaper The Observer that day. Although the report itself men-tioned that the article reacted to a situation that existed prior to the Soviet offensive, the ambiguous word-ing of the article, along with the even more misleading RFE commentary, could easily have been misun-derstood given the atmosphere in Hungary. It should also be mentioned that due to constant jamming, RFE broadcasts were often heard only in parts of Hungary, a fact that also contributed to the misinterpretation of the message in this case. Moreover, throughout the revolution the producers at RFE failed to make lis-teners aware of the difference between an opinion published in the press and the official U.S. government position. The Hungarian public had always believed that RFE's broadcasts constituted the authoritative views of Washington. This misapprehension, which had previously added to RFE's prestige in Eastern Europe, proved to be disastrous at the moment when the duality of the administration's "liberation rheto-ric" came into sharpest focus.

RADIO FREE EUROPE
MUNICH GERMANY
HUNGARIAN DESK
PROGRAM TITLE: SPECIAL SHORT WORLD PRESS NO. I–2
AIR DATE: NOVEMBER 4, 1956
AUTHOR: ZOLTÁN THURY
TRANSLATOR: L. MERAN

TRANSLATION OF A SCRIPT NOT CORRECTED AFTER BROADCAST[73]

ANNC: We have already reported several times that Western radio stations interrupt their broadcasts in order to report about the Hungarian events. In London, Paris, Washington and everywhere in the free countries the news of the Soviet attack has caused an immense indigna-tion. In several places the papers published special editions with reports on the Hungarian situ-ation. The Italian papers "Il Tempo" and "Il Messagero" and the British "Evening Standard," for example, had special editions. The three Paris radio stations publish proclamations for help for the Hungarians. The French radios emphasize that all Europe is looking toward the U.N. with anxiety. The General Assembly of the U.N. will meet tonight in order to discuss the Hungarian situation. Radio Stockholm says that the General Assembly of the U.N. will have to use sanc-tions against the SU [Soviet Union]. This morning the British "Observer" publishes a report of its Washington correspondent. This situation report was written before the Soviet attack early this morning. In spite of this the "Observer" correspondent writes that the Russians have prob-ably decided to beat down the Hungarian revolution with arms. The article goes on: "If the Soviet troops really attack Hungary, if this our apprehension should become true and the Hungarians will hold out for 3 or 4 days, then the pressure upon the government of the U.S. to send military help to the freedom fighters, will become irresistible."

---

[73] This rough translation is the version RFE officials used in evaluating the Radio's performance after the revolution. It
has been retained here despite its somewhat unfinished character.

This is what the Observer writes in today's number. The paper observes, that the American Congress cannot vote for war, as long as the presidential elections have not been held. The article continues:

"If the Hungarians continue to fight until Wednesday, we shall be closer to a world war than at any time since 1939."

The reports from London, Paris, Washington and other Western reports [sic] show that the world's reaction to the Hungarian events surpasses every imagination. In the Western capitals a practical manifestation of Western sympathy is expected at any hour.

[Source: Archives of the Hungarian Radio. Obtained by Judit Katona and György Vámos.]

DOCUMENT NO. 88: Yugoslav Foreign Ministry Instructions to Dalibor Soldatić, November 4, 1956

These Foreign Ministry instructions clearly spell out official Yugoslav policy in connection with Imre Nagy and his associates, who had just taken refuge inside the Yugoslav Embassy that morning. In the spirit of the Brioni agreement, the Ministry tried to use its influence to persuade Nagy and his followers to resign, thus contributing to the consolidation of the Kádár government. But the Hungarian prime minister and his colleagues unanimously refused. As this document shows, the Yugoslav leaders were somewhat taken aback: they informed Nagy that although it was not a precondition for granting asylum, a statement of the sort they were proposing would go a long way toward resolving the crisis. On November 5, Soldatić sent a telegram to Belgrade with Nagy's response, in which the prime minister gratefully accepted the offer of political asylum, promising to observe relevant international rules, and made the partial concession of not refusing to formulate an appropriate statement. Nevertheless, he repeated that his group wanted to travel to Yugoslavia as soon as possible. The Yugoslavs responded that in the current military situation Soviet approval was needed before they could leave Hungarian territory.

Inform Imre Nagy and his company of the following: When we agreed to give asylum to Imre Nagy and his company yesterday on the 3rd of this month, at Szántó's recommendation, we did not and we still do not condition it on providing a declaration. When we mentioned the possibility of a declaration that would support the Kádár government, we believed that it would be useful from the point of view of [encouraging] a more positive and painless development in the Hungarian events, and furthermore, with regard to his personal prestige, for the sake of his alienation from the reactionaries.

If Nagy wants to make such a declaration, he should do so while he is in Hungary, and immediately, because it would be neither useful nor possible to do so in Yugoslavia.

We are striving to get them out as soon as possible. At the same time, the well-known events of this morning have taken place since yesterday, while we were waiting for their reply and suggestion for how to get them out to Yugoslavia. Therefore, under these circumstances, getting them out depends on the guarantee we have to receive from the Russians.

We request an urgent reply.

[Source: KÜM Irattár (Hungarian Foreign Ministry Archives) (1956). Published in József Kiss, Zoltán Ripp and István Vida, eds., Magyar-jugoszláv kapcsolatok, 1956: Dokumentumok *(Budapest: MTA Jelenkor-kutató Bizottság, 1995), 161. Translated by Mónika Borbély.]*

Document No. 89: Notes from the CPSU CC Presidium Meeting Reflecting a CPSU Leadership Split, November 6, 1956

This CPSU Presidium session essentially marked the end of the Soviet leadership's discussions of the Hungarian crisis, which had been permanently on the agenda since October 23. The focus of this excerpt of Malin's notes is on the draft version of a proclamation to be made by the HSWP's Provisional Central Committee, which Kádár had worked on in Szolnok and sent to Moscow for approval the day before. Among the changes recommended was one by Molotov that branded the so-called Nagy-Losonczy group as traitors to the socialist cause; Kádár incorporated even harsher language in his final text.

In the extraordinary debate that flared up over how to evaluate Kádár's policies, those Presidium members who represented the "liberal" view on negotiations during the revolution (Mikoyan, Zhukov, Saburov) wanted to support the Hungarian leader. In addition, the hard-liners (Malenkov, Suslov and Bulganin) changed their earlier stance and withdrew their support from Molotov. Those who had no strong opinion on the matter (Furtseva, Pervukhin, Brezhnev, Aristov and Shvernik) also came down on Kádár's side. Against this background, Kaganovich and Voroshilov toned down their earlier comments, and while accepting Molotov's argument, found an opportunity to put in a few words of praise for Kádár, too. In his closing comments in the debate, Khrushchev himself approved the draft, and delivered a stinging attack on Molotov and Kaganovich whose views he associated with the discredited Stalinist past. The Presidium's subsequent virtually unanimous approval of the draft proclamation was a major victory for the first secretary who now seemed to have reasserted his control over the Presidium, once so strongly divided over Hungary.

Moscow's desire at least to pay lip service to the principles laid out in the October 30 government declaration (see Document No. 50) on relations with the socialist bloc can be seen in the inclusion of the following sentence: "Cdes. Mikoyan, Suslov, and Brezhnev are to transmit our changes and requests in a tactful manner" [emphasis added].

Participants: Bulganin, Malenkov, Mikoyan, Molotov, Kaganovich, Pervukhin, Saburov, Suslov, Khrushchev, Brezhnev, Zhukov, Shepilov, Shvernik, Furtseva, Aristov, Belyaev, Pospelov

I. On the Appeal of the Provisional CC of the Hungarian Socialist (Workers') Party[74]

(The text is read aloud by Cde. Malenkov.)[75]

Cde. Mikoyan—overall it should be adopted.

Cde. Molotov—in whose name is the document being issued (from the CC)? The composition of the CC is still unknown.[76] It is unclear what entity is supporting democratization if there is still a CC of the HWP. In actuality, the dissolution of the party is being proposed.

---

[74] The appeal, which was the Kádár government's first major statement since the radio address on November 4, was first published as a leaflet on November 6, then in *Szabad Nép* on the next day and finally in *Népszabadság* on November 8.

[75] The first draft of the appeal was sent to Moscow by V. S. Baikov (whose task in Budapest was to maintain communications between Kádár and the Soviet leadership) on November 5, with the following note: "At the request of cde. Kádár, I am forwarding the text, translated from Hungarian, of an appeal by the Provisional Central Committee of the Hungarian Socialist Workers' Party entitled 'To Hungarian Communists! To faithful members of the Hungarian Workers' Party!' Cde. Kádár requests the Soviet comrades to inform him of their views and observations regarding the text of the appeal by 10:00 a.m., November 6." (See, APRF, F. 3. Op. 64. D. 485. L. 132.) Before the start of the Presidium session, Mikoyan made a number of corrections and suggestions to the text. The most important of these were as follows: The section dealing with the responsibility of the Rákosi clique was to be supplemented by the following: "...in the same way we must break with the group of Imre Nagy, Losonczy and Donáth, which opened the way for the reaction and thus betrayed the cause of socialism." The third paragraph, he suggested, would end with the following: "we defend the state of the people's democracy and its foundation, the unbreakable alliance between workers and peasants." At the end of the text, Mikoyan proposed replacing the sentence "The most complete democracy should prevail in the life of the party organizations" with the phrase "Inner-party democracy, according to the principles of Leninism, must fully develop in the life of the party organizations." (For the marked-up draft, see, APRF, F. 3. Op. 64. D. 485. Ll. 136–8.)

A new party will be created on an unknown basis. Where will it lead?

In April 1956 there was an appeal from the CPSU CC. We sent greetings to the HWP CC (we acknowledged their services).[77]

They're talking about acknowledgment of Marxism-Leninism, but in reality everything can be acknowledged.

So far we have concurred in not resolving the question of the renaming of the party. We should not use the expression "the Rákosi clique."

Cde. Suslov—the draft of the appeal is correct—no one is talking about the dissolution of the HWP. The party's basic principles are being preserved.
We must support it. On the "clique"—the issue is not the name, but the mistakes that were made.[78] The Hungarian comrades again will have suspicions; let's dispel them.

Cde. Kaganovich: This is a step forward. Having discreet influence on Kádár. Overall it should be adopted.
We should try to suggest not changing the name of the party. We should suggest they speak about friendship with the USSR. We should suggest they decline mentioning both the name and the Rákosi clique.

Cde. Bulganin—The Declaration is fine. Cde. Mikoyan's changes are correct. As for the statements by Cdes. Molotov and Kaganovich: no one is talking about the dissolution of the HWP. That's a misleading argument.
There is no principled basis for Cde. Molotov to couch the matter that way.

On friendship with the USSR, we shouldn't mention it. Leave it as they propose (spoken about friendship).

Cde. Pervukhin—a proper document.
The HWP CC collapsed. It's not true that if we call something a "clique," we're condemning the whole party.

Cde. Malenkov—without harsh criticism of Rákosi we won't be able to strengthen the [Hungarian] leadership.
They're setting forth their own program. A CC plenum should not be convened (since Nagy is also a member of the CC).[79]

Cde. Zhukov—we must decisively support Cde. Kádár. Otherwise they won't understand us. Rákosi conducted an inapprop. policy, which must be condemned.

Cde. Saburov—I support Cde. Mikoyan.

Cde. Molotov—we must not forget that a change of names is a change of character. What's going on is the creation of a new Yugoslavia. We are responsible for Hungary (without Stalin). I vehemently object.

Cde. Furtseva—raises the question: where were the leaders?
The people fully support them.

Cde. Brezhnev: The Declaration is appropriate. It's pointless to theorize about it.

Cde. Saburov: Cdes. Molotov and Kaganovich are simplistically and dogmatically approach-

---

[76] Kádár announced the composition of the HSWP PCC at the November 13 meeting of the PCC. It was made public only in December 1956.

[77] See footnote 318 in Part Two.

[78] See footnote 65 above.

[79] This refers to the old HWP CC, which on the night of October 23 co-opted Nagy and elected him a member of the PC. Nagy was actually also a member of the Executive Committee of the HSWP, whose establishment Kádár announced in his radio address on November 1.

ing the question.
The party will be better.

Cde. Mikoyan—Cde. Molotov is completely ignoring the concrete situation—Cde. Molotov is dragging us backward. Speak about Nagy.

Cde. Voroshilov—Cde. Molotov's statements are fundamentally correct. But in this case it's impossible to adopt.

Cde. Aristov—we must endorse and support Cde. Kádár. The statements by Cdes. Molotov and Kaganovich—they clung to the cult of Stalin, and they're still clinging to it.

Cde. Shvernik—Cde. Molotov is incorrect. How can we not say something if Rákosi caused a great deal of harm?

Cde. Shepilov—the document is appropriate. Say—a condemnation of Nagy. On the "clique": we will leave a stain on the socialist past.

Cde. Khrushchev—a good draft.
We should make changes. Indicate which group is presenting it. If the CC is convened, it should be said then that we have faith in Kádár. For Cde. Molotov this is logical (Cde. Molotov doesn't come out and say it, but he's thinking of bringing back both Hegedüs and Rákosi).

Rákosi caused enormous damage, and for this he must be held accountable.
He must be excluded from the party.

Cde. Khrushchev:
Cde. Kaganovich, when will you mend your ways and stop all your toadying? Holding to some sort of hardened position. What Cde. Molotov and Kaganovich are proposing is the line of screeching and face-slapping. Speak about Nagy. About Losonczy and Donáth.

Cdes. Mikoyan, Suslov, and Brezhnev are to transmit our changes and requests in a tactful manner.[80]

II. Ciph. Tel. No. . . . from . . .[81]
(Zhukov, Shepilov)[82]

Affirm as an unfortunate event.[83]

[Source: TsKhSD, F. 3, Op. 12, D. 1006, Ll. 41–45ob, compiled by V. N. Malin. Originally published in the Cold War International History Project Bulletin, *no. 8/9 (Winter 1996/1997), pp. 399–400. Translated by Mark Kramer.]*

[80] Kádár accepted the changes made by the Soviets with one exception. He left out Donáth's name from the section condemning the Nagy-Losonczy group, but at the same time worded the sentence in a more critical way. The existing charges were supplemented with the crimes of "giving up the position of the working class and people's power," and "sinking into a nationalist-chauvinist position by calling for open anti-Soviet struggle."

[81] This was the telegram sent by Nikolai Firyubin on November 5 forwarding a formal protest by Yugoslav Foreign Minister Koèa Popović against the killing of Milenko Milovanov, third secretary of the Yugoslav Embassy. Milovanov had been hit by machine gun fire from a Soviet tank while he was inside a building at the embassy. "The Yugoslav government," said Popović, "is at a loss concerning what happened, especially since the Soviet government had been informed by the Yugoslav side of who, apart from the Yugoslav diplomats, was in the building." (For the telegram see, APRF, F. 3. Op. 64. D. 485. Ll. 143–144.)

[82] According to the official minutes of the meeting, Khrushchev also participated in the discussion and it is very likely that the draft resolution (the following sentence) was worded by him.

[83] Besides expressing "deep condolences" for the death of Milovanov, the response of the CPSU CC Presidium, sent by Foreign Minister Shepilov to Popović on November 6, promised a thorough investigation concerning the "unfortunate event." The results of this inquiry arrived in Moscow on November 7. While the Yugoslavs argued that the Soviet tank had no reason to open fire, members of the Soviet unit claimed that they were only responding to shots fired from a house next to the Yugoslav Embassy. According to their statement, one salvo accidentally hit the Embassy building and killed Milovanov who was standing at a window. The investigating committee accepted the latter version.

Document No. 90: Letter from Nikita Khrushchev to Josip Tito, November 7, 1956

The Yugoslav decision on November 4 to grant asylum to Imre Nagy and members of his government (and their families) in the Yugoslav Embassy outraged both Kádár and the Kremlin, who saw the move as directly undermining the goal of the invasion. It seemed particularly inexplicable after the lengthy session at Brioni where Tito had seemingly given his explicit agreement on the need to remove Nagy. In this letter to Tito, Khrushchev responds to a telegram from the Yugoslav leader in which he proposed a compromise solution—to send Nagy to Yugoslavia, thus removing him as a factor in Hungarian politics. Khrushchev and the CPSU Presidium brusquely reject the idea and warn Tito of the negative consequences of such a move not only in worsening the Hungarian situation but in harming Yugoslavia's position—and Yugoslav-Soviet relations in particular. Two days later, Tito responds with more counter-arguments (see Document No. 91).

NOVEMBER 6, 1956
STRICTLY SECRET

[....]

IV. Comrade Firyubin's Telegram from Belgrade of November 5, 1956
(Comrades Malenkov, Bulganin, Khrushchev, Molotov, Voroshilov, Suslov, Pervukhin, Kaganovich, Saburov)

1. To approve the draft response of the CPSU CC to Comrades Tito, Kardelj, and Ranković (attached).
2. To instruct Comrades Suslov and Shepilov to ensure the flow of information about the correspondence with the Yugoslavs to secretaries of the Central Committees of the fraternal parties of the countries of people's democracy and the Communist Parties of France and Italy via Soviet ambassadors.

SECRETARY OF THE CC CPSU

TO PARAGRAPH IV OF PROTOCOL NO. 53
    TOP SECRET

Dear Comrades Tito, Kardelj, Ranković!

We received your telegram, in which you presented your suggestion that we should not try to prevent the transfer of Imre Nagy and his co-conspirators to Yugoslavia.

The Presidium of the CPSU CC discussed your opinion and believes it is necessary to express the following considerations on this issue.

We will not hide the fact that your point of view regarding Nagy disappointed us.

When our delegation (Comrades Khrushchev, Malenkov) returned from Brioni and reported to the Presidium of our Central Committee about the complete similarity of our positions regarding the situation in Hungary, our central Committee was quite satisfied. It was very important that we made the same assessment of the situation on such a difficult issue, and both believed that Nagy cleared the way for counterrevolution and brought the reactionary [forces] to their victory. Members of the Presidium of the CPSU CC were impressed by Comrade Tito's words, "What kind of Communist Premier is it, under whom they can hang and execute Communists and workers and go unpunished."

We were united with respect to the measures for correcting the situation in Hungary in order to return it to the positions of socialism. The agreement on creating the Hungarian Revolutionary

Workers' and Peasants' government headed by Kádár, and on assistance from Soviet troops to this government was adopted unanimously.

We all believed that your proposal that the Yugoslav representatives should suggest to Nagy that he ought to resign on the grounds of his government's inability to deal with the forces of reaction, thus making it easier to establish the new Hungarian Revolutionary Workers' and Peasants' government, was correct. It is clear that it would have helped the cause of socialism in Hungary, while Nagy would have preserved some kind of a Communist face, and therefore, could count on a different general attitude toward him than the one that he experiences now.

However, it all worked out to the contrary. Nagy did not resign, he did not want to use the last opportunity left for an honest person, and continued to act in favor of the reaction up to the last moment. Just before his move underground, on the radio he called on Hungarian troops to resist the Soviet troops. And the whole world knows about his statement when he was prime minister: "In the early hours of this morning, Soviet troops ... launched an attack against our capital city with the obvious intention of overthrowing the lawful, democratic, Hungarian Government. Our troops are fighting. The Government is in its place. I inform the people of the country and world public opinion of this."

One cannot disregard the fact that Comrade Kádár and the entire new Hungarian party leadership, in the party declaration issued on behalf of the Provisional Central Committee of the Hungarian Socialist Workers' Party, announced to the entire world that it was necessary to "decisively break with the group of Nagy-Losonczy, which, having surrendered the positions of the working class, and having assumed the positions of nationalism and chauvinism, have opened the way for the counterrevolutionary forces, and thus betrayed the cause of socialism."[84]

In these circumstances, naturally, there can be no moral obligations towards Nagy and his group.

You give a positive appraisal of the fact that he took cover in the Yugoslav Embassy, and not in a capitalist one.

We are surprised by this argument. If Nagy went to, let us say, the American Embassy,[85] maybe it would have been even better—then he would have revealed himself in the eyes of the entire world as an agent of the western powers. In addition, no Embassy, including the American Embassy in this case, could hide someone, much less transport him out of Hungary, if there was no permission from the government of the country for that person to depart.

It is clear that no government with any self-respect, in this case the Hungarian Revolutionary government, would allow Nagy, who opened the way for the forces of reaction, and having been defeated now, to be transported to a neighboring friendly country.

You cannot disregard the fact that such a step would throw a certain shadow on Yugoslavia's relations with the new government of Hungary, and would make its situation more difficult, since the presence of Nagy and his co-conspirators outside the country would become a force for pulling together Hungarian counterrevolutionary elements. One also has to take into account that the presence of Nagy and his group abroad would be used by the imperialists to create problems with respect to Hungary's international situation.

One also has to foresee that the implementation of your proposal about transferring Nagy and his group to Yugoslavia would be interpreted everywhere to mean that they were Yugoslav agents, and, therefore, responsibility for the Hungarian events to some extent would be assigned to the Yugoslav side.

We should also state openly how it would be interpreted in our party, and how it could affect our relations.

Our party highly appreciates the rapprochement recently achieved between the CPSU and the Yugoslav League of Communists, and the sincere friendly relations that have been established between us. Therefore, we have to say openly that members of our party would not understand an incorrect decision on the issue of Nagy and his co-conspirators.

[84] This quotation is from the Kádár government's November 6 appeal. See footnote 74 above.

[85] The U.S. maintained a Legation, not an Embassy, at this time.

Our party is aware that those who held forth at the Petőfi Circle with statements to the effect that they were supporters of the Yugoslav way of development, later became leaders of the uprising. This important fact could be interpreted in such a way that all this was organized with the Yugoslavs' participation, but that they could not have restrained them, and the developments got out of hand.

In our party, it would be hard to understand how to combine this with the open, friendly relations between our parties. This will not be understood in other Communist parties either.

All these issues were removed by our unanimous agreement at Brioni to implement decisive measures to defeat the Hungarian counterrevolution and to create the Revolutionary Workers' and Peasants' government.

However, if now Nagy and his accomplices find refuge and protection in Yugoslavia, then the issue of assessing the sad events in Hungary with take a completely different turn. This fact will undoubtedly revive suspicions regarding our relations and will result in irreparable damage to those relations.

That is why the Presidium of our Central Committee, after discussing your letter, and having addressed this issue from all sides, believes that the only correct solution would be to transfer Nagy and his group to the authority of the Hungarian government.

In the interests of our common cause, which commenced so positively and unanimously, and which has been realized so successfully, it would be important to resolve this issue regarding Nagy unanimously as well, without complications.

We should resolve this issue as Communist duty requires us to do. The sooner Nagy and his group are transferred to the authority of the Hungarian government, the better it will be for all of us.

We thoroughly discussed all of these issues in the CPSU CC Presidium, and this letter represents the unanimous opinion of all members of the CPSU CC Presidium.

With comradely regards,

SECRETARY OF THE CPSU CC   N. KHRUSHCHEV

[TsKhSD, F. 3. Op. 64. D. 74. Ll. 2. 5–9. From the Protocol No. 53. APRF, F. 3. Op. 64. D. 485. Ll. 146–151. Extract from Protocol (P53/IV). Published in Sovietskii Soyuz i vengerskii krizis, 1956 goda: Dokumenty, *edited and compiled by E. D. Orekhova, Vyacheslav T. Sereda and Aleksandr. S. Stykhalin (Moscow: ROSSPEN, 1998), pp. 608–611. Translated by Svetlana Savranskaya.]*

Document No. 91: Josip Tito's Letter to Nikita Khrushchev, November 8, 1956

Following the Kremlin's rebuff of Belgrade's idea to transfer Imre Nagy to Yugoslavia, Tito offers a further response to Khrushchev, explaining the chain of events that led to his government's grant of asylum to Nagy and his colleagues, and reacting to Khrushchev's insinuations of Yugoslav involvement in the Hungarian revolution and to his threats about the possible consequences for Soviet-Yugoslav relations. Tito's letter provides fascinating details about his views of the Hungarian crisis, the talks at Brioni, and the dilemma his government faced at this delicate moment. His efforts to bring Khrushchev around ultimately failed, leading not only to the unexpected arrest of Nagy (notwithstanding promises of safe passage) but to a further deterioration in Belgrade's ties with Moscow.

NOVEMBER 8, 1956[86]

BRIONI

TO FIRST SECRETARY OF THE CPSU CC
COMRADE KHRUSHCHEV

Dear Comrades!

We received your letter, in which you presented the position of the Presidium of the CC CPSU on the issue of Imre Nagy and other [persons], who took refuge in our Embassy in Budapest. We understand some of your arguments presented in the above-mentioned letter, and [we] see them as logical; however, we still have to say openly that what deeply concerned us about your letter was the absence of your understanding of our situation, and especially the absence of understanding of our willingness to resolve this issue in the spirit of mutual friendly relations, and not to the detriment of Yugoslavia's international reputation as a sovereign country. You agreed with us that Yugoslavia played, and should continue to play, a very useful role in the world precisely due to the reputation that it has earned.

We will explain here in detail what circumstances led to the present situation, so that our position on this issue will become clearer to you.

It is true that during our conversations in Brioni, we agreed with the assessment that the weakness of Nagy's government, and a number of concessions made by that government to the forces of reaction, had led to the danger of destroying substantial socialist achievements in Hungary. We agreed that the Hungarian Communists should not remain in such a government any longer, and that they should rely on the working masses and give a most decisive rebuttal to the reaction. There is no need to remind you that from the very beginning, and throughout the entire conversation, we expressed our reservations regarding the consequences of the direct assistance provided by the Soviet Army. However, having in mind that according to your assessment such assistance had become unavoidable, we considered that nonetheless it was necessary to do everything in order to produce the least amount of harm to the cause of socialism. You remember that we were the first to express the opinion that in such a situation it would have been better to create a government comprised of people who had not compromised themselves under the Rákosi regime, which would be led by Comrade Kádár, who was a prominent Communist and enjoyed influence among the Hungarian working masses. We believed that it would have been better if that government issued a proclamation, which was done later. We agree with that

---

[86] This translation is of a Russian rendition from the Serbo-Croatian. According to the original translators, the Serbo-Croatian contained many grammatical errors which were not corrected for the publication.

proclamation, and therefore we gave full support to that government and to the program it presented. We believed, and you agreed, that only such a government could reestablish contact with the working masses and gradually repair at least the [more] grave consequences of the events in Hungary. Here you could see for yourself that in all our arguments we were led only by our deep concern that the achievements of socialism be preserved in Hungary, and to prevent the restoration of the old regime, which would have had significant repercussions for all the countries located in this part of Europe, including Yugoslavia. This is exactly why we presented our concerns, trying to turn the Communists, and maybe Nagy himself, away from that government, which already included various anti-socialist elements, and which, precisely for that reason, was not capable of stopping the forces of reaction in their drive to power. Comrades Khrushchev and Malenkov did not reject those concerns. To the contrary, they agreed with them, with some caveats concerning Nagy. We believed that there were honest Communists in that government and around it, who could be quite useful in creating a new government of János Kádár, and in eradicating the activity of anti-socialist forces. On the basis of a discussion [along those lines] in Brioni, we undertook some measures in Budapest on Saturday, November 3, around noon.

On November 2, Zoltán Szántó spoke with our representative in Budapest.[87] During that conversation, Szántó expressed a wish that he and several Communists might leave the government and the Central Committee building and take refuge in our Embassy, because their lives were in danger from the reactionary bands of thugs. In the spirit of that conversation, our representative responded to Szántó that we were ready to give them protection, if they did so immediately. We expected their answer on Sunday, the 4th of this month. However, on the morning of that day, the action of the Soviet Army had begun, and these conversations had not yet been concluded. Instead, in the early morning of that same day, Nagy and 15 other party and government leaders with their families arrived at our Embassy. When we received the first information about this development from Budapest, we did not know whether the statement that was read, which you mentioned in your letter, was indeed Nagy's statement, or if it had been published without his consent. Therefore, Nagy and his group came to us on the basis of conversations that had taken place earlier, before we in Belgrade could react to his statement—the authenticity of which we had no proof. As soon as we received the information that Nagy and the others had taken refuge in the Yugoslav Embassy, Comrade Kardelj invited the Soviet Embassy adviser in Belgrade, Comrade Gryaznov,[88] and told him of this fact. Despite the absence of detailed information, we then still believed that an appropriate statement by Nagy, which would have been essentially in favor of Kádár's government, could still help to alleviate the situation in Hungary, which is exactly what we proposed to you. Since we had not received the answer we urgently needed from you to this effect throughout November 4, we abstained from further action on this issue.

If you take all this into account, it becomes apparent that the issues had not been clarified and the problems that now have to be resolved were created only as a result of the great speed of events. We believe that now it is irrelevant whether our Embassy in Budapest acted correctly or incorrectly; it is important that we resolve this problem jointly, in the spirit of friendly relations, which we have already restored between our two countries and parties, since that problem ultimately emerged as a result of our conversation in Brioni—although events did not develop as we expected because of what transpired overnight from Saturday to Sunday. After this, all that is left to resolve, essentially, is the personal question of their request for asylum.

We do not question some of your arguments that granting asylum in Yugoslavia to members of the former Hungarian government, whose chairman has not resigned, could be negative; [please] do not think that we do not realize that all this has already brought us some unpleasant [moments] and problems. As we can see from your letter, you did not accept our proposal that Nagy and the rest of the

---

[87] In fact, this conversation took place the day before, see footnote 311 Part Two. In a memorandum written on November 16, Szántó clearly referred to November 1 as the date of this consultation. See Kiss, Ripp and Vida, *Magyar-jugoszláv kapcsolatok, 1956*, 228.

[88] F. N. Gryaznov was an adviser at the Soviet embassy from 1953 to 1957.

group be transported to Yugoslavia with your consent, and that, naturally, puts us in quite a difficult situation. It is precisely on this issue that we would like you to show some understanding for the efforts to find a joint solution, because on the basis of what is stated in our Constitution about granting the right of asylum, and on the basis of international custom, and on the basis of all other considerations presented above, we cannot violate our word and simply hand those people over. We must especially emphasize that such a step on our part would [have] led to serious consequences in our country.

In your letter, you stated that this could lead to adverse consequences in our relations, but we believe that this should not interfere with the development of friendly ties between our parties and countries, which have recently produced significant results. We believe that this question can be resolved in such a way as to bring no harm either to our country or to the Soviet Union, or to the development of socialism in Hungary. We think that it is precisely the existing friendship between our two countries that requires that the government of the Soviet Union looked at Yugoslavia's international reputation with more understanding, as it looks at the reputation of the Soviet Union itself. Had we acted differently, our masses would not have been able to understand either the policy of the Soviet Union or the policy of their own Yugoslav government. If one looks at the problem this way, then we must believe that with good will on both sides it is necessary to find a solution that would not exert a harmful influence on our friendly relations.

Having this situation in mind, we find it hard to believe that you are still not attempting to find another solution, especially because we believe that other opportunities to resolve this problem in accordance with international law—for instance, amnesty, or something similar—do exist. We hope that you will reconsider your position once again in light of the above.

In conclusion, we would like to return to one argument from your letter once again. Regardless of how some ill-intentioned people may interpret our attitude towards Nagy and the rest of the group in Budapest, we would like to emphasize that we have absolutely no connection either with that group or with the events in Hungary. Moreover, we reject the insinuation about our implied connection with the Petőfi Circle. Yugoslavia exists as it is, with all its revolutionary past, with its experience and understanding of the building of Socialism. If some people in Hungary have spoken about it [Yugoslavia], it still does give anyone the right to shift responsibility for their internal events, which had completely different origins, and different perpetrators, onto Yugoslavia. Precisely because we saw all the dangers of a stormy unfolding [of events] in Hungary, we were extremely reserved, and did all we could to act in a calm way. The arrival of the delegation of the Hungarian Workers' Party led by Gerő to Yugoslavia proves this point. For the same reason, we agreed with you on the assessment of the new course of events in Hungary, and we gave public support to the workers' and peasants' government led by Comrade Kádár from the very first day. Consequently, if anyone tries to blame Yugoslavia for the events in Hungary, for which it bears no responsibility whatsoever, we believe that in such a case it would be in our common interest, and in the interests of socialism, to refute such accusations.

WITH COMRADELY REGARDS
ON BEHALF OF THE CENTRAL COMMITTEE
OF THE YUGOSLAV LEAGUE OF COMMUNISTS   (J. B. TITO)

NOTE: "PROTOCOL NO. 54, SECTION I"

[Source: APRF, F. 3. Op. 64. D. 486. Ll. 61–67. Also in TsKhSD, F. 89. Per. 45. Dok. No. 38. Published in Sovietskii Soyuz i vengerskii krizis, 1956 goda: Dokumenty, edited and compiled by E. D. Orekhova, Vyacheslav T. Sereda and Aleksandr. S. Stykhalin (Moscow: ROSSPEN, 1998), pp. 622–625. Translated by Svetlana Savranskaya.]

DOCUMENT NO. 92: Memorandum of Discussion of the 303rd Meeting of the NSC, November 8, 1956 (Excerpts)

As surprising as it may seem, even though the Hungarian crisis was at its peak, a full week passed between the last meeting of the National Security Council (on November 1) and this session. Moreover, the previous meeting did not even deal with Hungary since Secretary of State John Foster Dulles convinced President Eisenhower that the situation had essentially been resolved, and that the group ought to discuss the more serious problems occurring in the Middle East (see Document No. 62). Here, the tone clearly reflects the participants' disgust and dismay at the Soviet attack. Several specific points are made during the discussion that give useful insights into the thinking of the president and his advisers. For one, Allen Dulles makes an interesting comparison between the newly installed János Kádár and Polish communist leader Władysław Gomułka, whom Dulles and others clearly admired for standing up to Khrushchev just days before. Another noteworthy point is Eisenhower's obvious frustration ("what can we do that is really constructive?") at Washington's inability to fundamentally alter the situation.

———

[....][89]

2. Significant World Developments Affecting U.S. Security

The Director of Central Intelligence said that he would first report briefly on the situation in Hungary. He said that the Soviet repression in Hungary had been ruthless and brutal to the last degree.... there were eye-witness accounts of what had happened from the U.S. Legation in Budapest. Mr. Dulles then reviewed what had happened in Hungary since the last meeting of the National Security Council[90], including reference to the Soviet admission that they had now 200,000 troops deployed in Hungary. Mr. Dulles also alluded to Janos Kadar, the head of the Hungarian Government. Mr. Dulles described Kadar as a potential Gomulka if his hands had not been so deeply stained by the blood of his own countrymen and if he had not acted in collaboration with the Soviets. Even so, he may yet turn out to be a Hungarian Gomulka—not, said Mr. Dulles, that he could put his trust in Kadar.

Mr. Dulles went on to describe briefly the European reaction to what the Soviets had done in Hungary, concluding that these Soviet actions had reduced Soviet prestige in Western Europe to its lowest point in many years. He ended with the prediction that the rebellion in Hungary would be extinguished in a matter of days, if not of hours. Nevertheless, the Soviets would be faced with a problem in Hungary for many, many years to come. In turn, the situation presents the United States with the problem of what more we can do, . . .

The President said that this was indeed a bitter pill for us to swallow. We say we are at the end of our patience, but what can we do that is really constructive? Should we break off diplomatic relations with the USSR? What would be gained by this action? The Soviets don't care. The whole business was shocking to the point of being unbelievable. And yet many people seemed unconvinced. For example, said the President, he had just had a message from Nehru—or was it a point he made in a recent speech? Wherever it came from, Nehru had said that what was really happening in Hungary was obscure[91]. Could anything be blinder? The President also

———

[89] This document begins with a list of the meeting's participants and a discussion of the impact of events in the Near East on the supply of oil in Europe.

[90] See Document No. 62.

[91] *The New York Times* reported on November 12 that in a speech delivered on November 9, Nehru had several times described the Hungarian situation as confusing. [Footnote from source text.]

cited Premier Bulganin's message to him received this morning[92], in which Bulganin stated in effect that what was going on in Hungary was none of the business of the United States.

The Vice President [Richard Nixon] inquired whether Soviet action in Hungary had produced any unfavorable reaction in Asian capitals. Had anything occurred there comparable to the demonstrations which Mr. Dulles had described as occurring in Western Europe? Mr. Dulles replied that not very much in the way of unfavorable reaction had occurred in Asia, although there were a few instances. The Vice President commented that this seemed to indicate that our own true story had not got across in Asia. Secretary Hoover[93] stated that if the British and French had not at this particular time decided to move into Suez, things would not have happened as they did in Hungary. If the British and French had stayed out of Egypt and the Soviets had nevertheless moved against Hungary, they would have been ruined in the eyes of world public opinion. Secretary Hoover doubted if they would under the circumstances have dared to move against Hungary. The President expressed his agreement.

[....][94]

Furthermore, the President said, it remained wholly inexplicable to him that any state in the world, Syria included, would play with the Russians after witnessing what had happened in Hungary. It is for this reason, continued the President, that we must go on playing up the situation in Hungary to the absolute maximum, so the whole world will see and understand.

The Vice President agreed with the President's proposal, and said that in carrying it out we should not neglect Asia. Mr. Dulles indicated that the Free Europe Committee was already engaged in preparing a White Paper which would give the world all the facts about what had happened in Hungary from the beginning.

The President proceeded to quote from his most recent message from Nehru[95], commenting that Nehru seemed to be falling for the Moscow line—buying their entire bill of goods.

The Vice President stated that the great message which we must get across to the rest of the world was that no state could afford to play in with the Soviet Union unless it wished to be taken over.

[....][96]

At this point the President interrupted Secretary Hoover to say that Admiral Strauss had just sent him a note stating that moving pictures had been taken of Soviet tanks killing Hungarians in the streets of Budapest. The President asked whether such movies should not immediately be disseminated through our Embassies all over the world. Mr. Streibert answered that the USIA was already engaged in doing precisely this, and was trying to get the story out just as fast as it could. The President said it would be a good idea to send one of the best reels to Nehru. The Vice President advised sending one to Sukarno[97] in Indonesia.

[....][98]

---

[92] For text, see Department of State *Bulletin*, November 19, 1956, 796–797. [Footnote from source text.]

[93] Since Secretary of State Dulles was hospitalized on November 3, Undersecretary of State Herbert C. Hoover took over temporarily as acting secretary.

[94] The following sections deals with the Middle East. See *FRUS, 1955–1957*, vol. 16 (Washington, D.C.: Government Printing Office, 1990), 1078–1086 passim.

[95] In his November 7 letter to the President, Nehru had written as follows: "You have referred in your letter to what I said about the situation in Hungary. I have, indeed, been greatly troubled by what has happened there, and I drew the attention of Mr. Bulganin to it. He has briefly replied and has promised to send a fuller reply later. Meanwhile, we have been told by the Russian Government that they had previously decided to withdraw their troops from Hungary and had declared their general policy on the 30th October. Subsequent events compelled them to intervene temporarily to protect the lives of their own people as governmental authority appeared to have vanished and, in fact, killings were taking place. I entirely agree with you that armed intervention of any country in another is highly objectionable and that people in every country must be free to choose their own governments without interference of others." (Eisenhower Library, Whitman File, International File) [Footnote from source text.]

[96] The following section deals with the Middle East.

[97] Ahmed Sukarno was president of Indonesia from 1945–1967.

[98] The following section deals with the Middle East.

The Vice President expressed the hope that while we must deal with the Near East problem, we should also give the Congressional leaders a good stiff talk on Hungary. There has been too great a tendency to allow developments in the Near East to divert attention from Hungary. Let's assure that the Congressional leaders do not leave without a knowledge of what had really happened in Hungary[99]. The Vice President thought this topic should come last in the briefing, and also suggested that the movies mentioned earlier should be shown to the Congressional leaders.

The President commented that the present Congressional leaders have been acting in a wholly admirable fashion.

The Attorney General warned the President that the Congressional leaders were very likely to ask him whether, in view of what had happened, the Government should not move now to exclude the Soviet Union from membership in the UN. The President replied that if he were asked this question he would say that we couldn't shoot from the hip, but state that this was certainly something to be considered.

[....][100]

Mr. Allen Dulles suggested that the Hungarian topic come first rather than last in the briefing of the leaders. The President and many other members of the Council thought this suggestion wise. The President went on to express the feeling that the Russians had jumped rapidly into the Near East situation not simply because the British and French had given them an opportunity, but because they have long hoped that somehow or other they could reach into the Middle East. Accordingly, we must be careful in briefing the Congressional leaders not to place all the blame for what had happened on Great Britain and France. Admiral Radford expressed warm agreement with the President's suggestion. It was unwise to blame overmuch the British and the French. We should instead put the Near East situation in its true perspective, and indicate clearly ultimate Communist responsibility for what has occurred in the Near East.

[....][101]

S. EVERETT GLEASON

[*Source:* Foreign Relations of the United States, 1955–1957, *Vol. 25 (Washington, D.C.: United States Government Printing Office, 1990), pp. 418–421.]*

---

[99] See Document 177, "Editorial Note," in *FRUS, 1955–1957, vol. 25, 423–424.*

[100] The following section deals with the Middle East.

[101] The following section deals with the Middle East.

DOCUMENT NO. 93: Message from Andrei Gromyko to János Kádár, November 9, 1956

In this message to Kádár, sent via Soviet Ambassador Andropov, the Soviet leadership hoped to strengthen Kádár's inclination not to let the Yugoslavs grant custody to Nagy and his group. In a telegram sent to Belgrade on November 4 (of whose contents Kádár was aware), the CPSU Presidium notified Tito about their revised position on the Brioni agreement. According to this new stance, after crushing the "counterrevolution" there was no need for any gesture by Nagy; therefore, it would be best to hand him to the Soviets who would then turn him over to the "Revolutionary Workers' and Peasants' Government" of Szolnok, i.e. Kádár's regime. Moscow attached such importance to settling the Nagy matter that, while hoping Tito would accept the fait accompli, they were willing to risk damaging Soviet-Yugoslav relations, which they had been steadily working to improve since 1955.

This document also illustrates the Kádár government's general weakness and its utter dependence on Soviet authorities, even to the extent of having to ask for Moscow's help in getting "Radio Kossuth" back on the air.

NOVEMBER 9, 1956

TOP SECRET. COPY NO. 3
TOP PRIORITY

Meet with Comrade Kádár and verbally pass the following to him from the CPSU CC:

"Dear Comrade Kádár!

1. Comrade Andropov informed us of your ideas on the measures to strengthen our fight against the groups of rebels. You think it is necessary to be more decisive in engaging the Hungarians themselves in this struggle, and that you should immediately create two regiments of the Hungarian Army from Communists and other loyal people. We completely agree with this proposal.

In accordance with your request to the Soviet Forces Command, we gave instructions to provide assistance to the Hungarian government in organizing the work of the Kossuth radio station and in putting in operation a printing press for publishing a newspaper, which is especially important today for improving political work among the masses.

2. Comrade Konev informed us on your behalf of your reception of the Yugoslav ambassador. We fully support your response to the ambassador to the effect that Imre Nagy and other individuals hiding in the Yugoslav Embassy should not be transferred to Yugoslavia under any conditions because they were organizers of the counterrevolutionary uprisings, and that you cannot allow two Hungarian governments to exist at the same time—one in Hungary, and one in Yugoslavia.

3. Some time earlier, before your reception of the Yugoslav ambassador, in your conversation with Comrade Andropov, you expressed the opinion that we probably should demand a document from Nagy, in which he would announce his resignation, and that Nagy and other persons who are currently with him, should present documents stating that they would not do any harm to the Workers' and Peasants' Government of Hungary. As a preliminary step, you expressed your own personal opinion that once the above-mentioned conditions are implemented, Nagy and the other individuals should be allowed to go to Yugoslavia so that we do not aggravate our relations with the Yugoslav leadership. At the same time, you noted correctly, that "apparently, the Yugoslavs were trying to save Nagy not because they needed him very much, but because of their concern that some 'things that are undesirable for them' could be revealed through him."

4. From your absolutely correct assessment of the genuine motives of the Yugoslav comrades in trying to save Nagy and get him to Yugoslavia, and also from your response to the Yugoslav ambassador, it is clear that we are in unison with you as far as the essence of the issue

is concerned—that Imre Nagy and his group should not be transferred to the Yugoslavs under any circumstances.

You have only some concerns regarding the possibility that relations with the Yugoslav comrades will be aggravated because of Nagy. In this regard, we have presented our position on the issue of Nagy and his group with full sincerity in the CPSU CC letter to Comrades Tito, Kardelj and Ranković.[102] You are familiar with that letter, and therefore we will not repeat the arguments that it contained.

We believe that the Yugoslav comrades will ultimately be convinced of the fairness of our joint point of view, and will understand that the interests of our common cause demand that we cannot do anything with Nagy other than what we have proposed.

We believe that the Yugoslavs' insistent demands regarding the transfer of Nagy and his group under their authority are unprecedented and violate Hungarian sovereignty. In reality, who can understand—in Hungary or in the rest of the world—why the Hungarian Revolutionary Workers' and Peasants' Government should allow Nagy and his group, who opened the way for the forces of reaction, to be transported to Yugoslavia after they were defeated?

The position of the Yugoslav leadership on this issue contradicts the Declaration on the Foundations for the Development and Further Strengthening of Friendship between the Soviet Union and Other Socialist Countries, which, as we know, enjoyed full approval in all the socialist countries.[103] This position grossly violates Hungarian sovereignty and represents interference in its internal affairs, which no self-respecting government can allow. We are convinced that if any other government assumed such a position toward Yugoslavia, then the Yugoslav leaders would not even talk about this issue.

The issue about Imre Nagy, which became the point of contention between the Yugoslav comrades and us, is an issue of high principles, touching on the core interests of Hungary and the common cause of socialism. Therefore, we cannot imagine that it would be possible to make concessions on this issue to the Yugoslav comrades when they are completely wrong, for fear of aggravating relations with them. To the contrary, we believe that we should show consistency and our principled position on this most important issue. The fairness of our position is completely obvious. Transferring Imre Nagy to Yugoslavia would bring instability to the position of the Hungarian revolutionary government and would result in irreparable damage to our common cause.

As far as the documents that should be requested from Nagy when he is under the authority of the Hungarian Workers' and Peasants' Government, we can return to this question later."

Inform by telegraph upon implementation.

A. GROMYKO

Notes: 1. "Copies: 1. Cde. Bulganin. 2. Cde. Khrushchev. 3. Cde. Khrushchev. 4. Cde. Shepilov. 5–7. Copies."

2. "Inform Cdes. Zorin, Patolichev, Semenov, Levychkin, Suzdalev."

[Source: APRF, Fond 3, Opis 64, Doc. 486, pp. 39–42. TsKhSD, Fond 89, Opis 45, Doc. 35. Published in Sovietskii Soyuz i vengerskii krizis, 1956 goda: Dokumenty, *edited and compiled by E. D. Orekhova, Vyacheslav T. Sereda and Aleksandr. S. Stykhalin (Moscow: ROSSPEN, 1998), pp. 627–629. Translated by Svetlana Savranskaya.]*

---

[102] See Document No. 90.
[103] See Document No. 50.

DOCUMENT NO. 94: Memoranda of Telephone Conversations between President Eisenhower and Henry Cabot Lodge, and between President Eisenhower and Secretary of State John Foster Dulles, November 9, 1956

At 4:48 in the afternoon of November 9, as reflected in the memo below, President Eisenhower spoke by telephone to U.N. Ambassador Henry Cabot Lodge, who raised an issue that lay at the heart of much of the domestic and international criticism of the administration at the time—that the U.S. appeared to have incited the Hungarians to revolt, only to "turn our backs on them" at the crucial moment. Lodge's comment exposes the gap between the administration's roll-back rhetoric and its conviction, very much down-played in public, that the U.S. could do little to help "liberate" the satellite states. Immediately after speaking with Lodge, Eisenhower calls his secretary of state, who is convalescing at Walter Reed Army Medical Center in Washington. After short references to a congressional briefing on Hungary which the president gave that morning, and to Dulles' suggestion that Eisenhower take a rest after the rigors of his recent re-election (on November 6), Eisenhower returns to Lodge's comment, which clearly rankled him and shows that he seemed to be unaware of the tremendous expectations his administration's public pronouncements had raised over the years.

4:48

Cabot Lodge, from UN, N.Y.

Resolution coming to the floor again tonight on Hungary. Amb. Lodge wondered if President could find his way clear to sending Bulganin another message, urging consideration of it. Lodge said there is the feeling at UN that for 10 years we have been exciting the Hungarians through our Radio Free Europe, and now that they are in trouble, we turn our backs on them.

The President insisted that is wrong—that we have never excited anybody to rebel. Said further that Lodge can check State and USIA. Amb. Lodge said that is what they are beginning to throw at him, and he is glad to know this from the President. He will call State Dept. and ask them to prepare something.

4:50

Secy. Dulles (in Walter Reed)

First, Secy. Dulles said he heard this morning's meeting went very well.

The President said it really did; and that afterwards, [then-Senate Majority Leader Lyndon] Johnson, [House Minority Leader Charles] Halleck and whole group of others said it was the best thing they ever saw. They were urged to just keep still.

About the week end, Secy. Dulles asked why didn't the President consider going to farm for a little longer period—after election strain, and all this. But the President won't.

The President told Dulles of Cabot Lodge's call. Second Hungarian resolution coming up, and they will pass it tonight. It seems that at the UN particularly many of our European friends are asking why we are so fretful about France and Britain with a few troops in Egypt, while we don't show as much concern about Hungary. Lodge wants President to send another message to Bulganin, saying this is before the Council again this evening, and urging them to consider and act on it. Again to say we would send in UN observer team, to determine needs for food and medicine, and getting out the wounded.

The President, however, feels there have already been too many messages. Dulles said he was not very enthusiastic about another to Bulganin. The President's question: Are we in danger of putting ourselves in wrong in that we will urge Ben-Gurion[104] and people like that if we don't try to put same pressure on this fellow?

---

[104] David Ben-Gurion, chairman of the Israeli Labor Party from 1930–1965, proclaimed the independent state of Israel in 1948 and served as prime minister and minister of defense from 1955–1963.

Dulles' reply was, I think, "Well, but you have."

The President repeated feeling that we have excited Hungarians for all these years, and now turning our backs to them when they are in a jam. Dulles said we always have been against violent rebellion. The President said he had told Lodge so, but was amazed that he was in ignorance of this fact.

The President said, finally, he might dictate a short message saying this is again before the Council, and he wants to point out again the great feeling of relief if he would support that Resolution and act upon it. Then give draft message to Herbert Hoover for an opinion.

The President doesn't want to let Cabot down. But hates to send messages back and forth, when we know they won't pay any attention to them . . .

Mr. Dulles said he doubts that the feeling about turning backs on Hungarians exists in any quarters but the French and British. President said that Lodge had mentioned France in particular.

[Here follows discussion of the Middle East.]

The President will go ahead with Bulganin draft message. He is sure it will have no influence on Bulganin; whether it has any influence on the UN, he is not sure.

[Source: Foreign Relations of the United States, 1955–1957, *Vol. 25 (Washington, D.C.: United States Government Printing Office, 1990) pp. 424–425.]*

DOCUMENT NO. 95: Minutes of the HSWP Provisional Central Committee Meeting, November 11, 1956 (Excerpts)

These minutes outline the main dilemma facing the early Kádár regime: how to break with the Rákosi era when the absence of popular support seemed to necessitate a resort to the "old methods" in order to hold onto power. This was the reason Kádár encouraged the establishment of a "military force loyal to the revolution" and enforcement of the police by the party. By calling on "people of all party affiliations" to "work together," he anticipates the concept made famous later by the dictum: "whoever is not against us is with us." György Aczél reflects an understanding of the party's shaky position when he adds, "We desperately need people whom the people consider credible." Noting that he believes Nagy to be a credible person, he urges his colleagues to begin negotiating with him. Interestingly, Kádár does not disapprove of Nagy at this point—consistent with the view he expressed to the CPSU Presidium a few days earlier—although by this time Moscow has come to see Nagy unambiguously as an enemy.

Comrade János Kádár: Allow me to inform the comrades about a few things that need to be stressed repeatedly. First of all, a few words about the events of last week. Events that the comrades are not familiar with in detail.

What happened to the government last week? I am personally convinced that Imre Nagy, Géza Losonczy and the other comrades who were previous members of the government had no intention whatsoever to support the counterrevolution. Imre Nagy, Losonczy and myself were the only ones who could influence decisions, there was only this cabinet,[105] while the Council of Ministers did not work the entire week. The real ringleaders in the Council of Ministers were not so much Imre Nagy as Tildy, Losonczy and to a certain extent Ferenc Erdei. With the increasingly aggravating situation, these people gradually took a position that is hard to define as anything other than nationalistic. They cared for nothing except to swim with the tide, and brought the issue of withdrawing Soviet troops into the focus of attention even within the government. With some uncertainty, Comrade Imre Nagy also jumped on the bandwagon, while Géza Losonczy embraced the issue with fervor. The comrades are well aware that in the meantime we made considerable political compromises—the most decisive one being recognition of the multiparty system.[106] I have to admit that I myself voted in favor of the proposition. On what grounds? With the ulterior motive that by ordering a cease-fire and making the utmost political compromise, we would manage to get out of the situation by political means. I also admit that at the same time I frequently consulted the Soviet comrades about these difficult issues, and that they asked for my opinion. In that situation, under pressure to decide whether we should accept a multiparty system, I told them that my impression was that if we continued in this way, the contradiction would destroy us, and with every Soviet unit that was deployed, we would become stronger in a military sense but correspondingly weaker politically. I also told them that within a few days the uprising would turn into a national war against the Soviet Union, because any increase in the number of Soviet units engaged in action would strengthen and deepen the nationalist position of the masses. What I mean by national war is that the government would order the people's army to fight against Soviet troops. The decision had to be made under these circumstances. My reasoning was that however difficult the situation becomes for us, we have the possibility of [creating] a solid political base, because in the past twelve years the party was characterized not just by negative features, but by positive ones as well. If we can bring to the

---

[105] This was the cabinet formed on October 30. See Document No. 46.

[106] According to the Council of Ministers' resolution of October 30, "[The Council of Ministers] permits the organization of parties on the basis of the coalition of 1945 and thus departs from the path of the one-party system." For the minutes of the meeting, see Glatz, "A kormány és a párt," 46–47.

foreground those things which constituted achievements over the past twelve years and in which the party played a large role—such as the nationalization of property, the redistribution of land and other fundamental issues—then we will be able to fight a political struggle with more or less success, and finally create a situation in which we will have a sustainable, or rather significant, influence in the government. Furthermore, we will be able to secure the principles of the people's democratic system and to enjoy the support of the masses.

Following that decision, the counterrevolution gained incredible momentum on both lines, and it became obvious that normal political means, political decisions, and persuasion are insufficient for resolving the situation. The armed conflict itself gradually took on a counterrevolutionary character, as it was joined by a great number of fascists and other subversive elements who up until now lived in the West and now somehow have trickled back.[107] In the sphere of politics, coalition partners that we had respected before as honest political players suddenly became all the more demanding, [a phenomenon] which can be described not so much as an open fight against the government, but rather as an attempt to realize their own goals in the turmoil. They demanded high office but never wanted to take the responsibility. When it came to negotiations with delegations, they pushed Imre Nagy to the forefront while they were busy organizing the party in a way that must be condemned most firmly: they intruded into the buildings and garages of the Hungarian Workers' Party, and into banks as well, laying their hands on millions of Forints. All in all, their behavior was a total disgrace. One of our political partners, the Social Democratic Party, headed by Anna Kéthly, [Gyula] Kelemen and others, declared to the people that they would not take any position in the coalition government. When we agreed on the multiparty system we had no contact with the social democrats, but we thought that they should delegate one member to the cabinet. Nonetheless, they refrained from appointing a delegate, obviously because they wanted the people to see that they had no intention of being part of that government.

At that time, the following happened concerning the party: there was a so-called Presidium. The party delayed taking a position during the fighting, mostly because the very concept of and opinion about the armed conflict was constantly changing. At the outbreak of the armed uprising, it seemed clearly to be a counterrevolutionary movement. Later, we saw that masses of workers and miners had joined forces (especially in the countryside), presenting claims—social demands, the withdrawal of Soviet troops, and the abolition of [compulsory] crop deliveries to the state—that were far from being counterrevolutionary. From then on, it was impossible to brand the entire movement as counterrevolutionary. The moment came in the coalition when a new idea and platform appeared to form a firm political base. The question arose: what should happen to the party? The unanimous opinion—which the Soviet comrades not only supported but also in a certain respect hastened—was that we should sharply distance ourselves from the political regime of Rákosi. The question was raised how this should be done. A suggestion came up in the Presidium, which five of us supported. What was the suggestion? That we condemn the politics of Rákosi in a political statement, and change the name of the party and the name of its central newspaper. By not going further than this, we could restructure the membership and organizations of the Hungarian Workers' Party. After some argument, Imre Nagy also embraced the idea. Later on, Zoltán Szántó came up with the idea that an entirely new party should be founded and new members admitted. We found this suggestion unacceptable.[108] Then the Presidium came under pressure from Donáth, Lukács, and Márton Horváth, who were proposing the same idea. After this, there were no more sessions, only a dozen people arguing and seriously influencing the Presidium with their hysterical attempt to change the tone [of the proceedings]. The essence of this campaign was to urge the formation of a new communist party, since writers and other social elements had already come together and they would certainly

---

[107] i.e. Hungarians who emigrated after WWII.

[108] Imre Nagy did not initiate the dissolution of the HWP; when Zoltán Szántó put forward the proposal in the Presidium on October 30, Nagy and other members objected to the idea.

organize the new party if we waited too long. It seemed that two or three communist parties were in the making at the same time, which could have led to serious political and ideological confusion within the working class. Given this situation, we all gave in, with the same motivation that drove us into the coalition. Namely, should the situation become consolidated and the armed confrontation stopped, then normal political activity could be resumed and the party could be reorganized from previous members of the Hungarian Workers' Party, ousting all politically discredited elements. The idea and the decision that we consequently made—which I announced in a radio broadcast[109]—were based on the given situation and on the assumption that we face a normal political struggle.[110]

So much for last week.

I do not wish to go into details about forming the new government and the declaration.[111] There is, however, an important event that the comrades should know about. Last weekend, unbeknownst to me—maybe comrade Köböl knows more about it—the events seemed to take a nationalist turn. Sunday morning, Imre Nagy, acting in the name of the government, stated that Soviet forces were attacking, and announced that the government was in office and ready for defense.[112] I must admit that Soviet troops and the Hungarian People's Army behaved very differently. Some units simply surrendered, while others exchanged fire, shooting once or twice. Some, however, decided to fight on and are still fighting, providing the rebels with medium-heavy armament. In connection with this, among several people the opinion was formed—which we have already expressed—that some people gave up the working class idea and shifted towards a nationalist standpoint.

There is one very concrete thing, which I would ask you to keep utterly confidential, because the whole question is extremely complex. After the broad resistance commenced, some started panicking, and quite a large group fled in panic from here: Imre Nagy, Lukács, Donáth, Haraszti, Vas, Jánosi,[113] Tánczos, Júlia Rajk[114] and Vásárhelyi asked and were granted asylum at the Yugoslav Embassy. This is a rather delicate and extremely complex issue. The Yugoslav ambassador was here the day before yesterday, and I had a talk with him. The ambassador gave me the list, and informed me that those named had asked and received political asylum.[115] I asked him whether they [the Yugoslav government] had an opinion about and position on the situation. The ambassador said that there was no opinion because first they would like to learn about the standpoint of the Hungarian

---

[109] This refers to Kádár's radio address on November 1. See footnote 247 Part Two.

[110] From November 1956 on, Kádár always referred to the very difficult circumstances in which the old party was dissolved, in an attempt to defend himself against the accusation, never explicitly stated, that he liquidated the party. (Kádár's sensitivity on this issue can be explained by the fact that when he was sentenced to prison in 1951, the main charge against him was that during WWII he had dissolved the party on orders of the Horthyite police.) His argument was that some officials had put heavy pressure on the Presidium and that there had also been a danger that further hesitation would result in a totally independent, new party being formed. According to available sources, the decision was indeed pressed from outside as well. Reformist intellectuals belonging to the former party opposition urged the party leadership to form a new organization, threatening otherwise to do it themselves. This challenge was passed on to the party leadership by the individuals Kádár mentioned: György Lukács, Márton Horváth, Ferenc Donáth and others.

[111] The "new government" refers to the formation of the Kádár government. For the declaration, see footnote 65 above.

[112] The radio address was broadcast on November 4, at 5.20 A.M. See Document No. 82.

[113] Ferenc Jánosi was a son-in-law of Imre Nagy and his assistant in the prime minister's office during the revolution. Sentenced to eight years in 1958, he was amnestied in 1960.

[114] As László Rajk's wife, Júlia Rajk was imprisoned between 1949–1954. After taking refugee at the Yugoslav Embassy on November 4, she was deported to Romania together with the other members of the Nagy group on November 23.

[115] This list has not yet been discovered. According to some sources, 43 people received asylum at the Yugoslav Embassy, including family members. Aside from those Kádár mentioned, György Fazekas (journalist, member of the former party opposition around Nagy), Géza Losonczy, Zoltán Szántó, József Szilágyi and Szilárd Ujhelyi also were part of this group.

government. The heart of the matter was that we should consent to that group being taken to Yugoslavia. I emphasized that I could only give him my personal opinion. I told him that we can in no way agree to their leaving the country. First of all, because the last public act of Nagy and Losonczy was their government declaration. The government fell apart, yet they never stated that they were no longer members of the government. I suggested that they tell them to put in writing that they had resigned from their ministerial offices and to state their opinion about the new government. They must by all means declare that they will not act against this government in any way. Unless they make this statement, it will not be possible to negotiate on any issue. I told them how unpleasant this is for us and particularly for the Yugoslav government. It is obvious to everyone that the spiritual leaders of the revolt are more or less identical to the ones that are now enjoying asylum. Were they to be admitted to Belgrade, it might seem as if the Yugoslav government was against the revolutionary government, which is not the case, and as if they [the Nagy group] were being held in reserve for a new government to come. I was rather blunt and outspoken; I told him that I am no diplomat and that this situation would be really difficult to explain to the workers of the world. The Yugoslav ambassador said that naturally this would not be the case and that they support the revolutionary workers' and peasants' government; nonetheless, because they asked for asylum as private individuals, international law is binding. I told him that they are not private individuals. This is now the most delicate issue in both international and party politics.

[....]

My personal impression is that the Soviet Union acted merely out of duty. After a certain time, we have to undertake negotiations concerning the withdrawal of Soviet troops from Hungary anyway.[116] As to the further prospects, there is no doubt that Soviet troops sooner or later must be withdrawn from Hungary. That is why we need our own forces. We have fragmentary ideas in this respect: instead of a huge army we need to maintain a voluntary army of twenty to thirty thousand troops, who are supplied in the same way as professional soldiers normally are. The main issue now, though, is that we should have our own military force loyal to the revolution, especially in Budapest. The same holds true of the police. It is as imperative, as it was in 1945. We must send to the police corps a few hundred communist revolutionaries, who are firmly loyal to the cause of the revolution and are ready to serve in these positions for several years, if necessary.

[....]

People want to know what political guarantees they can receive so that things will not continue as before.

[....]

People are concerned about the issue of what will happen to the coalition, what will happen with the people from other parties. These questions must given a definite answer. The answer we can give is that the matter now is not about having a people's democracy with single-party rule or with multi-party rule, but to have a people's democracy after all. Moreover, it has to be said that we, people of all party affiliations, should work together.

The situation has changed since last week. As the multiparty system looks now, we will only work with those—and maybe there will be independent party organizations as well—who join forces with us and can guarantee that they will not deliver the country into their hands [sic.].[117]

[....]

[116] The issue of Soviet troops stationed on Hungarian territory came up several times at party leadership meetings and during the Soviet-Hungarian negotiations. On May 27, 1957, an agreement was signed concerning the legal status of these Soviet units and in the summer of 1958 one division was withdrawn from the country. In the spring of 1958, Khrushchev raised the idea with Kádár of withdrawing all Soviet forces from the country, as had happened in Romania a few months later. Kádár, however, declined the offer, arguing that Hungary on its own would not be able to defend itself from external aggression.

[117] This somewhat confused sentence indicates that at this stage Kádár still was willing to consider allowing certain allied parties to exist, as some other Soviet bloc countries (e.g., Poland and East Germany) were doing, as long as they did not seek a real political role and did not question the leadership of the communist party.

There are other questions, such as the whole national issue, the use of the Kossuth coat of arms, the army uniform, and so on, that we have apparently handled carelessly so far, thus hurting national feelings. We must be determined and convince everybody to put aside any antagonism [in this respect] and help the [solution of the] most fundamental tasks instead: namely, the disarmament of paramilitary forces, surrendering arms, resuming work, and repressing the counterrevolution. After these [tasks], we can then make decisions concerning certain questions that we simply cannot put on the agenda right now. We decided to evacuate certain public buildings to ease the imminent housing shortage—the Ministry of Culture, for instance, is rather redundant right now. We offered some of the party center venues, without naming them specifically. Everything that can be done must be done. However, people must be reassured that there will be no functionaries in the party that members do not support. It must also be stated that in the future no fundamental question can be decided without asking and respecting the opinion of the masses. This will pacify the people. I explained that none of the leaders want to bring back the old regime, and if there were any, they would not be able to do so anyway.

[....]

Comrade József Köböl: Comrade Kádár asked me to give an account of the last few days of last week. Allow me to do so. Comrades who were in the party's Presidium and in the cabinet at the time became very uneasy concerning last Friday and Saturday. This unease was palpable in the Central Committee as well, among those still working there. We discussed this question in the Central Committee building, with the aim of forwarding our ideas to the Executive Committee.[118] One of the organizers of these discussions was comrade Zoltán Szántó. The following topic was on the agenda: it was a mistake to turn towards the U.N.[119] on issues of foreign policy because we almost entirely isolated ourselves from the socialist countries and started veering towards the western alliance under the excuse of neutrality. The general opinion was that we had made a grave mistake with this step and that it would have been more appropriate to ask other socialist states, such as Yugoslavia or China, to mediate instead of the U.N.

Another assertion of this kind was that what is going on under the label of communism is in fact a counterrevolutionary organization,[120] and the general opinion was that we should take firm steps so that the newly forming party stops this activity and the coalition parties present a united front in defense of democracy.

The third idea was that communists in the cabinet deploy all their influence to put an end to the atrocities committed by members of the national guard and other elements.[121] These thoughts, which were discussed in the presence of both comrades Sándor[122] and Orbán, were forwarded by comrade Szántó to the members of the Executive Committee, with the exception of Imre Nagy, who was usually absent from these sessions. Later, present members of the Executive Committee decided to inform Imre Nagy about the proposition, stating clearly that should he fail to fulfill these issues, they [the Communists] had better withdraw from the government. We tried, therefore, to back out of the unfortunate measure of the Hungarian government asking the U.N. for assistance. Let me add that at the time, if my memory serves me, unexplained departures of certain leading comrades caused much

[118] This refers to the Executive Committee of the new HSWP. Its members were Ferenc Donáth, János Kádár, Sándor Kopácsi, Géza Losonczy, György Lukács, Imre Nagy and Zoltán Szántó. It is worth mentioning that except for Kádár and Kopácsi (who had been arrested by Soviet forces) every member of the EC took refugee in the Yugoslav Embassy.

[119] The cabinet led by Nagy decided at its November 1 meeting to renounce the Warsaw Treaty, declare Hungary's independence, turn to the U.N. and ask the four great powers to guarantee the country's independence. See Document Nos. 64, 66, 67, and 68.

[120] This refers to the fact that certain members of the new HSWP were in contact with the armed insurgents.

[121] On October 30, the same József Köböl made the following appeal as the first secretary of the Budapest branch of the party: "The national guards are being formed. It is the duty of communists to participate to the best of their ability in the maintenance of order and the defense of workers' power. Therefore those communists fit for armed service should report immediately to the organizational centers of the national guards."

[122] József Sándor worked in the HWP CC Economics Department from 1948–1956. Beginning in November 1956, he was a member of the HSWP PCC and head of its Economics Department.

bitterness. I myself was unable to understand that comrade Kádár delivered a speech Wednesday evening last week,[123] if I am not mistaken, concerning the formation of the Hungarian Socialist Workers' Party, and then he disappeared a few hours later. Let me add that in so doing he unintentionally forced communist members of the cabinet into an awkward situation, when they were unable to explain to politicians—who were otherwise already well informed on the issue by that time—what had happened. Many of us, myself included, felt somewhat deceived, the more so as we later received news of other leading comrades leaving. Then and there we discussed what to do with ourselves, since we knew that counterrevolution was a real threat; we were not allowed to enter 17 Akadémia street,[124] and so on. For the sake of historical fidelity, let me add that we discussed what to do with different comrades, Zoltán Szántó among them, and the general opinion was to stay put, prepare for going underground, wait, and see what comes next. I have to tell you all this because—even though I consider the declaration that Imre Nagy made last Sunday to be entirely wrong and injurious—it is still necessary to make these things known, for all the comrades must see clearly what happened then and there. The other reason why I must tell you all this is because we have to do everything we can not to help the formation of such kinds of groups based on mistaken principles, such as we did with writers: instead of separating out those that we could have, we united them on an incorrect platform. We must be careful not to make the same mistake again. We must make a personal distinction for those who did not go abroad or elsewhere, but instead worked here throughout.

Although I agree with comrade Kádár on most issues, I do not share his view on the danger of nationalism in Hungary. He said that other problems have come to the forefront—I suppose he meant economic hardships and the ordeals of everyday life—whereas I think that nationalism and anti-Soviet behavior now cover everything; they overwhelmingly dominate politics. There are a host of symptoms that point in this direction. Of course, there are signs indicating that people have already begun to hate the saber-rattling youth, whose aimless shooting has often been irresponsible, yet nationalism is still all-pervasive. Yesterday I was walking the streets of Budapest around 6:30 in the evening, passing by the sites where battles had raged. The lights were out, and on Hunyadi Square, countless candles illuminated the makeshift graves. There are countless signs of overwhelming nationalism, particularly in Budapest. Part of this issue is that we have to be aware that just because we want to see unity in the leadership—on which I of course agree—we must not recruit the kind of front that isn't going to be effective.

The next thought is closely linked with the above. Comrade Kádár mentioned that no one in his right mind could think that the self-appointed provisional Central Committee could tread on the old path. This, however, is dependent on a number of factors, and I think the danger of treading on the old path is not to be underestimated, because actual conditions are pressing us in that direction. It must be noted that the power of the working class does not conform to the majority of the working class. Or rather let me put it this way: the government and the newly forming party rely on a minority of the working class and on certain armed forces. I strongly hope that we get over this phase in due course, but the situation with which we have to cope right now is that destruction is going on, people are tired and weary of everyday problems, the Soviet army is upon us, and everybody keeps their mouths shut. I walk around the city quite a lot, and my experience is that people tend to hold back and be rather reticent these days. There is the danger that our party members will withhold opposing opinions because their objections—which would ultimately express the opinion of the people—would differ considerably from what we say, and they themselves feel that what we need right now is unity. Consequently, we are pretty much compelled to resort to the old path and the old methods under the constraint of the present conditions. I only raise this issue so that we do not fool ourselves by assuming that we managed to abolish the methods of the past. The situation is fraught with controversy; the realization of democracy on a wide scale is difficult, yet imperative for recruiting the necessary mass support.

[123] Actually, the speech was on Thursday, November 1.

[124] This was the address of HWP headquarters.

Another relevant issue is the question of individual parties, which needs a clearer and more precise platform, in my opinion. Parties were strangled too quickly. They need more freedom—but to what extent is a question that has yet to be answered.

Another question that needs to be discussed is the question of the party. In my opinion we have to take advantage of the present political landslide and bring the party back to the basics that constitute its real task. In the last few years, the party played the role of the council of ministers but also functioned as a local authority and a host of other things; everything happened there. This is no longer tenable. I think now is the time that the party can and must return to being a leading political and propaganda organization, instead of being the administrator for affairs of all sorts. The idea that we communists are responsible for everything is rooted in the fact that we did everything ourselves. For instance, even kindergarten affairs had a separate administrator in the party center. I think we should deal with the national economy only in the sense that we discuss it in broad terms, and that actual decision-making should be left to the Council of Ministers.

Allow me another thought: the party needs to be pushed slightly into the background. So far it has been raised above everything: above the government and the trade unions, which is of course not a bad idea in principle but the way we did it was wrong. We have to establish and reinforce the reputation of the government and state organs by granting them due authority. We know that members of the government used to complain that the Council of Ministers meetings were all about sanctioning decisions that had been made in the party. I believe that the reputation of the trade unions needs to be raised to a great extent. First of all, elected bodies of the party must have a real function. Up to now, the party apparatus has been at the helm. The party apparatus needs downsizing and its auxiliary function has to be emphasized. A great number of communists must be selected and directed to state and social organizations to serve as reinforcement.

I do agree that we should not return to the system of individual admission to the party. To specify who the retarding forces are is only a marginal solution to the problem, which is unacceptable. I do agree that we have to rely on the forces of the HWP, yet it has to be noted that our huge but disintegrating mass party has to be taken over by a smaller party, a real vanguard. Our numbers will of course decrease anyway, but this shouldn't happen in such a way that we fail to get rid of the careerists while we "get rid" of those comrades we shouldn't get rid of. We must be extremely loyal and tolerant with comrades who were confused by the previous three weeks and the preceding few months—those who do not wish to be party members anymore. Let's not burn these bridges behind us, but rather let the valuable comrades find their way and join the party once again. [...]

Comrade György Aczél: [...] I do agree with what comrades Kádár, Marosán and Köböl said about the working class. Let me add, however, that never in history has a ruling class been treated so poorly as we treated the working class. Last year I talked to factory workers, and I tried to convince them as usual that they are the ruling class, that the sons of the working class represent the power in government, etc. One of them says, that's right, but once they are in the government, the next day they move into a villa in Pasarét,[125] and at the very best you see them waving from a car. That is why we have to fundamentally change the party apparatus and the behavior of functionaries.

The party has been ruined by the work done since 1949—this is what we have to correct. Upon my arrest in 1949, an officer of the State Security Authority told me that within a few years they would systematically rid the party of all those who might say no to any proposition. Such isolation and desolation of our own kind was extremely detrimental. It is the Hungarian people and the most devoted communists who must correct what has gone astray.

What comrade Köböl said about downsizing the apparatus and official revolutionaries I find to be a decisive factor. We should not bring party functionaries into the party. We need people who are, as Marx says, on the level of average workers and who live among average workers. We must not allow a party aristocracy to form again—this should be combatted most firmly, and we must tell this to the people as well.

[....]

---

[125] Pasarét is an affluent neighborhood of Budapest.

414

On the basis of the wide mass support [he has], it is essential that we start negotiations with Imre Nagy. From that group, my only personal friend is Szilárd Ujhelyi.[126] I do not know Imre Nagy personally, but I am convinced that at the core these are honest people and we must negotiate with them urgently. We have to admit that without them we are unable to win over the intellectuals and working masses to the party. The capital sin of the past years was that hundreds of communists were humiliated and dishonored in the eyes of the public. The policy of the last few months had catastrophic consequences, inasmuch as leading functionaries contradicted their previous statements. For instance, comrade Apró said that it was impossible to arrest Mihály Farkas, but just a few months later, news of his arrest was announced.[127] We desperately need people whom the people consider credible, and we must come to an agreement with them. For the writers, an acceptable platform would be to retain the land and factories for the people on the one hand, and fight against both Stalinist and fascist restoration on the other; to re-establish order, and regain independence and freedom. Writers will only accept this platform if it is presented by credible people. I think it is important to tell you all this because wide social layers of professionals and workers also share this opinion.

Unquestionably, it is necessary, as comrade Köböl has already mentioned, to work out in detail how we conceive of our national independence. Even if we had planned it systematically, we could not have ruined our reputation more effectively than we did. We should now establish a scheme of independence that the Soviet Union can accept as well; a neutrality [which is] not western neutrality on the model of Austria, but rather eastern neutrality on the model of Yugoslavia or any other example. I am not sure if you see what I mean—it is something, rather, that you feel. On the basis of such a platform, we could bring the workers back into the factories. [...]

These days, the danger of sectarianism is intensifying the following issue:[128] we are a very narrow layer who can only work with the help of orders and bayonets, despite the best intentions. We must do away with what was the major mistake of cadre policy in the past five years: the [placement of] untalented people in the leadership, [a situation] which also enhances the danger of sectarianism.

Let me get back to what the comrades said concerning the issue of parties. I spent a few years in prison with the leaders of [various] Hungarian political parties. We exercised two kinds of cadre policy. Some of the political leaders we discredited in the eyes of the public, while others we simply sent to prison. There are a lot of people who are undoubtedly ready to stand by the communists in certain theoretical and practical issues. I think it is advisable to advance some of them. Nonetheless, we must also note that there are a few who served many different regimes, and they are not popular with the people. For example, however well-meaning, honest, and upstanding a man István Dobi is, it is hard to imagine that peasants are lining up behind him. Or would you believe that social democrats are following Sándor Rónai? We should negotiate with Imre Nagy, even on the following basis: it is all right if they agree on fundamental questions, let them form their own party. The main thing, though, is that we have a substantial social basis with which we can co-operate without having to resort to swords and bayonets. Let there be parties with popular leaders who enjoy the support of their own masses. We must present the prospect that the Soviet troops will eventually withdraw from Hungary—but later, not now. Let us do away with the false and varnished assessment reports, let us try to step ahead of the mass base [sic], and let us give perspective to the masses.

I am not sure if I am personally suitable to be a member of this provisional executive committee,[129] as I think that we are still a narrow minority who is trying with the help of swords and bayonets to terrorize the working class and the masses of laborers into accepting a program that we might consider convenient. You know me, comrades, and you know that I have devoted my whole life to the working-class movement. All the same, I must say that I am not willing to take part in this. [....]

---

[126] Szilárd Ujhelyi belonged to the circle around Imre Nagy. Although he also took refuge at the Yugoslav embassy on November 4, he was not arrested later and was allowed to return to Hungary in 1958.

[127] The news of Mihály Farkas' arrest for offenses against socialist legality was published in the October 13 issue of *Szabad Nép*.

[128] Despite the wording, the intended meaning of this sentence is more likely that "the dangers of sectarianism are intensified by the following factors."

[129] Aczél means the Provisional Central Committee.

Decisions of the Provisional Central Committee of the HSWP, Made at the Meeting on November 11, 1956

1. The provisional Central Committee elected comrade Ferenc Münnich into the Executive Committee of the party.
2. [The CC] assigned comrades Jenő Fock[130] and István Tömpe[131] into the provisional Central Committee.
3. [The CC] decided that *Népszabadság* will be the official newspaper of the party, and agreed on the discontinuation of the publication of *Szabad Nép.*[132]
4. An organizing committee and an agitation committee are established, with broad political authorization.[133]
5. The Central Committee needs to be extended, with the admission of comrades from the party apparatus outside Budapest.
6. Small working committees have to be formed to work out topical problems of industry, agriculture and economics. Similar working committees have to be formed to work out the possibilities for cooperation with other parties.
7. With the participation of suitable experts, it must be determined how we can continue with state and planning affairs.
8. Comrade Lajos Fehér[134] presented the following suggestion to the provisional Central Committee, which the Central Committee recommended that the Executive Committee discuss immediately:
   a. He suggested that we appeal to the Presidium of the Communist Party of the Soviet Union, asking them to bring leaders of communist parties from all the people's democracies together for a conference where they could discuss future relations between the Soviet Union and the people's democracies.[135] The CPSU should send a party delegation to Hungary to study the present situation. Soviet military units should later be replaced with Polish or Yugoslav troops.
   b. We should start negotiating with Imre Nagy, perhaps with the mediation of comrade Tito.
   c. Imre Nagy should found a new worker-peasant party.
   d. Other members of the provisional Central Committee also stressed the necessity of negotiating with Imre Nagy.

BUDAPEST, NOVEMBER 11, 1956

---

[130] Jenő Fock was secretary, later deputy secretary general, of SZOT from 1955–1957, HSWP CC secretary from February 1957 and member of the PC from June 1957.

[131] István Tömpe was head of the National Directorate of Forestry from 1950–1956. He became a member of the HSWP PCC from November 1956 and first deputy minister of interior from December 8, 1956.

[132] Although *Népszabadság* replaced *Szabad Nép* on November 2 as the main HSWP daily, on November 6 another newspaper named *Szabad Nép* began publication in Szolnok, ostensibly as the organ of the Kádár government, although its editors actually followed a more old-style dogmatic line than even Kádár found acceptable. The two new dailies continued to be printed simultaneously until the Kádár-led CC decision clarified the situation.

[133] The Organizing Committee functioned between November 14, 1956, and February 26, 1957. It mainly dealt with practical political questions such as party organization, initiating the work of mass organizations and personnel and organizational problems related to building up the new party apparatus.

[134] Lajos Fehér was deputy editor-in-chief of *Szabad Nép* from 1954–1955 when he was dismissed for oppositional behavior; he was a member of the HWP CC Military Committee from October 23–31, 1956, editor-in-chief of *Népszabadság* from November 7–24, and a member of the HSWP PCC and PEC from November 1956.

[135] Hungarian, Bulgarian, Czechoslovak, Romanian and Soviet party and government leaders met for an extraordinary session in Budapest between January 1–4, 1957. However, the goals of that consultation turned out to be quite different from those outlined above. See Document Nos. 106, 107, and 108.

[Source: MOL, 288. f. 4/1. ő.e. Published in A Magyar Szocialista Munkáspárt ideiglenes vezető testületeinek jegyzőkönyvei, *vol. 1*, 1956. november 11–1957. január 14, *edited by Karola Némethné Vágyi and Levente Sipos (Budapest: Intera, 1993), pp. 25–50. Translated by Csaba Farkas.]*

DOCUMENT NO. 96: Speech by Josip Tito at Pula, November 11, 1956

Josip Tito's well-known speech at Pula, before the party aktiv at Istria, spells out his views on recent events in Hungary and Egypt. It is clear from other available records that these are his own opinions and not just party rhetoric. He sees the outbreak of revolution in Hungary as the justifiable result of popular indignation brought on by the mistakes of the Rákosi regime, but he believes that so-called reactionary forces (the frequently mentioned Horthy-ites, for example) then used the uprising for their own purposes. He blames the Nagy government for a lack of firmness. As at Brioni, he stands up for the Soviet intervention of November 4, even though he has difficulty reconciling the contradiction between precious national sovereignty and outside military intervention. The only justification in his mind, ultimately, is the need to defend socialism against "counterrevolution". This was why he ensured the Kádár regime of his support, even though he was in conflict with Kádár by this time over the future of Nagy and his companions. But Tito is also critical of the Soviet Union in this speech. He not only targets the Stalinist system but the politics of the current leadership, for example for delaying Rákosi's dismissal. As a result, Khrushchev, who was deeply concerned about the need to reconcile with Yugoslavia, nevertheless took these remarks as a personal insult. He rejected the accusation of Stalinism, and warned Tito that his actions might lead to a rupture of relations between the parties.

ADDRESS BY THE SECRETARY GENERAL OF THE YUGOSLAV LEAGUE OF COMMUNISTS, JOZIP BROZ TITO, BEFORE A MEETING OF THE LEAGUE MEMBERS, PULA, NOVEMBER 11, 1956

Comrades,

Yesterday I expressed the desire to make use of my stay on Brioni, while I am undergoing medical treatment, to come to you and present to you our outlook upon international problems which are today very tangled.

You read newspapers, but newspapers cannot present everything and completely shed light on it, and particularly there is no light shed in them on the causes of what is today happening in Hungary, as well as in Egypt, where it has come to Israeli-French-British aggression. It is quite a tangled situation today and we cannot say that a certain danger does not exist of major conflicts developing, but the peace-loving forces in the world, to which our country also belongs, have demonstrated in the United Nations that with their persevering and indefatigable efforts they can reduce the possibility of international conflict, and have already helped make it more possible for the world to be able to hope that peace will still be preserved.[136]

Above all, I would like to deal with what is happening today in Hungary and what took place in Poland, so that we may have an accurate idea of those events which are very complicated, notably in Hungary, where it came to this, that a large part of the working class and progressive men were fighting in the streets, with arms in their hands, against the Soviet armed forces. When the Hungarian workers and progressive elements began with demonstrations and then with resistance and armed action against the Rákosi method and against further continuation of that course, I am deeply convinced that one could not then speak of counterrevolutionary tendencies. One can say that it is regrettable and tragic that reaction was able to find highly fertile soil there and gradually to divert matters into its own channels, taking advantage for its own ends of the justified revolt which existed in Hungary.

---

[136] During the October 31 U.N. Security Council session, the Yugoslav delegate proposed convening an emergency session of the General Assembly to discuss the crisis in the Middle East. That session took place between November 1 and 10.

THE ROOTS OF THE EVENTS IN POLAND AND HUNGARY

You are aware, in the main, of the causes, which have led to the events in Poland and Hungary. It is necessary that we go back to the year 1948, when Yugoslavia was the first to give an energetic answer to Stalin and when she said that she desired to be independent, that she desired to build her life and socialism in accordance with the specific conditions in her country, and that she was permitting no one to interfere in her internal affairs. Of course, it did not then come to armed intervention, because Yugoslavia was already united. Various reactionary elements were not able to carry out various provocations because we had liquidated their main force already during the People's Liberation War. Second, we had a very strong, united, and monolithic Communist Party, steeled in both the prewar period and during the People's Liberation War. We also had a powerful and steeled Army, and most important, we had the unity of the people which personifies all these things.

Once the truth about our country had been victorious and the period of normalization of relations with the countries which had severed relations with us after the ill-famed resolution had begun, the leaders of Eastern countries expressed the desire that we no longer mention that which had been done to us, that we let bygones be bygones, and we accepted this only in order that relations with those countries might be improved as soon as possible. But you will see later that it is indeed necessary to remind certain people who are again today beginning to slander our country and who stand at the head of Communist Parties in the Eastern countries, and in certain Western countries, of what they had been doing to Yugoslavia during these last four or five years, and even longer, when Yugoslavia had stood entirely alone, face to face with a huge propaganda apparatus, when we had to struggle on all sides to preserve the achievements of our People's Revolution, to preserve that which we had already started to build—the foundations of socialism—in one word, to wipe off the disgrace which they had wanted to inflict upon us by various slanders and to prove where the real truth lay. We should remind them and state that these same men had then accused our country, using every possible means, saying that it was fascist, that we were bloodthirsty men and that we were destroying our people, that our working people were not with us, and so forth. We should remind them, they should remember this and keep this in mind today when they again wish to shift the blame for events in Poland and Hungary onto our shoulders. This perfidious tendency originates in those hard-bitten Stalinist elements in various parties who have still managed to maintain themselves in their posts and who would like to consolidate their rule again and impose those Stalinist leanings upon their peoples and on others. I am going to come back to this later. Just now I wish to tell you only that today we must view the events in Hungary in the light of this whole development.

IT IS A QUESTION NOT ONLY OF THE CULT OF PERSONALITY, BUT OF THE SYSTEM WHICH MADE POSSIBLE THE CREATION OF THE CULT OF PERSONALITY

Because of her desire and on her initiative, we have normalized relations with the Soviet Union. When Stalin died, the new Soviet leaders saw that, thanks to Stalin's madness, the Soviet Union found itself in a very difficult situation, in a blind alley both in foreign and internal policy and in the other countries of people's democracy as well, thanks to his nagging and by forcing his methods on them. They understood where the main cause of all these difficulties lay and at the 20th Congress they condemned Stalin's acts and his policy up to then, but they mistakenly made the whole matter a question of the cult of personality and not a question of the system. But the cult of personality is in fact the product of a system. They did not start the fight against that system, or if they have, they have done so rather tacitly, saying that on the whole everything has been all right but that of late, because Stalin had grown old, he had become a little mad and started to commit various mistakes.

From the very beginning we have been saying that here it was not a question of the cult of personality alone, but of a system which had made possible the creation of that cult, that therein lay the roots, that this is what should be struck at incessantly and tenaciously, and this is the most difficult thing to do. Where are those roots? In the bureaucratic apparatus, in the method of leadership and the so-called one man rule, and in the ignoring of the role and aspirations of the working masses, in different Enver Hoxhas, Shehus, and other leaders of certain Western and Eastern parties who are resisting democratization and the decisions of the 20th Congress and who have contributed a great deal to the consolidation of Stalin's system, and who are today working to revive it and to continue its rule. Therein lie the roots and this is what must be corrected.

THE MOSCOW DECLARATION IS INTENDED FOR A WIDER CIRCLE OF COUNTRIES THAN YUGOSLAVIA AND THE SOVIET UNION

As far as we are concerned, we have gone a considerable way in our relations with the Soviet Union. We have improved these relations and have concluded a whole series of economic arrangements, very useful for us, on very favorable terms, and so forth. Two declarations have also been adopted, one in Belgrade and the other in Moscow.[137] Both declarations should in fact be significant not only in our mutual relations but also in relations among all socialist countries. But, unfortunately, they have not been understood in this way. It was thought as follows: good, since the Yugoslavs are so stubborn we will respect and implement these declarations, but they do not concern the others because the situation there is, nevertheless, a little different than in Yugoslavia. Yugoslavia is an organized and disciplined state. The Yugoslavs have proved their worth because they have succeeded in maintaining themselves even in the most difficult times and in not allowing a restoration of the capitalist system, and so forth, to wit, they are something different from you in the Eastern countries where we brought you to power. And this was wrong, because those same elements which provoked such resistance on the part of Yugoslavia in 1948 also live in these Eastern countries, in Poland, Hungary, and in others, in some more and in some less. During the time that we were preparing the declaration in Moscow on our party relations, mainly on the relations between the Yugoslav League of Communists and the CPSU, this was a little difficult to settle. Here we could not completely agree, but, nevertheless, the declaration was issued which, in our opinion, is intended for a wider circle than Yugoslavia and the Soviet Union.[138] We warned that those tendencies which once provoked such strong resistance in Yugoslavia existed in all countries, and that one day they might find expression in other countries, too, when this would be far more difficult to correct.

You know that Khrushchev was here for a rest.[139] On that occasion, we had talks here and many more in Belgrade. Since I and comrades Ranković and Pucar[140] were invited to the Crimea, we went there and continued the talks.[141] We saw that it would be rather difficult going for other countries, since the Soviet leaders had a different attitude toward other countries. They had certain wrong and defective views on relations with these countries, with Poland, Hungary, and others. However, we did not take this too tragically, because we saw that this was not the attitude of the entire Soviet leadership, but only of a part which to some degree had imposed this attitude on others. We saw that this attitude was imposed rather by those people who took and still take a Stalinist position, but that there

---

[137] The joint declarations were signed in Belgrade on June 2, 1955, (see footnote 164 in Part One) and in Moscow on June 20, 1956.

[138] See Document Nos. 11 artd 14.

[139] Khrushchev arrived in Belgrade on September 19, 1956, and visited the Yugoslav president on the island of Brioni from September 22–26.

[140] Ðuro Pucar was chairman of the Parliament in Bosnia-Herzegovina between 1953 and 1963 and a member of the LCY Executive Committee.

[141] Tito, Ranković, and their delegation flew to the Crimea on September 27, where they held talks with Khrushchev, Bulganin and other Soviet leaders. The delegation returned to Yugoslavia on October 5.

420

were still possibilities that within the Soviet leadership those elements would win—through internal evolution—who stand for stronger and more rapid development in the direction of democratization, abandonment of all Stalinist methods, the creation of new relations among socialist states, and the development of foreign policy in this same direction as well. From certain signs and also from the conversations, we saw that these elements were not weak, that they were strong, but that this internal process of development in a progressive direction, in the direction of abandoning Stalinist methods, was also hindered by certain Western countries, which by their propaganda and ceaseless repetition of the need for the liberation of these countries were interfering in their internal affairs and hindering a rapid development and improvement in relations among these countries. The Soviet Union believes that in view of the fact that this interference in internal affairs has assumed rather extensive proportions through propaganda on the radio, the dispatch of material by balloons, and so forth, unpleasant consequences could result if it left these countries completely and gave them, say, a status such as that enjoyed by Yugoslavia. They are afraid that reactionary elements might then be victorious in these countries. In other words, this means that they lack sufficient confidence in the internal revolutionary forces of these countries. In my opinion, this is wrong, and the root of all later mistakes lies in insufficient confidence in the socialist forces of these peoples.

OUR COUNTRY HAS BEEN ACTING VERY POSITIVELY AND USEFULLY

When the Poznan affair happened—you know about it—there occurred among the Soviet people a sudden change of attitude toward us. They started to grow colder. They thought that we, the Yugoslavs, were to blame. Yes, we are to blame because we live in this world, for being such as we are, for having created a Yugoslavia such as she is, because her acts reverberate even beyond our country. Even if we did not desire it, our country still acts, and she does so very positively and usefully. Thanks to the fact that there still remained in Poland, in spite of all persecutions and Stalinist methods of destruction of cadres, a hard core of leaders with Gomułka at their head who at the Eighth Plenum managed to take matters strongly in their own hands, boldly to put their stamp on the new course, that is, the course toward democratization, toward their full independence, but also for good relations with the Soviet Union, resolutely to offer resistance to interference in their internal affairs—thanks to this, reactionary forces in Poland could not make themselves heard, although these forces certainly did exist and had hoped that they would be able to rise to the surface as a result of a clash between Communists. Thanks to the mature reasoning and attitude of the Soviet leaders, who stopped interfering in time, things have been stabilized considerably in Poland at present, and are developing quite well.

I cannot say that this positive development in Poland, which is very similar to ours, has met with much joy in the remaining countries of the "socialist camp." No, they criticize it secretly and among themselves but to some extent openly as well. Among these countries Poland did not even meet with as much support as she found among the Soviet leaders, who had agreed to such an attitude of Poland's. Among those various leading personalities in some countries of the "socialist camp," and even among some Communist Parties in the West, Poland did not meet with understanding because Stalinist elements are still sitting there.

When that would-be professor of history holds a lecture in France and says that Yugoslavia is a sly agent of imperialism when men are sitting in the Communist Party of France who at such a tragic and difficult time also come out with such a grave accusation before hundreds and hundreds of people, can this constitute a guarantee that the cause of socialism will develop correctly in the future? It cannot. For such excesses of such irresponsible and decadent elements the leaders of that Party are to blame. Or, for instance, when such a would-be Marxist as Enver Hoxha, who only knows how to utter "Marxism-Leninism" and not a word more, writes an article about Yugoslavia, without reference to her but hitting out at Yugoslavia and Poland, he resolutely condemns the tendencies of one's own path and development in accordance with the specific conditions and even goes against that which Khrushchev and other Soviet leaders have recognized—that there are spe-

421

cific roads to socialism. Such a type has dared not only to slander and stand up against Yugoslavia and still another great socialist country, but to strike even at the Soviet leaders themselves. Such Stalinist elements believe that men will be found in the Soviet Union of a Stalinist brand who will uphold them and help to maintain them on the backs of their people. This, comrades, is fatal.

When we were in Moscow there also was talk of Poland and Hungary and other countries.[142] We said that Rákosi's regime and Rákosi himself had no qualifications whatever to lead the Hungarian state and to bring about inner unity, but that, on the contrary, their actions could only bring about grave consequences. Unfortunately, the Soviet comrades did not believe us. They said that Rákosi was an old revolutionary, honest, and so forth. That he is old, this is granted, but that is not enough. That he is honest—this I could not say, inasmuch as I know him, especially after the Rajk trial and other things. To me, these are the most dishonest people in the world. The Soviet comrades said he was prudent, that he was going to succeed, and that they knew of no one else whom they could rely upon in that country. Just because our policy, both state and Party policy, is opposed to interference in the internal affairs of others, and in order not again to come into conflict with the Soviet comrades, we were not insistent enough with the Soviet leaders to have such a team as Rákosi and Gerő eliminated.

GERŐ DIFFERED IN NO WAY FROM RÁKOSI

When I went to Moscow, there was great surprise that I did not travel via Hungary. It was precisely because of Rákosi that I did not want to do so. I said that I would not go through Hungary even if it would have meant making the journey three times shorter. When increasingly strong dissatisfaction began to rise to the surface in the ranks of the Hungarian Communists themselves, and when they demanded that Rákosi should go, the Soviet leaders realized that it was impossible to continue in this way and agreed that he should be removed. But they committed a mistake by not also allowing the removal of Gerő and other Rákosi followers, who had compromised themselves in the eyes of the people. They made it a condition that Rákosi would go only if Gerő remained. And this was a mistake, because Gerő differed in no way from Rákosi. He pursued the same kind of policy and was to blame just as much as Rákosi was.

Well, comrades, what could we do? We saw that things were not going, as they should. When we were in the Crimea, Gerő "happened" to be there and we "accidentally" met him.[143] We talked with him. Gerő condemned the earlier policy and said that it had been a mistake, that they had slandered Yugoslavia; in short, he heaped ashes on his head and asked that good relations be established, promising that all previous errors would be corrected and that the old policy would never be used again. We wanted to prove that we were not vindictive and that we were not narrow-minded, and so we agreed to have talks with Gerő and a delegation of the HWP which was to come to Yugoslavia. We wanted to establish relations with the Hungarian Workers Party because we hoped that by not isolating the Hungarian Party we could more easily influence that country's proper internal development.[144]

However, matters had already gone pretty far, a fact which we did not know, so that Gerő's coming to Yugoslavia and our joint declaration could no longer help.[145] People in Hungary were absolutely against the Stalinist elements who were still in power, they demanded their removal

[142] Tito led a party and state delegation on an official visit to the Soviet Union from June 2–23, 1956.

[143] The meeting took place on September 30, 1956.

[144] In fact, in a letter to Gerő dated September 11, 1956, Tito had already agreed to receive a Hungarian delegation. The visit took place between October 14–23, 1956. On the rapprochement between Hungary and Yugoslavia, see Document Nos. 11, 14, and 18.

[145] Between October 15–22, the Hungarian party and government delegation led by Ernő Gerő held negotiations in Belgrade. On October 23, the two sides published a joint communiqué, which defined relations between the LCY and HWP according to the guidelines set by the Moscow declaration: thus, the Hungarian party leadership, like the Soviets, had to accept Yugoslavia's conditions on party independence, equality and non-interference. The communiqué was published in *Szabad Nép* on October 24. It was reprinted in Kiss, Ripp and Vida, *Magyar-jugoszláv kapcsolatok*, 1956, 125–127.

and the adoption of a policy of democratization. When the Hungarian delegation headed by Gerő returned to their country, Gerő, finding himself in a difficult situation, again showed his former face. He called the hundreds of thousands of demonstrators, who at that stage were still only demonstrators, a mob, and insulted nearly the whole nation.[146] Just imagine how blind he was and what kind of a leader he was. In such a critical moment, when all was in turmoil and when the whole nation was dissatisfied, he dared to fling the term "mob" at people among whom a huge number, perhaps even the majority, consisted of Communists and youth. This was enough to ignite the powder keg and to bring about the explosion. Thus the conflict began.

IT IS A GRAVE ERROR TO CALL UPON FOREIGN TROOPS TO TEACH ONE'S PEOPLE A LESSON

There is no point now in investigating who fired the first shot. The Army was called out by Gerő. It was a fatal mistake to call the Soviet Army at a time when the demonstrations were still in progress. It is a great mistake to call in the Army of another country to teach a lesson to the people of that country, even if there is some shooting. This angered the people even more, and thus a spontaneous revolt broke out in which the Communists found themselves, against their will, together with various reactionary elements. The reactionary elements got mixed up in this uprising and exploited it for their own ends. Are there not plenty of Horthyites there? Who has reeducated them? Could Rákosi be expected to have reeducated them? We all know that Horthy had large fascist forces in Hungary, those "Arrow Crossists,"[147] various other reactionary elements, the adherents of Ferenc Nagy, and so forth. In short, there were a large number of people who were not for Communism, who were not only against Rákosi but against socialism in general. And all this got mixed into the uprising. These reactionary forces did not dare raise their heads earlier, regardless of all the calls for an uprising from the outside, regardless of the aid which they got from abroad, nor did they have the strength or the courage to rise as long as they thought that the Party was united and monolithic. But as soon as they saw that the Party had split and that a huge section of the Party membership had risen against Rákosi's clique and the remnants of the past, they immediately intervened.

These reactionary forces revealed their true faces very quickly, within two or three days. Since in the general national revolt against everything which had happened in the past the then-existing leadership showed no desire to remove elements which disgusted the Hungarian people and to proceed along a truly Hungarian road of socialist development with all its internal peculiarities, events moved rapidly in the other direction, and the reactionaries began to dominate more and more. The justified revolt and uprising against a clique turned into an uprising of the whole nation against socialism and against the Soviet Union. And the Communists who were in the ranks of the rebels willy-nilly finally found themselves in a struggle not for socialism but for a return to the past, as soon as the reactionaries took matters into their own hands. Against their own will they found themselves in such a situation.

Was it now possible to prevent this? It seems that it was already late. Had Nagy's Government been more energetic, had it not wavered this way and that, had it stood firmly against anarchy and the killing of Communists by the reactionary elements, had it offered decisive resistance to the reactionaries, perhaps matters would have taken a correct turn and perhaps there would not have been any intervention by the Soviet Army. And what did Nagy do? He called the people to arms against the Soviet Army and appealed to the Western countries to intervene.[148]

---

[146] This expression does not appear in the surviving text of Gerő's October 23 speech although many contemporary listeners claim it was used. For the text of the speech, see Varga, *A forradalom hangja*, 23–26.

[147] See footnote 107 in Part Two.

[148] In fact, Nagy's speech, broadcast in the early morning of November 4, did not call for armed resistance, although he did declare that "our troops are fighting." In fact, Nagy was wrong—the Hungarian army had no orders to fight Soviet troops; only a few scattered military units were involved alongside the insurgents. See Document No. 82.

In the West this intervention was made full use of. It was exploited by the imperialists who could hardly wait to attack Egypt. They attacked it precisely in this phase of the Hungarian tragedy and attacked it hoping that the Soviet Union would be too preoccupied and would not be able to intervene against this aggression.[149] Thus renewed fighting broke out in Hungary. Soviet troops were reinforced. Nagy fled[150] and a new Government was set up. I can say to you, comrades, that I know these people in the new Government and that they, in my opinion, represent that which is most honest in Hungary. They were persecuted under Rákosi, they were in prisons and stand sincerely for a new kind of development. And the very program announced by Kádár, which you have read, proves this. But Soviet intervention weakens that whole program and the Government itself is in a very serious position.

ON SOVIET INTERVENTION IN HUNGARY

The question may now be asked whether Soviet intervention was necessary? The first intervention was not necessary. The first intervention, coming at the invitation of Gerő, was absolutely wrong. The second mistake consisted in the fact that the men responsible, instead of waiting for the second intervention, did not do at once what they did later on, when the second Soviet intervention took place, that is, form a new Government and issue a declaration. Had they first created a new Government and issued such a declaration, the worker and Communist elements would probably have separated themselves from the reactionary elements and it would have been easier to find a way out of this critical situation.

Before I deal with the second intervention of Soviet troops, I must say that the situation in Hungary assumed such proportions—and you have read a great deal about it—that it was clear that there would be a terrible massacre, a terrible civil war, in which socialism could be completely buried and in which a third world war could break out, because the Soviet Government could not tolerate interference from the West and the return to power of the Horthyites and the old reactionaries.

What did these reactionary elements do? I have already stated that they showed their true faces very early. It became clear that even among the top positions they were assuming more and more power as soon as they ordered that the word "comrade" could no longer be used, that the red star should be taken down. This became clear the moment a Communist could not say that he was a Communist or he would be done away with, and also by the fact that Communists were being hanged. Had there been only one such incident and had they hanged some member of the police who was known for his ill deeds, it might be said that this was the result of a spontaneous revolt of a group of people. But there was a general massacre. In Sopron they hanged twenty Communists. They caught people in the streets and killed them if they wore tan shoes because the police wore tan shoes.[151] They broke into homes and killed Communists. All this was done by the wild fascist and reactionary mobs.

Nagy's Government did nothing to prevent this. It continually cried over the radio and kept calling for help instead of fighting against this and showing in some way the will to put a halt to the massacre of Communists and progressive people. Instead it issued a manifesto, that is, a declaration in which it renounced the Warsaw Pact, proclaimed its independence, and so forth. As if that was the most important thing at the moment. As if its withdrawal from the Warsaw Pact meant something.

[149] In fact, as recent research has shown, there was no connection between the timing of the Suez attack, which the British, French and Israelis decided upon at Sèvres on October 22, and the outbreak of the Hungarian revolution the following day. See Békés, *The 1956 Hungarian Revolution*, 18.

[150] Tito's statement is inaccurate: Nagy and his associates took refuge in the Yugoslav Embassy at the latter's invitation. On November 16, Nagy and five others addressed a letter of protest to the Yugoslav leader objecting to his offensive statements. See Kiss, Ripp and Vida, *Magyar-jugoszláv kapcsolatok, 1956*, 226–227.

[151] In fact, it was the ÁVH, not the regular police force, that was known for wearing tan shoes. Moreover, although such lynchings did occur, they were rare.

Many people are now asking why the second Soviet intervention took place. It is clear, and we have said so and will continue to say it, that we are against interference and the use of foreign armed forces. Which was now the lesser evil? There could be either chaos, civil war, counterrevolution, and a new world war, or the intervention of Soviet troops which were there. The former would be a catastrophe and the latter a mistake. And, of course, if it meant saving socialism in Hungary, then, comrades, we can say, although we are against interference, Soviet intervention was necessary. But had they done everything that should have been done earlier, there would not have been any need for military intervention. This error was, unfortunately, a result of their idea that military power solves everything. And it does not solve everything. Just look how a barehanded and poorly armed people offers fierce resistance when it has one goal—to free itself and to be independent. It is no longer interested in the kind of independence it will gain, in whether there will be restored a bourgeois and reactionary system, but only that it should be nationally independent. It was this idea that prevailed among the people. Naturally, I can now say only that the first thing was the worst that could have happened and the second, the intervention of Soviet troops, was also bad, but if it leads to the preservation of socialism in Hungary, that is, to the further building up of socialism in that country, and to peace in the world, then one day this will become a positive thing, provided that the Soviet troops withdraw the moment the situation in that country is settled and quiet.

We said this to the Soviet comrades. We concealed nothing. The Soviet comrades stated that their troops would then leave. It should be borne in mind that the Soviet Union, too, is now in a very difficult situation. Their eyes have now been opened and they realize that not only are the Horthyites fighting but also workers in factories and mines, that the whole nation is fighting. Soviet soldiers go unwillingly, with heavy hearts. Therein lies the tragedy.

After my report, you can ask questions because I have perhaps not made everything clear. But you can rest assured that we have never advised them to go ahead and use the army. We never gave such advice and could not do so even in the present crisis. In this grave situation we can tell them nothing except that they should take care to correct their old mistakes. That is the crux of the matter. Therefore, we should combat those rumors in our country which see in the Soviet intervention a purely interventionist act. That is not correct. I, comrades, am deeply convinced of this.

I am deeply convinced that the bloodshed in Hungary and those dreadful sacrifices made by the Hungarian people will have a positive effect and that a little light will reach the eyes of the comrades in the Soviet Union, even those Stalinist elements, and that they will see that it is no longer possible to do things in this way. It is our tragedy—the tragedy of all of us—that socialism has been dealt such a terrible blow. It has been compromised. And do you not recall, comrades, that we often said that such methods would only compromise socialism? We did say it. I would not like us now to beat our chests and to take pleasure in all this and say, "We told you so."

EVENTS IN HUNGARY WILL PROBABLY MARK THE LAST TRAGEDY

In connection with this tragedy I want to say one thing—that these irresponsible elements in the various Communist Parties who are still in power thanks to Stalinist methods, that they are very poor support on the side of the Soviet Union if they advise it to act according to their ideas. I think that inside all these Parties there are honest Communists who see much further than these various Stalinists. They see much further. And if they want the situation there to improve not in the manner of Hungary but rather in a peaceful, Communist way, then they must criticize negative things and listen a bit to the voice of the masses, the voice of the Party members, and the entire nation. Because, if these prophets and advisers continue acting in a destructive way and if they find it necessary to do nothing but slander our country, to continue flinging mud at us, then, of course, socialism will still have a difficult time ahead of it. Yugoslavia stands so firmly on its own legs and has up to now withstood so many blows that these slanders from abroad will not make her deviate from her path. Although we are not as yet fully satisfied with our internal development, we will endeavor to make our people as satisfied as possible and, such as we are and such as we shall be, we will increase our efforts to prevent such prophets and advisers from succeeding in their plans, which are directed toward halting the process which began in 1948 in Yugoslavia, and is now continuing in Poland, and we will not allow them to divert this process onto a Stalinist track.

On one occasion I said to the Soviet comrades that this would have happened even if Stalin had not died, that this could have happened even more easily were he alive. They did not deny this. We cannot assume the right to tell them to do things this way or that, we can only point out the mistaken and negative results which may be caused by this or that act of theirs. I believe that the events in Hungary will probably be the last tragedy necessary to jolt the Soviet comrades and leaders who are still blind to this in other countries into doing everything in their power to prevent such a situation as now prevails in Hungary from arising in other countries as well.

In some countries and parties of Eastern Europe certain leaders are saying that this cannot happen to them, that they have a strong organization, a strong army, a powerful police force, that their membership is already informed of everything, and that everything is under control. Gerő said the same thing, and Rákosi, too. And what good does it do them? None at all if they do not change the methods which they have used and if the people one day revolt. Now they are reaping what they were sowing from 1948 onward. They sowed the wind and are reaping the storm. (Long Applause.)

THE OUTLOOK FOR OUR DEVELOPMENT AND IMMEDIATE TASKS

The events in Hungary have also stimulated somewhat various elements who still exist in our country. There are not many of them, but they babble a lot. Some of them indulge in wishful thinking, hoping for trouble in order to profit by it. I never said that we have liquidated and reeducated all the Ustashi,[152] Chetniks,[153] and those bigoted Vatican adherents. I always said that only the unity of the people will prevent them from attempting anything and achieving anything in our country. More than ever, the unity of the people and Party is necessary today, but not because we are afraid that anything could happen in this country, for Yugoslavia is still not the same as Hungary or any other country. We have carried out our revolution through the shedding of our blood, through the liberation struggle, and have cleaned our house thoroughly during the revolution. There is no such danger for us.

I will not say that our people are completely satisfied and that everything in our country is as it should be. Nor am I satisfied myself. But conditions are quite different in Yugoslavia; there is a perspective in our country, and working people in Yugoslavia are more and more productive in their labors. What does not yet satisfy me? You will remember, comrades, that I made a report last year in which I pointed out the necessity to change the course of our investment policy. I profoundly believed that the people who run our economy would take this to heart and that we should first and foremost really devote attention to the living standards of our people. In this regard a certain turning point has been reached, a certain stabilization in the market has been achieved, and the rapid rise in prices has been halted, the rise which threatened inflation, but all I expected has not been done. We have now decided to suppress again, even more energetically, the tendency to build and build. We must now see to it that the living standard is improved and that the defenses of our country are also strengthened. These two things have priority and we shall take care of them. That much I wanted to say about it.

---

[152] Formed in the late 1920's, the Ustaša was a Croatian nationalist underground organization that committed a number of terrorist activities in the 1930's. After the proclamation of the independent Croatian state in 1941 the movement became the leading political force in the country and was responsible for numerous atrocities against the Serbian population during World War II.

[153] The Chetniks (Četniks) were members of Serbian loyalist armed resistance groups established after the German invasion of Yugoslavia in 1941. Despite their mutual struggle against the invaders, political disagreements with Tito's partisans often led to armed conflicts between the two forces.

I would now like to say something about various elements which exist in our country. They think like this: "Now riots have occurred in Hungary, the Horthyites as well as the Vatican and others will come to power there, and here is a chance for us." In their opinion, Yugoslavia will again be cut off and encircled and they will be able to act more easily in it. There are still such elements but I say that they are very much mistaken. For in our Party there are not 800,000 members—Gerő said their Party had that many, and hearing this I looked at him a little doubtfully—but we have something over 600,000 Party members, cadres who have been steeled in the revolution and in struggle and who have not joined our Party along with various upstart elements or other tendencies, but are bearing on their shoulders the burden of building our country. They will always know in time how to prevent anybody from trying to undermine our country. We are a country in which there exists the League of Communists with over 600,000 members and the Socialist Alliance of Working People[154] with seven million members.

These seven million people are conscious builders of socialism, they have their program and know what they are aiming for. These seven million people can always give the word if they see that it is no longer possible to go this way any further, if they think that we can no longer invest such large funds in capital construction, or if this or that is necessary. Of course, nobody has the right, neither I nor the whole of our leadership, to oppose such a desire on the part of our people—namely, that our country be built at such a rate as is possible today. You know, comrades, when you are daily confronted with such questions, when you look and see that this or that factory, if built, would tomorrow produce such results that there would be an immediate improvement in the situation, when you then see that only a few millions of capital investments would be necessary in order to ensure so much more production, when you only see this, then the other thing—our man—fades away a little. You see only the factory and not the man.

It is clear that we are still in a difficult situation. We have a considerably unfavorable balance in foreign trade, which continues to increase despite the fact that during the last year and a half we have concluded rather good agreements, first of all with the Soviet Union for a considerable loan under very favorable terms at 2 percent interest. Secondly, we have concluded an agreement on the payment of reparations by Germany. The Czechs cancelled, that is, equalized 100 million dollars, while debts with Hungary will be settled in keeping with her possibilities. These agreements have eased the situation in the field of construction. Finally, we have wheat and raw materials on credit from America to a value of about 100 million dollars. Our situation is not as difficult as some would wish to make it. There will be food and bread. In our country the market is a little unorganized since people devote too little attention to the problem of assuring that it is sufficiently provided with supplies even though very favorable conditions exist throughout the entire country. Take Belgrade, for instance, a city which has the Pančevački Rit farms close by and where there are excellent conditions for growing vegetables. There are many districts and other communes where huge quantities of consumer goods could be prepared for the market, but they are not being prepared. Today, for example, vegetables are being transported from Ljubljana to Kopar. What kind of a policy is this since we know that Kopar formerly supplied Trieste. There are a number of such things in our country which cannot be considered as favorable.

WE MUST HELP THE CURRENT KÁDÁR GOVERNMENT

Comrades, I have digressed somewhat from the subject about which I was speaking. I wanted to tell you that, viewing current developments in Hungary from the perspective of socialism or counterrevolution, we must defend Kádár's present Government, we must help it. We must help it because it is in a very difficult situation. We must combat all those elements which now, in an irresponsible way, throw all the blame on the Russians. Yes, the Soviets comrades are

---

[154] The Socialist Alliance of Working People of Yugoslavia (Socialistićki Savez Radnog Naroda Jugoslavije, SSRNJ)— the Yugoslav people's front.

responsible because they failed to see and correct earlier the errors of the Rákosi regime, for not having made it possible for those men to come to power whom the working class and the entire people trusted. For one cannot impose a leader on a people; that is impossible.

In Poland the situation has become stabilized, but not entirely. The same elements are acting there, too, the elements which are against good relations between Poland and the Soviet Union. You know that those Poles who have reactionary leanings hate the Russians and the Soviet Union. It is necessary to lead the Polish people away from reaction which hates not only the USSR but also socialism as such. For the working class and Communists in Poland have a broad horizon, a wide outlook, and know that they can get support from the Soviet Union. For example, without the support of the Soviet Union, the Poles would hardly be able to defend the Oder-Neisse border, which the Germans never recognized and which will again be the subject of their claims. In brief, what is needed here is mutual aid and support.

Likewise, it is necessary that we act in closest contact with the Polish Government and Party and help them as much as we can. Together with the Polish comrades we shall have to fight such tendencies as may crop up in various other parties, whether in the Eastern countries or in the West. Comrades, this struggle will be difficult and long, for what is actually involved is whether the new trend will triumph in the Communist Parties—the trend which really began in Yugoslavia and was supported by a considerable number of factors originating in the decisions of the 20th Congress of the Communist Party of the Soviet Union. Now the question is, will this course be victorious or will the Stalinist course again prevail. Yugoslavia must not withdraw into her own shell, she must work in every direction, but not by undermining these countries from within, which would result in negative excesses, but in the ideological field, through contacts and talks, and thus to insure the victory of the new spirit. One should not refrain from criticizing what is bad in those parties. You have read the article in *Borba* which, in my opinion, is not bad as a first article, but it is not sufficient, and still more must be written about it. It is the duty of you Communists and leaders who work in the field to explain this to our members. I think that you will agree with my statements. (Prolonged Applause.)

ON AGGRESSION AGAINST EGYPT

Now permit me to refer briefly to the aggression which has taken place against Egypt. You have read about our position in the United Nations and the statement which I made in connection with that aggression, and you also read our newspapers. But I would like to go a little further back. When I met Nasser[155] for the first time, on my return voyage from India,[156] he gave me an exact account of all their difficulties in Egypt, which is an underdeveloped country without industry, with a very low standard of living, and without any strong internal organization — a party on which one could rely. Nasser said that the leaders of Egypt are soldiers who have taken power into their hands to serve their people, to create freedom for them, and to defend their independence. When he was setting forth all these difficulties, they really seemed almost insurmountable to us. Later, the second time we visited Egypt and Cairo,[157] we talked again and saw that these difficulties were enormous. But we observed that the people in that country had started to awaken, that they had started to acquire national consciousness, a people which had previously been suppressed and dormant due to prolonged occupation and the colonial activities of the British and French. We realized that Nasser and his team could rely on the people in the execution of their difficult tasks, under the condition that there be peace.

I openly expressed to Nasser my fears that I was hardly able to believe the imperialists would leave them in peace and he should take care not to offer them any possibility, not even the slight-

---

[155] Gamal Abdel Nasser was president of Egypt from 1954–1970.

[156] Tito visited India in February 1955. [Footnote from source text.]

[157] This visit took place in December 1955. [Footnote from source text.]

est pretext, to interfere in the affairs of the East. Of course I could not tell him in detail what he should do, but could only indicated the danger which lay ahead. I told him he should know that the imperialists are men without scruples, that they have not yet renounced their aspirations, that they consider Egypt, which is the strongest state in that part of the world, the most dangerous threat to imperialist and colonial possessions in Africa and Asia, and that the strong upsurge and development of Egypt might tempt the imperialist and colonial powers to block its efforts toward progress. It was our view, and I expressed it to Nasser, that they should first strengthen the country internally, that they should create an internal political organization, a strong and firm army, that they should raise themselves economically, endeavoring to get credits wherever they can, and straightaway let the people see something as a result of the new authority of the state, to let them feel a certain improvement. These were our suggestions and proposals, which they readily accepted.

During our first meeting Nasser already told us that he would have to nationalize the Suez Canal, since Egypt, an independent country, could not tolerate foreign administration of its own territory. Of course, they had full rights to nationalize it, and only the right moment had to be chosen. When the nationalization of the Suez Canal took place, the great colonial powers, England and France, reacted sharply, there were threats of armed attack to prevent nationalization. But thanks to the United Nations, this first threat of war was averted. It was decided to conduct negotiations and to settle this problem by peaceful means. Despite this, there was staged a sudden aggression. Egypt was first attacked by Israel and then by England and France. The entire aggression was probably planned jointly, and the moment of attack was chosen when the deplorable events in Hungary took place. The confusion in Hungary was welcomed by them because they had already prepared themselves. England and France used Israel's aggression as a motive, saying they must safeguard the Suez Canal.

ISRAEL SHOWED THAT IT WAS AN INSTRUMENT OF THE GREAT POWERS

This was typical aggression, which did not differ in any way from earlier classical aggressions on the part of the colonial powers. It is precisely the same. The men who brought about this aggression are today repenting, in my opinion, because they did not succeed. First, they imagined they would destroy Egypt in a few days and depose Nasser; second, they thought that such a state of mind reigned in the world that people would not interfere, and that the United Nations would not condemn them because they would get a majority in that organization. But they miscalculated. The opposite happened. Egypt was not ruined, although it suffered great losses; its army fought well and the interventionists did not succeed in occupying the whole of the Suez Canal, although they are still fighting. The Egyptian people did not depose Nasser, as Eden[158] expected. In England itself, the Laborites took a very sharp stand against the aggression and the Government's policy. In the United Nations, the vast majority condemned this act of aggression and the creation of an international police force for Egypt is now under way, for which we have also offered our own contingent. That is, the Egyptians themselves have requested this, and most probably we, too, will send a contingent from our army.

This time Israel showed that she was an instrument of the great powers and that as such she constituted a danger to peace. It is true that there exists a terrible opposition to Israel among the Arabs because nearly a million and a half Arabs have been expelled from that part of the world and these people now live under terribly difficult conditions. Egypt and other Arab countries did not want to conclude peace nor give a guarantee that they would respect Israel as a state, that is, they did not recognize her. They still refuse to recognize her, but this does not give Israel the right to undertake aggression. This does not give them such a right under any condition, as the English and others would like it to appear. Whether the Arabs will recognize Israel depends a great deal on peaceful talks and on persuasion, on the solution of all outstanding problems,

[158] Sir R. Anthony Eden was British prime minister from 1955–1957.

429

which have been hanging in mid air since the truce. What is here most tragic in my opinion, is that the French Socialist have disgraced them and shown again that they are faithful servants of the circles which are trying to retain the old classical forms of colonialism at all costs. They will never wash this stigma from their faces. By means of the aggression against Egypt they wished to settle not only the Algerian question but also to reap benefits in other Near East countries. They believed that this conflict would spread to other Arab countries and that they might thus strengthen their colonial positions. The English thought that after the occupation of the Suez Canal they would be in a firmer position in the East, that after the destruction of Egypt their interests in the Middle East would be secured. It is tragic that this aggression received the support of the majority of deputies in the French Assembly. Only the Communists and a small section of the Socialists were against it. This is very tragic.

And this, comrades, compels us to be cautious. For it has turned out that the upholders of so-called Western democracy, France and England, are for peace, justice, and democracy only in words, while actually they are hotbeds which can lead to extreme reaction and aggressive undertakings if an opportunity present itself. I am convinced that the unfortunate French people will have to pay dearly one day precisely because of this policy, which is pursued by the French Socialists, headed by Guy Mollet.

We wished to help the French on the Algerian question. We told Nasser that we considered it difficult for the French to leave Algeria and that it would be a good thing to find some solution in a union between France and Algeria. When we visited France,[159] we said the same thing to the French leaders. "Instead of spending a billion francs every day for the army which you are maintaining in Algeria, give one half of that sum for the improvement of the living standards of those people, for the construction of roads and other projects, and the Algerian people will have nothing against you, will not be against a solution in the form of a union with France. Instead of spending a billion francs a day, and that is thirty billions a month, you would be better off following that path." Some French leaders admitted this was correct while others said that the prestige of France was at stake. They have their prestige now! They have disgraced themselves before the whole world. The whole world condemns the act of the French Government, the act of aggression.

YUGOSLAVIA IS VERY ACTIVE AND ACTS IN A POSITIVE WAY IN THE UNITED NATIONS

Comrades, things have not yet been clarified. It is still not clear what they are planning and how far they will go. I doubt that the whole affair with the international police will run smoothly. The English will probably wish to see part of their army remain in Egypt as police, which is impossible both under the United Nations statute and because they are aggressors. They cannot stay in Egypt. Egypt would never agree to this, nor would any honest person. They can always find a motive to continue their aggressive actions. The fact that the Soviet Union took up this problem so forcefully startled them a little and compelled them to think.

More than ever before we must direct all our forces today toward preserving peace. Yugoslavia is very active and acts in a positive way in the United Nations. For our part we shall do everything in our power for the preservation of peace in the world. The vast majority of peoples do not want war. If anyone in the world values peace, I think it is our people who desire it in order to be able to build a better life in peace. We have suffered enough; we have shed enough blood in the last and in previous wars, and have reason enough to fight with all our might for the preservation of peace in the world. But this matter has now passed beyond our boundaries.

Our country is united, strong, and monolithic. There exists only the question of improving the life of our people as much as possible. Our unity, our monolithic character, cool headedness,

[159] Tito visited France in May 1956. [Footnote from source text.]

430

consideration of the gravest world events without becoming nervous, and levelheaded judgment are important for us. We must not permit the babbling of various doubtful elements. The people from below, the masses, must silence them and prevent them from sowing discord.

If anything is unclear to you, we are always at your disposal, we can always explain the situation to you. It is clear that there are sometimes things which cannot be told. You should not think that I said everything today, because I have not been able to do so. But one thing I can tell you, namely, that what I have not told you also is of great importance, and that it is in a great measure positive. Yugoslavia today plays a role in the world which is reckoned with. In order that she should continue to play this positive role, I think we must continue the policy, which we have consistently followed until now and preserve the strength which we have today.

This, comrades, is what I wanted to tell you. I have set forth, briefly, the basic outline and the most important things, which I thought could be useful to you in explaining the issues while doing your work in the field.

[Source: The speech was originally published in Borba, *November 16, 1956. This translation was published in Paul E. Zinner, ed.,* National Communism and Popular Revolt in Eastern Europe: A Selection of Documents on Events in Poland and Hungary, February–November, 1956 *(New York: Columbia University Press, 1956), pp. 516–541.]*

DOCUMENT NO. 97: Report by Soviet Deputy Interior Minister M. N. Holodkov to Interior Minister N. P. Dudorov, November 15, 1956

The following report from the Soviet deputy interior minister to the minister provides details about the arrest, imprisonment and deportation of Hungarians during the period of the Soviet intervention. The document was eventually submitted to the CPSU CC and presents exact data about the detainees, as well as describing the difficulties facing Soviet authorities in Hungary. Interestingly, the author assumes that some of the arrests were unjustified.

NOVEMBER 15, 1956

SPECIAL FOLDER
TOP SECRET
MINISTER OF THE INTERIOR OF THE USSR
COMRADE N. P. DUDOROV

I report that in accordance with your instructions I, along with a group of Ministry of the Interior officials and Defense Ministry representative Colonel Berezin, arrived in the city of Mukachevo on November 6 where I established contact with representative of Soviet Forces Command General Colonel Comrade Komarov, and agreed with him on the method and site for processing participants in the counterrevolutionary uprising in Hungary who were apprehended by units of the Soviet Army. It was decided that Soviet Army units would transport all detainees to Uzhgorod prison.

On November 7, during our conversation over secure line (VCh), Comrade Serov informed me that the number of detainees would reach 4,000 to 5,000 people. In this connection, I made a decision, together with representatives of the Ministry of the Interior of the Ukrainian SSR, that in addition to the Uzhgorod prison, the prisons in Stryy, Drogobych, Chernovtsy and Stanislav would be designated for placement of detainees.

The detainees began to arrive at Uzhgorod prison on November 8. On that day, 22 persons arrived from Debrecen and Miskolc.

By November 15, 1956, 846 arrestees had arrived in the Uzhgorod prison (among them 23 women), 463 of whom were transported on to the prison at Stryy, Drogobych Province. Subsequent groups of arrivals will be dispersed to prisons in Stanislav, Chernovtsy, and Drogobych.

The inmates are being held under the same conditions as those who are under investigation.

The largest number of arrestees has come from the areas of Budapest (548), Veszprém (90), Kaposvár (45), Szombathely (55), and Miskolc (20).

Among the arrestees are a substantial number of Hungarian Workers 'Party members servicemen of the Hungarian Army, and the student youth, as well as 68 underaged persons born between 1939 and 1942, including 9 girls. No excesses were registered during the processing of arrestees.

It is necessary to note that we do not have properly issued documents for a large number of arrestees. The materials that we have are mostly brief notes issued by local Hungarian authorities, the counterintelligence organs of the Soviet Army, reports of the military, or lists that mention only identifying [*ustanovochnykh*] information about the detainees.

Many of those arrested asked us why they, Hungarian citizens, found themselves on the territory of the Soviet Union. They claimed that they did not speak out against either the Hungarian Revolutionary Workers' and Peasants' Government, or the Soviet troops.

Hungarian Army servicemen Mihály Szepesi and László Szőlősi presented us with a letter (copy attached), in which they assert that they were honest Communists, and were very disappointed that they could not actively fight for the government of János Kádár at such a difficult time for Hungary.

Hungarian Army Lieutenant György Vig, brought in from Miskolc, stated that he did not take part in the uprising. In his capacity as interpreter for one of Hungarian Army units before his arrest, he maintained connections with the command of units of the Soviet Army, and on orders of his commanders assisted in their movement around the territory of Miskolc. He said that other Hungarians held in the same prison cell with him, in particular Rudolf Földvári (member of the Central Committee of the HWP), deputy of the Parliament, first secretary of the Borsod County Committee of the HWP) were supporters of János Kádár and friends of the Soviet Union, that their arrest was a mistake, and that Soviet comrades would be looking carefully at their cases and they would be rehabilitated. (Rudolf Földvári was sent to Debrecen according to Comrade I. A. Serov's instructions).

Among those brought to the Uzhgorod prison from Szolnok, there was the chief physician of the city clinic András Sebyk [Sebők], who was detained (according to the record) as an active participant in the riots, who spoke at a rebel rally with a proposal to appeal to the United States and the United Nations for help.

In a conversation with us, he reiterated his speech at the meeting, and stated that he was pursuing the sole purpose of dissuading a great crowd of agitated people gathered in the city square from mounting an armed uprising against units of the Soviet Army, which had surrounded and disarmed the Hungarian Army unit deployed in the city.

On November 13, 1956, András Sebyk was released from prison and sent back to Hungary.

Other inmates also proclaimed their innocence and asked that their cases be considered as soon as possible.

It is clear from our conversations with arrestees, and also from the fact that there are no properly prepared arrest documents for many of them—and in many cases not even lists of names—that Soviet Army units have to work in very difficult and complex conditions in locating and detaining the participants in the riots.

Stories of Soviet Army officers who have brought arrestees to Uzhgorod are evidence of that.

Having accompanied a group of arrestees from Debrecen and Miskolc, Counterintelligence officer Captain Zlygostev told us that when he personally took part in an operation to arrest rebels he had to face situations in a number of villages where there was such an absence of authority that there was nobody to ask who, among the local residents, had taken part in the counterrevolutionary activities.

The information cited above, and also the presence of underaged persons between 14 and 17 years of age, among them girls, gives grounds to suppose that there could have been some unjustified arrests.

It seems necessary to send responsible and competent officials (maybe even Hungarian ones), who would be able to quickly consider the cases of all imprisoned persons and release those who were arrested without sufficient grounds, to locations where arrested Hungarian citizens are being held.

This is even more necessary because, as is clear from the cable addressed to you from Minister of the Interior of the Ukrainian SSR Comrade Brovkin from November 15 of this year, the arrestees are demanding that consideration of their cases be expedited and are expressing their dissatisfaction with their imprisonment, while only eight investigators of the KGB and prosecutors office are currently investigating their cases.

Many inmates appealed to us and to the prison administration with requests to inform their relatives of their fate, to bring to their notice that they are alive, because, according to the inmates' statements, at the moment of their arrest rumors were spreading among the population to the effect that arrestees were being taken to Siberia, or to be executed.

The inmates also request that they be allowed to read newspapers and listen to the radio. Some of them are expressing dissatisfaction with the food.

Upon arrival, I issued orders to switch all arrestees to food norm No. 2, i.e. the same as for inmates serving a sentence [srochnykh zaklyuchennykh], along with a ration of tobacco, and also to trade the Forints that were confiscated from them for Soviet currency at the established exchange rate, as well as to give arrestees an opportunity to purchase first priority items (soap, toothbrushes, tooth powder, etc.) in the prison shop.

In addition, I would consider the following to be expedient:

1. To allow arrestees to read Hungarian newspapers published under the control of the Hungarian Revolutionary Workers' and Peasants' Government. In this connection, to organize delivery of such newspapers to the prisons via the Soviet Forces Command in Hungary.
2. To introduce proposals to the Hungarian government that the Hungarian authorities inform relatives of arrestees that the latter were detained by the Hungarian authorities and remain in good health (without mentioning where they are being detained).
3. The organs of internal affairs should transport Hungarian citizens who have been released and are subject to return to their homeland to the border checkpoint at Chop; from there they should be transferred to representatives of the Hungarian regime, in connection with which, the Soviet Forces Command should be required to work out an agreement with the government of the Hungarian People's Republic regarding the method for processing those persons by the Hungarian authorities in Chop, and their transportation to their final destinations.

HOLODKOV

[Source: APRF, F. 3, Op. 64, D. 486, Ll. 30–37. TsKhSD, F. 89, Op. 45, D. 46. Published in Russian in Sovietskii Soyuz i vengerskii krizis, 1956 goda: Dokumenty, *edited and compiled by E. D. Orekhova, Vyacheslav T. Sereda and Aleksandr. S. Stykhalin (Moscow: ROSSPEN, 1998), pp. 652–655. Translated by Svetlana Savranskaya.]*

DOCUMENT NO. 98: Report by Georgii Malenkov, Mikhail Suslov, and Averki Aristov on Hungarian-Yugoslav Negotiations, November 17, 1956

In this report, the high-ranking Kremlin envoys report on developments concerning the Imre Nagy group at the Yugoslav Embassy in Budapest. The day before, in a meeting with Dalibor Soldatić, Kádár agreed to a deal in which Nagy and his companions would distance themselves from the "counterrevolution" in return for having some members of the group leave the country for a period of three or four months, while the rest would return home and continue to take part in politics. Kádár promised to guarantee this in writing. However, on November 17, he withdrew the agreement, and in addition to raising new claims, again called for the Nagy group to be handed over to the Hungarian government. He declared that the Nagy group could not stay in Hungary, but he also made it clear that they could not go to Yugoslavia.

Unbeknownst to the Yugoslav ambassador, Kádár the day before had taken part in a secret meeting with Malenkov, Suslov, Aristov and Serov who told him about a plan to capture and deport Nagy and his colleagues to Romania. Without informing the Executive Committee of the HSWP or the government, Kádár readily agreed. Afterwards, the Soviet delegation wrote to Moscow urging the Kremlin to "[p]repare for and secure the arrest of Nagy and his group upon their exit from the Yugoslav Embassy." The arrest took place on 22 November.

NOVEMBER 17, 1956

CPSU CC

This morning, November 17, cde. Kádár received the Yugoslav ambassador and informed us of the following concerning his talks with the ambassador on the question of the Nagy group:

1. Kádár, as agreed yesterday, stated the position of the Hungarian government to the ambassador and told him that Imre Nagy and his group must be handed over to the Hungarian government; that this group could not remain in Hungary; that it must make a declaration to the Kádár government admitting its mistakes, offering support to the Revolutionary Workers' and Peasants' Government, and pledging not to carry out hostile acts against this government. In order not to complicate the situation with their presence in Hungary, they must pledge not to create obstacles to the rallying of revolutionary forces around the Workers' and Peasants' Government, and request permission to leave the country. At the same time, Kádár told the ambassador: if Nagy and his group want to go to Yugoslavia, no impediments will be raised.

2. The Yugoslav ambassador conducted the discussion with a raised voice, stating that, as a consequence of the above, the Yugoslav proposal "on the unimpeded stay of Nagy and his group in Hungary," had not been accepted, and that he would report on this to his government, but that he thought that the Yugoslav government would take the following steps:

   a) The Yugoslav government would produce an open declaration on the Nagy group presenting its position on this question;

   b) the Yugoslav Embassy would terminate its grant of asylum to Nagy and his group, discharge [*vypustit'*] the group from the Embassy, and bear no responsibility for any further consequences;

   c) The Yugoslav ambassador would leave for Belgrade because of the absence of normal working conditions;

We believe that the Yugoslavs are now compelled to withdraw the right of asylum to Nagy and his group, and are interested in getting rid of this group as quickly as possible. They are also forced to relinquish their demand for a guarantee for Nagy and his group from the Hungarian government—that is, in fact to renounce their previous position. However, they want to frame this renunciation in such a way as to preserve their own reputation, and consequently the forthcoming declaration of the Yugoslav government will undoubtedly be tendentious.

As far as the ambassador's statement about his departure for Belgrade, it must be kept in mind that he has thoroughly compromised himself throughout this affair by granting asylum to Nagy, and now it is in his interest to leave Hungary for a time. However, in his conversation with Kádár, the ambassador couched this as a kind of threat.

Our suggestions:

a) Prepare for and secure the arrest of Nagy and his group upon their exit from the Yugoslav Embassy;
b) Demand from Nagy and his group a statement admitting their mistakes and declaring that they will not carry out hostile activities with regard to the Kádár government;
c) Transfer Nagy and his group to Romania;
d) Immediately prepare the text of a declaration by the Hungarian government on the matter of Nagy and his group;

We explained our considerations to Kádár and he was in complete agreement with them.

MALENKOV
SUSLOV
ARISTOV

BUDAPEST

[Source: APRF, F. 3, Op. 64, D. 487, Ll. 79–80. Published in Sovietskii Soyuz i vengerskii krizis, 1956 goda: Dokumenty, *edited and compiled by E. D. Orekhova, Vyacheslav T. Sereda and Aleksandr. S. Stykhalin (Moscow: ROSSPEN, 1998), pp. 656–657. Translated by Malcolm Byrne.]*

DOCUMENT NO. 99: National Security Council Report NSC 5616/2, "Interim U.S. Policy on Developments in Poland and Hungary," November 19, 1956 (Excerpts)

This high-level policy review first appeared as a draft on October 31 when the crisis seemed on the verge of resolution in favor of the rebels. The National Security Council was supposed to consider it on November 1 but discussion of Hungary was postponed in order to concentrate on the Middle East. Almost three weeks later, and after the revolt had been completely crushed, President Eisenhower approved this report as official U.S. policy. What may be most surprising about the evolution of the document from draft to final version is how little it changed. United States goals remained the same, as did most of the methods proposed for achieving them. Among the more notable differences was the removal of an idea, probably suggested by Harold Stassen, to consider withdrawing some U.S. forces from Western Europe in return for a Soviet pull-out from Hungary. There was also generally a more pessimistic (or possibly realistic) tone to the final document that is evident in the realization that it would now take longer than previously expected for U.S. objectives to come to fruition. One interesting point that survived from the first draft was the idea of "reassuring the USSR that we do not look upon Hungary or the other satellites as potential military allies." Another, closely related, point was to consider whether to propose in the U.N. or elsewhere that Hungary adopt the Austrian model of neutrality. This transcript of NSC 5616/2 includes paragraphs 8, 10, 11b, 11c, and 15, which were omitted, ostensibly for security reasons, in the FRUS version.

NSC 5616/2   WASHINGTON, NOVEMBER 19, 1956.

INTERIM U.S. POLICY ON DEVELOPMENTS IN POLAND AND HUNGARY

General Considerations

1. Events of great magnitude in Poland and Hungary necessitate an appraisal of the situation and consideration of current U.S. policies, objectives, and courses of action toward those countries. Our initial objective toward the Eastern European satellite area has been to encourage, as a first step toward eventual full national independence and freedom, the emergence of "national" communist governments. While these governments might continue to be in close political and military alliance with the Soviet Union, they would be able to exercise to a much greater degree than in the past independent authority and control in the direction of their own affairs, primarily confined in the first stage to their internal affairs.

Poland

2. Developments in Poland appear favorable to the attainment of this objective. The Gomulka Government has proclaimed its "national independence and equality" and has asserted its right to pursue its own internal road to "socialism". At the same time it has declared continued loyalty to its alliance with the USSR and, though requesting the retirement of Soviet armed forces to their usual stations, has declared Soviet troops must remain in Poland and East Germany.

3. In Poland, as in Hungary, recent developments have revealed the strong anti-Russian and anti-communist sentiments of the population. Unlike Hungary, the existence of strong leadership in Poland at a critical moment, fear of a reunified Germany with irredentist claims, and the timely promise of reforms, together with an assertion of "national independence" linked with a closely calculated defiance of Russian pressure, evidently has served to enable a reconstituted Polish

communist government to set forth on its new course with the acquiescence, if not support, of the majority of Poles.

4. The United States has already indicated directly to the new Government that a Polish request for economic assistance, particularly for wheat or other surplus commodities, would be given sympathetic study.[160] Severe legal and administrative limits are imposed on such assistance.[161] On the other hand, opportunities exist for materially aiding Poland in the general area of trade with the free world.

Hungary

5. Developments in Hungary have differed significantly from those in Poland. In Hungary, a nationalist movement, similar to that in Poland, was triggered into national revolt by the intervention of Soviet troops called in by the Hungarian Government in the first hours of its difficulty. The subsequent demands of the people on the government went far beyond those originally sought and became anti-communist as well as anti-Soviet. Under Nagy, the Hungarians moved from a program of modest reforms to one in which the Nagy Government announced Hungary's withdrawal from the Warsaw Pact and appealed to the UN for aid in obtaining the cessation of Soviet intervention, the withdrawal of Soviet troops and the recognition of Hungarian neutrality.

6. The Soviet Government renewed on November 4 its efforts to suppress the Hungarian revolt by installing a new puppet regime headed by Kadar, and by the employment of greatly increased Soviet armed force. Soviet reaction to UN actions and to the President's appeal to Bulganin on November 4[162] have made clear Soviet determination to maintain its position there by force of arms. The Kadar regime has reverted to a program of modest reform promises including a promise to negotiate in the future for the withdrawal of Soviet forces while making it clear that the political and military alliance with the USSR must be maintained.

7. The direct intervention of Soviet troops in fighting the Hungarian population, and the threat of intervention of Soviet forces in Poland, illustrate that, at least in those countries where Soviet troops are stationed, the Soviet Union is willing to use its armed forces to prevent the coming into power of a non-communist government, or to prevent a communist government from altering a policy of close military and political alliance with the USSR. Moscow was apparently willing in the case of Poland to accept, however reluctantly, a communist government which, while remaining loyal to its military and political alliance with the USSR, asserts its "national independence" and its right to pursue its own internal road to communism.

Policy Conclusions

8. The events in Poland and Hungary have revealed to both the Soviet Union and the rest of the world how much the maintenance of Soviet control in East Germany and Eastern Europe depends upon the presence of Soviet forces in this area. It will be in the U.S. interest, therefore, through appropriate inducements and pressures, to encourage developments which may lead to reduction and withdrawal of Soviet forces from Eastern Europe.

9. It seems unlikely that U.S. action short of overt military intervention or obvious preparation for such intervention would lead the USSR deliberately to take steps which it believed would materially increase the risk of general war. Soviet suspicions of U.S. policy and present circumstances which involve Soviet troop movements and alerts probably increase the likelihood of a series of actions and counter-actions which might lead to war.

[160] See Document 109, Telegram from the Embassy in Poland to the Department of State, October 25, 1956, 1:00 p.m. in *FRUS, 1955–1957*, vol. 25, 287.

[161] See Annex C. [Footnote in the original]

[162] See Document 166, Telegram from the Department of State to the Embassy in the Soviet Union, November 4, 1956, 4:25 p.m. in *FRUS, 1955–1957*, vol. 25, 390–392.

10. Actions taken by the United States and other friendly governments in the present situation should strive to aid and encourage forces in the satellites moving toward U.S. objectives without provoking counter-action which would result in the suppression of "liberalizing" influences.

COURSES OF ACTION

Poland

11. Provided that the current situation with respect to Poland is not fundamentally altered:

    a. Make an early approach to the Polish Government in response to its note of October 8[163] indicating our willingness to discuss with it all problems affecting U.S.-Polish relations.

    b. Take appropriate steps to reorient Polish trade toward the West, and urge the countries of Western Europe, especially West Germany and the U.K., to offer economic assistance and trade inducements.

    c. Be prepared to make available at Polish request economic and technical assistance in moderate amounts sufficient to give the Poles an alternative to complete dependence on Moscow.

12. In the development of economic relations with Poland encourage the Poles to devote their energies to the satisfaction of consumer demands and peaceful trade.

13. While avoiding specific endorsement of the Gomulka Government, seek to influence the new Polish leaders to adhere to and fulfill its commitments[164] for reform made to the Polish people which will advance U.S. objectives.

14. Increase contacts and exchanges between Poland and the United States on economic, scientific and cultural bases in the context of NSC 5607. [165]

15. Studies should immediately be made to determine whether, if the USSR uses military force to repress the Gomulka regime or to reverse a further trend toward national independence, and if the Polish regime resists and makes a timely request to the UN, the United States should be prepared to support any UN action, including the use of force, necessary to prevent the USSR from successfully reimposing its control by force.

Hungary[166]

16. In pursuing our immediate objective of terminating harsh Soviet measures of repression and retaliation, mobilize all appropriate pressures, including UN action, on the USSR against such measures, while reassuring the USSR that we do not look upon Hungary or the other satellites as potential military allies. Such appropriate pressures might include the following as required:

---

[163] See footnote 7, Document 173, Despatch from the Embassy in Poland to the Department of State in *FRUS, 1955–1957*, vol. 25, 404–416.

[164] See SNIE 12–2–56. [Footnote in source text.] For the text of Special National Intelligence (SNIE) 12–2–56, "Probable Developments in East Europe and Implications for U.S. Policy," October 30, 1956, see *FRUS, 1955–1957*, vol. 25, 330–335.

[165] For text of NSC 5607, see *Foreign Relations of the United States, 1955–1957,* vol. 24 (Washington, D.C.: Government Printing Office, 1989), 243.

[166] One option not listed in this section but included in the draft document, NSC 5616 (paragraph 7), was to undertake: "A course of action ranging from immediate covert support of the rebels; through open recognition of their belligerent status; to overt military support and recognition of their government if one be formed and succeeds in holding a portion of the country." (See NSC 5616, October 31, 1956, in the National Security Archive's "Flashpoints" collection.)

a. Maintain constant pressure in the UN and elsewhere on the USSR for compliance with the UN Resolution of November 4, 1956.[167]

b. Initiate or support UN action designed to achieve free elections in Hungary under UN auspices, as soon as law and order have been restored.

c. In the event of continued Soviet defiance of UN Resolutions, consider:

(1) Initiating or supporting UN action for an embargo by member nations on all trade with the USSR.

(2) Initiating UN action or action with other nations outside the UN or unilateral action to obtain agreement to sever diplomatic relations with the USSR.

17. Consider whether it is advisable to make in the UN or elsewhere a proposal of Hungarian neutrality on the Austrian model.

18. Seek to keep alive the commitments for reform made to the Hungarian people which will advance U.S. objectives, including the total withdrawal of Soviet forces from Hungary.

19. Immediate relief assistance for the Hungarian people in the form of medical, food and other supplies has been offered through appropriate channels and should continue to be made available to supply their needs for the duration of the emergency.[168]

20. If a government comes to power in Hungary at least as independent as that in Poland:

a. Be prepared to make available at Hungarian request economic and technical assistance in moderate amounts sufficient to give the Hungarians an alternative to complete dependence on Moscow.

b. Increase contacts and exchanges between Hungary and the United States on economic, scientific and cultural bases in the context of NSC 5607.

c. Furnish disaster relief, especially for Budapest.

d. Take appropriate steps to reorient Hungarian trade toward the West, and urge the countries of Western Europe, especially West Germany and the United Kingdom, to offer economic assistance and trade inducements.

21. Encourage the Austrians to maintain their announced policy of granting asylum to Hungarians who may seek it. Aid the Austrians to meet the problem of an increased number of Hungarian refugees by financial and other material assistance from U.S. resources; and encourage the UN and friendly governments to assist. Should a considerable number of Hungarians seek refuge in Austria, urgent consideration will have to be given by the United States and other friendly governments to their immediate care and swift resettlement. Encourage the Yugoslav Government to grant asylum to Hungarians crossing over into Yugoslavia and to cooperate in international measures for their care and resettlement.

General

22. As a matter of high priority, exploit fully throughout the world propaganda opportunities afforded by recent events in Poland and Hungary.

23. The Planning Board should urgently undertake a study of policies and actions which will encourage or bring about withdrawal of Soviet forces from Eastern Germany and Eastern Europe.

---

[167] Reference is to Resolution 1004 (ES–II); see Document 164, Editorial Note in *FRUS, 1955–1957*, vol 25, 338–339.

[168] The U.S. Government was not planning to deal directly with the Hungarian Government on relief matters. The International Committee of the Red Cross (ICRC) had undertaken the responsibility of making relief arrangements and the United States was assessing the suitability of those arrangements. (Telegram 1402 to Bonn, November 21; Department of State, Central Files, 864.49/11–1656) The first Red Cross relief convoys had entered Hungary on November 11 and 14. [Footnote in source text.]

24. As soon as developments in the area can be adequately assessed, review "U.S. Policy Toward the Soviet Satellites in Eastern Europe" (NSC 5608/1),[169] and "U.S. Policy Toward Yugoslavia" (NSC 5601),[170] in the light of such developments.

25. As a matter of urgency, under currently organized governmental mechanisms, undertake a study of the situation in other European satellites to formulate plans and determine U.S. courses of action in the event of future revolutionary actions or uprisings, whether successful or unsuccessful, in those countries which indicate a movement away from control by the USSR.

[....][171]

Annex C

(Prepared by the International Cooperation Administration)

The extent to which U.S. assistance could be made available would vary according to whether or not the recipient country would agree to comply with the Battle Act.[172] (It should be noted that the President may grant exceptions to the applicability of the Battle Act with respect to certain shipments, but *not* in respect of arms, ammunition, implements of war, and atomic energy materials.)

I.

In case of non-agreement to comply with the Battle Act, assistance would be limited to the following:

(A) Mutual Security Assistance:

1. *Under Section 401* (up to $30 million in the case of either country) by Presidential Determination that such assistance is important to U.S. security.

2. *Under Sections 402 and 505,* sales of agricultural surplus or other commodities or services, but only if the local currency proceeds were used for concurrently developed programs for the purchase of commodities for third countries and appropriations for the benefit of such countries were charged.

(B) P.L. 480: surplus agricultural commodities:

1. *Under Title I.* Sales can be made only to "friendly nations," which requires a determination that these countries are no longer "dominated or controlled" by the USSR or a foreign organization controlling the world communist movement, and provided further that the local currency proceeds be used either by the U.S. or for the purchase of commodities for third countries.

2. *Under Title II.* Emergency Relief could be provided only to the *peoples*, not to the Government.

3. *Under Title III.* Commodities could be donated to *voluntary agencies* for use directly in the assistance of needy persons.

---

[169] Document 80, National Security Council Report, NSC 5608/1, 18 July 1956 in *FRUS, 1955–1957*, vol. 25, 216–221.

[170] Published in: *FRUS, 1955–1957*, vol. 26, 707–714.

[171] Annex A, "Statements by the President and the Secretary of State on Poland and Hungary," and Annex B, "United Nations Resolutions on Hungary," are lengthy summaries of publicly available information; they have been omitted here for reasons of space.

[172] The Battle Act, also known as the Mutual Defense Assistance Control Act, called for the termination of all U.S. economic, financial, and military assistance to any country trading embargoed items to the Soviet Union and its satellites.

II.

In case of agreement to comply with the Battle Act the following additional possibilities exist:

(A) Mutual Security Assistance:

1. *Under Section 131. Defense Support—commodities or services.* For assistance in this category the President would be required to find that such assistance will strengthen the security of the United States and promote world peace and the recipient country would be required to subscribe to the several undertakings and agreements specified in Section 142. Defense Support Assistance could be given wholly on a grant basis. However, funds for this purpose would have to be sought. (FY '57 Defense Support funds appropriated for Europe primarily Yugoslavia and Spain amounted to $68,700,000, to which might be added some "carry-over" from prior year funds. The amount for Europe could be augmented, up to 20 percent, by Presidential transfer of funds under Section 501.)

2. *Under Section 409,* ocean freight charges could be provided for shipments by voluntary agencies or the American Red Cross. (Total appropriated for this purpose is $3 million.)

(B) P.L. 480: Surplus agricultural commodities:

1. *Under Title I, sales* could be made for local currency, to be utilized by the countries involved for agreed purposes.

2. *Under Title II,* emergency relief could be provided directly to the Governments rather than limited to their needy people.

[Source: White House Office; Office of the Special Assistant for National Security Affairs: Records, 1953–61; NSC Series; Policy Papers Subseries; Box 19 A truncated version appears in Foreign Relations of the United States, 1955–1957, Vol. 25, Eastern Europe, (Washington, D.C.: United States Government Printing Office, 1990), pp. 463–469.]

DOCUMENT NO. 100: Notes of the Meeting between Dobrivoje Vidić and the Nagy Group, November 19, 1956

Dobrivoje Vidić, the Yugoslav deputy foreign minister, met with Kádár and the Nagy group in Budapest between November 19 and 22 to try to work out a deal to end the impasse at the Yugoslav Embassy. On the one hand, he tried to convince Kádár to provide a written guarantee of safe passage for the group, a proposal Yugoslav Vice President Edvard Kardelj had first made on November 18. On the other hand, as this note reports, the Yugoslav diplomat attempted to get Nagy, Losonczy, Donáth and Haraszti to come to terms with Kádár. He tried both ideological arguments, invoking the cause of socialism, and practical reasoning, pointing to "necessary realities," but was ultimately unable to persuade them. As long as Soviet influence prevailed in Hungary, Nagy saw no opportunity for compromise.

1. I informed them that to solve the question of political asylum we are making efforts which guarantee their personal security; thus they can leave the embassy freely and return to their homes. So far there has been no discussion with Kádár of demanding statements or of the possibility of political asylum in another socialist country. These two questions are the personal affairs of Imre Nagy and his companions. (Imre Nagy and his companions agree with this.) All that they asked was who participated apart from Kádár, but I did not want to tell them.

2. Imre Nagy expressed his view of why they demand his and Losonczy's resignation. In his opinion this question did not arise under any previous change of government; the Presidential Council simply dispensed with the previous government. In their case they are maintaining the possibility in order to condemn them of treachery, if at any given time there might be a need for this, and they will make them responsible for what happened in Pest. (I understood this to mean that he thinks that [the aim of the official explanation is to prove that] while Kádár's government was formed in a normal way, the government of Imre Nagy will not give up its mandate in a normal fashion, what can be seen from the fact that he will not hand in his resignation.) If they resigned, they would compromise themselves. In fact, he does not understand why they do not dispense with them, which under the terms of the Hungarian constitution had happened countless times before.

3. They asked me what our opinion is in Belgrade of the events in Hungary. I spoke about the starting point needing to be the protection of the achievements of socialist development. So not a return to capitalism, which would be achieved with free elections under the conditions of a multi-party system, especially given the current Hungarian circumstances.

They asked me what alternative there was to the Stalinist one-party system and to the multi-party system.

At this point I explained the system of direct democracy at length, our position that this is the real alternative to the one and to the other, and that this will basically be the road to socialist development. (I talked about the SAWPY[173], the Polish parties, and the Chinese case.)[174]

After that I talked about the need to understand the real Hungarian situation today. Time has come for the widespread gathering-together of all socialist forces, this is the only realistic path, only this can satisfy those conditions in Hungary, which by restructuring power and other questions (but on a new basis) might solve the weighty questions facing Hungarian national life, like their relationship with the Soviet Union and that with the USA. Given such a perspective and such results the military-strategic element, which is currently very significant, would take second place, and in such a situation the Russians would more readily accept withdrawal etc.

---

[173] See footnote 154 above.

[174] After communist parties came to power in Poland and China, just as in East Germany, some of the bourgeois parties survived but had to accept the dominant role of the Communist Party and had no real influence in the political life of the country.

Imre Nagy explained at length that Kádár is not his own boss, that the gathering-together of socialist forces is a fundamental question, that he is ready to do anything in the interests of cooperation with Kádár and others, but with the condition that they be freed from Soviet directives and Soviet monopoly. If the Soviet monopoly continues to remain, he could not struggle again for such a cause.

He asks whether after the article in "Pravda" those in Moscow are learning lessons from the events. He is afraid. I replied that it is one thing if everything stays as it was and it is another thing if in addition to the necessary realities they can generate a new situation. I also spoke of how, independent of the article in "Pravda,"[175] we have faith in the Soviet comrades learning the right lessons and sensing that they cannot be and remain outside the new trend.

They spoke a lot about the workers not supporting the Kádár government because of the Russians being invited in. Here I talked to them about the realities of life, about Kádár's program, his opportunities and the true possibility of him reaching understanding with the workers, and that he treats the relationship with the Soviet Union with a perspective in mind, in the same way that he has already started dealing [with] the Budapest workers' council. After this Imre Nagy spoke about how Rákosi had compromised the communists for twelve years, but that there are still a good number of believers in socialist progress in Hungary, of their own free will. He is thinking of himself and his group when he claims that despite their being communists, people still believe in them and are ready to follow them.

For this reason they do not wish to make a statement, do not want to leave the country, however obvious it might be that the Russians and Kádár want to send them away.

I told them that I had no idea what would happen, but it is not out of question that Kádár might change his mind.

[Source: KÜM Irattár (1956). Published in József Kiss, Zoltán Ripp and István Vida, eds. Magyar-jugoszláv kapcsolatok, 1956: Dokumentumok (Budapest: MTA Jelenkor-kutató Bizottság, 1995), pp. 257–258. Translated by David Evans.]

---

[175] A commentary on the Pula speech appeared in Pravda on November 19, 1956. For the speech and additional context, see Document Nos. 96 and 103, respectively.

DOCUMENT NO. 101: Hungarian Minutes of the Negotiations between János Kádár and Dobrivoje Vidić, November 20, 1956

The following record of conversation documents the tense atmosphere surrounding negotiations between the Kádár regime and the Yugoslav government on the fate of the Nagy group. The minutes reflect Yugoslav uneasiness about Nagy's asylum as well as Deputy Foreign Minister Vidić's insistence that the "Nagy group must receive a plausible guarantee so that they can leave freely." While Vidić admits that the "Nagy government is legally non-existent," he argues that members of Nagy's circle "could be involved in the political arena around the Kádár government." On November 21, Kádár signs a letter of safe conduct as requested by the Yugoslavs, but the group is arrested as soon as they leave the compound the following day. Later, in December, Kádár told the party leadership that the Yugoslavs had been informed verbally that the written guarantee would not be honored. He implied that, in effect, the guarantee had been meant only to provide the Yugoslavs with international cover.

BUDAPEST, NOVEMBER 20, 1956

The meeting [took] place in the Prime Minister's Office, attended by: János Kádár, István Sebes,[176] Yugoslav deputy foreign secretary Dobrivoje Vidić, Yugoslav ambassador in Budapest Soldatić, and the Yugoslav commercial counselor as interpreter.

Vidić presents Kádár with the letter of the Yugoslav government concerning Imre Nagy and his companions.

János Kádár reads through the letter.

Vidić: The conditions of November 17 caused further difficulties. The Hungarian suggestions are unacceptable for them. He asks repeatedly the Hungarian government for guarantee. The statement of Nagy and Losonczy is entirely our internal affair and they cannot influence them by any means.

Kádár: The facts of this letter are not entirely true. It seems as if he had agreed with Soldatić's suggestion of November 16, although he said that he welcomed the suggestion and thought that it would be possible to settle the matter after all, emphasizing though that it was his personal opinion and he still had to talk it over with other members of the government and he could only give a definite answer once he had done that. At the next meeting he presented how this solution would change the situation by and large. Later Soldatić mentioned that he passed on the news that Kádár agreed with the suggestions, but in actual fact it happened in a different way. Soldatić did not wait until the following day for the final answer, which resulted in misunderstanding. Furthermore, Kádár emphasizes that the solution would be urgent for us, especially as a question of home policy, something that Kádár has outlined earlier on. Before answering the letter, he would like to confer with the government.

Vidić: He knows the problem and says he is aware of what leading Yugoslav comrades think about the affair. He says he speaks sincerely. They are truly sorry that the affair has become a problem for both governments. They gave refuge and asylum to Nagy and his companions because they thought that it would help Hungary in that given situation. It was the only reason. They did not have any further opinion or intention apart from helping to resolve the situation which was taking shape on November 4. They have no specific reason to sustain Nagy as a substitute government. The Soviet comrades are familiar with the reasons that guided them. They were of the same opinion on November 4: that it would be desirable to provide Nagy and his companions with some kind of asylum in order to strengthen the Kádár regime. He supposes that

[176] István Sebes was deputy foreign minister from April 1956 to 1959.

this is known by comrade Kádár and the government. He assumes that their [the Soviets'] intention was only to clear the way for a new government to be organized, so that there would not be two governments at the same time.

Marosán interjects a remark, saying that de facto there are two governments. Kádár and Vidić disagree with the statement. Vidić explains that legally the situation is obvious.

Kádár: There is a Nagy government, which has collapsed, and there is a legitimate Kádár government. [Foreign] governments who want socialism are of this opinion. There is only one government according to Hungarian law as well. Nevertheless, the fact that Nagy, who has failed to declare that he is not Prime Minister any longer, is in asylum at the embassy of a friendly state has made it possible for some to take an unfair advantage of the situation. Anna Kéthly's appeal to the U.N. is a prime example. The situation makes it possible for foreign forces that are against Hungary to deny that there is only one legitimate government.

Vidić: He does not know Hungarian law in such detail but they all think that the Nagy government is legally non-existent. Yugoslavia accepts, together with all the friendly nations, that the Kádár regime is the only legitimate government in Hungary. As to those who want to take unfair advantage of the situation, he suggests that the Presidential Council pass a resolution in which they dismiss the Nagy government. It is a very simple legal solution as it corresponds to the actual facts. He emphasizes repeatedly that they did not have any ulterior motive in the Nagy affair. When they had negotiations with the Soviet comrades on November 4,[177] they were of the same opinion, i.e. that the Nagy government should be eliminated. The Yugoslav government had previously expressed their wish that the best solution would be if comrade Kádár formed a government. The Soviet comrades are aware of this. The Yugoslav government's opinion about János Kádár and attitude towards the Kádár government is obviously positive.

Kádár: He knows their opinion of November 3. For them the opinion of the fraternal parties and nations was not irrelevant. He and his colleagues' decision to initiate the formation of a new government was propelled by the fact that the leaders of other socialist states had expressed their agreement and consent. The Nagy affair, about which they were not in the know, was all the more embarrassing. He wishes to add that, contrary to all intentions, it was such a political move that caused great discomfort for Hungary internally and internationally alike. He has already discussed this with Soldatić.

Dobi: He wants to quote a specific case. When the multi-party system was announced, it seemed that the Smallholders' Party would be the strongest party. Their leader was Zoltán Tildy, a member of the Cabinet. The last night Tildy spent with Imre Nagy, and he asked Nagy to join him and they escape together. They set off with their luggage, when Nagy suddenly disappeared in a side corridor of the Parliament, leaving Tildy behind. Tildy stayed there crying and complained to Dobi that Nagy had left him in the lurch. It is quite interesting politically, because the Smallholders' Party was one of the strongest parties and now word spreads how Imre Nagy fled to the Yugoslav Embassy.

Vidić: In his speech comrade Tito has also referred to Nagy as a fugitive. He wants to refer back to what comrade Kádár said; how significant the support of the friendly states, Yugoslavia among them, was for [the Hungarians].

Kádár: It influenced his decision.

Vidić: Consequently, the Yugoslav government's opinion about the Kádár government is absolutely clear. Yugoslav leaders could not understand why the Nagy government supported the formation of several parties, which according to the Yugoslav leadership, would mean the end of socialism in the country.

Kádár: They would have restored capitalism by way of secret ballots.

Vidić: He agrees.

Marosán: The Nagy government was swimming with the tide of nationalism and chauvinism.

---

[177] Actually, this meeting took place from the evening of November 2 to the early hours of November 3. See Document No. 76.

446

Vidić: They would have dismissed Nagy very soon and would have eliminated communists afterwards. As neighbors, Yugoslavia understands the nature of chauvinism. It is their expressed interest that Hungary remains a friendly socialist country. The two nations have to solve the Nagy affair as promptly as possible, which they are certainly capable of, in their mutual interest as expressed above. It must be understood, however, that for them there is one problem of great moral significance; they are bound by their given word and the international law concerning political asylum. They understand Kádár's aspect of the issue as well. For instance, that Nagy and Losonczy should declare that they do not consider themselves ministers any longer, or the question of their leave for abroad. As regards this issue, they declare that it does not concern the Yugoslav government, they cannot influence Nagy and his companions. They have done every-thing to convince the Nagy group how wrong their whole concept was, that they were making wrong moves on the basis of fallacious opinions when in power, which was harmful for the development of socialism in Hungary. For instance, their hope to solve within a single day such cardinal questions as Hungary's resignation from the Warsaw Pact and the immediate with-drawal of Soviet troops, and so on. The Yugoslavs are glad that the Nagy group fully compre-hended the irrationality of these fallacies and how harmful their activities had been, and they [the Yugoslavs] are willingly sharing this with Kádár. They think that the questions of an official statement and the refugees' leave for abroad are easier to resolve; it is the business of the Hungarian government and does not concern Yugoslavia. They are concerned with one thing alone: that the refugees leave the embassy without breaching legal and moral requirements. Once again he emphasizes that as a state they cannot convince Nagy to make the above men-tioned statements but they think that it is entirely an internal affair of Hungary. They suggest that the Hungarian government make an effort in this respect. They think that it would be for the ben-efit of the country and of socialism in general if the Nagy group supported the political concept of the Kádár government and they made it apparent in a statement. This is an internal affair of Hungary. All the Yugoslav leaders think that Nagy and his companions are honest communists. It is very likely that, having left the embassy and confronted with the actual situation, in time they will abandon their quixotic attitude and realize that they have to contribute to and take part in the building of socialism.

Every effort has to be made in order to save these people for the cause of socialism. They think that a lot could be achieved with more patience and resolution in the long run. One must believe that, maybe not Nagy himself, but many of his adherents could be involved in the polit-ical arena around the Kádár government. They are striving for a solution which is honest and satisfactory both for the Yugoslav government and for the Kádár regime. The Nagy group must receive a plausible guarantee so that they can leave freely. The Yugoslav government thinks, out of moral and other considerations, that later, once they have returned to normal life, an attempt should be made to rescue these people for the benefit of socialism, in order to unite all demo-cratic forces. Nevertheless, they must emphasize again that they do not intend to intervene, as it is entirely an internal affair of Hungary. They are giving their friendly opinions because this is what serves the interest of socialism in this part of the world, where we live together and there-fore must help one another. Yugoslavia tries to help with all good intentions. They wish that we rescue Hungary for the cause of socialism.

Kádár: The issues that came up during the negotiation and concern state affairs he will dis-cuss with the government. As to the rest, he has one remark to be made. Not so long ago the Nagy group gained leading positions in the party and the government, representing communists. He gave his consent to this, as he voted for them. Nevertheless, the experiences were negative. This should not be forgotten when talking about political perspectives. He thinks that some of the Nagy group could cause more harm to us with their support than if they fight us. A lot has been said about morals—in relation to state affairs. He would like to say a few words about com-munist morals. Asking the Soviet troops for help was a very tough decision in both cases. We are convinced that it was not pleasant for the Soviet Union either. Still, it was our decision and we had thought it over thoroughly. He was present at every party and government meeting where they decided about the issue, but Imre Nagy was there as well and he voted in the same way. Yet it was the same person, Imre Nagy, who gave order to the Hungarian forces to shoot at Soviet troops.[178] What could our opinion be about Nagy after this? What perspectives can we talk about after all? He agrees that they have to be brought back to the communist platform but it is not an easy task because there are too many negative experiences.

Vidić: He would like to refer back to one specific issue, namely that the letter does not say exactly what comrade Kádár had said. Namely that comrade Kádár gave his consent to the suggested solution on November 16. I must add that Soldatić informed the Yugoslav government that it was merely Kádár's personal opinion and that they still have to wait for the official answer of the Hungarian government. The Yugoslav government, however, interpreted Kádár's words as proof that the affair had been settled.

Marosán: Tito's opinion about the Nagy government that he expressed in his speech in Pula and the Nagy group's being in asylum at the embassy created a peculiar situation and gave rise to contradictory opinions in Budapest.

Vidić: They want to solve the problem. It is the Hungarians' task to evaluate the situation and find the best possible solution. There is no turn-coat policy on the part of comrade Tito. It is merely a question of practicality that the Nagy group should leave the embassy.

Kádár: But how?

Vidić: We are both concerned in this issue.

[Source: MOL, XIX–J–1–j. 66. d. 4/j. 1956. First published in Tibor Zinner, "'...hogy megkönnyítsék a Nagy kormány likvidálását...': Három dokumentum Nagy Imre és köre 1956 november 4. utáni történetéhez," Társadalmi Szemle 44, No. 12 (1989): pp. 81–83. Translated by Csaba Farkas.]

---

[178] During his interrogation in 1957, Nagy stated that when the Soviet offensive began at dawn on November 4, he gave the order "not to offer any kind of resistance..., the Soviet troops must not be fired at." Quoted by Rainer, *Nagy Imre*, vol. 2, 330.

DOCUMENT NO. 102: Situation Report from Georgii Malenkov, Mikhail Suslov, and Averki Aristov, November 22, 1956

This report from the Malenkov group summarizes the political, military and economic situation in Hungary. The most topical issue at the time was the Hungarian-Yugoslav agreement on the Imre Nagy group, according to which they were supposed to leave the Yugoslav Embassy during the evening of November 22. A written guarantee from the Kádár government notwithstanding, the report refers to a plan to kidnap the group as soon as they leave the mission: "The necessary measures in this connection have been prepared together with comrades Serov and Münnich."[179]

On the state of play in Hungary, despite the Soviets' unquestionable military victory, Malenkov and his colleagues are forced to report that the consolidation process is moving slowly. They emphasize the "reactionary" role of the workers' councils as a major obstacle to the strengthening of the Kádár government. The Hungarian leader is seen fundamentally in a positive light: "Comrade Kádár gives the impression of a politically prepared and educated official." Yet, they voice some reservations as well, including the view that "[b]y his personality" he appears to be "somewhat soft."

Of particular interest in the document is the opinion of Kádár and his followers, on the "national question," which they suggest ought to be the main topic of discussion at the upcoming meeting of the socialist countries' communist parties.[180] "[T]he national question, in light of the Hungarian developments, is primarily a question of sovereignty and independence," Kádár declares, emphasizing the importance of elaborating Hungary's special approach to building socialism in order to strengthen communist rule in the country. The Soviet representatives in Budapest claimed that the CPSU CC supported the idea, but in fact the notion of a Yugoslav-style "Eastern neutrality," raised by György Aczél, was already unacceptable for Moscow.

NOVEMBER 22, 1956

CPSU CC

We are sending you the information about the situation in Hungary.

I.

In the course of the last several days we had to devote a lot of time to issues regarding the Imre Nagy group.

Late last night the negotiations between comrade Kádár and Vidić were concluded. As comrade Kádár informed us, as a result of the negotiations they reached agreement on removing the right of asylum for Imre Nagy and his group by the Yugoslavs.

In the letter to the Yugoslav government, the Hungarian government stated their position with regard to this affair. At the same time, [the latter] announced that in connection with the request of the Yugoslav government, it would guarantee the safety of the persons involved, and that it would not call them to justice for their past actions.

Today Vidić informed comrade Kádár that the Yugoslav government agreed with the results of the negotiations.

In the evening of November 22, Nagy and his group are supposed to leave the Yugoslav Embassy. The necessary measures in this connection have been prepared together with comrades Serov and Münnich.

[179] On the kidnap plan, see the headnote for Document No. 98.
[180] Concerning this meeting, see Document Nos. 106, 107, and 108.

II.

According to the information of the officials from the military commandant's office of the Committee on State Security, our Hungarian friends, and our own observations, the general situation in the country is gradually normalizing, although very slowly.

Since November 12, our troops have not been engaged in any military operations; only isolated units follow small bands of rebels into the countryside in order to eliminate them. During all this time, there have been no armed clashes in Budapest at all, not even small ones.

Most of the participants in the riot have either given up or abandoned their weapons. By November 20, according to comrades Konev and Serov's information, the following quantity of weapons was confiscated from the rebels and the population, or was abandoned: small arms—181,766; machine guns—3,172; various mortars—40 barrels, and 64,000 grenades. We repeatedly heard positive statements about the behavior of soldiers and commanders of the Soviet Army from our Hungarian friends both during the military operations and now.

The positions of the Revolutionary Workers' and Peasants' government are improving. However, this process is proceeding slowly and unevenly. In some locations and mainly in Budapest, the openly hostile attitudes toward the Kádár government are still quite strong. The counterrevolutionary elements are engaged in active work in order to compromise the revolutionary government in the eyes of the people by stating that it betrayed the national interests when it appealed to the Soviet government for military assistance.

The "Workers' Councils" created under the Nagy government still play a big role in the political life of the country. In many "Workers' Councils," which have substantial influence on the workers, the leading role belongs to the reactionary elements who are using the councils in their fight against the government.

Having lost the opportunity to fight by means of armed uprising, the reactionary forces use new methods to pursue their counterrevolutionary goals—primarily, strikes and sabotage.

Last week, the reaction attempted to involve a large segment of workers and service personnel in a general strike in the main branches of industry and on the railroad.

Exploiting the situation, where the party organizations at the enterprises were destroyed during the days of reaction and were being rebuilt very slowly, the reactionary elements began to infiltrate the plants and the mines. They try to undermine the work in various ways by inspiring the workers to go on strike until the government satisfies their demands for the withdrawal of Soviet troops, for bringing Imre Nagy back into the government, and for allowing a multiparty system. These demands were presented everywhere, and we tend to believe that they were disseminated from one center. Journalists, writers, and a segment of students play the most active role in the dissemination of the above-mentioned demands.

As a result of the political action and the repressive measures toward several of the organizers of the strikes beginning on Monday, November 19, the number of strikes has definitely declined. More and more industrial enterprises resumed operations. Almost all big industrial enterprises, a number of mines and railroads resumed work. It has to be noted though, that in a number of enterprises it is still the minority of workers who have returned to the job. In almost all big cities and industrial centers the public services, food industries, and retail network function normally. In Budapest, they began the work of cleaning the streets, and repairing buildings and transportation routes.

However, we have to note that as far as eliminating the strike movement at the enterprises, the situation is not yet stable. Yesterday, according to comrade Kádár, the Budapest Workers' Council decided to announce a two-day strike in all enterprises except the food enterprises. This time the main demands were the following: freedom for those arrested in connection with the riots and recognition of the Workers Council by the government. Today, workers in many Budapest enterprises stopped work again, and we are receiving information that the number of those participating in the strike is growing.

The Hungarian government is undertaking measures of a policing as well as political character. Our Hungarian comrades plan to influence the Budapest Workers' Council, relying on those of its members who are not negatively inclined toward the government and who expressed their desire to help get rid of those subversive elements in the Council. The Hungarian organs, with the help of our state security officials, will implement the police measures.

At the same time, today the Csepel Workers' Council of the biggest industrial complex in Budapest made the following decision: (1) To condemn the decision of the city of Budapest Workers' Council regarding the general strike. (2) To go back to work (3) To appeal to all workers of the country to go back to work (4) To create a new Workers Council of Budapest, because the current members of the Council do not represent the opinions of the workers.

The acute shortages of fuel and electric power present a serious danger to further stabilization of industry and transportation, and also to further normalization of national life. The country's coalmines, which under normal working conditions produced up to 80,000 tons of coal a day, produce only 2,000 to 3,000 tons at the present time. The majority of the mines work only at 10 to 15 percent of their capacity. There are practically no reserves of coal in industry and at the railroads. While the demand is 900 megawatts of electric power a day, only 300 megawatts is produced. Currently, the Hungarian comrades implement measures for organizing work at the coalmines and for increasing the extraction of coal.

Both in Budapest and on the periphery, the trade in food products is going well. There are sufficient reserves of flour, sugar, oils and meat. Out of 3,500 food stores in Budapest 3,100 are opened. The population of Budapest is worried about the possibility of inflation. Out of 1.2 billion forints in deposits, 400 million forints were withdrawn within several days. There are long lines at the consumer goods stores every day. Our Hungarian comrades proposed to resolve the situation by rapid cuts in investments, limitations on expenses for the army, and perhaps by credits from other countries.

In order to find and eliminate underground rebel centers, our security officials, together with the Hungarian police, worked on arresting and detaining persons who participated most actively in the armed riots. Altogether, 1,473 people were arrested in addition to 5,820 persons who were detained and remain under investigation. Leaders and organizers of the riots, persons who supplied the rebels with weapons and ammunition, and also members of the so-called revolutionary committees active during the riots are subject to arrest.

The following prominent organizers of the riots have been arrested: police Colonel Kopácsi, who is one of the most closely trusted of Imre Nagy's people, Dudás—one of the leaders of the rebellion, Szabó—the leader of the rebels in Széna Square, and others. So far, we have not been able to arrest the military leader of the rebellion General Király, and an important ideological leader of the rebels, the journalist Gimes. Our comrades, together with Hungarian comrades, are engaged in the search for those people.

Currently comrade Münnich is implementing measures for strengthening the organs of the political police. Comrade Serov and his officials are actively helping comrade Münnich.

III.

The Hungarian Workers' Party used to have more than 800,000 members. During the rage of the fascist terror, the party organs were either destroyed by the counterrevolution or fell apart. The majority of HWP members left active political life during the last days of the Nagy government as a result of the actions of the counterrevolution. A segment of party members turned to the rebel side and some of them fought with weapons in their hands.

As we know, even under the Nagy government, the Politburo of the Central Committee of HWP decided to transform the HWP into the Hungarian Socialist Workers' Party. On November 6 of this year, the provisional committee [sic] of the Hungarian Socialist Workers' Party published an appeal to all party members. It said: "Each member of the party who is relying on the masses, and is ready to fight for the power of working people, for the policy of our party, should immediately appear at his party organization and begin work!"

However, during the 15 days since that appeal was published, the process of party reunification is moving slowly and in a disorganized fashion. The Provisional Central Committee of the Socialist Workers' Party consists of 21 members, 15 of which are former members of the Central Committee of the HWP. The City Committee of the party works in Budapest and provisional party committees exist in almost all regions of the city. A portion of them were elected at conferences of the party *aktiv* and the Central Committee nominated anther part. District Committees of Budapest consist of five-to-eleven people each. In the majority of cases, secretaries of the district committees are new people because the former secretaries of the district committees were removed from their positions. So far, the district committees possess quite an insignificant *aktiv* (20–30 people) and have almost no political base in the enterprises and in the organizations.

In the last three or four days the district committees began re-registering party members more actively. According to our information, the largest number of those who were re-registered live in Csepel. More than 500 people have re-registered here (out of 12,000 HWP members counted before October 23); in the rest of the districts the number of those re-registered is still in the tens.

Local party organizations are beginning to emerge on the enterprises.

Several days ago, the Central Committee held a conference of the party *aktiv* of the city of Budapest. Approximately 200 people attended the conference. The speakers fully approved the program of the Kádár government and the measures implemented by it. Only one person spoke against it. Conferences of the party *aktiv* were held in the majority of Budapest districts.

County party committees were created in all the counties. However, we know very little about their constitution and size. The Provisional Central Committee of the Hungarian Socialist Workers' Party has sent their representatives to the county committees.

IV.

In the course of these days we met with comrade Kádár repeatedly, which allowed us to get to know him better. He leaves a good impression. As far as we can judge by his actions and his behavior in recent days, he began to realize much better the necessity of implementing a firmer line in the fight against the reaction. Now he is showing a much higher level of decisiveness in regard to arresting counterrevolutionaries, even though up until recently he was somewhat unsure in this regard under the pressure of those from his close circle who are not convinced. He is very firm in his position on the measures toward Imre Nagy and his group, and he upheld the party line very well during negotiations with Vidić and Soldatić.

Comrade Kádár gives the impression of a politically prepared and educated official. By his personality, he is somewhat soft; therefore in a number of cases we saw that some doubting persons from his close circle influence him. However, we have to say that on the issues of principle, which we had to decide with him, and on other issues, about which we know he was under another sort of influence, comrade Kádár was able to orient himself very quickly in the situation. He arrived at correct decisions, which he later practically always implemented in the Executive Committee, and in the government.

Comrade Kádár enjoys full support in the Executive Committee, and all the most important measures are implemented by consensus. Comrades Münnich, Marosán, Apró, Kis Károly and others behave very well.

At the same time, we have to say that two members of the Executive Committee—Lajos Fehér, editor of "Népszabadság" newspaper, and Béla Biszku, secretary of the Budapest city committee—are negatively disposed. One of them (Fehér) most clearly expresses feelings of dissatisfaction with the policy of the CPSU, and apparently completely shares the Yugoslav position, including what was stated in Tito's last speech at Pula. He does not agree with the "Pravda" criticism of that speech. Using his position as editor, Lajos Fehér is trying to get his views and feelings out through the press, and he manages to accomplish that when comrade Kádár does not have time to look after him or to show decisiveness when it is necessary.

We are aware of the fact that Lajos Fehér prepared a sharp polemical article against "Pravda" in connection with the known criticism of Tito's speech in "Pravda." It was only because of comrade Kádár's pressure that the article was not published. He, Fehér, allowed the article with a biased representation of the results of the Soviet-Polish negotiations to be published in the newspaper. We will have a substantive conversation with comrade Kádár and members of the Executive Committee about Lajos Fehér, having in mind that we can not tolerate his lack of discipline as editor.[181]

The pro-Yugoslav mood and the negative feelings toward the CPSU are quite strong among members of the Provisional Central Committee of the Hungarian Socialist Workers' Party.

V.

We had conversations regarding the conference of representatives of Communist and Workers' parties of socialist countries with comrade Kádár, and then with all members of the Executive Committee of the Socialist Workers' Party. Later we will prepare a special memorandum for the Central Committee, in which we will develop our suggestions on this issue. However, below we are reporting the most important information that we learned regarding the mood of the Hungarian comrades on the issue of the conference, how they see the idea and the substance of the conference.

The Hungarian comrades reiterated that it would be necessary to hold a conference of representatives of Communist and Workers' parties of the European countries of people's democracy, the Soviet Union, China and Yugoslavia in the nearest future, within the next three weeks. They do not have any proposals developed in final form, so they have outlined the goals and the tasks of the conference only in general form.

Comrade Kádár and other members of the Executive Committee believe that the main question that we should discuss at the conference is the national issue. In their opinion, this question took on special political importance in light of the Hungarian developments not only for the Hungarian Socialist Workers' Party, but also for other fraternal communist and workers' parties. Because of this, it is important to develop this question in principle and in practice. Our party, said comrade Kádár, should publish some kind of a program statement with the goal of winning the masses over to our side. The national issue, in the general sense of the word, should occupy the main place in such a program.

We asked our Hungarian comrades to tell us more concretely what they had in mind when they spoke about the national issue.

The Hungarian comrades responded that they were not going to raise territorial questions, of course. In our view, said comrade Kádár, the national question, in light of the Hungarian developments, is primarily a question of sovereignty and independence. In our speeches before the Hungarian people, we emphasized the issues of independence and sovereignty of Hungary, but we stated the question in a very general form, which is difficult to comprehend. The people are not sufficiently clear about it, and do not understand this very well. The masses want to know, what is it exactly that we are promising, and how is the question about relations between Hungary and the USSR, and also with other socialist countries, going to be decided in the future.

The problem is, said our Hungarian comrades, we spoke about the principles of sovereignty, independence and non-interference in each others' affairs, as principles, on which we were

[181] Lajos Fehér was relieved of his post as editor-in-chief of *Népszabadság* at the November 24 meeting of the HSWP Provisional Executive Committee. One of the main reasons for this decision was a strike by the newspaper's staff against the spiking of the article mentioned above. See, *A Magyar Szocialista Munkáspárt ideiglenes vezető testületeinek jegyzőkönyve*i, vol. 1, 119–122.

building relations between the USSR and the countries of people's democracy many times before. However, we did not always abide by those principles in practice. We made many mistakes. We should analyze those mistakes and learn the relevant lessons. We should tell the people, precisely, how these principles will be implemented in the future. We should bring clarity to the relations between the parties, and then to state relations, and we should present a clear perspective on these issues.

After fraternal parties discuss these questions, we could, said comrade Kádár, develop and make more concrete the Declaration of the Soviet government from October 30, 1956.[182] That would give the Hungarians and us an opportunity to present the program of the party and the government on the issue of the sovereignty and independence of Hungary in a positive way.

The Hungarian comrades believe that it is necessary to develop a program of building socialism that would be applicable to Hungarian conditions as soon as possible. Comrade Kádár said that at some point in the past it was stated that the people's democracy was a new form of dictatorship of the proletariat, but in practice they tried to build everything in Hungary after the Soviet model.[183] The main issue is to develop forms of building socialism that do not exist in the USSR but that fit Hungary's special conditions. Such specific forms that would be new for Hungary in comparison with the Soviet Union would help us attract all progressive forces of the country to our side.

We should mention that during the session of the Central Committee of the Hungarian Socialist Workers' Party, which took place on November 11 of this year,[184] some members of the Committee raised the issue of the sovereignty and independence of Hungary somewhat differently from the way it was presented by comrade Kádár and by other members of the Executive Committee in their conversations with us.

Thus, for example, György Aczél stated in his speech: "Unquestionably, it is necessary, as [comrade] Köböl has already mentioned, to work out in detail how we conceive of our national independence. Even if we had planned it systematically, we could not have ruined our reputation more effectively than we did. We should now establish a scheme of independence that the Soviet Union can accept as well; a neutrality [which is] not western neutrality on the model of Austria, but rather eastern neutrality on the model of Yugoslavia or any other example." Member of the Central Committee Miklós Somogyi[185] supported this statement of Aczél. László Földes[186] made a similar statement also.

From our conversation with the Executive Committee members, and from their speeches at the Central Committee session of November 11 of this year, we can draw the conclusion that some Hungarian comrades are inclined to subject to criticism the CPSU policy towards the countries of people's democracy, and also the internal policy of some of the communist and workers' parties of the European countries of people's democracy. The assessment of the policy of the CPSU toward the countries of people's democracy expressed by some Hungarian comrades, especially during the session of the Central Committee on November 11 of this year, repeated what Tito had said about it in his speech in Pula on many issues.

In our conversation with the Executive Committee members, we confirmed that the Central Committee of the CPSU was positively inclined toward holding the conference that they pro-

---

[182] See Document No. 50.

[183] The declaration that the "people's democratic system" was actually a form of "proletarian dictatorship" was first announced by Rákosi in an article in *Szabad Nép* on January 16, 1949. This signaled the end of the "popular front policy" followed from 1945 and the beginning of the final stage of the country's Sovietization.

[184] See Document No. 95.

[185] Miklós Somogyi was chairman of the National League of Hungarian Free Trade Unions and a member of the HSWP PCC from November 1956.

[186] László Földes was a candidate member of the HWP CC from July to October 28, 1956, and a member of the Military Committee between October 24–28. After the revolution he became a member of the HSWP PCC and was head of the Cadre Department from February to December 1957.

posed. We told them that we would report the opinions of the Hungarian comrades to the CPSU CC, and that we would additionally contact them later regarding the practical issue of convening the conference after we consult with the relevant fraternal parties.

During the same Executive Committee meeting, we spoke substantively with the Hungarian comrades about the pressing issues of political life in Hungary, and also about our assessment of the international situation.

During the conversation, on our part we paid special attention to the need for following a firm line on the necessity of a crushing defeat of the reactionary forces, the speediest rebuilding and strengthening of the party and party organizations, on correcting the mistakes that were made with regard to party personnel when party officials were defamed without discretion because of their work under Rákosi.

According to our impression, the Hungarian comrades agreed with us in their statements, with the exception of Fehér and Béla Biszku, who took an incorrect line toward the cadres who worked under Rákosi.

VI.

Romanian comrades Dej, Chivu Stoica, and Bodnăraş have just arrived. So far, we have only had a brief meeting with them since they were in a hurry to get to comrade Kádár's reception.[187]

MALENKOV
SUSLOV
ARISTOV

Note:
Received by the VCh (secure communications)
On November 22, 1956

[Source: APRF, F. 3. Op. 64. D. 488. Ll. 68–80. Published in Russian in Sovietskii Soyuz i vengerskii krizis, 1956 goda: Dokumenty, edited and compiled by E. D. Orekhova, Vyacheslav T. Sereda and Aleksandr. S. Stykhalin (Moscow: ROSSPEN, 1998), pp. 668–676. Translated by Svetlana Savranskaya.]

---

[187] The top-level Romanian delegation arrived in Budapest to discuss plans for transporting the Nagy group to Romania.

DOCUMENT NO. 103: Josip Tito's letter to Nikita Khrushchev on the Tensions between Belgrade and Moscow Caused by the Hungarian Revolution, December 3, 1956 (Excepts)

This letter from Tito to Khrushchev is part of the formerly secret record of the Yugoslav–Soviet divide, which had been sharpening once again since Tito's speech in Pula (see Document No. 96). The two countries carried on their quarrel largely in the pages of their respective party dailies, Pravda and Borba, but also in private communications between the two leaders. The Soviets translated this version of the letter into Russian and on December 10 sent it to their embassies in a dozen countries with instructions to inform the local party leaders orally of its contents.[188] In the letter, Tito refutes the various charges the USSR and other socialist countries had launched against Belgrade. He takes particular offense at the fact that certain parties are trying to shift responsibility for the Hungarian crisis on to Yugoslavia. He writes that he believes it was a mistake to deport Imre Nagy's group and their families to Romania and suggests that Nagy should be allowed to return home unharmed. He also tries to shed more light on aspects of his speech in Pula that had irritated the Soviets. The document is particularly helpful in casting light on the deepening Yugoslav–Soviet conflict, which was of primary importance to Hungarian–Yugoslav relations.

Strictly Confidential

CENTRAL COMMITTEE OF THE YUGOSLAV LEAGUE OF COMMUNISTS
BELGRADE, DECEMBER 3, 1956

CENTRAL COMMITTEE OF THE COMMUNIST PARTY OF THE SOVIET UNION
TO COMRADE N. S. KHRUSHCHEV

Dear Comrades,

It is true enough that the relationship between our two parties and governments has recently been somewhat aggravated, that this is contrary to our mutual aim as expressed in Moscow and Belgrade declarations[189] —namely to work with all our ability toward the strengthening and deepening of friendly relations between the Soviet Union and Yugoslavia. [...]

We do not intend to set out here in chronological order and in detail everything that has led us to the present situation. We would only like to touch on a few things that were in our opinion very significant moments that led to both a misunderstanding and to strains in our relations. [...]

You reacted abruptly and, in our opinion, erroneously to that part of Comrade Tito's speech at the party assembly in Pula, in which he assessed the current international situation and the events in Hungary. We are particularly offended that several excerpts of Tito's speech in Pula were later misinterpreted and even distorted. We are truly sorry that your press did not publish the complete text of Comrade Tito's speech because when it comes to an open debate, both sides have to approach the issue in the same way, so that party members and the people clearly see what the debate is about. This is what we indeed did, and we published word-for-word both *Pravda* articles which reacted to the Pula speech, notwithstanding the fact that several things were published a distorted way. This proves that we are not on equal terms in the discussion, and the concealment of our views from the Soviet public not only may cause damage to Yugoslavia, but could also harm our relations in general since one can understand that your people, insufficiently informed in this way, would form a very bad image of our relations.

---

[188] The countries were (in the order given) Poland, East Germany, Hungary, Czechoslovakia, Romania, Bulgaria, China, North Vietnam, North Korea, Mongolia, France and Italy.

[189] See footnote 137 above.

456

On the other hand, this form of discussion will not serve the [cause of] deepening trust and a sense of justice[190] among socialist countries in the eyes of Yugoslav public opinion and the world. For example, *Pravda* explains that whenever referring to the "regime," Tito meant the whole social order of the Soviet Union, i.e. when condemning the system—by which we mean different Stalinist methods—he condemned the entire social system of the Soviet Union, including the achievements of the Great October revolution. For us and for every communist this is an important matter and we must decisively renounce such an interpretation. For us, the word "system" in this particular case refers to the well-known negative methods that appeared in the guise of the system during the Stalinist era, and that we believe carries consequences to this day. When Tito spoke about the system, he meant the negative aspect that accumulated in the Stalinist period and found (established) deep roots not only in all the countries of the socialist camp but in the interpretation of leading communists of different communist parties [...]

We wish to emphasize here our deep conviction that the leaders and press of several communist parties, such as the French Communist Party, the Czechoslovak Communist Party, the Albanian Communist Party and the Bulgarian Communist Party, played and today continue to play a very negative role in this whole affair. More than that, they went even further beyond the bounds of your interpretation of the Pula speech. They went as far as to direct their entire campaign against us, accusing us incorrectly and even slanderously.

Moreover, some of the decisions of the Twentieth Congress of your party are also being subjected to indirect and even direct accusations, despite the fact that they make no mention of this. It is hard for us to believe that they are doing this on their own initiative, but it is just as hard to believe that you consider this to have a positive effect for socialist development world-wide. [....]

When the tragic Hungarian events happened, the above-mentioned parties expressed their dissatisfaction and started to accuse Yugoslavia in connection with this turn of events, inferring that leaders of the Yugoslav League of Communists had a finger in the pie. It is self-evident that we did not and could not tolerate these serious allegations and we had to firmly refute such insinuations.

We were much grieved by your shrill letter that we received in answer to our notice [informing you] that we granted asylum to Imre Nagy and that we believed that your consent would be most useful. The missive in question indicated for us that you think it is necessary to gear the Hungarian events in a different direction than we outlined when Comrades Malenkov and Khrushchev paid us a visit.

Further proof is the breach of the agreement between the Kádár government and the Yugoslav government concerning Imre Nagy.

It is indeed difficult for us that you utterly disregard the standpoint and obligations of our government on this issue—both in respect to our constitution and to international law. We think it would be most fortunate if you helped us to resolve the Imre Nagy situation. What is at stake here is not only that our government should get out of an awkward situation but that we must also find a solution that expedites the improvement of the dire Hungarian situation—a solution which suits Kádár and the Soviet Union alike. Strikes, the passive resistance of Hungarian workers and the enormous distrust of the Soviet Union and socialism in Hungary necessitates that we set aside petty problems and find a brave and constructive solution. You might raise the question of whether we insist on Nagy coming to Yugoslavia. We would rather put a different slant on this issue. First of all, one should have asked Nagy himself to which socialist country he wants to depart, instead of sending the whole group to Romania against their will. The Romanian comrades who were in Belgrade said that Nagy would have posed a danger at that time if he had stayed in Hungary. If this was so, what then was the point in rounding up and forcefully transferring to Romania children, women and communists who are well known in the country and could be useful for Hungary in the future? We think that was a mistake. Moreover, in our opin-

---

[190] The Russian translator of this document used the word "spravedlivost'" here, then followed with the paranthetical phrase: "(literally: love of truth [*pravdolyubie*])."

ion, Nagy could have been left in Budapest, at his home, without risk that he would intervene and disturb the work of the government. We think it is still possible to find a kind of solution to this issue. We do believe that it would be most beneficial if Nagy were allowed to return to, and continue to live in, Hungary. His declaration in itself—that he would return to Hungary with the government's accord and refrain from obstructing the government's attempt at the renewal of the country—would induce a very positive response from the Hungarian people, at the same time neutralizing all the arguments that are commonly adduced against the deportation of Imre Nagy world-wide.

All in all, the issue would be off the agenda at last, paving the way for the normalization of life in Hungary.

A further, more important motivation behind Tito's speech in Pula was the development of the Hungarian tragedy and its international reception, especially in our country. People were outraged even by the first intervention of Soviet troops, both within the League of Communists and among the great masses of the people. Upon news of the second Soviet intervention the tension mounted further, as people had no idea what was going on—they only saw that the internal affairs of Hungary were being intruded upon by military force. It is self-evident that certain elements in our country—enemies of the present social order in Yugoslavia—used this occasion to provoke disobedience against the authorities and the party leadership. We must say that this was the very reason why Tito raised the issue so sharply, and wanted to bring it to the people as soon as possible, despite the apparent likelihood that you would not interpret it the same way as we meant it; that is, we cannot deny and gloss over the facts, and we are not afraid of telling the people the truth, as this is the only way we can avoid in the future [the occurrence of] situations that have had such serious consequences in Hungary. Tito referred to these issues in his speech at Pula in a manner which he thought was the most appropriate and convincing. He considered the first intervention by the Soviet army a mishap, and referred to the second intervention as a lesser evil that only the positive nature of forthcoming events could justify. Members of the League of Communists and the people accepted this explanation unanimously. We presume that it is most expedient for the Soviet Union as well. With this, in a certain sense, we not only blunted the edge of the propaganda of international reaction, but also mitigated the outrage of well-intentioned people who saw only a negative phenomenon in this [intervention], which reminded them of the Stalinist era.

We are truly sorry that you emphasized only those passages in Tito's speech that international propaganda could exploit for capitalist purposes, instead of considering the text in its entirety, which facilitates the solution of the entire issue and a better understanding of what is happening in Hungary.

We believe that the Hungarian events dealt a terrible blow to the socialist world, and that we should not engage in a pointless and futile debate about this, but rather should boldly disentangle the cause of these events and make a joint effort to do away with them in the shortest possible time. [...]

Finally, let me inform you about a fact which you might already know, namely that Tito sent a letter to Mr. Nehru in which he explained the Hungarian situation. He did this in a way that he thought would be the most useful in allowing Nehru to take an objective position on the issue. As you know, he modified his opinion about Hungary soon afterwards. Unfortunately, though, his last letter to Tito expresses much concern and dissatisfaction with the turn of events in Hungary. The deportations from Hungary, especially the deportation of Imre Nagy and his group greatly embittered him. In his letter, Nehru asked Tito to intercede with you to prevent the deportation.

All of us here—not only leading politicians but the masses of people as well—believe that what is happening is incorrect and does not promote general esteem towards, and confidence in, the Soviet Union. On the contrary. In our opinion, such actions should have been avoided and we do not think that there was no place in Hungary for those people who could possibly pose a danger in such a situation. We believe that a more humane solution should be sought. Although we also say that there is a socialist and a capitalist world, we still must take account of international public opinion since there are progressive people in the capitalist world as well, there is a working class and there are progressive elements there, with regard to whom we must say that they are now much concerned about these matters.

Please do ponder these matters, casting aside your fear of losing face. Simply reconsider in a true communist manner what is useful and what is harmful, and get rid of all that is harmful.

We would like you to understand our sincere wish: that with [the aid of] our perspective we want to help untangle the latest events. We are not boasting that we hold the ultimate truth in every aspect. We are aware that our opinion is open to debate.

Yours fraternally,

IN THE NAME OF THE CENTRAL COMMITTEE OF YUGOSLAV COMMUNISTS
SECRETARY-GENERAL
J. B. TITO

[Source: TsKhSD, F. 89, Op.2, D. 4, Ll. 24–33. Published in Sereda, Vyacheslav T. and Aleksandr S. Stykhalin, eds., Hiányzó lapok 1956 történetéből: dokumentumok a volt SZKP KB levéltárából, *(Budapest: Móra Ferenc Könyvkiadó, 1993), pp. 252–256; and (in slightly different form) in Kiss, József, Zoltán Ripp and István Vida, eds.,* Magyar-jugoszláv kapcsolatok, 1956. december–1959 február: A magyar-jugoszláv kapcsolatok és a Nagy Imre csoport sorsa, Dokumentumok, *(Budapest: MTA Jelenkor-kutató Bizottság, 1995 [1997]), pp. 45–47. Translated by Csaba Farkas.]*

DOCUMENT NO. 104: Resolution of the Provisional Central Committee of the Hungarian Socialist Workers' Party, December 5, 1956. (Excerpts)

This resolution, passed by the HSWP Provisional CC after its December 2–5 meeting, was an extremely important document in the development of what later became the Kádár era. Besides offering an analysis of the reasons, precedents for, and course of the October–November events, it also evaluates the current political situation, and in the course of discussing the theoretical and political basis of the party's activities, outlines both a short- and long-term action program.

The excerpt published here lists the four main reasons for the "counterrevolution" from the point of view of the party leadership; these became the cornerstone of the official Kádár-era interpretation of the uprising, which survived for the next three decades. The first factor was the commission of grave mistakes, even crimes, by the Rákosi-Gerő clique. (The new leaders were hoping to gain some degree of popular support by distinguishing themselves from their predecessors.) The second factor—the policies of Nagy, who is still referred to as a "communist prime minister"—is said to be only a partial cause of the events, and Nagy himself is blamed more for being passive in the face of "counterrevolution" than for actively supporting it. Two more "logically" based factors supplement the two more basic causes: the role of the "Horthyite-fascist and Hungarian capitalist-landowner counterrevolution" and the role of "international imperialism." The main lesson the document offers is to emphasize the "disguised" appearance of the "counterrevolution," especially in the period before October 30, a formulation Kádár probably used to explain away his earlier cooperation with Nagy.

The December 5 Provisional CC resolution marks a clear dividing line in the history of the post-revolutionary consolidation process. After the hesitation, confusion and uncertainty that characterized the first few weeks following the uprising, the unambiguous formulation of the party's political platform indicated a rising level of confidence on the part of the HSWP leadership. Between the two opposing views within the party, the resolution signaled a victory for the group that favored restoring order by any means possible from the very start. From here on, the leadership gave up the tactical approach of gaining time with the workers' councils and national committees, and began to carry out a policy of brutal liquidation of the organized national resistance.

RESOLUTION OF THE PROVISIONAL CENTRAL COMMITTEE OF THE HUNGARIAN SOCIALIST WORKERS' PARTY

The Provisional Central Committee of the Hungarian Socialist Workers' Party met in continuous session on December 2, 3, and 5, 1956.[191] The agenda was the current political situation and the discussion of the upcoming tasks of the party. Comrade János Kádár proposed the agenda. In the course of intensive negotiations, 21 out of 23 comrades expressed their views. On the basis of these, the Provisional Central Committee made the following resolution:

I. The reasons and precedents for the events that started on October 23, 1956

In order to reveal precisely every aspect concerning the reasons and precedents for what happened on October 23, 1956, a systematic analysis of further data is needed. However, it is already entirely clear what kindled and motivated the events and what were its main characteristics.

Four main reasons and motivating factors influenced the course of events. These reasons and factors coexisted well before the outbreak of the October events, and their mutual interrelation led to the tragic outcome. The reasons and factors are the following:

---

[191] The document notes that the Provisional CC met in "continuous session" even though it omits the date December 4.

1. The clique of Rákosi and Gerő, which had a decisive influence in the Central Committee of the Hungarian Workers' Party and in the government of the Hungarian People's Republic, began to deviate from the principles of Marxism-Leninism after 1948. They initiated a sectarian and dogmatic policy in party, state, and economic affairs, and introduced peremptory, authoritarian, and bureaucratic methods of leadership. Their harmful methods resulted in serious mistakes and transgressions in both our party and state life. They impeded the expansion of democratization in party activities and social life, and severely offended socialist law and order. They imposed an economic policy on the people that disregarded Hungary's economic conditions and impeded the improvement of the workers' living standards. Neglecting Lenin's principle of voluntary participation, they gravely discredited the movement of collectivization in the eyes of most peasants. Mechanically copying the Soviet model, misinterpreting Soviet-Hungarian fraternity, suppressing national interests, and disparaging and ignoring our national values, they severely offended the national and patriotic feelings of the Hungarian people.

With their anti-Leninist methods of leadership, which are alien to the communist party, the clique of Rákosi and Gerő caused a split between the party leadership and membership, between the party and the working class, between the working class and its ally, the peasantry, as well as between the party and the intellectuals. They undermined and weakened the party's reputation.[192]

This leading clique was unable to admit and correct its serious mistakes and crimes. In fact, it failed to change its attitude and behavior even after the historic Twentieth Congress of the Communist Party of the Soviet Union, whose guidelines it disregarded. It continued to cling desperately to its power position even when—primarily from the beginning of March 1956 onward—the majority of the Central Committee and party functionaries, as well as practically the entire party membership, opposed it, thus reducing it to an isolated clique. Emphasizing party unity and condemning rightful criticism as dissension and factional policy, they [the members of the clique] hampered the democratic and party-minded correction of the questions [sic].

The sectarian policy of the old party leadership brought about the formation of a widespread democratic opposition movement after the summer of 1953,[193] first within the party and then later among the working masses, under the leadership of the very best communists. *Communists and democratic people outside the party, deeply embittered because of the [leadership's] grave mistakes, fought for the revision of these mistakes, while remaining faithful to the idea of communism, the socialist order of our society, and to the Hungarian People's Republic.*[194] Members of the broad democratic mass movement, faithful to the socialist ideal, gave unmistakable evidence of these views before, during, and after the October events.

2. Another crucial element that played a serious role in the rise of the October events and in their tragic turn was [the existence of] a dissenting wing within the party opposition, formed in earlier years and constantly expanding ever since, that chose Imre Nagy and Géza Losonczy as its emblem. The activity of this faction within the party opposition can be considered positive insofar as their fight was—together with the entire party opposition—directed against the fallacious policies of the Rákosi and Gerő clique. In the spring of 1956, however, a change ensued in their activity which fundamentally transformed the character of their behavior. They—incorrectly—took their criticism outside of the party and into the streets, where reactionary elements were able to join in.[195] In such a way, this criticism soon became deformed, no longer targeting the Rákosi-Gerő clique but rather undermining the party's remaining reputation and attacking the positions and foundations of the working class and the Hungarian people's democratic order.

---

[192] Emphasis in original.

[193] On the changes in Hungary during summer 1953, see the introductory essay to Part One and Document No. 2.

[194] Emphasis in original.

[195] This refers to the Petőfi Circle, a discussion group formed under the aegis of DISZ in 1955. The Circle soon became a forum for wide-ranging social and political debates that were unthinkable before. From spring 1956 on, the Circle's programs attracted an ever larger audience and nationwide attention.

This faction of party opposition, which failed to provide a positive program for correcting the mistakes, one-sidedly attacked only the party, and did not distance itself from reactionary forces.[196] Moreover, it encouraged reactionary forces and to a great extent contributed to the outbreak of the counterrevolution.

3. A fundamental factor in preparations for and the eventual outbreak of the October events were the forces of the Horthyite-fascist and Hungarian capitalist-landowner counterrevolution, a significant part of which worked underground in Hungary while the main forces gathered and organized themselves in West Germany. The objective of the Hungarian counterrevolution was to restore the capitalist and landowner regime, which they had never given up, even for a moment, since their defeat in 1945. On the contrary, they had been plotting ever since, waiting for the right moment to swoop down on our people's democracy and realize their counterrevolutionary aims.

4. Last but not least, international imperialism had a vital and fundamental role in the Hungarian events, with objectives that naturally went much further than the Hungarian question. The recent series of imperialist provocations in Vietnam, Korea, Taiwan, and Suez are well-known worldwide. These are all exemplary of the fact that international imperialism has not renounced the enslavement and exploitation of peoples, nor has it given up its plans to trigger local wars and a new, third world war. As evident and obvious proof that international imperialists had a share in preparing and meddling in the October events is that over the past twelve years their western radio stations (Voice of America and Free Europe) have not stopped instigating against the Hungarian People's Republic and its institutions, even for one minute.[197] They incited against land reform in 1945, then against the nationalization of factories, mines, and banks. In the past three years, they have used all their efforts to exaggerate in the extreme the actual mistakes and to employ them against the system. Their objective was to turn Hungarian communists and people with democratic attitudes against the socialist ideal, the regime of people's democracy, and against the Hungarian People's Republic. *Further proof of the iniquitous role that international imperialist circles, lurking and directing [events] in the background, played in the outbreak of the Hungarian events is the fact that years ago the émigré remnants of Horthy's army and gendarme forces, together with Hitler's fascists, were gathered in West Germany for counterrevolutionary purposes.*[198] They were uniformed, armed, trained, and paid with American dollars. Months before the October events, their vanguards were sent to Hungary in increasing numbers, so that they could continue their machinations against our people's democracy.

By backing the counterrevolution in Hungary, imperialist forces now intended to set up a new seat of war, this time right here—in the European region.

II. The events that started on October 23, 1956

The events which took place around the country differed from each other in terms of locale and chronological order, as well as in each of its phases [sic.].

In their despair over the mistakes and mismanagement of the Rákosi-Gerő clique, the majority of young protesters appearing on the streets of Budapest on October 23 were led by the goal that through the correction of these mistakes and the strengthening of the foundation of the people's democratic system, the country would advance on the road toward the building of socialism. The same attitude was even more apparent among workers who protested in the country-side.[199] [...]

---

[196] Emphasis in original.

[197] In case of RFE, this statement was incorrect since RFE began its Hungary program only in 1951. Voice of America, on the other hand, began its operations in 1942.

[198] Emphasis in original.

[199] Emphasis in original.

462

For a long time, however, counterrevolutionary forces carefully disguised themselves before the masses. They only revealed their true identity and cast off their masks after October 30, during the cease-fire. The counterrevolutionary forces, who now slaughtered communists and other progressive workers, peasants, and intellectuals in the streets, had participated in an organized fashion even in the very first hours of the uprising—the armed actions of the evening of October 23—and consciously influenced events to suit their own aims. [...]

It is quite evident that the purpose of the counterrevolution was not to correct mistakes, but rather to overthrow the people's power and the Hungarian People's Republic and destroy the achievements of socialism. In response to the question of whether the fundamental characteristic of the armed uprising that started on October 23 in Hungary was revolution or national revolution, in the face of plain facts we can give only one answer: it was neither of these, but rather a counterrevolution. This truth must be told, even though we are fully aware that the overwhelming majority of those who took part in the events all over the country were loyal citizens of the Hungarian People's Republic in their motivations, objectives, and innermost feelings— [they were] honest workers and good patriots, rather than counterrevolutionaries.

Those who took part in the October events with honest intentions must see the bitter truth that their armed uprising against the law and order of the people's republic unintentionally promoted the goals of the counterrevolution.

Similarly, those who were on strike and protested when the Hungarian People's Republic was under armed attack—even though they might have had rightful political and economic claims—must accept that their actions weakened the political system of the embattled Hungarian People's Republic and advanced the chances of the counterrevolution, which—as it is well known—was fighting to overthrow the rule of the working classes.[200]

In relation to the October events, attention must also be drawn to the deplorable role of the government of Imre Nagy at that time. The government's inadequacy and constant shifts to the right wing contributed to the advance of counterrevolutionary forces. This tendency is evident in their acceptance of such demands as the declaration of political neutrality without [proper international] guarantee, the immediate and unlawful withdrawal from the Warsaw Pact, the request for the United Nations to intervene, the call for resistance against Soviet troops who had been invited to subdue the counterrevolution,[201] the toleration of the activities and lawlessness of counterrevolutionary parties, and the declaration of a multi-party system in a way that was tantamount to the abandonment of the foundations of socialism.

By not acting openly against the counterrevolution, even in the days of the white terror's undisguised rage, and by shielding it under its name and reputation, the government of Imre Nagy—with a communist prime minister at its head—prevented the masses from realizing the actual danger posed by the counterrevolution.[202]

[...]

[*Source: Published in* Népszabadság, *December 8, 1956. Translated by Csaba Farkas.*]

---

[200] Emphasis in original.

[201] See footnote 178 above.

[202] Emphasis in original.

DOCUMENT NO. 105: "Policy Review of Voice for Free Hungary Programming, October 23–November 23, 1956," December 5, 1956

In the wake of the Soviet suppression of the Hungarian revolution, Radio Free Europe was widely accused of misleading the Hungarian people into believing that they could count on effective U.S. support in their opposition to the Soviets. This report by RFE political adviser William Griffith, published here for the first time, was part of an internal investigation of RFE broadcasts during the uprising. The document claims that there were only a "few genuine violations of policy" but reveals that RFE broadcasts in several cases had implied that foreign aid would be forthcoming if the Hungarians succeeded in establishing a "central military command." The broadcasts also appealed to the Hungarians to "continue to fight vigorously," and even gave specific tactical advice to the rebels. Significantly, the report also reveals serious flaws in the organizational structure and in the exercise of control over sections of RFE. It points out, for example, that there were important discrepancies between the program summaries submitted for review by émigré staff prior to broadcast and the substance of the broadcasts themselves.

MEMORANDUM

TO: MR. CONDON[203]

FROM: MR. GRIFFITH

SUBJECT: POLICY REVIEW OF VOICE FOR FREE HUNGARY PROGRAMMING, 23 OCTOBER – 23 NOVEMBER 1956

INTRODUCTION:

For the past three weeks we have been reviewing RFE's Hungarian broadcast output during the above period. We have conducted this review primarily for the purpose of determining the degree and effectiveness of compliance with and implementation of RFE policy of VFH scripts during this period. Inevitably, we have also had to consider problems of tone and technique, but I wish to emphasize that these aspects were neither the primary purpose of this review nor should our conclusions as to them be taken as more than provisional ones; they are included herein for what use they may be to the Program Department.

Our conclusions and recommendations have been made from the viewpoint of policy formulation and implementation only. I have not thought it proper or desirable in respect thereto, to go into personalities with the exception of an evaluation of the VFH Desk Chief from a policy viewpoint, and an appended evaluation of the output of each main writer for the period surveyed.

I. PROCEDURE

We have read for purposes of this policy survey a total of 187 programs in English translation; in addition Mr. Rademaekers has read 121 additional programs in the original Hungarian. Questionable passages from these latter he has translated orally to us verbatim and we have had him double-check the translations of sections of the English texts where serious errors of policy or techniques seem to have been committed. In a few cases tapes of the original broadcasts have also been checked but lack of time and personnel prevented us from doing this extensively. As you know, RFE/Munich translation facilities have proved inadequate to cope with the task of

---

[203] Richard J. Condon was European director of RFE.

translating programs rapidly after broadcast ever since the beginning of the Hungarian crisis (Oct 23). Only in the last week, as result of emergency measures, have we been able to obtain sufficient translation of programs from the 23 October–4 November period to have a good general impression of them. The lack of a Hungarian language summarizer-analyst in the Program Department (this position was eliminated last June) has also been keenly felt; we have not had a short daily summary of the main lines of programs as broadcast available to us during this time. (The Desk's summaries provided at morning meetings were inaccurate in many instances.)

VFH programming during the first month of the Hungarian Revolution falls naturally into two halves, with November 4 (the second Soviet military intervention) as the dividing line. Many commentaries were broadcast each day up to 4 November. After this date the number of commentaries was gradually restricted and programming emphasized press reviews, reports of Western demonstrations of sympathy with Hungary and accounts of UN developments. The Hungarian Desk apparently found it difficult to surpass its desire to comment, however, for toward the latter part of November a trend back toward more commentaries (since checked) again became evident.

The analysis which follows is based upon approximately 70% of all programming (excluding news) during the period of 24 October through 3 November, including not only commentaries but a large proportion of press reviews and special reports. For the period 4–23 November roughly 50% of all programming (excluding news) has been available for analysis. Relatively few news broadcasts are included in this analysis because very few have been translated. When means of translating them can be found, it would probably be useful to have a separate analysis done of them for the same period which this survey covers.

In general, we have found that the VFH did not measure up to our expectations during the first two weeks of the Hungarian Revolution. Although there were few genuine violations of policy and those did not occur in major political commentaries, the application of policy lines was more often than not crude and unimaginative. Many of the rules of effective broadcasting technique were violated. The tone of the broadcasts was over-excited. There was too much rhetoric, too much emotionalism, too much generalization. The great majority of programs were lacking in humility and subtlety. VFH output for the first two-week period in particular had a distinct "émigré" tone; too little specific reference was made to the desires and demands of the people in the country. An improvement is discernible toward the end of this first two-week period. By the first days of November considerably more frequent reference was made to the "freedom stations" in Hungary and the demands of the local revolutionary councils, and policy guidance on key questions such as the role of Imre Nagy was applied with greater refinement. The tendency to talk much too much continued into the period following the second Soviet intervention on 4 November. No serious policy violations have been discovered in this period and in some respects techniques also began to improve. Earlier faults remained evident, however, to the end of the period under survey.

II. POLICY VIOLATIONS AND DISTORTIONS

There were relatively few real policy violations. All of them occurred in the first period (before November 4). Of the four discovered out of the 308 programs read for this survey, none occurred in major political commentaries.

A rereading of the summaries originally presented at morning policy meetings for these programs makes it clear that the summaries often failed to reflect the content of the program as it was finally written (this is not the case only with programs where policy violation occurred; the summaries during the period under review in many other cases proved to be very inaccurate descriptions of the programs finally produced). In one instance, however, no summary of a program where a policy violation occurred was presented in advance, because this program was a press review and under normal circumstances would not have been checked in advance. The normal programming schedule of the desk was disrupted during the revolutionary crisis to a degree not justified, in our opinion, by the exigencies of the situation. Program distinctions tended to become meaningless and writers who would not ordinarily have been permitted to write political commentary apparently did so, as least during the period 23 October to 4 November, with very little supervision by those in charge of the desk.

A check of broadcast copies of the four programs which contain policy violations revealed that none of these programs bears the desk chief's (Gellert's)[204] initials as having approved them for broadcast. It can therefore be assumed that he did not read them in final form before broadcast.

Of 16 programs which involve distortions of policy or serious failure to employ constructive techniques of policy application, nine were approved by Marjas, three by Bery and five by Olvedi and one by Feketekuthy (again, none by Gellert). We were not aware at the time that Gellert was not editing and approving scripts before broadcast. As you will recall, Marjas very seldom, and Olvedi practically never, attended morning policy meetings during the most of the period under survey. Marjas' language and hearing difficulties make his attendance at meetings of doubtful value in any case. We had assumed, however, that Gellert would brief his subordinates on the conclusions of morning meetings and on policy guidance given him by us at other occasions during the day. If he did so, his briefing does not appear to have been effective.

A. Scripts Which in Themselves Constitute Policy Violations:

1. Borsanyi's "Armed Forces Special" #A1 of 27 October violates the letter and spirit of policy in effect at the time. The program gives detailed instructions as to how partisan and Hungarian armed forces should fight. It advises local authorities to secure stores of arms for the use of Freedom Fighters and tell the population to hide Freedom Fighters who become separated from their units. It advises the population to provide food and supplies for Freedom Fighters. The writer tells Hungarians to sabotage ("disconnect") railroad and telephone lines. It fairly clearly implies that foreign aid will be forthcoming if the resistance forces succeed in establishing a "central military command." The program is cast entirely in the form of advice from the outside; there is no reference to information coming from within the country. The program refers to the "Nagy puppet government" and states that Nagy is relying on the support of the Soviet armed forces. Although the writer is too categorical in his phraseology, his attacks on Nagy are in themselves not out of keeping with policy guidance in effect at the time. The program concludes with some rather complex formulations which could be interpreted by listeners as implying help from the outside.

The summary of this program presented at the morning meeting of the day it was broadcast stated:

> "Laws and experience of partisan war. Without inciting the participants of civil war, we tell them what are the experiences and techniques of partisan warfare, citing Russian, Yugoslav, etc., experiences. First rule, e.g., is that groups which are fighting dispersed should establish contact with one another and establish a political center, etc., etc.,"

I considered the program as summarized inappropriate when it was presented at the morning meeting. I pointed out that such a program could be permitted only if it dealt with the topic in purely theoretical terms without any reference to current events in Hungary. Gellert gave assur-

---

[204] The full name of the Hungarian editors mentioned in the text is as follows: Andor Gellért (chief of the Hungarian desk from September 1954 to June 1957), Viktor Márjás (deputy chief from January 1954 to December 1956); (other staff members on the Hungary desk in alphabetical order) Miklós Ajtay, László Béry, Tamás Bogyay, Gyula Borbándi, Júlián Borsányi, Emil Csonka, László Feketekúthy, Béla Horváth, Katalin Hunyadi, Sándor Körösi-Kirzsán, Gyula Litteráty-Loótz, László Mezőfy, Imre Mikes, József Molnár, Zoltán Németh, János Ölvedi, Zoltán Szabó, Károly Szakmáry, Zoltán Thury and Imre Vámos. László Bús-Fekete and T. Sebők were members of the New York staff.

ance that this could be done. This program was approved for broadcast by Bery. There is no evidence that Gellert read it in its completed form.

2. Borsanyi's "Armed Forces Special" #B1 of 28 October gives detailed instructions to Hungarian soldiers on the conduct of partisan warfare.[205] The author states at the beginning of the program that Hungarians must continue to fight vigorously because this will have a great effect on the handling of the Hungarian question by the Security Council of the UN. Without saying so directly, he implies that the UN will give active support to Hungarians if they keep on fighting. The program is over-optimistic in tone. The opening announcement states: "Colonel Bell will tell Hungarian soldiers how ingenious and smart leadership can counterbalance numerical and arms superiority". The conclusion states: "Colonel Bell has told Hungarian soldiers how to obstruct large forces by small ones and by simple means". In the light of subsequent events the program grossly underestimates the ability of the Soviets to move new troops into Hungary. Borsanyi implies that the most the Soviets can bring in is about four divisions and that it might take as long as two or three weeks for the Soviets to secure the Danube line if Hungarians fight effectively against them. The program makes a feeble effort at indirect propaganda by recounting a story about how Yugoslav partisans fought against much larger forces of Germans in South Serbia in 1943 and beat them; but the indirectness [sic] of this story is completely negated by the obvious comments at the beginning and end of it. This program of Borsanyi's constitutes a serious policy violation, for the author in no way makes any effort to demonstrate that he is basing his advice on opinions or even information coming from within the country. Here at its worst is the émigré on the outside, without responsibility or authority, giving detailed advice to the people fighting at home.

The summary of this program presented at the morning policy meeting of the day on which it was written was at the least misleading; it stated only:

"We review the success in November 1943 of the 500 Serb partisans who were able to hold back the 13,000-man German troop near the town of Nish".

The program was approved for broadcast by Olvedi.

3. Litterati's "Armed Forces Special #D1" of 30 October 1956,[206] like Borsanyi programs discussed above, gives detailed military instructions to the population of Hungary, this time on the techniques of anti-tank warfare. Litterati does not give his advice in quite as direct, categorical fashion as Borsanyi and makes repeated references to Soviet tactics in World War II. The intent of the program is nevertheless completely clear. A case would perhaps be made that this program is theoretically not a policy violation; in its effect, however, it must be considered as such, for the people of Hungary are not only encouraged to fight, but told how. There is a strong strain of over-optimism in the program; the author gives the impression that tanks are really very easy to destroy. The program is very skillfully written, contains little surplus rhetoric and gives on the whole, militarily sound advice. The summary of this program presented at the morning meeting on 30 October stated only:

"We explain the simple partisan means by which it is possible to avoid responsibility in connection with tanks".

Gellert assured me that this program, like others of its type would be written on a purely theoretical basis without specific reference to current events in Hungary. This program was approved for broadcast by Olvedi; there is no evidence that Gellert read it before broadcast.

4. Zoltan Thury's "Special Short World Press Review" #1 of 4 November probably constitutes the most serious violation of all.[207] At the conclusion of his press review, Thury quotes excerpts from a London *Observer* Washington dispatch of the same day as follows:

[205] See Document No. 45.

[206] Not included here, but for another program with similar content, see Document No. 45.

[207] See Document No. 87.

"If the Soviet troops really attack Hungary, if our expectations should hold true and Hungarians hold-out for three or four days, then the pressure upon the government of the United States to send military help to the Freedom Fighters will become irresistible!"

Thury then comments, paraphrasing the *Observer's* correspondent's words

"This is what the *Observer* writes in today's number. The paper observes that the American Congress cannot vote for war as long as the presidential elections have not been held. The article then continues: 'If the Hungarians can continue to fight until Wednesday we shall be closer to a world war than at any time since 1939.'"

Thury's own final comment in this program is:

"The reports from London, Paris, the U.S. and other Western reports show that the world's reaction to Hungarian events surpasses every imagination. In the Western capitals a practical manifestation of Western sympathy is expected at any hour."

The tapes of this program have been checked. It was broadcast in exactly the same form as written. The London *Observer* dispatch has been checked word for word. It is true that the normally cautious and realistic *Observer* printed the words Thury quotes (he did not alter them) on its front page. The passage must have been distributed through the Central Newsroom, having been telephoned in from London, since the *Observer* itself does not ordinarily reach Munich until Monday. It has been impossible, however, to track down the original item put out by the Central Newsroom. The fact that the *Observer* printed these words hardly gave Thury authorization to broadcast them to Hungary at a time when Hungarians were likely to be clutching for any straws of hope from the West. This program is undoubtedly the one several Hungarian refugees and correspondents have referred to as "the promise that help would come which RFE broadcast on the weekend of 4 November." The quotations from the *Observer* are bad enough; Thury's own comments are far worse since they clearly represented to the listener the editorial opinions of the VFH. He leads his listeners to believe that military intervention by the West can be expected within a few days. This is contrary to the entire RFE philosophy of broadcasting. To all desks throughout the years we have emphasized over and over again that RFE can never take the responsibility for promising something it cannot deliver. It was agreed with Gellert on 4 November that no promises of hope could be broadcast, that RFE could only attack Kadar and the Soviets for their treachery and give roundups of the reactions of the free world. It was agreed that any free world reactions which indicated promise of more than normal support and action undertaken by the UN General Assembly would be misleading and should not be put on the air.

Thury's press review was approved for broadcast by Olvedi. There is no evidence that Gellert saw it.

Another Thury program of the same day, a short special commentary, carried the same thesis as his press review, but in much more guarded form:

"Extraordinary cabinet meetings, a Security Council meeting, protest meetings to be held this afternoon by various parties and organizations prove the quick reaction of the West to the Soviet attack. It is believed in the free countries that the Hungarian Freedom Fight cannot be settled like a coup d'etat. Moscow did not sufficiently assess the echo of her action and the strength of Western possible support."

This record programs cannot be called a policy violation, but in light of Thury's press review it is clear what he was trying to get across to his listeners. It is difficult to understand how he could have wished to broadcast such false promi- [text cut off] thinking undoubtedly overcame his judgement. This hardly excuses his action, nor that of the editor who approved his script for broadcast.

In retrospect it appears to have been a mistake to have permitted the VFH to broadcast any programs on military topics during the revolution. As I recall, these programs were permitted because it was felt by Gellert and ourselves that to broadcast information on the theory of partisan warfare, tank defense techniques and elementary principles of civilian defense in a civil war situation might help save lives during the Revolution and at the least would remind Hungarian listeners to be cautious and avoid sacrificing themselves in foolish gestures of resistance. We were mistaken in assuming that the desk's military writers could write on, or the responsible editors edit, these delicate topics with sufficient cleverness and a proper sense of detachment to keep them theoretical while still offering relevant advice. As has been pointed out before, these programs, when presented in summary form at morning meetings were carefully discussed and Gellert gave full assurance that they would be kept entirely theoretical and would not resort to giving specific advice or instructions. Gellert did not take the necessary steps to make his assurances good. Our assumption that he would be able to was therefore also a mistake. We now see clearly that it would have been wiser never have to permitted such programs at all.

B. Groups of Programs which Reveal Serious Distortions of Policy or Failure to Apply Policy Guidance and Advice on Technique and Tone Constructively.

1. Programs Dealing with or Referring to the Political Position of the Nagy Government.

A summary of New York and Munich guidance on this and related topics is attached as Appendix III.[208] From this summary it can be seen that New York and Munich were in substantial agreement on the position to be taken in respect to the Nagy Government. New York tended perhaps to advocate slightly stronger questioning of Nagy's integrity and somewhat greater stress on the final goals of complete freedom (free elections, democratic freedoms as known in the West). It was agreed in both New York and Munich that RFE could not take a complete pro-Nagy position until he made the program of his government clear and rid his government of most of the communists associated with the previous regime. At the same time it was agreed that RFE should not take an irrevocably anti-Nagy position as long as no alternative figures capable of assuming leadership of the Revolution appeared. As the various Freedom Stations developed their activity, it was further agreed in both New York and Munich that the VFH should attempt to fit its line to whatever democratic common denominators the Freedom Station broadcasts contained. The Freedom Stations, of course, never developed a common line among themselves, and there is no evidence that they ever established effective contact among themselves. They attempted at first to take no clear position on Nagy and his government (for the first few days, e.g., there was speculation among correspondents and official quarter in Vienna as to whether Radio Free Gyor was not "a camouflaged Nagy station"). In the last days of October the Freedom Stations became increasingly vocal in their criticism of Nagy and his government, asking ever more pointed questions as to what Nagy's program would be and why so many discredited communists remained in positions of authority. On November 1, when Nagy declared that his government would permit free political activity and free elections, that Hungary was leaving the Warsaw Pact and would henceforth adhere to a policy of strict neutrality, the Freedom Stations swung over to complete support of him, still demanding that he reform his government on a broad multi-party basis.

RFE policy toward Nagy and his government followed much the same course. During the first three or four days after the Soviet military intervention it appeared that Nagy might actually have been involved in calling in Soviet troops, that the population could not judge his government or accept its program until he did so. It was agreed that RFE should attack the past records of particularly unsavory communists whether they were associated with the new government or not, but the RFE should not support actively any particular personalities until the attitudes of people inside Hungary became clearer (in this connection see NYC PREB 15, 28

---

[208] Not printed here.

October 56 and the Munich reply to it, MUN 292, 29 October 1956). The Hungarian Desk was constantly advised both from New York and in Munich to avoid giving the impression that the VFH was trying to direct the Revolution in Hungary. The VFH was likewise constantly advised by us to avoid discussing events in Hungary in too dogmatic terms, but instead to emphasize that our information was incomplete, that the situation was so complex that it could not be judged entirely from the outside. We urged the desk to phrase its own comments as much as possible in terms of lines taken by what seemed to be the more responsible commentaries over the Freedom Stations and the lines taken by the local Revolutionary Councils. Gellert indicated full agreement with this advice and complete understanding of the necessity for it. Program summaries presented at daily meetings generally reflected these principles.

A re-reading of the daily summaries of this period after a reading of the programs themselves often reveals wide disparity between the two. The disparity is more often than not one of tone. While the summaries presented in advance are measured, qualified, logical presentations of arguments and points of view, too many of the programs emerged in final form as bombastic, rhetorical, overly emotional blasts at the Nagy Government or certain members of it. The Freedom Stations were quoted too seldom (in many programs, not at all); little reference was made to the fact that the VFH lacked complete information and therefore was not really entitled to pass final judgment. In short, major mistakes of tone and techniques were made in many of these programs; the result was that policy was badly distorted in the final broadcasts. Nevertheless, the number of outstandingly good programs during the last week of October equals almost exactly the number of extremely bad programs. In reading through this programming, however, we found that the impression of the bad ones tended to cancel out the impression of the good ones; I wonder if the same may not have been the case with our listeners in Hungary. The worst programs are almost always those of Mikes; Bery runs Mikes a close second.

Gellert's two commentaries of 25 October and 2 November are the landmarks of the period. Both are written with consummate skill, richness of thought and logic and construction which makes most of the other commentaries produced by the desk during this period appear amateurish by comparison. The first (Gellert's "Special Commentary #IV," 25 Oct 56) asked a series of pointed questions about the role of Imre Nagy in the first phase of the revolution and particularly in connection with the calling in of Soviet troops. The commentary is an exact reflection of the line suggested in the Nathan Guidance received in Munich the afternoon before (see excerpt from Nathan's 24 October Guidance in Appendix III). In retrospect it can probably be said that both the commentary and guidance went too far in taking a dim view of Nagy. Gellert's commentary should at least have referred to the fact that there might be elements of complexity in Nagy's situation of which we were unaware and therefore our judgment could only be tentative. In terms of the way things looked at the time, however, Gellert insists that Nagy, who appears to have betrayed the trust the nation had in him, must explain himself very carefully and must be ready to take decisive action in favor of the revolution if he is to redeem himself in the eyes of his people and of the world.

Another program of the same day (Mezofy: "Special Commentary VII," 25 Oct 56) discusses Nagy's proclamation of martial law and the threats of the Government against revolutionaries who refused to surrender within the time limits set. In calm and factual fashion Mezofy takes issue with Nagy for calling the revolution "a revolt" and points out that the proclamation of martial law does not absolve a government or its members for responsibility or acts counter to the spirit of accepted principles of human rights.

The next day Mikes wrote a blast against Nagy and Kadar totally lacking in refinement, subtlety and humility (Mikes "Special Reflector #IV," 26 Oct 56), displaying no inclination to admit the differences in the situation faced by the two men, he attacks Nagy for not behaving like Gomulka and states: "Imre Nagy is no solution any more. . .the people backed him, they demanded his return and raised him from the political grave where he was thrown by his Moscow rivals in the eternal fight for power." The writer attacks Nagy for making promises but insisting that the revolution stop before they are implemented. Contradicting himself at the end, he declares "the premier should not make any promises, the people do not need his program now

. . . they only need his signature . . . to recall the Soviet Divisions" and in a final frenzied outburst shouts "The last moment was over long ago. It was over when the first martyr of the freedom fight died. Imre Nagy missed the last moment. Yet he still has an opportunity; to follow the will of the people and the nation—away with the Soviets if not away with him for ever!" Mikes's program is a distortion of the 24 October guidance mentioned above and of the Gellert program of the day before. The program was approved by Bery for broadcast.

The summary of this script presented at the morning meeting gave the impression of a much more moderate approach to the problem:

> "Imre Nagy's radio speech is crowded with foggy promises. Such promises: (1) *After* the riot is quelled, he will establish a wide-range People's Front; (2) *After* the riot is quelled, he will submit a reform program; (3) *After* the riot is quelled he will start negotiations with Moscow concerning the withdrawal of Soviet Troops. These tragic moments are not the time for promises; blood is being shed. Action is needed. First and foremost—and immediately—the withdrawal of Soviet troops. Conclusion: This is what the country expects, what it demands. This is the factor, which will decide the question of Imre Nagy's straightforwardness. If he acts promptly, then reforms may come. If Soviet troops continue to massacre the population, Imre Nagy will have forfeited himself, together with all his promises as far as the nation is concerned."

Another commentary of the same day (Bery: "Special Russia Commentary" (sic) 26 Oct 56) is less bombastic than Mikes, but indulges in the same kind of unrefined generalizations. It is full of rhetoric and pretends to full knowledge of the Hungarian situation but makes no specific reference to the demands of the Revolutionary Fighters. Bery takes too much of an all-or-nothing position toward Nagy, stating "there are only agents in Hungary who obey orders from Moscow." An excellent opportunity to apply the "golden bridge" theme was missed. This program was approved for broadcast by Feketekuthy. The morning meeting summary gave no indication that it would treat the position of the Nagy Government at all. It seems that Bery must have changed his plan for this commentary after the morning meeting had taken place.

Zoltan Nemeth declared that only the AVH supported the Nagy Government in his "Special Farmers Program #2['] of 27 October. The summary of this program presented at the morning meeting gave no indication that it would deal with this question at all:

> "Addressing the rural population, we tell them that the battle raging is already a victorious one. The world is watching anxiously, realizing that in this fight not one single stratum of society is backing the regime—the sole help on the aide of the latter is Soviet arms. The Communist economic system has been abolished in the rural areas, never to return. Hungarians are fighting for justified demands and fighting successfully."

The script was approved for broadcast by Bery.

The Vamos "Short Commentary #B2" of 28 October takes a somewhat less violent position on Nagy, but likewise displays a too unrefined attitude.

Bery wrote another commentary on 29 October (Bery: "Special Short Commentary #C3," 29 Oct 56) which has all the faults of his commentary of 26 October, and displays a perhaps even more pronounced and rather petulant "Nagy-is-no-damned-good" attitude. This commentary, too, is lacking in humility. No reference is made to the fact that we do not have enough information to judge Nagy's position and intentions with absolute finality. Bery's commentary could have been highly effective if he had confined himself to summing up the question about Nagy's position and intentions being asked at that very time by the Freedom Stations and the local National Councils. This commentary was approved by Marjas for broadcast.

The summary of this program presented in advance gives a totally different impression of it—in fact there is very little resemblance between the summary and the program as it was finally written. The reason may be that the summary was prepared by Gellert and the program by Bery without Gellert ever having seen the final product. The summary stated:

> "Reflections on Imre Nagy's speech—the speech promises the withdrawal of Soviet troops in case that a new police force is brought about. Who is to organize this force? What guarantee is there that this will not turn into a new AVH? When will it be organized? Soviet troops continue to remain in Budapest. Imre Nagy promises negotiations aiming at withdrawal of Soviet troops from the country. Is the Soviet Union willing to negotiate also? The speech does not include the two main announcements—the immediate withdrawal of Soviet troops and free elections. The Hungarian people evaluate Nagy's speech in accordance with these factors."

The programming of 30 October is particularly questionable in tone. This day was one of the most tense days of the whole revolution. Genuine victory appeared near, but nothing was yet clear—the position of the Nagy Government, the attitude of the Russian troops, whether there would be a cease-fire, whether Soviet troops would withdraw. The desk's programming inevitably reflects this tension, and because again there was too much said by the desk, many things were poorly said and many things were said which should not have been said at all. Some of the programming of this day will be dealt with under another heading in the sub-section following this one. Two of the programs bear upon the topic under discussions here:

Szakmary's "Youth Special #D1," 30 Oct 56, contains a feature rare in the programming of the VFH—a reminder at the beginning and at the end of the broadcast that the author is an émigré who feels to some extent ashamed to address people at home because he is not there fighting and does not really know what conditions there are like. This is excellent. But one wishes the writer had had a greater sense of shame, for in the body of the program he does exactly what he says he is ashamed to do. He gives emphatic impassioned advice in a flood of words and rhetoric. He urges fighters not to put down their arms, speaks over-optimistically about the "limited capabilities" of Soviet troops, tells his listeners that the promises of the Nagy government cannot be taken at face value. The program is chaotically organized. Though it is not a policy violation in terms of the policy in effect at the time, it is a poor application of it. No summary of this program had been presented at the morning meeting in advance of the broadcast. It was approved for broadcast by Marjas.

Borsanyi's "Armed Forces Special #D1," 30 October 1956, is devoted primarily to attacking the Defense Minister of the time, Karoly Janza. In the course of the program Borsanyi also attacks Nagy for having communists in his government, for calling in Soviet troops and implies that he has perfidious motives in misleading the people about the true situation. All these are issues with which the Freedom Stations at that time were dealing and many of them were attacking Nagy for the same reasons and asking him to rid his government of old communists and state his political program more clearly. Borsanyi finishes by telling soldiers that they must demand a democratic government, free elections and a multi-party system. These were also demands of the Freedom Stations of the time. *But Borsanyi never once makes any mention of the Freedom Stations.* His program, therefore, while not a violation of policy, is not a constructive implementation of it. This program was approved for broadcast by Olvedi.

Borsanyi made another crude attack on the Nagy Government in a short glossary on 31 October ("Special Glossary #E2") and two other programs, of those read for this survey, expressed misgivings about Nagy or his associates in milder form (Csonka, "Chronological Review of Week' Events #E1," 31 Oct 56; Vamos, "Special Commentary #E2," 31 Oct 56)[.] Mikes's "Reflector #E1," of the same day was one of the most tactless of all Mikes's poor programs. It is a supercilious polemic with the university youth and the revolutionary army paper *Igazsag* on the question of whether Nagy did or did not assent to calling in Soviet troops. For better or for worse, in view of the fact that the revolution was developing, the subject should have been left at that, and we should not have entered into argumentation with the revolutionary forces in Hungary, but instead simply said (as the summary indicated) Radio Budapest reports that Nagy had called them in. Incongruously, at the beginning of this program Mikes states "we do not intend to debate and we do not wish to stir up passions." The whole program does just this, except that one suspects such a program may well have stirred up more passions against RFE than against Nagy or any elements in the Revolutionary Forces. Like all of Mikes's programs this one is lavishly adorned with exaggerated phrases and rhetorical flourish. This program was approved for broadcast by Marjas.

A "Special Short Commentary #F3" by Szakmary, broadcast on 1 Nov., attacked Zoltan Tildy. After this date, however, no further attacks on Nagy or members of his government have been found in VFH broadcasts.

Gellert's well written commentary of 2 November associated the VFH with full support of Nagy.

2. Programs Urging Hungarians to Continue to Fight

Inasmuch as the VFH was in favor of the Hungarian Revolution it was by implication in favor of the Revolution's being carried to a successful conclusion. Policy on the extent to which RFE should indirectly urge Hungarians to continue fighting was never specifically formulated in writing; as the Revolution developed, it became increasingly clear that the best course to follow in judging this difficult question would be to let the Free Radios being heard in increasing volume from within Hungary be our guide. New York and Munich were in complete agreement on this point. As the end of October approached, this subject became increasingly important and was regularly discussed at length at morning policy meetings. It was agreed that programs should point out to listeners that there might be elements of deception in a cease-fire accepted without guarantee that the gains of the Revolution would be preserved and that Hungarians should be warned against attempts by the Communists to infiltrate local Revolutionary Councils. This particular topic was skillfully dealt with in indirect fashion by Korosi-Krizsan in his "Special Calling Communists #D1" of 30 October.

As for the general question of continuing the fighting, it was agreed that statements from the Freedom Stations, decisions of the local Revolutionary Councils and confirmed reports from journalists inside Hungary should be reported, summarized and analyzed. Gellert never expressed any disagreement with this approach. In this respect again, however, the desk's principal political commentators *were either unaware of this advice* (it is difficult to believe that Bery was, since he usually attended morning meetings regularly) *or failed to follow it.*

An overly excited Molnar program ("Special Workers Program #1" on 24 Oct 56) had included two sentences, one of which at least clearly urged Hungarians to fight: "No we cannot be pacified with words and half solutions any more . . . do not give up the struggle until you have received an answer to the most burning questions." As far as our survey indicates, this theme was not taken up again until 29 October.

A shrill, violent Mikes broadcast ("Special Reflector #01," 29 Oct 56) urged Freedom Fighters not to give up their arms. It did not directly urge them to continue fighting, as such. It lacked any reference to the fact that people in the country might be able to judge this delicate question better than émigrés on the outside and made no reference to the Freedom Stations or other opinion from within the country. This had been specifically advised and agreed upon at the morning meeting when a summary of the program had been presented. The program was approved for broadcast by Marjas.

In addition to the 30 October Litterati program discussed under sub-section A-1 above, which by implication urged Hungarians to continue fighting, three other programs dealt with this topic directly in the 30th of October: Mikes's Special Reflector #D2, Bery's Special Commentary #D1, and Szakmary's Youth Special #D1 (this last commentary has been partially discussed in Section A-1 above). Mikes made a shrill appeal to Hungarians to continue fighting or variously, at different points in the program, merely to retain their arms. (In this, as in many of Mike[s]'s programs, there are so many internal contradictions that it is often impossible to discover one singly consistent line; one gets the impression that these programs must often have sounded to listeners as emotional outpourings without any consistent line). No summary of this program which in any way reflects its contents seems to have been presented at either morning meeting of the days on which it was broadcast. According to the summary for 30 October, Mikes was to have written about the necessity for the Revolutionary Forces to organize their own police forces to replace the AVH and other discredited regime police elements. This would have been a quite acceptable topic, but in retrospect it is clear that no matter what topic he may have written about at this stage, Mikes would have produced a highly emotional program out of keeping with sound broadcast techniques. Mikes's 30 October program was likewise approved for broadcast by Marjas.

Bery's program of the same day was perhaps worse in its effects than Mikes's for it was much better written from a technical point of view. It clearly encouraged false hopes. Without identifying the source of his information Bery stated flatly that Soviet troops in Hungary were either not fighting or were only fighting half-[heartedly]. He grossly over-estimated the capabilities of the Hungarian Armed Forces:

"With comparatively small losses. . . they can stop for weeks a far greater armed force." Bery declared: "Hungarian soldiers. . . inactivity is treason." In the form in which these statements are made, without any reference to supporting opinion from within the country, they constitute a policy violation. No summary of this program was presented in advance. The Political Advisor's Office was not told that it was being written. There is no evidence that Gellert ever approved it, or for that matter never knew of its existence. It also was approved for broadcast by Marjas.

Like Bery, Szakmary in his Youth Special #D1 exhibits naïve and irresponsible over-optimism. He states: "It is evident that a putting down of the weapons based only on the irresponsible promises of Radio Budapest would represent giving up the results achieved so far by the Freedom Fight." As with the Bery program, no summary of Szakmary program was ever printed before broadcast.

On 31 October, as far as can be determined from scripts available for this survey, the "don't-stop-fighting" theme seems to be largely absent from VFH programming. It appeared again on 1 November in a Mikes program ("Special Reflector #F1") in what is probably the most emotional of all Mikes's broadcasts during this period. The bad technique, the extreme rhetoric, the violently nationalistic tone of this program must be read (still, better, I suppose, listened to) to be believed. As with all these other programs, there is no evidence that Gellert read it before it was broadcast. It was again approved for the air by Marjas.

The summary of this program presented at the 1 November morning meeting is very different from the final product:

> "There are sporadic signs and reports to the effect that the Stalinist remnants are trying to incite the revolutionary masses to irresponsible interference, thereby frustrating the victory and clean character of their fight for independence. It is this very clean nature of the fight which has brought about the admiration of the entire world, experience in the tremendous amount of assistance, medicines, etc. The arms could not be taken from the insurgents—now they try to take from them their word power, which they will be equally unable to do."

3. Programs Dealing with UN Security Council and General Assembly Sessions.

This category of programs, though on the whole well-done in terms of technique, tends too often to give listeners the impression that serious UN action is likely or imminent. Though no single program of this type can be termed a policy violation in itself, these programs as a group in the period before 3 November involve a distortion of policy which may have misled the population of Hungary and contributed to their later bitterness and disillusionment with the West in general.

Though a Bery program of 27 October ("Special Short Commentary #A2") warned listeners briefly not to expect any swift action from the UN, the first program to deal concretely with Security Council action on Hungary (T. Sebok (NY), "International Commentary #C524," 28 Oct 56) was shrill and rhetorical and could have given listeners the impression that *physical* UN intervention was imminent. The author chose UN intervention in the Iranian Azerbaijan case in 1946 as an example of successful UN action; this in itself was misleading because it automatically created the wishful hope that Soviet troops would be forced to withdraw from Hungary in the same way they had withdrawn from Iran in 1946. The author never once mentioned the *certain* Soviet veto that would prevent any real Security Council action on the Hungarian case. Instead of this poorly formulated and misleading script, it would have been more honest and in accord with policy to have broadcast a factual account of the actual workings of the UN Security Council. Since this script was written in New York, no summary of it was presented here in advance of the broadcast.

A less rhetorical, more informative program on the UN from the same day, written by Mezőfy, likewise failed to mention the possibility of a Soviet veto in the Security Council and concluded by implying that the UN might use force in Hungary. The summary of this program presented at the morning policy meeting gave the impression that the program would be written in a spirit of cold, clear objectivity and I repeatedly urged the desk to raise no false hopes in connection with UN action. The summary stated:

> "How is the Hungarian affair treated in the UN machinery? In connection with the fact that the question of Soviet aggression has come up before the Security Council we disclose just how and on what basis the question is discussed before the UN. We review the respective paragraphs of the UN Charter. Our aim is to inform the Hungarian population objectively and clearly on the operation of the UN and in particular the Security Council."

The following day's programming featured several programs consisting of long excerpts, in translation, of the previous night's Security Council debate. Four such programs have been read among the group selected for this survey. They are in no way objectionable in themselves, but many listeners may not have been able to judge the significance of many of the statements made by Western representatives and may have been inclined to over-interpret them in terms of expectation of action. It also appears that extensive simultaneous programming, in the form of running translation and comment, was done by the desk the night of the first Security Council Session. No scripts of this programming were made and a record of it exists only on tape; limitations of time and personnel prevented out checking it for this survey.

The same commentators in the same programs on 29 October repeated exactly the same errors they had made on the 28th. Sebok ("International Commentary #C525") gave a rhetorical and largely irrelevant account of the UN debate from New York. He made no mention of a Soviet veto. Mezőfy ("Special UN Program #C1") gave an over-optimistic account of the previous night's Security Council session, once again failing to mention the possibility of Soviet veto.

Apparently only one other program dealing with the UN's activities was broadcast during the remainder of October. It was "Special International Commentary (#D3)" sent from New York (author not indicated). It is more dramatic than factual.

The passage of time produced more realism in VFH commentaries on the UN's proceedings. Sebok's "International Commentary #H1" of 3 November was the first basically honest VFH commentary on UN developments. It mentioned the veto, Suez complications and procedural difficulties and pointed out that the UN did not have any armed forces of its own and therefore could not easily undertake military intervention. The New York Desk (author not indicated) gave a well written factual report of the 4 November early morning session of the UN Security Council devoid of promises, false implications or, on the other hand, excessive gloom.

Of five programs dealing with the UN and Hungary on 5 November, only one is relatively unsatisfactory—Bush-Fekete's "Special Short Commentary DJ1" is too excited in tone and uses too many florid phrases.

No objectionable programs on the UN have been discovered in the remainder of the programs for the period 4–23 November read for this survey.

4. Miscellaneous Shortcomings and Errors.

It would naturally be impossible here to go over the flaws and debatable points which can be found in many scripts read for this survey. Compared to the points discussed above many of them are not serious. Three which are serious will be taken up here, however:

Bogyay, a little known writer on the desk, included some rather peculiar references to Spain in a program which he wrote on 27 October ("Special Historical Report #B1"); "We are reminded of a great war 29 years ago. . . it took place on the Spanish Peninsula, but in part between the same forces which are now facing each other on Hungarian soil. Only in part because the. . . Spanish Civil War was much more than right wing Spaniards fighting against left wing." The meaning of the passage is not entirely clear, but it could be taken to imply that this commentator regarded the Hungarian Revolution as essentially a struggle of the right against the left, or as the Kremlin itself would have it, of fascists against Communists. This is certainly contrary to all RFE's principles. No summary of it was ever presented before broadcast, and a broadcast copy of this program cannot be found in the files; it is possible that it never went on the air; the desk has been unable to tell us whether it did or not.

Miss Hunyadi in a program dealing with the American reaction to Hungarian events on 29 October ("Special Report #C2") describes demonstrations before the UN Building in New York and in Cleveland in such a way as to give the impression that American public opinion will force the UN into action on Hungary. The program goes on to make reference to the fact that in Cleveland "Groups of Hungarians and Americans gave their names. . . they want to volunteer to go to Hungary so that they can fight together with the Freedom Fighters." It is no doubt true that people were giving their names to go to Hungary to fight. In the emotional context of this program, however, the subject was handled in such a way that wishful listeners could get the impression that American volunteers would soon be arriving in Hungary to fight against the Soviets. Miss Hunyadi's program was approved for broadcast by Olvedi. It was never submitted in summary from before broadcast.

A Bery program of 7 November ("Special Commentary #L1") commits a different kind of error, one which is unfortunately characteristic of the spirit of several scripts from the post-4 November period. Bery, obviously tired and depressed at the turn Hungarian events have taken, asks "Is there any sense in this fighting?" He then proceeds to answer the question in purely Western terms by pointing out that the Hungarian tragedy has awakened the West. Never once in the whole program does he make any reference to what is probably the most important aspect of the problem; the fact that the Hungarian Revolution has shaken the Communist system itself to its very roots. The script includes the ridiculous assertion that "the West could have done more for its freedom in Hungary with five divisions than with the 500 it is preparing to set up now." In making this irresponsible, ill-informed statement the author fails to point out to his listeners that any Western intervention in Hungary would have meant an atomic World War III and was for this reason out of the question. Bery misleads his listeners and caters to their delusions instead of informing them realistically.

When Bery's program summary was submitted at the morning meeting, Feketekuthy (in charge of morning meetings after Gellert collapsed) was advised to include reference to the effects of Hungarian events on the Communist movement everywhere, but this advice was not followed. This program was approved for broadcast by Marjas.

A Bery program of 23 November ("Special Commentary #D1") is almost identical in content and tone to Bery's program of 7 November. Marjas likewise approved it for broadcast, contrary to my advice as to what it should contain.

Since this time I have been requiring all commentaries dealing with Hungarian internal events or international reflections of them be presented to me in English translation before broadcast.

C. Cases of Poor Policy Implementation.

The basic problem is not so much that policy was violated as that it was not implemented with imagination, subtlety and cleverness. The incisive, dispassionate analyses of developments in Hungary which Gellert made daily at morning policy meetings are not reflected to the degree we were led to expect they would be (by Gellert himself and by the whole tenor of the morning meetings) in program output. Policy lines which were carefully discussed during these same morning meetings and which Gellert and other members of the desk who were present gave every indication of understanding clearly were frequently applied in crude and unrefined fashion in the programs as they were written. The all-too-frequent failure of program writers to implement policy imaginatively seems to have been merely another facet of their failure to employ effective techniques (see Section II below for a detailed discussion of errors of technique). It is remarkable that a group of Hungarians, most of whom have been with RFE for more than five years, should have absorbed so little of what has consistently been drummed into them—orally, in guidances, in listening sessions and meetings of many kinds—on radio broadcasting and political warfare techniques. Put to the severe test which they faced when the Hungarian Revolution began, the majority of Hungarian editors seem to have neglected to apply most of what they had ostensibly learned of the principles of sound broadcasting and effective political warfare which RFE stands for.

The most crucial failure of all was the failure of leadership within the desk. We over-estimated Gellert's ability to keep the desk under control. Without him, of course, the result would have been much worse. But he had just returned from a long and serious illness from which he had not yet totally recovered. The strain of the revolutionary events was so great that he collapsed at the end of the first week of November and has been seriously ill since. If Gellert had been in perfect health, he would no doubt have been able to maintain a greater degree of effective control over his desk. Bad health is nevertheless not a complete excuse, for Gellert's real shortcoming in leadership must be considered his failure to build up a sound leadership structure immediately under him. On taking over the desk two years ago, I had urged him to replace subordinates who had until then been kept in their positions but who, I felt, were not adequate for their tasks from a political and policy viewpoint. Gellert, instead of making serious efforts to replace these people, enabled them to become more consolidated in their positions and to the Olvedi-Marjas–Bery triumvirate added Ajtay, a man of excessively rightist political convictions and out of touch with developments in Hungary. Until recently we did not realize that he was exercising any supervisory functions in the desk. Marjas, an old journalist specializing in cultural matters, is apolitical but because of his past associations tends to gravitate toward the right. Hearing and language difficulties make it almost impossible to establish oral contact with him. Olvedi, politically more alert but definitely right of center, has likewise proved difficult to communicate with in English or German. Even though he has probably usually appreciated the techniques of political warfare and radio broadcasting which the desk has been expected to observe and has generally understood the main lines of policy guidance, he is (by his own admission) a rather weak person whose authority has not been respected by senior writers in the desk. He has consequently exercised very little authority over them.

Although sound guidance was given to the desk both from New York and in Munich (at morning meetings and frequently on an hour-by-hour basis orally and by phone) through the desk chief, the internal situation in the desk was such that the guidance was not effectively understood and much of the time improperly implemented or ignored. Guidance was understood in terms of prohibitions and elementary, unsubtle unimaginative general lines. This accounts for the fact that there were few actual policy violations, but that far too often policy was applied in a very unrefined form. Though the desk had been schooled in sound broadcasting techniques for years, the majority of writers do not seem to have absorbed this schooling to the extent that they were able to apply it under tense and critical circumstances when the desk lacked competent senior editors with the understanding and ability to require writers to observe good techniques in their programs.

D. Outstandingly Good Program.

As has been mentioned above, many excellent programs were written during the period before the second Russian military intervention on 4 November. In justice to the members of the desk who wrote them a few outstanding commentaries should at least be listed here, though lack of time makes it impossible to discuss them in detail. Interestingly enough even Bery, who wrote so many questionable programs, managed to write three good scripts:

477

Vamos	Special Commentary #3 – 24 October
B. Horvath	Special Commentary #VI – 25 October
Vamos	Special Commentary #5 – 25 October
Korosi-Krizsan	Calling Communists #C373 – 25 October
Bery	Special Commentary #VIII – 25 October
Bery	Special Commentary #B1 – 28 October
Molnar	Special Workers #C1 – 29 October
Molnar	Special Workers #D1 – 30 October
Korosi-Krizsan	Special Calling Communists #D1 – 30 October
Borbandy	International Commentary #A1 – 31 October
Molnar	Special Commentary #F2 – 1 November
Korosi-Krizsan	Special Calling Communists #D1 – 30 October
Borbandy	International Commentary #A1 – 31 October
Molnar	Special Commentary #F2 – 1 November
Korosi-Krizsan	Short Commentary #F5 – 1 November
Bery	Special Commentary #F4 – 1 November
Mezőfy	Special Warsaw Pact Program #F1 – 1 November
Csonka	Special Freedom Stations #F1 – 1 November
Gellert	Special Commentary – 2 November
Szabo	Special London Press Review #H1 – 3 November

(More detailed characterizations of these and all other programs are given in Appendix I)[209]

After the second Russian intervention the VFH, in response to continual requests from the Freedom Stations which still remained on the air for several days, continued its regular series of service programs and special announcements devoted to repeating messages from these Freedom Stations, as requested by them. In this way, the VFH undoubtedly served as a useful communications link between the Freedom Stations and groups of Freedom Fighters holding out in various parts of the country. Freedom Station messages were generally rebroadcast without comment.

At the same time, as the flow of refugees into Austria began, the VFH began a daily series of special programs devoted to repeating messages of safe arrival and greeting to their families and friends in Hungary from these refugees. This important service is continuing.

III. TECHNIQUE AND TONE

The previous section has been confined to a discussion of specific policy violations and policy implementation problems. It is difficult, however, to separate the question of policy implementation from the problem of application of sound techniques of radio broadcasting and political warfare. As I have stated in the Introduction, the following remarks on tone and technique are not presented as final, but as our impressions, for such value as they may be to the Program Department in their survey on this subject.

In general, reading of these 308 scripts indicates that the primary reason, in our opinion, why the VFH fell short of expectations during the first phase of the Hungarian Revolution was *not* that competent policy guidance was not given, nor that this guidance was not understood and implemented at least by the desk chief and a number of writers (though a sizable portion of other writers did not understand or agree with this guidance and the senior subordinates of the desk chief appear either to have failed to understand or were incapable of enforcing guidance in positive and constructive fashion) *but* that too many of the writers of the desk used bad techniques of writing and presenting the material over the air and were permitted to do so by the leadership of the desk. Instead of withstanding the emotional stresses of the time, the desk seems to have

---

[209] Not printed here.

478

succumbed to them. The principal errors and shortcomings of technique and tone, all of which are especially characteristic of the programming of the 23 October–4 November period seem to us to be as follows:

(1) *The VFH talked too much.* Too many original commentaries were broadcast. With so much being written and put on the air so hurriedly, it is not surprising that the desk chief and the senior editors had difficulty editing the output of the desk adequately. Many programs show no real evidence of having been edited at all. Except for insuring that general policy lines were at least formally complied with, the desk chief seems to have been unable either to infuse a common thread of basic ideas into VFH's programming or to enforce adherence to sound techniques of broadcasting. (His increasingly bad health during this period was certainly a contributing factor in this aspect.)

(2) *Many Hungarian editors show too little understanding for sound radio techniques.* Their programs are seldom written around a single idea or set of ideas. *The technique of repetition* is not constructively used. Writers tend to talk *at* their listeners or even *down to* them. A feeling of identification with the audience is too often lacking. Listeners are seldom encouraged to think or to draw their own conclusions on the basis of the information presented to them. Finally, VFH programming gives no impression of organic unity. If commentaries were intended to complement each other, press reviews to supplement and elaborate upon ideas put forth in newscasts and commentaries, this does not become evident from the reading of any single day's programs.

(3) *Probably the most serious fault of all is the tone of the broadcasts.* With some encouraging exceptions, writers sound too much like "emigrés" talking from a safe vantage point outside. There is violent denunciation of Communists and Russians and Rakosi but during the first week of the Revolution in particular there is relatively little reference to actual events in the country. The broadcasts tend to be too subjective. Many programs display no feeling of humility on the part of the VFH vis-a-vis the people in the country. Praise of the Hungarian people is too bombastic and rhetorical. Too few writers appear willing to admit that the situation inside the country may be so complex that they are not qualified to give listeners specific advise on what to do. They remind their listeners too rarely that they lack complete information about what is going on in the country. (One gets the impression that some VFH editors felt it beneath their dignity to admit that they were not omniscient about happenings in Hungary.) Since some writers were occasionally careless about using unconfirmed information—some of which we now know to have been wrong—this pose of omniscience is doubly unfortunate, for listeners in the country must sometimes have realized when hearing these programs that their writers did not know as much as they pretended to. If VFH editors had used caution and understatement more frequently, their broadcasts would have sounded less offensive to the critical ears of their countrymen.

(4) *Editors appear to have been reluctant to use the material from the "Freedom Stations"* during the first few days they were broadcasting, in spite of our urgings to them to do so. (It is to be hoped that this material was at least covered in the news.) A special program featuring material from the freedom stations was inaugurated on 31 October. After this time, reference to the broadcasts of the freedom stations and declarations of the local revolutionary councils was from time to time also made in commentaries, but by no means frequently enough. Careful quotations and repetition from broadcasts of the freedom stations and citation of the views of the revolutionary councils would have done much to remove the impression of émigré rhetoric which many political commentaries give, even when they are propagating ideas quite in accordance with policy guidance.

(5) Although there were relatively few programs which give instructions to the population in any direct way, *writers sometimes used imperative phraseology which might easily have given the impression that the VFH was trying to tell Hungarians what to do.* In some programs workers were urged to continue the strike, revolutionaries to continue fighting and farmers were advised to oppose Communist efforts to intimidate them. Writers obvious-

479

ly found it hard to avoid giving direct advice and the responsible editors in the desk seem to have been far less alert about changing such passages than they should have been. The most regrettable thing about this tendency to offer advice is the fact that such advice was probably unnecessary. When it was felt to be necessary, it should have been given (as we constantly advised) in the form of quotations from suitable material from the freedom stations, not on the responsibility of the VFH. Writers apparently failed to realize that the credibility of VFH broadcasts would have been greatly enhanced if listeners had been informed directly that the VFH was merely providing a louder voice for the desires and demands of the leading forces of the revolution in the homeland, rather then giving advice itself.

(6) *The propaganda arts of subtlety, insinuation, implication and understatement were too infrequently used* by VFH. Instead, the editors sometimes stated obvious and simple truths in bombastic fashion, telling listeners over and over again they could hardly help know better than anyone on the outside. Denunciations were all too often violent; irony when used was heavy; metaphors were crude. Scripts were replete with rhetorical clichés.

(7) *Certain programs tended to arouse false hopes and expectations of aid from the outside.* Many writers repeated promises of support made by Western officials and newspapers in such a way as to imply (albeit not to state) that more than moral support and medical aid was intended. This may not have been the intention of most of these writers—they projected their own wishful thinking into their programs. The leadership of the desk should have used more care in making clear to listeners that only moral support—and no military aid—was likely from the West under the circumstances. A relatively more pessimistic evaluation of the possibility of aid would have been less likely to be misunderstood and would have been in the long run more appropriate than over-optimism. Programs on the UN (many of them from the New York Desk) were too optimistic in tone; for several days they made no mention at all of the certainty of a Soviet veto in the Security Council. When the USSR vetoed the Hungarian issue in the Security Council, this development was also rather glossed over, and relatively exaggerated hopes for General A[ss]embly action were projected to Hungary. Only after 4 November did broadcasting on the UN possibilities become realistic. Press reviews of many kinds contributed to the impression that, variously, the UN, the US, or other elements in the West would find some concrete way to aid Hungarian revolutionaries.

(8) *The technique of some press reviews was bad.* Excessively long quotations of editorial opinion were given with no identification of the material except at the beginning of the excerpt and no further identification of the program as a press review, even at the end, was made. At least one program called a press review was devoted mostly to accounts of what domestic Western radio stations (less likely to be fully informed than RFE) were saying. Programs such as these could easily have led desperate listeners to have false hopes. It should be stressed, however, that actual assurances of Western military aid were *not* made. (It should be noted that some press reviewers employ outstandingly good technique, identifying their material repeatedly and selecting it skillfully.) False hopes and naively optimistic estimates of the military situation were directly encouraged by a group of commentaries (discussed in Section II above) broadcast at the end of October and beginning of November. (It should be kept in mind that the above listing of shortcomings is based almost exclusively on *reading* scripts; listening to tapes of these programs as actually broadcast might in some cases mitigate and in others accentuate some of the faults noted.) Fully half of the programs read for this survey from the 23 October–4 November period displayed a combination of several of the errors of tone and technique discussed above. VFH programming was probably at its worst in this respect from 26–30 October. Some improvement occurred on 31 October and continued through the first three days of November. Throughout this whole first period, it is a pleasure to observe,

several completely sound and acceptable programs were broadcast every day. Approximately 30% of the programs of this period can be classified as competent or extremely well done. This "minority group" of programs was almost devoid of the errors of tone and technique which characterized the dominant strain of programming during the period. The outstanding programs were more often than not written by writers who are not normally the major political commentators of the desk; they are also, as a group, predominantly "left-of-center" politically in terms of the desk political spectrum.

The fact that a minority of the desk's writers were able to produce excellent commentaries, many of which implemented policy in genuinely creative and imaginative fashion, makes the failure of the majority all the more serious. It is true that the whole Hungarian Desk was nervous, excited and subject to a dozen kinds of strains and stresses during these hectic days. However, to recognize that the desk was tense and excited is not to excuse it for performing ineffectively. As with a military unit, so in political warfare: the battle is the pay-off. An RFE desk should be organized so that it can successfully meet the severest test to which it is likely to be put, so that it can implement policy in constructive fashion, enforce good techniques and maintain sound tone in its broadcasts under the pressure of a crisis. The Hungarian Desk was not so organized and its leadership was not competent: for this reason it fell short of passing its supreme test.

On November 4, the day of the second Russian intervention, the VFH still broadcast too much original material (there were at least 21 commentaries of one sort or another). This happened in spite of the fact that Gellert had specifically agreed to my suggestion that morning that commentaries would be discontinued immediately and told me he had so ordered. During the period 4–23 November no serious policy violations occurred and techniques improved somewhat. Nearly half of the scripts read for this period can nevertheless be classified as still exhibiting some combination of the errors of technique listed above, while somewhat less than 40% of the programs for this period can be classed as good or excellent. A considerable proportion of the scripts from this period can be regarded as neither god nor bad, but inconsequential. Many of them ramble aimlessly, carry no particular message and come to no real conclusion. They would probably have been better not broadcast.

IV. CONCLUSIONS

(1) There is no evidence in the 308 scripts read in this survey that the VFH could have *incited* the Hungarian Revolution—i.e., caused it to begin. An additional 50 political programs from the period 1–22 October have been surveyed (See Appendix IV for a detailed discussion of these programs).[210] They reveal no policy violations, relatively few policy distortions and generally better technique than the VFH's later programming. There is *no evidence* from any of these programs *that the VFH had an inciting tone* during this period.

(2) The VFH (with one exception) made no *direct* promise or commitment of Western or UN military support or intervention. Its broadcasts may well, however, have encouraged Hungarians to have false hopes in this respect; they carefully did little or nothing to counteract them.

(3) Of the four policy violations and approximately 20 cases of misapplication or distortion of policy discovered in the 308 scripts read, three represent instructions on fighting which put the VFH in the position of attempting to direct its listeners; one uses western press comment in such a way as to imply, although not state, that western aid is coming. The other scripts which represent distortion and non-constructive application of policy, reveal an unrefined political viewpoint and poor technique (e.g., the frequent violent, "black and white" denunciation of Nagy; note, however, that General Crittenberger's[211] directive of 2 November ordering cessation of attacks on Nagy was followed).

(4) The VFH failed to measure up policy-wise to the challenge of the Hungarian Revolution primarily because of the predominance of incompetent personnel in positions of major

[210] Not printed here.

[211] Willis D. Crittenberger was chairman of the Free Europe Committee from October 1, 1956 to 1959.

importance on the desk. Most importantly, these desk personnel who approved scripts did not ensure that policy was implemented (or that proper broadcast technique and tone were used). This failure on their part arose, in my opinion, from their lack of sufficient powers of political analysis, propaganda ability, and radio technique.

(5) The Desk Chief, although a clear-headed analyst of events and a good originator of propaganda lines, failed to enforce the same degree of calm analytical approach on his chief subordinates. Though he throughout gave to us and others every indication of understanding and agreement with the policy given him, he failed to see that policy guidance was constructively enforced among his subordinates. The state of his health was apparently worse than he realized or admitted; this compounded his failure to exercise sufficient policy control. Though we were quite aware that the internal organization of the Hungarian Desk left much to be desired (and had in the past urged that more adequate top subordinates to the Desk Chief be found), we had assumed that the Desk Chief's return would mean that policy would be positively enforced (as it was in general in the period before October 23). This assumption was incorrect. In our opinion, the Desk Chief attempted to compromise with recalcitrant rightist forces in the Desk too frequently during the first stage of the Revolution (particularly in allowing to much and too violent denunciation of Nagy and in not enforcing the use and citation of Freedom Stations) and made impermissible concessions to some of his subordinates, in terms of policy application and adherence to sound techniques to avoid dissatisfaction. Our estimate of his capability to enforce policy must be revised downward.

(6) Senior political commentators of the VFH proved themselves unable to understand the nature of the revolutionary developments in Hungary or the role which the VFH would and should legitimately play in them. Policy violations and distortions centered in three senior editors.

(7) We did not detect policy violations and distortions as early as we should have. With few exceptions, there was no indication of them in the desk-prepared summaries for the morning policy meetings; in one case, my oral instructions to revise a program were not carried out. Lack of translation and summarizing facilities seriously handicapped us in detection of violations. There were and are too few Hungarian-speaking Americans in RFE/Munich capable of listening to and to some degree judging policy compliance and programming technique of programs in such a crisis period. Our one such person (Rademaekers) had to spend almost full time keeping us briefed on the rapidly changing Hungarian situation (from monitoring of regime-controlled and freedom stations); we would otherwise not have been able either to give proper policy guidance to the desk nor to have reported adequately to New York.

(8) Given the American personnel available and current responsible desk personnel, an imposition of a greater degree of American control during this period (e.g., pre-broadcast screening by us of all political commentaries) would have *helped somewhat* but would *not have prevented* most of the errors the VFH made during this period, since they very frequently did not occur in political commentaries. One way of avoiding many of the worst errors committed by the VFH during the Revolution would have been to order a drastic curtailment of its original programming as soon as the crisis began. Commentaries in particular should have been severely limited. If the desk had said less, what it did say probably would have been said much better.

(Note: The following conclusion (9) on technique and tone relates to the area of the Program Department, and is presented here for such use as it may be to them.)

(9) The *most* regrettable feature of most of the VFH programs was *not* their relatively few policy violations, but their *offense against the cannons of good political warfare and broadcasting technique*. They delivered in a bombastic and imperative tone a message

482

which could have been conveyed in the form of reports on and repetition of the information coming out of Hungary, particularly that from the Freedom Stations. The VFH told Hungarians things they either already knew or could not in any case have been taught at the last minute by radio. The mere fact that the VFH broadcast so much advice, whether it was needed or not, puts RFE in the position of appearing to have wanted to direct or supervise the Revolution.

(10) Generally (and there are exceptions), the VFH editors who transgressed the most against policy, tone and technique were "rightists" in terms of the VFH political spectrum. They, more than others, were incapable of grasping the true situation in the country and writing in accordance with it. Specifically, they attacked Nagy in a tone more violent than was justified by the Freedom Station broadcasts.

V. RECOMMENDATIONS

(1) A reorganization of the Hungarian Desk should be undertaken. Organizationally, it should aim to establish an internal structure of control within the desk, and competent personnel in the top positions, which will guarantee that policy guidance is effectively transmitted from the Desk Chief to the editors actually writing the programs (and that effective techniques of writing and production are uniformly adhered to in all the Desk's broadcasts). This can only take place if senior personnel responsible for advising writers on the political and propaganda content of their scripts are able to guide these writers on the basis of a correct analysis of the situation in Hungary and a proper implementation of policy (and use of propaganda techniques) in respect to it. From the policy viewpoint, I do not think that the present personnel exercising these functions fulfill these requirements. Politically, the reorganization should attempt to correct the imbalance to the "right" which has existed in the desk from its inception. The composition of the desk (particularly of its senior editors) should be made to reflect more accurately the actual political composition of Hungary as revealed during the Revolution, rather than (as up to now) that of the emigration as represented in the Hungarian National Council. This could be best done by employing the most qualified of the fresh refugees now pouring into Austria, while weeding out stale and incompetent writers and editors now in the desk.

(2) In view of the Desk Chief's health during this period, which certainly played a large part in his failure to enforce policy, consideration should be given to having him take a long leave of absence to recover his full energies. He is unlikely to be in sympathy with our policies in the period to come, particularly if the Kadar Government again becomes liberalized in the Nagy direction. More importantly, however, he will probably be unwilling to make the necessary personnel changes to insure policy implementation. Personnel changes are of course matters for you and the Program Department, not for us, to decide. However, I must advise you and them, from the policy viewpoint, that in my opinion the present Desk Chief has not been in the period since October 23, and is not likely to be in the future, an adequate guarantee for policy enforcement. It would be in my opinion advisable to begin a search for a replacement.

I append below some recommendation (3–5) which the Program Department may wish to consider; they relate to tone and broadcast technique.

(3) Original broadcasting time should be cut; specifically, political commentaries on internal Hungarian affairs should be restricted to no more than two per day.

(4) Editors writing press reviews should be schooled on proper technique for this kind of program. Press reviews should be more carefully checked for content and technique by competent senior editors before put on the air.

(5) The Hungarian program schedule should be revised and the broadcast techniques and prop-

aganda methods restudied so as to emphasize informative rather than polemic methods.

(6) Translation facilities should be expounded so that they will be able to satisfy RFE needs during emergencies without undue strain. All important scripts should be translated no later than 24 hours after broadcast.

(7) To assure rapid monitoring and policy control of broadcasts in such critical periods, the number of Hungarian-speaking Americans engaged in this work should be increased. Specifically, I recommend that our office be authorized to hire one additional Policy Assistant for this purpose.

(8) When doubt exists (as it must until new supervisory desk personnel have proved their competence), commentaries relating to Hungarian internal affairs must be read in translation and approved for broadcast by this office before broadcast. (This recommendation is already in effect).

[Source: From the collection of Simon Bourgin. On file at the National Security Archive, "Soviet Flashpoints" Collection.]

DOCUMENT NO. 106: Vladimir Baikov's Telegram to the CPSU CC Suggesting a Multilateral Meeting on the "Imre Nagy Group," December 28, 1956

At the very end of December 1956, Kádár found himself facing a new and unexpected challenge: he was informed by the Romanian leadership that Zoltán Szántó, one of the detainees from the Nagy group in Romania, would soon be returned to Hungary. By this time, Kádár was feeling more secure in his position since it was highly unlikely that either of his two main rivals, Rákosi or Nagy, could now replace him. Szántó, however was not only an experienced party leader (he had been a Communist since 1918), but a Muscovite who had worked for the Comintern in the 1930s. He thus might have seemed more reliable in Soviet eyes than Kádár, whom the Kremlin saw as a neophyte, who did not speak Russian, and who had spent time in jail, which was a black mark on anyone's record. Szántó on the other hand had done nothing blameworthy during the revolution; his main offense was having joined the Nagy group at the Yugoslav Embassy. The Romanian leadership's message was therefore somewhat alarming for Kádár since he was unsure whether the impetus for Szántó's return had originated in Moscow. In the document below, Kádár asks the Soviet leadership, through his liaison officer, to call a meeting of the three parties concerned to clarify matters, and to develop a joint strategy for dealing with the Nagy group.

DECEMBER 28, 1956

CPSU CC

Comrade Kádár asked me to inform you that at present he does not consider Zoltán Szántó's return to Hungary from Romania to be reasonable, as his presence would complicate the political situation in the country.

Comrade Kádár considers it necessary to inform the Soviet comrades of the fact that, according to the statement of Comrade Marosán (member of the HSWP CC Executive Committee, Minister of State), Comrade Gheorghiu-Dej and other Romanian leaders traveled from Bucharest especially to Transylvania where he [Marosán] spent the Christmas holidays. Comrade Dej informed Comrade Marosán of the fact that the Romanian comrades told Zoltán Szántó that he would soon be allowed to return to Hungary.[212]

According to Comrade Marosán's statement, Gheorghiu-Dej would like to invite György Lukács and his wife to a New Year's dinner.[213]

As Comrade Kádár is aware of the Soviet comrades' position, according to which the time has not yet come for Szántó to travel to Hungary, he requests that Gheorghiu-Dej, Walter Roman[214] and the other Romanian comrades be asked not to force Szántó's return home and to show special attentiveness toward the members of the Nagy group.

Comrade Kádár thinks that any one-sided act concerning the Imre Nagy group would only complicate the political situation in Hungary. In connection with this, Comrade Kádár requests that the Soviet comrades get acquainted with the statement of Zoltán Szántó, György Lukács and Zoltán Vas[215], and other materials to be found with other Romanian comrades concerning the Imre Nagy group. They should then discuss whether it would be reasonable to convene a con-

---

[212] Szántó was brought back to Hungary only for the period of the trial and remained in Romania until the autumn of 1958.

[213] Besides Szántó, the Romanian leadership tried to turn others against Imre Nagy, including György Lukács. But although Lukács disagreed with Nagy on many things, he was unwilling to testify against him.

[214] Walter Roman, a member of the RWP CC who knew Nagy from their time in the Soviet Union, maintained contacts—on party orders—with members of the Nagy group while they were in Romania.

[215] No joint statement by these individuals has yet been found. On December 17, 1956, Szántó nevertheless wrote a report to the Kádár government accusing Nagy and the others of maintaining secret contacts with the Yugoslav leadership long before the outbreak of the revolution, and claimed that they consciously prepared and led the uprising.

ference of accredited members of the CPSU, RSP[216] and the HSWP CC to debate common steps to be taken in connection with the "Imre Nagy group."[217]

Besides this, Comrade Kádár requests the Soviet comrades to discuss with Zhou Enlai that he should visit Hungary during his trip to Poland.[218]

BAIKOV

RECEPTION: HIGH-FREQUENCY TELEGRAM
DECEMBER 28, 1956

[Source: APRF, F. 3. Op. 64. D. 490. pp. 76–77. Document obtained and footnotes prepared by Vyacheslav Sereda. Translated by Attila Kolontári.]

[216] This should be RWP (Romanian Workers' Party)

[217] Khrushchev discussed this proposal with Kádár the next day. By then, Kádár was already talking about increasing the number of parties to be invited to the meeting, proposing to include the Bulgarian and Czechoslovak leaders as well. See the headnote for the next document.

[218] Following his visit to the Soviet Union and Poland, Chinese Prime Minister Zhou Enlai did indeed visit Hungary on January 16–17, 1957, to show Chinese support for the Kádár government. See Document No. 109.

DOCUMENT NO. 107: Memorandum from Boris Ponomarev to the CPSU CC on the Hungarian Government's Draft Declaration concerning "Major Tasks," December 29, 1956

This document reveals the main motivation behind the Soviet leadership's hasty call for a meeting of the five Communist countries in Budapest between January 1–4, 1957 (see Document No. 108). On December 29, the CPSU Presidium learned that a forthcoming Hungarian Government declaration was going to include a paragraph on legalizing the existence of non-Communist political parties. This prospect raised such alarms in Moscow that the Presidium immediately decided to send Khrushchev and Malenkov to Budapest on January 1. When Khrushchev called Kádár after the meeting to inform him of the visit, Kádár, who had asked for a trilateral meeting on the Nagy issue just the previous day (see Document No. 106), argued that the Czechoslovak, Romanian and Bulgarian parties should also be represented at the meeting.[219] Kádár was probably trying to widen the scope of the discussion in part to include the practical implications of the October 30 Soviet Government declaration (see Document No. 50). He apparently also wanted to use the occasion to come to a joint solution on the fate of the Nagy group.

DECEMBER 29, 1956

For the Central Committee of the CPSU

On behalf of Cde. Kádár, the text of the document entitled "The Declaration of the Revolutionary Workers' and Peasants' Government Concerning the Major Tasks" was dispatched from Budapest.

Cde. Kádár asked me to hand over this document to the Presidium of the CPSU CC.

In case there are any remarks from the CPSU CC, they will be considered by the Central Committee of the Hungarian Socialist Workers' Party.

Cde. Kádár asked me to convey that the text that is being delivered has not received a final edit.

The HSWP CC's plenum of December 28 this year had a preliminary look through the draft of the declaration, but it has not made a final decision concerning this matter. The final decision and the publication of the declaration are planned for January 5–6, 1957.[220]

Cde. Kádár also requested that I inform you that a point is missing from the draft declaration which describes the HSWP's relations with other parties and which says that the Hungarian government relies on the patriotic bloc of all those parties that acknowledge the policy of building socialism. In the same part of the declaration the government announces that they will allow an organization consisting only of the other parties' central organs and that the creation of some local organizations of these parties will not be allowed.[221]

This part of the declaration will be forwarded to the CPSU CC later.

---

[219] For the record of the telephone conversation, see *APRF F. 3. Op. 64. D. 490. L. 79.*

[220] Although the CC decided to meet again on January 3 to discuss the document further, the meeting was canceled and the issue was not raised again by either the HSWP CC or the government. The principal points of the "Resolution of the Hungarian Workers' Peasants' Government concerning the most important tasks" were thus determined by the meeting of communist party leaders on January 1–4, and the document was published on January 6, together with the communiqué of the latter meeting (see Document No. 108). For the minutes of the HSWP CC meeting on December 28, see A Magyar Szocialista Munkáspárt ideiglenes vezető testületeinek jegyzőkönyvei, vol. 1, 281–298.

[221] The published version of the government declaration eventually omitted the reference to a Patriotic Bloc and made no mention of any possibility for other parties to pursue their activities. The text made only a vague, and eventually broken, promise to "start negotiations with public factors [sic] of other party or non-party [affiliations]."

HEAD OF THE CPSU CC
DEPARTMENT FOR TIES WITH FOREIGN
COMMUNIST PARTIES
B. PONOMAREV

[Source: APRF, F. 3. Op. 64. D. 490. p. 85. Document obtained and footnotes written by Vyacheslav Sereda. Translated by Attila Kolontári.]

DOCUMENT NO. 108: Romanian and Czechoslovak Minutes on the Meeting of Five East European States' Leaders in Budapest (with Attached Final Communiqué), January 1–4, 1957

The following three documents deal with an extremely important Warsaw Pact summit meeting that had been called on very short notice to deal mainly with Hungary's internal situation. Despite the fact that it was originally proposed by the HSWP (see Document No. 106), and then insisted upon by Moscow (for different reasons), no Hungarian or Soviet minutes have yet been found. Nevertheless, the Czechoslovak memorandum and Romanian abstract presented below make it possible to reconstruct most of the issues that were discussed. (The latter memo was written in 1960 on the basis of a contemporary Romanian document.) As indicated above, the Kremlin's main reason for convening the summit was to discuss a forthcoming public declaration by the Kádár government, which alarmed Moscow because it contained a provision that would allow non-Communist parties a role, albeit a sharply limited one, in Hungary. Kádár had sent a draft version of the proposal to Moscow for approval, but had been ambiguous about this key passage which had become a political issue of some importance inside the Hungarian party (See Document No. 107). As these internal documents indicate, the Soviets and their colleagues at the meeting were insistent that the provision be struck before the declaration was due to be made public on January 5–6. Interestingly, the final communique made no mention of the multi-party issue. Another major topic discussed at the session—and the reason for Kádár's original request that it be convened—was the fate of the Imre Nagy group. While even these documents do not reveal the actual positions taken by the participants, it is clear that the meeting yielded crucial decisions, which opened the way for the trial and ultimately execution of the former prime minister. One of the most important points about this meeting was that it may have been the first time that the members of the Warsaw Pact[222] jointly and directly intervened into the internal politics of another member state. In this way, it recalls the later attempts by the Warsaw Pact—not just the Soviet Union alone—to put an end to the Prague Spring in Czechoslovakia in 1968.

[ROMANIAN MEMORANDUM]

Participants of the Conference among the Soviet Union, Bulgaria, Hungary and Romania.[223]

I. First session:

1. Information [provided] by comrade Kádár:
   - The situation of the party.
   - ca. 100,000 people were recruited.
   - The party has organizations in ca. 42 percent of the villages.
   - The lower party activists are more homogenous and active concerning the events and Nagy.
   - There is no unity within the Central Committee - 3–4 members have undesirable views:[224]

   a) There is no consolidation without Nagy
   b) The government must be enlarged
   c) The principal enemy is Rákosi
      They are talking of Rákosism and Stalinism
   d) They are supported by the Yugoslavs.

---

[222] Poland, the GDR and Albania were not invited to the session, at least partly because of the ad hoc nature of the meeting. In the case of Poland, there was also serious political mistrust of the Gomułka regime and a general intent to strengthen the "orthodox" communist line.

[223] Although omitted from this list, representatives from Czechoslovakia also participated in the meeting.

[224] Five officials within the Hungarian leadership at this time represented a more liberal policy line: József Köböl, György Aczél, Lajos Fehér, Antal Gyenes and Sándor Nógrádi.

- The above-mentioned 3–4 are rushing the enlargement of the government and pushing the new government to make a statement. This opinion is shared by others from the outside as well.
- Comrade Kádár maintains that the government in its present form should issue a statement.
- [The government] should convoke the parliament.
- Representatives should be co-opted.
- The presidium should be strengthened.[225]

2. The issue of the formation of two more parties is raised: the National Peasant Party and the Independent Peasant Party.[226]

- The formation of the Patriotic National Front,[227] with whom [the Party] could go together to the elections. (Some people would have liked to have the elections in May this year.)
- 20–25 percent more candidates should be nominated for the elections.
- The formation of the Peasant Union was proposed in the Central Committee; this was refused by saying that the party has organizations in only 42 percent of the villages.[228]
- There were attempts to activate the trade unions.
- The Social democrats will not openly take a stand against the government, but they are present in the trade unions in order to collect friends.
- They [the Politburo members] propose to organize the workers' councils along professional or occupational lines.

3. They will propose the restoration of constitutional activity [sic.] in the sense of setting up courts of law.

- There is no common standpoint concerning the fight against counterrevolution.
- They *are not* taking firm measures; they want unanimity (Münnich)[229]
- Some believe the principal danger to be Rákosi and "Rákosism"

4. Some economic problems:

- There is a shortage of commodities in the Public supply (in September they had commodities in the value of 13 billion, today they have only in the value of 3 billion and further 8 billion is needed).
- During the strikes, they gave 30 percent *extra* salaries.
- They have a 200 billion dollar debt to the West.[230]
- They propose the reexamination of the arms orders.
- There is a danger of inflation and unemployment.

II. Second session. (discussion concerning the program communiqué)[231]

- There are many improvements compared to the previous draft.
- Our comments and proposals.

[225] This probably refers to the HSWP Provisional Executive Committee, the equivalent of the Political Committee.

[226] The accurate name of the party referred to is: Független Kisgazdapárt (Independent Smallholders' Party).

[227] More accurately, the Patriotic People's Front.

[228] The Provisional Central Committee dealt with this issue at its December 28 session.

[229] This comment was probably added by Ferenc Münnich.

[230] This is obviously an error; Hungary's debt to Western countries never reached this amount. They probably meant to say 200 million.

[231] This refers to the detailed discussion of the Hungarian government declaration published in *Népszabadság* on January 6, 1957.

a) There should be an introductory part with the analysis of the past activities of Rákosi and Nagy; the perspectives and the tasks have to be outlined clearly.

b) It is not clear what kind of organizational forms they want, and why is it necessary to organize the workers' councils according professional or occupational lines.

c) The notion that culture should be national in form and content is incorrect.

d) University autonomy:

- The peasant problem
- The problem of small producers and tradesmen.
- The problem of the multiparty [system]
- The Nagy group.

5. The opinion of the rest of the delegates.

6. Consultations outside of the session.

- Trials of [Mihály] Farkas, Maléter, [János] Szabó, Dudás.
- The question of the return of the Nagy group.

Conclusion:
- The Hungarian comrades' evaluation of the conference.
- The perfecting of the proposed declaration.
- The Nagy case will be investigated.[232]
- They will send a delegate to speak with the Nagy group and they will answer to our government.[233]
- Their opinion on Szántó and Lukács.
- The Soviet comrades' conversations with the leadership of the Hungarian Party.[234]

8. Other problems:

- The cooperation between the Soviet Union and the socialist countries.
- Questions concerning Stalin.
- The Bulgarian comrades propose a conference between the two governments and the release of a joint statement.[235]

[Source: Archiva Birolului Politic al CC al PMR, Nr. 2/56, 1956. Document obtained by Mihai Retegan. Translated by József Litkei and István Török.]

***

[232] See the way this point appears in the Czechoslovak document: "The responsibility and accountability of Imre Nagy and others in the Hungarian events, and their legal consequences." Since the Hungarian sources currently available make no reference to any previous plan to put Nagy and his accomplices on trial, it seems very likely that the Hungarian leadership made this crucial decision during the summit, probably under pressure from the other communist parties.

[233] In January 1957, Kádár sent Gyula Kállai to Bucharest with a plan to divide the Nagy group and induce them, more than anything else, to practice self-criticism. While in Bucharest, Kállai also consulted with Romanian and Soviet leaders.

[234] No document on bilateral Hungarian-Soviet talks during the summit has yet been found.

[235] The two governments concerned are most likely Bulgaria and the Soviet Union, which did indeed issue a joint declaration on February 20, 1957.

Prompted by comrade Khrushchev, a meeting of party delegations was held in Budapest, between January 1 and 3, 1957.

Cde. Kádár asked the CPSU CC for a consultation about some problems of future development in Hungary.

Moscow and Bucharest were both suggested for hosting the meeting. On the proposal of the Soviet comrades, the meeting was held in Budapest with representatives of the following parties: Bulgaria, Romania, the Soviet Union, Czechoslovakia and Hungary.

Delegates present: comrades Zhivkov, Damyanov, Dej, Borilă, Moghioroş, Khrushchev, Malenkov, Novotný, Siroký, Kádár and Münnich.

Agenda:

1. Kádár provides information about the situation in Hungary.
2. Questions and problems concerning the election (prohlaseni) of the government of the Hungarian People's Republic.[237]
3. The responsibility and accountability of Imre Nagy and others in the Hungarian events, and their legal consequences. (zákonné závery)
4. Returning of some members of the Nagy-group to Hungary. (Szántó-Lukács)[238]
5. The Soviet comrades' information about Yugoslavia:
   a. the answer to Tito's letter[239]
   b. problems of the Soviet aid
   c. Yugoslav influence in Hungarian events.
6. Soviet information on the plenary session of the CC in December 1956.
7. Information about the negotiations with Poland.

[Hand-written notes, hardly legible, possibly by Siroký].
[by the name of Zoltán Szántó:]
   "dopis - ninal ?"
   Secretary-general

(concerning the 2nd point of the agenda)
   on convoking the parl[iament]
   decreasing state administration with 35%[240]

---

[236] Although the Czechoslovak memorandum indicates that negotiations occurred between January 1 and 3, the joint communiqué issued after the meeting lists the dates as January 1–4.

[237] This probably refers to the uncertain legality of the Kádár government's formation, which took place in Moscow on November 3, outside the provisions of the constitution. Although the new cabinet was sworn in on November 7 before István Dobi, president of the Presidential Council, the Presidential Council as a body never discussed the matter beforehand. News that the Presidential Council had dismissed the Nagy government and, with Decision No. 28, appointed the Kádár government in its place did not appear in the Hungarian Bulletin until November 12. From the perspective of the legitimacy of the Hungarian Revolutionary Workers' and Peasants' Government, Prime Minister Nagy and State Minister Losonczy's official resignations would therefore have been critically important.

[238] György Lukács and Zoltán Szántó were part of the group that sought asylum at the Yugoslav Embassy. They were forcibly taken to Romania, from where Lukács was allowed to return to Hungary in April 1957 and Szántó in 1958.

[239] This most probably refers to Tito's letter to Khrushchev on December 3, 1956, which the Soviet leader answered only on January 10, 1957. See Document No. 103.

[240] In December 1956, the Kádár government passed a decree that eliminated or merged certain ministries and organs with country-wide authority. It also made the decision to reduce the state apparatus by one-third during 1957.

about workers' councils
Party and people's front
                3 parties —   ours
                                  smallholders' party
                                  christian dem[ocratic] party[241]
reforms — permitting small-scale industry, peasant problem
autonomy of universities
crimes of Rákosi and others
crimes of the Nagy-group

signature: S. [Široký?]

[Source: AÚV KSČ, F. 07/16. Document obtained by Tibor Hajdú. Translated by Csaba Farkas.]

***

COMMUNIQUÉ ON THE MEETING OF REPRESENTATIVES OF THE GOVERNMENTS AND THE COMMUNIST AND WORKERS' PARTIES OF BULGARIA, CZECHOSLOVAKIA, HUNGARY, ROMANIA AND THE SOVIET UNION

BUDAPEST, JANUARY 6, 1957.

Invited by the leadership of the Hungarian Revolutionary Workers' and Peasants' Government and the Hungarian Socialist Workers' Party, Comrades Zhivkov and Damyanov representing the Bulgarian Communist Party and the government of the Bulgarian People's Republic; Comrades Novotný and Široký representing the Communist Party of Czechoslovakia and the government of the Czechoslovak Republic; Comrades Gheorghiu-Dej, Moghioroş and Borilă representing the Romanian Workers' Party and the government of the Romanian People's Republic; and Comrades Khrushchev and Malenkov representing the Communist Party of the Soviet Union and the government of the Soviet Union arrived in Budapest on January 1, 1957.

Between January 1–4 of this year, the representatives of the governments and parties of the above-mentioned nations conducted negotiations attended by Comrades Zhivkov and Damyanov (Bulgaria), Comrades Novotný and Široký (Czechoslovakia), Comrades Kádár and Münnich (Hungary), Comrades Gheorghiu-Dej, Moghioroş and Borilă (Romania) and Comrades Khrushchev and Malenkov (Soviet Union).

The participants conducted friendly and comradely negotiations on a number of political and economic issues of mutual interest as well as on questions concerning the situation of the parties and current international problems.

The meetings' participants each informed the others on the situation of their respective countries and parties.

The participants expressed their contentment with the fact that Bulgaria, Czechoslovakia, Romania and the Soviet Union, just as all the other socialist countries, had achieved new and great successes in building socialism and communism. The Hungarian economy had made successful [sic] progress on the socialist road of development. It was this development that was thwarted by

---

[241] In all probability, Kádár is referring here to the National Peasant Party, which appears in the text as third after the HSWP and the Smallholders' party. The Christian Democratic Party was not even a member of the governing coalition between 1945 and 1948, and in December 1956 and at the beginning of 1957 it was by no means considered at the level of a negotiating partner by the Kádár government.

the attack of the counterrevolutionary forces. At the moment, after having repressed the counter-revolution, the socialist economy of the Hungarian People's Republic has started developing again and is showing clear signs of strength. In the past few years the countries of the socialist camp have fulfilled the economic plans with success and achieved new results in enhancing the welfare of their people; there are clear signs of development in culture, science and technology. Under the mighty banner of Marxism-Leninism the peoples of these countries have further strengthened their unity with their communist and workers' parties and with their governments.

The participants of the meeting unanimously concluded that as a result of the efforts of the Hungarian workers, with the leadership of the Hungarian Revolutionary Workers' and Peasants' Government and with the support of the Soviet army, the attempts to eliminate the socialist achievements of the Hungarian people and their people's democratic system were successfully prevented. The danger of establishing a fascist dictatorship in Hungary was eliminated, and [the people] prevented the aggressive imperialist and counterrevolutionary circles from turning Hungary into the storm-center of a new war in Europe. They firmly shattered any attempts on the part of the imperialist circles to break the unity of the socialist camp.

The representatives of the communist and workers' parties and the governments participating at the meeting all expressed their satisfaction with the normalization of the Hungarian political situation and economic life. All the healthy and democratic forces of the country, led by the working class, are making united efforts to support the Hungarian Revolutionary Workers' and Peasants' Government and the Hungarian Socialist Workers' Party, support the policy and the economic course of the government and the party, and take an active and strong line against the anti-popular elements which, following the guidance of imperialist propaganda, conduct provocative and disruptive activities among the population. The Hungarian peasantry continues to work calmly, having rejected any attempt to be misled by the provocations of the imperialist and counterrevolutionary propaganda and having given an adequate response in the Hungarian villages to the attempts at restoring the land-owning system. Those Hungarian workers who were misled by the demagogic, provocative and nationalist slogans of the counterrevolution are becoming more and more convinced that they have been fooled, and they realize that for all this deception, for all of the counterrevolutionary activities [the country] now must pay with the blood of the best men, of the people who fell victim to the terror of the counterrevolutionary gangs. The working people of Hungary are realizing more and more how fatal the route was down which the adversary forces opposing the cause of socialism and the socialist system wanted to lead them.

The Hungarian working class, the peasantry and the intelligentsia can assess very well the situation of the country and the objectives set for the Hungarian people and the Revolutionary Workers' and Peasants' Government. The Hungarian workers understand more and more now that the increase in the standard of living and the strengthening of the people's democratic system can only be insured by restoring the normal economic situation and production, by the development of the economy of the country, by enhancing productivity in industry and agriculture, by decreasing the costs of production and by socialist accumulation.

In the course of exchanging ideas, the participants of the meeting have established that the Hungarian communists are beginning to realign their forces and are ready to make every effort to strengthen the people's democratic system and the achievements of socialism in Hungary and to further develop solid and friendly relations with all the countries of the socialist camp.

The representatives of Bulgaria, Romania, Czechoslovakia and the Soviet Union have insured the Hungarian comrades that the peoples of their respective countries will give all possible support and help to the Hungarian Revolutionary Workers' and Peasants' Government and the Hungarian Socialist Workers' Party so that they can strengthen the sovereignty and security of the country and the people's democratic state against the intrigues of the imperialist forces.

The participants of the meeting exchanged their views on the announcement of the Soviet government issued on October 30, 1956,[242] and have expressed their uniform conviction that this

---

[242] See Document No. 50.

declaration of the Soviet government fully corresponds to the interests of the socialist countries in strengthening their friendly relations based on respect for the interests and the equal rights of all peoples, and on the Leninist principles of non-interference and proletarian internationalism.

The representatives of the participating countries have established that the objectives issued in the declaration are being accomplished in the mutual relations of the socialist countries, further contributing in this way to the unity of the socialist camp, to the future success of these countries in developing the economy and culture of the socialist countries, to the reinforcement of friendly relations between the peoples of these countries and the broadening of mutual brotherly assistance.

After discussing current issues of the international situation, the participants of the meeting have established that the international situation has recently become more and more tense. This was largely due to the activities of the aggressive circles of the Western countries which intend to turn the world back to a state of cold war. This behavior is well reflected both in the English-French-Israeli aggression against Egypt and in the activities of the imperialist circles in Hungary.

The other reason for the increase in international tension can be seen in the activities of the United States, which has again launched a large-scale mission in order to subdue the states of the Middle East. These attempts at colonization are expressed in the so-called "Eisenhower-Dulles doctrine". An organic part of this "doctrine" is a special authorization for the president of the United States to use American armed forces in the Middle East at his own discretion.[243] The aggressive interference of American monopolist capital and its militarist circles into the matters of the Middle Eastern states would result in serious tensions in the region which recently became a military theater after the aggression on Egypt.[244]

In this situation all responsibility for the tensions in the Middle East and the ensuing consequences rests with the United States. The interests of the Middle Eastern peoples and the assurance of peace and stability in the region demand that every state make efforts to eliminate the consequences of the aggression against Egypt, to prevent any kind of external intervention into the affairs of the Middle Eastern countries and to insure the sovereignty and independence of these states.

The countries of the socialist camp, constantly protecting the cause of peace between nations, make every effort to prevent the world from returning to the cold war. These countries are determined to make use of the strength and power of the socialist system to counteract any attempt by aggressive circles to further increase international tensions, to widen the arms race and to inflame war fever. These countries are firmly convinced that the opportunities to improve relations between states and to insure genuine security for the nations are by no means being exploited fully. Under the present circumstances it would be especially important to take steps to reduce the armaments of the different states and to ban such weapons of mass destruction as the nuclear and the hydrogen bomb. The establishment of a collective European security system would correspond to the interests of all European nations and all countries of the world.

All participants at the meeting have expressed their firm resolution that the socialist countries will unite forces even more than before, protect their unbreakable unity and give a worthy response to any attempt at eliminating or weakening the socialist camp.

[Source: Népszabadság, January 6, 1957. Translated by András Bocz.]

---

[243] The "Eisenhower doctrine" was promulgated in a presidential message to Congress on January 5, 1957. It promised military or economic assistance to countries in the Middle East facing "Communist aggression," noting that "there is imperative need that any lack of power in the area should be made good."

[244] Israel, in collusion with Great Britain and France, invaded the Sinai Peninsula on October 29; the other two states then attacked Egypt directly on October 31.

DOCUMENT NO. 109: Minutes of a Meeting between the Hungarian and Chinese Delegations in Budapest, January 16, 1957

On January 16, at Kádár's request, a Chinese government delegation led by Prime Minister Zhou Enlai visited Budapest. The main purpose, as illustrated by the Hungarian minutes of these meetings, was to show demonstrative support for the Kádár regime. Among other activities while in Budapest, Zhou delivered a speech at a rally expressing his approval of Kádár's retaliatory measures. The Chinese had backed military action as early as October 30, one day before the Soviet decision to intervene; they also asked for the most severe punitive measures against the "counterrevolutionists".

At this meeting, a number of important topics are raised. The Chinese side comes out in favor of the intervention, stating flatly that "the situation [in Hungary] could not have been solved without the Soviet troops." Zhou agrees to take on the task of presenting Hungary's official position to the Third World. Both sides condemn Tito's role, and on the most important domestic issue for Hungary, the Nagy case, agree that treason was committed and discuss the merits of open versus closed trials, and the use of execution as punishment.

Held between 7:00 p.m. and 8:00 p.m., and between 10:15 p.m. and 1:30 a.m., in the Parliament and the residence of the Chinese Government delegation, respectively.

Chinese delegates in attendance:
Zhou Enlai, President of the State Council
He Long, Vice-President of the Council
Wang Jiaxiang, Deputy Foreign Minister[245]
Hao De-qing, Ambassador[246]
Qiao Guanhua, Assistant of Foreign Minister

Hungarian delegates in attendance:
János Kádár, Prime Minister
Dr. Ferenc Münnich, Deputy Prime Minister
György Marosán, Minister of State
Imre Horváth, Foreign Minister
Antal Apró, Minister of Industry
Sándor Rónai, Trade Minister

Zhou Enlai: What is the state of public order in Hungary? Are violent events still occurring?
Kádár: Order has basically been reestablished, but many unlicensed weapons are still in circulation. Our main problems tend to arise in the political sphere. The enemy exploits the severity of our situation, and attempts to gain the confidence of the masses with dishonest slogans. There are still problems concerning public order.
[He relates the murder of the Major][247]

---

[245] Wang Jiaxiang was ambassador to Moscow from 1949 to 1951, deputy foreign minister from 1949 to 1959 and a member of the CCP CC from 1956 to 1966.

[246] Hao De-qing was ambassador to Budapest from 1954 to 1961.

[247] On January 12, 1957, a major in the Hungarian armed forces was shot and killed in Budapest following a scuffle. The case was not a personal vendetta, as described by Kádár, but it was not an act of armed resistance either. Although the man with whom the officer (who was drunk at the time), picked a quarrel was active in underground activities, he was essentially a common criminal who murdered two elderly women during a break-in just a few days later. The sentence has been placed in brackets since it seems to be a remark made by the person writing the minutes and differs from the first-person singular mode of the rest of the text.

This was not so much a politically motivated murder as a personal vendetta.

Münnich: Since November we have collected more than 100,000 weapons from private individuals, which is a huge quantity in such a small country. We have not yet completed this task.

Marosán: When the Czechoslovak Government Delegation came to Budapest it still had to be escorted by tanks.[248] But by now our Chinese comrades must also be convinced that the situation has changed significantly.

Kádár: On November 20, the Yugoslav ambassador wanted to pay me a visit and asked for a tank to be sent to collect him.

I related the talks in Moscow[249] to the Hungarian Government, and the Hungarian leadership has reached complete agreement concerning the Chinese position.

At the airport, an Indian journalist asked: 'What is the aim of this visit, a gesture of friendship or negotiation?' I replied that we will negotiate, too, but that the friendship aspect of the visit is the most important. (Zhou Enlai agreed.) The Indian himself knows that one day is too short a time for large-scale negotiations.

The text of the declaration, which you would like to discuss, is not yet ready.[250]

Understandably, Chinese economic aid has given rise to much pleasure in Hungary.

Zhou Enlai: On my return journey I will make visits to Afghanistan and Nepal; the Hungarian question will also arise during my meeting with Nehru.

We also spoke about the Hungarian question with our comrades in the Polish leadership, and we told them that the characteristics of the Hungarian and Polish events were different.[251] Gomułka's leadership is fundamentally correct, while events in Hungary played out quite differently. Imre Nagy's traitorousness left its mark on the Hungarian situation. János Kádár could only save the socialist cause in Hungary by opposing Imre Nagy and with Soviet help. We have told the Poles and the leaders in Asia that the Hungarian government cannot solve the problems unless it employs the methods it is currently using.

Eisenhower told Nehru that he does not want war to break out because of the events in Hungary.[252] He realizes and accepts the fact that Hungary will remain in the socialist camp.

The South-Asian countries recognize that if the Soviet troops had not intervened, Hungary would now be in the Western camp and that this would represent a considerable risk of war breaking out. It was only with the help of the Soviet troops that Hungary managed to stay in the socialist camp.

Regarding the five-country Party leaders' summit,[253] the Poles asked why they were not invited: it seems that the socialist camp is separating into two groups. We discussed this question with comrade Khrushchev in Moscow, who said that there are quite a few questions on which the Poles' position differs from ours, but that they are also strongly confined by the imminent elections. There were therefore reasons for us to fear the participation of the Poles. It is not even sure that they would have come. Another argument is that the delegations coming to Hungary came from the four neighboring countries. This argument is a bit weak, because Bulgaria does not border Hungary. On no account did they want to exclude the Poles, and comrade Khrushchev advised that they take a stand in the Polish-Chinese declaration,[254] and condemn the U.N.'s intervention

---

[248] The Czechoslovak delegation led by Prime Minister Viliam Široký held talks in Budapest on November 16, 1956.

[249] Before coming to Budapest, Chinese Prime Minister Zhou Enlai was in Moscow for talks between January 7–11, 1957. Since the delegation planned only a two-day visit to Hungary, Kádár and György Marosán flew to Moscow to hold preliminary meetings with the Chinese and Soviet comrades on January 10.

[250] The joint communiqué was published in Népszabadság on January 18, 1957.

[251] Leaving Moscow, the Chinese delegation traveled to Warsaw where they held talks with the Polish leadership between January 11–16. For the notes on these talks, see, János Tischler, "Csou-Enlaj kínai miniszterelnök januári látogatása Varsóban," *Múltunk,* 44, no. 2 (1994): 141–175.

[252] Nehru paid an official visit to the United States in December 1956.

[253] See Document No. 108.

[254] This reference is to the joint communiqué published following the Polish-Chinese negotiations, see footnote 251 above.

in internal Hungarian affairs.[255] There wasn't actually a difference of opinion with the Poles on this question, who find the unity of the socialist countries important, and approve of negotiations between them.

In Moscow I will suggest that we arrange more meetings of this kind. We will communicate any potential dates via the Embassy.

The governments of the Asian countries recognized that objective circumstances made necessary the intervention of Soviet troops, but their leaders nevertheless contradict this when they pronounce that the Soviet army damaged the interests of the Hungarian people. This viewpoint is primarily based on the account of the Indian ambassador. It is a good thing [that] in the course of our visit I will be able to gain first-hand knowledge of this. In my opinion not just the current situation has to be examined, but its repercussions as well. The situation here could not have been solved without the Soviet troops. India is neutral, which explains its position. We should tell journalists more about how the situation in Hungary is improving.

Nehru raised a number of questions concerning Hungary:

1. Soviet troops sent more than 1,000 tanks to Hungary and more than 25,000 people died.[256] My impression now is that very little Soviet armed force is present here. The battles certainly generated casualties, but it would be good to inspect the figures more precisely.
2. He was informed that approximately 150,000 Hungarians escaped to the West.[257] (Comrade Kádár interrupted to note that the chief problem today is that the Western countries will not let them back into Hungary.)
3. There were rumors that the Hungarian government had been assassinated. I myself saw that every member of the government was present at the airport; it is clear that these rumors were started by hostile Western press sources. The leaders' security must be protected.
4. It is rumored that the Workers' Councils are all taking up positions against the Government. At the party assembly[258] the workers themselves reported that reactionary groups participate in the Workers' Councils, and so intervention against them is understandable.
5. Many agricultural cooperatives have disbanded—said Nehru. At lunch Comrade Dobi already explained the problems concerning the question of the agricultural cooperatives.
6. Before his journey to America, Nehru expressed his hope that János Kádár's government is consolidating itself. If we negotiate with neutral people, we must categorically abide by our opinion—this is the best method.
7. Concerning Imre Nagy, the Hungarian Government did not keep the promise it made to the Yugoslav Embassy.[259] In relation to this I noted to Nehru that he can understand our situation best—after all, he kept the Prime Minister of Kashmir in custody for three years. With regard to this and the other questions I would now like to gain first-hand information.

Kádár: The Polish-Chinese Declaration is a great help to us. Earlier, unfriendly articles had appeared in the Polish press. We did not keep Poland away from the Budapest Conference on purpose. Talks can be held on certain questions without lengthy preparation, for example the Moscow talks. The fact is that common problems emerged here. Three gov-

---

[255] From the beginning, the Soviet Union considered the U.N. resolutions concerning the Kádár government and the Hungarian revolution to be interference in Hungary's internal affairs. On January 10, 1957, the U.N. General Assembly established a Special Committee on Hungary with the participation of Australia, Ceylon, Denmark, Tunisia and Uruguay in order to investigate the Hungarian events.

[256] According a top-secret report by the Hungarian Central Statistical Office compiled in May 1957, the number of Hungarian casualties of the armed fighting was around 2,700 killed and 20,000 wounded. See, "Az október 23-i és az azt követő eseményekkel kapcsolatos sérülések és halálozások" (Injuries and deaths in relation to the events on October 23 and after), *Statisztikai Szemle 68*, no. 10 (1990): 797–815.

[257] In reality, the final number of emigrants was higher. See footnote 17 above.

[258] During its short visit in Budapest, the Chinese delegation participated in a meeting of the Budapest party aktiv.

[259] See Document No. 101.

ernments had an interest in the Imre Nagy affair, for example. We also invited our Czechoslovak and Bulgarian comrades, who had similarly expressed opinions on this subject. But we did not invite Poland, the GDR or Albania. The Poles were in any case occupied with other matters,[260] whose settlement we did not want to obstruct. If we had invited representatives from a greater number of countries, we would have had to widen the scope of the negotiations. We would nevertheless definitely like to meet and talk with our Polish comrades. Not in two or three months' time, but as soon as possible: for example, we must sit at the negotiating table with our Polish and Yugoslav comrades in February, lest our initial positions become overly rigid.[261]

Zhou Enlai: That is most sensible. After our arrival in Moscow I will immediately communicate this view to Comrade Mao Zedong by telephone.

Marosán: It would be good for the outside world if China initiated such a meeting.

Kádár: During the negotiations held with India, Minister Koshla[262] and Ambassador Menon[263] tried to put pressure on us concerning the question of inviting U.N. observers and the U.N. Secretary General. Koshla went as far as to threaten that they would not support us or stand by us if we do not satisfy their demands. They even invited the Indonesian ambassador in Belgrade to Budapest to give them support. They condemned us for sending Imre Nagy to Romania. They had obviously received information about this from the Yugoslav Government.

In response to the questions:

1. The number of tanks is not correct. The bulk of the Soviet tanks in Hungary were used to guard the Western border. The fighting had two focal points in Budapest: the area of the Corvin Cinema and Széna square. The fighting took place within about a half-kilometer radius; in such circumstances tanks could not have been deployed in such numbers. The number of casualties was between 1,700 and 2,000, with the number of injured above 13,000.[264] Previously we estimated the number of casualties to be 5,000, but we did not take into consideration the fact that 170 people die in Budapest every day under normal circumstances. For a protracted period there was no orderly registration of deaths, and those dying of illness, old age, etc. were not buried in the usual way, but in public squares, gardens, and other places, and we counted them amongst the casualties of the fighting.

2. Escapes to the West have not just slackened significantly, around 10,000 have already returned. The Western authorities are obstructing their return and are preventing official Hungarian institutions from establishing contact with the refugees.

3. Several attempts were made to challenge the government, but the Soviet troops offered adequate protection. In fact for the last month and a half order has been maintained completely by Hungarian security forces, without Soviet intervention.

4. Immediately after the events blew over, it was difficult to see the picture clearly. On November 15 I still declared to the mass public that Imre Nagy thought his intentions were good. His role as a traitor had not yet become clear then. As far as this question is concerned, we must bear in mind that the Yugoslavs of their own accord offered to convince Imre Nagy to resign—nevertheless they later protected him. At the end of the talks held with Vidić, the Yugoslav deputy foreign secretary, he declared that Yugoslavia wanted to aid the Hungarian Government's consolidation with Imre Nagy's removal. Later Yugoslav statements were completely at odds with this declaration.

---

[260] Kádár is referring to the upcoming general elections in Poland; however, this was only an excuse for deliberately not having invited the Polish leaders to the Budapest meeting.

[261] In fact, due to lingering tensions between the two leaderships, the first meeting took place only on May 9–12, 1958, when Gomułka and Prime Minister Cyrankiewicz visited Hungary.

[262] Jagan Nat Koshla was Indian minister in Prague in 1956.

[263] Kumara Pladmanabha Sivasankava Menon, Indian ambassador to Moscow, also representing India in both Poland and Hungary.

[264] In reality, the number of casualties was somewhat higher, see footnote 256 above.

5. Nehru's representatives wanted at all costs to persuade us to allow U.N. observers, or at least the U.N. Secretary General, to come to Hungary. I asked them whether the situation in Kashmir had improved over the last three years from the presence of U.N. observers. They were forced to admit that the situation had not improved at all, that in fact it had got worse. To this I asked why they wanted the situation here to get worse as well.

6. In regard to the Workers' Councils, we must bear in mind that they developed in the course of a counterrevolutionary surge and a climate of aggression and pogroms. Declassed [*deklasszált*][265] individuals had been working in factories for many years. They became the voice of the Workers' Councils. To legitimize themselves they rallied honest workers as well. The Regional and Central Workers' Councils, on the other hand, came into existence according to counterrevolutionary plans. The thinking of the imperialists and the Yugoslavs agrees on this point, and they asked us to explain why we do not rely on Regional Workers' Councils.

Zhou Enlai: This is open interference in internal Hungarian affairs. How many factory workers are there in Hungary?

Marosán: In Hungary there are a million-and-a-half factory workers and today there are approximately 2 million members of trade unions.

Kádár: Members of the Yugoslav Embassy and Yugoslav journalists used cars with diplomatic license plates to spread Kardelj's speech,[266] distributing it to Hungarian factories without saying anything about this to the Hungarian Government. When the Hungarian Government ordered a news black-out to the West, the Yugoslav News Agency's correspondent forwarded the enemy material from capitalist correspondents. The Hungarian Government was repeatedly attacked by the Yugoslav press.

Marosán: During this period there was hardly any difference between the Yugoslav and the American journalists.

Zhou Enlai: Has the tone of the Yugoslav press since changed?

Kádár: After *Renmin Ribao's* well-known article, *Borba* and *Politika* wrote something good about Hungary,[267] for the first time in a month-and-a-half, in the nature of the following: "It seems that the Kádár Government has found the road to consolidation." From that point on, open attacks in the press subsided. We did not argue about it openly because we did not want to make the situation any worse. In Yugoslavia they objected to our government declaration on the basis that it supposedly has a heavy tone and frequently mentions dictatorship. The Yugoslavs regard October 23 as an act of national heroism. In his speech in Pula,[268] Tito declared that it shows what a nation can achieve, bare-handed, if it knows what it wants. This effectively implies a condemnation of Soviet assistance, and contradicts the fact that most of the participants in the uprising did not know what they wanted. Only a small group, the deliberate counterrevolutionaries, were clear about what they wanted.

We can tell Nehru openly that the Soviet troops intervened at our request and in our interest.

---

[265] This term was used in communist jargon to denote people who held higher social status in the pre-1945 regime, but who lost their stature after 1948 and were typically required to take working-class jobs. The communist leadership, for obvious reasons, continued to look on them with suspicion.

[266] This refers to a speech Edvard Kardelj delivered before the Yugoslav Federal National Assembly on December 7, 1956. At the December 11 session of the Provisional Executive Committee Kádár voiced his disapproval of these activities. At an HSWP Central Committee session on February 26, 1957, he repeated his criticisms of Yugoslav journalists.

[267] A December 29 editorial in *Renmin Ribao* ("People's Daily"), the central daily of the Chinese Communist Party, described the revolution unequivocally as an attack by international imperialism, and inveighed against the speeches by Tito in Pula on November 11 (see Document No. 96) and Kardelj on December 7. For an English translation of the article, see "More on the Historical Experience of the Dictatorship of the Proletariat" in *Communist China 1955–1959: Policy Documents with Analysis*. (Cambridge, Massachusets: Harvard University Press, 1962), 257–272.

[268] See Document No. 96.

At that time 700 foreign journalists and the Diplomatic Corps were present in Budapest and other parts of the country. Thus nothing was kept secret from the outside world. The Western journalists themselves exposed the counterrevolutionary activities. What need is there for an investigating committee after that?

There are no deportations. It is true that unbeknownst to the Soviet and Hungarian Governments a subordinated[269] Soviet organ deported a carriage of prisoners captured during the fighting, but to the last man they were returned on our demand. This is no longer discussed.

The counterrevolutionaries took pains mainly to organize strikes in the coalmines, as they knew that would affect production and the country's life as a whole. Once we had arrested 25 or 20 leaders, production began again almost immediately. On Csepel Island, the Workers' Councils resigned with provocative intent, thinking that this would cause confusion.[270] It is typical that at the time of the resignation Western journalists were staying in Csepel, and the U.N. put the Hungarian question on its agenda. These events were no coincidence. They had deliberately planned to discredit the Hungarian Government.

Zhou Enlai: The enemy obviously does not propagate what isn't useful to it, while it exaggerates things that interest it. I agree with your position concerning Nehru. Two techniques can be used against Nehru: either ignore him, or make a carefully argued case, but the latter could take a very long time.

Kádár: In good faith, we supplied objective, detailed and honest information because we could see that Nehru was getting his information from inimical, or at least not well-intentioned, sources. The Indonesian ambassador listed the Indians' arguments in the same way, but after we had given our answer he did not insist on continuing the debate, and instead asked good naturedly: in what ways could they give us political help?

Zhou Enlai: With Nehru, the two methods we have mentioned have to be used flexibly. The information gained here was useful, and it can be used in the Asian countries against ill-intentioned information. The U.N. cannot do anything, though it is possible that they might expel Hungary, but there is no need to place too much significance on this possibility, as China exists pretty well outside the U.N., and then at least we would keep each other company—he remarked in jest.

Kádár: It is not easy to expel a country from the U.N.

Münnich: Menon said that the government's declaration had appealed to him, but immediately raised the question: when will there be democratic elections? I replied that they would receive a response in the government's declaration.

Zhou Enlai: Do not fall into the Indians' trap. Don't hurry the elections. At the reception the Indian chargé said that in his opinion, the situation in Hungary is improving and that there was probably need for the intervention of Soviet troops, and then added cunningly: at present the enlargement of the government is a big problem. In my opinion, though the government is small it works well, and it is just right for dictatorship.

Münnich: Unnavati, the Indian military attaché, asked how many Soviet troops were stationed in Hungary. I replied that we are on very friendly terms with the Soviets, and we speak often, but that I have never asked them this.

Horváth: It is very good that Zhou Enlai and Nehru discuss these questions, and the impre-

---

[269] The word Kádár uses here, "alantas," can also be translated as "base" or "mean". Although from the context it seems more likely that the sense used in the text is the right one, it is not impossible that Kádár had the secondary meaning in mind, or at least chose the word deliberately for its dual connotation. The Hungarian leader was indignant at the KGB for deporting Hungarian prisoners to the Soviet Union, an act that could seriously have undermined his efforts at consolidation. The available sources are somewhat ambiguous on the number of deportees—while one Interior Ministry document notes 846 prisoners on Soviet territory, a later report by Ivan Serov mentions 860 people taken to the Sub Carpathian region. In the end, all deportees were returned to Hungary. For the Interior Ministry report, see Document No. 97.

[270] On January 8, 1957, members of the Worker's Council of the Csepel Iron- and Metalworks announced their resignation following a government decree on January 5 that extended capital punishment to both the act of striking and the instigation to strike.

cise data is uncovered. They claim that the Soviet intervention was not justified and that the Soviet Union committed an act of aggression. They should prove it. In the U.N. Hungary was repeatedly slandered, and because of this our delegation walked out of the assembly.[271] On the other hand, it is not easy to exclude a member state from the organization, because this can be blocked by veto. But, with the help of the American electoral machine, it is relatively easy for them to exclude a state from the Assembly.

The Americans' bad intentions are demonstrated by the fact that their Minister has been in Hungary for three months now without presenting his credentials. He puts this down to not being able to maintain the necessary contact with his government.[272] This is the kind of political trickery they work with.

Zhou Enlai: I can refute Nehru with facts. It is clear to us that the Indians would like the nature of power in Hungary to change, via elections or by any other means.

Kádár: What they did not achieve with weapons, the enemy tries to achieve by other methods.

Zhou Enlai: Eisenhower is not starting a war either, but he did not say that he wouldn't continue their subversive activity.

Now it is not so much Nehru's question which is complicated, but rather Tito's. Can he be called a socialist at all? Outside negotiations, their attitude is not always socialist.

Kádár: Renmin Ribao's article is right when it points to phenomena like the Yugoslav conduct with Hungary, Bulgaria and Albania, a conduct which Yugoslavia would not want to be displayed vis-a-vis herself.

Zhou Enlai: They oppose Stalin, but in this they have learned from him.

Kádár: This side to the Yugoslavs has shown itself before. In January 1946 I participated in the secret meeting between the parties of our two countries. The Hungarian delegation supplied secret information about our party in full, but the Yugoslavs did not describe their internal affairs, they did not respond to our questions, or they started to talk about something else. They did not want to negotiate on an equal basis. There are those in Yugoslavia who think that reform of the socialist regime is possible, even by means of an uprising. The Yugoslavs are themselves conducting intelligence activities in the socialist countries. This came to light when they publicly quoted an internal Albanian party document, which was probably obtained with the help of agents. Such agents could be functioning in Hungary, too.

Zhou Enlai: The democratic character of the dictatorship must by all means be underlined. Comrade Marosán has said that Dudás was in close contact with Imre Nagy and executed his instructions.[273] His crime is unquestionably great, he deserves the death penalty, but the matter does not need to be rushed. It is better if we have living evidence in our hands. If he is executed, the enemy can later claim that false testimony was forced from him. If he lives, on the other hand, his punishment can be lessened if he makes a full confession. We have to recognize that there are three strata in society: the first consciously supports us, the second is the enemy, who are against us, and the third is neutral; this third stratum, which cannot see clearly, is the widest. It is in our interest to maintain the support of the masses. Ideally we can educate them with facts. We have to take especially great care with this, because we can only solve our problems with the support of the masses; it is not enough to rely on armed force [*karhatalom*]. If we sentence him to death as he deserves, we should at least not carry out the sentence, so that we can later use him as a living witness.

---

[271] The Hungarian delegation left the U.N. General Assembly on December 11, 1956, arguing that the body was not handling the Hungarian question in the spirit of the U.N. charter.

[272] U.S. Minister Edward T. Wailes arrived to Budapest on November 2, 1956. Following his government's instructions, he refused to present his credentials to the Kádár government. As a result, he was declared *persona non grata* and forced to leave the country on February 22, 1957.

[273] This statement is inaccurate. Although József Dudás did indeed meet with Imre Nagy on October 30, and accepted him as prime minister, he did not agree with Nagy's evaluation of the revolution's achievements and the emphasis on establishing peace and order as the top priority.

Kádár: Dudás was one of the organizers and military leaders of the armed uprising. There are many arguments to support his execution. Many smaller culprits have already been punished. At the same time the authorities have quite a few people in hand who can testify to Imre Nagy's role as a traitor. If the leaders are not punished, then the masses will not be shown that this government seriously wants to settle the score with the counterrevolution. Imre Nagy's role as a traitor is increasingly clear and increasingly demonstrable.

Zhou Enlai: Are you holding an open trial?

Kádár: No, we are holding a closed military trial.

Marosán: 47 witnesses have testified.

Zhou Enlai: Did Dudás recognize his guilt?

Kádár: Yes. During the trial a lot of information concerning Imre Nagy came to light, which we do not want to spread. There was a lot of information about Yugoslavia as well.

Zhou Enlai: Trustworthy cadres, like those who were at the assembly, could take part in the trials, and propagate suitable ideas among the masses. Of course, from our side this is merely advice; you know the situation better. Experience in China has shown that it is advantageous to divide the enemy. This way they can be defeated more easily. If you allow the leading counter-revolutionaries to live, you can accumulate more material, and public trials will have a more educative effect.

Kádár: There are other defendants who can perhaps testify to Imre Nagy's guilt even more effectively.

He Long: We also executed less important people, while keeping many leaders alive. When necessary we asked them for information; they were like a living encyclopedia.

Kádár: We have understood your thinking, but our situation is very complicated. Among those in custody is the former chief of police, whose relationship with Imre Nagy was even closer than that of Dudás.

Marosán: He [Dudás] led the attacks on the Foreign Ministry, the offices of *Szabad Nép*, and on Party Headquarters, and was the leader of one of the centers of the counterrevolution. We have not yet impeached any of the leaders of the attack on Party Headquarters.

Münnich: If the leading counterrevolutionaries are executed, then the strength of the counterrevolution would be considerably lessened, and weapons would be handed in much more quickly.

After this the discussion turned to the modification of certain phrases in the joint declaration, and with that the meeting drew to a close.

[Source: MOL, XIX–J–1–j. 4. d., pp. 1–8. Published in Tibor Zinner, "'...hogy megkönnyítsék a Nagy kormány likvidálását...': Három dokumentum Nagy Imre és köre 1956 november 4. utáni történetéhez," Társadalmi Szemle 44, No. 12 (1989): pp. 93–98. Translated by David Evans.]

DOCUMENT NO. 110: National Intelligence Estimate (NIE) 12–57, "Stability of the Soviet Satellite Structure," February 19, 1957

Written just over one year after the previous National Intelligence Estimate in this series on Eastern Europe (see Document No. 7), NIE 12–57 looks back at the tumultuous period that has just passed and draws conclusions about its significance for Soviet policy. The document's main points, while very general, as NIEs tended to be, are quite accurate. The authors state that recent events in the region will lead the Kremlin to accentuate internal security and Soviet control over the requirements for reform in Eastern Europe, but that tensions between local populations and their ruling regimes, as well as among the satellite states themselves, will grow over the next several years. This document, reproduced here in its entirety, appeared in significantly truncated form—leaving out the entire "Discussion" section—in the State Department's FRUS series.

STABILITY OF THE SOVIET SATELLITE STRUCTURE

THE PROBLEM

To estimate the prospects for stability in the Soviet Satellite structure over the next few years.

CONCLUSIONS

1. The long-latent conflict between Soviet interests and Satellite aspirations exploded into crisis last fall as a result of the progressive weakening of ideological authority and loosening of police control, following the death of Stalin. The Soviet leaders are experiencing great difficulty in formulating and putting info effect policies which will reduce this crisis to manageable proportions. *(Paras. 8, 12)*

2. We believe that the USSR will continue to regard the Satellite area as vital to its interests, and will not seriously entertain, at least for the next several years, the possibility of a general political or military withdrawal, even in return for a withdrawal of US forces from Europe. To the Soviet leaders, loss of control over Eastern Europe would constitute a severe setback for Communism. They would also view it as rendering them powerless to prevent German reunification, and as seriously impairing the USSR's strategic position. *(Paras. 11, 27).*

3. We believe that the Soviet leaders have concluded from the events of recent months that although reforms in certain fields were acceptable, concessions to nationalist pressures involve hazards to Soviet control. They apparently intend for some time to come to put primary emphasis on the internal security of the Satellite regimes and on Soviet control over them. *(Para. 29)*

4. Poland's success in maintaining its present limited degree of independence is a key factor affecting the future political developments in Eastern Europe. Should the USSR succeed in reimposing its complete control over Poland, it could more easily check dissident elements in other Satellites, particularly disruptive forces in the other Satellite Communist parties. If the USSR does not achieve its aim in Poland, its problems elsewhere will probably worsen. *(Para. 49)*

5. We believe that the Soviet leaders will try to undermine the special status which the Gomulka regime in Poland has acquired. However, the costs and risks of a military intervention would be great. Such action would almost certainly be resisted by the bulk of the Polish nation and armed forces and thus involved Soviet forces in large-scale military operations which could spread to East Germany and thus provoke a major international crisis. *(Paras. [illegible]).*

6. Soviet success in repairing its losses in Poland, however, would not remove the underlying causes of disaffection throughout the Satellites. Tensions between the Satellite populations and their regimes during the next several years probably will be higher that prior to the events

in Poland and Hungary, and the unity of Satellite parties will be subjected to greater strains. Soviet policy is not likely to reduce these tensions in Eastern Europe or even to restore the degree of acquiescence prevailing earlier. *(Paras. 47–49).*

DISCUSSION

7. The political stability of Communist regimes in the Satellite area depends upon the interplay of a variety of factors. The most basic of these are the nature and degree of the pressure applied by the USSR on behalf of its interest in the area and the degree of success attained by the local regimes in either controlling opposition forces or winning popular acceptance. Popular attitudes, in turn, depend on the extent to which the regimes can fulfill the strong popular aspirations for greater political and economic freedoms, national independence, and improved standards of living. Satellite expectations regarding Western policy also play a part. All these factors were at work in the crisis of recent months will continue to be present, and must be taken into account in assessing the future prospects for Satellite political stability.

SOVIET POLICY TOWARD THE SATELLITES

8. Basically it was the conflict between Soviet interests in the Satellites and the national aspirations of the individual countries which gave rise to the recent crisis in the Satellite area. The immediate cause of the crisis was the simultaneous weakening of ideological authority and loosening of police controls following the death of Stalin. These moves gave reign to opposition forces, the strength and determination of which were apparently underestimated by the Soviet leaders. The downgrading of Stalin was probably undertaken primarily with a view to internal Soviet conditions. On the other hand, the rapprochement with Tito was designed, as was the guarded endorsement of "separate roads to socialism," for foreign policy aims outside the Bloc. Insofar as the Soviet leaders considered the consequences of these moves within the Satellites, they apparently believed that these could be turned to their own advantage or at least contained. Accompanying moves to curb excesses of police terrorism were probably intended actually to broaden popular support for the Satellite regimes and to stimulate initiative and productivity.

9. Instead, the deterioration of Soviet authority and security controls in the Satellite weakened the prestige and the cohesiveness of some of the Satellite ruling groups and encouraged the emergence of nationalistic anti-Stalinist, and reformist tendencies within certain elements of the Satellite Communist parties. Intellectuals, workers, youth, and other discontented groups among the population felt it possible to speak out more openly against regimentation, economic burdens, and other grievances. These forces led to uneasiness throughout the Satellite area, to a breakdown of party unity and open expression of anti-Russian feeling in Poland and Hungary and, in the latter, to outright rebellion against the Communist system.

10. The upheavals in two Satellites and rumblings in others were not the result of organized resistance, which had become virtually impossible under Satellite police-state rule. Varying degrees of relaxation permitted by the regimes and their moderation of certain previous police-state practices led to a more open and spontaneous expression of reformist and even of some anti-Soviet sentiment, especially after the Soviet downgrading of Stalin. Even then, this occurred primarily among Communist party members; only in Poland and Hungary did wide segments of the basically anti-Communist population eventually become involved. With the probable exception of Hungary, there is at present no known widespread organization of anti-regime forces in the Satellites; articulate opposition has been largely confined to reformist elements within the Communist parties, the state bureaucracy and semiofficial organized groups such as journalists, artists, students, and trade unionists. So long as the Satellite leaderships remain united, maintain police controls, and stay closely aligned to Moscow, reformist sentiment can only express itself in cautious advocacy of the need for national variations from the Soviet pattern, and cannot openly attack Communist institutions as such. Developments in Poland and Hungary showed

that when a Communist regime permits the public expression of nationalist points of view, the resulting agitation can rapidly transform itself into political demands which are essentially anti-Communist, especially if the regime is divided and indecisive.

11. We believe that the Soviet leaders are determined to maintain their domination of the Satellite area. This determination continues despite their awareness of the potential strength of opposition forces and the reappraisal of the costs, especially in international prestige, of maintaining control forcibly, particularly in situations of open revolt. In the Soviet view, there are probably three main considerations which make control of the area vital:

a. The USSR's political and ideological investment in the myth of Communism's successful world advance is so great that defection from the "socialist camp" of any Satellite (except possibly Albania) would represent a severe setback for the world Communist movement. Such a defeat, especially if followed by uprisings in other Satellites, would not only impose severe handicaps on Soviet foreign policy everywhere, but would arouse Soviet fears of Western moves to exploit the situation. Even worse, it would probably give rise to unrest in the USSR itself which might lead to a challenge to the authority of the Soviet regime.

b. The Satellite area must continue to be available for Soviet military uses. Even if the Soviet leaders came in time to believe that they no longer needed to maintain large Soviet forces there to oppose a ground invasion or to mount offensive action, they would still insist on use of the area for Soviet air defense. They would almost certainly believe that they could not count upon the availability of the area as a forward or buffer zone if they permitted independent governments to replace the present Soviet-controlled regimes.

c. Loss of control over the Satellite area would make it impossible for the USSR to prevent unification of Germany or to exert major influence over the future policy of a reunited Germany. This would represent abandonment of one of the principal goals of Soviet postwar policy in Europe.

12. Confronted with the conflict between Soviet interests and Satellite aspirations, the Soviet leaders have found it difficult to formulate policies which reduce this conflict to manageable proportions. For a time they attempted a policy of lessening direct Soviet control and permitting, and in some cases encouraging, local regimes to make concessions to popular sentiment. The upheavals in Poland and Hungary have demonstrated to the Soviet leaders the dangers of such a course. They can return to a policy of rigid police terror by directly controlled local regimes in an effort to prevent the development of situations where resort to military force becomes unavoidable. But this course would give no hope of overcoming the problems which were inherited from Stalin, and would now in fact increase popular dissidence, further retard economic activity, and again damage the USSR's propaganda position.

13. The case of Poland brings into sharp focus continuing conflict between Soviet interests and security requirements on the one hand, and Polish nationalist aspirations and popular demands on the other. The success of Gomulka in the inner party struggle in October was due mainly to his pledges to abandon Poland's slavish adherence to Moscow, a position which commanded extensive popular support. In fact, the new leadership gained power by what was in effect a *coup d'etat* against pro-Soviet elements and against the Soviet power apparatus in Poland. Not only do the Soviet leaders mistrust Gomulka and his colleagues because of the experiences of October, but they must doubt the will and ability of the elements associated with him to maintain a regime acceptable to the USSR, especially in view of the involvement of almost the entire population in the open expression of anti-Soviet sentiments. Even in October, the Soviet leaders considered and came within an ace of actually undertaking the outright use of military force. They probably continue to be uneasy over the degree of independence which the current Polish leadership apparently intends to exercise.

506

ECONOMIC SITUATION OF THE SATELLITES

14. Underlying the general crisis in the European Satellites are economic difficulties which stem directly from the imposition of Soviet methods and policies. Although most Satellites are poorly endowed with the variety of resources needed for industrialization on the Soviet pattern, all have been required to imitate the USSR in giving first priority to heavy industry. This policy has resulted in rapid industrial growth, particularly in engineering industries, but at the expense of other sectors. Even in industry, production is high in cost, low in quality, and plagued by chronic shortages of raw materials. Soviet economic demands have imposed a further burden. These difficulties, coupled with poor planning and management, have subjected the Satellite economies to strains which now are increased by the pressure to raise living standards significantly.

15. The past high rate of defense outlays and investment in heavy industry was made possible by maintaining depressed living standards involving neglect of production of consumer goods and housing. The accompanying inflationary pressures required heavy taxes, forced saving, price controls, and in some instances outright rationing, all of which aggravated popular discontents and seriously reduced worker incentives.

16. Because of the neglect of agriculture in favor of industry and effects of collectivization, the area has moved from a food surplus to a food deficit position. Dependence on imports of food, difficulties in grain collection, and poor distribution in urban centers have created food stringencies and in many instances real hardship.

17. Economic difficulties have been aggravated by disruption of traditional trading relationships. Prewar exports of food products and industrial raw materials have given way to imports. Meanwhile, the consumer goods industries which formerly provided foreign earnings have been neglected in order to expand the engineering industries, which compete much less successfully in Western markets. Reorientation of Satellite trade towards dependence on the USSR, although it partially fulfilled Satellite needs for raw materials and markets, occurred on terms unfavorable to the Satellites. Trade difficulties were increased by the Satellite obligation to service debts incurred by their forced purchase from the USSR of so-called German assets in their territories which the USSR seized at the end of World War II. This combination of circumstances has further drained the Satellites of domestically produced goods and has weakened their foreign exchange position.

18. Since 1953 the Satellites have sought to revise national plans so as to reduce disproportions (a) between raw material availability and production capacity, (b) between industrial output of producer and consumer goods, and (c) between agricultural and industrial production. These efforts have been hampered by popular distrust and by the resistance of doctrinaire leaders intent upon adhering to the Soviet economic pattern. These revisions, which include an attempt to accelerate the integration of the Bloc economies, have now been overtaken by the disruptive political events in Poland and Hungary. The inability of these two countries to meet their commitments has probably invalidated existing economic plans in greater or lesser degree in all the Satellites. For the moment, the Satellites have been driven to rely upon Soviet credits and emergency bilateral trade agreements with the USSR to rescue their economies from critical raw material bottlenecks and at the same time to provide stop gap markets for machinery.

INTERNAL POLITICAL SITUATION OF THE VARIOUS SATELLITES

19. *Poland.* The Polish leadership is facing serious internal problems. Although the regime has maintained the substantial degree of internal autonomy it won from the USSR last October, the initial enthusiasm it aroused has probably been restrained by the necessity to emphasize solidarity with the USSR, to accept the continued presence of Soviet troops in Poland, and to halt political reforms short of the hopes aroused in October. The popular support given the regime in the recent elections rested mainly on the widespread belief that it is the only government which

507

can make some defense of Polish national interests and still not provoke Soviet military intervention. The regime appears to have made considerable progress in bringing the military and security organs under its effective control and in ousting many members of the pro-Soviet faction from party positions. Nevertheless it still has far to go in rebuilding a loyal party and administrative apparatus at the local level, and there are still many middle-level and politburo-level party figures who might be willing to support Soviet efforts to undermine Gomulka's position. His recent election success, however, has placed him in a stronger position to deal with opponents within his party.

20. The regime has not been able to overcome the effects of a deteriorating economic situation, which is characterized by a decrease in exports attendant on a decline in coal production, difficulties in collecting food from the peasants, and a partial industrial disorganization resulting from the weakening of central authority and the spontaneous establishment of workers' councils. Thus the regime has been faced with a weakened economy at a time when it is pledged to gratify long-contained popular desires for better standards of living.

21. *Hungary*. Most of the active resistance in Hungary has been weakened by attrition and suppressed by increasingly firm Soviet-sponsored security measures. Popular bitterness, however, remains undiminished and passive resistance and economic non-cooperation have abated only slightly. There is evidence that most government employees are not loyal to the regime and that organized anti-regime groups continue to exist and to maintain communication with each other. In its recent declaration of policy, the Kádár regime confirmed its complete puppet status and thus further reduced its chances of winning new adherents. The regime's main difficulty at present is in reconstituting dependable indigenous party cadres able to maintain its authority throughout the country without the presence or proximity of substantial Soviet armed strength. Its problems are complicated by severe economic dislocation in the wake of the almost complete breakdown in production discipline in mines and factories during the past few months. It has felt compelled to scrap the scheduled five-year plan altogether, and to concentrate its efforts on re-establishing a minimum level of economic activity.

22. *East Germany*. Popular disaffection in East Germany continues at a high level and has increased in the wake of developments in Poland and Hungary. Some unrest continues among the large urban working class, and increased anti-regime agitation among students and intellectuals has led recently to stern countermeasures. The regime's problems are increased by the failure to expand food supplies in the face of a promised end to rationing and by the decline in imports of Polish coal. Nevertheless, pressures for violent change in East Germany are still held in check by the presence of 22 Soviet divisions. Although there are probably differences of opinion in the leadership of the East German party on questions of economic policy and First Secretary Ulbricht's dictatorial role in the party, most party officials appear to have rallied around the leadership in response to the need for solidarity vis-à-vis a basically anti-Communist populace. Solidarity between Moscow and the Stalin installed East German leadership has been rearmed in the recent Soviet-East German communiqué. The populace at present appears disinclined to risk revolutionary action in view of the harsh Soviet repression of the June 1953 uprising and the more recent Soviet action in Hungary.

23. *Czechoslovakia*. Although there was some open agitation for liberalization and greater independence last spring, in recent months the only overt indications of unrest have been some cautiously stated criticism of the leadership in literary journals and some ferment in Slovak party organizations. The demands of local party organizations for a party congress and of students and intellectuals for greater freedom were rejected by the regime during the summer. Traditions of caution and accommodation to the existing authority as well as a relatively prosperous economic situation apparently dissuaded the populace from attempting any action against the regime in the wake of the Polish and Hungarian crises. Anti-Soviet elements exist within the Czech party but presently lack leadership on the national level. The absence of any important opposition political or religious figure to serve as a symbolic rallying point has aided the regime the fragmenting and dissipating popular opposition.

508

24. *Rumania.* While popular disaffection is only a little less widespread in Rumania than in Poland and Hungary, it appears to have no effective means of opposing the orthodox pro-Soviet regime of Gheorghiu-Dej. Sympathy for the Hungarian rebels was widespread, especially among the Hungarian minority. Agitation for change was vigorous among Rumanian students in the late autumn, and the chronic discontent of the predominantly peasant population was increased by poor crop returns. However, the lack of aggressive nationalistic traditions in Rumania, together with the uncompromising severity of the leadership and the intimidating presence of Soviet troops, has prevented the formation of effective pressures for change.

25. *Bulgaria.* Since Bulgaria traditionally has been closely linked to Russia, anti-Soviet feeling, while widespread, has tended to be less intense than in other Eastern European states. Nevertheless, popular disaffection with the Communist regime has remained strong during the past year, and there appears to be some factionalism within the party leadership and discontent among prominent military figures. In the face of these developments, the top Bulgarian leaders appear to have subordinated their differences for fear that disunity at the top would undermine them collectively. Solidarity with the USSR has been vigorously reaffirmed, and tightened security measures have been invoked, including some re-arrests of party figures pardoned of alleged Titoism. Thus, although Bulgaria has a national tradition which could serve as a basis for a national Communism movement, the top leadership appears to have united behind a policy of continued submission to the will of Moscow. Moreover, a common border with potentially hostile neighbors serves to some extent to balance desires for greater independence with interest in the protection afforded by the USSR.

26. *Albania.* Faced with a disaffected and economically depressed population and surrounded by unfriendly states, the Albanian Communist regime sustains itself by clinging to the ideological rigidity and police methods of the Stalin era. It is the only Satellite which has never recanted its anti-Titoist trials, and it seized upon recent Yugoslav-Soviet differences to renew direct attacks on Yugoslavia. The regime actively opposes internal liberalization or any greater autonomy, fearing that such tendencies would undermine the present leadership and lead to encroachments by Yugoslavia, Greece, or Italy. There is no known opposition within the party capable of effectively challenging the current leadership. However, the consistently harsh tone of the Albanian press since the Twentieth Party Congress and reports of some recent arrests and executions probably indicate apprehension about the extent of unrest in Albania and the firmness of Soviet protective guarantees.

PROBABLE DEVELOPMENTS

Soviet Policy

27. Because the Satellites will almost certainly continue to represent interests which the USSR considers vital to its security (see paragraph 11), we believe that Soviet policy will continue to be directed toward the maintenance of effective control over the area. Specifically, we believe that the Soviet leaders will not, at least during the next several years, seriously entertain the idea of a general political or military withdrawal from Eastern Europe, even in return for a withdrawal of US forces from Europe. It is possible, however, that there could eventually be some reduction or even complete withdrawal of Soviet troops stationed in one or another Satellite country if the USSR came to believe that the local regime was reliable and secure without such support.

28. Despite the firmness of the present Soviet attitude on control of Eastern Europe, contingencies could arise in which the USSR might be confronted with such serious alternatives that it could feel compelled to entertain the possibility of withdrawal. For example, in the unlikely event that the Soviet leaders believed themselves to be confronted with a choice between general war or withdrawal, it is possible that they would endeavor to negotiate the best possible terms for withdrawal. It is also conceivable that the political and economic costs of maintaining

control continue to rise, the USSR might eventually, given circumstances in which there was no immediate challenge to its prestige, consider withdrawal in return for substantial Western concessions with respect to European security, the German question, and the withdrawal of US forces. However, we do not believe that either these or any other combinations of circumstances which would alter the Soviet determination to retain control of Eastern Europe is likely to occur in the next several years.

29. We believe that the Soviet leaders have concluded from the events of recent months that allowing even limited concessions to nationalist pressures was unwise, and that they intend for some time to come to put primary emphasis on the internal security of the Satellite regimes and on Soviet control over them. This is indicated by the themes now being emphasized in Soviet propaganda: vigilance against reactionaries both at home and abroad, continuation of the class struggle, the dictatorship of the proletariat, and, above all, the unity of the socialist camp. Accordingly, there will probably be a further tightening of police controls and a renewed insistence upon Moscow's ideological authority. This renewed emphasis on repressive measures will probably be applied discreetly, however, with appropriate consideration for local requirements. A systematic, uniform, and provocative policy of repression would probably be regarded by the Communist leaders as disadvantageous, and possibly even dangerous in the wake of the Polish and Hungarian events. Nevertheless, the security of Communist regimes will clearly have priority in Soviet thinking, and all policies affecting the Satellites will be judged primarily for their effects on the security of those regimes.

30. The need to win broader popular acceptance for the Satellite regimes will continue to be felt, however, by both Satellite and Soviet leaders. They cannot achieve lasting stability for the regimes or make the desired progress toward their political and economic goals so long as the bulk of the populations remains disaffected. Nevertheless, for some time they will seek to avoid political concessions which would stimulate opposition. However, the Communist leaders evidently now believe that they can make some economic concessions without running this risk, and they will probably continue to make such concessions even at the cost of sacrificing earlier production goals.

31. A special Soviet policy is required in Poland, where the USSR no longer possesses direct control over Polish internal policy. The Soviet leaders are trying to regain this control, but the pro-Moscow faction in the Polish Communist party is not now strong enough to obtain compliance with Soviet views. The use of force by the USSR against the Gomulka regime would almost certainly be resisted by the bulk of the Polish nation and armed forces. The result would probably be the involvement of Soviet forces in large-scale military operations which could spread to East Germany and thus provoke a major international crisis.

32. Even though the costs and risks of military intervention are sufficiently high to convince the Soviet leaders that they must contain their dissatisfaction with Polish internal developments, the threat of such intervention nevertheless remains real enough to deter the Gomulka regime from encroaching on essential Soviet security interests. The regime will therefore continue to make its territory available for Soviet military uses, in particular a secure line of communication to East Germany, and to refrain from openly opposing the USSR and other Communist states on international issues. The Soviet leaders will probably accept the arrangement for the time being, since it meets their minimum security requirements and insures the continued existence of a Communist regime in Poland.

33. In our judgment, this arrangement will not, however, represent a long-run solution satisfactory to the Soviet leaders. It is possible that, at any time, they will conclude that their prospects for reimposing full authority by limited means are diminishing, and that developments in Poland are becoming increasingly dangerous to the Bloc. They might then decide to apply major political and economic pressures, and might eventually proceed to military measures. We believe it more likely that they will proceed more deliberately, hoping that, by taking advantage of Gomulka's economic and political difficulties and playing upon his dependence on the USSR for military supplies and economic help, they can rebuild the pro-Soviet faction within the Polish

party and armed forces and restore a more reliable Communist regime. As a part of this effort, other Communist parties have been employed to put ideological pressure on the Gomulka regime.

34. A major problem for the Soviet leaders, if the present more nationalist leadership in Poland consolidates its position, will be to prevent Polish deviationist tendencies from spreading to other Satellites. In many respects—press freedom, relations with the church, the role of trade unions and factory worker councils, agricultural collectivization and procurement policies, political activity by non-Party groups, the allocation of production to consumer needs—the Polish regime is already heretic in terms of some of the doctrines and practices which prevail elsewhere in the Bloc. The question which the Soviet leaders as well as the leaders of other Satellites must ask themselves is whether these departures from the hitherto imposed uniformity of Communist policy can be safely tolerated. Both groups of leaders must see the danger that the Polish experiments, if they succeed, will set afoot further factionalism within other Satellite parties. The Soviet leaders probably fear that acceptance of the innovations introduced in Poland could lead to variations of doctrine and practice elsewhere which would ultimately be very difficult for the authoritarian Communist creed to contain. Not least of all, the Soviet leaders would be concerned that the liberalizing heresy could spread rapidly to the USSR itself. Therefore, they will maintain a steady pressure on the Polish regime to keep its reformist tendencies within an acceptable margin of conformity.

35. It is this same concern with the danger of ideological deviation which has led the USSR to drop for the time being its effort to associate Yugoslavia more closely with the Bloc. The Soviet leaders probably believe that Yugoslavia's influence, while not a primary cause, contributed to the troubles in Warsaw and Budapest. They probably also believe that their willingness to receive Tito with high honors and their eager efforts to re-establish party relations encouraged the belief in the Satellite parties that the USSR was willing to tolerate independent nationalist tendencies. The polemics with Belgrade since the Hungarian events make it clear that the Soviet leaders intend to repair their previous error. They probably feel that it is essential to resume the ideological isolation of Titoism, but in order to avoid strengthening Yugoslav ties with the West and alienating neutralist opinion they will probably seek to avoid a new break in state relations.

36. The attitude of Communist China will also be an important factor affecting Soviet policy toward the Satellites. The unprecedented involvement of Communist China in Eastern European affairs through Chou En-lai's recent trip reflects the importance that Communist China attaches to Bloc stability as well as the seriousness of Soviet difficulties. This involvement has placed Communist China in a position to exert greater influence over Soviet policy. Because of ideological affinity and military and economic dependence, the Chinese Communists have given strong support to Soviet policy toward the Bloc. Concerned, however, with both their own independence from Moscow and Communism's image in neutralist Asia, they have stressed the dangers of "great power chauvinism" and the importance of "national peculiarities." While endorsing repression in Hungary, Communist China has not joined in Soviet criticisms of the Polish press, and there is some evidence of Sino-Soviet differences on the issue of Poland. The Soviet leaders' freedom of action in Eastern Europe may be limited by the desire to maintain the approval and cooperation of Communist China.

37. Soviet military policy toward the Satellites will probably be changed somewhat as a result of the Polish and Hungarian developments. The Polish army supported the nationalist opposition and most Hungarian soldiers either went over to the rebellion or did not oppose it. The Soviet leaders probably now believe that for many purposes the reliability of these forces cannot be counted upon, and that, in circumstances where internal uprisings or foreign war raised hopes of attaining national independence, they might become an actual danger to Communist regimes.

38. The USSR will probably not in the future pursue a uniform policy of supporting maintenance of large Satellite armed force, but will adapt its military programs to local conditions. Intensive efforts will be undertaken to improve security controls within the Satellite forces, especially among higher officers.

39. General economic development in the Satellites for the next several years will probably permit only small increases in living standards, even if there are no further outbreaks of popular resistance. Improvements substantial enough to alter political attitudes toward the USSR and local regimes would require a fundamental overhauling of some institutions and policies. This would include such measures as a reduction in total investment and a redirection of investment programs in favor of housing, consumers goods, and agriculture; abandonment of collectivization and state trade channels; the revival of small private industry; and some redirection of trade away from Bloc partners to the West. Except in Poland, sufficiently radical steps in these directions will be very difficult for Soviet and Satellite leaders to accept, and attempts to undertake them would probably lead to factional disputes.

40. Nevertheless, while the regimes would probably gain little politically from moderate increases in consumer welfare, they have much to lose if they aggravate discontent by failing to achieve such increases or by permitting declines. Thus grudging concessions will be made, although they probably will not be far-reaching enough to reduce significantly the underlying disaffection of the population. Other countries are likely to follow Poland, Hungary, and Rumania in revising their long-term economic plans to insure that some gains for the consumer are in fact achieved. Institutional changes will probably be adopted in an effort to remove specific causes of friction, but administrative decentralization and an active role for workers' councils in industry cannot be carried very far without jeopardizing political control and fulfillment of plans. Wage and pension increases have recently been instituted in most countries, but these add to inflationary pressure at a time when the supply of goods is inadequate. Several Satellite regimes have declared their intention to continue pressures for collectivization, a policy which will negate much of the effect of other concessions to the peasantry.

41. The general revision of Satellite plans, the impending revision of the USSR's Sixth Five-Year Plan, and the immediate economic dislocations caused by developments in Poland and Hungary will force the Bloc to take up again the difficult task of coordinating its economies. Poland will probably seek to direct a large share of its coal exports to Western countries, despite the needs of its Bloc trading partners. Other countries producing commodities readily marketable for hard currencies (such as Rumanian oil and Hungarian bauxite) might try to do the same, and several Satellites may seek to avoid those aspects of Bloc specialization which require them to develop uneconomic industries or to become unduly dependent upon their neighbors. Thus the effort through CEMA to subordinate national economic programs to an integration of the separate Bloc economies will probably be slowed.

42. Sufficient Soviet aid could, of course, help the Satellites through a period of readjustment. The USSR is waiving claims on many Satellite economies and bolstering them with hard currency loans and raw materials on long-term credit, concessions which thus far will cost it about $750,000,000 in 1957, and may be increased later in the year. Except for large grain shipments aimed at offsetting 1956 failures of Satellite harvests, these concessions will not produce important immediate results for Satellite peoples. The current re-examination in the USSR of its own five-year plan suggests that it could be reluctant to raise its aid to the Satellites much more. Thus, in addition to sanctioning or even suggesting a moderation of the industrialization effort in some Satellites, the Soviet leaders probably would not prevent the Satellites from expanding further their trade with the free world, particularly with the underdeveloped countries.

43. The Polish economy is presently plagued by general disorganization and low labor discipline. Provided these difficulties are removed, Polish long-range economic prospects will be somewhat better than those of most other Satellites because of Poland's potential for earning hard currency and its willingness to introduce radical economic reforms. The large majority of collective farms have already been dissolved, and many other measures of economic reform have been instituted or are being discussed. At best, these reforms will take time to produce improvements in living standards and additional external economic assistance would be neces-

sary to achieve prompt results. Poland has sought long-term credits from the West, although the Soviet leaders would almost certainly be uneasy if agreements for such credits on such a large scale were made. Large-scale Western assistance to Poland would tempt other Satellites to seek similar assistance and might tend to undermine Bloc unity.

Political Stability

44. Prospects for political stability in Poland, although remaining uncertain, have been improved by the recent elections. The degree of internal liberalization and independence from the USSR achieved thus far does not satisfy many Poles, who submit to the rule of native Communists only in order to avoid Soviet military intervention. Gomulka's election victory, however, has strengthened his hand vis-a-vis the USSR and pro-Soviet elements in his own party and will probably enable him to move further towards satisfying domestic aspirations. Nevertheless, the balance between Soviet requirements and Polish desires will remain susceptible to upset by such factors as serious economic deprivations, provocative Soviet acts, a renewal of the open struggle within the Polish party, or a flare-up of violence elsewhere in the Bloc. Political stability would be considerably enhanced by an early improvement in living standards, but this depends upon completion of extensive economic reforms, the restoration of labor discipline, and probably on foreign assistance as well.

45. In Hungary, the reimposition of political authority will continue to depend upon the regime's use of force. Fear of encouraging another uprising will prevent the regime from granting the kind of concessions likely to reduce the hatred of Soviet domination. This hatred will be strengthened by the decline in living standards which appears unavoidable in 1957. The regime will continue to be no more respected than its Stalinist predecessor, and its demands will encounter widespread apathy and evasion. However, exhaustion and the continued presence of Soviet troops will probably prevent another general uprising. Because anti-regime sentiment is so widely and consciously shared, however, passive resistance will probably continue and might at any time flare up into a general strike or other overt acts which could bring renewed violence.

46. While discontent is high in all the other Satellites, none seems likely to manifest that combination of party disunity and popular boldness which led to the Polish and Hungarian revolutions. A potential threat to political stability currently exists in East Germany, where a fuel shortage has caused difficulties which may lead to serious economic disruptions possibly followed by strikes, riots, or both. We believe, however, that Soviet forces there are sufficient to discourage a general rising or to suppress it quickly should it occur.

47. Over the next several years, tensions between the Satellite regimes and their populations are likely to be generally higher than prior to the events in Poland and Hungary. The intimidating effect of the repression in Hungary probably will be overshadowed by the disappointment of expectations for economic improvement, by the inability to grant meaningful political reforms without encouraging extreme demands, and by the continued employment of strict censorship and at least a modified form of police terror. While there will continue to be some danger of revolt in the Satellites during the next few years, we believe it more likely that major violence will be avoided and that, if it should break out, the USSR will move forcefully to suppress it.

48. The willingness of the Hungarians to oppose Soviet military force and their success in carrying out slowdowns and sit-down strikes have forced a new appraisal of the effectiveness of armed totalitarian power in intimidating opposition. The political, economic, and even military costs of armed intervention will lead the USSR to make every effort to prevent situations from arising in which this is the only Soviet alternative. On the other hand, the bloody reprisals in Hungary will give pause to rebellious elements there and in the other Satellites.

49. The success or failure of the Gomulka regime in Poland will greatly influence the future role of nationalist-oriented elements which continue to exist in most of the Satellite Communist parties. So long as Poland maintains its present course, nationalists in other Satellite Communist parties will be encouraged to seek substantial gains in autonomy, while the USSR will try to

suppress moves in this direction. In these circumstances nationalist elements may act not only to disrupt party unity but also, as in Hungary, to stimulate general resistance within the population, although the USSR would probably take whatever measures were necessary to maintain its control. It is also possible, however, that nationalist elements, for example in Czechoslovakia or Bulgaria, may act in less disruptive ways, and gradually achieve control of party organizations in a manner that would be difficult for the USSR to prevent. The reimposition by the USSR of complete control over Poland would probably not extinguish the forces of nationalism in the Satellite Communist parties, but these elements would be obliged to curtail their aspirations considerably and would for some time have to accept only such limited concessions as the USSR was willing to grant. In any case, we believe that the persistent sources of popular disaffection in the Satellites will continue to be present.

[Source: Published in Jeffrey Richelson, The Soviet Estimate: U.S. Analysis of the Soviet Union, 1947–1991 *(Washington, D.C.: National Security Archive and Chadwyck-Healey, 1995), document no. 00198. A truncated version (paragraphs 1–6) appears in* Foreign Relations of the United States, 1955–1957 *vol. 25, Eastern Europe, (Washington, D.C.: United States Government Printing Office, 1990), pp. 578–579.]*

DOCUMENT NO. 111: HSWP Provisional Central Committee Resolution concerning the Evaluation of the Nagy Group's Role, February 26, 1957 (Excerpts)

The February 26 session of the HSWP Provisional Central Committee was the most important political event in the country during the first quarter of 1957. The final resolution, published in Népszabadság the following day, clearly showed the party leadership's increasing self-confidence. One by one, the document deals with major questions of party-building, public administration, the economy, mass organizations and international inter-party relations. The resolution explains the regime's success partly as a result of the effectiveness of administrative measures (against the workers' councils and revolutionary committees), but mainly as a consequence of the party's clear separation from the "anti-Marxist" and "revisionist" views of the Nagy group, which the Central Committee is already describing unambiguously as traitorous. Naturally, the CC urges continuing this approach, which ultimately brings a new wave of administrative measures beginning in March 1957 that includes suppressing resistance by the church, eliminating alternative youth associations and carrying out mass arrests of revolutionaries.

The harsher tone of the February resolution did not entirely supplant the analysis in the December resolution, at least as far as its evaluation of the "October events" was concerned. The document reproduced here had a fairly specific purpose—to prepare for an upcoming visit to Moscow and to back up plans to take legal action against the Nagy group. Afterwards, the earlier interpretation resurfaced, becoming part of the ideological foundation of the Kádár era almost until the very end.[274]

THE "FEBRUARY 1957" RESOLUTION OF THE HSWP PROVISIONAL CENTRAL COMMITTEE CONCERNING CURRENT QUESTIONS AND TASKS.

The Provisional Central Committee of the Hungarian Socialist Workers' Party gathered on February 26, 1957. Following the reports of comrades János Kádár and Károly Kiss, the Central Committee discussed the following issues on the agenda: 1. Current questions and tasks; 2. Organizational and personnel questions. Besides the speakers, 17 comrades contributed to the joint discussion of the two issues. The Central Committee made several decisions regarding the items on the agenda.

The Central Committee found that the permanent battle against counterrevolutionary forces and the implementation of the party resolution of last December[275] has resulted in considerable success in the fields of politics, economics and culture, as well as in the development of party and mass organizations.

[....]

II. Uniting the forces of Socialism

Parallel with the further development of the party, significant advances were achieved regarding the unification and activation of the main forces of socialism for the fight against counterrevolution. The struggle for the successful and complete achievement of this objective began during a most complicated political situation, and it is still far from being over.

Since last December, when we crushed the open forces of counterrevolution (the armed squads and fascist and retrograde bourgeois parties and organizations that promptly cropped up after October 23), and forced their remaining fragments to go underground, a new phase of the

---

[274] For this interpretation of the February resolution, see Melinda Kalmár, *Ennivaló és Hozomány: A kora kádárizmus ideológiája* (Budapest: Magvető, 1998), 26.

[275] See Document No. 104.

struggle began. It is well known that, despite the protest of their honest members, the so-called "regional" and "central" workers' councils, the various "revolutionary committees," and the writers' and journalists' unions were the covert outposts of the defeated counterrevolution. The dissolution or suspension of some of these organizations proved to be a completely appropriate measure.

In order to eliminate the counterrevolutionary forces entirely, the consistent and firm use of the instruments of proletarian dictatorship is unavoidable, albeit insufficient on its own. In addition to retributive measures, the ideological and political exposure and isolation of the counterrevolution is absolutely necessary.

In its attempt to overthrow the Hungarian People's Republic, the counterrevolution directed its main attack against the leading force of the proletarian dictatorship—the party. They slandered the party, undermined its authority, ravaged party headquarters and institutions, and threatened, persecuted and physically annihilated party members, so that the socialist masses, bereft of their leaders, could be turned against the people's power—that is, against their own interests. The counterrevolution exploited the rightful indignation of one part of the masses, which was induced by the mistakes of the old party leadership. It attempted to confuse the class consciousness of the workers with chauvinist, nationalist, revisionist, anti-Semitic and other bourgeois counterrevolutionary ideas, as well as to win over the deluded masses and to launch an attack against the power of the people's state.

Besides expropriated industrialists, landowners, traders, kulaks, former fascist-Horthyite army officers, policemen and gendarmes, the counterrevolution possessed even in mid-December significant reserves in social strata which were temporarily confused and fell under the influence of counterrevolutionary ideas. [These strata were] made up in small measure by workers and peasants, in greater measure by certain intellectual circles, and most of all by young intellectuals (university and high-school students).

The ideological confusion among certain strata of workers and the paralyzing of the forces of socialism and the party were caused first and foremost by Imre Nagy and his followers with their anti-Marxist, revisionist views, which were in fact bourgeois, nationalist and anti-Soviet in nature and represented a rejection of the entire proletarian dictatorship. With their revisionist views, Imre Nagy and his followers were aligned with the imperialist bourgeoisie, thus playing the role of the counterrevolution's vanguard before October 23 and its rearguard after November 4.

Uniting the forces of socialism was a relatively speedy and successful process during the past two and a half months because the party openly condemned the revisionist views of the Imre Nagy group, and raised high the banner of Marxism-Leninism, proletarian dictatorship and the international proletariat—the banner betrayed by this group.

Regarding the evaluation of events in the recent past, organizations of the Hungarian Socialist Workers' Party have created a political and ideological consensus. The party membership sees more and more clearly the traitorous role of Imre Nagy, Losonczy and their accomplices, and believes that the prerequisite for our success and progress in the future is the final eradication of the anti-Marxist ideas that this group holds. The better we can cope with this task, the more the deluded strata of workers will be delivered from the political and ideological influence of the counterrevolution, and united to defend the people's power and build socialism. [...]

[Source: Népszabadság, *February 28, 1957. Translated by Csaba Farkas.]*

DOCUMENT NO. 112: Kádár's Report before the HSWP Provisional Executive Committee on the Soviet-Hungarian Negotiations in Moscow, April 2, 1957

Between March 21–28, a Hungarian party and government delegation visited Moscow. This document is an excerpt of the minutes of Kádár's report to the party afterwards. As the first official visit of the new Hungarian leadership after the revolution, it was of special significance. In his speech, Kádár emphasizes Rákosi's possible return to Hungary and the question of how to deal with the Nagy group. By this time, however, the Soviet leadership had given up on any political role for Rákosi and his circle in Hungary: they were "political corpses," according to the consensus. The only problem that threatened the stability of the Kádár government at this stage was the economy; yet, the report only marginally mentions the matter of Soviet economic aid—albeit in generous phrases despite the fact that in early 1957 Moscow promised barely one-third of the commodity credits Hungary was requesting. Kádár's report only briefly touches on the matter of Soviet troops "temporarily garrisoned in Hungary," as the standard phrase went, even though immediate legal clarification of the issue was equally important for both parties. One of the major points of significance of this document is that it reveals that it was Kádár and the Hungarians who initiated the court procedure against Nagy and his accomplices, and that the Soviets merely gave their consent.

MINUTES OF THE SESSION HELD ON APRIL 2, 1957, PREPARED BY THE EXECUTIVE COMMITTEE OF THE HSWP

1. Verbal account of the Party and Government delegations' experiences on their visit to Moscow.

Comrade *János Kádár:* As far as the Government delegation's visit to Moscow is concerned, I don't want to repeat what has already been made public. However what I can say about the negotiations is that they took place with fairly open diplomacy: the questions raised that were important appear in the report. At most it can be supplemented with a few elements that do not appear in the declaration.[276]

I would like to mention that the atmosphere of the negotiations was—it is fair to say—characterized by mutual trust and complete openness. Where opinions were not fully identical, we declared this openly.

Which questions deserve mention here?

The question of the former leaders was raised. On those occasions when ideas were exchanged about the former leaders, the comrades decisively and categorically declared that they (primarily Rákosi but the other former leaders as well) were—to use their words—political corpses, who would never return to power. In this regard the comrades also said that in their opinion it is not expedient to rebury the dead every week. This is clear and understandable and we agreed with it. The comrades said that they completely accept our resolution about this.[277] On one occasion I declared our position on this quite carefully and went on to justify it, because at first I thought that the comrades did not fully understand our resolution. I explained that for our part personal prejudice and vengeance would have no role to play, and that they should take note of this; on the other hand the way we see this question is that the return of a group of former leaders, and of

---

[276] The communiqué on the Hungarian-Soviet government and party negotiations appeared in *Népszabadság* on March 30, 1957. *Pravda* published the declaration on the front page of its March 29, 1957, edition.

[277] At its February 26, 1957, session, the HSWP Provisional CC decided on the possible repatriation of former Hungarian leaders currently living in the Soviet Union. Rákosi and Gerő were not allowed to return to Hungary for five years, while András Hegedüs, István Kovács, and others had to remain abroad for one year. József Révai, however, was permitted to return. In a March 5, 1957, letter, Károly Kiss informed the CPSU CC Presidium about these decisions.

course the return of Rákosi, would be tantamount to breaking up the newly organized party which can generally be described as unified. Quite simply, the very act of their return would be accompanied by the growth of factions within the party, and in response, as we have already witnessed, this would give birth to the right-wing as well, which would be an extremely dangerous thing for the party in the current period. The comrades regard this to be correct, support it, and will provide the assistance we asked for in this matter. They said that their position was no easier on this question, because these people are in contact with them. Actually I can mention by way of example that when we published Comrade Révai's article in *Népszabadság*, it received the predictable response[278] and met serious opposition; the debate within the party did not even concern Révai, rather the communists united in the party wanted to know what will happen to Rákosi, whether he will return and whether the others will return. Also connected to this question is the fact that Comrade [Károly] Kiss related our resolution to the comrades in exile. On one occasion he spoke to a group of comrades in exile and separately with Rákosi and Gerő. This conversation ended with negative results, because they declared in unison that they do not agree with our decision. They justified this with things that on their own are difficult to deny. E.g.: it was not in line with party principles for us to decide on their case without hearings; what party rule or law is there which empowers party leaders to keep citizens or communists out of the country? They made the point that this attitude is a very strange precedent, because it suggests that all communists who made mistakes must be sent to the Soviet Union, and Rákosi also made the point whether, according to this notion, Soviet communists who made mistakes should perhaps be sent to China? The point at issue, then, is that they did not agree with the resolution, which they see as seriously and exceptionally unfair. When the question was raised whether they should resign from certain public functions, they declared that they would not prepare any letters of resignation.

To this I should add that after Comrade Kiss spoke to them, Rákosi, Gerő and, separately, Hegedüs wrote a letter to the Presidium of the CPSU and a letter was written by László Piros as well. The CPSU Presidium told us about the letter, the essence of which was the same as what they had declared at the time of their talk with Comrade Kiss, and they asked the CPSU Presidium to revise our resolution.

Rákosi also wrote a particularly idiosyncratic letter, which said nothing about whether he could return home, but explained how the people of the country were actually waiting for him to come back.[279] He had received telegrams and letters saying that he should come home and in general—so he said—declaring that the situation in Hungary was strange, with followers of Imre Nagy and Tito in the leadership—like Kádár and Apró. This abnormal situation is also characterized by the nature of the party's growth: 200,000 have already joined the party in Hungary, but 600,000 former HWP members have not. From this it must be concluded that these 200,000 are followers of Kádár while the 600,000 are followers of Rákosi, and are waiting for him to come back. The Soviet comrades have seriously begun to think that there is something wrong in Rákosi's head. They renewed their support for our resolution.

The question arises of what else we should do. I suggest that we execute our resolution, that is, they should not come back and their resignation from public office should be arranged. It has

---

[278] In the March 7, 1957, issue of *Népszabadság*, József Révai's article entitled "Ideological Clarity" elicited considerable response. On the basis of county reports, the CC Agitation and Propaganda Department prepared a summary stating that some party members agreed with the article "to the last letter," while others agreed "only with the basic thought," and still others, "a strata (intellectuals, old HWP members)" reacted with "indignation." It is very likely that Kádár deliberately used Révai to test public opinion and to provoke a reaction that could be used to strengthen Kádár's own position. The dogmatic style with which Révai attempted to rehabilitate the Rákosi era and his vehement attacks on Nagy helped Kádár to create an atmosphere within the leadership that made it easier to settle the Nagy case. Also, the threat of Rákosi's possible return—for which the article became a symbol—helped Kádár by presenting him to party members and public alike as the lesser of two evils. See, Kalmár, *Ennivaló és Hozomány*, 30–45.

[279] Rákosi sent this letter to Khrushchev on March 27, 1957, after Károly Kiss informed him about the HSWP Provisional CC resolution. See footnote 277 above.

to be said that their behavior in this regard is not proper. The explanation for their behavior can only be that these comrades not only do not know what is happening at home, but they cannot examine their own situation with the necessary moderation and sobriety, and we particularly regret their behavior because if they follow this course these people will go to ruin. What their behavior suggests is that they think they were right, etc.

In addition to executing the resolution, I recommend that we examine a few questions. The question arises of the children of various ages of those in exile who have already lost a year of school and are going to miss another year. Their request is that their wives and children be able to return home and go to school in Hungary. In my opinion we must find a solution to this problem.

My other recommendation is that we write to the members of the group, and to Rákosi and Gerő separately, and show that their behavior is improper, and that even if they disagree with our decision, we will still execute it, and ask them please to refrain from any actions that would further inflame the problem. In the case of Rákosi, the Soviet comrades have themselves remarked that the question should be pondered as to whether he should not live in Moscow.[280] I have already said that within an hour and a half of the publication of the Révai article, Rákosi had telephoned Nemes[281] and told him that he wanted to write an article for *Népszabadság*.

In my opinion we should decide that, having heard the account of Comrade Kiss, the Executive Committee is of the opinion that it will execute its resolution, and that we will make a suggestion about the schooling of the children at the next session of the Executive Committee. The question is important from the party's point of view, of course, but also from the point of view of friendly relations with the CPSU, and we believe it to be a very positive result of our negotiations in the Soviet Union that the CPSU Presidium agrees with our proposal.

The matter of Mihály Farkas also arose during the discussions. At the time we were not aware of the sentence and I mentioned that since it was clear that the right-wing traitors must legally be called to account, it would strengthen the party's just position to a significant extent if it did not administer punishment in only one direction. I noted that the attitude towards Farkas has until now been very negative; it is not in accordance with the original decision and this must be corrected. The degree of punishment (which is exceptionally light, disregarding the fact that we did not want 20-year prison sentences) is at stake here. The course of the negotiations was such that those at the forefront turned against the party and the current leadership. Farkas' conduct and the timidity of the court contributed to this. The question arises what the Hungarian party will do with Farkas if we proclaim an amnesty. Will we present him [sic] to the Soviet Union, too? For the moment the thing to do is to condemn Farkas for what he has done, and we can and must deliver an appropriate sentence.[282]

The question of Imre Nagy and the others also arose. We raised it. The comrades think it proper that we call him to account with suitable severity. The opinion of the comrades is that the question of whether this proceeding happens sooner or later may be debated, but they endorse its execution. Those who have already dealt with this matter[283] say that criminal proceedings are inevitable—we are of course talking about a mass of genuine criminal acts. However many peo-

---

[280] In July 1957, Mátyás Rákosi and his wife were moved out of Moscow to the Black sea.

[281] Dezső Nemes was director of the Party College in 1956 and editor-in-chief of *Népszabadság* from January 1957–1961.

[282] Mihály Farkas, a member of the innermost circle of the leadership, bore the greatest share of responsibility, after Rákosi, for the illegalities and show trials of the late 1940s and early 1950s. Yet, the "Farkas case" had more to do with creating a scapegoat and with Rákosi's attempts to sacrifice him in order to divert attention from his own responsibility. In March 1956, the HWP CC launched an investigation of Farkas, which was followed by his demotion (from the rank of army general to private) and expulsion from the party in July. Farkas was arrested on October 12, 1956, and sentenced to 16 years in prison the following year. On April 5, 1960, he was released through a personal amnesty.

[283] The CPSU Presidium officials involved in the Nagy case were Nikolai Bulganin and Georgii Malenkov, as well as Boris Ponomarev, head of the CPSU CC Department for Ties with Foreign Communist Parties, who was sent to Bucharest on March 4, 1957.

ple we interview because they were traitors, they all declare that they got their instructions from Nagy, Losonczy, et al. Even Dudás referred to this group at the court proceeding. Of course, bearing our past experiences in mind, nothing can be invented—our starting point should be the facts known by hundreds of thousands of people. This matter demands conscientious preparatory work. As far as the political side of the matter is concerned, it is a more reasonable viewpoint to say that, depending on the amount of work the examination requires—not playing for time, of course—we must restore order to this problem. It is impossible to imagine the whole country's political situation without us establishing suitable order in this matter. Imre Nagy and his partners were proud during the "victorious days" that they had organized and initiated a "national revolution"; in my opinion, we must show the Hungarian people, the enemy of the Hungarian people, and the world, that a counterrevolution cannot be staged within the socialist system without being punished. I support starting work on this and making a decision within the foreseeable future; we cannot wait 8–10 months, or years, to pull out the bad tooth.[284]

Part of this matter is covered by another resolution of ours which must also be executed—the decision about György Lukács and Zoltán Vas, according to which they should be separated from the rest of the group.[285] Our opinion was that Lukács should return home, while Szántó and Vas should, from certain points of view, remain out of the country, because their return would have as strong an effect as the return of Hegedüs or István Kovács, although naturally the opposite one.

At the time we succeeded in reaching agreement with Zoltán Vas. Although he does not agree with the resolution that he cannot come home now, he recognizes it and as he said, he will work and behave in a way that will oblige us to allow him to return home early.

The letter Lukács wrote to the government has arrived. This letter is an interesting piece of work; it does not mention any kind of breaking away from the Nagy group, in fact there is even a twist in it, which in Lukács's case I do not think to be that significant. What is so interesting about this letter? Referring to the time of the events in October, it says that he is convinced that the tiny minority within the party leadership that wanted to distinguish politically between those fighting against Rákosi and Gerő and the counterrevolutionaries was right. Later he writes that serious mistakes were also made, like the declaration of neutrality and withdrawing from the Warsaw Pact, from which it is clear that he understands Nagy's group to be the "tiny minority". Lukács asks to return home on the pretext that he would like to finish a paper in suitable surroundings. In his earlier letter he said that on the basis of his conversation with Comrade Kállai he would agree to the solution according to which he would deal with his academic work, apolitically, for a suitable period of time in a convenient place. I think we must already allow Lukács's return. In my opinion the proper thing would be for me to declare at the Government's next session that such a letter has arrived from Lukács and that I recommend that the Government accept his return; then a two- to three-line article should appear in the newspaper, saying that the Government, at his request, allowed Lukács to return home. If Lukács keeps to his promise, there will be no further complications in this matter. There will of course be meddling and sensation-hunting.[286]

As far as Zoltán Szántó is concerned: he also wrote a letter, the essence of which is that he does not agree with our resolution, and wants to return home immediately. He refers to his merits, to the fact that he fought for a long time against Rákosi's mistakes, that he did not actually

---

[284] The Provisional Executive Committee accepted the proposal on the legal proceeding against the Nagy group and the Provisional CC approved the decision on April 5, 1957. On April 9, the Executive Committee introduced a resolution on "the arrest of" and "beginning of a legal procedure" against Nagy and his associates. Yet, the announcement of the sentences and the execution of the main defendants occurred only a year later. See Documents Nos. 116 and 117.

[285] The resolution on the separation of Zoltán Szántó, György Lukács and Zoltán Vas from the rest of the Nagy group was accepted by the HSWP Provisional Executive Committee on January 29, 1957. On February 26, the Provisional CC confirmed the decision.

[286] György Lukács returned to Hungary on April 11, 1957, the first of those detached from the rest of the Nagy group to be allowed to do so.

520

do anything wrong, that he even stood up against Nagy at the Yugoslav Embassy. He refers in his letter to two actions of his which he describes as positive. The first is that he recommended the creation of the HSWP, and only had this recommendation accepted after long debate.[287] Kádár and Münnich are to blame for the fact that he ended up at the Yugoslav Embassy, because they did not tell him what they wanted to do. He also refers to the previous falling out and says that he was in a very bad nervous state, regrets what he declared and did not even mean it. He states that he disagrees with the resolution. I recommend that we execute the resolution relating to him and that our envoy tell him that if he does not agree with it but is still willing to recognize and accommodate it, he can live in a free regime in Romania and can work somewhere as a contract employee. I only want to add that Szántó wrote a letter on December 14, in which he relates quite revealing facts about how they ended up at the Yugoslav Embassy.[288] Lukács also writes that they went there at the invitation of the Yugoslavs. Szántó criticizes us in connection with this for not yet having used the revealing material available to us.[289] In my opinion we must tell Szántó that if he really wants to fight against this group, he must reveal the relevant information at a news conference or similar forum.[290]

An aspect of the negotiations in the Soviet Union that is still very interesting—and which is not clear from the material that has been made public—is that the Soviets have altered their economic support in our favor and we can expect a commercial credit of about 200 million rubles. Comrade Khrushchev and his colleagues said that they were not in an easy situation either, what with their help for China, Poland and others. But they displayed very considerable understanding and the fact that they give us these things represents a serious effort on their part.

As far as Soviet troops are concerned—and this is included in the published agreement[291]—our opinion is that within the current conditions we must definitely remain within the Warsaw Pact. In this regard the Soviet comrades declared that on this question we have taken a defensive position to our own disadvantage, that we are not right to be defensive, and that our defensive propaganda does not correspond to the true nature of the international situation. The imperialists are steaming ahead: they have created a united command in Western Germany and in the Far East, and will do the same in the Middle East; they are building military bases around the countries of the socialist bloc, but we are still always on the defensive about whether Soviet troops should be based in Hungary or not. We should represent an opinion which strengthens the socialist bloc. Comrade Khrushchev suggested, a little ironically, that they have no objection to Hungarian troops being based in Moscow or perhaps guarding the Soviet border to Japan.

Another political question should be raised here, albeit not a very earth-shattering one: in the Soviet Union they will arrange a particularly large celebration on November 7 this year, which is the fortieth anniversary of the great October Socialist Revolution. We agreed at the negotiations that we will recommend to our various sister parties that military divisions from the socialist countries should participate symbolically in the military parade on November 7. I think this would in general have a beneficial effect as far as the strengthening of internationalism is concerned and as far as public opinion in Hungary is concerned as well. There is another similar

---

[287] It was indeed Szántó who, on October 30, first proposed to the HWP Presidium the idea of forming a new party called the Hungarian Socialist Workers' Party; the Presidium's initial response was negative.

[288] Szántó actually wrote the letter in question on December 17. On December 14, he produced a "Statement" on the circumstances of his entry into the Yugoslav Embassy.

[289] That is, the information sent by Szántó.

[290] Szántó was finally allowed to return to Hungary in 1958. During the investigation against the Nagy group, he produced incriminating evidence against the members of the group.

[291] The relevant part of the joint declaration states the following: "The two parties have agreed that they will conduct negotiations in the near future concerning the determination of the number and effective force of the Soviet troops' stationing in Hungary as well as the questions of their location and will sign an agreement for this purpose, which will regulate the legal status of the Soviet troops provisionally stationed on the territory of the Hungarian People's Republic." The agreement was signed in Budapest on May 27, 1957.

suggestion which I would also like to make, that workers' representatives from various countries participate in this demonstration and that they march under their own flag.[292]

The only other thing to say is that the whole reception—whether we were meeting or talking to the highest leaders or simple Soviet workers—was exceptionally warm-hearted, direct and friendly, and deserved great appreciation. The direct meetings with the Soviet workers were simply astonishing. There were occasions when hundreds of participants in the workers' meetings wept. This was not, of course, only for the delegation itself, but for the Hungarian people as a whole. Everywhere we heard cries of good wishes to the Hungarian people who have defended the cause of socialism. This is the sort of thing which cannot be arranged. To mark our stay in Leningrad, wherever we went crowds of people stood in minus 17 degree [temperatures] and gave the delegation a warm welcome. Such great confidence and affection even make one a bit nervous, because in our view it brings with it considerable obligations. They have such confidence in us that we feel an even more particular responsibility. So if we say that Soviet-Hungarian friendship was strengthened as a result of the delegation's visit, this is not just a phrase, this is genuinely true.

There is another aspect to this visit—namely the Yugoslav question. We spoke about this, in private, on many occasions, and it seems that the position the Information Bureau held in 1948, objecting to the overthrow of the party leadership, is in fact sound.[293] The later position, of course, is not. Regarding the Hungarian question and the general development of the situation in Hungary, the behavior of the leaders of the Yugoslav Party and the members of its Government has been troublesome. In the opinion of our Soviet comrades there is only one course of action, to debate the issues and defend our position, because there is nothing else we can do. We told them that the situation here is that the October counterrevolution's main ideological firepower was provided by the Nagy group, and the connection between their line and the general line of the Yugoslavs is as clear as day. We made some public appearances where we outlined our positions. The situation with the Yugoslavs was a rather strange one: the ambassador came out to the airport to meet us, he came to the reception given in honor of the Hungarian Embassy, but he did not come to the session in the Kremlin. What was interesting about the Kremlin meeting was that, in addition to ambassadors from friendly countries, the Finnish ambassador, the Swedish ambassador and ambassadors from the Far East were there, but the Yugoslav ambassador was not. We returned home on Sunday. On Monday morning the Yugoslav ambassador contacted Comrade Münnich. It was a formal visit and he said that he saw our delegation's mention of them as improper and that he regarded what we had said as insulting to Yugoslavia and unjust. He objected to the fact that we had repeatedly talked about them and the imperialists in the same breath, and that we had said that their positions were the same. They object to this and also to the fact that in relations between the socialist countries it is difficult to imagine a mechanical distinction between fighting ideologically and cooperating on a state-to-state basis. They objected to the fact that we are continually attacking them about the Nagy affair. But it was Comrade Bulganin who talked about this, not us.

With regard to this, I make the following recommendations: The Yugoslav comrades have sent a letter about Nagy. We should write to the Presidium of the Central Committee of the Yugoslav League of Communists, and make our observations.[294] Here we could possibly raise questions that do not have to be made public. The observations should be worked out properly.

[292] Although this idea, which probably came from Khrushchev himself, was accepted by the HSWP Provisional Central Committee, and the Soviets reacted positively to Kádár's official proposal, the plan was never put into effect. Because of changes on the international political scene, the Soviet leadership suddenly changed its mind in October 1957 in the belief that the parade might be interpreted by the West as a display of force that would threaten the normalization of East-West relations.

[293] On June 27, 1948, a Cominform resolution condemned the peasant policy of the Yugoslav Communist Party and branded its overall policy line as nationalist.

[294] Kádár is referring here to the letter written by the LCY CC on February 13, 1957, which also included the Soviet-Yugoslav correspondence on the Hungarian events. The Provisional Executive Committee assigned Kádár to prepare a response. Although a draft was completed, the letter was never sent.

It would not be right to use an aggressive tone, to insult, or to repeat statements, such as that they are not communists, etc.—but on important questions we must make our opinion clear. We could also use the method of systematically dealing with the question of proletarian internationalism in *Népszabadság*. Proletarian internationalism is a very important matter, and we have never had as much justification to talk about it as we do now. We can talk about this as a protective strength, and we can adequately reflect on disputed questions related to this. I say that in no way can we accept that there is East and there is West. For our purposes the outside world is not divided into regions. We have to state our opinion on these and similar questions. Proletarian internationalism can also be said to be related to the battle between the various peoples in the [Far] East and the keeping of the peace. [...]

[Source: MOL, 288. f. 5/20 ő.e. Published in A Magyar Szocialista Munkáspárt ideiglenes vezető testületeinek jegyzőkönyvei, *vol. 2, 1957. január 25.–1957. április 2, edited by Karola Némethné Vágyi and Károly Urbán, (Budapest: Intera, 1993), pp. 346–365. Translated by David Evans.]*

DOCUMENT NO. 113: Notes of Talks between the PPR Party-State Delegation and the USSR Party-State Delegation, Moscow, May 24–25, 1957

This fragmented record of talks between Soviet and Polish leaders covers an exchange in which members of the Polish delegation try to avert Imre Nagy's impending execution. Nikita Khrushchev dismisses their objections, in the process providing a glimpse of how the Soviets reached the decision to intervene and how events unfolded from the Kremlin's perspective. During the talks, Khrushchev pursues the question of whether Nagy was an "imperialist agent." "Was he an agent in a legal sense? Did he take money? This is not material. But he did the enemies' work." Noting his view that the Hungarian "counterrevolutionaries" had committed atrocities against the authorities, the Soviet leader concludes that "[f]or communists and workers it will not be comprehensible if Nagy is not tried."

First day of talks:

Soviet side present: Khrushchev, Bulganin, Zhukov, Mikoyan, Saburov, Kabanov,[295] Nikitin, Gundobin and Ponomarenko;

The Polish side: Gomułka, Cyrankiewicz, [Marian] Spychalski, [Eugeniusz] Szyr, Jędrychowski, Graniewski, Waluchowski.

(...)

Gomułka: We are considering going to Ulbricht on June 15–16 for a couple of days at their invitation. Kádár also invited us but we didn't have the time. Cyrankiewicz was in Asia, Czechoslovakia. Lately, we heard that the Hungarians want to begin proceedings against Nagy. He's sitting in a prison in Budapest. We believe, from a political perspective, that it may bring about a great deal of damage. It is their affair, of course, but it also affects us. We believe that if a trial began now against Nagy it would complicate affairs. We have not responded to the Hungarians because of a lack of time. In any case, officially they haven't said anything to us. Unofficially, we were informed by one of their comrades, and on the following day by the newspaper.

Khrushchev: And what should be done with him?

Mikoyan: Maybe send him to Warsaw?

Gomułka: That's not what this is about. We also had affairs concerning some of our people. We should do what is politically beneficial. A campaign will again begin against the Hungarians; again they [the West] will begin to return to these events. Of course, we don't have all the materials. We only know what was in our reports from Yugoslavia. He was not, with any degree of confidence, an imperialist agent. There will be an uproar.

Khrushchev: There will be.

Gomułka: But this is a mistake, politically.

Khrushchev: No. The enemy will scream but our friends will understand that his [Nagy's] role was treacherous. Was he an agent in the legal sense? Did he take money? This is not material. But he did the enemies' work.

Gomułka: Maybe there's something we do not know but even if he was a traitor he could not have decided on anything on his own. He could not decide.

Khrushchev: Yes, he was not alone but he was the standard bearer. Kopácsi—the chief of

---

[295] Ivan G. Kabanov was minister of foreign trade from 1952 to 1958.

police—carried out what Nagy ordered. And Kopácsi hung communists.[296] This is a complicated affair. And not only a Hungarian affair but we believe that those guilty of the putsch must be held responsible. Those are the privileges of battle. This is class war.

Mikoyan: You untangled your affairs correctly but your situation was different. He [Nagy] went against the authority of the people's democracy.

Khrushchev: He withdrew from the Warsaw Pact; declared neutrality like in Austria; trials against communists. (Zhukov: Without a trial and investigation.) What kind of dictatorship of the proletariat is this? If they [the insurgents] had won they would have hung Kádár long ago.

Cyrankiewicz: If the counterrevolution had been victorious they would also have hung Nagy.

Khrushchev: This not clear. The Americans were with Nagy.[297] They said that it was necessary to suspend the terror.

Gomułka: In any case, I believe that one person couldn't do this.

Khrushchev: There were others. The Yugoslavs played the wrong role. To some degree they incited it. And there are such examples from the history of the working class movement; for example Noske.[298]

Cyrankiewicz: The communists fought against Noske, the working class fought.

Gomułka: Nagy is not Noske.

Khrushchev: Let them [the Hungarians] decide what is needed but the Hungarian nation should understand that Rákosi made mistakes and Nagy took advantage of them.

After we visited you, we went to see Tito.[299] He was of the same mind. What kind of a communist is he [Nagy], if a communist Premier hangs communists. At Tito's there was also a split. What if Nagy resigned from the premiership after the counterrevolution was victorious? We said that he [Nagy] would have done very well. Tito (2.XI.[56]) promised that he would convince Nagy. Tito, Ranković, Kardelj, and, I think, Mićunović took part in the talks. We sat all night. There were no disagreements between us over any matter. Tito said: It's necessary that you in fact move in [to Hungary]. [Khrushchev:] [Hungary is] A big country. [There is] The Warsaw Pact. The Romanians wanted to, and the Bulgarians, the Czechs also—as volunteers helping the Soviet army. Tito said—it's not necessary, it's better if you go alone. It's necessary to destroy the counterrevolution. The following day at sunrise Tito personally took us to the port. I advised him to leave Brioni. (He was sick at the time.) I said that bombs could accidentally fall on the island. When we said farewell we kissed each other. Well then—we took action. But we did not tell him the timetable. Zhukov brought the estimates he had to have ready in three days. We made the decision before I departed. I arrived by air with Malenkov at 3 or 4 in the afternoon. Kádár as well. Bulganin called from Sofia, at the time he did not know Kádár. Waiting in Moscow were [Imre] Horváth, Bata, Münnich, Kádár. (Tito said that if Kádár left Nagy it suggests the position of the working class. It is the conscience of the working class.) They discussed who was to be the Premier. They decided on Kádár. When they asked the Hungarians, they all said: Kádár, although at first they thought Münnich or Kádár. And that's how we formed the [Hungarian] government in Moscow. At 4:15 am [November 4], Zhukov began to act. We waited, for Nagy to resign. Instead, he succumbed and called for a manifestation of support [for his government], in any case he decided to run to the Yugoslavian embassy. This ruined our plans and we sent a note to Tito. And now—[is Nagy] guilty or not guilty? Tito got scared. If we hadn't

---

[296] In reality, "organized" executions never occurred during the revolution. Defenders of the old regime who died either lost their lives during the fighting or were victims of mob violence. These occasional lynchings (which were usually reactions to atrocities committed by the other side) claimed 15 victims nation-wide. The only significant execution-like act occurred after the siege of the Budapest party headquarters at Köztársaság Square on October 30. Here the total number of killed was 27, but this figure included those who died during the siege. See the introduction to this part.

[297] As the American documents published in this volume make clear, this allegation was far from true.

[298] Gustav Noske was a Social Democratic minister of defense in the Weimar Republic who used military force against the workers in 1919–1920.

[299] This is a reference to Khrushchev and Malenkov's meeting with Tito on the island of Brioni on November 2–3, 1956. See Document No. 76.

moved in the fascists would have won. And they [the Yugoslavs] have 1,000 km of frontier with the Hungarians. He said it was an impossible problem for him. And now he accuses us and speaks of intervention. Historians will find it difficult to keep a grip on themselves. We have already told you that it will cost us too much time to heal wounds and, according to the Hungarian talks, we were told that a partisan war in Hungary will last a long time. But their nation did not support them. The army did not put up resistance. In two days Zhukov disarmed it and seized every armory. The longest resistance was in Budapest. And lastly, during the anniversary of the liberation of Hungary [from the Nazis on April 4.]—never have so many people to date ever gone to visit the graves of the soldiers of the Soviet Army and held so many rallies, as now. Our soldiers have absolutely no conflicts with the people [of Hungary]. Kádár asked us to send to him reinforcements—party workers, engineers, district committee [*raikom*] and county committee [*obkom*] secretaries. We sent them dressed in military uniforms. They went to factories. Kádár received from them [the Soviets] even better information than from his own people. Later he even asked for Mayors. The economy is improving, production of coal is nearing the level before the uprising. On the first day of the uprising, when the looters threw themselves at the factories, the workers fought them back and defended the factories. Had Gerő had any character, it would have been different. But he lay like a pancake. The [Hungarian] CC was dispersed—they would not have allowed it to happen. Nagy, Donáth, Losonczy and other writers incited [the situation]. After all, at the time of the rally [on October 23], arms were also distributed. After all, this was done by Horthy-ites. After all, from the first moment we supported Nagy. We decided to destroy the first group of insurgents. [Then] Mikoyan calls to say that Nagy will not agree to this. He [Nagy] said that the uprising committee came to him and that he surrendered to them. Then we decided not to act. As for Nagy—a traitor. Because this was the signal for the great fire. At the time, we moved our forces to the periphery. Nagy rescued these counterrevolutionaries. He came to terms with them, and betrayed us. They crushed the CC of the party. We have pictures of atrocities, taken by Hungarian film projectionists. For communists and workers it will not be comprehensible if Nagy is not tried. Not one sector of workers or peasants took part in the action against Soviet soldiers.[300]

Zhukov: The intelligentsia.

Khrushchev: Writers, journalists.

Jędrychowski: There were not that many writers there.

Khrushchev: It was an organization. You can't look at who participated, except who is he with and under what slogans does he act. Kolchak[301] and others also had sections of workers. The Hungarians will decide this, but that's how we see it.

Break until the following day [...]

[Source: Archiwum Akt Nowych (AAN), KC PZPR, paczka 112, tom 26. Materialy do stosunków partyjnych polsko-radzieckich z lat 1954–1957, k. 329, 250–253. Published in János Tischler, Rewolucja węgierska 1956 w polskich dokumentach *(Warszawa: Instýtut Studiów Politycznych PAN, 1995). Translated by L.W. Gluchowski.]*

[300] Although a thorough analysis of the armed resistance's social composition is not yet available, it can be stated that workers, especially younger ones, constituted the main base of the armed groups. This can be also inferred indirectly from statistic data which indicate that 60 percent of those who lost their lives during the revolution were physical laborers. Moreover, 70 percent of this group consisted of industrial workers and miners, a stratum traditionally considered by communists to be the most "conscious" segment of the working class. It is worth mentioning that almost 60 percent of the factory workers killed during this period were aged 29 or younger. See, "Az október 23-i és az azt követő eseményekkel kapcsolatos sérülések és halálozások," *Statisztikai Szemle* 68, no. 10 (1990): 805, 814. For a sociological study on the insurgents, see Gyula Kozák, "Szent Csőcselék" in *Évkönyv VII, 1999: Magyarország a Jelenkorban,* ed. Éva Standeisky and János M. Rainer (Budapest, 1956-os Intézet, 1999), 255–281.

[301] Admiral A.V. Kolchak was an anti-Bolshevik military leader during the Civil War in Russia (1918–1921).

DOCUMENT NO. 114: CPSU CC Plenum Transcript from June 24, 1957 (Excerpt from Evening Session)

The transcript below is taken from a crucial series of meetings of the CPSU Central Committee, which mark the final phase of the prolonged power struggle that followed Stalin's death. During the June Plenum, Khrushchev found himself being attacked for, among other things, undermining the concept of "collective leadership" by making unilateral decisions in foreign policy as well as economic affairs. In this excerpt, Anastas Mikoyan comes to Khrushchev's defense and points specifically to the Hungarian and Polish events as evidence of his international successes as first secretary—and thus confirming the continued relevance of these events to internal Kremlin politics. The Plenum ended with Khrushchev's victory—in personal and policy terms—over the hard-line "anti-party group" headed by Vyacheslav Molotov.

[....]

Mikoyan: Comrades, first of all I want to talk about some facts which have brought the party leadership chosen after the 20th party congress to its present state, when the plenum meets amidst the crisis of the party leadership. Now we have a crisis in the party leadership; that must be frankly stated.
Voice: No, there is no crisis.
Mikoyan: I am talking about the crisis in the CC Presidium.
Aristov: But the CC Presidium is not the leadership of our party. The leadership is the CC.
Mikoyan: Cde. Aristov has spoken correctly. After the 20th party congress showed ideological unity, we considered that collective leadership was the guarantee of the success of our party, and tried in every way to uphold that unity. It seemed that everyone tried. There were disagreements on separate issues, disputes, but insofar as they did not turn into a system, they did not harm the cause ...

The events in Poland and Hungary were a great test for our party and our leadership, [and] for the CC Presidium. I was very glad, [and] everyone else was very happy that in those days our CC Presidium was wholly unified and firm. On such serious issues, unity was gratifying.[302] It was pleasant for me that the comrades with whom we disagreed, like Molotov, Kaganovich, [and] Malenkov, in this matter behaved as was appropriate, although it should be noted that on the issue of the new Hungarian leadership, cde. Molotov did not agree. Malenkov behaved well in Hungary, and it was believed that he had come into line [*voshel v obshchuiu koleiu*]. That is how it was until recently.

After the February 1957 CC Plenum, from the point where the issue of the organization of the sovnarkhoz [large collective farms] was decided, the atmosphere began to worsen; an unstated dissatisfaction on the part of some members of the Presidium was evident; disagreement was noted, [and] it was felt that some people were not saying everything [they thought]. Then it was still bearable, but the atmosphere continued to poison the situation ...

Until recently there was no sign of the formation of a group in the CC Presidium, but there was some impression that cde. Molotov [and] cde. Kaganovich were sometimes silent, as if they had come to an understanding. They avoided arguing with one another. For instance, I did not avoid argument with Molotov or Kaganovich, but they avoided argument between themselves. Perhaps there were no grounds for disagreement? There were. Recently, Malenkov also began avoiding arguments with them. There was one case in which he agreed that he had not acted entirely properly; that was in relation to Yugoslavia. In connection with the incorrect speech by cde. Tito in Pula,[303] Soviet communists and the communist parties of other countries delivered a dignified rebuff. As a result, by its own

---

[302] Mikoyan talks about the Presidium's decision on October 31, 1956. It is worth mentioning that Mikoyan, who spoke so highly of leadership unity at the plenum, was the only member of the Presidium to vote against the use of Soviet forces on October 23, and to argue against the second intervention upon his return from Hungary at the November 1 Presidium meeting.

[303] See Document No. 96.

fault, the Yugoslav party ended up practically in isolation from the other communist parties. After this, the Yugoslav leadership began to speak out in conversations with our comrades and made known its desire to improve relations with us in its open statements.

At cde. Khrushchev's suggestion, we discussed this issue in the CC Presidium and decided to instruct [Soviet Ambassador to Yugoslavia] cde. [Nikolai] Firyubin to engage in an appropriate conversation with cde. Tito at the instructions of the CC Presidium.

Several days before this, information about the fact that one Yugoslav diplomat tried, albeit unsuccessfully, to win over one important leader of the Hungarian Socialist Workers' Party to the Yugoslav side, was sent around to the members of the CC Presidium. Thus, in connection with a discussion of measures to improve relations with Yugoslavia, cde. Molotov introduced a proposal that the CC CPSU inform all fraternal parties that Yugoslav diplomats were engaging in the recruitment of communists in fraternal parties. The adoption of cde. Molotov's proposal would have led, of course, to the disruption of the improvement of relations with Yugoslavia, because such an appeal by us to all parties could not be hidden from the Yugoslav leadership, and, in this, it would see duplicity in our policies and the absence of a true wish to reconcile. This was, in essence, Molotov's wish to put a fly in the ointment [*vlit' lozhku degtia v bochku meda*].

Then they talked very calmly about this; there were no insults. Khrushchev said: Vyacheslav, you again want to continue your line on disputes with Yugoslavia. I also calmly spoke twice, criticizing cde. Molotov; cde. Bulganin criticized him. Malenkov sat opposite and stayed silent. I know that Malenkov was against this; on many political issues he was not close to the views of Molotov and Kaganovich, but he sat and kept silent ...

Mikoyan: Generally there was unity in the Presidium on the Hungarian issue, but I must say that cde. Molotov held an incorrect line in relation to the new Hungarian leaders.

Imagine that tomorrow, on 4 November, our troops had to move out [*vystuplenie*] all over Hungary, but by this evening it was still unclear who would be at the head of the new government of Hungary, by whose summons and in support of whom our troops were mobilizing. Why? Khrushchev and Malenkov were in Yugoslavia meeting with the Romanians, Bulgarians, Hungarians, and Yugoslavs over the course of two days[304] in order to obtain their agreement for the use of our troops. I was busy with getting Kádár, Münnich, and others out of Budapest; there was still no government, [and] they were discussing whom to move into the government. We proposed Kádár. Molotov insisted that Hegedüs be at the head—the former prime minister. He asked: who is this Kádár? We, he implied [mol], did not know him and were slighting him. We could not agree on the composition of the government. Zhukov said: I cannot put off the operation; there is already an order to our troops to move out. Molotov insisted on reinstating the old leadership.

Molotov: That's not correct; we spoke about Münnich.

Mikoyan: You proposed Hegedüs; before his departure to Yugoslavia, Khrushchev proposed Münnich; others proposed Kádár—we argued all day. If there had been no argument, why not agree right away on the composition of the government? We had it out [*rugalis'*] with you, argued fiercely. Bulganin and other comrades should remember.

Khrushchev: Anastas Ivanovich [Mikoyan], when, during the Hungarian events, Malenkov and I returned from our trip to a series of people's democratic countries and Yugoslavia, we had formed the opinion that we must support Kádár's candidacy. Some called for Münnich 's candidacy. He is an honorable comrade who likes us; I did military training together with him in the Proletarian Division. He is an excellent comrade, but in the given situation, cde. Kádár is the best candidate.

Mikoyan: Only after cde. Khrushchev's arrival was it possible to specify the composition of

---

[304] Both scenes and nations are mixed up in this sentence. In fact, Khrushchev, Malenkov and Molotov met the Polish leaders in Brest, close to the Polish border on November 1, then Molotov returned to Moscow while Khrushchev and Malenkov flew to Bucharest to meet the Romanian and Czechoslovak leadership on November 2. The same day, they made a short visit to Sofia and then arrived by plane at Pula, meeting with Tito at his residency on the island of Brioni during the night of November 2–3. During this series of trips, however, no meetings were held with Hungarian leaders.

the government headed by Kádár. Cde. Kádár is from the working class and is a serious person, and that has now been justified. It is good that cde. Khrushchev reminded [us]. There was the following case: Molotov calls and proposes a meeting. On what topic? Rákosi wrote a letter to the HSWP, [saying] that they were not allowing him back into Hungary and requested that he remain here. Molotov asked: who decided, how, why? He considered that the convocation of a special session of the CC Presidium was called for. And when we met at the next regular meeting [i.e., no special session had been called], he insisted that Rákosi and Gerő be given the chance to work.

Molotov: Who insisted? That is not exact.

Mikoyan: After all, you demanded the convocation of a special session of the CC Presidium in order to discuss Rákosi's letter, which came to the CC CPSU Presidium with an accusation against the new leadership of the HSWP. Two days later [*cherez den'*], at the next meeting of the CC Presidium, you spoke with a criticism of the resolution of the CC Plenum of the HSWP that at present and in the near future, the interests of the HSWP demanded that Rákosi, Gerő, Hegedüs [be prevented from working] in Hungary, but remain in the Soviet Union for a specified period.[305] You demanded that Rákosi, Gerő, and Hegedüs return to Hungary. If we had heeded Molotov ['s advice], we would have lost the trust of the Hungarian party; the Hungarians would have thought that we were playing a double game. We argued with Molotov: Rákosi did not see what was happening, became detached from reality and led the party into a catastrophe. While located in Moscow, he called certain of his supporters in Budapest on the telephone and, essentially, led a group struggle against the new Hungarian leadership. In connection with this we told him: do not live in Moscow; live in another city, and don't mess things up [*ne port' dela*].

Khrushchev: When the Hungarian government delegation visited us, Molotov said to Kádár: why are you not taking Rákosi with you? This question once again upset the Hungarian leaders. They thought that we were supporting them [only] on a temporary basis, and that then Rákosi would once again come to power in Hungary.

Mikoyan: It's true; during the reception, cde. Molotov scolded Kádár [as to] why they weren't taking Rákosi back to work in Hungary. Such behavior by cde. Molotov was incorrect.

Molotov: We were talking not about Rákosi, but about Hegedüs.

Mikoyan: You were talking about Rákosi.

[....]

Mikoyan: In relation to the [Presidium] Saturday meeting, at which Bulganin said that Khrushchev acted incorrectly. What does that consist of?

The people's democratic countries request that, when we order equipment for the next year, the orders be given out at least six months' in advance, so that blueprints can be drawn up and inventories can be ordered. Otherwise, it is impossible to order in January and receive the products in January. This is an elementary thing. Not only our friends, but also the capitalists demand this.

This is an indisputable issue, but arguments have begun around it: will we be able to pay for the equipment? Here we order, but what will we pay with? I provide information: in all, we buy 16 billion rubles in goods, and now we are talking about a preliminary order for 3 billion rubles in equipment, and these are needed goods. Why should we not be able to pay? We will be able to. There is no issue here. The total volume of trade will be approximately the same as last year's.

Finally, what does this mean politically? On the whole, equipment is being supplied by the GDR and Czechoslovakia. If we do not strengthen East Germany, where workers are supporting their communist government, our army will end up in the fire. And, after all, there is an army of a half million [men] there. We cannot lose the sympathy of the German populace. If we lose their sympathy and trust-that will mean the loss of East Germany. And what would the loss of East

---

[305] See footnote 277 above.

Germany mean? We know what that would be, and for that reason operate on the basis that we must use the capacity of East German industry in full. Then the workers of the GDR will have work and will give us what we need; otherwise we will have to give the GDR both goods and food, without receiving equipment in return. I consider that our position is absolutely correct.

Voice: Correct.

Mikoyan: But we are told: you will order, but will we be able to pay? This is an issue unto itself—a great political issue. I kept calm, although I am also a quick-tempered person, but Nikita Sergeevich caught the scent of the whole political edge of the issue. Seeing that a majority against the draft was forming, he said the following phrase: "I would like on this issue in particular to hold a vote and to remain in the minority." The socialist camp has been created because it is important to strengthen it and not to permit wavering. If East Germany and Czechoslovakia today are left without orders, the whole socialist camp will crack. Who needs such a camp if we cannot ensure orders? After all, the issue stands as such: either feed the workers of the GDR for free, or provide orders, or otherwise lose the GDR entirely. That is why Nikita Sergeevich blew up [*vzorvalsia*]. I also almost blew up.

Voices: Blew up.

Khrushchev: Now it is clear that they had an understanding to fight us on this issue.

Mikoyan: I also think so ...

Comrades, after the Hungarian and Polish events, our prestige abroad temporarily weakened somewhat. First, we bared our teeth to the enemies, the Americans, for Hungary, and bared our teeth for Egypt and achieved a halt to the war which had started there.

Then they again conducted a policy of disarmament in order to turn the sympathy of the petty-bourgeois elements toward them. Molotov says that the Leninist policy of using the contradictions of the imperialist camp is not being put into practice. But he makes [only] one citation. First of all, he incorrectly interprets it. But even so, let us assume that he is correctly interpreting it. Look at our party's policy on splitting the bourgeois world. Our comrades went to India and to Burma, and managed to undermine the influence of the imperialist powers on the countries of Asia.

Voices: Correct.

Mikoyan: Earlier we had no access to the Arab countries; English influence had such a hold on the Muslim religion, that we had no access there. Three imperialist powers gathered together and decided all of the issues of the Near East without us. But when we sold arms to Egypt, we bared our teeth to our enemies, and Nasser turned out to be a strong leader, so that now they cannot any longer resolve the issues of the Near East without us. Is that not a realization of the Leninist policy on using the contradictions of the imperialist camp? In the given case we are supporting bourgeois nationalists against the imperialists.

Voices: Correct.

Mikoyan: Cde. Voroshilov went to Indonesia. Indonesia is a bourgeois state, in many ways feudal, even, which only recently won its political independence. They met Voroshilov triumphantly not only because he is a good person, but because he represents the Soviet Union. Remember the age we are living in, and the strength we have. The Indonesians are a 70-million-strong people; they have a smart President, Sukarno, but in order to strengthen his power with the people, he needs a visit from Voroshilov, in order to strengthen his influence through him. What strength we have and communism has ...

They accuse cde. Khrushchev of being hot-tempered and harsh [*goriach i rezok*]. But there they went and met without him. You can't imagine the precipitousness and fervor of cdes. Molotov and Kaganovich at the meeting of the Presidium! In the course of less than 10 days at three sessions of the CC Presidium on the three foreign-trade issues this now open grouping held trial battles, specifically on trade with Austria, on orders for equipment in people's democratic countries, on trade with Finland. After this, an attack started along the whole front. It is true, Finland is a bourgeois country and borders us, but is that really important to us? We know this through war with the Finns and the Germans. The Finnish people knows how to make war, and our task, not to make war, is the greatest task for our state. For that very reason cdes. Khrushchev and Bulganin travelled to Finland and succeeded there ...

Further, what did we do in foreign policy? Cde. Khrushchev proposed that a letter be written from cde. Bulganin to the Norwegians. At that time we had been arguing with the Norwegians after the Hungarian events, so let's now write a letter to the Norwegians, but say politely that if you meddle in military affairs, we will wipe you off the face of the earth [*sotrem s litsa zemli*]. We approved this, and it turned out to be a good idea.

Khrushchev: To speak about serious issues in a friendly tone.

Mikoyan: The people from MID[306] [*Midovtsy*] have now begun to write drafts of notes and letters. Well before, they put together documents very badly, in a criminal, crude way of speaking, stereotypically; it was impossible to read them.

That has made a huge impression. They sent letters to the English as well. They were influential. They addressed the French people. They didn't write to Eisenhower, not to everyone, but only to those of whom I have talked. Does this mean that we know how to see and use contradictions? We have been using the contradictions of capitalism everywhere in our foreign policy.

Molotov has picked on one sentence of cde. Khrushchev's: the USSR and the USA are the only possessors of atomic weapons, and now decide the questions of war and peace.

Khrushchev: Or the following fact: when we proposed to the President of the USA, Eisenhower, to call England and France to order during the English and French attack on Egypt. Was that not a use of contradictions?

Mikoyan: I am concerned about time, and for that reason do not talk about that. Remember the circumstances: there was an uprising in Hungary; our troops occupied Budapest, and the Anglo-French decided: the Russians are stuck in Hungary, [so] let's hit Egypt; they can't help; they can't fight on two fronts. We'll pour dirt on the Russians, they say, and we will thump Egypt; we will deprive the Soviet Union of influence in the Near East. That is what they decided, and we found both the strength to keep troops in Hungary and to threaten the imperialists that if they do not end the war in Egypt, it could lead to the use of missile weapons by us. Everyone recognizes that with that we decided the fate of Egypt.[307] Even before that, we made a move that cde. Khrushchev talked about. Since the Americans were conducting a different policy from the English, and did not want to dirty themselves with a colonial war, [or] that their "friends" be so dirtied, but to do in Egypt themselves [*a samim ukhlopat' Egipet*]. We said the following to the Americans: let's introduce American-Soviet troops together in order to restore peace in Egypt, which would accord with the goals of the United Nations. This produced a huge effect.

From the point of view of using the contradictions of imperialism in the interests of communist policy, there has never been such a broad practice, such rich results, as in recent years in our Central Committee with the participation of cde. Khrushchev...

Voice: Correct (Applause).

[Source: Istoricheskii arkhiv *3–6 (1993) and 1–2 (1994). Originally published in the* Cold War International History Project Bulletin *no. 10 (March 1998), pp. 52–55. Translated by Benjamin Aldrich-Moodie.]*

---

[306] The Soviet Foreign Ministry

[307] On November 5, 1956, Soviet Prime Minister Nikolai Bulganin sent telegrams to the British, French and Israeli governments demanding a halt to their military action against Egypt and threatening the possibility of nuclear missile attacks on London and Paris, and questioning the very existence of the state of Israel. We now know that this was no more than a bluff, which in fact did not have any significant impact on events: the British-French withdrew mainly because of the political intervention of the United States. At the time, however, this unprecedented Soviet step, presented as the espousal of the independence of Egypt—invaded by colonialist powers—made a great impression on many third World countries.

DOCUMENT NO. 115: Minutes of the HSWP Central Committee Meeting, December 21, 1957 (Excerpts)

During his visit to Moscow between March 21–28, 1957, Kádár and the Soviet leadership agreed to settle the Nagy issue within the framework of a criminal trial. On April 14, Nagy was arrested in Snagov, Romania (where he had been deported in November 1956), and transported back to Hungary.

During the following months, Minister of Interior Béla Biszku held further consultations with the Soviet leadership about plans for the trial, including discussing the text of the indictment. In the summer of 1957, Biszku told the Soviets that the HSWP leadership believed that Nagy and six others should be sentenced to capital punishment.

Because of the international significance of the case, the Kremlin followed it with special attention. The trial was originally scheduled for after the UNGA emergency session in September, but at the Soviets' request was later postponed so as not to tarnish the Moscow summit of communist parties planned for November. The summit, which targeted "revisionism" as the main threat to the communist movement, strengthened the hard-liners, brought about a deterioration in Soviet-Yugoslav relations, and fortified China's position, all of which helped Kádár in his goal of imposing a harsh sentence.

On December 16, the Political Investigation Department of the Ministry of Interior requested the party leadership's approval to begin the criminal process. That same day, the HSWP Political Committee agreed, and on December 21 a closed session of the Central Committee affirmed that the "[l]egal procedures must be allowed to take their course" in the cases of Nagy, Ferenc Donáth, József Szilágyi, Ferenc Jánosi, Miklós Vásárhelyi, György Fazekas,[308] Gábor Tánczos and Sándor Haraszti. Kádár based his presentation on two main charges: "class betrayal" (that Nagy had been preparing for years, as part of a secret master plan, to "give up the power positions of the working class, restore the coalition parties, and renounce the Warsaw Treaty"), and "betrayal of the People's Republic." If, as can be presumed, Kádár's aim in calling the meeting was to make the entire CC share responsibility for this crucial decision, then the course of the meeting did not disappoint his expectations. Of 51 members present, the 17 who spoke agreed unanimously with the decision; the only discussion was about who else should be sentenced. However, it is also clear from their statements that many of the members who supported Kádár's proposal did so in the belief that everyone who was to be sentenced would later be pardoned.

Based on the CC's resolution, the trial began on February 5, 1958. Although a renewed Soviet request for postponement delayed the procedure for a time, the May 27 PC and the June 6 CC meetings reinforced the December resolution. The trial began again on June 9, and the verdict came down on June 15. The death sentence against Imre Nagy, Pál Maléter and Miklós Gimes was carried out at dawn on June 16.

MINUTES OF THE CLOSED MEETING OF THE HSWP CENTRAL COMMITTEE, DECEMBER 21, 1957

[....]

Report by comrade János Kádár: At its 1957 spring meeting the Central Committee authorized the Political Committee to identify the decisive factors which launched the counter-revolution as well as all the culprits responsible for it without any regard to the persons involved. The Central Committee did not give any order to target specific individuals but it did instruct the Political Committee to specify the role of particular individuals based on what they had actually done.

Based on all this, the Political Committee submits the following proposals to the Central Committee, making a distinction between the assessment of specific groups or individuals:

---

[308] György Fazekas worked in Imre Nagy's secretariat from October 28, 1956. After taking refuge at the Yugoslav Embassy on November 4, he was deported to Romania and sentenced to 10 years imprisonment in 1958. He received an amnesty in 1961.

Legal procedures must be allowed to take their course against the following citizens: Imre Nagy, Ferenc Donáth, József Szilágyi, Ferenc Jánosi, Miklós Vásárhelyi, György Fazekas, Gábor Táncos and Sándor Haraszti.

Pardons must be granted for illegal acts, and no criminal procedure should be instituted against the following citizens: Zoltán Szántó, György Lukács, Zoltán Vas, Szilárd Ujhelyi and Mrs. László Rajk.

Others, who did not flee to the Yugoslav embassy but committed very serious crimes must also be prosecuted. These are: Zoltán Tildy, Pál Maléter, Sándor Kopácsi, Miklós Gimes, Péter Erdős and the fugitive Béla Király.

Pardons must be granted for lesser crimes, and no criminal procedure should be instituted against the following citizens: László Deszpot, former p[olice] major; József Vári, former s[tate] s[ecurity] major; István Kiss, former p[olice] lieutenant colonel; József Lantos, former p[olice] major; Miklós Szűcs, former a[rmy] colonel; and Tivadar Pártay,[309] former representative of the parliament. They were simply caught in the flow of events.

[....]

The entire matter will lead to a considerable struggle for us, both at home and abroad, including the U.N. It will also make consolidation rather creaky and cumbersome. But what is the foundation of the unity of the party, of consolidation? The fight that we have fought so far. We are still ready to fight. If we were to give up fighting now, our followers would be confused. This fight will line them up behind us even more than before. The most important issue for the enemy to fight about is amnesty. There are some 70–80 more people who must be held responsible for their deeds, and then the whole matter will be settled. Some 5–6,000 people have already been sentenced. There will be an amnesty, but it will be granted when it can make us stronger. If we introduced an amnesty now, it would involve those most guilty, and it would weaken our people's democracy. Amnesty is a very important question of prestige for the enemy. It is very important for their followers at home and for emigres abroad, and it is also important from the point of view of their own requirements [sic]. Furthermore, they fight in order to save their own cadres. They still believe that later they will be able to do something. Hungarian fascists, relying on the USA's promises, continued to fight, but the USA betrayed them and now it wants to give them some kind of a protection. We have to make the enemy understand that the more pressure they put on us the later we will introduce the amnesty.

The imperialists now want to unleash local wars. That's what they want to do here too, but if we continue to be consistent there will be no such local war here.

The Political Committee believes that this fight is very complex, thus we have to take measures which do not give any tactical advantage to the enemy. Therefore secrecy must be a priority; if something were to leak out, it would cause serious damage.

We were led by two principles: one is the principle of collective leadership within the Central Committee, the other is the interests of the country and the party.

This matter is very delicate because of its Yugoslav aspect. The question is what reaction it will evoke there. There is a valid bilateral agreement between us which was imposed on us.[310] We were in a difficult situation, and we were unaware of many things (e.g. the preliminary plans). They did not have the right to extend political asylum, but once they did so, they were obliged to prevent those people from having any contact with the outside world. This [obligation] they failed to meet. The Political Committee thinks that—since the investigation brought to light many new facts—we will denounce the agreement, not on the part of the government but trough party channels; but the time of denouncing it will be chosen by us. This is necessary so that the Western imperialists will not learn anything prematurely. If they [the Yugoslavs] make it public after we have informed them and start a dispute over it, then we will enter into this

---

[309] Tivadar Pártay was a member of the leadership of the Smallholders' Party and one of the editors of the newspaper *Magyar Nemzet* from October 26, 1956.

[310] See the headnote for Document No. 98.

debate and it will turn out to be worse for them. The position of the Political Committee is that in the course of the trial the Yugoslav aspects of this matter should not be mentioned; that is what is practical politically. We want to avoid an open dispute. We would rather not have a conflict between us, for the sake of the workers' movement.

Comrade Béla Biszku:[311] *They* [Biszku and Münnich] were given instructions to conduct the investigation and reveal—on the basis of facts that can be documented—who played a leading role in the preparation of counter-revolutionary acts. It has been established that Imre Nagy and his associates had a role in organizing the preparations. At the end of 1955 and the beginning of 1956 they worked out several different platforms and circulated them illegally. For instance: "Imre Nagy in defense of the people," "The country needs moral revival and a general 'changing of the guard'," "Words must be replaced by deeds". (Imre Nagy's own writing).[312]

They worked out the justification for withdrawal from the Warsaw Pact and passed it on to some foreign countries.[313]

They [Biszku and Münnich] managed to find Imre Nagy's own handwriting evaluating the events. Comrade Biszku cited passages from this assessment. They also found Géza Losonczy's own handwritten notes. On October 22 and 23, they [Losonczy and members of the Nagy group] had a meeting at their [sic] apartment and at SZÖVOSZ.[314] At this point comrade Biszku cited passages from Losonczy's writing. On the 23rd they again got together at Losonczy's flat. Comrade Biszku here again cited passages from those discussions.

The investigation was aimed at shedding light on the illegal acts committed after October 23. They were trying at any cost to paralyze and disorganize the armed forces, not only in the case of Corvin passage[315] but on other occasions too.

We have the minutes of the November 2 cabinet meeting at which a decision was made to supplement the composition of the government with the leaders of the counterrevolution.[316] They made a resolution as to who would choose the most suitable [new members] from among these people.

The investigation was conducted in an entirely legal manner. No physical force was used. The starting point was that a confession alone was not satisfactory, documents and witnesses were needed. They left out political interpretations of the facts. This is not their task, it must be done by the party. Some of those who were under criminal procedure admitted their guilt and stated that they were ready to take responsibility. Some only partially admitted their guilt and responsibility, while others denied any accusations and confessed only under pressure of the documents presented.

They were not only in political contact with foreign countries but they also had their own personal relations. This is, for instance, how Ferenc Jánosi nominated Béla Király. Losonczy had

---

[311] Although Biszku is the speaker, the note-taker, as was often the case, recorded his statement in the third person.

[312] These quotes are from studies Nagy wrote after his dismissal, during the period from June 1955–January 1956. In these writings, Nagy defended his reform policy and offered a comprehensive analysis and critique of the party's policies, ranging from politics and the economy to culture and foreign policy. Although by no means illegal, these studies were distributed only among a narrow circle of Nagy's adherents. In the spring of 1957, they were smuggled to the West with the assistance of László Kardos and Árpád Göncz, and were published in a book with the Hungarian title "A magyar nép védelmében" (In defense of the Hungarian people). For the English edition see, Imre Nagy, *On Communism: In Defense of the New Course* (London: Thames & Hudson, 1957).

[313] This presumably refers to one of Nagy's writings from January 1956 that discussed the principles of international relations and questions of Hungary's foreign policy. Inspired by the five principles of peaceful coexistence formulated in the *pancha sila*, Nagy advocated the dissolution of military blocs in the long term as the only way to avoid military conflicts, and envisaged Hungary's sovereignty as following a pattern of "active coexistence"—a form of neutrality similar to the Yugoslav model. See, Nagy, *On Communism*, 20–42.

[314] Szövetkezetek Országos Szövetsége (National League of Cooperatives).

[315] See footnote 127 in Part Two.

[316] See Document No. 71.

direct contact with several embassies and visited the Yugoslav embassy daily. A West German representative of Parliament, prince Löwenstein, visited him, then later spoke on the radio.[317]

Others broke their oath, for instance Maléter, who was given an order to clean up the Kilián barracks, but instead fought against the people's democracy and stayed in touch with the English military attaché too.

He [Biszku] concludes by saying that this is a matter that concerns the leaders of the Hungarian counterrevolution, a fact which increases tensions and also puts party unity to the test.

[....]

Comrade István Friss.[318] What we have to decide is that we should allow legal procedures to take their course freely. This was already done when we endorsed the policy of the party and the government. If we decided to stop here, we would be unable to justify and explain a number of sentences and [other] things." If we draw the conclusions from what we have done so far, we cannot take any other course of action. The Yugoslav aspect is very serious, but the situation is now more favorable in this respect too. Reading Imre Nagy's book published in the West,[319]— even if it may have been edited—makes it obvious what Imre Nagy's motives and views were. It is quite clear that he had decided in advance on certain things to do, for instance withdrawing from the Warsaw Pact. He wanted to follow the Yugoslav example, so it is quite obvious why he ended up at the Yugoslav embassy.

What he [Friss] heard today convinced him that it would be right to let the legal procedures take their course, but he does not agree that legal action should not be taken against Zoltán Vas and Márton Horváth. The discussion here today proves that they played a role in the preparations, so he believes it should be left up to the Political Committee who should be brought to account and under what kind of procedure.

He proposes that the "draft resolution" be modified in a way that allows the Central Committee to authorize the Political Committee to grant pardons after becoming thoroughly acquainted with the matter.

[....]

Comrade Dezső Kiss:[320] He agrees with the reports and the resolution. No such treachery has yet been witnessed in the history of a worker's party in power. In his view everybody's fate should be decided by the laws, on the basis of the facts, except for Mrs. Rajk. The sentences must be justified in detail, even if we later grant a pardon, because otherwise it will not be clear why certain individuals were not convicted for their political crimes [sic]. And state impeachment is just one thing. When socialism is a world system, then the party must not be attacked. This affair is a warning sign for the international workers' movement too. Imre Nagy is not the last of the traitors. The fight is extremely complex. We have to make fine distinctions, because it is a two-sided fight. The issue of the Muscovites[321] also engages the attention of the people. Those who are unwilling to acknowledge their mistakes should also be held responsible. The entire action must be conducted in such a way that the party emerges from this situation stronger and more united in Csepel[322] too.

He suggests that after the sentence the party should issue a detailed resolution, and then fur-

[317] Dr Hubertus von Löwenstein, parliamentary representative of the Free Democratic Party, visited Hungary as a representative of the West German Red Cross on November 2 and spoke on the radio at 10:30 p.m. See, Varga, *Forradalom hangja,* 420.

[318] István Friss was a member of the HWP CC from 1948 to October 30, 1956. Responsible mainly for economic affairs, he opposed Nagy's "new course" from the very beginning. He was a member of the HSWP PCC and head of the PCC's state-economy department from November 1956.

[319] See footnote 312 above.

[320] Dezső Kiss was head of the HSWP Executive Committee at the Csepel Iron Works from November 1956 and a member of the HSWP PCC beginning in February 1957.

[321] This is a reference to the earlier leadership of Rákosi, Gerő, Farkas and Révai, who were in exile in Moscow before 1945.

[322] Csepel Island was one of the most important industrial areas in Budapest, and a major symbol for factory workers.

ther political activity should be based on this.

[....]

Comrade Ferenc Nezvál: He does not think that legal procedures should be instituted and then pardons granted to certain individuals, because the people would not understand it. The Political Committee should examine again who should be brought under legal action, because we have [already] held responsible people who committed lesser crimes. Márton Horváth's article[323] caused serious damage.

Comrade Márton Valkó: He agrees with the reports and the resolution. The workers at our workplace also demand that those involved be called to account. The relatives of those arrested often question why the leaders were not called to account.

He proposes that all those who played an active role must be brought to legal account, but when the sentence is passed, their past merits must also be taken into account.

[....]

Summary by comrade János Kádár: All the comrades making a comment agreed that the fight should be fought to the finish based on its own logic. He believes that in the end we will be stronger.

Yet why have we brought [the issue] here [to the CC]? Because:

1. The resolution of the Central Committee obliged the Political Committee to do so.
2. Another, new method of granting pardons was raised. Retaliation would have been more justifiable between November 4–5, but it was then that we were the weakest. This [the retaliation] seemingly goes against consolidation, but last year we did not have enough power, it was then that retaliation would have been the right thing to do. Some leading circles of the USA indirectly, through the Austrian government, informed us that they would set the Hungarian issue aside and restore normal diplomatic relations, but only in return for an amnesty. We did not accept that.
3. It [the issue] had to be brought here [to this forum] because of its Yugoslav aspect too, because it bears the fact [sic] of a new conflict. But also because of the content of the trial, for what we want to punish is not the betrayal of the labor movement. In this sense this matter is different from the usual political trials. The subject matter of the charge is the betrayal of all people who love their country. We have to administer justice for the whole people. We have to stick with this aspect, so that the impeachment will be unassailable.

Comrade Révész[324] proposed that we include in our resolution the three high-ranking military officers. He proposes that these three soldiers be held responsible together with the other 60–70 people.

He [Kádár] agrees with the amendment proposed by comrade Friss. So the Political Committee should consider who should be charged in what form. It was mostly Zoltán Vas and Márton Horváth who were mentioned as those who should also be called to account. The Political Committee considered this [possibility]. They did not belong to the conspirators' group. These people had been communists and behaved accordingly for many years. Later they became careerists, that's what led them to this camp. They did not take the initiative in the most important things. Márton Horváth assisted them, which is condemnable. In addition, after November 4 we announced an amnesty for all those who were ready to lay down their arms. Zoltán Vas also left the embassy. Their past has to be taken into account too. For instance, Zoltán Vas' book was read by hundreds of thousands.[325] Yet he accepts the view of the Central Committee that the Political Committee should reconsider

---

[323] This most likely refers to the editorial in *Szabad Nép* on October 28 entitled "True to the truth."

[324] Géza Révész was military vice chairman of the National Planning Office from 1955–1957 and a member of the HSWP PCC from February 1957.

[325] Zoltán Vas' book, entitled "Sixteen years in prison," was an important contribution to the party's self-image of martyrdom, and was published in eight editions between 1944 and 1956.

536

the affairs of certain individuals.

Comrade Cservenka raised some important issues. Zoltán Szántó and Mrs. Rajk should not be left without any restrictions, they should not simply be allowed to go back to a normal life. When assessing Mrs. Rajk's situation, her husband's matters should be taken into consideration. What Mrs. Rajk had to go through was not a trifle. In 1955 she behaved decently. They made use of her confusion and involved her in their dealings. She was dragged to the Yugoslav embassy. But of course, she also has to comply with the laws.

The two-front struggle is very complex. Taking the enemy into consideration the first front includes the revisionists, but it is hard to fight against the enemy if we don't fight against sectarianism. This is not two fights but one, closely related. We have to discuss these matters within the party for a long time, but as for this particular matter, we don't need a long debate.

An amnesty will be introduced when it suits the needs and interests of the people's republic.

I agree with comrade Pothornyik[326] that there should be sanctions forbidding them from holding any office. Madarász's case is closed, it should not be re-examined.

Should we put these people in a morally impossible position? Yes, but it should not be contained in the sentence. For instance, Márton Horváth should not write a film script about Attila József,[327] because it is irreverent on his part.

What comrade Orbán said is valid indeed. An assault can be expected both from the right and from the left. When he should have tried to cooperate with Imre Nagy decently, comrade Rákosi was unable to do so. When he should have fought against him, he failed too. According to the Soviet and the Chinese comrades, that is his primary sin.

Several people have mentioned that there is a need for a thorough analysis. This is a sound demand. Concerning the way of the revisionists, for example, etc. They did not have deep roots either in the peasantry or in the working class. They relied first on the petty bourgeoisie and then on the bourgeoisie.

Some people at various organs of the Interior Ministry came to the opinion that the earlier trials were just. We had to explain to them that it was the unjust trials which pushed them [Nagy's group] into such directions. There were some among them who became angry with the party.

As for the question whether the situation will become strained or not: according to the Political Committee the struggle will get more intense, the right wing will become stiff, and certain layers will be hesitant. By the end of the struggle we will be more unified and stronger. The party will be purified in the course of our struggle. Further predictions are not needed. The position of the party will be complicated because a very tough repression will take place during the period of consolidation.

In addition, two further issues emerge: the separation of the double function,[328] and in February the issue of the Moscow group should be discussed. Naturally this issue will also be presented to the Central Committee. We have to be careful with the date, we should not give the enemy a good trump. What we should take as our starting point is not reverence, [or] the past; we have to subordinate everything to the interests of the Hungarian people. We want to ensure peace for the people.

With the amendment proposed by comrades Friss and Pothornyik let us adopt the "draft resolution."

Comrade Károly Kiss puts the "draft resolution" to vote. The members of the Central

---

[326] József Pothornyik was director of the Nógrág Mining Trust and became a member of the HSWP PCC in February 1957.

[327] Attila József (1905–1937) was a Hungarian poet who, because of his proletarian radicalism, was especially honored by the Communist Party.

[328] This refers to the separation of functions between the party leadership and the office of the premier, which was put into effect in 1958 when Münnich took over as premier.

Committee unanimously accept the report of the Political Committee and the "draft resolution" with the two amendments included.

DATED AS ABOVE

RECORDERS:

LÁSZLÓ FÖLDES [SIGNATURE]   ÁGNES BAKÓ [SIGNATURE]
PÁL ILKU [SIGNATURE]   ISTVÁN SZURDI [SIGNATURE]

[Source: MOL, 288. f. 4/14/1. ő.e. Published in Karola Némethné Vágyi, László Soós, György T. Varga and Gábor Ujváry, eds., A Magyar Szocialista Munkáspárt Központi Bizottságának 1957–1958. évi jegyzőkönyvei *(Budapest: Magyar Országos Levéltár, 1997), pp. 153–167. Translation by András Bocz]*

DOCUMENT NO. 116: Letter from Yurii Andropov to the CPSU CC regarding the Trial of Imre Nagy, August 26, 1957

The court procedure against Imre Nagy and his circle had been in train since April 1957. Soviet scrutiny of the case was intense, although no documents available so far indicate that they directly interfered in any way. The Kádár government did seek regular consultations with Moscow. The following secret note written by Andropov and two associates for the CPSU CC records the results of the first negotiation with Hungarian Interior Minister Béla Biszku, who visited Moscow in August 1957. Biszku informs his Soviet comrades about the contents of the inquiry brief against Nagy and the others, and about the Hungarian leadership's decisions in the case. He also hands over a draft of the indictment that the Hungarian Interior Ministry has prepared for the upcoming trial. The Soviet delegates respond that the document "is basically acceptable but needs more work," especially as far as laying out the relationship between "the treacherous Nagy group" and the "imperialists". Biszku also says that even though the HSWP leadership had made no decision yet about what sentences would be appropriate, there was a general opinion that Nagy and several others deserved "capital punishment."

TOP SECRET

To the Central Committee of the CPSU

In accordance with our instructions, we spoke with Minister of Interior of the Hungarian People's Republic cde. Béla Biszku, who informed us of the content of the Imre Nagy group's case and about the decisions the HSWP CC Politburo made with regard to this case.

As cde. Biszku reported, 74 active participants in the counterrevolutionary riot were arrested in connection with the aforementioned case, among whom we singled out the leading nucleus of the conspirators of 11 persons: Imre Nagy, Géza Losonczy, Ferenc Donáth, Miklós Gimes, Pál Maléter, Sándor Kopácsi, Zoltán Tildy, Ferenc Jánosi, Miklós Vásárhelyi, József Szilágyi, and also Béla Király, who escaped to the West and will be tried in absentia.

The Politburo made a decision to conduct a closed trial against this group at the end of September of this year. The Politburo gave instructions to the Minister of Interior to emphasize three main points in the indictment in the case of Nagy and his group: the violent seizure of power, the organization of a conspiracy directed at overthrowing the people's democratic regime, and the alliance with the imperialists. The Ministry of Interior possesses serious evidence, on the basis of which Nagy and his co-conspirators will be presented with the above charges.

According to cde. Biszku's information, the draft of the indictment, which was sent to Moscow by cde. Kádár earlier, was approved by the HSWP CC Politburo. The Politburo instructed the Ministry of Interior to prepare an investigation report, on the basis of which the Prosecutor's Office would draft a brief indictment. The Politburo has not made a decision as to punishment for Nagy and his group; however, in the course of discussions on this issue, opinions were expressed to the effect that they should adopt a differentiated approach toward the defendants in accordance with the degree of their guilt, and to sentence Nagy, Losonczy, Donáth, Gimes, Maléter, Szilágyi and Király to capital punishment;[329] the rest of the defendants should be sentenced to lighter punishments, depending on the charges pending against them and their conduct during the investigation and the trial.

Since during the investigation some facts compromising the government of Yugoslavia were established, the HSWP CC Politburo decided not to mention those facts during the court proceedings. At the same time, it was decided to prepare a special reference (report) on the role of

---

[329] Of those listed above, Imre Nagy, Miklós Gimes and Pál Maléter were executed on June 16, 1958; József Szilágyi (whose case was tried separately) on April 24. The case of Béla Király was also separated and it is not known whether a verdict was eventually reached. Géza Losonczy died in detention on December 21, 1957. Ferenc Donáth received 12 years in prison.

Yugoslavia in the counterrevolutionary events in Hungary, which would be included in the investigative materials on Nagy and his group.

The Politburo has also decided to prepare a draft note to the Yugoslav government regarding the grant of asylum by the Yugoslav Embassy in Budapest to Nagy and his co-conspirators, who used it to carry out their criminal activities. This note is intended to anticipate a possible accusation against the HPR government by the Yugoslavs to the effect that it violated the agreement not to bring Nagy and his co-conspirators to criminal trial. The intention is to hand the note to the Yugoslavs before the start of the trial.[330] It was also decided to prepare a political memorandum on all the materials compromising Yugoslavia that are available to the Ministry of Interior, which the HSWP CC might consider necessary to use later.

In order to prepare public opinion in the country and abroad for the trial of Nagy and his group, the Politburo made the decision to put on trial a group of writers closely connected with Nagy (Tibor Déry, Gyula Háy, and others). The trial of this group will be open.[331] Materials for this trial, in cde. Biszku's opinion, could be used for the purpose of refuting slanderous assertions from bourgeois propaganda about the events in Hungary.

Judging from cde. Biszku's report, and also from our reading of the indictment, which was sent to the CPSU CC by cde. Kádár, it appears expedient to hold two trials—one of Nagy and his accomplices, and the other of the writers' group. It would be correct—as decided by the HSWP CC Politburo—to hold a closed trial of Nagy's group after the discussion of the "Hungarian issue" at the U.N.[332]

The draft of the indictment in the case of Nagy and his group, prepared by the HPR Ministry of Interior, is basically acceptable but needs more work, especially on the part that deals with the treacherous Nagy group's connection with the imperialists, and the latter's role in the preparation and implementation of the counterrevolutionary riot.

We are asking for your permission, taking the aforementioned into account, to present our considerations to cde. Biszku. Cdes. Rudenko[333] and Ivashutin[334] will provide him with appropriate consultation on specific issues.

Yu. Andropov, R. Rudenko, P. Ivashutin
August 26, 1957
No. 15–D–619

[Source: Archive of the President of the Russian Federation. Published in Hungarian in Éva Gál, András B. Hegedűs, György Litván and János M. Rainer, eds., A "Jelcin Dosszié:" Szovjet dokumentumok 1956-ról (Budapest: Századvég Kiadó-1956-os Intézet, 1993), pp. 199–201. Also published in Rainer, M. János, "1956--The Other Side of the Story: Five Documents from the Yeltsin File," The Hungarian Quarterly 34, no. 129 (Spring 1993): 100–14. Translated by Svetlana Savranskaya.]

[330] The draft note was prepared but at the suggestion of the Soviet leadership was never sent. See Document No. 117.

[331] There were in fact two trials against the writers who were part of the intellectual ferment before the revolution, participated actively in it, and organized resistance afterwards. The first procedure, the so-called "small writers' trial" against Domonkos Varga, Gyula Fekete, Zoltán Molnár and Áron Tóbiás reached a guilty verdict for all defendants on October 9. The second, the trial "against Tibor Déry and his associates"—or the "great writers' trial," as it was called—was held in November and targeted some of the more prominent personalities in Hungarian literary life. On November 19, 1957, Tibor Déry was sentenced to nine years in prison, Gyula Háy to six years, Zoltán Zelk to three years and Tibor Tardos to one-and-a-half years. However, both of these trials were held in camera and not in public as planned earlier.

[332] The U.N. Special Committee, established on January 10, 1957, submitted its report on Hungary on June 20. It was discussed on September 10–14 by the Emergency Special Session of the U.N. General Assembly, which accepted it by a vote of 60–14 with 10 abstentions.

[333] Roman A. Rudenko was chief public prosecutor of the Soviet Union from 1953 and a candidate member of the CPSU CC between 1956–1961.

[334] P. I. Ivashutin was deputy head of the KGB at the Soviet Council of Ministers from 1954–1963.

DOCUMENT NO. 117: Memorandum from Yurii Andropov to the CPSU CC, August 29, 1957

After another meeting with Interior Minister Béla Biszku (see Document No. 116), Andropov writes this memorandum to the CPSU CC, specifying the points that the Soviet Union should take into account regarding the upcoming trial of Nagy and his associates. Andropov's main worry is that the case might jeopardize relations with Yugoslavia. He therefore argues that the Hungarian government should postpone the trial from September to December 1957 or January 1958. The Hungarian government agrees. The trial resumed in February 1958, but Moscow repeatedly proposed further delays, largely because of a hoped-for summit with the western powers. The court procedure finally concluded between June 9–15, 1958, with a guilty verdict that led to the execution of Nagy, Pál Maléter and Miklós Gimes on June 16, 1958.

To the Central Committee of the CPSU

As a supplement to the information sent earlier about the preparations for the trial of Imre Nagy and his group in Hungary,[335] we consider it necessary to inform you that during the August 27 discussion cde. Biszku told us about the decision of the HSWP CC Politburo to hold the trial in September of this year following the United Nations session that will examine the so-called "Hungarian question."[336]

Prior to this trial, the Hungarian comrades have in mind to send the Yugoslavs a note in which they intend to state that Hungary, in connection with recently discovered facts about the criminal activities of Nagy and his accomplices, considers itself to be free of the conditions it had accepted earlier (in an agreement with the Yugoslav side) not to bring Nagy and his group to account. In this way, the Hungarian friends want to prevent any possible statements by the Yugoslav side concerning Hungary's violation of conditions it had accepted, and to avoid a strain in relations with Yugoslavia.

It is known that during the recent meeting in Romania[337] the Yugoslav comrades objected to putting Nagy and his group on trial, stating that it would inevitably lead to a strain in relations between Yugoslavia and Hungary. Therefore, it would be very important to carry out this trial in such a way as to cause the least amount of harm to the emerging improvement in relations between Yugoslavia and the other socialist countries. In that regard, the correct choice of a date for the trial of Nagy and his group carries a great deal of significance.

In deciding this question, one may presume that it is necessary to take the following considerations into account:

1. Holding the Nagy trial before the upcoming meeting of representatives of communist and workers' parties, including the YLC, may have a negative influence on the position of the Yugoslav comrades with respect to their participation at this meeting.[338] On the other hand, it is not impossible that the participation of the Yugoslav comrades at the meeting of representatives of the fraternal parties may have a favorable effect on the reconsideration of their mistaken position on the Hungarian question as a whole. One may suppose that after the meeting the Yugoslavs would treat the fact of the Nagy trial with less sensitivity.

[335] See Document No. 116.

[336] See footnote 332 above.

[337] Prior to a planned international gathering of all communist parties (see next footnote), the Soviet and Chinese parties proposed a preliminary meeting, eventually held in August in Romania, in order to accept a resolution on the leading role of the Soviet Union and the CPSU within the socialist bloc. The Yugoslav delegation, however, refused to sign the document.

[338] The world conference of communist and worker's parties was organized between November 12–19, 1957, in Moscow. Here again, the Yugoslavs refused to sign the concluding joint declaration.

2. After the meeting between the delegations of the CPSU CC and the YLC CC in Romania at the beginning of August this year, a favorable tendency on the part of the Yugoslav state and party organs, and the press, towards the development of friendship and cooperation with the USSR and other socialist countries has been observed. As cde. Ranković stated not long ago in his conversation with a staff member of our embassy, the Yugoslav leadership intends seriously to reorient the YLC toward deepening the friendship and cooperation with the USSR. In this regard, the upcoming Seventh Congress of the Yugoslav League of Communists (November 1957),[339] the decisions of which will undoubtedly influence the further development of Yugoslav relations with the USSR and other socialist countries, especially along party lines, acquires a special importance. However, there is a danger that holding the Nagy proceeding before the YLC Congress might negatively affect the position of the Yugoslav leadership and in this sense influence the character of the Congress, its decisions and its assumptions.

3. With regard to the Nagy proceeding, imperialist reactionary propaganda will undoubtedly intensify its attacks against the USSR, the Hungarian People's Republic and the socialist system as a whole, and will try to exploit this event for purposes of provocation. This circumstance in some measure may unfavorably influence international public opinion, and weaken the effectiveness of measures by the CPSU and other fraternal parties in connection with the celebration of the 40th anniversary of the Great October Socialist Revolution.

All of these considerations ought to be taken into account when choosing a date for the Nagy trial.

In our opinion, it would be expedient, drawing on cde. Kádár's desire to discuss questions related to the Nagy proceeding on a high level, to advise our Hungarian friends to move the date of the Nagy trial to December 1957–January 1958.

It seems to us that in light of Hungary's domestic political conditions, moving the date of the trial back three or four months could not have a negative effect on the situation in the country.

We would assume that it would also be expedient to convey to our Hungarian friends our impression that it might be better not to send the Yugoslavs a note on the Nagy proceeding, but to inform them about it through party channels, explaining their motives, which make it necessary to hold the Nagy trial, and stating that this proceeding would not have an anti-Yugoslav character. In our opinion, this would make it possible to avoid a strain in relations between Hungary and Yugoslavia, which might emerge as a result of transmitting an official diplomatic note to the Yugoslavs on an issue that is extremely unpleasant for them.

HEAD, CPSU CC DEPARTMENT FOR RELATIONS
WITH COMMUNIST AND WORKERS' PARTIES OF THE
SOCIALIST COUNTRIES

YU. ANDROPOV
AUGUST 29, 1957
NO. 15–D–631

[Source: National Security Archive, "Soviet Flashpoints" collection (original archival citation from the Archive of the President of the Russian Federation does not appear on the document). Published in Hungarian in Éva Gál, András B. Hegedűs, György Litván and János M. Rainer, eds., A "Jelcin Dosszié:" Szovjet dokumentumok 1956-ról (Budapest: Századvég Kiadó-1956-os Intézet, 1993), pp. 202–204. Translated by Malcolm Byrne.]

[339] The Seventh Congress of the YLC was eventually held in April 1958.

DOCUMENT NO. 118: National Security Council Report 5811, "Policy Toward the Soviet-Dominated Nations in Eastern Europe," May 9, 1958

After the Hungarian revolution, the Eisenhower administration did not formally revise its policy toward the satellites immediately. But by 1958, a clear difference in approach could be detected, as evidenced by NSC 5811, which explicitly recognized that past experience had shown the limits of U.S. opportunities for fundamentally influencing events in Eastern Europe. Reversing the previous policy which had aimed to "ostracize the dominated regimes," the new approach called for a combination of trade, economic aid and "direct contact" with the satellite populations (in the form of cultural and scientific exchanges, visits by high-profile Americans and tourism), as a way to demonstrate U.S. interest in the region and generate "popular pressures upon the regimes for increased internal freedom and independence from Soviet control." The satellite governments themselves were also targets of the new policy, which included offers of economic, cultural and other blandishments in varying amounts depending at least in part on the behavior of each regime. This marked the beginning of the long-standing policy of "differentiation," a term officially coined by the Lyndon Johnson administration.[340] NSC 5811 remained in effect for the rest of the Eisenhower presidency.

U.S. POLICY TOWARD THE SOVIET-DOMINATED NATIONS IN EASTERN EUROPE

GENERAL CONSIDERATIONS

Regional Considerations

1. Soviet control over Albania, Bulgaria, Czechoslovakia, East Germany,[341] Hungary and Rumania (referred to hereafter as the dominated nations)[342] is a basic cause of international friction and, therefore, a threat to peace and to the security of the United States and Western Europe. Soviet determination to maintain control of these nations is also an obstacle to an overall European settlement and to a significant relaxation of international tensions, including a comprehensive disarmament agreement.

2. The principal impediment to Soviet efforts to impose an effective Communist political, economic and social system on the peoples of the dominated nations is the anti-Communist and anti-Russian attitude of the great majority of the population in each such nation. This attitude is intensified particularly by severe restriction of personal and religious freedom, a continued low standard of living, and strong nationalist sentiment among the people, especially the youth, and even among certain elements within the Communist parties. An additional impediment is the continued refusal of the West, particularly the United States and its principal NATO allies, to accept the permanence of Soviet-imposed regimes as compatible with the principles of human freedom and self-determination of nations.

3. Although Moscow has not incorporated the dominated nations into the state structure of the USSR as it did the Baltic Republics of Estonia, Latvia and Lithuania (see Annex B), Soviet physical control over these nations remains firm. The USSR maintains Soviet troops in much of the

---

[340] See Marchio, *Rhetoric and Reality*, 444.

[341] While many of the considerations set forth in this paper with respect to the Soviet-dominated nations of Eastern Europe also apply to East Germany, there are a number of respects in which special considerations are applicable to East Germany, owing to the fact that the United States regards it as under Soviet military occupation and not as a separate "nation." The specific problems of East Germany and Berlin are treated in the Supplements to NSC 5803. [Footnote in original.]

[342] U.S. Policy Toward Poland is treated separately in NSC 5808/1. [Footnote in original.]

area (see Annex A) and the Warsaw Pact formalized Soviet measures for coordination and control over the military forces of these nations. Political control is exerted both on a governmental level and through the Communist Party apparatus. Moscow also exercises control over the area's economy through such means as the Council of Economic Mutual Assistance (CEMA) and through bilateral trade and aid agreements. There are no known anti-regime groups capable of successfully organizing coordinated and sustained resistance to the Communist regimes in any of the dominated nations. The United States has not been prepared to resort to force or threat of force either to eliminate Soviet domination or to support revolutionary movements.

4. After Stalin's death in 1953, the stability of the Soviet political system in Eastern Europe was shaken by a succession of important developments, including: the elimination of a single source of ideological authority and the attacks on the cult of personality (denigration of Stalin); the reestablishment of Party primacy over the police; the growth of the concept of "different roads to socialism;" and, in the campaign to increase labor productivity, an increased use of economic incentives and a decreased reliance on arbitrary police and administrative methods. These developments, which gave rise to policy and doctrinal conflicts within the Soviet leadership, were reflected in the decisions of the 20th Congress of the CPSU in 1956; and their impact spread throughout the Bloc. These developments added to growing uncertainty and confusion in the Communist parties and strengthened the hand of party dissidents seeking democratization and greater national independence. Party and popular unrest reached the greatest heights in Poland and Hungary, where in October 1956 Soviet authority was seriously challenged for the first time since the Yugoslav break in 1948.

5. Although surface stability has been restored and will probably be preserved over the next few years, an atmosphere of change and ferment more highly charged than under Stalin will probably continue for some time. The forces of unrest which underlay the troubles of 1956 are manifest in discontent over current policies within the Communist parties, particularly at middle and lower levels; in intellectual and student ferment; in popular hostility to the regimes, stimulated by party and intellectual dissidents; and in economic discontent, common to all who do not enjoy privileged rank.

6. Additional factors adversely affecting Soviet control in Eastern Europe are:

a. The effects of the Hungarian revolt, which was a serious moral and ideological defeat for the USSR, will persist for some time. The revolt engendered an enduring hatred of the USSR. Future Soviet actions will be tempered by this demonstration of the risk of relying on indigenous armed forces and of failing to gain popular support for Communism.

b. Poland's ability to maintain the limited independence gained in October 1956 will be a key factor affecting future political developments in Eastern Europe. A Polish-type coup in the area is not likely soon, but if the Polish experiment is successful and Moscow's acquiescence in it continues, nationalist elements in the dominated nations may be encouraged to seek greater autonomy.

c. Similarly, the continued existence of Yugoslavia as a Communist nation independent of Moscow will tend to encourage nationalist elements in the area to seek greater autonomy.

7. In these circumstances, present Soviet policy appears to be one of experimentation in an effort to find a middle course between the alternatives of (a) placing primary reliance on policies of force and repression, and (b) granting increasing autonomy and independence to the Eastern European regimes. The first alternative would deny to these regimes the possibility of broadening their base of popular support. The second alternative would stimulate popular pressures for further concessions and might become extremely difficult to limit or control.

8. In this situation, Moscow may experience a diminished ability to exercise unilateral authority in the Communist world. The necessity for maintaining at least outward unity in the Sino-Soviet Bloc and the international Communist movement will, as in the past, lead the

Soviets to compromise on some issues and at least to consider the opinions of other Communist parties on others. However, while the memories of Hungary and Poland remain fresh, the security of the USSR's position will remain uppermost in Soviet minds and measures to insure it will be given first priority. This does not mean that Soviet leaders consider a return to Stalinist policies as either necessary or desirable. Rather, so long as Soviet hegemony and basic Communist tenets are not called into question, the USSR will continue to place major reliance on indirect methods of control, preferring to let the dominated regimes deal with their own internal problems unless these get out of hand.

9. In attempting to cope through flexible and pragmatic means with the complex problem of maintaining its position in the area, the USSR probably will:

a. Attempt to obtain some form of East-West ratification of the *status quo* in Eastern Europe in the hope of undermining the dominated peoples' hope of future U.S. support and thus reducing the likelihood of deviation and unrest.

b. Continue to maintain sizeable armed forces in the area, particularly in East Germany, not only for military reasons but as an essential element in maintaining control over the dominated nations.

c. Be prepared to use armed force to thwart any serious threat to its control in the area, although Soviet reaction to a Gomulka-type coup would depend on the circumstances of the moment; i.e. whether the threat to the Soviet position was sufficient to outweigh the disadvantages of military intervention.

d. Continue to provide economic aid to the dominated nations in order to reduce unrest by improving living standards, to maintain the area's dependence on the USSR, and to counter the appeal of increased trade between Eastern Europe and the West.

e. Permit the dominated nations to enter into increasing but selectively-controlled contacts with the West, in an attempt, among other things, to influence world opinion, to obtain technological data and ease economic strains, and to appease the desires of the intelligentsia in the area for wider associations throughout the world.

10. The current ferment in Eastern Europe offers new opportunities, though still limited, to influence the dominated regimes through greater U.S. activity, both private and official, in such fields as tourist travel, cultural exchange and economic relations, including of technical and commercial visitors. Experience has shown that a U.S. policy designed to ostracize the dominated regimes has had the concurrent effect of inhibiting increased direct U.S. contacts with the people of the dominated nations. It is now apparent that, as a practical matter, substantial expansion of direct U.S. contacts with the peoples of these nations, and the development through such contacts of popular pressures upon the regimes for increased internal freedom and independence from Soviet control, cannot be achieved without more active U.S. relationships with and through these governments. Such relationships would enable the United States to probe, within the party and governmental bureaucracy, for those individuals or groups who show signs of independent thought, nationalist aspirations, or willingness to use their influence to modify their nation's subservient relationship to the Soviet Union.

11. The West could have the greatest impact on Eastern Europe, and would run the greatest risk, through major East-West agreements which would fundamentally affect the European situation. The very fact of negotiations on any such issues as mutual troop withdrawals, German reunification, or the *status quo* in Europe would have some impact on Eastern Europe. To the extent that the West seemed to be confirming Soviet hegemony over Eastern Europe, morale among the peoples and potential party deviants would tend to be depressed. On the other hand, negotiations which appeared to offer hopes of a Soviet troop withdrawal, particularly if couples with convincing guarantees against their return, would have an opposite effect. An East-West agreement on German reunification which was interpreted in Eastern Europe as an abandonment by the USSR of East Germany would almost certainly have major repercussions throughout the

area. Unless countered by positive and vigorous Soviet action, these repercussions—in the form of increasing dissidence, ferment, Party factionalism, riots and strikes—might lead to upheavals or radical policy shifts toward greater external or internal freedom in Eastern Europe, especially in Poland.

12. With the passage of years during which Soviet domination of Eastern European nations has continued, emigre national committees have proved less productive. This situation has been aggravated by internal factional strife and lack of unified purpose. There is no evidence that emigre politicians have any significant following in their homelands or that in the foreseeable future they will be able to return there to assume a role of political leadership.

13. Flexible U.S. courses of action, involving inducements as well as probing actions and pressures, are required to exploit the Soviet dilemma and sensitivities in the dominated nations and to complicate the exercise of Soviet control over them. In order to take full advantage of existing opportunities in this area, U.S. courses of action toward the dominated nations must appropriately exploit their individual historical and cultural characteristics and the significant differences of their respective present situations.

Albania

14. Albania is unique among the dominated nations for its political, economic and cultural backwardness. Despite post-Stalin trends toward liberalization elsewhere in the Soviet Bloc, the Albanian regime has shown few signs of deviating from the Stalinist pattern. Albania presents special problem to U.S. policy because it has traditionally been subject to rival claims and ambitions by Greece, Italy and Yugoslavia. The Albanian Communists have posed as the indispensable champions of Albanian independence and territorial integrity.

15. Albania has never been a nation of primary importance to the United States. Immediately after World War II, U.S.-Albanian discussions on the establishment of diplomatic relations broke down as a result of Albanian refusal to affirm the validity of pre-war treaties and agreements between Albania and the United States. There have been some indications recently that the Albanian regime may desire to establish diplomatic relations with the United States.

Bulgaria

16. The Bulgarian regime, despite occasional top-level purges and discontent among intellectuals, appears relatively stable and able to maintain control of the nation. Communist efforts to make Bulgaria an industrial nation without the necessary resources base have produced serious economic problems. Large-scale unemployment has caused the Bulgarian regime to seek extensive economic aid from the Soviet Union and to adopt a new economic plan under which Bulgaria would specialize in light industry and truck-farming. The United States suspended diplomatic relations with Bulgaria in February 1950 after a series of harassments which culminated in Bulgarian action against the U.S. Minister as *persona non grata* on charges of subversion and espionage. Bulgarian leaders have several times indicated publicly and through diplomatic channels their desire for a resumption of relations.

Czechoslovakia

17. Except for a brief period of ferment in the spring of 1956 following the disclosures at the 20th Party Congress in Moscow, Czechoslovakia has been a submissive satellite. The Czech people, although traditionally Western-oriented and anti-Communist, have remained largely apathetic under Soviet domination. Specific grievances are probably allayed to some extent by the Czech standard of living, which is appreciably higher now than it was during the Stalin era and is the highest in Eastern Europe. Anti-Soviet sentiment exists within the Party, and there are certainly some in the Party who favor greater independence; but the Party leadership, so far as can be determined, is steadfast in its adherence to the Moscow line. The regime has failed to eliminate the thorny minority problem. The Communist Party continues to have less influence in Slovakia than in Bohemia-Moravia, and the Slovak potential for active resistance is higher.

Hungary

18. The present Communist regime in Hungary, in consolidating its physical control of the nation, has followed a policy of terror and intimidation clearly intended to wipe out all resistance. Although the Hungarian people continue to despise this regime, a surface calm prevails and the normal pattern of life under Soviet Communism has resumed.

19. A certain degree of moderation has been evident in the economic policy of the Hungarian regime. Collectivization of agriculture remains the ultimate goal, but Kadar has asserted that this will be achieved by "Leninist" persuasion rather than "Stalinist" coercion. A degree of private enterprise among artisans and small tradesmen has been tolerated though not encouraged, and there has been an effort to keep the market reasonably well supplied with consumer goods. With the aid of extensive grants and loans from the Soviet Union and other Communist nations, the Hungarian economy has recovered from the effects of the revolution more rapidly that had been anticipated, though grave economic problems remain.

20. The Hungarian regime has not granted any appreciable internal political concessions in order to improve its international standing. It has, however, made continuing efforts to overcome its isolation by other means. It has been energetic in negotiating trade agreements with the West, has shown interest in cultural exchanges, and appears to be prepared to permit a degree of contact between Hungarians and the West. The regime has continued publicly to condemn the excesses of Rakosi even while following a basically regressive policy. For public consumption, at least, it has pictured itself as determined to steer a "middle" course between the extremes of Nagy-ism and Rakosi-ism.

21. Because Hungary has become an important psychological factor in the world-wide struggle of the free nations against expansionist Soviet Communism, U.S. policy must maintain a delicate balance; it must seek to encourage the same evolutionary developments as in the other nations of Eastern Europe, without compromising the symbol which Hungary has become. More restraint will be required in dealing directly with regime officials than in certain other nations of the area and the timing of U.S. moves will be of great importance.

Rumania

22. The physical hold of the Communist regime on Rumania remains firm. Such personnel changes as have occurred in the Rumanian Communist Government and Party since the Polish and Hungarian events appear to have connected with internal Party differences, and have not been caused by overt public pressures for change.

23. One of the distinguishing marks of Rumanian Communist rule is an unwillingness to deviate too far from a moderate position in response to sudden changes of attitude in Moscow. The Rumanian Communists have consistently failed to attack Tito with the extreme fervor of some of the other Communist Parties while, on the other hand, they have never gone as far in the direction of liberalization as did the Hungarians prior to the 1956 uprising. Attempts both to pursue standard Communist goals and to allay the economic causes of popular discontent, have caused considerable economic strain.

24. Although unwilling to grant substantial political concessions to the population, the Rumanian leadership during the past year has sought an easing of relations and increased contacts with the United States in order to secure benefits in trade and technology and give substance to its claims of legitimacy and permanence in the eyes of its own people. The Rumanian regime is therefore exceptionally receptive to increased contacts with the West.

OBJECTIVES

25. *Short-range:* Promotion of the peaceful evolution of the dominated nations toward national independence and internal freedom, even though these nations may continue for some time under the close political and military control of the Soviet Union.

26. Reduction of the contribution of the dominated nations to Soviet strength, and weakening of the monolithic front and internal cohesiveness of the Soviet Bloc.

27. *Long-range*: Fulfillment of the right of the peoples in the dominated nations to enjoy representative governments resting upon the consent of the governed, exercising full national independence, and participating as peaceful members of the Free World community.

REGIONAL POLICY GUIDANCE[343]

Political and Diplomatic

28. In order to maintain and develop popular pressures on the present regime and accelerate evolution toward independence from Soviet control:

    a. Expand direct contacts with the dominated peoples to exploit their anti-Communist and anti-Russian attitudes.
    b. As a means toward accomplishing a. above, establish more active relations with the existing regimes, without creating the impression that the basic U.S. attitude toward those regimes has changed or will change in the absence of some significant modification in their character.
    c. Encourage the dominated peoples to seek their goals gradually {and without resort to premature violent actions.}[344] Avoid incitement or encouragement of violent uprisings, rioting or guerilla operations by the peoples of dominated nations, unless special circumstances arise in which there is a policy determination that such action would yield a net advantage in terms of U.S. policy objectives.
    d. Discreetly foster dissident and non-cooperative attitudes; and {do not discourage}[345] non-cooperative activities, including passive resistance.[346]

29. Review periodically Operations Coordinating Board contingency studies, and in addition maintain military contingency plans which would enable the United States to assist, should it be deemed desirable at the time, any revolutionary outbreak that may occur within the dominated nations.

30. To impair and weaken Soviet domination, exploit divisive forces by appropriate measures including:

    a. Fostering nationalist pride and aspirations among the people and within the regime leadership.
    b. Exacerbating areas of friction between the dominated nations and the USSR, and between the dominated regimes.
    c. Exploiting and fostering divisive tendencies within the dominated regimes.
    d. Publicizing evidences of unequal treatment by the USSR.
    e. Encouraging comparisons of the lot of the dominated nations with that of the USSR and with each other.

31. Emphasize on appropriate occasions the U.S. view that the people of each nation should be independent and free to choose their form of government; and avoid any action or statement which could reasonably be represented in the dominated nations as advocacy of a return to the authoritarian systems of government which existed prior to or during World War II.

---

[343] NSC policies on the Soviet Bloc (including NSC 5726/1, "U.S. Civil Aviation Policy Toward the Sino-Soviet Bloc," December 9, 1957, and NSC 5607, "East-West Exchanges" June 29, 1956) will continue to apply except as modified by this policy or by exceptions in the policies concerned. [Footnote in original.]

[344] JCS proposal. [Footnote in original.]

[345] State-Treasury-Budget proposal. [Footnote in original.]

[346] In the original, paragraph 28 d. is crossed out and the word "covertly" is written over the word "discreetly."

32. Reiterate on appropriate occasions in public statements that the United States does not look upon the dominated nations as potential military allies and supports their right to independence, not to encircle the Soviet Union with hostile forces, but so that they may take their rightful place as equal members in a peaceful European Community of nations.

33. Continue in official public statements:

a. To point out the evils and defects of the Soviet-Communist system.
b. To reiterate U.S. refusal to accept the domination of these nations by the USSR as an acceptable *status quo*.
c. To stress evolutionary change.

34.
a. Encourage the regimes in the dominated nations to take independent initiatives in foreign relations and domestic affairs.
b. Take advantage of every appropriate opportunity to demonstrate to these regimes how their national interests may be served by independent actions looking toward more normal relations with the West.

35. Be prepared to discuss and negotiate issues between the United States and the individual regimes. When complete solutions are not possible, be prepared to accept partial solutions which do not impair U.S. objectives.

36. Endeavor to bring the dominated nations increasingly into the activities of international technical and social organizations in order to contribute to their greater independence from Soviet influence and be to U.S. advantage.

37. Continue as appropriate to support selected emigres or emigre groups capable of making a positive contribution to U.S. objectives, while gradually phasing out support of less useful emigre organizations.

38. Exploit the benefits received by Yugoslavia and Poland from their relations with the United States as an inducement to the regimes of the dominated nations to seek closer relations with the West.

39. Continue application of "U.S. Policy on Defectors, Escapees and Refugees from Communist Areas" (NSC 5706/2) to nationals of the dominated nations, except that:

a. Efforts to induce the defection of leaders (paragraph 6–b of NSC 5706/2) should not be made unless the intelligence, operational or psychological contribution they could make would clearly result in a net advantage to the United States.
b. Avoid publicity concerning defectors, escapees and refugees unless such publicity would produce a net advantage to the United States.

Economic

40. Seek to establish between the United States and the dominated nations with which the United States has diplomatic relations, more normal economic relations thereby facilitating a gradual expansion of trade—consistent with "Basic National Security Policy" (NSC 5810/1) and "U.S. Economic Defense Policy" (NSC 5704/3)[347]—as a means of projecting U.S. influence and lessening the dominated nations' economic ties with and dependence on the Soviet Union.

41. Encourage voluntary relief agencies to undertake appropriate operations in the dominated nations if opportunities arise. Be prepared to offer food and other relief assistance, through voluntary agencies or otherwise, to the peoples of the dominated countries when emergency situations occur.

[347] NSC Action 1865-c directed the review of this policy; cf. NSC 5810/1 paragraph 37. For the Department of Commerce suggestions for expanding par. 40, see Annex C. [Footnote in original.]

42. Seek the alleviation or settlement of long-standing economic issues (nationalization claims, surplus property and other financial obligations) between the dominated nations and the United States.

Information and Exchange Activities

43.
   a. In dominated nations with which the United States maintains diplomatic relations, conduct as many information and cultural activities as are considered desirable and feasible.
   b. Continue radio broadcasting activities to all the dominated nations.
   c. Encourage private information and cultural activities in the dominated nations, recognizing that private media can engage in activities which would promote U.S. objectives but for which the United States would not wish to accept responsibility.
   d. Be prepared when necessary to permit information and cultural activities in the United States by the diplomatic missions of the dominated nations on an approximately reciprocal basis.

44. To promote expanded contacts and to revive and revitalize traditional bonds between the dominated nations and the United States, encourage, as circumstances in a particular nation may warrant:

   a. Contacts between U.S. individuals and individuals in dominated nations in religious, cultural, technical, business, and social fields.
   b. Contacts, between U.S. business and other organizations and organizations in the dominated nations in comparable fields, including the exchange of delegations of technical experts.
   c. Participation, where feasible and appropriate, in international trade fairs, film festivals, etc., organized by the dominated nations, inviting on a basis of general reciprocity their participation in such activities in the United States.
   d. An expanding exchange program of students and teachers and increasing numbers of leaders' and specialists' visits.
   e. Tourism, on an approximately reciprocal basis, particularly visits between relatives and friends.

Internal Security

45. Entries, visits, and activities in the United States of individuals or groups from Soviet-dominated nations shall take place under ICIS-approved internal security safeguards.

Policies of Other Free World Nations

46. Encourage Western European nations to adopt policies toward the dominated nations parallel to those of the United States, and in particular to concert together through established institutions such as NATO, OEEL, and the Council of Europe for the purposes of (a) taking all practicable steps to extend Western European influence among the dominated nations of Eastern Europe, and (b) exploiting the concept of an integrated, prosperous and stable European community.

47. Seek to counter Soviet efforts to use the dominated nations for penetration of less-developed nations.

SPECIAL COUNTRY POLICY GUIDANCE

Albania

48. Promote increased Western contacts with Albania and encourage other Western nations to establish diplomatic missions there. When appropriate, recognize and establish U.S. diplo-

matic relations with Albania, subject to certain conditions, including a guarantee of correct treatment of U.S. diplomatic personnel and satisfactory settlement of the question of the validity of pre-war treaties between Albania and the United States.

49. After U.S. recognition of Albania, permit travel of U.S. tourists in Albania.

Bulgaria

50. Seek through negotiations to re-establish diplomatic relations with Bulgaria in the near future, subject to appropriate conditions and suitable guarantees.

51. After U.S. resumption of relations with Bulgaria, permit travel of U.S. tourists in Bulgaria.

Czechoslovakia

52. Expand contacts and reporting opportunities in Slovakia. Be prepared to permit reciprocal reestablishment of Czech consulates in the United States on a on-for-one basis, despite the additional opportunity afforded for Communist espionage and subversion in the United States.

53. Seek to stimulate nationalist feeling by such means as references in U.S. propaganda to the Ruthenian territory annexed by the USSR in 1945 and frequent references to the Soviet Union's exploitation of Czechoslovakia's uranium resources.

54. Emphasize in U.S. propaganda past and present contributions of Czechoslovak intellectuals and scientists to demonstrate that the common interests and basic orientation of these groups is toward the Free World rather than toward the USSR.

Hungary

55. Continue to keep the Hungarian issue alive through diplomatic action, within the United Nations, through official and non-official U.S. media, and through the encouragement of public reactions and protests in Free World nations against repressive developments in Hungary.

56. Work toward the satisfactory integration of Hungarian refugees in the Free World through support of legislation aimed at regularizing the status of the parolees in this country and through continuing by the Escapee Program to assist in the solution of settlement problems in other nations.

57. In order to permit a substantial number of Americans to visit in Hungary, continue currently to interpret travel restrictions liberally, and for the next tourist season consider removing entirely the passport validation requirement.

58. Encourage cultural and scientific exchanges with Hungary on a case-by-case basis. Do not permit at this time the sending of larger prestige attractions to the United States, the exchange of official Government delegations, or visits to the United States by leading members of the Hungarian regime.

Rumania

59. Seek to exploit fully the opportunities which exist at present in Rumania because of the receptive attitude of the regime, particularly in economic and cultural relations.

ANNEX A

MILITARY FORCES IN THE SOVIET-DOMINATED NATIONS OF EASTERN EUROPE AND POLAND

	Albania	Bulgaria	Czechos-lovakia	Hungary	Rumania	Total	E. Germany	Poland	Total Incl. E. Germany and Poland
GROUND									
DIVISIONS	--	9	15	--	14	38	7	18	63
ARMY PERSONNEL	30,000	110,000	170,000	100,000	215,000	625,000	100,000	250,000	975,000
SECURITY FORCES	10,000	30,000	45,000	35,000	78,000	198,000	45,000	45,000	288,000
AIR									
PERSONNEL	1,500	16,000	23,000	5,500	13,500	59,500	8,000	34,000	101,500
JET DAY FIGHTERS	45	230	685	95	250	1,305	135	700	2,140
ALL-WEATHER JET FIGHTERS	--	10	40	--	--	50	--	20	70
JET ATTACK FIGHTERS	--	20	5	--	--	25	--	10	35
JET LIGHT BOMBERS	--	--	50	--	15	65	--	85	150
NAVY									
PERSONNEL	900	6,200	--	--	9,200	16,300	12,000	14,000	42,300
DESTROYERS	--	1	--	--	4	5	--	3	8
SUBMARINES	--	3	--	--	3	6	--	7	13
MINOR VESSELS	37	82	--	--	71	190	113	103	406
SOVIET FORCES									
GROUND									
DIVISIONS	--	--	--	4	2	6	20	2	28
ARMY PERSONNEL	--	--	--	55,000	35,000	90,000	315,000	35,000	440,000
SECURITY FORCES	--	--	--	1,500	2,000	3,500	13,500	1,000	18,000
AIR									
REGIMENTS	--	--	--	9	5	14	22	14	50
JET DAY FIGHTERS	--	--	--	185	170	355	525	210	1,090
ALL-WEATHER JET FIGHTERS	--	--		20	20	40	70	35	145
JET ATTACK FIGHTERS	--	--	--	--	--	--	--	90	90
JET LIGHT BOMBERS	--	--	--	90	--	90	90	60	240

[Source: DDEL; White House Office; Office of the Special Assistant for National Security Affairs, 1953–1961; NSC Series; NSC Subseries; Box 25.]

DOCUMENT NO. 119: Extraordinary Meeting of the HSWP Political Committee Discussing Imre Pozsgay's Declaration on 1956, January 31, 1989 (Excerpt)

On June 23, 1988, the HSWP Central Committee established a committee to analyze the political, economic and social development of the country during the preceding thirty years. It included the participation of party officials and social scientists alike, and was headed by Imre Pozsgay,[1] a member of the Political Committee and minister of state. The Historical Subcommittee (one of the four working groups), after several months of examining archival documents, prepared a formal report, which was discussed at its meeting on January 27, 1989. The report stated that what had occurred in 1956 in Hungary was not a counterrevolution but a popular uprising. This conclusion was first made public by Pozsgay in an interview on the morning news and on Hungarian Radio's most popular political magazine, "168 hours," the next day. He did this without prior consultation with the leadership. The issue caused a serious crisis in the party and eventually helped to accelerate the transition from communist rule. The following excerpt reflects the Politburo's first reactions to the new developments.

Imre Pozsgay: As regards the specific issue: the subcommittee, headed by Iván T. Berend,[2] held a debate on Friday morning, on the basis of a 102-page case study.

I had no chance to read the document before the debate, because it has just been given to me. All the same, let me point out only one aspect of the debate, namely that six members of the Central Committee were present, and the leaders of two party institutions. There was no argument about the objected assessment; on the contrary, the conclusion was that a minimal public consensus—I am merely interpreting this since I have no right to borrow other people's words— a minimal public consensus does no harm to the identity of the party, nor does it shatter the personal identity of those who tied their lives, careers, and behavior specifically to this struggle. Nonetheless, it can lead to social reconciliation and a national consensus on certain bitter and still all-too-distressing issues, such as the entire situation that has developed since 1948–49, and especially its pinnacle—or nadir, as others believe—the crisis and tragedy of 1956. The committee unanimously agreed on this issue. And finally we also agreed that this document, even before it is discussed by the Central Committee, has to be publicized, so that a scientific opinion, supported by wide masses of the party, could be used to set a political direction. These were the fundamental [issues] and basic motives of the committee. In a way it is an answer to the numerous questions that were in fact asked from many sides: why did the Central Committee not discuss the issue first? According to earlier procedures, it would indeed have been the way to handle such questions. However, I am convinced that this procedure is the very reason why the party was often hoisted on its own petard when it came to discussing similar issues.

Regarding further connections and problems that the questions raise: Certainly, or rather undoubtedly, the political impact that ensues—even if it achieves the minimal consensus I just mentioned—is expected to become a bone of contention within the party, something that divides people and induces political polemics, although it will not hurt even those who have won honor for the socialist homeland for their sacrifices. The committee was aware of this fact from the

---

[1] Imre Pozsgay was a leading figure of the reform movement inside the party and served as a member of the HSWP PC and a minister of state between 1988–1989.

[2] Iván T. Berend was a historian, president of the Hungarian Academy of Sciences, a member of the HSWP CC and chairman of the Advisory Board of the Council of Ministers. In 1990, he became a professor at the University of California, Los Angeles.

very beginning, knowing that we cannot get around this debate, that it has to happen. So, in a way, the cup of sorrows has to be taken up.

[....]

Mihály Jassó:[3] The vast majority is dumbfounded, and not because they have heard the results of an academic research project from the Historical Subcommittee, but because they feel that a pillar of the institutionalized political system is about to be uprooted. Party members feel that our political system is somehow based on 1956. And now they have the impression that this foundation is being removed from below. They think that this slice of the past—1956—has to be assessed with subtle differentiation. But now this assessment shows no sign of differentiation either. Figuratively speaking, they used to make a fine cabinet with an axe, and right now they are trying to do the same thing. I don't intend to be too poetic but I'm coming from an office where I got phone calls and letters today asking what we are going to call the monument on Köztársaság Square? Who sacrificed their lives there? Defenders of the people's power? Resistance fighters of the people's uprising, or their opponents? It is all confused. What shall we call Mező Imre Street? And so on. Because perhaps it was a people's uprising that started the whole thing but it led to something else. In that event, we need at least a subtle, differentiated assessment of the entire period. The present one is not differentiated at all. This is another extreme, which sets people wide apart. If we start a debate on the issue, which is now naturally unavoidable, I think it is only good for separating some of the party membership. It is a crude simplification but we divide party members into two groups on the basis of this: "pro uprising" and "pro counterrevolution" members. Obviously I refer to the underlying political content. Perhaps we cannot avoid the debate, but I am not sure that it has to be provoked so radically all at once.

[....]

Rezső Nyers[4]: The problem is greater, and we have to widen its scope. Is 1956 really the foundation of the Hungarian communist movement? If 1956 is our foundation, I will not expect the movement to hold out very long, because it is a weak foundation indeed. Our decisions and historical assessment of 1956 were driven by the spirit of the time and not without controversies. While things were going smoothly, people tolerated all this, but when times are hard, the same people seem discontented with what they tolerated before. Therefore we should not consider 1956 as a foundation. 1956 was a tragic event, a moment that manifested the prevailing crisis, and today we have to conclude that in fact 1956 signified a more serious crisis than we thought at the time, or even in 1957. We belittled the problem, but now we all agree—and I think there is a consensus about it in the party—that it was the materialization of a historical mistake.

[....]

Consequently, I have to point out that it would be a serious mistake—especially for the future of the party—to tie our policy to the 1956 bandwagon.

We have to conclude, having read the document—I have read the document and the material of the committee debate as well—that the declaration of Pozsgay and the exposé of the committee show a unanimous approach. They are in accord—which does not justify publicizing the declaration this way. I am still of the opinion that it [the presentation] was disadvantageous, hasty and inaccurate [*pontatlan*]. I hold to my opinion, even though there is no fundamental controversy between the standpoint of the committee and that of Pozsgay.

As to whether it was a "people's uprising" or "counterrevolution," my opinion is that a definition without controversy is impossible on this issue. Personally, I think that it was a people's uprising; our declaration in December 1956 acknowledged that in the first paragraph, labeling it the rightful dissatisfaction of the people.

[3] Mihály Jassó was a member of the HSWP CC, head of the Budapest branch of the HSWP and in April 1989 became a member of the HSWP PC.

[4] Rezső Nyers, a long-time politician, high official and leading pro-reform figure, was minister of state and member of the HSWP CC and PC at this time. He later became president of the HSWP and then of the Hungarian Socialist Party.

I do maintain, though, that hostile enemies gradually joined in, and they could have turned the wheel of history backwards, so the danger of counterrevolution was imminent. As to our opinion on 1956, I argue against the farfetched criticism of Imre Nagy and his circle, and the significance of revisionism.... I declare it with communist honesty, it was a mistake. It is not true that the revisionist group of Imre Nagy had such a vital role in the events ... At that time, I myself accepted this declaration. However, we get smarter, and now we see what went on. We now realize that the mistakes were more serious. We realize that it was wrong to think that between 1953 and 1956 Rákosi was a dime and Imre Nagy was a dozen, so to speak. In that debate, well, Imre Nagy was right. It is a matter of honesty, if someone thinks it over and believes that it is so, one should speak out all right. And I do speak out. Imre Nagy was not a counterrevolutionary; he was not. If a party ever, with their own ... One only has to read his speeches. Where the hell do we find counterrevolutionary ideas with Imre Nagy? Nowhere, absolutely nowhere! And these are matters of honor. He was rather a sectarian. If he was still among us now unchanged, he would be more of a Stalinist. His role in the 1956 events remains debatable, it cannot be clarified. The Soviets were mucking around, which we swept under the carpet. Even today we cannot see the truth. I already know, however, that the Soviets had a lion's share in the decision. János Kádár and the Political Committee of the time took full responsibility, for which I respect them. However, they are far from being the only ones to blame. Their responsibility is without question, because it also cannot be accepted that a decision was made in Moscow and was executed here. Unfortunately, though, I have to emphasize again that we won't be able to come to terms with the question of 1956. Legally, Imre Nagy was culpable, because he breached the law. It is not too moral, at a time when everyone was breaching the law—I was breaching it, and so was János Kádár—if the lawbreakers themselves accuse and convict the weaker one on the basis of a sectarian law. These are not righteous things. All the same, those who did not live in that situation are unable to imagine how it was—and this is the dramatic aspect. I think if we leave it in the focus of political debates it will result in the serious weakening of, and moral crisis in the communist movement. Consequently, we have to put history right; it can be corrected. Roughly according to the opinion of the committee, it can be corrected, but let me emphasize that the word "counterrevolution" should not be replaced with a single term, and it has to be decided who makes the correction. I think it is now time for us to try and come to some kind of political consensus. We cannot let the undulations of political life shatter the scarcely emerging unity and cooperation of the party and its leadership, so that other players take over while we eventually fall apart. I also mean that Pozsgay should not become the victim of this affair either. Yet, Pozsgay should show more discipline and more mutual responsibility as well.

All in all, we should not let ourselves confront each other to the extreme. What action do I think is possible to take? I believe that the Central Committee should be summoned and presented the material of the committee. The Pozsgay affair should not be presented on its own; it would be an impossible trial that would lead to nothing. I think that the documents of the Subcommittee have to be submitted for debate, and only then could it be discussed whether it was wise or not, what he did, and what action has to be taken in order to settle the debate. At the same time, principal issues of daily politics should be presented to the Central Committee, such as what should be done now on the question of the single party system and the multiparty system. Things have passed over our heads. I cannot see another option other than to accept the multiparty system. But we need to debate all this. And if we decide against the multiparty system, then that will be our decision, and everybody decides according to his conscience whether he takes the political responsibility for his decision. I do admit sincerely, I would take responsibility for both, even if I do not agree with the decision. It can be done intelligently. Retreat, however, is the worst one can do, it can only lead to our defeat. We have to do it sooner or later, anyway....

All in all, I say that we take seriously the committee's compilation, and consider their report worthy of being presented to the Central Committee. We suggest to the Central Committee that we publicize the committee's documents. We'll see if the Central Committee will accept the suggestion.

[....]

In fact, the most serious and sensitive issue of our policy is quite palpable here, namely how we relate to the Kádár era, to the Kádár regime. In my opinion, it would be a mistake for reformers to entirely do away with the Kádár regime. On the other hand, it would be a mistake to canonize the policy of the Kádár regime and battle to the last man standing in defense of what we have created since 1956. Some in the party lean toward the latter, while others are ready to prove and expose the mistakes. Neither of these should be embraced. We have to try to solve the problem with reason. If relevant circles, or the determining circle of the Central Committee put the issue on the agenda, a consensus is possible. We should start working out special programs for our activities [aimed at] preparing for the multiparty system. We need these projects for the purpose of creating a stabilizing program that addresses today's conditions, as well as more specific government programs.

[....]

[Source: MOL, M–KS–288. f. 5/1050. ő.e. Published in Csaba Békés and Malcolm Byrne, eds., Political Transition in Hungary, 1989–1990: A Compendium of Declassified Documents and Chronology of Events, *(National Security Archive, Cold War History Research Center, Institute for the History of the 1956 Hungarian Revolution, 1999). This documents reader was published for the international conference "Political Transition in Hungary, 1989–1990," Budapest, June 10–12, 1999. Translated By Csaba Farkas.]*

DOCUMENT NO. 120: Remarks on the Hungarian Revolution by Soviet President Mikhail Gorbachev, December 6, 1991, and Russian President Boris Yeltsin, November 11, 1992

By May 1990, Hungary had made the transition from a communist satellite of the Soviet Union to an independent country with a freely elected government. More than any other individual, the person responsible for the sea-change that occurred in Hungary and throughout Eastern Europe was then-Soviet President Mikhail Gorbachev. Although he initially hoped that the transformation he helped to bring about would strengthen the Soviet bloc, once he recognized that the process was moving out of control he broke dramatically with previous Soviet practice by choosing not to use violence to reverse the course of events. Within days of the collapse of the USSR itself, Gorbachev acknowledged publicly that the Soviet Union had committed an act of "interference" in Hungary in 1956. One year later, Boris Yeltsin, Russia's first democratically-elected president, went even further, referring to the upheaval as the "tragedy of 1956" but insisting that "the national uprising was not in vain." Declaring in an address to the Hungarian Parliament that "truth cannot be complete without documents," Yeltsin presented his Hungarian counterparts with a collection of previously secret records from Soviet archives describing the Kremlin's role in the revolution. Many of those crucial documents are included in this volume.

Gorbachev: [. . .]

I want to take this opportunity to say in the presence of this high-ranking Hungarian delegation that we cannot and indeed are not entitled on this day to fail to tell you . . . to give you our view of the events of 1956; to tell you that interference in Hungary's internal affairs was committed on the part of the Soviet Union. What we and you have done in recent times draws a line under the past, and I hope that we and you have now opened up the first page in the book of good relations between countries and people which have lived together and will live and cooperate fruitfully for [a] long to come.

[Source: Moscow Central Television First Program Network in Russian 1900 GMT 6 December 1991. Translated and reprinted as "Gorbachev on 1956 Hungarian 'Interference'," Foreign Broadcast Information Service *(SOV–91–237) 10 December 1991, 8.]*

***

Yelstin:

Mr. President,
Honorary deputies,
Ladies and gentlemen,

For the first time in the history of relations between our states the president of a democratic and free Russia has a chance to address parliamentarians of a democratic and free Hungary.

I pass you best wishes from Russians and their genuine desire to live in complete understanding and friendship with the Hungarian people.

There has always been a great and genuine interest in Russia to your country's life and culture. Russia and Hungary had maintained active political and trade contacts at the start of their statehood.

A friendly alliance struck by Peter the Great and Francis Rakoczy [Rákóczi] the Second[5] in 1707 was one of the brightest moments in the history of Russian-Hungarian relations.

---

[5] Prince Ferenc Rákóczi the Second was the leader of an anti-Habsburg uprising from 1703 to 1711.

Unfortunately, as it often happens in history, good times were replaced by darker times. I know that the Hungarian people remember the revolution of 1848 and 1849 and the sad role played by Tsarist Russia in it.

A little more than a hundred years later a very similar thing happened. I am now speaking about the tragedy of 1956.

It will forever remain an indelible spot on the Soviet regime. Traces of tracks, which ploughed the streets of Budapest have [been] forever imprinted on the souls of those who cherish the ideals of freedom and democracy. I am convinced these people constitute the majority in Hungary and Russia.

Mankind then got one more confirmation that totalitarianism, any tyranny never remain [sic] within the borders of one country. They strive to extend their poisonous tentacles as far as possible. They do not recognize borders and moral constraints.

It is bitter to think that Russian soldiers had been drawn in those tragic events on orders of the then Kremlin leaders. This happened only 10 years after they liberated Hungary from the brown plague of Fascism at the price of immense sacrifices. One violent ideology had been replaced by another.

I believe it is deeply symbolic that the Hungarian people were the first to rise against enslavement. The national uprising was not in vain. It showed that not only individuals, but entire nations were beginning to understand that there can be no future without the liberation from communist dictatorship.

Today we bow our heads before all victims of 1956. The revenge of the system that had been dealt a considerable strike was cruel. It extended outside Hungary. New prisoners of the gulag appeared in Russia and other countries of the so-called socialist camp.

The entire world saw that every country, every nation produces both heroes and henchmen. Unfortunately, there are no exclusions.

The citizens of Hungary and Russia should know all the truth about that tragic time. And they will know about it by all means. Very soon, rather than many years later.

Truth is needed not to prompt blind revenge. Justice cannot be restored and cleansing is impossible without full truth.

The court of conscience, repentance, and forgiveness are impossible without full truth.

An agreement on cooperation between our two countries in the archive sphere was signed today. It will shed new light on the events of 1956 and the archives of the KGB and the CPSU. It is clear that truth cannot be complete without documents kept in Staraya Square.[6] Russia is prepared for the broadest cooperation possible in studying them. All obstacles towards this have been removed.

The clamp on the revolution could not destroy your people's love of freedom.

During the decline of socialism, Hungary, more than any other East European country, tapped free-market experience. There was more openness and pluralism in your country, even in those tough conditions. Pragmatism always prevailed over ideological blindfolds.

Hungary was dubbed the most attractive barracks in the socialist camp. This is one of the saddest compliments I have ever heard in my life. However, it was justified.

[....]

[Source: Moscow ITAR-TASS *in English 1945 GMT, 11 November 1992. Reprinted in Foreign Broadcast Information Service (SOV–92–219) 12 November 1992, 19–22.]*

---

[6] "Staraya Ploshchad'" or "Old Square" in Moscow is the location of the Center for Preservation of Contemporary Documentation, the former CPSU CC archive containing records created after 1952.

MAIN ACTORS

AMORY, ROBERT, JR. (1915–1989): deputy director of intelligence, Central Intelligence Agency, 1953–1962.

ANDROPOV, YURII V. (1914–1984): Soviet ambassador to Hungary, 1954–1957; head of the CPSU CC Department for Relations with Communist and Workers' Parties of the Socialist Countries, 1957–1961.

APRÓ, ANTAL (1913–1994): member HWP PC, 1953–1956; deputy prime minister, 1953–November 3, 1956; member of the HWP Military Committee from October 26–31, 1956; member of the Presidium from October 28, 1957; minister of industry from November 7, 1956; deputy prime minister, May 1957–1971.

ARISTOV, AVERKI B. (1903–1973): secretary of the CPSU CC, 1955–1960; member CPSU CC Presidium, 1957–1961.

BATA, ISTVÁN (1910–1982): Hungarian minister of defense, 1953–October 27, 1956; member of the HWP CC and candidate member of the PC, 1953–October 27, 1956; fled to the Soviet Union on October 28, 1956 and returned only in 1958.

BEAM, JACOB D. (1908–1993): director, Office of Eastern European Affairs, Bureau of European Affairs, U.S. Department of State, March 1955–October 1955; deputy assistant secretary of state for European affairs from October 1955–June 1957; U.S. ambassador to Poland, August 1957–1961.

BIBÓ, ISTVÁN (1911–1979): minister of state for the Petőfi Party in Nagy's last cabinet; sentenced to life imprisonment in 1958 but freed in the amnesty of 1963.

BISZKU, BÉLA (1921–): secretary of the HWP Budapest 13th district committee, 1955–October 31, 1956; member of the HSWP PCC and PEC from November 4, 1956; minister of the interior from February 28, 1957.

BOHLEN, CHARLES E. (1904–1974): U.S. ambassador to the Soviet Union from 1953–April 1957.

BOWIE, ROBERT R. (1909–): director of the Policy Planning Staff, Department of State, until August 1955; assistant secretary of state for policy planning and Department of State representative on the NSC Planning Board, August 1955–October 1957.

BULGANIN, NIKOLAI A. (1895–1975): Soviet minister of defense, 1953–February 1955; chairman of the Council of Ministers, 1955–1958; member of the CPSU CC Presidium, 1948–1958.

DOBI, ISTVÁN (1898–1968): chairman of the Hungarian Presidential Council (president of Hungary), 1952–1967.

DONÁTH, FERENC (1913–1986): received 15 year sentence in a show trial in 1951; later rehabilitated and became supporter of Imre Nagy; member of the HWP CC Secretariat, October 24–November 4, 1956; forcibly interned in Romania in 1956 along with Nagy; sentenced to 12 years in prison in 1958; amnestied in 1960.

DUDÁS, JÓZSEF (1912–1957): Communist partisan during World War II; member of the Smallholders' party; founded the Hungarian National Revolutionary Committee; executed in January 1957.

DULLES, ALLEN W. (1893–1969): U.S. director of central intelligence, 1953–1961.

DULLES, JOHN FOSTER (1888–1959): U.S. secretary of state, 1953–1959.

EGRI, GYULA (1923–1972): deputy prime minister, 1954–1955; member of the HWP CC, 1954–1956; member of the HWP CC Secretariat, autumn 1954–October 24, 1956; fled to the Soviet Union November 16, 1956 and stayed there until March 1957.

EISENHOWER, DWIGHT D. (1890–1969): president of the United States, 1953–1961.

ERDEI, FERENC (1910–1971): co-founder and general secretary of the National Peasant Party; member of Imre Nagy's government during the revolution; arrested in Tököl on November 3, 1956, but released shortly thereafter.

FARKAS, MIHÁLY (1904–1965): member of HWP PC and deputy secretary general, then secretary of the CC, 1945–1955; minister of defense, 1948–1953; dismissed in 1956; sentenced to 16 years in prison in 1957; amnestied in 1960.

FIRYUBIN, NIKOLAI P. (1908–1983): Soviet ambassador to Yugoslavia, 1955–1957; candidate member of the CPSU CC, 1956–1966.

FÖLDVÁRI, RUDOLF (1921–): first secretary of the local HWP committee in Borsod County, 1954–1956; during the revolution, one of the leaders of the Workers' Council of Borsod County; deported to the USSR on November 5, 1956; sentenced to life imprisonment in 1958; amnestied in 1961.

GERŐ, ERNŐ (1898–1980): first secretary of the HWP, July 17–October 25, 1956; fled to Moscow with his family on October 28, 1956 where he stayed until 1960.

GHEORGHIU-DEJ, GHEORGHE (1901–1965): general, later first secretary of the RWP, 1945–1954 and 1955–1965; Romanian prime minister, 1952–1955.

GIMES, MIKLÓS (1917–1958): journalist; member of the Hungarian Communist (after 1948 Hungarian Workers') Party from 1945; fired from *Szabad Nép* and dropped from the party after Nagy's dismissal; one of the leading figures of the intellectual opposition after November 4, 1956; sentenced to death along with Nagy in June 1958.

GOMUŁKA, WŁADYSŁAW (1905–1982): top Polish party and government official, expelled from the party in 1949 and imprisoned, 1951–1954; rehabilitated and named first secretary of the PZPR CC, October 1956–December 1970.

GÖNCZ, ÁRPÁD (1922–): member of the Smallholders' Party from 1945; member of the intellectual opposition after November 4, 1956; member of the Hungarian Democratic Independence Movement; sentenced to life in prison in 1958, but freed in the general amnesty of 1963; president of the Hungarian Republic, 1990–2000.

GROMYKO, ANDREI A. (1909–1989): Soviet first deputy foreign minister until February 1957; thereafter foreign minister.

GROTEWOHL, OTTO (1894–1964): prime minister of the GDR, 1949–1960.

HAMMARSKJÖLD, DAG (1905–1961): United Nations secretary-general, 1953–1961.

HAYTER, WILLIAM G. (1906–1995): British ambassador to Moscow, 1953–1957.

HEGEDÜS, ANDRÁS (1922–1990): deputy prime minister of Hungary, 1953–1955; prime minister, April 1955–October 24, 1956; deputy prime minister, October 24–27, 1956; fled to the USSR on October 28, 1956.

HOOVER, HERBERT C. JR. (1903–1969): under secretary of state and chairman, Operations Coordinating Board, October 1954–February 1957.

HORVÁTH, IMRE (1901–1958): held various positions in the Hungarian foreign and diplomatic services prior to 1956; minister of foreign affairs, July 1956–1958; sent to the U.N. general assembly by Imre Nagy, but he fled to Moscow to join János Kádár.

HORVÁTH, MÁRTON (1906–1987): member of the HWP CC, 1944–1956; member of the HWP PC, 1944–1953; head of the Department for Agitation and Propaganda, 1950–1954; editor-in-chief of *Szabad Nép*, 1954–November 1956; was not allowed to join the HSWP due to his support for the revolution, but no legal procedure was launched against him.

IVÁN-KOVÁCS, LÁSZLÓ (1930–1957): participated in the armed uprising from October 23, 1956; commander of the Corvin Passage group, from October 25; member of the Revolutionary Armed Forces Committee and commandant of the national guard; sentenced to death and executed in 1957.

JACKSON, C.D. (1902–1964): special assistant to President Eisenhower for psychological warfare operations, February 1953–March 1954.

JACKSON, WILLIAM H. (1901–1971): special assistant to Secretary of State Dulles, September 1955–January 1956; special assistant to President Eisenhower, January–September 1956; acting special assistant to the President for national security affairs, September 1956–January 1957.

JANZA, KÁROLY (1914–): chief of the military supply service and deputy minister of defense, 1951–1956; minister of defense, October 27–31, 1956.

KÁDÁR, JÁNOS (1912–1989): Hungarian minister of the interior, 1948–1950; imprisoned from 1951–1954; regional party secretary, 1954–1956; elected HWP first secretary, October 25, 1956; minister of state in last Nagy cabinet; head of the HSWP, November 3, 1956–May 1988.

KAGANOVICH, LAZAR M. (1893–1991): member of the CPSU Presidium; first deputy of the prime minister, 1953 to 1957; relieved of all his positions in 1957.

KÁLLAI, GYULA (1910–1996): member of the HWP CC; imprisoned, 1951–1954; deputy minister of culture, 1955–October 31, 1956; member of the HWP CC and leader of the HWP CC department for science and culture, from July 1956; member HWP PC, from October 24, 1956; member of the HSWP PCC and PEC, from November 4, 1956; secretary of the HSWP CC and responsible for cultural affairs in the government from February 1957.

KARDELJ, EDVARD (1910–1979): leading ideologist of the YLC; member YLC CC and PC; vice-chairman of the Federal Executive Council, 1953–1963.

KÉTHLY, ANNA (1889–1976): chair of the Social Democratic Party in Hungary, 1956; minister of state in the Nagy government; chair of the Hungarian Revolutionary Council in exile in Strassbourg from 1957.

KHRUSHCHEV, NIKITA S. (1894–1971): first secretary of the CPSU, 1953–1964.

KIRÁLY, BÉLA (1912–): sentenced to life imprisonment during a show trial in 1952 and released in September 1956; commander of the National Guard (Revolutionary Armed Forces Committee) and the Revolutionary National Defense Commission during the revolution; emigrated to the United States in 1957 where he become a professor of history.

KISS, KÁROLY (1903–1983): member of the HWP PC, 1951–1953 and July–October 1956; member of the HWP Presidium from October 28; after November 4 HSWP PCC member, then member of the HSWP PEC; CC secretary, from February 1957.

KONEV, IVAN S. (1897–1973): Soviet first deputy minister of defense, 1955–1961; marshal and commander-in-chief of the Warsaw Pact Joint Armed Force; commander of the Soviet troops that invaded Hungary on November 4, 1956.

KOPÁCSI, SÁNDOR (1922–2001): chief of the Budapest police in 1956; member of the HSWP's PEC from October 31, 1956; sentenced to life imprisonment as part of the Nagy trial; released in 1963 under the general amnesty.

KOVÁCS, BÉLA (1908–1959): leader of the Smallholders' Party from 1945–1947 when sentenced to 20 years imprisonment in the USSR; released in 1956; head of the Smallholders' Party during the revolution; named a minister in the Nagy government

KOVÁCS, ISTVÁN (1911–): first secretary of the Budapest party committee, 1954–October 30, 1956; leader of the HWP Military Committee from October 23; on October 28, left Hungary for the USSR, returned in 1958.

KÖBÖL, JÓZSEF (1909–2000): member of the HWP CC, 1948–1956; PC member from October 24–28, 1956; HSWP PCC member, November 1956–June 1957; expelled in June 1957 because of his views concerning the trial of Imre Nagy.

LASHCHENKO, PIOTR N. (1910–1992): commander of the Soviet Special Army Corps, stationed in Hungary, 1955–1956.

LIU SHAQI (1898–1969): CPC secretary general, 1943–1967; member of the CPC's Politburo's Permanent Committee, 1956–1967.

LLOYD, SELWIN (1904–1978): British foreign minister, 1955–1960.

LODGE, HENRY CABOT JR. (1902–1985): permanent U.S. representative to the U.N., 1953–1960.

LOSONCZY, GÉZA (1917–1957): arrested and sentenced to 15 years imprisonment in a show trial in 1951, released in 1954; editor-in-chief of *Magyar Nemzet* during 1956; HWP CC member from October 24, 1956; minister of state in the Nagy government from October 30; arrested and interned with Nagy in Romania; died while on a hunger strike in detention in Budapest on December 21, 1957.

LUKÁCS, GYÖRGY (1885–1971): member of the HWP CC from October 24; minister of culture in the Nagy government from October 27–November 3; interned in Romania, returned in 1957; was not sentenced.

MALENKOV, GEORGII M. (1902–1988): member of the CPSU CC, 1937–1957; Politburo (later Presidium) member, 1946–1957; chairman of the Soviet Council of Ministers, 1953–February 1955; deputy prime minister, 1955–1957.

MALÉTER, PÁL (1917–1958): commander of the Killián Barracks from October 25, 1956; deputy minister of national defense from October 31, then named minister of national defense from November 3, 1956; arrested by KGB, November 3, 1956; co-defendant with Nagy, executed on June 16, 1958.

MALIN, VLADIMIR N. (1906–1982): head of the CPSU CC General Department (Secretariat), 1954–1965.

MALININ, MIKHAIL S. (1899–1960): first deputy of the chief of the General Staff of the Soviet Armed Forces, 1952–1960; directed the Soviet armed forces in Hungary from October 24, 1956; led negotiations for the withdrawal of Soviet troops on November 3.

MAO ZEDONG (1893–1976): chairman of the Chinese Communist Party, 1935–1976; president of the Chinese People's Republic, 1949–1959.

MAROSÁN, GYÖRGY (1908–1991): member of the HWP CC and PC from July 1956; deputy prime minister from July–October 27, 1956; member of the HSWP PEC (later PC); state minister from November 7, 1956–1960.

MECSÉRI, JÁNOS (1920–1958): army commander of the Buda district during the revolution; sentenced to death and executed in 1958.

MIĆUNOVIĆ, VELJKO (1916–1983): Yugoslav ambassador to the Soviet Union, March 1956–October 1958.

MIKOYAN, ANASTAS I. (1895–1978): member of the CPSU Politburo (Presidium), 1935–1966; first deputy chairman of the Soviet Council of Ministers, 1955–1957 and 1958–1964; traveled to Hungary as special envoy of the Presidium from October 24–31, 1956.

MINDSZENTY, CARDINAL JÓZSEF (1892–1975): primate of Hungary; arrested in 1948 and sentenced to life imprisonment in a show trial; placed under house arrest from July 1955–October 30, 1956; given refuge at U.S. Legation in Budapest, November 4, 1956–1971.

MOLOTOV, VYACHESLAV M. (1890–1986): member of the CPSU CC Politburo (Presidium), 1926–1957; Soviet foreign minister, 1953–June 1956; removed from main CPSU posts in June 1957.

MÜNNICH, FERENC (1886–1967): Hungarian ambassador to the USSR, September 1954–August 1956; ambassador to Yugoslavia, August 1956–October 25, 1956; member of the HWP CC from October 24; member of the Military Committee from October 26; member of the Presidium from October 28; minister of interior in Nagy's government form October 27–November 3; deputy premier in the Kádár government from November 4, 1956; prime minister from 1958–1961; member of the HSWP PEC, later PC, 1956–1966.

NAGY, IMRE (1896–1958): member of the HWP CC, 1945–1955 and October 23–31, 1956; member of the HWP PC, 1945–1949, 1951–1955, and October 23–30, 1956; prime minister, July 4, 1953–April 18, 1955; expelled from the party, December 1955; readmitted on October 13, 1956; renamed prime minister, October 23, 1956; took refuge in the Yugoslav Embassy, November 4; deported to Romania on November 22 and arrested on April 14, 1957; sentenced to death June 15, 1958; executed on June 16.

NEHRU, JAWAHARLAL (1889–1964): prime minister of India and minister of external affairs, 1947–1964.

NICKELSBURG, LÁSZLÓ (1924–1961): commander of the Baross square armed group during the revolution; sentenced to life imprisonment in 1957, then to the death penalty in 1961.

NOVOTNY, ANTONÍN (1904–1975): first secretary of the Czechoslovak Communist Party, 1953–1968; president of Czechoslovakia, 1957–1968.

PÉTER, GÁBOR (1906–1993): head of the ÁVO/ÁVH, 1945–1953; arrested in 1953 and sentenced to life in prison; retried and sentenced to 14 years following the revolution; released under an amnesty in 1960.

PINEAU, CHRISTIAN (1904–1995): French minister of foreign affairs, 1956–1958.

PIROS, LÁSZLÓ (1917–): candidate member and member of the HWP CC, 1948–October 1956; candidate member of the PC, April 1955–October 24, 1956; deputy minister of the interior and commander of the ÁVH, 1953–1954; minister of the interior, July 1954–October 26, 1956; traveled to the Soviet Union on October 28 with Gerő and Hegedüs, but returned on November 3 to participate in the arrest of the Hungarian delegation at Tököl; returned to the Soviet Union on November 10 and returned only in 1958.

PONGRÁTZ, GERGELY (1932–): commander of the Corvin passage group from November 1, 1956; fled to the United States after November 4.

RÁCZ, SÁNDOR (1933–): member of local factory workers' council, October 29, 1956; became member, then chairman, of the Greater Budapest Central Workers' Council, November 14; on December 11 arrived for negotiations at the Parliament building but was arrested; sentenced to life imprisonment in 1958; freed under the general amnesty, 1963.

RAJK, LÁSZLÓ (1909–1949): interior, then foreign minister in the immediate postwar Hungarian government; sentenced to death in a show trial and executed in 1949; rehabilitated in 1956 and reburied on October 6, 1956.

RÁKOSI, MÁTYÁS (1892–1971): general, later first secretary of the Hungarian Communist Party then HWP, 1945–July 18, 1956 when he was replaced by Ernő Gerő; prime minister, 1952–1953; lived out his life in the USSR.

RANKOVIĆ, ALEKSANDAR–LEKA (1909–1983): Yugoslav deputy prime minister, 1953–1963; member of the YLC CC Executive Committee, 1952–1966.

RÉVAI, JÓZSEF (1898–1959): member of the HWP CC and PC, 1945–1953; minister of education, 1949–1953; reelected as PC member July 1956 but dropped again on October 24, 1956; flees to Moscow, October 31–April 1957; returned to become HSWP PCC then CC member.

RÓNAI, SÁNDOR (1892–1965): member of the HWP PC, 1948–June 1953; member of the HWP CC, 1948–1956; chairman of the Parliament, 1952–1962; candidate member of the HWP PC and member of the Presidential Council from July 1956; minister in the Kádár government, November 4, 1956–February 1957; member of the HSWP PEC (later PC) until 1965.

SEROV, IVAN A. (1905–1991): head of the KGB, 1953–1958; sent to Hungary on October 24, 1956 to command Soviet state security forces until December 1956.

SHEPILOV, DMITRII T. (1905–1995): Editor-in-chief of *Pravda*, 1953–1956; CPSU CC member, 1952–1957; CPSU CC Presidium candidate member, 1956–1957; foreign minister, June 1956–February 1957; removed from main CPSU posts during June 1957 CC Plenum.

ŠIROKY, VILIAM (1902–1971): Czechoslovak foreign minister, 1950–1953; prime minister, 1953–1963.

SOBOLEV, ARKADII A. (1903–1964): Soviet representative to the U.N., 1955–1960.

SOLDATIĆ, DALIBOR (1909–): Yugoslav ambassador in Budapest, 1953–October 1956; remained in Hungary until December 1956.

STALIN, JOSEPH V. (1879–1953): general secretary of the CPSU, 1922–1953.

STASSEN, HAROLD E. (1907–2001): director, Foreign Operations Administration, 1953–1955; special assistant to President Eisenhower for disarmament matters, March 1955-1959.

SUSLOV, MIKHAIL A. (1902–1982): member of the CPSU Presidium, 1955–1982; traveled to Hungary on behalf of the CPSU Presidium, 24–31 October 1956 (although he took part in the CPSU session on 28–29 October).

SZABÓ, ISTVÁN B. (1893–1976): member of the reorganized Smallholders' Party's executive committee from October 30, 1956; minister of state in the last Nagy cabinet from November 3; sentenced to 3 years imprisonment in 1958; freed under an amnesty, 1959.

SZABÓ, JÁNOS (1897–1957): truck driver known as "Uncle Szabó;" commanded one of the armed groups at Széna Square; executed, January 1957.

SZÁNTÓ, ZOLTÁN (1893–1977): Hungarian ambassador to Warsaw, 1955–July 1956; member of the HWP PC from October 24, 1956, of the Directory from October 26, and of the Presidium from October 28; on November 4 joined the Nagy group at the Yugoslav embassy, left the premises on November 18, but was later deported to Romania; testified against members of the Nagy group at subsequent trial; returned to Hungary, 1958; joined the HSWP, 1964.

SZIGETHY, ATTILA (1912–1957): one of the leaders of the National Peasant Party and member of Parliament, 1947–1957; chairman of the Győr National Council and the Transdanubian National Council during the revolution; committed suicide after his arrest.

SZILÁGYI, JÓZSEF (1917–1958): member of Nagy's internal opposition group; headed Nagy's secretariat during the revolution; tried and executed, 1958.

TILDY, ZOLTÁN (1889–1961): founding member of the Smallholders' Party and president of Hungary, 1946–1948; kept under house arrest, 1948–1956; minister of state in the Nagy government from October 27–November 4, 1956; sentenced to 6 years imprisonment, 1958; released under an amnesty in 1959.

TITO, JOSIP BROZ (1892–1980): marshal, president of Yugoslavia, 1945–1980.

TOGLIATTI, PALMIRO (1893–1964): secretary general of the Italian Communist Party, 1927–1964.

ULBRICHT, WALTER (1893–1973): SED general secretary, 1950–1953; first secretary of the SED CC, 1953–1971; chairman of the GDR State Council (president), 1960–1973.

VAS, ZOLTÁN (1903–1983): head of the Council of Ministers' secretariat, 1954–January 1955; deputy minister for trade in 1955; government commissioner for public supply in the Nagy government; took refuge with Nagy in the Yugoslav embassy on November 4, subsequently deported to Romania; allowed to return to Hungary in 1958.

VÁSÁRHELYI, MIKLÓS (1917–2001): vice-chairman of the Information Bureau of the Council of Ministers, May 1954–1956; active leader of the internal party opposition; press chief of the Nagy government from November 1, 1956; sentenced to five years in prison in 1958; amnestied in 1960.

VIDIĆ, DOBRIVOJE (1918–): Yugoslav ambassador to Moscow, 1953–1956; deputy foreign minister, Spring 1956–1958.

VOROSHILOV, KLIMENT E. (1881–1969): chairman of the Allied Control Committee in Hungary, 1945–1946; deputy chairman of the USSR Council of Ministers, 1946–1953; chairman of the Presidium of the Supreme Soviet, 1953–1960.

WISNER, FRANK G. (1908–1965): deputy director of plans, Central Intelligence Agency, 1952–1961.

ZÁPOTOCKY, ANTONÍN (1884–1957): prime minister of Czechoslovakia, 1948–1953; president of Czechoslovakia, 1953–1957.

ZHOU ENLAI (1898–1976): prime minister of the PRC, 1949–1976; minister of foreign affairs, 1949–1958.

ZHUKOV, GEORGII K. (1896–1974): Soviet minister of defense, 1955–1957; candidate member of the CPSU Presidium, 1956–1957; senior commander of the Soviet Army during the second armed intervention.

ORGANIZATIONS

CENTRAL COMMITTEE: meeting between party congresses, the Central Committee was the official decision-making organ of the communist parties of the socialist camp. The real role of the CC (which usually had between 50 to 70 members) was to approve decisions handed down by the Political Committee (or Politburo) and the Secretariat.

CENTRAL WORKERS' COUNCIL OF GREATER BUDAPEST (KMT, *Nagybudapesti Központi Munkástanács*): founded on November 12, 1956 as a regional body representing the capital and large factories around the country. It threatened to become an alternative power center to the Kádár regime until it was forcibly dissolved and its leaders arrested on December 9.

COMMITTEE FOR STATE SECURITY (KGB): the main organ of Soviet state security since 1954, formerly known as the NKVD, among other titles.

DIRECTORY OF THE HWP CC (*Direktórium*): This term was used for naming two different HWP leading bodies, established during the revolution. See 1. Emergency Committee of the HWP CC; 2. Presidium of the HWP.

EMERGENCY COMMITTEE OF THE HWP CC (*Központi Vezetőség Rendkívüli Bizottsága*): formed on October 26, 1956, the Emergency Committee was established under the Central Committee to provide centralized management for the suppression of the revolution. However, its relationship to the already existing leading organs (CC, PC, Military Committee) was never made clear, which further confused the party's leadership system. The Committee's members were Antal Apró, András Hegedüs, János Kádár, Imre Nagy, Ferenc Münnich and Zoltán Szántó. It was replaced by the Presidium of the HWP on October 28.

HUNGARIAN SOCIALIST WORKERS' PARTY (HSWP, *Magyar Szocialista Munkáspárt*): founded on October 31, 1956 by members of the Hungarian Workers' Party who supported the goals of the uprising, it adopted an anti-Stalinist stance and was led by Imre Nagy and János Kádár. After November 4, 1956, Kádár assumed control and it remained the ruling party of Hungary until 1989.

HUNGARIAN WORKERS' PARTY (HWP, *Magyar Dolgozók Pártja*): Formed through the forced merger of the Social Democratic Party of Hungary and the Hungarian Communist Party in 1948; it was replaced by the HSWP on October 31, 1956.

MILITARY COMMITTEE (*Katonai Bizottság*): Established on the night of October 23, 1956 by members of the HWP CC, the task of this body was originally to coordinate between the party leadership and the Hungarian and Soviet armed forces, as well as to provide political leadership for the suppression of the revolution. Later, it became a nearly independent center of decision-making, representing a more hard-line position within the HWP leadership. Although it was never formally dissolved, after the political changes introduced beginning on October 28, the committee lost its importance.

NATIONAL SECURITY COUNCIL (U.S.): established under the National Security Act of 1947 as a top-level advisory body to the president on issues affecting national security, statutory members were the president, vice president, secretary of state, and secretary of defense; additional members served at the president's invitation.

NATIONAL GUARD (*Nemzetőrség*): formed on November 1, 1956 and staffed by freedom fighters, the National Guard assumed responsibility for maintaining public order when the ÁVH was dissolved. The concept harkened back to the Revolution of 1848–49, when similar organizations were formed across the country to preserve revolutionary order.

NATIONAL PEASANT PARTY (NPP, *Nemzeti Parasztpárt*): a radical, populist peasant party formed in 1945 and co-opted by the Hungarian Workers' Party in 1948. In October 1956 it was reestablished as the Petőfi Party, representing leftist intellectuals.

NATIONAL REVOLUTIONARY COMMITTEE (*Nemzeti Forradalmi Bizottmány*): a political group led by József Dudás that was critical of Imre Nagy for not seeking more fundamental reform.

NÉPSZABADSÁG (*"People's Freedom"*): The daily newspaper of the HSWP, beginning November 2, 1956.

PETŐFI CIRCLE (*Petőfi Kör*): a youth-oriented discussion group initially sanctioned by DISZ, it adopted an openly anti-Stalinist stance after Khrushchev's secret speech at the CPSU's Twentieth Party Congress in February 1956. It was closed down briefly, then resumed its activities in the fall of 1956 before being permanently dissolved the following year.

POLITICAL COMMITTEE: acted as the main decision-making body between the much less frequent sessions of the Central Committee. Although it consisted of 10–15 members, the PC's decisions were almost always determined by a few key members of the party leadership.

PRESIDIUM OF THE CPSU: The Presidium was the name given to the CPSU's Political Bureau (Politburo) between 1952 and 1966.

PRESIDIUM OF THE HWP (*Elnökség*): Established on October 28, 1956, the Presidium of the Hungarian Worker's Party was intended to serve as the party's leading organ. Although its composition (Antal Apró, János Kádár, Károly Kiss, Imre Nagy, Ferenc Münnich and Zoltán Szántó) did not differ significantly from that of the Emergency Committee it replaced, the Presidium had a much larger sphere of authority and relegated both the Political Committee and the Central Committee to *de facto* consultative roles.

PROVISIONAL EXECUTIVE COMMITTEE (*Ideiglenes Intéző Bizottság*): in the transitional period after the formation of the HSWP, the PEC corresponded to the Political Committee.

RADIO FREE EUROPE (RFE): an ostensibly non-governmental American radio station broadcasting from Munich, it operated with support from the U.S. government, including receiving guidance from the CIA, as a source of news and commentary broadcast into Eastern Europe. Broadcasts from the Hungary desk came under attack for aggressive commentary during the revolution.

REVOLUTIONARY COMMITTEE OF THE HUNGARIAN INTELLIGENTSIA (*Magyar Értelmiség Forradalmi Bizottsága*): founded on October 28, 1956, to press for reform and generate ideas for governance to the Nagy government; its successor, the Revolutionary Council of Hungarian Intelligentsia, was established after November 4, 1956, but banned in January 1957.

REVOLUTIONARY ARMED FORCES COMMITTEE (*Forradalmi Karhatalmi Bizottság*): founded on October 29, 1956, to coordinate the formation of the National Guard, it was headed by Béla Király.

REVOLUTIONARY WORKERS' AND PEASANTS' GOVERNMENT (*Magyar Forradalmi Munkás-Paraszt Kormány*): the name given to the "counter-government" established on November 4, 1956 by János Kádár, while he was still in the USSR and about to re-enter Hungary to challenge the Nagy government.

SMALLHOLDERS' PARTY (*Független Kisgazda Földmunkás és Polgári Párt*): founded in 1921, it became the leading political party in Hungary after the institution of free elections in 1945, but was undermined by the communists in 1946–1947. On October 30, 1956, after Nagy announced the end of the one-party system, its leaders formed a provisional executive body and began to publish *Kis Újság* (Small Newspaper) through November 4, 1956.

SOCIAL DEMOCRATIC PARTY (SZDP, *Szociáldemokrata Párt*): in existence since 1890, it was forced to merge with the Hungarian Communist Party in 1948. It resurfaced on October 30, 1956 but was declared illegal again in 1957.

STATE SECURITY AUTHORITY (ÁVH, *Államvédelmi Hatóság*): founded as the Department of State Security (ÁVO) in 1946, it was the Rákosi regime's main instrument for suppressing the population. Nagy dismantled it on October 28, 1956 in response to widespread public outcries.

SZABAD NÉP (*"Free People"*): The daily newspaper of the HWP (until October 29, 1956).

UNION OF WORKING YOUTH (DISZ, *Dolgozó Ifjúság Szövetsége*): a communist youth organization founded in 1950 and patterned after the Soviet Komsomol.

UNITED NATIONS SPECIAL COMMISSION ON HUNGARY: established on January 10, 1957 to provide the U.N. with a formal report on the revolution, because the Kádár regime refused to admit U.N. observers. It issued its findings on June 20, 1957.

WARSAW TREATY ORGANIZATION: a military alliance consisting of the USSR and its East European allies, also known as the Warsaw Pact. It was established on May 14, 1955 and dissolved in 1991.

WRITERS' UNION (*Írószövetség*): founded in 1945, and intended to ensure adherence to cultural priorities determined by the ruling communist party, most of its members supported the reform process beginning in 1953 and backed the revolution. Its activities were suspended in January 1957 and restored in 1959.

BIBLIOGRAPHY

Aczél, Tamás, ed. *Ten Years After: A Commemoration of the Tenth Anniversary of the Hungarian Revolution.* London: MacGibbon & Kee, 1966.

Aczél, Tamás and Tibor Méray. *The Revolt of the Mind: A Case Study of Intellectual Resistance Behind the Iron Curtain.* London: Thames & Hudson, 1960.

Ambrose, Steven E. *Ike's Spies: Eisenhower and the Espionage Establishment.* Garden City, N.Y.: Doubleday & Co., 1981.

American Friends of the Captive Nations. *Hungary Under Soviet Rule.* New York: American Friends of Captive Nations, 1957.

Anderson, A. *Hungary 1956.* London: Solidarity, 1964.

Aptheker, Herbert. *The Truth About Hungary.* New York: Mainstream Publishers, 1957.

Arendt, Hannah. *The Origins of Totalitarianism.* 2nd ed. New York: Meridian, c1958.

——, "Totalitarian Imperialism: Reflections on the Hungarian Revolution," *The Journal of Politics* 20 (1958): 5–43.

Bain, Leslie. *The Reluctant Satellites.* New York: Macmillan, 1960.

Balogh Sándor, ed. *Nehéz esztendők krónikája 1949–1953. Dokumentumok* (A Chronicle of difficult years 1949–1953: Documents). Budapest: Gondolat, 1986.

Barber, Noel. *A Handful of Ashes.* London: Allan Wingate, 1960.

——, *Seven Days of Freedom.* New York: Stein & Day, 1974.

Beke, László [pseud.]. *A Student's Diary: Budapest Oct 16–Nov 1, 1956.* Edited and translated by Leon Kosser and Ralph M. Zoltan. New York: Viking Press, 1957.

Békés, Csaba. *Az 1956-os magyar forradalom a világpolitikában: Tanulmány és válogatott dokumentumok* (The 1956 Hungarian Revolution in World Politics: Study and Selected Documents). Budapest: 1956-os Intézet, 1996.

——, *The 1956 Hungarian Revolution and World Politics.* Cold War International History Project Working Paper, no. 16. Washington, D.C.: Woodrow Wilson International Center for Scholars, 1996.

——, "The 1956 Hungarian Revolution and World Politics." *The Hungarian Quarterly* 35, no. 3 (1995): 109–21.

——, "Az Egyesült Államok és a magyar semlegesség 1956-ban" (The United States and Hungarian neutrality in 1956). In *Évkönyv III, 1994,* edited by János M. Bak, et al., 165–178. Budapest: 1956-os Intézet, 1994.

——, "Hidegháború, enyhülés és az 1956-os magyar forradalom" (Cold War, Détente and the 1956 Hungarian Revolution). In *Évkönyv V, 1996–1997,* edited by András B. Hegedűs, et al., 201–213. Budapest: 1956-os Intézet, 1997.

——, "A magyar kérdés az ENSZ-ben és a nyugati nagyhatalmak titkos tárgyalásai 1956. október 28.-november 4: Brit külügyi dokumentumok" (The Hungarian question in the U.N. and the secret negotiations of Western great powers between October 28 and November 4: British foriegn affairs documents). In *Évkönyv II, 1993,* edited by János M. Bak, et al., 39–71. Budapest: 1956-os Intézet, 1993.

——, "A magyar semlegesség 1956-ban" (Hungarian Neutrality in 1956). In *Semlegesség: Illúziók és Realitás* (Neutrality: Illusions and Reality), edited by Biztonságpolitikai és Honvédelmi Kutatások Központja, 111–130. Budapest: Biztonságpolitikai és Honvédelmi Kutatások Központja, [1997].

——, "New Findings on the 1956 Hungarian Revolution." *Cold War International History Project Bulletin,* no. 2 (Fall 1992): 1–3.

Belokov, A. and V. Tolstikov. *The Truth About Hungary: Facts and Eyewitness Accounts.* Moscow: Foreign Languages Publishing House, 1957.

Berecz, János. *1956 Counter-Revolution in Hungary: Words and Weapons*. Translated by István Butykay. Translation revised by Charles Coutts. Budapest: Akadémiai Kiadó, 1986.

Berki, Mihály. *Hadsereg vezetés nélkül, 1956* (Army without command, 1956). Budapest: Magyar Média, 1989.

Bibó, István. *Bibó István összegyűjtött munkái* (Collected works of István Bibó). 3 vols. Edited by István Kemény and Mátyás Sárközi. Bern: Európai Protestáns Magyar Szabadegyetem, 1993.

——, *Democracy, Revolution, Self-Determination*. Translated by András Boros-Kazai. Highland Lakes, N.J.: Social Science Monographs, Atlantic Research and Publications, 1991.

Bindorfferer, Györgyi, Pál Gyenes, and Gyula Kozák, eds. *Pesti utca-1956: Válogatás fegyveres felkelők visszaemlékezéseiből* (The Pest street-1956: Selection of recollections of armed insurgents). Budapest: Századvég Kiadó-1956-os Intézet, 1994.

Bone, Edith. *Seven Years' Solitary*. New York: Harcourt, Brace, 1957.

Borbándi, Gyula. *Magyarok az Angol Kertben: A Szabad Európa Rádió története* (Hungarians in the English garden: History of Radio Free Europe). Budapest: Európa Könyvkiadó, 1996.

Borhi, László. "Az Egyesült Államok Kelet-Európa politikájának néhány kérdése, 1948–1956" (Some questions concerning the U.S. policy toward Eastern Europe, 1948–1956). *Történelmi Szemle* 37, no. 3 (1995): 277–300.

——, "Franco és az 1956-os magyar forradalom: Dokumentumok a spanyol segítségnyújtás tervéről" (Franco and the 1956 Hungarian revolution: Documents on the plan of Spanish aid). *História* 20, no. 9–10 (1998): 60–62.

——, "Soviet Expansionism or American Imperialism? American Responses to the Sovietization of Hungary." In *Twentieth Century Hungary and the Great Powers*, edited by Ignác Romsics, 233–244. Highland Lakes, N.J.: Atlantic Research and Publications, 1995.

"A budapesti angol követség 1956. novemberi-decemberi jelentéseiből" (From the reports of the British Embassy in Budapest from November-December 1956), published by István Vida, *Társadalmi Szemle* 46, no. 1 (1991): 66–79.

Bursten, Martin A. *Escape From Fear*. Syracuse, N.Y.: Syracuse University Press, 1973.

Cable, James. "Britain and the Hungarian Revolution of 1956." *International Relations* 9 (1988): 317–33.

Calhoun, Daniel F. *Hungary and Suez, 1956: An Exploration of Who Makes History*. Lanham, Md.: University Press of America, 1991.

Campbell, John C. "Az Egyesült Államok kormánya és a magyar forradalom" (The U.S. government and the Hungarian revolution). *Világosság* 32, no. 10 (1991): 739–749.

——, "The Soviet Union, the United States and the Twin Crisis of Hungary and Suez." In *Suez 1956: The Crisis and its Consequences*, edited by W. M. Louis and R. Owen, 233–252. Oxford: Clarendon Press, 1989.

Cavendish, Anthony. *Inside Intelligence*. London: Collins, 1990.

Chubarian, A. O., ed. *Sovetskaya vesnaya politika v retrospective, 1917–1991* (Soviet foreign policy in retrospect 1917–1991). Moskva: Nauka, 1993.

Corson, William R. *The Armies of Ignorance*. New York: The Dial Press, 1977.

The Counter-Revolutionary Conspiracy of Imre Nagy and his Accomplices. Budapest: Information Bureau of the Council of Ministers of the Hungarian People's Republic, 1958.

The Counter-Revolutionary Forces in the October Events in Hungary. 4 vols. Budapest: Information Bureau of the Council of Ministers of the Hungarian People's Republic, 1956–1957.

Coutts, Charles. *Eyewitness in Hungary*. Daily Worker, 1957.

Cox, Terry, ed. *Hungary 1956—Forty Years On*. Portland, Ore.: Frank Cass, 1997.

Dávid, János, Sándor Geskó, and Pál Schiffer. *Forradalom, sortűz, megtorlás* (Revolution volleys, and reprisal). Budapest: Progresszió, 1990.

Davidson, Basil. *What Really Happened in Hungary: A Personal Record*. London: Union of Democratic Control, 1957.

Delaney, Robert Finley, ed. *This is Communist Hungary*. Chicago: Regnery, 1958.

Department of State, ed. *Foreign Relations of the United States, 1955–57*, vol. XXV. Washington, D.C.: Government Printing Office, 1990.

Dewar, Hugo and Daniel Norman. *Revolution and Counter-Revolution in Hungary*. London: Socialist Union of Central Eastern Europe, 1957.

Dornbach, Alajos, ed. *The Secret Trial of Imre Nagy*. Westport, Conn.: Prager, 1994.

Duco, Hellema. "The Relevance and Irrelevance of Dutch Anti-Communism: The Netherlands and the Hungarian Revolution, 1956–57." *Journal of Contemporary History* 30, no. 1 (Jan. 1995): 169–186.

Ekiert, Grzegorz. *The State Against Society: Political Crises and their Aftermath in East Central Europe*. Princeton, N.J.: Princeton University Press, 1996.

Eörsi, László. Corvinisták, 1956: A VIII. kerület fegyveres csoportjai (Corvinists, 1956: The armed groups of the 8th district). Budapest: 1956-os Intézet, 2001

——, *Ferencváros 1956: A kerület fegyveres csoportjai* (Ferencváros 1956: The armed groups of the discrict). Budapest: 1956-os Intézet, 1997.

Évkönyv I. 1992 (Yearbook). Edited by János M. Bak, Csaba Békés, András B. Hegedűs and György Litván. Budapest: 1956-os Intézet, 1992.

Évkönyv II. 1993 (Yearbook). Edited by János M. Bak, András B. Hegedűs, György Litván and Katalin S. Varga. Budapest: 1956-os Intézet, 1993.

Évkönyv III. 1994 (Yearbook). Edited by János M. Bak, András B. Hegedűs, György Litván, János M. Rainer and Katalin S. Varga. Budapest: 1956-os Intézet, 1994.

Évkönyv IV. 1995 (Yearbook). Edited by András B. Hegedűs, Péter Kende, György Litván, János M. Rainer and Katalin S. Varga. Budapest: 1956-os Intézet, 1995.

Évkönyv V, 1996–1997 (Yearbook). Edited by András B. Hegedűs, Péter Kende, Gyula Kozák, György Litván, János M. Rainer and János Bak. Budapest: 1956-os Intézet, 1997.

Évkönyv VI. 1998 (Yearbook). Edited by András B. Hegedűs, Péter Kende, Gyula Kozák, György Litván and János M. Rainer. Budapest: 1956-os Intézet, 1998.

Évkönyv VII, 1999: Magyarország a Jelenkorban (Yearbook 1999: Hungary in our age). Ed. Éva Standeisky and János M. Rainer. Budapest: 1956-os Intézet, 1999.

Évkönyv VIII, 2000: Magyarország a Jelenkorban (Yearbook 2000: Hungary in our age). Ed. Zsuzsanna Kőrösi, Éva Standeisky and János M. Rainer. Budapest: 1956-os Intézet, 2000.

Évkönyv IX, 2001: Magyarország a Jelenkorban (Yearbook 2001: Hungary in our age). Ed. Zsuzsanna Kőrösi, János M. Rainer and Éva Standeisky. Budapest: 1956-os Intézet, 2001

Faludy, György. *My Happy Days in Hell*. Translated by Kathleen Szasz. London: Andrew Deutsch, 1962.

Fehér, Ferenc and Ágnes Heller. *Hungary 1956 Revisited: The Message of a Revolution--a Quarter of a Century After*. Boston: Allen & Unwin, 1983.

Fejtő, Franois. *Behind the Rape of Hungary*. New York: McKay, 1957.

——, *A History of the Peoples' Democracies*. 2 vols. Translated by Daniel Weissbort. New York: Praeger, [1971].

Felkay, András. "Hungary and the Soviet Union in the Kadar Era, 1956–1988." In *Twentieth Century Hungary and the Great Powers*, edited by I. Romsics, 267–284. Highland Lakes, N.J.: Atlantic Research and Publications, 1995.

——, *Hungary and the USSR, 1956–1988: Kadar's Political Leadership*. New York: Greenwood Press, 1989.

Filep, Tibor. *A debreceni forradalom 1956 október: Tizenkét nap krónikája* (The revolution in Debrecen: Chronicle of twelve days). Debrecen: Piremon, 1990.

Fischer, George. "Twelve Days of Freedom." *Science and Freedom* 8 (April 1957): 25–41.

A forradalom előzményei, alakulása és utóélete: Tanulmányok és kronológia (The precedents, course and aftermath of the 1956 revolution: Studies and chronology). Paris: Magyar

Füzetek; Highland Lakes, N.J.: Atlantic Research and Publications, 1987.

Free Europe Committee. *The Revolt in Hungary.* New York: Free Europe Committee, 1956.

Fryer, Peter. *Hungarian Tragedy.* London: Dobson, 1956.

Gábor, Luca, ed. *Jalta és Szuez között: 1956 a világpolitikában* (Between Jalta and Suez: 1956 in world politics). Budapest: Tudósítások Kiadó, 1989.

Gadney, Reg. *Cry Hungary! Uprising 1956.* New York: Athenom, 1986.

Gál, Éva, András B. Hegedűs, György Litván and János M. Rainer, eds. *A 'Jelcin Dosszié.' Szovjet dokumentumok 1956-ról* (The 'Yeltsin Dossier': Soviet documents on 1956). Budapest: Századvég Kiadó-1956-os Intézet, 1993.

Garai, G. "Rakosi and the anti-Zionist campaign in Hungary." *Soviet Jewish Affairs* 12, no. 2 (1982): 19–36.

Garthoff, Raymond. " A magyar forradalom és Washington" (Hungary 1956: The Washington Reaction). In *Évkönyv V, 1996–1997* (Yearbook, 1996–1997), edited by András B. Hegedűs, et al. Budapest: 1956-os Intézet, 1997.

Garton Ash, Timothy. *History of the Present: Essays, Sketches, and Dispatches from Europe in the 1990s.* New York: Random House, 1999.

——, *Magic Lantern: The Revolutions of 1989 as Witnessed in Warsaw, Budapest, Berlin, and Prague.* New York: Random House, 1990.

——, *The Uses of Adversity: Essays on the Fate of Central Europe.* London: Penguin, 1989.

Gati, Charles. The Bloc that Failed: Soviet-East European Relations in Transition. Bloomington: Indiana University Press, 1990.

——, "The Democratic Interlude in Post-War Hungary." *Survey* 28, no. 2 (1984): 99–134.

——, *Hungary and the Soviet Bloc.* Durham, N.C.: Duke Univeristy Press, 1986.

——, "Imre Nagy and Moscow 1953–1956." *Problems of Communism* 33 (1986): 32–49.

Gecsényi, Lajos, ed. "Osztrák külügyi iratok Magyarország történetéhez, 1956 október–november" (Austrian foreign ministry documents concerning Hungarian history, October–November 1956). *Múltunk* 49, no. 2 (1996): 157–206.

Geréb, Sándor, comp. *Titkos jelentések, 1956 okt. 23.–nov. 4.* (Secret reports, October 23–November 4, 1956). [Budapest]: Hírlapkiadó, [1989].

Geza, Dr. [pseud.]. *Doctor in Revolt.* As told to Geoffrey Dias. London: F. Muller, 1958.

Gibianskii, Leonid. "Soviet-Yugoslav Relations and the Hungarian Revolution of 1956." *Cold War International History Project Bulletin,* no. 10 (March 1998): 139–148.

Glatz, Ferenc, ed. "A kormány és a párt vezető szerveinek dokumentumaiból, 1956. október 23–november 4." (From the documents of government and leading party bodies, 23 October–24 November 1956). *História* 11, nos. 4–5 (1989): 25–52.

Gleitman, Henry. *Youth in Revolt: the Failure of Communist Indoctrination in Hungary.* New York: Free Europe Press, 1957.

Gluchowski, L.W. "Poland, 1956: Khrushchev, Gomulka and the 'Polish October.'" *Cold War International History Project Bulletin,* no. 5 (Spring 1995): 1, 38–49.

Gorka, Paul. *Budapest Betrayed: A Prisoner's Story of the Betrayal of the Hungarian Resistance Movement to the Russians.* London: Oak Tree Press, 1986.

Gosztonyi, Péter. *Föltámadott a tenger... 1956: A magyar október története* (The Sea rose... 1956: History of the Hungarian October). 3rd ed. Budapest: Népszava, 1989.

Granville, Johanna. "Hungary 1956: The Yugoslav Connection." *Europe-Asia Studies* 50, no. 3 (May 1998).

——, "Imre Nagy, aka 'VOLODYA'—A Dent in the Martyr's Halo?" *Cold War International History Project Bulletin,* no. 5 (Fall 1995): 28, 34–36.

——, "Imre Nagy, Hesitant Revolutionary." *Cold War International History Project Bulletin,* no. 5 (Fall 1995): 23, 27–28.

——, "Tito and the Nagy Affair in 1956." *East European Quarterly* 32, no. 1 (Spring 1998): 23.

Griffith, W. E. "The revolt reconsidered." *East Europe* 9, no. 1 (1960): 12–20.

Grossman, Monica and William F. Robinson, eds. *The 1956 Revolution and Its Aftermath: A*

Collection of Documents. Washington, D.C.: Radio Free Europe Research and Analysis Department.

Guzner, Bridget and Ildiko Woliner. *Hungary 1956: A Catalogue of British Library Holdings*. London: British Library, Slavonic and East European Collections, 1997.

Győr Megyei Jogú Város Levéltára. *Győr 1956*, 2 vols. Győr: Győr Megyei Jogú Város Polgármesteri Hivatala, 1996.

Györkei, Jenő and Miklós Horváth, eds. *Soviet Military Intervention in Hungary, 1956*. Translated by Emma Roper-Evans. Budapest: Central European University Press, 1999.

Hahn, Hans Henning and Heinrich Olschowsky, eds. *Das Jahr 1956 in Ostmitteleuropa* (The year 1956 in East-Central Europe). Berlin: Akademie Verlag, 1996.

Hajdu, Tibor. "1956-Magyarország a szuperhatalmak játéketerében" (1956-Hungary in the game of superpowers). *Valóság* 33, no. 12 (1990): 40–53.

——, "1956 nemzetközi háttere" (The international background of 1956). *Társadalmi Szemle* 44, no. 8–9 (1989): 36–47.

——, "Soviet Foreign Policy towards Hungary, 1953–1956." In *Twentieth Century Hungary and the Great Powers*, edited by I. Romsics, 245–252. Highland Lakes, N.J.: Atlantic Research and Publications, 1995.

de Halasz, B.I.L. *A Bibliography of the Hungarian Revolution 1956*. Toronto: University of Toronto Press, 1963.

Hanrieder, Wolfram F. and Graeme P. Auton. *The Foreign Policies of West Germany, France & Britain*. Englewood Cliffs, N.J: Prentice-Hall Inc., 1980.

Haraszti-Taylor, Eva, comp. *The Hungarian Revolution of 1956: A Collection of Documents from the British Foreign Office*. Nottingham, U.K.: Astra Press, 1995.

Hay, Julius. *Born 1900*. Translated and abridged by J. A. Underwood. London: Hutchinson, 1974.

Hedli, D. J. "United States Involvement or Non-involvement in the Hungarian Revolution of 1956." *International Review of History and Political Science* 11 (1974): 72–78.

Hegedűs, András B. "Additional remarks by a major participant in the Hungarian Revolution of 1956." *Studies in Comparative Communism* 18 (1985): 115–23.

——, "The Petőfi Circle: The Forum of Reform in 1956." In *Hungary 1956--Forty Years On*, ed. Terry Cox, 108–134. Portland, Or: Frank Cass, 1997.

——, "Mikoyan's Overcoat: Discussions and Decisions in the Kremlin, 1956." In *Hungary 1956--Forty Years On*, ed. Terry Cox, 134–140. London–Portland, Ore.: Frank Cass, 1997.

——, ed. *1956 Kézikönyve*, 3 Vols. Budapest: 1956-os Intézet, 1996.

——, ed. *Ötvenhatról nyolcvanhatban: Az 1956-os magyar forradalom előzményei, alakulása és utóélete című, 1986. december 5–6-án Budapesten rendezett tanácskozás jegyzőkönyve* (On Fifty Six in Eithy Six: Minutes of the conference entitled "The precedents, course and aftermath of the 1956 revolution," organized in Budapest on December 5–6, 1986). Budapest: Századvég Kiadó—1956-os Intézet, 1992.

——, ed. *A Petőfi Kör vitái hiteles jegyzőkönyvek alapján* (The debates of the Petőfi circle based on authentic minutes). 7 vols. Budapest: Kelenföld-ELTE (vols. 1–3), 1956-os Intézet (vols.4–7), 1992–94.

Heinemann, Winfried and Norbert Wiggershaus, eds. *Das internationale Kriesenjahr 1956: Polen, Ungarn, Suez* (The interntional crisis-year 1956: Poland, Hungary and Suez). München: R. Oldenburg Verlag, 1999.

Held, Joseph, ed. *The Columbia History of Eastern Europe in the Twentieth Century*. New York: Columbia University Press, 1992.

Heller, Andor. *No More Comrades: A Message from the Freedom Fighters of Hungary*. Chicago: Regnery, 1957.

Helmreich, Ernst C., ed. *Hungary*. New York: Praeger, 1957.

Hihnala, Paula and Olli Vehvilainen, eds. *Hungary 1956*. Tampere: Tampereen Yliopisto, 1995.

Hodos, George H. *Show Trials: Stalinist Purges in Eastern Europe, 1949–1956*. New York: Praeger, 1987.

572

Horváth, Ibolya, Pál Solt, Győző Szabó, János Zanathy and Tibor Zinner, eds. *Iratok az igazságszolgáltatás történetéből* (Documents from the history of jurisdiction). 6 vols. Budapest: Közgazdasági és Jogi Jönyvkiadó, 1992–96.

Horváth, J. *Revolution for the Privilege to Tell the Truth*. New York: Kossuth Foundation, 1960.

Horváth, Julianna and Zoltán Ripp, eds. *Ötvenhat októbere és a hatalom: A Magyar Dolgozók Pártja vezető testületeinek dokumentumai, 1956. október 24–28* (October '56 and the power: documents of the leading bodies of the Hungarian Workers' Party, October 24–28, 1956). Budapest: Napvilág Kiadó, 1997.

Horváth, Miklós. *Maléter Pál*. Budapest: Osiris-Századvég-1956-os Intézet, 1995.

Hungaricus [Sándor Fekete]. *On a Few Lessons of the Hungarian National Democratic Revolution*. Brussels: Imre Nagy Institute for Political Research, 1959.

Ignotus, Paul. *Hungary*. New York: Praeger Publishers, 1972.

——, *Political Prisoner*. New York: Collier, 1964.

Immerman, Richard H. *John Foster Dulles and the Diplomacy of the Cold War*. Princeton, N.J.: Princeton University Press, 1990.

Imre, Robert J. "Post-Kadar Hungary: Three Approaches to the Challenge of Political and Economic Adjustment." Master's thesis, University of Victoria [Canada], 1992.

International Commission of Jurists. *The Hungarian Situation and the Rule of Law*. The Hague: The International Commission of Jurists, 1957.

International Confederation of Free Trade Unions. *Four Days of Freedom: The Uprising in Hungary and the Free Unions of the World*. Brussels: ICFTU, 1957.

International Research Associates. *Hungary and the 1956 Uprising: Personal Interviews: 1000 Hungarian Refugees in Austria*. New York: IRA, 1957.

International Union of Socialist Youth. *Why? The History of a Mass Revolt in Search of Freedom*. Vienna: IUSY, 1957.

Irving, David. *Uprising!* London: Hodder & Stoughton, 1981.

Izsák, Lajos. *Polgári pártok és programjaik Magyarországon, 1944–1956* (Bourgeois parties in Hungary and their programs, 1944–1956). Pécs: Baranya Megyei Könyvtár, 1994.

Izsák, Lajos and József Szabó, eds. *1956 a sajtó tükrében: 1956. október 22–november 5* (1956 in the mirror of the press). Budapest: Kossuth Kiadó, 1989.

Izsák, Lajos, József Szabó and Róbert Szabó, eds. *1956 plakátjai és röplapjai: Október 22–november 5.* (Posters and leaflets of 1956: 22 October–5 November). Budapest: Zrínyi Kiadó, 1991.

——, *1956 vidéki sajtója* (The Press of 1956 on the countryside). Budapest: Korona, 1996.

Jobbágyi, Gábor. *"Ez itt a vértanúk vére": Az 1956 utáni megtorlási eljárások* ("This is the blood of martyrs:" Reprisal after 1956). Budapest: Kairosz, 1998.

A jobboldali nézetektől az osztályárulásig: Adalékok Nagy Imrének és csoportjának elméleti és gyakorlati tevékenységéhez 1947–1956 (From right-wing ideas to class betrayal: Data on the theoretical and practical activities of Imre Nagy and his circle, 1947–1956). Budapest: Kossuth, 1957.

Juhász, Vilmos. *The Hungarian Revolution: The People's Demands*. New York: Free Europe Press, 1957.

——, ed. *Hungarian Social Science Reader: 1945–1963*. New York: Aurora, 1965.

Kabdebo, Thomas. *A Time for Everything: In Witness of the 1956 Hungarian Revolution*. Maynooth: Cardinal Press, 1996.

Kádár, János. *Socialist Construction in Hungary: Selected Speeches and Articles: 1957–1961*. Budapest: Corvina, 1962.

——, *Kádár János--végakarat*. Interviews by András Kanyó, documents complied and edited by Mária Veres. Budapest: Hírlapkiadó Vállalat, 1989.

Kahler, Frigyes. *Joghalál Magyarországon, 1945–1989* (Justitzmord in Hungary, 1945–1989). Budapest: Zrínyi, 1993.

——, ed. *Sortüzek 1956* (Volleys 1956). 2 Vols. Lakitelek: Antológia Kiadó, 1993–1994.

573

Kahler, Frigyes and M. Kiss Sándor. *Kinek a forradalma?* (Whose revolution?). Budapest: Püski-Kortárs, 1997.

Kajári, Erzsébet, ed. *Rendőrségi napi jelentések* (Daily Police reports). 2 vols. Annotated by Erzsébet Kaján and Attila Szakolczai. Budapest: Belügyminisztérium--1956-os Intézet, 1996-7.

——, "A magyarországi ellenforradalom a marxizmus-leninizmus fényében." *Társadalmi Szemle* 13, no. 1 (1957): 12–39.

Kalmár, Melinda. *Ennivaló és hozomány: A kora kádárizmus ideológiája* (Food and dowry: The ideology of early Kádárism). Budapest: Magvető, 1998.

Kapiller, Imre, ed. *'56 vidéken: Zalaegerszegen 1991. november 13-án rendezett Levéltári Napon elhangzott előadások* ('56 in the countryside: Papers presented during the day of archives on November 13, 1991 in Zalaegerszeg). Zalaegerszeg: Zala Megyei Levéltár, 1992.

Katona, P. "From Victory to Defeat." *Science and Freedom* 8 (April 1957): 42–48.

Kecskemeti, Paul. *The Unexpected Revolution: Social Forces in the Hungarian Uprising.* Stanford: Stanford University Press, 1961.

Kemény, István and Bill Lomax, eds. *Magyar Munkástanácsok 1956-ban* (Hungarian Workers' Councils in 1956). Paris: Magyar Füzetek, 1986.

Király, Béla K. "The aborted Soviet Military Plans against Yugoslavia." In *At the Brink of War and Peace: The Tito-Stalin Split in a Historic Perspective,* edited by W.S. Wucinich, 273–288. New York: Columbia University Press, 1982.

——, "From Death to Revolution." *Dissent* (1966): 709–724.

——, "Hungary's Army: Its part in the revolt." *East Europe* 7, no. 6 (1958): 3–15.

——, "Hungary's Army Under the Soviets." *East Europe* 7, no. 3 (1958): 3–14.

——, "The Hungarian Army Under Soviet Control." In *Twentieth Century Hungary and the Great Powers,* edited by I. Romsics, 285–306. Highland Lakes, N.J.: Atlantic Research and Publications, 1995.

Király, Béla K. and P. Jonas, eds. *The Hungarian Revolution of 1956 in Retrospect.* Boulder, Colo.: East European Monographs, 1977.

Király, Béla K., Barbara Lotze and Nándor Dreisziger, eds. *The First War Between Socialist States: The Hungarian Revolution of 1956 and its Impact.* Atlantic Studies on Society in Change. East European Monographs, vol. CLII. New York: Brooklyn College Press, 1984.

Kiroshev, G.F., ed. *Soviet Casualties and Combat Losses in the Twentieth Century.* Translated by Christine Barnard. Pennsylvania: Stackpole Books, 1997.

Kiss, József and Zoltán Ripp. "'Mi inkább az elnapolás mellett vagyunk, minthogy enyhe ítéletet hozzunk most.' Három dokumentum a Nagy Imre-per 1958. februári elhalasztásáról" ("We prefer postponing the trial to passing a light sentence right now." Three documents on the postponement of the Imre Nagy trial in February, 1958). *Társadalmi Szemle* 48, no. 4 (1993): 82–95.

Kiss, József, Zoltán Ripp and István Vida, eds. "Források a Nagy Imre-kormány külpolitikájának történetéhez" (Sources on the history of the Imre Nagy government). *Társadalmi Szemle* 48, no. 5, (1993): 78–94.

——, *Top Secret: Magyar-jugoszláv kapcsolatok. 1956. Dokumentumok* (Top Secret: Documents on Hungarian-Yugoslav relations, 1956). Budapest: MTA Jelenkor-kutató Bizottság, 1995

——, *Top Secret: Magyar-jugoszláv kapcsolatok. 1956. december-1959 február. A magyar-jugoszláv kapcsolatok és a Nagy Imre csoport sorsa: Dokumentumok* (Top Secret: Documents on Hungarian-Yugoslav Relations, December 1956-February 1959: Hungarian-Yugoslav relations and the fate of the Imre Nagy group). Budapest: MTA Jelenkor-kutató Bizottság, 1995 [1997].

Kissinger, Henry. *Diplomacy.* New York: Random House, 1944.

Klessmann, Christoph and Bernd Stöver, eds. *1953—Krisenjahr des Kaltes Krieges in Europa* (1953: Crisis Year of the Cold War in Europe). Vienna: Böhlau Verlag, 1999.

Kő, András and Lambert J. Nagy. *Kossuth Lajos tér, 1956* (Kossuth Lajos Square, 1956). Budapest: Teleki László Alapítvány, 2001.

——, *Tököl, 1956*. [Budapest]: Publica, 1992.

Kopácsi, Sándor. *In the Name of the Working Class*. Translated by Daniel and Judy Stoffman. New York: Grove Press, 1987.

Korányi, G. Tamás, ed. *Egy népfelkelés dokumentumaiból, 1956* (From documents of a popular uprising, 1956). Budapest: Tudósítások, 1989.

Kovács, Imre, ed. *Facts about Hungary*. New York: Hungarian Committee, 1959.

Kovács, Lajos Péter, ed. *A Nagy Imre vonal: Dokumentumválogatás* (The Imre Nagy line: Selection of documents). Budapest: Reform, 1989.

Kővágó, József. *You are All Alone*. New York: Praeger, 1959.

Kovrig, Bennett. *Communism in Hungary: From Kun to Kádár*. Stanford, Calif.: Hoover Institution Press, 1979.

——, *The Myth of Liberation: East Central Europe in U.S. Diplomacy and Politics Since 1941*. Baltimore: Johns Hopkins University Press, 1973.

——, *National Communism in Hungary*. Wisconsin: Marquette University Press, 1958.

——, *Of Walls and Bridges: The United States and Eastern Europe*. New York: New York University Press, 1991.

Kőrösi, Zsuzsanna and Pál Péter Tóth, eds. *Pártok, 1956. Válogatás 1956-os pártvezetők visszaemlékezéseiből* (Parties, 1956: Selection of recollections of party leaders in 1956). Budapest: 1956-os Intézet, 1997.

Kövér, György. *Losonczy Géza, 1917–1957*. Budapest: 1956-os Intézet, 1998.

Kozák, Gyula. "Szent Csőcselék" (Sacred mob). In *Évkönyv VII, 1999: Magyarország a Jelenkorban,* ed. Éva Standeisky and János M. Rainer, 255–281. Budapest: 1956-os Intézet, 1999.

——, ed. *Szemle: Válogatás a brüsszeli Nagy Imre Intézet Folyóiratából* (Review: Selected writings from the periodical of the Imre Nagy Institute in Brussels). Budapest: Századvég—1956-os Intézet, 1992.

Kozák, Gyula and Adrienn Molnár, eds. *"Szuronyok hegyén nem lehet dolgozni!" válogatás 1956-os munkástanácsvezetők visszaemlékezéseiből* ("You cannot work poked with bayonetts:" Recollections of Workers' Council leaders from 1956). Budapest: Századvég Kiadó—1956-os Intézet, 1993.

Kramer, Mark, ed. "Khrushchev's CPSU CC Presidium Meeting on East European Crises, 24 October 1956." *Cold War International History Project Bulletin,* no. 5 (Fall 1995): 1, 50–56.

——, "The 'Malin Notes' on the Crises in Hungary and Poland, 1956." *Cold War International History Project Bulletin,* no. 8/9 (Winter 1996/1997): 385–410.

——, "New Evidence on Soviet Decision-making and the 1956 Polish and Hungarian Crises." *Cold War International History Project Bulletin,* no. 8/9 (Winter 1996/1997): 358–84.

——, "Secret East German Report on Chinese Reactions to the 1956 Hungarian Revolt." *Cold War International History Project Bulletin,* no. 6/7 (Winter 1995/1996): 271.

——, "The Soviet Union and the 1956 Crises in Hungary and Poland: Reassessments and New Findings." *Journal of Contemporary History* 33, no. 2 (Apr. 1998): 163–214.

"A KSH nyilvánosságra nem került felmérése az 1956-os disszidálásról" (The unpublished report of the Central Statistical Office on defection in 1956). *Regio* 2, no. 4 (1991): 174–211.

Laping, Francis. and H. Knight. *Remember Hungary 1956*. New York: Alpha, 1975.

Lasky, Melvin J., ed. *The Hungarian Revolution: A White Book*. Secker & Warburg, 1957.

László, Péter. "Tolna megye 1956-ban" (Tolna county in 1956). In *Tolna Megyei Levéltári Füzetek,* no. 3., 71–102. Szekszárd : Tolna megyei Önkormányzat Levéltára, 1992.

The Legacy of the 1956 Hungarian Revolution. Five Participants, Forty Years Later: Andrew P. Fodor, Janos Horvath, Bela Kiraly, Kardy Nagy, and Laszlo Papp. New Brunswick, N.J.: Hungarian Alumni Association, 1996.

Leonov, V. *The Events in Hungary*. Moscow: Foreign Languages Publishing House, 1957.

Lettis, Richard and William E. Morris, eds. *The Hungarian Revolt: October 23–November 4, 1956*. New York: Scribner, 1961.

Litván, György. *Az 1956-os magyar forradalom hagyománya és irodalma* (The tradition and literature of the 1956 Hungarian revolution). Budapest: MTA Történettudományi Intézet, 1992.

——, "The political background of the Imre Nagy trial." In *The Secret Trial of Imre Nagy*, edited by A. Dornbach, 161–182. Westport, Conn.: Prager, 1994.

——, ed. "Francia dokumentumok 1956-ról" (French documents on 1956). In *Évkönyv III, 1994*, edited by János M. Bak et al., 139–147. Budapest: 1956-os Intézet, 1994.

Litván, György, János M. Bak and Lyman H. Legters, eds. *The Hungarian Revolution of 1956: Reform, Revolt and Repression, 1953–1963*. New York: Longman, 1996.

Lomax, Bill. "The Hungarian Revolution of 1956 and the origins of the Kadar regime." *Studies in Comparative Communism* 18, no. 23 (1985): 87–113.

——, *Hungary 1956*. London: Allen & Busby, 1976.

——, "The working class in the Hungarian revolution of 1956." *Critique* 13 (1980–81): 27–54.

——, ed. *Eye-Witness in Hungary: the Soviet Invasion of 1956*. Nottingham, U.K.: Spokesman, 1980.

——, ed. *Hungarian Workers' Councils in 1956*. Highland Lakes N.J.: Social Science Monographs, Atlantic Research and Publications, 1990.

Lukács, György. *Record of a Life*. London: Verso, 1983.

Lungu, Corneliu Mihai and Mihai Retegan, eds. *1956 Explozia: Percepţii române, iugoslave şi sovietice asupra evenimentelor din Polonia şi Ungaria* (1956 Explosion: Romanian, Yugoslav and Soviet perception of the events in Poland and Hungary). Bucharest: Editura Univers Enciclopedic, 1996.

Madariaga, S. de. "Suez and Hungary." *Swiss Review of World Affairs* 6 (1957): 10.

A Magyar Szocialista Munkáspárt ideiglenes vezető testületeinek jegyzőkönyvei (Minutes of the provisory leading bodies of the Hungarian Socialist Workers' Party). Vol. 1. *1956. november 11.–1957. január 14* (November 11, 1956–January 14, 1957). Edited by Karola Némethné Vágyi and Levente Sipos. Budapest: Intera, 1993.

——, Vol. 2, *1957. január 25.–1957. április 2* (January 25–April 2, 1957). Edited by Karola Némethné Vágyi and Károly Urbán. Budapest: Intera, 1993.

——, Vol. 3, *1957. április 5.–1957. május 17* (April 5–May 17, 1957). Edited by Magdolna Baráth and István Feitl. Budapest: Intera, 1993.

——, Vol. 4, *1957. május 21.–1957. június 24* (May 21–June 24, 1957). Edited by Magdolna Baráth and Zoltán Ripp. Budapest: Intera, 1994.

——, Vol. 5, *1956. november 14.–1957. június 26* (November 14, 1956–June 26, 1957). Edited by Magdolna Baráth, István Feitl, Karola Némethné Vágyi and Zoltán Ripp. Budapest: Napvilág, 1998.

Marchio, James David. "Resistance Potential and Rollback: U.S. Intelligence and the Eisenhower Administration's Policies Toward Eastern Europe, 1953–56." *Intelligence and National Security* 10, no. 2 (April 1995): 219–241.

——, "Rhetoric and Reality: The Eisenhower Administration and Unrest in Eastern Europe, 1953–1959." Ph.D. dissertation at American University, 1990. Ann Arbor, Mich.: UMI Dissertation Services, 1993.

Mastny, Vojtech. "'We are in a Bind': Polish and Czechoslovak Attempts at Reforming the Warsaw Pact." *Cold War International History Project*, no. 11 (Winter 1998): 230–250.

Matthews, John P. *Majales: The abortive Student Revolt in Czechoslovakia in 1956*. Cold War International History Project Working Paper, no. 24. Washington D.C.: Woodrow Wilson International Center for Scholars, 1998.

Maurer, Pierre. *La réconciliation sovéto-yougoslave 1954–1958: Illusions et désillusions de Tito* (The Soviet-Yugoslav reconciliation, 1954–1958: Illusions and disillusions of Tito). Cousset (Fribourg): Delval, 1991.

Márton, E. *The Forbidden Sky*. Boston: Little Brown, 1971.

McCauley, Brian. "Hungary and Suez 1956: The Limits of Soviet and American power." *Journal of Contemporary History* 16 (1981): 777–800.

Méray, Tibor. *Thirteen Days that Shook the Kremlin*. Translated by Howard L. Katsender. New York: Praeger, 1959.

Micunovic, Veljko. *Moscow Diary, 1956–1958*. Translated by David Floyd. Garden City, N.Y.: Doubleday, 1980.

Mikes, George. *The Hungarian Revolution*. London: Andre Deutsch, 1957.

Mindszenty, Cardinal József. *Memoirs*. Translated by Richard and Clara Winston. New York: Macmillan Publishing Co., 1974.

Ministère des Affaires Étrangères. *Documents Diplomatiques Français, 1956* (French diplomatic documents, 1956). Vol. 3. *24. Octobre–31. Décembre*. Paris: Imprimerie Nationale, 1990.

Molnár, Miklós. *Budapest 1956*. Translated by Jeannetta Ford. London: Allen & Unwin, 1971.

Musatov, Valerii L. *Predvestniki buri: Politicheskie krizisy v Vostochnoi Evrope* (Harbingers of the storm: Political crises in Eastern Europe). Moskva: Nauchnaya Kniga, 1996.

Nagy, Balázs. "The formation of the Central Workers Council of Greater Budapest in 1956." *International Socialism* 18 (1964): 24–30.

Nagy, Ferenc. *The Struggle Behind the Iron Curtain*. New York: Macmillan, 1948.

Nagy, Imre. *On Communism: In Defense of the New Course*. New York: Praeger, 1957.

Naumov, V.P. "Bor'ba N.S. Khrushcheva za edinolichnuyu vlast'" (Khrushchev's Struggle for One-Man Rule). *Novaya i Noveishaya Istoriya* 24, no. 2 (1996): 10–31.

Nemes, Dezső, ed. *Chapters from the Revolutionary Workers' Movement in Hungary: 1956–1962*. Budapest: Pannonia, 1971.

Némethné Vágyi, Karola, László Soós, György T. Varga and Gábor Ujváry, eds. *A Magyar Szocialista Munkáspárt Központi Bizottságának 1957–1958. évi jegyzőkönyvei* (Minutes of the Hungarian Socialist Workers' Party Central Committee in 1957–1958). Budapest: Magyar Országos Levéltár, 1997.

Nezhinskij, L.N. ed. *Sovetskaia vesnaja politika v godi khlodnoi voiny, 1945–1985* (Soviet Foreign Policy in the Cold War years 1945–1985). Moskva: Mezdunarodnaja Otnosheniia, 1995.

Novopashin, Y. S., ed. *Politicheskie krisisy i konflikty 50–60.h godov v "Vostochnoi Evrope"* (Political Crises and conflicts in Eastern Europe in the 1950–60s). Moscow: Institut Slavianovedenia i Balkanistiki RAN, 1993.

"Az október 23-i és az azt követő eseményekkel kapcsolatos sérülések és halálozások" (Injuries and deaths in relation to the events on October 23 and after). *Statisztikai Szemle* 68, no. 10 (1990): 797–815.

Ómolnár, Miklós. *Tizenkét nap, amely... :1956. október 23–november 4.: Események, emlékek, dokumentumok* (Twelve days that... : October 23–November 4, 1956: Events, Memories, Documents). Budapest: Szabad Tér, 1989.

Orekhova, Elena D., Viacheslav T. Sereda and Aleksandr. S. Stykalin, eds. *Sovetskii Soiuz i vengerskii krizis 1956 goda: Dokumenty* (The Soviet Union and the Hungarian Crisis in 1956: Documents). Moskva: Rossiiskaya Politicheskaya Enciklopedia, 1998.

Ostermann, Christian F. *The United States, the East German Uprising of 1953, and the Limits of Rollback*. Cold War International History Project Working Paper, no. 11. Washington, D.C.: Woodrow Wilson International Center for Scholars, 1994.

——, *Uprising in East Germany, 1953: The Cold War, the German Question, and the First Major Upheaval Behind the Iron Curtain*. Budapest: Central European Press, 2001

Pálóczi-Horváth, György. *The Undefeated*. London: Secker & Warburg, 1959.

——, ed. *One Sentence on Tyranny: Hungarian Literary Gazette Anthology*. Translated and supervised by Paul Tábor and John Sakeford. London: Waverley Press, 1957.

Pechatnov, Vladimir O. *The Big Three after World War II: New Documents on Soviet Thinking about Post War Relations with the United States and Great Britain.* Cold War International History Project Working Paper, no. 13. Washington, D.C.: Woodrow Wilson International Center for Scholars, 1995.

Pető, Iván and Sándor Szakács. *A hazai gazdaság négy évtizedének története* (History of four decades of the Hungarian national economy). Vol. 1. Budapest: Közgazdasági és Jogi Kiadó, 1985.

Pfeiffer, Ede. *Child of Communism.* Translated by Denise Goztola. New York: Crowell, 1958.

Pikhoya, Rudolf G. "O vnutripoliticheskoi bor'be v sovetskom rudovodstve 1945–1958 gg" (On the internal political struggles in the Soviet leadership, 1945–1958). *Novaya i Noveishchaya Istoriya* 23, no. 6 (1995): 3–14.

Pongrátz, Gergely. *Corvin köz-1956* (Corvin Passage, 1956). Budapest: Magyar Színkör Kisszövetkezet, 1989.

Porter, Suzanne Fuller, "The Promise: Pal Maleter and the 1956 Hungarian Revolution." Ph.D. diss., Georgetown University, 1996.

Pruessen, Ronald W. "John Foster Dulles and 1956." In *Évkönyv V, 1996–1997 (*Yearbook, 1996–1997), edited by András Hegedűs. Budapest: 1956-os Intézet, 1997.

Pryce-Jones, David. *The Hungarian Revolution.* London: Benn, 1969.

Rácz, Sándor. "Hungary 56: the workers' case." *Labour Focus on Eastern Europe* 7, no. 2 (1984): 2–17.

Radványi, János. *Hungary and the Superpowers: The 1956 Revolution and Realpolitik.* Stanford, Calif.: Hoover Institution Press, 1979.

Rainer, M. János. "1956. The Other Side of the Story. Five Documents from the Yeltsin File." *The Hungarian Quarterly* 34, no. 129 (1993): 100–114.

——, "The 1956 Revolution in the provinces." *Budapest Review of Books* 2, no. 2 (1992): 64–68.

——, "The City: Center of Post-Revolutionary Crisis, 1957–63." In *Budapest: A History from its Beginnings to 1998,* edited by András Gerő and János Poór, 233–250. Highland Lakes, N.J.: Atlantic Research and Publications, 1997.

——, Rainer, M. János. "The Malin Notes." In *Encounters: A Hungarian Quarterly Reader,* ed. Zsófia Zachár, 189–214. Budapest: Balassi Kiadó, c1999.

——, *Nagy Imre: Politikai életrajz* (Imre Nagy: A Political Biography). 2 vols. Budapest: 1956-os Intézet, 1996–1999.

——, The New Course in Hungary in 1953. Cold War International History Project Working Paper, no. 38. Washington D.C.: Woodrow Wilson International Center for Scholars, 2002.

——, "The Reprisals." *The New Hungarian Quarterly* 33, no. 127 (1992): 118–127.

——, "The Reprisals." In *Encounters: A Hungarian Quarterly Reader*, edited by Zsófia Zachár, 249–259. Budapest: Balassi Kiadó, 1999.

——, "Szovjet döntéshozatal Magyarországról 1956-ban" (Soviet decision making on Hungary in 1956). In *Évkönyv II, 1993,* ed. János M. Bak et al., 19–38. Budapest: 1956-os Intézet, 1993.

——, "The Yeltsin Dossier: Soviet Documents on Hungary, 1956." *Cold War International History Project Bulletin,* no. 5 (Fall 1995): 22, 24–27.

Rainer, M. János [Elek Fényes, pseud.]. "Adatok az 1956-os forradalmat követő megtorláshoz" (Further data on reprisal after the Revolution of 1956). *Beszélő,* no. 19 (1987): 43–63. Republished in *Beszélő összkiadás, 1981–1989* (Beszélő reprint, 1981–1989). Vol. 2. Edited by Fanny Havas, 649–663. Budapest: AB-Beszélő, 1992.

Rainer, M. János and Károly Urbán, eds. "'Konzultációk:' Dokumentumok a magyar és szovjet pártvezetők két moszkvai találkozójáról 1954–1955-ben" ("Consultations:" Documents relating to two meetings of Soviet and Hungarian party leaders in Moscow in 1954–1955). *Múltunk* 37, no. 4 (1992): 124–148.

Rákosi, Mátyás. *Visszaemlékezések, 1944–1956* (Memoirs, 1944–1956). 2 vols. Budapest: Napvilág Kiadó, 1997.

Reed, Daryl William, "Behind the Negotiated Revolution: Economic Reform, Social Change, and Legitimization in Hungary, 1956–1989." Ph.D. diss., University of Southern California, 1995.

"Reports on Agent 'Volodya': Russian Documents on Imre Nagy." Provided and translated by Johanna Granville. *Cold War International History Project Bulletin*, no. 5 (Fall 1995): 37.

Rév, István. "Counterrevolution." In *Between Past and Future*, edited by Sorin Antohi and Vladimir Tismaneanu, 247–271. Budapest: CEU Press, 2000.

Révai, Valéria, ed. *Törvénytelen szocializmus: A Tényfeltáró Bizottság jelentése* (Illegal Socialism: Report of the Investigation Committee). Budapest: Zrínyi Kiadó–Új Magyarország, 1993.

Richter, James. *Reexamining Soviet Policy During the Beria Interregnum*. Cold War International History Project Working Paper, no. 3. Washington, D.C.: Woodrow Wilson International Center for Scholars, 1992.

Ripp, Zoltán. *Belgrád és Moszkva között: A jugoszláv kapcsolat és a Nagy Imre-kérdés, 1956. november–1959. február* (Between Belgrad and Moscow: The Yugoslav connection and the Imre Nagy issue, November 1956–February 1959). Budapest: Politikatörténeti Alapítvány, 1994.

——, "Döntés a Nagy Imre-csoport ügyében: A Központi Bizottság zárt ülése 1957. dec. 21-én" (Decision on the case of the Imre Nagy group: Closed session of the Central Committee on December 21, 1957). *Múltunk* 35, no. 4 (1990): 159–178.

Romsics, Ignác, ed. *Twentieth Century Hungary and the Great Powers*. Highland Lakes, N.J.: Atlantic Research and Publications, 1995.

Ruff, Mihály. "Magyarország és az NDK kapcsolatairól, 1956. november–1958. március" (On the relations of Hungary and the GDR, November 1956–October 1958). *Múltunk* 40, no. 2 (1995): 30–66.

Sanderson, J. D. *Boy with a Gun*. New York: Henry Holt, 1958.

Sartre, Jean Paul. *The Spectre of Stalin*. Translated by Irene Clephane. London: Hamish Hamilton, 1969.

Scarlett, Dora. *Window Onto Hungary*. Broadacre, 1959.

Schöpflin, George. "Hungarian People's Republic." In *Marxist Governments: A World Survey*, edited by Bogdan Szajkowski. New York: Macmillan, 1981.

——, "Hungary." In *Communist Power in Europe 1944–1949*, edited by Martin MacCauley. New York: Macmillan, 1979.

Schramm, W. L., ed. *One Day in the World's Press*. Stanford, Calif.: Stanford University Press, 1959.

Schwartz, Martin Ben. "A New Look at the 1956 Hungarian Revolution: Soviet Opportunism, American Acquiescence." Ph.D. diss., Fletcher School of Law and Diplomacy, Tufts University, 1988. Ann Harbor, Mich.: University Microfilm International, 1988.

Sereda, Viacheslav and Aleksandr Stikalin, eds. *Hiányzó lapok 1956 történetéből: dokumentumok a volt SZKP KB levéltárából* (Missing pages from the history of 1956: Documents from the former archive of CPSU CC). Budapest: Móra Ferenc Könyvkiadó, 1993.

Sereda, Viacheslav and János M. Rainer, eds. *Döntés a Kremlben, 1956: A Szovjet pártelnökség vitái Magyarországról* (Decision in the Kremlin, 1956: The Debates of the Soviet Party Presidium on Hungary). Budapest: 1956-os Intézet, 1996.

Sereda, Vyacheslav and Elena D. Orekhova. "V. Sz. Bajkov naplójából: Feljegyzés Nemes Dezső et.-tel az MSZMP KB póttagjával folytatott beszélgetésről 1958 áprilisában" (From the diary of V. S. Baikov: Notes on the conversation with cde. Dezső Nemes, candidate member of the HSWP CC in April 1958). *Tekintet* 8, nos. 5–6 (1995): 200–207.

Shawcross, William. *Crime and Compromise: Janos Kádár and the Politics of Hungary Since Revolution*. New York: Dutton, 1974.

Simon, Zoltán, ed. *A vidék forradalma: Az 1991. október 22-én Debrecenben rendezett konferencia előadásai* (Revolution of the Countryside: Papers Delivered on the Conference Organized in Debrecen on October 22, 1991). Debrecen: Az 1956-os forradalom történetének Hajdú-Bihar

Megyei Kutatócsoportja, 1992.

Soós, Katalin. *1956 és Ausztria* (1956 and Austria). Szeged: JATE Bölcsészettudományi kara, 1999.

"Soviet Documents on the Hungarian Revolution, 24 October–4 November 1956." *Cold War International History Project Bulletin*, no. 5 (Fall 1995): 22, 29–34.

Spasowski, Romuald. *The Liberation of One*. New York: Harcourt Brace Jovanovich, 1986.

Standeisky, Éva. *Írók lázadása: 1956-os írószövetségi jegyzőkönyvek* (Revolt of the writers: Writers' Union minutes from 1956). Budapest: MTA Irodalomtudományi. Intézet, 1990.

——, *Írók és a hatalom, 1956–1963* (Writers and the power, 1956–1963). Budapest: 1956-os Intézet, 1996.

Steele, Jonathan, ed. *Eastern Europe since Stalin*. New York: Crane, Russak & Company, Inc., 1974.

Stillman, Edmund O. *The Ideology of Revolution: the People's Demands in Hungary, October–November 1956*. New York: Free Europe Press, 1957.

——, ed. *Bitter Harvest: The Intellectual Revolt Behind the Iron Curtain*. London: Thames & Hudson, 1958.

Szablya, Helen M. *The Fall of the Red Star*. Honesdale, P.A.: Boyds Mills Press, 1996.

Szabó, Tamás [pseud.]. *Boy on the Rooftop*. Translated by Davud Hughes. Toronto: Little Brown, 1958.

Szakolczai, Attila. az 1956-os forradalom és szabadságharc (The 1956 revolution and fight for independence). Budapest: 1956-os Intézet, 2001.

——, "A forradalmat követő megtorlás során kivégzettekről" (On people executed during the reprisal after the revolution). In *Évkönyv III, 1994*, edited by János M. Bak et al., 237–257. Budapest: 1956-os Intézet, 1994.

Szalay, Hanna, comp. *Napról napra: 1956 sajtója, október 23.–november 4.: Válogatás* (From day to day: The press of 1956, October 23–November 4: Selection). [Budapest]: Kolonel, 1989.

Szántó, Konrád. *Az 1956-os forradalom és a katolikus egyház* (The catholic church and the 1956 revolution). Miskolc: Szent Maximilian Lap- és Könyvkiadó, 1992.

Szász, Béla. *Volunteers for the Gallows*. Translated by Kathleen Szász. London: Chatto and Windus, 1971.

Sztáray, Zoltán. *Books on the Hungarian Revolution: A Bibliography*. Brussels: Imre Nagy Institute for Political Research, 1960.

Taylor, E. "The lessons of Hungary." *The Reporter* 27 (1956): 17–21.

Téglás, Csaba. *Budapest Exit: A Memoir of Fascism, Communism, and Freedom*. College Station, Tex.: Texas A&M Univeristy Press, 1998.

"Third World Reaction to Hungary and Suez, 1956: A Soviet Foreign Ministry Analysis." *Cold War International History Project Bulletin*, no. 4 (Fall 1994): 61–64.

Time-Life. *Hungary's Fight for Freedom—A Special Report in Pictures*. New York: Time-Life Magazine, 1956

Tischler, János. *Rewolucja węgierska 1956 w polskich dokumentach* (Polish documents on the 1956 Hungarian revolution). Warsaw: Instýtut Studiów Politycznych PAN, 1995.

——, "Csou-Enlaj kínai miniszterelnök januári látogatása Varsóban" (Prime Minister Zhou Enlai's January visit to Warsaw). *Múltunk* 44, no. 2 (1994): 141–175.

——, "A lengyel pártvezetés és az 1956-os magyar forradalom" (The Polish party leadership and the Hungarian revolution in 1956). In *Évkönyv III, 1994*, ed. János M. Bak et al., 179–195. Budapest: 1956-os Intézet, 1994.

——, ed. "Lengyel követjelentések és a budapesti lengyel nagykövetségnek Varsóból küldött táviratok az 1956-os magyar forradalom időszaka alatt" (Reports of the Polish ambassador and telegrams sent from Warsaw to the Polish Embassy during the period of the Hungarian revolution in 1956). *Társadalmi Szemle* 47, no. 10 (1992): 73–91.

Tóbiás, Áron, ed. *In memoriam Nagy Imre: Emlékezés egy miniszterelnökre* (In memoriam Imre

Nagy: Remembering a prime minister). Budapest: Szabad Tér, 1989.

"Togliatti on Nagy, 30 October 1956: Missing Cable Found." *Cold War International History Project Bulletin*, no. 8/9 (Winter 1996/1997): 357.

Trory, Ernie. *Hungary 1919 and 1956: the Anatomy of Counter-Revolution*. Hove, Sussex: Crabtree, 1981.

The Truth About the Nagy Affair, Facts. Documents. Comments. London: Secker & Warburg, 1959.

Tyekvicska, Árpád. *A bíboros és a katona: Mindszenty József és Pálinkás-Pallavicini Antal a forradalomban* (The cardinal and the soldier: József Mindszenty and Antal Pálinkás-Pallavicini in the revolution). Budapest: Századvég-1956-os Intézet, 1994.

Ulam, Adam B. *Expansion and Coexistence: Soviet Foreign Policy 1917–1973*. New York: Praeger, 1974.

United Nations. *Anatomy of Revolution: A Condensation of the United Nations Report on the Hungarian Uprising*. Washington, D.C.: Public Affairs Press, 1957.

——, *Report of the Special Committee on the Problem of Hungary*. New York: General Assembly Official Records, 1957.

Unwin, Peter. "The Hungarian Revolution of 1956: A Collection of Documents from the British Foreign Office." *Slavonic and East European Review* 75, no. 3 (July 1997): 571–2.

——, *Voice in the Wilderness: Imre Nagy and the Hungarian Revolution*. London: Macdonald, 1991.

Urbán, George R. *The Nineteen Days: A Broadcaster's Account of the Hungarian Revolution*. Heinemann, 1957.

——, *Radio Free Europe and the Pursuit of Democracy: My War Within the Cold War*. New Haven, Conn.: Yale University Press, 1997.

Urquhart, M. *Hungary Fights*. Brown Watson, 1957.

Váli, Ferenc A. *Rift and Revolt in Hungary*. Oxford: Oxford University Press, 1961.

Varga, György T. "Jegyzőkönyv a szovjet és a magyar párt- és állami vezetők tárgyalásairól (1953. június 13–16)" (Minutes of the Soviet-Hungarian party and state leaders' negotiations, Moscow 13–16 June 1953). *Múltunk* 37, no. 2–3 (1992): 234–269.

Varga, László. *Az elhagyott tömeg. Tanulmányok 1950–1956-ról* (The forsaken crowd: Studies on 1950–1956). Budapest: Cserépfalvi-Budapest Főváros Levéltára, 1994.

——, *Human Rights in Hungary*. Gainesville, Fla.: Danubian Research & Information Center, 1967.

——, "Moszkva-Belgrád-Budapest: A jugoszláv kapcsolat 1956. október–november" (Moscow-Belgrade-Budapest: The Yugoslav connection, October–November, 1956). In *Jalta és Szuez között* (Between Yalta and Suez), 142–175. Budapest: Tudósítások Kiadó, 1989.

——, "A Nagybudapesti Központi Munkástanács irataiból" (From the documents of the Budapest Central Workers' Council). Parts 1 and 2. *Társadalmi Szemle* 46, nos. 8–9 (1991): 142–155; no. 11 (1991): 79–93.

——, comp. *A forradalom hangja: Magyarországi rádióadások 1956. október 23–november 9* (The voice of the Revolution: Hungarian Broadcasts October 23–November 9, 1956). Edited and foreword by János Kenedi. Budapest: Századvég—Nyilvánosság Klub, 1989.

Vass, Henrik and Ságvári Ágnes, eds. *A Magyar Szocialista Munkáspárt határozatai és dokumentumai 1956–1962* (Resolutions and documents of the Hungarian Socialist Workers' Party, 1956–1962). 2nd ed. Budapest: Kossuth Könyvkiadó, 1979.

Vida, István, ed. *1956 és a politikai pártok : Politikai pártok az 1956-os forradalomban, 1956. október 23–november 4.: Válogatott dokumentumok* (1956 and the political parties: Political parties during the 1956 revolution, October 23–November 4, 1956). Budapest: MTA Jelenkorkutató Bizottság, 1998.

——, ed. "Amerikai követjelentések 1956-ból" (Reports of the U.S. minister in 1956). *Társadalmi Szemle* 47, no. 2 (1992): 77–93.

——, "A budapesti angol követség 1956. novemberi–decemberi jelentéseiből" (From the reports of the British embassy in Budapest from November–December 1956). *Társadalmi Szemle* 46, no. 1 (1991): 66–79.

Voneche Cardia, Isabelle. *L' Octobre Hongrois: Entre Croix Rouge et Drapeau Rouge: L'Action du Comité International de la Croix-Rouge en 1956* (The Hungarian October: Between the Red Cross and the red flag: The activity of the international committee of the Red Cross in 1956). Brussels: Buylant, 1996.

Wagner, Francis S., ed. *The Hungarian Revolution in Perspective*. Washington, DC: Freedom Fighters Memorial Foundation, 1967.

White, Brian: *Britain, Détente, and Changing East-West Relations*. London-New York: Routledge, 1992.

Woroszylski, Wiktor. *Diary of a Revolt: Budapest Through Polish Eyes*. London: Segal & Jenkins, 1957.

Zinner, Paul. E. *Revolution in Hungary*. New York: Columbia University Press, 1962.

——, ed. *National Communism and Popular Revolt in Eastern Europe: A Selection of Documents on Events in Poland and Hungary, February–November, 1956*. New York: Columbia University Press, 1956.

Zinner, Tibor, ed. "'...hogy megkönnyítsék a Nagy kormány likvidálását...': Három dokumentum Nagy Imre és köre 1956 november 4. utáni történetéhez" ("...to faciliate the liquidation of the Nagy government": Three documents concerning the history of Imre Nagy and his circle of followers after November 4, 1956). *Társadalmi Szemle* 44, no. 12 (1989): 72–98.

Zubok, Vladislav and Constantine Pleshakov. *Inside the Kremlin's Cold War. From Stalin to Khrushchev*. Boston: Harvard University Press, 1996.

INDEX

Page numbers in italics refer to biographical material on persons or actual text of document indicated.

Bulganin, Nikolai A., *(cont'd)*
  meetings with Hungarian leaders
    (1953–55), 17, 54, 57–58, 62–63
  and Nagy group, 519
  in Presidium power struggle, after revolu-
    tion, 392–94, 528, 529
  and Suez crisis, 531
  and uprising in Hungary, 217, 264,
    266–68, 296, 298, 317
  and Yugoslavia, 3, 142, 522
Bulgaria
  reaction to Hungarian revolution, 202,
    305–6
  at summit on Hungary (Jan. 1957), 487,
    489–95
  U.S. analyses of, 50–51, 509, 546
  U.S. policy toward (1958), 551
Bús-Fekete, László, 466, 475

C

Central Committee, *566*
Central Intelligence Agency (U.S.), 132, 215,
  216, 379. *See also* Dulles, Allen W.
Central Workers' Council of Greater
  Budapest (KMT), 367, *566*
China, 295, 378, 497, 511, 541
  and Hungarian crisis, 210, 299, 348, 352,
    498, 500
  state visit to Hungary (Jan. 1957),
    496–503
  and Twentieth Party Congress reforms,
    180–81
Christian Democratic Party, 493
Church/clergy, 10, 92–93, 98.
    See also Mindszenty, József
CIA. *See* Central Intelligence Agency
Committee for State Security (KGB; Soviet
  Union), 364, 366, *566*
communist party(ies). *See also* Hungarian
  Socialist Workers' Party; Hungarian
  Workers' Party; Soviet Union Communist
  Party
  Western European, 294, 311, 374
  world conference of (1957), 378
Corvin Passage rebel unit, 198, 201, 256,
  258, 262, 292, 384
Council of Mutual Economic Assistance, 377
CPSU. *See* Soviet Union Communist Party
CPSU CC Presidium. *See* Soviet Union
  Communist Party Central Committee

Presidium
Crittenberger, Willis D., *481*
Czechoslovakia
  and Hungarian crisis, 229–30, 327, 347
  in summit on Hungary (Jan. 1957), 487,
    489–95
  U.S. analyses of, 48–49, 508, 546
  U.S. policy toward (1958), 551
Czottner, Sándor, *279*

D

Debrecen, 193, 199, 217, 263
Dej, Gheorghe Gheorghiu. *See* Gheorghiu-
  Dej, Gheorghe
Déry, Tibor, *160–61*, 540
detainees. *See* prisoners
"differentiation policy", 543
"Directory" (Emergency/Extraordinary
  Committee), 201, 237, 253, 255, 257, 258,
  566
dissidence/resistance. *See also* nationalism
  in Eastern Europe, 4, 120, 202, 303–4,
    506–9
  in Hungary
    before 1956, 1, 86–101, 105
    on eve of uprising, 10–12, 143–47,
      159–72, 178–84, 187
    under Kádár government, 364–69,
      374–76, 450–51, 508, 513
    in Poland (*See* Poland, crisis in)
DISZ. *See* Union of Working Youth
Dobi, István, 20, 61, 162, 220, 273, 321,
  330–31, 415, 446, *560*
Dögei, Imre, *360*
Donáth, Ferenc, xvi, 443, *560*. *See also* Nagy
  group
  in Nagy government, 200, 225, 409
  trial of, 372–74, 532, 533, 539–40
  and uprising, 195–97, 199, 211, 225,
    237–38, 252
Dudás, József, 207, 323, 451, 502–3, 520,
  560
Dudorov, N.P., 432
Dulles, Allen W., *560*
  on Eastern Europe policy (July 1956),
    132, 133, 135
  and Hungarian revolution, 215, 231,
    240–41, 324
  on Radio Free Europe, 379
  and Soviet invasion, 401–403

Dulles, John Foster, *560*
  on Eastern Europe policy (July 1956),
    2, 129–34
  and Hungarian revolution, 209–10, 212,
    228, 242, 244–45, 324
  and Soviet invasion, 406–7

E

East Germany, 138–39, 202
  unrest in, 4, 508
  U.S. analyses of, 52–53, 112, 153–54,
    508, 513
Eastern Europe. *See also* Warsaw Treaty
  Organization; *specific countries*
  British policy analyses of (1956), *148–51,
    183–85*
  dissidence/resistance in, 4, 120, 202,
    303–4, 506–9
  economic conditions/policies in, 76–80,
    507, 512–13
  and Hungarian revolution, 202, 305
  nationalism in, 120, 121–23, 153, 175,
    505–6, 513–14
  and Soviet invasion of Hungary, 213, 214,
    347, 348, 528
  Soviet policy toward, xxiii, 3–4, 69–85,
    114–15, 119–24
    and friendship declaration, 210,
      295–99, *300–302,* 494–95
    NATO analysis of "thaw," 168,
      172–77
    after revolution, 376–78, 504–14,
      543–45
  Soviet troop withdrawals from, 377–78,
    437, 438, 440
  U.S. analyses of, 69–71, 74–85, 504–14
  U.S. policy toward, 2–3, 34–53, 124–35,
    152–56
    criticism of, after invasion, 378–79
    during and after revolution, 209–10,
      240, 242–45, 437–42, 543–52
economy. *See also* agriculture; industry; living standards
  of Eastern Europe, 76–80, 377, 507, 512–13
  of Hungary
    on eve of uprising (1956), 12, 172, 181
    under Kádár government, 367,
      450–51, 490, 512
    "New Course" reforms and, 4–6, 76–78
    Soviet criticism of (1954), 14–15, 18,

21, 22, 54–59
Eden, Anthony, 317
Egri, Gyula, 146, 225, *560*
Eisenhower, Dwight D.,
    2, 209, 212, 241–45, 437, *560*
  and Soviet invasion, 378–81, 401–403,
    406–7, 497
"Eisenhower doctrine," 495
Emergency/Extraordinary Committee. *See*
  "Directory" (Emergency/Extraordinary
  Committee)
émigrés/exiles, 124, 338, 369, 373, 381, 478,
  498, 499. *See also* Radio Free Europe
Erdei, Ferenc, 207, 215, 216, 278, 281,
  314–15, 330–31, 408, *560*
Erdős, Péter, 533
Erofeev, Vladimir, *363*
executions
  under Kádár government, 367, 375, 502–3
  of Nagy group defendants, 374, 496, 503,
    532, 539
  during revolution, 524

F

Farkas, Ferenc, *215,* 341
Farkas, Mihály, 14, 20, 58, 145, 178, 188, *561*
  arrest and trial of, 116, 118, 415, *519*
  criticism of (1953–55), 5, 10, 17, 20, 27,
    62, 64
Farkas, Vladimir, 352
Fazekas, György, 410, *532, 533.*
  See also Nagy group
Fehér, Lajos, 368, *416,* 450, 452–53, 489
Fekete, Gyula, 540
Feketekúthy, László, 466, 476
Field, Noel, 10
Firyubin, Nikolai P., 387, *561*
Földes, László, *454*
Földvári, Rudolf, 433, *561*
France, 203, 212, 250, 348, 363, 402.
  See also Suez crisis
Franco, Francisco, 379
Friss, István, *535*
Furtseva, Ekaterina A., *186,* 265, 308, 351,
  392–94

G

Gáspár, Sándor, *179,* 225, 254
Gellért, Andor, *466,* 467, 469–71, 473, 476–78

585

German Democratic Republic. *See* East
Germany
Gerő, Ernő, 20, 24, *561*
criticism of (1953-55), 10, 27, 28, 54, 64
Kádár government on, 460, 461
in meeting with CPSU CC Presidium
(June 1953), 14, 16, 19, 20
meetings with Soviets, on eve of uprising,
143–47, 161, 163–64, 166, 178–82
and plans for post-Nagy government, 309,
350, 359–60, 385–86, 529
regime of (1956), 11, 12, 171
after revolution, 517–19
during uprising, 191, 193–95, 197, 205,
219–22, 224–26, 238, 253–61
and Yugoslavia, 157–58, 162–64, 421–22
Gheorghiu-Dej, Gheorghe, 303–4, 318–20,
366, 455, 485, *561*
at Warsaw Pact summit on Hungary (Jan.
1957), 489–92
Gimes, Miklós, 10, 451, *561*
trial and execution of, 372–74, 532, 533,
539–40
Gollan, John, 374
Gomułka, Władysław, xxi, 13, 326, *561*
and Nagy group trials, 524–25
relations with Soviets, 13, 186, 222–24,
353, 497, 506–7, 510–11, 513
and Soviet invasion of Hungary, 213, 335
speech by (Oct. 1956), 13, 231, 232, 242
Göncz, Árpád, xxiv, 534, *561*
preface by, xiii–xiv
Gorbachev, Mikhail, 558
Griffith, William, xx–xxi, 464–84
Gromyko, Andrei A., 377, 404–5, *561*
Grősz, József, *10*, 92, 98
Grotewohl, Otto, *561*
Gryaznov, F. N., *399*
Gyenes, Antal, 280, 368, 489
Győr, 199, 204, 255, 327, 358

H

Hammarskjöld, Dag, 333, 386, *561*
Haraszti, Sándor, *330,* 443, 532, 533. *See
also* Nagy group
Háy, Gyula, 540
Hayter, William G., 317, *561*
He Long, 496, 503
Hegedüs, András, 9, 92, 163–64, 171, *561*
appeal for Soviet troops, *272*

in meeting with Mikoyan (July 1956),
143–45
and plans for post-Nagy government, 308,
529
after revolution, 517–19
during uprising, 191, 194, 220, 224, 225,
236, 252, 255–56, 258–61
Hidas, István, *20*
Holodkov, M.N., 432–34
Hoover, Herbert C., Jr., 388, 402, *561*
Horn, Gyula, xxiv
Horváth, Imre, 275–76, 356, 359, 496, 502,
561
Horváth, Márton, 64, 409, 535–37, *561*
HSWP. *See* Hungarian Socialist Workers'
Party
Humphrey, George, 130
Hungarian Army, 19–20, 103–5
and Soviet invasion, 215, 216, 364, 383,
432–33
and uprising, 192, 196–97, 199, 204–6,
220, 292
Hungarian revolution (1956), 191–216. *See
also* Nagy government (Oct.–Nov. 1956)
crushing of, 216, 364, 374–76, 384, 450,
451, 498, 499
Eastern European reaction to, 202,
229–30, 246–49, 303–6, 318–20,
326–27, 347, 398–400, 493–94, 509
Gorbachev on, 558
historical view of, xix–xxii
Kádár government's portrayal of, 370,
460–63, 515–16
Kádár's description to Soviets, 336–40,
358
Khrushchev's portrayal of (May 1957),
524–26
lynchings during, 208, 327, 524
Oct. 23, 191–93, 217–18, 224–25
Oct. 24, 194–95, 219–22, 224–26
Oct. 25, 195–98
Oct. 26, 198–200, 235, 237–39
Oct. 27, 200–201, 251–52
Oct. 28, 203–4, 253–61, 273–89
Oct. 29, 205
Oct. 30-Nov. 2, 206–8, 211–12, 292–93,
321–23, 326–27, 334
Nov. 2-3, 214–16
period leading to, 12–13
political unrest preceding, 10–12, 143–47,
159–72, 178–84, 187

Kádár, János, *(cont'd)*
  in Nagy government (Oct.–Nov. 1956),
    195, 198, 200, 201, 205, 211, 220,
    237–39, 252, 253–55, 260, 261, 297,
    313, 314–15, 326, 330–31
  before revolution, 7, 11, 12, 352
Kádár government, xix, xxiii, 364–76,
    567–68
  Chinese visit to, 496–503
  consolidation of power, 368–70, 452–55,
    460–63, 515–16
  early days of, 364–68, 408–16, 449–55
  early intentions of, 365, 368
  and multi-party political system, 370–71,
    411, 487, 489, 490, 493
  and Nagy, 365–66, 370, 395, 396, 404–5,
    408, 415, 460, 503
  and Nagy group, 365–66, 404–5, 410–11,
    485–87, 489, 499–500, 515, 516
    negotiations concerning, 445–49
  and Nagy group kidnapping, 366, 435–36,
    445
  and Nagy group trials, 370–74, 503,
    519–21, 532–42
  and Poland, 498–99
  portrayal of revolution/Nagy government,
    367, 370, 375, 392, 408–10, 460–63,
    515–16
  preparation of, 213, 214, 216, 307–10,
    348, 350–53, 355–61, 385–86,
    392–94, 525, 528–29
  public acceptance of, 369, 376, 508, 513
  radio address during invasion, 216
  and Rákosi-Gerő circle, 460, 461, 517–19
  reevaluation of (1989), 556, 557
  reforms under, 367, 370, 376
  relations with Soviet Union, 365, 411,
    453–55, 489, 517–22, 541–42
  repression under, 367–69, 374–76, 502–3,
    540
  resistance/dissent under, 366–69, 374–76,
    450–51, 508, 513
  shift to hard line, 367–68, 460–63,
    515–16
  and sovereignty/neutrality ("national
    question"), 449, 453–54, 521
  Soviet debates on (Nov. 1956), 376, 377,
    385–86, 392–94
  and U.N., 386, 499–502
  U.S. analyses of, 508, 513, 547
  and U.S., 379, 401, 502, 547, 551

Warsaw Pact summit on (Jan. 1957),
    370–71, 485–87, 489–95
  and Yugoslavia, 418, 427, 445–48, 500–2,
    522–23, 533–34, 540, 541–42
Kaganovich, Lazar M., 8, 54, 57, 61–62, *562*
  and invasion of Hungary, 340
  on post-revolution Hungary, 392–94
  in Presidium power struggle, after revolu-
    tion, 377, 392–94, 527–31
  and uprising in Hungary, 217, 263, 267,
    268, 296, 298
Kállai, Gyula, 225, 371, 491, *562*
Kardelj, Edvard, 387, 443, 500, *562*
Kardos, László, *199,* 251, 534
Kelemen, Gyula, *215*
Kenedi, János, xxiv
Keresztes, Mihály, *360*
Kéthly, Anna, 10, 206, 215, 327, 341, *562*
KGB. *See* Committee for State Security
    (KGB; Soviet Union)
Khrushchev, Nikita S., *562*
  decision to withdraw army, 295–302
  Eastern Europe policy, after revolution,
    376–78
  foreign policy, after revolution, 527–31
  on Hungarian leadership (1953-55), 8–9,
    14, 18, 22, 54–56, 58–60, 62–64
  and Hungary after revolution
    planning for, 213, 307–10, 348,
      350–61, 385–86, 392–94
    Warsaw Pact summit on (Jan. 1957),
      487, 489–95
  and invasion of Hungary, 210, 213, 214,
    217, 307–10, 348–54
  and Nagy group asylum in Yugoslav
    Embassy, 365, 395–400
  and Nagy group trial, 373–74, 524–25
  on Nagy/Nagy government, 213, 307,
    308, 354, 525–26
  and Poland, 13, 186, 222–24, 353, 497,
    524–26
  and post-Stalin reforms, xxvii, 4, 10
  power struggle with "hard-liners," after
    revolution, 376, 377, 385–86, 392–94
  on Soviet invasion (Nov. 1957), 525–26
  Twentieth Party Congress speech on
    Stalin, 10, 117–18, 135, 170
  and uprising in Hungary, xx, 181, 201,
    208, 210, 222, 224–26, 262–68,
    525–26
  and Yugoslavia, 3, 136–42, 348–54, 418,

O

Ölvedi, János, 466–68, 472, 476, 477
Operation Red Sox/Red Cap, *381*
Orbán, László, *368*

P

Papp, Simon, 10
Pártay, Tivadar, *533*
"Party Opposition"
  under Kádár government, 368
  before revolution, 9, 461–62
Patriotic People's Front ("popular front"),
  7–8, 10, 64, 490
peasantry, 6, 94–95, 204. *See also* agriculture
Péter, Gábor, 1, 7, 16, 23, 57, 98, *564*
Petőfi Circle, 10–11, 144, 160–61, 170, 461,
  567
Petőfi Party, 207, 215. *See also* National
  Peasant/Peasants' Party
Pineau, Christian, *564*
Piros, László, 225, 518, *564*
Poland. *See also* Gomułka, Władysław
  crisis in (1956), 11, 13, 174–75, 183–84,
    186–87, 222–24, 231, 232, 242, 353,
    421, 428, 505–6
  and Hungarian crisis, xxii, 326–27, 335,
    343, 524–26
  and Kádár government, 498–99
  Soviet troop withdrawal from, 378–79
  U.S. analyses of, 47–48, 169, 174–75,
    231, 232, 242, 504–8, 510–13
  U.S. policy toward, 129, 130, 380,
    437–39
  and Warsaw Pact summit (Jan. 1957),
    389, 497, 498–99
police forces
  secret (*See* Committee for State Security
    (KGB; Soviet Union); State Security
    Authority (ÁVH))
  in uprising, 192, 197, 206
political parties
  and Kádár government, 370–71, 487, 489,
    490, 493
  revival during revolution, 206–7, 327
political prisoners. *See* prisoners
political reforms. *See also* multi-party system
  and Kádár government, 370–71, 376
  in Nagy government (1956), 201, 203–7,
    290–91

in "New Course" period (1953–55),
  7–8
political repression. *See also* State Security
  Authority (ÁVH)
  in Hungary
    attempts to ease (1953–56), 6–7, 55,
      170, 173
    under Kádár government, 367–69,
      374–76, 540
    under Rákosi, 1, 5, 14–17, 21, 93–94,
      101
  in Soviet Eastern Europe policy, after
    Hungarian revolution, 510
  in Soviet Union, 202
political unrest. *See* dissidence/resistance;
  nationalism
Pongrátz, Gergely, 198, *564*
Ponomarev, Boris N., *371,* 487–88, 519
"popular front." *See* Patriotic People's Front
Pospelov, Piotr N., *186,* 265, 308, 351
Pozsgay, Imre, *554*
  reevaluation of revolution, 554–57
Preparatory Committee of the Revolutionary
  Armed Forces, 206
press, 321. *See also* Radio Free Europe;
  Szabad Nép
  under Kádár government, 416
  and "New Course" reforms, 9–10
  during revolution, 198, 207, 208, 321,
    322, 501
  Western, 373, 501
prisoners
  releases of, 6–7, 10, 211, 380
  during Soviet invasion and Kádár govern-
    ment, 432–34, 451, 501
propaganda campaigns
  under Kádár, on revolution, 375
  U.S., Eastern Europe, 2, 66–68, 132 (*See
    also* Radio Free Europe)

R

Rácz, Sándor, 367, *564*
Radio Free Europe (RFE), 2, 164, 203, 215, *567*
  criticism of role, xvi, xx–xxi, 379, 464
  internal investigation of, *464–84*
  Nov. 4 broadcast, *389–90*
  program advising on military tactics,
    286–89
Radio station (Budapest), 192, 193, 195
Rajk, Júlia, *410,* 533, 535, 537. *See also*

emissaries' reports on, *435–36, 449–55*
and multi-party system initiative,
370–71, 487, 489
and Nagy group kidnapping, 435–36,
449, 455
and Nagy group trials, 373–74, 519,
539–42
meetings with Hungarian leaders
(1953–55), 4, 8–9, 14–23, 54–64
and Nagy group asylum, 365–66, 387,
395–400, 404–5
and Polish crisis (1956), 186–87, 222–24
and political unrest before uprising,
reports on, 11, *143–47, 159–67, 178–82*
power struggle, after revolution, 376–77,
385–86, 392–94, 527–31
and Warsaw Pact summit on Hungary
(Jan. 1957), 370–71, 485–87, 489–95
and Yugoslavia, 420–21, 456–59, 511, 541
before Hungarian revolution, 3, 110,
123, 136–42
and Nagy group, 365–66, 387,
395–400, 404–5, 522, 540, 541–42
and Tito's speech at Pula, 418, 419–21,
425–28, 444, 453, 456–58, 500
Special Committee on Soviet and Related
Problems (U.S.), 231
Stalin, Joseph V., 1, *564*
and Rákosi, 353–54
Stalinism
Khrushchev's speech attacking, 10
Tito's criticism of, 419–21, 425, 457
Stassen, Harold E., 209, 240, 242–43, 437, *564*
State Security Authority (ÁVH), 1, *567.*
See also political repression
abolition of, 203, 256–59, 262–68,
284–85
in "New Course" period (1953–55), 7, 14,
15–16, 21, 29, 103
and uprising, 192, 193, 197, 208, 238
and U.S. leaflet propaganda campaign,
66–67
strikes
under Kádár government, 364, 367,
450–51, 501
during revolution, 326, 334
students, 12–13, 93, 95, 198
demonstrations by, 12–13, 191–93
"Sixteen Points" demands, 13, 188–90
Suez crisis, 212, 228, 349, 402, 495, 531
Tito on, 418, 424, 428–30

Suslov, Mikhail A., *564*
and Kádár government, 365, 392–94
reports to Presidium, *435–36,
449–55*
and Nagy group kidnapping, 366, 435–36,
449, 455
and uprising in Hungary, 194, 195, 201,
211, 217, 218, 253, 353
reports to Presidium, 195, 209,
211, *219–21, 237–39, 251–52,*
262, 265–66, 284, *292–93*
Svoboda, Jan, 222
Szabad Nép (newspaper), 64, *567*
under Kádár government, 416
Nagy's article in (1954), 8, 60–64
Soviet criticism of (1953), 28, 32
support for reform, 10, 13
and uprising, 191, 195, 208
Szabó, István B., 215, *564*
Szabó, János, 198, 362, 451, *564*
Szabó, Zoltán, 466
Szakmáry, Károly, 466, 472, 474
Szalai, Béla, *21,* 146, 225
Szantó, Zoltán, 8, 211, 219, 220, 225,
257–58, *565. See also* Nagy group
asylum request, 352, 399
in Nagy government, 260, 409, 412
separation from Nagy group, 370, 485,
492, 520–21, 533, 537
Szász, Béla, 12
SZDP. *See* Social Democratic Party
Széll, Jenő, *322*
Széna Square (Budapest), 198
Szigethy, Attila, 207, 255, *565*
Szilágyi, József, 199, 251, 315, *565.*
See also Nagy group
trial of, 372–74, 532, 539–40

T

Tamási, Áron, *199*
Tamási, Lajos, *322*
Tánczos, Gábor, *199,* 532, 533
Tardos, Tibor, 160–61, 540
Tausz, János, 274, 277
Thury, Zoltán, 466, 467–68
Tildy, Zoltán, 200, 201, 207, 220, 408, 446,
472, *565*
arrest of, 372
in Nagy government, 274, 275, 278–83,
314–15, 321, 330, 331, 338, 339, 341

PICTURE CREDITS

Photo 1 MTI, Hungarian News Agency
Photo 2 Historical Photograph Archive of the Hungarian National Museum
Photo 3 Historical Photograph Archive of the Hungarian National Museum
Photo 4 MTI, Hungarian News Agency
Photo 5 Historical Photograph Archive of the Hungarian National Museum
Photo 6 Tibor Szentpétery, Historical Photograph Archive of the Hungarian National Museum
Photo 7 MTI, Hungarian News Agency
Photo 8 Budapest Collection of the Municipal Szabó Ervin Library in Budapest
Photo 9 Jenő Virág, Historical Photograph Archive of the Hungarian National Museum
Photo 10 György Fábri, Photo Documentary Database of the Institute for the History of the 1956 Hungarian Revolution
Photo 11 Historical Photograph Archive of the Hungarian National Museum
Photo 12 MTI, Hungarian News Agency
Photo 13 Photo Documentary Database of the Institute for the History of the 1956 Hungarian Revolution
Photo 14 Tibor Szentpétery, Historical Photograph Archive of the Hungarian National Museum
Photo 15 Tibor Szentpétery
Photo 16 MTI, Hungarian News Agency
Photo 17 Sándor Bojár, Historical Photograph Archive of the Hungarian National Museum
Photo 18 Tibor Szentpétery, Historical Photograph Archive of the Hungarian National Museum
Photo 19 B. Takács, Photo Documentary Database of the Institute for the History of the 1956 Hungarian Revolution
Photo 20 Historical Photograph Archive of the Hungarian National Museum
Photo 21 Olivér Kiszely, Historical Photograph Archive of the Hungarian National Museum

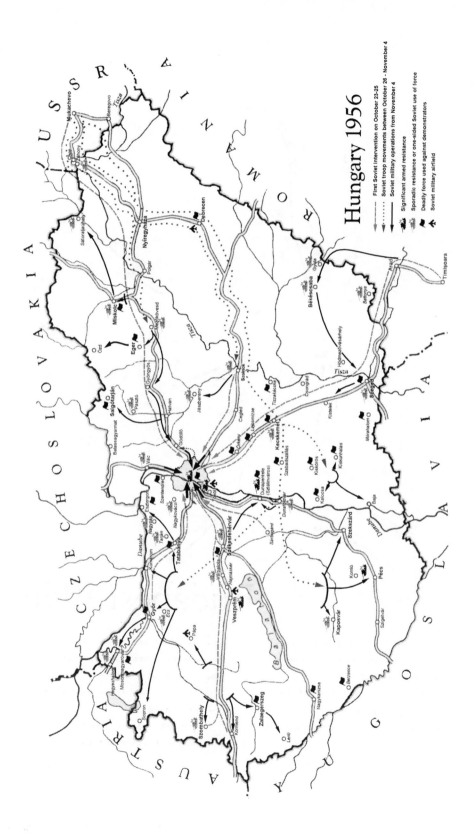

Hungary 1956

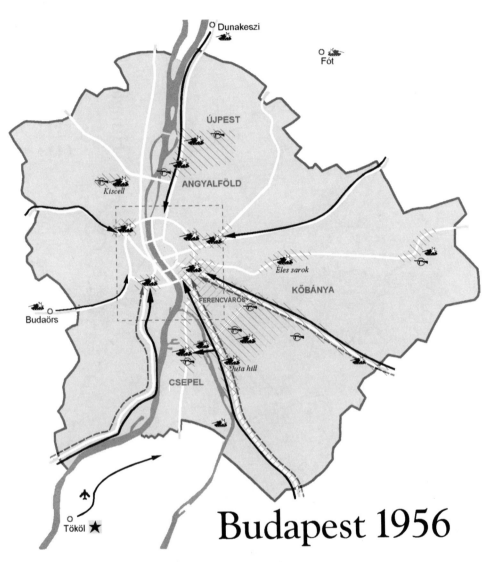

O Dunakeszi

O Fót

ÚJPEST

Kiscell

ANGYALFÖLD

Éles sarok

KŐBÁNYA

FERENCVÁROS

O Budaörs

Juta hill

CSEPEL

O Tököl ★

Budapest 1956

Route of the October 23 demonstrations	First Soviet intervention on October 23-29
Main sites of the October 23 demonstrations	Soviet military operations from November 4
Main revolutionary centers	Significant armed resistance
Deadly force used against demonstrators	Rebel siege of party or government facilities
Soviet military airfield	Armed groups
Headquarters of the Soviet Special Army Corps	Areas of fighting from October 23-29
	Areas of fighting from November 4

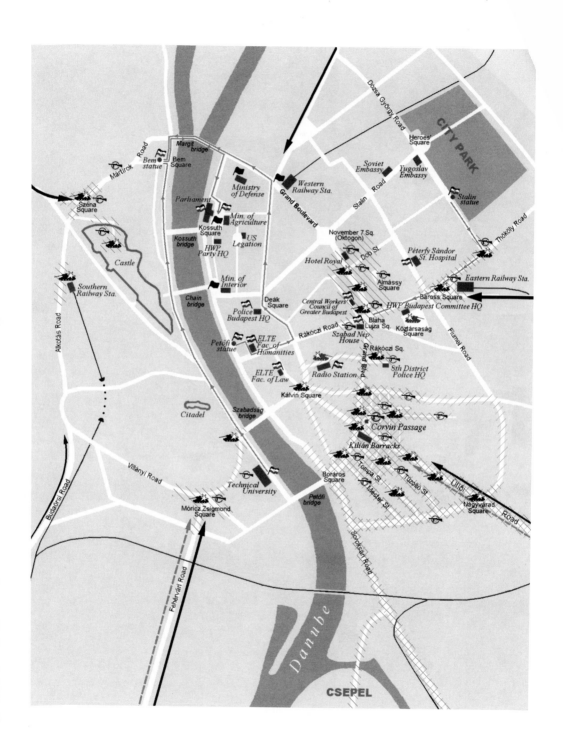